W9-BLY-466

PAULINE PARALLELS

PAULINE PARALLELS

Second Edition

Designed and Edited by

FRED O. FRANCIS

J. PAUL SAMPLEY

FORTRESS PRESS

First Edition Copyright © 1975 by the Society of Biblical Literature

Second Edition Copyright © 1984 by Fortress Press

First Fortress Press paperback edition 1987

Library of Congress Cataloging in Publication Data

Bible. N.T. Epistles of Paul. English. Revised
    standard. 1984
    Pauline parallels.

Includes indexes.
    1. Bible. N.T. Epistles of Paul—Harmonies, English.
I. Francis, Fred O. II. Sampley, J. Paul. III. Title.
IV. Series
BS2643.F7   1984   227′.065   83–48920
ISBN 0–8006–2094–1

3260I87   Printed in the United States of America   1–2094

to
NILS A. DAHL
for whom
we do not cease to give thanks

In Memoriam
FRED O. FRANCIS
1934–1984

Contents

We wish to record our hearty thanks for the efforts of the staffs of Fortress and Polebridge presses under the leadership of Norman A. Hjelm and Robert W. Funk.

Norman Hjelm has been committed to this project since its beginning. He deserves considerable credit for his willingness to undertake and see through to publication new approaches to scholarship.

To Robert Funk we owe a special debt of gratitude. He conceived of a new generation of publications and personally directed the preparation of this manuscript for printing. He made possible the book's appearance at this time.

Char Matejovsky has played a key role in styling and preparing camera ready copy. We thank her for her high standards and great energy.

We thank our wives.

On the Occasion of the
First Fortress Press Paperback Edition

From the outset Fred Francis and I viewed the *Pauline Parallels* as an aid, specifically as a workbook, for the study of Paul, and we hoped to make it accessible to as many students as possible. So it is appropriate that it now appear in paperback.

Special thanks go to Harold Rast for his continued interest in this volume and for his commitment to make it more available to a wider audience.

Fall, 1987   J. P. S.
Charlemont

The *Pauline Parallels* has been redesigned and revised in order to provide an improved practical tool for students seeking to understand the Pauline corpus of letters. In his letters, Paul echoes the structure of the common letter, he employs rhetorical devices, and he often repeats themes and images. The *Pauline Parallels* provides a ready, efficient, comprehensive way to study the letters structurally, formally, and thematically by gathering relevant passages from all the letters onto the page or folio for immediate comparison. The *Pauline Parallels* is the analog for the Pauline letters of a gospel parallels.

The *Pauline Parallels* is a sequential presentation of each of the ten chief letters attributed to Paul: Romans, 1 and 2 Corinthians, Galatians, Ephesians, Philippians, Colossians, 1 and 2 Thessalonians and Philemon. Each letter is divided into sense units or paragraphs of discourse; these paragraphs, as they are designated, are numbered consecutively from the salutation of Romans to the closing remarks of Philemon. Paragraph numbers are then used as the basis of the presentation of the materials in the *Pauline Parallels* and function effectively in a system of cross-referencing.

Each letter is arranged in canonical order in its entirety from salutation to final grace and closing remarks. A distinctive feature of this new design of the *Pauline Parallels* is that it highlights letter structure and formal elements in the Pauline letter collection. In order to indicate the full range of parallels, some paragraphs are printed several times.

Earlier Approaches

Prior to the first edition of the *Pauline Parallels*,[1] attempts to note common elements in Paul's letters have often taken the form of thematic tables that listed where Paul dealt with various subjects, such as the church or justification. The earliest extant effort of this kind seems to have been by an anonymous fourth century author.[2] Similar treatments continue into the modern era but sometimes suffer from the importation of non-pauline

---

[1] Fred O. Francis and J. Paul Sampley, *Pauline Parallels* (Philadelphia: Fortress Press; Missoula: Scholars Press, 1975).

[2] John Wordsworth and Henry J. White, and others, *Novum Testamentum Domini Nostri Jesu Christi Latine Secundum Editionem Sancti Hieronymi* (Oxford: Clarendon Press, 1889–1954), II, 12–16.

categories or a lack of comprehensiveness. Too frequently such treatments obscure or dissipate the discreteness of the letter occasions. A reductionist and simplistic "doctrinal" understanding of Paul is often the result.

The nearest modern analogy to what is here offered in the *Pauline Parallels* is the work of Goodspeed and Mitton on Ephesians,[3] but their efforts are marred by the severe fragmentation of the text into small phrases in an effort to demonstrate a use-hypothesis, namely, that Ephesians is a pastiche or mosaic of the other Pauline letters and is composed by a Paulinist. The *Pauline Parallels* presents the letters in discourse paragraphs and thus avoids fragmentation, and it supports no particular methodology or hypothesis. As a study instrument, it is designed to be as neutral as possible on all matters except the juxtaposition of related materials on the study page.

The reader familiar with various gospel parallels will see certain similarities in the layout of this volume. Comparable sense-units are collected for each numbered paragraph; smaller fragments and notes relevant to the primary text are provided at foot of each page. Letter structure gives the letters a common organization much as narrative structure results in a comparable plan among the gospels. Unlike the gospels, however, the letters of Paul manifest little or no literary interdependence. Further, each of the letters is wed to concrete historical circumstances and most nearly approximates one side of a written conversation.

Authorship

The *Pauline Parallels* entails no prejudgment concerning the authorship of 2 Thessalonians, Ephesians and Colossians. Persons who dispute the authorship of these three letters will have the occasion to test their judgment by examining paragraphs from these letters in relation to the other Pauline letters. Those who hold these three letters to be genuine will welcome the opportunity to study them alongside the remaining Pauline letters.

Table of Parallels

The following description of the volume's layout as well as the format of the individual paragraphs should facilitate the use of the *Pauline Parallels*. The detailed table of parallels divides each letter into sense-units and lists primary and secondary parallels for each passage. This table is the key to the entire volume. It shows what passages are associated with each other and is a direct means for readers to find their way to a given passage in its

---

[3] Edgar J. Goodspeed, *The Meaning of Ephesians* (Chicago: University of Chicago Press, 1933), and C. Leslie Mitton, *The Epistle to the Ephesians: Its Authorship, Origin and Purpose* (Oxford: Oxford University Press, 1951).

context. Familiarity with the table of parallels will enhance the usefulness of this working tool.

If, for example, one wishes to study a particular passage from one of the letters, he or she ought first to examine the passage "vertically" in that letter, that is, read the passage in its own literary context. Then the passage in question may be considered in its "horizontal" relationship to the other letters. Of course, one would want to examine the context of each of the parallel passages in the letters in which each is found—back to the "vertical" again. Finally, the notes and the index will indicate other possible parallels (See the *User's Guide* below for more detailed suggestions).

Layout of Paragraphs

The layout of each paragraph of the volume is separated into two parts. The upper section of each paragraph is composed of three columns (occasionally six across an entire folio) with the primary passage in bold type at the upper left. Primary and secondary parallels follow. These parallels are always printed in full sense-units. Our desire to avoid over-fragmentation is reflected in this decision to print whole units at every point in the upper section.

Criteria for Primary and Secondary Parallels

The criteria employed in the juxtaposition of passages alongside a particular Pauline text are fundamentally the following: 1) similarity of letter structure, 2) similarity of form, or 3) similarity of theme or image. In keeping with our view of this volume as a working tool, we encourage readers to use blank spaces in the text to include further passages they deem helpful.

Distinctions among Parallels

Letter-structure paragraphs and paragraphs containing formal elements are labeled and have structural and formal "primary" parallels. When there are additional, thematic parallels, they are included as "secondary" parallels. Paragraphs not labeled as structural or formal, namely thematic paragraphs, simply have primary parallels.

Varieties of Fragmentary Parallels and Notes

The lower section of each paragraph is devoted to smaller, fragmentary parallels and notes. All of the entries on this section of the page are keyed to the primary passage in bold type. In these notes there has been no effort to reproduce total sense-units. Insofar as space allows we have printed these verses rather than simply give references.

In this lower section of each paragraph, passages from Acts and the pastoral epistles (1 and 2 Timothy and Titus), a few references to other non-Pauline New Testament documents, and Old Testament quotations and strong allusions are cited. Textual variants and their manuscript witnesses are noted for those instances of some consequence (see "The Text" below). Selected verses have been included from the ten Pauline letters for the additional light they cast on the primary passage in question.

Indices

Indices are included at the end of the volume for convenience. There the reader will find an index to every occurrence of each paragraph in the Pauline letter corpus; there are also full indices to other scriptural references.

Though we have consistently tried to avoid imposing any particular methodology on the study of Paul by our construction of this volume, we are concerned that we do not contribute to a simplistic, conflationary or sythesizing methodology whereby fragments of Paul are recast in the thought patterns of the interpreter. It is our hope that a clearer notion of thought-units within a given letter and a stronger sense of context for a given passage might heighten the understanding of the diversity of occasions and communities that are represented in these different letters. Much as synoptic Gospel studies have moved away from a coalescing of the various parallels into one synthetic account towards an increased sensitivity to the idiosyncracies of a given gospel, we hope that the study of Paul may become more sophisticated by highlighting the diversity and complexity of Paul's letters.

J. Paul Sampley
School of Theology
Boston University

Fred O. Francis
Department of Religion
Chapman College

Many readers of the first edition of *Pauline Parallels* have reported ways in which they have found it useful. Scholars, pastors, and others have encouraged the editors by offering their suggestions, which are brought together here in this User's Guide.

Seeing Paul Whole

The parallel arrangement of materials has proved to be valuable to users in churches, seminaries, and colleges, as well as in private study and devotions. It is illuminating, for example, to have all of Paul's references to the faith of Abraham arranged alongside one another as one studies Paul's theology in the letter to the Romans (§§16-19). In analyzing 1 Cor 15, it is helpful to know that Paul draws out his Adam/Christ analogy elsewhere (cf. §133). Similarly, when readers encounter a Pauline notion such as the end of the ages (cf. §§287, 56), it is informative to see what Paul says on that subject in other letters. Further, in §287 a student of Paul can examine the evidence to determine whether the Apostle changed his mind about the proximity of the end. In all these cases one should ask how a variation in content is related to its specific epistolary context.

Seeing Paul Afresh

Many pastors have reported that the *Parallels* function as a productive resource for fresh views of Paul.

One may start with a given passage as the primary focus and then read through the primary and secondary parallels and notes for additional ideas. Related passages juxtaposed in this fashion often call attention to a feature or thread that had been overlooked; occasionally new light is cast on a familiar idea.

It is then wise to examine the context of each passage to see whether the thrust of each letter at the point of interest modifies the way Paul presents his subject.

In §307, for example, Paul foregoes a command in preference to an appeal. The other primary parallels (§51) show a range of content in Paul's appeals (Romans: present yourselves as a living sacrifice; 1 Corinthians: agree and be united in the same mind and judgment; Ephesians: lead a life worthy of your calling). As in Paul's major letters, so in Philemon, the appeal does not prescribe each detail of what Christians should do, but provides the symbolic ground on which the believers are expected to make their decisions. Each appeal is distinctive: it is correlated with the characteristics of the letter in which it is embedded.

Exploring the byways...

One can discover material in each of the Pauline letters that is incidental to the main purpose of the document. Philemon, for example, was not conceived as a vehicle through which Paul could advance his views on slavery. Rather, it deals with the return of a run-away slave. As a result, one can find in Philemon some indication of how Paul understood slavery as an institution. Indeed, Paul's view of slavery bears very much on what he thinks the slaveowner ought to do. Should Philemon free Onesimus? Should he retain Onesimus as a slave and recognize him as a new brother in Christ? Should the slave be sent back to Paul? If so, should he be sent back as a slave or as a freedman? The *Parallels* will be helpful in addressing these questions because (1) on the same page where Paul urges Philemon to receive Onesimus back as if he were Paul (cf. §308), there is printed 1 Cor 7:17–24, where Paul reflects his views of slavery as an institution; and (2) the references direct the reader to each appropriate letter to observe the context of the discussion of slavery.

The Structure and Arrangement of the Parallels

The editors have collected three kinds of parallels in this work: thematic, formal, and structural. The user will want to explore all three types.

Thematic Parallels

Many major parallels have been selected on the basis of thematic similarity. It is thus possible to trace a Pauline theme through all ten letters without turning a page. In §306, for example, one can study (1) other Pauline expressions of thankfulness to God; (2) the close connection of faith and love; (3) the interrelation of Christians to each other in faith, love, joy, comfort, and refreshment. (4) One can also take note of the repeated correlation of thanksgiving and prayer. In §307 and the parallels cited there, the user can observe the Pauline emphasis on the community context for what love requires from the believer. §309 reveals that Paul makes an apologia for sending a letter rather than making a visit, and his conviction that the prayers of others are a help to him.

Significant parallel themes are also represented in the notes at the bottom of each page. Taking Philemon once again as illustrative of these resources, the reader should observe: (1) Paul's selection of the parent-child metaphor to portray his relation to those converted by his gospel (see the note on v. 10 in §307); (2) Paul's tendency to add a personal comment to each letter at some point (§308); (3) and Paul's use of command in some circumstances and his rejection of it in others (§307).

Formal Parallels

Items that are comparable in form have also been collected in each of the letters.

Formal parallels include the vice lists (see §6) and lists of virtues (see §252). Are these lists ever tailored to fit the setting? Is Paul giving a comprehensive range of virtues and vices? Is he trying to establish common ground with his readers so that his argument can be based on that common ground?

One may also note the catalogs of suffering and hardship (e.g., §183) or the confessional or hymnic formulations (e.g., §131). What is the merit of having experienced difficult times? Are the readers familiar with a particular confessional statement, or is Paul introducing it to them for the first time? Are the Corinthians, to cite a specific case, already aware of the pre-Pauline formula that is reflected in Gal 3:28 (§118)? If they are, why is the whole formula not reflected in the passage in Corinthians?

Philemon offers additional formal parallels. Paul's reintroduction of the newly converted Onesimus to his master takes on the form of commendation, which can be observed, as a form, in other Pauline letters (§§307, 308). What does Paul see in these people as praiseworthy? Are the readers expected to emulate them? One may also observe in §§309, 63 the evidence for a formal element consisting of Paul's planned but delayed visits. In what ways does Paul employ this topic to respond to specific situations?

Structural Parallels

One of the most noticeable features of the *Pauline Parallels* are the structural similarities from letter to letter. Like the formal parallels, these structural items are noted in the headings to relevant sections. Among the structural items are the saluations (e.g., §305), the thanksgivings (e.g., §306), the appeals (e.g., §§307, 51), the greetings (e.g., §310), and the grace (e.g., §311).

The similarities of structural units may readily be observed when these units are laid out on the same page. In §305, for example, one may take note of the standard items in the Pauline salutation: the identification of Paul and those who join him in writing the letter, usually by reference to the calling in Christ; the identification of the recipients, usually by geographical reference and in connection with Christ; and finally the grace and peace.

The differences between and among these structural units stand out more clearly when one observes their basic similarities. In what salutation does Paul not identify himself as an apostle (see §305). Is that significant? Why are the salutations to the Romans and to the Galatians longer than the others? What are the distinctive ways in which Paul characterizes himself or others in these longer versions? Why is Paul the sole author of Romans and Ephesians?

Reading Between the Lines

Even "blanks" may be instructive: why are structural parallels sometimes lacking? Why does Paul not include a thanksgiving in the letter to the Galatians (§72)? Why are there no personal greetings in Galatians (§291)? Similarly, just how often does Paul admonish his readers to "imitate God" (§229)?

Each reader will want to develop his or her own ways to make use of the *Pauline Parallels*. In doing so, one should remember to read "up and down" in the letter, as well as across the letters. The format of *Pauline Parallels* permits the reader to do either with equal ease.

The indices provide a number of opportunities for creative study. The index of Pauline Letters lists all the sections in which each paragraph appears as a parallel. This device permits the user to begin to form a judgment about recurrent themes and arguments in Paul's letters. The Scripture Indices give one access to Paul's use of the Old Testament and make its possible to evaluate the portrait of Paul in Acts and the Pastorals.

The possibilities may be extended indefinitely by the user's creative imagination!

In the centuries prior to the invention of printing, hundreds and hundreds of copies of the Pauline epistles were produced by hand—copies written in Greek, Latin, Syriac, Coptic, and other languages, written on papyrus and vellum. In addition, Fathers of the early church quoted the letters and wrote commentaries on them, and lectionary texts were prepared for use in worship; these, too, had to be copied by hand.

In copying and re-copying the epistles over a period of several centuries, scribes made all the typical mistakes of eye and ear inherent in the production of handwritten documents. They also harmonized one portion of the text with another, and occasionally made theological or other modifications.

Textual criticism is employed to determine from this mass of manuscripts (MSS) what Paul originally wrote or at least the earliest form of the text available. The Revised Standard Version, which is used in this volume, is based on modern critical editions of the Greek New Testament, which are the result of the text-critical assessment of the best documentary evidence available to scholars.[1]

The notes in the *Pauline Parallels* contain a selection of textual variants, some of the more important cases when MSS differ on the wording of passages in the epistles.[2] Such notes approximately reflect the present combination of methods in textual criticism: an interest in the oldest MSS, the use of MSS to represent certain text types, and the eclectic weighing of individual cases.[3]

The main types of text represented in the notes in this volume are the Alexandrian (a short, but not highly polished text; circulated by the second century in Egypt and in the Eastern Church), the Western (a long text marked by striking "omissions" and "insertions"; circulated by the second century in the western Mediterranean with influence elsewhere), and the

---

[1] The two most important editions for the RSV text are Eberhard Nestle and Erwin Nestle, with Kurt Aland, Matthew Black, Carlo M. Martini, Bruce M. Metzger, Allen Wikgren, and Barbara Aland, *Novum Testamentum Graece* (26th edition, Stuttgart, 1979), and, behind that, B. F. Westcott and F. J. A. Hort, *The New Testament in the Original Greek* (Cambridge, 1881), 2 Vols. (2nd edition of Vol. 2, 1896).

[2] The Nestle text referred to in the preceding note was most useful to the editors in the preparation of textual notes.

[3] E. C. Colwell, *What is the Best New Testament?* (Chicago: University of Chicago Press, 1947). Cf. Bruce M. Metzger, *The Text of the New Testament: Its Transmission, Corruption, and Restoration* (New York: Oxford University Press, 1964).

Koine (a stylistically and linguistically smooth text that harmonizes parallel passages; circulated by the fourth century in the Byzantine Empire). Other types of text have been identified, such as the Caesarean and other families among medieval MSS. Readings from MSS of the Alexandrian type are generally given greatest weight, although editors at times favor readings of other textual families.

THE GREEK MANUSCRIPT EVIDENCE

Papyri cited

NUMBER	DATE	NAME	TEXT TYPE[4]	LOCATION
p[46]	ca. 200	Chester Beatty	Alexandrian	Dublin/Ann Arbor
p[61]	ca. 700	p.Colt 5	Alexandrian	New York
p[65]	III		Alexandrian	Florence

Other MSS and Versions Cited

S	IV	Sinaiticus	Alexandrian	London
A	V	Alexandrinus	Alexandrian	London
B	IV	Vaticanus	Alexandrian	Rome
C	V	Ephraemi Rescriptus	Alexandrian	Paris
D	VI	Claromontanus	Western	Paris
F	IX	Augiensis	Western	Cambridge
G	IX	Boernerianus	Western	Dresden
L	IX	Angelicus	Koine	Rome
P	IX	Porphyrianus	Alexandrian	Leningrad
Koine	III–XVI	the reading of a majority of Koine MSS[5]		
Lect	IX–XV	the reading of a majority of lectionaries		
it	II–IV	Itala or Old Latin	Western	
vg	IV	Vulgate	Western	
vg(clem)		Clementine edition (3rd edition, 1598; continued publication into this century) cited when differs from vg(w–w)		
vg(w–w)		Wordsworth and White, editors (3 Vols., 1889–1954) cited when differs from vg(clem)		
syr	V–VII	Syriac	mixed	
syr(pes)	V	The Peshitta		
syr(pal)	V	Palestinian		
syr(har)	616	Harclean		
cop	III–V	Coptic	Alexandrian	
cop(sa)	III	Sahidic		
cop(bo)	III or V	Bohairic		

---

[4] The classification of text types in this table applies only to the Pauline letter corpus in a MS.

[5] The received text, or Textus Receptus, was the common text of the Byzantine world. Medieval MSS of this text type were the ones readily available during the renewed interest in antiquity in the Renaissance. It has a number of other names: Koine (common)—the name used in the notes to the *Pauline Parallels* — Byzantine, Ecclesiastical, Traditional, etc.

Church Fathers cited

NAME	DATE	LOCATION
Ambrose	d.397	Milan
Ambrosiaster	IV	?
Chrysostom	d.407	Constantinople
Clement	d.215	Alexandria
Ephraem	d.373	Edessa
Hippolytus	d.235	Rome
Irenaeus	d.202	Lyons
Marcion	II	Rome
Origen	d.254	Alexandria/Caesarea
Pelagius	d.412	Rome
Tertullian	d.220	Carthage

The following symbols are used in connection with the citation of certain Greek MSS:

*	the original hand of a MS
c	corrector of a MS
c,2,3	multiple correctors of a MS
a,b,c	multiple correctors of MSS S and D

● Secondary Parallels

LETTER STRUCTURE: SALUTATION
FORMAL ELEMENT: CONFESSION

1 Paul, a servant of Jesus Christ, called to be an apostle, set apart for the gospel of God ²which he promised beforehand through his prophets in the holy scriptures, ³the gospel concerning his Son, who was descended from David according to the flesh ⁴and designated Son of God in power according to the Spirit of holiness by his resurrection from the dead, Jesus Christ our Lord, ⁵through whom we have received grace and apostleship to bring about the obedience of faith for the sake of his name among all the nations, ⁶including yourselves who are called to belong to Jesus Christ;

⁷To all God's beloved in Rome, who are called to be saints:

Grace to you and peace from God our Father and the Lord Jesus Christ.

PRIMARY

See §50 for CONFESSION

1 Cor 1:1–3 (§71)
¹Paul, called by the will of God to be an apostle of Christ Jesus, and our brother Sosthenes,

²To the church of God which is at Corinth, to those sanctified in Christ Jesus, called to be saints together with all those who in every place call on the name of our Lord Jesus Christ, both their Lord and ours:

³Grace to you and peace from God our Father and the Lord Jesus Christ.

2 Cor 1:1–2 (§146)
¹Paul, an apostle of Christ Jesus by the will of God, and Timothy our brother.

To the church of God which is at Corinth, with all the saints who are in the whole of Achaia:

²Grace to you and peace from God our Father and the Lord Jesus Christ.

Gal 1:1–5 (§193)
¹Paul an apostle—not from men nor through man, but through Jesus Christ and God the Father, who raised him from the dead— ²and all the brethren who are with me,

To the churches of Galatia:

³Grace to you and peace from God the Father and our Lord Jesus Christ, ⁴who gave himself for our sins to deliver us from the present evil age, according to the will of our God and Father; ⁵to whom be the glory for ever and ever. Amen.

Eph 1:1–2 (§218)
¹Paul, an apostle of Christ Jesus by the will of God,

To the saints who are also faithful in Christ Jesus:

²Grace to you and peace from God our Father and the Lord Jesus Christ.

Phil 1:1–2 (§237)
¹Paul and Timothy, servants of Christ Jesus,

To all the saints in Christ Jesus who are at Philippi, with the bishops and deacons:

²Grace to you and peace from God our Father and the Lord Jesus Christ.

Col 1:1–2 (§256)
¹Paul, an apostle of Christ Jesus by the will of God, and Timothy our brother,

²To the saints and faithful brethren in Christ at Colossae:

Grace to you and peace from God our Father.

1 Thess 1:1 (§275)
¹Paul, Silvanus, and Timothy,

To the church of the Thessalonians in God the Father and the Lord Jesus Christ:

Grace to you and peace.

2 Thess 1:1–2 (§294)
¹Paul, Silvanus, and Timothy,

To the church of the Thessalonians in God our Father and the Lord Jesus Christ:

²Grace to you and peace from God the Father and the Lord Jesus Christ.

Phlm 1–3 (§305)
¹Paul, a prisoner for Christ Jesus, and Timothy our brother,

To Philemon our beloved fellow worker ²and Apphia our sister and Archippus our fellow soldier, and the church in your house:

³Grace to you and peace from God our Father and the Lord Jesus Christ.

● **Rom 1:1–7**
Acts 9   ¹⁵But the Lord said to him, "Go, for he is a chosen instrument of mine to carry my name before the Gentiles and kings and the sons of Israel...."

Acts 22   ²¹"And he said to me, 'Depart; for I will send you far away to the Gentiles.'"

Acts 26   ¹⁶"But rise and stand upon your feet; for I have appeared to you for this purpose, to appoint you to serve and bear witness to the things in which you have seen me and to those in which I will appear to you, ¹⁷delivering you from the people and from the Gentiles—to whom I send you ¹⁸to open their eyes, that they may turn from darkness to light and from the power of Satan to God, that they may receive forgiveness of sins and a place among those who are sanctified by faith in me."

1 Tim 1   ¹Paul, an apostle of Christ Jesus by command of God our Savior and of Christ Jesus our hope, ²To Timothy, my true child in the faith:
Grace, mercy, and peace from God the Father and Christ Jesus our Lord.

2 Tim 1   ¹Paul, an apostle of Christ Jesus by the will of God according to the promise of the life which is in Christ Jesus, ²To Timothy, my beloved child:
Grace, mercy, and peace from God the Father and Christ Jesus our Lord.

Titus 1   ¹Paul, a servant of God and an apostle of Jesus Christ, to further the faith of God's elect and their knowledge of the truth which accords with godliness, ²in hope of eternal life which God, who never lies, promised ages ago ³and at the proper time manifested in his word through the preaching with which I have been entrusted by command of God our Savior; ⁴To Titus, my true child in a common faith:
Grace and peace from God the Father and Christ Jesus our Savior.

● **Rom 1:1**
Cf. 2 Cor 4:5

● **Rom 1:3–4**
1 Cor 15   ³For I delivered to you as of first importance what I also received, that Christ died for our sins in accordance with the scriptures, ⁴that he was buried, that he was raised on the third day in accordance with the scriptures, ⁵and that he appeared to Cephas, then to the twelve.

Cf. 2 Tim 2   ⁸Remember Jesus Christ, risen from the dead, descended from David, as preached in my gospel, ...

Cf. 1 Tim 3   ¹⁶Great indeed, we confess, is the mystery of our religion:
He was manifested in the flesh,
vindicated in the Spirit, seen by angels,
preached among the nations,
believed on in the world, taken up in glory.

● **Rom 1:3**
2 Cor 5   ¹⁶From now on, therefore, we regard no one from a human point of view; even though we once regarded Christ from a human point of view, we regard him thus no longer.

Cf. Gal 4:4

● **Rom 1:4**
1 Cor 15   ²⁴Then comes the end, when he delivers the kingdom to God the Father after destroying every rule and every authority and power. ²⁵For he must reign until he has put all his enemies under his feet.

Cf. Phil 3:10

● **Rom 1:5**
1 Cor 9   ¹Am I not free? Am I not an apostle? Have I not seen Jesus our Lord? Are not you my workmanship in the Lord? ²If to others I am not an apostle, at least I am to you; for you are the seal of my apostleship in the Lord.

1 Cor 15   ⁹For I am the least of the apostles, unfit to be called an apostle, because I persecuted the church of God. ¹⁰But by the grace of God I am what I am, and his grace toward me was not in vain. On the contrary, I worked harder than any of them, though it was not I, but the grace of God which is with me.

Gal 1   ¹⁵But when he who had set me apart before I was born, and had called me through his grace, ¹⁶was pleased to reveal his Son to me, in order that I might preach him among the Gentiles....

Cf. Rom 15:28; Rom 16:26; Eph 3:1–2; Col 2:24

● **Rom 1:7**
(Rome) *omit* in Rome: G. Origen

Letter Structure: Thanksgiving

[8]**First, I thank my God through Jesus Christ for all of you, because your faith is proclaimed in all the world.** [9]**For God is my witness, whom I serve with my spirit in the gospel of his Son, that without ceasing I mention you always in my prayers,** [10]**asking that somehow by God's will I may now at last succeed in coming to you.** [11]**For I long to see you, that I may impart to you some spiritual gift to strengthen you,** [12]**that is, that we may be mutually encouraged by each other's faith, both yours and mine.** [13]**I want you to know, brethren, that I have often intended to come to you (but thus far have been prevented), in order that I may reap some harvest among you as well as among the rest of the Gentiles.** [14]**I am under obligation both to Greeks and to barbarians, both to the wise and to the foolish:** [15]**so I am eager to preach the gospel to you also who are in Rome.**

Primary

1 Cor 1:4–9 (§72)

[4]I give thanks to God always for you because of the grace of God which was given you in Christ Jesus, [5]that in every way you were enriched in him with all speech and all knowledge— [6]even as the testimony to Christ was confirmed among you—[7]so that you are not lacking in any spiritual gift, as you wait for the revealing of our Lord Jesus Christ; [8]who will sustain you to the end, guiltless in the day of our Lord Jesus Christ. [9]God is faithful, by whom you were called into the fellowship of his Son, Jesus Christ our Lord.

Phil 1:3–11 (§238)

[3]I thank my God in all my remembrance of you, [4]always in every prayer of mine for you all making my prayer with joy, [5]thankful for your partnership in the gospel from the first day until now. [6]And I am sure that he who began a good work in you will bring it to completion at the day of Jesus Christ. [7]It is right for me to feel thus about you all, because I hold you in my heart, for you are all partakers with me of grace, both in my imprisonment and in the defense and confirmation of the gospel. [8]For God is my witness, how I yearn for you all with the affection of Christ Jesus. [9]And it is my prayer that your love may abound more and more, with

knowledge and all discernment, [10]so that you may approve what is excellent, and may be pure and blameless for the day of Christ, [11]filled with the fruits of righteousness which come through Jesus Christ, to the glory and praise of God.

Col 1:3–14 (§257)

[3]We always thank God, the Father of our Lord Jesus Christ, when we pray for you, [4]because we have heard of your faith in Christ Jesus and of the love which you have for all the saints, [5]because of the hope laid up for you in heaven. Of this you have heard before in the word of the truth, the gospel [6]which has come to you, as indeed in the whole world it is bearing fruit and growing—so among yourselves, from the day you heard and understood the grace of God in truth, [7]as you learned it from Epaphras our beloved fellow servant. He is a faithful minister of Christ on our behalf [8]and has made known to us your love in the Spirit.

[9]And so, from the day we heard of it, we have not ceased to pray for you, asking that you may be filled with the knowledge of his will in all spiritual wisdom and understanding, [10]to lead a life worthy of the Lord, fully pleasing to him, bearing fruit in every good work and increasing in the knowledge of God. [11]May you be strengthened with all power, according to his glorious might, for all endurance and patience with joy, [12]giving thanks to the Father, who has qualified us to share in the inheritance of the saints in light. [13]He has delivered us from the dominion of darkness and transferred us to the kingdom of his beloved Son, [14]in whom we have redemption, the forgiveness of sins.

1 Thess 1:2–10 (§276)

[2]We give thanks to God always for you all, constantly mentioning you in our prayers, [3]remembering before our God and Father your work of faith and labor of love and steadfastness of hope in our Lord Jesus Christ. [4]For we know, brethren beloved by God, that he has chosen you; [5]for our gospel came to you not only in word, but also in power and in the Holy Spirit and with full conviction. You know what kind of men we proved to be among you for your sake. [6]And you became imitators of us and of the Lord, for you received the word in much affliction, with joy inspired by the Holy Spirit; [7]so that you became an example to the all the believers in Macedonia and in Achaia. [8]For not only has the word of the Lord sounded forth

from you in Macedonia and Achaia, but your faith in God has gone forth everywhere, so that we need not say anything. [9]For they themselves report concerning us what a welcome we had among you, and how you turned to God from idols, to serve a living and true God, [10]and to wait for his Son from heaven, whom he raised from the dead, Jesus who delivers us from the wrath to come.

2 Thess 1:3–12 (§295)

[3]We are bound to give thanks to God always for you, brethren, as is fitting, because your faith is growing abundantly, and the love of every one of you for one another is increasing. [4]Therefore we ourselves boast of you in the churches of God for your steadfastness and faith in all your persecutions and in the afflictions which you are enduring.

[5]This is evidence of the righteous judgment of God, that you may be made worthy of the kingdom of God, for which you are suffering— [6]since indeed God deems it just to repay with affliction those who afflict you, [7]and to grant rest with us to you who are afflicted, when the Lord Jesus is revealed from heaven with his mighty angels in flaming fire, [8]inflicting vengeance upon those who do not know God and upon those who do not obey the gospel of our Lord Jesus. [9]They shall suffer the punishment of eternal destruction and exclusion from the presence of the Lord and from the glory of his might, [10]when he comes on that day to be glorified in his saints, and to be marveled at in all who have believed, because our testimony to you was believed. [11]To this end we always pray for you, that our God may make you worthy of his call, and may fulfil every good resolve and work of faith by his power, [12]so that the name of our Lord Jesus may be glorified in you, and you in him, according to the grace of our God and the Lord Jesus Christ.

Phlm 4–7 (§306)

[4]I thank my God always when I remember you in my prayers, [5]because I hear of your love and of the faith which you have toward the Lord Jesus and all the saints, [6]and I pray that the sharing of your faith may promote the knowledge of all the good that is ours in Christ. [7]For I have derived much joy and comfort from your love, my brother, because the hearts of the saints have been refreshed through you.

● **Rom 1:8**

1 Tim 1   [12]I thank him who has given me strength for this, Christ Jesus our Lord, because he judged me faithful by appointing me to his service, . . .

2 Tim 1   [3]I thank God whom I serve with a clear conscience, as did my fathers, when I remember you constantly in my prayers.

● **Rom 1:10**

Rom 15   [23]But now, since I no longer have any room for work in these regions, and since I have longed for many years to come to you, [24]I hope to see you in pass-

ing as I go to Spain, and to be sped on my journey there by you, once I have enjoyed your company for a little.

Rom 15   [32]so that by God's will I may come to you with joy and be refreshed in your company.

Cf. Acts 18:2

● **Rom 1:11**

Rom 12   [6]Having gifts that differ according to the grace given to us, let us use them: if prophecy, in proportion to our faith. . . .

1 Cor 12   [4]Now there are varieties of gifts, but the same Spirit. . . .

Cf. Acts 19:21

● **Rom 1:13**

Rom 15   [22]This is the reason why I have so often been hindered from coming to you.

● **Rom 1:14**

Cf. 1 Cor 9:16

● **Rom 1:15**

(Rome) *omit* in Rome: G. Origen

[16]For I am not ashamed of the gospel: it is the power of God for salvation to every one who has faith, to the Jew first and also to the Greek. [17]For in it the righteousness of God is revealed through faith for faith; as it is written, "He who through faith is righteous shall live."

PRIMARY

1 Cor 1:18–25 (§74)

[18]For the word of the cross is folly to those who are perishing, but to us who are being saved it is the power of God. [19]For it is written,

"I will destroy the wisdom of the wise,
and the cleverness of the clever I will thwart."

[20]Where is the wise man? Where is the scribe? Where is the debater of this age? Has not God made foolish the wisdom of the world? [21]For since, in the wisdom of God, the world did not know God through wisdom, it pleased God through the folly of what we preach to save those who believe. [22]For Jews demand signs and Greeks seek wisdom, [23]but we preach Christ crucified, a stumbling block to Jews and folly to Gentiles, [24]but to those who are called, both Jews and Greeks, Christ the power of God and the wisdom of God. [25]For the foolishness of God is wiser than men, and the weakness of God is stronger than men.

2 Cor 10:1–6 (§176)

[1]I, Paul, myself entreat you, by the meekness and gentleness of Christ—I who am humble when face to face with you, but bold to you when I am away!—[2]I beg of you that when I am present I may not have to show boldness with such confidence as I count on showing against some who suspect us of acting in worldly fashion. [3]For though we live in the world we are not carrying on a worldly war, [4]for the weapons of our warfare are not worldly but have divine power to destroy strongholds. [5]We destroy arguments and every proud obstacle to the knowledge of God, and take every thought captive to obey Christ, [6]being ready to punish every disobedience, when your obedience is complete.

Phil 1:12–18 (§239)

[12]I want you to know, brethren, that what has happened to me has really served to advance the gospel, [13]so that it has become known throughout the whole praetorian guard and to all the rest that my imprisonment is for Christ; [14]and most of the brethren have been made confident in the Lord because of my imprisonment, and are much more bold to speak the word of God without fear.

[15]Some indeed preach Christ from envy and rivalry, but others from good will. [16]The latter do it out of love, knowing that I am put here for the defense of the gospel; [17]the former proclaim Christ out of partisanship, not sincerely but thinking to afflict me in my imprisonment. [18]What then? Only that in every way, whether in pretense or in truth, Christ is proclaimed; and in that I rejoice.

● **Rom 1:16–17**

Cf. Rom 3 [21]But now the righteousness of God has been manifested apart from law, although the law and the prophets bear witness to it, [22]the righteousness of God through faith in Jesus Christ for all who believe. For there is no distinction; [23]since all have sinned and fall short of the glory of God, [24]they are justified by his grace as a gift, through the redemption which is in Christ Jesus, [25]whom God put forward as an expiation by his blood, to be received by faith. This was to show God's righteousness, because in his divine forbearance he had passed over former sins; [26]it was to prove at the present time that he himself is righteous and that he justifies him who has faith in Jesus.

● **Rom 1:16**

Phil 1 [20]as it is my eager expectation and hope that I shall not be at all ashamed, but that with full courage now as always Christ will be honored in my body, whether by life or by death.

2 Tim 1 [8]Do not be ashamed then of testifying to our Lord, nor of me his prisoner, but share in suffering for the gospel in the power of God, . . .

Cf. Rom 2 [9]There will be tribulation and distress for every human being who does evil, the Jew first and also the Greek, [10]but glory and honor and peace for every one who does good, the Jew first and also the Greek.

Cf. Rom 3 [9]What then? Are we Jews any better off? No, not at all; for I have already charged that all men, both Jews and Greeks, are under the power of sin. . . .

Cf. 2 Tim 1 [12]and therefore I suffer as I do. But I am not ashamed, for I know whom I have believed, and I am sure that he is able to guard until that Day what has been entrusted to me.

● **Rom 1:17**

Hab 2 [4]Behold, he whose soul is not upright in him shall fail,
but the righteous shall live by his faith.

[18]For the wrath of God is revealed from heaven against all ungodliness and wickedness of men who by their wickedness suppress the truth. [19]For what can be known about God is plain to them, because God has shown it to them. [20]Ever since the creation of the world his invisible nature, namely, his eternal power and deity, has been clearly perceived in the things that have been made. So they are without excuse; [21]for although they knew God they did not honor him as God or give thanks to him, but they became futile in their thinking and their senseless minds were darkened. [22]Claiming to be wise, they became fools, [23]and exchanged the glory of the immortal God for images resembling mortal man or birds or animals or reptiles.

PRIMARY

1 Cor 3:18–23 (§82)

[18]Let no one deceive himself. If any one among you thinks that he is wise in this age, let him become a fool that he may become wise. [19]For the wisdom of this world is folly with God. For it is written, "He catches the wise in their craftiness," [20]and again, "The Lord knows that the thoughts of the wise are futile." [21]So let no one boast of men. For all things are yours, [22]whether Paul or Apollos or Cephas or the world or life or death or the present or the future, all are yours; [23]and you are Christ's; and Christ is God's.

1 Cor 1:18–25 (§74)

[18]For the word of the cross is folly to those who are perishing, but to us who are being saved it is the power of God. [19]For it is written,
"I will destroy the wisdom of the wise,
and the cleverness of the clever I will
thwart."
[20]Where is the wise man? Where is the scribe? Where is the debater of this age? Has not God made foolish the wisdom of the world? [21]For since, in the wisdom of God, the world did not know God through wisdom, it pleased God through the folly of what we preach to save those who believe. [22]For Jews demand signs and Greeks seek wisdom, [23]but we preach Christ crucified, a stumbling block to Jews and folly to Gentiles, [24]but to those who are called, both Jews and Greeks, Christ the power of God and the wisdom of God. [25]For the foolishness of God is wiser than men, and the weakness of God is stronger than men.

2 Cor 11:16–21a (§182)

[16]I repeat, let no one think me foolish; but

even if you do, accept me as a fool, so that I too may boast a little. [17](What I am saying I say not with the Lord's authority but as a fool, in this boastful confidence; [18]since many boast of worldly things, I too will boast.) [19]For you gladly bear with fools, being wise yourselves! [20]For you bear it if a man makes slaves of you, or preys upon you, or takes advantage of you, or puts on airs, or strikes you in the face. [21]To my shame, I must say, we were too weak for that!

Gal 4:8–11 (§208)

[8]Formerly, when you did not know God, you were in bondage to beings that by nature are no gods; [9]but now that you have come to know God, or rather to be known by God, how can you turn back again to the weak and beggarly elemental spirits, whose slaves you want to be once more? [10]You observe days, and months, and seasons, and years! [11]I am afraid I have labored over you in vain.

Eph 3:1–13 (§222)

[1]For this reason I, Paul, a prisoner for Christ Jesus on behalf of you Gentiles—[2]assuming that you have heard of the stewardship of God's grace that was given to me for you, [3]how the mystery was made known to me by revelation, as I have written briefly. [4]When you read this you can perceive my insight into the mystery of Christ, [5]which was not made known to the sons of men in other generations as it has now been revealed to his holy apostles and prophets by the Spirit; [6]that is, how the Gentiles are fellow heirs, members of the same body, and partakers of the promise in Christ Jesus through the gospel. [7]Of this gospel I was made a minister according to the gift of God's grace which was given me by the working of his power. [8]To me, though I am the very least of all the saints, this grace was given, to preach to the Gentiles the unsearchable riches of Christ, [9]and to make all men see what is the plan of the mystery hidden for ages in God who created all things; [10]that through the church the manifold wisdom of God might now be made known to the principalities and powers in the heavenly places. [11]This was according to the eternal purpose which he has realized in Christ Jesus our Lord, [12]in whom we have boldness and confidence of access through our faith in him. [13]So I ask you not to lose heart over what I am suffering for you, which is your glory.

Col 1:24–2:3 (§260)

[24]Now I rejoice in my sufferings for your sake, and in my flesh I complete what is lacking in Christ's afflictions for the sake of his body,

that is, the church, [25]of which I became a minister according to the divine office which was given to me for you, to make the word of God fully known, [26]the mystery hidden for ages and generations but now made manifest to his saints. [27]To them God chose to make known how great among the Gentiles are the riches of the glory of this mystery, which is Christ in you, the hope of glory. [28]Him we proclaim warning every man and teaching every man in all wisdom, that we may present every man mature in Christ. [29]For this I toil, striving with all the energy which he mightily inspires within me.

2 [1]For I want you to know how greatly I strive for you, and for those at Laodicea, and for all who have not seen my face, [2]that their hearts may be encouraged as they are knit together in love, to have all the riches of assured understanding and the knowledge of God's mystery, of Christ, [3]in whom are hid all the treasures of wisdom and knowledge.

2 Thess 2:1–12 (§296)

[1]Now concerning the coming of our Lord Jesus Christ and our assembling to meet him, we beg you, brethren, [2]not to be quickly shaken in mind or excited, either by spirit or by word, or by letter purporting to be from us, to the effect that the day of the Lord has come. [3]Let no one deceive you in any way; for that day will not come, unless the rebellion comes first, and the man of lawlessness is revealed, the son of perdition, [4]who opposes and exalts himself against every so-called god or object of worship, so that he takes his seat in the temple of God, proclaiming himself to be God. [5]Do you not remember that when I was still with you I told you this? [6]And do you know what is restraining him now so that he may be revealed in his time. [7]For the mystery of lawlessness is already at work; only he who now restrains it will do so until he is out of the way. [8]And then the lawless one will be revealed, and the Lord Jesus will slay him with the breath of his mouth and destroy him by his appearing and his coming. [9]The coming of the lawless one by the activity of Satan will be with all power and with pretended signs and wonders, [10]and with all wicked deception for those who are to perish, because they refused to love the truth and so be saved. [11]Therefore God sends upon them a strong delusion, to make them believe what is false, [12]so that all may be condemned who did not believe the truth but had pleasure in unrighteousness.

● **Rom 1:18–23**
1 Thess 1   [9]For they themselves report concerning us what a welcome we had among you, and how you turned to God from idols, to serve a living and true God, [10]and to wait for his Son from heaven, whom he raised from the dead, Jesus who delivers us from the wrath to come.

Cf. 1 Thess 2:16; 2 Thess 1:7–8; 1 Cor 4:10

● **Rom 1:18**
Cf. 1 Thess 5:9; Acts 3:26; Acts 18:6

(God) *omit* God: Marcion.

● **Rom 1:19–20**
Cf. Rom 16:25–26

● **Rom 1:20**
Cf. 1 Tim 1:17

● **Rom 1:22**
Cf. Eph 5:15

● **Rom 1:23**
Acts 17   [29]"Being then God's offspring, we ought not to think that the Deity is like gold, or silver, or stone, a representation by the art and imagination of man."

24 Therefore God gave them up in the lusts of their hearts to impurity, to the dishonoring of their bodies among themselves, 25 because they exchanged the truth about God for a lie and worshiped and served the creature rather than the Creator, who is blessed for ever! Amen.

26 For this reason God gave them up to dishonorable passions. Their women exchanged natural relations for unnatural, 27 and the men likewise gave up natural relations with women and were consumed with passion for one another, men committing shameless acts with men and receiving in their own persons the due penalty for their error.

28 And since they did not see fit to acknowledge God, God gave them up to a base mind and to improper conduct.

PRIMARY

1 Cor 5:1–5 (§87)

1 It is actually reported that there is immorality among you, and of a kind that is not found even among pagans; for a man is living with his father's wife. 2 And you are arrogant! Ought you not rather to mourn? Let him who has done this be removed from among you.

3 For though absent in body I am present in spirit, and as if present, I have already pronounced judgment 4 in the name of the Lord Jesus on the man who has done such a thing. When you are assembled, and my spirit is present, with the power of our Lord Jesus, 5 you are to deliver this man to Satan for the destruction of the flesh, that his spirit may be saved in the day of the Lord Jesus.

1 Cor 5:9–13 (§89)

9 I wrote to you in my letter not to associate with immoral men; 10 not at all meaning the immoral of this world, or the greedy and robbers, or idolaters, since then you would need to go out of the world. 11 But rather I wrote to you not to associate with any one who bears the name of brother if he is guilty of immorality or greed, or is an idolater, reviler, drunkard, or robber—not even to eat with such a one. 12 For

what have I to do with judging outsiders? Is it not those inside the church whom you are to judge? 13 God judges those outside. "Drive out the wicked person from among you."

1 Cor 6:9–11 (§91)

9 Do you not know that the unrighteous will not inherit the kingdom of God? Do not be deceived; neither the immoral, nor idolaters, nor adulterers, nor sexual perverts, 10 nor thieves, nor the greedy, nor drunkards, nor revilers, nor robbers will inherit the kingdom of God. 11 And such were some of you. But you were washed, you were sanctified, you were justified in the name of the Lord Jesus Christ and in the Spirit of our God.

1 Cor 6:12–20 (§92)

12 "All things are lawful for me," but not all things are helpful. "All things are lawful for me," but I will not be enslaved by anything. 13 "Food is meant for the stomach and the stomach for food"—and God will destroy both one and the other. The body is not meant for immorality, but for the Lord, and the Lord for the body. 14 And God raised the Lord and will also raise us up by his power. 15 Do you not know that your bodies are members of Christ? Shall I therefore take the members of Christ and make them members of a prostitute? Never! 16 Do you not know that he who joins himself to a prostitute becomes one body with her? For, as it is written, "The two shall become one flesh." 17 But he who is united to the Lord becomes one spirit with him. 18 Shun immorality. Every other sin which a man commits is outside the body; but the immoral man sins against his own body. 19 Do you not know that your body is a temple of the Holy Spirit within you, which you have from God? You are not your own; 20 you were bought with a price. So glorify God in your body.

1 Thess 4:1–8 (§284)

1 Finally, brethren, we beseech and exhort you in the Lord Jesus, that as you learned from us how you ought to live and to please God, just as you are doing, you do so more and more. 2 For you know what instructions we gave you

through the Lord Jesus. 3 For this is the will of God, your sanctification: that you abstain from unchastity; 4 that each one of you know how to take a wife for himself in holiness and honor 5 not in the passion of lust like heathen who do not know God; 6 that no man transgress, and wrong his brother in this matter, because the Lord is an avenger in all these things, as we solemnly forewarned you. 7 For God has not called us for uncleanness, but in holiness. 8 Therefore whoever disregards this, disregards not man but God, who gives his Holy Spirit to you.

2 Thess 2:1–12 (§296)

1 Now concerning the coming of our Lord Jesus Christ and our assembling to meet him, we beg you, brethren, 2 not to be quickly shaken in mind or excited, either by spirit or by word, or by letter purporting to be from us, to the effect that the day of the Lord has come. 3 Let no one deceive you in any way; for that day will not come, unless the rebellion comes first, and the man of lawlessness is revealed, the son of perdition, 4 who opposes and exalts himself against every so-called god or object of worship, so that he takes his seat in the temple of God, proclaiming himself to be God. 5 Do you not remember that when I was still with you I told you this? 6 And you know what is restraining him now so that he may be revealed in his time. 7 For the mystery of lawlessness is already at work; only he who now restrains it will do so until he is out of the way. 8 And then the lawless one will be revealed, and the Lord Jesus will slay him with the breath of his mouth and destroy him by his appearing and his coming. 9 The coming of the lawless one by the activity of Satan will be with all power and with pretended signs and wonders, 10 and with all wicked deception for those who are to perish, because they refused to love the truth and so be saved. 11 Therefore God sends upon them a strong delusion, to make them believe what is false, 12 so that all may be condemned who did not believe the truth but had pleasure in unrighteousness.

● **Rom 1:24–28**
Cf. Rom 12   1 I appeal to you therefore, brethren, by the mercies of God, to present your bodies as a living sacrifice, holy and acceptable to God, which is your spiritual worship. 2 Do not be conformed to this world but be transformed by the renewal of your mind, that you may prove what is the will of God, what is good and acceptable and perfect.

● **Rom 1:24–25**
Rom 8   20 for the creation was subjected to futility, not of its own will but by the will of him who subjected it in hope; 21 because the creation itself will be set free from its bondage to decay and obtain the glorious liberty of the children of God. 22 We know that the

whole creation has been groaning in travail together until now; 23 and not only the creation, but we ourselves, who have the first fruits of the Spirit, groan inwardly as we wait for adoption as sons, the redemption of our bodies.

● **Rom 1:25**
1 Cor 8   6 yet for us there is one God, the Father, from whom are all things and for whom we exist, and one Lord, Jesus Christ, through whom are all things and through whom we exist.

Acts 17   24 The God who made the world and everything in it, being Lord of heaven and earth, does not live in shrines made by man. . . .

Cf. Eph 3   9 and to make all men see what is the plan of the mystery hidden for ages in God who created all things. . . .

Cf. Col 1   15 He is the image of the invisible God, the first-born of all creation; 16 for in him all things were created, in heaven and on earth, visible and invisible, whether thrones or dominions or principalities or authorities—all things were created through him and for him.

● **Rom 1:28**
Cf. Eph 5   10 and try to learn what is pleasing to the Lord.

FORMAL ELEMENT: VICE LIST

[29]**They were filled with all manner of wickedness, evil, covetousness, malice. Full of envy, murder, strife, deceit, malignity, they are gossips,** [30]**slanderers, haters of God, insolent, haughty, boastful, inventors of evil, disobedient to parents,** [31]**foolish, faithless, heartless, ruthless.** [32]**Though they know God's decree that those who do such things deserve to die, they not only do them but approve those who practice them.**

PRIMARY

1 Cor 5:9–13 (§89)

[9]I wrote to you in my letter not to associate with immoral men; [10]not at all meaning the immoral of this world, or the greedy and robbers, or idolaters, since then you would need to go out of the world. [11]But rather I wrote to you not to associate with any one who bears the name of brother if he is guilty of immorality or greed, or is an idolater, reviler, drunkard, or robber—not even to eat with such a one. [12]For what have I to do with judging outsiders? Is it not those inside the church whom you are to judge? [13]God judges those outside. "Drive out the wicked person from among you."

1 Cor 6:9–11 (§91)

[9]Do you not know that the unrighteous will not inherit the kingdom of God? Do not be deceived; neither the immoral, nor idolaters, nor adulterers, nor sexual perverts, [10]nor thieves, nor the greedy, nor drunkards, nor revilers, nor robbers will inherit the kingdom of God. [11]And such were some of you. But you were washed, you were sanctified, you were justified in the name of the Lord Jesus Christ and in the Spirit of our God.

2 Cor 12:19–21 (§188)

[19]Have you been thinking all along that we have been defending ourselves before you? It is in the sight of God that we have been speaking in Christ, and all for your upbuilding, beloved. [20]For I fear that perhaps I may come and find you not what I wish, and that you may find me not what you wish; that perhaps there may be quarreling, jealousy, anger, selfishness, slander, gossip, conceit, and disorder. [21]I fear that when I come again my God may humble me before you, and I may have to mourn over many of those who sinned before and have not repented of the impurity, immorality, and licentiousness which they have practiced.

Gal 5:16–26 (§213)

[16]But I say, walk by the Spirit, and do not gratify the desires of the flesh. [17]For the desires of the flesh are against the Spirit, and the desires of the Spirit are against the flesh; for these are opposed to each other, to prevent you from doing what you would. [18]But if you are led by the Spirit you are not under the law. [19]Now the works of the flesh are plain: fornication, impurity, licentiousness, [20]idolatry, sorcery, enmity, strife, jealousy, anger, selfishness, dissension, party spirit, [21]envy, drunkenness, carousing, and the like. I warn you, as I warned you before, that those who do such things shall not inherit the kingdom of God. [22]But the fruit of the Spirit is love, joy, peace, patience, kindness, goodness, faithfulness, [23]gentleness, self-control; against such there is no law. [24]And those who belong to Christ Jesus have crucified the flesh with its passions and desires.

[25]If we live by the Spirit, let us also walk by the Spirit. [26]Let us have no self-conceit, no provoking of one another, no envy of one another.

Eph 4:17–24 (§227)

[17]Now this I affirm and testify in the Lord, that you must no longer live as the Gentiles do, in the futility of their minds; [18]they are darkened in their understanding, alienated from the life of God because of the ignorance that is in them, due to their hardness of heart; [19]they have become callous and have given themselves up to licentiousness, greedy to practice every kind of uncleanness. [20]You did not so learn Christ!— [21]assuming that you have heard about him and were taught in him, as the truth is in Jesus. [22]Put off your old nature which belongs to your former manner of life and is corrupt through deceitful lusts, [23]and be renewed in the spirit of your minds, [24]and put on the new nature, created after the likeness of God in true righteousness and holiness.

Eph 4:25–32 (§228)

[25]Therefore, putting away falsehood, let every one speak the truth with his neighbor, for we are members one of another. [26]Be angry but do not sin; do not let the sun go down on your anger, [27]and give no opportunity to the devil. [28]Let the thief no longer steal, but rather let him labor, doing honest work with his hands, so that he may be able to give to those in need. [29]Let no evil talk come out of your mouths, but only such as is good for edifying, as fits the occasion, that it may impart grace to those who hear. [30]And do not grieve the Holy Spirit of God, in whom you were sealed for the day of redemption. [31]Let all bitterness and wrath and anger and clamor and slander be put away from you, with all malice, [32]and be kind to one another, tenderhearted, forgiving one another, as God in Christ forgave you.

Eph 5:3–14 (§230)

[3]But fornication and all impurity or covetousness must not even be named among you, as is fitting among saints. [4]Let there be no filthiness, nor silly talk, nor levity, which are not fitting; but instead let there be thanksgiving. [5]Be sure of this, that no fornicator or impure man, or one who is covetous (that is, an idolater), has any inheritance in the kingdom of Christ and of God. [6]Let no one deceive you with empty words, for it is because of these things that the wrath of God comes upon the sons of disobedience. [7]Therefore do not associate with them, [8]for once you were darkness, but now you are light in the Lord; walk as children of light [9](for the fruit of light is found in all that is good and right and true), [10]and try to learn what is pleasing to the Lord. [11]Take no part in the unfruitful works of darkness, but instead expose them. [12]For it is a shame even to speak of the things that they do in secret; [13]but when anything is exposed by the light it becomes visible, for anything that becomes visible is light. [14]Therefore it is said,

> "Awake, O sleeper, and arise from the dead,
> and Christ shall give you light."

Col 3:5–11 (§266)

[5]Put to death therefore what is earthly in you: fornication, impurity, passion, evil desire, and covetousness, which is idolatry. [6]On account of these the wrath of God is coming. [7]In these you once walked, when you lived in them. [8]But now put them all away: anger, wrath, malice, slander, and foul talk from your mouth. [9]Do not lie to one another, seeing that you have put off the old nature with its practices [10]and have put on the new nature, which is being renewed in knowledge after the image of its creator. [11]Here there cannot be Greek and Jew, circumcised and uncircumcised, barbarian, Scythian, slave, free man, but Christ is all, and in all.

• **Rom 1:29–32**

1 Tim 1   [9]understanding this, that the law is not laid down for the just but for the lawless and disobedient, for the ungodly and sinners, for the unholy and profane, for murderers of fathers and murderers of mothers, for manslayers, [10]immoral persons, sodomites, kidnappers, liars, perjurers, and whatever else is contrary to sound doctrine, . . .

Cf. 1 Tim 6   [4]he is puffed up with conceit, he knows nothing; he has a morbid craving for controversy and for disputes about words, which produce envy, dissension, slander, base suspicions, [5]and wrangling among men who are depraved in mind and bereft of the truth, imagining that godliness is a means of gain.

Cf. 2 Tim 3   [2]For men will be lovers of self, lovers of money, proud, arrogant, abusive, disobedient to their parents, ungrateful, unholy, [3]inhuman, implacable, slanderers, profligates, fierce, haters of good, [4]treacherous, reckless, swollen with conceit, lovers of pleasure rather than lovers of God, . . .

Cf. Titus 3   [3]For we ourselves were once foolish, disobedient, led astray, slaves to various passions and pleasures, passing our days in malice and envy, hated by men and hating one another; . . .

Cf. 1 Pet 4   [3]Let the time that is past suffice for doing what the Gentiles like to do, living in licentiousness, passions, drunkenness, revels, carousing, and lawless idolatry.

Cf. Rom 13:11–14

• **Rom 1:32**

Cf. Rom 5:16; Rom 5:18; Rom 8:4

2 Therefore you have no excuse, O man, whoever you are, when you judge another; for in passing judgment upon him you condemn yourself, because you, the judge, are doing the very same things. ²We know that the judgment of God rightly falls upon those who do such things. ³Do you suppose, O man, that when you judge those who do such things and yet do them yourself, you will escape the judgment of God? ⁴Or do you presume upon the riches of his kindness and forbearance and patience? Do you not know that God's kindness is meant to lead you to repentance? ⁵But by your hard and impenitent heart you are storing up wrath for yourself on the day of wrath when God's righteous judgment will be revealed.

PRIMARY

1 Cor 4:1–5 (§83)

¹This is how one should regard us, as servants of Christ and stewards of the mysteries of God. ²Moreover it is required of stewards that they be found trustworthy. ³But with me it is a very small thing that I should be judged by you or by any human court. I do not even judge myself. ⁴I am not aware of anything against myself, but I am not thereby acquitted. It is the Lord who judges me. ⁵Therefore do not pronounce judgment before the time, before the Lord comes, who will bring to light the things now hidden in darkness and will disclose the purposes of the heart. Then every man will receive his commendation from God.

1 Cor 5:1–5 (§87)

¹It is actually reported that there is immorality among you, and of a kind that is not found even among pagans; for a man is living with his father's wife. ²And you are arrogant! Ought you not rather to mourn? Let him who has done this be removed from among you.

³For though absent in body I am present in spirit, and as if present, I have already pro-

nounced judgment ⁴in the name of the Lord Jesus on the man who has done such a thing. When you are assembled, and my spirit is present, with the power of our Lord Jesus, ⁵you are to deliver this man to Satan for the destruction of the flesh, that his spirit may be saved in the day of the Lord Jesus.

1 Cor 6:1–8 (§90)

¹When one of you has a grievance against a brother, does he dare go to law before the unrighteous instead of the saints? ²Do you not know that the saints will judge the world? And if the world is to be judged by you, are you incompetent to try trivial cases? ³Do you not know that we are to judge angels? How much more, matters pertaining to this life! ⁴If then you have such cases, why do you lay them before those who are least esteemed by the church? ⁵I say this to your shame. Can it be that there is no man among you wise enough to decide between members of the brotherhood, ⁶but brother goes to law against brother, and that before unbelievers?

⁷To have lawsuits at all with one another is defeat for you. Why not rather suffer wrong? Why not rather be defrauded? ⁸But you yourselves wrong and defraud, and that even your own brethren.

2 Cor 2:5–11 (§151)

⁵But if any one has caused pain, he has caused it not to me, but in some measure—not to put it too severely— to you all. ⁶For such a one this punishment by the majority is enough; ⁷so you should rather turn to forgive and comfort him, or he may be overwhelmed by excessive sorrow. ⁸So I beg you to reaffirm your love for him. ⁹For this is why I wrote, that I might test you and know whether you are obedient in everything. ¹⁰Any one whom you forgive, I also forgive. What I have forgiven, if I have forgiven anything, has been for your sake in the presence of Christ, ¹¹to keep Satan from gaining the advantage over us; for we are not ignorant of his designs.

Gal 2:11–14 (§198)

¹¹But when Cephas came to Antioch I opposed him to his face, because he stood condemned. ¹²For before certain men came from James, he ate with the Gentiles; but when they came he drew back and separated himself, fearing the circumcision party. ¹³And with him the rest of the Jews acted insincerely, so that even Barnabas was carried away by their insincerity. ¹⁴But when I saw that they were not straightforward about the truth of the gospel, I said to Cephas before them all, "If you, though a Jew, live like a Gentile and not like a Jew, how can you compel the Gentiles to live like Jews?"

Phil 3:17–21 (§249)

¹⁷Brethren, join in imitating me, and mark those who so live as you have an example in us. ¹⁸For many, of whom I have often told you and now tell you even with tears, live as enemies of the cross of Christ. ¹⁹Their end is destruction, their god is the belly, and they glory in their shame, with minds set on earthly things. ²⁰But our commonwealth is in heaven, and from it we await a Savior, the Lord Jesus Christ, ²¹who will change our lowly body to be like his glorious body, by the power which enables him even to subject all things to himself.

Col 2:16–19 (§263)

¹⁶Therefore let no one pass judgment on you in questions of food and drink or with regard to a festival or a new moon or a sabbath. ¹⁷These are only a shadow of what is to come; but the substance belongs to Christ. ¹⁸Let no one disqualify you, insisting on self-abasement and worship of angels, taking his stand on visions, puffed up without reason by his sensuous mind, ¹⁹and not holding fast to the Head, from whom the whole body, nourished and knit together through its joints and ligaments, grows with a growth that is from God.

● **Rom 2:1–5**
Rom 14   ³Let not him who eats despise him who abstains, and let not him who abstains pass judgment on him who eats; for God has welcomed him. ⁴Who are you to pass judgment on the servant of another? It is before his own master that he stands or falls. And he will be upheld, for the Master is able to make him stand.

Rom 14   ¹⁰Why do you pass judgment on your brother? Or you, why do you despise your brother? For we shall all stand before the judgment seat of God;

● **Rom 2:1**
Cf. 1 Cor 6   ¹When one of you has a grievance against a brother, does he dare go to law before the unrighteous instead of the saints? ²Do you not know that the saints will judge the world? And if the world is to be judged by you, are you incompetent to try trivial cases? ³Do you not know that we are to judge angels? How much more, matters pertaining to this life!

Cf. 1 Cor 5   ¹²For what have I to do with judging outsiders? Is it not those inside the church whom you are to judge? ¹³God judges those outside. "Drive out the wicked person from among you."

Cf. 1 Cor 2   ¹⁵"The spiritual man judges all things, but is himself to be judged by no one. known the mind of the Lord so as to instruct him?" But we have the mind of Christ.

● **Rom 2:4**
Cf. 1 Tim 1   ¹⁶but I received mercy for this reason, that in me, as the foremost, Jesus Christ might display his perfect patience for an example to those who were to believe in him for eternal life.

Cf. Titus 3   ⁴but when the goodness and loving kindness of God our Savior appeared, ⁵he saved us, not because of deeds done by us in righteousness, but in virtue of his own mercy, . . .

Cf. 2 Tim 2   ²⁴And the Lord's servant must not be quarrelsome but kindly to every one, an apt teacher, forbearing, ²⁵correcting his opponents with gentleness.

Cf. 2 Cor 7   ⁹As it is, I rejoice, not because you were grieved, but because you were grieved into repenting; for you felt a godly grief, so that you suffered no loss through us. ¹⁰For godly grief produces a repentance that leads to salvation and brings no regret, but worldly grief produces death.

● **Rom 2:5**
Cf. Eph 5   ⁶Let no one deceive you with empty words, for it is because of these things that the wrath of God comes upon the sons of disobedience.

⁶For he will render to every man according to his works: ⁷to those who by patience in well-doing seek for glory and honor and immortality, he will give eternal life; ⁸but for those who are factious and do not obey the truth, but obey wickedness, there will be wrath and fury. ⁹There will be tribulation and distress for every human being who does evil, the Jew first and also the Greek, ¹⁰but glory and honor and peace for every one who does good, the Jew first and also the Greek. ¹¹For God shows no partiality.

PRIMARY

1 Cor 3:10–15 (§80)

¹⁰According to the grace of God given to me, like a skilled master builder I laid a foundation, and another man is building upon it. Let each man take care how he builds upon it. ¹¹For no other foundation can any one lay than that which is laid, which is Jesus Christ. ¹²Now if any one builds on the foundation with gold, silver, precious stones, wood, hay, straw— ¹³each man's work will become manifest; for the Day will disclose it, because it will be revealed with fire, and the fire will test what sort of work each one has done. ¹⁴If the work which any man has built on the foundation survives, he will receive a reward. ¹⁵If any man's work is burned up, he will suffer loss, though he himself will be saved, but only as through fire.

Phil 3:17–21 (§249)

¹⁷Brethren, join in imitating me, and mark those who so live as you have an example in us. ¹⁸For many, of whom I have often told you and now tell you even with tears, live as enemies of the cross of Christ. ¹⁹Their end is destruction, their god is the belly, and they glory in their shame, with minds set on earthly things. ²⁰But our commonwealth is in heaven, and from it we await a Savior, the Lord Jesus Christ, ²¹who will change our lowly body to be like his glorious body, by the power which enables him even to subject all things to himself.

1 Thess 4:1–8 (§284)

¹Finally, brethren, we beseech and exhort you in the Lord Jesus, that as you learned from us how you ought to live and to please God, just as you are doing, you do so more and more. ²For you know what instructions we gave you through the Lord Jesus. ³For this is the will of God, your sanctification: that you abstain from unchastity; ⁴that each one of you know how to take a wife for himself in holiness and honor ⁵not in the passion of lust like heathen who do not know God; ⁶that no man transgress, and wrong his brother in this matter, because the Lord is an avenger in all these things, as we solemnly forewarned you. ⁷For God has not called us for uncleanness, but in holiness. ⁸Therefore whoever disregards this, disregards not man but God, who gives his Holy Spirit to you.

2 Thess 1:3–12 (§295)

³We are bound to give thanks to God always for you, brethren, as is fitting, because your faith is growing abundantly, and the love of every one of you for one another is increasing. ⁴Therefore we ourselves boast of you in the churches of God for your steadfastness and faith in all your persecutions and in the afflictions which you are enduring.

⁵This is evidence of the righteous judgment of God, that you may be made worthy of the kingdom of God, for which you are suffering— ⁶since indeed God deems it just to repay with affliction those who afflict you, ⁷and to grant rest with us to you who are afflicted, when the Lord Jesus is revealed from heaven with his mighty angels in flaming fire, ⁸ inflicting vengeance upon those who do not know God and upon those who do not obey the gospel of our Lord Jesus. ⁹They shall suffer the punishment of eternal destruction and exclusion from the presence of the Lord and from the glory of his might, ¹⁰when he comes on that day to be glorified in his saints, and to be marveled at in all who have believed, because our testimony to you was believed. ¹¹To this end we always pray for you, that our God may make you worthy of his call, and may fulfil every good resolve and work of faith by his power, ¹²so that the name of our Lord Jesus may be glorified in you, and you in him, according to the grace of our God and the Lord Jesus Christ.

● **Rom 2:6–11**
Cf. 2 Cor 11   ¹⁵So it is not strange if his servants also disguise themselves as servants of righteousness. Their end will correspond to their deeds.

Cf. Eph 2   ⁸For by grace you have been saved through faith; and this is not your own doing, it is the gift of God— ⁹not because of works, lest any man should boast. ¹⁰For we are his workmanship, created in Christ Jesus for good works, which God prepared beforehand, that we should walk in them.

Cf. Eph 6   ⁸knowing that whatever good any one does, he will receive the same again from the Lord, whether he is a slave or free.

● **Rom 2:6**
2 Cor 5   ¹⁰For we must all appear before the judgment seat of Christ, so that each one may receive good or evil, according to what he has done in the body.

● **Rom 2:7**
2 Tim 1   ¹⁰and now has manifested through the appearing of our Savior Christ Jesus, who abolished death and brought life and immortality to light through the gospel.

● **Rom 2:8**
1 Cor 1   ¹⁰I appeal to you, brethren, by the name of our Lord Jesus Christ, that all of you agree and that

there be no dissensions among you, but that you be united in the same mind and the same judgment. ¹¹For it has been reported to me by Chloe's people that there is quarreling among you, my brethren.

Cf. Gal 1   ⁶I am astonished that you are so quickly deserting him who called you in the grace of Christ and turning to a different gospel— ⁷not that there is another gospel, but there are some who trouble you and want to pervert the gospel of Christ. ⁸But even if we, or an angel from heaven, should preach to you a gospel contrary to that which we preached to you, let him be accursed. ⁹As we have said before, so now I say again, If any one is preaching to you a gospel contrary to that which you received, let him be accursed.

Phil 1   ¹⁵Some indeed preach Christ from envy and rivalry, but others from good will. ¹⁶The latter do it out of love, knowing that I am put here for the defense of the gospel; ¹⁷the former proclaim Christ out of partisanship, not sincerely but thinking to afflict me in my imprisonment.

Cf. 2 Tim 4   ¹⁴Alexander the coppersmith did me great harm; the Lord will requite him for his deeds.

● **Rom 2:9–10**
Rom 3   ⁹What then? Are we Jews any better off? No, not at all; for I have already charged that all men, both Jews and Greeks, are under the power of sin, . . .

Rom 3   ²²the righteousness of God through faith in Jesus Christ for all who believe. For there is no distinction; . . .

2 Cor 10   ³For though we live in the world we are not carrying on a worldly war, ⁴for the weapons of our warfare are not worldly but have divine power to destroy strongholds. ⁵We destroy arguments and every proud obstacle to the knowledge of God, and take every thought captive to obey Christ, ⁶being ready to punish every disobedience, when your obedience is complete.

2 Thess 2   ⁷For the mystery of lawlessness is already at work; only he who now restrains it will do so until he is out of the way. ⁸And then the lawless one will be revealed, and the Lord Jesus will slay him with the breath of his mouth and destroy him by his appearing and his coming.

Cf. Rom 1   ¹⁶For I am not ashamed of the gospel: it is the power of God for salvation to every one who has faith, to the Jew first and also to the Greek.

● **Rom 2:9**
Acts 10   ³⁴And Peter opened his mouth and said: "Truly I perceive that God shows no partiality. . . ."

¹²All who have sinned without the law will also perish without the law, and all who have sinned under the law will be judged by the law. ¹³For it is not the hearers of the law who are righteous before God, but the doers of the law who will be justified. ¹⁴When Gentiles who have not the law do by nature what the law requires, they are a law to themselves, even though they do not have the law. ¹⁵They show that what the law requires is written on their hearts, while their conscience also bears witness and their conflicting thoughts accuse or perhaps excuse them ¹⁶on that day when, according to my gospel, God judges the secrets of men by Christ Jesus.

Primary

1 Cor 4:1–5 (§83)

¹This is how one should regard us, as servants of Christ and stewards of the mysteries of God. ²Moreover it is required of stewards that they be found trustworthy. ³But with me it is a very small thing that I should be judged by you or by any human court. I do not even judge myself. ⁴I am not aware of anything against myself, but I am not thereby acquitted. It is the Lord who judges me. ⁵Therefore do not pronounce judgment before the time, before the Lord comes, who will bring to light the things now hidden in darkness and will disclose the purposes of the heart. Then every man will receive his commendation from God.

1 Cor 8:7–13 (§104)

⁷However, not all possess this knowledge. But some, through being hitherto accustomed to idols, eat food as really offered to an idol; and their conscience, being weak, is defiled. ⁸Food will not commend us to God. We are no worse off if we do not eat, and no better off if we do. ⁹Only take care lest this liberty of yours somehow become a stumbling block to the weak. ¹⁰For if any one sees you, a man of knowledge, at table in an idol's temple, might he not be encouraged, if his conscience is weak, to eat food offered to idols? ¹¹And so by your knowledge this weak man is destroyed, the brother for whom Christ died. ¹²Thus, sinning against your brethren and wounding their conscience when it is weak, you sin against Christ. ¹³Therefore, if food is a cause of my brother's falling, I will never eat meat, lest I cause my brother to fall.

1 Cor 9:19–23 (§107)

¹⁹For though I am free from all men, I have made myself a slave to all, that I might win the more. ²⁰To the Jews I became as a Jew, in order to win Jews; to those under the law I became as one under the law—though not being myself under the law—that I might win those under the law. ²¹To those outside the law I became as one outside the law—not being without law toward God but under the law of Christ—that I might win those outside the law. ²²To the weak I became weak, that I might win the weak. I have become all things to all men, that I might by all means save some. ²³I do it all for the sake of the gospel, that I may share in its blessings.

1 Cor 10:23–11:1 (§111)

²³"All things are lawful," but not all things are helpful. "All things are lawful," but not all things build up. ²⁴Let no one seek his own good, but the good of his neighbor. ²⁵Eat whatever is sold in the meat market without raising any question on the ground of conscience. ²⁶For "the earth is the Lord's, and everything in it." ²⁷If one of the unbelievers invites you to dinner and you are disposed to go, eat whatever is set before you without raising any question on the ground of conscience. ²⁸(But if some one says to you, "This has been offered in sacrifice," then out of consideration for the man who informed you, and for conscience' sake— ²⁹I mean his conscience, not yours—do not eat it.) For why should my liberty be determined by another man's scruples? ³⁰If I partake with thankfulness, why am I denounced because of that for which I give thanks?

³¹So, whether you eat or drink, or whatever you do, do all to the glory of God. ³²Give no offense to Jews or to Greeks or to the church of God, ³³just as I try to please all men in everything I do, not seeking my own advantage, but that of many, that they may be saved. 11 ¹Be imitators of me, as I am of Christ.

● **Rom 2:12–16**

Rom 13 ⁵Therefore one must be subject, not only to avoid God's wrath but also for the sake of conscience.

Cf. Rom 13 ⁸Owe no one anything, except to love one another; for he who loves his neighbor has fulfilled the law. ⁹The commandments, "You shall not commit adultery, You shall not kill, You shall not steal, You shall not covet," and any other commandment, are summed up in this sentence, "You shall love your neighbor as yourself." ¹⁰Love does no wrong to a neighbor; therefore love is the fulfilling of the law.

Cf. 2 Cor 3 ³and you show that you are a letter from Christ delivered by us, written not with ink but with the Spirit of the living God, not on tablets of stone but on tablets of human hearts.

Cf. Gal 5 ¹³For you were called to freedom, brethren; only do not use your freedom as an opportunity for the flesh, but through love be servants of one another. ¹⁴For the whole law is fulfilled in one word, "You shall love your neighbor as yourself."

● **Rom 2:13ff.**

Acts 10 ³⁵". . . but in every nation any one who fears him and does what is right is acceptable to him."

Cf. Heb 8 ¹⁰I will put my laws into their minds,
and write them on their hearts,
and I will be their God,
and they shall be my people.

Cf. Heb 10 ¹⁶"This is the covenant that I will make with them
after those days, says the Lord:
I will put my laws on their hearts,
and write them on their minds."

● **Rom 2:13**

Gal 3 ¹⁰For all who rely on works of the law are under a curse; for it is written, "Cursed be every one who does not abide by all things written in the book of the law, and do them."

Gal 3 ²¹Is the law then against the promises of God? Certainly not; for if a law had been given which could make alive, then righteousness would indeed be by the law.

Gal 5 ³I testify again to every man who receives circumcision that he is bound to keep the whole law.

Cf. 2 Cor 5 ¹⁰For we must all appear before the judgment seat of Christ, so that each one may receive good or evil, according to what he has done in the body.

Rom 2:16

Acts 17 ³¹". . . because he has fixed a day on which he will judge the world in righteousness by a man whom he has appointed, and of this he has given assurance to all men by raising him from the dead."

Cf. Acts 10 ⁴²"And he commanded us to preach to the people, and to testify that he is the one ordained by God to be judge of the living and the dead."

[17]But if you call yourself a Jew and rely upon the law and boast of your relation to God [18]and know his will and approve what is excellent, because you are instructed in the law, [19]and if you are sure that you are a guide to the blind, a light to those who are in darkness, [20]a corrector of the foolish, a teacher of children, having in the law the embodiment of knowledge and truth— [21]you then who teach others, will you not teach yourself? While you preach against stealing, do you steal? [22]You who say that one must not commit adultery, do you commit adultery? You who abhor idols, do you rob temples? [23]You who boast in the law, do you dishonor God by breaking the law? [24]For, as it is written, "The name of God is blasphemed among the Gentiles because of you."

PRIMARY

2 Cor 11:21b–29 (§183)

But whatever any one dares to boast of—I am speaking as a fool—I also dare to boast of that. [22]Are they Hebrews? So am I. Are they Israelites? So am I. Are they descendants of Abraham? So am I. [23]Are they servants of Christ? I am a better one—I am talking like a madman—with far greater labors, far more imprisonments, with countless beatings, and often near death. [24]Five times I have received at the hands of the Jews the forty lashes less one. [25]Three times I have been beaten with rods; once I was stoned. Three times I have been shipwrecked; a night and a day I have been adrift at sea; [26]on frequent journeys, in danger from rivers, danger from robbers, danger from my own people, danger from Gentiles, danger in the city, danger in the wilderness, danger at sea, danger from false brethren; [27]in toil and hardship, through many a sleepless night, in hunger and thirst, often without food, in cold and exposure. [28]And, apart from other things, there is the daily pressure upon me of my anxiety for all the churches. [29]Who is weak, and I am not weak? Who is made to fall, and I am not indignant?

Gal 1:13–14 (§195)

[13]For you have heard of my former life in Judaism, how I persecuted the church of God violently and tried to destroy it; [14]and I advanced in Judaism beyond many of my own age among my people, so extremely zealous was I for the traditions of my fathers.

Gal 2:11–14 (§198)

[11]But when Cephas came to Antioch I opposed him to his face, because he stood condemned. [12]For before certain men came from James, he ate with the Gentiles; but when they came he drew back and separated himself, fearing the circumcision party. [13]And with him the rest of the Jews acted insincerely, so that even Barnabas was carried away by their insincerity. [14]But when I saw that they were not straightforward about the truth of the gospel, I said to Cephas before them all, "If you, though a Jew, live like a Gentile and not like a Jew, how can you compel the Gentiles to live like Jews?"

Phil 3:2–11 (§247)

[2]Look out for the dogs, look out for the evil-workers, look out for those who mutilate the flesh. [3]For we are the true circumcision, who worship God in spirit, and glory in Christ Jesus, and put no confidence in the flesh. [4]Though I myself have reason for confidence in the flesh also. If any other man thinks he has reason for confidence in the flesh, I have more: [5]circumcised on the eighth day, of the people of Israel, of the tribe of Benjamin, a Hebrew born of Hebrews; as to the law a Pharisee, [6]as to zeal a persecutor of the church, as to righteousness under the law blameless. [7]But whatever gain I had, I counted as loss for the sake of Christ. [8]Indeed I count everything as loss because of the surpassing worth of knowing Christ Jesus my Lord. For his sake I have suffered the loss of all things, and count them as refuse, in order that I may gain Christ [9]and be found in him, not having a righteousness of my own, based on law, but that which is through faith in Christ, the righteousness from God that depends on faith; [10]that I may know him and the power of his resurrection, and may share his sufferings, becoming like him in his death, [11]that if possible I may attain the resurrection from the dead.

● **Rom 2:17**

Cf. Rom 4   [2]For if Abraham was justified by works, he has something to boast about, but not before God.

● **Rom 2:20**

2 Tim 1   [13]Follow the pattern of the sound words which you have heard from me, in the faith and love which are in Christ Jesus;

● **Rom 2:23**

Gal 3   [10]For all who rely on works of the law are under a curse; for it is written, "Cursed be every one who does not abide by all things written in the book of the law, and do them."

Cf. Gal 5   [3]I testify again to every man who receives circumcision that he is bound to keep the whole law.

● **Rom 2:24**

Isa 52   [5]Now there what have I here, says the Lord, seeing that my people are taken away for nothing? Their rulers wail, says the Lord, and continually all the day my name is despised.

25Circumcision indeed is of value if you obey the law; but if you break the law, your circumcision becomes uncircumcision. 26So, if a man who is uncircumcised keeps the precepts of the law, will not his uncircumcision be regarded as circumcision? 27Then those who are physically uncircumcised but keep the law will condemn you who have the written code and circumcision but break the law. 28For he is not a real Jew who is one outwardly, nor is true circumcision something external and physical. 29He is a Jew who is one inwardly, and real circumcision is a matter of the heart, spiritual and not literal. His praise is not from men but from God.

Primary

1 Cor 7:17–24 (§97)
17Only, let every one lead the life which the Lord has assigned to him, and in which God has called him. This is my rule in all the churches. 18Was any one at the time of his call already circumcised? Let him not seek to remove the marks of circumcision. Was any one at the time of his call uncircumcised? Let him not seek circumcision. 19For neither circumcision counts for anything nor uncircumcision, but keeping the commandments of God. 20Every one should remain in the state in which he was called. 21Were you a slave when called? Never mind. But if you can gain your freedom, avail yourself of the opportunity. 22For he who was called in the Lord as a slave is a freedman of the Lord. Likewise he who was free when called is a slave of Christ. 23You were bought with a price; do not become slaves of men. 24So, brethren, in whatever state each was called, there let him remain with God.

Gal 3:10–14 (§202)
10For all who rely on works of the law are under a curse; for it is written, "Cursed be every one who does not abide by all things written in the book of the law, and do them." 11Now it is evident that no man is justified before God by the law; for "He who through faith is righteous shall live"; 12but the law does not rest on faith, for "He who does them shall live by them." 13Christ redeemed us from the curse of the law, having become a curse for us—for it is written, "Cursed be every one who hangs on a tree"— 14that in Christ Jesus the blessing of Abraham might come upon the Gentiles, that we might receive the promise of the Spirit through faith.

Gal 4:21–31 (§210)
21Tell me, you who desire to be under law, do you not hear the law? 22For it is written that Abraham had two sons, one by a slave and one by a free woman. 23But the son of the slave was born according to the flesh, the son of the free woman through promise. 24Now this is an allegory: these women are two covenants. One is from Mount Sinai, bearing children for slavery; she is Hagar. 25Now Hagar is Mount Sinai in Arabia; she corresponds to the present Jerusalem, for she is in slavery with her children. 26But the Jerusalem above is free, and she is our mother. 27For it is written,

"Rejoice, O barren one who does not bear;
break forth and shout, you who are not in travail;
for the children of the desolate one are many more
than the children of her that is married."

28Now we, brethren, like Isaac, are children of promise. 29But as at that time he who was born according to the flesh persecuted him who was born according to the Spirit, so it is now. 30But what does the scripture say? "Cast out the slave and her son; for the son of the slave shall not inherit with the son of the free woman." 31So, brethren, we are not children of the slave but of the free woman.

Gal 5:1–12 (§211)
1For freedom Christ has set us free; stand fast therefore, and do not submit again to a yoke of slavery.

2Now I, Paul, say to you that if you receive circumcision, Christ will be of no advantage to you. 3I testify again to every man who receives circumcision that he is bound to keep the whole law. 4You are severed from Christ, you who would be justified by the law; you have fallen away from grace. 5For through the Spirit, by faith, we wait for the hope of righteousness. 6For in Christ Jesus neither circumcision nor uncircumcision is of any avail, but faith working through love. 7You were running well; who hindered you from obeying the truth? 8This persuasion is not from him who called you. 9A little leaven leavens the whole lump. 10I have confidence in the Lord that you will take no other view than mine; and he who is troubling you will bear his judgment, whoever he is. 11But if I, brethren, still preach circumcision, why am I still persecuted? In that case the stumbling block of the cross has been removed. 12I wish those who unsettle you would mutilate themselves!

Gal 6:11–17 (§216)
11See with what large letters I am writing to you with my own hand. 12It is those who want to make a good showing in the flesh that would compel you to be circumcised, and only in order that they may not be persecuted for the cross of Christ. 13For even those who receive circumcision do not themselves keep the law, but they desire to have you circumcised that they may glory in your flesh. 14But far be it from me to glory except in the cross of our Lord Jesus Christ, by which the world has been crucified to me, and I to the world. 15For neither circumcision counts for anything, nor uncircumcision, but a new creation. 16Peace and mercy be upon all who walk by this rule, upon the Israel of God.

17Henceforth let no man trouble me; for I bear on my body the marks of Jesus.

Phil 3:2–11 (§247)
2Look out for the dogs, look out for the evil-workers, look out for those who mutilate the flesh. 3For we are the true circumcision, who worship God in spirit, and glory in Christ Jesus, and put no confidence in the flesh. 4Though I myself have reason for confidence in the flesh also. If any other man thinks he has reason for confidence in the flesh, I have more: 5circumcised on the eighth day, of the people of Israel, of the tribe of Benjamin, a Hebrew born of Hebrews; as to the law a Pharisee, 6as to zeal a persecutor of the church, as to righteousness under the law blameless. 7But whatever gain I had, I counted as loss for the sake of Christ. 8Indeed I count everything as loss because of the surpassing worth of knowing Christ Jesus my Lord. For his sake I have suffered the loss of all things, and count them as refuse, in order that I may gain Christ 9and be found in him, not having a righteousness of my own, based on law, but that which is through faith in Christ, the righteousness from God that depends on faith; 10that I may know him and the power of his resurrection, and may share his sufferings, becoming like him in his death, 11that if possible I may attain the resurrection from the dead.

Col 2:8–15 (§262)
8See to it that no one makes a prey of you by philosophy and empty deceit, according to human tradition, according to the elemental spirits of the universe, and not according to Christ. 9For in him the whole fulness of deity dwells bodily, 10and you have come to fulness of life in him, who is the head of all rule and authority. 11In him also you were circumcised with a circumcision made without hands, by putting off the body of flesh in the circumcision of Christ; 12and you were buried with him in baptism, in which you were also raised with him through faith in the working of God, who raised him from the dead. 13And you, who were dead in trespasses and the uncircumcision of your flesh, God made alive together with him, having forgiven us all our trespasses, 14having canceled the bond which stood against us with its legal demands; this he set aside, nailing it to the cross. 15He disarmed the principalities and powers and made a public example of them, triumphing over them in him.

● **Rom 2:25–29**
Rom 9   6But it is not as though the word of God had failed. For not all who are descended from Israel belong to Israel, 7and not all are children of Abraham because they are his descendants; but "Through Isaac shall your descendants be named." 8This means that it is not the children of the flesh who are the children of God, but the children of the promise are reckoned as descendants.

● **Rom 2:26**
Acts 10   35". . . but in every nation any one who fears him and does what is right is acceptable to him."

● **Rom 2:29**
Acts 7   51"You stiff-necked people, uncircumcised in heart and ears, you always resist the Holy Spirit. As your fathers did, so do you."

Cf. 1 Cor 4:5b

3 Then what advantage has the Jew? Or what is the value of circumcision? [2] Much in every way. To begin with, the Jews are entrusted with the oracles of God. [3] What if some were unfaithful? Does their faithlessness nullify the faithfulness of God? [4] By no means! Let God be true though every man be false, as it is written,

"That thou mayest be justified in thy words,

and prevail when thou art judged."

[5] But if our wickedness serves to show the justice of God, what shall we say? That God is unjust to inflict wrath on us? (I speak in a human way.) [6] By no means! For then how could God judge the world? [7] But if through my falsehood God's truthfulness abounds to his glory, why am I still being condemned as a sinner? [8] And why not do evil that good may come? —as some people slanderously charge us with saying. Their condemnation is just.

PRIMARY

Rom 9:1–5 (§35)

[1] I am speaking the truth in Christ, I am not lying; my conscience bears me witness in the Holy Spirit, [2] that I have great sorrow and unceasing anguish in my heart. [3] For I could wish that I myself were accursed and cut off from Christ for the sake of my brethren, my kinsmen by race. [4] They are Israelites, and to them belong the sonship, the glory, the covenants, the giving of the law, the worship, and the promises; [5] to them belong the patriarchs, and of their race, according to the flesh, is the Christ. God who is over all be blessed for ever. Amen.

2 Cor 3:7–11 (§156)

[7] Now if the dispensation of death, carved in letters on stone, came with such splendor that the Israelites could not look at Moses' face because of its brightness, fading as this was,

[8] will not the dispensation of the Spirit be attended with greater splendor? [9] For if there was splendor in the dispensation of condemnation, the dispensation of righteousness must far exceed it in splendor. [10] Indeed, in this case, what once had splendor has come to have no splendor at all, because of the splendor that surpasses it. [11] For if what faded away came with splendor, what is permanent must have much more splendor.

2 Cor 3:12–18 (§157)

[12] Since we have such a hope, we are very bold, [13] not like Moses, who put a veil over his face so that the Israelites might not see the end of the fading splendor. [14] But their minds were hardened; for to this day, when they read the old covenant, that same veil remains unlifted, because only through Christ is it taken away. [15] Yes, to this day whenever Moses is read a veil lies over their minds; [16] but when a man turns to the Lord the veil is removed. [17] Now the Lord is the Spirit, and where the Spirit of the Lord is, there is freedom. [18] And we all, with unveiled face, beholding the glory of the Lord, are being changed into his likeness from one degree of glory to another; for this comes from the Lord who is the Spirit.

Phil 3:2–11 (§247)

[2] Look out for the dogs, look out for the evilworkers, look out for those who mutilate the flesh. [3] For we are the true circumcision, who worship God in spirit, and glory in Christ Jesus, and put no confidence in the flesh. [4] Though I myself have reason for confidence in the flesh also. If any other man thinks he has reason for confidence in the flesh, I have more: [5] circumcised on the eighth day, of the people of Israel, of the tribe of Benjamin, a Hebrew born of Hebrews; as to the law a Pharisee, [6] as to zeal a persecutor of the church, as to righteousness under the law blameless. [7] But whatever gain I had, I counted as loss for the sake of Christ. [8] Indeed I count everything as loss because of

the surpassing worth of knowing Christ Jesus my Lord. For his sake I have suffered the loss of all things, and count them as refuse, in order that I may gain Christ [9] and be found in him, not having a righteousness of my own, based on law, but that which is through faith in Christ, the righteousness from God that depends on faith; [10] that I may know him and the power of his resurrection, and may share his sufferings, becoming like him in his death, [11] that if possible I may attain the resurrection from the dead.

2 Thess 1:3–12 (§295)

[3] We are bound to give thanks to God always for you, brethren, as is fitting, because your faith is growing abundantly, and the love of every one of you for one another is increasing. [4] Therefore we ourselves boast of you in the churches of God for your steadfastness and faith in all your persecutions and in the afflictions which you are enduring.

[5] This is evidence of the righteous judgment of God, that you may be made worthy of the kingdom of God, for which you are suffering— [6] since indeed God deems it just to repay with affliction those who afflict you, [7] and to grant rest with us to you who are afflicted, when the Lord Jesus is revealed from heaven with his mighty angels in flaming fire, [8] inflicting vengeance upon those who do not know God and upon those who do not obey the gospel of our Lord Jesus. [9] They shall suffer the punishment of eternal destruction and exclusion from the presence of the Lord and from the glory of his might, [10] when he comes on that day to be glorified in his saints, and to be marveled at in all who have believed, because our testimony to you was believed. [11] To this end we always pray for you, that our God may make you worthy of his call, and may fulfil every good resolve and work of faith by his power, [12] so that the name of our Lord Jesus may be glorified in you, and you in him, according to the grace of our God and the Lord Jesus Christ.

● **Rom 3:1–8**

Cf. Rom 1 [16] For I am not ashamed of the gospel: it is the power of God for salvation to every one who has faith, to the Jew first and also to the Greek.

Cf. Rom 2 [9] There will be tribulation and distress for every human being who does evil, the Jew first and also the Greek, [10] but glory and honor and peace for every one who does good, the Jew first and also the Greek. [11] For God shows no partiality.

Cf. Rom 3 [9] What then? Are we Jews any better off?

No, not at all; for I have already charged that all men, both Jews and Greeks, are under the power of sin, . . .

Cf. Rom 3 [22] the righteousness of God through faith in Jesus Christ for all who believe. For there is no distinction; . . .

● **Rom 3:1**

Rom 11 [28] As regards the gospel they are enemies of God, for your sake; but as regards election they are beloved for the sake of their forefathers. [29] For the gifts and the call of God are irrevocable.

● **Rom 3:3**

2 Tim 2 [13] if we are faithless, he remains faithful— for he cannot deny himself.

● **Rom 3:4**

Ps 51 [4] Against thee, thee only, have I sinned, and done that which is evil in thy sight, so that thou art justified in thy sentence and blameless in thy judgment.

[9]What then? Are we Jews any better off? No, not at all; for I have already charged that all men, both Jews and Greeks, are under the power of sin, [10]as it is written:

"None is righteous, no, not one;
[11]no one understands, no one seeks for God.
[12]All have turned aside, together they have gone wrong;
no one does good, not even one."
[13]"Their throat is an open grave,
they use their tongues to deceive."
"The venom of asps is under their lips."
[14]"Their mouth is full of curses and bitterness."
[15]"Their feet are swift to shed blood,
[16]in their paths are ruin and misery,
[17]and the way of peace they do not know."
[18]"There is no fear of God before their eyes."

Now we know that whatever the law says it speaks to those who are under the law, so that every mouth may be stopped, and the whole world may be held accountable to God. [20]For no human being will be justified in his sight by works of the law, since through the law comes knowledge of sin.

PRIMARY

Gal 2:15–21 (§199)

[15]We ourselves, who are Jews by birth and not Gentile sinners, [16]yet who know that a man is not justified by works of the law but through faith in Jesus Christ, even we have believed in Christ Jesus, in order to be justified by faith in Christ, and not by works of the law, because by works of the law shall no one be justified. [17]But if, in our endeavor to be justified in Christ, we ourselves were found to be sinners, is Christ then an agent of sin? Certainly not! [18]But if I build up again those things which I tore down, then I prove myself a transgressor. [19]For I through the law died to the law, that I might live to God. [20]I have been crucified with Christ; it is no longer I who live, but Christ who lives in me; and the life I now live in the flesh I live by faith in the Son of God, who loved me and gave himself for me. [21]I do not nullify the grace of God; for if justification were through the law, then Christ died to no purpose.

Gal 3:10–14 (§202)

[10]For all who rely on works of the law are under a curse; for it is written, "Cursed be every one who does not abide by all things written in the book of the law, and do them." [11]Now it is evident that no man is justified before God by the law; for "He who through faith is righteous shall live"; [12]but the law does not rest on faith, for "He who does them shall live by them." [13]Christ redeemed us from the curse of the law, having become a curse for us—for it is written, "Cursed be every one who hangs on a tree"— [14]that in Christ Jesus the blessing of Abraham might come upon the Gentiles, that we might receive the promise of the Spirit through faith.

Gal 3:21–25 (§205)

[21]Is the law then against the promises of God? Certainly not; for if a law had been given which could make alive, then righteousness would indeed be by the law. [22]But the scripture consigned all things to sin, that what was promised to faith in Jesus Christ might be given to those who believe. [23]Now before faith came, we were confined under the law, kept under restraint until faith should be revealed. [24]So that the law was our custodian until Christ came, that we might be justified by faith. [25]But now that faith has come, we are no longer under a custodian; . . .

● **Rom 3:9**
Cf. Rom 7   [7]What then shall we say? That the law is sin? By no means! Yet, if it had not been for the law, I should not have known sin. I should not have known what it is to covet if the law had not said, "You shall not covet."

Rom 11   [32]For God has consigned all men to disobedience, that he may have mercy upon all.

Cf. Rom 2   [11]For God shows no partiality.

● **Rom 3:10–12**
Ps 14   [1]The fool says in his heart,
"There is no God."
They are corrupt, they do abominable deeds,
there is none that does good.
[2]The Lord looks down from heaven
upon the children of men,
to see if there are any that act wisely,
that seek after God.

Ps 53   [1]The fool says in his heart,
"There is no God."
They are corrupt, doing abominable iniquity;

there is none that does good.
[2]The Lord looks down from heaven
upon the children of men,
to see if there are any that act wisely,
that seek after God.

● **Rom 3:13**
Cf. Ps 5   [9]For there is no truth in their mouth;
their heart is destruction,
their throat is an open sepulchre,
they flatter with their tongue.

Cf. Ps 140   [3]They make their tongue sharp as a serpent's,
and under their lips is the poison of vipers.

● **Rom 3:14**
Cf. Ps 10   [7]His mouth is filled with cursing and deceit and oppression;
under his tongue are mischief and iniquity.

● **Rom 3:15–17**
Cf. Isa 59   [7]Their feet run to evil,
and they make haste to shed innocent blood;
their thoughts are thoughts of iniquity,

desolation and destruction are in their highways.
[8]The way of peace they know not,
and there is no justice in their paths;
they have made their roads crooked,
no one who goes in them knows peace.

● **Rom 3:18**
Ps 36   [1]Transgression speaks to the wicked deep in his heart;
there is no fear of God before his eyes.

● **Rom 3:19**
Cf. 1 Cor 11   [32]But when we are judged by the Lord, we are chastened so that we may not be condemned along with the world.

● **Rom 3:20**
Acts 13   [39]". . . and by him every one that believes is freed from everything from which you could not be freed by the law of Moses."

Cf. Rom 2   [13]For it is not the hearers of the law who are righteous before God, but the doers of the law who will be justified.

[21] But now the righteousness of God has been manifested apart from law, although the law and the prophets bear witness to it, [22] the righteousness of God through faith in Jesus Christ for all who believe. For there is no distinction; [23] since all have sinned and fall short of the glory of God, [24] they are justified by his grace as a gift, through the redemption which is in Christ Jesus, [25] whom God put forward as an expiation by his blood, to be received by faith. This was to show God's righteousness, because in his divine forbearance he had passed over former sins; [26] it was to prove at the present time that he himself is righteous and that he justifies him who has faith in Jesus.

PRIMARY

1 Cor 4:6-7 (§84)

[6] I have applied all this to myself and Apollos for your benefit, brethren, that you may learn by us not to go beyond what is written, that none of you may be puffed up in favor of one against another. [7] For who sees anything different in you? What have you that you did not receive? If then you received it, why do you boast as if it were not a gift?

2 Cor 5:14-21 (§164)

[14] For the love of Christ controls us, because we are convinced that one has died for all; therefore all have died. [15] And he died for all, that those who live might live no longer for themselves but for him who for their sake died and was raised. [16] From now on, therefore, we regard no one from a human point of view; even though we once regarded Christ from a human point of view, we regard him thus no longer. [17] Therefore, if any one is in Christ, he is a new creation; the old has passed away, behold, the new has come. [18] All this is from God, who through Christ reconciled us to himself and gave us the ministry of reconciliation; [19] that is, in Christ God was reconciling the world to himself, not counting their trespasses against them, and entrusting to us the message of reconciliation. [20] So we are ambassadors for Christ, God making his appeal through us. We beseech you on behalf of Christ, be reconciled to God. [21] For our sake he made him to be sin who knew no sin, so that in him we might become the righteousness of God.

Gal 3:21-25 (§205)

[21] Is the law then against the promises of God? Certainly not; for if a law had been given which could make alive, then righteousness would indeed be by the law. [22] But the scripture consigned all things to sin, that what was promised to faith in Jesus Christ might be given to those who believe. [23] Now before faith came, we were confined under the law, kept under restraint until faith should be revealed. [24] So that the law was our custodian until Christ came, that we might be justified by faith. [25] But now that faith has come, we are no longer under a custodian;

Eph 2:1-10 (§220)

[1] And you he made alive, when you were dead through the trespasses and sins [2] in which you once walked, following the course of this world, following the prince of the power of the air, the spirit that is now at work in the sons of disobedience. [3] Among these we all once lived in the passions of our flesh, following the desires of body and mind, and so we were by nature children of wrath, like the rest of mankind. [4] But God, who is rich in mercy, out of the great love with which he loved us, [5] even when we were dead through our trespasses, made us alive together with Christ (by grace you have been saved), [6] and raised us up with him, and made us sit with him in the heavenly places in Christ Jesus, [7] that in the coming ages he might show the immeasurable riches of his grace in kindness toward us in Christ Jesus. [8] For by grace you have been saved through faith; and this is not your own doing, it is the gift of God— [9] not because of works, lest any man should boast. [10] For we are his workmanship, created in Christ Jesus for good works, which God prepared beforehand, that we should walk in them.

Phil 3:2-11 (§247)

[2] Look out for the dogs, look out for the evil-workers, look out for those who mutilate the flesh. [3] For we are the true circumcision, who worship God in spirit, and glory in Christ Jesus, and put no confidence in the flesh. [4] Though I myself have reason for confidence in the flesh also. If any other man thinks he has reason for confidence in the flesh, I have more: [5] circumcised on the eighth day, of the people of Israel, of the tribe of Benjamin, a Hebrew born of Hebrews; as to the law a Pharisee, [6] as to zeal a persecutor of the church, as to righteousness under the law blameless. [7] But whatever gain I had, I counted as loss for the sake of Christ. [8] Indeed I count everything as loss because of the surpassing worth of knowing Christ Jesus my Lord. For his sake I have suffered the loss of all things, and count them as refuse, in order that I may gain Christ [9] and be found in him, not having a righteousness of my own, based on law, but that which is through faith in Christ, the righteousness from God that depends on faith; [10] that I may know him and the power of his resurrection, and may share his sufferings, becoming like him in his death, [11] that if possible I may attain the resurrection from the dead.

Col 1:21-23 (§259)

[21] And you, who once were estranged and hostile in mind, doing evil deeds, [22] he has now reconciled in his body of flesh by his death, in order to present you holy and blameless and irreproachable before him, [23] provided that you continue in the faith, stable and steadfast, not shifting from the hope of the gospel which you heard, which has been preached to every creature under heaven, and of which I, Paul, became a minister.

● **Rom 3:21**

Rom 1   [17] For in it the righteousness of God is revealed through faith for faith; as it is written, "He who through faith is righteous shall live."

Gal 3   [8] And the scripture, foreseeing that God would justify the Gentiles by faith, preached the gospel beforehand to Abraham, saying, "In you shall all the nations be blessed."

● **Rom 3:22-23**

Cf. Rom 1   [16] For I am not ashamed of the gospel: it is the power of God for salvation to every one who has faith, to the Jew first and also to the Greek.

Cf. Rom 2   [9] There will be tribulation and distress for every human being who does evil, the Jew first and also the Greek, [10] but glory and honor and peace for every one who does good, the Jew first and also the Greek. [11] For God shows no partiality.

Cf. Rom 3   [9] What then? Are we Jews any better off? No, not at all; for I have already charged that all men, both Jews and Greeks, are under the power of sin, . . .

● **Rom 3:24-25**

Cf. Rom 5   [9] Since, therefore, we are now justified by his blood, much more shall we be saved by him from the wrath of God.

Cf. Eph 1   [7] In him we have redemption through his blood, the forgiveness of our trespasses, according to the riches of his grace . . .

Cf. Col 1   [13] He has delivered us from the dominion of darkness and transferred us to the kingdom of his beloved Son, [14] in whom we have redemption, the forgiveness of sins.

Cf. Col 1   [20] and through him to reconcile to himself all things, whether on earth or in heaven, making peace by the blood of his cross.

● **Rom 3:24**

Titus 3   [7] so that we might be justified by his grace and become heirs in hope of eternal life.

Cf. 1 Cor 15   [10] But by the grace of God I am what I am, and his grace toward me was not in vain. On the contrary, I worked harder than any of them, though it was not I, but the grace of God which is with me.

Cf. 1 Cor 1   [30] He is the source of your life in Christ Jesus, whom God made our wisdom, our righteousness and sanctification and redemption; . . .

● **Rom 3:25**

Cf. Acts 14   [16] "In past generations he allowed all the nations to walk in their own ways. . . ."

Cf. Acts 17   [30] "The times of ignorance God overlooked, but now he commands all men everywhere to repent. . . ."

● **Rom 3:26**

Gal 2   [16] yet who know that a man is not justified by works of the law but through faith in Jesus Christ, even we have believed in Christ Jesus, in order to be justified by faith in Christ, and not by works of the law, because by works of the law shall no one be justified.

²⁷Then what becomes of our boasting? It is excluded. On what principle? On the principle of works? No, but on the principle of faith. ²⁸For we hold that a man is justified by faith apart from works of law. ²⁹Or is God the God of Jews only? Is he not the God of Gentiles also? Yes, of Gentiles also, ³⁰since God is one; and he will justify the circumcised on the ground of their faith and the uncircumcised through their faith. ³¹Do we then overthrow the law by this faith? By no means! On the contrary, we uphold the law.

PRIMARY

1 Cor 1:26–31 (§75)
²⁶For consider your call, brethren; not many of you were wise according to worldly standards, not many were powerful, not many were of noble birth; ²⁷but God chose what is foolish in the world to shame the wise, God chose what is weak in the world to shame the strong, ²⁸God chose what is low and despised in the world, even things that are not, to bring to nothing things that are, ²⁹so that no human being might

boast in the presence of God. ³⁰He is the source of your life in Christ Jesus, whom God made our wisdom, our righteousness and sanctification and redemption; ³¹therefore, as it is written, "Let him who boasts, boast of the Lord."

2 Cor 10:13–18 (§178)
¹³But we will not boast beyond limit, but will keep to the limits God has apportioned us, to reach even to you. ¹⁴For we are not overextending ourselves, as though we did not reach you; we were the first to come all the way to you with the gospel of Christ. ¹⁵We do not boast beyond limit, in other men's labors; but our hope is that as your faith increases, our field among you may be greatly enlarged, ¹⁶so that we may preach the gospel in lands beyond you, without boasting of work already done in another's field. ¹⁷"Let him who boasts, boast of the Lord." ¹⁸For it is not the man who commends himself that is accepted, but the man whom the Lord commends.

Phil 3:2–11 (§247)
²Look out for the dogs, look out for the evil-

workers, look out for those who mutilate the flesh. ³For we are the true circumcision, who worship God in spirit, and glory in Christ Jesus, and put no confidence in the flesh. ⁴Though I myself have reason for confidence in the flesh also. If any other man thinks he has reason for confidence in the flesh, I have more: ⁵circumcised on the eighth day, of the people of Israel, of the tribe of Benjamin, a Hebrew born of Hebrews; as to the law a Pharisee, ⁶as to zeal a persecutor of the church, as to righteousness under the law blameless. ⁷But whatever gain I had, I counted as loss for the sake of Christ. ⁸Indeed I count everything as loss because of the surpassing worth of knowing Christ Jesus my Lord. For his sake I have suffered the loss of all things, and count them as refuse, in order that I may gain Christ ⁹and be found in him, not having a righteousness of my own, based on law, but that which is through faith in Christ, the righteousness from God that depends on faith; ¹⁰that I may know him and the power of his resurrection, and may share his sufferings, becoming like him in his death, ¹¹that if possible I may attain the resurrection from the dead.

● **Rom 3:27**
Rom 2   ¹⁷But if you call yourself a Jew and rely upon the law and boast of your relation to God . . .

2 Cor 11   ¹⁶I repeat, let no one think me foolish; but even if you do, accept me as a fool, so that I too may boast a little. ¹⁷(What I am saying I say not with the Lord's authority but as a fool, in this boastful confidence; ¹⁸since many boast of worldly things, I too will boast.)

2 Cor 11   ²¹ . . . But whatever any one dares to boast of—I am speaking as a fool—I also dare to boast of that. ²²Are they Hebrews? So am I. Are they Israelites? So am I. Are they descendants of Abraham? So am I.

2 Cor 11   ³⁰If I must boast, I will boast of the things that show my weakness.

2 Cor 12   ¹I must boast; there is nothing to be gained by it, but I will go on to visions and revelations of the Lord.

2 Cor 12   ⁸Three times I besought the Lord about this, that it should leave me; ⁹but he said to me, "My grace is sufficient for you, for my power is made perfect in weakness." I will all the more gladly boast of my weaknesses, that the power of Christ may rest upon me.

Eph 2   ⁸For by grace you have been saved through faith; and this is not your own doing, it is the gift of God— ⁹not because of works, lest any man should boast. ¹⁰For we are his workmanship, created in Christ Jesus for good works, which God prepared beforehand, that we should walk in them.

Cf. Rom 2   ²³You who boast in the law, do you dishonor God by breaking the law?

Cf. Rom 5   ²Through him we have obtained access to this grace in which we stand, and we rejoice in our hope of sharing the glory of God. ³More than that, we rejoice in our sufferings, knowing that suffering produces endurance, . . .

Cf. Rom 15   ¹⁷In Christ Jesus, then, I have reason to be proud of my work for God.

Cf. 1 Cor 3   ²¹So let no one boast of men. For all things are yours, . . .

Cf. 1 Cor 4   ⁷For who sees anything different in you? What have you that you did not receive? If then you received it, why do you boast as if it were not a gift?

Cf. 1 Cor 5   ⁶Your boasting is not good. Do you not know that a little leaven leavens the whole lump?

Cf. 1 Cor 9   ¹⁵ . . . For I would rather die than have any one deprive me of my ground for boasting. ¹⁶For if I preach the gospel, that gives me no ground for boasting. . . .

Cf. 1 Cor 19   ¹²What I mean is that each one of you says, "I belong to Paul," or "I belong to Apollos," or "I belong to Cephas," or "I belong to Christ." ¹³Is Christ divided? Was Paul crucified for you? Or where you baptized in the name of Paul? ¹⁴I am thankful that I baptized none of you except Crispus and Gaius; . . .

Cf. 2 Cor 5   ¹²We are not commending ourselves to you again but giving you cause to be proud of us, so that you may be able to answer those who pride themselves on a man's position and not on his heart.

Cf. 2 Cor 10   ⁸For even if I boast a little too much of our authority, which the Lord gave for building you up and not for destroying you, I shall not be put to shame.

Cf. Gal 6   ¹³For even those who receive circumcision do not themselves keep the law, but they desire to have you circumcised that they may glory in your flesh. ¹⁴But far be it from me to glory except in the cross of our Lord Jesus Christ, by which the world has been crucified to me, and I to the world.

Cf. 1 Thess 2   ¹⁹For what is our hope or joy or crown of boasting before our Lord Jesus at his coming? Is it not you?

● **Rom 3:28**
Acts 13   ³⁹". . . and by him every one that believes is

freed from everything from which you could not be freed by the law of Moses."

● **Rom 3:29**
Eph 2   ¹¹Therefore remember that at one time you Gentiles in the flesh, called the uncircumcision by what is called the circumcision, which is made in the flesh by hands— ¹²remember that you were at that time separated from Christ, alienated from the commonwealth of Israel, and strangers to the covenants of promise, having no hope and without God in the world. ¹³But now in Christ Jesus you who once were far off have been brought near in the blood of Christ. ¹⁴For he is our peace, who has made us both one, and has broken down the dividing wall of hostility, . . .

Cf. Acts 10   ³⁴And Peter opened his mouth and said: "Truly I perceive that God shows no partiality. . . ."

● **Rom 3:30**
Cf. Gal 3   ²⁰Now an intermediary implies more than one; but God is one.

● **Rom 3:31**
Rom 9   ³⁰What shall we say, then? That Gentiles who did not pursue righteousness have attained it, that is, righteousness through faith; ³¹but that Israel who pursued the righteousness which is based on law did not succeed in fulfilling that law. ³²Why? Because they did not pursue it through faith, but as if it were based on works. They have stumbled over the stumbling stone, . . .

Rom 13   ⁸Owe no one anything, except to love one another; for he who loves his neighbor has fulfilled the law.

Gal 5   ¹⁴For the whole law is fulfilled in one word, "You shall love your neighbor as yourself."

Cf. Rom 7   ⁷What then shall we say? That the law is sin? By no means! Yet, if it had not been for the law, I should not have known sin. I should not have known what it is to covet if the law had not said, "You shall not covet."

Cf. Rom 10   ⁴For Christ is the end of the law, that every one who has faith may be justified.

4 What then shall we say about Abraham, our forefather according to the flesh? [2]For if Abraham was justified by works, he has something to boast about, but not before God. [3]For what does the scripture say? "Abraham believed God, and it was reckoned to him as righteousness." [4]Now to one who works, his wages are not reckoned as a gift but as his due. [5]And to one who does not work but trusts him who justifies the ungodly, his faith is reckoned as righteousness. [6]So also David pronounces a blessing upon the man to whom God reckons righteousness apart from works:

[7]"Blessed are those whose iniquities are forgiven, and whose sins are covered;

[8]blessed is the man against whom the Lord will not reckon his sin."

PRIMARY

Gal 3:6–9 (§201)

[6]Thus Abraham "believed God, and it was reckoned to him as righteousness." [7]So you see that it is men of faith who are the sons of Abraham. [8]And the scripture, foreseeing that God would justify the Gentiles by faith, preached the gospel beforehand to Abraham, saying, "In you shall all the nations be blessed." [9]So then, those who are men of faith are blessed with Abraham who had faith.

● **Rom 4:1–8**

Jas 2 [21]Was not Abraham our father justified by works, when he offered his son Isaac upon the altar? [22]You see that faith was active along with his works, and faith was completed by works, [23]and the scripture was fulfilled which says, "Abraham believed God, and it was reckoned to him as righteousness"; and he was called the friend of God. [24]You see that a man is justified by works and not by faith alone. [25]And in the same way was not also Rahab the harlot justified by works when she received the messengers and sent them out another way? [26]For as the body apart from the spirit is dead, so faith apart from works is dead.

Cf. Rom 9 [6]But it is not as though the word of God had failed. For not all who are descended from Israel belong to Israel, [7]and not all are children of Abraham because they are his descendants; but "Through Isaac shall your descendants be named." [8]This means that it is not the children of the flesh who are the children of God, but the children of the promise are reckoned as descendants. [9]For this is what the promise said,

"About this time I will return and Sarah shall have a son." [10]And not only so, but also when Rebecca had conceived children by one man, our forefather Isaac, [11]though they were not yet born and had done nothing either good or bad, in order that God's purpose of election might continue, not because of works but because of his call, [12]she was told, "The elder will serve the younger." [13]As it is written, "Jacob I loved, but Esau I hated."

● **Rom 4:1**

(about) *read* was gained by: SACDG Koine Lect it vg syr(pal) cop(sa, bo); *text:* B Origen Ephraem

● **Rom 4:3**

Gen 15 [6]And he believed the Lord; and he reckoned it to him as righteousness.

● **Rom 4:4**

Rom 6 [23]For the wages of sin is death, but the free gift of God is eternal life in Christ Jesus our Lord.

Cf. Rom 2 [6]For he will render to every man according to his works: . . .

● **Rom 4:5**

Rom 1 [18]For the wrath of God is revealed from heaven against all ungodliness and wickedness of men who by their wickedness suppress the truth.

Rom 5 [6]While we were still weak, at the right time Christ died for the ungodly.

● **Rom 4:7**

Ps 32 [1]Blessed is he whose transgression is forgiven, whose sin is covered.
[2]Blessed is the man to whom the Lord imputes no iniquity,
and in whose spirit there is no deceit.

[9]Is this blessing pronounced only upon the circumcised, or also upon the uncircumcised? We say that faith was reckoned to Abraham as righteousness. [10]How then was it reckoned to him? Was it before or after he had been circumcised? It was not after, but before he was circumcised. [11]He received circumcision as a sign or seal of the righteousness which he had by faith while he was still uncircumcised. The purpose was to make him the father of all who believe without being circumcised and who thus have righteousness reckoned to them, [12]and likewise the father of the circumcised who are not merely circumcised but also follow the example of the faith which our father Abraham had before he was circumcised.

● **Rom 4:11**
Gen 17   [10]This is my covenant, which you shall keep, between me and you and your descendants after you: Every male among you shall be circumcised.

Gen 17   [24]Abraham was ninety-nine years old when he was circumcised in the flesh of his foreskin.

[13] The promise to Abraham and his descendants, that they should inherit the world, did not come through the law but through the righteousness of faith. [14] If it is the adherents of the law who are to be the heirs, faith is null and the promise is void. [15] For the law brings wrath, but where there is no law there is no transgression.

PRIMARY

Gal 3:15–20 (§203–204)

[15] To give a human example, brethren: no one annuls even a man's will, or adds to it, once it has been ratified. [16] Now the promises were made to Abraham and to his offspring. It does not say, "And to offsprings," referring to many; but, referring to one, "And to your offspring," which is Christ. [17] This is what I mean: the law, which came four hundred and thirty years afterward, does not annul a covenant previously ratified by God, so as to make the promise void. [18] For if the inheritance is by the law, it is no longer by promise; but God gave it to Abraham by a promise.

[19] Why then the law? It was added because of transgressions, till the offspring should come to whom the promise had been made; and it was ordained by angels through an intermediary. [20] Now an intermediary implies more than one; but God is one.

● **Rom 4:13–15**

Cf. Rom 9 [6] But it is not as though the word of God had failed. For not all who are descended from Israel belong to Israel, [7] and not all are children of Abraham because they are his descendants; but "Through Isaac shall your descendants be named." [8] This means that it is not the children of the flesh who are the children of God, but the children of the promise are reckoned as descendants. [9] For this is what the promise said, "About this time I will return and Sarah shall have a son." [10] And not only so, but also when Rebecca had conceived children by one man, our forefather Isaac, [11] though they were not yet born and had done nothing either good or bad, in order that God's purpose of election might continue, not because of works but because of his call, [12] she was told, "The elder will serve the younger." [13] As it is written, "Jacob I loved, but Esau I hated."

Gal 4 [22] For it is written that Abraham had two sons, one by a slave and one by a free woman. [23] But the son of the slave was born according to the flesh, the son of the free woman through promise.

Gal 4 [28] Now we, brethren, like Isaac, are children of promise.

● **Rom 4:13**

Gen 17 [4] "Behold, my covenant is with you, and you shall be the father of a multitude of nations. [5] No longer shall your name be Abram, but your name shall be Abraham; for I have made you the father of a multitude of nations. [6] I will make you exceedingly fruitful; and I will make nations of you, and kings shall come forth from you."

Cf. Rom 15 [8] For I tell you that Christ became a servant to the circumcised to show God's truthfulness, in order to confirm the promises given to the patriarchs, . . .

Cf. 2 Cor 1 [20] For all the promises of God find their Yes in him. That is why we utter the Amen through him, to the glory of God.

● **Rom 4:14**

Gal 3 [29] And if you are Christ's, then you are Abraham's offspring, heirs according to promise.

Cf. Rom 2 [12] All who have sinned without the law will also perish without the law, and all who have sinned under the law will be judged by the law. [13] For it is not the hearers of the law who are righteous before God, but the doers of the law who will be justified.

● **Rom 4:15**

Rom 5 [20] Law came in, to increase the trespass; but where sin increased, grace abounded all the more, . . .

Rom 7 [7] . . . Yet, if it had not been for the law, I should not have known sin. I should not have known what it is to covet if the law had not said, "You shall not covet."

¹⁶That is why it depends on faith, in order that the promise may rest on grace and be guaranteed to all his descendants—not only to the adherents of the law but also to those who share the faith of Abraham, for he is the father of us all, ¹⁷as it is written, "I have made you the father of many nations"—in the presence of the God in whom he believed, who gives life to the dead and calls into existence the things that do not exist. ¹⁸In hope he believed against hope, that he should become the father of many nations; as he had been told, "So shall your descendants be." ¹⁹He did not weaken in faith when he considered his own body, which was as good as dead because he was about a hundred years old, or when he considered the barrenness of Sarah's womb. ²⁰No distrust made him waver concerning the promise of God, but he grew strong in his faith as he gave glory to God, ²¹fully convinced that God was able to do what he had promised. ²²That is why his faith was "reckoned to him as righteousness." ²³But the words, "it was reckoned to him," were written not for his sake alone, ²⁴but for ours also. It will be reckoned to us who believe in him that raised from the dead Jesus our Lord, ²⁵who was put to death for our trespasses and raised for our justification.

● Rom 4:16–25
Cf. Gal 4   ²¹Tell me, you who desire to be under law, do you not hear the law? ²²For it is written that Abraham had two sons, one by a slave and one by a free woman. ²³But the son of the slave was born according to the flesh, the son of the free woman through promise. ²⁴Now this is an allegory: these women are two covenants. One is from Mount Sinai, bearing children for slavery; she is Hagar. ²⁵Now Hagar is Mount Sinai in Arabia; she corresponds to the present Jerusalem, for she is in slavery with her children. ²⁶But the Jerusalem above is free, and she is our mother. ²⁷For it is written,

"Rejoice, O barren one who does not bear;
  break forth and shout, you who are not in travail;
for the children of the desolate one are many more
  than the children of her that is married."

²⁸Now we, brethren, like Isaac, are children of promise. ²⁹But as at that time he who was born according to the flesh persecuted him who was born according to the Spirit, so it is now. ³⁰But what does the scripture say? "Cast out the slave and her son; for the son of the slave shall not inherit with the son of the free woman." ³¹So, brethren, we are not children of the slve but of the free woman.

● Rom 4:17
2 Cor 1   ⁹Why, we felt that we had received the sentence of death; but that was to make us rely not on ourselves but on God who raises the dead; . . .

Gen 17   ⁵No longer shall your name be Abram, but your name shall be Abraham; for I have made you the father of a multitude of nations.

● Rom 4:18
Rom 8   ²⁴For in this hope we were saved. Now hope that is seen is not hope. For who hopes for what he sees? ²⁵But if we hope for what we do not see, we wait for it with patience.

Gen 15   ⁵And he brought him outside and said, "Look toward heaven, and number the stars, if you are able to number them." Then he said to him, "So shall your descendants be."

● Rom 4:19
Gen 17   ¹⁷Then Abraham fell on his face and laughed, and said to himself, "Shall a child be born to a man who is a hundred years old? Shall Sarah, who is ninety years old, bear a child?"

Gen 18   ¹¹Now Abraham and Sarah were old, advanced in age; it had ceased to be with Sarah after the manner of women.

● Rom 4:21
Cf. Rom 14   ⁵. . . Let every one be fully convinced in his own mind.

Cf. Col 4   ¹²Epaphras, who is one of yourselves, a servant of Christ Jesus, greets you, always remembering you earnestly in his prayers, that you may stand mature and fully assured in all the will of God.

● Rom 4:22
Gen 15   ⁶And he believed the Lord; and he reckoned it to him as righteousness.

● Rom 4:23–24
Cf. 2 Tim 3   ¹⁶All scripture is inspired by God and profitable for teaching, for reproof, for correction, and for training in righteousness, ¹⁷that the man of God may be complete, equipped for every good work.

● Rom 4:24
Cf. Acts 2   ²⁴"But God raised him up, having loosed the pangs of death, because it was not possible for him to be held by it."

● Rom 4:25
1 Cor 15   ³For I delivered to you as of first importance what I also received, that Christ died for our sins in accordance with the scriptures, ⁴that he was buried, that he was raised on the third day in accordance with the scriptures, ⁵and that he appeared to Cephas, then to the twelve.

5 Therefore, since we are justified by faith, we have peace with God through our Lord Jesus Christ. [2]Through him we have obtained access to this grace in which we stand, and we rejoice in our hope of sharing the glory of God. [3]More than that, we rejoice in our sufferings, knowing that suffering produces endurance, [4]and endurance produces character, and character produces hope, [5]and hope does not disappoint us, because God's love has been poured into our hearts through the Holy Spirit which has been given to us.

PRIMARY

1 Cor 4:8–13 (§85)

[8]Already you are filled! Already you have become rich! Without us you have become kings! And would that you did reign, so that we might share the rule with you! [9]For I think that God has exhibited us apostles as last of all, like men sentenced to death; because we have become a spectacle to the world, to angels and to men. [10]We are fools for Christ's sake, but you are wise in Christ. We are weak, but you are strong. You are held in honor, but we in disrepute. [11]To the present hour we hunger and thirst, we are ill-clad and buffeted and homeless, [12]and we labor, working with our own hands. When reviled, we bless; when persecuted, we endure; [13]when slandered, we try to conciliate; we have become, and are now, as the refuse of the world, the off-scouring of all things.

2 Cor 1:3–11 (§147)

[3]Blessed be the God and Father of our Lord Jesus Christ, the Father of mercies and God of all comfort, [4]who comforts us in all our affliction, so that we may be able to comfort those who are in any affliction, with the comfort with which we ourselves are comforted by God. [5]For as we share abundantly in Christ's sufferings, so through Christ we share abundantly in comfort too. [6]If we are afflicted, it is for your comfort and salvation; and if we are comforted, it is for your comfort, which you experience when you patiently endure the same sufferings that we suffer. [7]Our hope for you is unshaken; for we know that as you share in our sufferings, you will also share in our comfort.

[8]For we do not want you to be ignorant, brethren, of the affliction we experienced in Asia; for we were so utterly, unbearably crushed that we despaired of life itself. [9]Why, we felt that we had received the sentence of death; but that was to make us rely not on ourselves but on God who raises the dead; [10]he delivered us from so deadly a peril, and he will deliver us; on him we have set our hope that he will deliver us again. [11]You also must help us by prayer, so that many will give thanks on our behalf for the blessing granted us in answer to many prayers.

2 Cor 4:7–12 (§159)

[7]But we have this treasure in earthen vessels, to show that the transcendent power belongs to God and not to us. [8]We are afflicted in every way, but not crushed; perplexed, but not driven to despair; [9]persecuted, but not forsaken; struck down, but not destroyed; [10]always carrying in the body the death of Jesus, so that the life of Jesus may also be manifested in our bodies. [11]For while we live we are always being given up to death for Jesus' sake, so that the life of Jesus may be manifested in our mortal flesh. [12]So death is at work in us, but life in you.

2 Cor 6:1–10 (§165)

[1]Working together with him, then, we entreat you not to accept the grace of God in vain. [2]For he says,

"At the acceptable time I have listened to you,

and helped you on the day of salvation."

Behold, now is the acceptable time; behold, now is the day of salvation. [3]We put no obstacle in any one's way, so that no fault may be found with our ministry, [4]but as servants of God we commend ourselves in every way: through great endurance, in afflictions, hardships, calamities, [5]beatings, imprisonments, tumults, labors, watching, hunger; [6]by purity, knowledge, forbearance, kindness, the Holy Spirit, genuine love, [7]truthful speech, and the power of God; with the weapons of righteousness for the right hand and for the left; [8]in honor and dishonor, in ill repute and good repute. We are treated as impostors, and yet are true; [9]as unknown, and yet well known; as dying, and behold we live; as punished, and yet not killed; [10]as sorrowful, yet always rejoicing; as poor, yet making many rich; as having nothing, and yet possessing everything.

2 Cor 11:21b–29 (§183)

But whatever any one dares to boast of—I am speaking as a fool—I also dare to boast of that. [22]Are they Hebrews? So am I. Are they Israelites? So am I. Are they descendants of Abraham? So am I. [23]Are they servants of Christ? I am a better one—I am talking like a madman—with far greater labors, far more imprisonments, with countless beatings, and often near death. [24]Five times I have received at the hands of the Jews the forty lashes less one. [25]Three times I have been beaten with rods; once I was stoned. Three times I have been shipwrecked; a night and a day I have been adrift at sea; [26]on frequent journeys, in danger from rivers, danger from robbers, danger from my own people, danger from Gentiles, danger in the city, danger in the wilderness, danger at sea, danger from false brethren; [27]in toil and hardship, through many a sleepless night, in hunger and thirst, often without food, in cold and exposure. [28]And, apart from other things, there is the daily pressure upon me of my anxiety for all the churches. [29]Who is weak, and I am not weak? Who is made to fall, and I am not indignant?

2 Cor 12:1–10 (§185)

[1]I must boast; there is nothing to be gained by it, but I will go on to visions and revelations of the Lord. [2]I know a man in Christ who fourteen years ago was caught up to the third heaven—whether in the body or out of the body I do not know, God knows. [3]And I know that this man was caught up into Paradise—whether in the body or out of the body I do not know, God knows— [4]and he heard things that cannot be told, which man may not utter. [5]On behalf of this man I will boast, but on my own behalf I will not boast, except of my weaknesses. [6]Though if I wish to boast, I shall not be a fool, for I shall be speaking the truth. But I refrain from it, so that no one may think more of me than he sees in me or hears from me. [7]And to keep me from being too elated by the abundance of revelations, a thorn was given me in the flesh, a messenger of Satan, to harass me, to keep me from being too elated. [8]Three times I besought the Lord about this, that it should leave me; [9]but he said to me, "My grace is sufficient for you, for my power is made perfect in weakness." I will all the more gladly boast of my weaknesses, that the power of Christ may rest upon me. [10]For the sake of Christ, then, I am content with weaknesses, insults, hardships, persecutions, and calamities; for when I am weak, then I am strong.

● **Rom 5:1–5**

Rom 8   [18]I consider that the sufferings of this present time are not worth comparing with the glory that is to be revealed to us.

● **Rom 5:1**

Cf. Rom 15:33

(we) *read* let us: S*AB*CD it(most) vg syr (pes pal) cop(bo) Marcion Tertullian; *text:* S*B³G (Greek) Koine Lect it(few) syr(har) cop(sa) Ephraem

● **Rom 5:2**

Col 1   [27]To them God chose to make known how great among the Gentiles are the riches of the glory of this mystery, which is Christ in you, the hope of glory.

(access) *add* by faith: S*C Koine Lect it(most) vg syr cop(bo) Chrysostom; *text:* BDG it(some) cop(sa) Ephraem

● **Rom 5:3**

Cf. Gal 5:22

● **Rom 5:5**

Acts 2   [17]"And in the last days it shall be, God declares,

that I will pour out my Spirit upon all flesh,

and your sons and your daughters shall prophesy,

and your young men shall see visions,

and your old men shall dream dreams;

[18]yea, and on my menservants and my maidservants in those days

I will pour out my Spirit; and they shall prophesy."

Acts 10   [45]And the believers from among the circumcised who came with Peter were amazed, because the gift of the Holy Spirit had been poured out even on the Gentiles.

Cf. Rom 12:11–12; 2 Cor 1:22; Gal 4:6; Titus 3:6; Acts 2:33

[6]While we were still weak, at the right time Christ died for the ungodly. [7]Why, one will hardly die for a righteous man—though perhaps for a good man one will dare even to die. [8]But God shows his love for us in that while we were yet sinners Christ died for us. [9]Since, therefore, we are now justified by his blood, much more shall we be saved by him from the wrath of God. [10]For if while we were enemies we were reconciled to God by the death of his Son, much more, now that we are reconciled, shall we be saved by his life. [11]Not only so, but we also rejoice in God through our Lord Jesus Christ, through whom we have now received our reconciliation.

PRIMARY

1 Cor 15:1-11 (§131)

[1]Now I would remind you, brethren, in what terms I preached to you the gospel, which you received, in which you stand, [2]by which you are saved, if you hold it fast —unless you believed in vain.

[3]For I delivered to you as of first importance what I also received, that Christ died for our sins in accordance with the scriptures, [4]that he was buried, that he was raised on the third day in accordance with the scriptures, [5]and that he appeared to Cephas, then to the twelve. [6]Then he appeared to more than five hundred brethren at one time, most of whom are still alive, though some have fallen asleep. [7]Then he appeared to James, then to all the apostles. [8]Last of all, as to one untimely born, he appeared also to me. [9]For I am the least of the apostles, unfit to be called an apostle, because I persecuted the church of God. [10]But by the grace of God I am what I am, and his grace toward me was not in vain. On the contrary, I worked harder than any of them, though it was not I, but the grace of God which is with me. [11]Whether then it was I or they, so we preach and so you believed.

2 Cor 5:14-21 (§164)

[14]For the love of Christ controls us, because we are convinced that one has died for all; there-fore all have died. [15]And he died for all, that those who live might live no longer for themselves but for him who for their sake died and was raised.

[16]From now on, therefore, we regard no one from a human point of view; even though we once regarded Christ from a human point of view, we regard him thus no longer. [17]Therefore, if any one is in Christ, he is a new creation; the old has passed away, behold, the new has come. [18]All this is from God, who through Christ reconciled us to himself and gave us the ministry of reconciliation; [19]that is, in Christ God was reconciling the world to himself, not counting their trespasses against them, and entrusting to us the message of reconciliation. [20]So we are ambassadors for Christ, God making his appeal through us. We beseech you on behalf of Christ, be reconciled to God. [21]For our sake he made him to be sin who knew no sin, so that in him we might become the right-eousness of God.

Eph 2:11-22 (§221)

[11]Therefore remember that at one time you Gentiles in the flesh, called the uncircumcision by what is called the circumcision, which is made in the flesh by hands— [12]remember that you were at that time separated from Christ, alienated from the commonwealth of Israel, and strangers to the covenants of promise, having no hope and without God in the world. [13]But now in Christ Jesus you who once were far off have been brought near in the blood of Christ. [14]For he is our peace, who has made us both one, and has broken down the dividing wall of hostility, [15]by abolishing in his flesh the law of commandments and ordinances, that he might create in himself one new man in place of the two, so making peace, [16]and might reconcile us both to God in one body through the cross, thereby bringing the hostility to an end. [17]And he came and preached peace to you who were far off and peace to those who were near; [18]for through him we both have access in one Spirit to the Father. [19]So then you are no longer strangers and sojourners, but you are fellow citizens with the saints and members of the household of God, [20]built upon the foundation of the apostles and prophets, Christ Jesus himself being the cornerstone, [21]in whom the whole structure is joined together and grows into a holy temple in the Lord; [22]in whom you also are built into it for a dwelling place of God in the Spirit.

Phil 3:17-21 (§249)

[17]Brethren, join in imitating me, and mark those who so live as you have an example in us. [18]For many, of whom I have often told you and now tell you even with tears, live as enemies of the cross of Christ. [19]Their end is destruction, their god is the belly, and they glory in their shame, with minds set on earthly things. [20]But our commonwealth is in heaven, and from it we await a Savior, the Lord Jesus Christ, [21]who will change our lowly body to be like his glorious body, by the power which enables him even to subject all things to himself.

Col 1:15-23 (§258-259)

[15]He is the image of the invisible God, the first-born of all creation; [16]for in him all things were created, in heaven and on earth, visible and invisible, whether thrones or dominions or principalities or authorities—all things were created through him and for him. [17]He is before all things, and in him all things hold together. [18]He is the head of the body, the church; he is the beginning, the first-born from the dead, that in everything he might be pre-eminent. [19]For in him all the fulness of God was pleased to dwell, [20]and through him to reconcile to himself all things, whether on earth or in heaven, making peace by the blood of his cross.

[21]And you, who once were estranged and hostile in mind, doing evil deeds, [22]he has now reconciled in his body of flesh by his death, in order to present you holy and blameless and irreproachable before him, [23]provided that you continue in the faith, stable and steadfast, not shifting from the hope of the gospel which you heard, which has been preached to every creature under heaven, and of which I, Paul, became a minister.

● **Rom 5:9**
Cf. Rom 1 [18]For the wrath of God is revealed from heaven against all ungodliness and wickedness of men who by their wickedness suppress the truth.

● **Rom 5:10**
2 Tim 2 [17]and their talk will eat its way like gangrene. Among them are Hymenaeus and Philetus, [18]who have swerved from the truth by holding that the resurrection is past already.

Cf. Rom 11 [28]As regards the gospel they are enemies of God, for your sake; but as regards election they are beloved for the sake of their forefathers.

[12]Therefore as sin came into the world through one man and death through sin, and so death spread to all men because all men sinned— [13]sin indeed was in the world before the law was given, but sin is not counted where there is no law. [14]Yet death reigned from Adam to Moses, even over those whose sins were not like the transgression of Adam, who was a type of the one who was to come.

[15]But the free gift is not like the trespass. For if many died through one man's trespass, much more have the grace of God and the free gift in the grace of that one man Jesus Christ abounded for many. [16]And the free gift is not like the effect of that one man's sin. For the judgment following one trespass brought condemnation, but the free gift following many trespasses brings justification. [17]If, because of one man's trespass, death reigned through that one man, much more will those who receive the abundance of grace and the free gift of righteousness reign in life through the one man Jesus Christ.

[18]Then as one man's trespass led to condemnation for all men, so one man's act of righteousness leads to acquittal and life for all men. [19]For as by one man's disobedience many were made sinners, so by one man's obedience many will be made righteous. [20]Law came in, to increase the trespass; but where sin increased, grace abounded all the more, [21]so that, as sin reigned in death, grace also might reign through righteousness to eternal life through Jesus Christ our Lord.

PRIMARY

1 Cor 15:20-28 (§133)

[20]But in fact Christ has been raised from the dead, the first fruits of those who have fallen asleep. [21]For as by a man came death, by a man has come also the resurrection of the dead. [22]For as in Adam all die, so also in Christ shall all be made alive. [23]But each in his own order: Christ the first fruits, then at his coming those who belong to Christ. [24]Then comes the end, when he delivers the kingdom to God the Father after destroying every rule and every authority and power. [25]For he must reign until he has put all his enemies under his feet. [26]The last enemy to be destroyed is death. [27]"For God has put all things in subjection under his feet." But when it says, "All things are put in subjection under him," it is plain that he is excepted who put all things under him. [28]When all things are subjected to him, then the Son himself will also be subjected to him who put all things under him, that God may be everything to every one.

2 Cor 3:7-11 (§156)

[7]Now if the dispensation of death, carved in letters on stone, came with such splendor that the Israelites could not look at Moses' face because of its brightness, fading as this was, [8]will not the dispensation of the Spirit be attended with greater splendor? [9]For if there was splendor in the dispensation of condemnation, the dispensation of righteousness must far exceed it in splendor. [10]Indeed, in this case, what once had splendor has come to have no splendor at all, because of the splendor that surpasses it. [11]For if what faded away came with splendor, what is permanent must have much more splendor.

Gal 3:19-20 (§204)

[19]Why then the law? It was added because of transgressions, till the offspring should come to whom the promise had been made; and it was ordained by angels through an intermediary. [20]Now an intermediary implies more than one; but God is one.

Eph 4:1-10 (§225)

[1]I therefore, a prisoner for the Lord, beg you to lead a life worthy of the calling to which you have been called, [2]with all lowliness and meekness, with patience, forbearing one another in love, [3]eager to maintain the unity of the Spirit in the bond of peace. [4]There is one body and one Spirit, just as you were called to the one hope that belongs to your call, [5]one Lord, one faith, one baptism, [6]one God and Father of us all, who is above all and through all and in all. [7]But grace was given to each of us according to the measure of Christ's gift. [8]Therefore it is said,

"When he ascended on high he led a host of captives,
and he gave gifts to men."

[9](In saying, "He ascended," what does it mean but that he had also descended into the lower parts of the earth? [10]He who descended is he who also ascended far above all the heavens, that he might fill all things.)

Phil 2:1-11 (§242)

[1]So if there is any encouragement in Christ, any incentive of love, any participation in the Spirit, any affection and sympathy, [2]complete my joy by being of the same mind, having the same love, being in full accord and of one mind. [3]Do nothing from selfishness or conceit, but in humility count others better than yourselves. [4]Let each of you look not only to his own interests, but also to the interests of others. [5]Have this mind among yourselves, which is yours in Christ Jesus, [6]who, though he was in the form of God, did not count equality with God a thing to be grasped, [7]but emptied himself, taking the form of a servant, being born in the likeness of men. [8]And being found in human form he humbled himself and became obedient unto death, even death on a cross. [9]Therefore God has highly exalted him and bestowed on him the name which is above every name, [10]that at the name of Jesus every knee should bow, in heaven and on earth and under the earth, [11]and every tongue confess that Jesus Christ is Lord, to the glory of God the Father.

● **Rom 5:12-21**
Eph 2   [8]For by grace you have been saved through faith; and this is not your own doing, it is the gift of God— [9]not because of works, lest any man should boast.

Cf. Rom 2   [6]For he will render to every man according to his works: . . .

Cf. Rom 6   [20]When you were slaves of sin, you were free in regard to righteousness. [21]But then what return did you get from the things of which you are now ashamed? The end of those things is death. [22]But now that you have been set free from sin and have become slaves of God, the return you get is sanctification and its end, eternal life. [23]For the wages of sin is death, but the free gift of God is eternal life in Christ Jesus our Lord.

● **Rom 5:15**
Acts 15   [11]"But we believe that we shall be saved through the grace of the Lord Jesus, just as they will."

1 Tim 2   [5]For there is one God, and there is one mediator between God and men, the man Christ Jesus, . . .

● **Rom 5:18**
Rom 11   [32]For God has consigned all men to disobedience, that he may have mercy upon all.

1 Thess 5   [9]For God has not destined us for wrath, but to obtain salvation through our Lord Jesus Christ, . . .

Cf. Gal 3   [22]But the scripture consigned all things to sin, that what was promised to faith in Jesus Christ might be given to those who believe.

Cf. 1 Cor 15   [51]Lo! I tell you a mystery. We shall not all sleep, but we shall all be changed, . . .

● **Rom 5:20**
Rom 7   [7]What then shall we say? That the law is sin? By no means! Yet, if it had not been for the law, I should not have known sin. I should not have known what it is to covet if the law had not said, "You shall not covet." [8]But sin, finding opportunity in the commandment, wrought in me all kinds of covetousness. Apart from the law sin lies dead. [9]I was once alive apart from the law, but when the commandment came, sin revived and I died; [10]the very commandment which promised life proved to be death to me. [11]For sin, finding opportunity in the commandment, deceived me and by it killed me. [12]So the law is holy, and the commandment is holy and just and good.

Cf. 1 Tim 1   [14]and the grace of our Lord overflowed for me with the faith and love that are in Christ Jesus.

6 What shall we say then? Are we to continue in sin that grace may abound? [2] By no means! How can we who died to sin still live in it? [3] Do you not know that all of us who have been baptized into Christ Jesus were baptized into his death? [4] We were buried therefore with him by baptism into death, so that as Christ was raised from the dead by the glory of the Father, we too might walk in newness of life.

[5] For if we have been united with him in a death like his, we shall certainly be united with him in a resurrection like his. [6] We know that our old self was crucified with him so that the sinful body might be destroyed, and we might no longer be enslaved to sin. [7] For he who has died is freed from sin. [8] But if we have died with Christ, we believe that we shall also live with him. [9] For we know that Christ being raised from the dead will never die again; death no longer has dominion over him. [10] The death he died he died to sin, once for all, but the life he lives he lives to God.

PRIMARY

2 Cor 4:13–15 (§160)

[13] Since we have the same spirit of faith as he had who wrote, "I believed, and so I spoke," we too believe, and so we speak, [14] knowing that he who raised the Lord Jesus will raise us also with Jesus and bring us with you into his presence. [15] For it is all for your sake, so that as grace extends to more and more people it may increase thanksgiving, to the glory of God.

Eph 2:1–10 (§220)

[1] And you he made alive, when you were dead through the trespasses and sins [2] in which you once walked, following the course of this world, following the prince of the power of the air, the spirit that is now at work in the sons of disobedience. [3] Among these we all once lived in the passions of our flesh, following the desires of body and mind, and so we were by nature children of wrath, like the rest of mankind. [4] But God, who is rich in mercy, out of the great love with which he loved us, [5] even when we were dead through our trespasses, made us alive together with Christ (by grace you have been saved), [6] and raised us up with him, and made us sit with him in the heavenly places in Christ Jesus, [7] that in the coming ages he might show the immeasurable riches of his grace in kindness toward us in Christ Jesus. [8] For by grace you have been saved through faith; and this is not your own doing, it is the gift of God—

[9] not because of works, lest any man should boast. [10] For we are his workmanship, created in Christ Jesus for good works, which God prepared beforehand, that we should walk in them.

Col 2:8–15 (§262)

[8] See to it that no one makes a prey of you by philosophy and empty deceit, according to human tradition, according to the elemental spirits of the universe, and not according to Christ. [9] For in him the whole fulness of deity dwells bodily, [10] and you have come to fulness of life in him, who is the head of all rule and authority. [11] In him also you were circumcised with a circumcision made without hands, by putting off the body of flesh in the circumcision of Christ; [12] and you were buried with him in baptism, in which you were also raised with him through faith in the working of God, who raised him from the dead. [13] And you, who were dead in trespasses and the uncircumcision of your flesh, God made alive together with him, having forgiven us all our trespasses, [14] having canceled the bond which stood against us with its legal demands; this he set aside, nailing it to the cross. [15] He disarmed the principalities and powers and made a public example of them, triumphing over them in him.

● **Rom 6:1–10**

Rom 3　[5] But if our wickedness serves to show the justice of God, what shall we say? That God is unjust to inflict wrath on us? (I speak in a human way.) [6] By no means! For then how could God judge the world? [7] But if through my falsehood God's truthfulness abounds to his glory, why am I still being condemned as a sinner? [8] And why not do evil that good may come?—as some people slanderously charge us with saying. Their condemnation is just.

Cf. 1 Cor 15　[3] For I delivered to you as of first importance what I also received, that Christ died for our sins in accordance with the scriptures, [4] that he was buried, that he was raised on the third day in accordance with the scriptures, [5] and that he appeared to Cephas, then to the twelve.

● **Rom 6:3**

Gal 3　[26] for in Christ Jesus you are all sons of God, through faith. [27] For as many of you as were baptized into Christ have put on Christ. [28] There is neither Jew nor Greek, there is neither slave nor free, there is neither male nor female; for you are all one in Christ Jesus. [29] And if you are Christ's, then you are Abraham's offspring, heirs according to promise.

Acts 2　[38] And Peter said to them, "Repent, and be baptized every one of you in the name of Jesus Christ for the forgiveness of your sins; and you shall receive the gift of the Holy Spirit."

Acts 8　[16] . . . for it had not yet fallen on any of them, but they had only been baptized in the name of the Lord Jesus.

Acts 19　[5] On hearing this, they were baptized in the name of the Lord Jesus.

● **Rom 6:5**

2 Cor 5　[14] For the love of Christ controls us, because we are convinced that one has died for all; therefore all have died. [15] And he died for all, that those who live might live no longer for themselves but for him who for their sake died and was raised.

Phil 3　[10] that I may know him and the power of his resurrection, and may share his sufferings, becoming like him in his death, [11] that if possible I may attain the resurrection from the dead.

● **Rom 6:8**

2 Tim 2　[11] The saying is sure:
　If we have died with him, we shall also live with him;
　[12] if we endure, we shall also reign with him;
　if we deny him, he also will deny us;
　[13] if we are faithless, he remains faithful—
　for he cannot deny himself.

● **Rom 6:9**

Acts 2　[24] "But God raised him up, having loosed the pangs of death, because it was not possible for him to be held by it."

¹¹ So you also must consider yourselves dead to sin and alive to God in Christ Jesus. ¹² Let not sin therefore reign in your mortal bodies, to make you obey their passions. ¹³ Do not yield your members to sin as instruments of wickedness, but yield yourselves to God as men who have been brought from death to life, and your members to God as instruments of righteousness. ¹⁴ For sin will have no dominion over you, since you are not under law but under grace.

PRIMARY

Gal 3:21–25 (§205)

²¹ Is the law then against the promises of God? Certainly not; for if a law had been given which could make alive, then righteousness would indeed be by the law. ²² But the scripture consigned all things to sin, that what was promised to faith in Jesus Christ might be given to those who believe.

²³ Now before faith came, we were confined under the law, kept under restraint until faith should be revealed. ²⁴ So that the law was our custodian until Christ came, that we might be justified by faith. ²⁵ But now that faith has come, we are no longer under a custodian; . . .

Col 2:20–3:11 (§264–266)

²⁰ If with Christ you died to the elemental spirits of the universe, why do you live as if you still belonged to the world? Why do you submit to regulations, ²¹ "Do not handle, Do not taste, Do not touch" ²² (referring to things which all perish as they are used), according to human precepts and doctrines? ²³ These have indeed an appearance of wisdom in promoting rigor of devotion and self-abasement and severity to the body, but they are of no value in checking the indulgence of the flesh.

3 If then you have been raised with Christ, seek the things that are above, where Christ is, seated at the right hand of God. ² Set your minds on things that are above, not on things that are on earth. ³ For you have died, and your life is hid with Christ in God. ⁴ When Christ who is our life appears, then you also will appear with him in glory.

⁵ Put to death therefore what is earthly in you: fornication, impurity, passion, evil desire, and covetousness, which is idolatry. ⁶ On account of these the wrath of God is coming. ⁷ In these you once walked, when you lived in them. ⁸ But now put them all away: anger, wrath, malice, slander, and foul talk from your mouth. ⁹ Do not lie to one another, seeing that you have put off the old nature with its practices ¹⁰ and have put on the new nature, which is being renewed in knowledge after the image of its creator. ¹¹ Here there cannot be Greek and Jew, circumcised and uncircumcised, barbarian, Scythian, slave, free man, but Christ is all, and in all.

● **Rom 6:11–14**

2 Cor 5   ¹⁴ For the love of Christ controls us, because we are convinced that one has died for all; therefore all have died. ¹⁵ And he died for all, that those who live might live no longer for themselves but for him who for their sake died and was raised.

Cf. 2 Cor 1   ⁹ Why, we felt that we had received the sentence of death; but that was to make us rely not on ourselves but on God who raises the dead; ¹⁰ he delivered us from so deadly a peril, and he will deliver us; on him we have set our hope that he will deliver us again.

● **Rom 6:12–14**

Rom 12   ¹ I appeal to you therefore, brethren, by the mercies of God, to present your bodies as a living sacrifice, holy and acceptable to God, which is your spiritual worship. ² Do not be conformed to this world but be transformed by the renewal of your mind, that you may prove what is the will of God, what is good and acceptable and perfect.

● **Rom 6:12**

(passions) *read* it: p⁴⁶DG it(some) Irenaeus(Latin) Tertullian; *text:* SABC* it(most) vg cop Origen Ambrosiaster

● **Rom 6:14**

Gal 4   ²¹ Tell me, you who desire to be under law, do you not hear the law?

Cf. 1 Cor 9   ²¹ To those outside the law I became as one outside the law—not being without law toward God but under the law of Christ —that I might win those outside the law.

Cf. Gal 5   ¹⁸ But if you are led by the Spirit you are not under the law.

15 What then? Are we to sin because we are not under law but under grace? By no means! 16 Do you not know that if you yield yourselves to any one as obedient slaves, you are slaves of the one whom you obey, either of sin, which leads to death, or of obedience, which leads to righteousness? 17 But thanks be to God, that you who were once slaves of sin have become obedient from the heart to the standard of teaching to which you were committed, 18 and, having been set free from sin, have become slaves of righteousness. 19 I am speaking in human terms, because of your natural limitations. For just as you once yielded your members to impurity and to greater and greater iniquity, so now yield your members to righteousness for sanctification.

20 When you were slaves of sin, you were free in regard to righteousness. 21 But then what return did you get from the things of which you are now ashamed? The end of those things is death. 22 But now that you have been set free from sin and have become slaves of God, the return you get is sanctification and its end, eternal life. 23 For the wages of sin is death, but the free gift of God is eternal life in Christ Jesus our Lord.

PRIMARY

1 Cor 6:12–20 (§92)

12 "All things are lawful for me," but not all things are helpful. "All things are lawful for me," but I will not be enslaved by anything. 13 "Food is meant for the stomach and the stomach for food"—and God will destroy both one and the other. The body is not meant for immorality, but for the Lord, and the Lord for the body. 14 And God raised the Lord and will also raise us up by his power. 15 Do you not know that your bodies are members of Christ? Shall I therefore take the members of Christ and make them members of a prostitute? Never! 16 Do you not know that he who joins himself to a prostitute becomes one body with her? For, as it is written, "The two shall become one flesh." 17 But he who is united to the Lord becomes one spirit with him. 18 Shun immorality. Every other sin which a man commits is outside the body; but the immoral man sins against his own body. 19 Do you not know that your body is a temple of the Holy Spirit within you, which you have from God? You are not your own; 20 you were bought with a price. So glorify God in your body.

1 Cor 7:17–24 (§97)

17 Only, let every one lead the life which the Lord has assigned to him, and in which God has called him. This is my rule in all the churches. 18 Was any one at the time of his call already circumcised? Let him not seek to remove the marks of circumcision. Was any one at the time of his call uncircumcised? Let him not seek circumcision. 19 For neither circumcision counts for anything nor uncircumcision, but keeping the commandments of God. 20 Every one should remain in the state in which he was called. 21 Were you a slave when called? Never mind. But if you can gain your freedom, avail yourself of the opportunity. 22 For he who was called in the Lord as a slave is a freedman of the Lord. Likewise he who was free when called is a slave of Christ. 23 You were bought with a price; do not become slaves of men. 24 So, brethren, in whatever state each was called, there let him remain with God.

Gal 4:1–7 (§207)

1 I mean that the heir, as long as he is a child, is no better than a slave, though he is the owner of all the estate; 2 but he is under guardians and trustees until the date set by the father. 3 So with us; when we were children, we were slaves to the elemental spirits of the universe. 4 But when the time had fully come, God sent forth his Son, born of woman, born under the law, 5 to redeem those who were under the law, so that we might receive adoption as sons. 6 And because you are sons, God has sent the Spirit of his Son into our hearts, crying, "Abba! Father!" 7 So through God you are no longer a slave but a son, and if a son then an heir.

Gal 5:1–12 (§211)

1 For freedom Christ has set us free; stand fast therefore, and do not submit again to a yoke of slavery.

2 Now I, Paul, say to you that if you receive circumcision, Christ will be of no advantage to you. 3 I testify again to every man who receives circumcision that he is bound to keep the whole law. 4 You are severed from Christ, you who would be justified by the law; you have fallen away from grace. 5 For through the Spirit, by faith, we wait for the hope of righteousness. 6 For in Christ Jesus neither circumcision nor uncircumcision is of any avail, but faith working through love. 7 You were running well; who hindered you from obeying the truth? 8 This persuasion is not from him who called you. 9 A little leaven leavens the whole lump. 10 I have confidence in the Lord that you will take no other view than mine; and he who is troubling you will bear his judgment, whoever he is. 11 But if I, brethren, still preach circumcision, why am I still persecuted? In that case the stumbling block of the cross has been removed. 12 I wish those who unsettle you would mutilate themselves!

Gal 5:13–15 (§212)

13 For you were called to freedom, brethren; only do not use your freedom as an opportunity for the flesh, but through love be servants of one another. 14 For the whole law is fulfilled in one word, "You shall love your neighbor as yourself." 15 But if you bite and devour one another take heed that you are not consumed by one another.

Gal 6:7–10 (§215)

7 Do not be deceived; God is not mocked, for whatever a man sows, that he will also reap. 8 For he who sows to his own flesh will from the flesh reap corruption; but he who sows to the Spirit will from the Spirit reap eternal life. 9 And let us not grow weary in well-doing, for in due season we shall reap, if we do not lose heart. 10 So then, as we have opportunity, let us do good to all men, and especially to those who are of the household of faith.

● **Rom 6:15–23**

1 Thess 1   9 For they themselves report concerning us what a welcome we had among you, and how you turned to God from idols, to serve a living and true God, . . .

Cf. Rom 7   25 Thanks be to God through Jesus Christ our Lord! So then, I of myself serve the law of God with my mind, but with my flesh I serve the law of sin.

Cf. Rom 14   18 he who thus serves Christ is acceptable to God and approved by men.

Cf. Rom 16   18 For such persons do not serve our Lord Christ, but their own appetites, and by fair and flattering words they deceive the hearts of the simpleminded.

Cf. Gal 4   9 but now that you have come to know God, or rather to be known by God, how can you turn back again to the weak and beggarly elemental spirits, whose slaves you want to be once more?

● **Rom 6:19**

1 Thess 4   3 For this is the will of God, your sanctification: that you abstain from unchastity; . . .

1 Thess 4   7 For God has not called us for uncleanness, but in holiness.

Cf. 1 Cor 1   30 He is the source of your life in Christ Jesus, whom God made our wisdom, our righteousness and sanctification and redemption; . . .

● **Rom 6:23**

Rom 5   15 But the free gift is not like the trespass. For if many died through one man's trespass, much more have the grace of God and the free gift in the grace of that one man Jesus Christ abounded for many.

Eph 2   8 For by grace you have been saved through faith; and this is not your own doing, it is the gift of God— 9 not because of works, lest any man should boast.

Jas 1   15 Then desire when it has conceived gives birth to sin; and sin when it is full-grown brings forth death.

Cf. Rom 2   6 For he will render to every man according to his works: . . .

7 Do you not know, brethren—for I am speaking to those who know the law—that the law is binding on a person only during his life? [2]Thus a married woman is bound by law to her husband as long as he lives; but if her husband dies she is discharged from the law concerning the husband. [3]Accordingly, she will be called an adulteress if she lives with another man while her husband is alive. But if her husband dies she is free from that law, and if she marries another man she is not an adulteress.

[4]Likewise, my brethren, you have died to the law through the body of Christ, so that you may belong to another, to him who has been raised from the dead in order that we may bear fruit for God. [5]While we were living in the flesh, our sinful passions, aroused by the law, were at work in our members to bear fruit for death. [6]But now we are discharged from the law, dead to that which held us captive, so that we serve not under the old written code but in the new life of the Spirit.

PRIMARY

1 Cor 7:8–9 (§94)

[8]To the unmarried and the widows I say that it is well for them to remain single as I do. [9]But if they cannot exercise self-control, they should marry. For it is better to marry than to be aflame with passion.

1 Cor 7:10–11 (§95)

[10]To the married I give charge, not I but the Lord, that the wife should not separate from her husband [11](but if she does, let her remain single or else be reconciled to her husband)—and that the husband should not divorce his wife.

1 Cor 7:39–40 (§101)

[39]A wife is bound to her husband as long as he lives. If the husband dies, she is free to be married to whom she wishes, only in the Lord. [40]But in my judgment she is happier if she remains as she is. And I think that I have the Spirit of God.

2 Cor 3:1–18 (§154–157)

[1]Are we beginning to commend ourselves again? Or do we need, as some do, letters of recommendation to you, or from you? [2]You yourselves are our letter of recommendation, written on your hearts, to be known and read by all men; [3]and you show that you are a letter from Christ delivered by us, written not with ink but with the Spirit of the living God, not on tablets of stone but on tablets of human hearts.

[4]Such is the confidence that we have through Christ toward God. [5]Not that we are competent of ourselves to claim anything as coming from us; our competence is from God, [6]who has made us competent to be ministers of a new covenant, not in a written code but in the Spirit; for the written code kills, but the Spirit gives life.

[7]Now if the dispensation of death, carved in letters on stone, came with such splendor that the Israelites could not look at Moses' face because of its brightness, fading as this was, [8]will not the dispensation of the Spirit be attended with greater splendor? [9]For if there was splendor in the dispensation of condemnation, the dispensation of righteousness must far exceed it in splendor. [10]Indeed, in this case, what once had splendor has come to have no splendor at all, because of the splendor that surpasses it. [11]For if what faded away came with splendor, what is permanent must have much more splendor.

[12]Since we have such a hope, we are very bold, [13]not like Moses, who put a veil over his face so that the Israelites might not see the end of the fading splendor. [14]But their minds were hardened; for to this day, when they read the old covenant, that same veil remains unlifted, because only through Christ is it taken away. [15]Yes, to this day whenever Moses is read a veil lies over their minds; [16]but when a man turns to the Lord the veil is removed. [17]Now the Lord is the Spirit, and where the Spirit of the Lord is, there is freedom. [18]And we all, with unveiled face, beholding the glory of the Lord, are being changed into his likeness from one degree of glory to another; for this comes from the Lord who is the Spirit.

Gal 2:15–21 (§199)

[15]We ourselves, who are Jews by birth and not Gentile sinners, [16]yet who know that a man is not justified by works of the law but through faith in Jesus Christ, even we have believed in Christ Jesus, in order to be justified by faith in Christ, and not by works of the law, because by works of the law shall no one be justified. [17]But if, in our endeavor to be justified in Christ, we ourselves were found to be sinners, is Christ then an agent of sin? Certainly not! [18]But if I build up again those things which I tore down, then I prove myself a transgressor. [19]For I through the law died to the law, that I might live to God. [20]I have been crucified with Christ; it is no longer I who live, but Christ who lives in me; and the life I now live in the flesh I live by faith in the Son of God, who loved me and gave himself for me. [21]I do not nullify the grace of God; for if justification were through the law, then Christ died to no purpose.

Gal 3:21–25 (§205)

[21]Is the law then against the promises of God? Certainly not; for if a law had been given which could make alive, then righteousness would indeed be by the law. [22]But the scripture consigned all things to sin, that what was promised to faith in Jesus Christ might be given to those who believe.

[23]Now before faith came, we were confined under the law, kept under restraint until faith should be revealed. [24]So that the law was our custodian until Christ came, that we might be justified by faith. [25]But now that faith has come, we are no longer under a custodian; is not irksome to me, and is safe for you.

Phil 3:2–11 (§247)

[2]Look out for the dogs, look out for the evil-workers, look out for those who mutilate the flesh. [3]For we are the true circumcision, who worship God in spirit, and glory in Christ Jesus, and put no confidence in the flesh. [4]Though I myself have reason for confidence in the flesh also. If any other man thinks he has reason for confidence in the flesh, I have more: [5]circumcised on the eighth day, of the people of Israel, of the tribe of Benjamin, a Hebrew born of Hebrews; as to the law a Pharisee, [6]as to zeal a persecutor of the church, as to righteousness under the law blameless. [7]But whatever gain I had, I counted as loss for the sake of Christ. [8]Indeed I count everything as loss because of the surpassing worth of knowing Christ Jesus my Lord. For his sake I have suffered the loss of all things, and count them as refuse, in order that I may gain Christ [9]and be found in him, not having a righteousness of my own, based on law, but that which is through faith in Christ, the righteousness from God that depends on faith; [10]that I may know him and the power of his resurrection, and may share his sufferings, becoming like him in his death, [11]that if possible I may attain the resurrection from the dead.

● **Rom 7:2**
1 Cor 7   [15]But if the unbelieving partner desires to separate, let it be so; in such a case the brother or sister is not bound. For God has called us to peace.

● **Rom 7:4**
Eph 2   [15]by abolishing in his flesh the law of commandments and ordinances, that he might create in himself one new man in place of the two, so making peace, . . .

● **Rom 7:5**
Rom 5   [20]Law came in, to increase the trespass; but where sin increased, grace abounded all the more, . . .

● **Rom 7:6**
(dead) *read* of death which: DG it vg(clem); *text:* SABC Koine Lect vg(w-w) syr cop Tertullian

[7] What then shall we say? That the law is sin? By no means! Yet, if it had not been for the law, I should not have known sin. I should not have known what it is to covet if the law had not said, "You shall not covet." [8] But sin, finding opportunity in the commandment, wrought in me all kinds of covetousness. Apart from the law sin lies dead. [9] I was once alive apart from the law, but when the commandment came, sin revived and I died; [10] the very commandment which promised life proved to be death to me. [11] For sin, finding opportunity in the commandment, deceived me and by it killed me. [12] So the law is holy, and the commandment is holy and just and good.

[13] Did that which is good, then, bring death to me? By no means! It was sin, working death in me through what is good, in order that sin might be shown to be sin, and through the commandment might become sinful beyond measure.

Primary

1 Cor 15:51–58 (§137)

[51] Lo! I tell you a mystery. We shall not all sleep, but we shall all be changed, [52] in a moment, in the twinkling of an eye, at the last trumpet. For the trumpet will sound, and the dead will be raised imperishable, and we shall be changed. [53] For this perishable nature must put on the imperishable, and this mortal nature must put on immortality. [54] When the perishable puts on the imperishable, and the mortal puts on immortality, then shall come to pass the saying that is written:

"Death is swallowed up in victory."
[55] "O death, where is thy victory?
O death, where is thy sting?" [56] The sting of death is sin, and the power of sin is the law. [57] But thanks be to God, who gives us the victory through our Lord Jesus Christ.

[58] Therefore, my beloved brethren, be steadfast, immovable, always abounding in the work of the Lord, knowing that in the Lord your labor is not in vain.

Gal 1:13–14 (§195)

[13] For you have heard of my former life in Judaism, how I persecuted the church of God violently and tried to destroy it; [14] and I advanced in Judaism beyond many of my own age among my people, so extremely zealous was I for the traditions of my fathers.

Gal 3:21–25 (§205)

[21] Is the law then against the promises of God? Certainly not; for if a law had been given which could make alive, then righteousness would indeed be by the law. [22] But the scripture consigned all things to sin, that what was promised to faith in Jesus Christ might be given to those who believe.

[23] Now before faith came, we were confined under the law, kept under restraint until faith should be revealed. [24] So that the law was our custodian until Christ came, that we might be justified by faith. [25] But now that faith has come, we are no longer under a custodian; . . .

Phil 3:2–11 (§247)

[2] Look out for the dogs, look out for the evil-workers, look out for those who mutilate the flesh. [3] For we are the true circumcision, who worship God in spirit, and glory in Christ Jesus, and put no confidence in the flesh. [4] Though I myself have reason for confidence in the flesh also. If any other man thinks he has reason for confidence in the flesh, I have more: [5] circumcised on the eighth day, of the people of Israel, of the tribe of Benjamin, a Hebrew born of Hebrews; as to the law a Pharisee, [6] as to zeal a persecutor of the church, as to righteousness under the law blameless. [7] But whatever gain I had, I counted as loss for the sake of Christ. [8] Indeed I count everything as loss because of the surpassing worth of knowing Christ Jesus my Lord. For his sake I have suffered the loss of all things, and count them as refuse, in order that I may gain Christ [9] and be found in him, not having a righteousness of my own, based on law, but that which is through faith in Christ, the righteousness from God that depends on faith; [10] that I may know him and the power of his resurrection, and may share his sufferings, becoming like him in his death, [11] that if possible I may attain the resurrection from the dead.

● **Rom 7:7**
Rom 4   [15] For the law brings wrath, but where there is no law there is no transgression.

Rom 5   [20] Law came in, to increase the trespass; but where sin increased, grace abounded all the more, . . .

Gal 3   [19] Why then the law? It was added because of transgressions, till the offspring should come to whom the promise had been made; and it was ordained by angels through an intermediary. [20] Now an intermediary implies more than one; but God is one.

Exod 20   [17] "You shall not covet your neighbor's house; you shall not covet your neighbor's wife, or his manservant, or his maidservant, or his ox, or his ass, or anything that is your neighbor's."

Deut 5   [21] "'Neither shall you covet your neighbor's wife; and you shall not desire your neighbor's house, his field, or his manservant, or his maidservant, his ox, or his ass, or anything that is your neighbor's.'"

● **Rom 7:10**
Cf. Gal 3   [12] but the law does not rest on faith, for "He who does them shall live by them."

● **Rom 7:12**
Rom 3   [31] Do we then overthrow the law by this faith? By no means! On the contrary, we uphold the law.

Rom 12   [2] Do not be conformed to this world but be transformed by the renewal of your mind, that you may prove what is the will of God, what is good and acceptable and perfect.

1 Tim 1   [8] Now we know that the law is good, if any one uses it lawfully, . . .

14 We know that the law is spiritual; but I am carnal, sold under sin. **15** I do not understand my own actions. For I do not do what I want, but I do the very thing I hate. **16** Now if I do what I do not want, I agree that the law is good. **17** So then it is no longer I that do it, but sin which dwells within me. **18** For I know that nothing good dwells within me, that is, in my flesh. I can will what is right, but I cannot do it. **19** For I do not do the good I want, but the evil I do not want is what I do. **20** Now if I do what I do not want, it is no longer I that do it, but sin which dwells within me.

21 So I find it to be a law that when I want to do right, evil lies close at hand. **22** For I delight in the law of God, in my inmost self, **23** but I see in my members another law at war with the law of my mind and making me captive to the law of sin which dwells in my members. **24** Wretched man that I am! Who will deliver me from this body of death? **25** Thanks be to God through Jesus Christ our Lord! So then, I of myself serve the law of God with my mind, but with my flesh I serve the law of sin.

PRIMARY

1 Cor 3:1–4 (§78)

1 But I, brethren, could not address you as spiritual men, but as men of the flesh, as babes in Christ. **2** I fed you with milk, not solid food; for you were not ready for it; and even yet you are not ready, **3** for you are still of the flesh. For while there is jealousy and strife among you, are you not of the flesh, and behaving like ordinary men? **4** For when one says, "I belong to Paul," and another, "I belong to Apollos," are you not merely men?

Gal 1:13–14 (§195)

13 For you have heard of my former life in Judaism, how I persecuted the church of God violently and tried to destroy it; **14** and I advanced in Judaism beyond many of my own age among my people, so extremely zealous was I for the traditions of my fathers.

Gal 5:16–26 (§213)

16 But I say, walk by the Spirit, and do not gratify the desires of the flesh. **17** For the desires of the flesh are against the Spirit, and the desires of the Spirit are against the flesh; for these are opposed to each other, to prevent you from doing what you would. **18** But if you are led by the Spirit you are not under the law. **19** Now the works of the flesh are plain: fornication, impurity, licentiousness, **20** idolatry, sorcery, enmity, strife, jealousy, anger, selfishness, dissension, party spirit, **21** envy, drunkenness, carousing, and the like. I warn you, as I warned you before, that those who do such things shall not inherit the kingdom of God. **22** But the fruit of the Spirit is love, joy, peace, patience, kindness, goodness, faithfulness, **23** gentleness, self-control; against such there is no law. **24** And those who belong to Christ Jesus have crucified the flesh with its passions and desires.

25 If we live by the Spirit, let us also walk by the Spirit. **26** Let us have no self-conceit, no provoking of one another, no envy of one another.

Phil 3:2–11 (§247)

2 Look out for the dogs, look out for the evil-workers, look out for those who mutilate the flesh. **3** For we are the true circumcision, who worship God in spirit, and glory in Christ Jesus, and put no confidence in the flesh. **4** Though I myself have reason for confidence in the flesh also. If any other man thinks he has reason for confidence in the flesh, I have more: **5** circumcised on the eighth day, of the people of Israel, of the tribe of Benjamin, a Hebrew born of Hebrews; as to the law a Pharisee, **6** as to zeal a persecutor of the church, as to righteousness under the law blameless. **7** But whatever gain I had, I counted as loss for the sake of Christ. **8** Indeed I count everything as loss because of the surpassing worth of knowing Christ Jesus my Lord. For his sake I have suffered the loss of all things, and count them as refuse, in order that I may gain Christ **9** and be found in him, not having a righteousness of my own, based on law, but that which is through faith in Christ, the righteousness from God that depends on faith; **10** that I may know him and the power of his resurrection, and may share his sufferings, becoming like him in his death, **11** that if possible I may attain the resurrection from the dead.

● **Rom 7:14**
Rom 8   **9** But you are not in the flesh, you are in the Spirit, if in fact the Spirit of God dwells in you. Any one who does not have the Spirit of Christ does not belong to him.

● **Rom 7:16**
1 Tim 1   **8** Now we know that the law is good, if any one uses it lawfully, . . .

● **Rom 7:22**
Eph 3   **16** that according to the riches of his glory he may grant you to be strengthened with might through his Spirit in the inner man, . . .

● **Rom 7:25**
1 Cor 9   **21** To those outside the law I became as one outside the law—not being without law toward God but under the law of Christ —that I might win those outside the law.

1 Cor 15   **57** But thanks be to God, who gives us the victory through our Lord Jesus Christ.

Gal 6   **2** Bear one another's burdens, and so fulfil the law of Christ.

Cf. Col 2   **18** Let no one disqualify you, insisting on self-abasement and worship of angels, taking his stand on visions, puffed up without reason by his sensuous mind, . . .

8 There is therefore now no condemnation for those who are in Christ Jesus. [2]For the law of the Spirit of life in Christ Jesus has set me free from the law of sin and death. [3]For God has done what the law, weakened by the flesh, could not do: sending his own Son in the likeness of sinful flesh and for sin, he condemned sin in the flesh, [4]in order that the just requirement of the law might be fulfilled in us, who walk not according to the flesh but according to the Spirit. [5]For those who live according to the flesh set their minds on the things of the flesh, but those who live according to the Spirit set their minds on the things of the Spirit. [6]To set the mind on the flesh is death, but to set the mind on the Spirit is life and peace. [7]For the mind that is set on the flesh is hostile to God; it does not submit to God's law, indeed it cannot; [8]and those who are in the flesh cannot please God.

PRIMARY

1 Cor 3:1–4 (§78)

[1]But I, brethren, could not address you as spiritual men, but as men of the flesh, as babes in Christ. [2]I fed you with milk, not solid food; for you were not ready for it; and even yet you are not ready, [3]for you are still of the flesh. For while there is jealousy and strife among you, are you not of the flesh, and behaving like ordinary men? [4]For when one says, "I belong to Paul," and another, "I belong to Apollos," are you not merely men?

2 Cor 3:7–11 (§156)

[7]Now if the dispensation of death, carved in letters on stone, came with such splendor that the Israelites could not look at Moses' face because of its brightness, fading as this was, [8]will not the dispensation of the Spirit be attended with greater splendor? [9]For if there was splendor in the dispensation of condemnation, the dispensation of righteousness must far exceed it in splendor. [10]Indeed, in this case, what once had splendor has come to have no splendor at all, because of the splendor that surpasses it. [11]For if what faded away came with splendor, what is permanent must have much more splendor.

Gal 5:16–26 (§213)

[16]But I say, walk by the Spirit, and do not gratify the desires of the flesh. [17]For the desires of the flesh are against the Spirit, and the desires of the Spirit are against the flesh; for these are opposed to each other, to prevent you from doing what you would. [18]But if you are led by the Spirit you are not under the law. [19]Now the works of the flesh are plain: fornication, impurity, licentiousness, [20]idolatry, sorcery, enmity, strife, jealousy, anger, selfishness, dissension, party spirit, [21]envy, drunkenness, carousing, and the like. I warn you, as I warned you before, that those who do such things shall not inherit the kingdom of God. [22]But the fruit of the Spirit is love, joy, peace, patience, kindness, goodness, faithfulness, [23]gentleness, self-control; against such there is no law. [24]And those who belong to Christ Jesus have crucified the flesh with its passions and desires.

[25]If we live by the Spirit, let us also walk by the Spirit. [26]Let us have no self-conceit, no provoking of one another, no envy of one another.

Eph 2:1–10 (§220)

[1]And you he made alive, when you were dead through the trespasses and sins [2]in which you once walked, following the course of this world, following the prince of the power of the air, the spirit that is now at work in the sons of disobedience. [3]Among these we all once lived in the passions of our flesh, following the desires of body and mind, and so we were by nature children of wrath, like the rest of mankind. [4]But God, who is rich in mercy, out of the great love with which he loved us, [5]even when we were dead through our trespasses, made us alive together with Christ (by grace you have been saved), [6]and raised us up with him, and made us sit with him in the heavenly places in Christ Jesus, [7]that in the coming ages he might show the immeasurable riches of his grace in kindness toward us in Christ Jesus. [8]For by grace you have been saved through faith; and this is not your own doing, it is the gift of God— [9]not because of works, lest any man should boast. [10]For we are his workmanship, created in Christ Jesus for good works, which God prepared beforehand, that we should walk in them.

Col 3:1–4 (§265)

[1]If then you have been raised with Christ, seek the things that are above, where Christ is, seated at the right hand of God. [2]Set your minds on things that are above, not on things that are on earth. [3]For you have died, and your life is hid with Christ in God. [4]When Christ who is our life appears, then you also will appear with him in glory.

- **Rom 8:1**
Rom 5   [8]But God shows his love for us in that while we were yet sinners Christ died for us.

(Jesus) *add* and do not walk according to the flesh: AD[b] it(most) vg Ephraem; *add* and do not walk according to the flesh but according to the Spirit: S[c]D[c] Koine Lect it (few) Theodoret; *text:* S*BC[2]D*G it (few) cop Marcion

- **Rom 8:2**
1 Cor 15   [45]Thus it is written, "The first man Adam became a living being"; the last Adam became a life-giving spirit.

(me) *read* you: SBG it(some) syr(pes) Tertullian Ephraem; *read* us: syr (pal) cop(bo) Marcion Origen; *text:* AD Koine Lect it(most) vg syr(har) cop(sa) Clement

- **Rom 8:3**
Rom 1   [3]the gospel concerning his Son, who was descended from David according to the flesh . . .

Gal 4   [4]But when the time had fully come, God sent forth his Son, born of woman, born under the law, . . .

2 Cor 5   [16]So we do not lose heart. Though our outer nature is wasting away, our inner nature is being renewed every day. [17]For this slight momentary affliction is preparing for us an eternal weight of glory beyond all comparison, . . .

Acts 13   [39]". . . and by him every one that believes is freed from everything from which you could not be freed by the law of Moses."

Col 1   [22]he has now reconciled in his body of flesh by his death, in order to present you holy and blameless and irreproachable before him, . . .

Cf. Phil 2   [6]who, though he was in the form of God, did not count equality with God a thing to be grasped, [7]but emptied himself, taking the form of a servant, being born in the likeness of men. [8]And being found in human form he humbled himself and became obedient unto death, even death on a cross. [9]Therefore God has highly exalted him and bestowed on him the name which is above every name, [10]that at the name of Jesus every knee should bow, in heaven and on earth and under the earth, [11]and every tongue confess that Jesus Christ is Lord, to the glory of God the Father.

- **Rom 8:4**
Rom 13   [8]Owe no one anything, except to love one another; for he who loves his neighbor has fulfilled the law.

Cf. Rom 13   [10]Love does no wrong to a neighbor; therefore love is the fulfilling of the law.

Cf. Eph 2   [15]by abolishing in his flesh the law of commandments and ordinances, that he might create in himself one new man in place of the two, so making peace, . . .

- **Rom 8:5**
Gal 5   [14]For the whole law is fulfilled in one word, "You shall love your neighbor as yourself."

Cf. Gal 6   [8]For he who sows to his own flesh will from the flesh reap corruption; but he who sows to the Spirit will from the Spirit reap eternal life.

[9]But you are not in the flesh, you are in the Spirit, if in fact the Spirit of God dwells in you. Any one who does not have the Spirit of Christ does not belong to him. [10]But if Christ is in you, although your bodies are dead because of sin, your spirits are alive because of righteousness. [11]If the Spirit of him who raised Jesus from the dead dwells in you, he who raised Christ Jesus from the dead will give life to your mortal bodies also through his Spirit which dwells in you.

[12]So then, brethren, we are debtors, not to the flesh, to live according to the flesh— [13]for if you live according to the flesh you will die, but if by the Spirit you put to death the deeds of the body you will live. [14]For all who are led by the Spirit of God are sons of God. [15]For you did not receive the spirit of slavery to fall back into fear, but you have received the spirit of sonship. When we cry, "Abba! Father!" [16]it is the Spirit himself bearing witness with our spirit that we are children of God, [17]and if children, then heirs, heirs of God and fellow heirs with Christ, provided we suffer with him in order that we may also be glorified with him.

PRIMARY

1 Cor 3:16-17 (§81)

[16]Do you not know that you are God's temple and that God's Spirit dwells in you? [17]If any one destroys God's temple, God will destroy him. For God's temple is holy, and that temple you are.

Gal 2:15-21 (§199)

[15]We ourselves, who are Jews by birth and not Gentile sinners, [16]yet who know that a man is not justified by works of the law but through faith in Jesus Christ, even we have believed in Christ Jesus, in order to be justified by faith in Christ, and not by works of the law, because by works of the law shall no one be justified. [17]But if, in our endeavor to be justified in Christ, we ourselves were found to be sinners, is Christ then an agent of sin? Certainly not! [18]But if I build up again those things which I tore down, then I prove myself a transgressor. [19]For I through the law died to the law, that I might live to God. [20]I have been crucified with Christ; it is no longer I who live, but Christ who lives in me; and the life I now live in the flesh I live by faith in the Son of God, who loved me and gave himself for me. [21]I do not nullify the grace of God; for if justification were through the law, then Christ died to no purpose.

Eph 2:11-22 (§221)

[11]Therefore remember that at one time you Gentiles in the flesh, called the uncircumcision by what is called the circumcision, which is made in the flesh by hands— [12]remember that you were at that time separated from Christ, alienated from the commonwealth of Israel, and strangers to the covenants of promise, having no hope and without God in the world. [13]But now in Christ Jesus you who once were far off have been brought near in the blood of Christ. [14]For he is our peace, who has made us both one, and has broken down the dividing wall of hostility, [15]by abolishing in his flesh the law of commandments and ordinances, that he might create in himself one new man in place of the two, so making peace, [16]and might reconcile us both to God in one body through the cross, thereby bringing the hostility to an end. [17]And he came and preached peace to you who were far off and peace to those who were near; [18]for through him we both have access in one Spirit to the Father. [19]So then you are no longer strangers and sojourners, but you are fellow citizens with the saints and members of the household of God, [20]built upon the foundation of the apostles and prophets, Christ Jesus himself being the cornerstone, [21]in whom the whole structure is joined together and grows into a holy temple in the Lord; [22]in whom you also are built into it for a dwelling place of God in the Spirit.

Phil 2:1-11 (§242)

[1]So if there is any encouragement in Christ, any incentive of love, any participation in the Spirit, any affection and sympathy, [2]complete my joy by being of the same mind, having the same love, being in full accord and of one mind. [3]Do nothing from selfishness or conceit, but in humility count others better than yourselves. [4]Let each of you look not only to his own interests, but also to the interests of others. [5]Have this mind among yourselves, which is yours in Christ Jesus, [6]who, though he was in the form of God, did not count equality with God a thing to be grasped, [7]but emptied himself, taking the form of a servant, being born in the likeness of men. [8]And being found in human form he humbled himself and became obedient unto death, even death on a cross. [9]Therefore God has highly exalted him and bestowed on him the name which is above every name, [10]that at the name of Jesus every knee should bow, in heaven and on earth and under the earth, [11]and every tongue confess that Jesus Christ is Lord, to the glory of God the Father.

Col 3:5-11 (§266)

[5]Put to death therefore what is earthly in you: fornication, impurity, passion, evil desire, and covetousness, which is idolatry. [6]On account of these the wrath of God is coming. [7]In these you once walked, when you lived in them. [8]But now put them all away: anger, wrath, malice, slander, and foul talk from your mouth. [9]Do not lie to one another, seeing that you have put off the old nature with its practices [10]and have put on the new nature, which is being renewed in knowledge after the image of its creator. [11]Here there cannot be Greek and Jew, circumcised and uncircumcised, barbarian, Scythian, slave, free man, but Christ is all, and in all.

1 Thess 5:23-24 (§289)

[23]May the God of peace himself sanctify you wholly; and may your spirit and soul and body be kept sound and blameless at the coming of our Lord Jesus Christ. [24]He who calls you is faithful, and he will do it.

• **Rom 8:9**
2 Tim 1   [14]guard the truth that has been entrusted to you by the Holy Spirit who dwells within us.

• **Rom 8:10**
2 Cor 13   [5]Examine yourselves, to see whether you are holding to your faith. Test yourselves. Do you not realize that Jesus Christ is in you?—unless indeed you fail to meet the test!

Cf. Gal 4   [19]My little children, with whom I am again in travail until Christ be formed in you!

• **Rom 8:13**
Gal 5   [24]And those who belong to Christ Jesus have crucified the flesh with its passions and desires.

• **Rom 8:15**
Cf. 2 Tim 1   [7]for God did not give us a spirit of timidity but a spirit of power and love and self-control.

• **Rom 8:16**
Acts 5   [32]"And we are witnesses to these things, and so is the Holy Spirit whom God has given to those who obey him."

Cf. 2 Cor 1   [22]he has put his seal upon us and given us his Spirit in our hearts as a guarantee.

• **Rom 8:17**
2 Cor 1   [5]For as we share abundantly in Christ's sufferings, so through Christ we share abundantly in comfort too.

2 Tim 2   [12]if we endure, we shall also reign with him;
    if we deny him, he also will deny us; . . .

Cf. Eph 3   [6]that is, how the Gentiles are fellow heirs, members of the same body, and partakers of the promise in Christ Jesus through the gospel.

Cf. Titus 3   [7]so that we might be justified by his grace and become heirs in hope of eternal life.

Cf. Acts 20   [32]"And now I commend you to God and to the word of his grace, which is able to build you up and to give you the inheritance among all those who are sanctified."

[18]I consider that the sufferings of this present time are not worth comparing with the glory that is to be revealed to us. [19]For the creation waits with eager longing for the revealing of the sons of God; [20]for the creation was subjected to futility, not of its own will but by the will of him who subjected it in hope; [21]because the creation itself will be set free from its bondage to decay and obtain the glorious liberty of the children of God. [22]We know that the whole creation has been groaning in travail together until now; [23]and not only the creation, but we ourselves, who have the first fruits of the Spirit, groan inwardly as we wait for adoption as sons, the redemption of our bodies. [24]For in this hope we were saved. Now hope that is seen is not hope. For who hopes for what he sees? [25]But if we hope for what we do not see, we wait for it with patience.

PRIMARY

1 Cor 15:42–50 (§136)

[42]So is it with the resurrection of the dead. What is sown is perishable, what is raised is imperishable. [43]It is sown in dishonor, it is raised in glory. It is sown in weakness, it is raised in power. [44]It is sown a physical body, it is raised a spiritual body. If there is a physical body, there is also a spiritual body. [45]Thus it is written, "The first man Adam became a living being"; the last Adam became a life-giving spirit. [46]But it is not the spiritual which is first but the physical, and then the spiritual. [47]The first man was from the earth, a man of dust; the second man is from heaven. [48]As was the man of dust, so are those who are of the dust; and as is the man of heaven, so are those who are of heaven. [49]Just as we have borne the image of the man of dust, we shall also bear the image of the man of heaven. [50]I tell you this, brethren: flesh and blood cannot inherit the kingdom of God, nor does the perishable inherit the imperishable.

2 Cor 4:16–5:5 (§161)

[16]So we do not lose heart. Though our outer nature is wasting away, our inner nature is being renewed every day. [17]For this slight momentary affliction is preparing for us an eternal weight of glory beyond all comparison, [18]because we look not to the things that are seen but to the things that are unseen; for the things that are seen are transient, but the things that are unseen are eternal.

5 [1]For we know that if the earthly tent we live in is destroyed, we have a building from God, a house not made with hands, eternal in the heavens. [2]Here indeed we groan, and long to put on our heavenly dwelling, [3]so that by putting it on we may not be found naked. [4]For while we are still in this tent, we sigh with anxiety; not that we would be unclothed, but that we would be further clothed, so that what is mortal may be swallowed up by life. [5]He who has prepared us for this very thing is God, who has given us the Spirit as a guarantee.

Gal 4:1–7 (§207)

[1]I mean that the heir, as long as he is a child, is no better than a slave, though he is the owner of all the estate; [2]but he is under guardians and trustees until the date set by the father. [3]So with us; when we were children, we were slaves to the elemental spirits of the universe. [4]But when the time had fully come, God sent forth his Son, born of woman, born under the law, [5]to redeem those who were under the law, so that we might receive adoption as sons. [6]And because you are sons, God has sent the Spirit of his Son into our hearts, crying, "Abba! Father!" [7]So through God you are no longer a slave but a son, and if a son then an heir.

● **Rom 8:18**
Titus 2   [13]awaiting our blessed hope, the appearing of the glory of our great God and Savior Jesus Christ, . . .

Cf. Col 3   [4]When Christ who is our life appears, then you also will appear with him in glory.

● **Rom 8:21**
Gal 5   [1]For freedom Christ has set us free; stand fast therefore, and do not submit again to a yoke of slavery.

Cf. Acts 3   [21]". . . whom heaven must receive until the time for establishing all that God spoke by the mouth of his holy prophets from of old."

● **Rom 8:22**
1 Thess 5   [3]When people say, "There is peace and security," then sudden destruction will come upon them as travail comes upon a woman with child, and there will be no escape.

Cf. Gal 4   [19]My little children, with whom I am again in travail until Christ be formed in you!

● **Rom 8:23**
2 Cor 1   [22]he has put his seal upon us and given us his Spirit in our hearts as a guarantee.

Gal 5   [5]For through the Spirit, by faith, we wait for the hope of righteousness.

(sons) *omit* adoption as sons: p[46] DG it(some) Ambrosiaster Ephraem; *text:* SABC Koine Lect it vg syr cop Origen(Latin)

Cf. Gal 5   [22]But the fruit of the Spirit is love, joy, peace, patience, kindness, goodness, faithfulness, [23]gentleness, self-control; against such there is no law.

● **Rom 8:24**
Rom 4   [18]In hope he believed against hope, that he should become the father of many nations; as he had been told, "So shall your descendants be."

2 Cor 5   [7]for we walk by faith, not by sight.

Titus 3   [7]so that we might be justified by his grace and become heirs in hope of eternal life.

Heb 11   [1]Now faith is the assurance of things hoped for, the conviction of things not seen.

Cf. 1 Thess 4   [13]But we would not have you ignorant, brethren, concerning those who are asleep, that you may not grieve as others do who have no hope.

[26] Likewise the Spirit helps us in our weakness; for we do not know how to pray as we ought, but the Spirit himself intercedes for us with sighs too deep for words. [27] And he who searches the hearts of men knows what is the mind of the Spirit, because the Spirit intercedes for the saints according to the will of God.

PRIMARY

1 Cor 2:6–16 (§77)

[6] Yet among the mature we do impart wisdom, although it is not a wisdom of this age or of the rulers of this age, who are doomed to pass away. [7] But we impart a secret and hidden wisdom of God, which God decreed before the ages for our glorification. [8] None of the rulers of this age understood this; for if they had, they would not have crucified the Lord of glory. [9] But, as it is written,

"What no eye has seen, nor ear heard,
nor the heart of man conceived,
what God has prepared for those who love him,"

[10] God has revealed to us through the Spirit. For the Spirit searches everything, even the depths of God. [11] For what person knows a man's thoughts except the spirit of the man which is in him? So also no one comprehends the thoughts of God except the Spirit of God. [12] Now we have received not the spirit of the world, but the Spirit which is from God, that we might understand the gifts bestowed on us by God. [13] And we impart this in words not taught by human wisdom but taught by the Spirit, interpreting spiritual truths to those who possess the Spirit.

[14] The unspiritual man does not receive the gifts of the Spirit of God, for they are folly to him, and he is not able to understand them because they are spiritually discerned. [15] The spiritual man judges all things, but is himself to be judged by no one. [16] "For who has known the mind of the Lord so as to instruct him?" But we have the mind of Christ.

1 Cor 4:1–5 (§83)

[1] This is how one should regard us, as servants of Christ and stewards of the mysteries of God. [2] Moreover it is required of stewards that they be found trustworthy. [3] But with me it is a very small thing that I should be judged by you or by any human court. I do not even judge myself. [4] I am not aware of anything against myself, but I am not thereby acquitted. It is the Lord who judges me. [5] Therefore do not pronounce judgment before the time, before the Lord comes, who will bring to light the things now hidden in darkness and will disclose the purposes of the heart. Then every man will receive his commendation from God.

2 Cor 3:4–6 (§155)

[4] Such is the confidence that we have through Christ toward God. [5] Not that we are competent of ourselves to claim anything as coming from us; our competence is from God, [6] who has made us competent to be ministers of a new covenant, not in a written code but in the Spirit; for the written code kills, but the Spirit gives life.

● **Rom 8:26–27**
1 Cor 14   [15] What am I to do? I will pray with the spirit and I will pray with the mind also; I will sing with the spirit and I will sing with the mind also.

Cf. Phil 1   [19] Yes, and I shall rejoice. For I know that through your prayers and the help of the Spirit of Jesus Christ this will turn out for my deliverance, . . .

● **Rom 8:26**
Rom 5   [6] While we were still weak, at the right time Christ died for the ungodly.

Gal 4   [6] And because you are sons, God has sent the Spirit of his Son into our hearts, crying, "Abba! Father!"

Cf. Rom 8   [15] . . . When we cry, "Abba! Father!" [16] it is the Spirit himself bearing witness with our spirit that we are children of God, . . .

● **Rom 8:27**
Acts 1   [24] And they prayed and said, "Lord, who knowest the hearts of all men, show which one of these two thou hast chosen. . . ."

[28]We know that in everything God works for good with those who love him, who are called according to his purpose. [29]For those whom he foreknew he also predestined to be conformed to the image of his Son, in order that he might be the first-born among many brethren. [30]And those whom he predestined he also called; and those whom he called he also justified; and those whom he justified he also glorified.

PRIMARY

Rom 5:1–5 (§20)

[1]Therefore, since we are justified by faith, we have peace with God through our Lord Jesus Christ. [2]Through him we have obtained access to this grace in which we stand, and we rejoice in our hope of sharing the glory of God. [3]More than that, we rejoice in our sufferings, knowing that suffering produces endurance, [4]and endurance produces character, and character produces hope, [5]and hope does not disappoint us, because God's love has been poured into our hearts through the Holy Spirit which has been given to us.

Eph 1:3–23 (§219)

[3]Blessed be the God and Father of our Lord Jesus Christ, who has blessed us in Christ with every spiritual blessing in the heavenly places, [4]even as he chose us in him before the foundation of the world, that we should be holy and blameless before him. [5]He destined us in love to be his sons through Jesus Christ, according to the purpose of his will, [6]to the praise of his glorious grace which he freely bestowed on us in the Beloved. [7]In him we have redemption through his blood, the forgiveness of our trespasses, according to the riches of his grace [8]which he lavished upon us. [9]For he has made known to us in all wisdom and insight the mystery of his will, according to his purpose which he set forth in Christ [10]as a plan for the fulness of time, to unite all things in him, things in heaven and things on earth.

[11]In him, according to the purpose of him who accomplishes all things according to the counsel of his will, [12]we who first hoped in Christ have been destined and appointed to live for the praise of his glory. [13]In him you also, who have heard the word of truth, the gospel of your salvation, and have believed in him, were sealed with the promised Holy Spirit, [14]which is the guarantee of our inheritance until we acquire possession of it, to the praise of his glory.

[15]For this reason, because I have heard of your faith in the Lord Jesus and your love toward all the saints, [16]I do not cease to give thanks for you, remembering you in my prayers, [17]that the God of our Lord Jesus Christ, the Father of glory, may give you a spirit of wisdom and of revelation in the knowledge of him, [18]having the eyes of your hearts enlightened, that you may know what is the hope to which he has called you, what are the riches of his glorious inheritance in the saints, [19]and what is the immeasurable greatness of his power in us who believe, according to the working of his great might [20]which he accomplished in Christ when he raised him from the dead and made him sit at his right hand in the heavenly places, [21]far above all rule and au-thority and power and dominion, and above every name that is named, not only in this age but also in that which is to come; [22]and he has put all things under his feet and has made him the head over all things for the church, [23]which is his body, the fulness of him who fills all in all.

Col 1:15–20 (§258)

[15]He is the image of the invisible God, the first-born of all creation; [16]for in him all things were created, in heaven and on earth, visible and invisible, whether thrones or dominions or principalities or authorities—all things were created through him and for him. [17]He is before all things, and in him all things hold together. [18]He is the head of the body, the church; he is the beginning, the first-born from the dead, that in everything he might be pre-eminent. [19]For in him all the fulness of God was pleased to dwell, [20]and through him to reconcile to himself all things, whether on earth or in heaven, making peace by the blood of his cross.

2 Thess 2:13–15 (§297)

[13]But we are bound to give thanks to God always for you, brethren beloved by the Lord, because God chose you from the beginning to be saved, through sanctification by the Spirit and belief in the truth. [14]To this he called you through our gospel, so that you may obtain the glory of our Lord Jesus Christ. [15]So then, brethren, stand firm and hold to the traditions which you were taught by us, either by word of mouth or by letter.

● **Rom 8:28–30**

2 Cor 1   [20]For all the promises of God find their Yes in him. That is why we utter the Amen through him, to the glory of God. [21]But it is God who establishes us with you in Christ, and has commissioned us; [22]he has put his seal upon us and given us his Spirit in our hearts as a guarantee.

Gal 1   [15]But when he who had set me apart before I was born, and had called me through his grace, . . .

Cf. Rom 9   [19]You will say to me then, "Why does he still find fault? For who can resist his will?" [20]But who are you, a man, to answer back to God? Will what is molded say to its molder, "Why have you made me thus?" [21]Has the potter no right over the clay, to make out of the same lump one vessel for beauty and another for menial use? [22]What if God, desiring to show his wrath and to make known his power, has endured with much patience the vessels of wrath made for destruction, [23]in order to make known the riches of his glory for the vessels of mercy, which he has prepared beforehand for glory, [24]even us whom he has called, not from the Jews only but also from the Gentiles? [25]As indeed he says in Hosea,

"Those who were not my people
    I will call 'my people,'
and her who was not beloved
    I will call 'my beloved.'"

[26]"And in the very place where it was said to them, 'You are not my people,'
they will be called 'sons of the living God.'"

[27]And Isaiah cries out concerning Israel: "Though the number of the sons of Israel be as the sand of the sea, only a remnant of them will be saved; [28]for the Lord will execute his sentence upon the earth with rigor and dispatch." [29]And as Isaiah predicted,
"If the Lord of hosts had not left us children,
    we would have fared like Sodom and been made like Gomorrah."

Cf. Rom 11   [25]Lest you be wise in your own conceits, I want you to understand this mystery, brethren: a hardening has come upon part of Israel, until the full number of the Gentiles come in, . . .

Cf. 1 Cor 1   [9]God is faithful, by whom you were called into the fellowship of his Son, Jesus Christ our Lord.

● **Rom 8:28**

(in every thing God) *omit* God: SCD G Koine Lect it vg syr cop(bo) Clement Origen(most); *text:* p46 AB cop(sa) Origen(some)

● **Rom 8:29**

2 Tim 1   [9]who saved us and called us with a holy calling, not in virtue of our works but in virtue of his own purpose and the grace which he gave us in Christ Jesus ages ago, . . .

Cf. Rom 11   [2]God has not rejected his people whom he foreknew. Do you not know what the scripture says of Elijah, how he pleads with God against Israel?

Cf. 1 Cor 2   [7]so that you are not lacking in any spiritual gift, as you wait for the revealing of our Lord Jesus Christ; . . .

Cf. Eph 3   [11]This was according to the eternal purpose which he has realized in Christ Jesus our Lord, . . .

Cf. Phil 3   [21]who will change our lowly body to be like his glorious body, by the power which enables him even to subject all things to himself.

Cf. Col 3   [9]Do not lie to one another, seeing that you have put off the old nature with its practices [10]and have put on the new nature, which is being renewed in knowledge after the image of its creator.

● **Rom 8:30**

1 Thess 5   [9]For God has not destined us for wrath, but to obtain salvation through our Lord Jesus Christ, . . .

FORMAL ELEMENT: HARDSHIPS LIST

[31]What then shall we say to this? If God is for us, who is against us? [32]He who did not spare his own Son but gave him up for us all, will he not also give us all things with him? [33]Who shall bring any charge against God's elect? It is God who justifies; [34]who is to condemn? Is it Christ Jesus, who died, yes, who was raised from the dead, who is at the right hand of God, who indeed intercedes for us? [35]Who shall separate us from the love of Christ? Shall tribulation, or distress, or persecution, or famine, or nakedness, or peril, or sword? [36]As it is written,

"For thy sake we are being killed all the day long;
we are regarded as sheep to be slaughtered."

[37]No, in all these things we are more than conquerors through him who loved us. [38]For I am sure that neither death, nor life, nor angels, nor principalities, nor things present, nor things to come, nor powers, [39]nor height, nor depth, nor anything else in all creation, will be able to separate us from the love of God in Christ Jesus our Lord.

PRIMARY

1 Cor 4:8–13 (§85)

[8]Already you are filled! Already you have become rich! Without us you have become kings! And would that you did reign, so that we might share the rule with you! [9]For I think that God has exhibited us apostles as last of all, like men sentenced to death; because we have become a spectacle to the world, to angels and to men. [10]We are fools for Christ's sake, but you are wise in Christ. We are weak, but you are strong. You are held in honor, but we in disrepute. [11]To the present hour we hunger and thirst, we are ill-clad and buffeted and homeless, [12]and we labor, working with our own hands. When reviled, we bless; when persecuted, we endure; [13]when slandered, we try to conciliate; we have become, and are now, as the refuse of the world, the off-scouring of all things.

2 Cor 4:7–12 (§159)

[7]But we have this treasure in earthen vessels, to show that the transcendent power belongs to God and not to us. [8]We are afflicted in every way, but not crushed; perplexed, but not driven to despair; [9]persecuted, but not forsaken; struck down, but not destroyed; [10]always carrying in the body the death of Jesus, so that the life of Jesus may also be manifested in our bodies. [11]For while we live we are always being given up to death for Jesus' sake, so that the life of Jesus may be manifested in our mortal flesh. [12]So death is at work in us, but life in you.

2 Cor 6:1–10 (§165)

[1]Working together with him, then, we entreat you not to accept the grace of God in vain. [2]For he says,

"At the acceptable time I have listened to you,
and helped you on the day of salvation."

Behold, now is the acceptable time; behold, now is the day of salvation. [3]We put no obstacle in any one's way, so that no fault may be found with our ministry, [4]but as servants of God we commend ourselves in every way: through great endurance, in afflictions, hardships, calamities, [5]beatings, imprisonments, tumults, labors, watching, hunger; [6]by purity, knowledge, forbearance, kindness, the Holy Spirit, genuine love, [7]truthful speech, and the power of God; with the weapons of righteousness for the right hand and for the left; [8]in honor and dishonor, in ill repute and good repute. We are treated as impostors, and yet are true; [9]as unknown, and yet well known; as dying, and behold we live; as punished, and yet not killed; [10]as sorrowful, yet always rejoicing; as poor, yet making many rich; as having nothing, and yet possessing everything.

2 Cor 11:21b–29 (§183)

But whatever any one dares to boast of—I am speaking as a fool—I also dare to boast of that. [22]Are they Hebrews? So am I. Are they Israelites? So am I. Are they descendants of Abraham? So am I. [23]Are they servants of Christ? I am a better one—I am talking like a madman—with far greater labors, far more imprisonments, with countless beatings, and often near death. [24]Five times I have received at the hands of the Jews the forty lashes less one. [25]Three times I have been beaten with rods; once I was stoned. Three times I have been shipwrecked; a night and a day I have been adrift at sea; [26]on frequent journeys, in danger from rivers, danger from robbers, danger from my own people, danger from Gentiles, danger in the city, danger in the wilderness, danger at sea, danger from false brethren; [27]in toil and hardship, through many a sleepless night, in hunger and thirst, often without food, in cold and exposure. [28]And, apart from other things, there is the daily pressure upon me of my anxiety for all the churches. [29]Who is weak, and I am not weak? Who is made to fall, and I am not indignant?

SECONDARY

1 Cor 4:1–5 (§83)

[1]This is how one should regard us, as servants of Christ and stewards of the mysteries of God. [2]Moreover it is required of stewards that they be found trustworthy. [3]But with me it is a very small thing that I should be judged by you or by any human court. I do not even judge myself. [4]I am not aware of anything against myself, but I am not thereby acquitted. It is the Lord who judges me. [5]Therefore do not pronounce judgment before the time, before the Lord comes, who will bring to light the things now hidden in darkness and will disclose the purposes of the heart. Then every man will receive his commendation from God.

2 Cor 1:3–11 (§147)

[3]Blessed be the God and Father of our Lord Jesus Christ, the Father of mercies and God of all comfort, [4]who comforts us in all our affliction, so that we may be able to comfort those who are in any affliction, with the comfort with which we ourselves are comforted by God. [5]For as we share abundantly in Christ's sufferings, so through Christ we share abundantly in comfort too. [6]If we are afflicted, it is for your comfort and salvation; and if we are comforted, it is for your comfort, which you experience

---

● **Rom 8:32**
Cf. Rom 4　[25]who was put to death for our trespasses and raised for our justification.

● **Rom 8:34**
Cf. Acts 2　[34]"But God raised him up, having loosed the pangs of death, because it was not possible for him to be held by it."

● **Rom 8:35**
(Christ) *read* God: S cop(sa) Origen(some); *read* God in Christ Jesus: B Origen(some); *text:* ACDG Koine Lect it vg syr cop(bo) Tertullian Origen(some)

● **Rom 8:36**
1 Cor 15　[30]Why am I in peril every hour?

Ps 44　[22]Nay, for thy sake we are slain all the day long,
and accounted as sheep for the slaughter.

when you patiently endure the same sufferings that we suffer. [7]Our hope for you is unshaken; for we know that as you share in our sufferings, you will also share in our comfort.

[8]For we do not want you to be ignorant, brethren, of the affliction we experienced in Asia; for we were so utterly, unbearably crushed that we despaired of life itself. [9]Why, we felt that we had received the sentence of death; but that was to make us rely not on ourselves but on God who raises the dead; [10]he delivered us from so deadly a peril, and he will deliver us; on him we have set our hope that he will deliver us again. [11]You also must help us by prayer, so that many will give thanks on our behalf for the blessing granted us in answer to many prayers.

2 Cor 12:1–10 (§185)

[1]I must boast; there is nothing to be gained by it, but I will go on to visions and revelations of the Lord. [2]I know a man in Christ who fourteen years ago was caught up to the third heaven—whether in the body or out of the body I do not know, God knows. [3]And I know that this man was caught up into Paradise—whether in the body or out of the body I do not know, God knows— [4]and he heard things that cannot be told, which man may not utter. [5]On behalf of this man I will boast, but on my own behalf I will not boast, except of my weaknesses. [6]Though if I wish to boast, I shall not be a fool, for I shall be speaking the truth. But I refrain from it, so that no one may think more of me than he sees in me or hears from me. [7]And to keep me from being too elated by the abundance of revelations, a thorn was given me in the flesh, a messenger of Satan, to harass me, to keep me from being too elated. [8]Three times I besought the Lord about this, that it should leave me; [9]but he said to me, "My grace is sufficient for you, for my power is made perfect in weakness." I will all the more gladly boast of my weaknesses, that the power of Christ may rest upon me. [10]For the sake of Christ, then, I am content with weaknesses, insults, hardships, persecutions, and calamities; for when I am weak, then I am strong.

Eph 3:14–19 (§223)

[14]For this reason I bow my knees before the Father, [15]from whom every family in heaven and on earth is named, [16]that according to the riches of his glory he may grant you to be strengthened with might through his Spirit in the inner man, [17]and that Christ may dwell in your hearts through faith; that you, being rooted and grounded in love, [18]may have power to comprehend with all the saints what is the breadth and length and height and depth, [19]and to know the love of Christ which surpasses knowledge, that you may be filled with all the fulness of God.

Phil 4:10–20 (§253)

[10]I rejoice in the Lord greatly that now at length you have revived your concern for me; you were indeed concerned for me, but you had no opportunity. [11]Not that I complain of want; for I have learned, in whatever state I am, to be content. [12]I know how to be abased, and I know how to abound; in any and all circumstances I have learned the secret of facing plenty and hunger, abundance and want. [13]I can do all things in him who strengthens me.

[14]Yet it was kind of you to share my trouble. [15]And you Philippians yourselves know that in the beginning of the gospel, when I left Macedonia, no church entered into partnership with me in giving and receiving except you only; [16]for even in Thessalonica you sent me help once and again. [17]Not that I seek the gift; but I seek the fruit which increases to your credit. [18]I have received full payment, and more; I am filled, having received from Epaphroditus the gifts you sent, a fragrant offering, a sacrifice acceptable and pleasing to God. [19]And my God will supply every need of yours according to his riches in glory in Christ Jesus. [20]To our God and Father be glory for ever and ever. Amen.

1 Thess 3:1–5 (§281)

[1]Therefore when we could bear it no longer, we were willing to be left behind at Athens alone, [2]and we sent Timothy, our brother and God's servant in the gospel of Christ, to establish you in your faith and to exhort you, [3]that no

one be moved by these afflictions. You yourselves know that this is to be our lot. [4]For when we were with you, we told you beforehand that we were to suffer affliction; just as it has come to pass, and as you know. [5]For this reason, when I could bear it no longer, I sent that I might know your faith, for fear that somehow the tempter had tempted you and that our labor would be in vain.

2 Thess 1:3–12 (§295)

[3]We are bound to give thanks to God always for you, brethren, as is fitting, because your faith is growing abundantly, and the love of every one of you for one another is increasing. [4]Therefore we ourselves boast of you in the churches of God for your steadfastness and faith in all your persecutions and in the afflictions which you are enduring.

[5]This is evidence of the righteous judgment of God, that you may be made worthy of the kingdom of God, for which you are suffering— [6]since indeed God deems it just to repay with affliction those who afflict you, [7]and to grant rest with us to you who are afflicted, when the Lord Jesus is revealed from heaven with his mighty angels in flaming fire, [8]inflicting vengeance upon those who do not know God and upon those who do not obey the gospel of our Lord Jesus. [9]They shall suffer the punishment of eternal destruction and exclusion from the presence of the Lord and from the glory of his might, [10]when he comes on that day to be glorified in his saints, and to be marveled at in all who have believed, because our testimony to you was believed. [11]To this end we always pray for you, that our God may make you worthy of his call, and may fulfil every good resolve and work of faith by his power, [12]so that the name of our Lord Jesus may be glorified in you, and you in him, according to the grace of our God and the Lord Jesus Christ.

Acts 20 [24]"But I do not account my life of any value nor as precious to myself, if only I may accomplish my course and the ministry which I received from the Lord Jesus, to testify to the gospel of the grace of God."

● **Rom 8:38–39**
1 Cor 3 [21]So let no one boast of men. For all things are yours, [22]whether Paul or Apollos or Cephas or the world or life or death or the present or the future, all are yours; [23]and you are Christ's; and Christ is God's.

1 Cor 15 [24]Then comes the end, when he delivers the kingdom to God the Father after destroying every rule and every authority and power.

9 I am speaking the truth in Christ, I am not lying; my conscience bears me witness in the Holy Spirit, ²that I have great sorrow and unceasing anguish in my heart. ³For I could wish that I myself were accursed and cut off from Christ for the sake of my brethren, my kinsmen by race. ⁴They are Israelites, and to them belong the sonship, the glory, the covenants, the giving of the law, the worship, and the promises; ⁵to them belong the patriarchs, and of their race, according to the flesh, is the Christ. God who is over all be blessed for ever. Amen.

PRIMARY

2 Cor 3:7–18 (§156–157)

⁷Now if the dispensation of death, carved in letters on stone, came with such splendor that the Israelites could not look at Moses' face because of its brightness, fading as this was, ⁸will not the dispensation of the Spirit be attended with greater splendor? ⁹For if there was splendor in the dispensation of condemnation, the dispensation of righteousness must far exceed it in splendor. ¹⁰Indeed, in this case, what once had splendor has come to have no splendor at all, because of the splendor that surpasses it. ¹¹For if what faded away came with splendor, what is permanent must have much more splendor.

¹²Since we have such a hope, we are very bold, ¹³not like Moses, who put a veil over his face so that the Israelites might not see the end of the fading splendor. ¹⁴But their minds were hardened; for to this day, when they read the old covenant, that same veil remains unlifted, because only through Christ is it taken away. ¹⁵Yes, to this day whenever Moses is read a veil lies over their minds; ¹⁶but when a man turns to the Lord the veil is removed. ¹⁷Now the Lord is the Spirit, and where the Spirit of the Lord is, there is freedom. ¹⁸And we all, with unveiled face, beholding the glory of the Lord, are being changed into his likeness from one degree of glory to another; for this comes from the Lord who is the Spirit.

2 Cor 11:21b–29 (§183)

But whatever any one dares to boast of—I am speaking as a fool—I also dare to boast of that. ²²Are they Hebrews? So am I. Are they Israelites? So am I. Are they descendants of Abraham? So am I. ²³Are they servants of Christ? I am a better one—I am talking like a madman—with far greater labors, far more imprisonments, with countless beatings, and often near death. ²⁴Five times I have received at the hands of the Jews the forty lashes less one. ²⁵Three times I have been beaten with rods; once I was stoned. Three times I have been shipwrecked; a night and a day I have been adrift at sea; ²⁶on frequent journeys, in danger from rivers, danger from robbers, danger from my own people, danger from Gentiles, danger in the city, danger in the wilderness, danger at sea, danger from false brethren; ²⁷in toil and hardship, through many a sleepless night, in hunger and thirst, often without food, in cold and exposure. ²⁸And, apart from other things, there is the daily pressure upon me of my anxiety for all the churches. ²⁹Who is weak, and I am not weak? Who is made to fall, and I am not indignant?

Gal 3:19–20 (§204)

¹⁹Why then the law? It was added because of transgressions, till the offspring should come to whom the promise had been made; and it was ordained by angels through an intermediary. ²⁰Now an intermediary implies more than one; but God is one.

● **Rom 9:1**

Gal 1 ²⁰(In what I am writing to you, before God, I do not lie!)

2 Cor 11 ³¹The God and Father of the Lord Jesus, he who is blessed for ever, knows that I do not lie.

1 Cor 4 ⁴I am not aware of anything against myself, but I am not thereby acquitted. It is the Lord who judges me.

Cf. 1 Tim 2 ⁷For this I was appointed a preacher and apostle (I am telling the truth, I am not lying), a teacher of the Gentiles in faith and truth.

● **Rom 9:2**

Cf. Rom 11 ¹³Now I am speaking to you Gentiles. Inasmuch then as I am an apostle to the Gentiles, I magnify my ministry ¹⁴in order to make my fellow Jews jealous, and thus save some of them.

Cf. 2 Cor 1 ²³But I call God to witness against me—it was to spare you that I refrained from coming to Corinth. ²⁴Not that we lord it over your faith; we work with you for your joy, for you stand firm in your faith.

● **Rom 9:3**

Cf. Gal 1 ⁸But even if we, or an angel from heaven, should preach to you a gospel contrary to that which we preached to you, let him be accursed.

● **Rom 9:4**

Rom 3 ¹Then what advantage has the Jew? Or what is the value of circumcision? ²Much in every way. To begin with, the Jews are entrusted with the oracles of God.

Eph 2:11-22 (§221)

[11]Therefore remember that at one time you Gentiles in the flesh, called the uncircumcision by what is called the circumcision, which is made in the flesh by hands— [12]remember that you were at that time separated from Christ, alienated from the commonwealth of Israel, and strangers to the covenants of promise, having no hope and without God in the world. [13]But now in Christ Jesus you who once were far off have been brought near in the blood of Christ. [14]For he is our peace, who has made us both one, and has broken down the dividing wall of hostility, [15]by abolishing in his flesh the law of commandments and ordinances, that he might create in himself one new man in place of the two, so making peace, [16]and might reconcile us both to God in one body through the cross, thereby bringing the hostility to an end. [17]And he came and preached peace to you who were far off and peace to those who were near; [18]for through him we both have access in one Spirit to the Father. [19]So then you are no longer strangers and sojourners, but you are fellow citizens with the saints and members of the household of God, [20]built upon the foundation of the apostles and prophets, Christ Jesus himself being the cornerstone, [21]in whom the whole structure is joined together and grows into a holy temple in the Lord; [22]in whom you also are built into it for a dwelling place of God in the Spirit.

Phil 3:2-11 (§247)

[2]Look out for the dogs, look out for the evilworkers, look out for those who mutilate the flesh. [3]For we are the true circumcision, who worship God in spirit, and glory in Christ Jesus, and put no confidence in the flesh. [4]Though I myself have reason for confidence in the flesh also. If any other man thinks he has reason for confidence in the flesh, I have more: [5]circumcised on the eighth day, of the people of Israel, of the tribe of Benjamin, a Hebrew born of Hebrews; as to the law a Pharisee, [6]as to zeal a persecutor of the church, as to righteousness under the law blameless. [7]But whatever gain I had, I counted as loss for the sake of Christ. [8]Indeed I count everything as loss because of the surpassing worth of knowing Christ Jesus my Lord. For his sake I have suffered the loss of all things, and count them as refuse, in order that I may gain Christ [9]and be found in him, not having a righteousness of my own, based on law, but that which is through faith in Christ, the righteousness from God that depends on faith; [10]that I may know him and the power of his resurrection, and may share his sufferings, becoming like him in his death, [11]that if possible I may attain the resurrection from the dead.

1 Thess 2:13-16 (§279)

[13]And we also thank God constantly for this, that when you received the word of God which you heard from us, you accepted it not as the word of men but as what it really is, the word of God, which is at work in you believers. [14]For you, brethren, became imitators of the churches of God in Christ Jesus which are in Judea; for you suffered the same things from your own countrymen as they did from the Jews, [15]who killed both the Lord Jesus and the prophets, and drove us out, and displease God and oppose all men [16]by hindering us from speaking to the Gentiles that they may be saved—so as always to fill up the measure of their sins. But God's wrath has come upon them at last!

Rom 3   [9]What then? Are we Jews any better off? No, not at all; for I have already charged that all men, both Jews and Greeks, are under the power of sin, . . .

Acts 2   [39]"For the promise is to you and to your children and to all that are far off, every one whom the Lord our God calls to him."

Acts 3   [25]"You are the sons of the prophets and of the covenant which God gave to your fathers, saying to Abraham, 'And in your posterity shall all the families of the earth be blessed.'"

Cf. Rom 11   [1]I ask, then, has God rejected his people? By no means! I myself am an Israelite, a descendant of Abraham, a member of the tribe of Benjamin. [2]God has not rejected his people whom he foreknew. Do you not know what the scripture says of Elijah, how he pleads with God against Israel?

Cf. Rom 15   [8]For I tell you that Christ became a servant to the circumcised to show God's truthfulness, in order to confirm the promises given to the patriarchs, . . .

Cf. Acts 13   [32]"And we bring you the good news that what God promised to the fathers. . . ."

● **Rom 9:5**
Rom 1   [3]the gospel concerning his Son, who was descended from David according to the flesh . . .

2 Cor 5   [16]So we do not lose heart. Though our outer nature is wasting away, our inner nature is being renewed every day.

Cf. Gal 4   [4]But when the time had fully come, God sent forth his Son, born of woman, born under the law, . . .

[6] But it is not as though the word of God had failed. For not all who are descended from Israel belong to Israel, [7] and not all are children of Abraham because they are his descendants; but "Through Isaac shall your descendants be named." [8] This means that it is not the children of the flesh who are the children of God, but the children of the promise are reckoned as descendants. [9] For this is what the promise said, "About this time I will return and Sarah shall have a son." [10] And not only so, but also when Rebecca had conceived children by one man, our forefather Isaac, [11] though they were not yet born and had done nothing either good or bad, in order that God's purpose of election might continue, not because of works but because of his call, [12] she was told, "The elder will serve the younger." [13] As it is written, "Jacob I loved, but Esau I hated."

PRIMARY

Gal 4:21–31 (§210)

[21] Tell me, you who desire to be under law, do you not hear the law? [22] For it is written that Abraham had two sons, one by a slave and one by a free woman. [23] But the son of the slave was born according to the flesh, the son of the free woman through promise. [24] Now this is an allegory: these women are two covenants. One is from Mount Sinai, bearing children for slavery; she is Hagar. [25] Now Hagar is Mount Sinai in Arabia; she corresponds to the present Jerusalem, for she is in slavery with her children. [26] But the Jerusalem above is free, and she is our mother. [27] For it is written,

"Rejoice, O barren one who does not bear;
break forth and shout, you who are not in travail;
for the children of the desolate one are many more
than the children of her that is married."

[28] Now we, brethren, like Isaac, are children of promise. [29] But as at that time he who was born according to the flesh persecuted him who was born according to the Spirit, so it is now. [30] But what does the scripture say? "Cast out the slave and her son; for the son of the slave shall not inherit with the son of the free woman." [31] So, brethren, we are not children of the slave but of the free woman.

Eph 1:3–23 (§219)

[3] Blessed be the God and Father of our Lord Jesus Christ, who has blessed us in Christ with every spiritual blessing in the heavenly places, [4] even as he chose us in him before the foundation of the world, that we should be holy and blameless before him. [5] He destined us in love to be his sons through Jesus Christ, according to the purpose of his will, [6] to the praise of his glorious grace which he freely bestowed on us in the Beloved. [7] In him we have redemption through his blood, the forgiveness of our trespasses, according to the riches of his grace [8] which he lavished upon us. [9] For he has made known to us in all wisdom and insight the mystery of his will, according to his purpose which he set forth in Christ [10] as a plan for the fulness of time, to unite all things in him, things in heaven and things on earth.

[11] In him, according to the purpose of him who accomplishes all things according to the counsel of his will, [12] we who first hoped in Christ have been destined and appointed to live for the praise of his glory. [13] In him you also, who have heard the word of truth, the gospel of your salvation, and have believed in him, were sealed with the promised Holy Spirit, [14] which is the guarantee of our inheritance until we acquire possession of it, to the praise of his glory.

[15] For this reason, because I have heard of your faith in the Lord Jesus and your love toward all the saints, [16] I do not cease to give thanks for you, remembering you in my prayers, [17] that the God of our Lord Jesus Christ, the Father of glory, may give you a spirit of wisdom and of revelation in the knowledge of him, [18] having the eyes of your hearts enlightened, that you may know what is the hope to which he has called you, what are the riches of his glorious inheritance in the saints, [19] and what is the immeasurable greatness of his power in us who believe, according to the working of his great might [20] which he accomplished in Christ when he raised him from the dead and made him sit at his right hand in the heavenly places, [21] far above all rule and authority and power and dominion, and above every name that is named, not only in this age but also in that which is to come; [22] and he has put all things under his feet and has made him the head over all things for the church, [23] which is his body, the fulness of him who fills all in all.

● **Rom 9:6**
Rom 2   [28] For he is not a real Jew who is one outwardly, nor is true circumcision something external and physical. [29] He is a Jew who is one inwardly, and real circumcision is a matter of the heart, spiritual and not literal. His praise is not from men but from God.

Cf. Gal 6   [16] Peace and mercy be upon all who walk by this rule, upon the Israel of God.

● **Rom 9:7**
Rom 4   [11] . . . The purpose was to make him the father of all who believe without being circumcised and who thus have righteousness reckoned to them, [12] and likewise the father of the circumcised who are not merely circumcised but also follow the example of the faith which our father Abraham had before he was circumcised.

Gen 21   [12] But God said to Abraham, "Be not displeased because of the lad and because of your slave woman; whatever Sarah says to you, do as she tells you, for through Isaac shall your descendants be named."

● **Rom 9:9**
Gen 18   [10] The Lord said, "I will surely return to you in the spring, and Sarah your wife shall have a son." And Sarah was listening at the tent door behind him.

● **Rom 9:10**
Gen 25   [21] And Isaac prayed to the Lord for his wife, because she was barren; and the Lord granted his prayer, and Rebekah his wife conceived.

● **Rom 9:11**
Rom 11   [28] As regards the gospel they are enemies of God, for your sake; but as regards election they are beloved for the sake of their forefathers.

Cf. Rom 8   [28] We know that in everything God works for good with those who love him, who are called according to his purpose. [29] For those whom he foreknew he also predestined to be conformed to the image of his Son, in order that he might be the first-born among many brethren. [30] And those whom he predestined he also called; and those whom he called he also justified; and those whom he justified he also glorified.

Cf. Rom 11   [7] What then? Israel failed to obtain what it sought. The elect obtained it, but the rest were hardened, . . .

Cf. Eph 1   [9] For he has made known to us in all wisdom and insight the mystery of his will, according to his purpose which he set forth in Christ [10] as a plan for the fulness of time, to unite all things in him, things in heaven and things on earth.

[11] In him, according to the purpose of him who accomplishes all things according to the counsel of his will, [12] we who first hoped in Christ have been destined and appointed to live for the praise of his glory.

Cf. 1 Thess 1   [4] For we know, brethren beloved by God, that he has chosen you; . . .

● **Rom 9:12**
Gen 25   [23] And the Lord said to her,
"Two nations are in your womb,
and two peoples, born of you, shall be divided;
the one shall be stronger than the other,
the elder shall serve the younger."

● **Rom 9:13**
Mal 1   [2] "I have loved you," says the Lord. But you say, "How hast thou loved us?" "Is not Esau Jacob's brother?" says the Lord. "Yet I have loved Jacob [3] but I have hated Esau; I have laid waste his hill country and left his heritage to jackals of the desert."

[14]What shall we say then? Is there injustice on God's part? By no means! [15]For he says to Moses, "I will have mercy on whom I have mercy, and I will have compassion on whom I have compassion." [16]So it depends not upon man's will or exertion, but upon God's mercy. [17]For the scripture says to Pharaoh, "I have raised you up for the very purpose of showing my power in you, so that my name may be proclaimed in all the earth." [18]So then he has mercy upon whomever he wills, and he hardens the heart of whomever he wills.

PRIMARY

Eph 2:1–10 (§220)

2 [1]And you he made alive, when you were dead through the trespasses and sins [2]in which you once walked, following the course of this world, following the prince of the power of the air, the spirit that is now at work in the sons of disobedience. [3]Among these we all once lived in the passions of our flesh, following the desires of body and mind, and so we were by nature children of wrath, like the rest of mankind. [4]But God, who is rich in mercy, out of the great love with which he loved us, [5]even when we were dead through our trespasses, made us alive together with Christ (by grace you have been saved), [6]and raised us up with him, and made us sit with him in the heavenly places in Christ Jesus, [7]that in the coming ages he might show the immeasurable riches of his grace in kindness toward us in Christ Jesus. [8]For by grace you have been saved through faith; and this is not your own doing, it is the gift of God— [9]not because of works, lest any man should boast. [10]For we are his workmanship, created in Christ Jesus for good works, which God prepared beforehand, that we should walk in them.

● **Rom 9:14–18**
Rom 11   [32]For God has consigned all men to disobedience, that he may have mercy upon all.

Cf. Rom 8   [28]We know that in everything God works for good with those who love him, who are called according to his purpose. [29]For those whom he foreknew he also predestined to be conformed to the image of his Son, in order that he might be the firstborn among many brethren. [30]And those whom he predestined he also called; and those whom he called he also justified; and those whom he justified he also glorified.

● **Rom 9:14**
Rom 3   [5]But if our wickedness serves to show the justice of God, what shall we say? That God is unjust to inflict wrath on us? (I speak in a human way.)

● **Rom 9:15**
Exod 33   [19]And he said, "I will make all my goodness pass before you, and will proclaim before you my name 'The Lord'; and I will be gracious to whom I will be gracious, and will show mercy on whom I will show mercy."

● **Rom 9:16**
Titus 3   [5]he saved us, not because of deeds done by us in righteousness, but in virtue of his own mercy, by the washing of regeneration and renewal in the Holy Spirit, . . .

● **Rom 9:17**
Exod 9   [16]but for this purpose have I let you live, to show you my power, so that my name may be declared throughout all the earth.

● **Rom 9:18**
Rom 11   [7]What then? Israel failed to obtain what it sought. The elect obtained it, but the rest were hardened, . . .

Rom 11   [25]Lest you be wise in your own conceits, I want you to understand this mystery, brethren: a hardening has come upon part of Israel, until the full number of the Gentiles come in, . . .

2 Cor 3   [14]But their minds were hardened; for to this day, when they read the old covenant, that same veil remains unlifted, because only through Christ is it taken away.

Cf. 2 Thess 2   [11]Therefore God sends upon them a strong delusion, to make them believe what is false, [12]so that all may be condemned who did not believe the truth but had pleasure in unrighteousness.

[19]You will say to me then, "Why does he still find fault? For who can resist his will?" [20]But who are you, a man, to answer back to God? Will what is molded say to its molder, "Why have you made me thus?" [21]Has the potter no right over the clay, to make out of the same lump one vessel for beauty and another for menial use? [22]What if God, desiring to show his wrath and to make known his power, has endured with much patience the vessels of wrath made for destruction, [23]in order to make known the riches of his glory for the vessels of mercy, which he has prepared beforehand for glory, [24]even us whom he has called, not from the Jews only but also from the Gentiles? [25]As indeed he says in Hosea,

"Those who were not my people
I will call 'my people,'
and her who was not beloved
I will call 'my beloved.'"

[26]"And in the very place where it was said to them, 'You are not my people,' they will be called 'sons of the living God.'"

[27]And Isaiah cries out concerning Israel: "Though the number of the sons of Israel be as the sand of the sea, only a remnant of them will be saved; [28]for the Lord will execute his sentence upon the earth with rigor and dispatch." [29]And as Isaiah predicted,

"If the Lord of hosts had not left us children,
we would have fared like Sodom and been made like Gomorrah."

PRIMARY

1 Cor 4:6–7 (§84)

[6]I have applied all this to myself and Apollos for your benefit, brethren, that you may learn by us not to go beyond what is written, that none of you may be puffed up in favor of one against another. [7]For who sees anything different in you? What have you that you did not receive? If then you received it, why do you boast as if it were not a gift?

2 Cor 3:4–6 (§155)

[4]Such is the confidence that we have through Christ toward God. [5]Not that we are competent of ourselves to claim anything as coming from us; our competence is from God, [6]who has made us competent to be ministers of a new covenant, not in a written code but in the Spirit; for the written code kills, but the Spirit gives life.

Gal 3:21–25 (§205)

[21]Is the law then against the promises of God? Certainly not; for if a law had been given which could make alive, then righteousness would indeed be by the law. [22]But the scripture consigned all things to sin, that what was promised to faith in Jesus Christ might be given to those who believe.

[23]Now before faith came, we were confined under the law, kept under restraint until faith should be revealed. [24]So that the law was our custodian until Christ came, that we might be justified by faith. [25]But now that faith has come, we are no longer under a custodian; . . .

Eph 1:3–23 (§219)

[3]Blessed be the God and Father of our Lord Jesus Christ, who has blessed us in Christ with every spiritual blessing in the heavenly places, [4]even as he chose us in him before the foundation of the world, that we should be holy and blameless before him. [5]He destined us in love to be his sons through Jesus Christ, according to the purpose of his will, [6]to the praise of his glorious grace which he freely bestowed on us in the Beloved. [7]In him we have redemption through his blood, the forgiveness of our trespasses, according to the riches of his grace [8]which he lavished upon us. [9]For he has made known to us in all wisdom and insight the mystery of his will, according to his purpose which he set forth in Christ [10]as a plan for the fulness of time, to unite all things in him, things in heaven and things on earth.

[11]In him, according to the purpose of him who accomplishes all things according to the counsel of his will, [12]we who first hoped in Christ have been destined and appointed to live for the praise of his glory. [13]In him you also, who have heard the word of truth, the gospel of your salvation, and have believed in him, were sealed with the promised Holy Spirit, [14]which is the guarantee of our inheritance until we acquire possession of it, to the praise of his glory.

[15]For this reason, because I have heard of your faith in the Lord Jesus and your love toward all the saints, [16]I do not cease to give thanks for you, remembering you in my prayers, [17]that the God of our Lord Jesus Christ, the Father of glory, may give you a spirit of wisdom and of revelation in the knowledge of him, [18]having the eyes of your hearts enlightened, that you may know what is the hope to which he has called you, what are the riches of his glorious inheritance in the saints,

---

● **Rom 9:19–29**

Cf. Rom 8   [28]We know that in everything God works for good with those who love him, who are called according to his purpose. [29]For those whom he foreknew he also predestined to be conformed to the image of his Son, in order that he might be the first-born among many brethren. [30]And those whom he predestined he also called; and those whom he called he also justified; and those whom he justified he also glorified.

Cf. Rom 16   [25]Now to him who is able to strengthen you according to my gospel and the preaching of Jesus Christ, according to the revelation of the mystery which was kept secret for long ages [26]but is now disclosed and through the prophetic writings is made known to all nations, according to the command of the eternal God, to bring about the obedience of faith— [27]to the only wise God be glory for evermore through Jesus Christ! Amen.

Cf. 2 Cor 11   [11] . . . But whatever any one dares to boast of—I am speaking as a fool—I also dare to boast of that. [22]Are they Hebrews? So am I. Are they Israelites? So am I. Are they descendants of Abraham? So am I. [23]Are they servants of Christ? I am a better one—I am talking like a madman—with far greater labors, far more imprisonments, with countless beatings, and often near death. [24]Five times I have received at the hands of the Jews the forty lashes less one. [25]Three times I have been beaten with rods; once I was stoned. Three times I have been shipwrecked; a night and a day I have been adrift at sea; [26]on frequent journeys, in danger from rivers, danger from robbers, danger from my own people, danger from Gentiles, danger in the city, danger in the wilderness, danger at sea, danger from false brethren; [27]in toil and hardship, through many a sleepless night, in hunger and thirst, often without food, in cold and exposure. [28]And, apart from other things, there is the daily pressure upon me of my anxiety for all the churches. [29]Who is weak, and I am not weak? Who is made to fall, and I am not indignant?

● **Rom 9:19**

Rom 3   [5]But if our wickedness serves to show the justice of God, what shall we say? That God is unjust to inflict wrath on us? (I speak in a human way.)

● **Rom 9:20**

Isa 29   [16]You turn things upside down!
Shall the potter be regarded as the clay;
that the thing made should say of its maker,
"He did not make me";
or the thing formed say of him who formed it,
"He has no understanding"?

Isa 45   [9]"Woe to him who strives with his Maker,
an earthen vessel with the potter!
Does the clay say to him who fashions it, 'What are you making'?
or 'Your work has no handles'?

[19]and what is the immeasurable greatness of his power in us who believe, according to the working of his great might [20]which he accomplished in Christ when he raised him from the dead and made him sit at his right hand in the heavenly places, [21]far above all rule and authority and power and dominion, and above every name that is named, not only in this age but also in that which is to come; [22]and he has put all things under his feet and has made him the head over all things for the church, [23]which is his body, the fulness of him who fills all in all.

Phil 3:17–21 (§249)

[17]Brethren, join in imitating me, and mark those who so live as you have an example in us. [18]For many, of whom I have often told you and now tell you even with tears, live as enemies of the cross of Christ. [19]Their end is destruction, their god is the belly, and they glory in their shame, with minds set on earthly things. [20]But our commonwealth is in heaven, and from it we await a Savior, the Lord Jesus Christ, [21]who will change our lowly body to be like his glorious body, by the power which enables him even to subject all things to himself.

Col 1:24–2:3 (§260)

[24]Now I rejoice in my sufferings for your sake, and in my flesh I complete what is lacking in Christ's afflictions for the sake of his body, that is, the church, [25]of which I became a minister according to the divine office which was given to me for you, to make the word of God fully known, [26]the mystery hidden for ages and generations but now made manifest to his saints. [27]To them God chose to make known how great among the Gentiles are the riches of the glory of this mystery, which is Christ in you,

the hope of glory. [28]Him we proclaim warning every man and teaching every man in all wisdom, that we may present every man mature in Christ. [29]For this I toil, striving with all the energy which he mightily inspires within me.

2 For I want you to know how greatly I strive for you, and for those at Laodicea, and for all who have not seen my face, [2]that their hearts may be encouraged as they are knit together in love, to have all the riches of assured understanding and the knowledge of God's mystery, of Christ, [3]in whom are hid all the treasures of wisdom and knowledge.

1 Thess 5:1–11 (§287)

[1]But as to the times and the seasons, brethren, you have no need to have anything written to you. [2]For you yourselves know well that the day of the Lord will come like a thief in the night. [3]When people say, "There is peace and security," then sudden destruction will come upon them as travail comes upon a woman with child, and there will be no escape. [4]But you are not in darkness, brethren, for that day to surprise you like a thief. [5]For you are all sons of light and sons of the day; we are not of the night or of darkness. [6]So then let us not sleep, as others do, but let us keep awake and be sober. [7]For those who sleep sleep at night, and those who get drunk are drunk at night. [8]But, since we belong to the day, let us be sober, and put on the breastplate of faith and love, and for a helmet the hope of salvation. [9]For God has not destined us for wrath, but to obtain salvation through our Lord Jesus Christ, [10]who died for us so that whether we wake or sleep we might live with him. [11]Therefore encourage one another and build one another up, just as you are doing.

2 Thess 2:1–12 (§296)

[1]Now concerning the coming of our Lord Jesus Christ and our assembling to meet him, we beg you, brethren, [2]not to be quickly shaken in mind or excited, either by spirit or by word, or by letter purporting to be from us, to the effect that the day of the Lord has come. [3]Let no one deceive you in any way; for that day will not come, unless the rebellion comes first, and the man of lawlessness is revealed, the son of perdition, [4]who opposes and exalts himself against every so-called god or object of worship, so that he takes his seat in the temple of God, proclaiming himself to be God. [5]Do you not remember that when I was still with you I told you this? [6]And you know what is restraining him now so that he may be revealed in his time. [7]For the mystery of lawlessness is already at work; only he who now restrains it will do so until he is out of the way. [8]And then the lawless one will be revealed, and the Lord Jesus will slay him with the breath of his mouth and destroy him by his appearing and his coming. [9]The coming of the lawless one by the activity of Satan will be with all power and with pretended signs and wonders, [10]and with all wicked deception for those who are to perish, because they refused to love the truth and so be saved. [11]Therefore God sends upon them a strong delusion, to make them believe what is false, [12]so that all may be condemned who did not believe the truth but had pleasure in unrighteousness.

● **Rom 9:21**
Cf. 2 Tim 2   [20]In a great house there are not only vessels of gold and silver but also of wood and earthenware, and some for noble use, some for ignoble.

● **Rom 9:22–23**
Rom 2   [4]Or do you presume upon the riches of his kindness and forbearance and patience? Do you not know that God's kindness is meant to lead you to repentance? [5]But by your hard and impenitent heart you are storing up wrath for yourself on the day of wrath when God's righteous judgment will be revealed.

● **Rom 9:23**
Cf. Phil 4   [19]And my God will supply every need of yours according to his riches in glory in Christ Jesus.

Cf. Eph 3   [16]that according to the riches of his glory he may grant you to be strengthened with might through his Spirit in the inner man, . . .

● **Rom 9:25**
Hos 2   [23]and I will sow him for myself in the land.
And I will have pity on Not pitied,
and I will say to Not my people, 'You are my people';
and he shall say, 'Thou art my God.'"

● **Rom 9:26**
Hos 1   [10]Yet the number of the people of Israel shall be like the sand of the sea, which can be neither measured nor numbered; and in the place where it was said to them, "You are not my people," it shall be said to them, "Sons of the living God."

● **Rom 9:27**
Isa 10   [22]For though your people Israel be as the sand of the sea, only a remnant of them will return. Destruction is decreed, overflowing with righteousness. [23]For the Lord, the Lord of hosts, will make a full end, as decreed, in the midst of all the earth.

Gen 22   [17]I will indeed bless you, and I will multiply your descendants as the stars of heaven and as the sand which is on the seashore. And your descendants shall possess the gate of their enemies.

Hos 1   [10]Yet the number of the people of Israel shall be like the sand of the sea, which can be neither measured nor numbered; and in the place where it was said to them, "You are not my people," it shall be said to them, "Sons of the living God."

● **Rom 9:29**
Isa 1   [9]If the Lord of hosts had not left us a few survivors,
we should have been like Sodom, and become like Gomorrah.

[30]What shall we say, then? That Gentiles who did not pursue righteousness have attained it, that is, righteousness through faith; [31]but that Israel who pursued the righteousness which is based on law did not succeed in fulfilling that law. [32]Why? Because they did not pursue it through faith, but as if it were based on works. They have stumbled over the stumbling stone, [33]as it is written,

"Behold, I am laying in Zion a stone that will make men stumble,

a rock that will make them fall;

and he who believes in him will not be put to shame."

PRIMARY

1 Cor 1:18–25 (§74)

[18]For the word of the cross is folly to those who are perishing, but to us who are being saved it is the power of God. [19]For it is written,

"I will destroy the wisdom of the wise,

and the cleverness of the clever I will thwart."

[20]Where is the wise man? Where is the scribe? Where is the debater of this age? Has not God made foolish the wisdom of the world? [21]For since, in the wisdom of God, the world did not know God through wisdom, it pleased God through the folly of what we preach to save those who believe. [22]For Jews demand signs and Greeks seek wisdom, [23]but we preach Christ crucified, a stumbling block to Jews and folly to Gentiles, [24]but to those who are called, both Jews and Greeks, Christ the power of God and the wisdom of God. [25]For the foolishness of God is wiser than men, and the weakness of God is stronger than men.

2 Cor 3:12–18 (§157)

[12]Since we have such a hope, we are very bold, [13]not like Moses, who put a veil over his face so that the Israelites might not see the end of the fading splendor. [14]But their minds were hardened; for to this day, when they read the old covenant, that same veil remains unlifted, because only through Christ is it taken away. [15]Yes, to this day whenever Moses is read a veil lies over their minds; [16]but when a man turns to the Lord the veil is removed. [17]Now the Lord is the Spirit, and where the Spirit of the Lord is, there is freedom. [18]And we all, with unveiled face, beholding the glory of the Lord, are being changed into his likeness from one degree of glory to another; for this comes from the Lord who is the Spirit.

Gal 2:15–21 (§199)

[15]We ourselves, who are Jews by birth and not Gentile sinners, [16]yet who know that a man is not justified by works of the law but through faith in Jesus Christ, even we have believed in Christ Jesus, in order to be justified by faith in Christ, and not by works of the law, because by works of the law shall no one be justified. [17]But if, in our endeavor to be justified in Christ, we ourselves were found to be sinners, is Christ then an agent of sin? Certainly not! [18]But if I build up again those things which I tore down, then I prove myself a transgressor. [19]For I through the law died to the law, that I might live to God. [20]I have been crucified with Christ; it is no longer I who live, but Christ who lives in me; and the life I now live in the flesh I live by faith in the Son of God, who loved me and gave himself for me. [21]I do not nullify the grace of God; for if justification were through the law, then Christ died to no purpose.

Gal 3:21–25 (§205)

[21]Is the law then against the promises of God? Certainly not; for if a law had been given which could make alive, then righteousness would indeed be by the law. [22]But the scripture consigned all things to sin, that what was promised to faith in Jesus Christ might be given to those who believe. [23]Now before faith came, we were confined under the law, kept under restraint until faith should be revealed. [24]So that the law was our custodian until Christ came, that we might be justified by faith. [25]But now that faith has come, we are no longer under a custodian; . . .

Gal 5:1–12 (§211)

[1]For freedom Christ has set us free; stand fast therefore, and do not submit again to a yoke of slavery.

[2]Now I, Paul, say to you that if you receive circumcision, Christ will be of no advantage to you. [3]I testify again to every man who receives circumcision that he is bound to keep the whole law. [4]You are severed from Christ, you who would be justified by the law; you have fallen away from grace. [5]For through the Spirit, by faith, we wait for the hope of righteousness. [6]For in Christ Jesus neither circumcision nor uncircumcision is of any avail, but faith working through love. [7]You were running well; who hindered you from obeying the truth? [8]This persuasion is not from him who called you. [9]A little leaven leavens the whole lump. [10]I have confidence in the Lord that you will take no other view than mine; and he who

is troubling you will bear his judgment, whoever he is. [11]But if I, brethren, still preach circumcision, why am I still persecuted? In that case the stumbling block of the cross has been removed. [12]I wish those who unsettle you would mutilate themselves!

Phil 3:2–11 (§247)

[2]Look out for the dogs, look out for the evil-workers, look out for those who mutilate the flesh. [3]For we are the true circumcision, who worship God in spirit, and glory in Christ Jesus, and put no confidence in the flesh. [4]Though I myself have reason for confidence in the flesh also. If any other man thinks he has reason for confidence in the flesh, I have more: [5]circumcised on the eighth day, of the people of Israel, of the tribe of Benjamin, a Hebrew born of Hebrews; as to the law a Pharisee, [6]as to zeal a persecutor of the church, as to righteousness under the law blameless. [7]But whatever gain I had, I counted as loss for the sake of Christ. [8]Indeed I count everything as loss because of the surpassing worth of knowing Christ Jesus my Lord. For his sake I have suffered the loss of all things, and count them as refuse, in order that I may gain Christ [9]and be found in him, not having a righteousness of my own, based on law, but that which is through faith in Christ, the righteousness from God that depends on faith; [10]that I may know him and the power of his resurrection, and may share his sufferings, becoming like him in his death, [11]that if possible I may attain the resurrection from the dead.

1 Thess 2:13–16 (§279)

[13]And we also thank God constantly for this, that when you received the word of God which you heard from us, you accepted it not as the word of men but as what it really is, the word of God, which is at work in you believers. [14]For you, brethren, became imitators of the churches of God in Christ Jesus which are in Judea; for you suffered the same things from your own countrymen as they did from the Jews, [15]who killed both the Lord Jesus and the prophets, and drove us out, and displease God and oppose all men [16]by hindering us from speaking to the Gentiles that they may be saved—so as always to fill up the measure of their sins. But God's wrath has come upon them at last!

● **Rom 9:30–33**

See Rom 2:12–16; Rom 3:31; Rom 13:8

Rom 7   [7]What then shall we say? That the law is sin? By no means! Yet, if it had not been for the law, I should not have known sin. I should not have known what it is to covet if the law had not said, "You shall not covet."

Gal 5   [14]For the whole law is fulfilled in one word, "You shall love your neighbor as yourself."

● **Rom 9:30–31**

1 Tim 6   [11]But as for you, man of God, shun all this; aim at righteousness, godliness, faith, love, steadfastness, gentleness.

2 Tim 2   [22]So shun youthful passions and aim at righteousness, faith, love, and peace, along with those who call upon the Lord from a pure heart.

● **Rom 9:32–33**

Eph 2   [8]For by grace you have been saved through faith; and this is not your own doing, it is the gift of

God— [9]not because of works, lest any man should boast.

Cf. 1 Cor 8:13; Rom 14:13

● **Rom 9:33**

Isa 28   [16]therefore thus says the Lord God,

"Behold, I am laying in Zion for a foundation a stone, a tested stone,

a precious cornerstone, of a sure foundation:

'He who believes will not be in haste.'"

10 Brethren, my heart's desire and prayer to God for them is that they may be saved. [2]I bear them witness that they have a zeal for God, but it is not enlightened. [3]For, being ignorant of the righteousness that comes from God, and seeking to establish their own, they did not submit to God's righteousness. [4]For Christ is the end of the law, that every one who has faith may be justified.

PRIMARY

2 Cor 3:12–18 (§157)

[12]Since we have such a hope, we are very bold, [13]not like Moses, who put a veil over his face so that the Israelites might not see the end of the fading splendor. [14]But their minds were hardened; for to this day, when they read the old covenant, that same veil remains unlifted, because only through Christ is it taken away. [15]Yes, to this day whenever Moses is read a veil lies over their minds; [16]but when a man turns to the Lord the veil is removed. [17]Now the Lord is the Spirit, and where the Spirit of the Lord is, there is freedom. [18]And we all, with unveiled face, beholding the glory of the Lord, are being changed into his likeness from one degree of glory to another; for this comes from the Lord who is the Spirit.

Gal 1:13–14 (§195)

[13]For you have heard of my former life in Judaism, how I persecuted the church of God violently and tried to destroy it; [14]and I advanced in Judaism beyond many of my own age among my people, so extremely zealous was I for the traditions of my fathers.

Gal 2:15–21 (§199)

[15]We ourselves, who are Jews by birth and not Gentile sinners, [16]yet who know that a man is not justified by works of the law but through faith in Jesus Christ, even we have believed in Christ Jesus, in order to be justified by faith in Christ, and not by works of the law, because by works of the law shall no one be justified. [17]But if, in our endeavor to be justified in Christ, we ourselves were found to be sinners, is Christ then an agent of sin? Certainly not! [18]But if I build up again those things which I tore down, then I prove myself a transgressor. [19]For I through the law died to the law, that I might live to God. [20]I have been crucified with Christ; it is no longer I who live, but Christ who lives in me; and the life I now live in the flesh I live by faith in the Son of God, who loved me and gave himself for me. [21]I do not nullify the grace of God; for if justification were through the law, then Christ died to no purpose.

Phil 3:2–11 (§247)

[2]Look out for the dogs, look out for the evil-workers, look out for those who mutilate the flesh. [3]For we are the true circumcision, who worship God in spirit, and glory in Christ Jesus, and put no confidence in the flesh. [4]Though I myself have reason for confidence in the flesh also. If any other man thinks he has reason for confidence in the flesh, I have more: [5]circumcised on the eighth day, of the people of Israel, of the tribe of Benjamin, a Hebrew born of Hebrews; as to the law a Pharisee, [6]as to zeal a persecutor of the church, as to righteousness under the law blameless. [7]But whatever gain I had, I counted as loss for the sake of Christ. [8]Indeed I count everything as loss because of the surpassing worth of knowing Christ Jesus my Lord. For his sake I have suffered the loss of all things, and count them as refuse, in order that I may gain Christ [9]and be found in him, not having a righteousness of my own, based on law, but that which is through faith in Christ, the righteousness from God that depends on faith; [10]that I may know him and the power of his resurrection, and may share his sufferings, becoming like him in his death, [11]that if possible I may attain the resurrection from the dead.

1 Thess 2:13–16 (§279)

[13]And we also thank God constantly for this, that when you received the word of God which you heard from us, you accepted it not as the word of men but as what it really is, the word of God, which is at work in you believers. [14]For you, brethren, became imitators of the churches of God in Christ Jesus which are in Judea; for you suffered the same things from your own countrymen as they did from the Jews, [15]who killed both the Lord Jesus and the prophets, and drove us out, and displease God and oppose all men [16]by hindering us from speaking to the Gentiles that they may be saved—so as always to fill up the measure of their sins. But God's wrath has come upon them at last!

● **Rom 10:1–4**

Rom 2   [17]But if you call yourself a Jew and rely upon the law and boast of your relation to God [18]and know his will and approve what is excellent, because you are instructed in the law, [19]and if you are sure that you are a guide to the blind, a light to those who are in darkness, [20]a corrector of the foolish, a teacher of children, having in the law the embodiment of knowledge and truth— [21]you then who teach others, will you not teach yourself? While you preach against stealing, do you steal? [22]You who say that one must not commit adultery, do you commit adultery? You who abhor idols, do you rob temples? [23]You who boast in the law, do you dishonor God by breaking the law? [24]For, as it is written, "The name of God is blasphemed among the Gentiles because of you."

Rom 6   [14]For sin will have no dominion over you, since you are not under law but under grace.

Rom 7   [4]Likewise, my brethren, you have died to the law through the body of Christ, so that you may belong to another, to him who has been raised from the dead in order that we may bear fruit for God. [5]While we were living in the flesh, our sinful passions, aroused by the law, were at work in our members to bear fruit for death. [6]But now we are discharged from the law, dead to that which held us captive, so that we serve not under the old written code but in the new life of the Spirit.

Rom 8   [3]For God has done what the law, weakened by the flesh, could not do: sending his own Son in the likeness of sinful flesh and for sin, he condemned sin in the flesh, [4]in order that the just requirement of the law might be fulfilled in us, who walk not according to the flesh but according to the Spirit.

Rom 9   [1]I am speaking the truth in Christ, I am not lying; my conscience bears me witness in the Holy Spirit, [2]that I have great sorrow and unceasing anguish in my heart. [3]For I could wish that I myself were accursed and cut off from Christ for the sake of my brethren, my kinsmen by race. [4]They are Israelites, and to them belong the sonship, the glory, the covenants, the giving of the law, the worship, and the promises; [5]to them belong the patriarchs, and of their race, according to the flesh, is the Christ. God who is over all be blessed for ever. Amen.

Rom 9   [32]Why? Because they did not pursue it through faith, but as if it were based on works. They have stumbled over the stumbling stone, . . .

Cf. Rom 7   [25]Thanks be to God through Jesus Christ our Lord! So then, I of myself serve the law of God with my mind, but with my flesh I serve the law of sin.

● **Rom 10:2**

Cf. Acts 22   [3]"I am a Jew, born at Tarsus in Cilicia, but brought up in this city at the feet of Gamaliel, educated according to the strict manner of the law of our fathers, being zealous for God as you all are this day."

● **Rom 10:4**

Rom 3   [31]Do we then overthrow the law by this faith? By no means! On the contrary, we uphold the law.

[5]Moses writes that the man who practices the righteousness which is based on the law shall live by it. [6]But the righteousness based on faith says, Do not say in your heart, "Who will ascend into heaven?" (that is, to bring Christ down) [7]or "Who will descend into the abyss?" (that is, to bring Christ up from the dead). [8]But what does it say? The word is near you, on your lips and in your heart (that is, the word of faith which we preach); [9]because, if you confess with your lips that Jesus is Lord and believe in your heart that God raised him from the dead, you will be saved. [10]For man believes with his heart and so is justified, and he confesses with his lips and so is saved. [11]The scripture says, "No one who believes in him will be put to shame." [12]For there is no distinction between Jew and Greek; the same Lord is Lord of all and bestows his riches upon all who call upon him. [13]For, "every one who calls upon the name of the Lord will be saved."

PRIMARY

1 Cor 12:1-3 (§116)

[1]Now concerning spiritual gifts, brethren, I do not want you to be uninformed. [2]You know that when you were heathen, you were led astray to dumb idols, however you may have been moved. [3]Therefore I want you to understand that no one speaking by the Spirit of God ever says "Jesus be cursed!" and no one can say "Jesus is Lord" except by the Holy Spirit.

1 Cor 12:12-13 (§118)

[12]For just as the body is one and has many members, and all the members of the body, though many, are one body, so it is with Christ. [13]For by one Spirit we were all baptized into one body— Jews or Greeks, slaves or free—and all were made to drink of one Spirit.

1 Cor 15:1-19 (§131-132)

[1]Now I would remind you, brethren, in what terms I preached to you the gospel, which you received, in which you stand, [2]by which you are saved, if you hold it fast —unless you believed in vain.

[3]For I delivered to you as of first importance what I also received, that Christ died for our sins in accordance with the scriptures, [4]that he was buried, that he was raised on the third day in accordance with the scriptures, [5]and that he appeared to Cephas, then to the twelve. [6]Then he appeared to more than five hundred brethren at one time, most of whom are still alive, though some have fallen asleep. [7]Then he appeared to James, then to all the apostles. [8]Last of all, as to one untimely born, he appeared also to me. [9]For I am the least of the apostles, unfit to be called an apostle, because I persecuted the church of God. [10]But by the grace of God I am what I am, and his grace toward me was not in vain. On the contrary, I worked harder than any of them, though it was not I, but the grace of God which is with me. [11]Whether then it was I or they, so we preach and so you believed.

[12]Now if Christ is preached as raised from the dead, how can some of you say that there is no resurrection of the dead? [13]But if there is no resurrection of the dead, then Christ has not been raised; [14]if Christ has not been raised, then our preaching is in vain and your faith is in vain. [15]We are even found to be misrepresenting God, because we testified of God that he raised Christ, whom he did not raise if it is true that the dead are not raised. [16]For if the dead are not raised, then Christ has not been raised. [17]If Christ has not been raised, your faith is futile and you are still in your sins. [18]Then those also who have fallen asleep in Christ have perished. [19]If for this life only we have hoped in Christ, we are of all men most to be pitied.

Gal 3:10-14 (§202)

[10]For all who rely on works of the law are under a curse; for it is written, "Cursed be every one who does not abide by all things written in the book of the law, and do them." [11]Now it is evident that no man is justified before God by the law; for "He who through faith is righteous shall live"; [12]but the law does not rest on faith, for "He who does them shall live by them." [13]Christ redeemed us from the curse of the law, having become a curse for us—for it is written, "Cursed be every one who hangs on a tree"— [14]that in Christ Jesus the blessing of Abraham might come upon the Gentiles, that we might receive the promise of the Spirit through faith.

Gal 3:26-29 (§206)

[26]for in Christ Jesus you are all sons of God, through faith. [27]For as many of you as were baptized into Christ have put on Christ. [28]There is neither Jew nor Greek, there is neither slave nor free, there is neither male nor female; for you are all one in Christ Jesus. [29]And if you are Christ's, then you are Abraham's offspring, heirs according to promise.

Phil 2:1-11 (§242)

2 [1]So if there is any encouragement in Christ, any incentive of love, any participation in the Spirit, any affection and sympathy, [2]complete my joy by being of the same mind, having the same love, being in full accord and of one mind. [3]Do nothing from selfishness or conceit, but in humility count others better than yourselves. [4]Let each of you look not only to his own interests, but also to the interests of others. [5]Have this mind among yourselves, which is yours in Christ Jesus, [6]who, though he was in the form of God, did not count equality with God a thing to be grasped, [7]but emptied himself, taking the form of a servant, being born in the likeness of men. [8]And being found in human form he humbled himself and became obedient unto death, even death on a cross. [9]Therefore God has highly exalted him and bestowed on him the name which is above every name, [10]that at the name of Jesus every knee should bow, in heaven and on earth and under the earth, [11]and every tongue confess that Jesus Christ is Lord, to the glory of God the Father.

Col 3:5-11 (§266)

[5]Put to death therefore what is earthly in you: fornication, impurity, passion, evil desire, and covetousness, which is idolatry. [6]On account of these the wrath of God is coming. [7]In these you once walked, when you lived in them. [8]But now put them all away: anger, wrath, malice, slander, and foul talk from your mouth. [9]Do not lie to one another, seeing that you have put off the old nature with its practices [10]and have put on the new nature, which is being renewed in knowledge after the image of its creator. [11]Here there cannot be Greek and Jew, circumcised and uncircumcised, barbarian, Scythian, slave, free man, but Christ is all, and in all.

● **Rom 10:5**

Gal 5 [3]I testify again to every man who receives circumcision that he is bound to keep the whole law.

Lev 18 [5]You shall therefore keep my statutes and my ordinances, by doing which a man shall live: I am the Lord.

● **Rom 10:6-7**

Cf. Eph 4:8-10

● **Rom 10:6**

Deut 30 [12]It is not in heaven, that you should say, 'Who will go up for us to heaven, and bring it to us, that we may hear it and do it?' [13]Neither is it beyond the sea, that you should say, 'Who will go over the sea for us, and bring it to us, that we may hear it and do it?'

● **Rom 10:8**

Deut 30 [14]But the word is very near you; it is in your mouth and in your heart, so that you can do it.

● **Rom 10:9**

Cf. 2 Cor 5:14-15

Acts 2 [24]"But God raised him up, having loosed the pangs of death, because it was not possible for him to be held by it."

Acts 16 [31]And they said, "Believe in the Lord Jesus, and you will be saved, you and your household."

● **Rom 10:11**

Isa 28 [16]therefore thus says the Lord God,
"Behold, I am laying in Zion for a foundation
a stone, a tested stone,

a precious cornerstone, of a sure foundation:
'He who believes will not be in haste.'"

● **Rom 10:12**

Acts 10 [36]"You know the word which he sent to Israel, preaching good news of peace by Jesus Christ (he is Lord of all). . . ."

Cf. Rom 2:11; Rom 3:22

● **Rom 10:13**

Acts 2 [21]'And it shall be that whoever calls on the name of the Lord shall be saved.'

Joel 2 [32]And it shall come to pass that all who call upon the name of the Lord shall be delivered; for in Mount Zion and in Jerusalem there shall be those who escape, as the Lord has said, and among the survivors shall be those whom the Lord calls.

[14]But how are men to call upon him in whom they have not believed? And how are they to believe in him of whom they have never heard? And how are they to hear without a preacher? [15]And how can men preach unless they are sent? As it is written, "How beautiful are the feet of those who preach good news!" [16]But they have not all obeyed the gospel; for Isaiah says, "Lord, who has believed what he has heard from us?" [17]So faith comes from what is heard, and what is heard comes by the preaching of Christ.

PRIMARY

1 Cor 14:6–12 (§125)

[6]Now, brethren, if I come to you speaking in tongues, how shall I benefit you unless I bring you some revelation or knowledge or prophecy or teaching? [7]If even lifeless instruments, such as the flute or the harp, do not give distinct notes, how will any one know what is played? [8]And if the bugle gives an indistinct sound, who will get ready for battle? [9]So with yourselves; if you in a tongue utter speech that is not intelligible, how will any one know what is said? For you will be speaking into the air. [10]There are doubtless many different languages in the world, and none is without meaning; [11]but if I do not know the meaning of the language, I shall be a foreigner to the speaker and the speaker a foreigner to me. [12]So with yourselves; since you are eager for manifestations of the Spirit, strive to excel in building up the church.

1 Cor 14:13–19 (§126)

[13]Therefore, he who speaks in a tongue should pray for the power to interpret. [14]For if I pray in a tongue, my spirit prays but my mind is unfruitful. [15]What am I to do? I will pray with the spirit and I will pray with the mind also; I will sing with the spirit and I will sing with the mind also. [16]Otherwise, if you bless with the spirit, how can any one in the position of an outsider say the "Amen" to your thanksgiving when he does not know what you are saying? [17]For you may give thanks well enough, but the other man is not edified. [18]I thank God that I speak in tongues more than you all; [19]nevertheless, in church I would rather speak five words with my mind, in order to instruct others, than ten thousand words in a tongue.

Gal 3:1–5 (§200)

[1]O foolish Galatians! Who has bewitched you, before whose eyes Jesus Christ was publicly portrayed as crucified? [2]Let me ask you only this: Did you receive the Spirit by works of the law, or by hearing with faith? [3]Are you so foolish? Having begun with the Spirit, are you now ending with the flesh? [4]Did you experience so many things in vain?—if it really is in vain. [5]Does he who supplies the Spirit to you and works miracles among you do so by works of the law, or by hearing with faith?

Phil 1:12–18 (§239)

[12]I want you to know, brethren, that what has happened to me has really served to advance the gospel, [13]so that it has become known throughout the whole praetorian guard and to all the rest that my imprisonment is for Christ; [14]and most of the brethren have been made confident in the Lord because of my imprisonment, and are much more bold to speak the word of God without fear. [15]Some indeed preach Christ from envy and rivalry, but others from good will. [16]The latter do it out of love, knowing that I am put here for the defense of the gospel; [17]the former proclaim Christ out of partisanship, not sincerely but thinking to afflict me in my imprisonment. [18]What then? Only that in every way, whether in pretense or in truth, Christ is proclaimed; and in that I rejoice.

Phil 4:8–9 (§252)

[8]Finally, brethren, whatever is true, whatever is honorable, whatever is just, whatever is pure, whatever is lovely, whatever is gracious, if there is any excellence, if there is anything worthy of praise, think about these things. [9]What you have learned and received and heard and seen in me, do; and the God of peace will be with you.

Col 1:21–23 (§259)

[21]And you, who once were estranged and hostile in mind, doing evil deeds, [22]he has now reconciled in his body of flesh by his death, in order to present you holy and blameless and irreproachable before him, [23]provided that you continue in the faith, stable and steadfast, not shifting from the hope of the gospel which you heard, which has been preached to every creature under heaven, and of which I, Paul, became a minister.

1 Thess 2:13–16 (§279)

[13]And we also thank God constantly for this, that when you received the word of God which you heard from us, you accepted it not as the word of men but as what it really is, the word of God, which is at work in you believers. [14]For you, brethren, became imitators of the churches of God in Christ Jesus which are in Judea; for you suffered the same things from your own countrymen as they did from the Jews, [15]who killed both the Lord Jesus and the prophets, and drove us out, and displease God and oppose all men [16]by hindering us from speaking to the Gentiles that they may be saved—so as always to fill up the measure of their sins. But God's wrath has come upon them at last!

● **Rom 10:14**

Acts 8 [31]And he said, "How can I, unless some one guides me?" And he invited Philip to come up and sit with him.

Cf. Titus 1 [3]and at the proper time manifested in his word through the preaching with which I have been entrusted by command of God our Savior; . . .

● **Rom 10:15**

Gal 4 [12]Brethren, I beseech you, become as I am, for I also have become as you are. You did me no wrong; [13]you know it was because of a bodily ailment that I preached the gospel to you at first; [14]and though my condition was a trial to you, you did not scorn or despise me, but received me as an angel of God, as Christ Jesus. [15]What has become of the satisfaction you felt? For I bear you witness that, if possible, you would have plucked out your eyes and given them to me.

Isa 52 [7]How beautiful upon the mountains are the feet of him who brings good tidings, who publishes peace, who brings good tidings of good, who publishes salvation, who says to Zion, "Your God reigns."

● **Rom 10:16**

Isa 53 [1]Who has believed what we have heard? And to whom has the arm of the Lord been revealed?

● **Rom 10:17**

Cf. Eph 2 [17]And he came and preached peace to you who were far off and peace to those who were near; . . .

[18]But I ask, have they not heard? Indeed they have; for

"Their voice has gone out to all the earth, and their words to the ends of the world."

[19]Again I ask, did Israel not understand? First Moses says,

"I will make you jealous of those who are not a nation;
with a foolish nation I will make you angry."

[20]Then Isaiah is so bold as to say,

"I have been found by those who did not seek me;
I have shown myself to those who did not ask for me."

[21]But of Israel he says, "All day long I have held out my hands to a disobedient and contrary people."

PRIMARY

Col 1:3–14 (§257)

[3]We always thank God, the Father of our Lord Jesus Christ, when we pray for you, [4]because we have heard of your faith in Christ Jesus and of the love which you have for all the saints, [5]because of the hope laid up for you in heaven. Of this you have heard before in the word of the truth, the gospel [6]which has come to you, as indeed in the whole world it is bearing fruit and growing—so among yourselves, from the day you heard and understood the grace of God in truth, [7]as you learned it from Epaphras our beloved fellow servant. He is a faithful minister of Christ on our behalf [8]and has made known to us your love in the Spirit.

[9]And so, from the day we heard of it, we have not ceased to pray for you, asking that you may be filled with the knowledge of his will in all spiritual wisdom and understanding, [10]to lead a life worthy of the Lord, fully pleasing to him, bearing fruit in every good work and increasing in the knowledge of God. [11]May you be strengthened with all power, according to his glorious might, for all endurance and patience with joy, [12]giving thanks to the Father, who has qualified us to share in the inheritance of the saints in light. [13]He has delivered us from the dominion of darkness and transferred us to the kingdom of his beloved Son, [14]in whom we have redemption, the forgiveness of sins.

1 Thess 1:2–10 (§276)

[2]We give thanks to God always for you all, constantly mentioning you in our prayers, [3]remembering before our God and Father your work of faith and labor of love and steadfastness of hope in our Lord Jesus Christ. [4]For we know, brethren beloved by God, that he has chosen you; [5]for our gospel came to you not only in word, but also in power and in the Holy Spirit and with full conviction. You know what kind of men we proved to be among you for your sake. [6]And you became imitators of us and of the Lord, for you received the word in much affliction, with joy inspired by the Holy Spirit; [7]so that you became an example to the all the believers in Macedonia and in Achaia. [8]For not only has the word of the Lord sounded forth from you in Macedonia and Achaia, but your faith in God has gone forth everywhere, so that we need not say anything. [9]For they themselves report concerning us what a welcome we had among you, and how you turned to God from idols, to serve a living and true God, [10]and to wait for his Son from heaven, whom he raised from the dead, Jesus who delivers us from the wrath to come.

1 Thess 2:13–16 (§279)

[13]And we also thank God constantly for this, that when you received the word of God which you heard from us, you accepted it not as the word of men but as what it really is, the word of God, which is at work in you believers. [14]For you, brethren, became imitators of the churches of God in Christ Jesus which are in Judea; for you suffered the same things from your own countrymen as they did from the Jews, [15]who killed both the Lord Jesus and the prophets, and drove us out, and displease God and oppose all men [16]by hindering us from speaking to the Gentiles that they may be saved—so as always to fill up the measure of their sins. But God's wrath has come upon them at last!

● Rom 10:18

Ps 19 [4]yet their voice goes out through all the earth, and their words to the end of the world.
In them he has set a tent for the sun, . . .

● Rom 10:19

Rom 11 [11]So I ask, have they stumbled so as to fall? By no means! But through their trespass salvation has come to the Gentiles, so as to make Israel jealous.

Deut 32 [21]They have stirred me to jealousy with what is no god;
they have provoked me with their idols.
So I will stir them to jealousy with those who are no people;
I will provoke them with a foolish nation.

● Rom 10:20

Rom 9 [30]What shall we say, then? That Gentiles who did not pursue righteousness have attained it, that is, righteousness through faith; [31]but that Israel who pursued the righteousness which is based on law did not succeed in fulfilling that law. [32]Why? Because they did not pursue it through faith, but as if it were based on works. They have stumbled over the stumbling stone, [33]as it is written,
"Behold, I am laying in Zion a stone that will make men stumble,
a rock that will make them fall;
and he who believes in him will not be put to shame."

Isa 65 [1]I was ready to be sought by those who did not ask for me;
I was ready to be found by those who did not seek me.
I said, "Here am I, here am I," to a nation that did not call on my name.

Cf. Rom 2 [14]When Gentiles who have not the law do by nature what the law requires, they are a law to themselves, even though they do not have the law.

● Rom 10:21

Isa 65 [2]I spread out my hands all the day to a rebellious people,
who walk in a way that is not good, following their own devices; . . .

11 I ask, then, has God rejected his people? By no means! I myself am an Israelite, a descendant of Abraham, a member of the tribe of Benjamin. [2] God has not rejected his people whom he foreknew. Do you not know what the scripture says of Elijah, how he pleads with God against Israel? [3] "Lord, they have killed thy prophets, they have demolished thy altars, and I alone am left, and they seek my life." [4] But what is God's reply to him? "I have kept for myself seven thousand men who have not bowed the knee to Baal." [5] So too at the present time there is a remnant, chosen by grace. [6] But if it is by grace, it is no longer on the basis of works; otherwise grace would no longer be grace.

PRIMARY

2 Cor 11:21b–29 (§183)

But whatever any one dares to boast of—I am speaking as a fool—I also dare to boast of that. [22] Are they Hebrews? So am I. Are they Israelites? So am I. Are they descendants of Abraham? So am I. [23] Are they servants of Christ? I am a better one—I am talking like a madman—with far greater labors, far more imprisonments, with countless beatings, and often near death. [24] Five times I have received at the hands of the Jews the forty lashes less one. [25] Three times I have been beaten with rods; once I was stoned. Three times I have been shipwrecked; a night and a day I have been adrift at sea; [26] on frequent journeys, in danger from rivers, danger from robbers, danger from my own people, danger from Gentiles, danger in the city, danger in the wilderness, danger at sea, danger from false brethren; [27] in toil and hardship, through many a sleepless night, in hunger and thirst, often without food, in cold and exposure. [28] And, apart from other things, there is the daily pressure upon me of my anxiety for all the churches. [29] Who is weak, and I am not weak? Who is made to fall, and I am not indignant?

Gal 1:13–14 (§195)

[13] For you have heard of my former life in Judaism, how I persecuted the church of God violently and tried to destroy it; [14] and I advanced in Judaism beyond many of my own age among my people, so extremely zealous was I for the traditions of my fathers.

Gal 2:15–21 (§199)

[15] We ourselves, who are Jews by birth and not Gentile sinners, [16] yet who know that a man is not justified by works of the law but through faith in Jesus Christ, even we have believed in Christ Jesus, in order to be justified by faith in Christ, and not by works of the law, because by works of the law shall no one be justified. [17] But if, in our endeavor to be justified in Christ, we ourselves were found to be sinners, is Christ then an agent of sin? Certainly not! [18] But if I build up again those things which I tore down, then I prove myself a transgressor. [19] For I through the law died to the law, that I might live to God. [20] I have been crucified with Christ; it is no longer I who live, but Christ who lives in me; and the life I now live in the flesh I live by faith in the Son of God, who loved me and gave himself for me. [21] I do not nullify the grace of God; for if justification were through the law, then Christ died to no purpose.

Eph 2:1–10 (§220)

[1] And you he made alive, when you were dead through the trespasses and sins [2] in which you once walked, following the course of this world, following the prince of the power of the air, the spirit that is now at work in the sons of disobedience. [3] Among these we all once lived in the passions of our flesh, following the desires of body and mind, and so we were by nature children of wrath, like the rest of mankind. [4] But God, who is rich in mercy, out of the great love with which he loved us, [5] even when we were dead through our trespasses, made us alive together with Christ (by grace you have been saved), [6] and raised us up with him, and made us sit with him in the heavenly places in Christ Jesus, [7] that in the coming ages he might show the immeasurable riches of his grace in kindness toward us in Christ Jesus. [8] For by grace you have been saved through faith; and this is not your own doing, it is the gift of God— [9] not because of works, lest any man should boast. [10] For we are his workmanship, created in Christ Jesus for good works, which God prepared beforehand, that we should walk in them.

Phil 3:2–11 (§247)

[2] Look out for the dogs, look out for the evil-workers, look out for those who mutilate the flesh. [3] For we are the true circumcision, who worship God in spirit, and glory in Christ Jesus, and put no confidence in the flesh. [4] Though I myself have reason for confidence in the flesh also. If any other man thinks he has reason for confidence in the flesh, I have more: [5] circumcised on the eighth day, of the people of Israel, of the tribe of Benjamin, a Hebrew born of Hebrews; as to the law a Pharisee, [6] as to zeal a persecutor of the church, as to righteousness under the law blameless. [7] But whatever gain I had, I counted as loss for the sake of Christ. [8] Indeed I count everything as loss because of the surpassing worth of knowing Christ Jesus my Lord. For his sake I have suffered the loss of all things, and count them as refuse, in order that I may gain Christ [9] and be found in him, not having a righteousness of my own, based on law, but that which is through faith in Christ, the righteousness from God that depends on faith; [10] that I may know him and the power of his resurrection, and may share his sufferings, becoming like him in his death, [11] that if possible I may attain the resurrection from the dead.

● **Rom 11:1–2**
Rom 8   [29] For those whom he foreknew he also predestined to be conformed to the image of his Son, in order that he might be the first-born among many brethren. [30] And those whom he predestined he also called; and those whom he called he also justified; and those whom he justified he also glorified.

Rom 9   [11] though they were not yet born and had done nothing either good or bad, in order that God's purpose of election might continue, not because of works but because of his call, . . .

Gal 1   [15] But when he who had set me apart before I was born, and had called me through his grace, . . .

● **Rom 11:1**
(people) *read* inheritance: p⁴⁶G it(few) Ambrosiaster Ambrose

Rom 11:2
Rom 11   [28] As regards the gospel they are enemies of God, for your sake; but as regards election they are beloved for the sake of their forefathers. [29] For the gifts and the call of God are irrevocable.

● **Rom 11:3**
1 Thess 2   [15] who killed both the Lord Jesus and the prophets, and drove us out, and displease God and oppose all men . . .

1 Kgs 19   [10] He said, "I have been very jealous for the Lord, the God of hosts; for the people of Israel have forsaken thy covenant, thrown down thy altars, and slain thy prophets with the sword; and I, even I only, am left; and they seek my life, to take it away."

● **Rom 11:4**
1 Kgs 19   [18] "Yet I will leave seven thousand in Israel, all the knees that have not bowed to Baal, and every mouth that has not kissed him."

7What then? Israel failed to obtain what it sought. The elect obtained it, but the rest were hardened, 8as it is written,

"God gave them a spirit of stupor,
eyes that should not see and ears that
    should not hear,
down to this very day."

9And David says,

"Let their table become a snare and a
    trap,
a pitfall and a retribution for them;
10let their eyes be darkened so that they
    cannot see,
and bend their backs for ever."

PRIMARY

2 Cor 3:12–18 (§157)

12Since we have such a hope, we are very bold, 13not like Moses, who put a veil over his face so that the Israelites might not see the end of the fading splendor. 14But their minds were hardened; for to this day, when they read the old covenant, that same veil remains unlifted, because only through Christ is it taken away. 15Yes, to this day whenever Moses is read a veil lies over their minds; 16but when a man turns to the Lord the veil is removed. 17Now the Lord is the Spirit, and where the Spirit of the Lord is, there is freedom. 18And we all, with unveiled face, beholding the glory of the Lord, are being changed into his likeness from one degree of glory to another; for this comes from the Lord who is the Spirit.

2 Thess 2:1–12 (§296)

1Now concerning the coming of our Lord Jesus Christ and our assembling to meet him, we beg you, brethren, 2not to be quickly shaken in mind or excited, either by spirit or by word, or by letter purporting to be from us, to the effect that the day of the Lord has come. 3Let no one deceive you in any way; for that day will not come, unless the rebellion comes first, and the man of lawlessness is revealed, the son of perdition, 4who opposes and exalts himself against every so-called god or object of worship, so that he takes his seat in the temple of God, proclaiming himself to be God. 5Do you not remember that when I was still with you I told you this? 6And you know what is restraining him now so that he may be revealed in his time. 7For the mystery of lawlessness is already at work; only he who now restrains it will do so until he is out of the way. 8And then the lawless one will be revealed, and the Lord Jesus will slay him with the breath of his mouth and destroy him by his appearing and his coming. 9The coming of the lawless one by the activity of Satan will be with all power and with pretended signs and wonders, 10and with all wicked deception for those who are to perish, because they refused to love the truth and so be saved. 11Therefore God sends upon them a strong delusion, to make them believe what is false, 12so that all may be condemned who did not believe the truth but had pleasure in unrighteousness.

● **Rom 11:7–10**

Rom 9   30What shall we say, then? That Gentiles who did not pursue righteousness have attained it, that is, righteousness through faith; 31but that Israel who pursued the righteousness which is based on law did not succeed in fulfilling that law. 32Why? Because they did not pursue it through faith, but as if it were based on works.

Rom 9   17For the scripture says to Pharaoh, "I have raised you up for the very purpose of showing my power in you, so that my name may be proclaimed in all the earth." 18So then he has mercy upon whomever he wills, and he hardens the heart of whomever he wills.

Rom 8   29For those whom he foreknew he also predestined to be conformed to the image of his Son, in order that he might be the first-born among many brethren. 30And those whom he predestined he also called; and those whom he called he also justified; and those whom he justified he also glorified.

● **Rom 11:8**

Isa 29   10For the Lord has poured out upon you a spirit of deep sleep, . . .

and has closed your eyes, the prophets,
    and covered your heads, the seers.

Deut 29   4but to this day the Lord has not given you a mind to understand, or eyes to see, or ears to hear.

● **Rom 11:9**

Ps 69   22Let their own table before them become a snare;
    let their sacrificial feasts be a trap.
   23Let their eyes be darkened, so that they cannot see;
    and make their loins tremble continually.

[11]So I ask, have they stumbled so as to fall? By no means! But through their trespass salvation has come to the Gentiles, so as to make Israel jealous. [12]Now if their trespass means riches for the world, and if their failure means riches for the Gentiles, how much more will their full inclusion mean!

PRIMARY

Eph 2:11–22 (§221)

[11]Therefore remember that at one time you Gentiles in the flesh, called the uncircumcision by what is called the circumcision, which is made in the flesh by hands— [12]remember that you were at that time separated from Christ, alienated from the commonwealth of Israel, and strangers to the covenants of promise, having no hope and without God in the world. [13]But now in Christ Jesus you who once were far off have been brought near in the blood of Christ. [14]For he is our peace, who has made us both one, and has broken down the dividing wall of hostility, [15]by abolishing in his flesh the law of commandments and ordinances, that he might create in himself one new man in place of the two, so making peace, [16]and might reconcile us both to God in one body through the cross, thereby bringing the hostility to an end. [17]And he came and preached peace to you who were far off and peace to those who were near; [18]for through him we both have access in one Spirit to the Father. [19]So then you are no longer strangers and sojourners, but you are fellow citizens with the saints and members of the household of God, [20]built upon the foundation of the apostles and prophets, Christ Jesus himself being the cornerstone, [21]in whom the whole structure is joined together and grows into a holy temple in the Lord; [22]in whom you also are built into it for a dwelling place of God in the Spirit.

● **Rom 11:11–12**
Rom 11   [1]I ask, then, has God rejected his people? By no means! I myself am an Israelite, a descendant of Abraham, a member of the tribe of Benjamin.

Cf. Rom 11   [15]For if their rejection means the reconciliation of the world, what will their acceptance mean but life from the dead?

Cf. Rom 11   [24]For if you have been cut from what is by nature a wild olive tree, and grafted, contrary to nature, into a cultivated olive tree, how much more will these natural branches be grafted back into their own olive tree.

Cf. Rom 11   [28]As regards the gospel they are enemies of God, for your sake; but as regards election they are beloved for the sake of their forefathers. [29]For the gifts and the call of God are irrevocable.

● **Rom 11:11**
Acts 13   [46]And Paul and Barnabas spoke out boldly, saying, "It was necessary that the word of God should be spoken first to you. Since you thrust it from you, and judge yourselves unworthy of eternal life, behold, we turn to the Gentiles."

Acts 28   [28]"Let it be known to you then that this salvation of God has been sent to the Gentiles; they will listen."

● **Rom 11:12**
Cf. Col 1   [27]To them God chose to make known how great among the Gentiles are the riches of the glory of this mystery, which is Christ in you, the hope of glory.

Cf. 1 Thess 2   [14]For you, brethren, became imitators of the churches of God in Christ Jesus which are in Judea; for you suffered the same things from your own countrymen as they did from the Jews, [15]who killed both the Lord Jesus and the prophets, and drove us out, and displease God and oppose all men [16]by hindering us from speaking to the Gentiles that they may be saved—so as always to fill up the measure of their sins. But God's wrath has come upon them at last!

[13]Now I am speaking to you Gentiles. Inasmuch then as I am an apostle to the Gentiles, I magnify my ministry [14]in order to make my fellow Jews jealous, and thus save some of them. [15]For if their rejection means the reconciliation of the world, what will their acceptance mean but life from the dead? [16]If the dough offered as first fruits is holy, so is the whole lump; and if the root is holy, so are the branches.

PRIMARY

1 Cor 9:19-23 (§107)

[19]For though I am free from all men, I have made myself a slave to all, that I might win the more. [20]To the Jews I became as a Jew, in order to win Jews; to those under the law I became as one under the law—though not being myself under the law—that I might win those under the law. [21]To those outside the law I became as one outside the law—not being without law toward God but under the law of Christ—that I might win those outside the law. [22]To the weak I became weak, that I might win the weak. I have become all things to all men, that I might by all means save some. [23]I do it all for the sake of the gospel, that I may share in its blessings.

2 Cor 5:14-21 (§164)

[14]For the love of Christ controls us, because we are convinced that one has died for all; therefore all have died. [15]And he died for all, that those who live might live no longer for themselves but for him who for their sake died and was raised.

[16]From now on, therefore, we regard no one from a human point of view; even though we once regarded Christ from a human point of view, we regard him thus no longer. [17]Therefore, if any one is in Christ, he is a new creation; the old has passed away, behold, the new has come. [18]All this is from God, who through Christ reconciled us to himself and gave us the ministry of reconciliation; [19]that is, in Christ God was reconciling the world to himself, not counting their trespasses against them, and entrusting to us the message of reconciliation. [20]So we are ambassadors for Christ, God making his appeal through us. We beseech you on behalf of Christ, be reconciled to God. [21]For our sake he made him to be sin who knew no sin, so that in him we might become the righteousness of God.

Gal 2:1-14 (§197-198)

[1]Then after fourteen years I went up again to Jerusalem with Barnabas, taking Titus along with me. [2]I went up by revelation; and I laid before them (but privately before those who were of repute) the gospel which I preach among the Gentiles, lest somehow I should be running or had run in vain. [3]But even Titus, who was with me, was not compelled to be circumcised, though he was a Greek. [4]But because of false brethren secretly brought in, who slipped in to spy out our freedom which we have in Christ Jesus, that they might bring us into bondage— [5]to them we did not yield submission even for a moment, that the truth of the gospel might be preserved for you. [6]And from those who were reputed to be something (what they were makes no difference to me; God shows no partiality)—those, I say, who were of repute added nothing to me; [7]but on the contrary, when they saw that I had been entrusted with the gospel to the uncircumcised, just as Peter had been entrusted with the gospel to the circumcised [8](for he who worked through Peter for the mission to the circumcised worked through me also for the Gentiles), [9]and when they perceived the grace that was given to me, James and Cephas and John, who were reputed to be pillars, gave to me and Barnabas the right hand of fellowship, that we should go to the Gentiles and they to the circumcised; [10]only they would have us remember the poor, which very thing I was eager to do.

[11]But when Cephas came to Antioch I opposed him to his face, because he stood condemned. [12]For before certain men came from James, he ate with the Gentiles; but when they came he drew back and separated himself, fearing the circumcision party. [13]And with him the rest of the Jews acted insincerely, so that even Barnabas was carried away by their insincerity. [14]But when I saw that they were not straightforward about the truth of the gospel, I said to Cephas before them all, "If you, though a Jew, live like a Gentile and not like a Jew, how can you compel the Gentiles to live like Jews?"

Eph 3:1-13 (§222)

[1]For this reason I, Paul, a prisoner for Christ Jesus on behalf of you Gentiles— [2]assuming that you have heard of the stewardship of God's grace that was given to me for you, [3]how the mystery was made known to me by revelation, as I have written briefly. [4]When you read this you can perceive my insight into the mystery of Christ, [5]which was not made known to the sons of men in other generations as it has now been revealed to his holy apostles and prophets by the Spirit; [6]that is, how the Gentiles are fellow heirs, members of the same body, and partakers of the promise in Christ Jesus through the gospel.

[7]Of this gospel I was made a minister according to the gift of God's grace which was given to me by the working of his power. [8]To me, though I am the very least of all the saints, this grace was given, to preach to the Gentiles the unsearchable riches of Christ, [9]and to make all men see what is the plan of the mystery hidden for ages in God who created all things; [10]that through the church the manifold wisdom of God might now be made known to the principalities and powers in the heavenly places. [11]This was according to the eternal purpose which he has realized in Christ Jesus our Lord, [12]in whom we have boldness and confidence of access through our faith in him. [13]So I ask you not to lose heart over what I am suffering for you, which is your glory.

Col 1:21-2:3 (§259-260)

[21]And you, who once were estranged and hostile in mind, doing evil deeds, [22]he has now reconciled in his body of flesh by his death, in order to present you holy and blameless and irreproachable before him, [23]provided that you continue in the faith, stable and steadfast, not shifting from the hope of the gospel which you heard, which has been preached to every creature under heaven, and of which I, Paul, became a minister.

[24]Now I rejoice in my sufferings for your sake, and in my flesh I complete what is lacking in Christ's afflictions for the sake of his body, that is, the church, [25]of which I became a minister according to the divine office which was given to me for you, to make the word of God fully known, [26]the mystery hidden for ages and generations but now made manifest to his saints. [27]To them God chose to make known how great among the Gentiles are the riches of the glory of this mystery, which is Christ in you, the hope of glory. [28]Him we proclaim, warning every man and teaching every man in all wisdom, that we may present every man mature in Christ. [29]For this I toil, striving with all the energy which he mightily inspires within me.

[2] [1]For I want you to know how greatly I strive for you, and for those at Laodicea, and for all who have not seen my face, [2]that their hearts may be encouraged as they are knit together in love, to have all the riches of assured understanding and the knowledge of God's mystery, of Christ, [3]in whom are hid all the treasures of wisdom and knowledge.

● **Rom 11:13**
Rom 1   [5]through whom we have received grace and apostleship to bring about the obedience of faith for the sake of his name among all the nations, . . .

Acts 9   [15]But the Lord said to him, "Go, for he is a chosen instrument of mine to carry my name before the Gentiles and kings and the sons of Israel. . . ."

Cf. Rom 15: 15-16; 1 Cor 15:9-10; 1 Thess 2:5-6; Eph 4:11

● **Rom 11:14**
1 Tim 2   [4]who desires all men to be saved and to come to the knowledge of the truth.

Cf. Acts 13   [45]But when the Jews saw the multitudes, they were filled with jealousy, and contradicted what was spoken by Paul, and reviled him.

Acts 17   [5]But the Jews were jealous, and taking some wicked fellows of the rabble, they gathered a crowd, set the city in an uproar, and attacked the house of Jason, seeking to bring them out to the people.

● **Rom 11:15**
Rom 5   [10]For if while we were enemies we were reconciled to God by the death of his Son, much more, now that we are reconciled, shall we be saved by his life.

● **Rom 11:16**
(and if) *omit* if: p46 G it(few) Chrysostom

[17]But if some of the branches were broken off, and you, a wild olive shoot, were grafted in their place to share the richness of the olive tree, [18]do not boast over the branches. If you do boast, remember it is not you that support the root, but the root that supports you. [19]You will say, "Branches were broken off so that I might be grafted in." [20]That is true. They were broken off because of their unbelief, but you stand fast only through faith. So do not become proud, but stand in awe. [21]For if God did not spare the natural branches, neither will he spare you. [22]Note then the kindness and the severity of God: severity toward those who have fallen, but God's kindness to you, provided you continue in his kindness; otherwise you too will be cut off. [23]And even the others, if they do not persist in their unbelief, will be grafted in, for God has the power to graft them in again. [24]For if you have been cut from what is by nature a wild olive tree, and grafted, contrary to nature, into a cultivated olive tree, how much more will these natural branches be grafted back into their own olive tree.

PRIMARY

1 Cor 4:6–7 (§84)

[6]I have applied all this to myself and Apollos for your benefit, brethren, that you may learn by us not to go beyond what is written, that none of you may be puffed up in favor of one against another. [7]For who sees anything different in you? What have you that you did not receive? If then you received it, why do you boast as if it were not a gift?

Eph 2:11–22 (§221)

[11]Therefore remember that at one time you Gentiles in the flesh, called the uncircumcision by what is called the circumcision, which is made in the flesh by hands— [12]remember that you were at that time separated from Christ, alienated from the commonwealth of Israel, and strangers to the covenants of promise, having no hope and without God in the world. [13]But now in Christ Jesus you who once were far off have been brought near in the blood of Christ. [14]For he is our peace, who has made us both one, and has broken down the dividing wall of hostility, [15]by abolishing in his flesh the law of commandments and ordinances, that he might create in himself one new man in place of the two, so making peace, [16]and might reconcile us both to God in one body through the cross, thereby bringing the hostility to an end. [17]And he came and preached peace to you who were far off and peace to those who were near; [18]for through him we both have access in one Spirit to the Father. [19]So then you are no longer strangers and sojourners, but you are fellow citizens with the saints and members of the household of God, [20]built upon the foundation of the apostles and prophets, Christ Jesus himself being the cornerstone, [21]in whom the whole structure is joined together and grows into a holy temple in the Lord; [22]in whom you also are built into it for a dwelling place of God in the Spirit.

● **Rom 11:17–18**
Rom 15   [27]they were pleased to do it, and indeed they are in debt to them, for if the Gentiles have come to share in their spiritual blessings, they ought also to be of service to them in material blessings.

● **Rom 11:17**
(richness) *read* rich root: S*BC; *read* root and richness: S^cAD^bc Koine Lect it(some) vg syr(pes har)

Origen(Latin); *text:* p^46D*G it(some) cop(bo) Irenaeus (Latin)

● **Rom 11:18**
Cf. 1 Tim 6   [17]As for the rich in this world, charge them not to be haughty, nor to set their hopes on uncertain riches but on God who richly furnishes us with everything to enjoy.

● **Rom 11:20**
Gal 5   [1]For freedom Christ has set us free; stand fast therefore, and do not submit again to a yoke of slavery.

● **Rom 11:22**
Rom 2   [4]Or do you presume upon the riches of his kindness and forbearance and patience? Do you not know that God's kindness is meant to lead you to repentance?

[25]Lest you be wise in your own conceits, I want you to understand this mystery, brethren: a hardening has come upon part of Israel, until the full number of the Gentiles come in, [26]and so all Israel will be saved; as it is written,

"The Deliverer will come from Zion,
he will banish ungodliness from Jacob";
[27]"and this will be my covenant with them
when I take away their sins."

[28]As regards the gospel they are enemies of God, for your sake; but as regards election they are beloved for the sake of their forefathers. [29]For the gifts and the call of God are irrevocable. [30]Just as you were once disobedient to God but now have received mercy because of their disobedience, [31]so they have now been disobedient in order that by the mercy shown to you they also may receive mercy. [32]For God has consigned all men to disobedience, that he may have mercy upon all.

PRIMARY

Eph 2:11–22 (§221)

[11]Therefore remember that at one time you Gentiles in the flesh, called the uncircumcision by what is called the circumcision, which is made in the flesh by hands— [12]remember that you were at that time separated from Christ, alienated from the commonwealth of Israel, and strangers to the covenants of promise, having no hope and without God in the world. [13]But now in Christ Jesus you who once were far off have been brought near in the blood of Christ. [14]For he is our peace, who has made us both one, and has broken down the dividing wall of hostility, [15]by abolishing in his flesh the law of commandments and ordinances, that he might create in himself one new man in place of the two, so making peace, [16]and might reconcile us both to God in one body through the cross, thereby bringing the hostility to an end. [17]And he came and preached peace to you who were far off and peace to those who were near; [18]for through him we both have access in one Spirit to the Father. [19]So then you are no longer strangers and sojourners, but you are fellow citizens with the saints and members of the household of God, [20]built upon the foundation of the apostles and prophets, Christ Jesus himself being the cornerstone, [21]in whom the whole structure is joined together and grows into a holy temple in the Lord; [22]in whom you also are built into it for a dwelling place of God in the Spirit.

Phil 3:17–21 (§249)

[17]Brethren, join in imitating me, and mark those who so live as you have an example in us. [18]For many, of whom I have often told you and now tell you even with tears, live as enemies of the cross of Christ. [19]Their end is destruction, their god is the belly, and they glory in their shame, with minds set on earthly things. [20]But our commonwealth is in heaven, and from it we await a Savior, the Lord Jesus Christ, [21]who will change our lowly body to be like his glorious body, by the power which enables him even to subject all things to himself.

Col 1:24–2:3 (§260)

[24]Now I rejoice in my sufferings for your sake, and in my flesh I complete what is lacking in Christ's afflictions for the sake of his body, that is, the church, [25]of which I became a minister according to the divine office which was given to me for you, to make the word of God fully known, [26]the mystery hidden for ages and generations but now made manifest to his saints. [27]To them God chose to make known how great among the Gentiles are the riches of the glory of this mystery, which is Christ in you, the hope of glory. [28]Him we proclaim warning every man and teaching every man in all wisdom, that we may present every man mature in Christ. [29]For this I toil, striving with all the energy which he mightily inspires within me.

2 [1]For I want you to know how greatly I strive for you, and for those at Laodicea, and for all who have not seen my face, [2]that their hearts may be encouraged as they are knit together in love, to have all the riches of assured understanding and the knowledge of God's mystery, of Christ, [3]in whom are hid all the treasures of wisdom and knowledge.

● **Rom 11:25**
Rom 9   [18]So then he has mercy upon whomever he wills, and he hardens the heart of whomever he wills.

Cf. 1 Cor 2   [7]But we impart a secret and hidden wisdom of God, which God decreed before the ages for our glorification. [8]None of the rulers of this age understood this; for if they had, they would not have crucified the Lord of glory. [9]But, as it is written,
"What no eye has seen, nor ear heard,
nor the heart of man conceived,
what God has prepared for those who love him,
. . ."

Cf. 2 Cor 3   [14]But their minds were hardened; for to this day, when they read the old covenant, that same veil remains unlifted, because only through Christ is it taken away. [15]Yes, to this day whenever Moses is read a veil lies over their minds; [16]but when a man turns to the Lord the veil is removed.

Cf. 2 Thess 1   [11]To this end we always pray for you, that our God may make you worthy of his call, and may fulfil every good resolve and work of faith by his power, . . .

Cf. 2 Thess 2   [11]Therefore God sends upon them a strong delusion, to make them believe what is false, [12]so that all may be condemned who did not believe the truth but had pleasure in unrighteousness.

● **Rom 11:26**
Isa 59   [20]"And he will come to Zion as Redeemer, to those in Jacob who turn from transgression, says the Lord."

● **Rom 11:27**
Jer 31   [33]But this is the covenant which I will make with the house of Israel after those days, says the Lord: I will put my law within them, and I will write it upon their hearts; and I will be their God, and they shall be my people.

Cf. 2 Tim 1   [9]who saved us and called us with a holy calling, not in virtue of our works but in virtue of his own purpose and the grace which he gave us in Christ Jesus ages ago, . . .

● **Rom 11:28**
Rom 5   [6]While we were still weak, at the right time Christ died for the ungodly.
[7]Why, one will hardly die for a righteous man— though perhaps for a good man one will dare even to die. [8]But God shows his love for us in that while we were yet sinners Christ died for us. [9]Since, therefore, we are now justified by his blood, much more shall we be saved by him from the wrath of God. [10]For if while we were enemies we were reconciled to God by the death of his Son, much more, now that we are reconciled, shall we be saved by his life.

● **Rom 11:31**
(may) *add* now: SBD(Greek) cop(bo)

● **Rom 11:32**
Rom 5   [19]For as by one man's disobedience many were made sinners, so by one man's obedience many will be made righteous.

Phil 2   [9]Therefore God has highly exalted him and bestowed on him the name which is above every name, [10]that at the name of Jesus every knee should bow, in heaven and on earth and under the earth, [11]and every tongue confess that Jesus Christ is Lord, to the glory of God the Father.

Cf. 1 Cor 15   [9]For I am the least of the apostles, unfit to be called an apostle, because I persecuted the church of God.

Cf. 1 Cor 15   [51]Lo! I tell you a mystery. We shall not all sleep, but we shall all be changed, . . .

Cf. Gal 3   [22]But the scripture consigned all things to sin, that what was promised to faith in Jesus Christ might be given to those who believe.

Cf. 1 Tim 2   [4]who desires all men to be saved and to come to the knowledge of the truth.

FORMAL ELEMENT: CONFESSION

33O the depth of the riches and wisdom and knowledge of God! How unsearchable are his judgments and how inscrutable his ways!
34"For who has known the mind of the Lord,
or who has been his counselor?"
35"Or who has given a gift to him
that he might be repaid?"
36For from him and through him and to him are all things. To him be glory for ever. Amen.

PRIMARY

1 Cor 8:4–6 (§103)

4Hence, as to the eating of food offered to idols, we know that "an idol has no real existence," and that "there is no God but one." 5For although there may be so-called gods in heaven or on earth—as indeed there are many "gods" and many "lords"— 6yet for us there is one God, the Father, from whom are all things and for whom we exist, and one Lord, Jesus Christ, through whom are all things and through whom we exist.

1 Cor 15:1–11 (§131)

1Now I would remind you, brethren, in what terms I preached to you the gospel, which you received, in which you stand, 2by which you are saved, if you hold it fast —unless you believed in vain.

3For I delivered to you as of first importance what I also received, that Christ died for our sins in accordance with the scriptures, 4that he was buried, that he was raised on the third day in accordance with the scriptures, 5and that he appeared to Cephas, then to the twelve. 6Then he appeared to more than five hundred brethren at one time, most of whom are still alive, though some have fallen asleep. 7Then he appeared to James, then to all the apostles. 8Last of all, as to one untimely born, he appeared also to me. 9For I am the least of the apostles, unfit to be called an apostle, because I persecuted the church of God. 10But by the grace of God I am what I am, and his grace

toward me was not in vain. On the contrary, I worked harder than any of them, though it was not I, but the grace of God which is with me. 11Whether then it was I or they, so we preach and so you believed.

Eph 4:1–10 (§225)

1I therefore, a prisoner for the Lord, beg you to lead a life worthy of the calling to which you have been called, 2with all lowliness and meekness, with patience, forbearing one another in love, 3eager to maintain the unity of the Spirit in the bond of peace. 4There is one body and one Spirit, just as you were called to the one hope that belongs to your call, 5one Lord, one faith, one baptism, 6one God and Father of us all, who is above all and through all and in all. 7But grace was given to each of us according to the measure of Christ's gift. 8Therefore it is said,
"When he ascended on high he led a host of captives,
and he gave gifts to men."
9(In saying, "He ascended," what does it mean but that he had also descended into the lower parts of the earth? 10He who descended is he who also ascended far above all the heavens, that he might fill all things.)

Phil 2:1–11 (§242)

1So if there is any encouragement in Christ, any incentive of love, any participation in the Spirit, any affection and sympathy, 2complete my joy by being of the same mind, having the same love, being in full accord and of one mind. 3Do nothing from selfishness or conceit, but in humility count others better than yourselves. 4Let each of you look not only to his own interests, but also to the interests of others. 5Have this mind among yourselves, which is yours in Christ Jesus, 6who, though he was in the form of God, did not count equality with God a thing to be grasped, 7but emptied himself, taking the form of a servant, being born in the likeness of men. 8And being found in human form he humbled himself and became obedient unto death, even death on a cross. 9Therefore God has highly exalted him and bestowed on him the name which is above every name, 10that at the name of Jesus every

knee should bow, in heaven and on earth and under the earth, 11and every tongue confess that Jesus Christ is Lord, to the glory of God the Father.

Col 1:15–20 (§258)

15He is the image of the invisible God, the first-born of all creation; 16for in him all things were created, in heaven and on earth, visible and invisible, whether thrones or dominions or principalities or authorities—all things were created through him and for him. 17He is before all things, and in him all things hold together. 18He is the head of the body, the church; he is the beginning, the first-born from the dead, that in everything he might be pre-eminent. 19For in him all the fulness of God was pleased to dwell, 20and through him to reconcile to himself all things, whether on earth or in heaven, making peace by the blood of his cross.

1 Thess 1:2–10 (§276)

2We give thanks to God always for you all, constantly mentioning you in our prayers, 3remembering before our God and Father your work of faith and labor of love and steadfastness of hope in our Lord Jesus Christ. 4For we know, brethren beloved by God, that he has chosen you; 5for our gospel came to you not only in word, but also in power and in the Holy Spirit and with full conviction. You know what kind of men we proved to be among you for your sake. 6And you became imitators of us and of the Lord, for you received the word in much affliction, with joy inspired by the Holy Spirit; 7so that you became an example to the all the believers in Macedonia and in Achaia. 8For not only has the word of the Lord sounded forth from you in Macedonia and Achaia, but your faith in God has gone forth everywhere, so that we need not say anything. 9For they themselves report concerning us what a welcome we had among you, and how you turned to God from idols, to serve a living and true God, 10and to wait for his Son from heaven, whom he raised from the dead, Jesus who delivers us from the wrath to come.

● **Rom 11:33–36**
Col 2　1For I want you to know how greatly I strive for you, and for those at Laodicea, and for all who have not seen my face, 2that their hearts may be encouraged as they are knit together in love, to have all the riches of assured understanding and the knowledge of God's mystery, of Christ, 3in whom are hid all the treasures of wisdom and knowledge.

Eph 3　4When you read this you can perceive my insight into the mystery of Christ, 5which was not made known to the sons of men in other generations as it has now been revealed to his holy apostles and prophets by the Spirit; . . .

Cf. 1 Cor 1:21; Rom 1:1-7

● **Rom 11:34**
Isa 40　13Who has directed the Spirit of the Lord,
or as his counselor has instructed him?
14Whom did he consult for his enlightenment,
and who taught him the path of justice,
and taught him knowledge,
and showed him the way of understanding?

● **Rom 11:35**
Job 35　7If you are righteous, what do you give to him;
or what does he receive from your hand?

Job 41　11Who has given to me, that I should repay him?
Whatever is under the whole heaven is mine.

● **Rom 11:36**
Rom 14　7None of us lives to himself, and none of us dies to himself. 8If we live, we live to the Lord, and if we die, we die to the Lord; so then, whether we live or whether we die, we are the Lord's. 9For to this end Christ died and lived again, that he might be Lord both of the dead and of the living.

1 Tim 2　5For there is one God, and there is one mediator between God and men, the man Christ Jesus, . . .

Acts 17　24The God who made the world and everything in it, being Lord of heaven and earth, does not live in shrines made by man. . . .

Cf. Rom 4:17

LETTER STRUCTURE: APPEAL

12 I appeal to you therefore, brethren, by the mercies of God, to present your bodies as a living sacrifice, holy and acceptable to God, which is your spiritual worship. [2] Do not be conformed to this world but be transformed by the renewal of your mind, that you may prove what is the will of God, what is good and acceptable and perfect.

PRIMARY

1 Cor 1:10–17 (§73)

[10] I appeal to you, brethren, by the name of our Lord Jesus Christ, that all of you agree and that there be no dissensions among you, but that you be united in the same mind and the same judgment. [11] For it has been reported to me by Chloe's people that there is quarreling among you, my brethren. [12] What I mean is that each one of you says, "I belong to Paul," or "I belong to Apollos," or "I belong to Cephas," or "I belong to Christ." [13] Is Christ divided? Was Paul crucified for you? Or were you baptized in the name of Paul? [14] I am thankful that I baptized none of you except Crispus and Gaius; [15] lest any one should say that you were baptized in my name. [16] (I did baptize also the household of Stephanas. Beyond that, I do not know whether I baptized any one else.) [17] For Christ did not send me to baptize but to preach the gospel, and not with eloquent wisdom, lest the cross of Christ be emptied of its power.

2 Cor 10:1–6 (§176)

10 [1] I, Paul, myself entreat you, by the meekness and gentleness of Christ—I who am humble when face to face with you, but bold to you when I am away!— [2] I beg of you that when I am present I may not have to show boldness with such confidence as I count on showing against some who suspect us of acting in worldly fashion. [3] For though we live in the world we are not carrying on a worldly war, [4] for the weapons of our warfare are not worldly but have divine power to destroy strongholds. [5] We destroy arguments and every proud obstacle to the knowledge of God, and take every thought captive to obey Christ, [6] being ready to punish every disobedience, when your obedience is complete.

Eph 4:1–10 (§225)

4 [1] I therefore, a prisoner for the Lord, beg you to lead a life worthy of the calling to which you have been called, [2] with all lowliness and meekness, with patience, forbearing one another in love, [3] eager to maintain the unity of the Spirit in the bond of peace. [4] There is one body and one Spirit, just as you were called to the one hope that belongs to your call, [5] one Lord, one faith, one baptism, [6] one God and Father of us all, who is above all and through all and in all. [7] But grace was given to each of us according to the measure of Christ's gift. [8] Therefore it is said,

"When he ascended on high he led a host of captives,

and he gave gifts to men."

[9] (In saying, "He ascended," what does it mean but that he had also descended into the lower parts of the earth? [10] He who descended is he who also ascended far above all the heavens, that he might fill all things.)

1 Thess 4:1–8 (§284)

4 [1] Finally, brethren, we beseech and exhort you in the Lord Jesus, that as you learned from us how you ought to live and to please God, just as you are doing, you do so more and more. [2] For you know what instructions we gave you through the Lord Jesus. [3] For this is the will of God, your sanctification: that you abstain from unchastity; [4] that each one of you know how to take a wife for himself in holiness and honor [5] not in the passion of lust like heathen who do not know God; [6] that no man transgress, and wrong his brother in this matter, because the Lord is an avenger in all these things, as we solemnly forewarned you. [7] For God has not called us for uncleanness, but in holiness. [8] Therefore whoever disregards this, disregards not man but God, who gives his Holy Spirit to you.

2 Thess 2:1–12 (§296)

2 [1] Now concerning the coming of our Lord Jesus Christ and our assembling to meet him, we beg you, brethren, [2] not to be quickly shaken in mind or excited, either by spirit or by word, or by letter purporting to be from us, to the effect that the day of the Lord has come. [3] Let no one deceive you in any way; for that day will not come, unless the rebellion comes first, and the man of lawlessness is revealed, the son of perdition, [4] who opposes and exalts himself

---

● **Rom 12:1**
Rom 11   [32] For God has consigned all men to disobedience, that he may have mercy upon all.

2 Cor 2   [15] For we are the aroma of Christ to God among those who are being saved and among those who are perishing, [16] to one a fragrance from death to death, to the other a fragrance from life to life. Who is sufficient for these things?

Eph 5   [2] And walk in love, as Christ loved us and gave himself up for us, a fragrant offering and sacrifice to God.

Cf. Rom 8   [10] But if Christ is in you, although your bodies are dead because of sin, your spirits are alive because of righteousness.

Cf. 2 Cor 1   [3] Blessed be the God and Father of our Lord Jesus Christ, the Father of mercies and God of all comfort, . . .

against every so-called god or object of worship, so that he takes his seat in the temple of God, proclaiming himself to be God. [5]Do you not remember that when I was still with you I told you this? [6]And you know what is restraining him now so that he may be revealed in his time. [7]For the mystery of lawlessness is already at work; only he who now restrains it will do so until he is out of the way. [8]And then the lawless one will be revealed, and the Lord Jesus will slay him with the breath of his mouth and destroy him by his appearing and his coming. [9]The coming of the lawless one by the activity of Satan will be with all power and with pretended signs and wonders, [10]and with all wicked deception for those who are to perish, because they refused to love the truth and so be saved. [11]Therefore God sends upon them a strong delusion, to make them believe what is false, [12]so that all may be condemned who did not believe the truth but had pleasure in unrighteousness.

Phlm 8–14 (§307)

[8]Accordingly, though I am bold enough in Christ to command you to do what is required, [9]yet for love's sake I prefer to appeal to you—I, Paul, an ambassador and now a prisoner also for Christ Jesus— [10]I appeal to you for my child, Onesimus, whose father I have become in my imprisonment. [11](Formerly he was useless to you, but now he is indeed useful to you and to me.) [12]I am sending him back to you, sending my very heart. [13]I would have been glad to keep him with me, in order that he might serve me on your behalf during my imprisonment for the gospel; [14]but I preferred to do nothing without your consent in order that your goodness might not be by compulsion but of your own free will.

SECONDARY

Phil 2:14–18 (§244)

[14]Do all things without grumbling or questioning, [15]that you may be blameless and innocent, children of God without blemish in the midst of a crooked and perverse generation, among whom you shine as lights in the world, [16]holding fast the word of life, so that in the day of Christ I may be proud that I did not run in vain or labor in vain. [17]Even if I am to be poured as a libation upon the sacrificial offering of your faith, I am glad and rejoice with you all. [18]Likewise you also should be glad and rejoice with me.

Phil 4:10–20 (§253)

[10]I rejoice in the Lord greatly that now at length you have revived your concern for me; you were indeed concerned for me, but you had no opportunity. [11]Not that I complain of want; for I have learned, in whatever state I am, to be content. [12]I know how to be abased, and I know how to abound; in any and all circumstances I have learned the secret of facing plenty and hunger, abundance and want. [13]I can do all things in him who strengthens me.

[14]Yet it was kind of you to share my trouble. [15]And you Philippians yourselves know that in the beginning of the gospel, when I left Macedonia, no church entered into partnership with me in giving and receiving except you only; [16]for even in Thessalonica you sent me help once and again. [17]Not that I seek the gift; but I seek the fruit which increases to your credit. [18]I have received full payment, and more; I am filled, having received from Epaphroditus the gifts you sent, a fragrant offering, a sacrifice acceptable and pleasing to God. [19]And my God will supply every need of yours according to his riches in glory in Christ Jesus. [20]To our God and Father be glory for ever and ever. Amen.

Col 1:21–23 (§259)

[21]And you, who once were estranged and hostile in mind, doing evil deeds, [22]he has now reconciled in his body of flesh by his death, in order to present you holy and blameless and irreproachable before him, [23]provided that you continue in the faith, stable and steadfast, not shifting from the hope of the gospel which you heard, which has been preached to every creature under heaven, and of which I, Paul, became a minister.

1 Thess 2:9–12 (§278)

[9]For you remember our labor and toil, brethren; we worked night and day, that we might not burden any of you, while we preached to you the gospel of God. [10]You are witnesses, and God also, how holy and righteous and blameless was our behavior to you believers; [11]for you know how, like a father with his children, we exhorted each one of you and encouraged you and charged you [12]to lead a life worthy of God, who calls you into his own kingdom and glory.

Cf. 1 Thess 5   [12]But we beseech you, brethren, to respect those who labor among you and are over you in the Lord and admonish you, . . .

Cf. 1 Thess 5   [23]May the God of peace himself sanctify you wholly; and may your spirit and soul and body be kept sound and blameless at the coming of our Lord Jesus Christ.

● **Rom 12:2**
Rom 7   [12]So the law is holy, and the commandment is holy and just and good.

Titus 3   [5]he saved us, not because of deeds done by us in righteousness, but in virtue of his own mercy, by the washing of regeneration and renewal in the Holy Spirit, . . .

[3]**For by the grace given to me I bid every one among you not to think of himself more highly than he ought to think, but to think with sober judgment, each according to the measure of faith which God has assigned him. [4]For as in one body we have many members, and all the members do not have the same function, [5]so we, though many, are one body in Christ, and individually members one of another. [6]Having gifts that differ according to the grace given to us, let us use them: if prophecy, in proportion to our faith; [7]if service, in our serving; he who teaches, in his teaching; [8]he who exhorts, in his exhortation; he who contributes, in liberality; he who gives aid, with zeal; he who does acts of mercy, with cheerfulness.**

PRIMARY

1 Cor 4:6–7 (§84)

[6]I have applied all this to myself and Apollos for your benefit, brethren, that you may learn by us not to go beyond what is written, that none of you may be puffed up in favor of one against another. [7]For who sees anything different in you? What have you that you did not receive? If then you received it, why do you boast as if it were not a gift?

1 Cor 12:4–31 (§117–120)

[4]Now there are varieties of gifts, but the same Spirit; [5]and there are varieties of service, but the same Lord; [6]and there are varieties of working, but it is the same God who inspires them all in every one. [7]To each is given the manifestation of the Spirit for the common good. [8]To one is given through the Spirit the utterance of wisdom, and to another the utterance of knowledge according to the same Spirit, [9]to another faith by the same Spirit, to another gifts of healing by the one Spirit, [10]to another the working of miracles, to another prophecy, to another the ability to distinguish between spirits, to another various kinds of tongues, to another the interpretation of tongues. [11]All these are inspired by one and the same Spirit, who apportions to each one individually as he wills.

[12]For just as the body is one and has many members, and all the members of the body, though many, are one body, so it is with Christ. [13]For by one Spirit we were all baptized into one body— Jews or Greeks, slaves or free—and all were made to drink of one Spirit.

[14]For the body does not consist of one member but of many. [15]If the foot should say, "Because I am not a hand, I do not belong to the body," that would not make it any less a part of the body. [16]And if the ear should say, "Because I am not an eye, I do not belong to the body," that would not make it any less a part of the body. [17]If the whole body were an eye, where would be the hearing? If the whole body were an ear, where would be the sense of smell? [18]But as it is, God arranged the organs in the body, each one of them, as he chose. [19]If all were a single organ, where would the body be? [20]As it is, there are many parts, yet one body. [21]The eye cannot say to the hand, "I have no need of you," nor again the head to the feet, "I have no need of you." [22]On the contrary, the parts of the body which seem to be weaker are indispensable, [23]and those parts of the body which we think less honorable we invest with the greater honor, and our unpresentable parts are treated with greater modesty, [24]which our more presentable parts do not require. But God has so composed the body, giving the greater honor to the inferior part, [25]that there may be no discord in the body, but that the members may have the same care for one another. [26]If one member suffers, all suffer together; if one member is honored, all rejoice together.

[27]Now you are the body of Christ and individually members of it. [28]And God has appointed in the church first apostles, second prophets, third teachers, then workers of miracles, then healers, helpers, administrators, speakers in various kinds of tongues. [29]Are all apostles? Are all prophets? Are all teachers? Do all work miracles? [30]Do all possess gifts of healing? Do all speak with tongues? Do all interpret? [31]But earnestly desire the higher gifts.

And I will show you a still more excellent way.

Eph 4:11–16 (§226)

[11]And his gifts were that some should be apostles, some prophets, some evangelists, some pastors and teachers, [12]to equip the saints for the work of ministry, for building up the body of Christ, [13]until we all attain to the unity of the faith and of the knowledge of the Son of God, to mature manhood, to the measure of the stature of the fulness of Christ; [14]so that we may no longer be children, tossed to and fro and carried about with every wind of doctrine, by the cunning of men, by their craftiness in deceitful wiles. [15]Rather, speaking the truth in love, we are to grow up in every way into him who is the head, into Christ, [16]from whom the whole body, joined and knit together by every joint with which it is supplied, when each part is working properly, makes bodily growth and upbuilds itself in love.

● **Rom 12:4**

Eph 4   [25]Therefore, putting away falsehood, let every one speak the truth with his neighbor, for we are members one of another.

Cf. 1 Cor 10   [17]Because there is one bread, we who are many are one body, for we all partake of the one bread.

● **Rom 12:5**

Eph 1   [23]which is his body, the fulness of him who fills all in all.

Col 1   [18]He is the head of the body, the church; he is the beginning, the first-born from the dead, that in everything he might be pre-eminent.

Col 2   [19]and not holding fast to the Head, from whom the whole body, nourished and knit together through its joints and ligaments, grows with a growth that is from God.

Eph 5   [30]because we are members of his body.

Cf. Col 3   [15]And let the peace of Christ rule in your hearts, to which indeed you were called in the one body. And be thankful.

● **Rom 12:6–8**

Cf. Phil 1   [1]Paul and Timothy, servants of Christ Jesus,

To all the saints in Christ Jesus who are at Philippi, with the bishops and deacons: . . .

● **Rom 12:6**

1 Tim 4   [14]Do not neglect the gift you have, which was given you by prophetic utterance when the council of elders laid their hands upon you.

● **Rom 12:7**

1 Tim 5   [17]As for the rich in this world, charge them not to be haughty, nor to set their hopes on uncertain riches but on God who richly furnishes us with everything to enjoy.

● **Rom 12:8**

Acts 13   [15]After the reading of the law and the prophets, the rulers of the synagogue sent to them, saying, "Brethren, if you have any word of exhortation for the people, say it."

Formal Element: Gnomic Sayings

[9] Let love be genuine; hate what is evil, hold fast to what is good; [10] love one another with brotherly affection; outdo one another in showing honor. [11] Never flag in zeal, be aglow with the Spirit, serve the Lord. [12] Rejoice in your hope, be patient in tribulation, be constant in prayer. [13] Contribute to the needs of the saints, practice hospitality.

[14] Bless those who persecute you; bless and do not curse them. [15] Rejoice with those who rejoice, weep with those who weep. [16] Live in harmony with one another; do not be haughty, but associate with the lowly; never be conceited. [17] Repay no one evil for evil, but take thought for what is noble in the sight of all. [18] If possible, so far as it depends upon you, live peaceably with all. [19] Beloved, never avenge yourselves, but leave it to the wrath of God; for it is written, "Vengeance is mine, I will repay, says the Lord." [20] No, "if your enemy is hungry, feed him; if he is thirsty, give him drink; for by so doing you will heap burning coals upon his head." [21] Do not be overcome by evil, but overcome evil with good.

Primary

1 Cor 13:4–7 (§122)

[4] Love is patient and kind; love is not jealous or boastful; [5] it is not arrogant or rude. Love does not insist on its own way; it is not irritable or resentful; [6] it does not rejoice at wrong, but rejoices in the right. [7] Love bears all things, believes all things, hopes all things, endures all things.

2 Cor 13:11–13 (§191)

[11] Finally, brethren, farewell. Mend your ways, heed my appeal, agree with one another, live in peace, and the God of love and peace will be with you. [12] Greet one another with a holy kiss. [13] All the saints greet you.

Eph 4:25–32 (§228)

[25] Therefore, putting away falsehood, let every one speak the truth with his neighbor, for we are members one of another. [26] Be angry but do not sin; do not let the sun go down on your anger, [27] and give no opportunity to the devil. [28] Let the thief no longer steal, but rather let him labor, doing honest work with his hands, so that he may be able to give to those in need. [29] Let no evil talk come out of your mouths, but only such as is good for edifying, as fits the occasion, that it may impart grace to those who

hear. [30] And do not grieve the Holy Spirit of God, in whom you were sealed for the day of redemption. [31] Let all bitterness and wrath and anger and clamor and slander be put away from you, with all malice, [32] and be kind to one another, tenderhearted, forgiving one another, as God in Christ forgave you.

Phil 2:1–11 (§242)

[1] So if there is any encouragement in Christ, any incentive of love, any participation in the Spirit, any affection and sympathy, [2] complete my joy by being of the same mind, having the same love, being in full accord and of one mind. [3] Do nothing from selfishness or conceit, but in humility count others better than yourselves. [4] Let each of you look not only to his own interests, but also to the interests of others. [5] Have this mind among yourselves, which is yours in Christ Jesus, [6] who, though he was in the form of God, did not count equality with God a thing to be grasped, [7] but emptied himself, taking the form of a servant, being born in the likeness of men. [8] And being found in human form he humbled himself and became obedient unto death, even death on a cross. [9] Therefore God has highly exalted him and bestowed on him the name which is above every name, [10] that at the name of Jesus every knee should bow, in heaven and on earth and under the earth, [11] and every tongue confess that Jesus Christ is Lord, to the glory of God the Father.

Phil 4:4–9 (§251–252)

[4] Rejoice in the Lord always; again I will say, Rejoice. [5] Let all men know your forbearance. The Lord is at hand. [6] Have no anxiety about anything, but in everything by prayer and supplication with thanksgiving let your requests be made known to God. [7] And the peace of God, which passes all understanding, will keep your hearts and your minds in Christ Jesus.

[8] Finally, brethren, whatever is true, whatever is honorable, whatever is just, whatever is pure, whatever is lovely, whatever is gracious, if there is any excellence, if there is anything worthy of praise, think about these things. [9] What you have learned and received and heard and seen in me, do; and the God of peace will be with you.

Col 3:12–17 (§267)

[12] Put on then, as God's chosen ones, holy and beloved, compassion, kindness, lowliness, meekness, and patience, [13] forbearing one another and, if one has a complaint against another, forgiving each other; as the Lord has forgiven you, so you also must forgive. [14] And above all these put on love, which binds every-

thing together in perfect harmony. [15] And let the peace of Christ rule in your hearts, to which indeed you were called in the one body. And be thankful. [16] Let the word of Christ dwell in you richly, as you teach and admonish one another in all wisdom, and as you sing psalms and hymns and spiritual songs with thankfulness in your hearts to God. [17] And whatever you do, in word or deed, do everything in the name of the Lord Jesus, giving thanks to God the Father through him.

1 Thess 4:9–12 (§285)

[9] But concerning love of the brethren you have no need to have any one write to you, for you yourselves have been taught by God to love one another; [10] and indeed you do love all the brethren throughout Macedonia. But we exhort you, brethren, to do so more and more, [11] to aspire to live quietly, to mind your own affairs, and to work with your hands, as we charged you; [12] so that you may command the respect of outsiders, and be dependent on nobody.

1 Thess 5:12–22 (§288)

[12] But we beseech you, brethren, to respect those who labor among you and are over you in the Lord and admonish you, [13] and to esteem them very highly in love because of their work. Be at peace among yourselves. [14] And we exhort you, brethren, admonish the idle, encourage the fainthearted, help the weak, be patient with them all. [15] See that none of you repays evil for evil, but always seek to do good to one another and to all. [16] Rejoice always, [17] pray constantly, [18] give thanks in all circumstances; for this is the will of God in Christ Jesus for you. [19] Do not quench the Spirit, [20] do not despise prophesying, [21] but test everything; hold fast what is good, [22] abstain from every form of evil.

Secondary

1 Thess 3:11–13 (§283)

[11] Now may our God and Father himself, and our Lord Jesus, direct our way to you; [12] and may the Lord make you increase and abound in love to one another and to all men, as we do to you, [13] so that he may establish your hearts unblamable in holiness before our God and Father, at the coming of our Lord Jesus with all his saints.

2 Thess 2:16–17 (§298)

[16] Now may our Lord Jesus Christ himself, and God our Father, who loved us and gave us eternal comfort and good hope through grace, [17] comfort your hearts and establish them in every good work and word.

● **Rom 12:9**
1 Tim 1   [5] whereas the aim of our charge is love that issues from a pure heart and a good conscience and sincere faith.

● **Rom 12:12**
1 Tim 2   [1] First of all, then, I urge that supplications, prayers, intercessions, and thanksgivings be made for all men, . . .

Acts 1   [14] All these with one accord devoted themselves to prayer, together with the women and Mary the mother of Jesus, and with his brothers.

● **Rom 12:19**
Lev 19   [18] You shall not take vengeance or bear any grudge against the sons of your own people, but you shall love your neighbor as yourself: I am the Lord.

Deut 32   [35] Vengeance is mine, and recompense,

for the time when their foot shall slip;
for the day of their calamity is at hand,
and their doom comes swiftly.

● **Rom 12:20**
Prov 25   [21] If your enemy is hungry, give him bread to eat;
and if he is thirsty, give him water to drink;
[22] for you will heap coals of fire on his head,
and the Lord will reward you.

13 Let every person be subject to the governing authorities. For there is no authority except from God, and those that exist have been instituted by God. [2]Therefore he who resists the authorities resists what God has appointed, and those who resist will incur judgment. [3]For rulers are not a terror to good conduct, but to bad. Would you have no fear of him who is in authority? Then do what is good, and you will receive his approval, [4]for he is God's servant for your good. But if you do wrong, be afraid, for he does not bear the sword in vain; he is the servant of God to execute his wrath on the wrongdoer. [5]Therefore one must be subject, not only to avoid God's wrath but also for the sake of conscience. [6]For the same reason you also pay taxes, for the authorities are ministers of God, attending to this very thing. [7]Pay all of them their dues, taxes to whom taxes are due, revenue to whom revenue is due, respect to whom respect is due, honor to whom honor is due.

PRIMARY

1 Cor 4:1-5 (§83)

[1]This is how one should regard us, as servants of Christ and stewards of the mysteries of God. [2]Moreover it is required of stewards that they be found trustworthy. [3]But with me it is a very small thing that I should be judged by you or by any human court. I do not even judge myself. [4]I am not aware of anything against myself, but I am not thereby acquitted. It is the Lord who judges me. [5]Therefore do not pronounce judgment before the time, before the Lord comes, who will bring to light the things now hidden in darkness and will disclose the purposes of the heart. Then every man will receive his commendation from God.

1 Cor 6:1-8 (§90)

[1]When one of you has a grievance against a brother, does he dare go to law before the unrighteous instead of the saints? [2]Do you not know that the saints will judge the world? And if the world is to be judged by you, are you incompetent to try trivial cases? [3]Do you not know that we are to judge angels? How much more, matters pertaining to this life! [4]If then you have such cases, why do you lay them before those who are least esteemed by the church? [5]I say this to your shame. Can it be that there is no man among you wise enough to decide between members of the brotherhood, [6]but brother goes to law against brother, and that before unbelievers?

[7]To have lawsuits at all with one another is defeat for you. Why not rather suffer wrong? Why not rather be defrauded? [8]But you yourselves wrong and defraud, and that even your own brethren.

Col 4:5-6 (§270)

[5]Conduct yourselves wisely toward outsiders, making the most of the time. [6]Let your speech always be gracious, seasoned with salt, so that you may know how you ought to answer every one.

● **Rom 13:1-7**
See §§83, 111 on the theme of conscience

1 Cor 2   [6]Yet among the mature we do impart wisdom, although it is not a wisdom of this age or of the rulers of this age, who are doomed to pass away. [7]But we impart a secret and hidden wisdom of God, which God decreed before the ages for our glorification. [8]None of the rulers of this age understood this; for if they had, they would not have crucified the Lord of glory.

See also Eph 5:21-6:9

Phil 1   [12]I want you to know, brethren, that what has happened to me has really served to advance the gospel, [13]so that it has become known throughout the whole praetorian guard and to all the rest that my imprisonment is for Christ; [14]and most of the brethren have been made confident in the Lord because of my imprisonment, and are much more bold to speak the word of God without fear.

Col 3   [18]Wives, be subject to your husbands, as is fitting in the Lord. [19]Husbands, love your wives, and do not be harsh with them. [20]Children, obey your parents in everything, for this pleases the Lord. [21]Fathers, do not provoke your children, lest they become discouraged. [22]Slaves, obey in everything those who are your earthly masters, not with eye-service, as men-pleasers, but in singleness of heart, fearing the Lord. [23]Whatever your task, work heartily, as serving the Lord and not men, [24]knowing that from the Lord you will receive the inheritance as your reward; you are serving the Lord Christ. [25]For the wrongdoer will be paid back for the wrong he has done, and there is no partiality.
4   [1]Masters, treat your slaves justly and fairly, knowing that you also have a Master in heaven.

1 Pet 2   [13]Be subject for the Lord's sake to every human institution, whether it be to the emperor as supreme, [14]or to governors as sent by him to punish those who do wrong and to praise those who do right. [15]For it is God's will that by doing right you should put to silence the ignorance of foolish men. [16]Live as free men, yet without using your freedom as a pretext for evil; but live as servants of God. [17]Honor all men. Love the brotherhood. Fear God. Honor the emperor. [18]Servants, be submissive to your masters with all respect, not only to the kind and gentle but also to the overbearing. [19]For one is approved if, mindful of God, he endures pain while suffering unjustly. [20]For what credit is it, if when you do wrong and are beaten for it you take it patiently? But if when you do right and suffer for it you take it patiently, you have God's approval. [21]For to this you have been called, because Christ also suffered for you, leaving you an example, that you should follow in his steps. [22]He committed no sin; no guile was found on his lips. [23]When he was reviled, he did not revile in return; when he suffered, he did not threaten; but he trusted to him who judges justly. [24]He himself bore our sins in his body on the tree, that we might die to sin and live to righteousness. By his wounds you have been healed. [25]For you were straying like sheep, but have now returned to the Shepherd and Guardian of your souls.
3   [1]Likewise you wives, be submissive to your husbands, so that some, though they do not obey the word, may be won without a word by the behavior of their wives, [2]when they see your reverent and chaste behavior. [3]Let not yours be the outward adorning with braiding of hair, decoration of gold, and wearing of fine clothing, [4]but let it be the hidden person of the heart with the imperishable jewel of a gentle and quiet spirit, which in God's sight is very precious. [5]So once the holy women who hoped in God used to adorn themselves and were submissive to their husbands, [6]as Sarah obeyed Abraham, calling him lord. And you are now her children if you do right and let nothing terrify you.
[7]Likewise you husbands, live considerately with your wives, bestowing honor on the woman as the weaker sex, since you are joint heirs of the grace of life, in order that your prayers may not be hindered.

1 Tim 6   [1]Let all who are under the yoke of slavery regard their masters as worthy of all honor, so that the name of God and the teaching may not be defamed. [2]Those who have believing masters must not be disrespectful on the ground that they are brethren; rather they must serve all the better since those who benefit by their service are believers and beloved.
Teach and urge these duties.

Titus 2   [1]But as for you, teach what befits sound doctrine. [2]Bid the older men be temperate, serious, sensible, sound in faith, in love, and in steadfastness. [3]Bid the older women likewise to be reverent in behavior, not to be slanderers or slaves to drink; they are to teach what is good, [4]and so train the young women to love their husbands and children, [5]to be sensible, chaste, domestic, kind, and submissive to their husbands, that the word of God may not be discredited. [6]Likewise urge the younger men to control themselves. [7]Show yourself in all respects a model of good deeds, and in your teaching show integrity, gravity, [8]and sound speech that cannot be censured, so that an opponent may be put to shame, having nothing evil to say of us. [9]Bid slaves to be submissive to their masters and to give satisfaction in every respect; they are not to be refractory, [10]nor to pilfer, but to show entire and true fidelity, so that in everything they may adorn the doctrine of God our Savior.

● **Rom 13:1**
Titus 3   [1]Remind them to be submissive to rulers and authorities, to be obedient, to be ready for any honest work, . . .

● **Rom 13:5**
Rom 2   [15]They show that what the law requires is written on their hearts, while their conscience also bears witness and their conflicting thoughts accuse or perhaps excuse them . . .

1 Cor 8   [7]However, not all possess this knowledge. But some, through being hitherto accustomed to idols, eat food as really offered to an idol; and their conscience, being weak, is defiled. [8]Food will not commend us to God. We are no worse off if we do not eat, and no better off if we do. [9]Only take care lest this liberty of yours somehow become a stumbling block to the weak. [10]For if any one sees you, a man of knowledge, at table in an idol's temple, might he not be encouraged, if his conscience is weak, to eat food offered to idols? [11]And so by your knowledge this weak man is destroyed, the brother for whom Christ died. [12]Thus, sinning against your brethren and wounding their conscience when it is weak, you sin against Christ. [13]Therefore, if food is a cause of my brother's falling, I will never eat meat, lest I cause my brother to fall.

1 Cor 10   [28](But if some one says to you, "This has been offered in sacrifice," then out of consideration for the man who informed you, and for conscience' sake— [29]I mean his conscience, not yours—do not eat it.) For why should my liberty be determined by another man's scruples?

[8]Owe no one anything, except to love one another; for he who loves his neighbor has fulfilled the law. [9]The commandments, "You shall not commit adultery, You shall not kill, You shall not steal, You shall not covet," and any other commandment, are summed up in this sentence, "You shall love your neighbor as yourself." [10]Love does no wrong to a neighbor; therefore love is the fulfilling of the law.

PRIMARY

1 Cor 13:1–3 (§121)

13 [1]If I speak in the tongues of men and of angels, but have not love, I am a noisy gong or a clanging cymbal. [2]And if I have prophetic powers, and understand all mysteries and all knowledge, and if I have all faith, so as to remove mountains, but have not love, I am nothing. [3]If I give away all I have, and if I deliver my body to be burned, but have not love, I gain nothing.

Gal 5:13–15 (§212)

[13]For you were called to freedom, brethren; only do not use your freedom as an opportunity for the flesh, but through love be servants of one another. [14]For the whole law is fulfilled in one word, "You shall love your neighbor as yourself." [15]But if you bite and devour one another take heed that you are not consumed by one another.

1 Thess 4:9–12 (§285)

[9]But concerning love of the brethren you have no need to have any one write to you, for you yourselves have been taught by God to love one another; [10]and indeed you do love all the brethren throughout Macedonia. But we exhort you, brethren, to do so more and more, [11]to aspire to live quietly, to mind your own affairs, and to work with your hands, as we charged you; [12]so that you may command the respect of outsiders, and be dependent on nobody.

Phlm 15–20 (§308)

[15]Perhaps this is why he was parted from you for a while, that you might have him back for ever, [16]no longer as a slave but more than a slave, as a beloved brother, especially to me but how much more to you, both in the flesh and in the Lord. [17]So if you consider me your partner, receive him as you would receive me. [18]If he has wronged you at all, or owes you anything, charge that to my account. [19]I, Paul, write this with my own hand, I will repay it—to say nothing of your owing me even your own self. [20]Yes, brother, I want some benefit from you in the Lord. Refresh my heart in Christ.

● **Rom 13:8**

Gal 6   [2]Bear one another's burdens, and so fulfil the law of Christ.

Eph 5   [2]And walk in love, as Christ loved us and gave himself up for us, a fragrant offering and sacrifice to God.

● **Rom 13:9**

Exod 20   [13]"You shall not kill."
[14]"You shall not commit adultery."

Deut 5   [17]"You shall not kill."
[18]"Neither shall you commit adultery."

Lev 19   [18]You shall not take vengeance or bear any grudge against the sons of your own people, but you shall love your neighbor as yourself: I am the Lord.

● **Rom 13:10**

Col 3   [14]And above all these put on love, which binds everything together in perfect harmony.

1 Tim 1   [5]whereas the aim of our charge is love that issues from a pure heart and a good conscience and sincere faith.

Formal Elements: Vice List, "Watch!" "Stand!"

11Besides this you know what hour it is, how it is full time now for you to wake from sleep. For salvation is nearer to us now than when we first believed; **12**the night is far gone, the day is at hand. Let us then cast off the works of darkness and put on the armor of light; **13**let us conduct ourselves becomingly as in the day, not in reveling and drunkenness, not in debauchery and licentiousness, not in quarreling and jealousy. **14**But put on the Lord Jesus Christ, and make no provision for the flesh, to gratify its desires.

Primary

See §6 for Vice Lists

1 Cor 16:13–14 (§141)
13Be watchful, stand firm in your faith, be courageous, be strong. **14**Let all that you do be done in love.

Eph 6:10–17 (§233)
10Finally, be strong in the Lord and in the strength of his might. **11**Put on the whole armor of God, that you may be able to stand against the wiles of the devil. **12**For we are not contending against flesh and blood, but against the principalities, against the powers, against the world rulers of this present darkness, against the spiritual hosts of wickedness in the heavenly places. **13**Therefore take the whole armor of God, that you may be able to withstand in the evil day, and having done all, to stand. **14**Stand therefore, having girded your loins with truth, and having put on the breastplate of righteousness, **15**and having shod your feet with the equipment of the gospel of peace; **16**besides all these, taking the shield of faith, with which you can quench all the flaming darts of the evil one. **17**And take the helmet of salvation, and the sword of the Spirit, which is the word of God.

Col 4:2–4 (§269)
2Continue steadfastly in prayer, being watchful in it with thanksgiving; **3**and pray for us also, that God may open to us a door for the word, to declare the mystery of Christ, on account of which I am in prison, **4**that I may make it clear, as I ought to speak.

1 Thess 5:1–11 (§287)
1But as to the times and the seasons, brethren, you have no need to have anything written to you. **2**For you yourselves know well that the day of the Lord will come like a thief in the night. **3**When people say, "There is peace and security," then sudden destruction will come upon them as travail comes upon a woman with child, and there will be no escape. **4**But you are not in darkness, brethren, for that day to surprise you like a thief. **5**For you are all sons of light and sons of the day; we are not of the night or of darkness. **6**So then let us not sleep, as others do, but let us keep awake and be sober. **7**For those who sleep sleep at night, and those who get drunk are drunk at night. **8**But, since we belong to the day, let us be sober, and put on the breastplate of faith and love, and for a helmet the hope of salvation. **9**For God has not destined us for wrath, but to obtain salvation through our Lord Jesus Christ, **10**who died for us so that whether we wake or sleep we might live with him. **11**Therefore encourage one another and build one another up, just as you are doing.

2 Thess 2:13–17 (§297–298)
13But we are bound to give thanks to God always for you, brethren beloved by the Lord, because God chose you from the beginning to be saved, through sanctification by the Spirit and belief in the truth. **14**To this he called you through our gospel, so that you may obtain the glory of our Lord Jesus Christ. **15**So then, brethren, stand firm and hold to the traditions which you were taught by us, either by word of mouth or by letter.

16Now may our Lord Jesus Christ himself, and God our Father, who loved us and gave us eternal comfort and good hope through grace, **17**comfort your hearts and establish them in every good work and word.

Secondary

Phil 2:14–18 (§244)
14Do all things without grumbling or questioning, **15**that you may be blameless and innocent, children of God without blemish in the midst of a crooked and perverse generation, among whom you shine as lights in the world, **16**holding fast the word of life, so that in the day of Christ I may be proud that I did not run in vain or labor in vain. **17**Even if I am to be poured as a libation upon the sacrificial offering of your faith, I am glad and rejoice with you all. **18**Likewise you also should be glad and rejoice with me.

● **Rom 13:11–12**
Cf. Phil 4   **5**Let all men know your forbearance. The Lord is at hand. **6**Have no anxiety about anything, but in everything by prayer and supplication with thanksgiving let your requests be made known to God.

● **Rom 13:11**
Cf. 1 Cor 7   **26**I think that in view of the present distress it is well for a person to remain as he is.

Cf. 1 Cor 7   **29**I mean, brethren, the appointed time has grown very short; from now on, let those who have wives live as though they had none, . . .

Cf. 1 Cor 7   **31**and those who deal with the world as though they had no dealings with it. For the form of this world is passing away.

● **Rom 13:12**
Cf. 2 Cor 6   **14**Do not be mismated with unbelievers. For what partnership have righteousness and iniquity? Or what fellowship has light with darkness?

● **Rom 13:13**
Rom 1   **29**They were filled with all manner of wickedness, evil, covetousness, malice. Full of envy, murder, strife, deceit, malignity, they are gossips, **30**slanderers, haters of God, insolent, haughty, boastful, inventors of evil, disobedient to parents, **31**foolish, faithless, heartless, ruthless. **32**Though they know God's decree that those who do such things deserve to die, they not only do them but approve those who practice them.

14 As for the man who is weak in faith, welcome him, but not for disputes over opinions. ²One believes he may eat anything, while the weak man eats only vegetables. ³Let not him who eats despise him who abstains, and let not him who abstains pass judgment on him who eats; for God has welcomed him. ⁴Who are you to pass judgment on the servant of another? It is before his own master that he stands or falls. And he will be upheld, for the Master is able to make him stand.

PRIMARY

1 Cor 10:23–11:1 (§111)

²³"All things are lawful," but not all things are helpful. "All things are lawful," but not all things build up. ²⁴Let no one seek his own good, but the good of his neighbor. ²⁵Eat whatever is sold in the meat market without raising any question on the ground of conscience. ²⁶For "the earth is the Lord's, and everything in it." ²⁷If one of the unbelievers invites you to dinner and you are disposed to go, eat whatever is set before you without raising any question on the ground of conscience. ²⁸(But if some one says to you, "This has been offered in sacrifice," then out of consideration for the man who informed you, and for conscience' sake — ²⁹I mean his conscience, not yours — do not eat it.) For why should my liberty be determined by another man's scruples? ³⁰If I partake with thankfulness, why am I denounced because of that for which I give thanks?

³¹So, whether you eat or drink, or whatever you do, do all to the glory of God. ³²Give no offense to Jews or to Greeks or to the church of God, ³³just as I try to please all men in everything I do, not seeking my own advantage, but that of many, that they may be saved. 11 ¹Be imitators of me, as I am of Christ.

1 Cor 11:17–22 (§113)

¹⁷But in the following instructions I do not commend you, because when you come together it is not for the better but for the worse. ¹⁸For, in the first place, when you assemble as a church, I hear that there are divisions among you; and I partly believe it, ¹⁹for there must be factions among you in order that those who are genuine among you may be recognized. ²⁰When you meet together, it is not the Lord's supper that you eat. ²¹For in eating, each one goes ahead with his own meal, and one is hungry and another is drunk. ²²What! Do you not have houses to eat and drink in? Or do you despise the church? of God and humiliate those who have nothing? What shall I say to you? Shall I commend you in this? No, I will not.

● **Rom 14:1–4**

1 Cor 8 ¹Now concerning food offered to idols: we know that "all of us possess knowledge." "Knowledge" puffs up, but love builds up. ²If any one imagines that he knows something, he does not yet know as he ought to know. ³But if one loves God, one is known by him.

Gal 2 ¹¹But when Cephas came to Antioch I opposed him to his face, because he stood condemned. ¹²For before certain men came from James, he ate with the Gentiles; but when they came he drew back and separated himself, fearing the circumcision party. ¹³And with him the rest of the Jews acted insincerely, so that even Barnabas was carried away by their insincerity. ¹⁴But when I saw that they were not straightforward about the truth of the gospel, I said to Cephas before them all, "If you, though a Jew, live like a Gentile and not like a Jew, how can you compel the Gentiles to live like Jews?"

● **Rom 14:1**

1 Cor 9 ²²To the weak I became weak, that I might win the weak. I have become all things to all men, that I might by all means save some.

● **Rom 14:3**

Col 2 ¹⁶Therefore let no one pass judgment on you in questions of food and drink or with regard to a festival or a new moon or a sabbath.

Col 2 ²⁰If with Christ you died to the elemental spirits of the universe, why do you live as if you still belonged to the world? Why do you submit to regulations, ²¹"Do not handle, Do not taste, Do not touch" . . .

● **Rom 14:4**

Rom 2 ¹Therefore you have no excuse, O man, whoever you are, when you judge another; for in passing judgment upon another you condemn yourself, because you, the judge, are doing the very same things. ²We know that the judgment of God rightly falls upon those who do such things. ³Do you suppose, O man, that when you judge those who do such things and yet do them yourself, you will escape the judgment of God?

[5]One man esteems one day as better than another, while another man esteems all days alike. Let every one be fully convinced in his own mind. [6]He who observes the day, observes it in honor of the Lord. He also who eats, eats in honor of the Lord, since he gives thanks to God; while he who abstains, abstains in honor of the Lord and gives thanks to God. [7]None of us lives to himself, and none of us dies to himself. [8]If we live, we live to the Lord, and if we die, we die to the Lord; so then, whether we live or whether we die, we are the Lord's. [9]For to this end Christ died and lived again, that he might be Lord both of the dead and of the living.

[10]Why do you pass judgment on your brother? Or you, why do you despise your brother? For we shall all stand before the judgment seat of God; [11]for it is written,

"As I live, says the Lord, every knee shall bow to me,

and every tongue shall give praise to God."

[12]So each of us shall give account of himself to God.

PRIMARY

1 Cor 4:1–5 (§83)

4 [1]This is how one should regard us, as servants of Christ and stewards of the mysteries of God. [2]Moreover it is required of stewards that they be found trustworthy. [3]But with me it is a very small thing that I should be judged by you or by any human court. I do not even judge myself. [4]I am not aware of anything against myself, but I am not thereby acquitted. It is the Lord who judges me. [5]Therefore do not pronounce judgment before the time, before the Lord comes, who will bring to light the things now hidden in darkness and will disclose the purposes of the heart. Then every man will receive his commendation from God.

1 Cor 7:17–24 (§97)

[17]Only, let every one lead the life which the Lord has assigned to him, and in which God has called him. This is my rule in all the churches. [18]Was any one at the time of his call already circumcised? Let him not seek to remove the marks of circumcision. Was any one at the time of his call uncircumcised? Let him not seek circumcision. [19]For neither circumcision counts for anything nor uncircumcision, but keeping the commandments of God. [20]Every one should remain in the state in which

he was called. [21]Were you a slave when called? Never mind. But if you can gain your freedom, avail yourself of the opportunity. [22]For he who was called in the Lord as a slave is a freedman of the Lord. Likewise he who was free when called is a slave of Christ. [23]You were bought with a price; do not become slaves of men. [24]So, brethren, in whatever state each was called, there let him remain with God.

Gal 4:8–11 (§208)

[8]Formerly, when you did not know God, you were in bondage to beings that by nature are no gods; [9]but now that you have come to know God, or rather to be known by God, how can you turn back again to the weak and beggarly elemental spirits, whose slaves you want to be once more? [10]You observe days, and months, and seasons, and years! [11]I am afraid I have labored over you in vain.

Eph 5:15–20 (§231)

[15]Look carefully then how you walk, not as unwise men but as wise, [16]making the most of the time, because the days are evil. [17]Therefore do not be foolish, but understand what the will of the Lord is. [18]And do not get drunk with wine, for that is debauchery; but be filled with the Spirit, [19]addressing one another in psalms and hymns and spiritual songs, singing and

---

● **Rom 14:5**
Cf. Rom 4   [21]fully convinced that God was able to do what he had promised.

● **Rom 14:8**
Cf. Gal 2   [20]I have been crucified with Christ; it is no longer I who live, but Christ who lives in me; and the life I now live in the flesh I live by faith in the Son of God, who loved me and gave himself for me.

● **Rom 14:9**
Rom 8   [38]For I am sure that neither death, nor life, nor angels, nor principalities, nor things present, nor

things to come, nor powers, [39]nor height, nor depth, nor anything else in all creation, will be able to separate us from the love of God in Christ Jesus our Lord.

Cf. 2 Cor 4   [11]For while we live we are always being given up to death for Jesus' sake, so that the life of Jesus may be manifested in our mortal flesh. [12]So death is at work in us, but life in you.

● **Rom 14:10**
Rom 2   [1]Therefore you have no excuse, O man, whoever you are, when you judge another; for in passing judgment upon another you condemn yourself,

because you, the judge, are doing the very same things. [2]We know that the judgment of God rightly falls upon those who do such things. [3]Do you suppose, O man, that when you judge those who do such things and yet do them yourself, you will escape the judgment of God?

1 Cor 5   [12]For what have I to do with judging outsiders? Is it not those inside the church whom you are to judge? [13]God judges those outside. "Drive out the wicked person from among you."

making melody to the Lord with all your heart, [20]always and for everything giving thanks in the name of our Lord Jesus Christ to God the Father.

Phil 1:19–26 (§240)

[19]Yes, and I shall rejoice. For I know that through your prayers and the help of the Spirit of Jesus Christ this will turn out for my deliverance, [20]as it is my eager expectation and hope that I shall not be at all ashamed, but that with full courage now as always Christ will be honored in my body, whether by life or by death. [21]For to me to live is Christ, and to die is gain. [22]If it is to be life in the flesh, that means fruitful labor for me. Yet which I shall choose I cannot tell. [23]I am hard pressed between the two. My desire is to depart and be with Christ, for that is far better. [24]But to remain in the flesh is more necessary on your account. [25]Convinced of this, I know that I shall remain and continue with you all, for your progress and joy in the faith, [26]so that in me you may have ample cause to glory in Christ Jesus, because of my coming to you again.

Col 2:16–19 (§263)

[16]Therefore let no one pass judgment on you in questions of food and drink or with regard to a festival or a new moon or a sabbath.

[17]These are only a shadow of what is to come; but the substance belongs to Christ. [18]Let no one disqualify you, insisting on self-abasement and worship of angels, taking his stand on visions, puffed up without reason by his sensuous mind, [19]and not holding fast to the Head, from whom the whole body, nourished and knit together through its joints and ligaments, grows with a growth that is from God.

Col 3:12–17 (§267)

[12]Put on then, as God's chosen ones, holy and beloved, compassion, kindness, lowliness, meekness, and patience, [13]forbearing one another and, if one has a complaint against another, forgiving each other; as the Lord has forgiven you, so you also must forgive. [14]And above all these put on love, which binds everything together in perfect harmony. [15]And let the peace of Christ rule in your hearts, to which indeed you were called in the one body. And be thankful. [16]Let the word of Christ dwell in you richly, as you teach and admonish one another in all wisdom, and as you sing psalms and hymns and spiritual songs with thankfulness in your hearts to God. [17]And whatever you do, in word or deed, do everything in the name of the Lord Jesus, giving thanks to God the Father through him.

1 Thess 5:1–11 (§287)

5 [1]But as to the times and the seasons, brethren, you have no need to have anything written to you. [2]For you yourselves know well that the day of the Lord will come like a thief in the night. [3]When people say, "There is peace and security," then sudden destruction will come upon them as travail comes upon a woman with child, and there will be no escape. [4]But you are not in darkness, brethren, for that day to surprise you like a thief. [5]For you are all sons of light and sons of the day; we are not of the night or of darkness. [6]So then let us not sleep, as others do, but let us keep awake and be sober. [7]For those who sleep sleep at night, and those who get drunk are drunk at night. [8]But, since we belong to the day, let us be sober, and put on the breastplate of faith and love, and for a helmet the hope of salvation. [9]For God has not destined us for wrath, but to obtain salvation through our Lord Jesus Christ, [10]who died for us so that whether we wake or sleep we might live with him. [11]Therefore encourage one another and build one another up, just as you are doing.

---

2 Cor 5   [10]For we must all appear before the judgment seat of Christ, so that each one may receive good or evil, according to what he has done in the body.

Col 1   [22]he has now reconciled in his body of flesh by his death, in order to present you holy and blameless and irreproachable before him, . . .

Acts 17   [31]". . . because he has fixed a day on which he will judge the world in righteousness by a man whom he has appointed, and of this he has given assurance to all men by raising him from the dead."

1 Cor 5   [3]For though absent in body I am present in spirit, and as if present, I have already pronounced judgment . . .

● **Rom 14:11**
Phil 2   [9]Therefore God has highly exalted him and bestowed on him the name which is above every name, [10]that at the name of Jesus every knee should bow, in heaven and on earth and under the earth, [11]and every tongue confess that Jesus Christ is Lord, to the glory of God the Father.

Isa 45   [23]By myself I have sworn,
from my mouth has gone forth in righteousness
a word that shall not return:
'To me every knee shall bow,
every tongue shall swear.'

● **Rom 14:12**
Rom 2   [16]on that day when, according to my gospel, God judges the secrets of men by Christ Jesus.

[13] Then let us no more pass judgment on one another, but rather decide never to put a stumbling block or hindrance in the way of a brother. [14] I know and am persuaded in the Lord Jesus that nothing is unclean in itself; but it is unclean for any one who thinks it unclean. [15] If your brother is being injured by what you eat, you are no longer walking in love. Do not let what you eat cause the ruin of one for whom Christ died. [16] So do not let your good be spoken of as evil. [17] For the kingdom of God is not food and drink but righteousness and peace and joy in the Holy Spirit; [18] he who thus serves Christ is acceptable to God and approved by men. [19] Let us then pursue what makes for peace and for mutual upbuilding. [20] Do not, for the sake of food, destroy the work of God. Everything is indeed clean, but it is wrong for any one to make others fall by what he eats; [21] it is right not to eat meat or drink wine or do anything that makes your brother stumble. [22] The faith that you have, keep between yourself and God; happy is he who has no reason to judge himself for what he approves. [23] But he who has doubts is condemned, if he eats, because he does not act from faith; for whatever does not proceed from faith is sin.

PRIMARY

1 Cor 4:1–5 (§83)

[1] This is how one should regard us, as servants of Christ and stewards of the mysteries of God. [2] Moreover it is required of stewards that they be found trustworthy. [3] But with me it is a very small thing that I should be judged by you or by any human court. I do not even judge myself. [4] I am not aware of anything against myself, but I am not thereby acquitted. It is the Lord who judges me. [5] Therefore do not pronounce judgment before the time, before the Lord comes, who will bring to light the things now hidden in darkness and will disclose the purposes of the heart. Then every man will receive his commendation from God.

1 Cor 8:7–13 (§104)

[7] However, not all possess this knowledge. But some, through being hitherto accustomed to idols, eat food as really offered to an idol; and their conscience, being weak, is defiled. [8] Food will not commend us to God. We are no worse off if we do not eat, and no better off if we do. [9] Only take care lest this liberty of yours somehow become a stumbling block to the weak. [10] For if any one sees you, a man of knowledge, at table in an idol's temple, might he not be encouraged, if his conscience is weak, to eat food offered to idols? [11] And so by your knowledge this weak man is destroyed, the brother for whom Christ died. [12] Thus, sinning against your brethren and wounding their conscience when it is weak, you sin against Christ. [13] Therefore, if food is a cause of my brother's falling, I will never eat meat, lest I cause my brother to fall.

1 Cor 10:23–11:1 (§111)

[23] "All things are lawful," but not all things are helpful. "All things are lawful," but not all things build up. [24] Let no one seek his own good, but the good of his neighbor. [25] Eat whatever is sold in the meat market without raising any question on the ground of conscience. [26] For "the earth is the Lord's, and everything in it." [27] If one of the unbelievers invites you to dinner and you are disposed to go, eat whatever is set before you without raising any question on the ground of conscience. [28] (But if some one says to you, "This has been offered in sacrifice," then out of consideration for the man who informed you, and for conscience' sake— [29] I mean his conscience, not yours—do not eat it.) For why should my liberty be determined by another man's scruples? [30] If I partake with thankfulness, why am I denounced because of that for which I give thanks?

[31] So, whether you eat or drink, or whatever you do, do all to the glory of God. [32] Give no offense to Jews or to Greeks or to the church of God, [33] just as I try to please all men in everything I do, not seeking my own advantage, but that of many, that they may be saved. 11 [1] Be imitators of me, as I am of Christ.

● **Rom 14:13**
Rom 2 [1] Therefore you have no excuse, O man, whoever you are, when you judge another; for in passing judgment upon him you condemn yourself, because you, the judge, are doing the very same things. [2] We know that the judgment of God rightly falls upon those who do such things. [3] Do you suppose, O man, that when you judge those who do such things and yet do them yourself, you will escape the judgment of God?

1 Cor 5 [3] For though absent in body I am present in spirit, and as if present, I have already pronounced judgment . . .

1 Cor 5 [12] For what have I to do with judging outsiders? Is it not those inside the church whom you are to judge? [13] God judges those outside. "Drive out the wicked person from among you."

Col 1 [22] he has now reconciled in his body of flesh by his death, in order to present you holy and blameless and irreproachable before him, . . .

● **Rom 14:14**
Titus 1 [5] This is why I left you in Crete, that you might amend what was defective, and appoint elders in every town as I directed you, . . .

Acts 10 [15] . . . and the voice came to him again a second time, "What God has cleansed, you must not call common."

Cf. Acts 10 [28] . . . and he said to them, "You yourselves know how unlawful it is for a Jew to associate with or to visit any one of another nation; but God has shown me that I should not call any man common or unclean."

● **Rom 14:17**
2 Tim 2 [22] So shun youthful passions and aim at righteousness, faith, love, and peace, along with those who call upon the Lord from a pure heart.

● **Rom 14:19**
1 Cor 8 [1] Now concerning food offered to idols: we know that "all of us possess knowledge." "Knowledge" puffs up, but love builds up.

1 Cor 10 [23] "All things are lawful," but not all things are helpful. "All things are lawful," but not all things build up. [24] Let no one seek his own good, but the good of his neighbor.

1 Cor 14 [12] So with yourselves; since you are eager for manifestations of the Spirit, strive to excel in building up the church.

(let us) *read* we: SABG (Greek); *text:* CD Koine Lect it vg syr cop Origen (Latin)

● **Rom 14:21**
(stumble) *read* be upset: S*; *add* or be weakened: syr (pal); *read* be upset or sin or be weakened: P; *add* sin or be weakened: S^cBDG Koine Lect it(most) vg syr(har)

● **Rom 14:22–23**
Rom 2 [15] They show that what the law requires is written on their hearts, while their conscience also bears witness and their conflicting thoughts accuse or perhaps excuse them [16] on that day when, according to my gospel, God judges the secrets of men by Christ Jesus.

● **Rom 14:23**
(sin) *add* 16:25–27 here only: L Koine Lect it(few) syr(har) Chrysostom; *add* 16:25–27 both here and at 16:25: AP; *text:* S BCD it(some) vg syr cop Clement Origen(Latin)

15 We who are strong ought to bear with the failings of the weak, and not to please ourselves; [2]let each of us please his neighbor for his good, to edify him. [3]For Christ did not please himself; but, as it is written, "The reproaches of those who reproached thee fell on me." [4]For whatever was written in former days was written for our instruction, that by steadfastness and by the encouragement of the scriptures we might have hope. [5]May the God of steadfastness and encouragement grant you to live in such harmony with one another, in accord with Christ Jesus, [6]that together you may with one voice glorify the God and Father of our Lord Jesus Christ.

PRIMARY

1 Cor 1:10-17 (§73)

[10]I appeal to you, brethren, by the name of our Lord Jesus Christ, that all of you agree and that there be no dissensions among you, but that you be united in the same mind and the same judgment. [11]For it has been reported to me by Chloe's people that there is quarreling among you, my brethren. [12]What I mean is that each one of you says, "I belong to Paul," or "I belong to Apollos," or "I belong to Cephas," or "I belong to Christ." [13]Is Christ divided? Was Paul crucified for you? Or were you baptized in the name of Paul? [14]I am thankful that I baptized none of you except Crispus and Gaius; [15]lest any one should say that you were baptized in my name. [16](I did baptize also the household of Stephanas. Beyond that, I do not know whether I baptized any one else.) [17]For Christ did not send me to baptize but to preach the gospel, and not with eloquent wisdom, lest the cross of Christ be emptied of its power.

1 Cor 14:1-5 (§124)

[1]Make love your aim, and earnestly desire the spiritual gifts, especially that you may prophesy. [2]For one who speaks in a tongue speaks not to men but to God; for no one understands him, but he utters mysteries in the Spirit.

[3]On the other hand, he who prophesies speaks to men for their upbuilding and encouragement and consolation. [4]He who speaks in a tongue edifies himself, but he who prophesies edifies the church. [5]Now I want you all to speak in tongues, but even more to prophesy. He who prophesies is greater than he who speaks in tongues, unless some one interprets, so that the church may be edified.

2 Cor 13:5-13 (§190-191)

[5]Examine yourselves, to see whether you are holding to your faith. Test yourselves. Do you not realize that Jesus Christ is in you?—unless indeed you fail to meet the test! [6]I hope you will find out that we have not failed. [7]But we pray God that you may not do wrong— not that we may appear to have met the test, but that you may do what is right, though we may seem to have failed. [8]For we cannot do anything against the truth, but only for the truth. [9]For we are glad when we are weak and you are strong. What we pray for is your improvement. [10]I write this while I am away from you, in order that when I come I may not have to be severe in my use of the authority which the Lord has given me for building up and not for tearing down.

[11]Finally, brethren, farewell. Mend your ways, heed my appeal, agree with one another, live in peace, and the God of love and peace will be with you. [12]Greet one another with a holy kiss. [13]All the saints greet you.

Gal 6:1-6 (§214)

[1]Brethren, if a man is overtaken in any trespass, you who are spiritual should restore him in a spirit of gentleness. Look to yourself, lest you too be tempted. [2]Bear one another's burdens, and so fulfil the law of Christ. [3]For if any one thinks he is something, when he is nothing, he deceives himself. [4]But let each one test his own work, and then his reason to boast will be in himself alone and not in his neighbor. [5]For each man will have to bear his own load.

[6]Let him who is taught the word share all good things with him who teaches.

Phil 2:1-11 (§242)

[1]So if there is any encouragement in Christ, any incentive of love, any participation in the Spirit, any affection and sympathy, [2]complete my joy by being of the same mind, having the same love, being in full accord and of one mind. [3]Do nothing from selfishness or conceit, but in humility count others better than yourselves. [4]Let each of you look not only to his own interests, but also to the interests of others. [5]Have this mind among yourselves, which is yours in Christ Jesus, [6]who, though he was in the form of God, did not count equality with God a thing to be grasped, [7]but emptied himself, taking the form of a servant, being born in the likeness of men. [8]And being found in human form he humbled himself and became obedient unto death, even death on a cross. [9]Therefore God has highly exalted him and bestowed on him the name which is above every name, [10]that at the name of Jesus every knee should bow, in heaven and on earth and under the earth, [11]and every tongue confess that Jesus Christ is Lord, to the glory of God the Father.

Col 3:12-17 (§267)

[12]Put on then, as God's chosen ones, holy and beloved, compassion, kindness, lowliness, meekness, and patience, [13]forbearing one another and, if one has a complaint against another, forgiving each other; as the Lord has forgiven you, so you also must forgive. [14]And above all these put on love, which binds everything together in perfect harmony. [15]And let the peace of Christ rule in your hearts, to which indeed you were called in the one body. And be thankful. [16]Let the word of Christ dwell in you richly, as you teach and admonish one another in all wisdom, and as you sing psalms and hymns and spiritual songs with thankfulness in your hearts to God. [17]And whatever you do, in word or deed, do everything in the name of the Lord Jesus, giving thanks to God the Father through him.

● **Rom 15:1**
1 Cor 1   [27]but God chose what is foolish in the world to shame the wise, God chose what is weak in the world to shame the strong, . . .

Cf. 1 Cor 8   [9]Only take care lest this liberty of yours somehow become a stumbling block to the weak.

1 Cor 14   [1]Make love your aim, and earnestly desire the spiritual gifts, especially that you may prophesy. [2]For one who speaks in a tongue speaks not to men but to God; for no one understands him, but he utters mysteries in the Spirit.

Cf. Gal 1   [10]Am I now seeking the favor of men, or of God? Or am I trying to please men? If I were still pleasing men, I should not be a servant of Christ.

● **Rom 15:2**
1 Thess 5   [11]Therefore encourage one another and build one another up, just as you are doing.

● **Rom 15:3**
Ps 69   [9]For zeal for thy house has consumed me, and the insults of those who insult thee have fallen on me.

● **Rom 15:4**
1 Cor 9   [10]Does he not speak entirely for our sake? It was written for our sake, because the plowman should plow in hope and the thresher thresh in hope of a share in the crop.

1 Cor 10   [6]Now these things are warnings for us, not to desire evil as they did.

1 Cor 10   [11]Now these things happened to them as a warning, but they were written down for our instruction, upon whom the end of the ages has come.

Cf. 2 Tim 3   [16]All scripture is inspired by God and profitable for teaching, for reproof, for correction, and for training in righteousness, [17]that the man of God may be complete, equipped for every good work.

7Welcome one another, therefore, as Christ has welcomed you, for the glory of God. 8For I tell you that Christ became a servant to the circumcised to show God's truthfulness, in order to confirm the promises given to the patriarchs, 9and in order that the Gentiles might glorify God for his mercy. As it is written,

"Therefore I will praise thee among the
Gentiles,
and sing to thy name";

10and again it is said,

"Rejoice, O Gentiles, with his peoples";

11and again,

"Praise the Lord, all Gentiles,
and let all the peoples praise him";

12and further Isaiah says,

"The root of Jesse shall come,
he who rises to rule the Gentiles;
in him shall the Gentiles hope."

13May the God of hope fill you with all joy and peace in believing, so that by the power of the Holy Spirit you may abound in hope.

PRIMARY

Gal 3:6-9 (§201)

6Thus Abraham "believed God, and it was reckoned to him as righteousness." 7So you see that it is men of faith who are the sons of Abraham. 8And the scripture, foreseeing that God would justify the Gentiles by faith, preached the gospel beforehand to Abraham, saying, "In you shall all the nations be blessed." 9So then, those who are men of faith are blessed with Abraham who had faith.

Phlm 15-20 (§308)

15Perhaps this is why he was parted from you for a while, that you might have him back for ever, 16no longer as a slave but more than a slave, as a beloved brother, especially to me but how much more to you, both in the flesh and in the Lord. 17So if you consider me your partner, receive him as you would receive me. 18If he has wronged you at all, or owes you anything, charge that to my account. 19I, Paul, write this with my own hand, I will repay it—to say nothing of your owing me even your own self. 20Yes, brother, I want some benefit from you in the Lord. Refresh my heart in Christ.

● **Rom 15:7**

Rom 14   1As for the man who is weak in faith, welcome him, but not for disputes over opinions. 2One believes he may eat anything, while the weak man eats only vegetables. 3Let not him who eats despise him who abstains, and let not him who abstains pass judgment on him who eats; for God has welcomed him.

● **Rom 15:8**

Rom 4   11He received circumcision as a sign or seal of the righteousness which he had by faith while he was still uncircumcised. The purpose was to make him the father of all who believe without being circumcised and who thus have righteousness reckoned to them, 12and likewise the father of the circumcised who are not merely circumcised but also follow the example of the faith which our father Abraham had before he was circumcised.

Rom 9   4They are Israelites, and to them belong the sonship, the glory, the covenants, the giving of the law, the worship, and the promises; 5to them belong the patriarchs, and of their race, according to the flesh, is the Christ. God who is over all be blessed for ever. Amen.

Acts 3   26"God, having raised up his servant, sent him to you first, to bless you in turning every one of you from your wickedness."

Cf. 2 Cor 1   20For all the promises of God find their Yes in him. That is why we utter the Amen through him, to the glory of God.

● **Rom 15:9**

Ps 18   49For this I will extol thee, O Lord, among the
nations,
and sing praises to thy name.

● **Rom 15:10**

Deut 32   43"Praise his people, O you nations;
for he avenges the blood of his servants,
and takes vengeance on his adversaries,
and makes expiation for the land of his people."

● **Rom 15:11**

Ps 117   1Praise the Lord, all nations!
Extol him, all peoples!

● **Rom 15:12**

Isa 11   10In that day the root of Jesse shall stand as an ensign to the peoples; him shall the nations seek, and his dwellings shall be glorious.

● **Rom 15:13**

Eph 2   12remember that you were at that time separated from Christ, alienated from the commonwealth of Israel, and strangers to the covenants of promise, having no hope and without God in the world.

1 Thess 1   5for our gospel came to you not only in word, but also in power and in the Holy Spirit and with full conviction. You know what kind of men we proved to be among you for your sake.

Cf. 1 Thess 2   19For what is our hope or joy or crown of boasting before our Lord Jesus at his coming? Is it not you?

1. The Jerusalem Conference (Galatians 2) = Acts 11:30

Date

33	Paul's conversion	
35	Paul's first Jerusalem visit	Acts 9:26
35–46	Paul in Syria and Cilicia	
46	Paul's conference visit to Jerusalem	Acts 11:27–30 (described as a famine visit)
47–48	Paul and Barnabas in Cyprus, Galatia (first missionary journey)	
?48	*Letter to the Galatians*	
49	Council at Jerusalem. Paul's third Jerusalem visit	Acts 15
49–50	Paul and Silas travel from Syrian Antioch through Asia Minor to Macedonia and back (second missionary journey)	
50	*Letters to the Thessalonians*	Claudius' edict (49) = Acts 18:2
50–52	Paul in Corinth	Gallio Inscription (51–52) = Acts 18:12
52	Paul's fourth Jerusalem visit	Acts 18:22
52–55	Paul in Ephesus	
55–56	*Letters to the Corinthians*	
55–57	Paul in Macedonia, Illyricum, Achaia	
57	*Letter to the Romans*	
57	Last visit to Jerusalem	Acts 21:17
57–59	Imprisonment at Caesarea	
60	Paul's arrival at Rome	
60–62	Paul under arrest in Rome ?Writes the *Captivity Letters*	
?65	Paul visits Spain	
?65	Paul dies	

Based on F. F. Bruce, *Paul: Apostle of the Heart Set Free* (Grand Rapids: Wm. B. Eerdmans, 1978), 475. Summary prepared by John A. Darr and published in: Daniel Patte, *Paul's Faith and the Power of the Gospel* (Philadelphia: Fortress Press, 1983), 352–60. Reprinted by permission of the publisher.
See pages 141, 175, 207, 223 for additional chronological sketches.

[14]I myself am satisfied about you, my brethren, that you yourselves are full of goodness, filled with all knowledge, and able to instruct one another. [15]But on some points I have written to you very boldly by way of reminder, because of the grace given me by God [16]to be a minister of Christ Jesus to the Gentiles in the priestly service of the gospel of God, so that the offering of the Gentiles may be acceptable, sanctified by the Holy Spirit. [17]In Christ Jesus, then, I have reason to be proud of my work for God. [18]For I will not venture to speak of anything except what Christ has wrought through me to win obedience from the Gentiles, by word and deed, [19]by the power of signs and wonders, by the power of the Holy Spirit, so that from Jerusalem and as far round as Illyricum I have fully preached the gospel of Christ, [20]thus making it my ambition to preach the gospel, not where Christ has already been named, lest I build on another man's foundation, [21]but as it is written,

"They shall see who have never been told of him,

and they shall understand who have never heard of him."

PRIMARY

1 Cor 2:1–5 (§76)

[1]When I came to you, brethren, I did not come proclaiming to you the testimony of God in lofty words or wisdom. [2]For I decided to know nothing among you except Jesus Christ and him crucified. [3]And I was with you in weakness and in much fear and trembling; [4]and my speech and my message were not in plausible words of wisdom, but in demonstration of the Spirit and of power, [5]that your faith might not rest in the wisdom of men but in the power of God.

1 Cor 3:10–15 (§80)

[10]According to the grace of God given to me, like a skilled master builder I laid a foundation, and another man is building upon it. Let each man take care how he builds upon it. [11]For no other foundation can any one lay than that which is laid, which is Jesus Christ. [12]Now if any one builds on the foundation with gold, silver, precious stones, wood, hay, straw — [13]each man's work will become manifest; for the Day will disclose it, because it will be revealed with fire, and the fire will test what sort of work each one has done. [14]If the work which any man has built on the foundation survives, he will receive a reward. [15]If any man's work is burned up, he will suffer loss, though he himself will be saved, but only as through fire.

2 Cor 4:1–6 (§158)

[1]Therefore, having this ministry by the mercy of God, we do not lose heart. [2]We have renounced disgraceful, underhanded ways; we refuse to practice cunning or to tamper with God's word, but by the open statement of the truth we would commend ourselves to every man's conscience in the sight of God. [3]And even if our gospel is veiled, it is veiled only to those who are perishing. [4]In their case the god of this world has blinded the minds of the unbelievers, to keep them from seeing the light of the gospel of the glory of Christ, who is the likeness of God. [5]For what we preach is not ourselves, but Jesus Christ as Lord, with ourselves as your servants for Jesus' sake. [6]For it is the God who said, "Let light shine out of darkness," who has shone in our hearts to give the light of the knowledge of the glory of God in the face of Christ.

2 Cor 10:13–18 (§178)

[13]But we will not boast beyond limit, but will keep to the limits God has apportioned us, to reach even to you. [14]For we are not over-extending ourselves, as though we did not reach you; we were the first to come all the way to you with the gospel of Christ. [15]We do not boast beyond limit, in other men's labors; but our hope is that as your faith increases, our field among you may be greatly enlarged, [16]so that we may preach the gospel in lands beyond you, without boasting of work already done in another's field. [17]"Let him who boasts, boast of the Lord." [18]For it is not the man who commends himself that is accepted, but the man whom the Lord commends.

2 Cor 12:11–13 (§186)

[11]I have been a fool! You forced me to it, for I ought to have been commended by you. For I was not at all inferior to these superlative apostles, even though I am nothing. [12]The signs of a true apostle were performed among you in all patience, with signs and wonders and mighty works. [13]For in what were you less favored than the rest of the churches, except that I myself did not burden you? Forgive me this wrong!

Gal 1:15–24 (§196)

[15]But when he who had set me apart before I was born, and had called me through his grace, [16]was pleased to reveal his Son to me, in order that I might preach him among the Gentiles, I did not confer with flesh and blood, [17]nor did I go up to Jerusalem to those who were apostles before me, but I went away into Arabia; and again I returned to Damascus.

[18]Then after three years I went up to Jerusalem to visit Cephas, and remained with him fifteen days. [19]But I saw none of the other apostles except James the Lord's brother. [20](In what I am writing to you, before God, I do not lie!) [21]Then I went into the regions of Syria and Cilicia. [22]And I was still not known by sight to the churches of Christ in Judea; [23]they only heard it said, "He who once persecuted us is

---

● **Rom 15:14–21**
Cf. 1 Cor 11   [2]I commend you because you remember me in everything and maintain the traditions even as I have delivered them to you.

● **Rom 15:16**
Acts 9   [15]But the Lord said to him, "Go, for he is a chosen instrument of mine to carry my name before the Gentiles and kings and the sons of Israel...."

Acts 26   [17]"delivering you from the people and from the Gentiles —to whom I send you [18]to open their eyes, that they may turn from darkness to light and from the power of Satan to God, that they may receive forgiveness of sins and a place among those who are sanctified by faith in me."

Cf. Phil 4   [18]I have received full payment, and more; I am filled, having received from Epaphroditus the gifts you sent, a fragrant offering, a sacrifice acceptable and pleasing to God.

Cf. 2 Cor 2   [14]But thanks be to God, who in Christ always leads us in triumph, and through us spreads the fragrance of the knowledge of him everywhere. [15]For we are the aroma of Christ to God among those who are being saved and among those who are perishing, [16]to one a fragrance from death to death, to the other a fragrance from life to life. Who is sufficient for these things? [17]For we are not, like so many, peddlers of God's word; but as men of sincerity, as commissioned by God, in the sight of God we speak in Christ.

Cf. Eph 5   [2]And walk in love, as Christ loved us and gave himself up for us, a fragrant offering and sacrifice to God.

● **Rom 15:18–19**
Acts 15   [12]And all the assembly kept silence; and

now preaching the faith he once tried to destroy." [24]And they glorified God because of me.

Eph 3:1-13 (§222)

[1]For this reason I, Paul, a prisoner for Christ Jesus on behalf of you Gentiles — [2]assuming that you have heard of the stewardship of God's grace that was given to me for you, [3]how the mystery was made known to me by revelation, as I have written briefly. [4]When you read this you can perceive my insight into the mystery of Christ, [5]which was not made known to the sons of men in other generations as it has now been revealed to his holy apostles and prophets by the Spirit; [6]that is, how the Gentiles are fellow heirs, members of the same body, and partakers of the promise in Christ Jesus through the gospel.

[7]Of this gospel I was made a minister according to the gift of God's grace which was given me by the working of his power. [8]To me, though I am the very least of all the saints, this grace was given, to preach to the Gentiles the unsearchable riches of Christ, [9]and to make all men see what is the plan of the mystery hidden for ages in God who created all things; [10]that through the church the manifold wisdom of God might now be made known to the principalities and powers in the heavenly places. [11]This was according to the eternal purpose which he has realized in Christ Jesus our Lord, [12]in whom we have boldness and confidence of access through our faith in him. [13]So I ask you not to lose heart over what I am suffering for you, which is your glory.

Phil 1:3-11 (§238)

[3]I thank my God in all my remembrance of you, [4]always in every prayer of mine for you all making my prayer with joy, [5]thankful for your partnership in the gospel from the first day until now. [6]And I am sure that he who began a good work in you will bring it to completion at the day of Jesus Christ. [7]It is right for me to feel thus about you all, because I hold you in my heart, for you are all partakers with me of grace, both in my imprisonment and in the defense and confirmation of the gospel. [8]For God is my witness, how I yearn for you all with the affection of Christ Jesus. [9]And it is my prayer that your love may abound more and more, with knowledge and all discernment, [10]so that you may approve what is excellent, and may be pure and blameless for the day of Christ, [11]filled with the fruits of righteousness which come through Jesus Christ, to the glory and praise of God.

Col 1:24-2:3 (§260)

[24]Now I rejoice in my sufferings for your sake, and in my flesh I complete what is lacking in Christ's afflictions for the sake of his body, that is, the church, [25]of which I became a minister according to the divine office which was given to me for you, to make the word of God fully known, [26]the mystery hidden for ages and generations but now made manifest to his saints. [27]To them God chose to make known how great among the Gentiles are the riches of the glory of this mystery, which is Christ in you, the hope of glory. [28]Him we proclaim warning every man and teaching every man in all wisdom, that we may present every man mature in Christ. [29]For this I toil, striving with all the energy which he mightily inspires within me.

2 [1]For I want you to know how greatly I strive for you, and for those at Laodicea, and for all who have not seen my face, [2]that their hearts may be encouraged as they are knit together in love, to have all the riches of assured understanding and the knowledge of God's mystery, of Christ, [3]in whom are hid all the treasures of wisdom and knowledge.

1 Thess 1:2-10 (§276)

[2]We give thanks to God always for you all, constantly mentioning you in our prayers, [3]remembering before our God and Father your work of faith and labor of love and steadfastness of hope in our Lord Jesus Christ. [4]For we know, brethren beloved by God, that he has chosen you; [5]for our gospel came to you not only in word, but also in power and in the Holy Spirit and with full conviction. You know what kind of men we proved to be among you for your sake. [6]And you became imitators of us and of the Lord, for you received the word in much affliction, with joy inspired by the Holy Spirit; [7]so that you became an example to the all the believers in Macedonia and in Achaia. [8]For not only has the word of the Lord sounded forth from you in Macedonia and Achaia, but your faith in God has gone forth everywhere, so that we need not say anything. [9]For they themselves report concerning us what a welcome we had among you, and how you turned to God from idols, to serve a living and true God, [10]and to wait for his Son from heaven, whom he raised from the dead, Jesus who delivers us from the wrath to come.

---

they listened to Barnabas and Paul as they related what signs and wonders God had done through them among the Gentiles.

Acts 22   [17]"When I had returned to Jerusalem and was praying in the temple, I fell into a trance [18]and saw him saying to me, 'Make haste and get quickly out of Jerusalem, because they will not accept your testimony about me.' [19]And I said, 'Lord, they themselves know that in every synagogue I imprisoned and beat those who believed in thee. [20]And when the blood of Stephen thy witness was shed, I also was

standing by and approving, and keeping the garments of those who killed him.' [21]And he said to me, 'Depart; for I will send you far away to the Gentiles.'"

● **Rom 15:18**

Acts 21   [19]After greeting them, he related one by one the things that God had done among the Gentiles through his ministry.

● **Rom 15:19**

2 Thess 2   [9]The coming of the lawless one will be by the activity of Satan will be with all power and with pretended signs and wonders, . . .

Cf. 2 Cor 10   [16]so that we may preach the gospel in lands beyond you, without boasting of work already done in another's field.

Cf. Acts 19   [11]And God did extraordinary miracles by the hands of Paul, . . .

● **Rom 15:21**

Isa 52   [15]so shall he startle many nations;
    kings shall shut their mouths because of him;
    for that which has not been told them they shall see,
    and that which they have not heard they shall
    understand.

FORMAL ELEMENT: APOSTOLIC VISIT

[22] **This is the reason why I have so often been hindered from coming to you.** [23] **But now, since I no longer have any room for work in these regions, and since I have longed for many years to come to you,** [24] **I hope to see you in passing as I go to Spain, and to be sped on my journey there by you, once I have enjoyed your company for a little.** [25] **At present, however, I am going to Jerusalem with aid for the saints.** [26] **For Macedonia and Achaia have been pleased to make some contribution for the poor among the saints at Jerusalem;** [27] **they were pleased to do it, and indeed they are in debt to them, for if the Gentiles have come to share in their spiritual blessings, they ought also to be of service to them in material blessings.** [28] **When therefore I have completed this, and have delivered to them what has been raised, I shall go on by way of you to Spain;** [29] **and I know that when I come to you I shall come in the fulness of the blessing of Christ.**

PRIMARY

1 Cor 4:14–21 (§86)

[14] I do not write this to make you ashamed, but to admonish you as my beloved children. [15] For though you have countless guides in Christ, you do not have many fathers. For I became your father in Christ Jesus through the gospel. [16] I urge you, then, be imitators of me. [17] Therefore I sent to you Timothy, my beloved and faithful child in the Lord, to remind you of my ways in Christ, as I teach them everywhere in every church. [18] Some are arrogant, as though I were not coming to you. [19] But I will come to you soon, if the Lord wills, and I will find out not the talk of these arrogant people but their power. [20] For the kingdom of God does not consist in talk but in power. [21] What do you wish? Shall I come to you with a rod, or with love in a spirit of gentleness?

1 Cor 16:1–4 (§138)

[1] Now concerning the contribution for the saints: as I directed the churches of Galatia, so you also are to do. [2] On the first day of every week, each of you is to put something aside and store it up, as he may prosper, so that contributions need not be made when I come. [3] And when I arrive, I will send those whom you accredit by letter to carry your gift to Jerusalem. [4] If it seems advisable that I should go also, they will accompany me.

1 Cor 16:5–9 (§139)

[5] I will visit you after passing through Macedonia, for I intend to pass through Macedonia, [6] and perhaps I will stay with you or even spend the winter, so that you may speed me on my journey, wherever I go. [7] For I do not want to see you now just in passing; I hope to spend some time with you, if the Lord permits. [8] But I will stay in Ephesus until Pentecost, [9] for a wide door for effective work has opened to me, and there are many adversaries.

2 Cor 1:15–22 (§149)

[15] Because I was sure of this, I wanted to come to you first, so that you might have a double pleasure; [16] I wanted to visit you on my way to Macedonia, and to come back to you from Macedonia and have you send me on my way to Judea. [17] Was I vacillating when I wanted to do this? Do I make my plans like a worldly man, ready to say Yes and No at once? [18] As surely as God is faithful, our word to you has not been Yes and No. [19] For the Son of God, Jesus Christ, whom we preached among you, Silvanus and Timothy and I, was not Yes and No; but in him it is always Yes. [20] For all the promises of God find their Yes in him. That is why we utter the Amen through him, to the glory of God. [21] But it is God who establishes us with you in Christ, and has commissioned us; [22] he has put his seal upon us and given us his Spirit in our hearts as a guarantee.

2 Cor 1:23–2:4 (§150)

[23] But I call God to witness against me—it was to spare you that I refrained from coming to Corinth. [24] Not that we lord it over your faith; we work with you for your joy, for you stand firm in your faith. 2 [1] For I made up my mind not to make you another painful visit. [2] For if I cause you pain, who is there to make me glad but the one whom I have pained? [3] And I wrote as I did, so that when I came I might not suffer pain from those who should have made me rejoice, for I felt sure of all of you, that my joy would be the joy of you all. [4] For I wrote you out of much affliction and anguish of heart and with many tears, not to cause you pain but to let you know the abundant love that I have for you.

2 Cor 9:1–5 (§174)

[1] Now it is superfluous for me to write to you about the offering for the saints, [2] for I know your readiness, of which I boast about you to the people of Macedonia, saying that Achaia has been ready since last year; and your zeal has stirred up most of them. [3] But I am sending the brethren so that our boasting about you may not prove vain in this case, so that you may be ready, as I said you would be; [4] lest if some Macedonians come with me and find that you are not ready, we be humiliated—to say nothing of you—for being so confident. [5] So I thought it necessary to urge the brethren to go on to you before me, and arrange in advance for this gift you have promised, so that it may be ready not as an exaction but as a willing gift.

2 Cor 12:14–13:10 (§187–190)

[14] Here for the third time I am ready to come to you. And I will not be a burden, for I seek not what is yours but you; for children ought not to lay up for their parents, but parents for their children. [15] I will most gladly spend and be spent for your souls. If I love you the more, am I to be loved the less? [16] But granting that I myself did not burden you, I was crafty, you say, and got the better of you by guile. [17] Did I take advantage of you through any of those whom I sent to you? [18] I urged Titus to go, and sent the brother with him. Did Titus take advantage of you? Did we not act in the same spirit? Did we not take the same steps?

[19] Have you been thinking all along that we have been defending ourselves before you? It is in the sight of God that we have been speaking in Christ, and all for your upbuilding, beloved. [20] For I fear that perhaps I may come and find you not what I wish, and that you may find me not what you wish; that perhaps there may be quarreling, jealousy, anger, selfishness, slander, gossip, conceit, and disorder. [21] I fear that when I come again my God may humble me before you, and I may have to mourn over many of those who sinned before and have not repented of the impurity, immorality, and licentiousness which they have practiced. 13 This is the third time I am coming to you. Any charge must be sustained by the evidence of two or three witnesses. [2] I warned those who sinned before and all the others, and I warn them now while absent, as I did when present on my second visit, that if I come again I will not spare them— [3] since you desire proof that Christ is speaking in me. He is not weak in dealing with you, but is powerful in you. [4] For he was crucified in weakness, but lives by the power of God. For we are weak in him, but in dealing with you we shall live with him by the power of God.

[5] Examine yourselves, to see whether you are holding to your faith. Test yourselves. Do you not realize that Jesus Christ is in you?—unless indeed you fail to meet the test! [6] I hope you will find out that we have not failed. [7] But we pray God that you may not do wrong— not

---

• **Rom 15:22**

Cf. Rom 1   [13] I want you to know, brethren, that I have often intended to come to you (but thus far have been prevented), in order that I may reap some harvest among you as well as among the rest of the Gentiles.

• **Rom 15:23**

Cf. 1 Thess 3   [6] But now that Timothy has come to us from you, and has brought us the good news of your faith and love and reported that you always remember us kindly and long to see us, as we long to see you. . . .

• **Rom 15:24–26**

Acts 19   [21] Now after these events Paul resolved in the Spirit to pass through Macedonia and Achaia and go to Jerusalem, saying, "After I have been there, I must also see Rome."

that we may appear to have met the test, but that you may do what is right, though we may seem to have failed. [8]For we cannot do anything against the truth, but only for the truth. [9]For we are glad when we are weak and you are strong. What we pray for is your improvement. [10]I write this while I am away from you, in order that when I come I may not have to be severe in my use of the authority which the Lord has given me for building up and not for tearing down.

1 Thess 2:17–20 (§280)

[17]But since we were bereft of you, brethren, for a short time, in person not in heart, we endeavored the more eagerly and with great desire to see you face to face; [18]because we wanted to come to you—I, Paul, again and again—but Satan hindered us. [19]For what is our hope or joy or crown of boasting before our Lord Jesus at his coming? Is it not you? [20]For you are our glory and joy.

Phlm 21–22 (§309)

[21]Confident of your obedience, I write to you, knowing that you will do even more than I say. [22]At the same time, prepare a guest room for me, for I am hoping through your prayers to be granted to you.

SECONDARY

2 Cor 8:1–24 (§171–173)

[1]We want you to know, brethren, about the grace of God which has been shown in the churches of Macedonia, [2]for in a severe test of affliction, their abundance of joy and their extreme poverty have overflowed in a wealth of liberality on their part. [3]For they gave according to their means, as I can testify, and beyond their means, of their own free will, [4]begging us earnestly for the favor of taking part in the relief of the saints— [5]and this, not as we expected, but first they gave themselves to the Lord and to us by the will of God. [6]Accordingly we have urged Titus that as he had already made a beginning, he should also complete among you this gracious work. [7]Now as you excel in everything—in faith, in utterance, in knowledge, in all earnestness, and in your love for us—see that you excel in this gracious work also.

[8]I say this not as a command, but to prove by the earnestness of others that your love also is genuine. [9]For you know the grace of our Lord Jesus Christ, that though he was rich, yet for your sake he became poor, so that by his poverty you might become rich. [10]And in this matter I give my advice: it is best for you now to complete what a year ago you began not only to do but to desire, [11]so that your readiness in desiring it may be matched by your completing it out of what you have. [12]For if the readiness is there, it is acceptable according to what a man has, not according to what he has not. [13]I do not mean that others should be eased and you burdened, [14]but that as a matter of equality your abundance at the present time should supply their want, so that their abundance may supply your want, that there may be equality. [15]As it is written, "He who gathered much had nothing over, and he who gathered little had no lack."

[16]But thanks be to God who puts the same earnest care for you into the heart of Titus. [17]For he not only accepted our appeal, but being himself very earnest he is going to you of his own accord. [18]With him we are sending the brother who is famous among all the churches for his preaching of the gospel; [19]and not only that, but he has been appointed by the churches to travel with us in this gracious work which we are carrying on, for the glory of the Lord and to show our good will. [20]We intend that no one should blame us about this liberal gift which we are administering, [21]for we aim at what is honorable not only in the Lord's sight but also in the sight of men. [22]And with them we are sending our brother whom we have often tested and found earnest in many matters, but who is now more earnest than ever because of his great confidence in you. [23]As for Titus, he is my partner and fellow worker in your service; and as for our brethren, they are messengers of the churches, the glory of Christ. [24]So give proof, before the churches, of your love and of our boasting about you to these men.

2 Cor 9:6–15 (§175)

[6]The point is this: he who sows sparingly will also reap sparingly, and he who sows bountifully will also reap bountifully. [7]Each one must do as he has made up his mind, not reluctantly or under compulsion, for God loves a cheerful giver. [8]And God is able to provide you with every blessing in abundance, so that you may always have enough of everything and may provide in abundance for every good work. [9]As it is written,

"He scatters abroad, he gives to the poor;
his righteousness endures for ever."

[10]He who supplies seed to the sower and bread for food will supply and multiply your resources and increase the harvest of your righteousness. [11]You will be enriched in every way for great generosity, which through us will produce thanksgiving to God; [12]for the rendering of this service not only supplies the wants of the saints but also overflows in many thanksgivings to God. [13]Under the test of this service, you will glorify God by your obedience in acknowledging the gospel of Christ, and by the generosity of your contribution for them and for all others; [14]while they long for you and pray for you, because of the surpassing grace of God in you. [15]Thanks be to God for his inexpressible gift!

Gal 2:1–10 (§197)

[1]Then after fourteen years I went up again to Jerusalem with Barnabas, taking Titus along with me. [2]I went up by revelation; and I laid before them (but privately before those who were of repute) the gospel which I preach among the Gentiles, lest somehow I should be running or had run in vain. [3]But even Titus, who was with me, was not compelled to be circumcised, though he was a Greek. [4]But because of false brethren secretly brought in, who slipped in to spy out our freedom which we have in Christ Jesus, that they might bring us into bondage— [5]to them we did not yield submission even for a moment, that the truth of the gospel might be preserved for you. [6]And from those who were reputed to be something (what they were makes no difference to me; God shows no partiality)—those, I say, who were of repute added nothing to me; [7]but on the contrary, when they saw that I had been entrusted with the gospel to the uncircumcised, just as Peter had been entrusted with the gospel to the circumcised [8](for he who worked through Peter for the mission to the circumcised worked through me also for the Gentiles), [9]and when they perceived the grace that was given to me, James and Cephas and John, who were reputed to be pillars, gave to me and Barnabas the right hand of fellowship, that we should go to the Gentiles and they to the circumcised; [10]only they would have us remember the poor, which very thing I was eager to do.

● **Rom 15:25**
Cf. Acts 11   [29]And the disciples determined, every one according to his ability, to send relief to the brethren who lived in Judea; [30]and they did so, sending it to the elders by the hand of Barnabas and Saul.

● **Rom 15:27**
Cf. 1 Cor 9   [11]If we have sown spiritual good among you, is it too much if we reap your material benefits?

● **Rom 15:29**
Cf. Phil 1   [26]so that in me you may have ample cause to glory in Christ Jesus, because of my coming to you again.

Cf. Phil 2   [24]and I trust in the Lord that shortly I myself shall come also.

(blessing) *add* of the gospel: S^c Koine Lect vg(clem) syr(pes har) Chrysostom

FORMAL ELEMENT:
REQUEST FOR PRAYER

[30] I appeal to you, brethren, by our Lord Jesus Christ and by the love of the Spirit, to strive together with me in your prayers to God on my behalf, [31] that I may be delivered from the unbelievers in Judea, and that my service for Jerusalem may be acceptble to the saints, [32] so that by God's will I may come to you with joy and be refreshed in your company. [33] The God of peace be with you all. Amen.

PRIMARY

Eph 6:18–20 (§234)
[18] Pray at all times in the Spirit, with all prayer and supplication. To that end keep alert with all perseverance, making supplication for all the saints, [19] and also for me, that utterance may be given me in opening my mouth boldly to proclaim the mystery of the gospel, [20] for which I am an ambassador in chains; that I may declare it boldly, as I ought to speak.

Col 4:2–4 (§269)
[2] Continue steadfastly in prayer, being watchful in it with thanksgiving; [3] and pray for us also, that God may open to us a door for the word, to declare the mystery of Christ, on account of which I am in prison, [4] that I may make it clear, as I ought to speak.

1 Thess 5:25 (§290)
[25] Brethren, pray for us.

2 Thess 3:1–5 (§299)
[1] Finally, brethren, pray for us, that the word of the Lord may speed on and triumph, as it did among you, [2] and that we may be delivered from wicked and evil men; for not all have faith. [3] But the Lord is faithful; he will strengthen you and guard you from evil. [4] And we have confidence in the Lord about you, that you are doing and will do the things which we command. [5] May the Lord direct your hearts to the love of God and to the steadfastness of Christ.

• **Rom 15:30**
2 Cor 1   [11] You also must help us by prayer, so that many will give thanks on our behalf for the blessing granted us in answer to many prayers.

Phil 4   [6] Have no anxiety about anything, but in everything by prayer and supplication with thanksgiving let your requests be made known to God.

Phlm [22] At the same time, prepare a guest room for me, for I am hoping through your prayers to be granted to you.

• **Rom 15:31**
Gal 2   [10] only they would have us remember the poor, which very thing I was eager to do.

1 Thess 2   [14] For you, brethren, became imitators of the churches of God in Christ Jesus which are in Judea; for you suffered the same things from your own countrymen as they did from the Jews, [15] who killed both the Lord Jesus and the prophets, and drove us out, and displease God and oppose all men [16] by hindering us from speaking to the Gentiles that they may be saved—so as always to fill up the measure of their sins. But God's wrath has come upon them at last!

Acts 9   [23] When many days had passed, the Jews plotted to kill him, [24] but their plot became known to Saul. They were watching the gates day and night, to kill him; . . .

Acts 20   [22] And now, behold, I am going to Jerusalem, bound in the Spirit, not knowing what shall befall me there; [23] except that the Holy Spirit testifies to me in every city that imprisonment and afflictions await me.

Acts 21   [4] . . . Through the Spirit they told Paul not to go on to Jerusalem.

• **Rom 15:32**
2 Tim 3   [11] my persecutions, my sufferings, what befell me at Antioch, at Iconium, and at Lystra, what persecutions I endured; yet from them all the Lord rescued me.

Acts 18   [21] but on taking leave of them he said, "I will return to you if God wills," and he set sail from Ephesus.

• **Rom 15:33**
(Amen) *omit* Amen: AG it(few); *omit* Amen *and add 16:25–27 here only:* p⁴⁶

FORMAL ELEMENT: COMMENDATION

16 I commend to you our sister Phoebe, a deaconess of the church at Cenchreae, ²that you may receive her in the Lord as befits the saints, and help her in whatever she may require from you, for she has been a helper of many and of myself as well.

PRIMARY

1 Cor 16:10–12 (§140)
¹⁰When Timothy comes, see that you put him at ease among you, for he is doing the work of the Lord, as I am. ¹¹So let no one despise him. Speed him on his way in peace, that he may return to me; for I am expecting him with the brethren.
¹²As for our brother Apollos, I strongly urged him to visit you with the other brethren, but it was not at all his will to come now. He will come when he has opportunity.

1 Cor 16:15–18 (§142)
¹⁵Now, brethren, you know that the household of Stephanas were the first converts in Achaia, and they have devoted themselves to the service of the saints; ¹⁶I urge you to be subject to such men and to every fellow worker and laborer. ¹⁷I rejoice at the coming of Stephanas and Fortunatus and Achaicus, because they have made up for your absence; ¹⁸for they refreshed my spirit as well as yours. Give recognition to such men.

2 Cor 3:1–3 (§154)
¹Are we beginning to commend ourselves again? Or do we need, as some do, letters of recommendation to you, or from you? ²You yourselves are our letter of recommendation, written on your hearts, to be known and read by all men; ³and you show that you are a letter from Christ delivered by us, written not with ink but with the Spirit of the living God, not on tablets of stone but on tablets of human hearts.

2 Cor 8:16–24 (§173)
¹⁶But thanks be to God who puts the same earnest care for you into the heart of Titus. ¹⁷For he not only accepted our appeal, but being himself very earnest he is going to you of his own accord. ¹⁸With him we are sending the brother who is famous among all the churches for his preaching of the gospel; ¹⁹and not only that, but he has been appointed by the churches to travel with us in this gracious work which we are carrying on, for the glory of the Lord and to show our good will. ²⁰We intend that no one should blame us about this liberal gift which we are administering, ²¹for we aim at what is honorable not only in the Lord's sight but also in the sight of men. ²²And with them we are sending our brother whom we have often tested and found earnest in many matters, but who is now more earnest than ever because of his great confidence in you. ²³As for Titus, he is my partner and fellow worker in your service; and as for our brethren, they are messengers of the churches, the glory of Christ. ²⁴So give proof, before the churches, of your love and of our boasting about you to these men.

Eph 6:21–22 (§235)
²¹Now that you also may know how I am and what I am doing, Tychicus the beloved brother and faithful minister in the Lord will tell you everything. ²²I have sent him to you for this very purpose, that you may know how we are, and that he may encourage your hearts.

Phil 2:19–24 (§245)
¹⁹I hope in the Lord Jesus to send Timothy to you soon, so that I may be cheered by news of you. ²⁰I have no one like him, who will be genuinely anxious for your welfare. ²¹They all look after their own interests, not those of Jesus Christ. ²²But Timothy's worth you know, how as a son with a father he has served with me in the gospel. ²³I hope therefore to send him just as soon as I see how it will go with me; ²⁴and I trust in the Lord that shortly I myself shall come also.

Phil 2:25–3:1 (§246)
²⁵I have thought it necessary to send to you Epaphroditus my brother and fellow worker and fellow soldier, and your messenger and minister to my need, ²⁶for he has been longing for you all, and has been distressed because you heard that he was ill. ²⁷Indeed he was ill, near to death. But God had mercy on him, and not only on him but on me also, lest I should have sorrow upon sorrow. ²⁸I am the more eager to send

him, therefore, that you may rejoice at seeing him again, and that I may be less anxious. ²⁹So receive him in the Lord with all joy; and honor such men, ³⁰for he nearly died for the work of Christ, risking his life to complete your service to me.

3 ¹Finally, my brethren, rejoice in the Lord. To write the same things to you is not irksome to me, and is safe for you.

Col 4:7–9 (§271)
⁷Tychicus will tell you all about my affairs; he is a beloved brother and faithful minister and fellow servant in the Lord. ⁸I have sent him to you for this very purpose, that you may know how we are and that he may encourage your hearts, ⁹and with him Onesimus, the faithful and beloved brother, who is one of yourselves. They will tell you of everything that has taken place here.

Phlm 8–20 (§307–308)
⁸Accordingly, though I am bold enough in Christ to command you to do what is required, ⁹yet for love's sake I prefer to appeal to you—I, Paul, an ambassador and now a prisoner also for Christ Jesus— ¹⁰I appeal to you for my child, Onesimus, whose father I have become in my imprisonment. ¹¹(Formerly he was useless to you, but now he is indeed useful to you and to me.) ¹²I am sending him back to you, sending my very heart. ¹³I would have been glad to keep him with me, in order that he might serve me on your behalf during my imprisonment for the gospel; ¹⁴but I preferred to do nothing without your consent in order that your goodness might not be by compulsion but of your own free will.
¹⁵Perhaps this is why he was parted from you for a while, that you might have him back for ever, ¹⁶no longer as a slave but more than a slave, as a beloved brother, especially to me but how much more to you, both in the flesh and in the Lord. ¹⁷So if you consider me your partner, receive him as you would receive me. ¹⁸If he has wronged you at all, or owes you anything, charge that to my account. ¹⁹I, Paul, write this with my own hand, I will repay it—to say nothing of your owing me even your own self. ²⁰Yes, brother, I want some benefit from you in the Lord. Refresh my heart in Christ.

● **Rom 16:1-2**
Phil 4 ²I entreat Euodia and I entreat Syntyche to agree in the Lord. ³And I ask you also, true yokefellow, help these women, for they have labored side by side with me in the gospel together with Clement and the rest of my fellow workers, whose names are in the book of life.

● **Rom 16:1**
Acts 18 ¹⁸After this Paul stayed many days longer, and then took leave of the brethren and sailed for Syria, and with him Priscilla and Aquila. At Cenchreae he cut his hair, for he had a vow.

LETTER STRUCTURE: GREETINGS

[3]Greet Prisca and Aquila, my fellow workers in Christ Jesus, [4]who risked their necks for my life, to whom not only I but also all the churches of the Gentiles give thanks; [5]greet also the church in their house. Greet my beloved Epaenetus, who was the first convert in Asia for Christ. [6]Greet Mary, who has worked hard among you. [7]Greet Andronicus and Junias, my kinsmen and my fellow prisoners; they are men of note among the apostles, and they were in Christ before me. [8]Greet Ampliatus, my beloved in the Lord. [9]Greet Urbanus, our fellow worker in Christ, and my beloved Stachys. [10]Greet Apelles, who is approved in Christ. Greet those who belong to the family of Aristobulus. [11]Greet my kinsman Herodion. Greet those in the Lord who belong to the family of Narcissus. [12]Greet those workers in the Lord, Tryphaena and Tryphosa. Greet the beloved Persis, who has worked hard in the Lord. [13]Greet Rufus, eminent in the Lord, also his mother and mine. [14]Greet Asyncritus, Phlegon, Hermes, Patrobas, Hermas, and the brethren who are with them. [15]Greet Philologus, Julia, Nereus and his sister, and Olympas, and all the saints who are with them. [16]Greet one another with a holy kiss. All the churches of Christ greet you.

PRIMARY

1 Cor 16:19–20 (§143)

[19]The churches of Asia send greetings. Aquila and Prisca, together with the church in their house, send you hearty greetings in the Lord. [20]All the brethren send greetings. Greet one another with a holy kiss.

2 Cor 13:11–13 (§191)

[11]Finally, brethren, farewell. Mend your ways, heed my appeal, agree with one another, live in peace, and the God of love and peace will be with you. [12]Greet one another with a holy kiss. [13]All the saints greet you.

Phil 4:21–22 (§254)

[21]Greet every saint in Christ Jesus. The brethren who are with me greet you. [22]All the saints greet you, especially those of Caesar's household.

Col 4:10–15 (§272)

[10]Aristarchus my fellow prisoner greets you, and Mark the cousin of Barnabas (concerning whom you have received instructions—if he comes to you, receive him), [11]and Jesus who is called Justus. These are the only men of the circumcision among my fellow workers for the kingdom of God, and they have been a comfort to me. [12]Epaphras, who is one of yourselves, a servant of Christ Jesus, greets you, always remembering you earnestly in his prayers, that you may stand mature and fully assured in all the will of God. [13]For I bear him witness that he has worked hard for you and for those in Laodicea and in Hierapolis. [14]Luke the beloved physician and Demas greet you. [15]Give my greetings to the brethren at Laodicea, and to Nympha and the church in her house.

1 Thess 5:26 (§291)

[26]Greet all the brethren with a holy kiss.

Phlm 23–24 (§310)

[23]Epaphras, my fellow prisoner in Christ Jesus, sends greetings to you, [24]and so do Mark, Aristarchus, Demas, and Luke, my fellow workers.

● **Rom 16:3–16**

2 Tim 4   [17]But the Lord stood by me and gave me strength to proclaim the message fully, that all the Gentiles might hear it. So I was rescued from the lion's mouth. [18]The Lord will rescue me from every evil and save me for his heavenly kingdom. To him be the glory for ever and ever. Amen.

[19]Greet Prisca and Aquila, and the household of Onesiphorus. [20]Erastus remained at Corinth; Trophimus I left ill at Miletus. [21]Do your best to come before winter. Eubulus sends greetings to you, as do Pudens and Linus and Claudia and all the brethren.

Titus 3   [15]All who are with me send greetings to you. Greet those who love us in the faith.
    Grace be with you all.

● **Rom 16:3**

Rom 16   [9]Greet Urbanus, our fellow worker in Christ, and my beloved Stachys.

Rom 16   [21]Timothy, my fellow worker, greets you; so do Lucius and Jason and Sosipater, my kinsmen.

1 Cor 3   [9]For we are God's fellow workers; you are God's field, God's building.

2 Cor 1   [24]Not that we lord it over your faith; we work with you for your joy, for you stand firm in your faith.

2 Cor 8   [23]As for Titus, he is my partner and fellow worker in your service; and as for our brethren, they are messengers of the churches, the glory of Christ.

Phil 2   [25]I have thought it necessary to send to you Epaphroditus my brother and fellow worker and fellow soldier, and your messenger and minister to my need, . . .

Phil 4   [3]And I ask you also, true yokefellow, help these women, for they have labored side by side with me in the gospel together with Clement and the rest of my fellow workers, whose names are in the book of life.

Col 4   [11]and Jesus who is called Justus. These are the only men of the circumcision among my fellow workers for the kingdom of God, and they have been a comfort to me.

1 Thess 3   [2]and we sent Timothy, our brother and God's servant in the gospel of Christ, to establish you in your faith and to exhort you, . . .

Phlm   [1]Paul, a prisoner for Christ Jesus, and Timothy our brother,
    To Philemon our beloved fellow worker . . .

Phlm   [24]and so do Mark, Aristarchus, Demas, and Luke, my fellow workers.

Acts 18   [2]"And he found a Jew named Aquila, a native of Pontus, lately come from Italy with his wife Priscilla, because Claudius had commanded all the Jews to leave Rome. And he went to see them. . . ."

Acts 18   [18]After this Paul stayed many days longer, and then took leave of the brethren and sailed for Syria, and with him Priscilla and Aquila. At Cenchreae he cut his hair, for he had a vow.

● **Rom 16:4**

Acts 15   [26]". . . men who have risked their lives for the sake of our Lord Jesus Christ."

[17]I appeal to you, brethren, to take note of those who create dissensions and difficulties, in opposition to the doctrine which you have been taught; avoid them. [18]For such persons do not serve our Lord Christ, but their own appetites, and by fair and flattering words they deceive the hearts of the simple-minded. [19]For while your obedience is known to all, so that I rejoice over you, I would have you wise as to what is good and guileless as to what is evil; [20]then the God of peace will soon crush Satan under your feet.

PRIMARY

1 Cor 5:1–5 (§87)

5 [1]It is actually reported that there is immorality among you, and of a kind that is not found even among pagans; for a man is living with his father's wife. [2]And you are arrogant! Ought you not rather to mourn? Let him who has done this be removed from among you.

[3]For though absent in body I am present in spirit, and as if present, I have already pronounced judgment [4]in the name of the Lord Jesus on the man who has done such a thing. When you are assembled, and my spirit is present, with the power of our Lord Jesus, [5]you are to deliver this man to Satan for the destruction of the flesh, that his spirit may be saved in the day of the Lord Jesus.

1 Cor 5:9–13 (§89)

[9]I wrote to you in my letter not to associate with immoral men; [10]not at all meaning the immoral of this world, or the greedy and robbers, or idolaters, since then you would need to go out of the world. [11]But rather I wrote to you not to associate with any one who bears the name of brother if he is guilty of immorality or greed, or is an idolater, reviler, drunkard, or robber—not even to eat with such a one. [12]For what have I to do with judging outsiders? Is it not those inside the church whom you are to judge? [13]God judges those outside. "Drive out the wicked person from among you."

2 Cor 6:14–7:1 (§167)

[14]Do not be mismated with unbelievers. For what partnership have righteousness and iniq-

uity? Or what fellowship has light with darkness? [15]What accord has Christ with Belial? Or what has a believer in common with an unbeliever? [16]What agreement has the temple of God with idols? For we are the temple of the living God; as God said,

"I will live in them and move among them,
and I will be their God,
and they shall be my people.
[17]Therefore come out from them,
and be separate from them, says the Lord,
and touch nothing unclean;
then I will welcome you,
[18]and I will be a father to you,
and you shall be my sons and daughters,
says the Lord Almighty."

7 [1]Since we have these promises, beloved, let us cleanse ourselves from every defilement of body and spirit, and make holiness perfect in the fear of God.

2 Cor 11:12–15 (§181)

[12]And what I do I will continue to do, in order to undermine the claim of those who would like to claim that in their boasted mission they work on the same terms as we do. [13]For such men are false apostles, deceitful workmen, disguising themselves as apostles of Christ. [14]And no wonder, for even Satan disguises himself as an angel of light. [15]So it is not strange if his servants also disguise themselves as servants of righteousness. Their end will correspond to their deeds.

Gal 1:6–12 (§194)

[6]I am astonished that you are so quickly deserting him who called you in the grace of Christ and turning to a different gospel— [7]not that there is another gospel, but there are some who trouble you and want to pervert the gospel of Christ. [8]But even if we, or an angel from heaven, should preach to you a gospel contrary to that which we preached to you, let him be accursed. [9]As we have said before, so now I say again, If any one is preaching to you a gospel contrary to that which you received, let him be accursed. [10]Am I now seeking the favor of men, or of God? Or am I trying to please men? If I were still pleasing men, I should not be a servant of Christ.

[11]For I would have you know, brethren, that the gospel which was preached by me is not man's gospel. [12]For I did not receive it from man, nor was I taught it, but it came through a revelation of Jesus Christ.

Phil 1:12–18 (§239)

[12]I want you to know, brethren, that what has happened to me has really served to advance the gospel, [13]so that it has become known throughout the whole praetorian guard and to all the rest that my imprisonment is for Christ; [14]and most of the brethren have been made confident in the Lord because of my imprisonment, and are much more bold to speak the word of God without fear.

[15]Some indeed preach Christ from envy and rivalry, but others from good will. [16]The latter do it out of love, knowing that I am put here for the defense of the gospel; [17]the former proclaim Christ out of partisanship, not sincerely but thinking to afflict me in my imprisonment. [18]What then? Only that in every way, whether in pretense or in truth, Christ is proclaimed; and in that I rejoice.

1 Thess 2:1–8 (§277)

[1]For you yourselves know, brethren, that our visit to you was not in vain; [2]but though we had already suffered and been shamefully treated at Philippi, as you know, we had courage in our God to declare to you the gospel of God in the face of great opposition. [3]For our appeal does not spring from error or uncleanness, nor is it made with guile; [4]but just as we have been approved by God to be entrusted with the gospel, so we speak, not to please men, but to please God who tests our hearts. [5]For we never used either words of flattery, as you know, or a cloak for greed, as God is witness; [6]nor did we seek glory from men, whether from you or from others, though we might have made demands as apostles of Christ. [7]But we were gentle among you, like a nurse taking care of her children. [8]So, being affectionately desirous of you, we were ready to share with you not only the gospel of God but also our own selves, because you had become very dear to us.

● **Rom 16:17**

1 Tim 1   [3]As I urged you when I was going to Macedonia, remain at Ephesus that you may charge certain persons not to teach any different doctrine, . . .

1 Tim 6   [3]If any one teaches otherwise and does not agree with the sound words of our Lord Jesus Christ and the teaching which accords with godliness, [4]he is puffed up with conceit, he knows nothing; he has a morbid craving for controversy and for disputes about words, which produce envy, dissension, slander, base suspicions, [5]and wrangling among men who are depraved in mind and bereft of the truth, imagining that godliness is a means of gain.

Titus 3   [10]As for a man who is factious, after admonishing him once or twice, have nothing more to do with him, . . .

Acts 19   [9]but when some were stubborn and disbelieved, speaking evil of the Way before the congregation, he withdrew from them, taking the disciples with him, and argued daily in the hall of Tyrannus.

● **Rom 16:19**

1 Cor 14   [20]Brethren, do not be children in your thinking; be babes in evil, but in thinking be mature.

Col 2   [4]I say this in order that no one may delude you with beguiling speech.

● **Rom 16:20**

1 Cor 15   [24]Then comes the end, when he delivers the kingdom to God the Father after destroying every rule and every authority and power. [25]For he must reign until he has put all his enemies under his feet. [26]The last enemy to be destroyed is death. [27]"For God has put all things in subjection under his feet." But when it says, "All things are put in subjection under him," it is plain that he is excepted who put all things under him. [28]When all things are subjected to him, then the Son himself will also be subjected to him who put all things under him, that God may be everything to every one.

LETTER STRUCTURE: CLOSING GRACE

The grace of our Lord Jesus Christ be with you.

PRIMARY

1 Cor 16:23–24 (§145)

[23]The grace of the Lord Jesus be with you. [24]My love be with you all in Christ Jesus. Amen.

2 Cor 13:14 (§192)

[14]The grace of the Lord Jesus Christ and the love of God and the fellowship of the Holy Spirit be with you all.

Gal 6:18 (§217)

[18]The grace of our Lord Jesus Christ be with your spirit, brethren. Amen.

Eph 6:23–24 (§236)

[23]Peace be to the brethren, and love with faith, from God the Father and the Lord Jesus Christ. [24]Grace be with all who love our Lord Jesus Christ with love undying.

Phil 4:23 (§255)

[23]The grace of the Lord Jesus Christ be with your spirit.

Col 4:18b (§274)

Grace be with you.

1 Thess 5:28 (§293)

[28]The grace of our Lord Jesus Christ be with you.

2 Thess 3:18 (§304)

[18]The grace of our Lord Jesus Christ be with you all.

Phlm 25 (§311)

[25]The grace of the Lord Jesus Christ be with your spirit.

● **Rom 16:20b**

1 Tim 6 [21]. . . Grace be with you.

2 Tim 4 [22]The Lord be with your spirit. Grace be with you.

Titus 3 [15]. . . Grace be with you all.

(you) *omit* Christ: p[46]SB; *omit 16:20b entirely:* DG it(some)

LETTER STRUCTURE: GREETINGS

[21]**Timothy, my fellow worker, greets you; so do Lucius and Jason and Sosipater, my kinsmen.** [22]**I Tertius, the writer of this letter, greet you in the Lord.** [23]**Gaius, who is host to me and to the whole church, greets you. Erastus, the city treasurer, and our brother Quartus, greet you.**

PRIMARY

1 Cor 16:19–20 (§143)

[19]The churches of Asia send greetings. Aquila and Prisca, together with the church in their house, send you hearty greetings in the Lord. [20]All the brethren send greetings. Greet one another with a holy kiss.

2 Cor 13:11–13 (§191)

[11]Finally, brethren, farewell. Mend your ways, heed my appeal, agree with one another, live in peace, and the God of love and peace will be with you. [12]Greet one another with a holy kiss. [13]All the saints greet you.

Phil 4:21–22 (§254)

[21]Greet every saint in Christ Jesus. The brethren who are with me greet you. [22]All the saints greet you, especially those of Caesar's household.

Col 4:10–15 (§272)

[10]Aristarchus my fellow prisoner greets you, and Mark the cousin of Barnabas (concerning whom you have received instructions—if he comes to you, receive him), [11]and Jesus who is called Justus. These are the only men of the circumcision among my fellow workers for the kingdom of God, and they have been a comfort to me. [12]Epaphras, who is one of yourselves, a servant of Christ Jesus, greets you, always remembering you earnestly in his prayers, that you may stand mature and fully assured in all the will of God. [13]For I bear him witness that he has worked hard for you and for those in Laodicea and in Hierapolis. [14]Luke the beloved physician and Demas greet you. [15]Give my greetings to the brethren at Laodicea, and to Nympha and the church in her house.

1 Thess 5:26 (§291)

[26]Greet all the brethren with a holy kiss.

Phlm 23–24 (§310)

[23]Epaphras, my fellow prisoner in Christ Jesus, sends greetings to you, [24]and so do Mark, Aristarchus, Demas, and Luke, my fellow workers.

● **Rom 16:21–23**
2 Tim 4 [19]Greet Prisca and Aquila, and the household of Onesiphorus. [20]Erastus remained at Corinth; Trophimus I left ill at Miletus. [21]Do your best to come before winter. Eubulus sends greetings to you, as do Pudens and Linus and Claudia and all the brethren.

Titus 3 [15]All who are with me send greetings to you. Greet those who love us in the faith.
　　Grace be with you all.

● **Rom 16:21**
Acts 13 [1]After the reading of the law and the prophets, the rulers of the synagogue sent to them, saying, "Brethren, if you have any word of exhortation for the people, say it."

Acts 16 [1]And he came also to Derbe and to Lystra. A disciple was there, named Timothy, the son of a Jewish woman who was a believer; but his father was a Greek.

● **Rom 16:23**
Acts 19 [29]So the city was filled with the confusion; and they rushed together into the theater, dragging with them Gaius and Aristarchus, Macedonians who were Paul's companions in travel.

Acts 20 [4]Sopater of Beroea, the son of Pyrrhus, accompanied him; and of the Thessalonians, Aristarchus and Secundus; and Gaius of Derbe, and Timothy; and the Asians, Tychicus and Trophimus.

(you) *add verse 24 here* (The grace of our Lord Jesus Christ be with you all. Amen): Koine Lect it (some) vg(clem) syr(har) Theodoret

Formal Element: Ascription

[25] Now to him who is able to strengthen you according to my gospel and the preaching of Jesus Christ, according to the revelation of the mystery which was kept secret for long ages [26] but is now disclosed and through the prophetic writings is made known to all nations, according to the command of the eternal God, to bring about the obedience of faith—[27] to the only wise God be glory for evermore through Jesus Christ! Amen.

Primary

Eph 3:20–21 (§224)

[20] Now to him who by the power at work within us is able to do far more abundantly than all that we ask or think, [21] to him be glory in the church and in Christ Jesus to all generations, for ever and ever. Amen.

Secondary

Col 1:24–2:3 (§260)

[24] Now I rejoice in my sufferings for your sake, and in my flesh I complete what is lacking in Christ's afflictions for the sake of his body, that is, the church, [25] of which I became a minister according to the divine office which was given to me for you, to make the word of God fully known, [26] the mystery hidden for ages and generations but now made manifest to his saints. [27] To them God chose to make known how great among the Gentiles are the riches of the glory of this mystery, which is Christ in you, the hope of glory. [28] Him we proclaim warning every man and teaching every man in all wisdom, that we may present every man mature in Christ. [29] For this I toil, striving with all the energy which he mightily inspires within me.

2 [1] For I want you to know how greatly I strive for you, and for those at Laodicea, and for all who have not seen my face, [2] that their hearts may be encouraged as they are knit together in love, to have all the riches of assured understanding and the knowledge of God's mystery, of Christ, [3] in whom are hid all the treasures of wisdom and knowledge.

● **Rom 16:25–26**

Rom 3   [21] But now the righteousness of God has been manifested apart from law, although the law and the prophets bear witness to it, . . .

Gal 3   [8] And the scripture, foreseeing that God would justify the Gentiles by faith, preached the gospel beforehand to Abraham, saying, "In you shall all the nations be blessed."

● **Rom 16:26**

Rom 1   [2] which he promised beforehand through his prophets in the holy scriptures, . . .

Rom 1   [5] through whom we have received grace and apostleship to bring about the obedience of faith for the sake of his name among all the nations, . . .

Rom 15   [18] For I will not venture to speak of anything except what Christ has wrought through me to win obedience from the Gentiles, by word and deed, . . .

● **Rom 16:27**

(Amen) *read 16:25–27 here and following 14:23:* AP; *omit 16:25–27 here and add following 15:33 only:* p[46]; *omit 16:25–27:* F(Greek)G few others; *text:* p[61] SBCD it(some) vg syr(pes) cop Clement Origen(Latin)

LETTER STRUCTURE: SALUTATION

1 **Paul, called by the will of God to be an apostle of Christ Jesus, and our brother Sosthenes,**
²To the church of God which is at Corinth, to those sanctified in Christ Jesus, called to be saints together with all those who in every place call on the name of our Lord Jesus Christ, both their Lord and ours:
³Grace to you and peace from God our Father and the Lord Jesus Christ.

PRIMARY

Rom 1:1–7 (§1)
¹Paul, a servant of Jesus Christ, called to be an apostle, set apart for the gospel of God ²which he promised beforehand through his prophets in the holy scriptures, ³the gospel concerning his Son, who was descended from David according to the flesh ⁴and designated Son of God in power according to the Spirit of holiness by his resurrection from the dead, Jesus Christ our Lord, ⁵through whom we have received grace and apostleship to bring about the obedience of faith for the sake of his name among all the nations, ⁶including yourselves who are called to belong to Jesus Christ;
⁷To all God's beloved in Rome, who are called to be saints:
Grace to you and peace from God our Father and the Lord Jesus Christ.

2 Cor 1:1–2 (§146)
¹Paul, an apostle of Christ Jesus by the will of God, and Timothy our brother.
To the church of God which is at Corinth, with all the saints who are in the whole of Achaia:
²Grace to you and peace from God our Father and the Lord Jesus Christ.

Gal 1:1–5 (§193)
¹Paul an apostle—not from men nor through man, but through Jesus Christ and God the Father, who raised him from the dead— ²and all the brethren who are with me,
To the churches of Galatia:
³Grace to you and peace from God the Father and our Lord Jesus Christ, ⁴who gave himself for our sins to deliver us from the present evil age, according to the will of our God and Father; ⁵to whom be the glory for ever and ever. Amen.

Eph 1:1–2 (§218)
¹Paul, an apostle of Christ Jesus by the will of God,
To the saints who are also faithful in Christ Jesus:
²Grace to you and peace from God our Father and the Lord Jesus Christ.

Phil 1:1–2 (§237)
¹Paul and Timothy, servants of Christ Jesus,
To all the saints in Christ Jesus who are at Philippi, with the bishops and deacons:

²Grace to you and peace from God our Father and the Lord Jesus Christ.

Col 1:1–2 (§256)
¹Paul, an apostle of Christ Jesus by the will of God, and Timothy our brother,
²To the saints and faithful brethren in Christ at Colossae:
Grace to you and peace from God our Father.

1 Thess 1:1 (§275)
¹Paul, Silvanus, and Timothy,
To the church of the Thessalonians in God the Father and the Lord Jesus Christ:
Grace to you and peace.

2 Thess 1:1–2 (§294)
¹Paul, Silvanus, and Timothy,
To the church of the Thessalonians in God our Father and the Lord Jesus Christ:
²Grace to you and peace from God the Father and the Lord Jesus Christ.

Phlm 1–3 (§305)
¹Paul, a prisoner for Christ Jesus, and Timothy our brother,
To Philemon our beloved fellow worker ²and Apphia our sister and Archippus our fellow soldier, and the church in your house:
³Grace to you and peace from God our Father and the Lord Jesus Christ.

● **1 Cor 1:1**
Acts 18 ¹⁷And they all seized Sosthenes, the ruler of the synagogue, and beat him in front of the tribunal. But Gallio paid no attention to this.

● **1 Cor 1:2**
1 Cor 1 ³⁰He is the source of your life in Christ Jesus, whom God made our wisdom, our righteousness and sanctification and redemption; ³¹therefore, as it is written, "Let him who boasts, boast of the Lord."

1 Cor 6 ¹¹And such were some of you. But you were washed, you were sanctified, you were justified in the name of the Lord Jesus Christ and in the Spirit of our God.

1 Cor 7 ¹⁴For the unbelieving husband is consecrated through his wife, and the unbelieving wife is consecrated through her husband. Otherwise, your children would be unclean, but as it is they are holy.

2 Tim 2 ²²So shun youthful passions and aim at righteousness, faith, love, and peace, along with those who call upon the Lord from a pure heart.

Acts 2 ²¹'And it shall be that whoever calls on the name of the Lord shall be saved.'

Acts 9 ¹⁴". . . and here he has authority from the chief priests to bind all who call upon thy name."

Acts 9 ²¹And all who heard him were amazed, and said, "Is not this the man who made havoc in Jerusalem of those who called on this name? And he has come here for this purpose, to bring them bound before the chief priests."

Acts 18 ¹After this he left Athens and went to Corinth.

LETTER STRUCTURE: THANKSGIVING

4I give thanks to God always for you because of the grace of God which was given you in Christ Jesus, 5that in every way you were enriched in him with all speech and all knowledge— 6even as the testimony to Christ was confirmed among you—7so that you are not lacking in any spiritual gift, as you wait for the revealing of our Lord Jesus Christ; 8who will sustain you to the end, guiltless in the day of our Lord Jesus Christ. 9God is faithful, by whom you were called into the fellowship of his Son, Jesus Christ our Lord.

PRIMARY

Rom 1:8–15 (§2)

8First, I thank my God through Jesus Christ for all of you, because your faith is proclaimed in all the world. 9For God is my witness, whom I serve with my spirit in the gospel of his Son, that without ceasing I mention you always in my prayers, 10asking that somehow by God's will I may now at last succeed in coming to you. 11For I long to see you, that I may impart to you some spiritual gift to strengthen you, 12that is, that we may be mutually encouraged by each other's faith, both yours and mine. 13I want you to know, brethren, that I have often intended to come to you (but thus far have been prevented), in order that I may reap some harvest among you as well as among the rest of the Gentiles. 14I am under obligation both to Greeks and to barbarians, both to the wise and to the foolish: 15so I am eager to preach the gospel to you also who are in Rome.

Phil 1:3–11 (§238)

3I thank my God in all my remembrance of you, 4always in every prayer of mine for you all making my prayer with joy, 5thankful for your partnership in the gospel from the first day until now. 6And I am sure that he who began a good work in you will bring it to completion at the day of Jesus Christ. 7It is right for me to feel thus about you all, because I hold you in my heart, for you are all partakers with me of grace, both in my imprisonment and in the defense and confirmation of the gospel. 8For God is my witness, how I yearn for you all with the affection of Christ Jesus. 9And it is my prayer that your love may abound more and more, with knowledge and all discernment, 10so that you may approve what is excellent, and may be pure and blameless for the day of Christ, 11filled with the fruits of righteousness which come through Jesus Christ, to the glory and praise of God.

Col 1:3–14 (§257)

3We always thank God, the Father of our Lord Jesus Christ, when we pray for you, 4because we have heard of your faith in Christ Jesus and of the love which you have for all the saints, 5because of the hope laid up for you in heaven. Of this you have heard before in the word of the truth, the gospel 6which has come to you, as indeed in the whole world it is bearing fruit and growing—so among yourselves, from the day you heard and understood the grace of God in truth, 7as you learned it from Epaphras our beloved fellow servant. He is a faithful minister of Christ on our behalf 8and has made known to us your love in the Spirit.

9And so, from the day we heard of it, we have not ceased to pray for you, asking that you may be filled with the knowledge of his will in all spiritual wisdom and understanding, 10to lead a life worthy of the Lord, fully pleasing to him, bearing fruit in every good work and increasing in the knowledge of God. 11May you be strengthened with all power, according to his glorious might, for all endurance and patience with joy, 12giving thanks to the Father, who has qualified us to share in the inheritance of the saints in light. 13He has delivered us from the dominion of darkness and transferred us to the kingdom of his beloved Son, 14in whom we have redemption, the forgiveness of sins.

1 Thess 1:2–10 (§276)

2We give thanks to God always for you all, constantly mentioning you in our prayers, 3remembering before our God and Father your work of faith and labor of love and steadfastness of hope in our Lord Jesus Christ. 4For we know, brethren beloved by God, that he has chosen you; 5for our gospel came to you not only in word, but also in power and in the Holy Spirit and with full conviction. You know what kind of men we proved to be among you for your sake. 6And you became imitators of us and of the Lord, for you received the word in much affliction, with joy inspired by the Holy Spirit; 7so that you became an example to the all the believers in Macedonia and in Achaia. 8For not only has the word of the Lord sounded forth from you in Macedonia and Achaia, but your faith in God has gone forth everywhere, so that we need not say anything. 9For they themselves report concerning us what a welcome we had among you, and how you turned to God from idols, to serve a living and true God, 10and to wait for his Son from heaven, whom he raised from the dead, Jesus who delivers us from the wrath to come.

2 Thess 1:3–12 (§295)

3We are bound to give thanks to God always for you, brethren, as is fitting, because your faith is growing abundantly, and the love of every one of you for one another is increasing. 4Therefore we ourselves boast of you in the churches of God for your steadfastness and faith in all your persecutions and in the afflictions which you are enduring.

5This is evidence of the righteous judgment of God, that you may be made worthy of the kingdom of God, for which you are suffering— 6since indeed God deems it just to repay with affliction those who afflict you, 7and to grant rest with us to you who are afflicted, when the Lord Jesus is revealed from heaven with his mighty angels in flaming fire, 8 inflicting vengeance upon those who do not know God and upon those who do not obey the gospel of our Lord Jesus. 9They shall suffer the punishment of eternal destruction and exclusion from the presence of the Lord and from the glory of his might, 10when he comes on that day to be glorified in his saints, and to be marveled at in all who have believed, because our testimony to you was believed. 11To this end we always pray for you, that our God may make you worthy of his call, and may fulfil every good resolve and work of faith by his power, 12so that the name of our Lord Jesus may be glorified in you, and you in him, according to the grace of our God and the Lord Jesus Christ.

Phlm 4–7 (§306)

4I thank my God always when I remember you in my prayers, 5because I hear of your love and of the faith which you have toward the Lord Jesus and all the saints, 6and I pray that the sharing of your faith may promote the knowledge of all the good that is ours in Christ. 7For I have derived much joy and comfort from your love, my brother, because the hearts of the saints have been refreshed through you.

● **1 Cor 1:4**

1 Tim 1   12I thank him who has given me strength for this, Christ Jesus our Lord, because he judged me faithful by appointing me to his service, . . .

2 Tim 1   3I thank God whom I serve with a clear conscience, as did my fathers, when I remember you constantly in my prayers.

(God) *read* my God: SᵃACDG it vg syr

● **1 Cor 1:5**

Rom 15   14I myself am satisfied about you, my brethren, that you yourselves are full of goodness, filled with all knowledge, and able to instruct one another.

● **1 Cor 1:6**

1 Tim 2   6who gave himself as a ransom for all, the testimony to which was borne at the proper time.

See 2 Tim 1:8; 2 Tim 1:12; Acts 18:5

● **1 Cor 1:7–8**

1 Thess 3   13so that he may establish your hearts unblamable in holiness before our God and Father, at the coming of our Lord Jesus with all his saints.

● **1 Cor 1:7**

Rom 12   6Having gifts that differ according to the grace given to us, let us use them: . . .

1 Cor 12   4Now there are varieties of gifts, but the same Spirit; . . .

Phil 3   20But our commonwealth is in heaven, and from it we await a Savior, the Lord Jesus Christ, . . .

● **1 Cor 1:9**

Rom 3   3What if some were unfaithful? Does their faithlessness nullify the faithfulness of God?

See 1 Cor 10:13

1 Thess 5   24He who calls you is faithful, and he will do it.

LETTER STRUCTURE: APPEAL

[10]I appeal to you, brethren, by the name of our Lord Jesus Christ, that all of you agree and that there be no dissensions among you, but that you be united in the same mind and the same judgment. [11]For it has been reported to me by Chloe's people that there is quarreling among you, my brethren. [12]What I mean is that each one of you says, "I belong to Paul," or "I belong to Apollos," or "I belong to Cephas," or "I belong to Christ." [13]Is Christ divided? Was Paul crucified for you? Or were you baptized in the name of Paul? [14]I am thankful that I baptized none of you except Crispus and Gaius; [15]lest any one should say that you were baptized in my name. [16](I did baptize also the household of Stephanas. Beyond that, I do not know whether I baptized any one else.) [17]For Christ did not send me to baptize but to preach the gospel, and not with eloquent wisdom, lest the cross of Christ be emptied of its power.

PRIMARY

See §51 for APPEAL

SECONDARY

Gal 5:13–15 (§212)

[13]For you were called to freedom, brethren; only do not use your freedom as an opportunity for the flesh, but through love be servants of one another. [14]For the whole law is fulfilled in one word, "You shall love your neighbor as yourself." [15]But if you bite and devour one another take heed that you are not consumed by one another.

Phil 4:1–3 (§250)

[1]Therefore, my brethren, whom I love and long for, my joy and crown, stand firm thus in the Lord, my beloved.
[2]I entreat Euodia and I entreat Syntyche to agree in the Lord. [3]And I ask you also, true yokefellow, help these women, for they have labored side by side with me in the gospel together with Clement and the rest of my fellow workers, whose names are in the book of life.

Col 2:16–19 (§263)

[16]Therefore let no one pass judgment on you in questions of food and drink or with regard to a festival or a new moon or a sabbath. [17]These are only a shadow of what is to come; but the substance belongs to Christ. [18]Let no one disqualify you, insisting on self-abasement and worship of angels, taking his stand on visions, puffed up without reason by his sensuous mind, [19]and not holding fast to the Head, from whom the whole body, nourished and knit together through its joints and ligaments, grows with a growth that is from God.

● 1 Cor 1:10

Rom 15   [5]May the God of steadfastness and encouragement grant you to live in such harmony with one another, in accord with Christ Jesus, [6]that together you may with one voice glorify the God and Father of our Lord Jesus Christ.

Phil 2   [1]So if there is any encouragement in Christ, any incentive of love, any participation in the Spirit, any affection and sympathy, [2]complete my joy by being of the same mind, having the same love, being in full accord and of one mind.

Phil 4   [2]I entreat Euodia and I entreat Syntyche to agree in the Lord.

● 1 Cor 1:11

1 Cor 11   [18]For, in the first place, when you assemble as a church, I hear that there are divisions among you; and I partly believe it, [19]for there must be factions among you in order that those who are genuine among you may be recognized.

Cf. 1 Cor 7   [1]Now concerning the matters about which you wrote.

Cf. 1 Cor 16   [17]I rejoice at the coming of Stephanas and Fortunatus and Achaicus, because they have made up for your absence; . . .

Cf. 1 Thess 3   [6]But now that Timothy has come to us from you, and has brought us the good news of your faith and love and reported that you always remember us kindly and long to see us, as we long to see you . . .

● 1 Cor 1:12

Cf. 1 Cor 3   [4]For when one says, "I belong to Paul," and another, "I belong to Apollos," are you not merely men?

Cf. 1 Cor 3   [21]So let no one boast of men. For all things are yours, [22]whether Paul or Apollos or Cephas or the world or life or death or the present or the future, all are yours; . . .

Cf. 1 Cor 4   [6]I have applied all this to myself and Apollos for your benefit, brethren, that you may learn by us not to go beyond what is written, that none of you may be puffed up in favor of one against another.

Cf. 2 Cor 10   [7]Look at what is before your eyes. If any one is confident that he is Christ's, let him remind himself that as he is Christ's, so are we.

● 1 Cor 1:13

Cf. Acts 18   [24]Now a Jew named Apollos, a native of Alexandria, came to Ephesus. He was an eloquent man, well versed in the scriptures. [25]He had been instructed in the way of the Lord; and being fervent in spirit, he spoke and taught accurately the things concerning Jesus, though he knew only the baptism of John. [26]He began to speak boldly in the synagogue; but when Priscilla and Aquila heard him, they took him and expounded to him the way of God more accurately. [27]And when he wished to cross to Achaia, the brethren encouraged him, and wrote to the disciples to receive him. When he arrived, he greatly helped those who through grace had believed, [28]for he powerfully confuted the Jews in public, showing by the scriptures that the Christ was Jesus.   19 [1]While

Apollos was at Corinth, Paul passed through the upper country and came to Ephesus. There he found some disciples.

● 1 Cor 1:14

Cf. Acts 2   [38]And Peter said to them, "Repent, and be baptized every one of you in the name of Jesus Christ for the forgiveness of your sins; and you shall receive the gift of the Holy Spirit."

Cf. Acts 18   [8]Crispus, the ruler of the synagogue, believed in the Lord, together with all his household; and many of the Corinthians hearing Paul believed and were baptized.

Cf. Acts 19   [29]So the city was filled with the confusion; and they rushed together into the theater, dragging with them Gaius and Aristarchus, Macedonians who were Paul's companions in travel.

(thankful) *read* I thank God: SᶜCDG Koine Lect it (some) vg syr(har) Tertullian Origen (Latin); *text:* S*B Clement Origen

● 1 Cor 1:16

Cf. 1 Cor 16   [15]Now, brethren, you know that the household of Stephanas were the first converts in Achaia, and they have devoted themselves to the service of the saints; [16]I urge you to be subject to such men and to every fellow worker and laborer.

● 1 Cor 1:17

1 Cor 2   [4]and my speech and my message were not in plausible words of wisdom, but in demonstration of the Spirit and of power, [5]that your faith might not rest in the wisdom of men but in the power of God.

18For the word of the cross is folly to those who are perishing, but to us who are being saved it is the power of God. **19**For it is written,

> "I will destroy the wisdom of the wise,
> and the cleverness of the clever I will thwart."

20Where is the wise man? Where is the scribe? Where is the debater of this age? Has not God made foolish the wisdom of the world? **21**For since, in the wisdom of God, the world did not know God through wisdom, it pleased God through the folly of what we preach to save those who believe. **22**For Jews demand signs and Greeks seek wisdom, **23**but we preach Christ crucified, a stumbling block to Jews and folly to Gentiles, **24**but to those who are called, both Jews and Greeks, Christ the power of God and the wisdom of God. **25**For the foolishness of God is wiser than men, and the weakness of God is stronger than men.

PRIMARY

Rom 1:16–17 (§3)

16For I am not ashamed of the gospel: it is the power of God for salvation to every one who has faith, to the Jew first and also to the Greek. **17**For in it the righteousness of God is revealed through faith for faith; as it is written, "He who through faith is righteous shall live."

Rom 1:18–23 (§4)

18For the wrath of God is revealed from heaven against all ungodliness and wickedness of men who by their wickedness suppress the truth. **19**For what can be known about God is plain to them, because God has shown it to them. **20**Ever since the creation of the world his invisible nature, namely, his eternal power and deity, has been clearly perceived in the things that have been made. So they are without excuse; **21**for although they knew God they did not honor him as God or give thanks to him, but they became futile in their thinking and their senseless minds were darkened. **22**Claiming to

be wise, they became fools, **23**and exchanged the glory of the immortal God for images resembling mortal man or birds or animals or reptiles.

Rom 9:30–33 (§39)

30What shall we say, then? That Gentiles who did not pursue righteousness have attained it, that is, righteousness through faith; **31**but that Israel who pursued the righteousness which is based on law did not succeed in fulfilling that law. **32**Why? Because they did not pursue it through faith, but as if it were based on works. They have stumbled over the stumbling stone, **33**as it is written,
"Behold, I am laying in Zion a stone that will make men stumble,
a rock that will make them fall;
and he who believes in him will not be put to shame."

Rom 11:33–36 (§50)

33O the depth of the riches and wisdom and knowledge of God! How unsearchable are his judgments and how inscrutable his ways!
34"For who has known the mind of the Lord, or who has been his counselor?"
35"Or who has given a gift to him that he might be repaid?"
36For from him and through him and to him are all things. To him be glory for ever. Amen.

2 Cor 11:16–21a (§182)

16I repeat, let no one think me foolish; but even if you do, accept me as a fool, so that I too may boast a little. **17**(What I am saying I say not with the Lord's authority but as a fool, in this boastful confidence; **18**since many boast of worldly things, I too will boast.) **19**For you gladly bear with fools, being wise yourselves! **20**For you bear it if a man makes slaves of you, or preys upon you, or takes advantage of you, or puts on airs, or strikes you in the face. **21**To my shame, I must say, we were too weak for that!

2 Cor 12:1–10 (§185)

1I must boast; there is nothing to be gained

by it, but I will go on to visions and revelations of the Lord. **2**I know a man in Christ who fourteen years ago was caught up to the third heaven—whether in the body or out of the body I do not know, God knows. **3**And I know that this man was caught up into Paradise—whether in the body or out of the body I do not know, God knows — **4**and he heard things that cannot be told, which man may not utter. **5**On behalf of this man I will boast, but on my own behalf I will not boast, except of my weaknesses. **6**Though if I wish to boast, I shall not be a fool, for I shall be speaking the truth. But I refrain from it, so that no one may think more of me than he sees in me or hears from me. **7**And to keep me from being too elated by the abundance of revelations, a thorn was given me in the flesh, a messenger of Satan, to harass me, to keep me from being too elated. **8**Three times I besought the Lord about this, that it should leave me; **9**but he said to me, "My grace is sufficient for you, for my power is made perfect in weakness." I will all the more gladly boast of my weaknesses, that the power of Christ may rest upon me. **10**For the sake of Christ, then, I am content with weaknesses, insults, hardships, persecutions, and calamities; for when I am weak, then I am strong.

1 Thess 2:13–16 (§279)

13And we also thank God constantly for this, that when you received the word of God which you heard from us, you accepted it not as the word of men but as what it really is, the word of God, which is at work in you believers. **14**For you, brethren, became imitators of the churches of God in Christ Jesus which are in Judea; for you suffered the same things from your own countrymen as they did from the Jews, **15**who killed both the Lord Jesus and the prophets, and drove us out, and displease God and oppose all men **16**by hindering us from speaking to the Gentiles that they may be saved—so as always to fill up the measure of their sins. But God's wrath has come upon them at last!

● **1 Cor 1:18**
2 Cor 2   **15**For we are the aroma of Christ to God among those who are being saved and among those who are perishing, . . .

2 Cor 4   **3**And even if our gospel is veiled, it is veiled only to those who are perishing.

2 Tim 1   **8**Do not be ashamed then of testifying to our Lord, nor of me his prisoner, but share in suffering for the gospel in the power of God, . . .

● **1 Cor 1:19**
Isa 29   **14**". . . therefore, behold, I will again do marvelous things with this people,

wonderful and marvelous;
and the wisdom of their wise men shall perish,
and the discernment of their discerning men shall be hid."

● **1 Cor 1:20**
Acts 6   **10**But they could not withstand the wisdom and the Spirit with which he spoke.

● **1 Cor 1:21**
1 Tim 4   **16**Take heed to yourself and to your teaching: hold to that, for by so doing you will save both yourself and your hearers.

● **1 Cor 1:23**
Gal 5   **11**But if I, brethren, still preach circumcision, why am I still persecuted? In that case the stumbling block of the cross has been removed.

● **1 Cor 1:25**
2 Cor 13   **3**. . . He is not weak in dealing with you, but is powerful in you. **4**For he was crucified in weakness, but lives by the power of God. For we are weak in him, but in dealing with you we shall live with him by the power of God.

26 For consider your call, brethren; not many of you were wise according to worldly standards, not many of you were powerful, not many were of noble birth; 27 but God chose what is foolish in the world to shame the wise, God chose what is weak in the world to shame the strong, 28 God chose what is low and despised in the world, even things that are not, to bring to nothing things that are, 29 so that no human being might boast in the presence of God. 30 He is the source of your life in Christ Jesus, whom God made our wisdom, our righteousness and sanctification and redemption; 31 therefore, as it is written, "Let him who boasts, boast of the Lord."

PRIMARY

Rom 3:27–31 (§15)

27 Then what becomes of our boasting? It is excluded. On what principle? On the principle of works? No, but on the principle of faith. 28 For we hold that a man is justified by faith apart from works of law. 29 Or is God the God of Jews only? Is he not the God of Gentiles also? Yes, of Gentiles also, 30 since God is one; and he will justify the circumcised on the ground of their faith and the uncircumcised through their faith. 31 Do we then overthrow the law by this faith? By no means! On the contrary, we uphold the law.

1 Cor 3:18–23 (§82)

18 Let no one deceive himself. If any one among you thinks that he is wise in this age, let him become a fool that he may become wise. 19 For the wisdom of this world is folly with God. For it is written, "He catches the wise in their craftiness," 20 and again, "The Lord knows that the thoughts of the wise are futile." 21 So let no one boast of men. For all things are yours, 22 whether Paul or Apollos or Cephas or the world or life or death or the present or the future, all are yours; 23 and you are Christ's; and Christ is God's.

1 Cor 4:6–13 (§84–85)

6 I have applied all this to myself and Apollos for your benefit, brethren, that you may learn by us not to go beyond what is written, that none of you may be puffed up in favor of one against another. 7 For who sees anything different in you? What have you that you did not receive? If then you received it, why do you boast as if it were not a gift?

8 Already you are filled! Already you have become rich! Without us you have become kings! And would that you did reign, so that we might share the rule with you! 9 For I think that God has exhibited us apostles as last of all, like men sentenced to death; because we have become a spectacle to the world, to angels and to men. 10 We are fools for Christ's sake, but you are wise in Christ. We are weak, but you are strong. You are held in honor, but we in disrepute. 11 To the present hour we hunger and thirst, we are ill-clad and buffeted and homeless, 12 and we labor, working with our own hands. When reviled, we bless; when persecuted, we endure; 13 when slandered, we try to conciliate; we have become, and are now, as the refuse of the world, the off-scouring of all things.

2 Cor 12:1–10 (§185)

1 I must boast; there is nothing to be gained by it, but I will go on to visions and revelations of the Lord. 2 I know a man in Christ who fourteen years ago was caught up to the third heaven—whether in the body or out of the body I do not know, God knows. 3 And I know that this man was caught up into Paradise—whether in the body or out of the body I do not know, God knows— 4 and he heard things that cannot be told, which man may not utter. 5 On behalf of this man I will boast, but on my own behalf I will not boast, except of my weak-nesses. 6 Though if I wish to boast, I shall not be a fool, for I shall be speaking the truth. But I refrain from it, so that no one may think more of me than he sees in me or hears from me. 7 And to keep me from being too elated by the abundance of revelations, a thorn was given me in the flesh, a messenger of Satan, to harass me, to keep me from being too elated. 8 Three times I besought the Lord about this, that it should leave me; 9 but he said to me, "My grace is sufficient for you, for my power is made perfect in weakness." I will all the more gladly boast of my weaknesses, that the power of Christ may rest upon me. 10 For the sake of Christ, then, I am content with weaknesses, insults, hardships, persecutions, and calamities; for when I am weak, then I am strong.

Phil 2:1–11 (§242)

1 So if there is any encouragement in Christ, any incentive of love, any participation in the Spirit, any affection and sympathy, 2 complete my joy by being of the same mind, having the same love, being in full accord and of one mind. 3 Do nothing from selfishness or conceit, but in humility count others better than yourselves. 4 Let each of you look not only to his own interests, but also to the interests of others. 5 Have this mind among yourselves, which is yours in Christ Jesus, 6 who, though he was in the form of God, did not count equality with God a thing to be grasped, 7 but emptied himself, taking the form of a servant, being born in the likeness of men. 8 And being found in human form he humbled himself and became obedient unto death, even death on a cross. 9 Therefore God has highly exalted him and bestowed on him the name which is above every name, 10 that at the name of Jesus every knee should bow, in heaven and on earth and under the earth, 11 and every tongue confess that Jesus Christ is Lord, to the glory of God the Father.

• **1 Cor 1:28**
Rom 4   17 as it is written, "I have made you the father of many nations"—in the presence of the God in whom he believed, who gives life to the dead and calls into existence the things that do not exist.

• **1 Cor 1:29**
1 Cor 5   6 Your boasting is not good. Do you not know that a little leaven leavens the whole lump?

2 Cor 11   30 If I must boast, I will boast of the things that show my weakness.

Eph 2   8 For by grace you have been saved through faith; and this is not your own doing, it is the gift of God— 9 not because of works, lest any man should boast.

• **1 Cor 1:31**
Jer 9   24 but let him who glories glory in this, that he understands and knows me, that I am the Lord who practice steadfast love, justice, and righteousness in the earth; for in these things I delight, says the Lord.

2 When I came to you, brethren, I did not come proclaiming to you the testimony of God in lofty words or wisdom. [2]For I decided to know nothing among you except Jesus Christ and him crucified. [3]And I was with you in weakness and in much fear and trembling; [4]and my speech and my message were not in plausible words of wisdom, but in demonstration of the Spirit and of power, [5]that your faith might not rest in the wisdom of men but in the power of God.

PRIMARY

2 Cor 10:7–12 (§177)

[7]Look at what is before your eyes. If any one is confident that he is Christ's, let him remind himself that as he is Christ's, so are we. [8]For even if I boast a little too much of our authority, which the Lord gave for building you up and not for destroying you, I shall not be put to shame. [9]I would not seem to be frightening you with letters. [10]For they say, "His letters are weighty and strong, but his bodily presence is weak, and his speech of no account." [11]Let such people understand that what we say by letter when absent, we do when present. [12]Not that we venture to class or compare ourselves with some of those who commend themselves. But when they measure themselves by one another and compare themselves with one another, they are without understanding.

2 Cor 12:11–13 (§186)

[11]I have been a fool! You forced me to it, for I ought to have been commended by you. For I was not at all inferior to these superlative apostles, even though I am nothing. [12]The signs of a true apostle were performed among you in all patience, with signs and wonders and mighty works. [13]For in what were you less favored than the rest of the churches, except that I myself did not burden you? Forgive me this wrong!

Gal 4:12–20 (§209)

[12]Brethren, I beseech you, become as I am, for I also have become as you are. You did me no wrong; [13]you know it was because of a bodily ailment that I preached the gospel to you at first; [14]and though my condition was a trial to you, you did not scorn or despise me, but received me as an angel of God, as Christ Jesus. [15]What has become of the satisfaction you felt? For I bear you witness that, if possible, you would have plucked out your eyes and given them to me. [16]Have I then become your enemy by telling you the truth? [17]They make much of you, but for no good purpose; they want to shut you out, that you may make much of them. [18]For a good purpose it is always good to be made much of, and not only when I am present with you. [19]My little children, with whom I am again in travail until Christ be formed in you! [20]I could wish to be present with you now and to change my tone, for I am perplexed about you.

Eph 3:1–13 (§222)

[1]For this reason I, Paul, a prisoner for Christ Jesus on behalf of you Gentiles — [2]assuming that you have heard of the stewardship of God's grace that was given to me for you, [3]how the mystery was made known to me by revelation, as I have written briefly. [4]When you read this you can perceive my insight into the mystery of Christ, [5]which was not made known to the sons of men in other generations as it has now been revealed to his holy apostles and prophets by the Spirit; [6]that is, how the Gentiles are fellow heirs, members of the same body, and partakers of the promise in Christ Jesus through the gospel. [7]Of this gospel I was made a minister according to the gift of God's grace which was given me by the working of his power. [8]To me, though I am the very least of all the saints, this grace was given, to preach to the Gentiles the unsearchable riches of Christ, [9]and to make all men see what is the plan of the mystery hidden for ages in God who created all things; [10]that through the church the manifold wisdom of God might now be made known to the principalities and powers in the heavenly places. [11]This was according to the eternal purpose which he has realized in Christ Jesus our Lord, [12]in whom we have boldness and confidence of access through our faith in him. [13]So I ask you not to lose heart over what I am suffering for you, which is your glory.

Phil 2:1–11 (§242)

[1]So if there is any encouragement in Christ, any incentive of love, any participation in the Spirit, any affection and sympathy, [2]complete my joy by being of the same mind, having the same love, being in full accord and of one mind. [3]Do nothing from selfishness or conceit, but in humility count others better than yourselves. [4]Let each of you look not only to his own interests, but also to the interests of others. [5]Have this mind among yourselves, which is yours in Christ Jesus, [6]who, though he was in the form of God, did not count equality with God a thing to be grasped, [7]but emptied himself, taking the form of a servant, being born in the likeness of men. [8]And being found in human form he humbled himself and became obedient unto death, even death on a cross. [9]Therefore God has highly exalted him and bestowed on him the name which is above every name, [10]that at the name of Jesus every knee should bow, in heaven and on earth and under the earth, [11]and every tongue confess that Jesus Christ is Lord, to the glory of God the Father.

1 Thess 1:2–10 (§276)

[2]We give thanks to God always for you all, constantly mentioning you in our prayers, [3]remembering before our God and Father your work of faith and labor of love and steadfastness of hope in our Lord Jesus Christ. [4]For we know, brethren beloved by God, that he has chosen you; [5]for our gospel came to you not only in word, but also in power and in the Holy Spirit and with full conviction. You know what kind of men we proved to be among you for your sake. [6]And you became imitators of us and of the Lord, for you received the word in much affliction, with joy inspired by the Holy Spirit; [7]so that you became an example to the all the believers in Macedonia and in Achaia. [8]For not only has the word of the Lord sounded forth from you in Macedonia and Achaia, but your faith in God has gone forth everywhere, so that we need not say anything. [9]For they themselves report concerning us what a welcome we had among you, and how you turned to God from idols, to serve a living and true God, [10]and to wait for his Son from heaven, whom he raised from the dead, Jesus who delivers us from the wrath to come.

● **1 Cor 2:1**

2 Cor 11   [6]Even if I am unskilled in speaking, I am not in knowledge; in every way we have made this plain to you in all things.

(testimony) *read* mystery: p[46] S*AC it (few) syr (pes) cop (bo) Hippolytus

● **1 Cor 2:2**

Gal 6   [14]But far be it from me to glory except in the cross of our Lord Jesus Christ, by which the world has been crucified to me, and I to the world.

● **1 Cor 2:3**

Acts 18   [1]After this he left Athens and went to Corinth.

● **1 Cor 2:4–5**

Rom 1   [16]For I am not ashamed of the gospel: it is the power of God for salvation to every one who has faith, to the Jew first and also to the Greek. [17]For in it the righteousness of God is revealed through faith for faith; as it is written, "He who through faith is righteous shall live."

2 Cor 13   [3]since you desire proof that Christ is speaking in me. He is not weak in dealing with you, but is powerful in you. [4]For he was crucified in weakness, but lives by the power of God. For we are weak in him, but in dealing with you we shall live with him by the power of God.

● **1 Cor 2:4**

Rom 15   [18]For I will not venture to speak of anything except what Christ has wrought through me to win obedience from the Gentiles, by word and deed, [19]by the power of signs and wonders, by the power of the Holy Spirit, so that from Jerusalem and as far round as Illyricum I have fully preached the gospel of Christ, . . .

1 Cor 4   [20]For the kingdom of God does not consist in talk but in power.

[6]Yet among the mature we do impart wisdom, although it is not a wisdom of this age or of the rulers of this age, who are doomed to pass away. [7]But we impart a secret and hidden wisdom of God, which God decreed before the ages for our glorification. [8]None of the rulers of this age understood this; for if they had, they would not have crucified the Lord of glory. [9]But, as it is written,

"What no eye has seen, nor ear heard, nor the heart of man conceived,

what God has prepared for those who love him," [10]God has revealed to us through the Spirit. For the Spirit searches everything, even the depths of God. [11]For what person knows a man's thoughts except the spirit of the man which is in him? So also no one comprehends the thoughts of God except the Spirit of God. [12]Now we have received not the spirit of the world, but the Spirit which is from God, that we might understand the gifts bestowed on us by God. [13]And we impart this in words not taught by human wisdom but taught by the Spirit, interpreting spiritual truths to those who possess the Spirit.

[14]The unspiritual man does not receive the gifts of the Spirit of God, for they are folly to him, and he is not able to understand them because they are spiritually discerned. [15]The spiritual man judges all things, but is himself to be judged by no one. [16]"For who has known the mind of the Lord so as to instruct him?" But we have the mind of Christ.

PRIMARY

Rom 8:26–27 (§32)
[26]Likewise the Spirit helps us in our weakness; for we do not know how to pray as we ought, but the Spirit himself intercedes for us with sighs too deep for words. [27]And he who searches the hearts of men knows what is the mind of the Spirit, because the Spirit intercedes for the saints according to the will of God.

Rom 11:33–36 (§50)
[33]O the depth of the riches and wisdom and knowledge of God! How unsearchable are his judgments and how inscrutable his ways!
[34]"For who has known the mind of the Lord, or who has been his counselor?"
[35]"Or who has given a gift to him that he might be repaid?"
[36]For from him and through him and to him are all things. To him be glory for ever. Amen.

Gal 6:1–6 (§214)
6 [1]Brethren, if a man is overtaken in any trespass, you who are spiritual should restore him in a spirit of gentleness. Look to yourself, lest you too be tempted. [2]Bear one another's burdens, and so fulfil the law of Christ. [3]For if any one thinks he is something, when he is nothing, he deceives himself. [4]But let each one test his own work, and then his reason to boast will be in himself alone and not in his neighbor. [5]For each man will have to bear his own load.

[6]Let him who is taught the word share all good things with him who teaches.

Eph 3:1–13 (§222)
3 [1]For this reason I, Paul, a prisoner for Christ Jesus on behalf of you Gentiles — [2]assuming that you have heard of the stewardship of God's grace that was given to me for you, [3]how the mystery was made known to me by revelation, as I have written briefly. [4]When you read this you can perceive my insight into the mystery of Christ, [5]which was not made known to the sons of men in other generations as it has now been revealed to his holy apostles and prophets by the Spirit; [6]that is, how the Gentiles are fellow heirs, members of the same body, and partakers of the promise in Christ Jesus through the gospel.

[7]Of this gospel I was made a minister according to the gift of God's grace which was given me by the working of his power. [8]To me, though I am the very least of all the saints, this grace was given, to preach to the Gentiles the unsearchable riches of Christ, [9]and to make all men see what is the plan of the mystery hidden for ages in God who created all things; [10]that through the church the manifold wisdom of God might now be made known to the principalities and powers in the heavenly places. [11]This was according to the eternal purpose which he has realized in Christ Jesus our Lord, [12]in whom we have boldness and confidence of access through our faith in him. [13]So I ask you not to lose heart over what I am suffering for you, which is your glory.

Eph 4:11–16 (§226)
[11]And his gifts were that some should be apostles, some prophets, some evangelists, some pastors and teachers, [12]to equip the saints for the work of ministry, for building up the body of Christ, [13]until we all attain to the unity of the faith and of the knowledge of the Son of God, to mature manhood, to the measure of the stature of the fulness of Christ; [14]so that we may no longer be children, tossed to and fro and carried about with every wind of doctrine, by the cunning of men, by their craftiness in deceitful wiles. [15]Rather, speaking the truth in love, we are to grow up in every way into him who is the head, into Christ, [16]from whom the whole body, joined and knit together by every joint with which it is supplied, when each part is working properly, makes bodily growth and upbuilds itself in love.

Col 1:24–2:3 (§260)
[24]Now I rejoice in my sufferings for your sake, and in my flesh I complete what is lacking in Christ's afflictions for the sake of his body, that is, the church, [25]of which I became a minister according to the divine office which was given to me for you, to make the word of God fully known, [26]the mystery hidden for ages and generations but now made manifest to his saints. [27]To them God chose to make known how great among the Gentiles are the riches of the glory of this mystery, which is Christ in you, the hope of glory. [28]Him we proclaim warning every man and teaching every man in all wisdom, that we may present every man mature in Christ. [29]For this I toil, striving with all the energy which he mightily inspires within me.

2 [1]For I want you to know how greatly I strive for you, and for those at Laodicea, and for all who have not seen my face, [2]that their hearts may be encouraged as they are knit together in love, to have all the riches of assured understanding and the knowledge of God's mystery, of Christ, [3]in whom are hid all the treasures of wisdom and knowledge.

● **1 Cor 2:7**
Rom 16   [25]Now to him who is able to strengthen you according to my gospel and the preaching of Jesus Christ, according to the revelation of the mystery which was kept secret for long ages . . .

● **1 Cor 2:8**
Acts 2   [17]"And in the last days it shall be, God declares,
that I will pour out my Spirit upon all flesh,
and your sons and your daughters shall prophesy,
and your young men shall see visions,
and your old men shall dream dreams; . . ."

Acts 13   [27]"For those who live in Jerusalem and their rulers, because they did not recognize him nor understand the utterances of the prophets which are read every sabbath, fulfilled these by condemning him."

Acts 17   [30]"The times of ignorance God overlooked, but now he commands all men everywhere to repent. . . ."

● **1 Cor 2:9**
Isa 64   [4]From of old no one has heard or perceived by the ear,
no eye has seen a God besides thee, who works for those who wait for him.

● **1 Cor 2:12**
1 Cor 1   [7]so that you are not lacking in any spiritual gift, as you wait for the revealing of our Lord Jesus Christ; . . .

1 Cor 12   [4]Now there are varieties of gifts, but the same Spirit; . . .

● **1 Cor 2:14**
1 Cor 15   [44]It is sown a physical body, it is raised a spiritual body. If there is a physical body, there is also a spiritual body.

1 Cor 15   [46]But it is not the spiritual which is first but the physical, and then the spiritual.

● **1 Cor 2:16**
Isa 40   [13]Who has directed the Spirit of the Lord, or as his counselor has instructed him?
[14]Whom did he consult for his enlightenment, and who taught him the path of justice,
and taught him knowledge,
and showed him the way of understanding?

3 But I, brethren, could not address you as spiritual men, but as men of the flesh, as babes in Christ. ²I fed you with milk, not solid food; for you were not ready for it; and even yet you are not ready, ³for you are still of the flesh. For while there is jealousy and strife among you, are you not of the flesh, and behaving like ordinary men? ⁴For when one says, "I belong to Paul," and another, "I belong to Apollos," are you not merely men?

PRIMARY

Rom 8:1-8 (§29)

¹There is therefore now no condemnation for those who are in Christ Jesus. ²For the law of the Spirit of life in Christ Jesus has set me free from the law of sin and death. ³For God has done what the law, weakened by the flesh, could not do: sending his own Son in the likeness of sinful flesh and for sin, he condemned sin in the flesh, ⁴in order that the just requirement of the law might be fulfilled in us, who walk not according to the flesh but according to the Spirit. ⁵For those who live according to the flesh set their minds on the things of the flesh, but those who live according to the Spirit set their minds on the things of the Spirit. ⁶To set the mind on the flesh is death, but to set the mind on the Spirit is life and peace. ⁷For the mind that is set on the flesh is hostile to God; it does not submit to God's law, indeed it cannot; ⁸and those who are in the flesh cannot please God.

Rom 8:9-17 (§30)

⁹But you are not in the flesh, you are in the Spirit, if in fact the Spirit of God dwells in you. Any one who does not have the Spirit of Christ does not belong to him. ¹⁰But if Christ is in you, although your bodies are dead because of sin, your spirits are alive because of righteousness. ¹¹If the Spirit of him who raised Jesus from the dead dwells in you, he who raised Christ Jesus from the dead will give life to your mortal bodies also through his Spirit which dwells in you.

¹²So then, brethren, we are debtors, not to the flesh, to live according to the flesh—¹³for if you live according to the flesh you will die, but if by the Spirit you put to death the deeds of the body you will live. ¹⁴For all who are led by the Spirit of God are sons of God. ¹⁵For you did not receive the spirit of slavery to fall back into fear, but you have received the spirit of sonship. When we cry, "Abba! Father!" ¹⁶it is the Spirit himself bearing witness with our spirit that we are children of God, ¹⁷and if children, then heirs, heirs of God and fellow heirs with Christ, provided we suffer with him in order that we may also be glorified with him.

2 Cor 5:14-21 (§164)

¹⁴For the love of Christ controls us, because we are convinced that one has died for all; therefore all have died. ¹⁵And he died for all, that those who live might live no longer for themselves but for him who for their sake died and was raised.

¹⁶From now on, therefore, we regard no one from a human point of view; even though we once regarded Christ from a human point of view, we regard him thus no longer. ¹⁷Therefore, if any one is in Christ, he is a new creation; the old has passed away, behold, the new has come. ¹⁸All this is from God, who through Christ reconciled us to himself and gave us the ministry of reconciliation; ¹⁹that is, in Christ God was reconciling the world to himself, not counting their trespasses against them, and entrusting to us the message of reconciliation. ²⁰So we are ambassadors for Christ, God making his appeal through us. We beseech you on behalf of Christ, be reconciled to God. ²¹For our sake he made him to be sin who knew no sin, so that in him we might become the righteousness of God.

Gal 5:16-26 (§213)

¹⁶But I say, walk by the Spirit, and do not gratify the desires of the flesh. ¹⁷For the desires of the flesh are against the Spirit, and the desires of the Spirit are against the flesh; for these are opposed to each other, to prevent you from doing what you would. ¹⁸But if you are led by the Spirit you are not under the law. ¹⁹Now the works of the flesh are plain: fornication, impurity, licentiousness, ²⁰idolatry, sorcery, enmity, strife, jealousy, anger, selfishness, dissension, party spirit, ²¹envy, drunkenness, carousing, and the like. I warn you, as I warned you before, that those who do such things shall not inherit the kingdom of God. ²²But the fruit of the Spirit is love, joy, peace, patience, kindness, goodness, faithfulness, ²³gentleness, self-control; against such there is no law. ²⁴And those who belong to Christ Jesus have crucified the flesh with its passions and desires.

²⁵If we live by the Spirit, let us also walk by the Spirit. ²⁶Let us have no self-conceit, no provoking of one another, no envy of one another.

Eph 2:1-10 (§220)

¹And you he made alive, when you were dead through the trespasses and sins ²in which you once walked, following the course of this world, following the prince of the power of the air, the spirit that is now at work in the sons of disobedience. ³Among these we all once lived in the passions of our flesh, following the desires of body and mind, and so we were by nature children of wrath, like the rest of mankind. ⁴But God, who is rich in mercy, out of the great love with which he loved us, ⁵even when we were dead through our trespasses, made us alive together with Christ (by grace you have been saved), ⁶and raised us up with him, and made us sit with him in the heavenly places in Christ Jesus, ⁷that in the coming ages he might show the immeasurable riches of his grace in kindness toward us in Christ Jesus. ⁸For by grace you have been saved through faith; and this is not your own doing, it is the gift of God— ⁹not because of works, lest any man should boast. ¹⁰For we are his workmanship, created in Christ Jesus for good works, which God prepared beforehand, that we should walk in them.

● **1 Cor 3:1-2**

1 Cor 4   ¹⁴I do not write this to make you ashamed, but to admonish you as my beloved children.

Gal 4   ¹⁹My little children, with whom I am again in travail until Christ be formed in you!

Phil 2   ²²But Timothy's worth you know, how as a son with a father he has served with me in the gospel.

Phlm   ¹²I am sending him back to you, sending my very heart.

Cf. 1 Cor 14   ²⁰Brethren, do not be children in your thinking; be babes in evil, but in thinking be mature.

Cf. 2 Cor 6   ¹³In return—I speak as to children—widen your hearts also.

Cf. Eph 5   ¹Therefore be imitators of God, as beloved children.

Cf. Heb 5   ¹³for every one who lives on milk is unskilled in the word of righteousness, for he is a child.
¹⁴But solid food is for the mature, for those who have their faculties trained by practice to distinguish good from evil.

Cf. 1 Pet 2   ²Like newborn babes, long for the pure spiritual milk, that by it you may grow up to salvation; . . .

● **1 Cor 3:1**

Rom 7   ¹⁴We know that the law is spiritual; but I am carnal, sold under sin.

● **1 Cor 3:3**

Col 3   ⁹Do not lie to one another, seeing that you have put off the old nature with its practices ¹⁰and have put on the new nature, which is being renewed in knowledge after the image of its creator.

● **1 Cor 3:4**

1 Cor 1   ¹²What I mean is that each one of you says, "I belong to Paul," or "I belong to Apollos," or "I belong to Cephas," or "I belong to Christ."

1 Cor 3   ²²whether Paul or Apollos or Cephas or the world or life or death or the present or the future, all are yours; . . .

1 Cor 4   ⁶I have applied all this to myself and Apollos for your benefit, brethren, that you may learn by us not to go beyond what is written, that none of you may be puffed up in favor of one against another.

⁵**What then is Apollos? What is Paul? Servants through whom you believed, as the Lord assigned to each.** ⁶**I planted, Apollos watered, but God gave the growth.** ⁷**So neither he who plants nor he who waters is anything, but only God who gives the growth.** ⁸**He who plants and he who waters are equal, and each shall receive his wages according to his labor.** ⁹**For we are God's fellow workers; you are God's field, God's building.**

PRIMARY

2 Cor 10:13–18 (§178)

¹³But we will not boast beyond limit, but will keep to the limits God has apportioned us, to reach even to you. ¹⁴For we are not overextending ourselves, as though we did not reach you; we were the first to come all the way to you with the gospel of Christ. ¹⁵We do not boast beyond limit, in other men's labors; but our hope is that as your faith increases, our field among you may be greatly enlarged, ¹⁶so that we may preach the gospel in lands beyond you, without boasting of work already done in another's field. ¹⁷"Let him who boasts, boast of the Lord." ¹⁸For it is not the man who commends himself that is accepted, but the man whom the Lord commends.

Gal 2:1–10 (§197)

¹Then after fourteen years I went up again to Jerusalem with Barnabas, taking Titus along with me. ²I went up by revelation; and I laid before them (but privately before those who were of repute) the gospel which I preach among the Gentiles, lest somehow I should be running or had run in vain. ³But even Titus, who was with me, was not compelled to be circumcised, though he was a Greek. ⁴But because of false brethren secretly brought in, who slipped in to spy out our freedom which we have in Christ Jesus, that they might bring us into bondage— ⁵to them we did not yield submission even for a moment, that the truth of the gospel might be preserved for you. ⁶And from those who were reputed to be something (what they were makes no difference to me; God shows no partiality)—those, I say, who were of repute added nothing to me; ⁷but on the contrary, when they saw that I had been entrusted with the gospel to the uncircumcised, just as Peter had been entrusted with the gospel to the circumcised ⁸(for he who worked through Peter for the mission to the circumcised worked through me also for the Gentiles), ⁹and when they perceived the grace that was given to me, James and Cephas and John, who were reputed to be pillars, gave to me and Barnabas the right hand of fellowship, that we should go to the Gentiles and they to the circumcised; ¹⁰only they would have us remember the poor, which very thing I was eager to do.

Eph 2:11–22 (§221)

¹¹Therefore remember that at one time you Gentiles in the flesh, called the uncircumcision by what is called the circumcision, which is made in the flesh by hands— ¹²remember that you were at that time separated from Christ, alienated from the commonwealth of Israel, and strangers to the covenants of promise, having no hope and without God in the world. ¹³But now in Christ Jesus you who once were far off have been brought near in the blood of Christ. ¹⁴For he is our peace, who has made us both one, and has broken down the dividing wall of hostility, ¹⁵by abolishing in his flesh the law of commandments and ordinances, that he might create in himself one new man in place of the two, so making peace, ¹⁶and might reconcile us both to God in one body through the cross, thereby bringing the hostility to an end. ¹⁷And he came and preached peace to you who were far off and peace to those who were near; ¹⁸for through him we both have access in one Spirit to the Father. ¹⁹So then you are no longer strangers and sojourners, but you are fellow citizens with the saints and members of the household of God, ²⁰built upon the foundation of the apostles and prophets, Christ Jesus himself being the cornerstone, ²¹in whom the whole structure is joined together and grows into a holy temple in the Lord; ²²in whom you also are built into it for a dwelling place of God in the Spirit.

● **1 Cor 3:5–9**
Gal 6 ⁷Do not be deceived; God is not mocked, for whatever a man sows, that he will also reap. ⁸For he who sows to his own flesh will from the flesh reap corruption; but he who sows to the Spirit will from the Spirit reap eternal life. ⁹And let us not grow weary in well-doing, for in due season we shall reap, if we do not lose heart.

● **1 Cor 3:5**
Acts 18 ²⁴Now a Jew named Apollos, a native of Alexandria, came to Ephesus. He was an eloquent man, well versed in the scriptures.

● **1 Cor 3:7**
Rom 9 ¹⁶So it depends not upon man's will or exertion, but upon God's mercy.

● **1 Cor 3:8**
1 Cor 4 ¹⁵For though you have countless guides in Christ, you do not have many fathers. For I became your father in Christ Jesus through the gospel.

● **1 Cor 3:9**
1 Cor 16 ¹⁰When Timothy comes, see that you put him at ease among you, for he is doing the work of the Lord, as I am.

2 Cor 6 ¹⁶What agreement has the temple of God with idols? For we are the temple of the living God; . . .

Phil 2 ²⁵I have thought it necessary to send to you Epaphroditus my brother and fellow worker and fellow soldier, and your messenger and minister to my need, . . .

Col 4 ¹¹and Jesus who is called Justus. These are the only men of the circumcision among my fellow workers for the kingdom of God, and they have been a comfort to me.

¹⁰According to the grace of God given to me, like a skilled master builder I laid a foundation, and another man is building upon it. Let each man take care how he builds upon it. ¹¹For no other foundation can any one lay than that which is laid, which is Jesus Christ. ¹²Now if any one builds on the foundation with gold, silver, precious stones, wood, hay, straw—¹³each man's work will become manifest; for the Day will disclose it, because it will be revealed with fire, and the fire will test what sort of work each one has done. ¹⁴If the work which any man has built on the foundation survives, he will receive a reward. ¹⁵If any man's work is burned up, he will suffer loss, though he himself will be saved, but only as through fire.

PRIMARY

Rom 2:1–11 (§7–8)

¹Therefore you have no excuse, O man, whoever you are, when you judge another; for in passing judgment upon him you condemn yourself, because you, the judge, are doing the very same things. ²We know that the judgment of God rightly falls upon those who do such things. ³Do you suppose, O man, that when you judge those who do such things and yet do them yourself, you will escape the judgment of God? ⁴Or do you presume upon the riches of his kindness and forbearance and patience? Do you not know that God's kindness is meant to lead you to repentance? ⁵But by your hard and impenitent heart you are storing up wrath for yourself on the day of wrath when God's righteous judgment will be revealed. ⁶For he will render to every man according to his works: ⁷to those who by patience in well-doing seek for glory and honor and immortality, he will give eternal life; ⁸but for those who are factious and do not obey the truth, but obey wickedness, there will be wrath and fury. ⁹There will be tribulation and distress for every human being

who does evil, the Jew first and also the Greek, ¹⁰but glory and honor and peace for every one who does good, the Jew first and also the Greek. ¹¹For God shows no partiality.

2 Cor 10:13–18 (§178)

¹³But we will not boast beyond limit, but will keep to the limits God has apportioned us, to reach even to you. ¹⁴For we are not overextending ourselves, as though we did not reach you; we were the first to come all the way to you with the gospel of Christ. ¹⁵We do not boast beyond limit, in other men's labors; but our hope is that as your faith increases, our field among you may be greatly enlarged, ¹⁶so that we may preach the gospel in lands beyond you, without boasting of work already done in another's field. ¹⁷"Let him who boasts, boast of the Lord." ¹⁸For it is not the man who commends himself that is accepted, but the man whom the Lord commends.

Eph 2:11–22 (§221)

¹¹Therefore remember that at one time you Gentiles in the flesh, called the uncircumcision by what is called the circumcision, which is made in the flesh by hands— ¹²remember that you were at that time separated from Christ, alienated from the commonwealth of Israel, and strangers to the covenants of promise, having no hope and without God in the world. ¹³But now in Christ Jesus you who once were far off have been brought near in the blood of Christ. ¹⁴For he is our peace, who has made us both one, and has broken down the dividing wall of hostility, ¹⁵by abolishing in his flesh the law of commandments and ordinances, that he might create in himself one new man in place of the two, so making peace, ¹⁶and might reconcile us both to God in one body through the cross, thereby bringing the hostility to an end. ¹⁷And he came and preached peace to you who were far off and peace to those who were near; ¹⁸for through him we both have access in one Spirit to the

Father. ¹⁹So then you are no longer strangers and sojourners, but you are fellow citizens with the saints and members of the household of God, ²⁰built upon the foundation of the apostles and prophets, Christ Jesus himself being the cornerstone, ²¹in whom the whole structure is joined together and grows into a holy temple in the Lord; ²²in whom you also are built into it for a dwelling place of God in the Spirit.

2 Thess 1:3–12 (§295)

³We are bound to give thanks to God always for you, brethren, as is fitting, because your faith is growing abundantly, and the love of every one of you for one another is increasing. ⁴Therefore we ourselves boast of you in the churches of God for your steadfastness and faith in all your persecutions and in the afflictions which you are enduring.

⁵This is evidence of the righteous judgment of God, that you may be made worthy of the kingdom of God, for which you are suffering— ⁶since indeed God deems it just to repay with affliction those who afflict you, ⁷and to grant rest with us to you who are afflicted, when the Lord Jesus is revealed from heaven with his mighty angels in flaming fire, ⁸inflicting vengeance upon those who do not know God and upon those who do not obey the gospel of our Lord Jesus. ⁹They shall suffer the punishment of eternal destruction and exclusion from the presence of the Lord and from the glory of his might, ¹⁰when he comes on that day to be glorified in his saints, and to be marveled at in all who have believed, because our testimony to you was believed. ¹¹To this end we always pray for you, that our God may make you worthy of his call, and may fulfil every good resolve and work of faith by his power, ¹²so that the name of our Lord Jesus may be glorified in you, and you in him, according to the grace of our God and the Lord Jesus Christ.

● **1 Cor 3:10–14**

Rom 15   ²⁰thus making it my ambition to preach the gospel, not where Christ has already been named, lest I build on another man's foundation, . . .

2 Cor 6   ¹⁶What agreement has the temple of God with idols? For we are the temple of the living God; . . .

Gal 3   ⁹So then, those who are men of faith are blessed with Abraham who had faith.

Eph 3   ⁷Of this gospel I was made a minister according to the gift of God's grace which was given me by the working of his power.

2 Tim 2   ¹⁹But God's firm foundation stands, bearing this seal: "The Lord knows those who are his,"

and, "Let every one who names the name of the Lord depart from iniquity."

²⁰In a great house there are not only vessels of gold and silver but also of wood and earthenware, and some for noble use, some for ignoble.

● **1 Cor 3:10**

Rom 1   ⁵through whom we have received grace and apostleship to bring about the obedience of faith for the sake of his name among all the nations, . . .

Gal 2   ⁹and when they perceived the grace that was given to me, James and Cephas and John, who were reputed to be pillars, gave to me and Barnabas the right hand of fellowship, that we should go to the Gentiles and they to the circumcised; . . .

(God) *omit* of God: p⁴⁶ it (few) Clement

● **1 Cor 3:13**

Rom 2   ¹⁶on that day when, according to my gospel, God judges the secrets of men by Christ Jesus.

1 Thess 5   ²For you yourselves know well that the day of the Lord will come like a thief in the night.

● **1 Cor 3:15**

1 Cor 5   ³For though absent in body I am present in spirit, and as if present, I have already pronounced judgment ⁴in the name of the Lord Jesus on the man who has done such a thing. When you are assembled, and my spirit is present, with the power of our Lord Jesus, ⁵you are to deliver this man to Satan for the destruction of the flesh, that his spirit may be saved in the day of the Lord Jesus.

[16] Do you not know that you are God's temple and that God's Spirit dwells in you? [17] If any one destroys God's temple, God will destroy him. For God's temple is holy, and that temple you are.

PRIMARY

2 Cor 6:14–7:1 (§167)

[14] Do not be mismated with unbelievers. For what partnership have righteousness and iniquity? Or what fellowship has light with darkness? [15] What accord has Christ with Belial? Or what has a believer in common with an unbeliever? [16] What agreement has the temple of God with idols? For we are the temple of the living God; as God said,

"I will live in them and move among them,
and I will be their God,
and they shall be my people.

[17] Therefore come out from them,
and be separate from them, says the Lord,
and touch nothing unclean;
then I will welcome you,
[18] and I will be a father to you,
and you shall be my sons and daughters,
says the Lord Almighty."

[1] Since we have these promises, beloved, let us cleanse ourselves from every defilement of body and spirit, and make holiness perfect in the fear of God.

Eph 2:11–22 (§221)

[11] Therefore remember that at one time you Gentiles in the flesh, called the uncircumcision by what is called the circumcision, which is made in the flesh by hands — [12] remember that you were at that time separated from Christ, alienated from the commonwealth of Israel, and strangers to the covenants of promise, having no hope and without God in the world. [13] But now in Christ Jesus you who once were far off have been brought near in the blood of Christ. [14] For he is our peace, who has made us both one, and has broken down the dividing wall of hostility, [15] by abolishing in his flesh the law of commandments and ordinances, that he might create in himself one new man in place of the two, so making peace, [16] and might reconcile us both to God in one body through the cross, thereby bringing the hostility to an end. [17] And he came and preached peace to you who were far off and peace to those who were near; [18] for through him we both have access in one Spirit to the Father. [19] So then you are no longer strangers and sojourners, but you are fellow citizens with the saints and members of the household of God, [20] built upon the foundation of the apostles and prophets, Christ Jesus himself being the cornerstone, [21] in whom the whole structure is joined together and grows into a holy temple in the Lord; [22] in whom you also are built into it for a dwelling place of God in the Spirit.

● **1 Cor 3:16–17**

1 Cor 6   [12] "All things are lawful for me," but not all things are helpful. "All things are lawful for me," but I will not be enslaved by anything. [13] "Food is meant for the stomach and the stomach for food"—and God will destroy both one and the other. The body is not meant for immorality, but for the Lord, and the Lord for the body. [14] And God raised the Lord and will also raise us up by his power. [15] Do you not know that your bodies are members of Christ? Shall I therefore take the members of Christ and make them members of a prostitute? Never! [16] Do you not know that he who joins himself to a prostitute becomes one body with her? For, as it is written, "The two shall become one flesh." [17] But he who is united to the Lord becomes one spirit with him. [18] Shun immorality. Every other sin which a man commits is outside the body; but the immoral man sins against his own body. [19] Do you not know that your body is a temple of the Holy Spirit within you, which you have from God? You are not your own; [20] you were bought with a price. So glorify God in your body.

● **1 Cor 3:16**

Rom 8   [9] But you are not in the flesh, you are in the Spirit, if in fact the Spirit of God dwells in you. Any one who does not have the Spirit of Christ does not belong to him. [10] But if Christ is in you, although your bodies are dead because of sin, your spirits are alive because of righteousness. [11] If the Spirit of him who raised Jesus from the dead dwells in you, he who raised Christ Jesus from the dead will give life to your mortal bodies also through his Spirit which dwells in you.

18 Let no one deceive himself. If any one among you thinks that he is wise in this age, let him become a fool that he may become wise. 19 For the wisdom of this world is folly with God. For it is written, "He catches the wise in their craftiness," 20 and again, "The Lord knows that the thoughts of the wise are futile." 21 So let no one boast of men. For all things are yours, 22 whether Paul or Apollos or Cephas or the world or life or death or the present or the future, all are yours; 23 and you are Christ's; and Christ is God's.

PRIMARY

Rom 8:31–39 (§34)

31 What then shall we say to this? If God is for us, who is against us? 32 He who did not spare his own Son but gave him up for us all, will he not also give us all things with him? 33 Who shall bring any charge against God's elect? It is God who justifies; 34 who is to condemn? Is it Christ Jesus, who died, yes, who was raised from the dead, who is at the right hand of God, who indeed intercedes for us? 35 Who shall separate us from the love of Christ? Shall tribulation, or distress, or persecution, or famine, or nakedness, or peril, or sword? 36 As it is written,

"For thy sake we are being killed all the day long;

we are regarded as sheep to be slaughtered."
37 No, in all these things we are more than conquerors through him who loved us. 38 For I am sure that neither death, nor life, nor angels, nor principalities, nor things present, nor things to come, nor powers, 39 nor height, nor depth, nor anything else in all creation, will be able to separate us from the love of God in Christ Jesus our Lord.

2 Cor 11:16–21a (§182)

16 I repeat, let no one think me foolish; but even if you do, accept me as a fool, so that I too may boast a little. 17 (What I am saying I say not with the Lord's authority but as a fool, in this boastful confidence; 18 since many boast of worldly things, I too will boast.) 19 For you gladly bear with fools, being wise yourselves! 20 For you bear it if a man makes slaves of you, or preys upon you, or takes advantage of you, or puts on airs, or strikes you in the face. 21 To my shame, I must say, we were too weak for that!

Eph 3:14–19 (§223)

14 For this reason I bow my knees before the Father, 15 from whom every family in heaven and on earth is named, 16 that according to the riches of his glory he may grant you to be strengthened with might through his Spirit in the inner man, 17 and that Christ may dwell in your hearts through faith; that you, being rooted and grounded in love, 18 may have power to comprehend with all the saints what is the breadth and length and height and depth, 19 and to know the love of Christ which surpasses knowledge, that you may be filled with all the fulness of God.

● 1 Cor 3:18–23

Rom 11   33 O the depth of the riches and wisdom and knowledge of God! How unsearchable are his judgments and how inscrutable his ways!

34 "For who has known the mind of the Lord, or who has been his counselor?"

35 "Or who has given a gift to him that he might be repaid?"

36 For from him and through him and to him are all things. To him be glory for ever. Amen.

1 Cor 1   18 For the word of the cross is folly to those who are perishing, but to us who are being saved it is the power of God. 19 For it is written,

"I will destroy the wisdom of the wise, and the cleverness of the clever I will thwart."

20 Where is the wise man? Where is the scribe? Where is the debater of this age? Has not God made foolish the wisdom of the world? 21 For since, in the wisdom of God, the world did not know God through wisdom, it pleased God through the folly of what we preach to save those who believe. 22 For Jews demand signs and Greeks seek wisdom, 23 but we preach Christ crucified, a stumbling block to Jews and folly to Gentiles, 24 but to those who are called, both Jews and Greeks, Christ the power of God and the wisdom of God. 25 For the foolishness of God is wiser than men, and the weakness of God is stronger than men.

26 For consider your call, brethren; not many of you were wise according to worldly standards, not many were powerful, not many were of noble birth; 27 but God chose what is foolish in the world to shame the wise, God chose what is weak in the world to shame the strong, 28 God chose what is low and despised in the world, even things that are not, to bring to nothing things that are, 29 so that no human being might boast in the presence of God. 30 He is the source of your life in Christ Jesus, whom God made our wisdom, our righteousness and sanctification and redemption; 31 therefore, as it is written, "Let him who boasts, boast of the Lord."

2 When I came to you, brethren, I did not come proclaiming to you the testimony of God in lofty words or wisdom. 2 For I decided to know nothing among you except Jesus Christ and him crucified. 3 And I was with you in weakness and in much fear and trembling; 4 and my speech and my message were not in plausible words of wisdom, but in demonstration of the Spirit and of power, 5 that your faith might not rest in the wisdom of men but in the power of God.

6 Yet among the mature we do impart wisdom, although it is not a wisdom of this age or of the rulers of this age, who are doomed to pass away. 7 But we impart a secret and hidden wisdom of God, which God decreed before the ages for our glorification. 8 None of the rulers of this age understood this; for if they had, they would not have crucified the Lord of glory. 9 But, as it is written,

"What no eye has seen, nor ear heard, nor the heart of man conceived,

what God has prepared for those who love him,"
. . .

2 Cor 11   12 And what I do I will continue to do, in order to undermine the claim of those who would like to claim that in their boasted mission they work on the same terms as we do. 13 For such men are false apostles, deceitful workmen, disguising themselves as apostles of Christ. 14 And no wonder, for even Satan disguises himself as an angel of light. 15 So it is not strange if his servants also disguise themselves as servants of righteousness. Their end will correspond to their deeds.

2 Thess 2   9 The coming of the lawless one by the activity of Satan will be with all power and with pretended signs and wonders, 10 and with all wicked deception for those who are to perish, because they refused to love the truth and so be saved. 11 Therefore God sends upon them a strong delusion, to make them believe what is false, . . .

● 1 Cor 3:18

2 Cor 11   3 But I am afraid that as the serpent deceived Eve by his cunning, your thoughts will be led astray from a sincere and pure devotion to Christ.

Gal 6   7 Do not be deceived; God is not mocked, for whatever a man sows, that he will also reap.

● 1 Cor 3:19

Rom 12   3 For by the grace given to me I bid every one among you not to think of himself more highly than he ought to think, but to think with sober judgment, each according to the measure of faith which God has assigned him.

Job 5   13 He takes the wise in their own craftiness; and the schemes of the wily are brought to a quick end.

● 1 Cor 3:20

Ps 94   11 the Lord, knows the thoughts of man, that they are but a breath.

● 1 Cor 3:21

Rom 3   27 Then what becomes of our boasting? It is excluded. On what principle? On the principle of works? No, but on the principle of faith.

● 1 Cor 3:22

1 Cor 1   12 What I mean is that each one of you says, "I belong to Paul," or "I belong to Apollos," or "I belong to Cephas," or "I belong to Christ." 13 Is Christ divided? Was Paul crucified for you? Or where you baptized in the name of Paul?

1 Cor 3   4 For when one says, "I belong to Paul," and another, "I belong to Apollos," are you not merely men?

1 Cor 4   6 I have applied all this to myself and Apollos for your benefit, brethren, that you may learn by us not to go beyond what is written, that none of you may be puffed up in favor of one against another.

● 1 Cor 3:23

1 Cor 11   3 But I want you to understand that the head of every man is Christ, the head of a woman is her husband, and the head of Christ is God.

4 This is how one should regard us, as servants of Christ and stewards of the mysteries of God. [2]Moreover it is required of stewards that they be found trustworthy. [3]But with me it is a very small thing that I should be judged by you or by any human court. I do not even judge myself. [4]I am not aware of anything against myself, but I am not thereby acquitted. It is the Lord who judges me. [5]Therefore do not pronounce judgment before the time, before the Lord comes, who will bring to light the things now hidden in darkness and will disclose the purposes of the heart. Then every man will receive his commendation from God.

PRIMARY

Rom 2:12–16 (§9)

[12]All who have sinned without the law will also perish without the law, and all who have sinned under the law will be judged by the law. [13]For it is not the hearers of the law who are righteous before God, but the doers of the law who will be justified. [14]When Gentiles who have not the law do by nature what the law requires, they are a law to themselves, even though they do not have the law. [15]They show that what the law requires is written on their hearts, while their conscience also bears witness and their conflicting thoughts accuse or perhaps excuse them [16]on that day when, according to my gospel, God judges the secrets of men by Christ Jesus.

Rom 13:1–7 (§54)

[1]Let every person be subject to the governing authorities. For there is no authority except from God, and those that exist have been instituted by God. [2]Therefore he who resists the authorities resists what God has appointed, and those who resist will incur judgment. [3]For rulers are not a terror to good conduct, but to bad. Would you have no fear of him who is in authority? Then do what is good, and you will receive his approval, [4]for he is God's servant for your good. But if you do wrong, be afraid, for he does not bear the sword in vain; he is the servant of God to execute his wrath on the wrongdoer. [5]Therefore one must be subject, not only to avoid God's wrath but also for the sake of conscience. [6]For the same reason you also pay taxes, for the authorities are ministers of God, attending to this very thing. [7]Pay all of them their dues, taxes to whom taxes are due, revenue to whom revenue is due, respect to whom respect is due, honor to whom honor is due.

Rom 14:13–23 (§59)

[13]Then let us no more pass judgment on one another, but rather decide never to put a stumbling block or hindrance in the way of a brother. [14]I know and am persuaded in the Lord Jesus that nothing is unclean in itself; but it is unclean for any one who thinks it unclean. [15]If your brother is being injured by what you eat, you are no longer walking in love. Do not let what you eat cause the ruin of one for whom Christ died. [16]So do not let your good be spoken of as evil. [17]For the kingdom of God is not food and drink but righteousness and peace and joy in the Holy Spirit; [18]he who thus serves Christ is acceptable to God and approved by men. [19]Let us then pursue what makes for peace and for mutual upbuilding. [20]Do not, for the sake of food, destroy the work of God. Everything is indeed clean, but it is wrong for any one to make others fall by what he eats; [21]it is right not to eat meat or drink wine or do anything that makes your brother stumble. [22]The faith that you have, keep between yourself and God; happy is he who has no reason to judge himself for what he approves. [23]But he who has doubts is condemned, if he eats, because he does not act from faith; for whatever does not proceed from faith is sin.

Col 1:24–2:3 (§260)

[24]Now I rejoice in my sufferings for your sake, and in my flesh I complete what is lacking in Christ's afflictions for the sake of his body, that is, the church, [25]of which I became a minister according to the divine office which was given to me for you, to make the word of God fully known, [26]the mystery hidden for ages and generations but now made manifest to his saints. [27]To them God chose to make known how great among the Gentiles are the riches of the glory of this mystery, which is Christ in you, the hope of glory. [28]Him we proclaim warning every man and teaching every man in all wisdom, that we may present every man mature in Christ. [29]For this I toil, striving with all the energy which he mightily inspires within me. [1]For I want you to know how greatly I strive for you, and for those at Laodicea, and for all who have not seen my face, [2]that their hearts may be encouraged as they are knit together in love, to have all the riches of assured understanding and the knowledge of God's mystery, of Christ, [3]in whom are hid all the treasures of wisdom and knowledge.

Col 2:16–19 (§263)

[16]Therefore let no one pass judgment on you in questions of food and drink or with regard to a festival or a new moon or a sabbath. [17]These are only a shadow of what is to come; but the substance belongs to Christ. [18]Let no one disqualify you, insisting on self-abasement and worship of angels, taking his stand on visions, puffed up without reason by his sensuous mind, [19]and not holding fast to the Head, from whom the whole body, nourished and knit together through its joints and ligaments, grows with a growth that is from God.

● **1 Cor 4:1–5**

1 Cor 8   [7]However, not all possess this knowledge. But some, through being hitherto accustomed to idols, eat food as really offered to an idol; and their conscience, being weak, is defiled. [8]Food will not commend us to God. We are no worse off if we do not eat, and no better off if we do. [9]Only take care lest this liberty of yours somehow become a stumbling block to the weak. [10]For if any one sees you, a man of knowledge, at table in an idol's temple, might he not be encouraged, if his conscience is weak, to eat food offered to idols?

1 Cor 10   [25]Eat whatever is sold in the meat market without raising any question on the ground of conscience. [26]For "the earth is the Lord's, and everything in it." [27]If one of the unbelievers invites you to dinner and you are disposed to go, eat whatever is set before you without raising any question on the ground of conscience. [28](But if some one says to you, "This has been offered in sacrifice," then out of consideration for the man who informed you, and for conscience' sake — [29]I mean his conscience, not yours—do not eat it.) For why should my liberty be determined by another man's scruples?

● **1 Cor 4:1**

Rom 11   [25]Lest you be wise in your own conceits, I want you to understand this mystery, brethren: a hardening has come upon part of Israel, until the full number of the Gentiles come in, . . .

Rom 16   [25]Now to him who is able to strengthen you according to my gospel and the preaching of Jesus Christ, according to the revelation of the mystery which was kept secret for long ages . . .

1 Cor 14   [2]For one who speaks in a tongue speaks not to men but to God; for no one understands him, but he utters mysteries in the Spirit.

Eph 3   [3]how the mystery was made known to me by revelation, as I have written briefly. [4]When you read this you can perceive my insight into the mystery of Christ, [5]which was not made known to the sons of men in other generations as it has now been revealed to his holy apostles and prophets by the Spirit; . . .

Col 1   [25]of which I became a minister according to the divine office which was given to me for you, to make the word of God fully known, . . .

2 Thess 2   [7]For the mystery of lawlessness is already at work; only he who now restrains it will do so until he is out of the way.

1 Tim 1   [7]desiring to be teachers of the law, without understanding either what they are saying or the things about which they make assertions.

See Eph 3:9; Eph 6:19; Col 2:2; Col 4:3

● **1 Cor 4:3**

1 Cor 6   [1]When one of you has a grievance against a brother, does he dare go to law before the unrighteous instead of the saints? [2]Do you not know that the saints will judge the world? And if the world is to be judged by you, are you incompetent to try trivial cases?

● **1 Cor 4:4**

Acts 23   [1]And Paul, looking intently at the council, said, "Brethren, I have lived before God in all good conscience up to this day."

● **1 Cor 4:5**

Col 2   [16]Therefore let no one pass judgment on you in questions of food and drink or with regard to a festival or a new moon or a sabbath.

⁶I have applied all this to myself and Apollos for your benefit, brethren, that you may learn by us not to go beyond what is written, that none of you may be puffed up in favor of one against another. ⁷For who sees anything different in you? What have you that you did not receive? If then you received it, why do you boast as if it were not a gift?

PRIMARY

Rom 3:21–26 (§14)

²¹But now the righteousness of God has been manifested apart from law, although the law and the prophets bear witness to it, ²²the righteousness of God through faith in Jesus Christ for all who believe. For there is no distinction; ²³since all have sinned and fall short of the glory of God, ²⁴they are justified by his grace as a gift, through the redemption which is in Christ Jesus, ²⁵whom God put forward as an expiation by his blood, to be received by faith. This was to show God's righteousness, because in his divine forbearance he had passed over former sins; ²⁶it was to prove at the present time that he himself is righteous and that he justifies him who has faith in Jesus.

Rom 11:17–24 (§48)

¹⁷But if some of the branches were broken off, and you, a wild olive shoot, were grafted in their place to share the richness of the olive tree, ¹⁸do not boast over the branches. If you do boast, remember it is not you that support the root, but the root that supports you. ¹⁹You will say, "Branches were broken off so that I might be grafted in." ²⁰That is true. They were broken off because of their unbelief, but you stand fast only through faith. So do not become proud, but stand in awe. ²¹For if God did not spare the natural branches, neither will he spare you. ²²Note then the kindness and the severity of God: severity toward those who have fallen, but God's kindness to you, provided you continue in his kindness; otherwise you too will be cut off. ²³And even the others, if they do not persist in their unbelief, will be grafted in, for God has the power to graft them in again. ²⁴For if you have been cut from what is by nature a wild olive tree, and grafted, contrary to nature, into a cultivated olive tree, how much more will these natural branches be grafted back into their own olive tree.

Rom 12:3–8 (§52)

³For by the grace given to me I bid every one among you not to think of himself more highly than he ought to think, but to think with sober judgment, each according to the measure of faith which God has assigned him. ⁴For as in one body we have many members, and all the members do not have the same function, ⁵so we, though many, are one body in Christ, and individually members one of another. ⁶Having gifts that differ according to the grace given to us, let us use them: if prophecy, in proportion to our faith; ⁷if service, in our serving; he who teaches, in his teaching; ⁸he who exhorts, in his exhortation; he who contributes, in liberality; he who gives aid, with zeal; he who does acts of mercy, with cheerfulness.

2 Cor 3:4–6 (§155)

⁴Such is the confidence that we have through Christ toward God. ⁵Not that we are competent of ourselves to claim anything as coming from us; our competence is from God, ⁶who has made us competent to be ministers of a new covenant, not in a written code but in the Spirit; for the written code kills, but the Spirit gives life.

Eph 2:1–10 (§220)

¹And you he made alive, when you were dead through the trespasses and sins ²in which you once walked, following the course of this world, following the prince of the power of the air, the spirit that is now at work in the sons of disobedience. ³Among these we all once lived in the passions of our flesh, following the desires of body and mind, and so we were by nature children of wrath, like the rest of mankind. ⁴But God, who is rich in mercy, out of the great love with which he loved us, ⁵even when we were dead through our trespasses, made us alive together with Christ (by grace you have been saved), ⁶and raised us up with him, and made us sit with him in the heavenly places in Christ Jesus, ⁷that in the coming ages he might show the immeasurable riches of his grace in kindness toward us in Christ Jesus. ⁸For by grace you have been saved through faith; and this is not your own doing, it is the gift of God— ⁹not because of works, lest any man should boast. ¹⁰For we are his workmanship, created in Christ Jesus for good works, which God prepared beforehand, that we should walk in them.

Phil 3:2–11 (§247)

²Look out for the dogs, look out for the evil workers, look out for those who mutilate the flesh. ³For we are the true circumcision, who worship God in spirit, and glory in Christ Jesus, and put no confidence in the flesh. ⁴Though I myself have reason for confidence in the flesh also. If any other man thinks he has reason for confidence in the flesh, I have more: ⁵circumcised on the eighth day, of the people of Israel, of the tribe of Benjamin, a Hebrew born of Hebrews; as to the law a Pharisee, ⁶as to zeal a persecutor of the church, as to righteousness under the law blameless. ⁷But whatever gain I had, I counted as loss for the sake of Christ. ⁸Indeed I count everything as loss because of the surpassing worth of knowing Christ Jesus my Lord. For his sake I have suffered the loss of all things, and count them as refuse, in order that I may gain Christ ⁹and be found in him, not having a righteousness of my own, based on law, but that which is through faith in Christ, the righteousness from God that depends on faith; ¹⁰that I may know him and the power of his resurrection, and may share his sufferings, becoming like him in his death, ¹¹that if possible I may attain the resurrection from the dead.

● **1 Cor 4:6**

1 Cor 1   ¹²What I mean is that each one of you says, "I belong to Paul," or "I belong to Apollos," or "I belong to Cephas," or "I belong to Christ." ¹³Is Christ divided? Was Paul crucified for you? Or where you baptized in the name of Paul?

1 Cor 3   ⁴For when one says, "I belong to Paul," and another, "I belong to Apollos," are you not merely men? ⁵What then is Apollos? What is Paul? Servants through whom you believed, as the Lord assigned to each. ⁶I planted, Apollos watered, but God gave the growth.

1 Cor 3   ²¹So let no one boast of men. For all things are yours, ²²whether Paul or Apollos or Cephas or the world or life or death or the present or the future, all are yours; ²³and you are Christ's; and Christ is God's.

Gal 2   ⁹and when they perceived the grace that was given to me, James and Cephas and John, who were reputed to be pillars, gave to me and Barnabas the right hand of fellowship, that we should go to the Gentiles and they to the circumcised; ¹⁰only they would have us remember the poor, which very thing I was eager to do.

Col 2   ¹⁸Let no one disqualify you, insisting on self-abasement and worship of angels, taking his stand on visions, puffed up without reason by his sensuous mind, . . .

● **1 Cor 4:7**

Rom 3   ²⁷Then what becomes of our boasting? It is excluded. On what principle? On the principle of works? No, but on the principle of faith.

1 Cor 1   ²⁶For consider your call, brethren; not many of you were wise according to worldly standards, not many were powerful, not many were of noble birth; . . .

Gal 6   ¹⁴But far be it from me to glory except in the cross of our Lord Jesus Christ, by which the world has been crucified to me, and I to the world.

FORMAL ELEMENT: HARDSHIPS LIST

8 Already you are filled! Already you have become rich! Without us you have become kings! And would that you did reign, so that we might share the rule with you! 9 For I think that God has exhibited us apostles as last of all, like men sentenced to death; because we have become a spectacle to the world, to angels and to men. 10 We are fools for Christ's sake, but you are wise in Christ. We are weak, but you are strong. You are held in honor, but we in disrepute. 11 To the present hour we hunger and thirst, we are ill-clad and buffeted and homeless, 12 and we labor, working with our own hands. When reviled, we bless; when persecuted, we endure; 13 when slandered, we try to conciliate; we have become, and are now, as the refuse of the world, the offscouring of all things.

PRIMARY

See §34 for HARDSHIPS LIST

SECONDARY

Rom 5:1–5 (§20)
1 Therefore, since we are justified by faith, we have peace with God through our Lord Jesus Christ. 2 Through him we have obtained access to this grace in which we stand, and we rejoice in our hope of sharing the glory of God. 3 More than that, we rejoice in our sufferings, knowing that suffering produces endurance, 4 and endurance produces character, and character produces hope, 5 and hope does not disappoint us, because God's love has been poured into our hearts through the Holy Spirit which has been given to us.

2 Cor 1:3–11 (§147)
3 Blessed be the God and Father of our Lord Jesus Christ, the Father of mercies and God of all comfort, 4 who comforts us in all our afflic-

tion, so that we may be able to comfort those who are in any affliction, with the comfort with which we ourselves are comforted by God. 5 For as we share abundantly in Christ's sufferings, so through Christ we share abundantly in comfort too. 6 If we are afflicted, it is for your comfort and salvation; and if we are comforted, it is for your comfort, which you experience when you patiently endure the same sufferings that we suffer. 7 Our hope for you is unshaken; for we know that as you share in our sufferings, you will also share in our comfort.

8 For we do not want you to be ignorant, brethren, of the affliction we experienced in Asia; for we were so utterly, unbearably crushed that we despaired of life itself. 9 Why, we felt that we had received the sentence of death; but that was to make us rely not on ourselves but on God who raises the dead; 10 he delivered us from so deadly a peril, and he will deliver us; on him we have set our hope that he will deliver us again. 11 You also must help us by prayer, so that many will give thanks on our behalf for the blessing granted us in answer to many prayers.

2 Cor 12:1–10 (§185)
1 I must boast; there is nothing to be gained by it, but I will go on to visions and revelations of the Lord. 2 I know a man in Christ who fourteen years ago was caught up to the third heaven—whether in the body or out of the body I do not know, God knows. 3 And I know that this man was caught up into Paradise—whether in the body or out of the body I do not know, God knows— 4 and he heard things that cannot be told, which man may not utter. 5 On behalf of this man I will boast, but on my own behalf I will not boast, except of my weaknesses. 6 Though if I wish to boast, I shall not be a fool, for I shall be speaking the truth. But I refrain from it, so that no one may think more of me than he sees in me or hears from me. 7 And to keep me from being too elated by the abundance of revelations, a thorn was given me in the flesh, a messenger of Satan, to harass me,

to keep me from being too elated. 8 Three times I besought the Lord about this, that it should leave me; 9 but he said to me, "My grace is sufficient for you, for my power is made perfect in weakness." I will all the more gladly boast of my weaknesses, that the power of Christ may rest upon me. 10 For the sake of Christ, then, I am content with weaknesses, insults, hardships, persecutions, and calamities; for when I am weak, then I am strong.

1 Thess 2:9–12 (§278)
9 For you remember our labor and toil, brethren; we worked night and day, that we might not burden any of you, while we preached to you the gospel of God. 10 You are witnesses, and God also, how holy and righteous and blameless was our behavior to you believers; 11 for you know how, like a father with his children, we exhorted each one of you and encouraged you and charged you 12 to lead a life worthy of God, who calls you into his own kingdom and glory.

2 Thess 3:6–13 (§300)
6 Now we command you, brethren, in the name of our Lord Jesus Christ, that you keep away from any brother who is living in idleness and not in accord with the tradition that you received from us. 7 For you yourselves know how you ought to imitate us; we were not idle when we were with you, 8 we did not eat any one's bread without paying, but with toil and labor we worked night and day, that we might not burden any of you. 9 It was not because we have not that right, but to give you in our conduct an example to imitate. 10 For even when we were with you, we gave you this command: If any one will not work, let him not eat. 11 For we hear that some of you are living in idleness, mere busybodies, not doing any work. 12 Now such persons we command and exhort in the Lord Jesus Christ to do their work in quietness and to earn their own living. 13 Brethren, do not be weary in well-doing.

● **1 Cor 4:8**
2 Cor 11   7 Did I commit a sin in abasing myself so that you might be exalted, because I preached God's gospel without cost to you?

● **1 Cor 4:9**
2 Cor 12   11 I have been a fool! You forced me to it, for I ought to have been commended by you. For I was not at all inferior to these superlative apostles, even though I am nothing. 12 The signs of a true apostle were performed among you in all patience, with signs and wonders and mighty works. 13 For in what were you less favored than the rest of the churches, except that I myself did not burden you? Forgive me this wrong!

Phil 4   11 Not that I complain of want; for I have learned, in whatever state I am, to be content. 12 I know how to be abased, and I know how to abound; in any and all circumstances I have learned the secret of facing plenty and hunger, abundance and want.

Col 1   24 Now I rejoice in my sufferings for your sake, and in my flesh I complete what is lacking in Christ's afflictions for the sake of his body, that is, the church, . . .

Acts 5   40 So they took his advice, and when they had called in the apostles, they beat them and charged them not to speak in the name of Jesus, and let them go.

Cf. 1 Cor 15   7 Then he appeared to James, then to all the apostles. 8 Last of all, as to one untimely born, he appeared also to me. 9 For I am the least of the apostles, unfit to be called an apostle, because I persecuted the church of God. 10 But by the grace of God I am what I am, and his grace toward me was not in vain. On the contrary, I worked harder than any of them, though it was not I, but the grace of God which is with me. 11 Whether then it was I or they, so we preach and so you believed.

Cf. Gal 1:17

Cf. 1 Thess 3   1 Therefore when we could bear it no longer, we were willing to be left behind at Athens alone, 2 and we sent Timothy, our brother and God's servant in the gospel of Christ, to establish you in your faith and to exhort you, 3 that no one be moved by these afflictions. You yourselves know that this is to be our lot. 4 For when we were with you, we told you beforehand that we were to suffer affliction; just as it has come to pass, and as you know. 5 For this reason,

when I could bear it no longer, I sent that I might know your faith, for fear that somehow the tempter had tempted you and that our labor would be in vain.

● **1 Cor 4:10**
Acts 17   18 Some also of the Epicurean and Stoic philosophers met him. And some said, "What would this babbler say?" Others said, "He seems to be a preacher of foreign divinities"—because he preached Jesus and the resurrection. . . .

Cf. Acts 26   24 And as he thus made his defense, Festus said with a loud voice, "Paul, you are mad; your great learning is turning you mad."

● **1 Cor 4:12**
1 Cor 9   6 Or is it only Barnabas and I who have no right to refrain from working for a living?

Acts 20   34 "You yourselves know that these hands ministered to my necessities, and to those who were with me."

Cf. Acts 18   3 and because he was of the same trade he stayed with them, and they worked, for by trade they were tentmakers.

FORMAL ELEMENT: APOSTOLIC VISIT

I do not write this to make you ashamed, but to admonish you as my beloved children. ¹⁵For though you have countless guides in Christ, you do not have many fathers. For I became your father in Christ Jesus through the gospel. ¹⁶I urge you, then, be imitators of me. ¹⁷Therefore I sent to you Timothy, my beloved and faithful child in the Lord, to remind you of my ways in Christ, as I teach them everywhere in every church. ¹⁸Some are arrogant, as though I were not coming to you. ¹⁹But I will come to you soon, if the Lord wills, and I will find out not the talk of these arrogant people but their power. ²⁰For the kingdom of God does not consist in talk but in power. ²¹What do you wish? Shall I come to you with a rod, or with love in a spirit of gentleness?

PRIMARY

Rom 1:8–15 (§2)

⁸First, I thank my God through Jesus Christ for all of you, because your faith is proclaimed in all the world. ⁹For God is my witness, whom I serve with my spirit in the gospel of his Son, that without ceasing I mention you always in my prayers, ¹⁰asking that somehow by God's will I may now at last succeed in coming to you. ¹¹For I long to see you, that I may impart to you some spiritual gift to strengthen you, ¹²that is, that we may be mutually encouraged by each other's faith, both yours and mine. ¹³I want you to know, brethren, that I have often intended to come to you (but thus far have been prevented), in order that I may reap some harvest among you as well as among the rest of the Gentiles. ¹⁴I am under obligation both to Greeks and to barbarians, both to the wise and to the foolish: ¹⁵so I am eager to preach the gospel to you also who are in Rome.

Rom 15:22–29 (§63)

²²This is the reason why I have so often been hindered from coming to you. ²³But now, since I no longer have any room for work in these regions, and since I have longed for many years to come to you, ²⁴I hope to see you in passing as I go to Spain, and to be sped on my journey there by you, once I have enjoyed your company for a little. ²⁵At present, however, I am going to Jerusalem with aid for the saints. ²⁶For Macedonia and Achaia have been pleased to make some contribution for the poor among the saints at Jerusalem; ²⁷they were pleased to do it, and indeed they are in debt to them, for if the Gentiles have come to share in their spiritual blessings, they ought also to be of service to them in material blessings. ²⁸When therefore I have completed this, and have delivered to them what has been raised, I shall go on by way of you to Spain; ²⁹and I know that when I come to you I shall come in the fulness of the blessing of Christ.

1 Cor 16:1–4 (§138)

¹Now concerning the contribution for the saints: as I directed the churches of Galatia, so you also are to do. ²On the first day of every week, each of you is to put something aside and store it up, as he may prosper, so that contributions need not be made when I come. ³And when I arrive, I will send those whom you accredit by letter to carry your gift to Jerusalem. ⁴If it seems advisable that I should go also, they will accompany me.

1 Cor 16:5–9 (§139)

⁵I will visit you after passing through Macedonia, for I intend to pass through Macedonia, ⁶and perhaps I will stay with you or even spend the winter, so that you may speed me on my journey, wherever I go. ⁷For I do not want to see you now just in passing; I hope to spend some time with you, if the Lord permits. ⁸But I will stay in Ephesus until Pentecost, ⁹for a wide door for effective work has opened to me, and there are many adversaries.

2 Cor 1:15–2:4 (§149–150)

¹⁵Because I was sure of this, I wanted to come to you first, so that you might have a double pleasure; ¹⁶I wanted to visit you on my way to Macedonia, and to come back to you from Macedonia and have you send me on my way to Judea. ¹⁷Was I vacillating when I wanted to do this? Do I make my plans like a worldly man, ready to say Yes and No at once? ¹⁸As surely as God is faithful, our word to you has not been Yes and No. ¹⁹For the Son of God, Jesus Christ, whom we preached among you, Silvanus and Timothy and I, was not Yes and No; but in him it is always Yes. ²⁰For all the promises of God find their Yes in him. That is why we utter the Amen through him, to the glory of God. ²¹But it is God who establishes us with you in Christ, and has commissioned us; ²²he has put his seal upon us and given us his Spirit in our hearts as a guarantee.

²³But I call God to witness against me—it was to spare you that I refrained from coming to Corinth. ²⁴Not that we lord it over your faith; we work with you for your joy, for you stand firm in your faith. 2 ¹For I made up my mind not to make you another painful visit. ²For if I cause you pain, who is there to make me glad but the one whom I have pained? ³And I wrote as I did, so that when I came I might not suffer pain from those who should have made me rejoice, for I felt sure of all of you, that my joy would be the joy of you all. ⁴For I wrote you out of much affliction and anguish of heart and with many tears, not to cause you pain but to let you know the abundant love that I have for you.

2 Cor 9:1–5 (§174)

¹Now it is superfluous for me to write to you about the offering for the saints, ²for I know your readiness, of which I boast about you to the people of Macedonia, saying that Achaia has been ready since last year; and your zeal has stirred up most of them. ³But I am sending the brethren so that our boasting about you may not prove vain in this case, so that you may be ready, as I said you would be; ⁴lest if some Macedonians come with me and find that you are not ready, we be humiliated—to say nothing of you—for being so confident. ⁵So I thought it necessary to urge the brethren to go on to you before me, and arrange in advance for this gift you have promised, so that it may be ready not as an exaction but as a willing gift.

2 Cor 12:14–13:10 (§187–190)

¹⁴Here for the third time I am ready to come to you. And I will not be a burden, for I seek not what is yours but you; for children ought not to lay up for their parents, but parents for their children. ¹⁵I will most gladly spend and be spent for your souls. If I love you the more, am I to be loved the less? ¹⁶But granting that I myself did not burden you, I was crafty, you say, and got the better of you by guile. ¹⁷Did I take advantage of you through any of those whom I sent to you? ¹⁸I urged Titus to go, and sent the brother with him. Did Titus take advantage of you? Did we not act in the same spirit? Did we not take the same steps?

¹⁹Have you been thinking all along that we have been defending ourselves before you? It is in the sight of God that we have been speaking in Christ, and all for your upbuilding, beloved. ²⁰For I fear that perhaps I may come and find you not what I wish, and that you may find me not what you wish; that perhaps there may be quarreling, jealousy, anger, selfishness, slander, gossip, conceit, and disorder. ²¹I fear that when I come again my God may humble me before you, and I may have to mourn over many of those who sinned before and have not repented of the impurity, immorality, and licentiousness which they have practiced.

13 ¹This is the third time I am coming to you. Any charge must be sustained by the evidence of two or three witnesses. ²I warned those who sinned before and all the others, and I warn them now while absent, as I did when

---

● **Rom 4:14**
Cf. 1 Cor 14:20; 2 Cor 6:13; Gal 4:19; Eph 5:1; Phlm 10

● **Rom 4:15**
Cf. 1 Cor 3:8

● **Rom 4:16**
1 Cor 11 ¹Be imitators of me, as I am of Christ.

Phil 3 ¹⁷Brethren, join in imitating me, and mark those who so live as you have an example in us.

Cf. Gal 4:12; 1 Thess 1:6; 1 Thess 2:14a

● **Rom 4:17**
Acts 16 ¹And he came also to Derbe and to Lystra. A disciple was there, named Timothy, the son of a Jewish woman who was a believer; but his father was a Greek.

Cf. 1 Cor 7:17; 1 Cor 11:16; 1 Cor 14:33b

present on my second visit, that if I come again I will not spare them— ³since you desire proof that Christ is speaking in me. He is not weak in dealing with you, but is powerful in you. ⁴For he was crucified in weakness, but lives by the power of God. For we are weak in him, but in dealing with you we shall live with him by the power of God.

⁵Examine yourselves, to see whether you are holding to your faith. Test yourselves. Do you not realize that Jesus Christ is in you?— unless indeed you fail to meet the test! ⁶I hope you will find out that we have not failed. ⁷But we pray God that you may not do wrong— not that we may appear to have met the test, but that you may do what is right, though we may seem to have failed. ⁸For we cannot do anything against the truth, but only for the truth. ⁹For we are glad when we are weak and you are strong. What we pray for is your improvement. ¹⁰I write this while I am away from you, in order that when I come I may not have to be severe in my use of the authority which the Lord has given me for building up and not for tearing down.

1 Thess 2:17–20(§280)

¹⁷But since we were bereft of you, brethren, for a short time, in person not in heart, we endeavored the more eagerly and with great desire to see you face to face; ¹⁸because we wanted to come to you—I, Paul, again and again—but Satan hindered us. ¹⁹For what is our hope or joy or crown of boasting before our Lord Jesus at his coming? Is it not you? ²⁰For you are our glory and joy.

Phlm 21–22(§309)

²¹Confident of your obedience, I write to you, knowing that you will do even more than I say. ²²At the same time, prepare a guest room for me, for I am hoping through your prayers to be granted to you.

SECONDARY

2 Cor 10:1–6(§176)

¹I, Paul, myself entreat you, by the meekness and gentleness of Christ—I who am humble when face to face with you, but bold to you when I am away!—²I beg of you that when I am present I may not have to show boldness with such confidence as I count on showing against some who suspect us of acting in worldly fashion. ³For though we live in the world we are not carrying on a worldly war, ⁴for the weapons of our warfare are not worldly but have divine power to destroy strongholds. ⁵We destroy arguments and every proud obstacle to the knowledge of God, and take every thought captive to obey Christ, ⁶being ready to punish

every disobedience, when your obedience is complete.

Phil 1:19–30(§240–241)

¹⁹Yes, and I shall rejoice. For I know that through your prayers and the help of the Spirit of Jesus Christ this will turn out for my deliverance, ²⁰as it is my eager expectation and hope that I shall not be at all ashamed, but that with full courage now as always Christ will be honored in my body, whether by life or by death. ²¹For to me to live is Christ, and to die is gain. ²²If it is to be life in the flesh, that means fruitful labor for me. Yet which I shall choose I cannot tell. ²³I am hard pressed between the two. My desire is to depart and be with Christ, for that is far better. ²⁴But to remain in the flesh is more necessary on your account. ²⁵Convinced of this, I know that I shall remain and continue with you all, for your progress and joy in the faith, ²⁶so that in me you may have ample cause to glory in Christ Jesus, because of my coming to you again.

²⁷Only let your manner of life be worthy of the gospel of Christ, so that whether I come and see you or am absent, I may hear of you that you stand firm in one spirit, with one mind striving side by side for the faith of the gospel, ²⁸and not frightened in anything by your opponents. This is a clear omen to them of their destruction, but of your salvation, and that from God. ²⁹For it has been granted to you that for the sake of Christ you should not only believe in him but also suffer for his sake, ³⁰engaged in the same conflict which you saw and now hear to be mine.

Phil 2:19–24(§245)

¹⁹I hope in the Lord Jesus to send Timothy to you soon, so that I may be cheered by news of you. ²⁰I have no one like him, who will be genuinely anxious for your welfare. ²¹They all look after their own interests, not those of Jesus Christ. ²²But Timothy's worth you know, how as a son with a father he has served with me in the gospel. ²³I hope therefore to send him just as soon as I see how it will go with me; ²⁴and I trust in the Lord that shortly I myself shall come also.

1 Thess 2:1–12(§277–278)

¹For you yourselves know, brethren, that our visit to you was not in vain; ²but though we had already suffered and been shamefully treated at Philippi, as you know, we had courage in our God to declare to you the gospel of God in the face of great opposition. ³For our appeal does not spring from error or uncleanness, nor is it made with guile; ⁴but just as we have been approved by God to be entrusted with the gospel, so we speak, not to please men,

but to please God who tests our hearts. ⁵For we never used either words of flattery, as you know, or a cloak for greed, as God is witness; ⁶nor did we seek glory from men, whether from you or from others, though we might have made demands as apostles of Christ. ⁷But we were gentle among you, like a nurse taking care of her children. ⁸So, being affectionately desirous of you, we were ready to share with you not only the gospel of God but also our own selves, because you had become very dear to us.

⁹For you remember our labor and toil, brethren; we worked night and day, that we might not burden any of you, while we preached to you the gospel of God. ¹⁰You are witnesses, and God also, how holy and righteous and blameless was our behavior to you believers; ¹¹for you know how, like a father with his children, we exhorted each one of you and encouraged you and charged you ¹²to lead a life worthy of God, who calls you into his own kingdom and glory.

1 Thess 3:1–5(§281)

¹Therefore when we could bear it no longer, we were willing to be left behind at Athens alone, ²and we sent Timothy, our brother and God's servant in the gospel of Christ, to establish you in your faith and to exhort you, ³that no one be moved by these afflictions. You yourselves know that this is to be our lot. ⁴For when we were with you, we told you beforehand that we were to suffer affliction; just as it has come to pass, and as you know. ⁵For this reason, when I could bear it no longer, I sent that I might know your faith, for fear that somehow the tempter had tempted you and that our labor would be in vain.

2 Thess 3:6–13(§300)

⁶Now we command you, brethren, in the name of our Lord Jesus Christ, that you keep away from any brother who is living in idleness and not in accord with the tradition that you received from us. ⁷For you yourselves know how you ought to imitate us; we were not idle when we were with you, ⁸we did not eat any one's bread without paying, but with toil and labor we worked night and day, that we might not burden any of you. ⁹It was not because we have not that right, but to give you in our conduct an example to imitate. ¹⁰For even when we were with you, we gave you this command: If any one will not work, let him not eat. ¹¹For we hear that some of you are living in idleness, mere busybodies, not doing any work. ¹²Now such persons we command and exhort in the Lord Jesus Christ to do their work in quietness and to earn their own living. ¹³Brethren, do not be weary in well-doing.

● **Rom 4:19**
Cf. 1 Cor 16:1–4; 1 Cor 16:5–9

● **Rom 4:20**
Cf. Rom 14:17

● **Rom 4:21**
Cf. Gal 6:1

5 It is actually reported that there is immorality among you, and of a kind that is not found even among pagans; for a man is living with his father's wife. [2] And you are arrogant! Ought you not rather to mourn? Let him who has done this be removed from among you.

[3] For though absent in body I am present in spirit, and as if present, I have already pronounced judgment [4] in the name of the Lord Jesus on the man who has done such a thing. When you are assembled, and my spirit is present, with the power of our Lord Jesus, [5] you are to deliver this man to Satan for the destruction of the flesh, that his spirit may be saved in the day of the Lord Jesus.

PRIMARY

Rom 16:17–20a (§67)

[17] I appeal to you, brethren, to take note of those who create dissensions and difficulties, in opposition to the doctrine which you have been taught; avoid them. [18] For such persons do not serve our Lord Christ, but their own appetites, and by fair and flattering words they deceive the hearts of the simple-minded. [19] For while your obedience is known to all, so that I rejoice over you, I would have you wise as to what is good and guileless as to what is evil; [20] then the God of peace will soon crush Satan under your feet.

2 Cor 2:5–11 (§151)

[5] But if any one has caused pain, he has caused it not to me, but in some measure—not to put it too severely— to you all. [6] For such a one this punishment by the majority is enough; [7] so you should rather turn to forgive and comfort him, or he may be overwhelmed by excessive sorrow. [8] So I beg you to reaffirm your love for him. [9] For this is why I wrote, that I might test you and know whether you are obedient in everything. [10] Any one whom you forgive, I also forgive. What I have forgiven, if I have forgiven anything, has been for your sake in the presence of Christ, [11] to keep Satan from gaining the advantage over us; for we are not ignorant of his designs.

2 Cor 6:14–7:1 (§167)

[14] Do not be mismated with unbelievers. For what partnership have righteousness and iniquity? Or what fellowship has light with darkness? [15] What accord has Christ with Belial? Or what has a believer in common with an unbeliever? [16] What agreement has the temple of God with idols? For we are the temple of the living God; as God said,

"I will live in them and move among them,
and I will be their God,
and they shall be my people.
[17] Therefore come out from them,
and be separate from them, says the Lord,
and touch nothing unclean;
then I will welcome you,
[18] and I will be a father to you,
and you shall be my sons and daughters,
says the Lord Almighty."

7 [1] Since we have these promises, beloved, let us cleanse ourselves from every defilement of body and spirit, and make holiness perfect in the fear of God.

2 Thess 3:14–15 (§301)

[14] If any one refuses to obey what we say in this letter, note that man, and have nothing to do with him, that he may be ashamed. [15] Do not look on him as an enemy, but warn him as a brother.

● **1 Cor 5:1–5**

1 Cor 5   [9] I wrote to you in my letter not to associate with immoral men; [10] not at all meaning the immoral of this world, or the greedy and robbers, or idolaters, since then you would need to go out of the world. [11] But rather I wrote to you not to associate with any one who bears the name of brother if he is guilty of immorality or greed, or is an idolater, reviler, drunkard, or robber—not even to eat with such a one. [12] For what have I to do with judging outsiders? Is it not those inside the church whom you are to judge? [13] God judges those outside. "Drive out the wicked person from among you."

● **1 Cor 5:3–5**

2 Cor 10   [2] I beg of you that when I am present I may not have to show boldness with such confidence as I count on showing against some who suspect us of acting in worldly fashion.

2 Cor 13   [2] I warned those who sinned before and all the others, and I warn them now while absent, as I did when present on my second visit, that if I come again I will not spare them— [3] since you desire proof that Christ is speaking in me. He is not weak in dealing with you, but is powerful in you.

2 Cor 13   [10] I write this while I am away from you, in order that when I come I may not have to be severe in my use of the authority which the Lord has given me for building up and not for tearing down.

Col 2   [5] For though I am absent in body, yet I am with you in spirit, rejoicing to see your good order and the firmness of your faith in Christ.

● **1 Cor 5:5**

1 Tim 1   [20] among them Hymenaeus and Alexander, whom I have delivered to Satan that they may learn not to blaspheme.

(Jesus) *omit* Jesus: p⁴⁶ B Marcion Tertullian; *add* Christ: ADG it vg(clem) syr(pes) cop; *text:* S Koine Lect vg(w-w) syr(har) Origen(Latin)

6 Your boasting is not good. Do you not know that a little leaven leavens the whole lump? 7 Cleanse out the old leaven that you may be a new lump, as you really are unleavened. For Christ, our paschal lamb, has been sacrificed. 8 Let us, therefore, celebrate the festival, not with the old leaven, the leaven of malice and evil, but with the unleavened bread of sincerity and truth.

PRIMARY

Eph 5:1–2 (§229)
1 Therefore be imitators of God, as beloved children. 2 And walk in love, as Christ loved us and gave himself up for us, a fragrant offering and sacrifice to God.

● **1 Cor 5:6**
Gal 5   9 A little leaven leavens the whole lump.

● **1 Cor 5:7–8**
Rom 12   1 I appeal to you therefore, brethren, by the mercies of God, to present your bodies as a living sacrifice, holy and acceptable to God, which is your spiritual worship. 2 Do not be conformed to this world but be transformed by the renewal of your mind, that you may prove what is the will of God, what is good and acceptable and perfect.

Phil 4   18 I have received full payment, and more; I am filled, having received from Epaphroditus the gifts you sent, a fragrant offering, a sacrifice acceptable and pleasing to God.

● **1 Cor 5:7**
Rom 15   16 to be a minister of Christ Jesus to the Gentiles in the priestly service of the gospel of God, so that the offering of the Gentiles may be acceptable, sanctified by the Holy Spirit.

2 Cor 2   15 For we are the aroma of Christ to God among those who are being saved and among those who are perishing, 16 to one a fragrance from death to death, to the other a fragrance from life to life. Who is sufficient for these things?

● **1 Cor 5:8**
Rom 14   5 One man esteems one day as better than another, while another man esteems all days alike. Let every one be fully convinced in his own mind. 6 He who observes the day, observes it in honor of the Lord. He also who eats, eats in honor of the Lord, since he gives thanks to God; while he who abstains, abstains in honor of the Lord and gives thanks to God. 7 None of us lives to himself, and none of us dies to himself. 8 If we live, we live to the Lord, and if we die, we die to the Lord; so then, whether we live or whether we die, we are the Lord's. 9 For to this end Christ died and lived again, that he might be Lord both of the dead and of the living.

Gal 4   10 You observe days, and months, and seasons, and years! 11 I am afraid that I have labored over you in vain.

Phil 2   17 Even if I am to be poured as a libation upon the sacrificial offering of your faith, I am glad and rejoice with you all. 18 Likewise you also should be glad and rejoice with me.

Col 2   16 Therefore let no one pass judgment on you in questions of food and drink or with regard to a festival or a new moon or a sabbath.

FORMAL ELEMENT: VICE LIST

⁹I wrote to you in my letter not to associate with immoral men; ¹⁰not at all meaning the immoral of this world, or the greedy and robbers, or idolaters, since then you would need to go out of the world. ¹¹But rather I wrote to you not to associate with any one who bears the name of brother if he is guilty of immorality or greed, or is an idolater, reviler, drunkard, or robber—not even to eat with such a one. ¹²For what have I to do with judging outsiders? Is it not those inside the church whom you are to judge? ¹³God judges those outside. "Drive out the wicked person from among you."

PRIMARY

See §6 for VICE LIST

SECONDARY

Rom 16:17-20a (§67)

¹⁷I appeal to you, brethren, to take note of those who create dissensions and difficulties, in opposition to the doctrine which you have been taught; avoid them. ¹⁸For such persons do not serve our Lord Christ, but their own appetites, and by fair and flattering words they deceive the hearts of the simple-minded. ¹⁹For while your obedience is known to all, so that I rejoice over you, I would have you wise as to what is good and guileless as to what is evil; ²⁰then the God of peace will soon crush Satan under your feet.

2 Cor 6:14–7:1 (§167)

¹⁴Do not be mismated with unbelievers. For what partnership have righteousness and iniquity? Or what fellowship has light with darkness? ¹⁵What accord has Christ with Belial? Or what has a believer in common with an unbeliever? ¹⁶What agreement has the temple of God with idols? For we are the temple of the living God; as God said,

"I will live in them and move among them,
and I will be their God,
and they shall be my people.
¹⁷Therefore come out from them,
and be separate from them, says the Lord,
and touch nothing unclean;
then I will welcome you,
¹⁸and I will be a father to you,
and you shall be my sons and daughters,
says the Lord Almighty."

7 ¹Since we have these promises, beloved, let us cleanse ourselves from every defilement of body and spirit, and make holiness perfect in the fear of God.

2 Thess 3:14–15 (§301)

¹⁴If any one refuses to obey what we say in this letter, note that man, and have nothing to do with him, that he may be ashamed. ¹⁵Do not look on him as an enemy, but warn him as a brother.

● **1 Cor 5:9-13**

1 Cor 11　³¹So, whether you eat or drink, or whatever you do, do all to the glory of God. ³²Give no offense to Jews or to Greeks or to the church of God, . . .

Phil 3　¹⁸For many, of whom I have often told you and now tell you even with tears, live as enemies of the cross of Christ. ¹⁹Their end is destruction, their god is the belly, and they glory in their shame, with minds set on earthly things.

1 Tim 1　⁹understanding this, that the law is not laid down for the just but for the lawless and disobedient, for the ungodly and sinners, for the unholy and profane, for murderers of fathers and murderers of mothers, for manslayers, ¹⁰immoral persons, sodomites, kidnappers, liars, perjurers, and whatever else is contrary to sound doctrine, . . .

1 Tim 6　⁴he is puffed up with conceit, he knows nothing; he has a morbid craving for controversy and for disputes about words, which produce envy, dissension, slander, base suspicions, ⁵and wrangling among men who are depraved in mind and bereft of the truth, imagining that godliness is a means of gain.

2 Tim 3　²For men will be lovers of self, lovers of money, proud, arrogant, abusive, disobedient to their parents, ungrateful, unholy, ³inhuman, implacable, slanderers, profligates, fierce, haters of good, ⁴treacherous, reckless, swollen with conceit, lovers of pleasure rather than lovers of God, . . .

Titus 3　³For we ourselves were once foolish, disobedient, led astray, slaves to various passions and pleasures, passing our days in malice and envy, hated by men and hating one another; . . .

● **1 Cor 5:9-11**

1 Cor 6　⁹I wrote to you in my letter not to associate with immoral men; ¹⁰not at all meaning the immoral of this world, or the greedy and robbers, or idolaters, since then you would need to go out of the world.

1 Cor 10　⁷Do not be idolaters as some of them were; as it is written, "The people sat down to eat and drink and rose up to dance." ⁸We must not indulge in immorality as some of them did, and twenty-three thousand fell in a single day.

2 Thess 3　⁶Now we command you, brethren, in the name of our Lord Jesus Christ, that you keep away from any brother who is living in idleness and not in accord with the tradition that you received from us.

6 When one of you has a grievance against a brother, does he dare go to law before the unrighteous instead of the saints? [2] Do you not know that the saints will judge the world? And if the world is to be judged by you, are you incompetent to try trivial cases? [3] Do you not know that we are to judge angels? How much more, matters pertaining to this life! [4] If then you have such cases, why do you lay them before those who are least esteemed by the church? [5] I say this to your shame. Can it be that there is no man among you wise enough to decide between members of the brotherhood, [6] but brother goes to law against brother, and that before unbelievers?

[7] To have lawsuits at all with one another is defeat for you. Why not rather suffer wrong? Why not rather be defrauded? [8] But you yourselves wrong and defraud, and that even your own brethren.

PRIMARY

Rom 13:1–7 (§54)

[1] Let every person be subject to the governing authorities. For there is no authority except from God, and those that exist have been instituted by God. [2] Therefore he who resists the authorities resists what God has appointed, and those who resist will incur judgment. [3] For rulers are not a terror to good conduct, but to bad. Would you have no fear of him who is in authority? Then do what is good, and you will receive his approval, [4] for he is God's servant for your good. But if you do wrong, be afraid, for he does not bear the sword in vain; he is the servant of God to execute his wrath on the wrongdoer. [5] Therefore one must be subject, not only to avoid God's wrath but also for the sake of conscience. [6] For the same reason you also pay taxes, for the authorities are ministers of God, attending to this very thing. [7] Pay all of them their dues, taxes to whom taxes are due, revenue to whom revenue is due, respect to whom respect is due, honor to whom honor is due.

2 Cor 11:30–33 (§184)

[30] If I must boast, I will boast of the things that show my weakness. [31] The God and Father of the Lord Jesus, he who is blessed for ever, knows that I do not lie. [32] At Damascus, the governor under King Aretas guarded the city of Damascus in order to seize me, [33] but I was let down in a basket through a window in the wall, and escaped his hands.

Col 4:5–6 (§270)

[5] Conduct yourselves wisely toward outsiders, making the most of the time. [6] Let your speech always be gracious, seasoned with salt, so that you may know how you ought to answer every one.

Phlm 15–20 (§308)

[15] Perhaps this is why he was parted from you for a while, that you might have him back for ever, [16] no longer as a slave but more than a slave, as a beloved brother, especially to me but how much more to you, both in the flesh and in the Lord. [17] So if you consider me your partner, receive him as you would receive me. [18] If he has wronged you at all, or owes you anything, charge that to my account. [19] I, Paul, write this with my own hand, I will repay it—to say nothing of your owing me even your own self. [20] Yes, brother, I want some benefit from you in the Lord. Refresh my heart in Christ.

● **1 Cor 6:1–8**

1 Cor 4   [1] This is how one should regard us, as servants of Christ and stewards of the mysteries of God. [2] Moreover it is required of stewards that they be found trustworthy. [3] But with me it is a very small thing that I should be judged by you or by any human court. I do not even judge myself. [4] I am not aware of anything against myself, but I am not thereby acquitted. It is the Lord who judges me. [5] Therefore do not pronounce judgment before the time, before the Lord comes, who will bring to light the things now hidden in darkness and will disclose the purposes of the heart. Then every man will receive his commendation from God.

● **1 Cor 6:1–2**

1 Tim 5   [19] Never admit any charge against an elder except on the evidence of two or three witnesses. [20] As for those who persist in sin, rebuke them in the presence of all, so that the rest may stand in fear. [21] In the presence of God and of Christ Jesus and of the elect angels I charge you to keep these rules without favor, doing nothing from partiality.

● **1 Cor 6:4–5**

2 Cor 13   [1] This is the third time I am coming to you. Any charge must be sustained by the evidence of two or three witnesses.

1 Thess 4   [9] But concerning love of the brethren you have no need to have any one write to you, for you yourselves have been taught by God to love one another; [10] and indeed you do love all the brethren throughout Macedonia. But we exhort you, brethren, to do so more and more, [11] to aspire to live quietly, to mind your own affairs, and to work with your hands, as we charged you; [12] so that you may command the respect of outsiders, and be dependent on nobody.

Phlm   [18] If he has wronged you at all, or owes you anything, charge that to my account. [19] I, Paul, write this with my own hand, I will repay it—to say nothing of your owing me even your own self.

● **1 Cor 6:7**

Gal 6   [10] So then, as we have opportunity, let us do good to all men, and especially to those who are of the household of faith.

1 Thess 5   [15] See that none of you repays evil for evil, but always seek to do good to one another and to all.

FORMAL ELEMENT: VICE LIST

⁹Do you not know that the unrighteous will not inherit the kingdom of God? Do not be deceived; neither the immoral, nor idolaters, nor adulterers, nor sexual perverts, ¹⁰nor thieves, nor the greedy, nor drunkards, nor revilers, nor robbers will inherit the kingdom of God. ¹¹And such were some of you. But you were washed, you were sanctified, you were justified in the name of the Lord Jesus Christ and in the Spirit of our God.

PRIMARY

Rom 1:29–32 (§6)

²⁹They were filled with all manner of wickedness, evil, covetousness, malice. Full of envy, murder, strife, deceit, malignity, they are gossips, ³⁰slanderers, haters of God, insolent, haughty, boastful, inventors of evil, disobedient to parents, ³¹foolish, faithless, heartless, ruthless. ³²Though they know God's decree that those who do such things deserve to die, they not only do them but approve those who practice them.

Rom 13:11–14 (§56)

¹¹Besides this you know what hour it is, how it is full time now for you to wake from sleep. For salvation is nearer to us now than when we first believed; ¹²the night is far gone, the day is at hand. Let us then cast off the works of darkness and put on the armor of light; ¹³let us conduct ourselves becomingly as in the day, not in reveling and drunkenness, not in debauchery and licentiousness, not in quarreling and jealousy. ¹⁴But put on the Lord Jesus Christ, and make no provision for the flesh, to gratify its desires.

2 Cor 12:19–21 (§188)

¹⁹Have you been thinking all along that we have been defending ourselves before you? It is in the sight of God that we have been speaking in Christ, and all for your upbuilding, beloved. ²⁰For I fear that perhaps I may come and find you not what I wish, and that you may find me not what you wish; that perhaps there may be quarreling, jealousy, anger, selfishness, slander, gossip, conceit, and disorder. ²¹I fear that when I come again my God may humble me before you, and I may have to mourn over many of those who sinned before and have not repented of the impurity, immorality, and licentiousness which they have practiced.

Gal 5:16–26 (§213)

¹⁶But I say, walk by the Spirit, and do not gratify the desires of the flesh. ¹⁷For the desires of the flesh are against the Spirit, and the desires of the Spirit are against the flesh; for these are opposed to each other, to prevent you from doing what you would. ¹⁸But if you are led by the Spirit you are not under the law. ¹⁹Now the works of the flesh are plain: fornication, impurity, licentiousness, ²⁰idolatry, sorcery, enmity, strife, jealousy, anger, selfishness, dissension, party spirit, ²¹envy, drunkenness, carousing, and the like. I warn you, as I warned you before, that those who do such things shall not inherit the kingdom of God. ²²But the fruit of the Spirit is love, joy, peace, patience, kindness, goodness, faithfulness, ²³gentleness, self-control; against such there is no law. ²⁴And those who belong to Christ Jesus have crucified the flesh with its passions and desires.

²⁵If we live by the Spirit, let us also walk by the Spirit. ²⁶Let us have no self-conceit, no provoking of one another, no envy of one another.

Eph 4:17–32 (§227–228)

¹⁷Now this I affirm and testify in the Lord, that you must no longer live as the Gentiles do, in the futility of their minds; ¹⁸they are darkened in their understanding, alienated from the life of God because of the ignorance that is in them, due to their hardness of heart; ¹⁹they have become callous and have given themselves up to licentiousness, greedy to practice every kind of uncleanness. ²⁰You did not so learn Christ!— ²¹assuming that you have heard about him and were taught in him, as the truth is in Jesus. ²²Put off your old nature which belongs to your former manner of life and is corrupt through deceitful lusts, ²³and be renewed in the spirit of your minds, ²⁴and put on the new nature, created after the likeness of God in true righteousness and holiness.

²⁵Therefore, putting away falsehood, let every one speak the truth with his neighbor, for we are members one of another. ²⁶Be angry but do not sin; do not let the sun go down on your anger, ²⁷and give no opportunity to the devil. ²⁸Let the thief no longer steal, but rather let him labor, doing honest work with his hands, so that he may be able to give to those in need. ²⁹Let no evil talk come out of your mouths, but only such as is good for edifying, as fits the occasion, that it may impart grace to those who hear. ³⁰And do not grieve the Holy Spirit of God, in whom you were sealed for the day of redemption. ³¹Let all bitterness and wrath and anger and clamor and slander be put away from you, with all malice, ³²and be kind to one another, tenderhearted, forgiving one another, as God in Christ forgave you.

Eph 5:3–14 (§230)

³But fornication and all impurity or covetousness must not even be named among you, as is fitting among saints. ⁴Let there be no filthiness, nor silly talk, nor levity, which are not fitting; but instead let there be thanksgiving. ⁵Be sure of this, that no fornicator or impure man, or one who is covetous (that is, an idolater), has any inheritance in the kingdom of Christ and of God. ⁶Let no one deceive you with empty words, for it is because of these things that the wrath of God comes upon the sons of disobedience. ⁷Therefore do not associate with them, ⁸for once you were darkness, but now you are light in the Lord; walk as children of light ⁹(for the fruit of light is found in all that is good and right and true), ¹⁰and try to learn what is pleasing to the Lord. ¹¹Take no part in the unfruitful works of darkness, but instead expose them. ¹²For it is a shame even to speak of the things that they do in secret; ¹³but when anything is exposed by the light it becomes visible, for anything that becomes visible is light. ¹⁴Therefore it is said,

　"Awake, O sleeper, and arise from the dead,
　and Christ shall give you light."

Col 3:5–11 (§266)

⁵Put to death therefore what is earthly in you: fornication, impurity, passion, evil desire, and covetousness, which is idolatry. ⁶On account of these the wrath of God is coming. ⁷In these you once walked, when you lived in them. ⁸But now put them all away: anger, wrath, malice, slander, and foul talk from your mouth. ⁹Do not lie to one another, seeing that you have put off the old nature with its practices ¹⁰and have put on the new nature, which is being renewed in knowledge after the image of its creator. ¹¹Here there cannot be Greek and Jew, circumcised and uncircumcised, barbarian, Scythian, slave, free man, but Christ is all, and in all.

● **1 Cor 6:9–10**
See 1 Cor 5:10–11; 1 Cor 15:50

● **1 Cor 6:9**
1 Tim 1　⁹understanding this, that the law is not laid down for the just but for the lawless and disobedient, for the ungodly and sinners, for the unholy and profane, for murderers of fathers and murderers of mothers, for manslayers, ¹⁰immoral persons, sodomites, kidnappers, liars, perjurers, and whatever else is contrary to sound doctrine, . . .

1 Tim 6　⁴he is puffed up with conceit, he knows nothing; he has a morbid craving for controversy and for disputes about words, which produce envy, dissension, slander, base suspicions, ⁵and wrangling among men who are depraved in mind and bereft of the truth, imagining that godliness is a means of gain.

2 Tim 3　²For men will be lovers of self, lovers of money, proud, arrogant, abusive, disobedient to their parents, ungrateful, unholy, ³inhuman, implacable, slanderers, profligates, fierce, haters of good, ⁴treacherous, reckless, swollen with conceit, lovers of pleasure rather than lovers of God, . . .

Titus 3　³For we ourselves were once foolish, disobedient, led astray, slaves to various passions and pleasures, passing our days in malice and envy, hated by men and hating one another; . . .

● **1 Cor 6:11**
Acts 22　¹⁶"And now why do you wait? Rise and be baptized, and wash away your sins, calling on his name."

See Rom 3:21–26; 1 Cor 1: 30; 2 Thess 2:13

[12]"All things are lawful for me," but not all things are helpful. "All things are lawful for me," but I will not be enslaved by anything. [13]"Food is meant for the stomach and the stomach for food"—and God will destroy both one and the other. The body is not meant for immorality, but for the Lord, and the Lord for the body. [14]And God raised the Lord and will also raise us up by his power. [15]Do you not know that your bodies are members of Christ? Shall I therefore take the members of Christ and make them members of a prostitute? Never! [16]Do you not know that he who joins himself to a prostitute becomes one body with her? For, as it is written, "The two shall become one flesh." [17]But he who is united to the Lord becomes one spirit with him. [18]Shun immorality. Every other sin which a man commits is outside the body; but the immoral man sins against his own body. [19]Do you not know that your body is a temple of the Holy Spirit within you, which you have from God? You are not your own; [20]you were bought with a price. So glorify God in your body.

PRIMARY

Rom 6:1–23 (§23–25)

[1]What shall we say then? Are we to continue in sin that grace may abound? [2]By no means! How can we who died to sin still live in it? [3]Do you not know that all of us who have been baptized into Christ Jesus were baptized into his death? [4]We were buried therefore with him by baptism into death, so that as Christ was raised from the dead by the glory of the Father, we too might walk in newness of life.

[5]For if we have been united with him in a death like his, we shall certainly be united with him in a resurrection like his. [6]We know that our old self was crucified with him so that the sinful body might be destroyed, and we might no longer be enslaved to sin. [7]For he who has died is freed from sin. [8]But if we have died with Christ, we believe that we shall also live with him. [9]For we know that Christ being raised from the dead will never die again; death no longer has dominion over him. [10]The death he died he died to sin, once for all, but the life he lives he lives to God.

[11]So you also must consider yourselves dead to sin and alive to God in Christ Jesus.

[12]Let not sin therefore reign in your mortal bodies, to make you obey their passions. [13]Do not yield your members to sin as instruments of wickedness, but yield yourselves to God as men who have been brought from death to life, and your members to God as instruments of righteousness. [14]For sin will have no dominion over you, since you are not under law but under grace.

[15]What then? Are we to sin because we are not under law but under grace? By no means! [16]Do you not know that if you yield yourselves to any one as obedient slaves, you are slaves of the one whom you obey, either of sin, which leads to death, or of obedience, which leads to righteousness? [17]But thanks be to God, that you who were once slaves of sin have become obedient from the heart to the standard of teaching to which you were committed, [18]and, having been set free from sin, have become slaves of righteousness. [19]I am speaking in human terms, because of your natural limitations. For just as you once yielded your members to impurity and to greater and greater iniquity, so now yield your members to righteousness for sanctification.

[20]When you were slaves of sin, you were free in regard to righteousness. [21]But then what return did you get from the things of which you are now ashamed? The end of those things is death. [22]But now that you have been set free from sin and have become slaves of God, the return you get is sanctification and its end, eternal life. [23]For the wages of sin is death, but the free gift of God is eternal life in Christ Jesus our Lord.

Eph 2:11–22 (§221)

[11]Therefore remember that at one time you Gentiles in the flesh, called the uncircumcision by what is called the circumcision, which is made in the flesh by hands— [12]remember that you were at that time separated from Christ, alienated from the commonwealth of Israel, and strangers to the covenants of promise, having no hope and without God in the world. [13]But now in Christ Jesus you who once were far off have been brought near in the blood of Christ. [14]For he is our peace, who has made us both one, and has broken down the dividing wall of hostility, [15]by abolishing in his flesh the law of commandments and ordinances, that he might create in himself one new man in place of the two, so making peace, [16]and might reconcile us both to God in one body through the cross, thereby bringing the hostility to an end. [17]And he came and preached peace to you who were far off and peace to those who were near; [18]for through him we both have access in one Spirit to the Father. [19]So then you are no longer strangers and sojourners, but you are fellow citizens with the saints and members of the household of God, [20]built upon the foundation of the apostles and prophets, Christ Jesus himself being the cornerstone, [21]in whom the whole structure is joined together and grows into a holy temple in the Lord; [22]in whom you also are built into it for a dwelling place of God in the Spirit.

1 Thess 4:1–8 (§284)

[1]Finally, brethren, we beseech and exhort you in the Lord Jesus, that as you learned from us how you ought to live and to please God, just as you are doing, you do so more and more. [2]For you know what instructions we gave you through the Lord Jesus. [3]For this is the will of God, your sanctification: that you abstain from unchastity; [4]that each one of you know how to take a wife for himself in holiness and honor [5]not in the passion of lust like heathen who do not know God; [6]that no man transgress, and wrong his brother in this matter, because the Lord is an avenger in all these things, as we solemnly forewarned you. [7]For God has not called us for uncleanness, but in holiness. [8]Therefore whoever disregards this, disregards not man but God, who gives his Holy Spirit to you.

● **1 Cor 6:12**

1 Cor 10   [23]"All things are lawful," but not all things are helpful. "All things are lawful," but not all things build up.

● **1 Cor 6:13**

Rom 14   [17]For the kingdom of God is not food and drink but righteousness and peace and joy in the Holy Spirit; . . .

2 Cor 4   [10]always carrying in the body the death of Jesus, so that the life of Jesus may also be manifested in our bodies.

Cf. 1 Cor 8   [8]Food will not commend us to God. We are no worse off if we do not eat, and no better off if we do.

● **1 Cor 6:14**

Cf. 1 Cor 15   [20]But in fact Christ has been raised from the dead, the first fruits of those who have fallen asleep.

Cf. 2 Cor 4   [14]knowing that he who raised the Lord Jesus will raise us also with Jesus and bring us with you into his presence.

Cf. Phil 3   [10]that I may know him and the power of his resurrection, and may share his sufferings, becoming like him in his death, [11]that if possible I may attain the resurrection from the dead.

Cf. Col 2   [12]and you were buried with him in baptism, in which you were also raised with him through faith in the working of God, who raised him from the dead.

Cf. Acts 2   [24]"But God raised him up, having loosed the pangs of death, because it was not possible for him to be held by it."

● **1 Cor 6:17**

Rom 8   [9]But you are not in the flesh, you are in the Spirit, if in fact the Spirit of God dwells in you. Any one who does not have the Spirit of Christ does not belong to him.

Gal 2   [20]I have been crucified with Christ; it is no longer I who live, but Christ who lives in me; and the life I now live in the flesh I live by faith in the Son of God, who loved me and gave himself for me.

● **1 Cor 6:18–19**

Cf. Phil 1   [20]as it is my eager expectation and hope that I shall not be at all ashamed, but that with full courage now as always Christ will be honored in my body, whether by life or by death.

● **1 Cor 6:19**

1 Cor 3   [16]Do you not know that you are God's temple and that God's Spirit dwells in you?

● **1 Cor 6:20**

Cf. Acts 20   [28]"Take heed to yourselves and to all the flock, in which the Holy Spirit has made you overseers, to care for the church of God which he obtained with the blood of his own Son."

7 Now concerning the matters about which you wrote. It is well for a man not to touch a woman. [2] But because of the temptation to immorality, each man should have his own wife and each woman her own husband. [3] The husband should give to his wife her conjugal rights, and likewise the wife to her husband. [4] For the wife does not rule over her own body, but the husband does; likewise the husband does not rule over his own body, but the wife does. [5] Do not refuse one another except perhaps by agreement for a season, that you may devote yourselves to prayer; but then come together again, lest Satan tempt you through lack of self-control. [6] I say this by way of concession, not of command. [7] I wish that all were as I myself am. But each has his own special gift from God, one of one kind and one of another.

PRIMARY

1 Thess 4:1-8 (§284)

[1] Finally, brethren, we beseech and exhort you in the Lord Jesus, that as you learned from us how you ought to live and to please God, just as you are doing, you do so more and more. [2] For you know what instructions we gave you through the Lord Jesus. [3] For this is the will of God, your sanctification: that you abstain from unchastity; [4] that each one of you know how to take a wife for himself in holiness and honor [5] not in the passion of lust like heathen who do not know God; [6] that no man transgress, and wrong his brother in this matter, because the Lord is an avenger in all these things, as we solemnly forewarned you. [7] For God has not called us for uncleanness, but in holiness. [8] Therefore whoever disregards this, disregards not man but God, who gives his Holy Spirit to you.

● **1 Cor 7:1-2**

1 Cor 6   [12] "All things are lawful for me," but not all things are helpful. "All things are lawful for me," but I will not be enslaved by anything.

1 Cor 10   [23] "All things are lawful," but not all things are helpful. "All things are lawful," but not all things build up.

● **1 Cor 7:1**

Rom 5   [1] Therefore, since we are justified by faith, we have peace with God through our Lord Jesus Christ.

1 Cor 7   [25] Now concerning the unmarried, I have no command of the Lord, but I give my opinion as one who by the Lord's mercy is trustworthy.

1 Cor 8   [1] Now concerning food offered to idols: we know that "all of us possess knowledge." "Knowledge" puffs up, but love builds up.

1 Cor 12   [1] Now concerning spiritual gifts, brethren, I do not want you to be uninformed.

1 Cor 16   [1] Now concerning the contribution for the saints: as I directed the churches of Galatia, so you also are to do.

1 Thess 4   [9] But concerning love of the brethren you have no need to have any one write to you, for you yourselves have been taught by God to love one another; . . .

1 Thess 4   [13] But we would not have you ignorant, brethren, concerning those who are asleep, that you may not grieve as others do who have no hope.

● **1 Cor 7:4**

Eph 5   [28] Even so husbands should love their wives as their own bodies. He who loves his wife loves himself. [29] For no man ever hates his own flesh, but nourishes and cherishes it, as Christ does the church, . . .

● **1 Cor 7:5**

2 Cor 2   [11] to keep Satan from gaining the advantage over us; for we are not ignorant of his designs.

2 Cor 11   [14] And no wonder, for even Satan disguises himself as an angel of light.

(paryer) *add* fasting: S[c] Koine Lect syr Ephraeum

● **1 Cor 7:6**

1 Cor 7   [25] Now concerning the unmarried, I have no command of the Lord, but I give my opinion as one who by the Lord's mercy is trustworthy.

1 Cor 7   [35] I say this for your own benefit, not to lay any restraint upon you, but to promote good order and to secure your undivided devotion to the Lord.

1 Cor 14   [37] If any one thinks that he is a prophet, or spiritual, he should acknowledge that what I am writing to you is a command of the Lord.

2 Cor 8   [8] I say this not as a command, but to prove by the earnestness of others that your love also is genuine.

2 Cor 11   [17] (What I am saying I say not with the Lord's authority but as a fool, in this boastful confidence; . . .)

Phlm   [8] Accordingly, though I am bold enough in Christ to command you to do what is required, [9] yet for love's sake I prefer to appeal to you—I, Paul, an ambassador and now a prisoner also for Christ Jesus . . .

● **1 Cor 7:7**

Rom 12   [6] Having gifts that differ according to the grace given to us, let us use them: if prophecy, in proportion to our faith; . . .

1 Cor 12   [11] All these are inspired by one and the same Spirit, who apportions to each one individually as he wills.

[8]To the unmarried and the widows I say that it is well for them to remain single as I do. [9]But if they cannot exercise self-control, they should marry. For it is better to marry than to be aflame with passion.

P<small>RIMARY</small>

1 Thess 4:1–8 (§284)

[1]Finally, brethren, we beseech and exhort you in the Lord Jesus, that as you learned from us how you ought to live and to please God, just as you are doing, you do so more and more. [2]For you know what instructions we gave you through the Lord Jesus. [3]For this is the will of God, your sanctification: that you abstain from unchastity; [4]that each one of you know how to take a wife for himself in holiness and honor [5]not in the passion of lust like heathen who do not know God; [6]that no man transgress, and wrong his brother in this matter, because the Lord is an avenger in all these things, as we solemnly forewarned you. [7]For God has not called us for uncleanness, but in holiness. [8]Therefore whoever disregards this, disregards not man but God, who gives his Holy Spirit to you.

• **1 Cor 7:8–9**

1 Tim 5   [14]So I would have younger widows marry, bear children, rule their households, and give the enemy no occasion to revile us.

• **1 Cor 7:9**

1 Cor 9   [25]Every athlete exercises self-control in all things. They do it to receive a perishable wreath, but we an imperishable.

Gal 5   [16]But I say, walk by the Spirit, and do not gratify the desires of the flesh. [17]For the desires of the flesh are against the Spirit, and the desires of the Spirit are against the flesh; for these are opposed to each other, to prevent you from doing what you would. [18]But if you are led by the Spirit you are not under the law. [19]Now the works of the flesh are plain: fornication, impurity, licentiousness, [20]idolatry, sorcery, enmity, strife, jealousy, anger, selfishness, dissension, party spirit, [21]envy, drunkenness, carousing, and the like. I warn you, as I warned you before, that those who do such things shall not inherit the kingdom of God. [22]But the fruit of the Spirit is love, joy, peace, patience, kindness, goodness, faithfulness, [23]gentleness, self-control; against such there is no law.

¹⁰To the married I give charge, not I but the Lord, that the wife should not separate from her husband ¹¹(but if she does, let her remain single or else be reconciled to her husband)—and that the husband should not divorce his wife.

Primary

Rom 7:1–6 (§26)

¹Do you not know, brethren—for I am speaking to those who know the law—that the law is binding on a person only during his life? ²Thus a married woman is bound by law to her husband as long as he lives; but if her husband dies she is discharged from the law concerning the husband. ³Accordingly, she will be called an adulteress if she lives with another man while her husband is alive. But if her husband dies she is free from that law, and if she marries another man she is not an adulteress. ⁴Likewise, my brethren, you have died to the law through the body of Christ, so that you may belong to another, to him who has been raised from the dead in order that we may bear fruit for God. ⁵While we were living in the flesh, our sinful passions, aroused by the law, were at work in our members to bear fruit for death. ⁶But now we are discharged from the law, dead to that which held us captive, so that we serve not under the old written code but in the new life of the Spirit.

● **1 Cor 7:10-11**

Mark 10   ²And Pharisees came up and in order to test him asked, "Is it lawful for a man to divorce his wife?" ³He answered them, "What did Moses command you?" ⁴They said, "Moses allowed a man to write a certificate of divorce, and to put her away." ⁵But Jesus said to them, "For your hardness of heart he wrote you this commandment. ⁶But from the beginning of creation, 'God made them male and female.' ⁷'For this reason a man shall leave his father and mother and be joined to his wife, ⁸and the two shall become one flesh.' So they are no longer two but one flesh. ⁹What therefore God has joined together, let not man put asunder."

¹⁰And in the house the disciples asked him again about this matter. ¹¹And he said to them, "Whoever divorces his wife and marries another, commits adultery against her; ¹²and if she divorces her husband and marries another, she commits adultery."

● **1 Cor 7:10**

1 Cor 7   ¹²To the rest I say, not the Lord, that if any brother has a wife who is an unbeliever, and she consents to live with him, he should not divorce her.

1 Cor 7   ²⁵Now concerning the unmarried, I have no command of the Lord, but I give my opinion as one who by the Lord's mercy is trustworthy.

12To the rest I say, not the Lord, that if any brother has a wife who is an unbeliever, and she consents to live with him, he should not divorce her. **13**If any woman has a husband who is an unbeliever, and he consents to live with her, she should not divorce him. **14**For the unbelieving husband is consecrated through his wife, and the unbelieving wife is consecrated through her husband. Otherwise, your children would be unclean, but as it is they are holy. **15**But if the unbelieving partner desires to separate, let it be so; in such a case the brother or sister is not bound. For God has called us to peace. **16**Wife, how do you know whether you will save your husband? Husband, how do you know whether you will save your wife?

PRIMARY

Rom 7:1–6 (§26)

1Do you not know, brethren—for I am speaking to those who know the law—that the law is binding on a person only during his life? **2**Thus a married woman is bound by law to her husband as long as he lives; but if her husband dies she is discharged from the law concerning the husband. **3**Accordingly, she will be called an adulteress if she lives with another man while her husband is alive. But if her husband dies she is free from that law, and if she marries another man she is not an adulteress.

4Likewise, my brethren, you have died to the law through the body of Christ, so that you may belong to another, to him who has been raised from the dead in order that we may bear fruit for God. **5**While we were living in the flesh, our sinful passions, aroused by the law, were at work in our members to bear fruit for death. **6**But now we are discharged from the law, dead to that which held us captive, so that we serve not under the old written code but in the new life of the Spirit.

2 Cor 6:14–7:1 (§167)

14Do not be mismated with unbelievers. For what partnership have righteousness and iniquity? Or what fellowship has light with darkness? **15**What accord has Christ with Belial? Or what has a believer in common with an unbeliever? **16**What agreement has the temple of God with idols? For we are the temple of the living God; as God said,

"I will live in them and move among them,
and I will be their God,
and they shall be my people."

17Therefore come out from them,
and be separate from them, says the Lord,
and touch nothing unclean;

then I will welcome you,
18and I will be a father to you,
and you shall be my sons and daughters,
says the Lord Almighty."

7 **1**Since we have these promises, beloved, let us cleanse ourselves from every defilement of body and spirit, and make holiness perfect in the fear of God.

1 Thess 4:1–8 (§284)

1Finally, brethren, we beseech and exhort you in the Lord Jesus, that as you learned from us how you ought to live and to please God, just as you are doing, you do so more and more. **2**For you know what instructions we gave you through the Lord Jesus. **3**For this is the will of God, your sanctification: that you abstain from unchastity; **4**that each one of you know how to take a wife for himself in holiness and honor **5**not in the passion of lust like heathen who do not know God; **6**that no man transgress, and wrong his brother in this matter, because the Lord is an avenger in all these things, as we solemnly forewarned you. **7**For God has not called us for uncleanness, but in holiness. **8**Therefore whoever disregards this, disregards not man but God, who gives his Holy Spirit to you.

● 1 Cor 7:12–16
Mark 10   **10**And in the house the disciples asked him again about this matter. **11**And he said to them, "Whoever divorces his wife and marries another, commits adultery against her; **12**and if she divorces her husband and marries another, she commits adultery."

● 1 Cor 7:12
1 Cor 7   **10**To the married I give charge, not I but the Lord, that the wife should not separate from her husband . . .

1 Cor 7   **25**Now concerning the unmarried, I have no command of the Lord, but I give my opinion as one who by the Lord's mercy is trustworthy.

2 Cor 11   **17**(What I am saying I say not with the Lord's authority but as a fool, in this boastful confidence; . . .)

● 1 Cor 7:14
Rom 11   **16**If the dough offered as first fruits is holy, so is the whole lump; and if the root is holy, so are the branches.

1 Thess 4   **4**that each one of you know how to take a wife for himself in holiness and honor . . .

● 1 Cor 7:15
Rom 14   **19**Let us then pursue what makes for peace and for mutual upbuilding.

1 Cor 7   **39**A wife is bound to her husband as long as he lives. If the husband dies, she is free to be married to whom she wishes, only in the Lord.

(us) *read* you: S*AC cop(bo) Pelagius

● 1 Cor 7:16
Eph 5   **21**Be subject to one another out of reverence for Christ. **22**Wives, be subject to your husbands, as to the Lord. **23**For the husband is the head of the wife as Christ is the head of the church, his body, and is himself its Savior.

[17]Only, let every one lead the life which the Lord has assigned to him, and in which God has called him. This is my rule in all the churches. [18]Was any one at the time of his call already circumcised? Let him not seek to remove the marks of circumcision. Was any one at the time of his call uncircumcised? Let him not seek circumcision. [19]For neither circumcision counts for anything nor uncircumcision, but keeping the commandments of God. [20]Every one should remain in the state in which he was called. [21]Were you a slave when called? Never mind. But if you can gain your freedom, avail yourself of the opportunity. [22]For he who was called in the Lord as a slave is a freedman of the Lord. Likewise he who was free when called is a slave of Christ. [23]You were bought with a price; do not become slaves of men. [24]So, brethren, in whatever state each was called, there let him remain with God.

PRIMARY

Rom 2:25–29 (§11)

[25]Circumcision indeed is of value if you obey the law; but if you break the law, your circumcision becomes uncircumcision. [26]So, if a man who is uncircumcised keeps the precepts of the law, will not his uncircumcision be regarded as circumcision? [27]Then those who are physically uncircumcised but keep the law will condemn you who have the written code and circumcision but break the law. [28]For he is not a real Jew who is one outwardly, nor is true circumcision something external and physical. [29]He is a Jew who is one inwardly, and real circumcision is a matter of the heart, spiritual and not literal. His praise is not from men but from God.

Rom 6:15–23 (§25)

[15]What then? Are we to sin because we are not under law but under grace? By no means! [16]Do you not know that if you yield yourselves to any one as obedient slaves, you are slaves of the one whom you obey, either of sin, which leads to death, or of obedience, which leads to righteousness? [17]But thanks be to God, that you who were once slaves of sin have become obedient from the heart to the standard of teaching to which you were committed, [18]and, having been set free from sin, have become slaves of righteousness. [19]I am speaking in human terms, because of your natural limitations. For just as you once yielded your members to impurity and to greater and greater iniquity, so now yield your members to righteousness for sanctification.

[20]When you were slaves of sin, you were free in regard to righteousness. [21]But then what return did you get from the things of which you are now ashamed? The end of those things is death. [22]But now that you have been set free from sin and have become slaves of God, the return you get is sanctification and its end, eternal life. [23]For the wages of sin is death, but the free gift of God is eternal life in Christ Jesus our Lord.

Gal 5:1–12 (§211)

[1]For freedom Christ has set us free; stand fast therefore, and do not submit again to a yoke of slavery.

[2]Now I, Paul, say to you that if you receive circumcision, Christ will be of no advantage to you. [3]I testify again to every man who receives circumcision that he is bound to keep the whole law. [4]You are severed from Christ, you who would be justified by the law; you have fallen away from grace. [5]For through the Spirit, by faith, we wait for the hope of righteousness. [6]For in Christ Jesus neither circumcision nor uncircumcision is of any avail, but faith working through love. [7]You were running well; who hindered you from obeying the truth? [8]This persuasion is not from him who called you. [9]A little leaven leavens the whole lump. [10]I have confidence in the Lord that you will take no other view than mine; and he who is troubling you will bear his judgment, whoever he is. [11]But if I, brethren, still preach circumcision, why am I still persecuted? In that case the stumbling block of the cross has been removed. [12]I wish those who unsettle you would mutilate themselves!

Gal 6:11–17 (§216)

[11]See with what large letters I am writing to you with my own hand. [12]It is those who want to make a good showing in the flesh that would compel you to be circumcised, and only in order that they may not be persecuted for the cross of Christ. [13]For even those who receive circumcision do not themselves keep the law, but they desire to have you circumcised that they may glory in your flesh. [14]But far be it from me to glory except in the cross of our Lord Jesus Christ, by which the world has been crucified to me, and I to the world. [15]For neither circumcision counts for anything, nor uncircumcision, but a new creation. [16]Peace and mercy be upon all who walk by this rule, upon the Israel of God.

[17]Henceforth let no man trouble me; for I bear on my body the marks of Jesus.

Phlm 8–20 (§307–308)

[8]Accordingly, though I am bold enough in Christ to command you to do what is required, [9]yet for love's sake I prefer to appeal to you—I, Paul, an ambassador and now a prisoner also for Christ Jesus— [10]I appeal to you for my child, Onesimus, whose father I have become in my imprisonment. [11](Formerly he was useless to you, but now he is indeed useful to you and to me.) [12]I am sending him back to you, sending my very heart. [13]I would have been glad to keep him with me, in order that he might serve me on your behalf during my imprisonment for the gospel; [14]but I preferred to do nothing without your consent in order that your goodness might not be by compulsion but of your own free will.

[15]Perhaps this is why he was parted from you for a while, that you might have him back for ever, [16]no longer as a slave but more than a slave, as a beloved brother, especially to me but how much more to you, both in the flesh and in the Lord. [17]So if you consider me your partner, receive him as you would receive me. [18]If he has wronged you at all, or owes you anything, charge that to my account. [19]I, Paul, write this with my own hand, I will repay it—to say nothing of your owing me even your own self. [20]Yes, brother, I want some benefit from you in the Lord. Refresh my heart in Christ.

● **1 Cor 7:17**
Rom 12 [3]For by the grace given to me I bid every one among you not to think of himself more highly than he ought to think, but to think with sober judgment, each according to the measure of faith which God has assigned him.

1 Cor 4 [17]Therefore I sent to you Timothy, my beloved and faithful child in the Lord, to remind you of my ways in Christ, as I teach them everywhere in every church.

1 Cor 11 [16]If any one is disposed to be contentious, we recognize no other practice, nor do the churches of God.

2 Cor 8 [18]With him we are sending the brother who is famous among all the churches for his preaching of the gospel; . . .

2 Cor 11 [28]And, apart from other things, there is the daily pressure upon me of my anxiety for all the churches.

● **1 Cor 7:18**
Acts 15 [1]But some men came down from Judea and were teaching the brethren, "Unless you are circumcised according to the custom of Moses, you cannot be saved." [2]And when Paul and Barnabas had no small dissension and debate with them, Paul and Barnabas and some of the others were appointed to go up to Jerusalem to the apostles and the elders about this question.

● **1 Cor 7:21**
See Eph 6:5–8; Col 3:22–25

1 Tim 6 [1]Let all who are under the yoke of slavery regard their masters as worthy of all honor, so that the name of God and the teaching may not be defamed.

Titus 2 [4]and so train the young women to love their husbands and children, [5]to be sensible, chaste, domestic, kind, and submissive to their husbands, that the word of God may not be discredited. [6]Likewise urge the younger men to control themselves. [7]Show yourself in all respects a model of good deeds, and in your teaching show integrity, gravity, [8]and sound speech that cannot be censured, so that an opponent may be put to shame, having nothing evil to say of us. [9]Bid slaves to be submissive to their masters and to give satisfaction in every respect; they are not to be refractory, [10]nor to pilfer, but to show entire and true fidelity, so that in everything they may adorn the doctrine of God our Savior.

● **1 Cor 7:23**
1 Cor 6 [20]you were bought with a price. So glorify God in your body.

25 Now concerning the unmarried, I have no command of the Lord, but I give my opinion as one who by the Lord's mercy is trustworthy. **26** I think that in view of the present distress it is well for a person to remain as he is. **27** Are you bound to a wife? Do not seek to be free. Are you free from a wife? Do not seek marriage. **28** But if you marry, you do not sin, and if a girl marries she does not sin. Yet those who marry will have worldly troubles, and I would spare you that. **29** I mean, brethren, the appointed time has grown very short; from now on, let those who have wives live as though they had none, **30** and those who mourn as though they were not mourning, and those who rejoice as though they were not rejoicing, and those who buy as though they had no goods, **31** and those who deal with the world as though they had no dealings with it. For the form of this world is passing away.

PRIMARY

Rom 13:11–14 (§56)

11 Besides this you know what hour it is, how it is full time now for you to wake from sleep. For salvation is nearer to us now than when we first believed; **12** the night is far gone, the day is at hand. Let us then cast off the works of darkness and put on the armor of light; **13** let us conduct ourselves becomingly as in the day, not in reveling and drunkenness, not in debauchery and licentiousness, not in quarreling and jealousy. **14** But put on the Lord Jesus Christ, and make no provision for the flesh, to gratify its desires.

1 Thess 5:1–11 (§287)

1 But as to the times and the seasons, brethren, you have no need to have anything written to you. **2** For you yourselves know well that the day of the Lord will come like a thief in the night. **3** When people say, "There is peace and security," then sudden destruction will come upon them as travail comes upon a woman with child, and there will be no escape. **4** But you are not in darkness, brethren, for that day to surprise you like a thief. **5** For you are all sons of light and sons of the day; we are not of the night or of darkness. **6** So then let us not sleep, as others do, but let us keep awake and be sober. **7** For those who sleep sleep at night, and those who get drunk are drunk at night. **8** But, since we belong to the day, let us be sober, and put on the breastplate of faith and love, and for a helmet the hope of salvation. **9** For God has not destined us for wrath, but to obtain salvation through our Lord Jesus Christ, **10** who died for us so that whether we wake or sleep we might live with him. **11** Therefore encourage one another and build one another up, just as you are doing.

2 Thess 2:1–12 (§296)

1 Now concerning the coming of our Lord Jesus Christ and our assembling to meet him, we beg you, brethren, **2** not to be quickly shaken in mind or excited, either by spirit or by word, or by letter purporting to be from us, to the effect that the day of the Lord has come. **3** Let no one deceive you in any way; for that day will not come, unless the rebellion comes first, and the man of lawlessness is revealed, the son of perdition, **4** who opposes and exalts himself against every so-called god or object of worship, so that he takes his seat in the temple of God, proclaiming himself to be God. **5** Do you not remember that when I was still with you I told you this? **6** And you know what is restraining him now so that he may be revealed in his time. **7** For the mystery of lawlessness is already at work; only he who now restrains it will do so until he is out of the way. **8** And then the lawless one will be revealed, and the Lord Jesus will slay him with the breath of his mouth and destroy him by his appearing and his coming. **9** The coming of the lawless one by the activity of Satan will be with all power and with pretended signs and wonders, **10** and with all wicked deception for those who are to perish, because they refused to love the truth and so be saved. **11** Therefore God sends upon them a strong delusion, to make them believe what is false, **12** so that all may be condemned who did not believe the truth but had pleasure in unrighteousness.

● **1 Cor 7:25**
1 Cor 7 **10** To the married I give charge, not I but the Lord, that the wife should not separate from her husband . . .

1 Cor 7 **12** To the rest I say, not the Lord, that if any brother has a wife who is an unbeliever, and she consents to live with him, he should not divorce her.

1 Tim 1 **12** I thank him who has given me strength for this, Christ Jesus our Lord, because he judged me faithful by appointing me to his service, . . .

● **1 Cor 7:26**
1 Cor 10 **11** Now these things happened to them as a warning, but they were written down for our instruction, upon whom the end of the ages has come.

● **1 Cor 7:31**
Rom 8 **18** I consider that the sufferings of this present time are not worth comparing with the glory that is to be revealed to us. **19** For the creation waits with eager longing for the revealing of the sons of God; **20** for the creation was subjected to futility, not of its own will but by the will of him who subjected it in hope; **21** because the creation itself will be set free from its bondage to decay and obtain the glorious liberty of the children of God. **22** We know that the whole creation has been groaning in travail together until now; **23** and not only the creation, but we ourselves, who have the first fruits of the Spirit, groan inwardly as we wait for adoption as sons, the redemption of our bodies. **24** For in this hope we were saved. Now hope that is seen is not hope. For who hopes for what he sees? **25** But if we hope for what we do not see, we wait for it with patience.

Phil 4 **5** Let all men know your forbearance. The Lord is at hand.

[32]I want you to be free from anxieties. The unmarried man is anxious about the affairs of the Lord, how to please the Lord; [33]but the married man is anxious about worldly affairs, how to please his wife, [34]and his interests are divided. And the unmarried woman or girl is anxious about the affairs of the Lord, how to be holy in body and spirit; but the married woman is anxious about worldly affairs, how to please her husband. [35]I say this for your own benefit, not to lay any restraint upon you, but to promote good order and to secure your undivided devotion to the Lord.

PRIMARY

Eph 5:21–6:9 (§232)

[21]Be subject to one another out of reverence for Christ. [22]Wives, be subject to your husbands, as to the Lord. [23]For the husband is the head of the wife as Christ is the head of the church, his body, and is himself its Savior. [24]As the church is subject to Christ, so let wives also be subject in everything to their husbands. [25]Husbands, love your wives, as Christ loved the church and gave himself up for her, [26]that he might sanctify her, having cleansed her by the washing of water with the word, [27]that he might present the church to himself in splendor, without spot or wrinkle or any such thing, that she might be holy and without blemish. [28]Even so husbands should love their wives as their own bodies. He who loves his wife loves himself. [29]For no man ever hates his own flesh, but nourishes and cherishes it, as Christ does the church, [30]because we are members of his body. [31]"For this reason a man shall leave his father and mother and be joined to his wife, and the two shall become one flesh." [32]This mystery is a profound one, and I am saying that it refers to Christ and the church; [33]however, let each one of you love his wife as himself, and let the wife see that she respects her husband.

6 [1]Children, obey your parents in the Lord, for this is right. [2]"Honor your father and mother" (this is the first commandment with a promise), [3]"that it may be well with you and that you may live long on the earth." [4]Fathers, do not provoke your children to anger, but bring them up in the discipline and instruction of the Lord.

[5]Slaves, be obedient to those who are your earthly masters, with fear and trembling, in singleness of heart, as to Christ; [6]not in the way of eyeservice, as men-pleasers, but as servants of Christ, doing the will of God from the heart, [7]rendering service with a good will as to the Lord and not to men, [8]knowing that whatever good any one does, he will receive the same again from the Lord, whether he is a slave or free. [9]Masters, do the same to them, and forbear threatening, knowing that he who is both their Master and yours is in heaven, and that there is no partiality with him.

Phil 4:4–7 (§251)

[4]Rejoice in the Lord always; again I will say, Rejoice. [5]Let all men know your forbearance. The Lord is at hand. [6]Have no anxiety about anything, but in everything by prayer and supplication with thanksgiving let your requests be made known to God. [7]And the peace of God, which passes all understanding, will keep your hearts and your minds in Christ Jesus.

Col 2:4–7 (§261)

[4]I say this in order that no one may delude you with beguiling speech. [5]For though I am absent in body, yet I am with you in spirit, rejoicing to see your good order and the firmness of your faith in Christ.

[6]As therefore you received Christ Jesus the Lord, so live in him, [7]rooted and built up in him and established in the faith, just as you were taught, abounding in thanksgiving.

Col 3:18–4:1 (§268)

[18]Wives, be subject to your husbands, as is fitting in the Lord. [19]Husbands, love your wives, and do not be harsh with them. [20]Children, obey your parents in everything, for this pleases the Lord. [21]Fathers, do not provoke your children, lest they become discouraged. [22]Slaves, obey in everything those who are your earthly masters, not with eyeservice, as men-pleasers, but in singleness of heart, fearing the Lord. [23]Whatever your task, work heartily, as serving the Lord and not men, [24]knowing that from the Lord you will receive the inheritance as your reward; you are serving the Lord Christ. [25]For the wrongdoer will be paid back for the wrong he has done, and there is no partiality.

4 [1]Masters, treat your slaves justly and fairly, knowing that you also have a Master in heaven.

1 Thess 4:1–8 (§284)

[1]Finally, brethren, we beseech and exhort you in the Lord Jesus, that as you learned from us how you ought to live and to please God, just as you are doing, you do so more and more. [2]For you know what instructions we gave you through the Lord Jesus. [3]For this is the will of God, your sanctification: that you abstain from unchastity; [4]that each one of you know how to take a wife for himself in holiness and honor [5]not in the passion of lust like heathen who do not know God; [6]that no man transgress, and wrong his brother in this matter, because the Lord is an avenger in all these things, as we solemnly forewarned you. [7]For God has not called us for uncleanness, but in holiness. [8]Therefore whoever disregards this, disregards not man but God, who gives his Holy Spirit to you.

● **1 Cor 7:32–34**
1 Cor 7   [14]For the unbelieving husband is consecrated through his wife, and the unbelieving wife is consecrated through her husband. Otherwise, your children would be unclean, but as it is they are holy.

1 Cor 12   [25]that there may be no discord in the body, but that the members may have the same care for one another.

2 Cor 11   [28]And, apart from other things, there is the daily pressure upon me of my anxiety for all the churches.

● **1 Cor 7:32**
Rom 8   [8]and those who are in the flesh cannot please God.

1 Tim 5   [5]She who is a real widow, and is left all alone, has set her hope on God and continues in supplications and prayers night and day; . . .

● **1 Cor 7:35**
1 Cor 7   [6]I say this by way of concession, not of command.

Phlm   [8]Accordingly, though I am bold enough in Christ to command you to do what is required, [9]yet for love's sake I prefer to appeal to you—I, Paul, an ambassador and now a prisoner also for Christ Jesus . . .

Phlm   [14]but I preferred to do nothing without your consent in order that your goodness might not be by compulsion but of your own free will.

[36]If any one thinks that he is not behaving properly toward his betrothed, if his passions are strong, and it has to be, let him do as he wishes: let them marry—it is no sin. [37]But whoever is firmly established in his heart, being under no necessity but having his desire under control, and has determined this in his heart, to keep her as his betrothed, he will do well. [38]So that he who marries his betrothed does well; and he who refrains from marriage will do better.

PRIMARY

1 Thess 4:1–8 (§284)

[1]Finally, brethren, we beseech and exhort you in the Lord Jesus, that as you learned from us how you ought to live and to please God, just as you are doing, you do so more and more. [2]For you know what instructions we gave you through the Lord Jesus. [3]For this is the will of God, your sanctification: that you abstain from unchastity; [4]that each one of you know how to take a wife for himself in holiness and honor [5]not in the passion of lust like heathen who do not know God; [6]that no man transgress, and wrong his brother in this matter, because the Lord is an avenger in all these things, as we solemnly forewarned you. [7]For God has not called us for uncleanness, but in holiness. [8]Therefore whoever disregards this, disregards not man but God, who gives his Holy Spirit to you.

● **1 Cor 7:36–38**

1 Cor 7   [8]To the unmarried and the widows I say that it is well for them to remain single as I do. [9]But if they cannot exercise self-control, they should marry. For it is better to marry than to be aflame with passion.

1 Cor 7   [25]Now concerning the unmarried, I have no command of the Lord, but I give my opinion as one who by the Lord's mercy is trustworthy. [26]I think that in view of the present distress it is well for a person to remain as he is. [27]Are you bound to a wife? Do not seek to be free. Are you free from a wife? Do not seek marriage. [28]But if you marry, you do not sin, and if a girl marries she does not sin. Yet those who marry will have worldly troubles, and I would spare you that. [29]I mean, brethren, the appointed time has grown very short; from now on, let those who have wives live as though they had none, [30]and those who mourn as though they were not mourning, and those who rejoice as though they were not rejoicing, and those who buy as though they had no goods, [31]and those who deal with the world as though they had no dealings with it. For the form of this world is passing away.

[39] A wife is bound to her husband as long as he lives. If the husband dies, she is free to be married to whom she wishes, only in the Lord. [40] But in my judgment she is happier if she remains as she is. And I think that I have the Spirit of God.

PRIMARY

Rom 7:1–6 (§26)

[1] Do you not know, brethren—for I am speaking to those who know the law—that the law is binding on a person only during his life? [2] Thus a married woman is bound by law to her husband as long as he lives; but if her husband dies she is discharged from the law concerning the husband. [3] Accordingly, she will be called an adulteress if she lives with another man while her husband is alive. But if her husband dies she is free from that law, and if she marries another man she is not an adulteress.

[4] Likewise, my brethren, you have died to the law through the body of Christ, so that you may belong to another, to him who has been raised from the dead in order that we may bear fruit for God. [5] While we were living in the flesh, our sinful passions, aroused by the law, were at work in our members to bear fruit for death. [6] But now we are discharged from the law, dead to that which held us captive, so that we serve not under the old written code but in the new life of the Spirit.

● **1 Cor 7:39**

1 Cor 7   [12] To the rest I say, not the Lord, that if any brother has a wife who is an unbeliever, and she consents to live with him, he should not divorce her. [13] If any woman has a husband who is an unbeliever, and he consents to live with her, she should not divorce him.

1 Cor 7   [15] But if the unbelieving partner desires to separate, let it be so; in such a case the brother or sister is not bound. For God has called us to peace.

● **1 Cor 7:40**

1 Cor 2   [16] "For who has known the mind of the Lord so as to instruct him?" But we have the mind of Christ.

1 Cor 7   [8] To the unmarried and the widows I say that it is well for them to remain single as I do.

1 Cor 7   [25] Now concerning the unmarried, I have no command of the Lord, but I give my opinion as one who by the Lord's mercy is trustworthy.

2 Cor 10   [7] Look at what is before your eyes. If any one is confident that he is Christ's, let him remind himself that as he is Christ's, so are we.

8 Now concerning food offered to idols: we know that "all of us possess knowledge." "Knowledge" puffs up, but love builds up. ²If any one imagines that he knows something, he does not yet know as he ought to know. ³But if one loves God, one is known by him.

PRIMARY

Eph 3:14–19 (§223)
¹⁴For this reason I bow my knees before the Father, ¹⁵from whom every family in heaven and on earth is named, ¹⁶that according to the riches of his glory he may grant you to be strengthened with might through his Spirit in the inner man, ¹⁷and that Christ may dwell in your hearts through faith; that you, being rooted and grounded in love, ¹⁸may have power to comprehend with all the saints what is the breadth and length and height and depth, ¹⁹and to know the love of Christ which surpasses knowledge, that you may be filled with all the fulness of God.

● **1 Cor 8:1**
Rom 14   ¹As for the man who is weak in faith, welcome him, but not for disputes over opinions. ²One believes he may eat anything, while the weak man eats only vegetables. ³Let not him who eats despise him who abstains, and let not him who abstains pass judgment on him who eats; for God has welcomed him. ⁴Who are you to pass judgment on the servant of another? It is before his own master that he stands or falls. And he will be upheld, for the Master is able to make him stand.

Rom 15   ¹⁴I myself am satisfied about you, my brethren, that you yourselves are full of goodness, filled with all knowledge, and able to instruct one another.

Acts 15   ²⁰". . . but should write to them to abstain from the pollutions of idols and from unchastity and from what is strangled and from blood."

Acts 15   ²⁹". . . that you abstain from what has been sacrificed to idols and from blood and from what is strangled and from unchastity. If you keep yourselves from these, you will do well. Farewell."

● **1 Cor 8:2–3**
Col 2   ²that their hearts may be encouraged as they are knit together in love, to have all the riches of assured understanding and the knowledge of God's mystery, of Christ, ³in whom are hid all the treasures of wisdom and knowledge.

● **1 Cor 8:2**
Gal 6   ³For if any one thinks he is something, when he is nothing, he deceives himself.

1 Tim 6   ⁴he is puffed up with conceit, he knows nothing; he has a morbid craving for controversy and for disputes about words, which produce envy, dissension, slander, base suspicions, ⁵and wrangling among men who are depraved in mind and bereft of the truth, imagining that godliness is a means of gain.

(something) *omit* something: p⁴⁶ Tertullian Origen

● **1 Cor 8:3**
1 Cor 13   ¹²For now we see in a mirror dimly, but then face to face. Now I know in part; then I shall understand fully, even as I have been fully understood.

Gal 4   ⁹but now that you have come to know God, or rather to be known by God, how can you turn back again to the weak and beggarly elemental spirits, whose slaves you want to be once more?

(God) *omit* God: p⁴⁶ S* Clement; (him) *omit* by him: p⁴⁶ S* Clement

FORMAL ELEMENT: CONFESSION

[4]Hence, as to the eating of food offered to idols, we know that "an idol has no real existence," and that "there is no God but one." [5]For although there may be so-called gods in heaven or on earth—as indeed there are many "gods" and many "lords"—[6]yet for us there is one God, the Father, from whom are all things and for whom we exist, and one Lord, Jesus Christ, through whom are all things and through whom we exist.

PRIMARY

Rom 1:1-7 (§1)

[1]Paul, a servant of Jesus Christ, called to be an apostle, set apart for the gospel of God [2]which he promised beforehand through his prophets in the holy scriptures, [3]the gospel concerning his Son, who was descended from David according to the flesh [4]and designated Son of God in power according to the Spirit of holiness by his resurrection from the dead, Jesus Christ our Lord, [5]through whom we have received grace and apostleship to bring about the obedience of faith for the sake of his name among all the nations, [6]including yourselves who are called to belong to Jesus Christ;

[7]To all God's beloved in Rome, who are called to be saints:

Grace to you and peace from God our Father and the Lord Jesus Christ.

Rom 11:33-36 (§50)

[33]O the depth of the riches and wisdom and knowledge of God! How unsearchable are his judgments and how inscrutable his ways!

[34]"For who has known the mind of the Lord, or who has been his counselor?"

[35]"Or who has given a gift to him that he might be repaid?"

[36]For from him and through him and to him are all things. To him be glory for ever. Amen.

Eph 4:1-10 (§225)

[1]I therefore, a prisoner for the Lord, beg you to lead a life worthy of the calling to which you have been called, [2]with all lowliness and meekness, with patience, forbearing one another in love, [3]eager to maintain the unity of the Spirit in the bond of peace. [4]There is one body and one Spirit, just as you were called to the one hope that belongs to your call, [5]one Lord, one faith, one baptism, [6]one God and Father of us all, who is above all and through all and in all. [7]But grace was given to each of us according to the measure of Christ's gift. [8]Therefore it is said,

"When he ascended on high he led a host of captives,

and he gave gifts to men."

[9](In saying, "He ascended," what does it mean but that he had also descended into the lower parts of the earth? [10]He who descended is he who also ascended far above all the heavens, that he might fill all things.)

Phil 2:1-11 (§242)

[1]So if there is any encouragement in Christ, any incentive of love, any participation in the Spirit, any affection and sympathy, [2]complete my joy by being of the same mind, having the same love, being in full accord and of one mind. [3]Do nothing from selfishness or conceit, but in humility count others better than yourselves. [4]Let each of you look not only to his own interests, but also to the interests of others. [5]Have this mind among yourselves, which is yours in Christ Jesus, [6]who, though he was in the form of God, did not count equality with God a thing to be grasped, [7]but emptied himself, taking the form of a servant, being born in the likeness of men. [8]And being found in human form he humbled himself and became obedient unto death, even death on a cross. [9]Therefore God has highly exalted him and bestowed on him the name which is above every name, [10]that at the name of Jesus every knee should bow, in heaven and on earth and under the earth, [11]and every tongue confess that Jesus Christ is Lord, to the glory of God the Father.

Col 1:15-20 (§258)

[15]He is the image of the invisible God, the first-born of all creation; [16]for in him all things were created, in heaven and on earth, visible and invisible, whether thrones or dominions or principalities or authorities—all things were created through him and for him. [17]He is before all things, and in him all things hold together. [18]He is the head of the body, the church; he is the beginning, the first-born from the dead, that in everything he might be pre-eminent. [19]For in him all the fulness of God was pleased to dwell, [20]and through him to reconcile to himself all things, whether on earth or in heaven, making peace by the blood of his cross.

1 Thess 1:2-10 (§276)

[2]We give thanks to God always for you all, constantly mentioning you in our prayers, [3]remembering before our God and Father your work of faith and labor of love and steadfastness of hope in our Lord Jesus Christ. [4]For we know, brethren beloved by God, that he has chosen you; [5]for our gospel came to you not only in word, but also in power and in the Holy Spirit and with full conviction. You know what kind of men we proved to be among you for your sake. [6]And you became imitators of us and of the Lord, for you received the word in much affliction, with joy inspired by the Holy Spirit; [7]so that you became an example to the all the believers in Macedonia and in Achaia. [8]For not only has the word of the Lord sounded forth from you in Macedonia and Achaia, but your faith in God has gone forth everywhere, so that we need not say anything. [9]For they themselves report concerning us what a welcome we had among you, and how you turned to God from idols, to serve a living and true God, [10]and to wait for his Son from heaven, whom he raised from the dead, Jesus who delivers us from the wrath to come.

SECONDARY

Gal 3:19-20 (§204)

[19]Why then the law? It was added because of transgressions, till the offspring should come to whom the promise had been made; and it was ordained by angels through an intermediary. [20]Now an intermediary implies more than one; but God is one.

Gal 4:8-11 (§208)

[8]Formerly, when you did not know God, you were in bondage to beings that by nature are no gods; [9]but now that you have come to know God, or rather to be known by God, how can you turn back again to the weak and beggarly elemental spirits, whose slaves you want to be once more? [10]You observe days, and months, and seasons, and years! [11]I am afraid I have labored over you in vain.

● **1 Cor 8:4-5**

Rom 1   [22]Claiming to be wise, they became fools, [23]and exchanged the glory of the immortal God for images resembling mortal man or birds or animals or reptiles.

● **1 Cor 8:4**

1 Cor 10   [19]What do I imply then? That food offered to idols is anything, or that an idol is anything? [20]No, I imply that what pagans sacrifice they offer to demons and not to God. I do not want you to be partners with demons.

1 Thess 1   [9]For they themselves report concerning us what a welcome we had among you, and how you turned to God from idols, to serve a living and true God, . . .

Acts 14   [15]"Men, why are you doing this? We also are men, of like nature with you, and bring you good news, that you should turn from these vain things to a living God who made the heaven and the earth and the sea and all that is in them."

● **1 Cor 8:5-6**

Cf. 1 Cor 15:1-11

● **1 Cor 8:5**

2 Thess 2   [4]who opposes and exalts himself against every so-called god or object of worship, so that he takes his seat in the temple of God, proclaiming himself to be God.

● **1 Cor 8:6**

Cf. Rom 4:17; Rom 14:8

[7]However, not all possess this knowledge. But some, through being hitherto accustomed to idols, eat food as really offered to an idol; and their conscience, being weak, is defiled. [8]Food will not commend us to God. We are no worse off if we do not eat, and no better off if we do. [9]Only take care lest this liberty of yours somehow become a stumbling block to the weak. [10]For if any one sees you, a man of knowledge, at table in an idol's temple, might he not be encouraged, if his conscience is weak, to eat food offered to idols? [11]And so by your knowledge this weak man is destroyed, the brother for whom Christ died. [12]Thus, sinning against your brethren and wounding their conscience when it is weak, you sin against Christ. [13]Therefore, if food is a cause of my brother's falling, I will never eat meat, lest I cause my brother to fall.

PRIMARY

Rom 2:12–16 (§9)

[12]All who have sinned without the law will also perish without the law, and all who have sinned under the law will be judged by the law. [13]For it is not the hearers of the law who are righteous before God, but the doers of the law who will be justified. [14]When Gentiles who have not the law do by nature what the law requires, they are a law to themselves, even though they do not have the law. [15]They show that what the law requires is written on their hearts, while their conscience also bears witness and their conflicting thoughts accuse or perhaps excuse them [16]on that day when, according to my gospel, God judges the secrets of men by Christ Jesus.

Rom 14:13–23 (§59)

[13]Then let us no more pass judgment on one another, but rather decide never to put a stumbling block or hindrance in the way of a brother. [14]I know and am persuaded in the Lord Jesus that nothing is unclean in itself; but it is unclean for any one who thinks it unclean. [15]If your brother is being injured by what you eat, you are no longer walking in love. Do not let what you eat cause the ruin of one for whom Christ died. [16]So do not let your good be spoken of as evil. [17]For the kingdom of God is not food and drink but righteousness and peace and joy in the Holy Spirit; [18]he who thus serves Christ is acceptable to God and approved by men. [19]Let us then pursue what makes for peace and for mutual upbuilding. [20]Do not, for the sake of food, destroy the work of God. Everything is indeed clean, but it is wrong for any one to make others fall by what he eats; [21]it is right not to eat meat or drink wine or do anything that makes your brother stumble. [22]The faith that you have, keep between yourself and God; happy is he who has no reason to judge himself for what he approves. [23]But he who has doubts is condemned, if he eats, because he does not act from faith; for whatever does not proceed from faith is sin.

● **1 Cor 8:7–13**

1 Cor 4   [1]This is how one should regard us, as servants of Christ and stewards of the mysteries of God. [2]Moreover it is required of stewards that they be found trustworthy. [3]But with me it is a very small thing that I should be judged by you or by any human court. I do not even judge myself. [4]I am not aware of anything against myself, but I am not thereby acquitted. It is the Lord who judges me. [5]Therefore do not pronounce judgment before the time, before the Lord comes, who will bring to light the things now hidden in darkness and will disclose the purposes of the heart. Then every man will receive his commendation from God.

1 Cor 10   [23]"All things are lawful," but not all things are helpful. "All things are lawful," but not all things build up. [24]Let no one seek his own good, but the good of his neighbor. [25]Eat whatever is sold in the meat market without raising any question on the ground of conscience. [26]For "the earth is the Lord's, and everything in it." [27]If one of the unbelievers invites you to dinner and you are disposed to go, eat whatever is set before you without raising any question on the ground of conscience. [28](But if some one says to you, "This has been offered in sacrifice," then out of consideration for the man who informed you, and for conscience' sake — [29]I mean his conscience, not yours—do not eat it.) For why should my liberty be determined by another man's scruples? [30]If I partake with thankfulness, why am I denounced because of that for which I give thanks?

[31]So, whether you eat or drink, or whatever you do, do all to the glory of God. [32]Give no offense to Jews or to Greeks or to the church of God, [33]just as I try to please all men in everything I do, not seeking my own advantage, but that of many, that they may be saved. 11 [1]Be imitators of me, as I am of Christ.

● **1 Cor 8:7**

1 Cor 10   [19]What do I imply then? That food offered to idols is anything, or that an idol is anything? [20]No, I imply that what pagans sacrifice they offer to demons and not to God. I do not want you to be partners with demons.

● **1 Cor 8:8**

Rom 12   [1]I appeal to you therefore, brethren, by the mercies of God, to present your bodies as a living sacrifice, holy and acceptable to God, which is your spiritual worship.

Rom 14   [10]Why do you pass judgment on your brother? Or you, why do you despise your brother? For we shall all stand before the judgment seat of God; . . .

2 Cor 4   [14]knowing that he who raised the Lord Jesus will raise us also with Jesus and bring us with you into his presence.

Col 1   [22]he has now reconciled in his body of flesh by his death, in order to present you holy and blameless and irreproachable before him, . . .

● **1 Cor 8:10**

Acts 15   [20]". . . but should write to them to abstain from the pollutions of idols and from unchastity and from what is strangled and from blood."

● **1 Cor 8:11–13**

1 Cor 9   [22]To the weak I became weak, that I might win the weak. I have become all things to all men, that I might by all means save some.

9 Am I not free? Am I not an apostle? Have I not seen Jesus our Lord? Are not you my workmanship in the Lord? [2]If to others I am not an apostle, at least I am to you; for you are the seal of my apostleship in the Lord.

[3]This is my defense to those who would examine me. [4]Do we not have the right to our food and drink? [5]Do we not have the right to be accompanied by a wife, as the other apostles and the brothers of the Lord and Cephas? [6]Or is it only Barnabas and I who have no right to refrain from working for a living? [7]Who serves as a soldier at his own expense? Who plants a vineyard without eating any of its fruit? Who tends a flock without getting some of the milk?

[8]Do I say this on human authority? Does not the law say the same? [9]For it is written in the law of Moses, "You shall not muzzle an ox when it is treading out the grain." Is it for oxen that God is concerned? [10]Does he not speak entirely for our sake? It was written for our sake, because the plowman should plow in hope and the thresher thresh in hope of a share in the crop. [11]If we have sown spiritual good among you, is it too much if we reap your material benefits? [12]If others share this rightful claim upon you, do not we still more?

Nevertheless, we have not made use of this right, but we endure anything rather than put an obstacle in the way of the gospel of Christ. [13]Do you not know that those who are employed in the temple service get their food from the temple, and those who serve at the altar share in the sacrificial offerings? [14]In the same way, the Lord commanded that those who proclaim the gospel should get their living by the gospel.

PRIMARY

2 Cor 3:1–3 (§154)

[1]Are we beginning to commend ourselves again? Or do we need, as some do, letters of recommendation to you, or from you? [2]You yourselves are our letter of recommendation, written on your hearts, to be known and read by all men; [3]and you show that you are a letter from Christ delivered by us, written not with ink but with the Spirit of the living God, not on tablets of stone but on tablets of human hearts.

2 Cor 11:7–11 (§180)

[7]Did I commit a sin in abasing myself so that you might be exalted, because I preached God's gospel without cost to you? [8]I robbed other churches by accepting support from them in order to serve you. [9]And when I was with you and was in want, I did not burden any one, for my needs were supplied by the brethren who came from Macedonia. So I refrained and will refrain from burdening you in any way. [10]As the truth of Christ is in me, this boast of mine shall not be silenced in the regions of Achaia. [11]And why? Because I do not love you? God knows I do!

2 Cor 12:14–18 (§187)

[14]Here for the third time I am ready to come to you. And I will not be a burden, for I seek not what is yours but you; for children ought not to lay up for their parents, but parents for their children. [15]I will most gladly spend and be spent for your souls. If I love you the more, am I to be loved the less? [16]But granting that I myself did not burden you, I was crafty, you say, and got the better of you by guile. [17]Did I take advantage of you through any of those whom I sent to you? [18]I urged Titus to go, and sent the brother with him. Did Titus take advantage of you? Did we not act in the same spirit? Did we not take the same steps?

Gal 1:15–24 (§196)

[15]But when he who had set me apart before I was born, and had called me through his grace, [16]was pleased to reveal his Son to me, in order that I might preach him among the Gentiles, I did not confer with flesh and blood, [17]nor did I go up to Jerusalem to those who were apostles before me, but I went away into Arabia; and again I returned to Damascus.

[18]Then after three years I went up to Jerusalem to visit Cephas, and remained with him fifteen days. [19]But I saw none of the other apostles except James the Lord's brother. [20](In what I am writing to you, before God, I do not lie!) [21]Then I went into the regions of Syria and Cilicia. [22]And I was still not known by sight to the churches of Christ in Judea; [23]they only heard it said, "He who once persecuted us is now preaching the faith he once tried to destroy." [24]And they glorified God because of me.

Phil 4:10–20 (§253)

[10]I rejoice in the Lord greatly that now at length you have revived your concern for me; you were indeed concerned for me, but you had no opportunity. [11]Not that I complain of want; for I have learned, in whatever state I am, to be content. [12]I know how to be abased, and I know how to abound; in any and all circumstances I have learned the secret of facing plenty and hunger, abundance and want. [13]I can do all things in him who strengthens me.

[14]Yet it was kind of you to share my trouble. [15]And you Philippians yourselves know that in the beginning of the gospel, when I left Macedonia, no church entered into partnership with me in giving and receiving except you only; [16]for even in Thessalonica you sent me help once and again. [17]Not that I seek the gift; but I seek the fruit which increases to your credit. [18]I have received full payment, and more; I am filled, having received from Epaphroditus the gifts you sent, a fragrant offering, a sacrifice acceptable and pleasing to God. [19]And my God will supply every need of yours according to his riches in glory in Christ Jesus. [20]To our God and Father be glory for ever and ever. Amen.

1 Thess 2:9–12 (§278)

[9]For you remember our labor and toil, brethren; we worked night and day, that we might not burden any of you, while we preached to you the gospel of God. [10]You are witnesses, and God also, how holy and righteous and blameless was our behavior to you believers; [11]for you know how, like a father with his children, we exhorted each one of you and encouraged you and charged you [12]to lead a life worthy of God, who calls you into his own kingdom and glory.

2 Thess 3:6–13 (§300)

[6]Now we command you, brethren, in the name of our Lord Jesus Christ, that you keep away from any brother who is living in idleness and not in accord with the tradition that you received from us. [7]For you yourselves know how you ought to imitate us; we were not idle when we were with you, [8]we did not eat any one's bread without paying, but with toil and labor we worked night and day, that we might not burden any of you. [9]It was not because we have not that right, but to give you in our conduct an example to imitate. [10]For even when we were with you, we gave you this command: If any one will not work, let him not eat. [11]For we hear that some of you are living in idleness, mere busybodies, not doing any work. [12]Now such persons we command and exhort in the Lord Jesus Christ to do their work in quietness and to earn their own living. [13]Brethren, do not be weary in well-doing.

● **1 Cor 9:1–2**
Cf. Rom 1:1; 1 Cor 15:8

● **1 Cor 9:1**
1 Tim 2   [7]For this I was appointed a preacher and apostle (I am telling the truth, I am not lying), a teacher of the Gentiles in faith and truth.

2 Tim 1   [11]For this gospel I was appointed a preacher and apostle and teacher, . . .

Cf. 1 Cor 3:6; Acts 9:3; Acts 9:17; Acts 22:14; Acts 26:19

● **1 Cor 9:6**
Acts 20   [34]"You yourselves know that these hands ministered to my necessities, and to those who were with me."

● **1 Cor 9:7**
Cf. 2 Tim 2:4–6

● **1 Cor 9:9**
1 Tim 5   [18]for the scripture says, "You shall not muzzle an ox when it is treading out the grain," and, "The laborer deserves his wages."

Deut 25   [4]"You shall not muzzle an ox when it treads out the grain."

● **1 Cor 9:11**
Cf. Rom 15:27, Gal 6:7

● **1 Cor 9:12**
2 Cor 11   [20]For you bear it if a man makes slaves of you, or preys upon you, or takes advantage of you, or puts on airs, or strikes you in the face. [21]To my shame, I must say, we were too weak for that!

● **1 Cor 9:14**
Gal 6   [6]Let him who is taught the word share all good things with him who teaches.

Cf. Luke 10:7

15But I have made no use of any of these rights, nor am I writing this to secure any such provision. For I would rather die than have any one deprive me of my ground for boasting. 16For if I preach the gospel, that gives me no ground for boasting. For necessity is laid upon me. Woe to me if I do not preach the gospel! 17For if I do this of my own will, I have a reward; but if not of my own will, I am entrusted with a commission. 18What then is my reward? Just this: that in my preaching I may make the gospel free of charge, not making full use of my right in the gospel.

PRIMARY

2 Cor 11:7–11 (§180)

7Did I commit a sin in abasing myself so that you might be exalted, because I preached God's gospel without cost to you? 8I robbed other churches by accepting support from them in order to serve you. 9And when I was with you and was in want, I did not burden any one, for my needs were supplied by the brethren who came from Macedonia. So I refrained and will refrain from burdening you in any way. 10As the truth of Christ is in me, this boast of mine shall not be silenced in the regions of Achaia. 11And why? Because I do not love you? God knows I do!

2 Cor 11:12–15 (§181)

12And what I do I will continue to do, in order to undermine the claim of those who would like to claim that in their boasted mission they work on the same terms as we do. 13For such men are false apostles, deceitful workmen, disguising themselves as apostles of Christ. 14And no wonder, for even Satan disguises himself as an angel of light. 15So it is not strange if his servants also disguise themselves as servants of righteousness. Their end will correspond to their deeds.

Eph 3:1–13 (§222)

1For this reason I, Paul, a prisoner for Christ Jesus on behalf of you Gentiles — 2assuming that you have heard of the stewardship of God's grace that was given to me for you, 3how the mystery was made known to me by revelation, as I have written briefly. 4When you read this you can perceive my insight into the mystery of Christ, 5which was not made known to the sons of men in other generations as it has now been revealed to his holy apostles and prophets by the Spirit; 6that is, how the Gentiles are fellow heirs, members of the same body, and partakers of the promise in Christ Jesus through the gospel.

7Of this gospel I was made a minister according to the gift of God's grace which was given me by the working of his power. 8To me, though I am the very least of all the saints, this grace was given, to preach to the Gentiles the unsearchable riches of Christ, 9and to make all men see what is the plan of the mystery hidden for ages in God who created all things; 10that through the church the manifold wisdom of God might now be made known to the principalities and powers in the heavenly places. 11This was according to the eternal purpose which he has realized in Christ Jesus our Lord, 12in whom we have boldness and confidence of access through our faith in him. 13So I ask you not to lose heart over what I am suffering for you, which is your glory.

Phil 4:10–20 (§253)

10I rejoice in the Lord greatly that now at length you have revived your concern for me; you were indeed concerned for me, but you had no opportunity. 11Not that I complain of want; for I have learned, in whatever state I am, to be content. 12I know how to be abased, and I know how to abound; in any and all circumstances I have learned the secret of facing plenty and hunger, abundance and want. 13I can do all things in him who strengthens me.

14Yet it was kind of you to share my trouble. 15And you Philippians yourselves know that in the beginning of the gospel, when I left Macedonia, no church entered into partnership with me in giving and receiving except you only; 16for even in Thessalonica you sent me help once and again. 17Not that I seek the gift; but I seek the fruit which increases to your credit. 18I have received full payment, and more; I am filled, having received from Epaphroditus the gifts you sent, a fragrant offering, a sacrifice acceptable and pleasing to God. 19And my God will supply every need of yours according to his riches in glory in Christ Jesus. 20To our God and Father be glory for ever and ever. Amen.

1 Thess 2:1–8 (§277)

1For you yourselves know, brethren, that our visit to you was not in vain; 2but though we had already suffered and been shamefully treated at Philippi, as you know, we had courage in our God to declare to you the gospel of God in the face of great opposition. 3For our appeal does not spring from error or uncleanness, nor is it made with guile; 4but just as we have been approved by God to be entrusted with the gospel, so we speak, not to please men, but to please God who tests our hearts. 5For we never used either words of flattery, as you know, or a cloak for greed, as God is witness; 6nor did we seek glory from men, whether from you or from others, though we might have made demands as apostles of Christ. 7But we were gentle among you, like a nurse taking care of her children. 8So, being affectionately desirous of you, we were ready to share with you not only the gospel of God but also our own selves, because you had become very dear to us.

● **1 Cor 9:15**

2 Cor 1 12For our boast is this, the testimony of our conscience that we have behaved in the world, and still more toward you, with holiness and godly sincerity, not by earthly wisdom but by the grace of God.

2 Cor 11 10As the truth of Christ is in me, this boast of mine shall not be silenced in the regions of Achaia.

Phil 4 11Not that I complain of want; for I have learned, in whatever state I am, to be content.

Phil 4 17Not that I seek the gift; but I seek the fruit which increases to your credit.

● **1 Cor 9:16**

2 Cor 4 5For what we preach is not ourselves, but Jesus Christ as Lord, with ourselves as your servants for Jesus' sake.

● **1 Cor 9:17**

Eph 3 7Of this gospel I was made a minister according to the gift of God's grace which was given me by the working of his power. 8To me, though I am the very least of all the saints, this grace was given, to preach to the Gentiles the unsearchable riches of Christ, . . .

● **1 Cor 9:18**

Phlm 8Accordingly, though I am bold enough in Christ to command you to do what is required, . . .

Phlm 18If he has wronged you at all, or owes you anything, charge that to my account.

Phlm 22At the same time, prepare a guest room for me, for I am hoping through your prayers to be granted to you.

Acts 18 3and because he was of the same trade he stayed with them, and they worked, for by trade they were tentmakers.

¹⁹For though I am free from all men, I have made myself a slave to all, that I might win the more. ²⁰To the Jews I became as a Jew, in order to win Jews; to those under the law I became as one under the law—though not being myself under the law—that I might win those under the law. ²¹To those outside the law I became as one outside the law—not being without law toward God but under the law of Christ—that I might win those outside the law. ²²To the weak I became weak, that I might win the weak. I have become all things to all men, that I might by all means save some. ²³I do it all for the sake of the gospel, that I may share in its blessings.

PRIMARY

Rom 2:12-16 (§9)

¹²All who have sinned without the law will also perish without the law, and all who have sinned under the law will be judged by the law. ¹³For it is not the hearers of the law who are righteous before God, but the doers of the law who will be justified. ¹⁴When Gentiles who have not the law do by nature what the law requires, they are a law to themselves, even though they do not have the law. ¹⁵They show that what the law requires is written on their hearts, while their conscience also bears witness and their conflicting thoughts accuse or perhaps excuse them ¹⁶on that day when, according to my gospel, God judges the secrets of men by Christ Jesus.

Rom 11:13-16 (§47)

¹³Now I am speaking to you Gentiles. Inasmuch then as I am an apostle to the Gentiles, I magnify my ministry ¹⁴in order to make my fellow Jews jealous, and thus save some of them. ¹⁵For if their rejection means the reconciliation of the world, what will their acceptance mean but life from the dead? ¹⁶If the dough offered as first fruits is holy, so is the whole lump; and if the root is holy, so are the branches.

Rom 15:1-6 (§60)

¹We who are strong ought to bear with the failings of the weak, and not to please ourselves; ²let each of us please his neighbor for his good, to edify him. ³For Christ did not please himself; but, as it is written, "The reproaches of those who reproached thee fell on me." ⁴For whatever was written in former days was written for our instruction, that by steadfastness and by the encouragement of the scriptures we might have hope. ⁵May the God of steadfastness and encouragement grant you to live in such harmony with one another, in accord with Christ Jesus, ⁶that together you may with one voice glorify the God and Father of our Lord Jesus Christ.

Gal 2:1-10 (§197)

¹Then after fourteen years I went up again to Jerusalem with Barnabas, taking Titus along with me. ²I went up by revelation; and I laid before them (but privately before those who were of repute) the gospel which I preach among the Gentiles, lest somehow I should be running or had run in vain. ³But even Titus, who was with me, was not compelled to be circumcised, though he was a Greek. ⁴But because of false brethren secretly brought in, who slipped in to spy out our freedom which we have in Christ Jesus, that they might bring us into bondage—⁵to them we did not yield submission even for a moment, that the truth of the gospel might be preserved for you. ⁶And from those who were reputed to be something (what they were makes no difference to me; God shows no partiality)—those, I say, who were of repute added nothing to me; ⁷but on the contrary, when they saw that I had been entrusted with the gospel to the uncircumcised, just as Peter had been entrusted with the gospel to the circumcised ⁸(for he who worked through Peter for the mission to the circumcised worked through me also for the Gentiles), ⁹and when they perceived the grace that was given to me, James and Cephas and John, who were reputed to be pillars, gave to me and Barnabas the right hand of fellowship, that we should go to the Gentiles and they to the circumcised; ¹⁰only they would have us remember the poor, which very thing I was eager to do.

Gal 5:13-15 (§212)

¹³For you were called to freedom, brethren; only do not use your freedom as an opportunity for the flesh, but through love be servants of one another. ¹⁴For the whole law is fulfilled in one word, "You shall love your neighbor as yourself." ¹⁵But if you bite and devour one another take heed that you are not consumed by one another.

● 1 Cor 9:19

1 Cor 9 ¹Am I not free? Am I not an apostle? Have I not seen Jesus our Lord? Are not you my workmanship in the Lord?

● 1 Cor 9:20

Gal 2 ¹¹But when Cephas came to Antioch I opposed him to his face, because he stood condemned. ¹²For before certain men came from James, he ate with the Gentiles; but when they came he drew back and separated himself, fearing the circumcision party. ¹³And with him the rest of the Jews acted insincerely, so that even Barnabas was carried away by their insincerity. ¹⁴But when I saw that they were not straightforward about the truth of the gospel, I said to Cephas before them all, "If you, though a Jew, live like a Gentile and not like a Jew, how can you compel the Gentiles to live like Jews?"

Gal 3 ¹¹Now it is evident that no man is justified before God by the law; for "He who through faith is righteous shall live"; . . .

Acts 16 ³Paul wanted Timothy to accompany him; and he took him and circumcised him because of the Jews that were in those places, for they all knew that his father was a Greek.

Acts 21 ²³"Do therefore what we tell you. We have four men who are under a vow; ²⁴take these men and purify yourself along with them and pay their expenses, so that they may shave their heads. Thus all will know that there is nothing in what they have been told about you but that you yourself live in observance of the law. ²⁵But as for the Gentiles who have believed, we have sent a letter with our judgment that they should abstain from what has been sacrificed to idols and from blood and from what is strangled and from unchastity." ²⁶Then Paul took the men, and the next day he purified himself with them and went into the temple, to give notice when the days of purification would be fulfilled and the offering presented for every one of them.

● 1 Cor 9:21

1 Cor 7 ¹⁹For neither circumcision counts for anything nor uncircumcision, but keeping the commandments of God.

Gal 6 ²Bear one another's burdens, and so fulfil the law of Christ.

Eph 2 ¹²remember that you were at that time separated from Christ, alienated from the commonwealth of Israel, and strangers to the covenants of promise, having no hope and without God in the world.

● 1 Cor 9:22

Rom 14 ¹As for the man who is weak in faith, welcome him, but not for disputes over opinions.

1 Cor 8 ¹¹And so by your knowledge this weak man is destroyed, the brother for whom Christ died. ¹²Thus, sinning against your brethren and wounding their conscience when it is weak, you sin against Christ. ¹³Therefore, if food is a cause of my brother's falling, I will never eat meat, lest I cause my brother to fall.

1 Cor 10 ³³just as I try to please all men in everything I do, not seeking my own advantage, but that of many, that they may be saved.

2 Cor 1 ¹⁷Was I vacillating when I wanted to do this? Do I make my plans like a worldly man, ready to say Yes and No at once?

2 Cor 11 ²⁹Who is weak, and I am not weak? Who is made to fall, and I am not indignant?

Gal 1 ¹⁰Am I now seeking the favor of men, or of God? Or am I trying to please men? If I were still pleasing men, I should not be a servant of Christ.

1 Thess 2 ⁴but just as we have been approved by God to be entrusted with the gospel, so we speak, not to please men, but to please God who tests our hearts.

● 1 Cor 9:23

Phil 1 ⁵For we never used either words of with joy, ⁵thankful for your partnership in the gospel from the first day until now.

²⁴Do you not know that in a race all the runners compete, but only one receives the prize? So run that you may obtain it. ²⁵Every athlete exercises self-control in all things. They do it to receive a perishable wreath, but we an imperishable. ²⁶Well, I do not run aimlessly, I do not box as one beating the air; ²⁷but I pommel my body and subdue it, lest after preaching to others I myself should be disqualified.

PRIMARY

Phil 3:12–16 (§248)

¹²Not that I have already obtained this or am already perfect; but I press on to make it my own, because Christ Jesus has made me his own. ¹³Brethren, I do not consider that I have made it my own; but one thing I do, forgetting what lies behind and straining forward to what lies ahead, ¹⁴I press on toward the goal for the prize of the upward call of God in Christ Jesus. ¹⁵Let those of us who are mature be thus minded; and if in anything you are otherwise minded, God will reveal that also to you. ¹⁶Only let us hold true to what we have attained.

● **1 Cor 9:24–27**
2 Tim 4   ⁷I have fought the good fight, I have finished the race, I have kept the faith. ⁸Henceforth there is laid up for me the crown of righteousness, which the Lord, the righteous judge, will award to me on that Day, and not only to me but also to all who have loved his appearing.

● **1 Cor 9:24**
Gal 2   ²I went up by revelation; and I laid before them (but privately before those who were of repute) the gospel which I preach among the Gentiles, lest somehow I should be running or had run in vain.

● **1 Cor 9:25**
1 Cor 7   ⁵Do not refuse one another except perhaps by agreement for a season, that you may devote yourselves to prayer; but then come together again, lest Satan tempt you through lack of self-control.

1 Cor 7   ⁹But if they cannot exercise self-control, they should marry. For it is better to marry than to be aflame with passion.

1 Cor 7   ³⁷But whoever is firmly established in his heart, being under no necessity but having his desire under control, and has determined this in his heart, to keep her as his betrothed, he will do well.

Gal 5   ²³gentleness, self-control; against such there is no law.

2 Tim 2   ⁵An athlete is not crowned unless he competes according to the rules.

Jas 1   ¹²Blessed is the man who endures trial, for when he has stood the test he will receive the crown of life which God has promised to those who love him.

Heb 12   ¹Therefore, since we are surrounded by so great a cloud of witnesses, let us also lay aside every weight, and sin which clings so closely, and let us run with perseverance the race that is set before us, ²looking to Jesus the pioneer and perfecter of our faith, who for the joy that was set before him endured the cross, despising the shame, and is seated at the right hand of the throne of God.

2 Pet 1   ⁶and knowledge with self-control, and self-control with steadfastness, and steadfastness with godliness, . . .

● **1 Cor 9:26**
Phil 2   ¹⁶holding fast the word of life, so that in the day of Christ I may be proud that I did not run in vain or labor in vain.

● **1 Cor 9:27**
Col 2   ¹⁸Let no one disqualify you, insisting on self-abasement and worship of angels, taking his stand on visions, puffed up without reason by his sensuous mind, . . .

10 I want you to know, brethren, that our fathers were all under the cloud, and all passed through the sea, [2]and all were baptized into Moses in the cloud and in the sea, [3]and all ate the same supernatural food [4]and all drank the same supernatural drink. For they drank from the supernatural Rock which followed them, and the Rock was Christ. [5]Nevertheless with most of them God was not pleased; for they were overthrown in the wilderness.

[6]Now these things are warnings for us, not to desire evil as they did. [7]Do not be idolaters as some of them were; as it is written, "The people sat down to eat and drink and rose up to dance." [8]We must not indulge in immorality as some of them did, and twenty-three thousand fell in a single day. [9]We must not put the Lord to the test, as some of them did and were destroyed by serpents; [10]nor grumble, as some of them did and were destroyed by the Destroyer. [11]Now these things happened to them as a warning, but they were written down for our instruction, upon whom the end of the ages has come. [12]Therefore let any one who thinks that he stands take heed lest he fall. [13]No temptation has overtaken you that is not common to man. God is faithful, and he will not let you be tempted beyond your strength, but with the temptation will also provide the way of escape, that you may be able to endure it.

PRIMARY

Rom 6:11–14 (§24)

[11]So you also must consider yourselves dead to sin and alive to God in Christ Jesus.

[12]Let not sin therefore reign in your mortal bodies, to make you obey their passions. [13]Do not yield your members to sin as instruments of wickedness, but yield yourselves to God as men who have been brought from death to life, and your members to God as instruments of righteousness. [14]For sin will have no dominion over you, since you are not under law but under grace.

Gal 5:16–26 (§213)

[16]But I say, walk by the Spirit, and do not gratify the desires of the flesh. [17]For the desires of the flesh are against the Spirit, and the desires of the Spirit are against the flesh; for these are opposed to each other, to prevent you from doing what you would. [18]But if you are led by the Spirit you are not under the law. [19]Now the works of the flesh are plain: fornication, impurity, licentiousness, [20]idolatry, sorcery, enmity, strife, jealousy, anger, selfishness, dissension, party spirit, [21]envy, drunkenness, carousing, and the like. I warn you, as I warned you before, that those who do such things shall not inherit the kingdom of God. [22]But the fruit of the Spirit is love, joy, peace, patience, kindness, goodness, faithfulness, [23]gentleness, self-control; against such there is no law. [24]And those who belong to Christ Jesus have crucified the flesh with its passions and desires.

[25]If we live by the Spirit, let us also walk by the Spirit. [26]Let us have no self-conceit, no provoking of one another, no envy of one another.

Col 3:5–11 (§266)

[5]Put to death therefore what is earthly in you: fornication, impurity, passion, evil desire, and covetousness, which is idolatry. [6]On account of these the wrath of God is coming. [7]In these you once walked, when you lived in them. [8]But now put them all away: anger, wrath, malice, slander, and foul talk from your mouth. [9]Do not lie to one another, seeing that you have put off the old nature with its practices [10]and have put on the new nature, which is being renewed in knowledge after the image of its creator. [11]Here there cannot be Greek and Jew, circumcised and uncircumcised, barbarian, Scythian, slave, free man, but Christ is all, and in all.

2 Thess 2:1–12 (§296)

[1]Now concerning the coming of our Lord Jesus Christ and our assembling to meet him, we beg you, brethren, [2]not to be quickly shaken in mind or excited, either by spirit or by word, or by letter purporting to be from us, to the effect that the day of the Lord has come. [3]Let no one deceive you in any way; for that day will not come, unless the rebellion comes first, and the man of lawlessness is revealed, the son of perdition, [4]who opposes and exalts himself against every so-called god or object of worship, so that he takes his seat in the temple of God, proclaiming himself to be God. [5]Do you not remember that when I was still with you I told you this? [6]And you know what is restraining him now so that he may be revealed in his time. [7]For the mystery of lawlessness is already at work; only he who now restrains it will do so until he is out of the way. [8]And then the lawless one will be revealed, and the Lord Jesus will slay him with the breath of his mouth and destroy him by his appearing and his coming. [9]The coming of the lawless one by the activity of Satan will be with all power and with pretended signs and wonders, [10]and with all wicked deception for those who are to perish, because they refused to love the truth and so be saved. [11]Therefore God sends upon them a strong delusion, to make them believe what is false, [12]so that all may be condemned who did not believe the truth but had pleasure in unrighteousness.

● **1 Cor 10:2**
Cf. Gal 3:27

● **1 Cor 10:3**
Exod 16   [4]Then the Lord said to Moses, "Behold, I will rain bread from heaven for you; and the people shall go out and gather a day's portion every day, that I may prove them, whether they will walk in my law or not."

Exod 16   [25]Moses said, "Eat it today, for today is a sabbath to the Lord; today you will not find it in the field."

● **1 Cor 10:4**
Exod 17   [6]"Behold, I will stand before you there on the rock at Horeb; and you shall strike the rock, and water shall come out of it, that the people may drink." And Moses did so, in the sight of the elders of Israel.

Num 20   [11]And Moses lifted up his hand and struck the rock with his rod twice; and water came forth abundantly, and the congregation drank, and their cattle.

● **1 Cor 10:5**
Num 14   [29]your dead bodies shall fall in this wilderness; and of all your number, numbered from twenty years old and upward, who have murmured against me, [30]not one shall come into the land where I swore that I would make you dwell, except Caleb the son of Jephunneh and Joshua the son of Nun.

● **1 Cor 10:6**
Num 11   [4]Now the rabble that was among them had a strong craving; and the people of Israel also wept again, and said, "O that we had meat to eat!"

Cf. Num 11:34

● **1 Cor 10:7**
Exod 32   [4]And he received the gold at their hand, and fashioned it with a graving tool, and made a molten calf; and they said, "These are your gods, O Israel, who brought you up out of the land of Egypt!"

Exod 32   [6]And they rose up early on the morrow, and offered burnt offerings and brought peace offerings; and the people sat down to eat and drink, and rose up to play.

● **1 Cor 10:8**
Num 25   [1]While Israel dwelt in Shittim the people began to play the harlot with the daughters of Moab.

Num 25   [9]Nevertheless those that died by the plague were twenty-four thousand.

● **1 Cor 10:9**
Num 21   [5]And the people spoke against God and against Moses, "Why have you brought us up out of Egypt to die in the wilderness? For there is no food and no water, and we loathe this worthless food." [6]Then the Lord sent fiery serpents among the people, and they bit the people, so that many people of Israel died.

(Lord) *read* Christ: p[46] DG Koine Lect it vg syr cop Marcion Irenaeus (Latin)

● **1 Cor 10:10**
Num 16   [41]But on the morrow all the congregation of the people of Israel murmured against Moses and against Aaron, saying, "You have killed the people of the Lord."

Num 16   [49]Now those who died by the plague were fourteen thousand seven hundred, besides those who died in the affair of Korah.

Cf. Phil 2:14

● **1 Cor 10:11**
Cf. Rom 15:4; 1 Cor 9:10; Rom 4:23–24; 2 Tim 3:16

● **1 Cor 10:12**
Cf. Rom 11:20

● **1 Cor 10:13**
Cf. 1 Cor 1:9; 2 Cor 1:18; 1 Thess 5:24; 2 Thess 3:3; 2 Tim 2:13

FORMAL ELEMENT:
EUCHARISTIC LITURGY

14 Therefore, my beloved, shun the worship of idols. **15** I speak as to sensible men; judge for yourselves what I say. **16** The cup of blessing which we bless, is it not a participation in the blood of Christ? The bread which we break, is it not a participation in the body of Christ? **17** Because there is one bread, we who are many are one body, for we all partake of the one bread.

18 Consider the people of Israel; are not those who eat the sacrifices partners in the altar? **19** What do I imply then? That food offered to idols is anything, or that an idol is anything? **20** No, I imply that what pagans sacrifice they offer to demons and not to God. I do not want you to be partners with demons. **21** You cannot drink the cup of the Lord and the cup of demons. You cannot partake of the table of the Lord and the table of demons. **22** Shall we provoke the Lord to jealousy? Are we stronger than he?

PRIMARY

1 Cor 11:23–26 (§114)

23 For I received from the Lord what I also delivered to you, that the Lord Jesus on the night when he was betrayed took bread, **24** and when he had given thanks, he broke it, and said, "This is my body which is for you. Do this in remembrance of me." **25** In the same way also the cup, after supper, saying, "This cup is the

new covenant in my blood. Do this, as often as you drink it, in remembrance of me." **26** For as often as you eat this bread and drink the cup, you proclaim the Lord's death until he comes.

SECONDARY

2 Cor 6:14–7:1 (§167)

14 Do not be mismated with unbelievers. For what partnership have righteousness and iniquity? Or what fellowship has light with darkness? **15** What accord has Christ with Belial? Or what has a believer in common with an unbeliever? **16** What agreement has the temple of God with idols? For we are the temple of the living God; as God said,

"I will live in them and move among them,
and I will be their God,
and they shall be my people.
17 Therefore come out from them,
and be separate from them, says the Lord,
and touch nothing unclean;
then I will welcome you,
18 and I will be a father to you,
and you shall be my sons and daughters,
says the Lord Almighty."

7 **1** Since we have these promises, beloved, let us cleanse ourselves from every defilement of body and spirit, and make holiness perfect in the fear of God.

Gal 4:8–11 (§208)

8 Formerly, when you did not know God, you were in bondage to beings that by nature are no gods; **9** but now that you have come to

know God, or rather to be known by God, how can you turn back again to the weak and beggarly elemental spirits, whose slaves you want to be once more? **10** You observe days, and months, and seasons, and years! **11** I am afraid I have labored over you in vain.

1 Thess 1:2–10 (§276)

2 We give thanks to God always for you all, constantly mentioning you in our prayers, **3** remembering before our God and Father your work of faith and labor of love and steadfastness of hope in our Lord Jesus Christ. **4** For we know, brethren beloved by God, that he has chosen you; **5** for our gospel came to you not only in word, but also in power and in the Holy Spirit and with full conviction. You know what kind of men we proved to be among you for your sake. **6** And you became imitators of us and of the Lord, for you received the word in much affliction, with joy inspired by the Holy Spirit; **7** so that you became an example to the all the believers in Macedonia and in Achaia. **8** For not only has the word of the Lord sounded forth from you in Macedonia and Achaia, but your faith in God has gone forth everywhere, so that we need not say anything. **9** For they themselves report concerning us what a welcome we had among you, and how you turned to God from idols, to serve a living and true God, **10** and to wait for his Son from heaven, whom he raised from the dead, Jesus who delivers us from the wrath to come.

● **1 Cor 10:16**
1 Thess 1 **9** For they themselves report concerning us what a welcome we had among you, and how you turned to God from idols, to serve a living and true God, . . .

Acts 2 **42** And they devoted themselves to the apostles' teaching and fellowship, to the breaking of bread and the prayers.

● **1 Cor 10:17**
Rom 1 **5** so we, though many, are one body in Christ, and individually members one of another.

1 Cor 12 **12** For just as the body is one and has many members, and all the members of the body, though many, are one body, so it is with Christ. **13** For by one Spirit we were all baptized into one body— Jews or Greeks, slaves or free—and all were made to drink of one Spirit.

● **1 Cor 10:18**
Lev 7 **6** Every male among the priests may eat of it; it shall be eaten in a holy place; it is most holy.

● **1 Cor 10:19–21**
1 Cor 8 **4** Hence, as to the eating of food offered to idols, we know that "an idol has no real existence," and

that "there is no God but one." **5** For although there may be so-called gods in heaven or on earth—as indeed there are many "gods" and many "lords"—**6** yet for us there is one God, the Father, from whom are all things and for whom we exist, and one Lord, Jesus Christ, through whom are all things and through whom we exist.

● **1 Cor 10:21**
1 Cor 10 **27** If one of the unbelievers invites you to dinner and you are disposed to go, eat whatever is set before you without raising any question on the ground of conscience.

[23]"All things are lawful," but not all things are helpful. "All things are lawful," but not all things build up. [24]Let no one seek his own good, but the good of his neighbor. [25]Eat whatever is sold in the meat market without raising any question on the ground of conscience. [26]For "the earth is the Lord's, and everything in it." [27]If one of the unbelievers invites you to dinner and you are disposed to go, eat whatever is set before you without raising any question on the ground of conscience. [28](But if some one says to you, "This has been offered in sacrifice," then out of consideration for the man who informed you, and for conscience' sake— [29]I mean his conscience, not yours—do not eat it.) For why should my liberty be determined by another man's scruples? [30]If I partake with thankfulness, why am I denounced because of that for which I give thanks?

[31]So, whether you eat or drink, or whatever you do, do all to the glory of God. [32]Give no offense to Jews or to Greeks or to the church of God, [33]just as I try to please all men in everything I do, not seeking my own advantage, but that of many, that they may be saved. 11 [1]Be imitators of me, as I am of Christ.

PRIMARY

Rom 2:12–16 (§9)

[12]All who have sinned without the law will also perish without the law, and all who have sinned under the law will be judged by the law. [13]For it is not the hearers of the law who are righteous before God, but the doers of the law who will be justified. [14]When Gentiles who have not the law do by nature what the law requires, they are a law to themselves, even though they do not have the law. [15]They show that what the law requires is written on their hearts, while their conscience also bears witness and their conflicting thoughts accuse or perhaps excuse them [16]on that day when, according to my gospel, God judges the secrets of men by Christ Jesus.

Rom 14:5–12 (§58)

[5]One man esteems one day as better than another, while another man esteems all days alike. Let every one be fully convinced in his own mind. [6]He who observes the day, observes it in honor of the Lord. He also who eats, eats in honor of the Lord, since he gives thanks to God; while he who abstains, abstains in honor of the Lord and gives thanks to God. [7]None of us lives to himself, and none of us dies to himself. [8]If we live, we live to the Lord, and if we die, we die to the Lord; so then, whether we live or whether we die, we are the Lord's. [9]For to this end Christ died and lived again, that he might be Lord both of the dead and of the living.

[10]Why do you pass judgment on your brother? Or you, why do you despise your brother? For we shall all stand before the judgment seat of God; [11]for it is written,

"As I live, says the Lord, every knee shall bow to me,

and every tongue shall give praise to God." [12]So each of us shall give account of himself to God.

Rom 14:13–23 (§59)

[13]Then let us no more pass judgment on one another, but rather decide never to put a stumbling block or hindrance in the way of a brother. [14]I know and am persuaded in the Lord Jesus that nothing is unclean in itself; but it is unclean for any one who thinks it unclean. [15]If your brother is being injured by what you eat, you are no longer walking in love. Do not let what you eat cause the ruin of one for whom Christ died. [16]So do not let your good be spoken of as evil. [17]For the kingdom of God is not food and drink but righteousness and peace and joy in the Holy Spirit; [18]he who thus serves Christ is acceptable to God and approved by men. [19]Let us then pursue what makes for peace and for mutual upbuilding. [20]Do not, for the sake of food, destroy the work of God. Everything is indeed clean, but it is wrong for any one to

---

● 1 Cor 10:23

1 Cor 6   [12]"All things are lawful for me," but not all things are helpful. "All things are lawful for me," but I will not be enslaved by anything.

● 1 Cor 10:24

Gal 6   [2]Bear one another's burdens, and so fulfil the law of Christ.

● 1 Cor 10:25

1 Cor 4   [3]But with me it is a very small thing that I should be judged by you or by any human court. I do not even judge myself. [4]I am not aware of anything against myself, but I am not thereby acquitted. It is the Lord who judges me.

1 Cor 8   [7]However, not all possess this knowledge. But some, through being hitherto accustomed to idols, eat food as really offered to an idol; and their conscience, being weak, is defiled. [8]Food will not commend us to God. We are no worse off if we do not

eat, and no better off if we do. [9]Only take care lest this liberty of yours somehow become a stumbling block to the weak. [10]For if any one sees you, a man of knowledge, at table in an idol's temple, might he not be encouraged, if his conscience is weak, to eat food offered to idols? [11]And so by your knowledge this weak man is destroyed, the brother for whom Christ died. [12]Thus, sinning against your brethren and wounding their conscience when it is weak, you sin against Christ. [13]Therefore, if food is a cause of my brother's falling, I will never eat meat, lest I cause my brother to fall.

● 1 Cor 10:26

1 Tim 4   [4]For everything created by God is good, and nothing is to be rejected if it is received with thanksgiving; . . .

Ps 24   [1]The earth is the Lord's and the fulness thereof,
   the world and those who dwell therein; . . .

● 1 Cor 10:27

1 Cor 5   [9]I wrote to you in my letter not to associate with immoral men; [10]not at all meaning the immoral of this world, or the greedy and robbers, or idolaters, since then you would need to go out of the world. [11]But rather I wrote to you not to associate with any one who bears the name of brother if he is guilty of immorality or greed, or is an idolater, reviler, drunkard, or robber—not even to eat with such a one. [12]For what have I to do with judging outsiders? Is it not those inside the church whom you are to judge? [13]God judges those outside. "Drive out the wicked person from among you."

● 1 Cor 10:30

Cf. Gal 5   [11]But if I, brethren, still preach circumcision, why am I still persecuted? In that case the stumbling block of the cross has been removed.

Cf. Phil 4   [6]Have no anxiety about anything, but in

make others fall by what he eats; [21] it is right not to eat meat or drink wine or do anything that makes your brother stumble. [22] The faith that you have, keep between yourself and God; happy is he who has no reason to judge himself for what he approves. [23] But he who has doubts is condemned, if he eats, because he does not act from faith; for whatever does not proceed from faith is sin.

Rom 15:1–6 (§60)

[1] We who are strong ought to bear with the failings of the weak, and not to please ourselves; [2] let each of us please his neighbor for his good, to edify him. [3] For Christ did not please himself; but, as it is written, "The reproaches of those who reproached thee fell on me." [4] For whatever was written in former days was written for our instruction, that by steadfastness and by the encouragement of the scriptures we might have hope. [5] May the God of steadfastness and encouragement grant you to live in such harmony with one another, in accord with Christ Jesus, [6] that together you may with one voice glorify the God and Father of our Lord Jesus Christ.

2 Cor 6:14–7:1 (§167)

[14] Do not be mismated with unbelievers. For what partnership have righteousness and iniquity? Or what fellowship has light with darkness? [15] What accord has Christ with Belial? Or what has a believer in common with an unbe-liever? [16] What agreement has the temple of God with idols? For we are the temple of the living God; as God said,

"I will live in them and move among them,
and I will be their God,
and they shall be my people.
[17] Therefore come out from them,
and be separate from them, says the Lord,
and touch nothing unclean;
then I will welcome you,
[18] and I will be a father to you,
and you shall be my sons and daughters,
says the Lord Almighty."

7 [1] Since we have these promises, beloved, let us cleanse ourselves from every defilement of body and spirit, and make holiness perfect in the fear of God.

Gal 2:11–14 (§198)

[11] But when Cephas came to Antioch I opposed him to his face, because he stood condemned. [12] For before certain men came from James, he ate with the Gentiles; but when they came he drew back and separated himself, fearing the circumcision party. [13] And with him the rest of the Jews acted insincerely, so that even Barnabas was carried away by their insincerity. [14] But when I saw that they were not straightforward about the truth of the gospel, I said to Cephas before them all, "If you, though a Jew, live like a Gentile and not like a Jew, how can you compel the Gentiles to live like Jews?"

Eph 5:15–20 (§231)

[15] Look carefully then how you walk, not as unwise men but as wise, [16] making the most of the time, because the days are evil. [17] Therefore do not be foolish, but understand what the will of the Lord is. [18] And do not get drunk with wine, for that is debauchery; but be filled with the Spirit, [19] addressing one another in psalms and hymns and spiritual songs, singing and making melody to the Lord with all your heart, [20] always and for everything giving thanks in the name of our Lord Jesus Christ to God the Father.

Col 3:12–17 (§267)

[12] Put on then, as God's chosen ones, holy and beloved, compassion, kindness, lowliness, meekness, and patience, [13] forbearing one another and, if one has a complaint against another, forgiving each other; as the Lord has forgiven you, so you also must forgive. [14] And above all these put on love, which binds everything together in perfect harmony. [15] And let the peace of Christ rule in your hearts, to which indeed you were called in the one body. And be thankful. [16] Let the word of Christ dwell in you richly, as you teach and admonish one another in all wisdom, and as you sing psalms and hymns and spiritual songs with thankfulness in your hearts to God. [17] And whatever you do, in word or deed, do everything in the name of the Lord Jesus, giving thanks to God the Father through him.

---

everything by prayer and supplication with thanksgiving let your requests be made known to God.

● **1 Cor 10:32**
Acts 24   [16] "So I always take pains to have a clear conscience toward God and toward men."

Rom 11   [13] Now I am speaking to you Gentiles. Inasmuch then as I am an apostle to the Gentiles, I magnify my ministry [14] in order to make my fellow Jews jealous, and thus save some of them.

1 Cor 9   [19] For though I am free from all men, I have made myself a slave to all, that I might win the more. [20] To the Jews I became as a Jew, in order to win Jews; to those under the law I became as one under the law—though not being myself under the law—that I might win those under the law. [21] To those outside the law I became as one outside the law—not being without law toward God but under the law of Christ—that I might win those outside the law. [22] To the weak I became weak, that I might win the weak. I have become all things to all men, that I might by all means save some. [23] I do it all for the sake of the gospel, that I may share in its blessings.

● **1 Cor 10:33**
Phil 2   [4] Let each of you look not only to his own interests, but also to the interests of others.

● **1 Cor 11:1**
Cf. 1 Cor 4   [16] I urge you, then, be imitators of me.

Cf. Gal 4   [12] Brethren, I beseech you, become as I am, for I also have become as you are. You did me no wrong; . . .

Cf. Eph 5   [1] Therefore be imitators of God, as beloved children.

Cf. Phil 3   [17] Brethren, join in imitating me, and mark those who so live as you have an example in us.

Cf. Phil 4   [8] Finally, brethren, whatever is true, whatever is honorable, whatever is just, whatever is pure, whatever is lovely, whatever is gracious, if there is any excellence, if there is anything worthy of praise, think about these things. [9] What you have learned and received and heard and seen in me, do; and the God of peace will be with you.

Cf. 1 Thess 1   [6] And you became imitators of us and of the Lord, for you received the word in much affliction, with joy inspired by the Holy Spirit; . . .

Cf. 1 Thess 2   [14] For you, brethren, became imitators of the churches of God in Christ Jesus which are in Judea; for you suffered the same things from your own countrymen as they did from the Jews, . . .

Cf. 2 Thess 3   [7] For you yourselves know how you ought to imitate us; we were not idle when we were with you, . . .

²I commend you because you remember me in everything and maintain the traditions even as I have delivered them to you. ³But I want you to understand that the head of every man is Christ, the head of a woman is her husband, and the head of Christ is God. ⁴Any man who prays or prophesies with his head covered dishonors his head, ⁵but any woman who prays or prophesies with her head unveiled dishonors her head—it is the same as if her head were shaven. ⁶For if a woman will not veil herself, then she should cut off her hair; but if it is disgraceful for a woman to be shorn or shaven, let her wear a veil. ⁷For a man ought not to cover his head, since he is the image and glory of God; but woman is the glory of man. ⁸(For man was not made from woman, but woman from man. ⁹Neither was man created for woman, but woman for man.) ¹⁰That is why a woman ought to have a veil on her head, because of the angels. ¹¹(Nevertheless, in the Lord woman is not independent of man nor man of woman; ¹²for as woman was made from man, so man is now born of woman. And all things are from God.) ¹³Judge for yourselves; is it proper for a woman to pray to God with her head uncovered? ¹⁴Does not nature itself teach you that for a man to wear long hair is degrading to him, ¹⁵but if a woman has long hair, it is her pride? For her hair is given to her for a covering. ¹⁶If any one is disposed to be contentious, we recognize no other practice, nor do the churches of God.

Primary

Eph 5:21–6:9 (§232)

²¹Be subject to one another out of reverence for Christ. ²²Wives, be subject to your husbands, as to the Lord. ²³For the husband is the head of the wife as Christ is the head of the church, his body, and is himself its Savior. ²⁴As the church is subject to Christ, so let wives also be subject in everything to their husbands. ²⁵Husbands, love your wives, as Christ loved the church and gave himself up for her, ²⁶that he might sanctify her, having cleansed her by the washing of water with the word, ²⁷that he might present the church to himself in splendor, without spot or wrinkle or any such thing, that she might be holy and without blemish. ²⁸Even so husbands should love their wives as their own bodies. He who loves his wife loves himself. ²⁹For no man ever hates his own flesh, but nourishes and cherishes it, as Christ does the church, ³⁰because we are members of his body. ³¹"For this reason a man shall leave his father and mother and be joined to his wife, and the two shall become one flesh." ³²This mystery is a profound one, and I am saying that it refers to Christ and the church; ³³however, let each one of you love his wife as himself, and let the wife see that she respects her husband.

6 ¹Children, obey your parents in the Lord, for this is right. ²"Honor your father and mother" (this is the first commandment with a promise), ³"that it may be well with you and that you may live long on the earth." ⁴Fathers, do not provoke your children to anger, but bring them up in the discipline and instruction of the Lord.

⁵Slaves, be obedient to those who are your earthly masters, with fear and trembling, in singleness of heart, as to Christ; ⁶not in the way of eyeservice, as men-pleasers, but as servants of Christ, doing the will of God from the heart, ⁷rendering service with a good will as to the Lord and not to men, ⁸knowing that whatever good any one does, he will receive the same again from the Lord, whether he is a slave or free. ⁹Masters, do the same to them, and forbear threatening, knowing that he who is both their Master and yours is in heaven, and that there is no partiality with him.

Phil 4:8–9 (§252)

⁸Finally, brethren, whatever is true, whatever is honorable, whatever is just, whatever is pure, whatever is lovely, whatever is gracious, if there is any excellence, if there is anything worthy of praise, think about these things. ⁹What you have learned and received and heard and seen in me, do; and the God of peace will be with you.

2 Thess 3:14–15 (§301)

¹⁴If any one refuses to obey what we say in this letter, note that man, and have nothing to do with him, that he may be ashamed. ¹⁵Do not look on him as an enemy, but warn him as a brother.

● 1 Cor 11:2

Cf. Rom 6   ¹⁷But thanks be to God, that you who were once slaves of sin have become obedient from the heart to the standard of teaching to which you were committed, . . .

Cf. 1 Cor 11   ²³"All things are lawful," but not all things are helpful. "All things are lawful," but not all things build up.

Cf. 1 Cor 15   ¹Now I would remind you, brethren, in what terms I preached to you the gospel, which you received, in which you stand, ²by which you are saved, if you hold it fast —unless you believed in vain.
³For I delivered to you as of first importance what I also received, that Christ died for our sins in accordance with the scriptures, . . .

Cf. 1 Thess 2   ¹³And we also thank God constantly for this, that when you received the word of God which you heard from us, you accepted it not as the word of men but as what it really is, the word of God, which is at work in you believers. ¹⁴For you, brethren, became imitators of the churches of God in Christ Jesus which are in Judea; . . .

● 1 Cor 11:3

1 Cor 3   ²³and you are Christ's; and Christ is God's.

Eph 1   ²²and he has put all things under his feet and has made him the head over all things for the church, . . .

Col 2   ¹⁹and not holding fast to the Head, from whom the whole body, nourished and knit together through its joints and ligaments, grows with a growth that is from God.

Cf. Eph 4   ¹⁵Rather, speaking the truth in love, we are to grow up in every way into him who is the head, into Christ, . . .

● 1 Cor 11:5

1 Cor 14   ³³. . . As in all the churches of the saints, ³⁴the women should keep silence in the churches. For they are not permitted to speak, but should be subordinate, as even the law says. ³⁵If there is anything they desire to know, let them ask their husbands at home. For it is shameful for a woman to speak in church. ³⁶What! Did the word of God originate with you, or are you the only ones it has reached?

Cf. Rom 16   ¹I commend to you our sister Phoebe, a deaconess of the church at Cenchreae, . . .

Cf. Acts 21   ⁹And he had four unmarried daughters, who prophesied.

● 1 Cor 11:8

Cf. 1 Tim 2   ¹¹Let a woman learn in silence with all submissiveness. ¹²I permit no woman to teach or to have authority over men; she is to keep silent. ¹³For Adam was formed first, then Eve; ¹⁴and Adam was not deceived, but the woman was deceived and became a transgressor.

● 1 Cor 11:10

Cf. 1 Cor 6   ³Do you not know that we are to judge angels? How much more, matters pertaining to this life!

● 1 Cor 11:11

1 Cor 7   ⁴For the wife does not rule over her own body, but the husband does; likewise the husband does not rule over his own body, but the wife does.

● 1 Cor 11:14

Rom 1   ²⁶For this reason God gave them up to dishonorable passions. Their women exchanged natural relations for unnatural, . . .

● 1 Cor 11:16

1 Cor 7   ¹⁷Only, let every one lead the life which the Lord has assigned to him, and in which God has called him. This is my rule in all the churches.

Cf. 1 Cor 14   ³⁸If any one does not recognize this, he is not recognized.

¹⁷But in the following instructions I do not commend you, because when you come together it is not for the better but for the worse. ¹⁸For, in the first place, when you assemble as a church, I hear that there are divisions among you; and I partly believe it, ¹⁹for there must be factions among you in order that those who are genuine among you may be recognized. ²⁰When you meet together, it is not the Lord's supper that you eat. ²¹For in eating, each one goes ahead with his own meal, and one is hungry and another is drunk. ²²What! Do you not have houses to eat and drink in? Or do you despise the church of God and humiliate those who have nothing? What shall I say to you? Shall I commend you in this? No, I will not.

PRIMARY

Rom 14:1–4 (§57)

¹As for the man who is weak in faith, welcome him, but not for disputes over opinions. ²One believes he may eat anything, while the weak man eats only vegetables. ³Let not him who eats despise him who abstains, and let not him who abstains pass judgment on him who eats; for God has welcomed him. ⁴Who are you to pass judgment on the servant of another? It is before his own master that he stands or falls. And he will be upheld, for the Master is able to make him stand.

● **1 Cor 11:17**

1 Cor 11   ²I commend you because you remember me in everything and maintain the traditions even as I have delivered them to you.

● **1 Cor 11:18–19**

1 Cor 1   ¹⁰I appeal to you, brethren, by the name of our Lord Jesus Christ, that all of you agree and that there be no dissensions among you, but that you be united in the same mind and the same judgment. ¹¹For it has been reported to me by Chloe's people that there is quarreling among you, my brethren. ¹²What I

mean is that each one of you says, "I belong to Paul," or "I belong to Apollos," or "I belong to Cephas," or "I belong to Christ." ¹³Is Christ divided? Was Paul crucified for you? Or were you baptized in the name of Paul?

Phil 2   ²complete my joy by being of the same mind, having the same love, being in full accord and of one mind.

● **1 Cor 11:20**

1 Cor 10   ¹⁶The cup of blessing which we bless, is it

not a participation in the blood of Christ? The bread which we break, is it not a participation in the body of Christ? ¹⁷Because there is one bread, we who are many are one body, for we all partake of the one bread.

● **1 Cor 11:22**

1 Cor 11   ³³So then, my brethren, when you come together to eat, wait for one another — ³⁴if any one is hungry, let him eat at home—lest you come together to be condemned. About the other things I will give directions when I come.

FORMAL ELEMENT:
EUCHARISTIC LITURGY

23 For I received from the Lord what I also delivered to you, that the Lord Jesus on the night when he was betrayed took bread, 24 and when he had given thanks, he broke it, and said, "This is my body which is for you. Do this in remembrance of me." 25 In the same way also the cup, after supper, saying, "This cup is the new covenant in my blood. Do this, as often as you drink it, in remembrance of me." 26 For as often as you eat this bread and drink the cup, you proclaim the Lord's death until he comes.

PRIMARY

1 Cor 10:14–22 (§110)
14 Therefore, my beloved, shun the worship of idols. 15 I speak as to sensible men; judge for yourselves what I say. 16 The cup of blessing which we bless, is it not a participation in the blood of Christ? The bread which we break, is it not a participation in the body of Christ? 17 Because there is one bread, we who are many are one body, for we all partake of the one bread.

18 Consider the people of Israel; are not those who eat the sacrifices partners in the altar? 19 What do I imply then? That food offered to idols is anything, or that an idol is anything? 20 No, I imply that what pagans sacrifice they offer to demons and not to God. I do not want you to be partners with demons. 21 You cannot drink the cup of the Lord and the cup of demons. You cannot partake of the table of the Lord and the table of demons. 22 Shall we provoke the Lord to jealousy? Are we stronger than he?

● **1 Cor 11:23–26**
1 Cor 7   10 To the married I give charge, not I but the Lord, that the wife should not separate from her husband . . .

1 Cor 15   3 For I delivered to you as of first importance what I also received, that Christ died for our sins in accordance with the scriptures, 4 that he was buried, that he was raised on the third day in accordance with the scriptures, 5 and that he appeared to Cephas, then to the twelve.

Gal 1   12 For I did not receive it from man, nor was I taught it, but it came through a revelation of Jesus Christ.

Mark 14   22 And as they were eating, he took bread, and blessed, and broke it, and gave it to them, and said, "Take; this is my body." 23 And he took a cup, and when he had given thanks he gave it to them, and they all drank of it. 24 And he said to them, "This is my blood of the covenant, which is poured out for many.

25 Truly, I say to you, I shall not drink again of the fruit of the vine until that day when I drink it new in the kingdom of God."

Acts 2   42 And they devoted themselves to the apostles' teaching and fellowship, to the breaking of bread and the prayers.

● **1 Cor 11:24**
(for) *read* broken for: S^{c}C^{3}D^{bc}G Koine Lect it (few) sy Ambrosiaster: *read* given for: cop; broken up for: D*; *text:* p^{46} S*ABC*

● **1 Cor 11:26**
Rom 13   11 Besides this you know what hour it is, how it is full time now for you to wake from sleep. For salvation is nearer to us now than when we first believed; 12 the night is far gone, the day is at hand. Let us then cast off the works of darkness and put on the armor of light; . . .

1 Cor 1   23 but we preach Christ crucified, a stumbling block to Jews and folly to Gentiles, . . .

1 Cor 2   1 When I came to you, brethren, I did not come proclaiming to you the testimony of God in lofty words or wisdom. 2 For I decided to know nothing among you except Jesus Christ and him crucified.

Gal 6   14 But far be it from me to glory except in the cross of our Lord Jesus Christ, by which the world has been crucified to me, and I to the world.

1 Thess 4   15 For this we declare to you by the word of the Lord, that we who are alive, who are left until the coming of the Lord, shall not precede those who have fallen asleep.

1 Thess 5   2 For you yourselves know well that the day of the Lord will come like a thief in the night.

2 Thess 2   1 Now concerning the coming of our Lord Jesus Christ and our assembling to meet him, we beg you, brethren, 2 not to be quickly shaken in mind or excited, either by spirit or by word, or by letter purporting to be from us, to the effect that the day of the Lord has come.

[27]Whoever, therefore, eats the bread or drinks the cup of the Lord in an unworthy manner will be guilty of profaning the body and blood of the Lord. [28]Let a man examine himself, and so eat of the bread and drink of the cup. [29]For any one who eats and drinks without discerning the body eats and drinks judgment upon himself. [30]That is why many of you are weak and ill, and some have died. [31]But if we judged ourselves truly, we should not be judged. [32]But when we are judged by the Lord, we are chastened so that we may not be condemned along with the world.

[33]So then, my brethren, when you come together to eat, wait for one another— [34]if any one is hungry, let him eat at home—lest you come together to be condemned. About the other things I will give directions when I come.

Rom 14:13–23 (§59)

[13]Then let us no more pass judgment on one another, but rather decide never to put a stumbling block or hindrance in the way of a brother. [14]I know and am persuaded in the Lord Jesus that nothing is unclean in itself; but it is unclean for any one who thinks it unclean. [15]If your brother is being injured by what you eat, you are no longer walking in love. Do not let what you eat cause the ruin of one for whom Christ died. [16]So do not let your good be spoken of as evil. [17]For the kingdom of God is not food and drink but righteousness and peace and joy in the Holy Spirit; [18]he who thus serves Christ is acceptable to God and approved by men. [19]Let us then pursue what makes for peace and for mutual upbuilding. [20]Do not, for the sake of food, destroy the work of God. Everything is indeed clean, but it is wrong for any one to make others fall by what he eats; [21]it is right not to eat meat or drink wine or do anything that makes your brother stumble. [22]The faith that you have, keep between yourself and God; happy is he who has no reason to judge himself for what he approves. [23]But he who has doubts is condemned, if he eats, because he does not act from faith; for whatever does not proceed from faith is sin.

2 Cor 13:5–10 (§190)

[5]Examine yourselves, to see whether you are holding to your faith. Test yourselves. Do you not realize that Jesus Christ is in you?— unless indeed you fail to meet the test! [6]I hope you will find out that we have not failed. [7]But we pray God that you may not do wrong— not that we may appear to have met the test, but that you may do what is right, though we may seem to have failed. [8]For we cannot do anything against the truth, but only for the truth. [9]For we are glad when we are weak and you are strong. What we pray for is your improvement. [10]I write this while I am away from you, in order that when I come I may not have to be severe in my use of the authority which the Lord has given me for building up and not for tearing down.

• **1 Cor 11:28**
Gal 6   [4]But let each one test his own work, and then his reason to boast will be in himself alone and not in his neighbor.

• **1 Cor 11:29**
1 Cor 10   [16]The cup of blessing which we bless, is it not a participation in the blood of Christ? The bread which we break, is it not a participation in the body of Christ? [17]Because there is one bread, we who are many are one body, for we all partake of the one bread.

• **1 Cor 11:30**
Acts 5   [5]When Ananias heard these words, he fell down and died. And great fear came upon all who heard of it.

• **1 Cor 11:31–32**
1 Cor 4   [3]But with me it is a very small thing that I should be judged by you or by any human court. I do not even judge myself. [4]I am not aware of anything against myself, but I am not thereby acquitted. It is the Lord who judges me.

• **1 Cor 11:32**
1 Pet 4   [17]For the time has come for judgment to begin with the household of God; and if it begins with us, what will be the end of those who do not obey the gospel of God?

12 Now concerning spiritual gifts, brethren, I do not want you to be uninformed. ²You know that when you were heathen, you were led astray to dumb idols, however you may have been moved. ³Therefore I want you to understand that no one speaking by the Spirit of God ever says "Jesus be cursed!" and no one can say "Jesus is Lord" except by the Holy Spirit.

PRIMARY

Gal 4:8-11 (§208)

⁸Formerly, when you did not know God, you were in bondage to beings that by nature are no gods; ⁹but now that you have come to know God, or rather to be known by God, how can you turn back again to the weak and beggarly elemental spirits, whose slaves you want to be once more? ¹⁰You observe days, and months, and seasons, and years! ¹¹I am afraid I have labored over you in vain.

Eph 2:11-22 (§221)

¹¹Therefore remember that at one time you Gentiles in the flesh, called the uncircumcision by what is called the circumcision, which is made in the flesh by hands— ¹²remember that you were at that time separated from Christ, alienated from the commonwealth of Israel, and strangers to the covenants of promise, having no hope and without God in the world. ¹³But now in Christ Jesus you who once were far off have been brought near in the blood of Christ. ¹⁴For he is our peace, who has made us both one, and has broken down the dividing wall of hostility, ¹⁵by abolishing in his flesh the law of commandments and ordinances, that he might create in himself one new man in place of the two, so making peace, ¹⁶and might reconcile us both to God in one body through the cross, thereby bringing the hostility to an end. ¹⁷And he came and preached·peace to you who were far off and peace to those who were near; ¹⁸for through him we both have access in one Spirit to the Father. ¹⁹So then you are no longer strangers and sojourners, but you are fellow citizens with the saints and members of the household of God, ²⁰built upon the foundation of the apostles and prophets, Christ Jesus himself being the cornerstone, ²¹in whom the whole structure is joined together and grows into a holy temple in the Lord; ²²in whom you also are built into it for a dwelling place of God in the Spirit.

1 Thess 1:2-10 (§276)

²We give thanks to God always for you all, constantly mentioning you in our prayers, ³remembering before our God and Father your work of faith and labor of love and steadfastness of hope in our Lord Jesus Christ. ⁴For we know, brethren beloved by God, that he has chosen you; ⁵for our gospel came to you not only in word, but also in power and in the Holy Spirit and with full conviction. You know what kind of men we proved to be among you for your sake. ⁶And you became imitators of us and of the Lord, for you received the word in much affliction, with joy inspired by the Holy Spirit; ⁷so that you became an example to the all the believers in Macedonia and in Achaia. ⁸For not only has the word of the Lord sounded forth from you in Macedonia and Achaia, but your faith in God has gone forth everywhere, so that we need not say anything. ⁹For they themselves report concerning us what a welcome we had among you, and how you turned to God from idols, to serve a living and true God, ¹⁰and to wait for his Son from heaven, whom he raised from the dead, Jesus who delivers us from the wrath to come.

● **1 Cor 12:1**

1 Cor 1   ⁷so that you are not lacking in any spiritual gift, as you wait for the revealing of our Lord Jesus Christ; . . .

1 Cor 2   ¹²Now we have received not the spirit of the world, but the Spirit which is from God, that we might understand the gifts bestowed on us by God.

● **1 Cor 12:2**

Acts 17   ²⁹"Being then God's offspring, we ought not to think that the Deity is like gold, or silver, or stone, a representation by the art and imagination of man."

● **1 Cor 12:3**

Rom 10   ⁹because, if you confess with your lips that Jesus is Lord and believe in your heart that God raised him from the dead, you will be saved.

Phil 2   ¹¹and every tongue confess that Jesus Christ is Lord, to the glory of God the Father.

⁴Now there are varieties of gifts, but the same Spirit; ⁵and there are varieties of service, but the same Lord; ⁶and there are varieties of working, but it is the same God who inspires them all in every one. ⁷To each is given the manifestation of the Spirit for the common good. ⁸To one is given through the Spirit the utterance of wisdom, and to another the utterance of knowledge according to the same Spirit, ⁹to another faith by the same Spirit, to another gifts of healing by the one Spirit, ¹⁰to another the working of miracles, to another prophecy, to another the ability to distinguish between spirits, to another various kinds of tongues, to another the interpretation of tongues. ¹¹All these are inspired by one and the same Spirit, who apportions to each one individually as he wills.

PRIMARY

Rom 12:3–8 (§52)

³For by the grace given to me I bid every one among you not to think of himself more highly than he ought to think, but to think with sober judgment, each according to the measure of faith which God has assigned him. ⁴For as in one body we have many members, and all the members do not have the same function, ⁵so we, though many, are one body in Christ, and individually members one of another. ⁶Having gifts that differ according to the grace given to us, let us use them: if prophecy, in proportion to our faith; ⁷if service, in our serving; he who teaches, in his teaching; ⁸he who exhorts, in his exhortation; he who contributes, in liberality; he who gives aid, with zeal; he who does acts of mercy, with cheerfulness.

Eph 4:1–10 (§225)

¹I therefore, a prisoner for the Lord, beg you to lead a life worthy of the calling to which you have been called, ²with all lowliness and meekness, with patience, forbearing one another in love, ³eager to maintain the unity of the Spirit in the bond of peace. ⁴There is one body and one Spirit, just as you were called to the one hope that belongs to your call, ⁵one Lord, one faith, one baptism, ⁶one God and Father of us all, who is above all and through all and in all. ⁷But grace was given to each of us according to the measure of Christ's gift. ⁸Therefore it is said,

"When he ascended on high he led a host of
   captives,
   and he gave gifts to men."

⁹(In saying, "He ascended," what does it mean but that he had also descended into the lower parts of the earth? ¹⁰He who descended is he who also ascended far above all the heavens, that he might fill all things.)

● **1 Cor 12:4**
Gal 5   ²²But the fruit of the Spirit is love, joy, peace, patience, kindness, goodness, faithfulness, . . .

● **1 Cor 12:7**
1 Cor 6   ¹²"All things are lawful for me," but not all things are helpful. "All things are lawful for me," but I will not be enslaved by anything.

1 Cor 10   ³³just as I try to please all men in everything I do, not seeking my own advantage, but that of many, that they may be saved.

1 Cor 14   ²⁶What then, brethren? When you come together, each one has a hymn, a lesson, a revelation, a tongue, or an interpretation. Let all things be done for edification. ²⁷If any speak in a tongue, let there be only two or at most three, and each in turn; and let one interpret. ²⁸But if there is no one to interpret, let each of them keep silence in church and speak to himself and to God. ²⁹Let two or three prophets speak, and let the others weigh what is said. ³⁰If a revelation is made to another sitting by, let the first be silent. ³¹For you can all prophesy one by one, so that all may learn and all be encouraged; ³²and the spirits of prophets are subject to prophets. ³³For God is not a God of confusion but of peace.

● **1 Cor 12:10**
1 Thess 5   ¹⁹Do not quench the Spirit, ²⁰do not despise prophesying, ²¹but test everything; hold fast what is good, . . .

Acts 2   ³And there appeared to them tongues as of fire, distributed and resting on each one of them. ⁴And they were all filled with the Holy Spirit and began to speak in other tongues, as the Spirit gave them utterance.

Formal Element: Baptismal Liturgy

12For just as the body is one and has many members, and all the members of the body, though many, are one body, so it is with Christ. 13For by one Spirit we were all baptized into one body— Jews or Greeks, slaves or free—and all were made to drink of one Spirit.

Primary

Gal 3:26–29 (§206)
26for in Christ Jesus you are all sons of God, through faith. 27For as many of you as were baptized into Christ have put on Christ. 28There is neither Jew nor Greek, there is neither slave nor free, there is neither male nor female; for you are all one in Christ Jesus. 29And if you are Christ's, then you are Abraham's offspring, heirs according to promise.

Eph 2:11–22 (§221)
11Therefore remember that at one time you Gentiles in the flesh, called the uncircumcision by what is called the circumcision, which is made in the flesh by hands — 12remember that you were at that time separated from Christ, alienated from the commonwealth of Israel, and strangers to the covenants of promise, having no hope and without God in the world. 13But now in Christ Jesus you who once were far off have been brought near in the blood of Christ. 14For he is our peace, who has made us both one, and has broken down the dividing wall of hostility, 15by abolishing in his flesh the law of commandments and ordinances, that he might create in himself one new man in place of the two, so making peace, 16and might reconcile us both to God in one body through the cross, thereby bringing the hostility to an end. 17And he came and preached peace to you who were far off and peace to those who were near; 18for through him we both have access in one Spirit to the Father. 19So then you are no longer strangers and sojourners, but you are fellow citizens with the saints and members of the household of God, 20built upon the foundation of the apostles and prophets, Christ Jesus himself being the cornerstone, 21in whom the whole structure is joined together and grows into a holy temple in the Lord; 22in whom you also are built into it for a dwelling place of God in the Spirit.

Col 3:5–11 (§266)
5Put to death therefore what is earthly in you: fornication, impurity, passion, evil desire, and covetousness, which is idolatry. 6On account of these the wrath of God is coming. 7In these you once walked, when you lived in them. 8But now put them all away: anger, wrath, malice, slander, and foul talk from your mouth. 9Do not lie to one another, seeing that you have put off the old nature with its practices 10and have put on the new nature, which is being renewed in knowledge after the image of its creator. 11Here there cannot be Greek and Jew, circumcised and uncircumcised, barbarian, Scythian, slave, free man, but Christ is all, and in all.

● **1 Cor 12:12–13**
Rom 12　4For as in one body we have many members, and all the members do not have the same function, 5so we, though many, are one body in Christ, and individually members one of another.

1 Cor 10　16The cup of blessing which we bless, is it not a participation in the blood of Christ? The bread which we break, is it not a participation in the body of Christ? 17Because there is one bread, we who are many are one body, for we all partake of the one bread.

● **1 Cor 12:13**
Rom 6　4We were buried therefore with him by baptism into death, so that as Christ was raised from the dead by the glory of the Father, we too might walk in newness of life.

1 Cor 1　17For Christ did not send me to baptize but to preach the gospel, and not with eloquent wisdom, lest the cross of Christ be emptied of its power.

Eph 4　4There is one body and one Spirit, just as you were called to the one hope that belongs to your call, . . .

Col 2　11In him also you were circumcised with a circumcision made without hands, by putting off the body of flesh in the circumcision of Christ; 12and you were buried with him in baptism, in which you were also raised with him through faith in the working of God, who raised him from the dead.

Phil 2　1So if there is any encouragement in Christ, any incentive of love, any participation in the Spirit, any affection and sympathy, 2complete my joy by being of the same mind, having the same love, being in full accord and of one mind.

Acts 19　5On hearing this, they were baptized in the name of the Lord Jesus. 6And when Paul had laid his hands upon them, the Holy Spirit came on them; and they spoke with tongues and prophesied.

¹⁴For the body does not consist of one member but of many. ¹⁵If the foot should say, "Because I am not a hand, I do not belong to the body," that would not make it any less a part of the body. ¹⁶And if the ear should say, "Because I am not an eye, I do not belong to the body," that would not make it any less a part of the body. ¹⁷If the whole body were an eye, where would be the hearing? If the whole body were an ear, where would be the sense of smell? ¹⁸But as it is, God arranged the organs in the body, each one of them, as he chose. ¹⁹If all were a single organ, where would the body be? ²⁰As it is, there are many parts, yet one body. ²¹The eye cannot say to the hand, "I have no need of you," nor again the head to the feet, "I have no need of you." ²²On the contrary, the parts of the body which seem to be weaker are indispensable, ²³and those parts of the body which we think less honorable we invest with the greater honor, and our unpresentable parts are treated with greater modesty, ²⁴which our more presentable parts do not require. But God has so composed the body, giving the greater honor to the inferior part, ²⁵that there may be no discord in the body, but that the members may have the same care for one another. ²⁶If one member suffers, all suffer together; if one member is honored, all rejoice together.

PRIMARY

Rom 11:17–24 (§48)

¹⁷But if some of the branches were broken off, and you, a wild olive shoot, were grafted in their place to share the richness of the olive tree, ¹⁸do not boast over the branches. If you do boast, remember it is not you that support the root, but the root that supports you. ¹⁹You will say, "Branches were broken off so that I might be grafted in." ²⁰That is true. They were broken off because of their unbelief, but you stand fast only through faith. So do not become proud, but stand in awe. ²¹For if God did not spare the natural branches, neither will he spare you. ²²Note then the kindness and the severity of God: severity toward those who have fallen, but God's kindness to you, provided you continue in his kindness; otherwise you too will be cut off. ²³And even the others, if they do not persist in their unbelief, will be grafted in, for God has the power to graft them in again. ²⁴For if you have been cut from what is by nature a wild olive tree, and grafted, contrary to nature, into a cultivated olive tree, how much more will these natural branches be grafted back into their own olive tree.

2 Cor 1:3–11 (§147)

³Blessed be the God and Father of our Lord Jesus Christ, the Father of mercies and God of all comfort, ⁴who comforts us in all our affliction, so that we may be able to comfort those who are in any affliction, with the comfort with which we ourselves are comforted by God. ⁵For as we share abundantly in Christ's suffer-ings, so through Christ we share abundantly in comfort too. ⁶If we are afflicted, it is for your comfort and salvation; and if we are comforted, it is for your comfort, which you experience when you patiently endure the same sufferings that we suffer. ⁷Our hope for you is unshaken; for we know that as you share in our sufferings, you will also share in our comfort.

⁸For we do not want you to be ignorant, brethren, of the affliction we experienced in Asia; for we were so utterly, unbearably crushed that we despaired of life itself. ⁹Why, we felt that we had received the sentence of death; but that was to make us rely not on our-selves but on God who raises the dead; ¹⁰he delivered us from so deadly a peril, and he will deliver us; on him we have set our hope that he will deliver us again. ¹¹You also must help us by prayer, so that many will give thanks on our behalf for the blessing granted us in answer to many prayers.

2 Cor 4:7–12 (§159)

⁷But we have this treasure in earthen ves-sels, to show that the transcendent power be-longs to God and not to us. ⁸We are afflicted in every way, but not crushed; perplexed, but not driven to despair; ⁹persecuted, but not for-saken; struck down, but not destroyed; ¹⁰always carrying in the body the death of Jesus, so that the life of Jesus may also be manifested in our bodies. ¹¹For while we live we are always being given up to death for Jesus' sake, so that the life of Jesus may be manifested in our mortal flesh. ¹²So death is at work in us, but life in you.

● **1 Cor 12:18**

1 Cor 15 ³⁸But God gives it a body as he has chosen, and to each kind of seed its own body.

● **1 Cor 12:22–26**

Phlm ¹⁵Perhaps this is why he was parted from you for a while, that you might have him back for ever, ¹⁶no longer as a slave but more than a slave, as a beloved brother, especially to me but how much more to you, both in the flesh and in the Lord. ¹⁷So if you consider me your partner, receive him as you would receive me. ¹⁸If he has wronged you at all, or owes you anything, charge that to my account. ¹⁹I, Paul, write this with my own hand, I will repay it—to say nothing of your owing me even your own self. ²⁰Yes, brother, I want some benefit from you in the Lord. Refresh my heart in Christ.

● **1 Cor 12:24**

1 Cor 1 ²⁶For consider your call, brethren; not many of you were wise according to worldly standards, not many were powerful, not many were of noble birth; ²⁷but God chose what is foolish in the world to shame the wise, God chose what is weak in the world to shame the strong, ²⁸God chose what is low and de-spised in the world, even things that are not, to bring to nothing things that are, ²⁹so that no human being might boast in the presence of God. ³⁰He is the source of your life in Christ Jesus, whom God made our wisdom, our righteousness and sanctification and re-demption; ³¹therefore, as it is written, "Let him who boasts, boast of the Lord."

● **1 Cor 12:26**

Rom 12 ¹⁵Rejoice with those who rejoice, weep with those who weep.

2 Cor 11 ²⁸And, apart from other things, there is the daily pressure upon me of my anxiety for all the churches. ²⁹Who is weak, and I am not weak? Who is made to fall, and I am not indignant?

27 Now you are the body of Christ and individually members of it. 28 And God has appointed in the church first apostles, second prophets, third teachers, then workers of miracles, then healers, helpers, administrators, speakers in various kinds of tongues. 29 Are all apostles? Are all prophets? Are all teachers? Do all work miracles? 30 Do all possess gifts of healing? Do all speak with tongues? Do all interpret? 31 But earnestly desire the higher gifts.

And I will show you a still more excellent way.

PRIMARY

Rom 12:3–8 (§52)
3 For by the grace given to me I bid every one among you not to think of himself more highly than he ought to think, but to think with sober judgment, each according to the measure of faith which God has assigned him. 4 For as in one body we have many members, and all the members do not have the same function, 5 so we, though many, are one body in Christ, and individually members one of another. 6 Having gifts that differ according to the grace given to us, let us use them: if prophecy, in proportion to our faith; 7 if service, in our serving; he who teaches, in his teaching; 8 he who exhorts, in his exhortation; he who contributes, in liberality; he who gives aid, with zeal; he who does acts of mercy, with cheerfulness.

1 Cor 12:4–11 (§117)
4 Now there are varieties of gifts, but the same Spirit; 5 and there are varieties of service, but the same Lord; 6 and there are varieties of working, but it is the same God who inspires them all in every one. 7 To each is given the manifestation of the Spirit for the common good. 8 To one is given through the Spirit the utterance of wisdom, and to another the utterance of knowledge according to the same Spirit, 9 to another faith by the same Spirit, to another gifts of healing by the one Spirit, 10 to another the working of miracles, to another prophecy, to another the ability to distinguish between spirits, to another various kinds of tongues, to another the interpretation of tongues. 11 All these are inspired by one and the same Spirit, who apportions to each one individually as he wills.

Eph 4:11–16 (§226)
11 And his gifts were that some should be apostles, some prophets, some evangelists, some pastors and teachers, 12 to equip the saints for the work of ministry, for building up the body of Christ, 13 until we all attain to the unity of the faith and of the knowledge of the Son of God, to mature manhood, to the measure of the stature of the fulness of Christ; 14 so that we may no longer be children, tossed to and fro and carried about with every wind of doctrine, by the cunning of men, by their craftiness in deceitful wiles. 15 Rather, speaking the truth in love, we are to grow up in every way into him who is the head, into Christ, 16 from whom the whole body, joined and knit together by every joint with which it is supplied, when each part is working properly, makes bodily growth and upbuilds itself in love.

● **1 Cor 12:27**
Rom 7   4 Likewise, my brethren, you have died to the law through the body of Christ, so that you may belong to another, to him who has been raised from the dead in order that we may bear fruit for God.

1 Cor 10   16 The cup of blessing which we bless, is it not a participation in the blood of Christ? The bread which we break, is it not a participation in the body of Christ? 17 Because there is one bread, we who are many are one body, for we all partake of the one bread.

1 Cor 11   27 If one of the unbelievers invites you to dinner and you are disposed to go, eat whatever is set before you without raising any question on the ground of conscience.

Eph 1   22 and he has put all things under his feet and has made him the head over all things for the church, 23 which is his body, the fulness of him who fills all in all.

Col 1   22 he has now reconciled in his body of flesh by his death, in order to present you holy and blameless and irreproachable before him, . . .

Col 2   17 These are only a shadow of what is to come; but the substance belongs to Christ.

● **1 Cor 12:28–30**
1 Tim 5   17 As for the rich in this world, charge them not to be haughty, nor to set their hopes on uncertain riches but on God who richly furnishes us with everything to enjoy.

Acts 2   3 And there appeared to them tongues as of fire, distributed and resting on each one of them. 4 And they were all filled with the Holy Spirit and began to speak in other tongues, as the Spirit gave them utterance.

Acts 6   3 "Therefore, brethren, pick out from among you seven men of good repute, full of the Spirit and of wisdom, whom we may appoint to this duty. 4 But we will devote ourselves to prayer and to the ministry of the word."

Acts 13   15 After the reading of the law and the prophets, the rulers of the synagogue sent to them, saying, "Brethren, if you have any word of exhortation for the people, say it."

Acts 19   11 And God did extraordinary miracles by the hands of Paul, 12 so that handkerchiefs or aprons were carried away from his body to the sick, and diseases left them and the evil spirits came out of them.

● **1 Cor 12:28**
Phil 1   1 Paul and Timothy, servants of Christ Jesus,
To all the saints in Christ Jesus who are at Philippi, with the bishops and deacons: . . .

13

If I speak in the tongues of men and of angels, but have not love, I am a noisy gong or a clanging cymbal. [2] And if I have prophetic powers, and understand all mysteries and all knowledge, and if I have all faith, so as to remove mountains, but have not love, I am nothing. [3] If I give away all I have, and if I deliver my body to be burned, but have not love, I gain nothing.

PRIMARY

Rom 16:25–27 (§70)

[25] Now to him who is able to strengthen you according to my gospel and the preaching of Jesus Christ, according to the revelation of the mystery which was kept secret for long ages [26] but is now disclosed and through the prophetic writings is made known to all nations, according to the command of the eternal God, to bring about the obedience of faith— [27] to the only wise God be glory for evermore through Jesus Christ! Amen.

Eph 3:1–13 (§222)

[1] For this reason I, Paul, a prisoner for Christ Jesus on behalf of you Gentiles— [2] assuming that you have heard of the stewardship of God's grace that was given to me for you, [3] how the mystery was made known to me by revelation, as I have written briefly. [4] When you read this you can perceive my insight into the mystery of Christ, [5] which was not made known to the sons of men in other generations as it has now been revealed to his holy apostles and prophets by the Spirit; [6] that is, how the Gentiles are fellow heirs, members of the same body, and partakers of the promise in Christ Jesus through the gospel. [7] Of this gospel I was made a minister according to the gift of God's grace which was given me by the working of his power. [8] To me, though I am the very least of all the saints, this grace was given, to preach to the Gentiles the unsearchable riches of Christ, [9] and to make all men see what is the plan of the mystery hidden for ages in God who created all things; [10] that through the church the manifold wisdom of God might now be made known to the principalities and powers in the heavenly places. [11] This was according to the eternal purpose which he has realized in Christ Jesus our Lord, [12] in whom we have boldness and confidence of access through our faith in him. [13] So I ask you not to lose heart over what I am suffering for you, which is your glory.

Col 1:24–2:3 (§260)

[24] Now I rejoice in my sufferings for your sake, and in my flesh I complete what is lacking in Christ's afflictions for the sake of his body, that is, the church, [25] of which I became a minister according to the divine office which was given to me for you, to make the word of God fully known, [26] the mystery hidden for ages and generations but now made manifest to his saints. [27] To them God chose to make known how great among the Gentiles are the riches of the glory of this mystery, which is Christ in you, the hope of glory. [28] Him we proclaim warning every man and teaching every man in all wisdom, that we may present every man mature in Christ. [29] For this I toil, striving with all the energy which he mightily inspires within me.

2 [1] For I want you to know how greatly I strive for you, and for those at Laodicea, and for all who have not seen my face, [2] that their hearts may be encouraged as they are knit together in love, to have all the riches of assured understanding and the knowledge of God's mystery, of Christ, [3] in whom are hid all the treasures of wisdom and knowledge.

● **1 Cor 13:1–3**

1 Cor 14   [1] Make love your aim, and earnestly desire the spiritual gifts, especially that you may prophesy. [2] For one who speaks in a tongue speaks not to men but to God; for no one understands him, but he utters mysteries in the Spirit.

● **1 Cor 13:1**

Acts 2   [3] And there appeared to them tongues as of fire, distributed and resting on each one of them. [4] And they were all filled with the Holy Spirit and began to speak in other tongues, as the Spirit gave them utterance.

● **1 Cor 13:2**

1 Cor 8   [1] Now concerning food offered to idols: we know that "all of us possess knowledge." "Knowledge" puffs up, but love builds up.

Gal 5   [6] For in Christ Jesus neither circumcision nor uncircumcision is of any avail, but faith working through love.

Eph 3   [19] and to know the love of Christ which surpasses knowledge, that you may be filled with all the fulness of God.

● **1 Cor 13:3**

1 Cor 15   [30] Why am I in peril every hour? [31] I protest, brethren, by my pride in you which I have in Christ Jesus our Lord, I die every day! [32] What do I gain if, humanly speaking, I fought with beasts at Ephesus? If the dead are not raised, "Let us eat and drink, for tomorrow we die."

(burned) *read* body that I may glory: p⁴⁶SAB cop Clement Origen: *text:* CDG Koine it vg syr Tertullian Origen

FORMAL ELEMENT: GNOMIC SAYINGS

[4]Love is patient and kind; love is not jealous or boastful; [5]it is not arrogant or rude. Love does not insist on its own way; it is not irritable or resentful; [6]it does not rejoice at wrong, but rejoices in the right. [7]Love bears all things, believes all things, hopes all things, endures all things.

PRIMARY

See §53 for GNOMIC SAYINGS

SECONDARY

Rom 13:8–10 (§55)

[8]Owe no one anything, except to love one another; for he who loves his neighbor has fulfilled the law. [9]The commandments, "You shall not commit adultery, You shall not kill, You shall not steal, You shall not covet," and any other commandment, are summed up in this sentence, "You shall love your neighbor as yourself." [10]Love does no wrong to a neighbor; therefore love is the fulfilling of the law.

Gal 5:13–15 (§212)

[13]For you were called to freedom, brethren; only do not use your freedom as an opportunity for the flesh, but through love be servants of one another. [14]For the whole law is fulfilled in one word, "You shall love your neighbor as yourself." [15]But if you bite and devour one another take heed that you are not consumed by one another.

Phlm 8–20 (§307–308)

[8]Accordingly, though I am bold enough in Christ to command you to do what is required, [9]yet for love's sake I prefer to appeal to you—I, Paul, an ambassador and now a prisoner also for Christ Jesus—[10]I appeal to you for my child, Onesimus, whose father I have become in my imprisonment. [11](Formerly he was useless to you, but now he is indeed useful to you and to me.) [12]I am sending him back to you, sending my very heart. [13]I would have been glad to keep him with me, in order that he might serve me on your behalf during my imprisonment for the gospel; [14]but I preferred to do nothing without your consent in order that your goodness might not be by compulsion but of your own free will.

[15]Perhaps this is why he was parted from you for a while, that you might have him back for ever, [16]no longer as a slave but more than a slave, as a beloved brother, especially to me but how much more to you, both in the flesh and in the Lord. [17]So if you consider me your partner, receive him as you would receive me. [18]If he has wronged you at all, or owes you anything, charge that to my account. [19]I, Paul, write this with my own hand, I will repay it—to say nothing of your owing me even your own self. [20]Yes, brother, I want some benefit from you in the Lord. Refresh my heart in Christ.

● **1 Cor 13:4–7**
Col 3 [14]And above all these put on love, which binds everything together in perfect harmony.

● **1 Cor 13:4–6**
Tit 3 [2]to speak evil of no one, to avoid quarreling, to be gentle, and to show perfect courtesy toward all men.

● **1 Cor 13:4–5**
Eph 4 [2]with all lowliness and meekness, with patience, forbearing one another in love, . . .

[8]Love never ends; as for prophecies, they will pass away; as for tongues, they will cease; as for knowledge, it will pass away. [9]For our knowledge is imperfect and our prophecy is imperfect; [10]but when the perfect comes, the imperfect will pass away. [11]When I was a child, I spoke like a child, I thought like a child, I reasoned like a child; when I became a man, I gave up childish ways. [12]For now we see in a mirror dimly, but then face to face. Now I know in part; then I shall understand fully, even as I have been fully understood. [13]So faith, hope, love abide, these three; but the greatest of these is love.

PRIMARY

Eph 4:11–16 (§226)

[11]And his gifts were that some should be apostles, some prophets, some evangelists, some pastors and teachers, [12]to equip the saints for the work of ministry, for building up the body of Christ, [13]until we all attain to the unity of the faith and of the knowledge of the Son of God, to mature manhood, to the measure of the stature of the fulness of Christ; [14]so that we may no longer be children, tossed to and fro and carried about with every wind of doctrine, by the cunning of men, by their craftiness in deceitful wiles. [15]Rather, speaking the truth in love, we are to grow up in every way into him who is the head, into Christ, [16]from whom the whole body, joined and knit together by every joint with which it is supplied, when each part is working properly, makes bodily growth and upbuilds itself in love.

Phlm 4–7 (§306)

[4]I thank my God always when I remember you in my prayers, [5]because I hear of your love and of the faith which you have toward the Lord Jesus and all the saints, [6]and I pray that the sharing of your faith may promote the knowledge of all the good that is ours in Christ. [7]For I have derived much joy and comfort from your love, my brother, because the hearts of the saints have been refreshed through you.

● **1 Cor 13:8**

Phil 1   [9]And it is my prayer that your love may abound more and more, with knowledge and all discernment, . . .

Col 2   [2]that their hearts may be encouraged as they are knit together in love, to have all the riches of assured understanding and the knowledge of God's mystery, of Christ, . . .

1 Thess 5   [20]do not despise prophesying, . . .

1 Tim 4   [14]Do not neglect the gift you have, which was given you by prophetic utterance when the council of elders laid their hands upon you.

● **1 Cor 13:9–10**

1 Cor 8   [1]Now concerning food offered to idols: we know that "all of us possess knowledge." "Knowledge" puffs up, but love builds up. [2]If any one imagines that he knows something, he does not yet know as he ought to know. [3]But if one loves God, one is known by him.

● **1 Cor 13:11**

1 Cor 3   [1]But I, brethren, could not address you as spiritual men, but as men of the flesh, as babes in Christ. [2]I fed you with milk, not solid food; for you were not ready for it; and even yet you are not ready, [3]for you are still of the flesh. For while there is jealousy and strife among you, are you not of the flesh, and behaving like ordinary men? [4]For when one says, "I belong to Paul," and another, "I belong to Apollos," are you not merely men?

1 Cor 14   [20]Brethren, do not be children in your thinking; be babes in evil, but in thinking be mature.

2 Tim 2   [22]So shun youthful passions and aim at righteousness, faith, love, and peace, along with those who call upon the Lord from a pure heart.

● **1 Cor 13:12**

2 Cor 1   [13]For we write you nothing but what you can read and understand; I hope you will understand fully, [14]as you have understood in part, that you can be proud of us as we can be of you, on the day of the Lord Jesus.

2 Cor 5   [7]for we walk by faith, not by sight.

● **1 Cor 13:13**

Rom 5   [1]Therefore, since we are justified by faith, we have peace with God through our Lord Jesus Christ. [2]Through him we have obtained access to this grace in which we stand, and we rejoice in our hope of sharing the glory of God. [3]More than that, we rejoice in our sufferings, knowing that suffering produces endurance, [4]and endurance produces character, and character produces hope, [5]and hope does not disappoint us, because God's love has been poured into our hearts through the Holy Spirit which has been given to us.

Gal 5   [5]For through the Spirit, by faith, we wait for the hope of righteousness. [6]For in Christ Jesus neither circumcision nor uncircumcision is of any avail, but faith working through love.

Col 1   [3]We always thank God, the Father of our Lord Jesus Christ, when we pray for you, [4]because we have heard of your faith in Christ Jesus and of the love which you have for all the saints, [5]because of the hope laid up for you in heaven. Of this you have heard before in the word of the truth, the gospel . . .

1 Thess 1   [3]remembering before our God and Father your work of faith and labor of love and steadfastness of hope in our Lord Jesus Christ.

1 Thess 5   [8]But, since we belong to the day, let us be sober, and put on the breastplate of faith and love, and for a helmet the hope of salvation.

14 Make love your aim, and earnestly desire the spiritual gifts, especially that you may prophesy. [2]For one who speaks in a tongue speaks not to men but to God; for no one understands him, but he utters mysteries in the Spirit. [3]On the other hand, he who prophesies speaks to men for their upbuilding and encouragement and consolation. [4]He who speaks in a tongue edifies himself, but he who prophesies edifies the church. [5]Now I want you all to speak in tongues, but even more to prophesy. He who prophesies is greater than he who speaks in tongues, unless some one interprets, so that the church may be edified.

PRIMARY

Rom 15:1–6 (§60)
[1]We who are strong ought to bear with the failings of the weak, and not to please ourselves; [2]let each of us please his neighbor for his good, to edify him. [3]For Christ did not please himself; but, as it is written, "The reproaches of those who reproached thee fell on me." [4]For whatever was written in former days was written for our instruction, that by steadfastness and by the encouragement of the scriptures we might have hope. [5]May the God of steadfastness and encouragement grant you to live in such harmony with one another, in accord with Christ Jesus, [6]that together you may with one voice glorify the God and Father of our Lord Jesus Christ.

● **1 Cor 14:1–5**
1 Cor 8   [1]Now concerning food offered to idols: we know that "all of us possess knowledge." "Knowledge" puffs up, but love builds up.

Acts 2   [4]And they were all filled with the Holy Spirit and began to speak in other tongues, as the Spirit gave them utterance. [5]Now there were dwelling in Jerusalem Jews, devout men from every nation under heaven. [6]And at this sound the multitude came together, and they were bewildered, because each one heard them speaking in his own language. [7]And they were amazed and wondered, saying, "Are not all these who are speaking Galileans? [8]And how is it that we hear, each of us in his own native language?"

Acts 2   [17]"And in the last days it shall be, God declares,
    that I will pour out my Spirit upon all flesh,
    and your sons and your daughters shall prophesy,
    and your young men shall see visions,
    and your old men shall dream dreams; . . ."

● **1 Cor 14:1**
1 Thess 5   [19]Do not quench the Spirit, [20]do not despise prophesying, . . .

● **1 Cor 14:2–3**
1 Cor 1   [3]Grace to you and peace from God our Father and the Lord Jesus Christ.

[4]I give thanks to God always for you because of the grace of God which was given you in Christ Jesus, [5]that in every way you were enriched in him with all speech and all knowledge— [6]even as the testimony to Christ was confirmed among you . . .

1 Cor 14   [31]For you can all prophesy one by one, so that all may learn and all be encouraged; . . .

1 Thess 2   [12]to lead a life worthy of God, who calls you into his own kingdom and glory.

1 Thess 5   [14]And we exhort you, brethren, admonish the idle, encourage the fainthearted, help the weak, be patient with them all.

● **1 Cor 14:2**
Rom 16   [25]Now to him who is able to strengthen you according to my gospel and the preaching of Jesus Christ, according to the revelation of the mystery which was kept secret for long ages [26]but is now disclosed and through the prophetic writings is made known to all nations, according to the command of the eternal God, to bring about the obedience of faith . . .

Eph 3   [4]When you read this you can perceive my insight into the mystery of Christ, [5]which was not made known to the sons of men in other generations as it has now been revealed to his holy apostles and prophets by the Spirit; . . .

Eph 3   [9]and to make all men see what is the plan of the mystery hidden for ages in God who created all things; . . .

Col 1   [26]the mystery hidden for ages and generations but now made manifest to his saints.

● **1 Cor 14:4**
1 Cor 10   [23]"All things are lawful," but not all things are helpful. "All things are lawful," but not all things build up.

1 Cor 14   [26]What then, brethren? When you come together, each one has a hymn, a lesson, a revelation, a tongue, or an interpretation. Let all things be done for edification.

2 Cor 10   [8]For even if I boast a little too much of our authority, which the Lord gave for building you up and not for destroying you, I shall not be put to shame.

2 Cor 13   [10]I write this while I am away from you, in order that when I come I may not have to be severe in my use of the authority which the Lord has given me for building up and not for tearing down.

[6]Now, brethren, if I come to you speaking in tongues, how shall I benefit you unless I bring you some revelation or knowledge or prophecy or teaching? [7]If even lifeless instruments, such as the flute or the harp, do not give distinct notes, how will any one know what is played? [8]And if the bugle gives an indistinct sound, who will get ready for battle? [9]So with yourselves; if you in a tongue utter speech that is not intelligible, how will any one know what is said? For you will be speaking into the air. [10]There are doubtless many different languages in the world, and none is without meaning; [11]but if I do not know the meaning of the language, I shall be a foreigner to the speaker and the speaker a foreigner to me. [12]So with yourselves; since you are eager for manifestations of the Spirit, strive to excel in building up the church.

PRIMARY

Rom 1:8-15 (§2)

[8]First, I thank my God through Jesus Christ for all of you, because your faith is proclaimed in all the world. [9]For God is my witness, whom I serve with my spirit in the gospel of his Son, that without ceasing I mention you always in my prayers, [10]asking that somehow by God's will I may now at last succeed in coming to you. [11]For I long to see you, that I may impart to you some spiritual gift to strengthen you, [12]that is, that we may be mutually encouraged by each other's faith, both yours and mine. [13]I want you to know, brethren, that I have often intended to come to you (but thus far have been prevented), in order that I may reap some harvest among you as well as among the rest of the Gentiles. [14]I am under obligation both to Greeks and to barbarians, both to the wise and to the foolish: [15]so I am eager to preach the gospel to you also who are in Rome.

Rom 10:14-17 (§42)

[14]But how are men to call upon him in whom they have not believed? And how are they to believe in him of whom they have never heard? And how are they to hear without a preacher? [15]And how can men preach unless they are sent? As it is written, "How beautiful are the feet of those who preach good news!" [16]But they have not all obeyed the gospel; for Isaiah says, "Lord, who has believed what he has heard from us?" [17]So faith comes from what is heard, and what is heard comes by the preaching of Christ.

2 Cor 1:12-14 (§148)

[12]For our boast is this, the testimony of our conscience that we have behaved in the world, and still more toward you, with holiness and godly sincerity, not by earthly wisdom but by the grace of God. [13]For we write you nothing but what you can read and understand; I hope you will understand fully, [14]as you have understood in part, that you can be proud of us as we can be of you, on the day of the Lord Jesus.

● **1 Cor 14:9**

1 Cor 9   [26]Well, I do not run aimlessly, I do not box as one beating the air; . . .

● **1 Cor 14:10**

Acts 2   [5]Now there were dwelling in Jerusalem Jews, devout men from every nation under heaven. [6]And at this sound the multitude came together, and they were bewildered, because each one heard them speaking in his own language.

● **1 Cor 14:12**

1 Cor 10   [23]"All things are lawful," but not all things are helpful. "All things are lawful," but not all things build up.

1 Cor 14   [26]What then, brethren? When you come together, each one has a hymn, a lesson, a revelation, a tongue, or an interpretation. Let all things be done for edification.

2 Cor 10   [8]For even if I boast a little too much of our authority, which the Lord gave for building you up and not for destroying you, I shall not be put to shame.

2 Cor 13   [10]I write this while I am away from you, in order that when I come I may not have to be severe in my use of the authority which the Lord has given me for building up and not for tearing down.

Eph 4   [12]to equip the saints for the work of ministry, for building up the body of Christ, . . .

1 Thess 5   [11]Therefore encourage one another and build one another up, just as you are doing.

¹³Therefore, he who speaks in a tongue should pray for the power to interpret. ¹⁴For if I pray in a tongue, my spirit prays but my mind is unfruitful. ¹⁵What am I to do? I will pray with the spirit and I will pray with the mind also; I will sing with the spirit and I will sing with the mind also. ¹⁶Otherwise, if you bless with the spirit, how can any one in the position of an outsider say the "Amen" to your thanksgiving when he does not know what you are saying? ¹⁷For you may give thanks well enough, but the other man is not edified. ¹⁸I thank God that I speak in tongues more than you all; ¹⁹nevertheless, in church I would rather speak five words with my mind, in order to instruct others, than ten thousand words in a tongue.

PRIMARY

Rom 8:26–27 (§32)

²⁶Likewise the Spirit helps us in our weakness; for we do not know how to pray as we ought, but the Spirit himself intercedes for us with sighs too deep for words. ²⁷And he who searches the hearts of men knows what is the mind of the Spirit, because the Spirit intercedes for the saints according to the will of God.

Rom 10:14–17 (§42)

¹⁴But how are men to call upon him in whom they have not believed? And how are they to believe in him of whom they have never heard? And how are they to hear without a preacher? ¹⁵And how can men preach unless they are sent? As it is written, "How beautiful are the feet of those who preach good news!" ¹⁶But they have not all obeyed the gospel; for Isaiah says, "Lord, who has believed what he has heard from us?" ¹⁷So faith comes from what is heard, and what is heard comes by the preaching of Christ.

Eph 5:15–20 (§231)

¹⁵Look carefully then how you walk, not as unwise men but as wise, ¹⁶making the most of the time, because the days are evil. ¹⁷Therefore do not be foolish, but understand what the will of the Lord is. ¹⁸And do not get drunk with wine, for that is debauchery; but be filled with the Spirit, ¹⁹addressing one another in psalms and hymns and spiritual songs, singing and making melody to the Lord with all your heart, ²⁰always and for everything giving thanks in the name of our Lord Jesus Christ to God the Father.

Col 3:12–17 (§267)

¹²Put on then, as God's chosen ones, holy and beloved, compassion, kindness, lowliness, meekness, and patience, ¹³forbearing one another and, if one has a complaint against another, forgiving each other; as the Lord has forgiven you, so you also must forgive. ¹⁴And above all these put on love, which binds everything together in perfect harmony. ¹⁵And let the peace of Christ rule in your hearts, to which indeed you were called in the one body. And be thankful. ¹⁶Let the word of Christ dwell in you richly, as you teach and admonish one another in all wisdom, and as you sing psalms and hymns and spiritual songs with thankfulness in your hearts to God. ¹⁷And whatever you do, in word or deed, do everything in the name of the Lord Jesus, giving thanks to God the Father through him.

● **1 Cor 14:15**
Acts 22   ¹⁷"When I had returned to Jerusalem and was praying in the temple, I fell into a trance ¹⁸and saw him saying to me, 'Make haste and get quickly out of Jerusalem, because they will not accept your testimony about me.'"

● **1 Cor 14:16**
2 Cor 1   ²⁰For all the promises of God find their Yes in him. That is why we utter the Amen through him, to the glory of God.

● **1 Cor 14:17**
1 Cor 10   ²³"All things are lawful," but not all things are helpful. "All things are lawful," but not all things build up.

1 Cor 14   ¹²So with yourselves; since you are eager for manifestations of the Spirit, strive to excel in building up the church.

1 Cor 14   ¹⁷For you may give thanks well enough, but the other man is not edified.

1 Cor 14   ²⁶What then, brethren? When you come together, each one has a hymn, a lesson, a revelation, a tongue, or an interpretation. Let all things be done for edification.

2 Cor 10   ⁸For even if I boast a little too much of our authority, which the Lord gave for building you up and not for destroying you, I shall not be put to shame.

2 Cor 13   ¹⁰I write this while I am away from you, in order that when I come I may not have to be severe in my use of the authority which the Lord has given me for building up and not for tearing down.

Eph 4   ¹²to equip the saints for the work of ministry, for building up the body of Christ, . . .

Col 1   ⁹And so, from the day we heard of it, we have not ceased to pray for you, asking that you may be filled with the knowledge of his will in all spiritual wisdom and understanding, ¹⁰to lead a life worthy of the Lord, fully pleasing to him, bearing fruit in every good work and increasing in the knowledge of God. ¹¹May you be strengthened with all power, according to his glorious might, for all endurance and patience with joy, ¹²giving thanks to the Father, who has qualified us to share in the inheritance of the saints in light.

1 Thess 5   ¹¹Therefore encourage one another and build one another up, just as you are doing.

²⁰Brethren, do not be children in your thinking; be babes in evil, but in thinking be mature. ²¹In the law it is written, "By men of strange tongues and by the lips of foreigners will I speak to this people, and even then they will not listen to me, says the Lord." ²²Thus, tongues are a sign not for believers but for unbelievers, while prophecy is not for unbelievers but for believers. ²³If, therefore, the whole church assembles and all speak in tongues, and outsiders or unbelievers enter, will they not say that you are mad? ²⁴But if all prophesy, and an unbeliever or outsider enters, he is convicted by all, he is called to account by all, ²⁵the secrets of his heart are disclosed; and so, falling on his face, he will worship God and declare that God is really among you.

Primary

Eph 4:11–16 (§226)
¹¹And his gifts were that some should be apostles, some prophets, some evangelists, some pastors and teachers, ¹²to equip the saints for the work of ministry, for building up the body of Christ, ¹³until we all attain to the unity of the faith and of the knowledge of the Son of God, to mature manhood, to the measure of the stature of the fulness of Christ; ¹⁴so that we may no longer be children, tossed to and fro and carried about with every wind of doctrine, by the cunning of men, by their craftiness in deceitful wiles. ¹⁵Rather, speaking the truth in love, we are to grow up in every way into him who is the head, into Christ, ¹⁶from whom the whole body, joined and knit together by every joint with which it is supplied, when each part is working properly, makes bodily growth and upbuilds itself in love.

Col 4:5–6 (§270)
⁵Conduct yourselves wisely toward outsiders, making the most of the time. ⁶Let your speech always be gracious, seasoned with salt, so that you may know how you ought to answer every one.

● **1 Cor 14:20**
Rom 16 ¹⁹For while your obedience is known to all, so that I rejoice over you, I would have you wise as to what is good and guileless as to what is evil; . . .

1 Cor 2 ⁶Yet among the mature we do impart wisdom, although it is not a wisdom of this age or of the rulers of this age, who are doomed to pass away. ⁷But we impart a secret and hidden wisdom of God, which God decreed before the ages for our glorification.

1 Cor 13 ¹¹When I was a child, I spoke like a child, I thought like a child, I reasoned like a child; when I became a man, I gave up childish ways.

Phil 3 ¹⁵Let those of us who are mature be thus minded; and if in anything you are otherwise minded, God will reveal that also to you.

Col 4 ¹²Epaphras, who is one of yourselves, a servant of Christ Jesus, greets you, always remembering you earnestly in his prayers, that you may stand mature and fully assured in all the will of God.

● **1 Cor 14:21**
Isa 28 ¹¹Nay, but by men of strange lips
  and with an alien tongue
 the Lord will speak to this people,
  ¹²to whom he has said,
 "This is rest;
  give to the weary;
 and this is repose";
  yet they would not hear.

● **1 Cor 14:23–24**
1 Thess 4 ¹²so that you may command the respect of outsiders, and be dependent on nobody.

1 Tim 3 ⁷moreover he must be well thought of by outsiders, or he may fall into reproach and the snare of the devil.

● **1 Cor 14:23**
Acts 22 ¹³". . . came to me, and standing by me said to me, 'Brother Saul, receive your sight.' And in that very hour I received my sight and saw him."

● **1 Cor 14:25**
Eph 5 ¹³but when anything is exposed by the light it becomes visible, for anything that becomes visible is light. ¹⁴Therefore it is said,
 "Awake, O sleeper, and arise from the dead,
 and Christ shall give you light."

26 What then, brethren? When you come together, each one has a hymn, a lesson, a revelation, a tongue, or an interpretation. Let all things be done for edification. 27 If any speak in a tongue, let there be only two or at most three, and each in turn; and let one interpret. 28 But if there is no one to interpret, let each of them keep silence in church and speak to himself and to God. 29 Let two or three prophets speak, and let the others weigh what is said. 30 If a revelation is made to another sitting by, let the first be silent. 31 For you can all prophesy one by one, so that all may learn and all be encouraged; 32 and the spirits of prophets are subject to prophets. 33 For God is not a God of confusion but of peace.

PRIMARY

Rom 12:3–8 (§52)

3 For by the grace given to me I bid every one among you not to think of himself more highly than he ought to think, but to think with sober judgment, each according to the measure of faith which God has assigned him. 4 For as in one body we have many members, and all the members do not have the same function, 5 so we, though many, are one body in Christ, and individually members one of another. 6 Having gifts that differ according to the grace given to us, let us use them: if prophecy, in proportion to our faith; 7 if service, in our serving; he who teaches, in his teaching; 8 he who exhorts, in his exhortation; he who contributes, in liberality; he who gives aid, with zeal; he who does acts of mercy, with cheerfulness.

Eph 5:15–20 (§231)

15 Look carefully then how you walk, not as unwise men but as wise, 16 making the most of the time, because the days are evil. 17 Therefore do not be foolish, but understand what the will of the Lord is. 18 And do not get drunk with wine, for that is debauchery; but be filled with the Spirit, 19 addressing one another in psalms and hymns and spiritual songs, singing and making melody to the Lord with all your heart, 20 always and for everything giving thanks in the name of our Lord Jesus Christ to God the Father.

Col 3:12–17 (§267)

12 Put on then, as God's chosen ones, holy and beloved, compassion, kindness, lowliness, meekness, and patience, 13 forbearing one another and, if one has a complaint against another, forgiving each other; as the Lord has forgiven you, so you also must forgive. 14 And above all these put on love, which binds everything together in perfect harmony. 15 And let the peace of Christ rule in your hearts, to which indeed you were called in the one body. And be thankful. 16 Let the word of Christ dwell in you richly, as you teach and admonish one another in all wisdom, and as you sing psalms and hymns and spiritual songs with thankfulness in your hearts to God. 17 And whatever you do, in word or deed, do everything in the name of the Lord Jesus, giving thanks to God the Father through him.

1 Thess 5:12–22 (§288)

12 But we beseech you, brethren, to respect those who labor among you and are over you in the Lord and admonish you, 13 and to esteem them very highly in love because of their work. Be at peace among yourselves. 14 And we exhort you, brethren, admonish the idle, encourage the fainthearted, help the weak, be patient with them all. 15 See that none of you repays evil for evil, but always seek to do good to one another and to all. 16 Rejoice always, 17 pray constantly, 18 give thanks in all circumstances; for this is the will of God in Christ Jesus for you. 19 Do not quench the Spirit, 20 do not despise prophesying, 21 but test everything; hold fast what is good, 22 abstain from every form of evil.

2 Thess 3:16 (§302)

16 Now may the Lord of peace himself give you peace at all times in all ways. The Lord be with you all.

● **1 Cor 14:26**.

Rom 14   19 Let us then pursue what makes for peace and for mutual upbuilding.

Rom 15   2 let each of us please his neighbor for his good, to edify him.

Gal 2   18 But if I build up again those things which I tore down, then I prove myself a transgressor.

1 Thess 5   11 Therefore encourage one another and build one another up, just as you are doing.

● **1 Cor 14:33**

Rom 15   33 The God of peace be with you all. Amen.

Rom 16   20 then the God of peace will soon crush Satan under your feet.

1 Cor 7   15 But if the unbelieving partner desires to separate, let it be so; in such a case the brother or sister is not bound. For God has called us to peace.

1 Cor 7   35 I say this for your own benefit, not to lay any restraint upon you, but to promote good order and to secure your undivided devotion to the Lord.

1 Thess 5   23 May the God of peace himself sanctify you wholly; . . .

As in all the churches of the saints, [34] the women should keep silence in the churches. For they are not permitted to speak, but should be subordinate, as even the law says. [35] If there is anything they desire to know, let them ask their husbands at home. For it is shameful for a woman to speak in church. [36] What! Did the word of God originate with you, or are you the only ones it has reached?

PRIMARY

1 Cor 11:2–16 (§112)
[2] I commend you because you remember me in everything and maintain the traditions even as I have delivered them to you. [3] But I want you to understand that the head of every man is Christ, the head of a woman is her husband, and the head of Christ is God. [4] Any man who prays or prophesies with his head covered dishonors his head, [5] but any woman who prays or prophesies with her head unveiled dishonors her head—it is the same as if her head were shaven. [6] For if a woman will not veil herself, then she should cut off her hair; but if it is disgraceful for a woman to be shorn or shaven, let her wear a veil. [7] For a man ought not to cover his head, since he is the image and glory of God; but woman is the glory of man. [8] (For man was not made from woman, but woman from man. [9] Neither was man created for woman, but woman for man.) [10] That is why a woman ought to have a veil on her head, because of the angels. [11] (Nevertheless, in the Lord woman is not independent of man nor man of woman; [12] for as woman was made from man, so man is now born of woman. And all things are from God.) [13] Judge for yourselves; is it proper for a woman to pray to God with her head uncovered? [14] Does not nature itself teach you that for a man to wear long hair is degrading to him, [15] but if a woman has long hair, it is her pride? For her hair is given to her for a covering. [16] If any one is disposed to be contentious, we recognize no other practice, nor do the churches of God.

● **1 Cor 14:34–35**
(church(*omit 14:34–35 here and add following 14:40:* DG it (some) Ambrosiaster

● **1 Cor 14:34**
1 Tim 2   [11] Let a woman learn in silence with all submissiveness. [12] I permit no woman to teach or to have authority over men; she is to keep silent.

Titus 2   [5] to be sensible, chaste, domestic, kind, and submissive to their husbands, that the word of God may not be discredited.

● **1 Cor 14:35**
Eph 5   [22] Wives, be subject to your husbands, as to the Lord. [23] For the husband is the head of the wife as Christ is the head of the church, his body, and is himself its Savior.

Col 3   [18] Wives, be subject to your husbands, as is fitting in the Lord.

● **1 Cor 14:36**
Col 1   [5] because of the hope laid up for you in heaven. Of this you have heard before in the word of the truth, the gospel [6] which has come to you, as indeed in the whole world it is bearing fruit and growing—so among yourselves, from the day you heard and understood the grace of God in truth, . . .

FORMAL ELEMENT:
ENFORCEMENT STATEMENT

37 If any one thinks that he is a prophet, or spiritual, he should acknowledge that what I am writing to you is a command of the Lord. 38 If any one does not recognize this, he is not recognized. 39 So, my brethren, earnestly desire to prophesy, and do not forbid speaking in tongues; 40 but all things should be done decently and in order.

PRIMARY

Col 4:16–18a (§273)
16 And when this letter has been read among you, have it read also in the church of the Laodiceans; and see that you read also the letter from Laodicea. 17 And say to Archippus, "See that you fulfil the ministry which you have received in the Lord."

18 I, Paul, write this greeting with my own hand. Remember my fetters.

1 Thess 5:27 (§292)
27 I adjure you by the Lord that this letter be read to all the brethren.

2 Thess 3:14–15 (§301)
14 If any one refuses to obey what we say in this letter, note that man, and have nothing to do with him, that he may be ashamed. 15 Do not look on him as an enemy, but warn him as a brother.

SECONDARY

Phlm 8–14 (§307)
8 Accordingly, though I am bold enough in Christ to command you to do what is required, 9 yet for love's sake I prefer to appeal to you—I, Paul, an ambassador and now a prisoner also for Christ Jesus— 10 I appeal to you for my child,

Onesimus, whose father I have become in my imprisonment. 11 (Formerly he was useless to you, but now he is indeed useful to you and to me.) 12 I am sending him back to you, sending my very heart. 13 I would have been glad to keep him with me, in order that he might serve me on your behalf during my imprisonment for the gospel; 14 but I preferred to do nothing without your consent in order that your goodness might not be by compulsion but of your own free will.

Phlm 21–22 (§309)
21 Confident of your obedience, I write to you, knowing that you will do even more than I say. 22 At the same time, prepare a guest room for me, for I am hoping through your prayers to be granted to you.

● **1 Cor 14:37**
1 Cor 3   1 But I, brethren, could not address you as spiritual men, but as men of the flesh, as babes in Christ. 2 I fed you with milk, not solid food; for you were not ready for it; and even yet you are not ready, 3 for you are still of the flesh. For while there is jealousy and strife among you, are you not of the flesh, and behaving like ordinary men? 4 For when one says, "I belong to Paul," and another, "I belong to Apollos," are you not merely men?

1 Cor 7   6 I say this by way of concession, not of command.

1 Cor 7   10 To the married I give charge, not I but the Lord, that the wife should not separate from her husband . . .

1 Cor 7   12 To the rest I say, not the Lord, that if any brother has a wife who is an unbeliever, and she consents to live with him, he should not divorce her.

1 Cor 7   25 Now concerning the unmarried, I have no command of the Lord, but I give my opinion as one who by the Lord's mercy is trustworthy.

2 Cor 8   8 I say this not as a command, but to prove by the earnestness of others that your love also is genuine.

2 Cor 8   10 And in this matter I give my advice: it is best for you now to complete what a year ago you began not only to do but to desire, . . .

● **1 Cor 14:40**
1 Cor 7   35 I say this for your own benefit, not to lay any restraint upon you, but to promote good order and to secure your undivided devotion to the Lord.

Col 2   5 For though I am absent in body, yet I am with you in spirit, rejoicing to see your good order and the firmness of your faith in Christ.

(order) *add 14:34–35 here only:* DG it (some) Ambrosiaster

2. The Jerusalem Conference (Galatians 2) = Acts 15

Date
35	Paul's conversion	Acts 9
38	Paul's first Jerusalem visit	Acts 9:26
38–47	Paul in Syria and Cilicia	
46	Famine relief visit to Jerusalem	Acts 11:30, ?12:25
47–48	First missionary journey (Cyprus and Galatia)	Acts 13, 14
48	Council at Jerusalem (conference visit)	Gal 2:1–10 = Acts 15
49–52	Second missionary journey (Asia Minor, Macedonia, Caesarea)	Acts 15:36–18:22
49	Jews expelled from Rome	Claudius' edict (49); Acts 18:2
50	Paul reaches Corinth	
50	*Letters to the Thessalonians*	
51	Gallio becomes proconsul of Corinth	Gallio inscription 51–52
52	*Letter to the Galatians*	
52–56	Third missionary journey (Macedonia and Achaia)	Acts 18:23–21:15
52–55	Three years spent at Ephesus	
55	*Letters to the Corinthians*	
56	*Epistle to the Romans*	
56	Arrival at Jerusalem	
56–58	Imprisonment at Caesarea	Acts 24:27
59	Paul reaches Rome	Acts 28:16
59–61	Paul at Rome	
	Philippians, Philemon, Colossians, Ephesians	
61(64)	Paul's martyrdom	Neronian persecution (64)

Based on B. W. Robinson, *The Life of Paul*, 2nd edition (Chicago: University of Chicago Press, 1928), 240–41. Summary prepared by John A. Darr and published in: Daniel Patte, *Paul's Faith and the Power of the Gospel* (Philadelphia: Fortress Press, 1983), 352–60. Reprinted by permission of the publisher.
See pages 67, 175, 207, 223 for other views of the chronology of Paul's life and letters.

FORMAL ELEMENT: CONFESSION

15 Now I would remind you, brethren, in what terms I preached to you the gospel, which you received, in which you stand, ²by which you are saved, if you hold it fast —unless you believed in vain.

³For I delivered to you as of first importance what I also received, that Christ died for our sins in accordance with the scriptures, ⁴that he was buried, that he was raised on the third day in accordance with the scriptures, ⁵and that he appeared to Cephas, then to the twelve. ⁶Then he appeared to more than five hundred brethren at one time, most of whom are still alive, though some have fallen asleep. ⁷Then he appeared to James, then to all the apostles. ⁸Last of all, as to one untimely born, he appeared also to me. ⁹For I am the least of the apostles, unfit to be called an apostle, because I persecuted the church of God. ¹⁰But by the grace of God I am what I am, and his grace toward me was not in vain. On the contrary, I worked harder than any of them, though it was not I, but the grace of God which is with me. ¹¹Whether then it was I or they, so we preach and so you believed.

PRIMARY

See §50 for CONFESSION

SECONDARY

Rom 5:6-11 (§21)

⁶While we were still weak, at the right time Christ died for the ungodly.

⁷Why, one will hardly die for a righteous man—though perhaps for a good man one will dare even to die. ⁸But God shows his love for us in that while we were yet sinners Christ died for us. ⁹Since, therefore, we are now justified by his blood, much more shall we be saved by him from the wrath of God. ¹⁰For if while we were enemies we were reconciled to God by the death of his Son, much more, now that we are reconciled, shall we be saved by his life. ¹¹Not only so, but we also rejoice in God through our Lord Jesus Christ, through whom we have now received our reconciliation.

Rom 6:1-10 (§23)

¹What shall we say then? Are we to continue in sin that grace may abound? ²By no means! How can we who died to sin still live in it? ³Do you not know that all of us who have been baptized into Christ Jesus were baptized into his death? ⁴We were buried therefore with him by baptism into death, so that as Christ was raised from the dead by the glory of the Father, we too might walk in newness of life.

⁵For if we have been united with him in a death like his, we shall certainly be united with him in a resurrection like his. ⁶We know that our old self was crucified with him so that the sinful body might be destroyed, and we might no longer be enslaved to sin. ⁷For he who has died is freed from sin. ⁸But if we have died with Christ, we believe that we shall also live with him. ⁹For we know that Christ being raised from the dead will never die again; death no longer has dominion over him. ¹⁰The death he died he died to sin, once for all, but the life he lives he lives to God.

2 Cor 5:14-21 (§164)

¹⁴For the love of Christ controls us, because we are convinced that one has died for all; therefore all have died. ¹⁵And he died for all, that those who live might live no longer for themselves but for him who for their sake died and was raised.

¹⁶From now on, therefore, we regard no one from a human point of view; even though we once regarded Christ from a human point of view, we regard him thus no longer. ¹⁷There-fore, if any one is in Christ, he is a new creation; the old has passed away, behold, the new has come. ¹⁸All this is from God, who through Christ reconciled us to himself and gave us the ministry of reconciliation; ¹⁹that is, in Christ God was reconciling the world to himself, not counting their trespasses against them, and entrusting to us the message of reconciliation. ²⁰So we are ambassadors for Christ, God making his appeal through us. We beseech you on behalf of Christ, be reconciled to God. ²¹For our sake he made him to be sin who knew no sin, so that in him we might become the righteousness of God.

2 Cor 10:7-12 (§177)

⁷Look at what is before your eyes. If any one is confident that he is Christ's, let him remind himself that as he is Christ's, so are we. ⁸For even if I boast a little too much of our authority, which the Lord gave for building you up and not for destroying you, I shall not be put to shame. ⁹I would not seem to be frightening you with letters. ¹⁰For they say, "His letters are weighty and strong, but his bodily presence is weak, and his speech of no account." ¹¹Let such people understand that what we say by letter when absent, we do when present. ¹²Not that we venture to class or compare ourselves with some of those who commend themselves. But when they measure themselves by one another and compare themselves with one another, they are without understanding.

Gal 1:15-24 (§196)

¹⁵But when he who had set me apart before I was born, and had called me through his grace, ¹⁶was pleased to reveal his Son to me, in order that I might preach him among the Gentiles, I did not confer with flesh and blood, ¹⁷nor did I go up to Jerusalem to those who were apostles before me, but I went away into Arabia; and again I returned to Damascus.

● **1 Cor 15:1-3**
Cf. 1 Cor 10 ²³"All things are lawful," but not all things are helpful. "All things are lawful," but not all things build up.

● **1 Cor 15:3-5**
Cf. 1 Tim 3 ¹⁶Great indeed, we confess, is the mystery of our religion:
He was manifested in the flesh,
vindicated in the Spirit, . . .

● **1 Cor 15:3-4**
1 Thess 1 ⁹For they themselves report concerning us what a welcome we had among you, and how you turned to God from idols, to serve a living and true God, ¹⁰and to wait for his Son from heaven, whom he raised from the dead, Jesus who delivers us from the wrath to come.

1 Thess 4 ¹⁴For since we believe that Jesus died and rose again, even so, through Jesus, God will bring with him those who have fallen asleep.

Acts 26 ²²"To this day I have had the help that comes from God, and so I stand here testifying both to small and great, saying nothing but what the prophets and Moses said would come to pass: ²³that the Christ must suffer, and that, by being the first to rise from the dead, he would proclaim light both to the people and to the Gentiles."

● **1 Cor 15:3**
Acts 17 ²And Paul went in, as was his custom, and for three weeks he argued with them from the scriptures, ³explaining and proving that it was necessary for the Christ to suffer and to rise from the dead, and saying, "This Jesus, whom I proclaim to you, is the Christ."

● **1 Cor 15:4**
Acts 2 ²⁴"But God raised him up, having loosed the pangs of death, because it was not possible for him to be held by it."

Acts 2 ³¹". . . he foresaw and spoke of the resurrection of the Christ, that he was not abandoned to Hades, nor did his flesh see corruption."

● **1 Cor 15:7**
Acts 1 ³To them he presented himself alive after his passion by many proofs, appearing to them during forty days, and speaking of the kingdom of God. ⁴And while staying with them he charged them not to depart from Jerusalem, but to wait for the promise of the Father, which, he said, "you heard from me. . . ."

● **1 Cor 15:8-9**
Acts 9 ³Now as he journeyed he approached Damascus, and suddenly a light from heaven flashed about him. ⁴And he fell to the ground and heard a voice saying to him, "Saul, Saul, why do you persecute me?"

[18]Then after three years I went up to Jerusalem to visit Cephas, and remained with him fifteen days. [19]But I saw none of the other apostles except James the Lord's brother. [20](In what I am writing to you, before God, I do not lie!) [21]Then I went into the regions of Syria and Cilicia. [22]And I was still not known by sight to the churches of Christ in Judea; [23]they only heard it said, "He who once persecuted us is now preaching the faith he once tried to destroy." [24]And they glorified God because of me.

Gal 2:1–10 (§197)

[1]Then after fourteen years I went up again to Jerusalem with Barnabas, taking Titus along with me. [2]I went up by revelation; and I laid before them (but privately before those who were of repute) the gospel which I preach among the Gentiles, lest somehow I should be running or had run in vain. [3]But even Titus, who was with me, was not compelled to be circumcised, though he was a Greek. [4]But because of false brethren secretly brought in, who slipped in to spy out our freedom which we have in Christ Jesus, that they might bring us into bondage — [5]to them we did not yield submission even for a moment, that the truth of the gospel might be preserved for you. [6]And from those who were reputed to be something (what they were makes no difference to me; God shows no partiality)—those, I say, who were of repute added nothing to me; [7]but on the contrary, when they saw that I had been entrusted with the gospel to the uncircumcised, just as Peter had been entrusted with the gospel to the circumcised [8](for he who worked through Peter for the mission to the circumcised worked through me also for the Gentiles), [9]and when they perceived the grace that was given to me, James and Cephas and John, who were reputed to be pillars, gave to me and Barnabas the right hand of fellowship, that we should go to the Gentiles and they to the cir-

cumcised; [10]only they would have us remember the poor, which very thing I was eager to do.

Eph 2:1–10 (§220)

[1]And you he made alive, when you were dead through the trespasses and sins [2]in which you once walked, following the course of this world, following the prince of the power of the air, the spirit that is now at work in the sons of disobedience. [3]Among these we all once lived in the passions of our flesh, following the desires of body and mind, and so we were by nature children of wrath, like the rest of mankind. [4]But God, who is rich in mercy, out of the great love with which he loved us, [5]even when we were dead through our trespasses, made us alive together with Christ (by grace you have been saved), [6]and raised us up with him, and made us sit with him in the heavenly places in Christ Jesus, [7]that in the coming ages he might show the immeasurable riches of his grace in kindness toward us in Christ Jesus. [8]For by grace you have been saved through faith; and this is not your own doing, it is the gift of God— [9]not because of works, lest any man should boast. [10]For we are his workmanship, created in Christ Jesus for good works, which God prepared beforehand, that we should walk in them.

Eph 3:1–13 (§222)

[1]For this reason I, Paul, a prisoner for Christ Jesus on behalf of you Gentiles — [2]assuming that you have heard of the stewardship of God's grace that was given to me for you, [3]how the mystery was made known to me by revelation, as I have written briefly. [4]When you read this you can perceive my insight into the mystery of Christ, [5]which was not made known to the sons of men in other generations as it has now been revealed to his holy apostles and prophets by the Spirit; [6]that is, how the Gentiles are fellow heirs, members of the same body, and partakers

of the promise in Christ Jesus through the gospel.

[7]Of this gospel I was made a minister according to the gift of God's grace which was given me by the working of his power. [8]To me, though I am the very least of all the saints, this grace was given, to preach to the Gentiles the unsearchable riches of Christ, [9]and to make all men see what is the plan of the mystery hidden for ages in God who created all things; [10]that through the church the manifold wisdom of God might now be made known to the principalities and powers in the heavenly places. [11]This was according to the eternal purpose which he has realized in Christ Jesus our Lord, [12]in whom we have boldness and confidence of access through our faith in him. [13]So I ask you not to lose heart over what I am suffering for you, which is your glory.

Col 2:8–15 (§262)

[8]See to it that no one makes a prey of you by philosophy and empty deceit, according to human tradition, according to the elemental spirits of the universe, and not according to Christ. [9]For in him the whole fulness of deity dwells bodily, [10]and you have come to fulness of life in him, who is the head of all rule and authority. [11]In him also you were circumcised with a circumcision made without hands, by putting off the body of flesh in the circumcision of Christ; [12]and you were buried with him in baptism, in which you were also raised with him through faith in the working of God, who raised him from the dead. [13]And you, who were dead in trespasses and the uncircumcision of your flesh, God made alive together with him, having forgiven us all our trespasses, [14]having canceled the bond which stood against us with its legal demands; this he set aside, nailing it to the cross. [15]He disarmed the principalities and powers and made a public example of them, triumphing over them in him.

Acts 22   [6]"As I made my journey and drew near to Damascus, about noon a great light from heaven suddenly shone about me. [7]And I fell to the ground and heard a voice saying to me, 'Saul, Saul, why do you persecute me?'"

Acts 26   [12]"Thus I journeyed to Damascus with the authority and commission of the chief priests. [13]At midday, O king, I saw on the way a light from heaven, brighter than the sun, shining round me and those who journeyed with me. [14]And when we had all fallen to the ground, I heard a voice saying to me in the Hebrew language, 'Saul, Saul, why do you persecute me? It hurts you to kick against the goads.' [15]And I said, 'Who are you, Lord?' And the Lord said, 'I am Jesus whom you are persecuting. [16]But rise and stand upon your feet; for I have appeared to you for this purpose, to appoint you to serve and bear witness to the things in which you have seen me and to those in which I will appear to you.'. . ."

Cf. 1 Tim 1   [15]The saying is sure and worthy of full acceptance, that Christ Jesus came into the world to save sinners. And I am the foremost of sinners; . . .

● **1 Cor 15:9**
Cf. 2 Cor 11   [5]I think that I am not in the least inferior to these superlative apostles.

● **1 Cor 15:10**
Rom 1   [1]Paul, a servant of Jesus Christ, called to be an apostle, set apart for the gospel of God [2]which he promised beforehand through his prophets in the holy scriptures, [3]the gospel concerning his Son, who was descended from David according to the flesh [4]and designated Son of God in power according to the Spirit of holiness by his resurrection from the dead, Jesus Christ our Lord, [5]through whom we have received grace and apostleship to bring about the obedience of faith for the sake of his name among all

the nations, [6]including yourselves who are called to belong to Jesus Christ; . . .

2 Cor 11   [21]. . . But whatever any one dares to boast of—I am speaking as a fool—I also dare to boast of that. [22]Are they Hebrews? So am I. Are they Israelites? So am I. Are they descendants of Abraham? So am I. [23]Are they servants of Christ? I am a better one—I am talking like a madman—with far greater labors, far more imprisonments, with countless beatings, and often near death.

● **1 Cor 15:11**
Cf. Phil 1   [16]The latter do it out of love, knowing that I am put here for the defense of the gospel; [17]the former proclaim Christ out of partisanship, not sincerely but thinking to afflict me in my imprisonment. [18]What then? Only that in every way, whether in pretense or in truth, Christ is proclaimed; and in that I rejoice.

¹²Now if Christ is preached as raised from the dead, how can some of you say that there is no resurrection of the dead? ¹³But if there is no resurrection of the dead, then Christ has not been raised; ¹⁴if Christ has not been raised, then our preaching is in vain and your faith is in vain. ¹⁵We are even found to be misrepresenting God, because we testified of God that he raised Christ, whom he did not raise if it is true that the dead are not raised. ¹⁶For if the dead are not raised, then Christ has not been raised. ¹⁷If Christ has not been raised, your faith is futile and you are still in your sins. ¹⁸Then those also who have fallen asleep in Christ have perished. ¹⁹If for this life only we have hoped in Christ, we are of all men most to be pitied.

Primary

Rom 5:1–5 (§20)

¹Therefore, since we are justified by faith, we have peace with God through our Lord Jesus Christ. ²Through him we have obtained access to this grace in which we stand, and we rejoice in our hope of sharing the glory of God. ³More than that, we rejoice in our sufferings, knowing that suffering produces endurance, ⁴and endurance produces character, and character produces hope, ⁵and hope does not disappoint us, because God's love has been poured into our hearts through the Holy Spirit which has been given to us.

Rom 6:1–10 (§23)

¹What shall we say then? Are we to continue in sin that grace may abound? ²By no means! How can we who died to sin still live in it? ³Do you not know that all of us who have been baptized into Christ Jesus were baptized into his death? ⁴We were buried therefore with him by baptism into death, so that as Christ was raised from the dead by the glory of the Father, we too might walk in newness of life. ⁵For if we have been united with him in a death like his, we shall certainly be united with him in a resurrection like his. ⁶We know that our old self was crucified with him so that the sinful body might be destroyed, and we might no longer be enslaved to sin. ⁷For he who has died is freed from sin. ⁸But if we have died with Christ, we believe that we shall also live with him. ⁹For we know that Christ being raised from the dead will never die again; death no longer has dominion over him. ¹⁰The death he died he died to sin, once for all, but the life he lives he lives to God.

2 Cor 5:14–21 (§164)

¹⁴For the love of Christ controls us, because we are convinced that one has died for all; therefore all have died. ¹⁵And he died for all, that those who live might live no longer for themselves but for him who for their sake died and was raised.

¹⁶From now on, therefore, we regard no one from a human point of view; even though we once regarded Christ from a human point of view, we regard him thus no longer. ¹⁷Therefore, if any one is in Christ, he is a new creation; the old has passed away, behold, the new has come. ¹⁸All this is from God, who through Christ reconciled us to himself and gave us the ministry of reconciliation; ¹⁹that is, in Christ God was reconciling the world to himself, not counting their trespasses against them, and entrusting to us the message of reconciliation. ²⁰So we are ambassadors for Christ, God making his appeal through us. We beseech you on behalf of Christ, be reconciled to God. ²¹For our sake he made him to be sin who knew no sin, so that in him we might become the righteousness of God.

Eph 2:1–10 (§220)

¹And you he made alive, when you were dead through the trespasses and sins ²in which

---

● **1 Cor 15:12**
Acts 17   ³²Now when they heard of the resurrection of the dead, some mocked; but others said, "We will hear you again about this."

Cf. Acts 4   ²annoyed because they were teaching the people and proclaiming in Jesus the resurrection from the dead.

Cf. Acts 23   ⁸For the Sadducees say that there is no resurrection, nor angel, nor spirit; but the Pharisees acknowledge them all.

● **1 Cor 15:15**
Cf. Acts 2   ²⁴"But God raised him up, having loosed the pangs of death, because it was not possible for him to be held by it."

● **1 Cor 15:19**
Rom 8   ²⁴For in this hope we were saved. Now hope that is seen is not hope. For who hopes for what he sees?

Rom 15   ¹³May the God of hope fill you with all joy and peace in believing, so that by the power of the Holy Spirit you may abound in hope.

you once walked, following the course of this world, following the prince of the power of the air, the spirit that is now at work in the sons of disobedience. [3]Among these we all once lived in the passions of our flesh, following the desires of body and mind, and so we were by nature children of wrath, like the rest of mankind. [4]But God, who is rich in mercy, out of the great love with which he loved us, [5]even when we were dead through our trespasses, made us alive together with Christ (by grace you have been saved), [6]and raised us up with him, and made us sit with him in the heavenly places in Christ Jesus, [7]that in the coming ages he might show the immeasurable riches of his grace in kindness toward us in Christ Jesus. [8]For by grace you have been saved through faith; and this is not your own doing, it is the gift of God— [9]not because of works, lest any man should boast. [10]For we are his workmanship, created in Christ Jesus for good works, which God prepared beforehand, that we should walk in them.

Phil 3:17–21 (§249)

[17]Brethren, join in imitating me, and mark those who so live as you have an example in us. [18]For many, of whom I have often told you and now tell you even with tears, live as enemies of the cross of Christ. [19]Their end is destruction,

their god is the belly, and they glory in their shame, with minds set on earthly things. [20]But our commonwealth is in heaven, and from it we await a Savior, the Lord Jesus Christ, [21]who will change our lowly body to be like his glorious body, by the power which enables him even to subject all things to himself.

Col 2:8–15 (§262)

[8]See to it that no one makes a prey of you by philosophy and empty deceit, according to human tradition, according to the elemental spirits of the universe, and not according to Christ. [9]For in him the whole fulness of deity dwells bodily, [10]and you have come to fulness of life in him, who is the head of all rule and authority. [11]In him also you were circumcised with a circumcision made without hands, by putting off the body of flesh in the circumcision of Christ; [12]and you were buried with him in baptism, in which you were also raised with him through faith in the working of God, who raised him from the dead. [13]And you, who were dead in trespasses and the uncircumcision of your flesh, God made alive together with him, having forgiven us all our trespasses, [14]having canceled the bond which stood against us with its legal demands; this he set aside, nailing it to the cross. [15]He disarmed the principalities and

powers and made a public example of them, triumphing over them in him.

1 Thess 4:13–18 (§286)

[13]But we would not have you ignorant, brethren, concerning those who are asleep, that you may not grieve as others do who have no hope. [14]For since we believe that Jesus died and rose again, even so, through Jesus, God will bring with him those who have fallen asleep. [15]For this we declare to you by the word of the Lord, that we who are alive, who are left until the coming of the Lord, shall not precede those who have fallen asleep. [16]For the Lord himself will descend from heaven with a cry of command, with the archangel's call, and with the sound of the trumpet of God. And the dead in Christ will rise first; [17]then we who are alive, who are left, shall be caught up together with them in the clouds to meet the Lord in the air; and so we shall always be with the Lord. [18]Therefore comfort one another with these words.

Eph 2   [12]remember that you were at that time separated from Christ, alienated from the commonwealth of Israel, and strangers to the covenants of promise, having no hope and without God in the world.

Col 1   [5]because of the hope laid up for you in heaven. Of this you have heard before in the word of the truth, the gospel . . .

1 Thess 1   [10]and to wait for his Son from heaven, whom he raised from the dead, Jesus who delivers us from the wrath to come.

2 Thess 1   [10]when he comes on that day to be glorified in his saints, and to be marveled at in all who have believed, because our testimony to you was believed.

[20]But in fact Christ has been raised from the dead, the first fruits of those who have fallen asleep. [21]For as by a man came death, by a man has come also the resurrection of the dead. [22]For as in Adam all die, so also in Christ shall all be made alive. [23]But each in his own order: Christ the first fruits, then at his coming those who belong to Christ. [24]Then comes the end, when he delivers the kingdom to God the Father after destroying every rule and every authority and power. [25]For he must reign until he has put all his enemies under his feet. [26]The last enemy to be destroyed is death. [27]"For God has put all things in subjection under his feet." But when it says, "All things are put in subjection under him," it is plain that he is excepted who put all things under him. [28]When all things are subjected to him, then the Son himself will also be subjected to him who put all things under him, that God may be everything to every one.

Primary

Rom 5:12–21 (§22)

[12]Therefore as sin came into the world through one man and death through sin, and so death spread to all men because all men sinned— [13]sin indeed was in the world before the law was given, but sin is not counted where there is no law. [14]Yet death reigned from Adam to Moses, even over those whose sins were not like the transgression of Adam, who was a type of the one who was to come.

[15]But the free gift is not like the trespass. For if many died through one man's trespass, much more have the grace of God and the free gift in the grace of that one man Jesus Christ abounded for many. [16]And the free gift is not like the effect of that one man's sin. For the judgment following one trespass brought condemnation, but the free gift following many trespasses brings justification. [17]If, because of one man's trespass, death reigned through that one man, much more will those who receive the abundance of grace and the free gift of righteousness reign in life through the one man Jesus Christ.

[18]Then as one man's trespass led to condemnation for all men, so one man's act of righteousness leads to acquittal and life for all men. [19]For as by one man's disobedience many were made sinners, so by one man's obedience many will be made righteous. [20]Law came in, to increase the trespass; but where sin increased, grace abounded all the more, [21]so that, as sin reigned in death, grace also might reign through righteousness to eternal life through Jesus Christ our Lord.

2 Cor 10:1–6 (§176)

[1]I, Paul, myself entreat you, by the meekness and gentleness of Christ—I who am humble when face to face with you, but bold to you when I am away!— [2]I beg of you that when I am present I may not have to show boldness with such confidence as I count on showing against some who suspect us of acting in worldly fashion. [3]For though we live in the world we are not carrying on a worldly war, [4]for the weapons of our warfare are not worldly but have divine power to destroy strongholds. [5]We destroy arguments and every proud obstacle to the knowledge of God, and take every thought captive to obey Christ, [6]being ready to punish every disobedience, when your obedience is complete.

Eph 1:3–23 (§219)

[3]Blessed be the God and Father of our Lord Jesus Christ, who has blessed us in Christ with every spiritual blessing in the heavenly places, [4]even as he chose us in him before the foundation of the world, that we should be holy and blameless before him. [5]He destined us in love to be his sons through Jesus Christ, according to the purpose of his will, [6]to the praise of his glorious grace which he freely bestowed on us in the Beloved. [7]In him we have redemption through his blood, the forgiveness of our trespasses, according to the riches of his grace [8]which he lavished upon us. [9]For he has made known to us in all wisdom and insight the mystery of his will, according to his purpose which he set forth in Christ [10]as a plan for the fulness of time, to unite all things in him, things in heaven and things on earth.

[11]In him, according to the purpose of him who accomplishes all things according to the counsel of his will, [12]we who first hoped in Christ have been destined and appointed to live for the praise of his glory. [13]In him you also, who have heard the word of truth, the gospel of your salvation, and have believed in him, were sealed with the promised Holy Spirit, [14]which is the guarantee of our inheritance until we acquire possession of it, to the praise of his glory.

● **1 Cor 15:20–23**

Rom 8   [23]and not only the creation, but we ourselves, who have the first fruits of the Spirit, groan inwardly as we wait for adoption as sons, the redemption of our bodies.

● **1 Cor 15:20**

Acts 2   [24]"But God raised him up, having loosed the pangs of death, because it was not possible for him to be held by it."

Acts 26   [22]"To this day I have had the help that comes from God, and so I stand here testifying both to small and great, saying nothing but what the prophets and Moses said would come to pass: [23]that the Christ must suffer, and that, by being the first to rise from the dead, he would proclaim light both to the people and to the Gentiles."

● **1 Cor 15:24**

1 Thess 5   [3]When people say, "There is peace and security," then sudden destruction will come upon them as travail comes upon a woman with child, and there will be no escape.

[15]For this reason, because I have heard of your faith in the Lord Jesus and your love toward all the saints, [16]I do not cease to give thanks for you, remembering you in my prayers, [17]that the God of our Lord Jesus Christ, the Father of glory, may give you a spirit of wisdom and of revelation in the knowledge of him, [18]having the eyes of your hearts enlightened, that you may know what is the hope to which he has called you, what are the riches of his glorious inheritance in the saints, [19]and what is the immeasurable greatness of his power in us who believe, according to the working of his great might [20]which he accomplished in Christ when he raised him from the dead and made him sit at his right hand in the heavenly places, [21]far above all rule and authority and power and dominion, and above every name that is named, not only in this age but also in that which is to come; [22]and he has put all things under his feet and has made him the head over all things for the church, [23]which is his body, the fulness of him who fills all in all.

Phil 3:17–21 (§249)

[17]Brethren, join in imitating me, and mark those who so live as you have an example in us. [18]For many, of whom I have often told you and now tell you even with tears, live as enemies of the cross of Christ. [19]Their end is destruction, their god is the belly, and they glory in their shame, with minds set on earthly things. [20]But our commonwealth is in heaven, and from it we await a Savior, the Lord Jesus Christ, [21]who will change our lowly body to be like his glorious body, by the power which enables him even to subject all things to himself.

Col 1:15–20 (§258)

[15]He is the image of the invisible God, the first-born of all creation; [16]for in him all things were created, in heaven and on earth, visible and invisible, whether thrones or dominions or principalities or authorities—all things were created through him and for him. [17]He is before all things, and in him all things hold together. [18]He is the head of the body, the church; he is the beginning, the first-born from the dead, that in everything he might be pre-eminent. [19]For in him all the fulness of God was pleased to dwell, [20]and through him to reconcile to himself all things, whether on earth or in heaven, making peace by the blood of his cross.

1 Thess 4:13–18 (§286)

[13]But we would not have you ignorant, brethren, concerning those who are asleep, that you may not grieve as others do who have no hope. [14]For since we believe that Jesus died and rose again, even so, through Jesus, God will bring with him those who have fallen asleep. [15]For this we declare to you by the word of the Lord, that we who are alive, who are left until the coming of the Lord, shall not precede those who have fallen asleep. [16]For the Lord himself will descend from heaven with a cry of command, with the archangel's call, and with the sound of the trumpet of God. And the dead in Christ will rise first; [17]then we who are alive, who are left, shall be caught up together with them in the clouds to meet the Lord in the air; and so we shall always be with the Lord. [18]Therefore comfort one another with these words.

2 Thess 2:1–12 (§296)

[1]Now concerning the coming of our Lord Jesus Christ and our assembling to meet him, we beg you, brethren, [2]not to be quickly shaken in mind or excited, either by spirit or by word, or by letter purporting to be from us, to the effect that the day of the Lord has come. [3]Let no one deceive you in any way; for that day will not come, unless the rebellion comes first, and the man of lawlessness is revealed, the son of perdition, [4]who opposes and exalts himself against every so-called god or object of worship, so that he takes his seat in the temple of God, proclaiming himself to be God. [5]Do you not remember that when I was still with you I told you this? [6]And you know what is restraining him now so that he may be revealed in his time. [7]For the mystery of lawlessness is already at work; only he who now restrains it will do so until he is out of the way. [8]And then the lawless one will be revealed, and the Lord Jesus will slay him with the breath of his mouth and destroy him by his appearing and his coming. [9]The coming of the lawless one by the activity of Satan will be with all power and with pretended signs and wonders, [10]and with all wicked deception for those who are to perish, because they refused to love the truth and so be saved. [11]Therefore God sends upon them a strong delusion, to make them believe what is false, [12]so that all may be condemned who did not believe the truth but had pleasure in unrighteousness.

● **1 Cor 15:27**
Ps 8   [6]Thou hast given him dominion over the works of thy hands;
    thou hast put all things under his feet, . . .

Cf. Phil 2   [9]Therefore God has highly exalted him and bestowed on him the name which is above every name, [10]that at the name of Jesus every knee should bow, in heaven and on earth and under the earth, [11]and every tongue confess that Jesus Christ is Lord, to the glory of God the Father.

● **1 Cor 15:28**
Cf. 1 Cor 3   [21]So let no one boast of men. For all things are yours, [22]whether Paul or Apollos or Cephas or the world or life or death or the present or the future, all are yours; [23]and you are Christ's; and Christ is God's.

²⁹Otherwise, what do people mean by being baptized on behalf of the dead? If the dead are not raised at all, why are people baptized on their behalf? ³⁰Why am I in peril every hour? ³¹I protest, brethren, by my pride in you which I have in Christ Jesus our Lord, I die every day! ³²What do I gain if, humanly speaking, I fought with beasts at Ephesus? If the dead are not raised, "Let us eat and drink, for tomorrow we die." ³³Do not be deceived: "Bad company ruins good morals." ³⁴Come to your right mind, and sin no more. For some have no knowledge of God. I say this to your shame.

PRIMARY

2 Cor 4:7–12 (§159)

⁷But we have this treasure in earthen vessels, to show that the transcendent power belongs to God and not to us. ⁸We are afflicted in every way, but not crushed; perplexed, but not driven to despair; ⁹persecuted, but not forsaken; struck down, but not destroyed; ¹⁰always carrying in the body the death of Jesus, so that the life of Jesus may also be manifested in our bodies. ¹¹For while we live we are always being given up to death for Jesus' sake, so that the life of Jesus may be manifested in our mortal flesh. ¹²So death is at work in us, but life in you.

2 Cor 6:1–10 (§165)

¹Working together with him, then, we entreat you not to accept the grace of God in vain. ²For he says,

"At the acceptable time I have listened to you,
and helped you on the day of salvation."

Behold, now is the acceptable time; behold, now is the day of salvation. ³We put no obstacle in any one's way, so that no fault may be found with our ministry, ⁴but as servants of God we commend ourselves in every way: through great endurance, in afflictions, hardships, calamities, ⁵beatings, imprisonments, tumults, labors, watching, hunger; ⁶by purity, knowledge, forbearance, kindness, the Holy Spirit, genuine love, ⁷truthful speech, and the power of God; with the weapons of righteousness for the right hand and for the left; ⁸in honor and dishonor, in ill repute and good repute. We are treated as impostors, and yet are true; ⁹as unknown, and yet well known; as dying, and behold we live; as punished, and yet not killed; ¹⁰as sorrowful, yet always rejoicing; as poor, yet making many rich; as having nothing, and yet possessing everything.

2 Cor 11:21b–29 (§183)

But whatever any one dares to boast of—I am speaking as a fool—I also dare to boast of that. ²²Are they Hebrews? So am I. Are they Israelites? So am I. Are they descendants of Abraham? So am I. ²³Are they servants of Christ? I am a better one—I am talking like a madman—with far greater labors, far more imprisonments, with countless beatings, and often near death. ²⁴Five times I have received at the hands of the Jews the forty lashes less one. ²⁵Three times I have been beaten with rods; once I was stoned. Three times I have been shipwrecked; a night and a day I have been adrift at sea; ²⁶on frequent journeys, in danger from rivers, danger from robbers, danger from my own people, danger from Gentiles, danger in the city, danger in the wilderness, danger at sea, danger from false brethren; ²⁷in toil and hardship, through many a sleepless night, in hunger and thirst, often without food, in cold and exposure. ²⁸And, apart from other things, there is the daily pressure upon me of my anxiety for all the churches. ²⁹Who is weak, and I am not weak? Who is made to fall, and I am not indignant?

Phil 1:19–26 (§240)

¹⁹Yes, and I shall rejoice. For I know that through your prayers and the help of the Spirit of Jesus Christ this will turn out for my deliverance, ²⁰as it is my eager expectation and hope that I shall not be at all ashamed, but that with full courage now as always Christ will be honored in my body, whether by life or by death. ²¹For to me to live is Christ, and to die is gain. ²²If it is to be life in the flesh, that means fruitful labor for me. Yet which I shall choose I cannot tell. ²³I am hard pressed between the two. My desire is to depart and be with Christ, for that is far better. ²⁴But to remain in the flesh is more necessary on your account. ²⁵Convinced of this, I know that I shall remain and continue with you all, for your progress and joy in the faith, ²⁶so that in me you may have ample cause to glory in Christ Jesus, because of my coming to you again.

Col 1:24–2:3 (§260)

²⁴Now I rejoice in my sufferings for your sake, and in my flesh I complete what is lacking in Christ's afflictions for the sake of his body, that is, the church, ²⁵of which I became a minister according to the divine office which was given to me for you, to make the word of God fully known, ²⁶the mystery hidden for ages and generations but now made manifest to his saints. ²⁷To them God chose to make known how great among the Gentiles are the riches of the glory of this mystery, which is Christ in you, the hope of glory. ²⁸Him we proclaim warning every man and teaching every man in all wisdom, that we may present every man mature in Christ. ²⁹For this I toil, striving with all the energy which he mightily inspires within me.

¹For I want you to know how greatly I strive for you, and for those at Laodicea, and for all who have not seen my face, ²that their hearts may be encouraged as they are knit together in love, to have all the riches of assured understanding and the knowledge of God's mystery, of Christ, ³in whom are hid all the treasures of wisdom and knowledge.

1 Thess 3:1–5 (§281)

¹Therefore when we could bear it no longer, we were willing to be left behind at Athens alone, ²and we sent Timothy, our brother and God's servant in the gospel of Christ, to establish you in your faith and to exhort you, ³that no one be moved by these afflictions. You yourselves know that this is to be our lot. ⁴For when we were with you, we told you beforehand that we were to suffer affliction; just as it has come to pass, and as you know. ⁵For this reason, when I could bear it no longer, I sent that I might know your faith, for fear that somehow the tempter had tempted you and that our labor would be in vain.

● **1 Cor 15:30**

Gal 5   ¹¹But if I, brethren, still preach circumcision, why am I still persecuted? In that case the stumbling block of the cross has been removed.

2 Cor 1   ⁸For we do not want you to be ignorant, brethren, of the affliction we experienced in Asia; for we were so utterly, unbearably crushed that we despaired of life itself.

2 Cor 12   ¹⁰For the sake of Christ, then, I am content with weaknesses, insults, hardships, persecutions, and calamities; for when I am weak, then I am strong.

● **1 Cor 15:32**

Isa 22   ¹³and behold, joy and gladness, slaying oxen and killing sheep, eating flesh and drinking wine. "Let us eat and drink, for tomorrow we die."

Acts 18   ¹⁹And they came to Ephesus, and he left them there; but he himself went into the synagogue and argued with the Jews.

Acts 19   ³²Now some cried one thing, some another; for the assembly was in confusion, and most of them did not know why they had come together.

● **1 Cor 15:33**

Meander, *Thais.*

● **1 Cor 15:34**

Gal 4   ⁹but now that you have come to know God, or rather to be known by God, how can you turn back again to the weak and beggarly elemental spirits, whose slaves you want to be once more?

Gal 4   ¹⁴and though my condition was a trial to you, you did not scorn or despise me, but received me as an angel of God, as Christ Jesus.

[35]But some one will ask, "How are the dead raised? With what kind of body do they come?" [36]You foolish man! What you sow does not come to life unless it dies. [37]And what you sow is not the body which is to be, but a bare kernel, perhaps of wheat or of some other grain. [38]But God gives it a body as he has chosen, and to each kind of seed its own body. [39]For not all flesh is alike, but there is one kind for men, another for animals, another for birds, and another for fish. [40]There are celestial bodies and there are terrestrial bodies; but the glory of the celestial is one, and the glory of the terrestrial is another. [41]There is one glory of the sun, and another glory of the moon, and another glory of the stars; for star differs from star in glory.

PRIMARY

Rom 8:18–25 (§31)

[18]I consider that the sufferings of this present time are not worth comparing with the glory that is to be revealed to us. [19]For the creation waits with eager longing for the re-vealing of the sons of God; [20]for the creation was subjected to futility, not of its own will but by the will of him who subjected it in hope; [21]because the creation itself will be set free from its bondage to decay and obtain the glorious liberty of the children of God. [22]We know that the whole creation has been groaning in travail together until now; [23]and not only the creation, but we ourselves, who have the first fruits of the Spirit, groan inwardly as we wait for adoption as sons, the redemption of our bodies. [24]For in this hope we were saved. Now hope that is seen is not hope. For who hopes for what he sees? [25]But if we hope for what we do not see, we wait for it with patience.

2 Cor 4:16–5:5 (§161)

[16]So we do not lose heart. Though our outer nature is wasting away, our inner nature is being renewed every day. [17]For this slight momentary affliction is preparing for us an eternal weight of glory beyond all comparison, [18]because we look not to the things that are seen but to the things that are unseen; for the things that are seen are transient, but the things that are unseen are eternal.

5 [1]For we know that if the earthly tent we live in is destroyed, we have a building from God, a house not made with hands, eternal in the heavens. [2]Here indeed we groan, and long to put on our heavenly dwelling, [3]so that by putting it on we may not be found naked. [4]For while we are still in this tent, we sigh with anxiety; not that we would be unclothed, but that we would be further clothed, so that what is mortal may be swallowed up by life. [5]He who has prepared us for this very thing is God, who has given us the Spirit as a guarantee.

Phil 3:17–21 (§249)

[17]Brethren, join in imitating me, and mark those who so live as you have an example in us. [18]For many, of whom I have often told you and now tell you even with tears, live as enemies of the cross of Christ. [19]Their end is destruction, their god is the belly, and they glory in their shame, with minds set on earthly things. [20]But our commonwealth is in heaven, and from it we await a Savior, the Lord Jesus Christ, [21]who will change our lowly body to be like his glorious body, by the power which enables him even to subject all things to himself.

● **1 Cor 15:35–41**
Rom 8   [9]But you are not in the flesh, you are in the Spirit, if in fact the Spirit of God dwells in you. Any one who does not have the Spirit of Christ does not belong to him. [10]But if Christ is in you, although your bodies are dead because of sin, your spirits are alive because of righteousness. [11]If the Spirit of him who raised Jesus from the dead dwells in you, he who raised Christ Jesus from the dead will give life to your mortal bodies also through his Spirit which dwells in you.

● **1 Cor 15:35**
Acts 26   [8]"Why is it thought incredible by any of you that God raises the dead?"

[42]So is it with the resurrection of the dead. What is sown is perishable, what is raised is imperishable. [43]It is sown in dishonor, it is raised in glory. It is sown in weakness, it is raised in power. [44]It is sown a physical body, it is raised a spiritual body. If there is a physical body, there is also a spiritual body. [45]Thus it is written, "The first man Adam became a living being"; the last Adam became a life-giving spirit. [46]But it is not the spiritual which is first but the physical, and then the spiritual. [47]The first man was from the earth, a man of dust; the second man is from heaven. [48]As was the man of dust, so are those who are of the dust; and as is the man of heaven, so are those who are of heaven. [49]Just as we have borne the image of the man of dust, we shall also bear the image of the man of heaven. [50]I tell you this, brethren: flesh and blood cannot inherit the kingdom of God, nor does the perishable inherit the imperishable.

PRIMARY

Rom 5:12-21 (§22)

[12]Therefore as sin came into the world through one man and death through sin, and so death spread to all men because all men sinned— [13]sin indeed was in the world before the law was given, but sin is not counted where there is no law. [14]Yet death reigned from Adam to Moses, even over those whose sins were not like the transgression of Adam, who was a type of the one who was to come.

[15]But the free gift is not like the trespass. For if many died through one man's trespass, much more have the grace of God and the free gift in the grace of that one man Jesus Christ abounded for many. [16]And the free gift is not like the effect of that one man's sin. For the judgment following one trespass brought condemnation, but the free gift following many trespasses brings justification. [17]If, because of one man's trespass, death reigned through that one man, much more will those who receive the abundance of grace and the free gift of righteousness reign in life through the one man Jesus Christ.

[18]Then as one man's trespass led to condemnation for all men, so one man's act of righteousness leads to acquittal and life for all men. [19]For as by one man's disobedience many were made sinners, so by one man's obedience many will be made righteous. [20]Law came in, to increase the trespass; but where sin increased, grace abounded all the more, [21]so that, as sin reigned in death, grace also might reign through righteousness to eternal life through Jesus Christ our Lord.

Gal 6:7-10 (§215)

[7]Do not be deceived; God is not mocked, for whatever a man sows, that he will also reap. [8]For he who sows to his own flesh will from the flesh reap corruption; but he who sows to the Spirit will from the Spirit reap eternal life. [9]And let us not grow weary in well-doing, for in due season we shall reap, if we do not lose heart. [10]So then, as we have opportunity, let us do good to all men, and especially to those who are of the household of faith.

Phil 3:17-21 (§249)

[17]Brethren, join in imitating me, and mark those who so live as you have an example in us. [18]For many, of whom I have often told you and now tell you even with tears, live as enemies of the cross of Christ. [19]Their end is destruction, their god is the belly, and they glory in their shame, with minds set on earthly things. [20]But our commonwealth is in heaven, and from it we await a Savior, the Lord Jesus Christ, [21]who will change our lowly body to be like his glorious body, by the power which enables him even to subject all things to himself.

Col 1:15-20 (§258)

[15]He is the image of the invisible God, the first-born of all creation; [16]for in him all things were created, in heaven and on earth, visible and invisible, whether thrones or dominions or principalities or authorities—all things were created through him and for him. [17]He is before all things, and in him all things hold together. [18]He is the head of the body, the church; he is the beginning, the first-born from the dead, that in everything he might be pre-eminent. [19]For in him all the fulness of God was pleased to dwell, [20]and through him to reconcile to himself all things, whether on earth or in heaven, making peace by the blood of his cross.

● 1 Cor 15:44

1 Cor 2   [14]The unspiritual man does not receive the gifts of the Spirit of God, for they are folly to him, and he is not able to understand them because they are spiritually discerned.

● 1 Cor 15:45

Rom 8   [11]If the Spirit of him who raised Jesus from the dead dwells in you, he who raised Christ Jesus from the dead will give life to your mortal bodies also through his Spirit which dwells in you.

Gen 2   [7]then the Lord God formed man of dust from the ground, and breathed into his nostrils the breath of life; and man became a living being.

● 1 Cor 15:49

Rom 8   [29]For those whom he foreknew he also predestined to be conformed to the image of his Son, in order that he might be the first-born among many brethren.

1 Cor 3   [10]According to the grace of God given to me, like a skilled master builder I laid a foundation, and another man is building upon it. Let each man take care how he builds upon it.

1 Cor 11   [7]For a man ought not to cover his head, since he is the image and glory of God; but woman is the glory of man.

2 Cor 3   [18]And we all, with unveiled face, beholding the glory of the Lord, are being changed into his likeness from one degree of glory to another; for this comes from the Lord who is the Spirit.

2 Cor 4   [4]In their case the god of this world has blinded the minds of the unbelievers, to keep them from seeing the light of the gospel of the glory of Christ, who is the likeness of God.

(shall) *read* let us: p[46]SACDG Koine it vg cop(bo) Marcion Clement; *text:* B Lect cop(sa) Irenaeus Origen

● 1 Cor 15:50

Col 2   [11]In him also you were circumcised with a circumcision made without hands, by putting off the body of flesh in the circumcision of Christ; . . .

[51]Lo! I tell you a mystery. We shall not all sleep, but we shall all be changed, [52]in a moment, in the twinkling of an eye, at the last trumpet. For the trumpet will sound, and the dead will be raised imperishable, and we shall be changed. [53]For this perishable nature must put on the imperishable, and this mortal nature must put on immortality. [54]When the perishable puts on the imperishable, and the mortal puts on immortality, then shall come to pass the saying that is written:

"Death is swallowed up in victory."

[55]"O death, where is thy victory?

O death, where is thy sting?" [56]The sting of death is sin, and the power of sin is the law. [57]But thanks be to God, who gives us the victory through our Lord Jesus Christ.

[58]Therefore, my beloved brethren, be steadfast, immovable, always abounding in the work of the Lord, knowing that in the Lord your labor is not in vain.

PRIMARY

2 Cor 4:16–5:5 (§161)

[16]So we do not lose heart. Though our outer nature is wasting away, our inner nature is being renewed every day. [17]For this slight momentary affliction is preparing for us an eternal weight of glory beyond all comparison, [18]because we look not to the things that are seen but to the things that are unseen; for the things that are seen are transient, but the things that are unseen are eternal.

[1]For we know that if the earthly tent we live in is destroyed, we have a building from God, a house not made with hands, eternal in the heavens. [2]Here indeed we groan, and long to put on our heavenly dwelling, [3]so that by putting it on we may not be found naked. [4]For while we are still in this tent, we sigh with anxiety; not that we would be unclothed, but that we would be further clothed, so that what is mortal may be swallowed up by life. [5]He who has prepared us for this very thing is God, who has given us the Spirit as a guarantee.

Eph 4:17–24 (§227)

[17]Now this I affirm and testify in the Lord, that you must no longer live as the Gentiles do, in the futility of their minds; [18]they are darkened in their understanding, alienated from the life of God because of the ignorance that is in them, due to their hardness of heart; [19]they have become callous and have given themselves up to licentiousness, greedy to practice every kind of uncleanness. [20]You did not so learn Christ!— [21]assuming that you have heard about him and were taught in him, as the truth is in Jesus. [22]Put off your old nature which belongs to your former manner of life and is corrupt through deceitful lusts, [23]and be renewed in the spirit of your minds, [24]and put on the new nature, created after the likeness of God in true righteousness and holiness.

Col 3:1–4 (§265)

[1]If then you have been raised with Christ, seek the things that are above, where Christ is, seated at the right hand of God. [2]Set your minds on things that are above, not on things that are on earth. [3]For you have died, and your life is hid with Christ in God. [4]When Christ who is our life appears, then you also will appear with him in glory.

Col 3:5–11 (§266)

[5]Put to death therefore what is earthly in you: fornication, impurity, passion, evil desire, and covetousness, which is idolatry. [6]On account of these the wrath of God is coming. [7]In these you once walked, when you lived in them. [8]But now put them all away: anger, wrath, malice, slander, and foul talk from your mouth. [9]Do not lie to one another, seeing that you have put off the old nature with its practices [10]and have put on the new nature, which is being renewed in knowledge after the image of its creator. [11]Here there cannot be Greek and Jew, circumcised and uncircumcised, barbarian, Scythian, slave, free man, but Christ is all, and in all.

1 Thess 4:13–18 (§286)

[13]But we would not have you ignorant, brethren, concerning those who are asleep, that you may not grieve as others do who have no hope. [14]For since we believe that Jesus died and rose again, even so, through Jesus, God will bring with him those who have fallen asleep. [15]For this we declare to you by the word of the Lord, that we who are alive, who are left until the coming of the Lord, shall not precede those who have fallen asleep. [16]For the Lord himself will descend from heaven with a cry of command, with the archangel's call, and with the sound of the trumpet of God. And the dead in Christ will rise first; [17]then we who are alive, who are left, shall be caught up together with them in the clouds to meet the Lord in the air; and so we shall always be with the Lord. [18]Therefore comfort one another with these words.

● **1 Cor 15:51**

Rom 5   [18]Then as one man's trespass led to condemnation for all men, so one man's act of righteousness leads to acquittal and life for all men.

(changed) *read* we shall not all sleep but we shall not all be changed: p46 Ac Origen; *read* we shall sleep but we shall not all be changed: SCG (Greek) Origen; *read* we shall rise but we shall not all be changed: D* it (most) vg Marcion Tertullian; *text:* BDc Koine Lect syr cop Tertullian Origen

Cf. Rom 11   [32]For God has consigned all men to disobedience, that he may have mercy upon all.

● **1 Cor 15:54**

Isa 25   [8]He will swallow up death for ever, and the Lord God will wipe away tears from all faces, and the reproach of his people he will take away from all the earth, for the Lord has spoken.

● **1 Cor 15:55**

Hos 13   [14]Shall I ransom them from the power of Sheol?

Shall I redeem them from Death?

O Death, where are your plagues?

O Sheol, where is your destruction?

Compassion is hid from my eyes.

● **1 Cor 15:56**

Rom 7   [10]the very commandment which promised life proved to be death to me. [11]For sin, finding opportunity in the commandment, deceived me and by it killed me.

Cf. Rom 7   [25]Thanks be to God through Jesus Christ our Lord! So then, I of myself serve the law of God with my mind, but with my flesh I serve the law of sin.

● **1 Cor 15:58**

Phil 2   [16]holding fast the word of life, so that in the day of Christ I may be proud that I did not run in vain or labor in vain.

Col 2   [5]For though I am absent in body, yet I am with you in spirit, rejoicing to see your good order and the firmness of your faith in Christ.

[6]As therefore you received Christ Jesus the Lord, so live in him, [7]rooted and built up in him and established in the faith, just as you were taught, abounding in thanksgiving.

Cf. Gal 2   [2]I went up by revelation; and I laid before them (but privately before those who were of repute) the gospel which I preach among the Gentiles, lest somehow I should be running or had run in vain.

Cf. 1 Thess 3   [5]For this reason, when I could bear it no longer, I sent that I might know your faith, for fear that somehow the tempter had tempted you and that our labor would be in vain.

FORMAL ELEMENT: APOSTOLIC VISIT

16 Now concerning the contribution for the saints: as I directed the churches of Galatia, so you also are to do. ²On the first day of every week, each of you is to put something aside and store it up, as he may prosper, so that contributions need not be made when I come. ³And when I arrive, I will send those whom you accredit by letter to carry your gift to Jerusalem. ⁴If it seems advisable that I should go also, they will accompany me.

PRIMARY

See §63 for APOSTOLIC VISIT

SECONDARY

2 Cor 8:1–24 (§171–173)

¹We want you to know, brethren, about the grace of God which has been shown in the churches of Macedonia, ²for in a severe test of affliction, their abundance of joy and their extreme poverty have overflowed in a wealth of liberality on their part. ³For they gave according to their means, as I can testify, and beyond their means, of their own free will, ⁴begging us earnestly for the favor of taking part in the relief of the saints— ⁵and this, not as we expected, but first they gave themselves to the Lord and to us by the will of God. ⁶Accordingly we have urged Titus that as he had already made a beginning, he should also complete among you this gracious work. ⁷Now as you excel in everything—in faith, in utterance, in knowledge, in all earnestness, and in your love

for us—see that you excel in this gracious work also.

⁸I say this not as a command, but to prove by the earnestness of others that your love also is genuine. ⁹For you know the grace of our Lord Jesus Christ, that though he was rich, yet for your sake he became poor, so that by his poverty you might become rich. ¹⁰And in this matter I give my advice: it is best for you now to complete what a year ago you began not only to do but to desire, ¹¹so that your readiness in desiring it may be matched by your completing it out of what you have. ¹²For if the readiness is there, it is acceptable according to what a man has, not according to what he has not. ¹³I do not mean that others should be eased and you burdened, ¹⁴but that as a matter of equality your abundance at the present time should supply their want, so that their abundance may supply your want, that there may be equality. ¹⁵As it is written, "He who gathered much had nothing over, and he who gathered little had no lack."

¹⁶But thanks be to God who puts the same earnest care for you into the heart of Titus. ¹⁷For he not only accepted our appeal, but being himself very earnest he is going to you of his own accord. ¹⁸With him we are sending the brother who is famous among all the churches for his preaching of the gospel; ¹⁹and not only that, but he has been appointed by the churches to travel with us in this gracious work which we are carrying on, for the glory of the Lord and to show our good will. ²⁰We intend that no one should blame us about this liberal gift which we are administering, ²¹for we aim at what is honorable not only in the Lord's sight but also in the sight of men. ²²And with them we are sending our brother whom we have often tested

and found earnest in many matters, but who is now more earnest than ever because of his great confidence in you. ²³As for Titus, he is my partner and fellow worker in your service; and as for our brethren, they are messengers of the churches, the glory of Christ. ²⁴So give proof, before the churches, of your love and of our boasting about you to these men.

2 Cor 9:6–15 (§175)

⁶The point is this: he who sows sparingly will also reap sparingly, and he who sows bountifully will also reap bountifully. ⁷Each one must do as he has made up his mind, not reluctantly or under compulsion, for God loves a cheerful giver. ⁸And God is able to provide you with every blessing in abundance, so that you may always have enough of everything and may provide in abundance for every good work. ⁹As it is written,

"He scatters abroad, he gives to the poor;
his righteousness endures for ever."

¹⁰He who supplies seed to the sower and bread for food will supply and multiply your resources and increase the harvest of your righteousness. ¹¹You will be enriched in every way for great generosity, which through us will produce thanksgiving to God; ¹²for the rendering of this service not only supplies the wants of the saints but also overflows in many thanksgivings to God. ¹³Under the test of this service, you will glorify God by your obedience in acknowledging the gospel of Christ, and by the generosity of your contribution for them and for all others; ¹⁴while they long for you and pray for you, because of the surpassing grace of God in you. ¹⁵Thanks be to God for his inexpressible gift!

● **1 Cor 16:1–4**

1 Cor 4   ¹⁴I do not write this to make you ashamed, but to admonish you as my beloved children. ¹⁵For though you have countless guides in Christ, you do not have many fathers. For I became your father in Christ Jesus through the gospel. ¹⁶I urge you, then, be imitators of me. ¹⁷Therefore I sent to you Timothy, my beloved and faithful child in the Lord, to remind you of my ways in Christ, as I teach them everywhere in every church. ¹⁸Some are arrogant, as though I were not coming to you. ¹⁹But I will come to you soon, if the Lord wills, and I will find out not the talk of these arrogant people but their power. ²⁰For the kingdom of

God does not consist in talk but in power. ²¹What do you wish? Shall I come to you with a rod, or with love in a spirit of gentleness?

1 Cor 16   ⁵I will visit you after passing through Macedonia, for I intend to pass through Macedonia, ⁶and perhaps I will stay with you or even spend the winter, so that you may speed me on my journey, wherever I go. ⁷For I do not want to see you now just in passing; I hope to spend some time with you, if the Lord permits. ⁸But I will stay in Ephesus until Pentecost, ⁹for a wide door for effective work has opened to me, and there are many adversaries.

● **1 Cor 16:1**

Rom 15   ¹⁶to be a minister of Christ Jesus to the Gentiles in the priestly service of the gospel of God, so that the offering of the Gentiles may be acceptable, sanctified by the Holy Spirit.

Acts 11   ²⁹And the disciples determined, every one according to his ability, to send relief to the brethren who lived in Judea; . . .

Acts 24   ¹⁷"Now after some years I came to bring to my nation alms and offerings."

FORMAL ELEMENT: APOSTOLIC VISIT

[5]I will visit you after passing through Macedonia, for I intend to pass through Macedonia, [6]and perhaps I will stay with you or even spend the winter, so that you may speed me on my journey, wherever I go. [7]For I do not want to see you now just in passing; I hope to spend some time with you, if the Lord permits. [8]But I will stay in Ephesus until Pentecost, [9]for a wide door for effective work has opened to me, and there are many adversaries.

PRIMARY

See §63 for APOSTOLIC VISIT

SECONDARY

2 Cor 8:1–7 (§171)
[1]We want you to know, brethren, about the grace of God which has been shown in the churches of Macedonia, [2]for in a severe test of affliction, their abundance of joy and their extreme poverty have overflowed in a wealth of liberality on their part. [3]For they gave according to their means, as I can testify, and beyond their means, of their own free will, [4]begging us earnestly for the favor of taking part in the relief of the saints — [5]and this, not as we expected, but first they gave themselves to the Lord and to us by the will of God. [6]Accordingly we have urged Titus that as he had already made a beginning, he should also complete among you this gracious work. [7]Now as you excel in everything—in faith, in utterance, in knowledge, in all earnestness, and in your love for us—see that you excel in this gracious work also.

1 Thess 1:2–10 (§276)
[2]We give thanks to God always for you all, constantly mentioning you in our prayers, [3]remembering before our God and Father your work of faith and labor of love and steadfastness of hope in our Lord Jesus Christ. [4]For we know, brethren beloved by God, that he has chosen you; [5]for our gospel came to you not only in word, but also in power and in the Holy Spirit and with full conviction. You know what kind of men we proved to be among you for your sake. [6]And you became imitators of us and of the Lord, for you received the word in much affliction, with joy inspired by the Holy Spirit; [7]so that you became an example to the all the believers in Macedonia and in Achaia. [8]For not only has the word of the Lord sounded forth from you in Macedonia and Achaia, but your faith in God has gone forth everywhere, so that we need not say anything. [9]For they themselves report concerning us what a welcome we had among you, and how you turned to God from idols, to serve a living and true God, [10]and to wait for his Son from heaven, whom he raised from the dead, Jesus who delivers us from the wrath to come.

● **1 Cor 5–9**
1 Cor 4　[14]I do not write this to make you ashamed, but to admonish you as my beloved children. [15]For though you have countless guides in Christ, you do not have many fathers. For I became your father in Christ Jesus through the gospel. [16]I urge you, then, be imitators of me. [17]Therefore I sent to you Timothy, my beloved and faithful child in the Lord, to remind you of my ways in Christ, as I teach them everywhere in every church. [18]Some are arrogant, as though I were not coming to you. [19]But I will come to you soon, if the Lord wills, and I will find out not the talk of these arrogant people but their power. [20]For the kingdom of God does not consist in talk but in power. [21]What do you wish? Shall I come to you with a rod, or with love in a spirit of gentleness?

Cf. 1 Cor 16　[1]Now concerning the contribution for the saints: as I directed the churches of Galatia, so you also are to do. [2]On the first day of every week, each of you is to put something aside and store it up, as he may prosper, so that contributions need not be made when I come. [3]And when I arrive, I will send those whom you accredit by letter to carry your gift to Jerusalem. [4]If it seems advisable that I should go also, they will accompany me.

Cf. Phil 1　[27]Only let your manner of life be worthy of the gospel of Christ, so that whether I come and see you or am absent, I may hear of you that you stand firm in one spirit, with one mind striving side by side for the faith of the gospel, . . .

● **1 Cor 16:5**
Acts 19　[21]Now after these events Paul resolved in the Spirit to pass through Macedonia and Achaia and go to Jerusalem, saying, "After I have been there, I must also see Rome."

● **1 Cor 16:7**
Acts 18　[21]but on taking leave of them he said, "I will return to you if God wills," and he set sail from Ephesus.

● **1 Cor 16:8**
Acts 18　[19]And they came to Ephesus, and he left them there; but he himself went into the synagogue and argued with the Jews.

● **1 Cor 16:9**
Acts 14　[27]And when they arrived, they gathered the church together and declared all that God had done with them, and how he had opened a door of faith to the Gentiles.

Acts 19　[9]but when some were stubborn and disbelieved, speaking evil of the Way before the congregation, he withdrew from them, taking the disciples with him, and argued daily in the hall of Tyrannus.

Cf. 2 Cor 2　[12]When I came to Troas to preach the gospel of Christ, a door was opened for me in the Lord; . . .

Cf. Col 4　[3]and pray for us also, that God may open to us a door for the word, to declare the mystery of Christ, on account of which I am in prison, . . .

FORMAL ELEMENT: COMMENDATION

[10]**When Timothy comes, see that you put him at ease among you, for he is doing the work of the Lord, as I am.** [11]**So let no one despise him. Speed him on his way in peace, that he may return to me; for I am expecting him with the brethren.**

[12]**As for our brother Apollos, I strongly urged him to visit you with the other brethren, but it was not at all his will to come now. He will come when he has opportunity.**

PRIMARY

Rom 16:1–2 (§65)

[1]I commend to you our sister Phoebe, a deaconess of the church at Cenchreae, [2]that you may receive her in the Lord as befits the saints, and help her in whatever she may require from you, for she has been a helper of many and of myself as well.

1 Cor 16:15–18 (§142)

[15]Now, brethren, you know that the household of Stephanas were the first converts in Achaia, and they have devoted themselves to the service of the saints; [16]I urge you to be subject to such men and to every fellow worker and laborer. [17]I rejoice at the coming of Stephanas and Fortunatus and Achaicus, because they have made up for your absence; [18]for they refreshed my spirit as well as yours. Give recognition to such men.

2 Cor 3:1–3 (§154)

[1]Are we beginning to commend ourselves again? Or do we need, as some do, letters of recommendation to you, or from you? [2]You yourselves are our letter of recommendation, written on your hearts, to be known and read by all men; [3]and you show that you are a letter from Christ delivered by us, written not with ink but with the Spirit of the living God, not on tablets of stone but on tablets of human hearts.

2 Cor 8:16–24 (§173)

[16]But thanks be to God who puts the same earnest care for you into the heart of Titus. [17]For he not only accepted our appeal, but being himself very earnest he is going to you of his own accord. [18]With him we are sending the brother who is famous among all the churches for his preaching of the gospel; [19]and not only that, but he has been appointed by the churches to travel with us in this gracious work which we are carrying on, for the glory of the Lord and to show our good will. [20]We intend that no one should blame us about this liberal gift which we are administering, [21]for we aim at what is honorable not only in the Lord's sight but also in the sight of men. [22]And with them we are sending our brother whom we have often tested and found earnest in many matters, but who is now more earnest than ever because of his great confidence in you. [23]As for Titus, he is my partner and fellow worker in your service; and as for our brethren, they are messengers of the churches, the glory of Christ. [24]So give proof, before the churches, of your love and of our boasting about you to these men.

Eph 6:21–22 (§235)

[21]Now that you also may know how I am and what I am doing, Tychicus the beloved brother and faithful minister in the Lord will tell you everything. [22]I have sent him to you for this very purpose, that you may know how we are, and that he may encourage your hearts.

● **1 Cor 16:10**

1 Cor 4   [17]Therefore I sent to you Timothy, my beloved and faithful child in the Lord, to remind you of my ways in Christ, as I teach them everywhere in every church.

Acts 16   [1]And he came also to Derbe and to Lystra. A disciple was there, named Timothy, the son of a Jewish woman who was a believer; but his father was a Greek.

Cf. 1 Cor 16   [15]Now, brethren, you know that the household of Stephanas were the first converts in Achaia, and they have devoted themselves to the service of he saints; [16]I urge you to be subject to such men and to every fellow worker and laborer. [17]I rejoice at the coming of Stephanas and Fortunatus and Achaicus, because they have made up for your absence; [18]for they refreshed my spirit as well as yours. Give recognition to such men. Jesus.

Cf. 2 Cor 1   [19]For the Son of God, Jesus Christ, whom we preached among you, Silvanus and Timothy and I, was not Yes and No; but in him it is always Yes.

Cf. 1 Thess 3   [2]and we sent Timothy, our brother and God's servant in the gospel of Christ, to establish you in your faith and to exhort you, . . .

Phil 2:19–24 (§245)

[19]I hope in the Lord Jesus to send Timothy to you soon, so that I may be cheered by news of you. [20]I have no one like him, who will be genuinely anxious for your welfare. [21]They all look after their own interests, not those of Jesus Christ. [22]But Timothy's worth you know, how as a son with a father he has served with me in the gospel. [23]I hope therefore to send him just as soon as I see how it will go with me; [24]and I trust in the Lord that shortly I myself shall come also.

Phil 2:25–3:1 (§246)

[25]I have thought it necessary to send to you Epaphroditus my brother and fellow worker and fellow soldier, and your messenger and minister to my need, [26]for he has been longing for you all, and has been distressed because you heard that he was ill. [27]Indeed he was ill, near to death. But God had mercy on him, and not only on him but on me also, lest I should have sorrow upon sorrow. [28]I am the more eager to send him, therefore, that you may rejoice at seeing him again, and that I may be less anxious. [29]So receive him in the Lord with all joy; and honor such men, [30]for he nearly died for the work of Christ, risking his life to complete your service to me.

[3] [1]Finally, my brethren, rejoice in the Lord. To write the same things to you is not irksome to me, and is safe for you.

Col 4:7–9 (§271)

[7]Tychicus will tell you all about my affairs; he is a beloved brother and faithful minister and fellow servant in the Lord. [8]I have sent him to you for this very purpose, that you may know how we are and that he may encourage your hearts, [9]and with him Onesimus, the faithful and beloved brother, who is one of yourselves. They will tell you of everything that has taken place here.

Phlm 8–20 (§307–308)

[8]Accordingly, though I am bold enough in Christ to command you to do what is required, [9]yet for love's sake I prefer to appeal to you—I, Paul, an ambassador and now a prisoner also for Christ Jesus— [10]I appeal to you for my child, Onesimus, whose father I have become in my imprisonment. [11](Formerly he was useless to you, but now he is indeed useful to you and to me.) [12]I am sending him back to you, sending my very heart. [13]I would have been glad to keep him with me, in order that he might serve me on your behalf during my imprisonment for the gospel; [14]but I preferred to do nothing without your consent in order that your goodness might not be by compulsion but of your own free will.

[15]Perhaps this is why he was parted from you for a while, that you might have him back for ever, [16]no longer as a slave but more than a slave, as a beloved brother, especially to me but how much more to you, both in the flesh and in the Lord. [17]So if you consider me your partner, receive him as you would receive me. [18]If he has wronged you at all, or owes you anything, charge that to my account. [19]I, Paul, write this with my own hand, I will repay it—to say nothing of your owing me even your own self. [20]Yes, brother, I want some benefit from you in the Lord. Refresh my heart in Christ.

Cf. 1 Thess 3   [6]But now that Timothy has come to us from you, and has brought us the good news of your faith and love and reported that you always remember us kindly and long to see us, as we long to see you . . .

● **1 Cor 16:12**
1 Cor 3   [4]For when one says, "I belong to Paul," and another, "I belong to Apollos," are you not merely men?
[5]What then is Apollos? What is Paul? Servants through whom you believed, as the Lord assigned to each. [6]I planted, Apollos watered, but God gave the growth.

1 Cor 4   [6]I have applied all this to myself and Apollos for your benefit, brethren, that you may learn by us not to go beyond what is written, that none of you may be puffed up in favor of one against another.

Acts 18   [24]Now a Jew named Apollos, a native of Alexandria, came to Ephesus. He was an eloquent man, well versed in the scriptures.

Cf. 1 Cor 1   [12]What I mean is that each one of you says, "I belong to Paul," or "I belong to Apollos," or "I belong to Cephas," or "I belong to Christ."

Cf. 1 Cor 3   [22]whether Paul or Apollos or Cephas or the world or life or death or the present or the future, all are yours; [23]and you are Christ's; and Christ is God's.

Formal Element: "Watch!" "Stand!"

13Be watchful, stand firm in your faith, be courageous, be strong. 14Let all that you do be done in love.

Primary

Rom 13:11–14 (§56)

11Besides this you know what hour it is, how it is full time now for you to wake from sleep. For salvation is nearer to us now than when we first believed; 12the night is far gone, the day is at hand. Let us then cast off the works of darkness and put on the armor of light; 13let us conduct ourselves becomingly as in the day, not in reveling and drunkenness, not in debauchery and licentiousness, not in quarreling and jealousy. 14But put on the Lord Jesus Christ, and make no provision for the flesh, to gratify its desires.

Eph 6:10–17 (§233)

10Finally, be strong in the Lord and in the strength of his might. 11Put on the whole armor of God, that you may be able to stand against the wiles of the devil. 12For we are not contending against flesh and blood, but against the principalities, against the powers, against the world rulers of this present darkness, against the spiritual hosts of wickedness in the heavenly places. 13Therefore take the whole armor of God, that you may be able to withstand in the evil day, and having done all, to stand. 14Stand therefore, having girded your loins with truth, and having put on the breastplate of righteousness, 15and having shod your feet with the equipment of the gospel of peace; 16besides all these, taking the shield of faith, with which you can quench all the flaming darts of the evil one. 17And take the helmet of salvation, and the sword of the Spirit, which is the word of God.

Col 4:2–4 (§269)

2Continue steadfastly in prayer, being watchful in it with thanksgiving; 3and pray for us also, that God may open to us a door for the word, to declare the mystery of Christ, on account of which I am in prison, 4that I may make it clear, as I ought to speak.

1 Thess 5:1–11 (§287)

1But as to the times and the seasons, brethren, you have no need to have anything written to you. 2For you yourselves know well that the day of the Lord will come like a thief in the night. 3When people say, "There is peace and security," then sudden destruction will come upon them as travail comes upon a woman with child, and there will be no escape. 4But you are not in darkness, brethren, for that day to surprise you like a thief. 5For you are all sons of light and sons of the day; we are not of the night or of darkness. 6So then let us not sleep, as others do, but let us keep awake and be sober. 7For those who sleep sleep at night, and those who get drunk are drunk at night. 8But, since we belong to the day, let us be sober, and put on the breastplate of faith and love, and for a helmet the hope of salvation. 9For God has not destined us for wrath, but to obtain salvation through our Lord Jesus Christ, 10who died for us so that whether we wake or sleep we might live with him. 11Therefore encourage one another and build one another up, just as you are doing.

2 Thess 2:13–17 (§297–298)

13But we are bound to give thanks to God always for you, brethren beloved by the Lord, because God chose you from the beginning to be saved, through sanctification by the Spirit and belief in the truth. 14To this he called you through our gospel, so that you may obtain the glory of our Lord Jesus Christ. 15So then, brethren, stand firm and hold to the traditions which you were taught by us, either by word of mouth or by letter.

16Now may our Lord Jesus Christ himself, and God our Father, who loved us and gave us eternal comfort and good hope through grace, 17comfort your hearts and establish them in every good work and word.

Secondary

Rom 13:8–10 (§55)

8Owe no one anything, except to love one another; for he who loves his neighbor has fulfilled the law. 9The commandments, "You shall not commit adultery, You shall not kill, You shall not steal, You shall not covet," and any other commandment, are summed up in this sentence, "You shall love your neighbor as yourself." 10Love does no wrong to a neighbor; therefore love is the fulfilling of the law.

● **1 Cor 16:13**

1 Cor 15　58Therefore, my beloved brethren, be steadfast, immovable, always abounding in the work of the Lord, knowing that in the Lord your labor is not in vain.

Gal 5　1For freedom Christ has set us free; stand fast therefore, and do not submit again to a yoke of slavery.

Phil 1　27Only let your manner of life be worthy of the gospel of Christ, so that whether I come and see you or am absent, I may hear of you that you stand firm in one spirit, with one mind striving side by side for the faith of the gospel, . . .

Col 1　23provided that you continue in the faith, stable and steadfast, not shifting from the hope of the gospel which you heard, which has been preached to every creature under heaven, and of which I, Paul, became a minister.

1 Thess 3　6But now that Timothy has come to us from you, and has brought us the good news of your faith and love and reported that you always remember us kindly and long to see us, as we long to see you—7for this reason, brethren, in all our distress and affliction we have been comforted about you through your faith; 8for now we live, if you stand fast in the Lord. 9For what thanksgiving can we render to God for you, for all the joy which we feel for your sake before our God, 10praying earnestly night and day that we may see you face to face and supply what is lacking in your faith?

FORMAL ELEMENT: COMMENDATION

15Now, brethren, you know that the household of Stephanas were the first converts in Achaia, and they have devoted themselves to the service of the saints; 16 I urge you to be subject to such men and to every fellow worker and laborer. 17I rejoice at the coming of Stephanas and Fortunatus and Achaicus, because they have made up for your absence; 18for they refreshed my spirit as well as yours. Give recognition to such men.

PRIMARY

Rom 16:1–2 (§65)

1I commend to you our sister Phoebe, a deaconess of the church at Cenchreae, 2that you may receive her in the Lord as befits the saints, and help her in whatever she may require from you, for she has been a helper of many and of myself as well.

2 Cor 3:1–3 (§154)

1Are we beginning to commend ourselves again? Or do we need, as some do, letters of recommendation to you, or from you? 2You yourselves are our letter of recommendation, written on your hearts, to be known and read by all men; 3and you show that you are a letter from Christ delivered by us, written not with ink but with the Spirit of the living God, not on tablets of stone but on tablets of human hearts.

2 Cor 8:16–24 (§173)

16But thanks be to God who puts the same earnest care for you into the heart of Titus. 17For he not only accepted our appeal, but being himself very earnest he is going to you of his own accord. 18With him we are sending the brother who is famous among all the churches for his preaching of the gospel; 19and not only that, but he has been appointed by the churches to travel with us in this gracious work which we are carrying on, for the glory of the Lord and to show our good will. 20We intend that no one should blame us about this liberal gift which we are administering, 21for we aim at what is honorable not only in the Lord's sight but also in the sight of men. 22And with them we are sending our brother whom we have often tested and found earnest in many matters, but who is now more earnest than ever because of his great confidence in you. 23As for Titus, he is my partner and fellow worker in your service; and as for our brethren, they are messengers of the churches, the glory of Christ. 24So give proof, before the churches, of your love and of our boasting about you to these men.

Eph 6:21–22 (§235)

21Now that you also may know how I am and what I am doing, Tychicus the beloved brother and faithful minister in the Lord will tell you everything. 22I have sent him to you for this very purpose, that you may know how we are, and that he may encourage your hearts.

Phil 2:19–24 (§245)

19I hope in the Lord Jesus to send Timothy to you soon, so that I may be cheered by news of you. 20I have no one like him, who will be genuinely anxious for your welfare. 21They all look after their own interests, not those of Jesus Christ. 22But Timothy's worth you know, how as a son with a father he has served with me in the gospel. 23I hope therefore to send him just as soon as I see how it will go with me; 24and I trust in the Lord that shortly I myself shall come also.

Phil 2:25–3:1 (§246)

25I have thought it necessary to send to you Epaphroditus my brother and fellow worker and fellow soldier, and your messenger and minister to my need, 26for he has been longing for you all, and has been distressed because you heard that he was ill. 27Indeed he was ill, near to death. But God had mercy on him, and not only on him but on me also, lest I should have sorrow upon sorrow. 28I am the more eager to send him, therefore, that you may rejoice at seeing him again, and that I may be less anxious. 29So receive him in the Lord with all joy; and honor such men, 30for he nearly died for the work of Christ, risking his life to complete your service to me.

3 1Finally, my brethren, rejoice in the Lord. To write the same things to you is not irksome to me, and is safe for you.

Col 4:7–9 (§271)

7Tychicus will tell you all about my affairs; he is a beloved brother and faithful minister and fellow servant in the Lord. 8I have sent him to you for this very purpose, that you may know how we are and that he may encourage your hearts, 9and with him Onesimus, the faithful and beloved brother, who is one of yourselves. They will tell you of everything that has taken place here.

1 Thess 5:12–22 (§288)

12But we beseech you, brethren, to respect those who labor among you and are over you in the Lord and admonish you, 13and to esteem them very highly in love because of their work. Be at peace among yourselves. 14And we exhort you, brethren, admonish the idle, encourage the fainthearted, help the weak, be patient with them all. 15See that none of you repays evil for evil, but always seek to do good to one another and to all. 16Rejoice always, 17pray constantly, 18give thanks in all circumstances; for this is the will of God in Christ Jesus for you. 19Do not quench the Spirit, 20do not despise prophesying, 21but test everything; hold fast what is good, 22abstain from every form of evil.

Phlm 8–20 (§307–308)

8Accordingly, though I am bold enough in Christ to command you to do what is required, 9yet for love's sake I prefer to appeal to you—I, Paul, an ambassador and now a prisoner also for Christ Jesus— 10I appeal to you for my child, Onesimus, whose father I have become in my imprisonment. 11(Formerly he was useless to you, but now he is indeed useful to you and to me.) 12I am sending him back to you, sending my very heart. 13I would have been glad to keep him with me, in order that he might serve me on your behalf during my imprisonment for the gospel; 14but I preferred to do nothing without your consent in order that your goodness might not be by compulsion but of your own free will. 15Perhaps this is why he was parted from you for a while, that you might have him back for ever, 16no longer as a slave but more than a slave, as a beloved brother, especially to me but how much more to you, both in the flesh and in the Lord. 17So if you consider me your partner, receive him as you would receive me. 18If he has wronged you at all, or owes you anything, charge that to my account. 19I, Paul, write this with my own hand, I will repay it—to say nothing of your owing me even your own self. 20Yes, brother, I want some benefit from you in the Lord. Refresh my heart in Christ.

● 1 Cor 16:15–18

1 Cor 16　　10When Timothy comes, see that you put him at ease among you, for he is doing the work of the Lord, as I am. 11So let no one despise him. Speed him on his way in peace, that he may return to me; for I am expecting him with the brethren.

12As for our brother Apollos, I strongly urged him to visit you with the other brethren, but it was not at all his will to come now. He will come when he has opportunity.

● 1 Cor 16:17

1 Thess 2　　17But since we were bereft of you, brethren, for a short time, in person not in heart, we endeavored the more eagerly and with great desire to see you face to face; 18because we wanted to come to you—I, Paul, again and again—but Satan hindered us. 19For what is our hope or joy or crown of boasting before our Lord Jesus at his coming? Is it not you? 20For you are our glory and joy.

3 1Therefore when we could bear it no longer, we were willing to be left behind at Athens alone, 2and we sent Timothy, our brother and God's servant in the gospel of Christ, to establish you in your faith and to exhort you, . . .

● 1 Cor 16:18

Phlm　　7For I have derived much joy and comfort from your love, my brother, because the hearts of the saints have been refreshed through you.

LETTER STRUCTURE: GREETINGS

[19]The churches of Asia send greetings. Aquila and Prisca, together with the church in their house, send you hearty greetings in the Lord. [20]All the brethren send greetings. Greet one another with a holy kiss.

PRIMARY

Rom 16:3–16 (§66)

[3]Greet Prisca and Aquila, my fellow workers in Christ Jesus, [4]who risked their necks for my life, to whom not only I but also all the churches of the Gentiles give thanks; [5]greet also the church in their house. Greet my beloved Epaenetus, who was the first convert in Asia for Christ. [6]Greet Mary, who has worked hard among you. [7]Greet Andronicus and Junias, my kinsmen and my fellow prisoners; they are men of note among the apostles, and they were in Christ before me. [8]Greet Ampliatus, my beloved in the Lord. [9]Greet Urbanus, our fellow worker in Christ, and my beloved Stachys. [10]Greet Apelles, who is approved in Christ. Greet those who belong to the family of Aristobulus. [11]Greet my kinsman Herodion. Greet those in the Lord who belong to the family of Narcissus. [12]Greet those workers in the Lord, Tryphaena and Tryphosa. Greet the beloved Persis, who has worked hard in the Lord. [13]Greet Rufus, eminent in the Lord, also his mother and mine. [14]Greet Asyncritus, Phlegon, Hermes, Patrobas, Hermas, and the brethren who are with them. [15]Greet Philologus, Julia, Nereus and his sister, and Olympas, and all the saints who are with them. [16]Greet one another with a holy kiss. All the churches of Christ greet you.

Rom 16:21–23 (§69)

[21]Timothy, my fellow worker, greets you; so do Lucius and Jason and Sosipater, my kinsmen.

[22]I Tertius, the writer of this letter, greet you in the Lord.

[23]Gaius, who is host to me and to the whole church, greets you. Erastus, the city treasurer, and our brother Quartus, greet you.

2 Cor 13:11–13 (§191)

[11]Finally, brethren, farewell. Mend your ways, heed my appeal, agree with one another, live in peace, and the God of love and peace will be with you. [12]Greet one another with a holy kiss. [13]All the saints greet you.

Phil 4:21–22 (§254)

[21]Greet every saint in Christ Jesus. The brethren who are with me greet you. [22]All the saints greet you, especially those of Caesar's household.

Col 4:10–15 (§272)

[10]Aristarchus my fellow prisoner greets you, and Mark the cousin of Barnabas (concerning whom you have received instructions—if he comes to you, receive him), [11]and Jesus who is called Justus. These are the only men of the circumcision among my fellow workers for the kingdom of God, and they have been a comfort to me. [12]Epaphras, who is one of yourselves, a servant of Christ Jesus, greets you, always remembering you earnestly in his prayers, that you may stand mature and fully assured in all the will of God. [13]For I bear him witness that he has worked hard for you and for those in Laodicea and in Hierapolis. [14]Luke the beloved physician and Demas greet you. [15]Give my greetings to the brethren at Laodicea, and to Nympha and the church in her house.

1 Thess 5:26 (§291)

[26]Greet all the brethren with a holy kiss.

Phlm 23–24 (§310)

[23]Epaphras, my fellow prisoner in Christ Jesus, sends greetings to you, [24]and so do Mark, Aristarchus, Demas, and Luke, my fellow workers.

● **1 Cor 16:19–20**

2 Tim 4   [19]Greet Prisca and Aquila, and the household of Onesiphorus. [20]Erastus remained at Corinth; Trophimus I left ill at Miletus. [21]Do your best to come before winter. Eubulus sends greetings to you, as do Pudens and Linus and Claudia and all the brethren.

Titus 3   [15]All who are with me send greetings to you. Greet those who love us in the faith.

● **1 Cor 16:19**

Acts 18   [2]"And he found a Jew named Aquila, a native of Pontus, lately come from Italy with his wife Priscilla, because Claudius had commanded all the Jews to leave Rome. And he went to see them. . . ."

Formal Element: Signature Device

²¹I, Paul, write this greeting with my own hand. ²²If any one has no love for the Lord, let him be accursed. Our Lord, come!

Primary

Gal 6:11–17 (§216)

¹¹See with what large letters I am writing to you with my own hand. ¹²It is those who want to make a good showing in the flesh that would compel you to be circumcised, and only in order that they may not be persecuted for the cross of Christ. ¹³For even those who receive circumcision do not themselves keep the law, but they desire to have you circumcised that they may glory in your flesh. ¹⁴But far be it from me to glory except in the cross of our Lord Jesus Christ, by which the world has been crucified to me, and I to the world. ¹⁵For neither circumcision counts for anything, nor uncircumcision, but a new creation. ¹⁶Peace and mercy be upon all who walk by this rule, upon the Israel of God.

¹⁷Henceforth let no man trouble me; for I bear on my body the marks of Jesus.

Col 4:16–18a (§273)

¹⁶And when this letter has been read among you, have it read also in the church of the Laodiceans; and see that you read also the letter from Laodicea. ¹⁷And say to Archippus, "See that you fulfil the ministry which you have received in the Lord."

¹⁸I, Paul, write this greeting with my own hand. Remember my fetters.

2 Thess 3:17 (§303)

¹⁷I, Paul, write this greeting with my own hand. This is the mark in every letter of mine; it is the way I write.

● **1 Cor 16:22**

1 Cor 12 ¹Now concerning spiritual gifts, brethren, I do not want you to be uninformed. ²You know that when you were heathen, you were led astray to dumb idols, however you may have been moved. ³Therefore I want you to understand that no one speaking by the Spirit of God ever says "Jesus be cursed!" and no one can say "Jesus is Lord" except by the Holy Spirit.

Gal 1 ⁸But even if we, or an angel from heaven, should preach to you a gospel contrary to that which we preached to you, let him be accursed. ⁹As we have said before, so now I say again, If any one is preaching to you a gospel contrary to that which you received, let him be accursed.

LETTER STRUCTURE: CLOSING GRACE

[23] The grace of the Lord Jesus be with you. [24] My love be with you all in Christ Jesus. Amen.

PRIMARY

Rom 16:20b (§68)

The grace of our Lord Jesus Christ be with you.

2 Cor 13:14 (§192)

[14] The grace of the Lord Jesus Christ and the love of God and the fellowship of the Holy Spirit be with you all.

Gal 6:18 (§217)

[18] The grace of our Lord Jesus Christ be with your spirit, brethren. Amen.

Eph 6:23–24 (§236)

[23] Peace be to the brethren, and love with faith, from God the Father and the Lord Jesus Christ. [24] Grace be with all who love our Lord Jesus Christ with love undying.

Phil 4:23 (§255)

[23] The grace of the Lord Jesus Christ be with your spirit.

Col 4:18b (§274)

Grace be with you.

1 Thess 5:28 (§293)

[28] The grace of our Lord Jesus Christ be with you.

2 Thess 3:18 (§304)

[18] The grace of our Lord Jesus Christ be with you all.

Phlm 25 (§311)

[25] The grace of the Lord Jesus Christ be with your spirit.

● **1 Cor 16:23**

1 Tim 6   [21] . . . Grace be with you.

2 Tim 4   [22] The Lord be with your spirit. Grace be with you.

Titus 3   [15] Grace be with you all.

Letter Structure: Salutation

1 Paul, an apostle of Christ Jesus by the will of God, and Timothy our brother.
To the church of God which is at Corinth, with all the saints who are in the whole of Achaia:
2 Grace to you and peace from God our Father and the Lord Jesus Christ.

Primary

Rom 1:1–7 (§1)
[1] Paul, a servant of Jesus Christ, called to be an apostle, set apart for the gospel of God [2] which he promised beforehand through his prophets in the holy scriptures, [3] the gospel concerning his Son, who was descended from David according to the flesh [4] and designated Son of God in power according to the Spirit of holiness by his resurrection from the dead, Jesus Christ our Lord, [5] through whom we have received grace and apostleship to bring about the obedience of faith for the sake of his name among all the nations, [6] including yourselves who are called to belong to Jesus Christ; [7] To all God's beloved in Rome, who are called to be saints:
Grace to you and peace from God our Father and the Lord Jesus Christ.

1 Cor 1:1–3 (§71)
[1] Paul, called by the will of God to be an apostle of Christ Jesus, and our brother Sosthenes,

[2] To the church of God which is at Corinth, to those sanctified in Christ Jesus, called to be saints together with all those who in every place call on the name of our Lord Jesus Christ, both their Lord and ours: [3] Grace to you and peace from God our Father and the Lord Jesus Christ.

Gal 1:1–5 (§193)
[1] Paul an apostle—not from men nor through man, but through Jesus Christ and God the Father, who raised him from the dead — [2] and all the brethren who are with me,
To the churches of Galatia:
[3] Grace to you and peace from God the Father and our Lord Jesus Christ, [4] who gave himself for our sins to deliver us from the present evil age, according to the will of our God and Father; [5] to whom be the glory for ever and ever. Amen.

Eph 1:1–2 (§218)
[1] Paul, an apostle of Christ Jesus by the will of God,
To the saints who are also faithful in Christ Jesus:
[2] Grace to you and peace from God our Father and the Lord Jesus Christ.

Phil 1:1–2 (§237)
[1] Paul and Timothy, servants of Christ Jesus,
To all the saints in Christ Jesus who are at Philippi, with the bishops and deacons:
[2] Grace to you and peace from God our Father and the Lord Jesus Christ.

Col 1:1–2 (§256)
[1] Paul, an apostle of Christ Jesus by the will of God, and Timothy our brother,
[2] To the saints and faithful brethren in Christ at Colossae:
Grace to you and peace from God our Father.

1 Thess 1:1 (§275)
[1] Paul, Silvanus, and Timothy,
To the church of the Thessalonians in God the Father and the Lord Jesus Christ:
Grace to you and peace.

2 Thess 1:1–2 (§294)
[1] Paul, Silvanus, and Timothy,
To the church of the Thessalonians in God our Father and the Lord Jesus Christ:
[2] Grace to you and peace from God the Father and the Lord Jesus Christ.

Phlm 1–3 (§305)
[1] Paul, a prisoner for Christ Jesus, and Timothy our brother,
To Philemon our beloved fellow worker [2] and Apphia our sister and Archippus our fellow soldier, and the church in your house:
[3] Grace to you and peace from God our Father and the Lord Jesus Christ.

● **2 Cor 1:1**
Acts 16   [1] And he came also to Derbe and to Lystra. A disciple was there, named Timothy, the son of a Jewish woman who was a believer; but his father was a Greek.

Acts 18   [1] After this he left Athens and went to Corinth.

1 Tim 1   [1] Paul, an apostle of Christ Jesus by command of God our Savior and of Christ Jesus our hope,

[2] To Timothy, my true child in the faith:
Grace, mercy, and peace from God the Father and Christ Jesus our Lord.

2 Tim 1   [1] Paul, an apostle of Christ Jesus by the will of God according to the promise of the life which is in Christ Jesus,
[2] To Timothy, my beloved child:
Grace, mercy, and peace from God the Father and Christ Jesus our Lord.

Titus 1   [1] Paul, a servant of God and an apostle of Jesus Christ, to further the faith of God's elect and their knowledge of the truth which accords with godliness, [2] in hope of eternal life which God, who never lies, promised ages ago [3] and at the proper time manifested in his word through the preaching with which I have been entrusted by command of God our Savior;
[4] To Titus, my true child in a common faith:
Grace and peace from God the Father and Christ Jesus our Savior.

LETTER STRUCTURE: BLESSING

[3]Blessed be the God and Father of our Lord Jesus Christ, the Father of mercies and God of all comfort, [4]who comforts us in all our affliction, so that we may be able to comfort those who are in any affliction, with the comfort with which we ourselves are comforted by God. [5]For as we share abundantly in Christ's sufferings, so through Christ we share abundantly in comfort too. [6]If we are afflicted, it is for your comfort and salvation; and if we are comforted, it is for your comfort, which you experience when you patiently endure the same sufferings that we suffer. [7]Our hope for you is unshaken; for we know that as you share in our sufferings, you will also share in our comfort.

[8]For we do not want you to be ignorant, brethren, of the affliction we experienced in Asia; for we were so utterly, unbearably crushed that we despaired of life itself. [9]Why, we felt that we had received the sentence of death; but that was to make us rely not on ourselves but on God who raises the dead; [10]he delivered us from so deadly a peril, and he will deliver us; on him we have set our hope that he will deliver us again. [11]You also must help us by prayer, so that many will give thanks on our behalf for the blessing granted us in answer to many prayers.

PRIMARY

Eph 1:3–23 (§219)

[3]Blessed be the God and Father of our Lord Jesus Christ, who has blessed us in Christ with every spiritual blessing in the heavenly places, [4]even as he chose us in him before the foundation of the world, that we should be holy and blameless before him. [5]He destined us in love to be his sons through Jesus Christ, according to the purpose of his will, [6]to the praise of his glorious grace which he freely bestowed on us in the Beloved. [7]In him we have redemption through his blood, the forgiveness of our trespasses, according to the riches of his grace [8]which he lavished upon us. [9]For he has made known to us in all wisdom and insight the mystery of his will, according to his purpose which he set forth in Christ [10]as a plan for the fulness of time, to unite all things in him, things in heaven and things on earth.

[11]In him, according to the purpose of him who accomplishes all things according to the counsel of his will, [12]we who first hoped in Christ have been destined and appointed to live for the praise of his glory. [13]In him you also, who have heard the word of truth, the gospel of your salvation, and have believed in him, were sealed with the promised Holy Spirit, [14]which is the guarantee of our inheritance until we acquire possession of it, to the praise of his glory.

[15]For this reason, because I have heard of your faith in the Lord Jesus and your love toward all the saints, [16]I do not cease to give thanks for you, remembering you in my prayers, [17]that the God of our Lord Jesus Christ, the Father of glory, may give you a spirit of wisdom and of revelation in the knowledge of him, [18]having the eyes of your hearts enlightened, that you may know what is the hope to which he has called you, what are the riches of his glorious inheritance in the saints, [19]and what is the immeasurable greatness of his power in us who believe, according to the working of his great might [20]which he accomplished in Christ when he raised him from the dead and made him sit at his right hand in the heavenly places, [21]far above all rule and authority and power and dominion, and above every name that is named, not only in this age but also in that which is to come; [22]and he has put all things under his feet and has made him the head over all things for the church, [23]which is his body, the fulness of him who fills all in all.

SECONDARY

Rom 5:1–5 (§20)

[1]Therefore, since we are justified by faith, we have peace with God through our Lord Jesus Christ. [2]Through him we have obtained access to this grace in which we stand, and we rejoice in our hope of sharing the glory of God. [3]More than that, we rejoice in our sufferings, knowing that suffering produces endurance, [4]and endurance produces character, and character produces hope, [5]and hope does not dis-

---

● **2 Cor 1:3–11**

2 Cor 4   [7]But we have this treasure in earthen vessels, to show that the transcendent power belongs to God and not to us. [8]We are afflicted in every way, but not crushed; perplexed, but not driven to despair; [9]persecuted, but not forsaken; struck down, but not destroyed; [10]always carrying in the body the death of Jesus, so that the life of Jesus may also be manifested in our bodies. [11]For while we live we are always being given up to death for Jesus' sake, so that the life of Jesus may be manifested in our mortal flesh. [12]So death is at work in us, but life in you.

2 Cor 6   [1]Working together with him, then, we entreat you not to accept the grace of God in vain. [2]For he says,

"At the acceptable time I have listened to you,
  and helped you on the day of salvation."

Behold, now is the acceptable time; behold, now is the day of salvation. [3]We put no obstacle in any one's way, so that no fault may be found with our ministry, [4]but as servants of God we commend ourselves in every way: through great endurance, in afflictions, hardships, calamities, [5]beatings, imprisonments, tumults, labors, watching, hunger; [6]by purity, knowledge, forbearance, kindness, the Holy Spirit, genuine love, [7]truthful speech, and the power of God; with the weapons of righteousness for the right hand and for the left; [8]in honor and dishonor, in ill repute and good repute. We are treated as impostors, and yet are true; [9]as unknown, and yet well known; as dying, and behold we live; as punished, and yet not killed; [10]as sorrowful, yet always rejoicing; as poor, yet making many rich; as having nothing, and yet possessing everything.

● **2 Cor 1:3–7**

Rom 15   [1]We who are strong ought to bear with the failings of the weak, and not to please ourselves; [2]let each of us please his neighbor for his good, to edify him. [3]For Christ did not please himself; but, as it is written, "The reproaches of those who reproached thee fell on me." [4]For whatever was written in former days was written for our instruction, that by steadfastness and by the encouragement of the scriptures we might have hope. [5]May the God of steadfastness and encouragement grant you to live in such harmony with one another, in accord with Christ Jesus, [6]that together you may with one voice glorify the God and Father of our Lord Jesus Christ.

[7]Welcome one another, therefore, as Christ has welcomed you, for the glory of God. [8]For I tell you that Christ became a servant to the circumcised to show God's truthfulness, in order to confirm the promises given to the patriarchs, [9]and in order that the Gentiles might glorify God for his mercy. As it is written,

"Therefore I will praise thee among the Gentiles,
  and sing to thy name";

[10]and again it is said,

"Rejoice, O Gentiles, with his peoples";

[11]and again,

"Praise the Lord, all Gentiles,
  and let all the peoples praise him";

[12]and further Isaiah says,

"The root of Jesse shall come,
  he who rises to rule the Gentiles;
  in him shall the Gentiles hope."

[13]May the God of hope fill you with all joy and peace in believing, so that by the power of the Holy Spirit you may abound in hope.

[14]I myself am satisfied about you, my brethren, that you yourselves are full of goodness, filled with all knowledge, and able to instruct one another. [15]But on some points I have written to you very boldly by way of reminder, because of the grace given me by God [16]to be a minister of Christ Jesus to the Gentiles in the priestly service of the gospel of God, so that the offering of the Gentiles may be acceptable, sanctified by the Holy Spirit.

1 Cor 4   [13]when slandered, we try to conciliate; we have become, and are now, as the refuse of the world, the off-scouring of all things.

Cf. 2 Cor 7   [6]But God, who comforts the downcast, comforted us by the coming of Titus, . . .

Cf. 2 Cor 7   [13]Therefore we are comforted.

Cf. Eph 6   [22]Wives, be subject to your husbands, as to the Lord.

Cf. 1 Thess 4   [18]Therefore comfort one another with these words.

appoint us, because God's love has been poured into our hearts through the Holy Spirit which has been given to us.

1 Thess 3:1–10 (§281–282)

[1]Therefore when we could bear it no longer, we were willing to be left behind at Athens alone, [2]and we sent Timothy, our brother and God's servant in the gospel of Christ, to establish you in your faith and to exhort you, [3]that no one be moved by these afflictions. You yourselves know that this is to be our lot. [4]For when we were with you, we told you beforehand that we were to suffer affliction; just as it has come to pass, and as you know. [5]For this reason, when I could bear it no longer, I sent that I might know your faith, for fear that somehow the tempter had tempted you and that our labor would be in vain.

[6]But now that Timothy has come to us from you, and has brought us the good news of your faith and love and reported that you always remember us kindly and long to see us, as we long to see you— [7]for this reason, brethren, in all our distress and affliction we have been comforted about you through your faith; [8]for now we live, if you stand fast in the Lord. [9]For what thanksgiving can we render to God for you, for all the joy which we feel for your sake before our God, [10]praying earnestly night and day that we may see you face to face and supply what is lacking in your faith?

2 Thess 1:3–12 (§295)

[3]We are bound to give thanks to God always for you, brethren, as is fitting, because your faith is growing abundantly, and the love of every one of you for one another is increasing. [4]Therefore we ourselves boast of you in the churches of God for your steadfastness and faith in all your persecutions and in the afflictions which you are enduring.

[5]This is evidence of the righteous judgment of God, that you may be made worthy of the kingdom of God, for which you are suffering— [6]since indeed God deems it just to repay with affliction those who afflict you, [7]and to grant rest with us to you who are afflicted, when the Lord Jesus is revealed from heaven with his mighty angels in flaming fire, [8] inflicting vengeance upon those who do not know God and upon those who do not obey the gospel of our Lord Jesus. [9]They shall suffer the punishment of eternal destruction and exclusion from the presence of the Lord and from the glory of his might, [10]when he comes on that day to be glorified in his saints, and to be marveled at in all who have believed, because our testimony to you was believed. [11]To this end we always pray for you, that our God may make you worthy of his call, and may fulfil every good resolve and work of faith by his power, [12]so that the name of our Lord Jesus may be glorified in you, and you in him, according to the grace of our God and the Lord Jesus Christ.

2 Thess 2:16–17 (§298)

[16]Now may our Lord Jesus Christ himself, and God our Father, who loved us and gave us eternal comfort and good hope through grace, [17]comfort your hearts and establish them in every good work and word.

- **2 Cor 1:3**

1 Pet 1   [3]Blessed be the God and Father of our Lord Jesus Christ! By his great mercy we have been born anew to a living hope through the resurrection of Jesus Christ from the dead, . . .

- **2 Cor 1:7**

Phil 3   [10]that I may know him and the power of his resurrection, and may share his sufferings, becoming like him in his death, . . .

Col 1   [24]Now I rejoice in my sufferings for your sake, and in my flesh I complete what is lacking in Christ's afflictions for the sake of his body, that is, the church, . . .

Eph 3   [13]So I ask you not to lose heart over what I am suffering for you, which is your glory.

- **2 Cor 1:8**

1 Cor 15   [32]What do I gain if, humanly speaking, I fought with beasts at Ephesus? If the dead are not raised, "Let us eat and drink, for tomorrow we die."

Acts 16   [6]And they went through the region of Phrygia and Galatia, having been forbidden by the Holy Spirit to speak the word in Asia.

Cf. Acts 19   [23]About that time there arose no little stir concerning the Way. [24]For a man named Demetrius, a silversmith, who made silver shrines of Artemis, brought no little busines to the craftsmen. [25]These he gathered together, with the workmen of

like occupation, with the workmen of like occupation, and said, "Men, you know that from this business we have our wealth. [26]And you see and hear that not only at Ephesus but almost throughout all Asia this Paul has persuaded and turned away a considerable company of people, saying that gods made with hands are not gods. [27]And there is danger not only that this trade of ours may come into disrepute but also that the temple of the great goddess Artemis may count for nothing, and that she may even be deposed from her magnificence, she whom all Asia and the world worship."

[28]When they heard this they were enraged, and cried out, "Great is Artemis of the Ephesians!" [29]So the city was filled with the confusion; and they rushed together into the theater, dragging with them Gaius and Aristarchus, Macedonians who were Paul's companions in travel. [30]Paul wished to go in among the crowd, but the disciples would not let him; [31]some of the Asiarchs also, who were friends of his, sent to him and begged him not to venture into the theater. [32]Now some cried one thing, some another; for the assembly was in confusion, and most of them did not know why they had come together. [33]Some of the crowd prompted Alexander, whom the Jews had put forward. And Alexander motioned with his hand, wishing to make a defense to the people. [34]But when they recognized that he was Jew, for about two hours they all with one voice cried out, "Great is Artemis of the Ephesians!" [35]And when the town clerk had quieted the crowd, he said, "Men of Ephesus, what man is there who does not know that the city of the Ephesians is temple keeper of the great Artemis, and of the

sacred stone that fell from the sky? [36]Seeing then that these things cannot be contradicted, you ought to be quiet and do nothing rash. [37]For you have brought these men here who are neither sacrilegious nor blasphemers of our goddess. [38]If therefore Demetrius and the craftsmen with him have a complaint against any one, the courts are open, and there are proconsuls; let them bring charges against one another. [39]But if you seek anything further, it shall be settled in the regular assembly. [40]For we are in danger of being charged with rioting today, there being no cause that we can give to justify this commotion." [41]And when he had said this, he dismissed the assembly.

- **2 Cor 1:9**

Rom 4   [17]as it is written, "I have made you the father of many nations" — in the presence of the God in whom he believed, who gives life to the dead and calls into existence the things that do not exist.

- **2 Cor 1:10**

1 Tim 4   [10]For to this end we toil and strive, because we have our hope set on the living God, who is the Savior of all men, especially of those who believe.

Cf. 2 Tim 4   [18]The Lord will rescue me from every evil and save me for his heavenly kingdom. To him be the glory for ever and ever. Amen.

- **2 Cor 1:11**

Phil 1   [19]Yes, and I shall rejoice. For I know that through your prayers and the help of the Spirit of Jesus Christ this will turn out for my deliverance, . . .

[12] For our boast is this, the testimony of our conscience that we have behaved in the world, and still more toward you, with holiness and godly sincerity, not by earthly wisdom but by the grace of God. [13] For we write you nothing but what you can read and understand; I hope you will understand fully, [14] as you have understood in part, that you can be proud of us as we can be of you, on the day of the Lord Jesus.

PRIMARY

1 Cor 4:1–5 (§83)

[1] This is how one should regard us, as servants of Christ and stewards of the mysteries of God. [2] Moreover it is required of stewards that they be found trustworthy. [3] But with me it is a very small thing that I should be judged by you or by any human court. I do not even judge myself. [4] I am not aware of anything against myself, but I am not thereby acquitted. It is the Lord who judges me. [5] Therefore do not pronounce judgment before the time, before the Lord comes, who will bring to light the things now hidden in darkness and will disclose the purposes of the heart. Then every man will receive his commendation from God.

1 Thess 2:1–8 (§277)

[1] For you yourselves know, brethren, that our visit to you was not in vain; [2] but though we had already suffered and been shamefully treated at Philippi, as you know, we had courage in our God to declare to you the gospel of God in the face of great opposition. [3] For our appeal does not spring from error or uncleanness, nor is it made with guile; [4] but just as we have been approved by God to be entrusted with the gospel, so we speak, not to please men, but to please God who tests our hearts. [5] For we never used either words of flattery, as you know, or a cloak for greed, as God is witness; [6] nor did we seek glory from men, whether from you or from others, though we might have made demands as apostles of Christ. [7] But we were gentle among you, like a nurse taking care of her children. [8] So, being affectionately desirous of you, we were ready to share with you not only the gospel of God but also our own selves, because you had become very dear to us.

1 Thess 2:9–12 (§278)

[9] For you remember our labor and toil, brethren; we worked night and day, that we might not burden any of you, while we preached to you the gospel of God. [10] You are witnesses, and God also, how holy and righteous and blameless was our behavior to you believers; [11] for you know how, like a father with his children, we exhorted each one of you and encouraged you and charged you [12] to lead a life worthy of God, who calls you into his own kingdom and glory.

● **2 Cor 1:12**

Rom 13   [5] Therefore one must be subject, not only to avoid God's wrath but also for the sake of conscience.

Rom 14   [22] The faith that you have, keep between yourself and God; happy is he who has no reason to judge himself for what he approves. [23] But he who has doubts is condemned, if he eats, because he does not act from faith; for whatever does not proceed from faith is sin.

1 Cor 9   [5] Do we not have the right to be accompanied by a wife, as the other apostles and the brothers of the Lord and Cephas?

2 Cor 2   [17] For we are not, like so many, peddlers of God's word; but as men of sincerity, as commissioned by God, in the sight of God we speak in Christ.

2 Cor 10   [13] But we will not boast beyond limit, but will keep to the limits God has apportioned us, to reach even to you. [14] For we are not overextending ourselves, as though we did not reach you; we were the first to come all the way to you with the gospel of Christ. [15] We do not boast beyond limit, in other men's labors; but our hope is that as your faith increases, our field among you may be greatly enlarged, [16] so that we may preach the gospel in lands beyond you, without boasting of work already done in another's field. [17] "Let him who boasts, boast of the Lord." [18] For it is not the man who commends himself that is accepted, but the man whom the Lord commends.

2 Cor 11   [2] I feel a divine jealousy for you, for I betrothed you to Christ to present you as a pure bride to her one husband.

Gal 6   [13] For even those who receive circumcision do not themselves keep the law, but they desire to have you circumcised that they may glory in your flesh. [14] But far be it from me to glory except in the cross of our Lord Jesus Christ, by which the world has been crucified to me, and I to the world.

Acts 23   [1] And Paul, looking intently at the council, said, "Brethren, I have lived before God in all good conscience up to this day."

● **2 Cor 1:13–14**

1 Cor 8   [2] If any one imagines that he knows something, he does not yet know as he ought to know. [3] But if one loves God, one is known by him.

1 Cor 13   [12] For now we see in a mirror dimly, but then face to face. Now I know in part; then I shall understand fully, even as I have been fully understood.

● **2 Cor 1:14**

1 Cor 1   [8] who will sustain you to the end, guiltless in the day of our Lord Jesus Christ.

2 Cor 5   [5] He who has prepared us for this very thing is God, who has given us the Spirit as a guarantee.

Phil 1   [6] And I am sure that he who began a good work in you will bring it to completion at the day of Jesus Christ.

Phil 1   [10] so that you may approve what is excellent, and may be pure and blameless for the day of Christ, . . .

1 Thess 5   [2] For you yourselves know well that the day of the Lord will come like a thief in the night.

2 Thess 2   [2] not to be quickly shaken in mind or excited, either by spirit or by word, or by letter purporting to be from us, to the effect that the day of the Lord has come.

FORMAL ELEMENT: APOSTOLIC VISIT

[15] Because I was sure of this, I wanted to come to you first, so that you might have a double pleasure; [16] I wanted to visit you on my way to Macedonia, and to come back to you from Macedonia and have you send me on my way to Judea. [17] Was I vacillating when I wanted to do this? Do I make my plans like a worldly man, ready to say Yes and No at once? [18] As surely as God is faithful, our word to you has not been Yes and No. [19] For the Son of God, Jesus Christ, whom we preached among you, Silvanus and Timothy and I, was not Yes and No; but in him it is always Yes. [20] For all the promises of God find their Yes in him. That is why we utter the Amen through him, to the glory of God. [21] But it is God who establishes us with you in Christ, and has commissioned us; [22] he has put his seal upon us and given us his Spirit in our hearts as a guarantee.

PRIMARY

Rom 15:22–29 (§63)

[22] This is the reason why I have so often been hindered from coming to you. [23] But now, since I no longer have any room for work in these regions, and since I have longed for many years to come to you, [24] I hope to see you in passing as I go to Spain, and to be sped on my journey there by you, once I have enjoyed your company for a little. [25] At present, however, I am going to Jerusalem with aid for the saints. [26] For Macedonia and Achaia have been pleased to make some contribution for the poor among the saints at Jerusalem; [27] they were pleased to do it, and indeed they are in debt to them, for if the Gentiles have come to share in their spiritual blessings, they ought also to be of service to them in material blessings. [28] When therefore I have completed this, and have delivered to them what has been raised, I shall go on by way of you to Spain; [29] and I know that when I come to you I shall come in the fulness of the blessing of Christ.

1 Cor 4:14–21 (§86)

[14] I do not write this to make you ashamed, but to admonish you as my beloved children. [15] For though you have countless guides in Christ, you do not have many fathers. For I became your father in Christ Jesus through the gospel. [16] I urge you, then, be imitators of me. [17] Therefore I sent to you Timothy, my beloved and faithful child in the Lord, to remind you of my ways in Christ, as I teach them everywhere in every church. [18] Some are arrogant, as though I were not coming to you. [19] But I will come to you soon, if the Lord wills, and I will find out not the talk of these arrogant people but their power. [20] For the kingdom of God does not consist in talk but in power. [21] What do you wish? Shall I come to you with a rod, or with love in a spirit of gentleness?

1 Cor 16:1–4 (§138)

[1] Now concerning the contribution for the saints: as I directed the churches of Galatia, so you also are to do. [2] On the first day of every week, each of you is to put something aside and store it up, as he may prosper, so that contributions need not be made when I come. [3] And when I arrive, I will send those whom you accredit by letter to carry your gift to Jerusalem. [4] If it seems advisable that I should go also, they will accompany me.

1 Cor 16:5–9 (§139)

[5] I will visit you after passing through Macedonia, for I intend to pass through Macedonia, [6] and perhaps I will stay with you or even spend the winter, so that you may speed me on my journey, wherever I go. [7] For I do not want to see you now just in passing; I hope to spend some time with you, if the Lord permits. [8] But I will stay in Ephesus until Pentecost, [9] for a wide door for effective work has opened to me, and there are many adversaries.

1 Thess 2:17–20 (§280)

[17] But since we were bereft of you, brethren, for a short time, in person not in heart, we endeavored the more eagerly and with great desire to see you face to face; [18] because we wanted to come to you—I, Paul, again and again—but Satan hindered us. [19] For what is our hope or joy or crown of boasting before our Lord Jesus at his coming? Is it not you? [20] For you are our glory and joy.

Phlm 21–22 (§309)

[21] Confident of your obedience, I write to you, knowing that you will do even more than I say. [22] At the same time, prepare a guest room for me, for I am hoping through your prayers to be granted to you.

● **2 Cor 1:15–22**

2 Cor 1 [23] But I call God to witness against me—it was to spare you that I refrained from coming to Corinth. [24] Not that we lord it over your faith; we work with you for your joy, for you stand firm in your faith. 2 [1] For I made up my mind not to make you another painful visit. [2] For if I cause you pain, who is there to make me glad but the one whom I have pained? [3] And I wrote as I did, so that when I came I might not suffer pain from those who should have made me rejoice, for I felt sure of all of you, that my joy would be the joy of you all. [4] For I wrote you out of much affliction and anguish of heart and with many tears, not to cause you pain but to let you know the abundant love that I have for you.

2 Cor 9 [1] Now it is superfluous for me to write to you about the offering for the saints, [2] for I know your readiness, of which I boast about you to the people of Macedonia, saying that Achaia has been ready since last year; and your zeal has stirred up most of them. [3] But I am sending the brethren so that our boasting about you may not prove vain in this case, so that you may be ready, as I said you would be; [4] lest if some Macedonians come with me and find that you are not ready, we be humiliated—to say nothing of you—for being so confident. [5] So I thought it necessary to urge the brethren to go on to you before me, and arrange in advance for this gift you have promised, so that it may be ready not as an exaction but as a willing gift.

2 Cor 12 [14] Here for the third time I am ready to come to you. And I will not be a burden, for I seek not what is yours but you; for children ought not to lay up for their parents, but parents for their children. [15] I will most gladly spend and be spent for your souls. If I love you the more, am I to be loved the less? [16] But granting that I myself did not burden you, I was crafty, you say, and got the better of you by guile. [17] Did I take advantage of you through any of those whom I sent to you? [18] I urged Titus to go, and sent the brother with him. Did Titus take advantage of you? Did we not act in the same spirit? Did we not take the same steps?

[19] Have you been thinking all along that we have been defending ourselves before you? It is in the sight of God that we have been speaking in Christ, and all for your upbuilding, beloved. [20] For I fear that perhaps I may come and find you not what I wish, and that you may find me not what you wish; that perhaps there may be quarreling, jealousy, anger, selfishness, slander, gossip, conceit, and disorder. [21] I fear that when I come again my God may humble me before you, and I may have to mourn over many of those who sinned before and have not repented of the impurity, immorality, and licentiousness which they have practiced.

13 [1] This is the third time I am coming to you. Any charge must be sustained by the evidence of two or three witnesses. [2] I warned those who sinned before and all the others, and I warn them now while absent, as I did when present on my second visit, that if I come again I will not spare them— [3] since you desire proof that Christ is speaking in me. He is not weak in dealing with you, but is powerful in you. [4] For he was crucified in weakness, but lives by the power of God. For we are weak in him, but in dealing with you we shall live with him by the power of God.

[5] Examine yourselves, to see whether you are holding to your faith. Test yourselves. Do you not realize that Jesus Christ is in you?—unless indeed you fail to meet the test! [6] I hope you will find out that we have not failed. [7] But we pray God that you may not do wrong— not that we may appear to have met the test, but that you may do what is right, though we may seem to have failed. [8] For we cannot do anything against the truth, but only for the truth. [9] For we are glad when we are weak and you are strong. What we pray for is your improvement. [10] I write this while I am away from you, in order that when I come I may not have to be severe in my use of the authority which the Lord has given me for building up and not for tearing down.

● **2 Cor 1:15**

(pleasure) *read* favor: S*ACDG Koine Lect it vg syr cop(sa); *text:* S^{c}BP cop(bo) Theodoret

● **2 Cor 1:16**

Acts 19 [21] Now after these events Paul resolved in the Spirit to pass through Macedonia and Achaia and go to Jerusalem, saying, "After I have been there, I must also see Rome."

● **2 Cor 1:19**

Cf. Acts 15:22

● **2 Cor 1:20–21**

Cf. Eph 1:13–14

● **2 Cor 1:20**

Cf. Rom 15:8; 1 Cor 14:16; Gal 3:17–18; Gal 3:22

● **2 Cor 1:22**

Rom 8 [23] and not only the creation, but we ourselves, who have the first fruits of the Spirit, groan inwardly as we wait for adoption as sons, the redemption of our bodies.

2 Cor 5 [5] He who has prepared us for this very thing is God, who has given us the Spirit as a guarantee.

Cf. Rom 8:16; Rom 5:5

FORMAL ELEMENT: APOSTOLIC VISIT

23 But I call God to witness against me— it was to spare you that I refrained from coming to Corinth. **24** Not that we lord it over your faith; we work with you for your joy, for you stand firm in your faith. **2 1** For I made up my mind not to make you another painful visit. **2** For if I cause you pain, who is there to make me glad but the one whom I have pained? **3** And I wrote as I did, so that when I came I might not suffer pain from those who should have made me rejoice, for I felt sure of all of you, that my joy would be the joy of you all. **4** For I wrote you out of much affliction and anguish of heart and with many tears, not to cause you pain but to let you know the abundant love that I have for you.

PRIMARY

See §149 for APOSTOLIC VISIT

SECONDARY

Gal 5:1–12 (§211)

1 For freedom Christ has set us free; stand fast therefore, and do not submit again to a yoke of slavery.

2 Now I, Paul, say to you that if you receive circumcision, Christ will be of no advantage to you. **3** I testify again to every man who receives circumcision that he is bound to keep the whole law. **4** You are severed from Christ, you who would be justified by the law; you have fallen away from grace. **5** For through the Spirit, by faith, we wait for the hope of righteousness. **6** For in Christ Jesus neither circumcision nor uncircumcision is of any avail, but faith working through love. **7** You were running well; who hindered you from obeying the truth? **8** This persuasion is not from him who called you. **9** A little leaven leavens the whole lump. **10** I have confidence in the Lord that you will take no other view than mine; and he who is troubling you will bear his judgment, whoever he is. **11** But if I, brethren, still preach circumcision, why am I still persecuted? In that case the stumbling block of the cross has been removed. **12** I wish those who unsettle you would mutilate themselves!

Phil 1:27–30 (§241)

27 Only let your manner of life be worthy of the gospel of Christ, so that whether I come and see you or am absent, I may hear of you that you stand firm in one spirit, with one mind striving side by side for the faith of the gospel, **28** and not frightened in anything by your opponents. This

is a clear omen to them of their destruction, but of your salvation, and that from God. **29** For it has been granted to you that for the sake of Christ you should not only believe in him but also suffer for his sake, **30** engaged in the same conflict which you saw and now hear to be mine.

1 Thess 3:6–10 (§282)

6 But now that Timothy has come to us from you, and has brought us the good news of your faith and love and reported that you always remember us kindly and long to see us, as we long to see you— **7** for this reason, brethren, in all our distress and affliction we have been comforted about you through your faith; **8** for now we live, if you stand fast in the Lord. **9** For what thanksgiving can we render to God for you, for all the joy which we feel for your sake before our God, **10** praying earnestly night and day that we may see you face to face and supply what is lacking in your faith?

● **2 Cor 1:23–24**

1 Cor 15 **1** Now I would remind you, brethren, in what terms I preached to you the gospel, which you received, in which you stand, **2** by which you are saved, if you hold it fast —unless you believed in vain.

2 Cor 1 **15** Because I was sure of this, I wanted to come to you first, so that you might have a double pleasure; **16** I wanted to visit you on my way to Macedonia, and to come back to you from Macedonia and have you send me on my way to Judea. **17** Was I vacillating when I wanted to do this? Do I make my plans like a worldly man, ready to say Yes and No at once? **18** As surely as God is faithful, our word to you has not been Yes and No. **19** For the Son of God, Jesus Christ, whom we preached among you, Silvanus and Timothy and I, was not Yes and No; but in him it is always Yes. **20** For all the promises of God find their Yes in him. That is why we utter the Amen through him, to the glory of God. **21** But it is God who establishes us with you in Christ, and has commissioned us; **22** he has put his seal upon us and given us his Spirit in our hearts as a guarantee.

2 Cor 9 **3** But I am sending the brethren so that our boasting about you may not prove vain in this case, so that you may be ready, as I said you would be; **4** lest if some Macedonians come with me and find that you are not ready, we be humiliated—to say nothing of you—for being so confident.

2 Cor 12 **14** Here for the third time I am ready to come to you. And I will not be a burden, for I seek not what is yours but you; for children ought not to lay up for their parents, but parents for their children. **15** I will most gladly spend and be spent for your souls. If I love you the more, am I to be loved the less? **16** But granting that I myself did not burden you, I was crafty, you say, and got the better of you by guile. **17** Did I take

advantage of you through any of those whom I sent to you? **18** I urged Titus to go, and sent the brother with him. Did Titus take advantage of you? Did we not act in the same spirit? Did we not take the same steps?

19 Have you been thinking all along that we have been defending ourselves before you? It is in the sight of God that we have been speaking in Christ, and all for your upbuilding, beloved. **20** For I fear that perhaps I may come and find you not what I wish, and that you may find me not what you wish; that perhaps there may be quarreling, jealousy, anger, selfishness, slander, gossip, conceit, and disorder. **21** I fear that when I come again my God may humble me before you, and I may have to mourn over many of those who sinned before and have not repented of the impurity, immorality, and licentiousness which they have practiced.

13 1 This is the third time I am coming to you. Any charge must be sustained by the evidence of two or three witnesses. **2** I warned those who sinned before and all the others, and I warn them now while absent, as I did when present on my second visit, that if I come again I will not spare them— **3** since you desire proof that Christ is speaking in me. He is not weak in dealing with you, but is powerful in you. **4** For he was crucified in weakness, but lives by the power of God. For we are weak in him, but in dealing with you we shall live with him by the power of God.

5 Examine yourselves, to see whether you are holding to your faith. Test yourselves. Do you not realize that Jesus Christ is in you?—unless indeed you fail to meet the test! **6** I hope you will find out that we have not failed. **7** But we pray God that you may not do wrong—not that we may appear to have met the test, but that you may do what is right, though we may seem to have failed. **8** For we cannot do anything against the truth, but only for the truth. **9** For we are glad when we are weak and you are strong. What we pray for is your improvement. **10** I write this while I am away from you, in order that when I come I may not have to be severe

in my use of the authority which the Lord has given me for building up and not for tearing down.

● **2 Cor 1:23**

Rom 1 **13** I want you to know, brethren, that I have often intended to come to you (but thus far have been prevented), in order that I may reap some harvest among you as well as among the rest of the Gentiles.

Rom 15 **22** This is the reason why I have so often been hindered from coming to you.

2 Cor 11 **31** The God and Father of the Lord Jesus, he who is blessed for ever, knows that I do not lie.

Gal 1 **20** (In what I am writing to you, before God, I do not lie!)

● **2 Cor 1:24**

Gal 5 **1** For freedom Christ has set us free; stand fast therefore, and do not submit again to a yoke of slavery.

Phil 4 **1** Therefore, my brethren, whom I love and long for, my joy and crown, stand firm thus in the Lord, my beloved.

● **2 Cor 2:3**

2 Cor 7 **16** What agreement has the temple of God with idols? For we are the temple of the living God; as God said,
"I will live in them and move among them,
and I will be their God,
and they shall be my people."

● **2 Cor 2:4**

Acts 20 **31** "Therefore be alert, remembering that for three years I did not cease night or day to admonish every one with tears."

[5]But if any one has caused pain, he has caused it not to me, but in some measure—not to put it too severely— to you all. [6]For such a one this punishment by the majority is enough; [7]so you should rather turn to forgive and comfort him, or he may be overwhelmed by excessive sorrow. [8]So I beg you to reaffirm your love for him. [9]For this is why I wrote, that I might test you and know whether you are obedient in everything. [10]Any one whom you forgive, I also forgive. What I have forgiven, if I have forgiven anything, has been for your sake in the presence of Christ, [11]to keep Satan from gaining the advantage over us; for we are not ignorant of his designs.

PRIMARY

Rom 16:17-20a (§67)
[17]I appeal to you, brethren, to take note of those who create dissensions and difficulties, in opposition to the doctrine which you have been taught; avoid them. [18]For such persons do not serve our Lord Christ, but their own appetites, and by fair and flattering words they deceive the hearts of the simple-minded. [19]For while your obedience is known to all, so that I rejoice over you, I would have you wise as to what is good and guileless as to what is evil; [20]then the God of peace will soon crush Satan under your feet.

1 Cor 5:1-5 (§87)
[1]It is actually reported that there is immorality among you, and of a kind that is not found even among pagans; for a man is living with his father's wife. [2]And you are arrogant! Ought you not rather to mourn? Let him who has done this be removed from among you.
[3]For though absent in body I am present in spirit, and as if present, I have already pronounced judgment [4]in the name of the Lord Jesus on the man who has done such a thing. When you are assembled, and my spirit is present, with the power of our Lord Jesus, [5]you are to deliver this man to Satan for the destruction of the flesh, that his spirit may be saved in the day of the Lord Jesus.

Gal 6:1-6 (§214)
[1]Brethren, if a man is overtaken in any trespass, you who are spiritual should restore him in a spirit of gentleness. Look to yourself, lest you too be tempted. [2]Bear one another's burdens, and so fulfil the law of Christ. [3]For if any one thinks he is something, when he is nothing, he deceives himself. [4]But let each one test his own work, and then his reason to boast will be in himself alone and not in his neighbor. [5]For each man will have to bear his own load.
[6]Let him who is taught the word share all good things with him who teaches.

2 Thess 3:14-15 (§301)
[14]If any one refuses to obey what we say in this letter, note that man, and have nothing to do with him, that he may be ashamed. [15]Do not look on him as an enemy, but warn him as a brother.

Phlm 15-20 (§308)
[15]Perhaps this is why he was parted from you for a while, that you might have him back for ever, [16]no longer as a slave but more than a slave, as a beloved brother, especially to me but how much more to you, both in the flesh and in the Lord. [17]So if you consider me your partner, receive him as you would receive me. [18]If he has wronged you at all, or owes you anything, charge that to my account. [19]I, Paul, write this with my own hand, I will repay it—to say nothing of your owing me even your own self. [20]Yes, brother, I want some benefit from you in the Lord. Refresh my heart in Christ.

● **2 Cor 2:5-11**
2 Cor 6   [14]Do not be mismated with unbelievers. For what partnership have righteousness and iniquity? Or what fellowship has light with darkness? [15]What accord has Christ with Belial? Or what has a believer in common with an unbeliever? [16]What agreement has the temple of God with idols? For we are the temple of the living God; as God said,
"I will live in them and move among them,
and I will be their God,
and they shall be my people.
[17]Therefore come out from them,
and be separate from them, says the Lord,
and touch nothing unclean;
then I will welcome you,
[18]and I will be a father to you,
and you shall be my sons and daughters,
says the Lord Almighty."
7 [1]Since we have these promises, beloved, let us cleanse ourselves from every defilement of body and spirit, and make holiness perfect in the fear of God.

● **2 Cor 2:7-8**
Eph 4   [32]and be kind to one another, tenderhearted, forgiving one another, as God in Christ forgave you.

Col 3   [13]forbearing one another and, if one has a complaint against another, forgiving each other; as the Lord has forgiven you, so you also must forgive. [14]And above all these put on love, which binds everything together in perfect harmony.

● **2 Cor 2:8**
Phil 4   [3]And I ask you also, true yokefellow, help these women, for they have labored side by side with me in the gospel together with Clement and the rest of my fellow workers, whose names are in the book of life.

● **2 Cor 2:10-11**
2 Cor 4   [3]And even if our gospel is veiled, it is veiled only to those who are perishing. [4]In their case the god of this world has blinded the minds of the unbelievers, to keep them from seeing the light of the gospel of the glory of Christ, who is the likeness of God. [5]For what we preach is not ourselves, but Jesus Christ as Lord, with ourselves as your servants for Jesus' sake. [6]For it is the God who said, "Let light shine out of darkness," who has shone in our hearts to give the light of the knowledge of the glory of God in the face of Christ.

¹²When I came to Troas to preach the gospel of Christ, a door was opened for me in the Lord; ¹³but my mind could not rest because I did not find my brother Titus there. So I took leave of them and went on to Macedonia.

PRIMARY

Col 4:2–4 (§269)

²Continue steadfastly in prayer, being watchful in it with thanksgiving; ³and pray for us also, that God may open to us a door for the word, to declare the mystery of Christ, on account of which I am in prison, ⁴that I may make it clear, as I ought to speak.

● **2 Cor 2:12**

Acts 14   ²⁷And when they arrived, they gathered the church together and declared all that God had done with them, and how he had opened a door of faith to the Gentiles.

Acts 16   ⁸so, passing by Mysia, they went down to Troas.

● **2 Cor 2:13**

Gal 2   ¹Then after fourteen years I went up again to Jerusalem with Barnabas, taking Titus along with me. ²I went up by revelation; and I laid before them (but privately before those who were of repute) the gospel which I preach among the Gentiles, lest somehow I should be running or had run in vain. ³But even Titus, who was with me, was not compelled to be circumcised, though he was a Greek.

Titus 1   ⁴To Titus, my true child in a common faith: Grace and peace from God the Father and Christ Jesus our Savior.

¹⁴But thanks be to God, who in Christ always leads us in triumph, and through us spreads the fragrance of the knowledge of him everywhere. ¹⁵For we are the aroma of Christ to God among those who are being saved and among those who are perishing, ¹⁶to one a fragrance from death to death, to the other a fragrance from life to life. Who is sufficient for these things? ¹⁷For we are not, like so many, peddlers of God's word; but as men of sincerity, as commissioned by God, in the sight of God we speak in Christ.

Primary

Rom 12:1–2 (§51)

¹I appeal to you therefore, brethren, by the mercies of God, to present your bodies as a living sacrifice, holy and acceptable to God, which is your spiritual worship. ²Do not be conformed to this world but be transformed by the renewal of your mind, that you may prove what is the will of God, what is good and acceptable and perfect.

1 Cor 9:15–18 (§106)

¹⁵But I have made no use of any of these rights, nor am I writing this to secure any such provision. For I would rather die than have any one deprive me of my ground for boasting. ¹⁶For if I preach the gospel, that gives me no ground for boasting. For necessity is laid upon me. Woe to me if I do not preach the gospel! ¹⁷For if I do this of my own will, I have a reward; but if not of my own will, I am entrusted with a commission. ¹⁸What then is my reward? Just this: that in my preaching I may make the gospel free of charge, not making full use of my right in the gospel.

Phil 1:12–18 (§239)

¹²I want you to know, brethren, that what has happened to me has really served to advance the gospel, ¹³so that it has become known throughout the whole praetorian guard and to all the rest that my imprisonment is for Christ; ¹⁴and most of the brethren have been made confident in the Lord because of my imprisonment, and are much more bold to speak the word of God without fear. ¹⁵Some indeed preach Christ from envy and rivalry, but others from good will. ¹⁶The latter do it out of love, knowing that I am put here for the defense of the gospel; ¹⁷the former proclaim Christ out of partisanship, not sincerely but thinking to afflict me in my imprisonment. ¹⁸What then? Only that in every way, whether in pretense or in truth, Christ is proclaimed; and in that I rejoice.

Phil 4:10–20 (§253)

¹⁰I rejoice in the Lord greatly that now at length you have revived your concern for me; you were indeed concerned for me, but you had no opportunity. ¹¹Not that I complain of want; for I have learned, in whatever state I am, to be content. ¹²I know how to be abased, and I know how to abound; in any and all circumstances I have learned the secret of facing plenty and hunger, abundance and want. ¹³I can do all things in him who strengthens me.

¹⁴Yet it was kind of you to share my trouble. ¹⁵And you Philippians yourselves know that in the beginning of the gospel, when I left Macedonia, no church entered into partnership with me in giving and receiving except you only; ¹⁶for even in Thessalonica you sent me help once and again. ¹⁷Not that I seek the gift; but I seek the fruit which increases to your credit. ¹⁸I have received full payment, and more; I am filled, having received from Epaphroditus the gifts you sent, a fragrant offering, a sacrifice acceptable and pleasing to God. ¹⁹And my God will supply every need of yours according to his riches in glory in Christ Jesus. ²⁰To our God and Father be glory for ever and ever. Amen.

1 Thess 2:1–8 (§277)

¹For you yourselves know, brethren, that our visit to you was not in vain; ²but though we had already suffered and been shamefully treated at Philippi, as you know, we had courage in our God to declare to you the gospel of God in the face of great opposition. ³For our appeal does not spring from error or uncleanness, nor is it made with guile; ⁴but just as we have been approved by God to be entrusted with the gospel, so we speak, not to please men, but to please God who tests our hearts. ⁵For we never used either words of flattery, as you know, or a cloak for greed, as God is witness; ⁶nor did we seek glory from men, whether from you or from others, though we might have made demands as apostles of Christ. ⁷But we were gentle among you, like a nurse taking care of her children. ⁸So, being affectionately desirous of you, we were ready to share with you not only the gospel of God but also our own selves, because you had become very dear to us.

● **2 Cor 2:14**
1 Cor 15   ⁵⁷But thanks be to God, who gives us the victory through our Lord Jesus Christ.

Col 2   ¹⁵He disarmed the principalities and powers and made a public example of them, triumphing over them in him.

● **2 Cor 2:15–16**
Eph 5   ²And walk in love, as Christ loved us and gave himself up for us, a fragrant offering and sacrifice to God.

Phil 2   ¹⁷Even if I am to be poured as a libation upon the sacrificial offering of your faith, I am glad and rejoice with you all.

● **2 Cor 2:15**
1 Cor 1   ¹⁸For the word of the cross is folly to those who are perishing, but to us who are being saved it is the power of God.

● **2 Cor 2:16**
2 Cor 3   ⁵Not that we are competent of ourselves to claim anything as coming from us; our competence is from God, . . .

● **2 Cor 2:17**
2 Cor 12   ¹⁹Have you been thinking all along that we have been defending ourselves before you? It is in the sight of God that we have been speaking in Christ, and all for your upbuilding, beloved.

FORMAL ELEMENT: COMMENDATION

3 Are we beginning to commend ourselves again? Or do we need, as some do, letters of recommendation to you, or from you? [2] You yourselves are our letter of recommendation, written on your hearts, to be known and read by all men; [3] and you show that you are a letter from Christ delivered by us, written not with ink but with the Spirit of the living God, not on tablets of stone but on tablets of human hearts.

PRIMARY

Rom 16:1–2 (§65)

[1] I commend to you our sister Phoebe, a deaconess of the church at Cenchreae, [2] that you may receive her in the Lord as befits the saints, and help her in whatever she may require from you, for she has been a helper of many and of myself as well.

1 Cor 16:10–12 (§140)

[10] When Timothy comes, see that you put him at ease among you, for he is doing the work of the Lord, as I am. [11] So let no one despise him. Speed him on his way in peace, that he may return to me; for I am expecting him with the brethren. [12] As for our brother Apollos, I strongly urged him to visit you with the other brethren, but it was not at all his will to come now. He will come when he has opportunity.

1 Cor 16:15–18 (§142)

[15] Now, brethren, you know that the household of Stephanas were the first converts in Achaia, and they have devoted themselves to the service of the saints; [16] I urge you to be subject to such men and to every fellow worker and laborer. [17] I rejoice at the coming of Stephanas and Fortunatus and Achaicus, because they have made up for your absence; [18] for they refreshed my spirit as well as yours. Give recognition to such men.

2 Cor 8:16–24 (§173)

[16] But thanks be to God who puts the same earnest care for you into the heart of Titus. [17] For he not only accepted our appeal, but being himself very earnest he is going to you of his own accord. [18] With him we are sending the brother who is famous among all the churches for his preaching of the gospel; [19] and not only that, but he has been appointed by the churches to travel with us in this gracious work which we are carrying on, for the glory of the Lord and to show our good will. [20] We intend that no one should blame us about this liberal gift which we are administering, [21] for we aim at what is honorable not only in the Lord's sight but also in the sight of men. [22] And with them we are sending our brother whom we have often tested and found earnest in many matters, but who is now more earnest than ever because of his great confidence in you. [23] As for Titus, he is my partner and fellow worker in your service; and as for our brethren, they are messengers of the churches, the glory of Christ. [24] So give proof, before the churches, of your love and of our boasting about you to these men.

Eph 6:21–22 (§235)

[21] Now that you also may know how I am and what I am doing, Tychicus the beloved brother and faithful minister in the Lord will tell you everything. [22] I have sent him to you for this very purpose, that you may know how we are, and that he may encourage your hearts.

Phil 2:19–24 (§245)

[19] I hope in the Lord Jesus to send Timothy to you soon, so that I may be cheered by news of you. [20] I have no one like him, who will be genuinely anxious for your welfare. [21] They all look after their own interests, not those of Jesus Christ. [22] But Timothy's worth you know, how as a son with a father he has served with me in the gospel. [23] I hope therefore to send him just as soon as I see how it will go with me; [24] and I trust in the Lord that shortly I myself shall come also.

Phil 2:25–3:1 (§246)

[25] I have thought it necessary to send to you Epaphroditus my brother and fellow worker and fellow soldier, and your messenger and minister to my need, [26] for he has been longing for you all, and has been distressed because you heard that he was ill. [27] Indeed he was ill, near to death. But God had mercy on him, and not only on him but on me also, lest I should have sorrow upon sorrow. [28] I am the more eager to send him, therefore, that you may rejoice at seeing him again, and that I may be less anxious. [29] So receive him in the Lord with all joy; and honor such men, [30] for he nearly died for the work of Christ, risking his life to complete your service to me.

3 [1] Finally, my brethren, rejoice in the Lord. To write the same things to you is not irksome to me, and is safe for you.

Col 4:7–9 (§271)

[7] Tychicus will tell you all about my affairs; he is a beloved brother and faithful minister and fellow servant in the Lord. [8] I have sent him to you for this very purpose, that you may know how we are and that he may encourage your hearts, [9] and with him Onesimus, the faithful and beloved brother, who is one of yourselves. They will tell you of everything that has taken place here.

Phlm 8–20 (§307–308)

[8] Accordingly, though I am bold enough in Christ to command you to do what is required, [9] yet for love's sake I prefer to appeal to you—I, Paul, an ambassador and now a prisoner also for Christ Jesus— [10] I appeal to you for my child, Onesimus, whose father I have become in my imprisonment. [11] (Formerly he was useless to you, but now he is indeed useful to you and to me.) [12] I am sending him back to you, sending my very heart. [13] I would have been glad to keep him with me, in order that he might serve me on your behalf during my imprisonment for the gospel; [14] but I preferred to do nothing without your consent in order that your goodness might not be by compulsion but of your own free will. [15] Perhaps this is why he was parted from you for a while, that you might have him back for ever, [16] no longer as a slave but more than a slave, as a beloved brother, especially to me but how much more to you, both in the flesh and in the Lord. [17] So if you consider me your partner, receive him as you would receive me. [18] If he has wronged you at all, or owes you anything, charge that to my account. [19] I, Paul, write this with my own hand, I will repay it—to say nothing of your owing me even your own self. [20] Yes, brother, I want some benefit from you in the Lord. Refresh my heart in Christ.

● **2 Cor 3:1**

Acts 18   [27] And when he wished to cross to Achaia, the brethren encouraged him, and wrote to the disciples to receive him. When he arrived, he greatly helped those who through grace had believed.

● **2 Cor 3:2**

(your) *read* our: p⁴⁶ ABCDG Koine Lect it vg syr cop; *text:* S

● **2 Cor 3:3**

Rom 2   [25] Circumcision indeed is of value if you obey the law; but if you break the law, your circumcision becomes uncircumcision. [26] So, if a man who is uncircumcised keeps the precepts of the law, will not his uncircumcision be regarded as circumcision? [27] Then those who are physically uncircumcised but keep the law will condemn you who have the written code and circumcision but break the law. [28] For he is not a real Jew who is one outwardly, nor is true circumcision something external and physical. [29] He is a Jew who is one inwardly, and real circumcision is a matter of the heart, spiritual and not literal. His praise is not from men but from God.

Rom 7   [6] But now we are discharged from the law, dead to that which held us captive, so that we serve not under the old written code but in the new life of the Spirit.

4Such is the confidence that we have through Christ toward God. **5**Not that we are competent of ourselves to claim anything as coming from us; our competence is from God, **6**who has made us competent to be ministers of a new covenant, not in a written code but in the Spirit; for the written code kills, but the Spirit gives life.

PRIMARY

Rom 12:3–8 (§52)

3For by the grace given to me I bid every one among you not to think of himself more highly than he ought to think, but to think with sober judgment, each according to the measure of faith which God has assigned him. **4**For as in one body we have many members, and all the members do not have the same function, **5**so we, though many, are one body in Christ, and individually members one of another. **6**Having gifts that differ according to the grace given to us, let us use them: if prophecy, in proportion to our faith; **7**if service, in our serving; he who teaches, in his teaching; **8**he who exhorts, in his exhortation; he who contributes, in liberality; he who gives aid, with zeal; he who does acts of mercy, with cheerfulness.

1 Cor 4:6–7 (§84)

6I have applied all this to myself and Apollos for your benefit, brethren, that you may learn by us not to go beyond what is written, that none of you may be puffed up in favor of one against another. **7**For who sees anything different in you? What have you that you did not receive? If then you received it, why do you boast as if it were not a gift?

Gal 2:15–21 (§199)

15We ourselves, who are Jews by birth and not Gentile sinners, **16**yet who know that a man is not justified by works of the law but through faith in Jesus Christ, even we have believed in Christ Jesus, in order to be justified by faith in Christ, and not by works of the law, because by works of the law shall no one be justified. **17**But if, in our endeavor to be justified in Christ, we ourselves were found to be sinners, is Christ then an agent of sin? Certainly not! **18**But if I build up again those things which I tore down, then I prove myself a transgressor. **19**For I through the law died to the law, that I might live to God. **20**I have been crucified with Christ; it is no longer I who live, but Christ who lives in me; and the life I now live in the flesh I live by faith in the Son of God, who loved me and gave himself for me. **21**I do not nullify the grace of God; for if justification were through the law, then Christ died to no purpose.

Gal 5:1–12 (§211)

1For freedom Christ has set us free; stand fast therefore, and do not submit again to a yoke of slavery.

2Now I, Paul, say to you that if you receive circumcision, Christ will be of no advantage to you. **3**I testify again to every man who receives circumcision that he is bound to keep the whole law. **4**You are severed from Christ, you who would be justified by the law; you have fallen away from grace. **5**For through the Spirit, by faith, we wait for the hope of righteousness. **6**For in Christ Jesus neither circumcision nor uncircumcision is of any avail, but faith working through love. **7**You were running well; who hindered you from obeying the truth? **8**This persuasion is not from him who called you. **9**A little leaven leavens the whole lump. **10**I have confidence in the Lord that you will take no other view than mine; and he who is troubling you will bear his judgment, whoever he is. **11**But if I, brethren, still preach circumcision, why am I still persecuted? In that case the stumbling block of the cross has been removed. **12**I wish those who unsettle you would mutilate themselves!

Phil 3:2–11 (§247)

2Look out for the dogs, look out for the evil-workers, look out for those who mutilate the flesh. **3**For we are the true circumcision, who worship God in spirit, and glory in Christ Jesus, and put no confidence in the flesh. **4**Though I myself have reason for confidence in the flesh also. If any other man thinks he has reason for confidence in the flesh, I have more: **5**circumcised on the eighth day, of the people of Israel, of the tribe of Benjamin, a Hebrew born of Hebrews; as to the law a Pharisee, **6**as to zeal a persecutor of the church, as to righteousness under the law blameless. **7**But whatever gain I had, I counted as loss for the sake of Christ. **8**Indeed I count everything as loss because of the surpassing worth of knowing Christ Jesus my Lord. For his sake I have suffered the loss of all things, and count them as refuse, in order that I may gain Christ **9**and be found in him, not having a righteousness of my own, based on law, but that which is through faith in Christ, the righteousness from God that depends on faith; **10**that I may know him and the power of his resurrection, and may share his sufferings, becoming like him in his death, **11**that if possible I may attain the resurrection from the dead.

Phil 3:12–16 (§248)

12Not that I have already obtained this or am already perfect; but I press on to make it my own, because Christ Jesus has made me his own. **13**Brethren, I do not consider that I have made it my own; but one thing I do, forgetting what lies behind and straining forward to what lies ahead, **14**I press on toward the goal for the prize of the upward call of God in Christ Jesus. **15**Let those of us who are mature be thus minded; and if in anything you are otherwise minded, God will reveal that also to you. **16**Only let us hold true to what we have attained.

1 Thess 2:1–8 (§277)

1For you yourselves know, brethren, that our visit to you was not in vain; **2**but though we had already suffered and been shamefully treated at Philippi, as you know, we had courage in our God to declare to you the gospel of God in the face of great opposition. **3**For our appeal does not spring from error or uncleanness, nor is it made with guile; **4**but just as we have been approved by God to be entrusted with the gospel, so we speak, not to please men, but to please God who tests our hearts. **5**For we never used either words of flattery, as you know, or a cloak for greed, as God is witness; **6**nor did we seek glory from men, whether from you or from others, though we might have made demands as apostles of Christ. **7**But we were gentle among you, like a nurse taking care of her children. **8**So, being affectionately desirous of you, we were ready to share with you not only the gospel of God but also our own selves, because you had become very dear to us.

● **2 Cor 3:4**
Eph 3   **12**in whom we have boldness and confidence of access through our faith in him.

● **2 Cor 3:5**
1 Cor 15   **10**But by the grace of God I am what I am, and his grace toward me was not in vain. On the contrary, I worked harder than any of them, though it was not I, but the grace of God which is with me.

Gal 3   **2**Let me ask you only this: Did you receive the Spirit by works of the law, or by hearing with faith?

● **2 Cor 3:6**
Rom 2   **29**He is a Jew who is one inwardly, and real circumcision is a matter of the heart, spiritual and not literal. His praise is not from men but from God.

Rom 7   **6**But now we are discharged from the law, dead to that which held us captive, so that we serve not under the old written code but in the new life of the Spirit.

1 Cor 11   **25**Eat whatever is sold in the meat market without raising any question on the ground of conscience.

Eph 2   **15**by abolishing in his flesh the law of commandments and ordinances, that he might create in himself one new man in place of the two, so making peace, . . .

Gal 3   **15**To give a human example, brethren: no one annuls even a man's will, or adds to it, once it has been ratified.

Gal 3   **21**Is the law then against the promises of God? Certainly not; for if a law had been given which could make alive, then righteousness would indeed be by the law.

[7]Now if the dispensation of death, carved in letters on stone, came with such splendor that the Israelites could not look at Moses' face because of its brightness, fading as this was, [8]will not the dispensation of the Spirit be attended with greater splendor? [9]For if there was splendor in the dispensation of condemnation, the dispensation of righteousness must far exceed it in splendor. [10]Indeed, in this case, what once had splendor has come to have no splendor at all, because of the splendor that surpasses it. [11]For if what faded away came with splendor, what is permanent must have much more splendor.

PRIMARY

Rom 3:21–26 (§14)

[21]But now the righteousness of God has been manifested apart from law, although the law and the prophets bear witness to it, [22]the righteousness of God through faith in Jesus Christ for all who believe. For there is no distinction; [23]since all have sinned and fall short of the glory of God, [24]they are justified by his grace as a gift, through the redemption which is in Christ Jesus, [25]whom God put forward as an expiation by his blood, to be received by faith. This was to show God's righteousness, because in his divine forbearance he had passed over former sins; [26]it was to prove at the present time that he himself is righteous and that he justifies him who has faith in Jesus.

Rom 5:6–21 (§21–22)

[6]While we were still weak, at the right time Christ died for the ungodly. [7]Why, one will hardly die for a righteous man—though perhaps for a good man one will dare even to die. [8]But God shows his love for us in that while we were yet sinners Christ died for us. [9]Since, therefore, we are now justified by his blood, much more shall we be saved by him from the wrath of God. [10]For if while we were enemies we were reconciled to God by the death of his Son, much more, now that we are reconciled, shall we be saved by his life. [11]Not only so, but we also rejoice in God through our Lord Jesus Christ, through whom we have now received our reconciliation.

[12]Therefore as sin came into the world through one man and death through sin, and so death spread to all men because all men sinned— [13]sin indeed was in the world before the law was given, but sin is not counted where there is no law. [14]Yet death reigned from Adam to Moses, even over those whose sins were not like the transgression of Adam, who was a type of the one who was to come.

[15]But the free gift is not like the trespass. For if many died through one man's trespass, much more have the grace of God and the free gift in the grace of that one man Jesus Christ abounded for many. [16]And the free gift is not like the effect of that one man's sin. For the judgment following one trespass brought condemnation, but the free gift following many trespasses brings justification. [17]If, because of one man's trespass, death reigned through that one man, much more will those who receive the abundance of grace and the free gift of righteousness reign in life through the one man Jesus Christ.

[18]Then as one man's trespass led to condemnation for all men, so one man's act of righteousness leads to acquittal and life for all men. [19]For as by one man's disobedience many were made sinners, so by one man's obedience many will be made righteous. [20]Law came in, to increase the trespass; but where sin increased, grace abounded all the more, [21]so that, as sin reigned in death, grace also might reign through righteousness to eternal life through Jesus Christ our Lord.

Rom 8:1–8 (§29)

[1]There is therefore now no condemnation for those who are in Christ Jesus. [2]For the law of the Spirit of life in Christ Jesus has set me free from the law of sin and death. [3]For God has done what the law, weakened by the flesh, could not do: sending his own Son in the likeness of sinful flesh and for sin, he condemned sin in the flesh, [4]in order that the just requirement of the law might be fulfilled in us, who walk not according to the flesh but according to the Spirit. [5]For those who live according to the flesh set their minds on the things of the flesh, but those who live according to the Spirit set their minds on the things of the Spirit. [6]To set the mind on the flesh is death, but to set the mind on the Spirit is life and peace. [7]For the

mind that is set on the flesh is hostile to God; it does not submit to God's law, indeed it cannot; [8]and those who are in the flesh cannot please God.

Rom 9:1–5 (§35)

[1]I am speaking the truth in Christ, I am not lying; my conscience bears me witness in the Holy Spirit, [2]that I have great sorrow and unceasing anguish in my heart. [3]For I could wish that I myself were accursed and cut off from Christ for the sake of my brethren, my kinsmen by race. [4]They are Israelites, and to them belong the sonship, the glory, the covenants, the giving of the law, the worship, and the promises; [5]to them belong the patriarchs, and of their race, according to the flesh, is the Christ. God who is over all be blessed for ever. Amen.

Rom 15:7–13 (§61)

[7]Welcome one another, therefore, as Christ has welcomed you, for the glory of God. [8]For I tell you that Christ became a servant to the circumcised to show God's truthfulness, in order to confirm the promises given to the patriarchs, [9]and in order that the Gentiles might glorify God for his mercy. As it is written,

"Therefore I will praise thee among the Gentiles,
and sing to thy name";
[10]and again it is said,
"Rejoice, O Gentiles, with his peoples";
[11]and again,
"Praise the Lord, all Gentiles,
and let all the peoples praise him";
[12]and further Isaiah says,
"The root of Jesse shall come,
he who rises to rule the Gentiles;
in him shall the Gentiles hope."
[13]May the God of hope fill you with all joy and peace in believing, so that by the power of the Holy Spirit you may abound in hope.

2 Cor 5:14–21 (§164)

[14]For the love of Christ controls us, because we are convinced that one has died for all; therefore all have died. [15]And he died for all, that those who live might live no longer for themselves but for him who for their sake died and was raised.

[16]From now on, therefore, we regard no one

● **2 Cor 3:7–11**

Rom 1   [18]For the wrath of God is revealed from heaven against all ungodliness and wickedness of men who by their wickedness suppress the truth. [19]For what can be known about God is plain to them, because God has shown it to them. [20]Ever since the creation of the world his invisible nature, namely, his eternal power and deity, has been clearly perceived in the things that have been made. So they are without excuse; [21]for although they knew God they did not honor him as God or give thanks to him, but they became futile in their thinking and their senseless minds were darkened. [22]Claiming to be wise, they became fools, [23]and exchanged the glory of the immortal God for images resembling mortal man or birds or animals or reptiles.

Rom 9   [22]What if God, desiring to show his wrath and to make known his power, has endured with much patience the vessels of wrath made for destruction, [23]in order to make known the riches of his glory for the vessels of mercy, which he has prepared beforehand for glory, . . .

1 Cor 15   [40]There are celestial bodies and there are

from a human point of view; even though we once regarded Christ from a human point of view, we regard him thus no longer. [17]Therefore, if any one is in Christ, he is a new creation; the old has passed away, behold, the new has come. [18]All this is from God, who through Christ reconciled us to himself and gave us the ministry of reconciliation; [19]that is, in Christ God was reconciling the world to himself, not counting their trespasses against them, and entrusting to us the message of reconciliation. [20]So we are ambassadors for Christ, God making his appeal through us. We beseech you on behalf of Christ, be reconciled to God. [21]For our sake he made him to be sin who knew no sin, so that in him we might become the righteousness of God.

Gal 3:6–18 (§201–203)

[6]Thus Abraham "believed God, and it was reckoned to him as righteousness." [7]So you see that it is men of faith who are the sons of Abraham. [8]And the scripture, foreseeing that God would justify the Gentiles by faith, preached the gospel beforehand to Abraham, saying, "In you shall all the nations be blessed." [9]So then, those who are men of faith are blessed with Abraham who had faith.

[10]For all who rely on works of the law are under a curse; for it is written, "Cursed be every one who does not abide by all things written in the book of the law, and do them." [11]Now it is evident that no man is justified before God by the law; for "He who through faith is righteous shall live"; [12]but the law does not rest on faith, for "He who does them shall live by them." [13]Christ redeemed us from the curse of the law, having become a curse for us—for it is written, "Cursed be every one who hangs on a tree"— [14]that in Christ Jesus the blessing of Abraham might come upon the Gentiles, that we might receive the promise of the Spirit through faith.

[15]To give a human example, brethren: no one annuls even a man's will, or adds to it, once it has been ratified. [16]Now the promises were made to Abraham and to his offspring. It does not say, "And to offsprings," referring to many; but, referring to one, "And to your offspring," which is Christ. [17]This is what I mean: the law, which came four hundred and thirty years afterward, does not annul a covenant previously ratified by God, so as to make the promise

void. [18]For if the inheritance is by the law, it is no longer by promise; but God gave it to Abraham by a promise.

Gal 3:21–25 (§205)

[21]Is the law then against the promises of God? Certainly not; for if a law had been given which could make alive, then righteousness would indeed be by the law. [22]But the scripture consigned all things to sin, that what was promised to faith in Jesus Christ might be given to those who believe.

[23]Now before faith came, we were confined under the law, kept under restraint until faith should be revealed. [24]So that the law was our custodian until Christ came, that we might be justified by faith. [25]But now that faith has come, we are no longer under a custodian;

Eph 2:11–22 (§221)

[11]Therefore remember that at one time you Gentiles in the flesh, called the uncircumcision by what is called the circumcision, which is made in the flesh by hands— [12]remember that you were at that time separated from Christ, alienated from the commonwealth of Israel, and strangers to the covenants of promise, having no hope and without God in the world. [13]But now in Christ Jesus you who once were far off have been brought near in the blood of Christ. [14]For he is our peace, who has made us both one, and has broken down the dividing wall of hostility, [15]by abolishing in his flesh the law of commandments and ordinances, that he might create in himself one new man in place of the two, so making peace, [16]and might reconcile us both to God in one body through the cross, thereby bringing the hostility to an end. [17]And he came and preached peace to you who were far off and peace to those who were near; [18]for through him we both have access in one Spirit to the Father. [19]So then you are no longer strangers and sojourners, but you are fellow citizens with the saints and members of the household of God, [20]built upon the foundation of the apostles and prophets, Christ Jesus himself being the cornerstone, [21]in whom the whole structure is joined together and grows into a holy temple in the Lord; [22]in whom you also are built into it for a dwelling place of God in the Spirit.

Phil 3:2–11 (§247)

[2]Look out for the dogs, look out for the evilworkers, look out for those who mutilate the flesh. [3]For we are the true circumcision, who worship God in spirit, and glory in Christ Jesus, and put no confidence in the flesh. [4]Though I myself have reason for confidence in the flesh also. If any other man thinks he has reason for confidence in the flesh, I have more: [5]circumcised on the eighth day, of the people of Israel, of the tribe of Benjamin, a Hebrew born of Hebrews; as to the law a Pharisee, [6]as to zeal a persecutor of the church, as to righteousness under the law blameless. [7]But whatever gain I had, I counted as loss for the sake of Christ. [8]Indeed I count everything as loss because of the surpassing worth of knowing Christ Jesus my Lord. For his sake I have suffered the loss of all things, and count them as refuse, in order that I may gain Christ [9]and be found in him, not having a righteousness of my own, based on law, but that which is through faith in Christ, the righteousness from God that depends on faith; [10]that I may know him and the power of his resurrection, and may share his sufferings, becoming like him in his death, [11]that if possible I may attain the resurrection from the dead.

Col 1:21–23 (§259)

[21]And you, who once were estranged and hostile in mind, doing evil deeds, [22]he has now reconciled in his body of flesh by his death, in order to present you holy and blameless and irreproachable before him, [23]provided that you continue in the faith, stable and steadfast, not shifting from the hope of the gospel which you heard, which has been preached to every creature under heaven, and of which I, Paul, became a minister.

---

terrestrial bodies; but the glory of the celestial is one, and the glory of the terrestrial is another. [41]There is one glory of the sun, and another glory of the moon, and another glory of the stars; for star differs from star in glory.

● **2 Cor 3:7**

Exod 34   [29]When Moses came down from Mount Sinai, with the two tables of the testimony in his hand

as he came down from the mountain, Moses did not know that the skin of his face shone because he had been talking with God. [30]And when Aaron and all the people of Israel saw Moses, behold, the skin of his face shone, and they were afraid to come near him. [31]But Moses called to them; and Aaron and all the leaders of the congregation returned to him, and Moses talked with them. [32]And afterward all the people of Israel came near, and he gave them in commandment all

that the Lord had spoken with him in Mount Sinai. [33]And when Moses had finished speaking with them, he put a veil on his face; [34]but whenever Moses went in before the Lord to speak with him, he took the veil off, until he came out; and when he came out, and told the people of Israel what he was commanded, [35]the people of Israel saw the face of Moses, that the skin of Moses' face shone; and Moses would put the veil upon his face again, until he went in to speak with him.

¹²Since we have such a hope, we are very bold, ¹³not like Moses, who put a veil over his face so that the Israelites might not see the end of the fading splendor. ¹⁴But their minds were hardened; for to this day, when they read the old covenant, that same veil remains unlifted, because only through Christ is it taken away. ¹⁵Yes, to this day whenever Moses is read a veil lies over their minds; ¹⁶but when a man turns to the Lord the veil is removed. ¹⁷Now the Lord is the Spirit, and where the Spirit of the Lord is, there is freedom. ¹⁸And we all, with unveiled face, beholding the glory of the Lord, are being changed into his likeness from one degree of glory to another; for this comes from the Lord who is the Spirit.

PRIMARY

Rom 7:1–6 (§26)

¹Do you not know, brethren—for I am speaking to those who know the law—that the law is binding on a person only during his life? ²Thus a married woman is bound by law to her husband as long as he lives; but if her husband dies she is discharged from the law concerning the husband. ³Accordingly, she will be called an adulteress if she lives with another man while her husband is alive. But if her husband dies she is free from that law, and if she marries another man she is not an adulteress. ⁴Likewise, my brethren, you have died to the law through the body of Christ, so that you may belong to another, to him who has been raised from the dead in order that we may bear fruit for God. ⁵While we were living in the flesh, our sinful passions, aroused by the law, were at work in our members to bear fruit for death. ⁶But now we are discharged from the law, dead to that which held us captive, so that we serve not under the old written code but in the new life of the Spirit.

Rom 9:30–33 (§39)

³⁰What shall we say, then? That Gentiles who did not pursue righteousness have attained it, that is, righteousness through faith; ³¹but that Israel who pursued the righteousness which is based on law did not succeed in fulfilling that law. ³²Why? Because they did not pursue it through faith, but as if it were based on works. They have stumbled over the stumbling stone, ³³as it is written,

"Behold, I am laying in Zion a stone that will make men stumble,

a rock that will make them fall;

and he who believes in him will not be put to shame."

Rom 10:1–4 (§40)

¹Brethren, my heart's desire and prayer to God for them is that they may be saved. ²I bear them witness that they have a zeal for God, but it is not enlightened. ³For, being ignorant of the righteousness that comes from God, and seeking to establish their own, they did not submit to God's righteousness. ⁴For Christ is the end of the law, that every one who has faith may be justified.

Rom 11:7–10 (§45)

⁷What then? Israel failed to obtain what it sought. The elect obtained it, but the rest were hardened, ⁸as it is written,

"God gave them a spirit of stupor,

eyes that should not see and ears that should not hear,

down to this very day."

⁹And David says,

"Let their table become a snare and a trap,

a pitfall and a retribution for them;

¹⁰let their eyes be darkened so that they cannot see,

and bend their backs for ever."

Gal 3:21–25 (§205)

²¹Is the law then against the promises of God? Certainly not; for if a law had been given which could make alive, then righteousness would indeed be by the law. ²²But the scripture consigned all things to sin, that what was promised to faith in Jesus Christ might be given to those who believe.

²³Now before faith came, we were confined under the law, kept under restraint until faith should be revealed. ²⁴So that the law was our custodian until Christ came, that we might be justified by faith. ²⁵But now that faith has come, we are no longer under a custodian; . . .

Gal 4:21–31 (§210)

²¹Tell me, you who desire to be under law, do you not hear the law? ²²For it is written that Abraham had two sons, one by a slave and one by a free woman. ²³But the son of the slave was born according to the flesh, the son of the free woman through promise. ²⁴Now this is an allegory: these women are two covenants. One is

from Mount Sinai, bearing children for slavery; she is Hagar. ²⁵Now Hagar is Mount Sinai in Arabia; she corresponds to the present Jerusalem, for she is in slavery with her children. ²⁶But the Jerusalem above is free, and she is our mother. ²⁷For it is written,

"Rejoice, O barren one who does not bear;

break forth and shout, you who are not in travail;

for the children of the desolate one are many more

than the children of her that is married."

²⁸Now we, brethren, like Isaac, are children of promise. ²⁹But as at that time he who was born according to the flesh persecuted him who was born according to the Spirit, so it is now. ³⁰But what does the scripture say? "Cast out the slave and her son; for the son of the slave shall not inherit with the son of the free woman." ³¹So, brethren, we are not children of the slave but of the free woman.

Phil 3:2–11 (§247)

²Look out for the dogs, look out for the evilworkers, look out for those who mutilate the flesh. ³For we are the true circumcision, who worship God in spirit, and glory in Christ Jesus, and put no confidence in the flesh. ⁴Though I myself have reason for confidence in the flesh also. If any other man thinks he has reason for confidence in the flesh, I have more: ⁵circumcised on the eighth day, of the people of Israel, of the tribe of Benjamin, a Hebrew born of Hebrews; as to the law a Pharisee, ⁶as to zeal a persecutor of the church, as to righteousness under the law blameless. ⁷But whatever gain I had, I counted as loss for the sake of Christ. ⁸Indeed I count everything as loss because of the surpassing worth of knowing Christ Jesus my Lord. For his sake I have suffered the loss of all things, and count them as refuse, in order that I may gain Christ ⁹and be found in him, not having a righteousness of my own, based on law, but that which is through faith in Christ, the righteousness from God that depends on faith; ¹⁰that I may know him and the power of his resurrection, and may share his sufferings, becoming like him in his death, ¹¹that if possible I may attain the resurrection from the dead.

● 2 Cor 3:12

Acts 4   ¹³Now when they saw the boldness of Peter and John, and perceived that they were uneducated, common men, they wondered; and they recognized that they had been with Jesus.

● 2 Cor 3:14

Rom 9   ¹⁸So then he has mercy upon whomever he wills, and he hardens the heart of whomever he wills.

Rom 11   ²⁵Lest you be wise in your own conceits, I want you to understand this mystery, brethren: a hardening has come upon part of Israel, until the full number of the Gentiles come in, . . .

Eph 3   ⁴When you read this you can perceive my insight into the mystery of Christ, ⁵which was not made known to the sons of men in other generations as it has now been revealed to his holy apostles and prophets by the Spirit; . . .

● 2 Cor 3:15

Acts 15   ²¹"For from early generations Moses has had in every city those who preach him, for he is read every sabbath in the synagogues."

● 2 Cor 3:17

Gal 5   ¹For freedom Christ has set us free; stand fast therefore, and do not submit again to a yoke of slavery.

● 2 Cor 3:18

1 Cor 6   ¹⁷But he who is united to the Lord becomes one spirit with him.

3. The Jerusalem Conference (Galatians 2) = Acts 15 = Acts 11:30

Date
30–32   Paul's conversion
32–34   Paul's first Jerusalem visit
45/45   Paul's conference visit   Gal 2:1–10 = Acts 15/11:30
46   Mission Cyprus and Asia Minor
46/47   Quarrel with Barnabas   Gal 2:13
47–51   Mission to Macedonia and Achaia
        1 Thessalonians
52–58   Mission in Galatia, Phrygia, and Asia; collection journey
        Galatians
        Letters to the Corinthians
        Romans
58   Arrest in Jerusalem and Caesarean imprisonment
        Philemon
60   Journey to Rome
60–   Roman imprisonment
        ?Philippians

A. J. M. Wedderburn, "Keeping up with Recent Studies, VIII, Some Recent Pauline Chronologies,"
    Expository Times (January, 1981), 107. Summary prepared by John A. Darr and published in: Daniel Patte,
    Paul's Faith and the Power of the Gospel (Philadelphia: Fortress Press, 1983), 352–60. Reprinted by
    permission of the publisher.
See pages 67, 141, 207, 223 for other versions of the Pauline chronology.

4 Therefore, having this ministry by the mercy of God, we do not lose heart. [2]We have renounced disgraceful, underhanded ways; we refuse to practice cunning or to tamper with God's word, but by the open statement of the truth we would commend ourselves to every man's conscience in the sight of God. [3]And even if our gospel is veiled, it is veiled only to those who are perishing. [4]In their case the god of this world has blinded the minds of the unbelievers, to keep them from seeing the light of the gospel of the glory of Christ, who is the likeness of God. [5]For what we preach is not ourselves, but Jesus Christ as Lord, with ourselves as your servants for Jesus' sake. [6]For it is the God who said, "Let light shine out of darkness," who has shone in our hearts to give the light of the knowledge of the glory of God in the face of Christ.

PRIMARY

Rom 1:1–7 (§1)

[1]Paul, a servant of Jesus Christ, called to be an apostle, set apart for the gospel of God [2]which he promised beforehand through his prophets in the holy scriptures, [3]the gospel concerning his Son, who was descended from David according to the flesh [4]and designated Son of God in power according to the Spirit of holiness by his resurrection from the dead, Jesus Christ our Lord, [5]through whom we have received grace and apostleship to bring about the obedience of faith for the sake of his name among all the nations, [6]including yourselves who are called to belong to Jesus Christ;

[7]To all God's beloved in Rome, who are called to be saints:

Grace to you and peace from God our Father and the Lord Jesus Christ.

Rom 10:14–17 (§42)

[14]But how are men to call upon him in whom they have not believed? And how are they to believe in him of whom they have never heard? And how are they to hear without a preacher? [15]And how can men preach unless they are sent? As it is written, "How beautiful are the feet of those who preach good news!" [16]But they have not all obeyed the gospel; for Isaiah says, "Lord, who has believed what he has heard from us?" [17]So faith comes from what is heard, and what is heard comes by the preaching of Christ.

Rom 15:14–21 (§62)

[14]I myself am satisfied about you, my brethren, that you yourselves are full of goodness, filled with all knowledge, and able to instruct one another. [15]But on some points I have written to you very boldly by way of reminder, because of the grace given me by God [16]to be a minister of Christ Jesus to the Gentiles in the priestly service of the gospel of God, so that the offering of the Gentiles may be acceptable, sanctified by the Holy Spirit. [17]In Christ Jesus, then, I have reason to be proud of my work for God. [18]For I will not venture to speak of anything except what Christ has wrought through me to win obedience from the Gentiles, by word and deed, [19]by the power of signs and wonders, by the power of the Holy Spirit, so that from Jerusalem and as far round as Illyricum I have fully preached the gospel of Christ, [20]thus making it my ambition to preach the gospel, not where Christ has already been named, lest I build on another man's foundation, [21]but as it is written,

"They shall see who have never been told of him,

and they shall understand who have never heard of him."

1 Cor 2:1–5 (§76)

[1]When I came to you, brethren, I did not come proclaiming to you the testimony of God in lofty words or wisdom. [2]For I decided to know nothing among you except Jesus Christ and him crucified. [3]And I was with you in weakness and in much fear and trembling; [4]and my speech and my message were not in plausible words of wisdom, but in demonstration of the Spirit and of power, [5]that your faith might not rest in the wisdom of men but in the power of God.

Gal 6:11–17 (§216)

[11]See with what large letters I am writing to you with my own hand. [12]It is those who want to make a good showing in the flesh that would compel you to be circumcised, and only in order that they may not be persecuted for the cross of Christ. [13]For even those who receive circumcision do not themselves keep the law, but they desire to have you circumcised that they may glory in your flesh. [14]But far be it from me to glory except in the cross of our Lord Jesus Christ, by which the world has been crucified to me, and I to the world. [15]For neither circumcision counts for anything, nor uncircumcision, but a new creation. [16]Peace

---

● **2 Cor 4:1**

1 Cor 7　[25]Now concerning the unmarried, I have no command of the Lord, but I give my opinion as one who by the Lord's mercy is trustworthy.

● **2 Cor 4:3**

1 Cor 1　[18]For the word of the cross is folly to those who are perishing, but to us who are being saved it is the power of God.

● **2 Cor 4:4–6**

Col 1　[15]He is the image of the invisible God, the first-born of all creation; [16]for in him all things were created, in heaven and on earth, visible and invisible, whether thrones or dominions or principalities or authorities—all things were created through him and for him.

● **2 Cor 4:4**

Rom 11　[7]What then? Israel failed to obtain what it sought. The elect obtained it, but the rest were har-

and mercy be upon all who walk by this rule, upon the Israel of God.

[17] Henceforth let no man trouble me; for I bear on my body the marks of Jesus.

Eph 3:1–13 (§222)

[1] For this reason I, Paul, a prisoner for Christ Jesus on behalf of you Gentiles— [2] assuming that you have heard of the stewardship of God's grace that was given to me for you, [3] how the mystery was made known to me by revelation, as I have written briefly. [4] When you read this you can perceive my insight into the mystery of Christ, [5] which was not made known to the sons of men in other generations as it has now been revealed to his holy apostles and prophets by the Spirit; [6] that is, how the Gentiles are fellow heirs, members of the same body, and partakers of the promise in Christ Jesus through the gospel.

[7] Of this gospel I was made a minister according to the gift of God's grace which was given me by the working of his power. [8] To me, though I am the very least of all the saints, this grace was given, to preach to the Gentiles the unsearchable riches of Christ, [9] and to make all men see what is the plan of the mystery hidden for ages in God who created all things; [10] that through the church the manifold wisdom of God might now be made known to the principalities and powers in the heavenly places. [11] This was according to the eternal purpose which he has realized in Christ Jesus our Lord, [12] in whom we have boldness and confidence of access through our faith in him. [13] So I ask you not to lose heart over what I am suffering for you, which is your glory.

Phil 1:12–18 (§239)

[12] I want you to know, brethren, that what has happened to me has really served to advance the gospel, [13] so that it has become known throughout the whole praetorian guard and to all the rest that my imprisonment is for Christ; [14] and most of the brethren have been made confident in the Lord because of my imprisonment, and are much more bold to speak the word of God without fear.

[15] Some indeed preach Christ from envy and rivalry, but others from good will. [16] The latter do it out of love, knowing that I am put here for the defense of the gospel; [17] the former proclaim Christ out of partisanship, not sincerely but thinking to afflict me in my imprisonment. [18] What then? Only that in every way, whether in pretense or in truth, Christ is proclaimed; and in that I rejoice.

Col 1:24–2:3 (§260)

[24] Now I rejoice in my sufferings for your sake, and in my flesh I complete what is lacking in Christ's afflictions for the sake of his body, that is, the church, [25] of which I became a minister according to the divine office which was given to me for you, to make the word of God fully known, [26] the mystery hidden for ages and generations but now made manifest to his saints. [27] To them God chose to make known how great among the Gentiles are the riches of the glory of this mystery, which is Christ in you, the hope of glory. [28] Him we proclaim warning every man and teaching every man in all wisdom, that we may present every man mature in Christ. [29] For this I toil, striving with all the energy which he mightily inspires within me.

2 [1] For I want you to know how greatly I strive for you, and for those at Laodicea, and for all who have not seen my face, [2] that their hearts may be encouraged as they are knit together in love, to have all the riches of assured understanding and the knowledge of God's mystery, of Christ, [3] in whom are hid all the treasures of wisdom and knowledge.

1 Thess 2:1–8 (§277)

[1] For you yourselves know, brethren, that our visit to you was not in vain; [2] but though we had already suffered and been shamefully treated at Philippi, as you know, we had courage in our God to declare to you the gospel of God in the face of great opposition. [3] For our appeal does not spring from error or uncleanness, nor is it made with guile; [4] but just as we have been approved by God to be entrusted with the gospel, so we speak, not to please men, but to please God who tests our hearts. [5] For we never used either words of flattery, as you know, or a cloak for greed, as God is witness; [6] nor did we seek glory from men, whether from you or from others, though we might have made demands as apostles of Christ. [7] But we were gentle among you, like a nurse taking care of her children. [8] So, being affectionately desirous of you, we were ready to share with you not only the gospel of God but also our own selves, because you had become very dear to us.

---

dened, [8] as it is written,

> "God gave them a spirit of stupor,
> eyes that should not see and ears that should not hear,
> down to this very day."

[9] And David says,

> "Let their table become a snare and a trap,

a pitfall and a retribution for them;
[10] let their eyes be darkened so that they cannot see, and bend their backs for ever."

Eph 2   [1] And you he made alive, when you were dead through the trespasses and sins [2] in which you once walked, following the course of this world, following the prince of the power of the air, the spirit that is now at work in the sons of disobedience.

2 Thess 2   [11] Therefore God sends upon them a strong delusion, to make them believe what is false, [12] so that all may be condemned who did not believe the truth but had pleasure in unrighteousness.

FORMAL ELEMENT: HARDSHIPS LIST

7But we have this treasure in earthen vessels, to show that the transcendent power belongs to God and not to us. 8We are afflicted in every way, but not crushed; perplexed, but not driven to despair; 9persecuted, but not forsaken; struck down, but not destroyed; 10always carrying in the body the death of Jesus, so that the life of Jesus may also be manifested in our bodies. 11For while we live we are always being given up to death for Jesus' sake, so that the life of Jesus may be manifested in our mortal flesh. 12So death is at work in us, but life in you.

PRIMARY

Rom 8:31–39 (§34)

31What then shall we say to this? If God is for us, who is against us? 32He who did not spare his own Son but gave him up for us all, will he not also give us all things with him? 33Who shall bring any charge against God's elect? It is God who justifies; 34who is to condemn? Is it Christ Jesus, who died, yes, who was raised from the dead, who is at the right hand of God, who indeed intercedes for us? 35Who shall separate us from the love of Christ? Shall tribulation, or distress, or persecution, or famine, or nakedness, or peril, or sword? 36As it is written,

"For thy sake we are being killed all the day long;

we are regarded as sheep to be slaughtered."

37No, in all these things we are more than conquerors through him who loved us. 38For I am sure that neither death, nor life, nor angels, nor principalities, nor things present, nor things to come, nor powers, 39nor height, nor depth, nor anything else in all creation, will be able to separate us from the love of God in Christ Jesus our Lord.

1 Cor 4:8–13 (§85)

8Already you are filled! Already you have become rich! Without us you have become kings! And would that you did reign, so that we might share the rule with you! 9For I think that God has exhibited us apostles as last of all, like men sentenced to death; because we have become a spectacle to the world, to angels and to men. 10We are fools for Christ's sake, but you are wise in Christ. We are weak, but you are strong. You are held in honor, but we in disrepute. 11To the present hour we hunger and thirst, we are ill-clad and buffeted and homeless, 12and we labor, working with our own hands. When reviled, we bless; when persecuted, we endure; 13when slandered, we try to conciliate; we have become, and are now, as the refuse of the world, the off-scouring of all things.

SECONDARY

Rom 5:1–5 (§20)

1Therefore, since we are justified by faith, we have peace with God through our Lord Jesus Christ. 2Through him we have obtained access to this grace in which we stand, and we rejoice in our hope of sharing the glory of God. 3More than that, we rejoice in our sufferings, knowing that suffering produces endurance, 4and endurance produces character, and character produces hope, 5and hope does not disappoint us, because God's love has been poured into our hearts through the Holy Spirit which has been given to us.

Phil 1:12–18 (§239)

12I want you to know, brethren, that what has happened to me has really served to advance the gospel, 13so that it has become known throughout the whole praetorian guard and to all the rest that my imprisonment is for Christ;

● **2 Cor 4:7–12**

2 Cor 6 1Working together with him, then, we entreat you not to accept the grace of God in vain. 2For he says,

"At the acceptable time I have listened to you,
and helped you on the day of salvation."

Behold, now is the acceptable time; behold, now is the day of salvation. 3We put no obstacle in any one's way, so that no fault may be found with our ministry, 4but as servants of God we commend ourselves in every way: through great endurance, in afflictions, hardships, calamities, 5beatings, imprisonments, tumults, labors, watching, hunger; 6by purity, knowledge, forbearance, kindness, the Holy Spirit, genuine love, 7truthful speech, and the power of God; with the weapons of righteousness for the right hand and for the left; 8in honor and dishonor, in ill repute and good repute. We are treated as impostors, and yet are true; 9as unknown, and yet well known; as dying, and behold we live; as punished, and yet not killed; 10as sorrowful, yet always rejoicing; as poor, yet making many rich; as having nothing, and yet possessing everything.

2 Cor 11 21. . . But whatever any one dares to boast of—I am speaking as a fool—I also dare to boast of that. 22Are they Hebrews? So am I. Are they Israelites? So am I. Are they descendants of Abraham? So am I. 23Are they servants of Christ? I am a better one—I am talking like a madman—with far greater labors, far more imprisonments, with countless beatings, and often near death. 24Five times I have received at the hands of the Jews the forty lashes less one. 25Three times I have been beaten with rods; once I was stoned. Three times I have been shipwrecked; a night and a day I have been adrift at sea; 26on frequent journeys, in danger from rivers, danger from robbers, danger from my own people, danger from Gentiles, danger in the city, danger in the wilderness, danger at sea, danger from false brethren; 27in toil and hardship, through many a sleepless night, in hunger and thirst, often without food, in cold and exposure. 28And, apart from other things, there is the daily pressure upon me of my anxiety for all the churches. 29Who is weak, and I am not weak? Who is made to fall, and I am not indignant?

[14]and most of the brethren have been made confident in the Lord because of my imprisonment, and are much more bold to speak the word of God without fear.

[15]Some indeed preach Christ from envy and rivalry, but others from good will. [16]The latter do it out of love, knowing that I am put here for the defense of the gospel; [17]the former proclaim Christ out of partisanship, not sincerely but thinking to afflict me in my imprisonment. [18]What then? Only that in every way, whether in pretense or in truth, Christ is proclaimed; and in that I rejoice.

Phil 1:19–26 (§240)

[19]Yes, and I shall rejoice. For I know that through your prayers and the help of the Spirit of Jesus Christ this will turn out for my deliverance, [20]as it is my eager expectation and hope that I shall not be at all ashamed, but that with full courage now as always Christ will be honored in my body, whether by life or by death. [21]For to me to live is Christ, and to die is gain. [22]If it is to be life in the flesh, that means fruitful labor for me. Yet which I shall choose I cannot tell. [23]I am hard pressed between the two. My desire is to depart and be with Christ, for that is far better. [24]But to remain in the flesh is more necessary on your account. [25]Con-vinced of this, I know that I shall remain and continue with you all, for your progress and joy in the faith, [26]so that in me you may have ample cause to glory in Christ Jesus, because of my coming to you again.

Phil 4:10–20 (§253)

[10]I rejoice in the Lord greatly that now at length you have revived your concern for me; you were indeed concerned for me, but you had no opportunity. [11]Not that I complain of want; for I have learned, in whatever state I am, to be content. [12]I know how to be abased, and I know how to abound; in any and all circumstances I have learned the secret of facing plenty and hunger, abundance and want. [13]I can do all things in him who strengthens me.

[14]Yet it was kind of you to share my trouble. [15]And you Philippians yourselves know that in the beginning of the gospel, when I left Macedonia, no church entered into partnership with me in giving and receiving except you only; [16]for even in Thessalonica you sent me help once and again. [17]Not that I seek the gift; but I seek the fruit which increases to your credit. [18]I have received full payment, and more; I am filled, having received from Epaphroditus the gifts you sent, a fragrant offering, a sacrifice acceptable and pleasing to God. [19]And my God will supply every need of yours according to his riches in glory in Christ Jesus. [20]To our God and Father be glory for ever and ever. Amen.

1 Thess 2:1–8 (§277)

[1]For you yourselves know, brethren, that our visit to you was not in vain; [2]but though we had already suffered and been shamefully treated at Philippi, as you know, we had courage in our God to declare to you the gospel of God in the face of great opposition. [3]For our appeal does not spring from error or uncleanness, nor is it made with guile; [4]but just as we have been approved by God to be entrusted with the gospel, so we speak, not to please men, but to please God who tests our hearts. [5]For we never used either words of flattery, as you know, or a cloak for greed, as God is witness; [6]nor did we seek glory from men, whether from you or from others, though we might have made demands as apostles of Christ. [7]But we were gentle among you, like a nurse taking care of her children. [8]So, being affectionately desirous of you, we were ready to share with you not only the gospel of God but also our own selves, because you had become very dear to us.

---

2 Cor 12   [10]For the sake of Christ, then, I am content with weaknesses, insults, hardships, persecutions, and calamities; for when I am weak, then I am strong.

Phil 3   [10]that I may know him and the power of his resurrection, and may share his sufferings, becoming like him in his death, [11]that if possible I may attain the resurrection from the dead.

● **2 Cor 4:7**
2 Tim 2   [20]In a great house there are not only vessels of gold and silver but also of wood and earthenware, and some for noble use, some for ignoble.

● **2 Cor 4:8**
2 Cor 1   [8]For we do not want you to be ignorant, brethren, of the affliction we experienced in Asia; for we were so utterly, unbearably crushed that we de-spaired of life itself. [9]Why, we felt that we had received the sentence of death; but that was to make us rely not on ourselves but on God who raises the dead; [10]he delivered us from so deadly a peril, and he will deliver us; on him we have set our hope that he will deliver us again.

● **2 Cor 4:10**
1 Cor 15   [31]I protest, brethren, by my pride in you which I have in Christ Jesus our Lord, I die every day!

Col 1   [24]Now I rejoice in my sufferings for your sake, and in my flesh I complete what is lacking in Christ's afflictions for the sake of his body, that is, the church, . . .

● **2 Cor 4:11**
Phil 3   [21]who will change our lowly body to be like his glorious body, by the power which enables him even to subject all things to himself.

¹³Since we have the same spirit of faith as he had who wrote, "I believed, and so I spoke," we too believe, and so we speak, ¹⁴knowing that he who raised the Lord Jesus will raise us also with Jesus and bring us with you into his presence. ¹⁵For it is all for your sake, so that as grace extends to more and more people it may increase thanksgiving, to the glory of God.

PRIMARY

Rom 6:1–10 (§23)

¹What shall we say then? Are we to continue in sin that grace may abound? ²By no means! How can we who died to sin still live in it? ³Do you not know that all of us who have been baptized into Christ Jesus were baptized into his death? ⁴We were buried therefore with him by baptism into death, so that as Christ was raised from the dead by the glory of the Father, we too might walk in newness of life.

⁵For if we have been united with him in a death like his, we shall certainly be united with him in a resurrection like his. ⁶We know that our old self was crucified with him so that the sinful body might be destroyed, and we might no longer be enslaved to sin. ⁷For he who has died is freed from sin. ⁸But if we have died with Christ, we believe that we shall also live with him. ⁹For we know that Christ being raised from the dead will never die again; death no longer has dominion over him. ¹⁰The death he died he died to sin, once for all, but the life he lives he lives to God.

1 Cor 15:12–19 (§132)

¹²Now if Christ is preached as raised from the dead, how can some of you say that there is no resurrection of the dead? ¹³But if there is no resurrection of the dead, then Christ has not been raised; ¹⁴if Christ has not been raised, then our preaching is in vain and your faith is in vain. ¹⁵We are even found to be misrepresenting God, because we testified of God that he raised Christ, whom he did not raise if it is true that the dead are not raised. ¹⁶For if the dead are not raised, then Christ has not been raised. ¹⁷If Christ has not been raised, your

faith is futile and you are still in your sins. ¹⁸Then those also who have fallen asleep in Christ have perished. ¹⁹If for this life only we have hoped in Christ, we are of all men most to be pitied.

Gal 2:15–21 (§199)

¹⁵We ourselves, who are Jews by birth and not Gentile sinners, ¹⁶yet who know that a man is not justified by works of the law but through faith in Jesus Christ, even we have believed in Christ Jesus, in order to be justified by faith in Christ, and not by works of the law, because by works of the law shall no one be justified. ¹⁷But if, in our endeavor to be justified in Christ, we ourselves were found to be sinners, is Christ then an agent of sin? Certainly not! ¹⁸But if I build up again those things which I tore down, then I prove myself a transgressor. ¹⁹For I through the law died to the law, that I might live to God. ²⁰I have been crucified with Christ; it is no longer I who live, but Christ who lives in me; and the life I now live in the flesh I live by faith in the Son of God, who loved me and gave himself for me. ²¹I do not nullify the grace of God; for if justification were through the law, then Christ died to no purpose.

Eph 2:1–10 (§220)

¹And you he made alive, when you were dead through the trespasses and sins ²in which you once walked, following the course of this world, following the prince of the power of the air, the spirit that is now at work in the sons of disobedience. ³Among these we all once lived in the passions of our flesh, following the desires of body and mind, and so we were by nature children of wrath, like the rest of mankind. ⁴But God, who is rich in mercy, out of the great love with which he loved us, ⁵even when we were dead through our trespasses, made us alive together with Christ (by grace you have been saved), ⁶and raised us up with him, and made us sit with him in the heavenly places in Christ Jesus, ⁷that in the coming ages he might show the immeasurable riches of his grace in kindness toward us in Christ Jesus. ⁸For by grace you have been saved through faith; and this is not your own doing, it is the gift of God—

⁹not because of works, lest any man should boast. ¹⁰For we are his workmanship, created in Christ Jesus for good works, which God prepared beforehand, that we should walk in them.

Phil 3:17–21 (§249)

¹⁷Brethren, join in imitating me, and mark those who so live as you have an example in us. ¹⁸For many, of whom I have often told you and now tell you even with tears, live as enemies of the cross of Christ. ¹⁹Their end is destruction, their god is the belly, and they glory in their shame, with minds set on earthly things. ²⁰But our commonwealth is in heaven, and from it we await a Savior, the Lord Jesus Christ, ²¹who will change our lowly body to be like his glorious body, by the power which enables him even to subject all things to himself.

Col 3:1–4 (§265)

¹If then you have been raised with Christ, seek the things that are above, where Christ is, seated at the right hand of God. ²Set your minds on things that are above, not on things that are on earth. ³For you have died, and your life is hid with Christ in God. ⁴When Christ who is our life appears, then you also will appear with him in glory.

1 Thess 4:13–18 (§286)

¹³But we would not have you ignorant, brethren, concerning those who are asleep, that you may not grieve as others do who have no hope. ¹⁴For since we believe that Jesus died and rose again, even so, through Jesus, God will bring with him those who have fallen asleep. ¹⁵For this we declare to you by the word of the Lord, that we who are alive, who are left until the coming of the Lord, shall not precede those who have fallen asleep. ¹⁶For the Lord himself will descend from heaven with a cry of command, with the archangel's call, and with the sound of the trumpet of God. And the dead in Christ will rise first; ¹⁷then we who are alive, who are left, shall be caught up together with them in the clouds to meet the Lord in the air; and so we shall always be with the Lord. ¹⁸Therefore comfort one another with these words.

● **2 Cor 4:13–15**
Rom 8 　¹¹If the Spirit of him who raised Jesus from the dead dwells in you, he who raised Christ Jesus from the dead will give life to your mortal bodies also through his Spirit which dwells in you.

1 Thess 1 　⁹For they themselves report concerning us what a welcome we had among you, and how you turned to God from idols, to serve a living and true God, ¹⁰and to wait for his Son from heaven, whom he

raised from the dead, Jesus who delivers us from the wrath to come.

● **2 Cor 4:13**
Ps 116 　¹⁰I kept my faith, even when I said, "I am greatly afflicted"; . . .

● **2 Cor 4:14**
Phil 3 　¹⁰that I may know him and the power of his resurrection, and may share his sufferings, becoming

like him in his death, ¹¹that if possible I may attain the resurrection from the dead.

Col 1 　²²he has now reconciled in his body of flesh by his death, in order to present you holy and blameless and irreproachable before him, . . .

Acts 2 　²⁴"But God raised him up, having loosed the pangs of death, because it was not possible for him to be held by it."

16So we do not lose heart. Though our outer nature is wasting away, our inner nature is being renewed every day. **17**For this slight momentary affliction is preparing for us an eternal weight of glory beyond all comparison, **18**because we look not to the things that are seen but to the things that are unseen; for the things that are seen are transient, but the things that are unseen are eternal.

5 1 For we know that if the earthly tent we live in is destroyed, we have a building from God, a house not made with hands, eternal in the heavens. **2**Here indeed we groan, and long to put on our heavenly dwelling, **3**so that by putting it on we may not be found naked. **4**For while we are still in this tent, we sigh with anxiety; not that we would be unclothed, but that we would be further clothed, so that what is mortal may be swallowed up by life. **5**He who has prepared us for this very thing is God, who has given us the Spirit as a guarantee.

PRIMARY

Rom 8:18–25 (§31)

18I consider that the sufferings of this present time are not worth comparing with the glory that is to be revealed to us. **19**For the creation waits with eager longing for the revealing of the sons of God; **20**for the creation was subjected to futility, not of its own will but by the will of him who subjected it in hope; **21**because the creation itself will be set free from its bondage to decay and obtain the glorious liberty of the children of God. **22**We know that the whole creation has been groaning in travail together until now; **23**and not only the creation, but we ourselves, who have the first fruits of the Spirit, groan inwardly as we wait for adoption as sons, the redemption of our bodies. **24**For in this hope we were saved. Now hope that is seen is not hope. For who hopes for what he sees? **25**But if we hope for what we do not see, we wait for it with patience.

1 Cor 15:51–58 (§137)

51Lo! I tell you a mystery. We shall not all sleep, but we shall all be changed, **52**in a moment, in the twinkling of an eye, at the last trumpet. For the trumpet will sound, and the dead will be raised imperishable, and we shall be changed. **53**For this perishable nature must put on the imperishable, and this mortal nature must put on immortality. **54**When the perishable puts on the imperishable, and the mortal puts on immortality, then shall come to pass the saying that is written:

"Death is swallowed up in victory."
55"O death, where is thy victory?
O death, where is thy sting?" **56**The sting of death is sin, and the power of sin is the law. **57**But thanks be to God, who gives us the victory through our Lord Jesus Christ.

58Therefore, my beloved brethren, be steadfast, immovable, always abounding in the work of the Lord, knowing that in the Lord your labor is not in vain.

Eph 3:14–19 (§223)

14For this reason I bow my knees before the Father, **15**from whom every family in heaven and on earth is named, **16**that according to the riches of his glory he may grant you to be strengthened with might through his Spirit in the inner man, **17**and that Christ may dwell in your hearts through faith; that you, being rooted and grounded in love, **18**may have power to comprehend with all the saints what is the breadth and length and height and depth, **19**and to know the love of Christ which surpasses knowledge, that you may be filled with all the fulness of God.

Phil 3:17–21 (§249)

17Brethren, join in imitating me, and mark those who so live as you have an example in us. **18**For many, of whom I have often told you and now tell you even with tears, live as enemies of the cross of Christ. **19**Their end is destruction, their god is the belly, and they glory in their shame, with minds set on earthly things. **20**But our commonwealth is in heaven, and from it we await a Savior, the Lord Jesus Christ, **21**who will change our lowly body to be like his glorious body, by the power which enables him even to subject all things to himself.

Col 3:1–4 (§265)

1If then you have been raised with Christ, seek the things that are above, where Christ is, seated at the right hand of God. **2**Set your minds on things that are above, not on things that are on earth. **3**For you have died, and your life is hid with Christ in God. **4**When Christ who is our life appears, then you also will appear with him in glory.

Col 3:5–11 (§266)

5Put to death therefore what is earthly in you: fornication, impurity, passion, evil desire, and covetousness, which is idolatry. **6**On account of these the wrath of God is coming. **7**In these you once walked, when you lived in them. **8**But now put them all away: anger, wrath, malice, slander, and foul talk from your mouth. **9**Do not lie to one another, seeing that you have put off the old nature with its practices **10**and have put on the new nature, which is being renewed in knowledge after the image of its creator. **11**Here there cannot be Greek and Jew, circumcised and uncircumcised, barbarian, Scythian, slave, free man, but Christ is all, and in all.

1 Thess 4:13–18 (§286)

13But we would not have you ignorant, brethren, concerning those who are asleep, that you may not grieve as others do who have no hope. **14**For since we believe that Jesus died and rose again, even so, through Jesus, God will bring with him those who have fallen asleep. **15**For this we declare to you by the word of the Lord, that we who are alive, who are left until the coming of the Lord, shall not precede those who have fallen asleep. **16**For the Lord himself will descend from heaven with a cry of command, with the archangel's call, and with the sound of the trumpet of God. And the dead in Christ will rise first; **17**then we who are alive, who are left, shall be caught up together with them in the clouds to meet the Lord in the air; and so we shall always be with the Lord. **18**Therefore comfort one another with these words.

● **2 Cor 4:18**
Col 1   **15**He is the image of the invisible God, the first-born of all creation; **16**for in him all things were created, in heaven and on earth, visible and invisible, whether thrones or dominions or principalities or authorities—all things were created through him and for him.

● **2 Cor 5:1–2**
1 Cor 6   **15**Do you not know that your bodies are members of Christ? Shall I therefore take the members of Christ and make them members of a prostitute? Never!

1 Cor 6   **19**Do you not know that your body is a temple of the Holy Spirit within you, which you have from God? You are not your own; . . .

1 Cor 6   **16**What agreement has the temple of God with idols? For we are the temple of the living God; as God said,

"I will live in them and move among them,
and I will be their God,
and they shall be my people."

● **2 Cor 5:1**
Acts 7   **48**"Yet the Most High does not dwell in houses made with hands; as the prophet says. . . ."

● **2 Cor 5:2**
Phil 1   **23**I am hard pressed between the two. My desire is to depart and be with Christ, for that is far better. **24**But to remain in the flesh is more necessary on your account.

● **2 Cor 5:3**
Eph 6   **11**Put on the whole armor of God, that you may be able to stand against the wiles of the devil.

● **2 Cor 5:5**
Rom 8   **23**and not only the creation, but we ourselves, who have the first fruits of the Spirit, groan inwardly as we wait for adoption as sons, the redemption of our bodies.

2 Cor 1   **22**he has put his seal upon us and given us his Spirit in our hearts as a guarantee.

⁶So we are always of good courage; we know that while we are at home in the body we are away from the Lord, ⁷for we walk by faith, not by sight. ⁸We are of good courage, and we would rather be away from the body and at home with the Lord. ⁹So whether we are at home or away, we make it our aim to please him. ¹⁰For we must all appear before the judgment seat of Christ, so that each one may receive good or evil, according to what he has done in the body.

PRIMARY

Rom 2:6–16 (§8–9)
⁶For he will render to every man according to his works: ⁷to those who by patience in well-doing seek for glory and honor and immortality, he will give eternal life; ⁸but for those who are factious and do not obey the truth, but obey wickedness, there will be wrath and fury.

⁹There will be tribulation and distress for every human being who does evil, the Jew first and also the Greek, ¹⁰but glory and honor and peace for every one who does good, the Jew first and also the Greek. ¹¹For God shows no partiality.

¹²All who have sinned without the law will also perish without the law, and all who have sinned under the law will be judged by the law. ¹³For it is not the hearers of the law who are righteous before God, but the doers of the law who will be justified. ¹⁴When Gentiles who have not the law do by nature what the law requires, they are a law to themselves, even though they do not have the law. ¹⁵They show that what the law requires is written on their hearts, while their conscience also bears witness and their conflicting thoughts accuse or perhaps excuse them ¹⁶on that day when, according to my gospel, God judges the secrets of men by Christ Jesus.

Phil 1:19–26 (§240)
¹⁹Yes, and I shall rejoice. For I know that through your prayers and the help of the Spirit of Jesus Christ this will turn out for my deliverance, ²⁰as it is my eager expectation and hope that I shall not be at all ashamed, but that with full courage now as always Christ will be honored in my body, whether by life or by death. ²¹For to me to live is Christ, and to die is gain. ²²If it is to be life in the flesh, that means fruitful labor for me. Yet which I shall choose I cannot tell. ²³I am hard pressed between the two. My desire is to depart and be with Christ, for that is far better. ²⁴But to remain in the flesh is more necessary on your account. ²⁵Convinced of this, I know that I shall remain and continue with you all, for your progress and joy in the faith, ²⁶so that in me you may have ample cause to glory in Christ Jesus, because of my coming to you again.

● **2 Cor 5:6–10**
Rom 14   ¹⁰Why do you pass judgment on your brother? Or you, why do you despise your brother? For we shall all stand before the judgment seat of God; ¹¹for it is written,
"As I live, says the Lord, every knee shall bow to me, and every tongue shall give praise to God."
¹²So each of us shall give account of himself to God.

● **2 Cor 5:7**
Rom 8   ²⁴For in this hope we were saved. Now hope that is seen is not hope. For who hopes for what he sees? ²⁵But if we hope for what we do not see, we wait for it with patience.

1 Cor 13   ¹²For now we see in a mirror dimly, but then face to face. Now I know in part; then I shall understand fully, even as I have been fully understood.

● **2 Cor 5:9**
Rom 12   ¹I appeal to you therefore, brethren, by the mercies of God, to present your bodies as a living sacrifice, holy and acceptable to God, which is your spiritual worship.

Rom 14   ¹⁸he who thus serves Christ is acceptable to God and approved by men.

Gal 1   ¹⁰Am I now seeking the favor of men, or of God? Or am I trying to please men? If I were still pleasing men, I should not be a servant of Christ.

Eph 5   ¹⁰and try to learn what is pleasing to the Lord.

Col 1   ¹⁰to lead a life worthy of the Lord, fully pleasing to him, bearing fruit in every good work and increasing in the knowledge of God.

● **2 Cor 5:10**
1 Cor 3   ⁸He who plants and he who waters are equal, and each shall receive his wages according to his labor.

Eph 6   ⁸knowing that whatever good any one does, he will receive the same again from the Lord, whether he is a slave or free.

Acts 10   ⁴²"And he commanded us to preach to the people, and to testify that he is the one ordained by God to be judge of the living and the dead."

¹¹**Therefore, knowing the fear of the Lord, we persuade men; but what we are is known to God, and I hope it is known also to your conscience.** ¹²**We are not commending ourselves to you again but giving you cause to be proud of us, so that you may be able to answer those who pride themselves on a man's position and not on his heart.** ¹³**For if we are beside ourselves, it is for God; if we are in our right mind, it is for you.**

PRIMARY

1 Cor 4:1–5 (§83)

¹This is how one should regard us, as servants of Christ and stewards of the mysteries of God. ²Moreover it is required of stewards that they be found trustworthy. ³But with me it is a very small thing that I should be judged by you or by any human court. I do not even judge myself. ⁴I am not aware of anything against myself, but I am not thereby acquitted. It is the Lord who judges me. ⁵Therefore do not pronounce judgment before the time, before the Lord comes, who will bring to light the things now hidden in darkness and will disclose the purposes of the heart. Then every man will receive his commendation from God.

Eph 3:1–13 (§222)

¹For this reason I, Paul, a prisoner for Christ Jesus on behalf of you Gentiles— ²assuming that you have heard of the stewardship of God's grace that was given to me for you, ³how the mystery was made known to me by revelation, as I have written briefly. ⁴When you read this you can perceive my insight into the mystery of Christ, ⁵which was not made known to the sons of men in other generations as it has now been revealed to his holy apostles and prophets by the Spirit; ⁶that is, how the Gentiles are fellow heirs, members of the same body, and partakers of the promise in Christ Jesus through the gospel.

⁷Of this gospel I was made a minister according to the gift of God's grace which was given me by the working of his power. ⁸To me, though I am the very least of all the saints, this grace was given, to preach to the Gentiles the unsearchable riches of Christ, ⁹and to make all men see what is the plan of the mystery hidden for ages in God who created all things; ¹⁰that through the church the manifold wisdom of God might now be made known to the principalities and powers in the heavenly places. ¹¹This was according to the eternal purpose which he has realized in Christ Jesus our Lord, ¹²in whom we have boldness and confidence of access through our faith in him. ¹³So I ask you not to lose heart over what I am suffering for you, which is your glory.

Col 1:24–2:3 (§260)

²⁴Now I rejoice in my sufferings for your sake, and in my flesh I complete what is lacking in Christ's afflictions for the sake of his body, that is, the church, ²⁵of which I became a minister according to the divine office which was given to me for you, to make the word of God fully known, ²⁶the mystery hidden for ages and generations but now made manifest to his saints. ²⁷To them God chose to make known how great among the Gentiles are the riches of the glory of this mystery, which is Christ in you, the hope of glory. ²⁸Him we proclaim warning every man and teaching every man in all wisdom, that we may present every man mature in Christ. ²⁹For this I toil, striving with all the energy which he mightily inspires within me.

2 ¹For I want you to know how greatly I strive for you, and for those at Laodicea, and for all who have not seen my face, ²that their hearts may be encouraged as they are knit together in love, to have all the riches of assured understanding and the knowledge of God's mystery, of Christ, ³in whom are hid all the treasures of wisdom and knowledge.

1 Thess 2:1–8 (§277)

¹For you yourselves know, brethren, that our visit to you was not in vain; ²but though we had already suffered and been shamefully treated at Philippi, as you know, we had courage in our God to declare to you the gospel of God in the face of great opposition. ³For our appeal does not spring from error or uncleanness, nor is it made with guile; ⁴but just as we have been approved by God to be entrusted with the gospel, so we speak, not to please men, but to please God who tests our hearts. ⁵For we never used either words of flattery, as you know, or a cloak for greed, as God is witness; ⁶nor did we seek glory from men, whether from you or from others, though we might have made demands as apostles of Christ. ⁷But we were gentle among you, like a nurse taking care of her children. ⁸So, being affectionately desirous of you, we were ready to share with you not only the gospel of God but also our own selves, because you had become very dear to us.

● **2 Cor 5:12**

2 Cor 3   ¹Are we beginning to commend ourselves again? Or do we need, as some do, letters of recommendation to you, or from you?

2 Cor 10   ¹²Not that we venture to class or compare ourselves with some of those who commend themselves. But when they measure themselves by one another and compare themselves with one another, they are without understanding.

Gal 6   ¹²It is those who want to make a good showing in the flesh that would compel you to be circumcised, and only in order that they may not be persecuted for the cross of Christ. ¹³For even those who receive circumcision do not themselves keep the law, but they desire to have you circumcised that they may glory in your flesh. ¹⁴But far be it from me to glory except in the cross of our Lord Jesus Christ, by which the world has been crucified to me, and I to the world.

Phil 1   ²⁵Convinced of this, I know that I shall remain and continue with you all, for your progress and joy in the faith, ²⁶so that in me you may have ample cause to glory in Christ Jesus, because of my coming to you again.

● **2 Cor 5:13**

1 Cor 14   ¹Make love your aim, and earnestly desire the spiritual gifts, especially that you may prophesy. ²For one who speaks in a tongue speaks not to men but to God; for no one understands him, but he utters mysteries in the Spirit. ³On the other hand, he who prophesies speaks to men for their upbuilding and encouragement and consolation. ⁴He who speaks in a tongue edifies himself, but he who prophesies edifies the church. ⁵Now I want you all to speak in tongues, but even more to prophesy. He who prophesies is greater than he who speaks in tongues, unless some one interprets, so that the church may be edified.

1 Cor 14   ¹⁸I thank God that I speak in tongues more than you all; . . .

2 Cor 12   ¹¹I have been a fool! You forced me to it, for I ought to have been commended by you. For I was not at all inferior to these superlative apostles, even though I am nothing. ¹²The signs of a true apostle were performed among you in all patience, with signs and wonders and mighty works. ¹³For in what were you less favored than the rest of the churches, except that I myself did not burden you? Forgive me this wrong!

[14]For the love of Christ controls us, because we are convinced that one has died for all; therefore all have died. [15]And he died for all, that those who live might live no longer for themselves but for him who for their sake died and was raised.

[16]From now on, therefore, we regard no one from a human point of view; even though we once regarded Christ from a human point of view, we regard him thus no longer. [17]Therefore, if any one is in Christ, he is a new creation; the old has passed away, behold, the new has come. [18]All this is from God, who through Christ reconciled us to himself and gave us the ministry of reconciliation; [19]that is, in Christ God was reconciling the world to himself, not counting their trespasses against them, and entrusting to us the message of reconciliation. [20]So we are ambassadors for Christ, God making his appeal through us. We beseech you on behalf of Christ, be reconciled to God. [21]For our sake he made him to be sin who knew no sin, so that in him we might become the righteousness of God.

PRIMARY

Rom 5:6–11 (§21)

[6]While we were still weak, at the right time Christ died for the ungodly.

[7]Why, one will hardly die for a righteous man—though perhaps for a good man one will dare even to die. [8]But God shows his love for us in that while we were yet sinners Christ died for us. [9]Since, therefore, we are now justified by his blood, much more shall we be saved by him from the wrath of God. [10]For if while we were enemies we were reconciled to God by the death of his Son, much more, now that we are reconciled, shall we be saved by his life. [11]Not only so, but we also rejoice in God through our Lord Jesus Christ, through whom we have now received our reconciliation.

Rom 6:1–10 (§23)

[1]What shall we say then? Are we to continue in sin that grace may abound? [2]By no means! How can we who died to sin still live in it? [3]Do you not know that all of us who have been baptized into Christ Jesus were baptized into his death? [4]We were buried therefore with him by baptism into death, so that as Christ was raised from the dead by the glory of the Father, we too might walk in newness of life. [5]For if we have been united with him in a death like his, we shall certainly be united with him in a resurrection like his. [6]We know that our old self was crucified with him so that the sinful body might be destroyed, and we might no longer be enslaved to sin. [7]For he who has died is freed from sin. [8]But if we have died with Christ, we believe that we shall also live with him. [9]For we know that Christ being raised from the dead will never die again; death no longer has dominion over him. [10]The death he died he died to sin, once for all, but the life he lives he lives to God.

Rom 6:11–14 (§24)

[11]So you also must consider yourselves dead to sin and alive to God in Christ Jesus.

[12]Let not sin therefore reign in your mortal bodies, to make you obey their passions. [13]Do not yield your members to sin as instruments of wickedness, but yield yourselves to God as men who have been brought from death to life, and your members to God as instruments of righteousness. [14]For sin will have no dominion over you, since you are not under law but under grace.

Rom 11:13–16 (§47)

[13]Now I am speaking to you Gentiles. Inasmuch then as I am an apostle to the Gentiles, I magnify my ministry [14]in order to make my fellow Jews jealous, and thus save some of them. [15]For if their rejection means the reconciliation of the world, what will their acceptance mean but life from the dead? [16]If the dough offered as first fruits is holy, so is the whole lump; and if the root is holy, so are the branches.

1 Cor 15:1–11 (§131)

[1]Now I would remind you, brethren, in what terms I preached to you the gospel, which you received, in which you stand, [2]by which you are saved, if you hold it fast —unless you believed in vain.

[3]For I delivered to you as of first importance what I also received, that Christ died for our sins in accordance with the scriptures, [4]that he was buried, that he was raised on the third day in accordance with the scriptures, [5]and that he appeared to Cephas, then to the twelve. [6]Then he appeared to more than five hundred brethren at one time, most of whom are still alive, though some have fallen asleep. [7]Then he appeared to James, then to all the apostles. [8]Last of all, as to one untimely born, he appeared also to me. [9]For I am the least of the apostles, unfit to be called an apostle, because I persecuted the church of God. [10]But by the grace of God I am what I am, and his grace toward me was not in vain. On the contrary, I worked harder than any of them, though it was not I, but the grace of God which is with me. [11]Whether then it was I or they, so we preach and so you believed.

2 Cor 3:7–11 (§156)

[7]Now if the dispensation of death, carved in letters on stone, came with such splendor that the Israelites could not look at Moses' face because of its brightness, fading as this was, [8]will not the dispensation of the Spirit be attended with greater splendor? [9]For if there was splendor in the dispensation of condemnation, the dispensation of righteousness must far exceed it in splendor. [10]Indeed, in this case, what once had splendor has come to have no splendor at all, because of the splendor that surpasses it. [11]For if what faded away came with splendor, what is permanent must have much more splendor.

Gal 2:15–21 (§199)

[15]We ourselves, who are Jews by birth and not Gentile sinners, [16]yet who know that a man is not justified by works of the law but through faith in Jesus Christ, even we have believed in

---

● **2 Cor 5:14–15**
Rom 7   [14]We know that the law is spiritual; but I am carnal, sold under sin.

● **2 Cor 5:15**
Phil 3   [8]Indeed I count everything as loss because of the surpassing worth of knowing Christ Jesus my Lord. For his sake I have suffered the loss of all things, and count them as refuse, in order that I may gain Christ . . .

● **2 Cor 5:16**
1 Cor 3   [1]But I, brethren, could not address you as spiritual men, but as men of the flesh, as babes in Christ. [2]I fed you with milk, not solid food; for you were not ready for it; and even yet you are not ready, [3]for you are still of the flesh. For while there is jealousy and strife among you, are you not of the flesh, and behaving like ordinary men? [4]For when one says, "I belong to Paul," and another, "I belong to Apollos," are you not merely men?

● **2 Cor 5:17**
Gal 6   [15]For neither circumcision counts for anything, nor uncircumcision, but a new creation.

Eph 4   [24]and put on the new nature, created after the likeness of God in true righteousness and holiness.

● **2 Cor 5:18**
Acts 20   [24]"But I do not account my life of any value nor as precious to myself, if only I may accomplish my

Christ Jesus, in order to be justified by faith in Christ, and not by works of the law, because by works of the law shall no one be justified. [17]But if, in our endeavor to be justified in Christ, we ourselves were found to be sinners, is Christ then an agent of sin? Certainly not! [18]But if I build up again those things which I tore down, then I prove myself a transgressor. [19]For I through the law died to the law, that I might live to God. [20]I have been crucified with Christ; it is no longer I who live, but Christ who lives in me; and the life I now live in the flesh I live by faith in the Son of God, who loved me and gave himself for me. [21]I do not nullify the grace of God; for if justification were through the law, then Christ died to no purpose.

Eph 3:1–13 (§222)

[1]For this reason I, Paul, a prisoner for Christ Jesus on behalf of you Gentiles— [2]assuming that you have heard of the stewardship of God's grace that was given to me for you, [3]how the mystery was made known to me by revelation, as I have written briefly. [4]When you read this you can perceive my insight into the mystery of Christ, [5]which was not made known to the sons of men in other generations as it has now been revealed to his holy apostles and prophets by the Spirit; [6]that is, how the Gentiles are fellow heirs, members of the same body, and partakers of the promise in Christ Jesus through the gospel.

[7]Of this gospel I was made a minister according to the gift of God's grace which was given me by the working of his power. [8]To me, though I am the very least of all the saints, this grace was given, to preach to the Gentiles the unsearchable riches of Christ, [9]and to make all men see what is the plan of the mystery hidden for ages in God who created all things; [10]that through the church the manifold wisdom of God might now be made known to the principalities and powers in the heavenly places. [11]This was according to the eternal purpose which he has realized in Christ Jesus our Lord, [12]in whom we have boldness and confidence of access through our faith in him. [13]So I ask you not to lose heart over what I am suffering for you, which is your glory.

Eph 4:17–24 (§227)

[17]Now this I affirm and testify in the Lord, that you must no longer live as the Gentiles do, in the futility of their minds; [18]they are darkened in their understanding, alienated from the life of God because of the ignorance that is in them, due to their hardness of heart; [19]they have become callous and have given themselves up to licentiousness, greedy to practice every kind of uncleanness. [20]You did not so learn Christ!— [21]assuming that you have heard about him and were taught in him, as the truth is in Jesus. [22]Put off your old nature which belongs to your former manner of life and is corrupt through deceitful lusts, [23]and be renewed in the spirit of your minds, [24]and put on the new nature, created after the likeness of God in true righteousness and holiness.

Col 1:15–20 (§258)

[15]He is the image of the invisible God, the first-born of all creation; [16]for in him all things were created, in heaven and on earth, visible and invisible, whether thrones or dominions or principalities or authorities—all things were created through him and for him. [17]He is before all things, and in him all things hold together. [18]He is the head of the body, the church; he is the beginning, the first-born from the dead, that in everything he might be preeminent. [19]For in him all the fulness of God was pleased to dwell, [20]and through him to reconcile to himself all things, whether on earth or in heaven, making peace by the blood of his cross.

Col 1:21–23 (§259)

[21]And you, who once were estranged and hostile in mind, doing evil deeds, [22]he has now reconciled in his body of flesh by his death, in order to present you holy and blameless and irreproachable before him, [23]provided that you continue in the faith, stable and steadfast, not shifting from the hope of the gospel which you heard, which has been preached to every creature under heaven, and of which I, Paul, became a minister.

Col 2:8–15 (§262)

[8]See to it that no one makes a prey of you by philosophy and empty deceit, according to human tradition, according to the elemental spirits of the universe, and not according to Christ. [9]For in him the whole fulness of deity dwells bodily, [10]and you have come to fulness of life in him, who is the head of all rule and authority. [11]In him also you were circumcised with a circumcision made without hands, by putting off the body of flesh in the circumcision of Christ; [12]and you were buried with him in baptism, in which you were also raised with him through faith in the working of God, who raised him from the dead. [13]And you, who were dead in trespasses and the uncircumcision of your flesh, God made alive together with him, having forgiven us all our trespasses, [14]having canceled the bond which stood against us with its legal demands; this he set aside, nailing it to the cross. [15]He disarmed the principalities and powers and made a public example of them, triumphing over them in him.

Col 3:5–11 (§266)

[5]Put to death therefore what is earthly in you: fornication, impurity, passion, evil desire, and covetousness, which is idolatry. [6]On account of these the wrath of God is coming. [7]In these you once walked, when you lived in them. [8]But now put them all away: anger, wrath, malice, slander, and foul talk from your mouth. [9]Do not lie to one another, seeing that you have put off the old nature with its practices [10]and have put on the new nature, which is being renewed in knowledge after the image of its creator. [11]Here there cannot be Greek and Jew, circumcised and uncircumcised, barbarian, Scythian, slave, free man, but Christ is all, and in all.

---

course and the ministry which I received from the Lord Jesus, to testify to the gospel of the grace of God."

● **2 Cor 5:19**

Eph 2   [16]and might reconcile us both to God in one body through the cross, thereby bringing the hostility to an end.

● **2 Cor 5:20**

Eph 6   [20]for which I am an ambassador in chains; that I may declare it boldly, as I ought to speak.

● **2 Cor 5:21**

1 Cor 1   [30]He is the source of your life in Christ Jesus, whom God made our wisdom, our righteousness and sanctification and redemption; [31]therefore, as it is written, "Let him who boasts, boast of the Lord."

Gal 3   [10]For all who rely on works of the law are under a curse; for it is written, "Cursed be every one who does not abide by all things written in the book of the law, and do them." [11]Now it is evident that no man is justified before God by the law; for "He who

through faith is righteous shall live"; [12]but the law does not rest on faith, for "He who does them shall live by them." [13]Christ redeemed us from the curse of the law, having become a curse for us—for it is written, "Cursed be every one who hangs on a tree" . . .

Acts 3   [14]"But you denied the Holy and Righteous One, and asked for a murderer to be granted to you. . . ."

FORMAL ELEMENTS: VIRTUE LIST
& HARDSHIPS LIST

6 **Working together with him, then, we entreat you not to accept the grace of God in vain. ²For he says,**

"At the acceptable time I have listened to you,

and helped you on the day of salvation."
Behold, now is the acceptable time; behold, now is the day of salvation. ³We put no obstacle in any one's way, so that no fault may be found with our ministry, ⁴but as servants of God we commend ourselves in every way: through great endurance, in afflictions, hardships, calamities, ⁵beatings, imprisonments, tumults, labors, watchings, hunger; ⁶by purity, knowledge, forbearance, kindness, the Holy Spirit, genuine love, ⁷truthful speech, and the power of God; with the weapons of righteousness for the right hand and for the left; ⁸in honor and dishonor, in ill repute and good repute. We are treated as impostors, and yet are true; ⁹as unknown, and yet well known; as dying, and behold we live; as punished, and yet not killed; ¹⁰as sorrowful, yet always rejoicing; as poor, yet making many rich; as having nothing, and yet possessing everything.

PRIMARY

Rom 5:1–5 (§20)

¹Therefore, since we are justified by faith, we have peace with God through our Lord Jesus Christ. ²Through him we have obtained access to this grace in which we stand, and we rejoice in our hope of sharing the glory of God. ³More than that, we rejoice in our sufferings, knowing that suffering produces endurance, ⁴and endurance produces character, and character produces hope, ⁵and hope does not disappoint us, because God's love has been poured into our hearts through the Holy Spirit which has been given to us.

Rom 8:31–39 (§34)

³¹What then shall we say to this? If God is for us, who is against us? ³²He who did not spare his own Son but gave him up for us all, will he not also give us all things with him? ³³Who shall bring any charge against God's elect? It is God who justifies; ³⁴who is to condemn? Is it Christ Jesus, who died, yes, who was raised from the dead, who is at the right hand of God, who indeed intercedes for us? ³⁵Who shall separate us from the love of Christ? Shall tribulation, or distress, or persecution, or famine, or nakedness, or peril, or sword? ³⁶As it is written,

"For thy sake we are being killed all the day long;

we are regarded as sheep to be slaughtered."
³⁷No, in all these things we are more than conquerors through him who loved us. ³⁸For I am sure that neither death, nor life, nor angels, nor principalities, nor things present, nor things to come, nor powers, ³⁹nor height, nor depth, nor anything else in all creation, will be able to separate us from the love of God in Christ Jesus our Lord.

1 Cor 4:8–13 (§85)

⁸Already you are filled! Already you have become rich! Without us you have become kings! And would that you did reign, so that we might share the rule with you! ⁹For I think that God has exhibited us apostles as last of all, like men sentenced to death; because we have become a spectacle to the world, to angels and to men. ¹⁰We are fools for Christ's sake, but you are wise in Christ. We are weak, but you are strong. You are held in honor, but we in disrepute. ¹¹To the present hour we hunger and thirst, we are ill-clad and buffeted and homeless, ¹²and we labor, working with our own hands. When reviled, we bless; when persecuted, we endure; ¹³when slandered, we try to conciliate; we have become, and are now, as the refuse of the world, the off-scouring of all things.

Gal 5:16–26 (§213)

¹⁶But I say, walk by the Spirit, and do not gratify the desires of the flesh. ¹⁷For the desires of the flesh are against the Spirit, and the desires of the Spirit are against the flesh; for these are opposed to each other, to prevent you from doing what you would. ¹⁸But if you are led by the Spirit you are not under the law. ¹⁹Now the works of the flesh are plain: fornication, impurity, licentiousness, ²⁰idolatry, sorcery, enmity, strife, jealousy, anger, selfishness, dissension, party spirit, ²¹envy, drunkenness, carousing, and the like. I warn you, as I warned you before, that those who do such things shall not inherit the kingdom of God. ²²But the fruit of the Spirit is love, joy, peace, patience, kindness, goodness, faithfulness, ²³gentleness, self-control; against such there is no law. ²⁴And those who belong to Christ Jesus have crucified the flesh with its passions and desires.

²⁵If we live by the Spirit, let us also walk by

● **2 Cor 6:2**

Isa 49　　⁸Thus says the Lord:
"In a time of favor I have answered you,
in a day of salvation I have helped you;
I have kept you and given you as a covenant to the people
to establish the land, to apportion the desolate heritages. . .".

● **2 Cor 6:4**

2 Tim 2　　²⁴And the Lord's servant must not be quarrelsome but kindly to every one, an apt teacher, forbearing, ²⁵correcting his opponents with gentleness. God may perhaps grant that they will repent and come to know the truth, . . .

Cf. Acts 9　　¹⁶". . . for I will show him how much he must suffer for the sake of my name."

● **2 Cor 6:5**

Acts 16　　²³And when they had inflicted many blows upon them, they threw them into prison, charging the jailer to keep them safely.

● **2 Cor 6:6–10**

2 Cor 1　　⁸For we do not want you to be ignorant, brethren, of the affliction we experienced in Asia; for we were so utterly, unbearably crushed that we despaired of life itself. ⁹Why, we felt that we had received the sentence of death; but that was to make us rely not on ourselves but on God who raises the dead; ¹⁰he delivered us from so deadly a peril, and he will deliver us; on him we have set our hope that he will deliver us again. ¹¹You also must help us by prayer, so that many will give thanks on our behalf for the blessing granted us in answer to many prayers.

2 Cor 4　　⁷But we have this treasure in earthen vessels, to show that the transcendent power belongs to God and not to us. ⁸We are afflicted in every way, but not crushed; perplexed, but not driven to despair; ⁹persecuted, but not forsaken; struck down, but not destroyed; ¹⁰always carrying in the body the death of Jesus, so that the life of Jesus may also be manifested in our bodies. ¹¹For while we live we are always being given up to death for Jesus' sake, so that the life of Jesus may be manifested in our mortal flesh. ¹²So death is at work in us, but life in you.

the Spirit. ²⁶Let us have no self-conceit, no provoking of one another, no envy of one another.

Eph 4:1–10 (§225)

¹I therefore, a prisoner for the Lord, beg you to lead a life worthy of the calling to which you have been called, ²with all lowliness and meekness, with patience, forbearing one another in love, ³eager to maintain the unity of the Spirit in the bond of peace. ⁴There is one body and one Spirit, just as you were called to the one hope that belongs to your call, ⁵one Lord, one faith, one baptism, ⁶one God and Father of us all, who is above all and through all and in all. ⁷But grace was given to each of us according to the measure of Christ's gift. ⁸Therefore it is said,

"When he ascended on high he led a host of captives,

and he gave gifts to men."

⁹(In saying, "He ascended," what does it mean but that he had also descended into the lower parts of the earth? ¹⁰He who descended is he who also ascended far above all the heavens, that he might fill all things.)

Phil 4:8–20 (§252–253)

⁸Finally, brethren, whatever is true, whatever is honorable, whatever is just, whatever is pure, whatever is lovely, whatever is gracious, if there is any excellence, if there is anything worthy of praise, think about these things. ⁹What you have learned and received and heard and seen in me, do; and the God of peace will be with you.

¹⁰I rejoice in the Lord greatly that now at length you have revived your concern for me; you were indeed concerned for me, but you had no opportunity. ¹¹Not that I complain of want; for I have learned, in whatever state I am, to be content. ¹²I know how to be abased, and I know how to abound; in any and all circumstances I have learned the secret of facing plenty and hunger, abundance and want. ¹³I can do all things in him who strengthens me.

¹⁴Yet it was kind of you to share my trouble. ¹⁵And you Philippians yourselves know that in the beginning of the gospel, when I left Macedonia, no church entered into partnership with me in giving and receiving except you only; ¹⁶for even in Thessalonica you sent me help once and again. ¹⁷Not that I seek the gift; but I seek the fruit which increases to your credit. ¹⁸I have received full payment, and more; I am filled, having received from Epaphroditus the gifts you sent, a fragrant offering, a sacrifice acceptable and pleasing to God. ¹⁹And my God will supply every need of yours according to his riches in glory in Christ Jesus. ²⁰To our God and Father be glory for ever and ever. Amen.

Col 3:12–17 (§267)

¹²Put on then, as God's chosen ones, holy and beloved, compassion, kindness, lowliness, meekness, and patience, ¹³forbearing one another and, if one has a complaint against another, forgiving each other; as the Lord has forgiven you, so you also must forgive. ¹⁴And above all these put on love, which binds everything together in perfect harmony. ¹⁵And let the peace of Christ rule in your hearts, to which indeed you were called in the one body. And be thankful. ¹⁶Let the word of Christ dwell in you richly, as you teach and admonish one another in all wisdom, and as you sing psalms and hymns and spiritual songs with thankfulness in your hearts to God. ¹⁷And whatever you do, in word or deed, do everything in the name of the Lord Jesus, giving thanks to God the Father through him.

1 Thess 2:1–8 (§277)

¹For you yourselves know, brethren, that our visit to you was not in vain; ²but though we had already suffered and been shamefully treated at Philippi, as you know, we had courage in our God to declare to you the gospel of God in the face of great opposition. ³For our appeal does not spring from error or uncleanness, nor is it made with guile; ⁴but just as we have been approved by God to be entrusted with the gospel, so we speak, not to please men, but to please God who tests our hearts. ⁵For we never used either words of flattery, as you know, or a cloak for greed, as God is witness; ⁶nor did we seek glory from men, whether from you or from others, though we might have made demands as apostles of Christ. ⁷But we were gentle among you, like a nurse taking care of her children. ⁸So, being affectionately desirous of you, we were ready to share with you not only the gospel of God but also our own selves, because you had become very dear to us.

---

2 Cor 8   ⁷Now as you excel in everything—in faith, in utterance, in knowledge, in all earnestness, and in your love for us—see that you excel in this gracious work also.

2 Cor 11   ²¹. . . But whatever any one dares to boast of—I am speaking as a fool—I also dare to boast of that. ²²Are they Hebrews? So am I. Are they Israelites? So am I. Are they descendants of Abraham? So am I. ²³Are they servants of Christ? I am a better one—I am talking like a madman—with far greater labors, far more imprisonments, with countless beatings, and often near death. ²⁴Five times I have received at the hands of the Jews the forty lashes less one. ²⁵Three times I have been beaten with rods; once I was stoned. Three times I have been shipwrecked; a night and a day I have been adrift at sea; ²⁶on frequent journeys, in danger from rivers, danger from robbers, danger from my own people, danger from Gentiles, danger in the city, danger in the wilderness, danger at sea, danger from false brethren; ²⁷in toil and hardship, through many a sleepless night, in hunger and thirst, often without food, in cold and exposure. ²⁸And, apart from other things, there is the daily pressure upon me of my anxiety for all the churches. ²⁹Who is weak, and I am not weak? Who is made to fall, and I am not indignant?

● **2 Cor 6:6**
Cf. Eph 4   ³²and be kind to one another, tenderhearted, forgiving one another, as God in Christ forgave you.

● **2 Cor 6:7**
Eph 6   ¹¹Put on the whole armor of God, that you may be able to stand against the wiles of the devil.

1 Thess 5   ⁸But, since we belong to the day, let us be sober, and put on the breastplate of faith and love, and for a helmet the hope of salvation.

● **2 Cor 6:10**
1 Cor 3   ²¹So let no one boast of men. For all things are yours, ²²whether Paul or Apollos or Cephas or the world or life or death or the present or the future, all are yours; ²³and you are Christ's; and Christ is God's.

[11]Our mouth is open to you, Corinthians; our heart is wide. [12]You are not restricted by us, but you are restricted in your own affections. [13]In return—I speak as to children—widen your hearts also.

PRIMARY

1 Cor 3:1–4 (§78)

[1]But I, brethren, could not address you as spiritual men, but as men of the flesh, as babes in Christ. [2]I fed you with milk, not solid food; for you were not ready for it; and even yet you are not ready, [3]for you are still of the flesh. For while there is jealousy and strife among you, are you not of the flesh, and behaving like ordinary men? [4]For when one says, "I belong to Paul," and another, "I belong to Apollos," are you not merely men?

1 Cor 4:14–21 (§86)

[14]I do not write this to make you ashamed, but to admonish you as my beloved children. [15]For though you have countless guides in Christ, you do not have many fathers. For I became your father in Christ Jesus through the gospel. [16]I urge you, then, be imitators of me. [17]Therefore I sent to you Timothy, my beloved and faithful child in the Lord, to remind you of my ways in Christ, as I teach them everywhere in every church. [18]Some are arrogant, as though I were not coming to you. [19]But I will come to you soon, if the Lord wills, and I will find out not the talk of these arrogant people but their power. [20]For the kingdom of God does not consist in talk but in power. [21]What do you wish? Shall I come to you with a rod, or with love in a spirit of gentleness?

● **2 Cor 6:11–13**

2 Cor 7　[2]Open your hearts to us; we have wronged no one, we have corrupted no one, we have taken advantage of no one. [3]I do not say this to condemn you, for I said before that you are in our hearts, to die together and to live together. [4]I have great confidence in you; I have great pride in you; I am filled with comfort. With all our affliction, I am overjoyed.

● **2 Cor 6:13**

1 Cor 14　[20]Brethren, do not be children in your thinking; be babes in evil, but in thinking be mature.

Gal 4　[19]My little children, with whom I am again in travail until Christ be formed in you!

Eph 5　[1]Therefore be imitators of God, as beloved children.

Phil 2　[22]But Timothy's worth you know, how as a son with a father he has served with me in the gospel.

Phlm　[10]I appeal to you for my child, Onesimus, whose father I have become in my imprisonment.

1 Pet 2　[2]Like newborn babes, long for the pure spiritual milk, that by it you may grow up to salvation; . . .

Heb 5　[13]for every one who lives on milk is unskilled in the word of righteousness, for he is a child. [14]But solid food is for the mature, for those who have their faculties trained by practice to distinguish good from evil.

14Do not be mismated with unbelievers. For what partnership have righteousness and iniquity? Or what fellowship has light with darkness? **15**What accord has Christ with Belial? Or what has a believer in common with an unbeliever? **16**What agreement has the temple of God with idols? For we are the temple of the living God; as God said,

"I will live in them and move among them,
and I will be their God,
and they shall be my people.
17Therefore come out from them,
and be separate from them, says the Lord,
and touch nothing unclean;
then I will welcome you,
18and I will be a father to you,
and you shall be my sons and daughters, says the Lord Almighty."

7 **1**Since we have these promises, beloved, let us cleanse ourselves from every defilement of body and spirit, and make holiness perfect in the fear of God.

PRIMARY

1 Cor 3:16–17 (§81)

16Do you not know that you are God's temple and that God's Spirit dwells in you? **17**If any one destroys God's temple, God will destroy him. For God's temple is holy, and that temple you are.

1 Cor 5:1–5 (§87)

1It is actually reported that there is immorality among you, and of a kind that is not found even among pagans; for a man is living with his father's wife. **2**And you are arrogant! Ought you not rather to mourn? Let him who has done this be removed from among you.

3For though absent in body I am present in spirit, and as if present, I have already pronounced judgment **4**in the name of the Lord Jesus on the man who has done such a thing.

When you are assembled, and my spirit is present, with the power of our Lord Jesus, **5**you are to deliver this man to Satan for the destruction of the flesh, that his spirit may be saved in the day of the Lord Jesus.

1 Cor 5:9–13 (§89)

9I wrote to you in my letter not to associate with immoral men; **10**not at all meaning the immoral of this world, or the greedy and robbers, or idolaters, since then you would need to go out of the world. **11**But rather I wrote to you not to associate with any one who bears the name of brother if he is guilty of immorality or greed, or is an idolater, reviler, drunkard, or robber—not even to eat with such a one. **12**For what have I to do with judging outsiders? Is it not those inside the church whom you are to judge? **13**God judges those outside. "Drive out the wicked person from among you."

1 Cor 6:12–20 (§92)

12"All things are lawful for me," but not all things are helpful. "All things are lawful for me," but I will not be enslaved by anything. **13**"Food is meant for the stomach and the stomach for food"—and God will destroy both one and the other. The body is not meant for immorality, but for the Lord, and the Lord for the body. **14**And God raised the Lord and will also raise us up by his power. **15**Do you not know that your bodies are members of Christ? Shall I therefore take the members of Christ and make them members of a prostitute? Never! **16**Do you not know that he who joins himself to a prostitute becomes one body with her? For, as it is written, "The two shall become one flesh." **17**But he who is united to the Lord becomes one spirit with him. **18**Shun immorality. Every other sin which a man commits is outside the body; but the immoral man sins against his own body. **19**Do you not know that your body is a temple of the Holy Spirit within you, which you have from God? You are not your own; **20**you were bought with a price. So glorify God in your body.

1 Cor 7:12–16 (§96)

12To the rest I say, not the Lord, that if any brother has a wife who is an unbeliever, and she consents to live with him, he should not divorce her. **13**If any woman has a husband who is an unbeliever, and he consents to live with her, she should not divorce him. **14**For the unbelieving husband is consecrated through his wife, and the unbelieving wife is consecrated through her husband. Otherwise, your children would be unclean, but as it is they are holy. **15**But if the unbelieving partner desires to separate, let it be so; in such a case the brother or sister is not bound. For God has called us to peace. **16**Wife, how do you know whether you will save your husband? Husband, how do you know whether you will save your wife?

Eph 5:3–14 (§230)

3But fornication and all impurity or covetousness must not even be named among you, as is fitting among saints. **4**Let there be no filthiness, nor silly talk, nor levity, which are not fitting; but instead let there be thanksgiving. **5**Be sure of this, that no fornicator or impure man, or one who is covetous (that is, an idolater), has any inheritance in the kingdom of Christ and of God. **6**Let no one deceive you with empty words, for it is because of these things that the wrath of God comes upon the sons of disobedience. **7**Therefore do not associate with them, **8**for once you were darkness, but now you are light in the Lord; walk as children of light **9**(for the fruit of light is found in all that is good and right and true), **10**and try to learn what is pleasing to the Lord. **11**Take no part in the unfruitful works of darkness, but instead expose them. **12**For it is a shame even to speak of the things that they do in secret; **13**but when anything is exposed by the light it becomes visible, for anything that becomes visible is light. **14**Therefore it is said,

"Awake, O sleeper, and arise from the dead,
and Christ shall give you light."

● **2 Cor 6:14**

2 Cor 4 **6**For it is the God who said, "Let light shine out of darkness," who has shone in our hearts to give the light of the knowledge of the glory of God in the face of Christ.

2 Cor 5 **1**For we know that if the earthly tent we live in is destroyed, we have a building from God, a house not made with hands, eternal in the heavens. **2**Here indeed we groan, and long to put on our heavenly dwelling, . . .

● **2 Cor 6:16**

1 Cor 6 **15**Do you not know that your bodies are members of Christ? Shall I therefore take the members of Christ and make them members of a prostitute? Never!

1 Cor 6 **19**Do you not know that your body is a temple of the Holy Spirit within you, which you have from God? You are not your own; . . .

1 Cor 10 **19**What do I imply then? That food offered to idols is anything, or that an idol is anything? **20**No, I imply that what pagans sacrifice they offer to demons

and not to God. I do not want you to be partners with demons. **21**You cannot drink the cup of the Lord and the cup of demons. You cannot partake of the table of the Lord and the table of demons. **22**Shall we provoke the Lord to jealousy? Are we stronger than he?

1 Thess 1 **9**For they themselves report concerning us what a welcome we had among you, and how you turned to God from idols, to serve a living and true God, . . .

Exod 25 **8**And let them make me a sanctuary, that I may dwell in their midst.

Exod 29 **45**And I will dwell among the people of Israel, and will be their God.

Lev 26 **12**And I will walk among you, and will be your God, and you shall be my people.

Jer 31 **1**"At that time, says the Lord, I will be the God of all the families of Israel, and they shall be my people."

Ezek 37 **27**My dwelling place shall be with them; and I will be their God, and they shall be my people.

● **2 Cor 6:17**

1 Thess 2 **3**For our appeal does not spring from error or uncleanness, nor is it made with guile; . . .

Acts 19 **9**but when some were stubborn and disbelieved, speaking evil of the Way before the congregation, he withdrew from them, taking the disciples with him, and argued daily in the hall of Tyrannus.

Isa 52 **11** Depart, depart, go out thence, touch no unclean thing;
go out from the midst of her, purify yourselves, you who bear the vessels of the Lord.

● **2 Cor 6:18**

Hos 1 **10**Yet the number of the people of Israel shall be like the sand of the sea, which can be neither measured nor numbered; and in the place where it was said to them, "You are not my people," it shall be said to them, "Sons of the living God."

Isa 43 **6** I will say to the north, Give up,
and to the south, Do not withhold;
bring my sons from afar
and my daughters from the end of the earth, . . .

²Open your hearts to us; we have wronged no one, we have corrupted no one, we have taken advantage of no one. ³I do not say this to condemn you, for I said before that you are in our hearts, to die together and to live together. ⁴I have great confidence in you; I have great pride in you; I am filled with comfort. With all our affliction, I am overjoyed.

PRIMARY

Phil 4:10–20 (§253)

¹⁰I rejoice in the Lord greatly that now at length you have revived your concern for me; you were indeed concerned for me, but you had no opportunity. ¹¹Not that I complain of want; for I have learned, in whatever state I am, to be content. ¹²I know how to be abased, and I know how to abound; in any and all circumstances I have learned the secret of facing plenty and hunger, abundance and want. ¹³I can do all things in him who strengthens me.

¹⁴Yet it was kind of you to share my trouble. ¹⁵And you Philippians yourselves know that in the beginning of the gospel, when I left Macedonia, no church entered into partnership with me in giving and receiving except you only; ¹⁶for even in Thessalonica you sent me help once and again. ¹⁷Not that I seek the gift; but I seek the fruit which increases to your credit. ¹⁸I have received full payment, and more; I am filled, having received from Epaphroditus the gifts you sent, a fragrant offering, a sacrifice acceptable and pleasing to God. ¹⁹And my God will supply every need of yours according to his

riches in glory in Christ Jesus. ²⁰To our God and Father be glory for ever and ever. Amen.

1 Thess 2:1–8 (§277)

¹For you yourselves know, brethren, that our visit to you was not in vain; ²but though we had already suffered and been shamefully treated at Philippi, as you know, we had courage in our God to declare to you the gospel of God in the face of great opposition. ³For our appeal does not spring from error or uncleanness, nor is it made with guile; ⁴but just as we have been approved by God to be entrusted with the gospel, so we speak, not to please men, but to please God who tests our hearts. ⁵For we never used either words of flattery, as you know, or a cloak for greed, as God is witness; ⁶nor did we seek glory from men, whether from you or from others, though we might have made demands as apostles of Christ. ⁷But we were gentle among you, like a nurse taking care of her children. ⁸So, being affectionately desirous of you, we were ready to share with you not only the gospel of God but also our own selves, because you had become very dear to us.

2 Thess 1:3–12 (§295)

³We are bound to give thanks to God always for you, brethren, as is fitting, because your faith is growing abundantly, and the love of every one of you for one another is increasing. ⁴Therefore we ourselves boast of you in the churches of God for your steadfastness and faith in all your persecutions and in the afflictions which you are enduring.

⁵This is evidence of the righteous judgment

of God, that you may be made worthy of the kingdom of God, for which you are suffering— ⁶since indeed God deems it just to repay with affliction those who afflict you, ⁷and to grant rest with us to you who are afflicted, when the Lord Jesus is revealed from heaven with his mighty angels in flaming fire, ⁸ inflicting vengeance upon those who do not know God and upon those who do not obey the gospel of our Lord Jesus. ⁹They shall suffer the punishment of eternal destruction and exclusion from the presence of the Lord and from the glory of his might, ¹⁰when he comes on that day to be glorified in his saints, and to be marveled at in all who have believed, because our testimony to you was believed. ¹¹To this end we always pray for you, that our God may make you worthy of his call, and may fulfil every good resolve and work of faith by his power, ¹²so that the name of our Lord Jesus may be glorified in you, and you in him, according to the grace of our God and the Lord Jesus Christ.

Phlm 4–7 (§306)

⁴I thank my God always when I remember you in my prayers, ⁵because I hear of your love and of the faith which you have toward the Lord Jesus and all the saints, ⁶and I pray that the sharing of your faith may promote the knowledge of all the good that is ours in Christ. ⁷For I have derived much joy and comfort from your love, my brother, because the hearts of the saints have been refreshed through you.

● **2 Cor 7:2**

2 Cor 6   ¹¹Our mouth is open to you, Corinthians; our heart is wide. ¹²You are not restricted by us, but you are restricted in your own affections. ¹³In return—I speak as to children—widen your hearts also.

2 Cor 11   ⁷Did I commit a sin in abasing myself so that you might be exalted, because I preached God's gospel without cost to you? ⁸I robbed other churches by accepting support from them in order to serve you. ⁹And when I was with you and was in want, I did not burden any one, for my needs were supplied by the brethren who came from Macedonia. So I refrained and will refrain from burdening you in any way. ¹⁰As

the truth of Christ is in me, this boast of mine shall not be silenced in the regions of Achaia. ¹¹And why? Because I do not love you? God knows I do!

1 Thess 2   ⁹For you remember our labor and toil, brethren; we worked night and day, that we might not burden any of you, while we preached to you the gospel of God.

Acts 20   ³³"I coveted no one's silver or gold or apparel."

● **2 Cor 7:4**

2 Cor 1   ³Blessed be the God and Father of our Lord

Jesus Christ, the Father of mercies and God of all comfort, ⁴who comforts us in all our affliction, so that we may be able to comfort those who are in any affliction, with the comfort with which we ourselves are comforted by God. ⁵For as we share abundantly in Christ's sufferings, so through Christ we share abundantly in comfort too. ⁶If we are afflicted, it is for your comfort and salvation; and if we are comforted, it is for your comfort, which you experience when you patiently endure the same sufferings that we suffer. ⁷Our hope for you is unshaken; for we know that as you share in our sufferings, you will also share in our comfort.

⁵For even when we came into Macedonia, our bodies had no rest but we were afflicted at every turn— fighting without and fear within. ⁶But God, who comforts the downcast, comforted us by the coming of Titus, ⁷and not only by his coming but also by the comfort with which he was comforted in you, as he told us of your longing, your mourning, your zeal for me, so that I rejoiced still more. ⁸For even if I made you sorry with my letter, I do not regret it (though I did regret it), for I see that that letter grieved you, though only for a while. ⁹As it is, I rejoice, not because you were grieved, but because you were grieved into repenting; for you felt a godly grief, so that you suffered no loss through us. ¹⁰For godly grief produces a repentance that leads to salvation and brings no regret, but worldly grief produces death. ¹¹For see what earnestness this godly grief has produced in you, what eagerness to clear yourselves, what indignation, what alarm, what longing, what zeal, what punishment! At every point you have proved yourselves guiltless in the matter. ¹²So although I wrote to you, it was not on account of the one who did the wrong, nor on account of the one who suffered the wrong, but in order that your zeal for us might be revealed to you in the sight of God. ¹³Therefore we are comforted.

PRIMARY

Rom 5:1–5 (§20)

¹Therefore, since we are justified by faith, we have peace with God through our Lord Jesus Christ. ²Through him we have obtained access to this grace in which we stand, and we rejoice in our hope of sharing the glory of God. ³More than that, we rejoice in our sufferings, knowing that suffering produces endurance, ⁴and endurance produces character, and character produces hope, ⁵and hope does not disappoint us, because God's love has been poured into our hearts through the Holy Spirit which has been given to us.

1 Thess 3:1–5 (§281)

¹Therefore when we could bear it no longer, we were willing to be left behind at Athens alone, ²and we sent Timothy, our brother and God's servant in the gospel of Christ, to establish you in your faith and to exhort you, ³that no one be moved by these afflictions. You yourselves know that this is to be our lot. ⁴For when we were with you, we told you beforehand that we were to suffer affliction; just as it has come to pass, and as you know. ⁵For this reason, when I could bear it no longer, I sent that I might know your faith, for fear that somehow the tempter had tempted you and that our labor would be in vain.

2 Thess 2:16–17 (§298)

¹⁶Now may our Lord Jesus Christ himself, and God our Father, who loved us and gave us eternal comfort and good hope through grace, ¹⁷comfort your hearts and establish them in every good work and word.

• 2 Cor 7:5–13a

2 Cor 1 ³Blessed be the God and Father of our Lord Jesus Christ, the Father of mercies and God of all comfort, ⁴who comforts us in all our affliction, so that we may be able to comfort those who are in any affliction, with the comfort with which we ourselves are comforted by God. ⁵For as we share abundantly in Christ's sufferings, so through Christ we share abundantly in comfort too. ⁶If we are afflicted, it is for your comfort and salvation; and if we are comforted, it is for your comfort, which you experience when you patiently endure the same sufferings that we suffer. ⁷Our hope for you is unshaken; for we know that as you share in our sufferings, you will also share in our comfort.

• 2 Cor 7:5

Acts 20 ¹After the uproar ceased, Paul sent for the disciples and having exhorted them took leave of them and departed for Macedonia. ²When he had gone through these parts and had given them much encouragement, he came to Greece. ³There he spent three months, and when a plot was made against him by the Jews as he was about to set sail for Syria, he determined to return through Macedonia.

• 2 Cor 7:8

2 Cor 13 ¹This is the third time I am coming to you. Any charge must be sustained by the evidence of two or three witnesses. ²I warned those who sinned before

and all the others, and I warn them now while absent, as I did when present on my second visit, that if I come again I will not spare them— ³since you desire proof that Christ is speaking in me. He is not weak in dealing with you, but is powerful in you. ⁴For he was crucified in weakness, but lives by the power of God. For we are weak in him, but in dealing with you we shall live with him by the power of God.

⁵Examine yourselves, to see whether you are holding to your faith. Test yourselves. Do you not realize that Jesus Christ is in you?—unless indeed you fail to meet the test! ⁶I hope you will find out that we have not failed. ⁷But we pray God that you may not do wrong— not that we may appear to have met the test, but that you may do what is right, though we may seem to have failed. ⁸For we cannot do anything against the truth, but only for the truth. ⁹For we are glad when we are weak and you are strong. What we pray for is your improvement. ¹⁰I write this while I am away from you, in order that when I come I may not have to be severe in my use of the authority which the Lord has given me for building up and not for tearing down.

Cf. 1 Cor 5 ⁹I wrote to you in my letter not to associate with immoral men; . . .

• 2 Cor 7:10

Acts 11 ¹⁸When they heard this they were silenced. And they glorified God, saying, "Then to the Gentiles also God has granted repentance unto life."

• 2 Cor 7:12

1 Cor 5 ¹It is actually reported that there is immorality among you, and of a kind that is not found even among pagans; for a man is living with his father's wife. ²And you are arrogant! Ought you not rather to mourn? Let him who has done this be removed from among you.

³For though absent in body I am present in spirit, and as if present, I have already pronounced judgment ⁴in the name of the Lord Jesus on the man who has done such a thing. When you are assembled, and my spirit is present, with the power of our Lord Jesus, ⁵you are to deliver this man to Satan for the destruction of the flesh, that his spirit may be saved in the day of the Lord Jesus.

2 Cor 2 ⁵But if any one has caused pain, he has caused it not to me, but in some measure—not to put it too severely—to you all. ⁶For such a one this punishment by the majority is enough; ⁷so you should rather turn to forgive and comfort him, or he may be overwhelmed by excessive sorrow. ⁸So I beg you to reaffirm your love for him. ⁹For this is why I wrote, that I might test you and know whether you are obedient in everything. ¹⁰Any one whom you forgive, I also forgive. What I have forgiven, if I have forgiven anything, has been for your sake in the presence of Christ, ¹¹to keep Satan from gaining the advantage over us; for we are not ignorant of his designs.

And besides our own comfort we rejoiced still more at the joy of Titus, because his mind has been set at rest by you all. [14]For if I have expressed to him some pride in you, I was not put to shame; but just as everything we said to you was true, so our boasting before Titus has proved true. [15]And his heart goes out all the more to you, as he remembers the obedience of you all, and the fear and trembling with which you received him. [16]I rejoice, because I have perfect confidence in you.

PRIMARY

Phil 2:12–13 (§243)

[12]Therefore, my beloved, as you have always obeyed, so now, not only as in my presence but much more in my absence, work out your own salvation with fear and trembling; [13]for God is at work in you, both to will and to work for his good pleasure.

1 Thess 3:6–10 (§282)

[6]But now that Timothy has come to us from you, and has brought us the good news of your faith and love and reported that you always remember us kindly and long to see us, as we long to see you— [7]for this reason, brethren, in all our distress and affliction we have been comforted about you through your faith; [8]for now we live, if you stand fast in the Lord. [9]For what thanksgiving can we render to God for you, for all the joy which we feel for your sake before our God, [10]praying earnestly night and day that we may see you face to face and supply what is lacking in your faith?

2 Thess 3:1–5 (§299)

[1]Finally, brethren, pray for us, that the word of the Lord may speed on and triumph, as it did among you, [2]and that we may be delivered from wicked and evil men; for not all have faith. [3]But the Lord is faithful; he will strengthen you and guard you from evil. [4]And we have confidence in the Lord about you, that you are doing and will do the things which we command. [5]May the Lord direct your hearts to the love of God and to the steadfastness of Christ.

Phlm 21–22 (§309)

[21]Confident of your obedience, I write to you, knowing that you will do even more than I say. [22]At the same time, prepare a guest room for me, for I am hoping through your prayers to be granted to you.

● **2 Cor 7:14**

2 Cor 7 [4]I have great confidence in you; I have great pride in you; I am filled with comfort. With all our affliction, I am overjoyed.

2 Cor 8 [23]As for Titus, he is my partner and fellow worker in your service; and as for our brethren, they are messengers of the churches, the glory of Christ. [24]So give proof, before the churches, of your love and of our boasting about you to these men.

2 Cor 9 [2]for I know your readiness, of which I boast about you to the people of Macedonia, saying that Achaia has been ready since last year; and your zeal has stirred up most of them. [3]But I am sending the brethren so that our boasting about you may not prove vain in this case, so that you may be ready, as I said you would be; . . .

2 Cor 12 [18]I urged Titus to go, and sent the brother with him. Did Titus take advantage of you? Did we not act in the same spirit? Did we not take the same steps?

Gal 2 [1]Then after fourteen years I went up again to Jerusalem with Barnabas, taking Titus along with me. [2]I went up by revelation; and I laid before them (but privately before those who were of repute) the gospel which I preach among the Gentiles, lest somehow I should be running or had run in vain. [3]But even Titus, who was with me, was not compelled to be circumcised, though he was a Greek.

Phil 2 [16]holding fast the word of life, so that in the day of Christ I may be proud that I did not run in vain or labor in vain.

● **1 Cor 7:15**

1 Cor 2 [3]And I was with you in weakness and in much fear and trembling; . . .

● **2 Cor 7:16**

Gal 5 [10]I have confidence in the Lord that you will take no other view than mine; and he who is troubling you will bear his judgment, whoever he is.

FORMAL ELEMENT: VIRTUE LIST

8 We want you to know, brethren, about the grace of God which has been shown in the churches of Macedonia, [2]for in a severe test of affliction, their abundance of joy and their extreme poverty have overflowed in a wealth of liberality on their part. [3]For they gave according to their means, as I can testify, and beyond their means, of their own free will, [4]begging us earnestly for the favor of taking part in the relief of the saints—[5]and this, not as we expected, but first they gave themselves to the Lord and to us by the will of God. [6]Accordingly we have urged Titus that as he had already made a beginning, he should also complete among you this gracious work. [7]Now as you excel in everything—in faith, in utterance, in knowledge, in all earnestness, and in your love for us—see that you excel in this gracious work also.

PRIMARY

Gal 5:16–26 (§213)

[16]But I say, walk by the Spirit, and do not gratify the desires of the flesh. [17]For the desires of the flesh are against the Spirit, and the desires of the Spirit are against the flesh; for these are opposed to each other, to prevent you from doing what you would. [18]But if you are led by the Spirit you are not under the law. [19]Now the works of the flesh are plain: fornication, impurity, licentiousness, [20]idolatry, sorcery, enmity, strife, jealousy, anger, selfishness, dissension, party spirit, [21]envy, drunkenness, carousing, and the like. I warn you, as I warned you before, that those who do such things shall not inherit the kingdom of God. [22]But the fruit of the Spirit is love, joy, peace, patience, kindness, goodness, faithfulness, [23]gentleness, self-control; against such there is no law. [24]And those who belong to Christ Jesus have crucified the flesh with its passions and desires.

[25]If we live by the Spirit, let us also walk by the Spirit. [26]Let us have no self-conceit, no provoking of one another, no envy of one another.

Eph 4:1–10 (§225)

[1]I therefore, a prisoner for the Lord, beg you to lead a life worthy of the calling to which you have been called, [2]with all lowliness and meekness, with patience, forbearing one another in love, [3]eager to maintain the unity of the Spirit in the bond of peace. [4]There is one body and one Spirit, just as you were called to the one hope that belongs to your call, [5]one Lord, one faith, one baptism, [6]one God and Father of us all, who is above all and through all and in all. [7]But grace was given to each of us according to the measure of Christ's gift. [8]Therefore it is said,

"When he ascended on high he led a host of captives,

and he gave gifts to men."

[9](In saying, "He ascended," what does it mean but that he had also descended into the lower parts of the earth? [10]He who descended is he who also ascended far above all the heavens, that he might fill all things.)

Phil 4:8–9 (§252)

[8]Finally, brethren, whatever is true, whatever is honorable, whatever is just, whatever is pure, whatever is lovely, whatever is gracious, if there is any excellence, if there is anything worthy of praise, think about these things. [9]What you have learned and received and heard and seen in me, do; and the God of peace will be with you.

Col 3:12–17 (§267)

[12]Put on then, as God's chosen ones, holy and beloved, compassion, kindness, lowliness, meekness, and patience, [13]forbearing one another and, if one has a complaint against another, forgiving each other; as the Lord has forgiven you, so you also must forgive. [14]And above all these put on love, which binds everything together in perfect harmony. [15]And let the peace of Christ rule in your hearts, to which indeed you were called in the one body. And be thankful. [16]Let the word of Christ dwell in you richly, as you teach and admonish one another in all wisdom, and as you sing psalms and hymns and spiritual songs with thankfulness in your hearts to God. [17]And whatever you do, in word or deed, do everything in the name of the Lord Jesus, giving thanks to God the Father through him.

● **2 Cor 8:1**

Rom 15   [26]For Macedonia and Achaia have been pleased to make some contribution for the poor among the saints at Jerusalem; . . .

Eph 4   [7]But grace was given to each of us according to the measure of Christ's gift.

Phil 4   [15]And you Philippians yourselves know that in the beginning of the gospel, when I left Macedonia, no church entered into partnership with me in giving and receiving except you only; [16]for even in Thessalonica you sent me help once and again.

1 Thess 1   [7]so that you became an example to the all the believers in Macedonia and in Achaia.

● **2 Cor 8:2**

Rom 12   [8]he who exhorts, in his exhortation; he who contributes, in liberality; he who gives aid, with zeal; he who does acts of mercy, with cheerfulness.

● **2 Cor 8:3**

Rom 12   [8]he who exhorts, in his exhortation; he who contributes, in liberality; he who gives aid, with zeal; he who does acts of mercy, with cheerfulness.

Phlm   [14]but I preferred to do nothing without your consent in order that your goodness might not be by compulsion but of your own free will.

● **2 Cor 8:4**

Gal 2   [10]only they would have us remember the poor, which very thing I was eager to do.

Acts 11   [29]And the disciples determined, every one according to his ability, to send relief to the brethren who lived in Judea; . . .

● **2 Cor 8:7**

1 Cor 1   [5]that in every way you were enriched in him with all speech and all knowledge . . .

2 Cor 6   [6]by purity, knowledge, forbearance, kindness, the Holy Spirit, genuine love, [7]truthful speech, and the power of God; with the weapons of righteousness for the right hand and for the left; [8]in honor and dishonor, in ill repute and good repute.

Eph 4   [2]with all lowliness and meekness, with patience, forbearing one another in love, [3]eager to maintain the unity of the Spirit in the bond of peace.

Eph 4   [32]and be kind to one another, tenderhearted, forgiving one another, as God in Christ forgave you.

1 Thess 1   [3]remembering before our God and Father your work of faith and labor of love and steadfastness of hope in our Lord Jesus Christ.

(us) *read* our love for you: p[46] B syr(pes) cop Origen (Latin); *text*: SCDG Koine Lect it vg syr(har) Ambrosiaster

⁸I say this not as a command, but to prove by the earnestness of others that your love also is genuine. ⁹For you know the grace of our Lord Jesus Christ, that though he was rich, yet for your sake he became poor, so that by his poverty you might become rich. ¹⁰And in this matter I give my advice: it is best for you now to complete what a year ago you began not only to do but to desire, ¹¹so that your readiness in desiring it may be matched by your completing it out of what you have. ¹²For if the readiness is there, it is acceptable according to what a man has, not according to what he has not. ¹³I do not mean that others should be eased and you burdened, ¹⁴but that as a matter of equality your abundance at the present time should supply their want, so that their abundance may supply your want, that there may be equality. ¹⁵As it is written, "He who gathered much had nothing over, and he who gathered little had no lack."

PRIMARY

Rom 15:22–29 (§63)

²²This is the reason why I have so often been hindered from coming to you. ²³But now, since I no longer have any room for work in these regions, and since I have longed for many years to come to you, ²⁴I hope to see you in passing as I go to Spain, and to be sped on my journey there by you, once I have enjoyed your company for a little. ²⁵At present, however, I am going to Jerusalem with aid for the saints. ²⁶For Macedonia and Achaia have been pleased to make some contribution for the poor among the saints at Jerusalem; ²⁷they were pleased to do it, and indeed they are in debt to them, for if the Gentiles have come to share in their spiritual blessings, they ought also to be of service to them in material blessings. ²⁸When therefore I have completed this, and have delivered to them what has been raised, I shall go on by way of you to Spain; ²⁹and I know that when I come to you I shall come in the fulness of the blessing of Christ.

1 Cor 16:1–4 (§138)

¹Now concerning the contribution for the saints: as I directed the churches of Galatia, so you also are to do. ²On the first day of every week, each of you is to put something aside and store it up, as he may prosper, so that contributions need not be made when I come. ³And when I arrive, I will send those whom you accredit by letter to carry your gift to Jerusalem. ⁴If it seems advisable that I should go also, they will accompany me.

Gal 2:1–10 (§197)

¹Then after fourteen years I went up again to Jerusalem with Barnabas, taking Titus along with me. ²I went up by revelation; and I laid before them (but privately before those who were of repute) the gospel which I preach among the Gentiles, lest somehow I should be running or had run in vain. ³But even Titus, who was with me, was not compelled to be circumcised, though he was a Greek. ⁴But because of false brethren secretly brought in, who slipped in to spy out our freedom which we have in Christ Jesus, that they might bring us into bondage— ⁵to them we did not yield submission even for a moment, that the truth of the gospel might be preserved for you. ⁶And from those who were reputed to be something (what they were makes no difference to me; God shows no partiality)—those, I say, who were of repute added nothing to me; ⁷but on the contrary, when they saw that I had been entrusted with the gospel to the uncircumcised, just as Peter had been entrusted with the gospel to the circumcised ⁸(for he who worked through Peter for the mission to the circumcised worked through me also for the Gentiles), ⁹and when they perceived the grace that was given to me, James and Cephas and John, who were reputed to be pillars, gave to me and Barnabas the right hand of fellowship, that we should go to the Gentiles and they to the circumcised; ¹⁰only they would have us remember the poor, which very thing I was eager to do.

Gal 6:1–6 (§214)

¹Brethren, if a man is overtaken in any trespass, you who are spiritual should restore him in a spirit of gentleness. Look to yourself, lest you too be tempted. ²Bear one another's burdens, and so fulfil the law of Christ. ³For if any one thinks he is something, when he is nothing, he deceives himself. ⁴But let each one test his own work, and then his reason to boast will be in himself alone and not in his neighbor. ⁵For each man will have to bear his own load. ⁶Let him who is taught the word share all good things with him who teaches.

Phil 2:1–11 (§242)

¹So if there is any encouragement in Christ, any incentive of love, any participation in the Spirit, any affection and sympathy, ²complete my joy by being of the same mind, having the same love, being in full accord and of one mind. ³Do nothing from selfishness or conceit, but in humility count others better than yourselves. ⁴Let each of you look not only to his own interests, but also to the interests of others. ⁵Have this mind among yourselves, which is yours in Christ Jesus, ⁶who, though he was in the form of God, did not count equality with God a thing to be grasped, ⁷but emptied himself, taking the form of a servant, being born in the likeness of men. ⁸And being found in human form he humbled himself and became obedient unto death, even death on a cross. ⁹Therefore God has highly exalted him and bestowed on him the name which is above every name, ¹⁰that at the name of Jesus every knee should bow, in heaven and on earth and under the earth, ¹¹and every tongue confess that Jesus Christ is Lord, to the glory of God the Father.

1 Thess 2:9–12 (§278)

⁹For you remember our labor and toil, brethren; we worked night and day, that we might not burden any of you, while we preached to you the gospel of God. ¹⁰You are witnesses, and God also, how holy and righteous and blameless was our behavior to you believers; ¹¹for you know how, like a father with his children, we exhorted each one of you and encouraged you and charged you ¹²to lead a life worthy of God, who calls you into his own kingdom and glory.

● **2 Cor 8:8**
Rom 12 ⁹Let love be genuine; hate what is evil, hold fast to what is good; . . .

1 Cor 7 ⁶I say this by way of concession, not of command.

1 Cor 7 ¹⁰To the married I give charge, not I but the Lord, that the wife should not separate from her husband . . .

1 Cor 7 ¹²To the rest I say, not the Lord, that if any brother has a wife who is an unbeliever, and she consents to live with him, he should not divorce her.

1 Cor 7 ²⁵Now concerning the unmarried, I have no command of the Lord, but I give my opinion as one who by the Lord's mercy is trustworthy.

1 Cor 7 ³⁵I say this for your own benefit, not to lay any restraint upon you, but to promote good order and to secure your undivided devotion to the Lord.

Phlm ⁸Accordingly, though I am bold enough in Christ to command you to do what is required, ⁹yet for love's sake I prefer to appeal to you—I, Paul, an ambassador and now a prisoner also for Christ Jesus . . .

● **2 Cor 8:15**
Exod 16 ¹⁸But when they measured it with an omer, he that gathered much had nothing over, and he that gathered little had no lack; each gathered according to what he could eat.

FORMAL ELEMENT: COMMENDATION

[16]But thanks be to God who puts the same earnest care for you into the heart of Titus. [17]For he not only accepted our appeal, but being himself very earnest he is going to you of his own accord. [18]With him we are sending the brother who is famous among all the churches for his preaching of the gospel; [19]and not only that, but he has been appointed by the churches to travel with us in this gracious work which we are carrying on, for the glory of the Lord and to show our good will. [20]We intend that no one should blame us about this liberal gift which we are administering, [21]for we aim at what is honorable not only in the Lord's sight but also in the sight of men. [22]And with them we are sending our brother whom we have often tested and found earnest in many matters, but who is now more earnest than ever because of his great confidence in you. [23]As for Titus, he is my partner and fellow worker in your service; and as for our brethren, they are messengers of the churches, the glory of Christ. [24]So give proof, before the churches, of your love and of our boasting about you to these men.

PRIMARY

See §65 for COMMENDATION

SECONDARY

Rom 15:22–29 (§63)

[22]This is the reason why I have so often been hindered from coming to you. [23]But now, since I no longer have any room for work in these regions, and since I have longed for many years to come to you, [24]I hope to see you in passing as I go to Spain, and to be sped on my journey there by you, once I have enjoyed your company for a little. [25]At present, however, I am going to Jerusalem with aid for the saints. [26]For Macedonia and Achaia have been pleased to make some contribution for the poor among the saints at Jerusalem; [27]they were pleased to do it, and indeed they are in debt to them, for if the Gentiles have come to share in their spiritual blessings, they ought also to be of service to them in material blessings. [28]When therefore I have completed this, and have delivered to them what has been raised, I shall go on by way of you to Spain; [29]and I know that when I come to you I shall come in the fulness of the blessing of Christ.

1 Cor 16:1–4 (§138)

[1]Now concerning the contribution for the saints: as I directed the churches of Galatia, so you also are to do. [2]On the first day of every week, each of you is to put something aside and store it up, as he may prosper, so that contributions need not be made when I come. [3]And when I arrive, I will send those whom you accredit by letter to carry your gift to Jerusalem. [4]If it seems advisable that I should go also, they will accompany me.

Gal 2:1–10 (§197)

[1]Then after fourteen years I went up again to Jerusalem with Barnabas, taking Titus along with me. [2]I went up by revelation; and I laid before them (but privately before those who were of repute) the gospel which I preach among the Gentiles, lest somehow I should be running or had run in vain. [3]But even Titus, who was with me, was not compelled to be circumcised, though he was a Greek. [4]But because of false brethren secretly brought in, who slipped in to spy out our freedom which we have in Christ Jesus, that they might bring us into bondage— [5]to them we did not yield submission even for a moment, that the truth of the gospel might be preserved for you. [6]And from those who were reputed to be something (what they were makes no difference to me; God shows no partiality)—those, I say, who were of repute added nothing to me; [7]but on the contrary, when they saw that I had been entrusted with the gospel to the uncircumcised, just as Peter had been entrusted with the gospel to the circumcised [8](for he who worked through Peter for the mission to the circumcised worked through me also for the Gentiles), [9]and when they perceived the grace that was given to me, James and Cephas and John, who were reputed to be pillars, gave to me and Barnabas the right hand of fellowship, that we should go to the Gentiles and they to the circumcised; [10]only they would have us remember the poor, which very thing I was eager to do.

● **2 Cor 8:16–24**

2 Cor 3 [1]Are we beginning to commend ourselves again? Or do we need, as some do, letters of recommendation to you, or from you? [2]You yourselves are our letter of recommendation, written on your hearts, to be known and read by all men; [3]and you show that you are a letter from Christ delivered by us, written not with ink but with the Spirit of the living God, not on tablets of stone but on tablets of human hearts.

● **2 Cor 8:24**

1 Cor 15 [31]I protest, brethren, by my pride in you which I have in Christ Jesus our Lord, I die every day!

2 Cor 7 [4]I have great confidence in you; I have great pride in you; I am filled with comfort. With all our affliction, I am overjoyed.

2 Cor 7 [14]For if I have expressed to him some pride in you, I was not put to shame; but just as everything

we said to you was true, so our boasting before Titus has proved true.

2 Cor 9 [2]for I know your readiness, of which I boast about you to the people of Macedonia, saying that Achaia has been ready since last year; and your zeal has stirred up most of them. [3]But I am sending the brethren so that our boasting about you may not prove vain in this case, so that you may be ready, as I said you would be; . . .

FORMAL ELEMENT: APOSTOLIC VISIT

9 Now it is superfluous for me to write to you about the offering for the saints, [2]for I know your readiness, of which I boast about you to the people of Macedonia, saying that Achaia has been ready since last year; and your zeal has stirred up most of them. [3]But I am sending the brethren so that our boasting about you may not prove vain in this case, so that you may be ready, as I said you would be; [4]lest if some Macedonians come with me and find that you are not ready, we be humiliated—to say nothing of you—for being so confident. [5]So I thought it necessary to urge the brethren to go on to you before me, and arrange in advance for this gift you have promised, so that it may be ready not as an exaction but as a willing gift.

PRIMARY

See §63 for APOSTOLIC VISIT

SECONDARY

1 Thess 1:2–10 (§276)
[2]We give thanks to God always for you all, constantly mentioning you in our prayers, [3]remembering before our God and Father your work of faith and labor of love and steadfastness of hope in our Lord Jesus Christ. [4]For we know, brethren beloved by God, that he has chosen you; [5]for our gospel came to you not only in word, but also in power and in the Holy Spirit and with full conviction. You know what kind of men we proved to be among you for your sake. [6]And you became imitators of us and of the Lord, for you received the word in much affliction, with joy inspired by the Holy Spirit; [7]so that you became an example to the all the believers in Macedonia and in Achaia. [8]For not only has the word of the Lord sounded forth from you in Macedonia and Achaia, but your faith in God has gone forth everywhere, so that we need not say anything. [9]For they themselves report concerning us what a welcome we had among you, and how you turned to God from idols, to serve a living and true God, [10]and to wait for his Son from heaven, whom he raised from the dead, Jesus who delivers us from the wrath to come.

Gal 2:1–10 (§197)
[1]Then after fourteen years I went up again to Jerusalem with Barnabas, taking Titus along with me. [2]I went up by revelation; and I laid before them (but privately before those who were of repute) the gospel which I preach among the Gentiles, lest somehow I should be running or had run in vain. [3]But even Titus, who was with me, was not compelled to be circumcised, though he was a Greek. [4]But because of false brethren secretly brought in, who slipped in to spy out our freedom which we have in Christ Jesus, that they might bring us into bondage— [5]to them we did not yield submission even for a moment, that the truth of the gospel might be preserved for you. [6]And from those who were reputed to be something (what they were makes no difference to me; God shows no partiality)—those, I say, who were of repute added nothing to me; [7]but on the contrary, when they saw that I had been entrusted with the gospel to the uncircumcised, just as Peter had been entrusted with the gospel to the circumcised [8](for he who worked through Peter for the mission to the circumcised worked through me also for the Gentiles), [9]and when they perceived the grace that was given to me, James and Cephas and John, who were reputed to be pillars, gave to me and Barnabas the right hand of fellowship, that we should go to the Gentiles and they to the circumcised; [10]only they would have us remember the poor, which very thing I was eager to do.

● 2 Cor 9:1–5
2 Cor 1   [15]Because I was sure of this, I wanted to come to you first, so that you might have a double pleasure; [16]I wanted to visit you on my way to Macedonia, and to come back to you from Macedonia and have you send me on my way to Judea. [17]Was I vacillating when I wanted to do this? Do I make my plans like a worldly man, ready to say Yes and No at once? [18]As surely as God is faithful, our word to you has not been Yes and No. [19]For the Son of God, Jesus Christ, whom we preached among you, Silvanus and Timothy and I, was not Yes and No; but in him it is always Yes. [20]For all the promises of God find their Yes in him. That is why we utter the Amen through him, to the glory of God. [21]But it is God who establishes us with you in Christ, and has commissioned us; [22]he has put his seal upon us and given us his Spirit in our hearts as a guarantee.
[23]But I call God to witness against me—it was to spare you that I refrained from coming to Corinth. [24]Not that we lord it over your faith; we work with you for your joy, for you stand firm in your faith. 2 [1]For I made up my mind not to make you another painful visit. [2]For if I cause you pain, who is there to make me glad but the one whom I have pained? [3]And I wrote as I did, so that when I came I might not suffer pain from those who should have made me rejoice, for I felt sure of all of you, that my joy would be the joy of you all. [4]For I wrote you out of much affliction and anguish of heart and with many tears, not to cause you pain but to let you know the abundant love that I have for you.

2 Cor 12   [14]Here for the third time I am ready to come to you. And I will not be a burden, for I seek not what is yours but you; for children ought not to lay up for their parents, but parents for their children. [15]I will most gladly spend and be spent for your souls. If I love you the more, am I to be loved the less? [16]But granting that I myself did not burden you, I was crafty, you say, and got the better of you by guile. [17]Did I take advantage of you through any of those whom I sent to you? [18]I urged Titus to go, and sent the brother with him. Did Titus take advantage of you? Did we not act in the same spirit? Did we not take the same steps?
[19]Have you been thinking all along that we have been defending ourselves before you? It is in the sight of God that we have been speaking in Christ, and all for your upbuilding, beloved. [20]For I fear that perhaps I may come and find you not what I wish, and that you may find me not what you wish; that perhaps there may be quarreling, jealousy, anger, selfishness, slander, gossip, conceit, and disorder. [21]I fear that when I come again my God may humble me before you, and I may have to mourn over many of those who sinned before and have not repented of the impurity, immorality, and licentiousness which they have practiced.
13 [1]This is the third time I am coming to you. Any charge must be sustained by the evidence of two or three witnesses. [2]I warned those who sinned before and all the others, and I warn them now while absent, as I did when present on my second visit, that if I come again I will not spare them— [3]since you desire proof that Christ is speaking in me. He is not weak in dealing with you, but is powerful in you. [4]For he was crucified in weakness, but lives by the power of God. For we are weak in him, but in dealing with you we shall live with him by the power of God.
[5]Examine yourselves, to see whether you are holding to your faith. Test yourselves. Do you not realize that Jesus Christ is in you?—unless indeed you fail to meet the test! [6]I hope you will find out that we have not failed. [7]But we pray God that you may not do wrong—not that we may appear to have met the test, but that you may do what is right, though we may seem to have failed. [8]For we cannot do anything against the truth, but only for the truth. [9]For we are glad when we are weak and you are strong. What we pray for is your improvement. [10]I write this while I am away from you, in order that when I come I may not have to be severe in my use of the authority which the Lord has given me for building up and not for tearing down.

● 2 Cor 9:1
Phil 3   [1]Finally, my brethren, rejoice in the Lord. To write the same things to you is not irksome to me, and is safe for you.

● 2 Cor 9:2–3
1 Cor 15   [31]I protest, brethren, by my pride in you which I have in Christ Jesus our Lord, I die every day!

2 Cor 7   [4]I have great confidence in you; I have great pride in you; I am filled with comfort. With all our affliction, I am overjoyed.

2 Cor 7   [14]For if I have expressed to him some pride in you, I was not put to shame; but just as everything we said to you was true, so our boasting before Titus has proved true.

2 Cor 8   [24]So give proof, before the churches, of your love and of our boasting about you to these men.

Phil 2   [16]holding fast the word of life, so that in the day of Christ I may be proud that I did not run in vain or labor in vain.

[6] The point is this: he who sows sparingly will also reap sparingly, and he who sows bountifully will also reap bountifully. [7] Each one must do as he has made up his mind, not reluctantly or under compulsion, for God loves a cheerful giver. [8] And God is able to provide you with every blessing in abundance, so that you may always have enough of everything and may provide in abundance for every good work. [9] As it is written,

"He scatters abroad, he gives to the poor; his righteousness endures for ever."

[10] He who supplies seed to the sower and bread for food will supply and multiply your resources and increase the harvest of your righteousness. [11] You will be enriched in every way for great generosity, which through us will produce thanksgiving to God; [12] for the rendering of this service not only supplies the wants of the saints but also overflows in many thanksgivings to God. [13] Under the test of this service, you will glorify God by your obedience in acknowledging the gospel of Christ, and by the generosity of your contribution for them and for all others; [14] while they long for you and pray for you, because of the surpassing grace of God in you. [15] Thanks be to God for his inexpressible gift!

Primary

Rom 15:22-29 (§63)

[22] This is the reason why I have so often been hindered from coming to you. [23] But now, since I no longer have any room for work in these regions, and since I have longed for many years to come to you, [24] I hope to see you in passing as I go to Spain, and to be sped on my journey there by you, once I have enjoyed your company for a little. [25] At present, however, I am going to Jerusalem with aid for the saints. [26] For Macedonia and Achaia have been pleased to make some contribution for the poor among the saints at Jerusalem; [27] they were pleased to do it, and indeed they are in debt to them, for if the Gentiles have come to share in their spiritual blessings, they ought also to be of service to them in material blessings. [28] When therefore I have completed this, and have delivered to them what has been raised, I shall go on by way of you to Spain; [29] and I know that when I come to you I shall come in the fulness of the blessing of Christ.

1 Cor 9:1-14 (§105)

[1] Am I not free? Am I not an apostle? Have I not seen Jesus our Lord? Are not you my workmanship in the Lord? [2] If to others I am not an apostle, at least I am to you; for you are the seal of my apostleship in the Lord.

[3] This is my defense to those who would examine me. [4] Do we not have the right to our food and drink? [5] Do we not have the right to be accompanied by a wife, as the other apostles and the brothers of the Lord and Cephas? [6] Or is it only Barnabas and I who have no right to refrain from working for a living? [7] Who serves as a soldier at his own expense? Who plants a vineyard without eating any of its fruit? Who tends a flock without getting some of the milk?

[8] Do I say this on human authority? Does not the law say the same? [9] For it is written in the law of Moses, "You shall not muzzle an ox when it is treading out the grain." Is it for oxen that God is concerned? [10] Does he not speak entirely for our sake? It was written for our sake, because the plowman should plow in hope and the thresher thresh in hope of a share in the crop. [11] If we have sown spiritual good among you, is it too much if we reap your material benefits? [12] If others share this rightful claim upon you, do not we still more?

Nevertheless, we have not made use of this right, but we endure anything rather than put an obstacle in the way of the gospel of Christ. [13] Do you not know that those who are employed in the temple service get their food from the temple, and those who serve at the altar share in the sacrificial offerings? [14] In the same way, the Lord commanded that those who proclaim the gospel should get their living by the gospel.

1 Cor 16:1-4 (§138)

[1] Now concerning the contribution for the saints: as I directed the churches of Galatia, so you also are to do. [2] On the first day of every week, each of you is to put something aside and store it up, as he may prosper, so that contributions need not be made when I come. [3] And when I arrive, I will send those whom you accredit by letter to carry your gift to Jerusalem. [4] If it seems advisable that I should go also, they will accompany me.

Gal 2:1-10 (§197)

[1] Then after fourteen years I went up again to Jerusalem with Barnabas, taking Titus along with me. [2] I went up by revelation; and I laid before them (but privately before those who were of repute) the gospel which I preach among the Gentiles, lest somehow I should be running or had run in vain. [3] But even Titus, who was with me, was not compelled to be circumcised, though he was a Greek. [4] But because of false brethren secretly brought in, who slipped in to spy out our freedom which we have in Christ Jesus, that they might bring us into bondage— [5] to them we did not yield submission even for a moment, that the truth of the gospel might be preserved for you. [6] And from those who were reputed to be something (what they were makes no difference to me; God shows no partiality)—those, I say, who were of repute added nothing to me; [7] but on the contrary, when they saw that I had been entrusted with the gospel to the uncircumcised, just as Peter had been entrusted with the gospel to the circumcised [8] (for he who worked through Peter for the mission to the circumcised worked through me also for the Gentiles), [9] and when they perceived the grace that was given to me, James and Cephas and John, who were reputed to be pillars, gave to me and Barnabas the right hand of fellowship, that we should go to the Gentiles and they to the circumcised; [10] only they would have us remember the poor, which very thing I was eager to do.

Eph 3:20-21 (§224)

[20] Now to him who by the power at work within us is able to do far more abundantly than all that we ask or think, [21] to him be glory in the church and in Christ Jesus to all generations, for ever and ever. Amen.

● **2 Cor 9:6**
Gal 6 [7] Do not be deceived; God is not mocked, for whatever a man sows, that he will also reap. [8] For he who sows to his own flesh will from the flesh reap corruption; but he who sows to the Spirit will from the Spirit reap eternal life. [9] And let us not grow weary in well-doing, for in due season we shall reap, if we do not lose heart.

● **2 Cor 9:7**
Phlm [14] but I preferred to do nothing without your consent in order that your goodness might not be by compulsion but of your own free will.

● **2 Cor 9:8**
Rom 12 [8] he who exhorts, in his exhortation; he who contributes, in liberality; he who gives aid, with zeal; he who does acts of mercy, with cheerfulness.

● **2 Cor 9:9**
Ps 112 [9] He has distributed freely, he has given to the poor;
his righteousness endures for ever;
his horn is exalted in honor.

● **2 Cor 9:12**
2 Cor 4 [15] For it is all for your sake, so that as grace extends to more and more people it may increase thanksgiving, to the glory of God.

Eph 5 [20] always and for everything giving thanks in the name of our Lord Jesus Christ to God the Father.

Col 3 [15] ... And be thankful. [16] Let the word of Christ dwell in you richly, as you teach and admonish one another in all wisdom, and as you sing psalms and hymns and spiritual songs with thankfulness in your hearts to God. [17] And whatever you do, in word or deed, do everything in the name of the Lord Jesus, giving thanks to God the Father through him.

Letter Structure: Appeal

10 I, Paul, myself entreat you, by the meekness and gentleness of Christ—I who am humble when face to face with you, but bold to you when I am away!—[2] I beg of you that when I am present I may not have to show boldness with such confidence as I count on showing against some who suspect us of acting in worldly fashion. [3] For though we live in the world we are not carrying on a worldly war, [4] for the weapons of our warfare are not worldly but have divine power to destroy strongholds. [5] We destroy arguments and every proud obstacle to the knowledge of God, and take every thought captive to obey Christ, [6] being ready to punish every disobedience, when your obedience is complete.

Primary

Rom 12:1–2 (§51)

[1] I appeal to you therefore, brethren, by the mercies of God, to present your bodies as a living sacrifice, holy and acceptable to God, which is your spiritual worship. [2] Do not be conformed to this world but be transformed by the renewal of your mind, that you may prove what is the will of God, what is good and acceptable and perfect.

1 Cor 1:10–17 (§73)

[10] I appeal to you, brethren, by the name of our Lord Jesus Christ, that all of you agree and that there be no dissensions among you, but that you be united in the same mind and the same judgment. [11] For it has been reported to me by Chloe's people that there is quarreling among you, my brethren. [12] What I mean is that each one of you says, "I belong to Paul," or "I belong to Apollos," or "I belong to Cephas," or "I belong to Christ." [13] Is Christ divided? Was Paul crucified for you? Or were you baptized in the name of Paul? [14] I am thankful that I baptized none of you except Crispus and Gaius; [15] lest any one should say that you were baptized in my name. [16] (I did baptize also the household of Stephanas. Beyond that, I do not know whether I baptized any one else.) [17] For Christ did not send me to baptize but to preach the gospel, and not with eloquent wisdom, lest the cross of Christ be emptied of its power.

Eph 4:1–10 (§225)

[1] I therefore, a prisoner for the Lord, beg you to lead a life worthy of the calling to which you have been called, [2] with all lowliness and meekness, with patience, forbearing one another in love, [3] eager to maintain the unity of the Spirit in the bond of peace. [4] There is one body and one Spirit, just as you were called to the one hope that belongs to your call, [5] one Lord, one faith, one baptism, [6] one God and Father of us all, who is above all and through all and in all. [7] But grace was given to each of us according to the measure of Christ's gift. [8] Therefore it is said,

"When he ascended on high he led a host of captives,

and he gave gifts to men."

[9] (In saying, "He ascended," what does it mean but that he had also descended into the lower parts of the earth? [10] He who descended is he who also ascended far above all the heavens, that he might fill all things.)

1 Thess 4:1–8 (§284)

[1] Finally, brethren, we beseech and exhort you in the Lord Jesus, that as you learned from us how you ought to live and to please God, just as you are doing, you do so more and more. [2] For you know what instructions we gave you through the Lord Jesus. [3] For this is the will of God, your sanctification: that you abstain from unchastity; [4] that each one of you know how to take a wife for himself in holiness and honor [5] not in the passion of lust like heathen who do not know God; [6] that no man transgress, and wrong his brother in this matter, because the Lord is an avenger in all these things, as we solemnly forewarned you. [7] For God has not called us for uncleanness, but in holiness. [8] Therefore whoever disregards this, disregards not man but God, who gives his Holy Spirit to you.

2 Thess 2:1–12 (§296)

[1] Now concerning the coming of our Lord Jesus Christ and our assembling to meet him, we beg you, brethren, [2] not to be quickly shaken in mind or excited, either by spirit or by word, or by letter purporting to be from us, to the effect that the day of the Lord has come. [3] Let no one deceive you in any way; for that day will not come, unless the rebellion comes first, and the man of lawlessness is revealed, the son of perdition, [4] who opposes and exalts himself against every so-called god or object of worship, so that he takes his seat in the temple of God, proclaiming himself to be God. [5] Do you not remember that when I was still with you I told you this? [6] And you know what is restraining him now so that he may be revealed in his time. [7] For the mystery of lawlessness is already at work; only he who now restrains it will do so until he is out of the way. [8] And then the lawless one will be revealed, and the Lord Jesus will slay him with the breath of his mouth and destroy him by his appearing and his coming. [9] The coming of the lawless one by the activity of Satan will be with all power and with pretended signs and wonders, [10] and with all wicked deception for those who are to perish, because they refused to love the truth and so be saved. [11] Therefore God sends upon them a strong delusion, to make them believe what is false, [12] so that all may be condemned who did not believe the truth but had pleasure in unrighteousness.

Phlm 8–14 (§307)

[8] Accordingly, though I am bold enough in Christ to command you to do what is required, [9] yet for love's sake I prefer to appeal to you—I, Paul, an ambassador and now a prisoner also for Christ Jesus— [10] I appeal to you for my child, Onesimus, whose father I have become in my imprisonment. [11] (Formerly he was useless to you, but now he is indeed useful to you and to me.) [12] I am sending him back to you, sending my very heart. [13] I would have been glad to keep him with me, in order that he might serve me on your behalf during my imprisonment for the gospel; [14] but I preferred to do nothing without your consent in order that your goodness might not be by compulsion but of your own free will.

● **2 Cor 10:1–6**

2 Cor 13   [10] I write this while I am away from you, in order that when I come I may not have to be severe in my use of the authority which the Lord has given me for building up and not for tearing down.

● **2 Cor 10:1**

1 Cor 2   [3] And I was with you in weakness and in much fear and trembling; . . .

2 Cor 10   [10] For they say, "His letters are weighty and strong, but his bodily presence is weak, and his speech of no account."

Gal 1   [8] But even if we, or an angel from heaven, should preach to you a gospel contrary to that which we preached to you, let him be accursed. [9] As we have said before, so now I say again, If any one is preaching to you a gospel contrary to that which you received, let him be accursed.

Gal 4   [13] you know it was because of a bodily ailment that I preached the gospel to you at first; [14] and though my condition was a trial to you, you did not scorn or despise me, but received me as an angel of God, as Christ Jesus.

● **2 Cor 10:2**

Rom 16   [17] I appeal to you, brethren, to take note of those who create dissensions and difficulties, in opposition to the doctrine which you have been taught;

SECONDARY

Rom 1:16–17 (§3)

[16] For I am not ashamed of the gospel: it is the power of God for salvation to every one who has faith, to the Jew first and also to the Greek. [17] For in it the righteousness of God is revealed through faith for faith; as it is written, "He who through faith is righteous shall live."

Rom 13:11–14 (§56)

[11] Besides this you know what hour it is, how it is full time now for you to wake from sleep. For salvation is nearer to us now than when we first believed; [12] the night is far gone, the day is at hand. Let us then cast off the works of darkness and put on the armor of light; [13] let us conduct ourselves becomingly as in the day, not in reveling and drunkenness, not in debauchery and licentiousness, not in quarreling and jealousy. [14] But put on the Lord Jesus Christ, and make no provision for the flesh, to gratify its desires.

1 Cor 4:14–21 (§86)

[14] I do not write this to make you ashamed, but to admonish you as my beloved children. [15] For though you have countless guides in Christ, you do not have many fathers. For I became your father in Christ Jesus through the gospel. [16] I urge you, then, be imitators of me. [17] Therefore I sent to you Timothy, my beloved and faithful child in the Lord, to remind you of my ways in Christ, as I teach them everywhere in every church. [18] Some are arrogant, as though I were not coming to you. [19] But I will come to you soon, if the Lord wills, and I will find out not the talk of these arrogant people but their power. [20] For the kingdom of God does not consist in talk but in power. [21] What do you wish? Shall I come to you with a rod, or with love in a spirit of gentleness?

Gal 1:13–14 (§195)

[13] For you have heard of my former life in Judaism, how I persecuted the church of God violently and tried to destroy it; [14] and I advanced in Judaism beyond many of my own age among my people, so extremely zealous was I for the traditions of my fathers.

Eph 6:10–17 (§233)

[10] Finally, be strong in the Lord and in the strength of his might. [11] Put on the whole armor of God, that you may be able to stand against the wiles of the devil. [12] For we are not contending against flesh and blood, but against the principalities, against the powers, against the world rulers of this present darkness, against the spiritual hosts of wickedness in the heavenly places. [13] Therefore take the whole armor of God, that you may be able to withstand in the evil day, and having done all, to stand. [14] Stand therefore, having girded your loins with truth, and having put on the breastplate of righteousness, [15] and having shod your feet with the equipment of the gospel of peace; [16] besides all these, taking the shield of faith, with which you can quench all the flaming darts of the evil one. [17] And take the helmet of salvation, and the sword of the Spirit, which is the word of God.

Phil 1:12–18 (§239)

[12] I want you to know, brethren, that what has happened to me has really served to advance the gospel, [13] so that it has become known throughout the whole praetorian guard and to all the rest that my imprisonment is for Christ; [14] and most of the brethren have been made confident in the Lord because of my imprisonment, and are much more bold to speak the word of God without fear. [15] Some indeed preach Christ from envy and rivalry, but others from good will. [16] The latter do it out of love, knowing that I am put here for the defense of the gospel; [17] the former proclaim Christ out of partisanship, not sincerely but thinking to afflict me in my imprisonment. [18] What then? Only that in every way, whether in pretense or in truth, Christ is proclaimed; and in that I rejoice.

Col 2:20–23 (§264)

[20] If with Christ you died to the elemental spirits of the universe, why do you live as if you still belonged to the world? Why do you submit to regulations, [21] "Do not handle, Do not taste, Do not touch" [22] (referring to things which all perish as they are used), according to human precepts and doctrines? [23] These have indeed an appearance of wisdom in promoting rigor of devotion and self-abasement and severity to the body, but they are of no value in checking the indulgence of the flesh.

1 Thess 2:1–8 (§277)

[1] For you yourselves know, brethren, that our visit to you was not in vain; [2] but though we had already suffered and been shamefully treated at Philippi, as you know, we had courage in our God to declare to you the gospel of God in the face of great opposition. [3] For our appeal does not spring from error or uncleanness, nor is it made with guile; [4] but just as we have been approved by God to be entrusted with the gospel, so we speak, not to please men, but to please God who tests our hearts. [5] For we never used either words of flattery, as you know, or a cloak for greed, as God is witness; [6] nor did we seek glory from men, whether from you or from others, though we might have made demands as apostles of Christ. [7] But we were gentle among you, like a nurse taking care of her children. [8] So, being affectionately desirous of you, we were ready to share with you not only the gospel of God but also our own selves, because you had become very dear to us.

1 Thess 5:1–11 (§287)

[1] But as to the times and the seasons, brethren, you have no need to have anything written to you. [2] For you yourselves know well that the day of the Lord will come like a thief in the night. [3] When people say, "There is peace and security," then sudden destruction will come upon them as travail comes upon a woman with child, and there will be no escape. [4] But you are not in darkness, brethren, for that day to surprise you like a thief. [5] For you are all sons of light and sons of the day; we are not of the night or of darkness. [6] So then let us not sleep, as others do, but let us keep awake and be sober. [7] For those who sleep sleep at night, and those who get drunk are drunk at night. [8] But, since we belong to the day, let us be sober, and put on the breastplate of faith and love, and for a helmet the hope of salvation. [9] For God has not destined us for wrath, but to obtain salvation through our Lord Jesus Christ, [10] who died for us so that whether we wake or sleep we might live with him. [11] Therefore encourage one another and build one another up, just as you are doing.

---

avoid them. [18] For such persons do not serve our Lord Christ, but their own appetites, and by fair and flattering words they deceive the hearts of the simpleminded. [19] For while your obedience is known to all, so that I rejoice over you, I would have you wise as to what is good and guileless as to what is evil; [20] then the God of peace will soon crush Satan under your feet.

1 Cor 3 [3] for you are still of the flesh. For while there is jealousy and strife among you, are you not of the flesh, and behaving like ordinary men?

2 Cor 2 [17] For we are not, like so many, peddlers of God's word; but as men of sincerity, as commissioned by God, in the sight of God we speak in Christ.

2 Cor 4 [2] We have renounced disgraceful, underhanded ways; we refuse to practice cunning or to tamper with God's word, but by the open statement of the truth we would commend ourselves to every man's conscience in the sight of God.

● **2 Cor 10:3**

2 Cor 6 [7] truthful speech, and the power of God; with the weapons of righteousness for the right hand and for the left; . . .

● **2 Cor 10:4**

Cf. 1 Tim 1 [18] This charge I commit to you, Timothy, my son, in accordance with the prophetic utterances which pointed to you, that inspired by them you may wage the good warfare, . . .

⁷Look at what is before your eyes. If any one is confident that he is Christ's, let him remind himself that as he is Christ's, so are we. ⁸For even if I boast a little too much of our authority, which the Lord gave for building you up and not for destroying you, I shall not be put to shame. ⁹I would not seem to be frightening you with letters. ¹⁰For they say, "His letters are weighty and strong, but his bodily presence is weak, and his speech of no account." ¹¹Let such people understand that what we say by letter when absent, we do when present. ¹²Not that we venture to class or compare ourselves with some of those who commend themselves. But when they measure themselves by one another and compare themselves with one another, they are without understanding.

Primary

Rom 1:1–7 (§1)

¹Paul, a servant of Jesus Christ, called to be an apostle, set apart for the gospel of God ²which he promised beforehand through his prophets in the holy scriptures, ³the gospel concerning his Son, who was descended from David according to the flesh ⁴and designated Son of God in power according to the Spirit of holiness by his resurrection from the dead, Jesus Christ our Lord, ⁵through whom we have received grace and apostleship to bring about the obedience of faith for the sake of his name among all the nations, ⁶including yourselves who are called to belong to Jesus Christ;

⁷To all God's beloved in Rome, who are called to be saints:

Grace to you and peace from God our Father and the Lord Jesus Christ.

Rom 15:14–21 (§62)

¹⁴I myself am satisfied about you, my brethren, that you yourselves are full of goodness, filled with all knowledge, and able to instruct one another. ¹⁵But on some points I have written to you very boldly by way of reminder, because of the grace given me by God ¹⁶to be a minister of Christ Jesus to the Gentiles in the priestly service of the gospel of God, so that the offering of the Gentiles may be acceptable, sanctified by the Holy Spirit. ¹⁷In Christ Jesus, then, I have reason to be proud of my work for God. ¹⁸For I will not venture to speak of anything except what Christ has wrought through me to win obedience from the Gentiles, by word and deed, ¹⁹by the power of signs and wonders, by the power of the Holy Spirit, so that from Jerusalem and as far round as Illyricum I have fully preached the gospel of Christ, ²⁰thus making it my ambition to preach the gospel, not where Christ has already been named, lest I build on another man's foundation, ²¹but as it is written,

"They shall see who have never been told of him,
and they shall understand who have never heard of him."

1 Cor 2:1–5 (§76)

¹When I came to you, brethren, I did not come proclaiming to you the testimony of God in lofty words or wisdom. ²For I decided to know nothing among you except Jesus Christ and him crucified. ³And I was with you in weakness and in much fear and trembling; ⁴and my speech and my message were not in plausible words of wisdom, but in demonstration of the Spirit and of power, ⁵that your faith might not rest in the wisdom of men but in the power of God.

1 Cor 3:18–23 (§82)

¹⁸Let no one deceive himself. If any one among you thinks that he is wise in this age, let him become a fool that he may become wise. ¹⁹For the wisdom of this world is folly with God. For it is written, "He catches the wise in their craftiness," ²⁰and again, "The Lord knows that the thoughts of the wise are futile." ²¹So let no one boast of men. For all things are yours, ²²whether Paul or Apollos or Cephas or the world or life or death or the present or the future, all are yours; ²³and you are Christ's; and Christ is God's.

1 Cor 4:1–5 (§83)

¹This is how one should regard us, as servants of Christ and stewards of the mysteries of God. ²Moreover it is required of stewards that they be found trustworthy. ³But with me it is a very small thing that I should be judged by you or by any human court. I do not even judge myself. ⁴I am not aware of anything against myself, but I am not thereby acquitted. It is the Lord who judges me. ⁵Therefore do not pronounce judgment before the time, before the Lord comes, who will bring to light the things now hidden in darkness and will disclose the purposes of the heart. Then every man will receive his commendation from God.

1 Cor 15:1–11 (§131)

¹Now I would remind you, brethren, in what terms I preached to you the gospel, which you received, in which you stand, ²by which you are saved, if you hold it fast —unless you believed in vain.

³For I delivered to you as of first importance what I also received, that Christ died for our sins in accordance with the scriptures, ⁴that he was buried, that he was raised on the third day

---

● 2 Cor 10:7

1 Cor 4   ²³You were bought with a price; do not become slaves of men.

2 Cor 11   ²¹. . . But whatever any one dares to boast of—I am speaking as a fool—I also dare to boast of that. ²²Are they Hebrews? So am I. Are they Israelites? So am I. Are they descendants of Abraham? So am I. ²³Are they servants of Christ? I am a better one—I am talking like a madman—with far greater labors, far more imprisonments, with countless beatings, and often near death.

● 2 Cor 10:8

Rom 1   ¹⁶For I am not ashamed of the gospel: it is the power of God for salvation to every one who has

faith, to the Jew first and also to the Greek. ¹⁷For in it the righteousness of God is revealed through faith for faith; as it is written, "He who through faith is righteous shall live."

1 Cor 5   ⁴in the name of the Lord Jesus on the man who has done such a thing. When you are assembled, and my spirit is present, with the power of our Lord Jesus, . . .

1 Cor 13   ¹⁰I write this while I am away from you, in order that when I come I may not have to be severe in my use of the authority which the Lord has given me for building up and not for tearing down.

Gal 2   ¹⁸But if I build up again those things which I tore down, then I prove myself a transgressor.

Phlm   ⁸Accordingly, though I am bold enough in Christ to command you to do what is required, ⁹yet for love's sake I prefer to appeal to you—I, Paul, an ambassador and now a prisoner also for Christ Jesus . . .

● 2 Cor 10:10–12

2 Cor 12   ¹¹I have been a fool! You forced me to it, for I ought to have been commended by you. For I was not at all inferior to these superlative apostles, even though I am nothing. ¹²The signs of a true apostle were performed among you in all patience, with signs and wonders and mighty works.

● 2 Cor 10:10

2 Cor 1   ¹³For we write you nothing but what you

in accordance with the scriptures, ⁵and that he appeared to Cephas, then to the twelve. ⁶Then he appeared to more than five hundred brethren at one time, most of whom are still alive, though some have fallen asleep. ⁷Then he appeared to James, then to all the apostles. ⁸Last of all, as to one untimely born, he appeared also to me. ⁹For I am the least of the apostles, unfit to be called an apostle, because I persecuted the church of God. ¹⁰But by the grace of God I am what I am, and his grace toward me was not in vain. On the contrary, I worked harder than any of them, though it was not I, but the grace of God which is with me. ¹¹Whether then it was I or they, so we preach and so you believed.

Eph 3:1-13 (§222)

¹For this reason I, Paul, a prisoner for Christ Jesus on behalf of you Gentiles— ²assuming that you have heard of the stewardship of God's grace that was given to me for you, ³how the mystery was made known to me by revelation, as I have written briefly. ⁴When you read this you can perceive my insight into the mystery of Christ, ⁵which was not made known to the sons of men in other generations as it has now been revealed to his holy apostles and prophets by the Spirit; ⁶that is, how the Gentiles are fellow heirs, members of the same body, and partakers of the promise in Christ Jesus through the gospel. ⁷Of this gospel I was made a minister according to the gift of God's grace which was given me by the working of his power. ⁸To me, though I am the very least of all the saints, this grace was given, to preach to the Gentiles the unsearchable riches of Christ, ⁹and to make all men see what is the plan of the mystery hidden for ages in God who created all things; ¹⁰that

through the church the manifold wisdom of God might now be made known to the principalities and powers in the heavenly places. ¹¹This was according to the eternal purpose which he has realized in Christ Jesus our Lord, ¹²in whom we have boldness and confidence of access through our faith in him. ¹³So I ask you not to lose heart over what I am suffering for you, which is your glory.

Phil 1:12-18 (§239)

¹²I want you to know, brethren, that what has happened to me has really served to advance the gospel, ¹³so that it has become known throughout the whole praetorian guard and to all the rest that my imprisonment is for Christ; ¹⁴and most of the brethren have been made confident in the Lord because of my imprisonment, and are much more bold to speak the word of God without fear. ¹⁵Some indeed preach Christ from envy and rivalry, but others from good will. ¹⁶The latter do it out of love, knowing that I am put here for the defense of the gospel; ¹⁷the former proclaim Christ out of partisanship, not sincerely but thinking to afflict me in my imprisonment. ¹⁸What then? Only that in every way, whether in pretense or in truth, Christ is proclaimed; and in that I rejoice.

Col 1:24-2:3 (§260)

²⁴Now I rejoice in my sufferings for your sake, and in my flesh I complete what is lacking in Christ's afflictions for the sake of his body, that is, the church, ²⁵of which I became a minister according to the divine office which was given me for you, to make the word of God fully known, ²⁶the mystery hidden for ages and generations but now made manifest to his saints. ²⁷To them God chose to make known

how great among the Gentiles are the riches of the glory of this mystery, which is Christ in you, the hope of glory. ²⁸Him we proclaim warning every man and teaching every man in all wisdom, that we may present every man mature in Christ. ²⁹For this I toil, striving with all the energy which he mightily inspires within me.

2 ¹For I want you to know how greatly I strive for you, and for those at Laodicea, and for all who have not seen my face, ²that their hearts may be encouraged as they are knit together in love, to have all the riches of assured understanding and the knowledge of God's mystery, of Christ, ³in whom are hid all the treasures of wisdom and knowledge.

1 Thess 2:1-8 (§277)

¹For you yourselves know, brethren, that our visit to you was not in vain; ²but though we had already suffered and been shamefully treated at Philippi, as you know, we had courage in our God to declare to you the gospel of God in the face of great opposition. ³For our appeal does not spring from error or uncleanness, nor is it made with guile; ⁴but just as we have been approved by God to be entrusted with the gospel, so we speak, not to please men, but to please God who tests our hearts. ⁵For we never used either words of flattery, as you know, or a cloak for greed, as God is witness; ⁶nor did we seek glory from men, whether from you or from others, though we might have made demands as apostles of Christ. ⁷But we were gentle among you, like a nurse taking care of her children. ⁸So, being affectionately desirous of you, we were ready to share with you not only the gospel of God but also our own selves, because you had become very dear to us.

---

can read and understand; I hope you will understand fully, . . .

2 Cor 10　¹I, Paul, myself entreat you, by the meekness and gentleness of Christ—I who am humble when face to face with you, but bold to you when I am away!

2 Cor 11　⁶Even if I am unskilled in speaking, I am not in knowledge; in every way we have made this plain to you in all things.

2 Cor 12　⁷And to keep me from being too elated by the abundance of revelations, a thorn was given me in the flesh, a messenger of Satan, to harass me, to keep me from being too elated.

Gal 4　¹²Brethren, I beseech you, become as I am, for I also have become as you are. You did me no wrong; ¹³you know it was because of a bodily ailment that I preached the gospel to you at first; ¹⁴and though my condition was a trial to you, you did not scorn or despise me, but received me as an angel of God, as Christ Jesus. ¹⁵What has become of the satisfaction you felt? For I bear you witness that, if possible, you would have plucked out your eyes and given them to me. ¹⁶Have I then become your enemy by telling you the truth? ¹⁷They make much of you, but for no good purpose; they want to shut you out, that you may make much of them. ¹⁸For a good purpose it is always good to be made much of, and not only when I am present with you. ¹⁹My little children, with whom I am again in travail until Christ be formed in you! ²⁰I could wish

to be present with you now and to change my tone, for I am perplexed about you.

● **2 Cor 10:11**
2 Cor 1　¹⁷Was I vacillating when I wanted to do this? Do I make my plans like a worldly man, ready to say Yes and No at once? ¹⁸As surely as God is faithful, our word to you has not been Yes and No.

● **1 Cor 10:12**
Gal 2　⁶And from those who were reputed to be something (what they were makes no difference to me; God shows no partiality)—those, I say, who were of repute added nothing to me; . . .

¹³But we will not boast beyond limit, but will keep to the limits God has apportioned us, to reach even to you. ¹⁴For we are not overextending ourselves, as though we did not reach you; we were the first to come all the way to you with the gospel of Christ. ¹⁵We do not boast beyond limit, in other men's labors; but our hope is that as your faith increases, our field among you may be greatly enlarged, ¹⁶so that we may preach the gospel in lands beyond you, without boasting of work already done in another's field. ¹⁷"Let him who boasts, boast of the Lord." ¹⁸For it is not the man who commends himself that is accepted, but the man whom the Lord commends.

PRIMARY

Rom 3:27–31 (§15)

²⁷Then what becomes of our boasting? It is excluded. On what principle? On the principle of works? No, but on the principle of faith. ²⁸For we hold that a man is justified by faith apart from works of law. ²⁹Or is God the God of Jews only? Is he not the God of Gentiles also? Yes, of Gentiles also, ³⁰since God is one; and he will justify the circumcised on the ground of their faith and the uncircumcised through their faith. ³¹Do we then overthrow the law by this faith? By no means! On the contrary, we uphold the law.

Rom 15:14–21 (§62)

¹⁴I myself am satisfied about you, my brethren, that you yourselves are full of goodness, filled with all knowledge, and able to instruct one another. ¹⁵But on some points I have written to you very boldly by way of reminder, because of the grace given me by God ¹⁶to be a minister of Christ Jesus to the Gentiles in the priestly service of the gospel of God, so that the offering of the Gentiles may be acceptable, sanctified by the Holy Spirit. ¹⁷In Christ Jesus, then, I have reason to be proud of my work for God. ¹⁸For I will not venture to speak of anything except what Christ has wrought through me to win obedience from the Gentiles, by

word and deed, ¹⁹by the power of signs and wonders, by the power of the Holy Spirit, so that from Jerusalem and as far round as Illyricum I have fully preached the gospel of Christ, ²⁰thus making it my ambition to preach the gospel, not where Christ has already been named, ²¹but as it is written,
"They shall see who have never been told of him,
and they shall understand who have never heard of him."

1 Cor 3:5–9 (§79)

⁵What then is Apollos? What is Paul? Servants through whom you believed, as the Lord assigned to each. ⁶I planted, Apollos watered, but God gave the growth. ⁷So neither he who plants nor he who waters is anything, but only God who gives the growth. ⁸He who plants and he who waters are equal, and each shall receive his wages according to his labor. ⁹For we are God's fellow workers; you are God's field, God's building.

1 Cor 3:10–15 (§80)

¹⁰According to the grace of God given to me, like a skilled master builder I laid a foundation, and another man is building upon it. Let each man take care how he builds upon it. ¹¹For no other foundation can any one lay than that which is laid, which is Jesus Christ. ¹²Now if any one builds on the foundation with gold, silver, precious stones, wood, hay, straw— ¹³each man's work will become manifest; for the Day will disclose it, because it will be revealed with fire, and the fire will test what sort of work each one has done. ¹⁴If the work which any man has built on the foundation survives, he will receive a reward. ¹⁵If any man's work is burned up, he will suffer loss, though he himself will be saved, but only as through fire.

1 Cor 4:14–21 (§86)

¹⁴I do not write this to make you ashamed, but to admonish you as my beloved children. ¹⁵For though you have countless guides in Christ, you do not have many fathers. For I

became your father in Christ Jesus through the gospel. ¹⁶I urge you, then, be imitators of me. ¹⁷Therefore I sent to you Timothy, my beloved and faithful child in the Lord, to remind you of my ways in Christ, as I teach them everywhere in every church. ¹⁸Some are arrogant, as though I were not coming to you. ¹⁹But I will come to you soon, if the Lord wills, and I will find out not the talk of these arrogant people but their power. ²⁰For the kingdom of God does not consist in talk but in power. ²¹What do you wish? Shall I come to you with a rod, or with love in a spirit of gentleness?

Gal 2:1–10 (§197)

¹Then after fourteen years I went up again to Jerusalem with Barnabas, taking Titus along with me. ²I went up by revelation; and I laid before them (but privately before those who were of repute) the gospel which I preach among the Gentiles, lest somehow I should be running or had run in vain. ³But even Titus, who was with me, was not compelled to be circumcised, though he was a Greek. ⁴But because of false brethren secretly brought in, who slipped in to spy out our freedom which we have in Christ Jesus, that they might bring us into bondage— ⁵to them we did not yield submission even for a moment, that the truth of the gospel might be preserved for you. ⁶And from those who were reputed to be something (what they were makes no difference to me; God shows no partiality)—those, I say, who were of repute added nothing to me; ⁷but on the contrary, when they saw that I had been entrusted with the gospel to the uncircumcised, just as Peter had been entrusted with the gospel to the circumcised ⁸(for he who worked through Peter for the mission to the circumcised worked through me also for the Gentiles), ⁹and when they perceived the grace that was given to me, James and Cephas and John, who were reputed to be pillars, gave to me and Barnabas the right hand of fellowship, that we should go to the Gentiles and they to the circumcised; ¹⁰only they would have us remember the poor, which very thing I was eager to do.

● **2 Cor 10:13**

Rom 12   ³For by the grace given to me I bid every one among you not to think of himself more highly than he ought to think, but to think with sober judgment, each according to the measure of faith which God has assigned him.

● **2 Cor 10:16**

Acts 19   ²¹Now after these events Paul resolved in the Spirit to pass through Macedonia and Achaia and

go to Jerusalem, saying, "After I have been there, I must also see Rome."

● **2 Cor 10:17**

1 Cor 1   ³¹therefore, as it is written, "Let him who boasts, boast of the Lord."

Jer 9   ²⁴but let him who glories glory in this, that he understands and knows me, that I am the Lord who

practice steadfast love, justice, and righteousness in the earth; for in these things I delight, says the Lord.

● **2 Cor 10:18**

1 Cor 4   ⁵Therefore do not pronounce judgment before the time, before the Lord comes, who will bring to light the things now hidden in darkness and will disclose the purposes of the heart. Then every man will receive his commendation from God.

11 I wish you would bear with me in a little foolishness. Do bear with me! [2]I feel a divine jealousy for you, for I betrothed you to Christ to present you as a pure bride to her one husband. [3]But I am afraid that as the serpent deceived Eve by his cunning, your thoughts will be led astray from a sincere and pure devotion to Christ. [4]For if some one comes and preaches another Jesus than the one we preached, or if you receive a different spirit from the one you received, or if you accept a different gospel from the one you accepted, you submit to it readily enough. [5]I think that I am not in the least inferior to these superlative apostles. [6]Even if I am unskilled in speaking, I am not in knowledge; in every way we have made this plain to you in all things.

PRIMARY

1 Cor 2:1–5 (§76)

[1]When I came to you, brethren, I did not come proclaiming to you the testimony of God in lofty words or wisdom. [2]For I decided to know nothing among you except Jesus Christ and him crucified. [3]And I was with you in weakness and in much fear and trembling; [4]and my speech and my message were not in plausible words of wisdom, but in demonstration of the Spirit and of power, [5]that your faith might not rest in the wisdom of men but in the power of God.

Gal 1:6–12 (§194)

[6]I am astonished that you are so quickly deserting him who called you in the grace of Christ and turning to a different gospel— [7]not that there is another gospel, but there are some who trouble you and want to pervert the gospel of Christ. [8]But even if we, or an angel from heaven, should preach to you a gospel contrary to that which we preached to you, let him be accursed. [9]As we have said before, so now I say again, If any one is preaching to you a gospel contrary to that which you received, let him be accursed.

[10]Am I now seeking the favor of men, or of God? Or am I trying to please men? If I were still pleasing men, I should not be a servant of Christ.

[11]For I would have you know, brethren, that the gospel which was preached by me is not man's gospel. [12]For I did not receive it from man, nor was I taught it, but it came through a revelation of Jesus Christ.

Eph 5:21–6:9 (§232)

[21]Be subject to one another out of reverence for Christ. [22]Wives, be subject to your husbands, as to the Lord. [23]For the husband is the head of the wife as Christ is the head of the church, his body, and is himself its Savior. [24]As the church is subject to Christ, so let wives also be subject in everything to their husbands. [25]Husbands, love your wives, as Christ loved the church and gave himself up for her, [26]that he might sanctify her, having cleansed her by the washing of water with the word, [27]that he might present the church to himself in splendor, without spot or wrinkle or any such thing, that she might be holy and without blemish. [28]Even so husbands should love their wives as their own bodies. He who loves his wife loves himself. [29]For no man ever hates his own flesh, but nourishes and cherishes it, as Christ does the church, [30]because we are members of his body. [31]"For this reason a man shall leave his father and mother and be joined to his wife, and the two shall become one flesh." [32]This mystery is a profound one, and I am saying that it refers to Christ and the church; [33]however, let each one of you love his wife as himself, and let the wife see that she respects her husband.

[6] [1]Children, obey your parents in the Lord, for this is right. [2]"Honor your father and mother" (this is the first commandment with a promise), [3]"that it may be well with you and that you may live long on the earth." [4]Fathers, do not provoke your children to anger, but bring them up in the discipline and instruction of the Lord.

[5]Slaves, be obedient to those who are your earthly masters, with fear and trembling, in singleness of heart, as to Christ; [6]not in the way of eyeservice, as men-pleasers, but as servants of Christ, doing the will of God from the heart, [7]rendering service with a good will as to the Lord and not to men, [8]knowing that whatever good any one does, he will receive the same again from the Lord, whether he is a slave or free. [9]Masters, do the same to them, and forbear threatening, knowing that he who is both their Master and yours is in heaven, and that there is no partiality with him.

● **2 Cor 11:3**
1 Tim 2   [14]and Adam was not deceived, but the woman was deceived and became a transgressor.

● **2 Cor 11:4**
2 Cor 11   [19]For you gladly bear with fools, being wise yourselves! [20]For you bear it if a man makes slaves of you, or preys upon you, or takes advantage of you, or puts on airs, or strikes you in the face.

Phil 1   [18]What then? Only that in every way, whether in pretense or in truth, Christ is proclaimed; and in that I rejoice.

● **2 Cor 11:5**
2 Cor 12   [11]I have been a fool! You forced me to it, for I ought to have been commended by you. For I was not at all inferior to these superlative apostles, even though I am nothing.

● **2 Cor 11:6**
2 Cor 10   [10]For they say, "His letters are weighty and strong, but his bodily presence is weak, and his speech of no account."

[7]Did I commit a sin in abasing myself so that you might be exalted, because I preached God's gospel without cost to you? [8]I robbed other churches by accepting support from them in order to serve you. [9]And when I was with you and was in want, I did not burden any one, for my needs were supplied by the brethren who came from Macedonia. So I refrained and will refrain from burdening you in any way. [10]As the truth of Christ is in me, this boast of mine shall not be silenced in the regions of Achaia. [11]And why? Because I do not love you? God knows I do!

PRIMARY

1 Cor 4:8–13 (§85)

[8]Already you are filled! Already you have become rich! Without us you have become kings! And would that you did reign, so that we might share the rule with you! [9]For I think that God has exhibited us apostles as last of all, like men sentenced to death; because we have become a spectacle to the world, to angels and to men. [10]We are fools for Christ's sake, but you are wise in Christ. We are weak, but you are strong. You are held in honor, but we are in disrepute. [11]To the present hour we hunger and thirst, we are ill-clad and buffeted and homeless, [12]and we labor, working with our own hands. When reviled, we bless; when persecuted, we endure; [13]when slandered, we try to conciliate; we have become, and are now, as the refuse of the world, the off-scouring of all things.

1 Cor 9:1–14 (§105)

[1]Am I not free? Am I not an apostle? Have I not seen Jesus our Lord? Are not you my workmanship in the Lord? [2]If to others I am not an apostle, at least I am to you; for you are the seal of my apostleship in the Lord. [3]This is my defense to those who would examine me. [4]Do we not have the right to our food and drink? [5]Do we not have the right to be accompanied by a wife, as the other apostles and the brothers of the Lord and Cephas? [6]Or is it only Barnabas and I who have no right to refrain from working for a living? [7]Who serves as a soldier at his own expense? Who plants a vineyard without eating any of its fruit? Who tends a flock without getting some of the milk? [8]Do I say this on human authority? Does not the law say the same? [9]For it is written in the law of Moses, "You shall not muzzle an ox when it is treading out the grain." Is it for oxen that God is concerned? [10]Does he not speak entirely for our sake? It was written for our sake, because the plowman should plow in hope and the thresher thresh in hope of a share in the crop. [11]If we have sown spiritual good among you, is it too much if we reap your material benefits? [12]If others share this rightful claim upon you, do not we still more?

Nevertheless, we have not made use of this right, but we endure anything rather than put an obstacle in the way of the gospel of Christ. [13]Do you not know that those who are employed in the temple service get their food from the temple, and those who serve at the altar share in the sacrificial offerings? [14]In the same way, the Lord commanded that those who proclaim the gospel should get their living by the gospel.

1 Cor 9:15–18 (§106)

[15]But I have made no use of any of these rights, nor am I writing this to secure any such provision. For I would rather die than have any one deprive me of my ground for boasting. [16]For if I preach the gospel, that gives me no ground for boasting. For necessity is laid upon me. Woe to me if I do not preach the gospel! [17]For if I do this of my own will, I have a reward; but if not of my own will, I am entrusted with a commission. [18]What then is my reward? Just this: that in my preaching I may make the gospel free of charge, not making full use of my right in the gospel.

Phil 4:10–20 (§253)

[10]I rejoice in the Lord greatly that now at length you have revived your concern for me; you were indeed concerned for me, but you had no opportunity. [11]Not that I complain of want; for I have learned, in whatever state I am, to be content. [12]I know how to be abased, and I know how to abound; in any and all circumstances I have learned the secret of facing plenty and hunger, abundance and want. [13]I can do all things in him who strengthens me.

[14]Yet it was kind of you to share my trouble. [15]And you Philippians yourselves know that in the beginning of the gospel, when I left Macedonia, no church entered into partnership with me in giving and receiving except you only; [16]for even in Thessalonica you sent me help once and again. [17]Not that I seek the gift; but I seek the fruit which increases to your credit. [18]I have received full payment, and more; I am filled, having received from Epaphroditus the gifts you sent, a fragrant offering, a sacrifice acceptable and pleasing to God. [19]And my God will supply every need of yours according to his riches in glory in Christ Jesus. [20]To our God and Father be glory for ever and ever. Amen.

1 Thess 2:9–12 (§278)

[9]For you remember our labor and toil, brethren; we worked night and day, that we might not burden any of you, while we preached to you the gospel of God. [10]You are witnesses, and God also, how holy and righteous and blameless was our behavior to you believers; [11]for you know how, like a father with his children, we exhorted each one of you and encouraged you and charged you [12]to lead a life worthy of God, who calls you into his own kingdom and glory.

2 Thess 3:6–13 (§300)

[6]Now we command you, brethren, in the name of our Lord Jesus Christ, that you keep away from any brother who is living in idleness and not in accord with the tradition that you received from us. [7]For you yourselves know how you ought to imitate us; we were not idle when we were with you, [8]we did not eat any one's bread without paying, but with toil and labor we worked night and day, that we might not burden any of you. [9]It was not because we have not that right, but to give you in our conduct an example to imitate. [10]For even when we were with you, we gave you this command: If any one will not work, let him not eat. [11]For we hear that some of you are living in idleness, mere busybodies, not doing any work. [12]Now such persons we command and exhort in the Lord Jesus Christ to do their work in quietness and to earn their own living. [13]Brethren, do not be weary in well-doing.

● 2 Cor 11:7–9

2 Cor 11   [19]For you gladly bear with fools, being wise yourselves! [20]For you bear it if a man makes slaves of you, or preys upon you, or takes advantage of you, or puts on airs, or strikes you in the face. [21]To my shame, I must say, we were too weak for that!

¹²And what I do I will continue to do, in order to undermine the claim of those who would like to claim that in their boasted mission they work on the same terms as we do. ¹³For such men are false apostles, deceitful workmen, disguising themselves as apostles of Christ. ¹⁴And no wonder, for even Satan disguises himself as an angel of light. ¹⁵So it is not strange if his servants also disguise themselves as servants of righteousness. Their end will correspond to their deeds.

PRIMARY

Rom 16:17–20a (§67)

¹⁷I appeal to you, brethren, to take note of those who create dissensions and difficulties, in opposition to the doctrine which you have been taught; avoid them. ¹⁸For such persons do not serve our Lord Christ, but their own appetites, and by fair and flattering words they deceive the hearts of the simple-minded. ¹⁹For while your obedience is known to all, so that I rejoice over you, I would have you wise as to what is good and guileless as to what is evil; ²⁰then the God of peace will soon crush Satan under your feet.

1 Cor 9:15–18 (§106)

¹⁵But I have made no use of any of these rights, nor am I writing this to secure any such provision. For I would rather die than have any one deprive me of my ground for boasting. ¹⁶For if I preach the gospel, that gives me no ground for boasting. For necessity is laid upon me. Woe to me if I do not preach the gospel! ¹⁷For if I do this of my own will, I have a reward; but if not of my own will, I am entrusted with a commission. ¹⁸What then is my reward? Just this: that in my preaching I may make the gospel free of charge, not making full use of my right in the gospel.

Gal 1:6–12 (§194)

⁶I am astonished that you are so quickly deserting him who called you in the grace of Christ and turning to a different gospel— ⁷not that there is another gospel, but there are some who trouble you and want to pervert the gospel of Christ. ⁸But even if we, or an angel from heaven, should preach to you a gospel contrary to that which we preached to you, let him be accursed. ⁹As we have said before, so now I say again, If any one is preaching to you a gospel contrary to that which you received, let him be accursed.

¹⁰Am I now seeking the favor of men, or of God? Or am I trying to please men? If I were still pleasing men, I should not be a servant of Christ.

¹¹For I would have you know, brethren, that the gospel which was preached by me is not man's gospel. ¹²For I did not receive it from man, nor was I taught it, but it came through a revelation of Jesus Christ.

1 Thess 2:1–8 (§277)

¹For you yourselves know, brethren, that our visit to you was not in vain; ²but though we had already suffered and been shamefully treated at Philippi, as you know, we had courage in our God to declare to you the gospel of God in the face of great opposition. ³For our appeal does not spring from error or uncleanness, nor is it made with guile; ⁴but just as we have been approved by God to be entrusted with the gospel, so we speak, not to please men, but to please God who tests our hearts. ⁵For we never used either words of flattery, as you know, or a cloak for greed, as God is witness; ⁶nor did we seek glory from men, whether from you or from others, though we might have made demands as apostles of Christ. ⁷But we were gentle among you, like a nurse taking care of her children. ⁸So, being affectionately desirous of you, we were ready to share with you not only the gospel of God but also our own selves, because you had become very dear to us.

2 Thess 2:1–12 (§296)

¹Now concerning the coming of our Lord Jesus Christ and our assembling to meet him, we beg you, brethren, ²not to be quickly shaken in mind or excited, either by spirit or by word, or by letter purporting to be from us, to the effect that the day of the Lord has come. ³Let no one deceive you in any way; for that day will not come, unless the rebellion comes first, and the man of lawlessness is revealed, the son of perdition, ⁴who opposes and exalts himself against every so-called god or object of worship, so that he takes his seat in the temple of God, proclaiming himself to be God. ⁵Do you not remember that when I was still with you I told you this? ⁶And you know what is restraining him now so that he may be revealed in his time. ⁷For the mystery of lawlessness is already at work; only he who now restrains it will do so until he is out of the way. ⁸And then the lawless one will be revealed, and the Lord Jesus will slay him with the breath of his mouth and destroy him by his appearing and his coming. ⁹The coming of the lawless one by the activity of Satan will be with all power and with pretended signs and wonders, ¹⁰and with all wicked deception for those who are to perish, because they refused to love the truth and so be saved. ¹¹Therefore God sends upon them a strong delusion, to make them believe what is false, ¹²so that all may be condemned who did not believe the truth but had pleasure in unrighteousness.

● **2 Cor 11:12**

1 Cor 9   ³This is my defense to those who would examine me. ⁴Do we not have the right to our food and drink? ⁵Do we not have the right to be accompanied by a wife, as the other apostles and the brothers of the Lord and Cephas? ⁶Or is it only Barnabas and I who have no right to refrain from working for a living?

● **2 Cor 11:13**

Phil 3   ²Look out for the dogs, look out for the evil-workers, look out for those who mutilate the flesh.

Acts 20   ²⁹"I know that after my departure fierce wolves will come in among you, not sparing the flock; ³⁰and from among your own selves will arise men speaking perverse things, to draw away the disciples after them."

● **2 Cor 11:15**

Rom 2   ⁶For he will render to every man according to his works: . . .

Rom 6   ²³For the wages of sin is death, but the free gift of God is eternal life in Christ Jesus our Lord.

Gal 6   ⁷Do not be deceived; God is not mocked, for whatever a man sows, that he will also reap.

1 Thess 2   ¹⁶by hindering us from speaking to the Gentiles that they may be saved—so as always to fill up the measure of their sins. But God's wrath has come upon them at last!

2 Tim 4   ¹⁴Alexander the coppersmith did me great harm; the Lord will requite him for his deeds.

¹⁶I repeat, let no one think me foolish; but even if you do, accept me as a fool, so that I too may boast a little. ¹⁷(What I am saying I say not with the Lord's authority but as a fool, in this boastful confidence; ¹⁸since many boast of worldly things, I too will boast.) ¹⁹For you gladly bear with fools, being wise yourselves! ²⁰For you bear it if a man makes slaves of you, or preys upon you, or takes advantage of you, or puts on airs, or strikes you in the face. ²¹To my shame, I must say, we were too weak for that!

PRIMARY

Rom 1:18–23 (§4)

¹⁸For the wrath of God is revealed from heaven against all ungodliness and wickedness of men who by their wickedness suppress the truth. ¹⁹For what can be known about God is plain to them, because God has shown it to them. ²⁰Ever since the creation of the world his invisible nature, namely, his eternal power and deity, has been clearly perceived in the things that have been made. So they are without excuse; ²¹for although they knew God they did not honor him as God or give thanks to him, but they became futile in their thinking and their senseless minds were darkened. ²²Claiming to be wise, they became fools, ²³and exchanged the glory of the immortal God for images resembling mortal man or birds or animals or reptiles.

Rom 3:27–31 (§15)

²⁷Then what becomes of our boasting? It is excluded. On what principle? On the principle of works? No, but on the principle of faith. ²⁸For we hold that a man is justified by faith apart from works of law. ²⁹Or is God the God of Jews only? Is he not the God of Gentiles also? Yes, of Gentiles also, ³⁰since God is one; and he

will justify the circumcised on the ground of their faith and the uncircumcised through their faith. ³¹Do we then overthrow the law by this faith? By no means! On the contrary, we uphold the law.

1 Cor 1:18–25 (§74)

¹⁸For the word of the cross is folly to those who are perishing, but to us who are being saved it is the power of God. ¹⁹For it is written,

"I will destroy the wisdom of the wise,
and the cleverness of the clever I will thwart."

²⁰Where is the wise man? Where is the scribe? Where is the debater of this age? Has not God made foolish the wisdom of the world? ²¹For since, in the wisdom of God, the world did not know God through wisdom, it pleased God through the folly of what we preach to save those who believe. ²²For Jews demand signs and Greeks seek wisdom, ²³but we preach Christ crucified, a stumbling block to Jews and folly to Gentiles, ²⁴but to those who are called, both Jews and Greeks, Christ the power of God and the wisdom of God. ²⁵For the foolishness of God is wiser than men, and the weakness of God is stronger than men.

1 Cor 1:26–31 (§75)

²⁶For consider your call, brethren; not many of you were wise according to worldly standards, not many were powerful, not many were of noble birth; ²⁷but God chose what is foolish in the world to shame the wise, God chose what is weak in the world to shame the strong, ²⁸God chose what is low and despised in the world, even things that are not, to bring to nothing things that are, ²⁹so that no human being might boast in the presence of God. ³⁰He is the source of your life in Christ Jesus, whom God made our wisdom, our righteousness and sanctification and redemption; ³¹therefore, as it is written, "Let him who boasts, boast of the Lord."

1 Cor 4:8–13 (§85)

⁸Already you are filled! Already you have become rich! Without us you have become kings! And would that you did reign, so that we might share the rule with you! ⁹For I think that God has exhibited us apostles as last of all, like men sentenced to death; because we have become a spectacle to the world, to angels and to men. ¹⁰We are fools for Christ's sake, but you are wise in Christ. We are weak, but you are strong. You are held in honor, but we are in disrepute. ¹¹To the present hour we hunger and thirst, we are ill-clad and buffeted and homeless, ¹²and we labor, working with our own hands. When reviled, we bless; when persecuted, we endure; ¹³when slandered, we try to conciliate; we have become, and are now, as the refuse of the world, the off-scouring of all things.

1 Thess 2:1–8 (§277)

¹For you yourselves know, brethren, that our visit to you was not in vain; ²but though we had already suffered and been shamefully treated at Philippi, as you know, we had courage in our God to declare to you the gospel of God in the face of great opposition. ³For our appeal does not spring from error or uncleanness, nor is it made with guile; ⁴but just as we have been approved by God to be entrusted with the gospel, so we speak, not to please men, but to please God who tests our hearts. ⁵For we never used either words of flattery, as you know, or a cloak for greed, as God is witness; ⁶nor did we seek glory from men, whether from you or from others, though we might have made demands as apostles of Christ. ⁷But we were gentle among you, like a nurse taking care of her children. ⁸So, being affectionately desirous of you, we were ready to share with you not only the gospel of God but also our own selves, because you had become very dear to us.

● **2 Cor 11:16–21a**
2 Cor 12   ¹¹I have been a fool! You forced me to it, for I ought to have been commended by you. For I was not at all inferior to these superlative apostles, even though I am nothing. ¹²The signs of a true apostle were performed among you in all patience, with signs and wonders and mighty works. ¹³For in what were you less favored than the rest of the churches, except that I myself did not burden you? Forgive me this wrong!

1 Cor 3   ¹⁸Let no one deceive himself. If any one among you thinks that he is wise in this age, let him become a fool that he may become wise.

● **2 Cor 11:17**
1 Cor 7   ⁶I say this by way of concession, not of command.

1 Cor 7   ¹⁰To the married I give charge, not I but the Lord, that the wife should not separate from her husband . . .

1 Cor 7   ¹²To the rest I say, not the Lord, that if any brother has a wife who is an unbeliever, and she consents to live with him, he should not divorce her.

1 Cor 7   ²⁵Now concerning the unmarried, I have no command of the Lord, but I give my opinion as one who by the Lord's mercy is trustworthy.

1 Cor 7   ³⁵I say this for your own benefit, not to lay any restraint upon you, but to promote good order and to secure your undivided devotion to the Lord.

Phlm   ⁸Accordingly, though I am bold enough in Christ to command you to do what is required, ⁹yet for love's sake I prefer to appeal to you—I, Paul, an ambassador and now a prisoner also for Christ Jesus . . .

● **2 Cor 11:18**
Cf. 2 Cor 10:13–18

2 Cor 11   ²¹. . . But whatever any one dares to boast of—I am speaking as a fool—I also dare to boast of that. ²²Are they Hebrews? So am I. Are they Israelites? So am I. Are they descendants of Abraham? So am I. ²³Are they servants of Christ?

2 Cor 11   ³⁰If I must boast, I will boast of the things that show my weakness.

2 Cor 12   ¹I must boast; there is nothing to be gained

by it, but I will go on to visions and revelations of the Lord.

2 Cor 12   ⁵On behalf of this man I will boast, but on my own behalf I will not boast, except of my weaknesses. ⁶Though if I wish to boast, I shall not be a fool, for I shall be speaking the truth. But I refrain from it, so that no one may think more of me than he sees in me or hears from me.

2 Cor 12   ⁹but he said to me, "My grace is sufficient for you, for my power is made perfect in weakness." I will all the more gladly boast of my weaknesses, that the power of Christ may rest upon me.

Eph 2   ⁸For by grace you have been saved through faith; and this is not your own doing, it is the gift of God— ⁹not because of works, lest any man should boast.

Phil 3   ⁴Though I myself have reason for confidence in the flesh also. If any other man thinks he has reason for confidence in the flesh, I have more: . . .

● **2 Cor 11:20–21**
Gal 4   ¹⁵What has become of the satisfaction you felt? For I bear you witness that, if possible, you would have plucked out your eyes and given them to me.

4. The Jerusalem Conference (Galatians 2) = Acts 18:22

Date		
33/34	Paul's conversion	Gal 1:15, 16; 2 Cor 12:2
36/37	Paul's first Jerusalem visit	Gal 1:18
36–38/	Mission activity in Syria,	
37–39	Cilicia and Galatia	Gal 1:21
38–50/	Pauline missionary activity in	
39–51	Macedonia, Achaia, perhaps elsewhere	
41	Paul in Corinth	Claudius' edict (41) = Acts 18:22
	1 Thessalonians	
	Aquila and Priscilla come to Corinth from Rome	
50/51	Conference visit to Jerusalem	Gal 2:1 = Acts 18:22
	[Acts 15 is misplaced]	
50–54/	Collection for the Jerusalem church;	
51–55	Other missionary activity in Asia Minor and Greece	
51	Paul in Galatia	
51–53	Paul based in Ephesus	
52	*1 Corinthians*	
52	Quick trip to Corinth and return	Gallio inscription (51–52); Acts 18:12
53	Paul travels to Troas and Macedonia	
	2 Corinthians	
	Galatians	
54	Paul arrives in Corinth	
	Romans	
54/55	Final journey to Jerusalem	
	[Hard evidence is lacking after this point]	

This table is a conflation of two near versions of the Pauline chronology: J. Knox, *Chapters in a Life of Paul* (Nashville: Abingdon Press, 1950), 83–88; G. Lüdemann, *Paul, Apostle to the Gentiles* (Philadelphia: Fortress Press, 1984), chap. 6. Summary prepared by John A. Darr and published in: Daniel Patte, *Paul's Faith and the Power of the Gospel* (Philadelphia: Fortress Press, 1983), 352–60. Reprinted by permission of the publisher.
See pages 67, 141, 175, 223 for other versions of the Pauline chronology.

Formal Element: Hardships List

But whatever any one dares to boast of—I am speaking as a fool—I also dare to boast of that. 22 Are they Hebrews? So am I. Are they Israelites? So am I. Are they descendants of Abraham? So am I. 23 Are they servants of Christ? I am a better one—I am talking like a madman—with far greater labors, far more imprisonments, with countless beatings, and often near death. 24 Five times I have received at the hands of the Jews the forty lashes less one. 25 Three times I have been beaten with rods; once I was stoned. Three times I have been shipwrecked; a night and a day I have been adrift at sea; 26 on frequent journeys, in danger from rivers, danger from robbers, danger from my own people, danger from Gentiles, danger in the city, danger in the wilderness, danger at sea, danger from false brethren; 27 in toil and hardship, through many a sleepless night, in hunger and thirst, often without food, in cold and exposure. 28 And, apart from other things, there is the daily pressure upon me of my anxiety for all the churches. 29 Who is weak, and I am not weak? Who is made to fall, and I am not indignant?

Primary

Rom 8:31–39 (§34)

31 What then shall we say to this? If God is for us, who is against us? 32 He who did not spare his own Son but gave him up for us all, will he not also give us all things with him? 33 Who shall bring any charge against God's elect? It is God who justifies; 34 who is to condemn? Is it Christ Jesus, who died, yes, who was raised from the dead, who is at the right hand of God, who indeed intercedes for us? 35 Who shall separate us from the love of Christ? Shall tribulation, or distress, or persecution, or famine, or nakedness, or peril, or sword? 36 As it is written,

"For thy sake we are being killed all the day long;
we are regarded as sheep to be slaughtered."

37 No, in all these things we are more than conquerors through him who loved us. 38 For I am sure that neither death, nor life, nor angels, nor principalities, nor things present, nor things to come, nor powers, 39 nor height, nor depth, nor anything else in all creation, will be able to separate us from the love of God in Christ Jesus our Lord.

1 Cor 4:8–13 (§85)

8 Already you are filled! Already you have become rich! Without us you have become kings! And would that you did reign, so that we might share the rule with you! 9 For I think that God has exhibited us apostles as last of all, like men sentenced to death; because we have become a spectacle to the world, to angels and to men. 10 We are fools for Christ's sake, but you are wise in Christ. We are weak, but you are strong. You are held in honor, but we in disrepute. 11 To the present hour we hunger and thirst, we are ill-clad and buffeted and homeless, 12 and we labor, working with our own hands. When reviled, we bless; when persecuted, we endure; 13 when slandered, we try to conciliate; we have become, and are now, as the refuse of the world, the off-scouring of all things.

Secondary

Rom 2:17–24 (§10)

17 But if you call yourself a Jew and rely upon the law and boast of your relation to God 18 and know his will and approve what is excellent, because you are instructed in the law, 19 and if you are sure that you are a guide to the blind, a light to those who are in darkness, 20 a corrector of the foolish, a teacher of children, having in the law the embodiment of knowledge and truth— 21 you then who teach others, will you not teach yourself? While you preach against stealing, do you steal? 22 You who say that one

must not commit adultery, do you commit adultery? You who abhor idols, do you rob temples? 23 You who boast in the law, do you dishonor God by breaking the law? 24 For, as it is written, "The name of God is blasphemed among the Gentiles because of you."

Rom 3:27–31 (§15)

27 Then what becomes of our boasting? It is excluded. On what principle? On the principle of works? No, but on the principle of faith. 28 For we hold that a man is justified by faith apart from works of law. 29 Or is God the God of Jews only? Is he not the God of Gentiles also? Yes, of Gentiles also, 30 since God is one; and he will justify the circumcised on the ground of their faith and the uncircumcised through their faith. 31 Do we then overthrow the law by this faith? By no means! On the contrary, we uphold the law.

Rom 9:1–5 (§35)

1 I am speaking the truth in Christ, I am not lying; my conscience bears me witness in the Holy Spirit, 2 that I have great sorrow and unceasing anguish in my heart. 3 For I could wish that I myself were accursed and cut off from Christ for the sake of my brethren, my kinsmen by race. 4 They are Israelites, and to them belong the sonship, the glory, the covenants, the giving of the law, the worship, and the promises; 5 to them belong the patriarchs, and of their race, according to the flesh, is the Christ. God who is over all be blessed for ever. Amen.

Rom 11:1–6 (§44)

1 I ask, then, has God rejected his people? By no means! I myself am an Israelite, a descendant of Abraham, a member of the tribe of Benjamin. 2 God has not rejected his people whom he foreknew. Do you not know what the scripture says of Elijah, how he pleads with God against Israel? 3 "Lord, they have killed thy prophets, they have demolished thy altars, and I alone am left, and they seek my life." 4 But

---

● **2 Cor 11:21b–29**

2 Cor 1 3 Blessed be the God and Father of our Lord Jesus Christ, the Father of mercies and God of all comfort, 4 who comforts us in all our affliction, so that we may be able to comfort those who are in any affliction, with the comfort with which we ourselves are comforted by God. 5 For as we share abundantly in Christ's sufferings, so through Christ we share abundantly in comfort too. 6 If we are afflicted, it is for your comfort and salvation; and if we are comforted, it is for your comfort, which you experience when you patiently endure the same sufferings that we suffer. 7 Our hope for you is unshaken; for we know that as you share in our sufferings, you will also share in our comfort.

8 For we do not want you to be ignorant, brethren, of the affliction we experienced in Asia; for we were so utterly, unbearably crushed that we despaired of life itself. 9 Why, we felt that we had received the sentence

of death; but that was to make us rely not on ourselves but on God who raises the dead; 10 he delivered us from so deadly a peril, and he will deliver us; on him we have set our hope that he will deliver us again. 11 You also must help us by prayer, so that many will give thanks on our behalf for the blessing granted us in answer to many prayers.

2 Cor 4 7 But we have this treasure in earthen vessels, to show that the transcendent power belongs to God and not to us. 8 We are afflicted in every way, but not crushed; perplexed, but not driven to despair; 9 persecuted, but not forsaken; struck down, but not destroyed; 10 always carrying in the body the death of Jesus, so that the life of Jesus may also be manifested in our bodies. 11 For while we live we are always being given up to death for Jesus' sake, so that the life of Jesus may be manifested in our mortal flesh. 12 So death is at work in us, but life in you.

2 Cor 6 4 but as servants of God we commend ourselves in every way: through great endurance, in afflictions, hardships, calamities, 5 beatings, imprisonments, tumults, labors, watching, hunger; 6 by purity, knowledge, forbearance, kindness, the Holy Spirit, genuine love, 7 truthful speech, and the power of God; with the weapons of righteousness for the right hand and for the left; 8 in honor and dishonor, in ill repute and good repute. We are treated as impostors, and yet are true; 9 as unknown, and yet well known; as dying, and behold we live; as punished, and yet not killed; 10 as sorrowful, yet always rejoicing; as poor, yet making many rich; as having nothing, and yet possessing everything.

2 Cor 12 10 For the sake of Christ, then, I am content with weaknesses, insults, hardships, persecutions, and calamities; for when I am weak, then I am strong.

what is God's reply to him? "I have kept for myself seven thousand men who have not bowed the knee to Baal." ⁵So too at the present time there is a remnant, chosen by grace. ⁶But if it is by grace, it is no longer on the basis of works; otherwise grace would no longer be grace.

Phil 3:2–11 (§247)

²Look out for the dogs, look out for the evil-workers, look out for those who mutilate the flesh. ³For we are the true circumcision, who worship God in spirit, and glory in Christ Jesus, and put no confidence in the flesh. ⁴Though I myself have reason for confidence in the flesh also. If any other man thinks he has reason for confidence in the flesh, I have more: ⁵circumcised on the eighth day, of the people of Israel, of the tribe of Benjamin, a Hebrew born of Hebrews; as to the law a Pharisee, ⁶as to zeal a persecutor of the church, as to righteousness under the law blameless. ⁷But whatever gain I had, I counted as loss for the sake of Christ. ⁸Indeed I count everything as loss because of the surpassing worth of knowing Christ Jesus my Lord. For his sake I have suffered the loss of all things, and count them as refuse, in order that I may gain Christ ⁹and be found in him, not having a righteousness of my own, based on law, but that which is through faith in Christ, the righteousness from God that depends on faith; ¹⁰that I may know him and the power of his resurrection, and may share his sufferings, becoming like him in his death, ¹¹that if possible I may attain the resurrection from the dead.

Phil 4:10–20 (§253)

¹⁰I rejoice in the Lord greatly that now at length you have revived your concern for me; you were indeed concerned for me, but you had no opportunity. ¹¹Not that I complain of want; for I have learned, in whatever state I am, to be content. ¹²I know how to be abased, and I know how to abound; in any and all circumstances I have learned the secret of facing plenty and hunger, abundance and want. ¹³I can do all things in him who strengthens me.

¹⁴Yet it was kind of you to share my trouble. ¹⁵And you Philippians yourselves know that in the beginning of the gospel, when I left Macedonia, no church entered into partnership with me in giving and receiving except you only; ¹⁶for even in Thessalonica you sent me help once and again. ¹⁷Not that I seek the gift; but I seek the fruit which increases to your credit. ¹⁸I have received full payment, and more; I am filled, having received from Epaphroditus the gifts you sent, a fragrant offering, a sacrifice acceptable and pleasing to God. ¹⁹And my God will supply every need of yours according to his riches in glory in Christ Jesus. ²⁰To our God and Father be glory for ever and ever. Amen.

Col 1:24–2:3 (§260)

²⁴Now I rejoice in my sufferings for your sake, and in my flesh I complete what is lacking in Christ's afflictions for the sake of his body, that is, the church, ²⁵of which I became a minister according to the divine office which was given to me for you, to make the word of God fully known, ²⁶the mystery hidden for ages and generations but now made manifest to his saints. ²⁷To them God chose to make known how great among the Gentiles are the riches of the glory of this mystery, which is Christ in you, the hope of glory. ²⁸Him we proclaim warning every man and teaching every man in all wisdom, that we may present every man mature in Christ. ²⁹For this I toil, striving with all the energy which he mightily inspires within me.

2 ¹For I want you to know how greatly I strive for you, and for those at Laodicea, and for all who have not seen my face, ²that their hearts may be encouraged as they are knit together in love, to have all the riches of assured understanding and the knowledge of God's mystery, of Christ, ³in whom are hid all the treasures of wisdom and knowledge.

1 Thess 2:1–8 (§277)

¹For you yourselves know, brethren, that our visit to you was not in vain; ²but though we had already suffered and been shamefully treated at Philippi, as you know, we had courage in our God to declare to you the gospel of God in the face of great opposition. ³For our appeal does not spring from error or uncleanness, nor is it made with guile; ⁴but just as we have been approved by God to be entrusted with the gospel, so we speak, not to please men, but to please God who tests our hearts. ⁵For we never used either words of flattery, as you know, or a cloak for greed, as God is witness; ⁶nor did we seek glory from men, whether from you or from others, though we might have made demands as apostles of Christ. ⁷But we were gentle among you, like a nurse taking care of her children. ⁸So, being affectionately desirous of you, we were ready to share with you not only the gospel of God but also our own selves, because you had become very dear to us.

1 Thess 3:1–5 (§281)

¹Therefore when we could bear it no longer, we were willing to be left behind at Athens alone, ²and we sent Timothy, our brother and God's servant in the gospel of Christ, to establish you in your faith and to exhort you, ³that no one be moved by these afflictions. You yourselves know that this is to be our lot. ⁴For when we were with you, we told you beforehand that we were to suffer affliction; just as it has come to pass, and as you know. ⁵For this reason, when I could bear it no longer, I sent that I might know your faith, for fear that somehow the tempter had tempted you and that our labor would be in vain.

● **2 Cor 11:23**

1 Cor 15   ¹⁰But by the grace of God I am what I am, and his grace toward me was not in vain. On the contrary, I worked harder than any of them, though it was not I, but the grace of God which is with me.

Acts 9   ¹⁶". . . for I will show him how much he must suffer for the sake of my name."

Acts 16   ²³And when they had inflicted many blows upon them, they threw them into prison, charging the jailer to keep them safely.

● **2 Cor 11:25–26**

Acts 14   ¹⁹But Jews came there from Antioch and Iconium; and having persuaded the people, they stoned Paul and dragged him out of the city, supposing that he was dead.

Acts 27   ⁴¹But striking a shoal they ran the vessel aground; the bow stuck and remained immovable, and

the stern was broken up by the surf. ⁴²The soldiers' plan was to kill the prisoners, lest any should swim away and escape; . . .

● **2 Cor 11:25**

Acts 16   ²²The crowd joined in attacking them; and the magistrates tore the garments off them and gave orders to beat them with rods.

● **2 Cor 11:26**

Acts 9   ²³When many days had passed, the Jews plotted to kill him, . . .

Acts 13   ⁴⁵But when the Jews saw the multitudes, they were filled with jealousy, and contradicted what was spoken by Paul, and reviled him.

Acts 13   ⁵⁰But the Jews incited the devout women of high standing and the leading men of the city, and stirred up persecution against Paul and Barnabas, and drove them out of their district.

Acts 17   ⁵But the Jews were jealous, and taking some wicked fellows of the rabble, they gathered a crowd, set the city in an uproar, and attacked the house of Jason, seeking to bring them out to the people.

Acts 17   ¹³But when the Jews of Thessalonica learned that the word of God was proclaimed by Paul at Beroea also, they came there too, stirring up and inciting the crowds.

Acts 18   ¹²But when Gallio was proconsul of Achaia, the Jews made a united attack upon Paul and brought him before the tribunal, . . .

Acts 21   ³¹And as they were trying to kill him, word came to the tribune of the cohort that all Jerusalem was in confusion.

● **2 Cor 11:28**

Acts 18   ²⁸but on taking leave of them he said, "I will return to you if God wills," and he set sail from Ephesus.

³⁰If I must boast, I will boast of the things that show my weakness. ³¹The God and Father of the Lord Jesus, he who is blessed for ever, knows that I do not lie. ³²At Damascus, the governor under King Aretas guarded the city of Damascus in order to seize me, ³³but I was let down in a basket through a window in the wall, and escaped his hands.

PRIMARY

1 Cor 1:26–31 (§75)
²⁶For consider your call, brethren; not many of you were wise according to worldly standards, not many were powerful, not many were of noble birth; ²⁷but God chose what is foolish in the world to shame the wise, God chose what is weak in the world to shame the strong, ²⁸God chose what is low and despised in the world, even things that are not, to bring to nothing things that are, ²⁹so that no human being might boast in the presence of God. ³⁰He is the source of your life in Christ Jesus, whom God made our wisdom, our righteousness and sanctification and redemption; ³¹therefore, as it is written, "Let him who boasts, boast of the Lord."

SECONDARY

Gal 1:15–24 (§196)
¹⁵But when he who had set me apart before I was born, and had called me through his grace, ¹⁶was pleased to reveal his Son to me, in order that I might preach him among the Gentiles, I did not confer with flesh and blood, ¹⁷nor did I go up to Jerusalem to those who were apostles before me, but I went away into Arabia; and again I returned to Damascus.

¹⁸Then after three years I went up to Jerusalem to visit Cephas, and remained with him fifteen days. ¹⁹But I saw none of the other apostles except James the Lord's brother. ²⁰(In what I am writing to you, before God, I do not lie!) ²¹Then I went into the regions of Syria and Cilicia. ²²And I was still not known by sight to the churches of Christ in Judea; ²³they only heard it said, "He who once persecuted us is now preaching the faith he once tried to destroy." ²⁴And they glorified God because of me.

● **2 Cor 11:30–33**
Acts 9   ²⁴but their plot became known to Saul. They were watching the gates day and night, to kill him; ²⁵but his disciples took him by night and let him down over the wall, lowering him in a basket.

● **2 Cor 1:23**
2 Cor 1   ²³But I call God to witness against me—it was to spare you that I refrained from coming to Corinth.

12

I must boast; there is nothing to be gained by it, but I will go on to visions and revelations of the Lord. ²I know a man in Christ who fourteen years ago was caught up to the third heaven—whether in the body or out of the body I do not know, God knows. ³And I know that this man was caught up into Paradise—whether in the body or out of the body I do not know, God knows—⁴and he heard things that cannot be told, which man may not utter. ⁵On behalf of this man I will boast, but on my own behalf I will not boast, except of my weaknesses. ⁶Though if I wish to boast, I shall not be a fool, for I shall be speaking the truth. But I refrain from it, so that no one may think more of me than he sees in me or hears from me. ⁷And to keep me from being too elated by the abundance of revelations, a thorn was given me in the flesh, a messenger of Satan, to harass me, to keep me from being too elated. ⁸Three times I besought the Lord about this, that it should leave me; ⁹but he said to me, "My grace is sufficient for you, for my power is made perfect in weakness." I will all the more gladly boast of my weaknesses, that the power of Christ may rest upon me. ¹⁰For the sake of Christ, then, I am content with weaknesses, insults, hardships, persecutions, and calamities; for when I am weak, then I am strong.

PRIMARY

Rom 5:1–5 (§20)

¹Therefore, since we are justified by faith, we have peace with God through our Lord Jesus Christ. ²Through him we have obtained access to this grace in which we stand, and we rejoice in our hope of sharing the glory of God. ³More than that, we rejoice in our sufferings, knowing that suffering produces endurance, ⁴and endurance produces character, and character produces hope, ⁵and hope does not disappoint us, because God's love has been poured into our hearts through the Holy Spirit which has been given to us.

1 Cor 1:26–31 (§75)

²⁶For consider your call, brethren; not many of you were wise according to worldly standards, not many were powerful, not many were of noble birth; ²⁷but God chose what is foolish in the world to shame the wise, God chose what is weak in the world to shame the strong, ²⁸God chose what is low and despised in the world,

even things that are not, to bring to nothing things that are, ²⁹so that no human being might boast in the presence of God. ³⁰He is the source of your life in Christ Jesus, whom God made our wisdom, our righteousness and sanctification and redemption; ³¹therefore, as it is written, "Let him who boasts, boast of the Lord."

1 Cor 4:8–13 (§85)

⁸Already you are filled! Already you have become rich! Without us you have become kings! And would that you did reign, so that we might share the rule with you! ⁹For I think that God has exhibited us apostles as last of all, like men sentenced to death; because we have become a spectacle to the world, to angels and to men. ¹⁰We are fools for Christ's sake, but you are wise in Christ. We are weak, but you are strong. You are held in honor, but we in disrepute. ¹¹To the present hour we hunger and thirst, we are ill-clad and buffeted and homeless, ¹²and we labor, working with our own hands. When reviled, we bless; when persecuted, we endure; ¹³when slandered, we try to conciliate; we have become, and are now, as the refuse of the world, the off-scouring of all things.

Phil 4:10–20 (§253)

¹⁰I rejoice in the Lord greatly that now at length you have revived your concern for me; you were indeed concerned for me, but you had no opportunity. ¹¹Not that I complain of want; for I have learned, in whatever state I am, to be content. ¹²I know how to be abased, and I know how to abound; in any and all circumstances I have learned the secret of facing plenty and hunger, abundance and want. ¹³I can do all things in him who strengthens me.

¹⁴Yet it was kind of you to share my trouble. ¹⁵And you Philippians yourselves know that in the beginning of the gospel, when I left Macedonia, no church entered into partnership with me in giving and receiving except you only; ¹⁶for even in Thessalonica you sent me help once and again. ¹⁷Not that I seek the gift; but I seek the fruit which increases to your credit. ¹⁸I have received full payment, and more; I am filled, having received from Epaphroditus the gifts you sent, a fragrant offering, a sacrifice acceptable and pleasing to God. ¹⁹And my God will supply every need of yours according to his riches in glory in Christ Jesus. ²⁰To our God and Father be glory for ever and ever. Amen.

1 Thess 1:2–10 (§276)

²We give thanks to God always for you all, constantly mentioning you in our prayers, ³re-

membering before our God and Father your work of faith and labor of love and steadfastness of hope in our Lord Jesus Christ. ⁴For we know, brethren beloved by God, that he has chosen you; ⁵for our gospel came to you not only in word, but also in power and in the Holy Spirit and with full conviction. You know what kind of men we proved to be among you for your sake. ⁶And you became imitators of us and of the Lord, for you received the word in much affliction, with joy inspired by the Holy Spirit; ⁷so that you became an example to the all the believers in Macedonia and in Achaia. ⁸For not only has the word of the Lord sounded forth from you in Macedonia and Achaia, but your faith in God has gone forth everywhere, so that we need not say anything. ⁹For they themselves report concerning us what a welcome we had among you, and how you turned to God from idols, to serve a living and true God, ¹⁰and to wait for his Son from heaven, whom he raised from the dead, Jesus who delivers us from the wrath to come.

2 Thess 1:3–12 (§295)

³We are bound to give thanks to God always for you, brethren, as is fitting, because your faith is growing abundantly, and the love of every one of you for one another is increasing. ⁴Therefore we ourselves boast of you in the churches of God for your steadfastness and faith in all your persecutions and in the afflictions which you are enduring.

⁵This is evidence of the righteous judgment of God, that you may be made worthy of the kingdom of God, for which you are suffering—⁶since indeed God deems it just to repay with affliction those who afflict you, ⁷and to grant rest with us to you who are afflicted, when the Lord Jesus is revealed from heaven with his mighty angels in flaming fire, ⁸ inflicting vengeance upon those who do not know God and upon those who do not obey the gospel of our Lord Jesus. ⁹They shall suffer the punishment of eternal destruction and exclusion from the presence of the Lord and from the glory of his might, ¹⁰when he comes on that day to be glorified in his saints, and to be marveled at in all who have believed, because our testimony to you was believed. ¹¹To this end we always pray for you, that our God may make you worthy of his call, and may fulfil every good resolve and work of faith by his power, ¹²so that the name of our Lord Jesus may be glorified in you, and you in him, according to the grace of our God and the Lord Jesus Christ.

● **2 Cor 12:1**
1 Cor 9   ¹Am I not free? Am I not an apostle? Have I not seen Jesus our Lord? Are not you my workmanship in the Lord?

1 Cor 15   ⁸Last of all, as to one untimely born, he appeared also to me.

Gal 2   ²I went up by revelation; and I laid before them (but privately before those who were of repute) the gospel which I preach among the Gentiles, lest somehow I should be running or had run in vain.

Cf. 2 Cor 5:16; Gal 1:12

● **2 Cor 12:2**
Acts 8   ³⁹And when they came up out of the water, the Spirit of the Lord caught up Philip; and the eunuch saw him no more, and went on his way rejoicing.

● **2 Cor 12:5**
2 Cor 11   ³⁰If I must boast, I will boast of the things that show my weakness.

● **2 Cor 12:9**
Deut 3   ²⁶But the Lord was angry with me on your account, and would not hearken to me; and the Lord said to me, 'Let it suffice you; speak no more to me of this matter.'

Cf. Rom 8   ³⁷No, in all these things we are more than conquerors through him who loved us.

● **2 Cor 12:10**
See 2 Cor 11:21b–29

11I have been a fool! You forced me to it, for I ought to have been commended by you. For I was not at all inferior to these superlative apostles, even though I am nothing. **12**The signs of a true apostle were performed among you in all patience, with signs and wonders and mighty works. **13**For in what were you less favored than the rest of the churches, except that I myself did not burden you? Forgive me this wrong!

PRIMARY

Rom 15:14–21 (§62)

14I myself am satisfied about you, my brethren, that you yourselves are full of goodness, filled with all knowledge, and able to instruct one another. **15**But on some points I have written to you very boldly by way of reminder, because of the grace given me by God **16**to be a minister of Christ Jesus to the Gentiles in the priestly service of the gospel of God, so that the offering of the Gentiles may be acceptable, sanctified by the Holy Spirit. **17**In Christ Jesus, then, I have reason to be proud of my work for God. **18**For I will not venture to speak of anything except what Christ has wrought through me to win obedience from the Gentiles, by word and deed, **19**by the power of signs and wonders, by the power of the Holy Spirit, so that from Jerusalem and as far round as Illyr-icum I have fully preached the gospel of Christ, **20**thus making it my ambition to preach the gospel, not where Christ has already been named, lest I build on another man's foundation, **21**but as it is written,

"They shall see who have never been told of him,
and they shall understand who have never heard of him."

1 Cor 2:1–5 (§76)

1When I came to you, brethren, I did not come proclaiming to you the testimony of God in lofty words or wisdom. **2**For I decided to know nothing among you except Jesus Christ and him crucified. **3**And I was with you in weakness and in much fear and trembling; **4**and my speech and my message were not in plausible words of wisdom, but in demonstration of the Spirit and of power, **5**that your faith might not rest in the wisdom of men but in the power of God.

Phil 4:10–20 (§253)

10I rejoice in the Lord greatly that now at length you have revived your concern for me; you were indeed concerned for me, but you had no opportunity. **11**Not that I complain of want; for I have learned, in whatever state I am, to be content. **12**I know how to be abased, and I know how to abound; in any and all circumstances I have learned the secret of facing plenty and hunger, abundance and want. **13**I can do all things in him who strengthens me.

14Yet it was kind of you to share my trouble. **15**And you Philippians yourselves know that in the beginning of the gospel, when I left Macedonia, no church entered into partnership with me in giving and receiving except you only; **16**for even in Thessalonica you sent me help once and again. **17**Not that I seek the gift; but I seek the fruit which increases to your credit. **18**I have received full payment, and more; I am filled, having received from Epaphroditus the gifts you sent, a fragrant offering, a sacrifice acceptable and pleasing to God. **19**And my God will supply every need of yours according to his riches in glory in Christ Jesus. **20**To our God and Father be glory for ever and ever. Amen.

1 Thess 2:9–12 (§278)

9For you remember our labor and toil, brethren; we worked night and day, that we might not burden any of you, while we preached to you the gospel of God. **10**You are witnesses, and God also, how holy and righteous and blameless was our behavior to you believers; **11**for you know how, like a father with his children, we exhorted each one of you and encouraged you and charged you **12**to lead a life worthy of God, who calls you into his own kingdom and glory.

● **2 Cor 12:11–13**

2 Cor 11   **16**I repeat, let no one think me foolish; but even if you do, accept me as a fool, so that I too may boast a little. **17**(What I am saying I say not with the Lord's authority but as a fool, in this boastful confidence; **18**since many boast of worldly things, I too will boast.) **19**For you gladly bear with fools, being wise yourselves! **20**For you bear it if a man makes slaves of you, or preys upon you, or takes advantage of you, or puts on airs, or strikes you in the face. **21**To my shame, I must say, we were too weak for that!

● **2 Cor 12:11–12**

2 Cor 10   **10**For they say, "His letters are weighty and strong, but his bodily presence is weak, and his speech is of no account." **11**Let such people understand that what we say by letter when absent, we do when present. **12**Not that we venture to class or compare ourselves with some of those who commend themselves. But when they measure themselves by one another and compare themselves with one another, they are without understanding.

● **2 Cor 12:11**

2 Cor 5   **12**We are not commending ourselves to you again but giving you cause to be proud of us, so that you may be able to answer those who pride themselves on a man's position and not on his heart.

2 Cor 11   **5**I think that I am not in the least inferior to these superlative apostles.

● **2 Cor 12:12**

1 Thess 1   **5**for our gospel came to you not only in word, but also in power and in the Holy Spirit and with full conviction. You know what kind of men we proved to be among you for your sake.

2 Thess 2   **9**The coming of the lawless one by the activity of Satan will be with all power and with pretended signs and wonders, . . .

Acts 5   **12**Now many signs and wonders were done among the people by the hands of the apostles. And they were all together in Solomon's Portico.

FORMAL ELEMENT: APOSTOLIC VISIT

¹⁴**Here for the third time I am ready to come to you. And I will not be a burden, for I seek not what is yours but you; for children ought not to lay up for their parents, but parents for their children. ¹⁵I will most gladly spend and be spent for your souls. If I love you the more, am I to be loved the less? ¹⁶But granting that I myself did not burden you, I was crafty, you say, and got the better of you by guile. ¹⁷Did I take advantage of you through any of those whom I sent to you? ¹⁸I urged Titus to go, and sent the brother with him. Did Titus take advantage of you? Did we not act in the same spirit? Did we not take the same steps?**

PRIMARY

See §63 for APOSTOLIC VISIT

SECONDARY

1 Thess 2:1–8 (§277)
¹For you yourselves know, brethren, that our visit to you was not in vain; ²but though we had already suffered and been shamefully treated at Philippi, as you know, we had courage in our God to declare to you the gospel of God in the face of great opposition. ³For our appeal does not spring from error or uncleanness, nor is it made with guile; ⁴but just as we have been approved by God to be entrusted with the gospel, so we speak, not to please men, but to please God who tests our hearts. ⁵For we never used either words of flattery, as you know, or a cloak for greed, as God is witness; ⁶nor did we seek glory from men, whether from you or from others, though we might have made demands as apostles of Christ. ⁷But we were gentle among you, like a nurse taking care of her children. ⁸So, being affectionately desirous of you, we were ready to share with you not only the gospel of God but also our own selves, because you had become very dear to us.

● **2 Cor 12:14–18**
Rom 16 ¹⁷I appeal to you, brethren, to take note of those who create dissensions and difficulties, in opposition to the doctrine which you have been taught; avoid them. ¹⁸For such persons do not serve our Lord Christ, but their own appetites, and by fair and flattering words they deceive the hearts of the simpleminded. ¹⁹For while your obedience is known to all, so that I rejoice over you, I would have you wise as to what is good and guileless as to what is evil; ²⁰then the God of peace will soon crush Satan under your feet.

2 Cor 9 ¹Now it is superfluous for me to write to you about the offering for the saints, ²for I know your readiness, of which I boast about you to the people of Macedonia, saying that Achaia has been ready since last year; and your zeal has stirred up most of them. ³But I am sending the brethren so that our boasting about you may not prove vain in this case, so that you may be ready, as I said you would be; ⁴lest if some Macedonians come with me and find that you are not ready, we be humiliated—to say nothing of you—for being so confident. ⁵So I thought it necessary to urge the brethren to go on to you before me, and arrange in advance for this gift you have promised, so that it may be ready not as an exaction but as a willing gift.

2 Cor 12 ¹⁹Have you been thinking all along that we have been defending ourselves before you? It is in the sight of God that we have been speaking in Christ, and all for your upbuilding, beloved. ²⁰For I fear that perhaps I may come and find you not what I wish, and that you may find me not what you wish; that perhaps there may be quarreling, jealousy, anger, selfishness, slander, gossip, conceit, and disorder. ²¹I fear that when I come again my God may humble me before you, and I may have to mourn over many of those who sinned before and have not repented of the impurity, immorality, and licentiousness which they have practiced.

2 Cor 13 ¹This is the third time I am coming to you. Any charge must be sustained by the evidence of two or three witnesses. ²I warned those who sinned before and all the others, and I warn them now while absent, as I did when present on my second visit, that if I come again I will not spare them— ³since you desire proof that Christ is speaking in me. He is not weak in dealing with you, but is powerful in you. ⁴For he was crucified in weakness, but lives by the power of God. For we are weak in him, but in dealing with you we shall live with him by the power of God.

⁵Examine yourselves, to see whether you are holding to your faith. Test yourselves. Do you not realize that Jesus Christ is in you?—unless indeed you fail to meet the test! ⁶I hope you will find out that we have not failed. ⁷But we pray God that you may not do wrong—not that we may appear to have met the test, but that you may do what is right, though we may seem to have failed. ⁸For we cannot do anything against the truth, but only for the truth. ⁹For we are glad when we are weak and you are strong. What we pray for is your improvement. ¹⁰I write this while I am away from you, in order that when I come I may not have to be severe in my use of the authority which the Lord has given me for building up and not for tearing down.

● **2 Cor 12:14**
2 Cor 1 ¹⁵Because I was sure of this, I wanted to come to you first, so that you might have a double pleasure; ¹⁶I wanted to visit you on my way to Macedonia, and to come back to you from Macedonia and have you send me on my way to Judea. ¹⁷Was I vacillating when I wanted to do this? Do I make my plans like a worldly man, ready to say Yes and No at once? ¹⁸As surely as God is faithful, our word to you has not been Yes and No.

2 Cor 2 ¹For I made up my mind not to make you another painful visit.

2 Cor 13 ¹This is the third time I am coming to you. Any charge must be sustained by the evidence of two or three witnesses.

● **2 Cor 12:15**
Phil 2 ¹⁷Even if I am to be poured as a libation upon the sacrificial offering of your faith, I am glad and rejoice with you all.

2 Tim 2 ¹⁰Therefore I endure everything for the sake of the elect, that they also may obtain salvation in Christ Jesus with its eternal glory.

● **2 Cor 12:16**
2 Cor 11 ⁹And when I was with you and was in want, I did not burden any one, for my needs were supplied by the brethren who came from Macedonia. So I refrained and will refrain from burdening you in any way.

● **2 Cor 12:18**
2 Cor 8 ⁶Accordingly we have urged Titus that as he had already made a beginning, he should also complete among you this gracious work.

2 Cor 8 ¹⁶But thanks be to God who puts the same earnest care for you into the heart of Titus. ¹⁷For he not only accepted our appeal, but being himself very earnest he is going to you of his own accord. ¹⁸With him we are sending the brother who is famous among all the churches for his preaching of the gospel; ¹⁹and not only that, but he has been appointed by the churches to travel with us in this gracious work which we are carrying on, for the glory of the Lord and to show our good will.

Formal Elements: Vice List & Apostolic Visit

[19] Have you been thinking all along that we have been defending ourselves before you? It is in the sight of God that we have been speaking in Christ, and all for your upbuilding, beloved. [20] For I fear that perhaps I may come and find you not what I wish, and that you may find me not what you wish; that perhaps there may be quarreling, jealousy, anger, selfishness, slander, gossip, conceit, and disorder. [21] I fear that when I come again my God may humble me before you, and I may have to mourn over many of those who sinned before and have not repented of the impurity, immorality, and licentiousness which they have practiced.

Primary

See §6 for Vice List

See §63 for Apostolic Visit

Secondary

1 Cor 1:10–17 (§73)

[10] I appeal to you, brethren, by the name of our Lord Jesus Christ, that all of you agree and that there be no dissensions among you, but that you be united in the same mind and the same judgment. [11] For it has been reported to me by Chloe's people that there is quarreling among you, my brethren. [12] What I mean is that each one of you says, "I belong to Paul," or "I belong to Apollos," or "I belong to Cephas," or "I belong to Christ." [13] Is Christ divided? Was Paul crucified for you? Or were you baptized in the name of Paul? [14] I am thankful that I baptized none of you except Crispus and Gaius; [15] lest any one should say that you were baptized in my name. [16] (I did baptize also the household of Stephanas. Beyond that, I do not know whether I baptized any one else.) [17] For Christ did not send me to baptize but to preach the gospel, and not with eloquent wisdom, lest the cross of Christ be emptied of its power.

2 Cor 3:1–3 (§154)

3 [1] Are we beginning to commend ourselves again? Or do we need, as some do, letters of recommendation to you, or from you? [2] You yourselves are our letter of recommendation, written on your hearts, to be known and read by all men; [3] and you show that you are a letter from Christ delivered by us, written not with ink but with the Spirit of the living God, not on tablets of stone but on tablets of human hearts.

● 2 Cor 12:19–21

2 Cor 9 [1] Now it is superfluous for me to write to you about the offering for the saints, [2] for I know your readiness, of which I boast about you to the people of Macedonia, saying that Achaia has been ready since last year; and your zeal has stirred up most of them. [3] But I am sending the brethren so that our boasting about you may not prove vain in this case, so that you may be ready, as I said you would be; [4] lest if some Macedonians come with me and find that you are not ready, we be humiliated—to say nothing of you—for being so confident. [5] So I thought it necessary to urge the brethren to go on to you before me, and arrange in advance for this gift you have promised, so that it may be ready not as an exaction but as a willing gift.

2 Cor 12 [1] I must boast; there is nothing to be gained by it, but I will go on to visions and revelations of the Lord. [2] I know a man in Christ who fourteen years ago was caught up to the third heaven—whether in the body or out of the body I do not know, God knows. [3] And I know that this man was caught up into Paradise—whether in the body or out of the body I do not know, God knows— [4] and he heard things that cannot be told, which man may not utter. [5] On behalf of this man I will boast, but on my own behalf I will not boast, except of my weaknesses. [6] Though if I wish to boast, I shall not be a fool, for I shall be speaking the truth. But I refrain from it, so that no one may think more of me than he sees in me or hears from me. [7] And to keep me from being too elated by the abundance of revelations, a thorn was given me in the flesh, a messenger of Satan, to harass me, to keep me from being too elated. [8] Three times I besought the Lord about this, that it should leave me; [9] but he said to me, "My grace is sufficient for you, for my power is made perfect in weakness." I will all the more gladly boast of my weaknesses, that the power of Christ may rest upon me. [10] For the sake of Christ, then, I am content with weaknesses, insults, hardships, persecutions, and calamities; for when I am weak, then I am strong.

2 Cor 12 [14] Here for the third time I am ready to come to you. And I will not be a burden, for I seek not what is yours but you; for children ought not to lay up for their parents, but parents for their children. [15] I will most gladly spend and be spent for your souls. If I love you the more, am I to be loved the less? [16] But granting that I myself did not burden you, I was crafty, you say, and got the better of you by guile. [17] Did I take advantage of you through any of those whom I sent to you? [18] I urged Titus to go, and sent the brother with him.

Did Titus take advantage of you? Did we not act in the same spirit? Did we not take the same steps?

● 2 Cor 12:19

1 Cor 10 [23] "All things are lawful," but not all things are helpful. "All things are lawful," but not all things build up.

2 Cor 2 [17] For we are not, like so many, peddlers of God's word; but as men of sincerity, as commissioned by God, in the sight of God we speak in Christ.

2 Cor 3 [1] Are we beginning to commend ourselves again? Or do we need, as some do, letters of recommendation to you, or from you?

2 Cor 10 [18] For it is not the man who commends himself that is accepted, but the man whom the Lord commends.

1 Thess 5 [4] But you are not in darkness, brethren, for that day to surprise you like a thief.

● 2 Cor 12:20

2 Cor 10 [11] Let such people understand that what we say by letter when absent, we do when present.

FORMAL ELEMENT: APOSTOLIC VISIT

13 This is the third time I am coming to you. Any charge must be sustained by the evidence of two or three witnesses. ²I warned those who sinned before and all the others, and I warn them now while absent, as I did when present on my second visit, that if I come again I will not spare them— ³since you desire proof that Christ is speaking in me. He is not weak in dealing with you, but is powerful in you. ⁴For he was crucified in weakness, but lives by the power of God. For we are weak in him, but in dealing with you we shall live with him by the power of God.

PRIMARY

See §63 for APOSTOLIC VISIT

SECONDARY

Rom 1:16–17 (§3)

¹⁶For I am not ashamed of the gospel: it is the power of God for salvation to every one who has faith, to the Jew first and also to the Greek. ¹⁷For in it the righteousness of God is revealed through faith for faith; as it is written, "He who through faith is righteous shall live."

1 Cor 1:18–25 (§74)

¹⁸For the word of the cross is folly to those who are perishing, but to us who are being saved it is the power of God. ¹⁹For it is written,

"I will destroy the wisdom of the wise,
and the cleverness of the clever I will thwart."

²⁰Where is the wise man? Where is the scribe? Where is the debater of this age? Has not God made foolish the wisdom of the world? ²¹For since, in the wisdom of God, the world did not know God through wisdom, it pleased God through the folly of what we preach to save those who believe. ²²For Jews demand signs and Greeks seek wisdom, ²³but we preach Christ crucified, a stumbling block to Jews and folly to Gentiles, ²⁴but to those who are called, both Jews and Greeks, Christ the power of God and the wisdom of God. ²⁵For the foolishness of God is wiser than men, and the weakness of God is stronger than men.

1 Cor 5:1–5 (§87)

¹It is actually reported that there is immorality among you, and of a kind that is not found even among pagans; for a man is living with his father's wife. ²And you are arrogant! Ought you not rather to mourn? Let him who has done this be removed from among you.

³For though absent in body I am present in spirit, and as if present, I have already pronounced judgment ⁴in the name of the Lord Jesus on the man who has done such a thing. When you are assembled, and my spirit is present, with the power of our Lord Jesus, ⁵you are to deliver this man to Satan for the destruction of the flesh, that his spirit may be saved in the day of the Lord Jesus.

● **2 Cor 13:1–4**

2 Cor 1   ¹⁵Because I was sure of this, I wanted to come to you first, so that you might have a double pleasure; ¹⁶I wanted to visit you on my way to Macedonia, and to come back to you from Macedonia and have you send me on my way to Judea. ¹⁷Was I vacillating when I wanted to do this? Do I make my plans like a worldly man, ready to say Yes and No at once? ¹⁸As surely as God is faithful, our word to you has not been Yes and No. ¹⁹For the Son of God, Jesus Christ, whom we preached among you, Silvanus and Timothy and I, was not Yes and No; but in him it is always Yes. ²⁰For all the promises of God find their Yes in him. That is why we utter the Amen through him, to the glory of God. ²¹But it is God who establishes us with you in Christ, and has commissioned us; ²²he has put his seal upon us and given us his Spirit in our hearts as a guarantee.

²³But I call God to witness against me—it was to spare you that I refrained from coming to Corinth. ²⁴Not that we lord it over your faith; we work with you for your joy, for you stand firm in your faith. 2 ¹For I made up my mind not to make you another painful visit. ²For if I cause you pain, who is there to make me glad but the one whom I have pained? ³And I wrote as I did, so that when I came I might not suffer pain from those who should have made me rejoice, for I felt sure of all of you, that my joy would be the joy of you all. ⁴For I wrote you out of much affliction and anguish of heart and with many tears, not to cause you pain but to let you know the abundant love that I have for you.

2 Cor 9   ¹Now it is superfluous for me to write to you about the offering for the saints, ²for I know your readiness, of which I boast about you to the people of Macedonia, saying that Achaia has been ready since last year; and your zeal has stirred up most of them. ³But I am sending the brethren so that our boasting about you may not prove vain in this case, so that you may be ready, as I said you would be; ⁴lest if some Macedonians come with me and find that you are not ready, we be humiliated—to say nothing of you—for being so confident. ⁵So I thought it necessary to urge the brethren to go on to you before me, and arrange in advance for this gift you have promised, so that it may be ready not as an exaction but as a willing gift.

2 Cor 12   ¹⁴Here for the third time I am ready to come to you. And I will not be a burden, for I seek not what is yours but you; for children ought not to lay up for their parents, but parents for their children. ¹⁵I will most gladly spend and be spent for your souls. If I love you the more, am I to be loved the less? ¹⁶But granting that I myself did not burden you, I was crafty, you say, and got the better of you by guile. ¹⁷Did I take advantage of you through any of those whom I sent to you? ¹⁸I urged Titus to go, and sent the brother with him. Did Titus take advantage of you? Did we not act in the same spirit? Did we not take the same steps?

¹⁹Have you been thinking all along that we have been defending ourselves before you? It is in the sight of God that we have been speaking in Christ, and all for your upbuilding, beloved. ²⁰For I fear that perhaps I may come and find you not what I wish, and that you may find me not what you wish; that perhaps there may be quarreling, jealousy, anger, selfishness, slander, gossip, conceit, and disorder. ²¹I fear that when I come again my God may humble me before you, and I may have to mourn over many of those who sinned before and have not repented of the impurity, immorality, and licentiousness which they have practiced.

2 Cor 13   ⁵Examine yourselves, to see whether you are holding to your faith. Test yourselves. Do you not realize that Jesus Christ is in you?—unless indeed you fail to meet the test! ⁶I hope you will find out that we have not failed. ⁷But we pray God that you may not do wrong—not that we may appear to have met the test, but that you may do what is right, though we may seem to have failed. ⁸For we cannot do anything against the truth, but only for the truth. ⁹For we are glad when we are weak and you are strong. What we pray for is your improvement. ¹⁰I write this while I am away from you, in order that when I come I may not have to be severe in my use of the authority which the Lord has given me for building up and not for tearing down.

● **2 Cor 13:1**

1 Cor 6   ⁴If then you have such cases, why do you lay them before those who are least esteemed by the church? ⁵I say this to your shame. Can it be that there is no man among you wise enough to decide between members of the brotherhood, . . .

2 Cor 12   ¹⁴Here for the third time I am ready to come to you. And I will not be a burden, for I seek not what is yours but you; for children ought not to lay up for their parents, but parents for their children.

● **2 Cor 13:3**

1 Thess 2   ¹³And we also thank God constantly for this, that when you received the word of God which you heard from us, you accepted it not as the word of men but as what it really is, the word of God, which is at work in you believers.

● **2 Cor 13:4**

Rom 1   ³the gospel concerning his Son, who was descended from David according to the flesh ⁴and designated Son of God in power according to the Spirit of holiness by his resurrection from the dead, Jesus Christ our Lord, . . .

1 Cor 2   ¹When I came to you, brethren, I did not come proclaiming to you the testimony of God in lofty words or wisdom. ²For I decided to know nothing among you except Jesus Christ and him crucified. ³And I was with you in weakness and in much fear and trembling; ⁴and my speech and my message were not in plausible words of wisdom, but in demonstration of the Spirit and of power, ⁵that your faith might not rest in the wisdom of men but in the power of God.

Phil 2   ⁷but emptied himself, taking the form of a servant, being born in the likeness of men.

FORMAL ELEMENT: APOSTOLIC VISIT

[5]Examine yourselves, to see whether you are holding to your faith. Test yourselves. Do you not realize that Jesus Christ is in you?—unless indeed you fail to meet the test! [6]I hope you will find out that we have not failed. [7]But we pray God that you may not do wrong— not that we may appear to have met the test, but that you may do what is right, though we may seem to have failed. [8]For we cannot do anything against the truth, but only for the truth. [9]For we are glad when we are weak and you are strong. What we pray for is your improvement. [10]I write this while I am away from you, in order that when I come I may not have to be severe in my use of the authority which the Lord has given me for building up and not for tearing down.

PRIMARY

See §63 for APOSTOLIC VISIT

SECONDARY

Rom 15:1–6 (§60)

[1]We who are strong ought to bear with the failings of the weak, and not to please ourselves; [2]let each of us please his neighbor for his good, to edify him. [3]For Christ did not please himself; but, as it is written, "The reproaches of those who reproached thee fell on me." [4]For whatever was written in former days was written for our instruction, that by steadfastness and by the encouragement of the scriptures we might have hope. [5]May the God of steadfastness and encouragement grant you to live in such harmony with one another, in accord with Christ Jesus, [6]that together you may with one voice glorify the God and Father of our Lord Jesus Christ.

● **2 Cor 13:5–10**

2 Cor 1 [15]Because I was sure of this, I wanted to come to you first, so that you might have a double pleasure; [16]I wanted to visit you on my way to Macedonia, and to come back to you from Macedonia and have you send me on my way to Judea. [17]Was I vacillating when I wanted to do this? Do I make my plans like a worldly man, ready to say Yes and No at once? [18]As surely as God is faithful, our word to you has not been Yes and No. [19]For the Son of God, Jesus Christ, whom we preached among you, Silvanus and Timothy and I, was not Yes and No; but in him it is always Yes. [20]For all the promises of God find their Yes in him. That is why we utter the Amen through him, to the glory of God. [21]But it is God who establishes us with you in Christ, and has commissioned us; [22]he has put his seal upon us and given us his Spirit in our hearts as a guarantee.

[23]But I call God to witness against me—it was to spare you that I refrained from coming to Corinth. [24]Not that we lord it over your faith; we work with you for your joy, for you stand firm in your faith. **2** [1]For I made up my mind not to make you another painful visit. [2]For if I cause you pain, who is there to make me glad but the one whom I have pained? [3]And I wrote as I did, so that when I came I might not suffer pain from those who should have made me rejoice, for I felt sure of all of you, that my joy would be the joy of you all. [4]For I wrote you out of much affliction and anguish of heart and with many tears, not to cause you pain but to let you know the abundant love that I have for you.

2 Cor 9 [1]Now it is superfluous for me to write to you about the offering for the saints, [2]for I know your readiness, of which I boast about you to the people of Macedonia, saying that Achaia has been ready since last year; and your zeal has stirred up most of them. [3]But I am sending the brethren so that our boasting about you may not prove vain in this case, so that you may be ready, as I said you would be; [4]lest if some Macedonians come with me and find that you are not ready, we be humiliated—to say nothing of you—for being so confident. [5]So I thought it necessary to urge the brethren to go on to you before me, and arrange in advance for this gift you have promised, so that it may be ready not as an exaction but as a willing gift.

2 Cor 12 [14]Here for the third time I am ready to come to you. And I will not be a burden, for I seek not what is yours but you; for children ought not to lay up for their parents, but parents for their children. [15]I will most gladly spend and be spent for your souls. If I love you the more, am I to be loved the less? [16]But granting that I myself did not burden you, I was crafty, you say, and got the better of you by guile. [17]Did I take advantage of you through any of those whom I sent to you? [18]I urged Titus to go, and sent the brother with him. Did Titus take advantage of you? Did we not act in the same spirit? Did we not take the same steps?

[19]Have you been thinking all along that we have been defending ourselves before you? It is in the sight of God that we have been speaking in Christ, and all for your upbuilding, beloved. [20]For I fear that perhaps I may come and find you not what I wish, and that you may find me not what you wish; that perhaps there may be quarreling, jealousy, anger, selfishness, slander, gossip, conceit, and disorder. [21]I fear that when I come again my God may humble me before you, and I may have to mourn over many of those who sinned before and have not repented of the impurity, immorality, and licentiousness which they have practiced.

13 [1]This is the third time I am coming to you. Any charge must be sustained by the evidence of two or three witnesses. [2]I warned those who sinned before and all the others, and I warn them now while absent, as I did when present on my second visit, that if I come again I will not spare them— [3]since you desire proof that Christ is speaking in me. He is not weak in dealing with you, but is powerful in you. [4]For he was crucified in weakness, but lives by the power of God. For we are weak in him, but in dealing with you we shall live with him by the power of God.

● **2 Cor 13:5–6**

2 Cor 2 [9]For this is why I wrote, that I might test you and know whether you are obedient in everything.

2 Cor 7 [11]For see what earnestness this godly grief has produced in you, what eagerness to clear yourselves, what indignation, what alarm, what longing, what zeal, what punishment! At every point you have proved yourselves guiltless in the matter.

● **2 Cor 13:5**

1 Cor 11 [28](But if some one says to you, "This has been offered in sacrifice," then out of consideration for the man who informed you, and for conscience' sake . . .

Gal 6 [4]But let each one test his own work, and then his reason to boast will be in himself alone and not in his neighbor.

● **2 Cor 3:8**

1 Cor 3 [13]each man's work will become manifest; for the Day will disclose it, because it will be revealed with fire, and the fire will test what sort of work each one has done.

● **2 Cor 13:9**

1 Cor 4 [10]We are fools for Christ's sake, but you are wise in Christ. We are weak, but you are strong. You are held in honor, but we in disrepute.

● **2 Cor 13:10**

2 Cor 10 [1]I, Paul, myself entreat you, by the meekness and gentleness of Christ—I who am humble when face to face with you, but bold to you when I am away!— [2]I beg of you that when I am present I may not have to show boldness with such confidence as I count on showing against some who suspect us of acting in worldly fashion. [3]For though we live in the world we are not carrying on a worldly war, [4]for the weapons of our warfare are not worldly but have divine power to destroy strongholds. [5]We destroy arguments and every proud obstacle to the knowledge of God, and take every thought captive to obey Christ, [6]being ready to punish every disobedience, when your obedience is complete.

2 Cor 10 [8]For even if I boast a little too much of our authority, which the Lord gave for building you up and not for destroying you, I shall not be put to shame.

Gal 2 [18]But if I build up again those things which I tore down, then I prove myself a transgressor.

Titus 1 [13]This testimony is true. Therefore rebuke them sharply, that they may be sound in the faith, . . .

LETTER STRUCTURE: GREETINGS
FORMAL ELEMENT: GNOMIC SAYINGS

¹¹Finally, brethren, farewell. Mend your ways, heed my appeal, agree with one another, live in peace, and the God of love and peace will be with you. ¹²Greet one another with a holy kiss. ¹³All the saints greet you.

PRIMARY

See §53 for GNOMIC SAYINGS

Rom 16:3–16 (§66)
³Greet Prisca and Aquila, my fellow workers in Christ Jesus, ⁴who risked their necks for my life, to whom not only I but also all the churches of the Gentiles give thanks; ⁵greet also the church in their house. Greet my beloved Epaenetus, who was the first convert in Asia for Christ. ⁶Greet Mary, who has worked hard among you. ⁷Greet Andronicus and Junias, my kinsmen and my fellow prisoners; they are men of note among the apostles, and they were in Christ before me. ⁸Greet Ampliatus, my beloved in the Lord. ⁹Greet Urbanus, our fellow worker in Christ, and my beloved Stachys. ¹⁰Greet Apelles, who is approved in Christ. Greet those who belong to the family of Aristobulus. ¹¹Greet my kinsman Herodion. Greet those in the Lord who belong to the family of Narcissus. ¹²Greet those workers in the Lord, Tryphaena and Tryphosa. Greet the beloved Persis, who has worked hard in the Lord. ¹³Greet Rufus, eminent in the Lord, also

his mother and mine. ¹⁴Greet Asyncritus, Phlegon, Hermes, Patrobas, Hermas, and the brethren who are with them. ¹⁵Greet Philologus, Julia, Nereus and his sister, and Olympas, and all the saints who are with them. ¹⁶Greet one another with a holy kiss. All the churches of Christ greet you.

Rom 16:21–23 (§69)
²¹Timothy, my fellow worker, greets you; so do Lucius and Jason and Sosipater, my kinsmen.
²²I Tertius, the writer of this letter, greet you in the Lord.
²³Gaius, who is host to me and to the whole church, greets you. Erastus, the city treasurer, and our brother Quartus, greet you.

1 Cor 16:19–20 (§143)
¹⁹The churches of Asia send greetings. Aquila and Prisca, together with the church in their house, send you hearty greetings in the Lord. ²⁰All the brethren send greetings. Greet one another with a holy kiss.

Phil 4:21–22 (§254)
²¹Greet every saint in Christ Jesus. The brethren who are with me greet you. ²²All the saints greet you, especially those of Caesar's household.

Col 4:10–15 (§272)
¹⁰Aristarchus my fellow prisoner greets you, and Mark the cousin of Barnabas (concerning whom you have received instructions—if he comes to you, receive him), ¹¹and Jesus who is

called Justus. These are the only men of the circumcision among my fellow workers for the kingdom of God, and they have been a comfort to me. ¹²Epaphras, who is one of yourselves, a servant of Christ Jesus, greets you, always remembering you earnestly in his prayers, that you may stand mature and fully assured in all the will of God. ¹³For I bear him witness that he has worked hard for you and for those in Laodicea and in Hierapolis. ¹⁴Luke the beloved physician and Demas greet you. ¹⁵Give my greetings to the brethren at Laodicea, and to Nympha and the church in her house.

1 Thess 5:23–24 (§289)
²³May the God of peace himself sanctify you wholly; and may your spirit and soul and body be kept sound and blameless at the coming of our Lord Jesus Christ. ²⁴He who calls you is faithful, and he will do it.

1 Thess 5:26 (§291)
²⁶Greet all the brethren with a holy kiss.

2 Thess 3:16 (§302)
¹⁶Now may the Lord of peace himself give you peace at all times in all ways. The Lord be with you all.

Phlm 23–24 (§310)
²³Epaphras, my fellow prisoner in Christ Jesus, sends greetings to you, ²⁴and so do Mark, Aristarchus, Demas, and Luke, my fellow workers.

● **2 Cor 13:11-13**
2 Tim 4   ¹⁹Greet Prisca and Aquila, and the household of Onesiphorus. ²⁰Erastus remained at Corinth; Trophimus I left ill at Miletus. ²¹Do your best to come before winter. Eubulus sends greetings to you, as do Pudens and Linus and Claudia and all the brethren.

Titus 3   ¹⁵All who are with me send greetings to you. Greet those who love us in the faith.

● **2 Cor 13:11**
Rom 12   ¹⁶Live in harmony with one another; do not be haughty, but associate with the lowly; never be conceited.

Rom 12   ¹⁸If possible, so far as it depends upon you, live peaceably with all.

Lᴇᴛᴛᴇʀ Sᴛʀᴜᴄᴛᴜʀᴇ: Cʟᴏsɪɴɢ Gʀᴀᴄᴇ

¹⁴The grace of the Lord Jesus Christ and the love of God and the fellowship of the Holy Spirit be with you all.

Pʀɪᴍᴀʀʏ

Rom 16:20b (§68)
The grace of our Lord Jesus Christ be with you.

1 Cor 16:23–24 (§145)
²³The grace of the Lord Jesus be with you. ²⁴My love be with you all in Christ Jesus. Amen.

Gal 6:18 (§217)
¹⁸The grace of our Lord Jesus Christ be with your spirit, brethren. Amen.

Eph 6:23–24 (§236)
²³Peace be to the brethren, and love with faith, from God the Father and the Lord Jesus Christ. ²⁴Grace be with all who love our Lord Jesus Christ with love undying.

Phil 4:23 (§255)
²³The grace of the Lord Jesus Christ be with your spirit.

Col 4:18b (§274)
Grace be with you.

1 Thess 5:28 (§293)
²⁸The grace of our Lord Jesus Christ be with you.

2 Thess 3:18 (§304)
¹⁸The grace of our Lord Jesus Christ be with you all.

Phlm 25 (§311)
²⁵The grace of the Lord Jesus Christ be with your spirit.

● **2 Cor 13:14**
1 Tim 6   ²¹. . . Grace be with you.

2 Tim 4   ²²The Lord be with your spirit. Grace be with you.

Titus 3   ¹⁵. . . Grace be with you all.

LETTER STRUCTURE: SALUTATION

1 Paul an apostle–not from men nor through man, but through Jesus Christ and God the Father, who raised him from the dead—[2]and all the brethren who are with me,

To the churches of Galatia:

[3]Grace to you and peace from God the Father and our Lord Jesus Christ, [4]who gave himself for our sins to deliver us from the present evil age, according to the will of our God and Father; [5]to whom be the glory for ever and ever. Amen.

PRIMARY

Rom 1:1–7 (§1)

[1]Paul, a servant of Jesus Christ, called to be an apostle, set apart for the gospel of God [2]which he promised beforehand through his prophets in the holy scriptures, [3]the gospel concerning his Son, who was descended from David according to the flesh [4]and designated Son of God in power according to the Spirit of holiness by his resurrection from the dead, Jesus Christ our Lord, [5]through whom we have received grace and apostleship to bring about the obedience of faith for the sake of his name among all the nations, [6]including yourselves who are called to belong to Jesus Christ;

[7]To all God's beloved in Rome, who are called to be saints:

Grace to you and peace from God our Father and the Lord Jesus Christ.

1 Cor 1:1–3 (§71)

[1]Paul, called by the will of God to be an apostle of Christ Jesus, and our brother Sosthenes,

[2]To the church of God which is at Corinth, to those sanctified in Christ Jesus, called to be saints together with all those who in every place call on the name of our Lord Jesus Christ, both their Lord and ours:

[3]Grace to you and peace from God our Father and the Lord Jesus Christ.

2 Cor 1:1–2 (§146)

[1]Paul, an apostle of Christ Jesus by the will of God, and Timothy our brother.

To the church of God which is at Corinth, with all the saints who are in the whole of Achaia:

[2]Grace to you and peace from God our Father and the Lord Jesus Christ.

Eph 1:1–2 (§218)

[1]Paul, an apostle of Christ Jesus by the will of God,

To the saints who are also faithful in Christ Jesus:

[2]Grace to you and peace from God our Father and the Lord Jesus Christ.

Phil 1:1–2 (§237)

[1]Paul and Timothy, servants of Christ Jesus,

To all the saints in Christ Jesus who are at Philippi, with the bishops and deacons:

[2]Grace to you and peace from God our Father and the Lord Jesus Christ.

Col 1:1–2 (§256)

[1]Paul, an apostle of Christ Jesus by the will of God, and Timothy our brother,

[2]To the saints and faithful brethren in Christ at Colossae:

Grace to you and peace from God our Father.

1 Thess 1:1 (§275)

[1]Paul, Silvanus, and Timothy,

To the church of the Thessalonians in God the Father and the Lord Jesus Christ:

Grace to you and peace.

2 Thess 1:1–2 (§294)

[1]Paul, Silvanus, and Timothy,

To the church of the Thessalonians in God our Father and the Lord Jesus Christ:

[2]Grace to you and peace from God the Father and the Lord Jesus Christ.

Phlm 1–3 (§305)

[1]Paul, a prisoner for Christ Jesus, and Timothy our brother,

To Philemon our beloved fellow worker [2]and Apphia our sister and Archippus our fellow soldier, and the church in your house:

[3]Grace to you and peace from God our Father and the Lord Jesus Christ.

● **Gal 1:1–5**

1 Cor 15　[3]For I delivered to you as of first importance what I also received, that Christ died for our sins in accordance with the scriptures, [4]that he was buried, that he was raised on the third day in accordance with the scriptures, [5]and that he appeared to Cephas, then to the twelve.

1 Tim 1　[1]Paul, an apostle of Christ Jesus by command of God our Savior and of Christ Jesus our hope, [2]To Timothy, my true child in the faith:

Grace, mercy, and peace from God the Father and Christ Jesus our Lord.

2 Tim 1　[1]Paul, an apostle of Christ Jesus by the will of God according to the promise of the life which is in Christ Jesus, [2]To Timothy, my beloved child:

Grace, mercy, and peace from God the Father and Christ Jesus our Lord.

Titus 1　[1]Paul, a servant of God and an apostle of Jesus Christ, to further the faith of God's elect and their knowledge of the truth which accords with godliness, [2]in hope of eternal life which God, who never lies, promised ages ago [3]and at the proper time manifested in his word through the preaching with which I have been entrusted by command of God our Savior;

[4]To Titus, my true child in a common faith:

Grace and peace from God the Father and Christ Jesus our Savior.

● **Gal 1:1**

Acts 2　[24]"But God raised him up, having loosed the pangs of death, because it was not possible for him to be held by it."

Acts 9　[15]But the Lord said to him, "Go, for he is a chosen instrument of mine to carry my name before the Gentiles and kings and the sons of Israel. . . ."

Acts 20　[24]"But I do not account my life of any value nor as precious to myself, if only I may accomplish my course and the ministry which I received from the Lord Jesus, to testify to the gospel of the grace of God."

Acts 22　[21]"And he said to me, 'Depart; for I will send you far away to the Gentiles.'"

Acts 26　[16]"But rise and stand upon your feet; for I have appeared to you for this purpose, to appoint you to serve and bear witness to the things in which you have seen me and to those in which I will appear to you, . . ."

● **Gal 1:2**

Acts 16　[6]And they went through the region of Phrygia and Galatia, having been forbidden by the Holy Spirit to speak the word in Asia.

● **Gal 1:4**

Col 1　[13]He has delivered us from the dominion of darkness and transferred us to the kingdom of his beloved Son, . . .

1 Tim 2　[6]who gave himself as a ransom for all, the testimony to which was borne at the proper time.

Acts 2　[40]And he testified with many other words and exhorted them, saying, "Save yourselves from this crooked generation."

LETTER STRUCTURE: ASTONISHMENT

[6] I am astonished that you are so quickly deserting him who called you in the grace of Christ and turning to a different gospel— [7] not that there is another gospel, but there are some who trouble you and want to pervert the gospel of Christ. [8] But even if we, or an angel from heaven, should preach to you a gospel contrary to that which we preached to you, let him be accursed. [9] As we have said before, so now I say again, If any one is preaching to you a gospel contrary to that which you received, let him be accursed.

[10] Am I now seeking the favor of men, or of God? Or am I trying to please men? If I were still pleasing men, I should not be a servant of Christ.

[11] For I would have you know, brethren, that the gospel which was preached by me is not man's gospel. [12] For I did not receive it from man, nor was I taught it, but it came through a revelation of Jesus Christ.

PRIMARY

Rom 16:17–20a (§67)

[17] I appeal to you, brethren, to take note of those who create dissensions and difficulties, in opposition to the doctrine which you have been taught; avoid them. [18] For such persons do not serve our Lord Christ, but their own appetites, and by fair and flattering words they deceive the hearts of the simple-minded. [19] For while your obedience is known to all, so that I rejoice over you, I would have you wise as to what is good and guileless as to what is evil; [20] then the God of peace will soon crush Satan under your feet.

1 Cor 15:1–11 (§131)

[1] Now I would remind you, brethren, in what terms I preached to you the gospel, which you received, in which you stand, [2] by which you are saved, if you hold it fast —unless you believed in vain.

[3] For I delivered to you as of first importance what I also received, that Christ died for our sins in accordance with the scriptures, [4] that he was buried, that he was raised on the third day in accordance with the scriptures, [5] and that he appeared to Cephas, then to the twelve. [6] Then he appeared to more than five hundred brethren at one time, most of whom are still alive, though some have fallen asleep. [7] Then he appeared to James, then to all the apostles. [8] Last of all, as to one untimely born, he appeared also to me. [9] For I am the least of the apostles, unfit to be called an apostle, because I persecuted the church of God. [10] But by the grace of God I am what I am, and his grace toward me was not in vain. On the contrary, I worked harder than any of them, though it was not I, but the grace of God which is with me. [11] Whether then it was I or they, so we preach and so you believed.

2 Cor 5:11–13 (§163)

[11] Therefore, knowing the fear of the Lord, we persuade men; but what we are is known to God, and I hope it is known also to your conscience. [12] We are not commending ourselves to you again but giving you cause to be proud of us, so that you may be able to answer those who pride themselves on a man's position and not on his heart. [13] For if we are beside ourselves, it is for God; if we are in our right mind, it is for you.

2 Cor 11:1–6 (§179)

[1] I wish you would bear with me in a little foolishness. Do bear with me! [2] I feel a divine jealousy for you, for I betrothed you to Christ to present you as a pure bride to her one husband. [3] But I am afraid that as the serpent deceived Eve by his cunning, your thoughts will be led astray from a sincere and pure devotion to Christ. [4] For if some one comes and preaches another Jesus than the one we preached, or if

---

● **Gal 1:6**

1 Cor 11   [23] "All things are lawful," but not all things are helpful. "All things are lawful," but not all things build up.

1 Cor 15   [1] Now I would remind you, brethren, in what terms I preached to you the gospel, which you received, in which you stand, [2] by which you are saved, if you hold it fast —unless you believed in vain.
[3] For I delivered to you as of first importance what I also received, that Christ died for our sins in accordance with the scriptures, . . .

Eph 5   [6] Let no one deceive you with empty words, for it is because of these things that the wrath of God comes upon the sons of disobedience.

Phil 1   [27] Only let your manner of life be worthy of the gospel of Christ, so that whether I come and see you or am absent, I may hear of you that you stand firm in one spirit, with one mind striving side by side for the faith of the gospel, . . .

Cf. Gal 3   [1] O foolish Galatians! Who has bewitched you, before whose eyes Jesus Christ was publicly portrayed as crucified? [2] Let me ask you only this: Did you receive the Spirit by works of the law, or by hearing with faith? [3] Are you so foolish? Having begun with the Spirit, are you now ending with the flesh? [4] Did you experience so many things in vain?—if it really is in vain. [5] Does he who supplies the Spirit to you and works miracles among you do so by works of the law, or by hearing with faith?

Cf. Gal 6   [7] Do not be deceived; God is not mocked, for whatever a man sows, that he will also reap.

Cf. Gal 6   [17] Henceforth let no man trouble me; for I bear on my body the marks of Jesus.

● **Gal 1:7**

Cf. 2 Cor 12   [11] I have been a fool! You forced me to it, for I ought to have been commended by you. For I was not at all inferior to these superlative apostles, even though I am nothing.

Cf. Gal 4   [17] They make much of you, but for no good purpose; they want to shut you out, that you may make much of them.

you receive a different spirit from the one you received, or if you accept a different gospel from the one you accepted, you submit to it readily enough. [5]I think that I am not in the least inferior to these superlative apostles. [6]Even if I am unskilled in speaking, I am not in knowledge; in every way we have made this plain to you in all things.

2 Cor 11:12–21a (§181–182)

[12]And what I do I will continue to do, in order to undermine the claim of those who would like to claim that in their boasted mission they work on the same terms as we do. [13]For such men are false apostles, deceitful workmen, disguising themselves as apostles of Christ. [14]And no wonder, for even Satan disguises himself as an angel of light. [15]So it is not strange if his servants also disguise themselves as servants of righteousness. Their end will correspond to their deeds.

[16]I repeat, let no one think me foolish; but even if you do, accept me as a fool, so that I too may boast a little. [17](What I am saying I say not with the Lord's authority but as a fool, in this boastful confidence; [18]since many boast of worldly things, I too will boast.) [19]For you gladly bear with fools, being wise yourselves! [20]For you bear it if a man makes slaves of you, or preys upon you, or takes advantage of you, or puts on airs, or strikes you in the face. [21]To my shame, I must say, we were too weak for that!

Col 2:4–7 (§261)

[4]I say this in order that no one may delude you with beguiling speech. [5]For though I am absent in body, yet I am with you in spirit, rejoicing to see your good order and the firmness of your faith in Christ.

[6]As therefore you received Christ Jesus the Lord, so live in him, [7]rooted and built up in him and established in the faith, just as you were taught, abounding in thanksgiving.

1 Thess 2:1–8 (§277)

[1]For you yourselves know, brethren, that our visit to you was not in vain; [2]but though we had already suffered and been shamefully treated at Philippi, as you know, we had courage in our God to declare to you the gospel of God in the face of great opposition. [3]For our appeal does not spring from error or uncleanness, nor is it made with guile; [4]but just as we have been approved by God to be entrusted with the gospel, so we speak, not to please men, but to please God who tests our hearts. [5]For we never used either words of flattery, as you know, or a cloak for greed, as God is witness; [6]nor did we seek glory from men, whether from you or from others, though we might have made demands as apostles of Christ. [7]But we were gentle among you, like a nurse taking care of her children. [8]So, being affectionately desirous of you, we were ready to share with you not only the gospel of God but also our own selves, because you had become very dear to us.

2 Thess 2:13–15 (§297)

[13]But we are bound to give thanks to God always for you, brethren beloved by the Lord, because God chose you from the beginning to be saved, through sanctification by the Spirit and belief in the truth. [14]To this he called you through our gospel, so that you may obtain the glory of our Lord Jesus Christ. [15]So then, brethren, stand firm and hold to the traditions which you were taught by us, either by word of mouth or by letter.

2 Thess 3:14–15 (§301)

[14]If any one refuses to obey what we say in this letter, note that man, and have nothing to do with him, that he may be ashamed. [15]Do not look on him as an enemy, but warn him as a brother.

● **Gal 1:8**
Phil 1 [15]Some indeed preach Christ from envy and rivalry, but others from good will. [16]The latter do it out of love, knowing that I am put here for the defense of the gospel; [17]the former proclaim Christ out of partisanship, not sincerely but thinking to afflict me in my imprisonment. [18]What then? Only that in every way, whether in pretense or in truth, Christ is proclaimed; and in that I rejoice.

Cf. Gal 4 [14]and though my condition was a trial to you, you did not scorn or despise me, but received me as an angel of God, as Christ Jesus.

● **Gal 1:9**
Gal 5 [4]You are severed from Christ, you who would be justified by the law; you have fallen away from grace.

Cf. 1 Cor 16 [22]If any one has no love for the Lord, let him be accursed. Our Lord, come!

● **Gal 1:10**
Cf. Rom 8 [8]and those who are in the flesh cannot please God.

Cf. Rom 15 [1]We who are strong ought to bear with the failings of the weak, and not to please ourselves; [2]let each of us please his neighbor for his good, to edify him. [3]For Christ did not please himself; . . .

Cf. 1 Thess 4 [1]Finally, brethren, we beseech and exhort you in the Lord Jesus, that as you learned from us how you ought to live and to please God, just as you are doing, you do so more and more.

● **Gal 1:12**
1 Cor 9 [1]Am I not free? Am I not an apostle? Have I not seen Jesus our Lord? Are not you my workmanship in the Lord?

2 Cor 12 [1]I must boast; there is nothing to be gained by it, but I will go on to visions and revelations of the Lord.

13For you have heard of my former life in Judaism, how I persecuted the church of God violently and tried to destroy it; **14**and I advanced in Judaism beyond many of my own age among my people, so extremely zealous was I for the traditions of my fathers.

PRIMARY

Rom 2:17–24 (§10)

17But if you call yourself a Jew and rely upon the law and boast of your relation to God **18**and know his will and approve what is excellent, because you are instructed in the law, **19**and if you are sure that you are a guide to the blind, a light to those who are in darkness, **20**a corrector of the foolish, a teacher of children, having in the law the embodiment of knowledge and truth— **21**you then who teach others, will you not teach yourself? While you preach against stealing, do you steal? **22**You who say that one must not commit adultery, do you commit adultery? You who abhor idols, do you rob temples? **23**You who boast in the law, do you dishonor God by breaking the law? **24**For, as it is written, "The name of God is blasphemed among the Gentiles because of you."

Rom 9:1–13 (§35–36)

1I am speaking the truth in Christ, I am not lying; my conscience bears me witness in the Holy Spirit, **2**that I have great sorrow and unceasing anguish in my heart. **3**For I could wish that I myself were accursed and cut off from Christ for the sake of my brethren, my kinsmen by race. **4**They are Israelites, and to them belong the sonship, the glory, the covenants, the giving of the law, the worship, and the promises; **5**to them belong the patriarchs, and of their race, according to the flesh, is the Christ. God who is over all be blessed for ever. Amen.

6But it is not as though the word of God had failed. For not all who are descended from Israel belong to Israel, **7**and not all are children of Abraham because they are his descendants; but "Through Isaac shall your descendants be named." **8**This means that it is not the children of the flesh who are the children of God, but the children of the promise are reckoned as descendants. **9**For this is what the promise said, "About this time I will return and Sarah shall have a son." **10**And not only so, but also when Rebecca had conceived children by one man, our forefather Isaac, **11**though they were not yet born and had done nothing either good or bad, in order that God's purpose of election might continue, not because of works but because of his call, **12**she was told, "The elder will serve the younger." **13**As it is written, "Jacob I loved, but Esau I hated."

Rom 10:1–4 (§40)

1Brethren, my heart's desire and prayer to God for them is that they may be saved. **2**I bear them witness that they have a zeal for God, but it is not enlightened. **3**For, being ignorant of the righteousness that comes from God, and seeking to establish their own, they did not submit to God's righteousness. **4**For Christ is the end of the law, that every one who has faith may be justified.

Rom 11:1–6 (§44)

1I ask, then, has God rejected his people? By no means! I myself am an Israelite, a descendant of Abraham, a member of the tribe of Benjamin. **2**God has not rejected his people whom he foreknew. Do you not know what the scripture says of Elijah, how he pleads with God against Israel? **3**"Lord, they have killed thy prophets, they have demolished thy altars, and I alone am left, and they seek my life." **4**But what is God's reply to him? "I have kept for myself seven thousand men who have not bowed the knee to Baal." **5**So too at the present time there is a remnant, chosen by grace. **6**But if it is by grace, it is no longer on the basis of works; otherwise grace would no longer be grace.

2 Cor 11:21b–29 (§183)

But whatever any one dares to boast of—I am speaking as a fool—I also dare to boast of that. **22**Are they Hebrews? So am I. Are they Israelites? So am I. Are they descendants of Abraham? So am I. **23**Are they servants of Christ? I am a better one—I am talking like a madman—with far greater labors, far more imprisonments, with countless beatings, and often near death. **24**Five times I have received at the hands of the Jews the forty lashes less one. **25**Three times I have been beaten with rods; once I was stoned. Three times I have been shipwrecked; a night and a day I have been adrift at sea; **26**on frequent journeys, in danger from rivers, danger from robbers, danger from my own people, danger from Gentiles, danger in the city, danger in the wilderness, danger at sea, danger from false brethren; **27**in toil and hardship, through many a sleepless night, in hunger and thirst, often without food, in cold and exposure. **28**And, apart from other things, there is the daily pressure upon me of my anxiety for all the churches. **29**Who is weak, and I am not weak? Who is made to fall, and I am not indignant?

Phil 3:2–11 (§247)

2Look out for the dogs, look out for the evil-workers, look out for those who mutilate the flesh. **3**For we are the true circumcision, who worship God in spirit, and glory in Christ Jesus, and put no confidence in the flesh. **4**Though I myself have reason for confidence in the flesh also. If any other man thinks he has reason for confidence in the flesh, I have more: **5**circumcised on the eighth day, of the people of Israel, of the tribe of Benjamin, a Hebrew born of Hebrews; as to the law a Pharisee, **6**as to zeal a persecutor of the church, as to righteousness under the law blameless. **7**But whatever gain I had, I counted as loss for the sake of Christ. **8**Indeed I count everything as loss because of the surpassing worth of knowing Christ Jesus my Lord. For his sake I have suffered the loss of all things, and count them as refuse, in order that I may gain Christ **9**and be found in him, not having a righteousness of my own, based on law, but that which is through faith in Christ, the righteousness from God that depends on faith; **10**that I may know him and the power of his resurrection, and may share his sufferings, becoming like him in his death, **11**that if possible I may attain the resurrection from the dead.

● **Gal 1:13–14**

1 Thess 2   **14**For you, brethren, became imitators of the churches of God in Christ Jesus which are in Judea; for you suffered the same things from your own countrymen as they did from the Jews, **15**who killed both the Lord Jesus and the prophets, and drove us out, and displease God and oppose all men **16**by hindering us from speaking to the Gentiles that they may be saved—so as always to fill up the measure of their sins. But God's wrath has come upon them at last!

● **Gal 1:13**

1 Cor 15   **9**For I am the least of the apostles, unfit to be called an apostle, because I persecuted the church of God.

Gal 1   **23**they only heard it said, "He who once persecuted us is now preaching the faith he once tried to destroy."

Acts 19   **21**Now after these events Paul resolved in the Spirit to pass through Macedonia and Achaia and go to Jerusalem, saying, "After I have been there, I must also see Rome."

Acts 26   **4**"My manner of life from my youth, spent from the beginning among my own nation and at Jerusalem, is known by all the Jews. **5**They have known for a long time, if they are willing to testify, that according to the strictest party of our religion I have lived as a Pharisee."

● **Gal 1:14**

Acts 8   **31**And he said, "How can I, unless some one guides me?" And he invited Philip to come up and sit with him.

Acts 22   **3**"I am a Jew, born at Tarsus in Cilicia, but brought up in this city at the feet of Gamaliel, educated according to the strict manner of the law of our fathers, being zealous for God as you all are this day."

5. The Jerusalem Conference (Galatians 2) = Acts 18:22

Date

34	Paul's conversion	
35–37	Activities in Arabia; return to Damascus	
37	Escape from Aretas IV; first Jerusalem visit	2 Cor 11:32–33; Acts 9:23–26
37–46	Activities in Syria and Cilicia	
43–45	First missionary journey: Antioch, Cyprus, Pamphylia, and South Galatia	
46–51	Second missionary journey: Antioch, North Galatia, Troas, Philippi, Thessalonica, Berea, Athens, Corinth	Claudius' edict (49)
	Letters to the Thessalonians	
51	Hearing before Gallio at Corinth	Gallio inscription
51	Second Jerusalem visit: apostolic conference	Acts 18:22/Gal 2:1–10
52	Conflict with Peter	Gal 2:14–17
52–57	Third missionary journey: North Galatia	
52–54	Ephesus: *Galatians*	
54/55	Ephesian imprisonment: *Philippians*	
55	Visit to Corinth; return to Macedonia and Asia	
	Letters to the Corinthians	
56/57	Return to Corinth: *Romans*	
57	Philippi to Jerusalem; arrest	
57–59	Imprisonment in Caesarea	
61	Imprisonment in Rome	
62	Execution in Rome	

R. Jewett, *A Chronology of Paul's Life* (Philadelphia: Fortress Press, 1979), endpaper foldout. This chart is a greatly simplified version of the Jewett chronology. Summary prepared by John A. Darr and published in: Daniel Patte, *Paul's Faith and the Power of the Gospel* (Philadelphia: Fortress Press, 1983), 352–60. Reprinted by permission of the publisher.
See pages 67, 141, 175, 207 for other sketches of the Pauline chronology.

[15]But when he who had set me apart before I was born, and had called me through his grace, [16]was pleased to reveal his Son to me, in order that I might preach him among the Gentiles, I did not confer with flesh and blood, [17]nor did I go up to Jerusalem to those who were apostles before me, but I went away into Arabia; and again I returned to Damascus.

[18]Then after three years I went up to Jerusalem to visit Cephas, and remained with him fifteen days. [19]But I saw none of the other apostles except James the Lord's brother. [20](In what I am writing to you, before God, I do not lie!) [21]Then I went into the regions of Syria and Cilicia. [22]And I was still not known by sight to the churches of Christ in Judea; [23]they only heard it said, "He who once persecuted us is now preaching the faith he once tried to destroy." [24]And they glorified God because of me.

PRIMARY

Rom 15:14–21 (§62)

[14]I myself am satisfied about you, my brethren, that you yourselves are full of goodness, filled with all knowledge, and able to instruct one another. [15]But on some points I have written to you very boldly by way of reminder, because of the grace given me by God [16]to be a minister of Christ Jesus to the Gentiles in the priestly service of the gospel of God, so that the offering of the Gentiles may be acceptable, sanctified by the Holy Spirit. [17]In Christ Jesus, then, I have reason to be proud of my work for God. [18]For I will not venture to speak of anything except what Christ has wrought through me to win obedience from the Gentiles, by word and deed, [19]by the power of signs and wonders, by the power of the Holy Spirit, so that from Jerusalem and as far round as Illyricum I have fully preached the gospel of Christ, [20]thus making it my ambition to preach the gospel, not where Christ has already been named, lest I build on another man's foundation, [21]but as it is written,

"They shall see who have never been told of him,

and they shall understand who have never heard of him."

1 Cor 1:10–17 (§73)

[10]I appeal to you, brethren, by the name of our Lord Jesus Christ, that all of you agree and that there be no dissensions among you, but that you be united in the same mind and the same judgment. [11]For it has been reported to me by Chloe's people that there is quarreling among you, my brethren. [12]What I mean is that each one of you says, "I belong to Paul," or "I belong to Apollos," or "I belong to Cephas," or "I belong to Christ." [13]Is Christ divided? Was Paul crucified for you? Or were you baptized in the name of Paul? [14]I am thankful that I baptized none of you except Crispus and Gaius; [15]lest any one should say that you were baptized in my name. [16](I did baptize also the household of Stephanas. Beyond that, I do not know whether I baptized any one else.) [17]For Christ did not send me to baptize but to preach the gospel, and not with eloquent wisdom, lest the cross of Christ be emptied of its power.

1 Cor 9:1–14 (§105)

[1]Am I not free? Am I not an apostle? Have I not seen Jesus our Lord? Are not you my workmanship in the Lord? [2]If to others I am not an apostle, at least I am to you; for you are the seal of my apostleship in the Lord.

[3]This is my defense to those who would examine me. [4]Do we not have the right to our food and drink? [5]Do we not have the right to be accompanied by a wife, as the other apostles and the brothers of the Lord and Cephas? [6]Or is it only Barnabas and I who have no right to refrain from working for a living? [7]Who serves as a soldier at his own expense? Who plants a vineyard without eating any of its fruit? Who tends a flock without getting some of the milk?

[8]Do I say this on human authority? Does not the law say the same? [9]For it is written in the law of Moses, "You shall not muzzle an ox when it is treading out the grain." Is it for oxen that God is concerned? [10]Does he not speak entirely for our sake? It was written for our sake, because the plowman should plow in hope and the thresher thresh in hope of a share in the crop. [11]If we have sown spiritual good among you, is it too much if we reap your material benefits? [12]If others share this rightful claim upon you, do not we still more?

Nevertheless, we have not made use of this right, but we endure anything rather than put an obstacle in the way of the gospel of Christ. [13]Do you not know that those who are employed in the temple service get their food from the temple, and those who serve at the altar share in the sacrificial offerings? [14]In the same way, the Lord commanded that those who proclaim the gospel should get their living by the gospel.

1 Cor 15:1–11 (§131)

[1]Now I would remind you, brethren, in what terms I preached to you the gospel, which you received, in which you stand, [2]by which you are saved, if you hold it fast —unless you believed in vain.

[3]For I delivered to you as of first importance what I also received, that Christ died for our sins in accordance with the scriptures, [4]that he

---

● **Gal 1:15–24**

Acts 9   [1]But Saul, still breathing threats and murder against the disciples of the Lord, went to the high priest [2]and asked him for letters to the synagogues at Damascus, so that if he found any belonging to the Way, men or women, he might bring them bound to Jerusalem. [3]Now as he journeyed he approached Damascus, and suddenly a light from heaven flashed about him. [4]And he fell to the ground and heard a voice saying to him, "Saul, Saul, why do you persecute me?" [5]And he said, "Who are you, Lord?" And he said, "I am Jesus, whom you are persecuting; [6]but rise and enter the city, and you will be told what you are to do."

Acts 9   [10]Now there was a disciple at Damascus named Ananias. The Lord said to him in a vision, "Ananias." And he said, "Here I am, Lord."

Acts 9   [15]But the Lord said to him, "Go, for he is a chosen instrument of mine to carry my name before the Gentiles and kings and the sons of Israel. [16]For I will show him how much he must suffer for the sake of my name."

Acts 22   [6]"As I made my journey and drew near to Damascus, about noon a great light from heaven suddenly shone about me. [7]And I fell to the ground and heard a voice saying to me, 'Saul, Saul, why do you persecute me?' [8]And I answered, 'Who are you, Lord?' And he said to me, 'I am Jesus of Nazareth whom you are persecuting.' [9]Now those who were with me saw the light but did not hear the voice of the one who was speaking to me. [10]And I said, 'What shall I do, Lord?' And the Lord said to me, 'Rise, and go into Damascus, and there you will be told all that is appointed for you to do.'"

Acts 22   [17]"When I had returned to Jerusalem and was praying in the temple, I fell into a trance [18]and saw him saying to me, 'Make haste and get quickly out of Jerusalem, because they will not accept your testimony about me.' [19]And I said, 'Lord, they themselves know that in every synagogue I imprisoned and beat those who believed in thee. [20]And when the blood of Stephen thy witness was shed, I also was standing by and approving, and keeping the garments of those who killed him.' [21]And he said to me, 'Depart; for I will send you far away to the Gentiles.'"

Acts 26   [12]"Thus I journeyed to Damascus with the authority and commission of the chief priests. [13]At midday, O king, I saw on the way a light from heaven, brighter than the sun, shining round me and those who journeyed with me. [14]And when we had all fallen to the ground, I heard a voice saying to me in the Hebrew language, 'Saul, Saul, why do you persecute me? It hurts you to kick against the goads.' [15]And I said, 'Who are you, Lord?' And the Lord said, 'I am Jesus whom you are persecuting. [16]But rise and stand upon your feet; for I have appeared to you for this purpose, to appoint you to serve and bear witness to the things in which you have seen me and to those in which I will appear to you, [17]delivering you from the people and from the Gentiles —to whom I send you [18]to open their eyes, that they may turn from darkness to light and from the power of Satan to God, that they may receive forgiveness of sins and a place among those who are sanctified by faith in me.'"

was buried, that he was raised on the third day in accordance with the scriptures, [5]and that he appeared to Cephas, then to the twelve. [6]Then he appeared to more than five hundred brethren at one time, most of whom are still alive, though some have fallen asleep. [7]Then he appeared to James, then to all the apostles. [8]Last of all, as to one untimely born, he appeared also to me. [9]For I am the least of the apostles, unfit to be called an apostle, because I persecuted the church of God. [10]But by the grace of God I am what I am, and his grace toward me was not in vain. On the contrary, I worked harder than any of them, though it was not I, but the grace of God which is with me. [11]Whether then it was I or they, so we preach and so you believed.

Eph 3:1–13 (§222)

[1]For this reason I, Paul, a prisoner for Christ Jesus on behalf of you Gentiles— [2]assuming that you have heard of the stewardship of God's grace that was given to me for you, [3]how the mystery was made known to me by revelation, as I have written briefly. [4]When you read this you can perceive my insight into the mystery of Christ, [5]which was not made known to the sons of men in other generations as it has now been revealed to his holy apostles and prophets by the Spirit; [6]that is, how the Gentiles are fellow heirs, members of the same body, and partakers of the promise in Christ Jesus through the gospel.

[7]Of this gospel I was made a minister according to the gift of God's grace which was given to me by the working of his power. [8]To me, though I am the very least of all the saints, this grace was given, to preach to the Gentiles the unsearchable riches of Christ, [9]and to make all men see what is the plan of the mystery hidden for ages in God who created all things; [10]that through the church the manifold wisdom of God might now be made known to the principalities and powers in the heavenly places. [11]This was according to the eternal purpose which he has realized in Christ Jesus our Lord, [12]in whom we have boldness and confidence of access through our faith in him. [13]So I ask you not to lose heart over what I am suffering for you, which is your glory.

Phil 3:2–11 (§247)

[2]Look out for the dogs, look out for the evil-workers, look out for those who mutilate the flesh. [3]For we are the true circumcision, who worship God in spirit, and glory in Christ Jesus, and put no confidence in the flesh. [4]Though I myself have reason for confidence in the flesh also. If any other man thinks he has reason for confidence in the flesh, I have more: [5]circumcised on the eighth day, of the people of Israel, of the tribe of Benjamin, a Hebrew born of Hebrews; as to the law a Pharisee, [6]as to zeal a persecutor of the church, as to righteousness under the law blameless. [7]But whatever gain I had, I counted as loss for the sake of Christ. [8]Indeed I count everything as loss because of the surpassing worth of knowing Christ Jesus my Lord. For his sake I have suffered the loss of all things, and count them as refuse, in order that I may gain Christ [9]and be found in him, not having a righteousness of my own, based on law, but that which is through faith in Christ, the righteousness from God that depends on faith; [10]that I may know him and the power of his resurrection, and may share his sufferings, becoming like him in his death, [11]that if possible I may attain the resurrection from the dead.

Phil 3:12–16 (§248)

[12]Not that I have already obtained this or am already perfect; but I press on to make it my own, because Christ Jesus has made me his own. [13]Brethren, I do not consider that I have made it my own; but one thing I do, forgetting what lies behind and straining forward to what lies ahead, [14]I press on toward the goal for the prize of the upward call of God in Christ Jesus. [15]Let those of us who are mature be thus minded; and if in anything you are otherwise minded, God will reveal that also to you. [16]Only let us hold true to what we have attained.

Col 1:24–2:3 (§260)

[24]Now I rejoice in my sufferings for your sake, and in my flesh I complete what is lacking in Christ's afflictions for the sake of his body, that is, the church, [25]of which I became a minister according to the divine office which was given to me for you, to make the word of God fully known, [26]the mystery hidden for ages and generations but now made manifest to his saints. [27]To them God chose to make known how great among the Gentiles are the riches of the glory of this mystery, which is Christ in you, the hope of glory. [28]Him we proclaim warning every man and teaching every man in all wisdom, that we may present every man mature in Christ. [29]For this I toil, striving with all the energy which he mightily inspires within me.

2 [1]For I want you to know how greatly I strive for you, and for those at Laodicea, and for all who have not seen my face, [2]that their hearts may be encouraged as they are knit together in love, to have all the riches of assured understanding and the knowledge of God's mystery, of Christ, [3]in whom are hid all the treasures of wisdom and knowledge.

● **Gal 1:15–16**
Rom 1   [6]including yourselves who are called to belong to Jesus Christ; . . .

● **Gal 1:15**
Acts 13   [27]"For those who live in Jerusalem and their rulers, because they did not recognize him nor understand the utterances of the prophets which are read every sabbath, fulfilled these by condemning him."

Jer 1   [5]"Before I formed you in the womb I knew you.
and before you were born I consecrated you;
I appointed you a prophet to the nations."

● **Gal 1:17**
2 Cor 11   [5]I think that I am not in the least inferior to these superlative apostles.

2 Cor 11   [30]If I must boast, I will boast of the things that show my weakness. [31]The God and Father of the Lord Jesus, he who is blessed for ever, knows that I do not lie. [32]At Damascus, the governor under King Aretas guarded the city of Damascus in order to seize me, [33]but I was let down in a basket through a window in the wall, and escaped his hands.

2 Cor 12   [11]I have been a fool! You forced me to it, for I ought to have been commended by you. For I was not at all inferior to these superlative apostles, even though I am nothing.

Gal 2   [2]I went up by revelation; and I laid before them (but privately before those who were of repute) the gospel which I preach among the Gentiles, lest somehow I should be running or had run in vain.

Gal 2   [6]And from those who were reputed to be something (what they were makes no difference to me; God shows no partiality)—those, I say, who were of repute added nothing to me; . . .

Gal 2   [9]and when they perceived the grace that was given to me, James and Cephas and John, who were reputed to be pillars, gave to me and Barnabas the right hand of fellowship, that we should go to the Gentiles and they to the circumcised; . . .

● **Gal 1:20**
2 Cor 1   [23]But I call God to witness against me—it was to spare you that I refrained from coming to Corinth.

2 Cor 11   [31]The God and Father of the Lord Jesus, he who is blessed for ever, knows that I do not lie.

2 Then after fourteen years I went up again to Jerusalem with Barnabas, taking Titus along with me. [2]I went up by revelation; and I laid before them (but privately before those who were of repute) the gospel which I preach among the Gentiles, lest somehow I should be running or had run in vain. [3]But even Titus, who was with me, was not compelled to be circumcised, though he was a Greek. [4]But because of false brethren secretly brought in, who slipped in to spy out our freedom which we have in Christ Jesus, that they might bring us into bondage— [5]to them we did not yield submission even for a moment, that the truth of the gospel might be preserved for you. [6]And from those who were reputed to be something (what they were makes no difference to me; God shows no partiality)—those, I say, who were of repute added nothing to me; [7]but on the contrary, when they saw that I had been entrusted with the gospel to the uncircumcised, just as Peter had been entrusted with the gospel to the circumcised [8](for he who worked through Peter for the mission to the circumcised worked through me also for the Gentiles), [9]and when they perceived the grace that was given to me, James and Cephas and John, who were reputed to be pillars, gave to me and Barnabas the right hand of fellowship, that we should go to the Gentiles and they to the circumcised; [10]only they would have us remember the poor, which very thing I was eager to do.

PRIMARY

Rom 11:13–16 (§47)

[13]Now I am speaking to you Gentiles. Inasmuch then as I am an apostle to the Gentiles, I magnify my ministry [14]in order to make my fellow Jews jealous, and thus save some of them. [15]For if their rejection means the reconciliation of the world, what will their acceptance mean but life from the dead? [16]If the dough offered as first fruits is holy, so is the whole lump; and if the root is holy, so are the branches.

Rom 15:22–29 (§63)

[22]This is the reason why I have so often been hindered from coming to you. [23]But now, since I no longer have any room for work in these regions, and since I have longed for many years to come to you, [24]I hope to see you in passing as I go to Spain, and to be sped on my journey there by you, once I have enjoyed your company for a little. [25]At present, however, I am going to Jerusalem with aid for the saints. [26]For Macedonia and Achaia have been pleased to make some contribution for the poor among the saints at Jerusalem; [27]they were pleased to do it, and indeed they are in debt to them, for if the Gentiles have come to share in their spiritual blessings, they ought also to be of service to them in material blessings. [28]When therefore I have completed this, and have delivered to them what has been raised, I shall go on by way of you to Spain; [29]and I know that when I come to you I shall come in the fulness of the blessing of Christ.

1 Cor 4:6–7 (§84)

[6]I have applied all this to myself and Apollos

for your benefit, brethren, that you may learn by us not to go beyond what is written, that none of you may be puffed up in favor of one against another. [7]For who sees anything different in you? What have you that you did not receive? If then you received it, why do you boast as if it were not a gift?

1 Cor 9:19–23 (§107)

[19]For though I am free from all men, I have made myself a slave to all, that I might win the more. [20]To the Jews I became as a Jew, in order to win Jews; to those under the law I became as one under the law—though not being myself under the law—that I might win those under the law. [21]To those outside the law I became as one outside the law—not being without law toward God but under the law of Christ—that I might win those outside the law. [22]To the weak I became weak, that I might win the weak. I have become all things to all men, that I might by all means save some. [23]I do it all for the sake of the gospel, that I may share in its blessings.

1 Cor 15:1–11 (§131)

[1]Now I would remind you, brethren, in what terms I preached to you the gospel, which you received, in which you stand, [2]by which you are saved, if you hold it fast —unless you believed in vain.

[3]For I delivered to you as of first importance what I also received, that Christ died for our sins in accordance with the scriptures, [4]that he was buried, that he was raised on the third day in accordance with the scriptures, [5]and that he appeared to Cephas, then to the twelve. [6]Then he appeared to more than five hundred brethren at one time, most of whom are still alive, though some have fallen asleep. [7]Then he

---

● **Gal 2:1–10**

Acts 11   [29]And the disciples determined, every one according to his ability, to send relief to the brethren who lived in Judea; [30]and they did so, sending it to the elders by the hand of Barnabas and Saul.

Acts 12   [25]And Barnabas and Saul returned from Jerusalem when they had fulfilled their mission, bringing with them John whose other name was Mark.

Acts 15   [1]But some men came down from Judea and were teaching the brethren, "Unless you are circumcised according to the custom of Moses, you cannot be saved." [2]And when Paul and Barnabas had no small dissension and debate with them, Paul and Barnabas and some of the others were appointed to go up to Jerusalem to the apostles and the elders about this question.

Acts 15   [6]The apostles and the elders were gathered together to consider this matter. [7]And after there had been much debate, Peter rose and said to them, "Brethren, you know that in the early days God made choice among you, that by my mouth the Gentiles should hear the word of the gospel and believe.

Acts 15   [12]And all the assembly kept silence; and they listened to Barnabas and Paul as they related what signs and wonders God had done through them among the Gentiles. [13]Ater they finished speaking, James replied, "Brethren, listen to me.

Acts 15   [19]"Therefore my judgment is that we should not trouble those of the Gentiles who turn to God, [20]But should write to them to abstain from the pollutions of idols and from unchastity and from what is strangled and from blood. [21]For from early generations Moses has had in every city those who preach

him, for he is read every sabbath in the synagogues."
[22]Then it seemed good to the apostles and the elders, with the whole church, to choose men from among them and send them to Antioch with Paul and Barnabas.

● **Gal 2:2**

2 Cor 11   [23]Are they servants of Christ? I am a better one—I am talking like a madman—with far greater labors, far more imprisonments, with countless beatings, and often near death.

Gal 1   [17]nor did I go up to Jerusalem to tnose who were apostles before me, but I went away into Arabia; and again I returned to Damascus.

Phil 2   [16]holding fast the word of life, so that in the day of Christ I may be proud that I did not run in vain or labor in vain.

appeared to James, then to all the apostles. [8]Last of all, as to one untimely born, he appeared also to me. [9]For I am the least of the apostles, unfit to be called an apostle, because I persecuted the church of God. [10]But by the grace of God I am what I am, and his grace toward me was not in vain. On the contrary, I worked harder than any of them, though it was not I, but the grace of God which is with me. [11]Whether then it was I or they, so we preach and so you believed.

2 Cor 8:1–7 (§171)

[1]We want you to know, brethren, about the grace of God which has been shown in the churches of Macedonia, [2]for in a severe test of affliction, their abundance of joy and their extreme poverty have overflowed in a wealth of liberality on their part. [3]For they gave according to their means, as I can testify, and beyond their means, of their own free will, [4]begging us earnestly for the favor of taking part in the relief of the saints— [5]and this, not as we expected, but first they gave themselves to the Lord and to us by the will of God. [6]Accordingly we have urged Titus that as he had already made a beginning, he should also complete among you this gracious work. [7]Now as you excel in everything—in faith, in utterance, in knowledge, in all earnestness, and in your love for us—see that you excel in this gracious work also.

2 Cor 9:1–5 (§174)

[1]Now it is superfluous for me to write to you about the offering for the saints, [2]for I know your readiness, of which I boast about you to the people of Macedonia, saying that Achaia has been ready since last year; and your zeal has stirred up most of them. [3]But I am sending the brethren so that our boasting about you may not prove vain in this case, so that you may be ready, as I said you would be; [4]lest if some Macedonians come with me and find that you are not ready, we be humiliated—to say nothing of you—for being so confident. [5]So I thought it necessary to urge the brethren to go on to you before me, and arrange in advance for this gift you have promised, so that it may be ready not as an exaction but as a willing gift.

Eph 3:1–13 (§222)

[1]For this reason I, Paul, a prisoner for Christ Jesus on behalf of you Gentiles— [2]assuming that you have heard of the stewardship of God's grace that was given to me for you, [3]how the mystery was made known to me by revelation, as I have written briefly. [4]When you read this you can perceive my insight into the mystery of Christ, [5]which was not made known to the sons of men in other generations as it has now been revealed to his holy apostles and prophets by the Spirit; [6]that is, how the Gentiles are fellow heirs, members of the same body, and partakers of the promise in Christ Jesus through the gospel.

[7]Of this gospel I was made a minister according to the gift of God's grace which was given me by the working of his power. [8]To me, though I am the very least of all the saints, this grace was given, to preach to the Gentiles the unsearchable riches of Christ, [9]and to make all men see what is the plan of the mystery hidden for ages in God who created all things; [10]that through the church the manifold wisdom of God might now be made known to the principalities and powers in the heavenly places. [11]This is according to the eternal purpose which he has realized in Christ Jesus our Lord, [12]in whom we have boldness and confidence of access through our faith in him. [13]So I ask you not to lose heart over what I am suffering for you, which is your glory.

Col 1:24–2:3 (§260)

[24]Now I rejoice in my sufferings for your sake, and in my flesh I complete what is lacking in Christ's afflictions for the sake of his body, that is, the church, [25]of which I became a minister according to the divine office which was given to me for you, to make the word of God fully known, [26]the mystery hidden for ages and generations but now made manifest to his saints. [27]To them God chose to make known how great among the Gentiles are the riches of the glory of this mystery, which is Christ in you, the hope of glory. [28]Him we proclaim warning every man and teaching every man in all wisdom, that we may present every man mature in Christ. [29]For this I toil, striving with all the energy which he mightily inspires within me.

2 [1]For I want you to know how greatly I strive for you, and for those at Laodicea, and for all who have not seen my face, [2]that their hearts may be encouraged as they are knit together in love, to have all the riches of assured understanding and the knowledge of God's mystery, of Christ, [3]in whom are hid all the treasures of wisdom and knowledge.

Cf. 1 Cor 15   [58]Therefore, my beloved brethren, be steadfast, immovable, always abounding in the work of the Lord, knowing that in the Lord your labor is not in vain.

Cf. 2 Cor 11   [5]I think that I am not in the least inferior to these superlative apostles.

Cf. 2 Cor 12   [11]I have been a fool! You forced me to it, for I ought to have been commended by you. For I was not at all inferior to these superlative apostles, even though I am nothing.

Cf. 1 Thess 3   [5]For this reason, when I could bear it no longer, I sent that I might know your faith, for fear that somehow the tempter had tempted you and that our labor would be in vain.

● **Gal 2:3**
Acts 16   [3]Paul wanted Timothy to accompany him;

and he took him and circumcised him because of the Jews that were in those places, for they all knew that his father was a Greek.

● **Gal 2:4**
1 Cor 9   [1]Am I not free? Am I not an apostle? Have I not seen Jesus our Lord? Are not you my workmanship in the Lord? [2]If to others I am not an apostle, at least I am to you; for you are the seal of my apostleship in the Lord.

● **Gal 2:6**
Rom 2   [11]For God shows no partiality.

Acts 10   [34]And Peter opened his mouth and said: "Truly I perceive that God shows no partiality. . . ."

● **Gal 2:7**
Rom 1   [5]through whom we have received grace and

apostleship to bring about the obedience of faith for the sake of his name among all the nations, . . .

1 Tim 2   [7]For this I was appointed a preacher and apostle (I am telling the truth, I am not lying), a teacher of the Gentiles in faith and truth.

Acts 9   [15]But the Lord said to him, "Go, for he is a chosen instrument of mine to carry my name before the Gentiles and kings and the sons of Israel. . . ."

● **Gal 2:9**
Rom 1   [15]so I am eager to preach the gospel to you also who are in Rome.

1 Cor 3   [10]According to the grace of God given to me, like a skilled master builder I laid a foundation, and another man is building upon it. Let each man take care how he builds upon it.

[11]But when Cephas came to Antioch I opposed him to his face, because he stood condemned. [12]For before certain men came from James, he ate with the Gentiles; but when they came he drew back and separated himself, fearing the circumcision party. [13]And with him the rest of the Jews acted insincerely, so that even Barnabas was carried away by their insincerity. [14]But when I saw that they were not straightforward about the truth of the gospel, I said to Cephas before them all, "If you, though a Jew, live like a Gentile and not like a Jew, how can you compel the Gentiles to live like Jews?"

PRIMARY

Rom 2:1–5 (§7)

[1]Therefore you have no excuse, O man, whoever you are, when you judge another; for in passing judgment upon him you condemn yourself, because you, the judge, are doing the very same things. [2]We know that the judgment of God rightly falls upon those who do such things. [3]Do you suppose, O man, that when you judge those who do such things and yet do them yourself, you will escape the judgment of God? [4]Or do you presume upon the riches of his kindness and forbearance and patience? Do you not know that God's kindness is meant to lead you to repentance? [5]But by your hard and impenitent heart you are storing up wrath for yourself on the day of wrath when God's righteous judgment will be revealed.

Rom 2:17–24 (§10)

[17]But if you call yourself a Jew and rely upon the law and boast of your relation to God [18]and know his will and approve what is excellent, because you are instructed in the law, [19]and if you are sure that you are a guide to the blind, a light to those who are in darkness, [20]a corrector of the foolish, a teacher of children, having in the law the embodiment of knowledge and truth— [21]you then who teach others, will you not teach yourself? While you preach against stealing, do you steal? [22]You who say that one must not commit adultery, do you commit adultery? You who abhor idols, do you rob temples? [23]You who boast in the law, do you dishonor God by breaking the law? [24]For, as it is written, "The name of God is blasphemed among the Gentiles because of you."

1 Cor 10:23–11:1 (§111)

[23]"All things are lawful," but not all things are helpful. "All things are lawful," but not all things build up. [24]Let no one seek his own good, but the good of his neighbor. [25]Eat whatever is sold in the meat market without raising any question on the ground of conscience. [26]For "the earth is the Lord's, and everything in it." [27]If one of the unbelievers invites you to dinner and you are disposed to go, eat whatever is set before you without raising any question on the ground of conscience. [28](But if some one says to you, "This has been offered in sacrifice," then out of consideration for the man who informed you, and for conscience' sake— [29]I mean his conscience, not yours—do not eat it.) For why should my liberty be determined by another man's scruples? [30]If I partake with thankfulness, why am I denounced because of that for which I give thanks?

[31]So, whether you eat or drink, or whatever you do, do all to the glory of God. [32]Give no offense to Jews or to Greeks or to the church of God, [33]just as I try to please all men in everything I do, not seeking my own advantage, but that of many, that they may be saved. 11 [1]Be imitators of me, as I am of Christ.

2 Cor 11:1–6 (§179)

[1]I wish you would bear with me in a little foolishness. Do bear with me! [2]I feel a divine jealousy for you, for I betrothed you to Christ to present you as a pure bride to her one husband. [3]But I am afraid that as the serpent deceived Eve by his cunning, your thoughts will be led astray from a sincere and pure devotion to Christ. [4]For if some one comes and preaches another Jesus than the one we preached, or if you receive a different spirit from the one you received, or if you accept a different gospel from the one you accepted, you submit to it readily enough. [5]I think that I am not in the least inferior to these superlative apostles.

[6]Even if I am unskilled in speaking, I am not in knowledge; in every way we have made this plain to you in all things.

Eph 2:11–22 (§221)

[11]Therefore remember that at one time you Gentiles in the flesh, called the uncircumcision by what is called the circumcision, which is made in the flesh by hands— [12]remember that you were at that time separated from Christ, alienated from the commonwealth of Israel, and strangers to the covenants of promise, having no hope and without God in the world. [13]But now in Christ Jesus you who once were far off have been brought near in the blood of Christ. [14]For he is our peace, who has made us both one, and has broken down the dividing wall of hostility, [15]by abolishing in his flesh the law of commandments and ordinances, that he might create in himself one new man in place of the two, so making peace, [16]and might reconcile us both to God in one body through the cross, thereby bringing the hostility to an end. [17]And he came and preached peace to you who were far off and peace to those who were near; [18]for through him we both have access in one Spirit to the Father. [19]So then you are no longer strangers and sojourners, but you are fellow citizens with the saints and members of the household of God, [20]built upon the foundation of the apostles and prophets, Christ Jesus himself being the cornerstone, [21]in whom the whole structure is joined together and grows into a holy temple in the Lord; [22]in whom you also are built into it for a dwelling place of God in the Spirit.

Col 1:21–23 (§259)

[21]And you, who once were estranged and hostile in mind, doing evil deeds, [22]he has now reconciled in his body of flesh by his death, in order to present you holy and blameless and irreproachable before him, [23]provided that you continue in the faith, stable and steadfast, not shifting from the hope of the gospel which you heard, which has been preached to every creature under heaven, and of which I, Paul, became a minister.

● **Gal 2:11**

1 Tim 5   [20]As for those who persist in sin, rebuke them in the presence of all, so that the rest may stand in fear.

Acts 11   [25]So Barnabas went to Tarsus to look for Saul; [26]and when he had found him, he brought him to Antioch.

● **Gal 2:12**

Gal 6   [12]It is those who want to make a good showing in the flesh that would compel you to be circumcised, and only in order that they may not be persecuted for the cross of Christ. [13]For even those who receive circumcision do not themselves keep the law, but they desire to have you circumcised that they may glory in your flesh.

Phil 3   [2]Look out for the dogs, look out for the evil-workers, look out for those who mutilate the flesh.

Acts 10   [28]and he said to them, "You yourselves know how unlawful it is for a Jew to associate with or to visit any one of another nation; but God has shown me that I should not call any man common or unclean."

Acts 11   [2]So when Peter went up to Jerusalem, the circumcision party criticized him, . . .

Acts 15   [1]But some men came down from Judea and were teaching the brethren, "Unless you are circumcised according to the custom of Moses, you cannot be saved."

● **Gal 2:14**

Gal 5   [11]But if I, brethren, still preach circumcision, why am I still persecuted? In that case the stumbling block of the cross has been removed.

¹⁵We ourselves, who are Jews by birth and not Gentile sinners, ¹⁶yet who know that a man is not justified by works of the law but through faith in Jesus Christ, even we have believed in Christ Jesus, in order to be justified by faith in Christ, and not by works of the law, because by works of the law shall no one be justified. ¹⁷But if, in our endeavor to be justified in Christ, we ourselves were found to be sinners, is Christ then an agent of sin? Certainly not! ¹⁸But if I build up again those things which I tore down, then I prove myself a transgressor. ¹⁹For I through the law died to the law, that I might live to God. ²⁰I have been crucified with Christ; it is no longer I who live, but Christ who lives in me; and the life I now live in the flesh I live by faith in the Son of God, who loved me and gave himself for me. ²¹I do not nullify the grace of God; for if justification were through the law, then Christ died to no purpose.

PRIMARY

See §14 on the theme Justification

Rom 5:6–11 (§21)

⁶While we were still weak, at the right time Christ died for the ungodly.

⁷Why, one will hardly die for a righteous man—though perhaps for a good man one will dare even to die. ⁸But God shows his love for us in that while we were yet sinners Christ died for us. ⁹Since, therefore, we are now justified by his blood, much more shall we be saved by him from the wrath of God. ¹⁰For if while we were enemies we were reconciled to God by the death of his Son, much more, now that we are reconciled, shall we be saved by his life. ¹¹Not only so, but we also rejoice in God through our Lord Jesus Christ, through whom we have now received our reconciliation.

Rom 6:1–14 (§23–24)

¹What shall we say then? Are we to continue in sin that grace may abound? ²By no means! How can we who died to sin still live in it? ³Do you not know that all of us who have been baptized into Christ Jesus were baptized into his death? ⁴We were buried therefore with him by baptism into death, so that as Christ was raised from the dead by the glory of the Father, we too might walk in newness of life.

⁵For if we have been united with him in a death like his, we shall certainly be united with him in a resurrection like his. ⁶We know that our old self was crucified with him so that the sinful body might be destroyed, and we might no longer be enslaved to sin. ⁷For he who has died is freed from sin. ⁸But if we have died with Christ, we believe that we shall also live with him. ⁹For we know that Christ being raised from the dead will never die again; death no longer has dominion over him. ¹⁰The death he died he died to sin, once for all, but the life he lives he lives to God.

¹¹So you also must consider yourselves dead to sin and alive to God in Christ Jesus.

¹²Let not sin therefore reign in your mortal bodies, to make you obey their passions. ¹³Do not yield your members to sin as instruments of wickedness, but yield yourselves to God as men who have been brought from death to life, and your members to God as instruments of righteousness. ¹⁴For sin will have no dominion over you, since you are not under law but under grace.

Rom 8:9–17 (§30)

⁹But you are not in the flesh, you are in the Spirit, if in fact the Spirit of God dwells in you. Any one who does not have the Spirit of Christ does not belong to him. ¹⁰But if Christ is in you, although your bodies are dead because of sin, your spirits are alive because of righteousness. ¹¹If the Spirit of him who raised Jesus from the dead dwells in you, he who raised Christ Jesus from the dead will give life to your mortal bodies also through his Spirit which dwells in you.

¹²So then, brethren, we are debtors, not to the flesh, to live according to the flesh—¹³for if you live according to the flesh you will die, but if by the Spirit you put to death the deeds of the body you will live. ¹⁴For all who are led by the Spirit of God are sons of God. ¹⁵For you did not receive the spirit of slavery to fall back into fear, but you have received the spirit of sonship. When we cry, "Abba! Father!" ¹⁶it is the Spirit himself bearing witness with our spirit that we are children of God, ¹⁷and if children, then heirs, heirs of God and fellow heirs with Christ, provided we suffer with him in order that we may also be glorified with him.

Rom 9:30–33 (§39)

³⁰What shall we say, then? That Gentiles who did not pursue righteousness have attained it, that is, righteousness through faith; ³¹but that Israel who pursued the righteousness which is based on law did not succeed in fulfilling that law. ³²Why? Because they did not pursue it through faith, but as if it were based on works. They have stumbled over the stumbling stone, ³³as it is written,

"Behold, I am laying in Zion a stone that will make men stumble,
a rock that will make them fall;
and he who believes in him will not be put to shame."

Col 2:8–15 (§262)

⁸See to it that no one makes a prey of you by philosophy and empty deceit, according to human tradition, according to the elemental spirits of the universe, and not according to Christ. ⁹For in him the whole fulness of deity dwells bodily, ¹⁰and you have come to fulness of life in him, who is the head of all rule and authority. ¹¹In him also you were circumcised with a circumcision made without hands, by putting off the body of flesh in the circumcision of Christ; ¹²and you were buried with him in baptism, in which you were also raised with him through faith in the working of God, who raised him from the dead. ¹³And you, who were dead in trespasses and the uncircumcision of your flesh, God made alive together with him, having forgiven us all our trespasses, ¹⁴having canceled the bond which stood against us with its legal demands; this he set aside, nailing it to the cross. ¹⁵He disarmed the principalities and powers and made a public example of them, triumphing over them in him.

● **Gal 2:15**

Rom 9   ³For I could wish that I myself were accursed and cut off from Christ for the sake of my brethren, my kinsmen by race.

Eph 2   ¹¹Therefore remember that at one time you Gentiles in the flesh, called the uncircumcision by what is called the circumcision, which is made in the flesh by hands— ¹²remember that you were at that time separated from Christ, alienated from the commonwealth of Israel, and strangers to the covenants of promise, having no hope and without God in the world.

Eph 4   ¹⁷Now this I affirm and testify in the Lord, that you must no longer live as the Gentiles do, in the futility of their minds; . . .

● **Gal 2:16**

Rom 3   ²⁰For no human being will be justified in his sight by works of the law, since through the law comes knowledge of sin.

Rom 3   ²⁸For we hold that a man is justified by faith apart from works of law.

Rom 4   ⁵And to one who does not work but trusts him who justifies the ungodly, his faith is reckoned as righteousness.

Rom 11   ⁶But if it is by grace, it is no longer on the basis of works; otherwise grace would no longer be grace.

Acts 13   ³⁹"and by him every one that believes is freed from everything from which you could not be freed by the law of Moses."

Acts 15   ¹¹"But we believe that we shall be saved through the grace of the Lord Jesus, just as they will."

Jas 2   ²⁴You see that a man is justified by works and not by faith alone.

● **Gal 2:17**

Cf. Rom 3:3; Rom 7:13

● **Gal 2:18**

Cf. 2 Cor 10:8; 2 Cor 13:10; Eph 2:14–16

● **Gal 2:20**

Rom 14   ⁸If we live, we live to the Lord, and if we die, we die to the Lord; so then, whether we live or whether we die, we are the Lord's.

Gal 5   ²⁴And those who belong to Christ Jesus have crucified the flesh with its passions and desires.

Gal 6   ¹⁴But far be it from me to glory except in the cross of our Lord Jesus Christ, by which the world has been crucified to me, and I to the world.

Cf. Eph 5:2; Eph 5:25

(God) *read* in God and Christ: p⁴⁶BD*G it (few) Pelagius

3 O foolish Galatians! Who has bewitched you, before whose eyes Jesus Christ was publicly portrayed as crucified? [2] Let me ask you only this: Did you receive the Spirit by works of the law, or by hearing with faith? [3] Are you so foolish? Having begun with the Spirit, are you now ending with the flesh? [4] Did you experience so many things in vain?—if it really is in vain. [5] Does he who supplies the Spirit to you and works miracles among you do so by works of the law, or by hearing with faith?

PRIMARY

Rom 8:9–17 (§30)

[9] But you are not in the flesh, you are in the Spirit, if in fact the Spirit of God dwells in you. Any one who does not have the Spirit of Christ does not belong to him. [10] But if Christ is in you, although your bodies are dead because of sin, your spirits are alive because of righteousness. [11] If the Spirit of him who raised Jesus from the dead dwells in you, he who raised Christ Jesus from the dead will give life to your mortal bodies also through his Spirit which dwells in you.

[12] So then, brethren, we are debtors, not to the flesh, to live according to the flesh— [13] for if you live according to the flesh you will die, but if by the Spirit you put to death the deeds of the body you will live. [14] For all who are led by the Spirit of God are sons of God. [15] For you did not receive the spirit of slavery to fall back into fear, but you have received the spirit of sonship. When we cry, "Abba! Father!" [16] it is the Spirit himself bearing witness with our spirit that we are children of God, [17] and if children, then heirs, heirs of God and fellow heirs with Christ, provided we suffer with him in order that we may also be glorified with him.

Rom 10:14–17 (§42)

[14] But how are men to call upon him in whom they have not believed? And how are they to believe in him of whom they have never heard? And how are they to hear without a preacher? [15] And how can men preach unless they are sent? As it is written, "How beautiful are the feet of those who preach good news!" [16] But they have not all obeyed the gospel; for Isaiah says, "Lord, who has believed what he has heard from us?" [17] So faith comes from

what is heard, and what is heard comes by the preaching of Christ.

1 Cor 2:1–5 (§76)

[1] When I came to you, brethren, I did not come proclaiming to you the testimony of God in lofty words or wisdom. [2] For I decided to know nothing among you except Jesus Christ and him crucified. [3] And I was with you in weakness and in much fear and trembling; [4] and my speech and my message were not in plausible words of wisdom, but in demonstration of the Spirit and of power, [5] that your faith might not rest in the wisdom of men but in the power of God.

1 Cor 3:1–4 (§78)

[1] But I, brethren, could not address you as spiritual men, but as men of the flesh, as babes in Christ. [2] I fed you with milk, not solid food; for you were not ready for it; and even yet you are not ready, [3] for you are still of the flesh. For while there is jealousy and strife among you, are you not of the flesh, and behaving like ordinary men? [4] For when one says, "I belong to Paul," and another, "I belong to Apollos," are you not merely men?

Eph 2:1–10 (§220)

[1] And you he made alive, when you were dead through the trespasses and sins [2] in which you once walked, following the course of this world, following the prince of the power of the air, the spirit that is now at work in the sons of disobedience. [3] Among these we all once lived in the passions of our flesh, following the desires of body and mind, and so we were by nature children of wrath, like the rest of mankind. [4] But God, who is rich in mercy, out of the great love with which he loved us, [5] even when we were dead through our trespasses, made us alive together with Christ (by grace you have been saved), [6] and raised us up with him, and made us sit with him in the heavenly places in Christ Jesus, [7] that in the coming ages he might show the immeasurable riches of his grace in kindness toward us in Christ Jesus. [8] For by grace you have been saved through faith; and this is not your own doing, it is the gift of God— [9] not because of works, lest any man should boast. [10] For we are his workmanship, created in Christ Jesus for good works, which God prepared beforehand, that we should walk in them.

Phil 3:2–11 (§247)

[2] Look out for the dogs, look out for the evil-workers, look out for those who mutilate the flesh. [3] For we are the true circumcision, who worship God in spirit, and glory in Christ Jesus, and put no confidence in the flesh. [4] Though I myself have reason for confidence in the flesh also. If any other man thinks he has reason for confidence in the flesh, I have more: [5] circumcised on the eighth day, of the people of Israel, of the tribe of Benjamin, a Hebrew born of Hebrews; as to the law a Pharisee, [6] as to zeal a persecutor of the church, as to righteousness under the law blameless. [7] But whatever gain I had, I counted as loss for the sake of Christ. [8] Indeed I count everything as loss because of the surpassing worth of knowing Christ Jesus my Lord. For his sake I have suffered the loss of all things, and count them as refuse, in order that I may gain Christ [9] and be found in him, not having a righteousness of my own, based on law, but that which is through faith in Christ, the righteousness from God that depends on faith; [10] that I may know him and the power of his resurrection, and may share his sufferings, becoming like him in his death, [11] that if possible I may attain the resurrection from the dead.

Col 2:8–15 (§262)

[8] See to it that no one makes a prey of you by philosophy and empty deceit, according to human tradition, according to the elemental spirits of the universe, and not according to Christ. [9] For in him the whole fulness of deity dwells bodily, [10] and you have come to fulness of life in him, who is the head of all rule and authority. [11] In him also you were circumcised with a circumcision made without hands, by putting off the body of flesh in the circumcision of Christ; [12] and you were buried with him in baptism, in which you were also raised with him through faith in the working of God, who raised him from the dead. [13] And you, who were dead in trespasses and the uncircumcision of your flesh, God made alive together with him, having forgiven us all our trespasses, [14] having canceled the bond which stood against us with its legal demands; this he set aside, nailing it to the cross. [15] He disarmed the principalities and powers and made a public example of them, triumphing over them in him.

● **Gal 3:1**

Rom 11   [7] What then? Israel failed to obtain what it sought. The elect obtained it, but the rest were hardened, [8] as it is written,

"God gave them a spirit of stupor,
    eyes that should not see and ears that should not
       hear,
    down to this very day."

[9] And David says,

"Let their table become a snare and a trap,
    a pitfall and a retribution for them;
[10] let their eyes be darkened so that they cannot see,
    and bend their backs for ever."

Gal 1   [6] I am astonished that you are so quickly deserting him who called you in the grace of Christ and turning to a different gospel . . .

Gal 5   [12] I wish those who unsettle you would mutilate themselves!

● **Gal 3:2**

Heb 4   [2] For good news came to us just as to them; but the message which they heard did not benefit them, because it did not meet with faith in the hearers.

● **Gal 3:5**

2 Cor 12   [12] The signs of a true apostle were performed among you in all patience, with signs and wonders and mighty works.

⁶Thus Abraham "believed God, and it was reckoned to him as righteousness." ⁷So you see that it is men of faith who are the sons of Abraham. ⁸And the scripture, foreseeing that God would justify the Gentiles by faith, preached the gospel beforehand to Abraham, saying, "In you shall all the nations be blessed." ⁹So then, those who are men of faith are blessed with Abraham who had faith.

PRIMARY

Rom 4:1–8 (§16)

¹What then shall we say about Abraham, our forefather according to the flesh? ²For if Abraham was justified by works, he has something to boast about, but not before God. ³For what does the scripture say? "Abraham believed God, and it was reckoned to him as righteousness." ⁴Now to one who works, his wages are not reckoned as a gift but as his due. ⁵And to one who does not work but trusts him who justifies the ungodly, his faith is reckoned as righteousness. ⁶So also David pronounces a blessing upon the man to whom God reckons righteousness apart from works:

⁷"Blessed are those whose iniquities are forgiven, and whose sins are covered;
⁸blessed is the man against whom the Lord will not reckon his sin."

Rom 9:6–13 (§36)

⁶But it is not as though the word of God had failed. For not all who are descended from Israel belong to Israel, ⁷and not all are children of Abraham because they are his descendants; but "Through Isaac shall your descendants be named." ⁸This means that it is not the children of the flesh who are the children of God, but the children of the promise are reckoned as descendants. ⁹For this is what the promise said, "About this time I will return and Sarah shall have a son." ¹⁰And not only so, but also when Rebecca had conceived children by one man, our forefather Isaac, ¹¹though they were not yet born and had done nothing either good or bad, in order that God's purpose of election might continue, not because of works but because of his call, ¹²she was told, "The elder will serve the younger." ¹³As it is written, "Jacob I loved, but Esau I hated."

Rom 15:7–13 (§61)

⁷Welcome one another, therefore, as Christ has welcomed you, for the glory of God. ⁸For I tell you that Christ became a servant to the circumcised to show God's truthfulness, in order to confirm the promises given to the patriarchs, ⁹and in order that the Gentiles might glorify God for his mercy. As it is written,

"Therefore I will praise thee among the Gentiles,
and sing to thy name";
¹⁰and again it is said,
"Rejoice, O Gentiles, with his peoples";
¹¹and again,
"Praise the Lord, all Gentiles,
and let all the peoples praise him";
¹²and further Isaiah says,
"The root of Jesse shall come,
he who rises to rule the Gentiles;
in him shall the Gentiles hope."
¹³May the God of hope fill you with all joy and peace in believing, so that by the power of the Holy Spirit you may abound in hope.

● **Gal 3:6**
Gen 15   ⁶And he believed the Lord; and he reckoned it to him as righteousness.

● **Gal 3:7**
Gal 3   ²⁹And if you are Christ's, then you are Abraham's offspring, heirs according to promise.

Gal 4   ⁷So through God you are no longer a slave but a son, and if a son then an heir.

Gal 4   ³¹So, brethren, we are not children of the slave but of the free woman.

● **Gal 3:8**
Rom 3   ²¹But now the righteousness of God has been manifested apart from law, although the law and the prophets bear witness to it, . . .

Acts 3   ²⁵"You are the sons of the prophets and of the covenant which God gave to your fathers, saying to Abraham, 'And in your posterity shall all the families of the earth be blessed.'"

Gen 12   ³I will bless those who bless you, and him who curses you I will curse; and by you all the families of the earth shall bless themselves.

Gen 18   ¹⁸seeing that Abraham shall become a great and mighty nation, and all the nations of the earth shall bless themselves by him?

[10]For all who rely on works of the law are under a curse; for it is written, "Cursed be every one who does not abide by all things written in the book of the law, and do them." [11]Now it is evident that no man is justified before God by the law; for "He who through faith is righteous shall live"; [12]but the law does not rest on faith, for "He who does them shall live by them." [13]Christ redeemed us from the curse of the law, having become a curse for us—for it is written, "Cursed be every one who hangs on a tree"— [14]that in Christ Jesus the blessing of Abraham might come upon the Gentiles, that we might receive the promise of the Spirit through faith.

PRIMARY

Rom 1:16–17 (§3)

[16]For I am not ashamed of the gospel: it is the power of God for salvation to every one who has faith, to the Jew first and also to the Greek. [17]For in it the righteousness of God is revealed through faith for faith; as it is written, "He who through faith is righteous shall live."

Rom 2:25–29 (§11)

[25]Circumcision indeed is of value if you obey the law; but if you break the law, your circumcision becomes uncircumcision. [26]So, if a man who is uncircumcised keeps the precepts of the law, will not his uncircumcision be regarded as circumcision? [27]Then those who are physically uncircumcised but keep the law will condemn you who have the written code and circumcision but break the law. [28]For he is not a real Jew who is one outwardly, nor is true circumcision something external and physical. [29]He is a Jew who is one inwardly, and real circumcision is a matter of the heart, spiritual and not literal. His praise is not from men but from God.

Rom 3:9–20 (§13)

[9]What then? Are we Jews any better off? No, not at all; for I have already charged that all men, both Jews and Greeks, are under the power of sin, [10]as it is written:

"None is righteous, no, not one;
[11]no one understands, no one seeks for God.
[12]All have turned aside, together they have gone wrong;
no one does good, not even one."
[13]"Their throat is an open grave,
they use their tongues to deceive."
"The venom of asps is under their lips."
[14]"Their mouth is full of curses and bitterness."
[15]"Their feet are swift to shed blood,
[16]in their paths are ruin and misery,
[17]and the way of peace they do not know."
[18]"There is no fear of God before their eyes."

Now we know that whatever the law says it speaks to those who are under the law, so that every mouth may be stopped, and the whole world may be held accountable to God. [20]For no human being will be justified in his sight by works of the law, since through the law comes knowledge of sin.

Rom 10:5–13 (§41)

[5]Moses writes that the man who practices the righteousness which is based on the law shall live by it. [6]But the righteousness based on faith says, Do not say in your heart, "Who will ascend into heaven?" (that is, to bring Christ down) [7] or "Who will descend into the abyss?" (that is, to bring Christ up from the dead). [8]But what does it say? The word is near you, on your lips and in your heart (that is, the word of faith which we preach); [9]because, if you confess with your lips that Jesus is Lord and believe in your heart that God raised him from the dead, you will be saved. [10]For man believes with his heart and so is justified, and he confesses with his lips and so is saved. [11]The scripture says, "No one who believes in him will be put to shame." [12]For there is no distinction between Jew and Greek; the same Lord is Lord of all and bestows his riches upon all who call upon him. [13]For, "every one who calls upon the name of the Lord will be saved."

2 Cor 3:7–11 (§156)

[7]Now if the dispensation of death, carved in letters on stone, came with such splendor that the Israelites could not look at Moses' face because of its brightness, fading as this was, [8]will not the dispensation of the Spirit be attended with greater splendor? [9]For if there was splendor in the dispensation of condemnation, the dispensation of righteousness must far exceed it in splendor. [10]Indeed, in this case, what once had splendor has come to have no splendor at all, because of the splendor that surpasses it. [11]For if what faded away came with splendor, what is permanent must have much more splendor.

SECONDARY

Rom 7:7–13 (§27)

[7]What then shall we say? That the law is sin? By no means! Yet, if it had not been for the law, I should not have known sin. I should not have known what it is to covet if the law had not said, "You shall not covet." [8]But sin, finding opportunity in the commandment, wrought in me all kinds of covetousness. Apart from the law sin lies dead. [9]I was once alive apart from the law, but when the commandment came, sin revived and I died; [10]the very commandment which promised life proved to be death to me. [11]For sin, finding opportunity in the commandment, deceived me and by it killed me. [12]So the law is holy, and the commandment is holy and just and good.

[13]Did that which is good, then, bring death to me? By no means! It was sin, working death in me through what is good, in order that sin might be shown to be sin, and through the commandment might become sinful beyond measure.

● **Gal 3:10–14**
Rom 10   [4]For Christ is the end of the law, that every one who has faith may be justified.

Phil 3   [2]Look out for the dogs, look out for the evil-workers, look out for those who mutilate the flesh. [3]For we are the true circumcision, who worship God in spirit, and glory in Christ Jesus, and put no confidence in the flesh. [4]Though I myself have reason for confidence in the flesh also. If any other man thinks he has reason for confidence in the flesh, I have more: [5]circumcised on the eighth day, of the people of Israel, of the tribe of Benjamin, a Hebrew born of Hebrews; as to the law a Pharisee, [6]as to zeal a persecutor of the church, as to righteousness under the law blameless. [7]But whatever gain I had, I counted as loss for the sake of Christ. [8]Indeed I count everything as loss because of the surpassing worth of knowing Christ Jesus my Lord. For his sake I have suffered the loss of all things, and count them as refuse, in order that I may gain Christ [9]and be found in him, not having a righteousness of my own, based on law, but that which is through faith in Christ, the righteousness from God that depends on faith; [10]that I may know him and the power of his resurrection, and may share his sufferings, becoming like him in his death, [11]that if possible I may attain the resurrection from the dead.

● **Gal 3:10**
Gal 5   [3]I testify again to every man who receives circumcision that he is bound to keep the whole law.

Deut 27   [26]"Cursed be he who does not confirm the words of this law by doing them.' And all the people shall say, 'Amen.'"

● **Gal 3:11**
Hab 2   [4]Behold, he whose soul is not upright in him shall fail,
but the righteous shall live by his faith.

● **Gal 3:13**
Rom 8   [3]For God has done what the law, weakened by the flesh, could not do: sending his own Son in the likeness of sinful flesh and for sin, he condemned sin in the flesh, . . .

2 Cor 5   [21]For our sake he made him to be sin who knew no sin, so that in him we might become the righteousness of God.

Acts 5   [30]"The God of our fathers raised Jesus whom you killed by hanging him on a tree."

Deut 21   [23]his body shall not remain all night upon the tree, but you shall bury him the same day, for a hanged man is accursed by God; you shall not defile your land which the Lord your God gives you for an inheritance.

● **Gal 3:14**
Acts 2   [33]"Being therefore exalted at the right hand of God, and having received from the Father the promise of the Holy Spirit, he has poured out this which you see and hear."

[15]To give a human example, brethren: no one annuls even a man's will, or adds to it, once it has been ratified. [16]Now the promises were made to Abraham and to his offspring. It does not say, "And to offsprings," referring to many; but, referring to one, "And to your offspring," which is Christ. [17]This is what I mean: the law, which came four hundred and thirty years afterward, does not annul a covenant previously ratified by God, so as to make the promise void. [18]For if the inheritance is by the law, it is no longer by promise; but God gave it to Abraham by a promise.

PRIMARY

Rom 4:13–15 (§18)

[13]The promise to Abraham and his descendants, that they should inherit the world, did not come through the law but through the right-eousness of faith. [14]If it is the adherents of the law who are to be the heirs, faith is null and the promise is void. [15]For the law brings wrath, but where there is no law there is no transgression.

Rom 9:6–13 (§36)

[6]But it is not as though the word of God had failed. For not all who are descended from Israel belong to Israel, [7]and not all are children of Abraham because they are his descendants; but "Through Isaac shall your descendants be named." [8]This means that it is not the children of the flesh who are the children of God, but the children of the promise are reckoned as descendants. [9]For this is what the promise said, "About this time I will return and Sarah shall have a son." [10]And not only so, but also when Rebecca had conceived children by one man, our forefather Isaac, [11]though they were not yet born and had done nothing either good or bad, in order that God's purpose of election might continue, not because of works but because of his call, [12]she was told, "The elder will serve the younger." [13]As it is written, "Jacob I loved, but Esau I hated."

2 Cor 3:7–11 (§156)

[7]Now if the dispensation of death, carved in letters on stone, came with such splendor that the Israelites could not look at Moses' face because of its brightness, fading as this was, [8]will not the dispensation of the Spirit be attended with greater splendor? [9]For if there was splendor in the dispensation of condemnation, the dispensation of righteousness must far exceed it in splendor. [10]Indeed, in this case, what once had splendor has come to have no splendor at all, because of the splendor that surpasses it. [11]For if what faded away came with splendor, what is permanent must have much more splendor.

● **Gal 3:16**
Gen 12　[7]Then the Lord appeared to Abram, and said, "To your descendants I will give this land." So he built there an altar to the Lord, who had appeared to him.

● **Gal 3:17–18**
Rom 15　[8]For I tell you that Christ became a servant to the circumcised to show God's truthfulness, in order to confirm the promises given to the patriarchs, [9]and in order that the Gentiles might glorify God for his mercy.

2 Cor 1　[20]For all the promises of God find their Yes in him. That is why we utter the Amen through him, to the glory of God.

● **Gal 3:17**
Acts 7　[6]"And God spoke to this effect, that his posterity would be aliens in a land belonging to others, who would enslave them and ill-treat them four hundred years."

Exod 12　[40]The time that the people of Israel dwelt in Egypt was four hundred and thirty years.

● **Gal 3:18**
Rom 7　[6]But now we are discharged from the law, dead to that which held us captive, so that we serve not under the old written code but in the new life of the Spirit.

Rom 8　[3]For God has done what the law, weakened by the flesh, could not do: sending his own Son in the likeness of sinful flesh and for sin, he condemned sin in the flesh, [4]in order that the just requirement of the law might be fulfilled in us, who walk not according to the flesh but according to the Spirit.

Col 2　[13]And you, who were dead in trespasses and the uncircumcision of your flesh, God made alive together with him, having forgiven us all our trespasses, [14]having canceled the bond which stood against us with its legal demands; this he set aside, nailing it to the cross.

[19]Why then the law? It was added because of transgressions, till the offspring should come to whom the promise had been made; and it was ordained by angels through an intermediary. [20]Now an intermediary implies more than one; but God is one.

PRIMARY

Rom 4:13-15 (§18)

[13]The promise to Abraham and his descendants, that they should inherit the world, did not come through the law but through the righteousness of faith. [14]If it is the adherents of the law who are to be the heirs, faith is null and the promise is void. [15]For the law brings wrath, but where there is no law there is no transgression.

Rom 5:12-21 (§22)

[12]Therefore as sin came into the world through one man and death through sin, and so death spread to all men because all men sinned— [13]sin indeed was in the world before the law was given, but sin is not counted where there is no law. [14]Yet death reigned from Adam to Moses, even over those whose sins were not like the transgression of Adam, who was a type of the one who was to come.

[15]But the free gift is not like the trespass. For if many died through one man's trespass, much more have the grace of God and the free gift in the grace of that one man Jesus Christ abounded for many. [16]And the free gift is not like the effect of that one man's sin. For the judgment following one trespass brought condemnation, but the free gift following many trespasses brings justification. [17]If, because of one man's trespass, death reigned through that one man, much more will those who receive the abundance of grace and the free gift of righteousness reign in life through the one man Jesus Christ.

[18]Then as one man's trespass led to condemnation for all men, so one man's act of righteousness leads to acquittal and life for all men. [19]For as by one man's disobedience many were made sinners, so by one man's obedience many will be made righteous. [20]Law came in, to increase the trespass; but where sin increased, grace abounded all the more, [21]so that, as sin reigned in death, grace also might reign · through righteousness to eternal life through Jesus Christ our Lord.

Rom 9:1-5 (§35)

[1]I am speaking the truth in Christ, I am not lying; my conscience bears me witness in the Holy Spirit, [2]that I have great sorrow and unceasing anguish in my heart. [3]For I could wish that I myself were accursed and cut off from Christ for the sake of my brethren, my kinsmen by race. [4]They are Israelites, and to them belong the sonship, the glory, the covenants, the giving of the law, the worship, and the promises; [5]to them belong the patriarchs, and of their race, according to the flesh, is the Christ. God who is over all be blessed for ever. Amen.

Rom 10:1-4 (§40)

[1]Brethren, my heart's desire and prayer to God for them is that they may be saved. [2]I bear them witness that they have a zeal for God, but it is not enlightened. [3]For, being ignorant of the righteousness that comes from God, and seeking to establish their own, they did not submit to God's righteousness. [4]For Christ is the end of the law, that every one who has faith may be justified.

1 Cor 8:4-6 (§103)

[4]Hence, as to the eating of food offered to idols, we know that "an idol has no real existence," and that "there is no God but one." [5]For although there may be so-called gods in heaven or on earth—as indeed there are many "gods" and many "lords"— [6]yet for us there is one God, the Father, from whom are all things and for whom we exist, and one Lord, Jesus Christ, through whom are all things and through whom we exist.

● **Gal 3:19**

Gal 4   [4]But when the time had fully come, God sent forth his Son, born of woman, born under the law, . . .

Acts 7   [53]"you who received the law as delivered by angels and did not keep it."

Heb 9   [15]Therefore he is the mediator of a new covenant, so that those who are called may receive the promised eternal inheritance, since a death has occurred which redeems them from the transgressions under the first covenant.

● **Gal 3:20**

Eph 4   [5]one Lord, one faith, one baptism, [6]one God and Father of us all, who is above all and through all and in all.

1 Tim 2   [5]For there is one God, and there is one mediator between God and men, the man Christ Jesus, . . .

21 Is the law then against the promises of God? Certainly not; for if a law had been given which could make alive, then righteousness would indeed be by the law. **22** But the scripture consigned all things to sin, that what was promised to faith in Jesus Christ might be given to those who believe.

23 Now before faith came, we were confined under the law, kept under restraint until faith should be revealed. **24** So that the law was our custodian until Christ came, that we might be justified by faith. **25** But now that faith has come, we are no longer under a custodian;

PRIMARY

Rom 3:9–20 (§13)

9 What then? Are we Jews any better off? No, not at all; for I have already charged that all men, both Jews and Greeks, are under the power of sin, **10** as it is written:

"None is righteous, no, not one;
11 no one understands, no one seeks for God.
12 All have turned aside, together they have gone wrong;
no one does good, not even one."
13 "Their throat is an open grave,
they use their tongues to deceive."
"The venom of asps is under their lips."
14 "Their mouth is full of curses and bitterness."
15 "Their feet are swift to shed blood,
16 in their paths are ruin and misery,
17 and the way of peace they do not know."
18 "There is no fear of God before their eyes."

Now we know that whatever the law says it speaks to those who are under the law, so that every mouth may be stopped, and the whole world may be held accountable to God. **20** For no human being will be justified in his sight by works of the law, since through the law comes knowledge of sin.

Rom 6:11–14 (§24)

11 So you also must consider yourselves dead to sin and alive to God in Christ Jesus.

12 Let not sin therefore reign in your mortal bodies, to make you obey their passions. **13** Do not yield your members to sin as instruments of wickedness, but yield yourselves to God as men who have been brought from death to life, and your members to God as instruments of righteousness. **14** For sin will have no dominion over

you, since you are not under law but under grace.

Rom 7:7–13 (§27)

7 What then shall we say? That the law is sin? By no means! Yet, if it had not been for the law, I should not have known sin. I should not have known what it is to covet if the law had not said, "You shall not covet." **8** But sin, finding opportunity in the commandment, wrought in me all kinds of covetousness. Apart from the law sin lies dead. **9** I was once alive apart from the law, but when the commandment came, sin revived and I died; **10** the very commandment which promised life proved to be death to me. **11** For sin, finding opportunity in the commandment, deceived me and by it killed me. **12** So the law is holy, and the commandment is holy and just and good.

13 Did that which is good, then, bring death to me? By no means! It was sin, working death in me through what is good, in order that sin might be shown to be sin, and through the commandment might become sinful beyond measure.

Rom 11:25–32 (§49)

25 Lest you be wise in your own conceits, I want you to understand this mystery, brethren: a hardening has come upon part of Israel, until the full number of the Gentiles come in, **26** and so all Israel will be saved; as it is written,

"The Deliverer will come from Zion,
he will banish ungodliness from Jacob";
27 "and this will be my covenant with them
when I take away their sins."

28 As regards the gospel they are enemies of God, for your sake; but as regards election they are beloved for the sake of their forefathers. **29** For the gifts and the call of God are irrevocable. **30** Just as you were once disobedient to God but now have received mercy because of their disobedience, **31** so they have now been disobedient in order that by the mercy shown to you they also may receive mercy. **32** For God has consigned all men to disobedience, that he may have mercy upon all.

2 Cor 3:7–11 (§156)

7 Now if the dispensation of death, carved in letters on stone, came with such splendor that the Israelites could not look at Moses' face because of its brightness, fading as this was, **8** will not the dispensation of the Spirit be attended with greater splendor? **9** For if there was

splendor in the dispensation of condemnation, the dispensation of righteousness must far exceed it in splendor. **10** Indeed, in this case, what once had splendor has come to have no splendor at all, because of the splendor that surpasses it. **11** For if what faded away came with splendor, what is permanent must have much more splendor.

2 Cor 3:12–18 (§157)

12 Since we have such a hope, we are very bold, **13** not like Moses, who put a veil over his face so that the Israelites might not see the end of the fading splendor. **14** But their minds were hardened; for to this day, when they read the old covenant, that same veil remains unlifted, because only through Christ is it taken away. **15** Yes, to this day whenever Moses is read a veil lies over their minds; **16** but when a man turns to the Lord the veil is removed. **17** Now the Lord is the Spirit, and where the Spirit of the Lord is, there is freedom. **18** And we all, with unveiled face, beholding the glory of the Lord, are being changed into his likeness from one degree of glory to another; for this comes from the Lord who is the Spirit.

Phil 3:2–11 (§247)

2 Look out for the dogs, look out for the evil-workers, look out for those who mutilate the flesh. **3** For we are the true circumcision, who worship God in spirit, and glory in Christ Jesus, and put no confidence in the flesh. **4** Though I myself have reason for confidence in the flesh also. If any other man thinks he has reason for confidence in the flesh, I have more: **5** circumcised on the eighth day, of the people of Israel, of the tribe of Benjamin, a Hebrew born of Hebrews; as to the law a Pharisee, **6** as to zeal a persecutor of the church, as to righteousness under the law blameless. **7** But whatever gain I had, I counted as loss for the sake of Christ. **8** Indeed I count everything as loss because of the surpassing worth of knowing Christ Jesus my Lord. For his sake I have suffered the loss of all things, and count them as refuse, in order that I may gain Christ **9** and be found in him, not having a righteousness of my own, based on law, but that which is through faith in Christ, the righteousness from God that depends on faith; **10** that I may know him and the power of his resurrection, and may share his sufferings, becoming like him in his death, **11** that if possible I may attain the resurrection from the dead.

● **Gal 3:21**

Rom 8   **2** For the law of the Spirit of life in Christ Jesus has set me free from the law of sin and death.

Gal 2   **21** I do not nullify the grace of God; for if justification were through the law, then Christ died to no purpose.

(God) *omit* of God: p⁴⁶ B it (few) Ambrosiaster

● **Gal 3:22**

2 Cor 1   **20** For all the promises of God find their Yes in him. That is why we utter the Amen through him, to the glory of God.

Gal 4   **30** But what does the scripture say? "Cast out the slave and her son; for the son of the slave shall not inherit with the son of the free woman." **31** So, brethren, we are not children of the slve but of the free woman.

● **Gal 3:23–25**

2 Cor 5   **16** So we do not lose heart. Though our outer nature is wasting away, our inner nature is being renewed every day. **17** For this slight momentary affliction is preparing for us an eternal weight of glory beyond all comparison, . . .

● **Gal 3:25**

Rom 3   **31** Do we then overthrow the law by this faith? By no means! On the contrary, we uphold the law.

Rom 10   **4** For Christ is the end of the law, that every one who has faith may be justified.

Acts 21   **21** "and they have been told about you that you teach all the Jews who are among the Gentiles to forsake Moses, telling them not to circumcise their children or observe the customs."

FORMAL ELEMENT: BAPTISMAL LITURGY

26for in Christ Jesus you are all sons of God, through faith. 27For as many of you as were baptized into Christ have put on Christ. 28There is neither Jew nor Greek, there is neither slave nor free, there is neither male nor female; for you are all one in Christ Jesus. 29And if you are Christ's, then you are Abraham's offspring, heirs according to promise.

PRIMARY

1 Cor 12:12–13 (§118)
12For just as the body is one and has many members, and all the members of the body, though many, are one body, so it is with Christ. 13For by one Spirit we were all baptized into one body— Jews or Greeks, slaves or free—and all were made to drink of one Spirit.

Col 3:5–11 (§266)
5Put to death therefore what is earthly in you: fornication, impurity, passion, evil desire, and covetousness, which is idolatry. 6On account of these the wrath of God is coming. 7In these you once walked, when you lived in them. 8But now put them all away: anger, wrath, malice, slander, and foul talk from your mouth. 9Do not lie to one another, seeing that you have put off the old nature with its practices 10and have put on the new nature, which is being renewed in knowledge after the image of its creator. 11Here there cannot be Greek and Jew, circumcised and uncircumcised, barbarian, Scythian, slave, free man, but Christ is all, and in all.

SECONDARY

Rom 10:5–13 (§41)
5Moses writes that the man who practices the righteousness which is based on the law shall live by it. 6But the righteousness based on faith says, Do not say in your heart, "Who will ascend into heaven?" (that is, to bring Christ down) 7 or "Who will descend into the abyss?" (that is, to bring Christ up from the dead). 8But what does it say? The word is near you, on your lips and in your heart (that is, the word of faith which we preach); 9because, if you confess with your lips that Jesus is Lord and believe in your heart that God raised him from the dead, you will be saved. 10For man believes with his heart and so is justified, and he confesses with his lips and so is saved. 11The scripture says, "No one who believes in him will be put to shame." 12For there is no distinction between Jew and Greek; the same Lord is Lord of all and bestows his riches upon all who call upon him. 13For, "every one who calls upon the name of the Lord will be saved."

Eph 2:11–22 (§221)
11Therefore remember that at one time you Gentiles in the flesh, called the uncircumcision by what is called the circumcision, which is made in the flesh by hands— 12remember that you were at that time separated from Christ, alienated from the commonwealth of Israel, and strangers to the covenants of promise, having no hope and without God in the world. 13But now in Christ Jesus you who once were far off have been brought near in the blood of Christ. 14For he is our peace, who has made us both one, and has broken down the dividing wall of hostility, 15by abolishing in his flesh the law of commandments and ordinances, that he might create in himself one new man in place of the two, so making peace, 16and might reconcile us both to God in one body through the cross, thereby bringing the hostility to an end. 17And he came and preached peace to you who were far off and peace to those who were near; 18for through him we both have access in one Spirit to the Father. 19So then you are no longer strangers and sojourners, but you are fellow citizens with the saints and members of the household of God, 20built upon the foundation of the apostles and prophets, Christ Jesus himself being the cornerstone, 21in whom the whole structure is joined together and grows into a holy temple in the Lord; 22in whom you also are built into it for a dwelling place of God in the Spirit.

● **Gal 3:27**
Rom 13   14But put on the Lord Jesus Christ, and make no provision for the flesh, to gratify its desires.

2 Cor 5   12We are not commending ourselves to you again but giving you cause to be proud of us, so that you may be able to answer those who pride themselves on a man's position and not on his heart.

Gal 2   20I have been crucified with Christ; it is no longer I who live, but Christ who lives in me; and the life I now live in the flesh I live by faith in the Son of God, who loved me and gave himself for me.

Eph 4   24and put on the new nature, created after the likeness of God in true righteousness and holiness.

● **Gal 3:29**
Gal 3   7So you see that it is men of faith who are the sons of Abraham.

Gal 4   7So through God you are no longer a slave but a son, and if a son then an heir.

Gal 4   31So, brethren, we are not children of the slave but of the free woman.

4 I mean that the heir, as long as he is a child, is no better than a slave, though he is the owner of all the estate; ²but he is under guardians and trustees until the date set by the father. ³So with us; when we were children, we were slaves to the elemental spirits of the universe. ⁴But when the time had fully come, God sent forth his Son, born of woman, born under the law, ⁵to redeem those who were under the law, so that we might receive adoption as sons. ⁶And because you are sons, God has sent the Spirit of his Son into our hearts, crying, "Abba! Father!" ⁷So through God you are no longer a slave but a son, and if a son then an heir.

PRIMARY

Rom 5:1-5 (§20)

¹Therefore, since we are justified by faith, we have peace with God through our Lord Jesus Christ. ²Through him we have obtained access to this grace in which we stand, and we rejoice in our hope of sharing the glory of God. ³More than that, we rejoice in our sufferings, knowing that suffering produces endurance, ⁴and endurance produces character, and character produces hope, ⁵and hope does not disappoint us, because God's love has been poured into our hearts through the Holy Spirit which has been given to us.

Rom 6:15-23 (§25)

¹⁵What then? Are we to sin because we are not under law but under grace? By no means! ¹⁶Do you not know that if you yield yourselves to any one as obedient slaves, you are slaves of the one whom you obey, either of sin, which leads to death, or of obedience, which leads to righteousness? ¹⁷But thanks be to God, that you who were once slaves of sin have become obedient from the heart to the standard of teaching to which you were committed, ¹⁸and, having been set free from sin, have become slaves of righteousness. ¹⁹I am speaking in human terms, because of your natural limitations. For just as you once yielded your members to impurity and to greater and greater iniquity, so now yield your members to righteousness for sanctification. ²⁰When you were slaves of sin, you were free in regard to righteousness. ²¹But then what return did you get from the things of which you are now ashamed? The end of those things is death. ²²But now that you have been set free from sin and have become slaves of God, the return you get is sanctification and its end, eternal life. ²³For the wages of sin is death, but the free gift of God is eternal life in Christ Jesus our Lord.

Rom 8:9-17 (§30)

⁹But you are not in the flesh, you are in the Spirit, if in fact the Spirit of God dwells in you. Any one who does not have the Spirit of Christ does not belong to him. ¹⁰But if Christ is in you, although your bodies are dead because of sin, your spirits are alive because of righteousness. ¹¹If the Spirit of him who raised Jesus from the dead dwells in you, he who raised Christ Jesus from the dead will give life to your mortal bodies also through his Spirit which dwells in you.

¹²So then, brethren, we are debtors, not to the flesh, to live according to the flesh—¹³for if you live according to the flesh you will die, but if by the Spirit you put to death the deeds of the body you will live. ¹⁴For all who are led by the Spirit of God are sons of God. ¹⁵For you did not receive the spirit of slavery to fall back into fear, but you have received the spirit of sonship. When we cry, "Abba! Father!" ¹⁶it is the Spirit himself bearing witness with our spirit that we are children of God, ¹⁷and if children, then heirs, heirs of God and fellow heirs with Christ, provided we suffer with him in order that we may also be glorified with him.

● **Gal 4:3**

Col 2 ⁸See to it that no one makes a prey of you by philosophy and empty deceit, according to human tradition, according to the elemental spirits of the universe, and not according to Christ.

Col 2 ²⁰If with Christ you died to the elemental spirits of the universe, why do you live as if you still belonged to the world? Why do you submit to regulations, . . .

● **Gal 4:4**

Rom 1 ³the gospel concerning his Son, who was descended from David according to the flesh ⁴and designated Son of God in power according to the Spirit of holiness by his resurrection from the dead, Jesus Christ our Lord, . . .

Gal 3 ¹⁹Why then the law? It was added because of transgressions, till the offspring should come to whom the promise had been made; and it was ordained by angels through an intermediary.

Eph 1 ¹⁰as a plan for the fulness of time, to unite all things in him, things in heaven and things on earth.

● **Gal 4:7**

1 Cor 6 ²⁰you were bought with a price. So glorify God in your body.

1 Cor 7 ²⁰Every one should remain in the state in which he was called. ²¹Were you a slave when called? Never mind. But if you can gain your freedom, avail yourself of the opportunity. ²²For he who was called in the Lord as a slave is a freedman of the Lord. Likewise he who was free when called is a slave of Christ. ²³You were bought with a price; do not become slaves of men. ²⁴So, brethren, in whatever state each was called, there let him remain with God.

Gal 3 ⁷So you see that it is men of faith who are the sons of Abraham.

Gal 3 ²⁹And if you are Christ's, then you are Abraham's offspring, heirs according to promise.

Gal 4 ³¹So, brethren, we are not children of the slave but of the free woman.

Eph 1 ¹⁴which is the guarantee of our inheritance until we acquire possession of it, to the praise of his glory.

Eph 1 ¹⁸having the eyes of your hearts enlightened, that you may know what is the hope to which he has called you, what are the riches of his glorious inheritance in the saints, . . .

[8]Formerly, when you did not know God, you were in bondage to beings that by nature are no gods; [9]but now that you have come to know God, or rather to be known by God, how can you turn back again to the weak and beggarly elemental spirits, whose slaves you want to be once more? [10]You observe days, and months, and seasons, and years! [11]I am afraid I have labored over you in vain.

PRIMARY

Rom 1:18–23 (§4)

[18]For the wrath of God is revealed from heaven against all ungodliness and wickedness of men who by their wickedness suppress the truth. [19]For what can be known about God is plain to them, because God has shown it to them. [20]Ever since the creation of the world his invisible nature, namely, his eternal power and deity, has been clearly perceived in the things that have been made. So they are without excuse; [21]for although they knew God they did not honor him as God or give thanks to him, but they became futile in their thinking and their senseless minds were darkened. [22]Claiming to be wise, they became fools, [23]and exchanged the glory of the immortal God for images resembling mortal man or birds or animals or reptiles.

Rom 14:5–12 (§58)

[5]One man esteems one day as better than another, while another man esteems all days alike. Let every one be fully convinced in his own mind. [6]He who observes the day, observes it in honor of the Lord. He also who eats, eats in honor of the Lord, since he gives thanks to God; while he who abstains, abstains in honor of the Lord and gives thanks to God. [7]None of us lives to himself, and none of us dies to himself. [8]If we live, we live to the Lord, and if we die, we die to the Lord; so then, whether we live or whether we die, we are the Lord's. [9]For to this end Christ died and lived again, that he might be Lord both of the dead and of the living.
[10]Why do you pass judgment on your brother? Or you, why do you despise your brother? For we shall all stand before the judgment seat of God; [11]for it is written,

"As I live, says the Lord, every knee shall bow to me,
and every tongue shall give praise to God."
[12]So each of us shall give account of himself to God.

1 Cor 8:4–6 (§103)

[4]Hence, as to the eating of food offered to idols, we know that "an idol has no real existence," and that "there is no God but one." [5]For although there may be so-called gods in heaven or on earth—as indeed there are many "gods" and many "lords"— [6]yet for us there is one God, the Father, from whom are all things and for whom we exist, and one Lord, Jesus Christ, through whom are all things and through whom we exist.

1 Cor 10:14–22 (§110)

[14]Therefore, my beloved, shun the worship of idols. [15]I speak as to sensible men; judge for yourselves what I say. [16]The cup of blessing which we bless, is it not a participation in the blood of Christ? The bread which we break, is it not a participation in the body of Christ? [17]Because there is one bread, we who are many are one body, for we all partake of the one bread.
[18]Consider the people of Israel; are not those who eat the sacrifices partners in the altar? [19]What do I imply then? That food offered to idols is anything, or that an idol is anything? [20]No, I imply that what pagans sacrifice they offer to demons and not to God. I do not want you to be partners with demons. [21]You cannot drink the cup of the Lord and the cup of demons. You cannot partake of the table of the Lord and the table of demons. [22]Shall we provoke the Lord to jealousy? Are we stronger than he?

1 Cor 12:1–3 (§116)

[1]Now concerning spiritual gifts, brethren, I do not want you to be uninformed. [2]You know that when you were heathen, you were led astray to dumb idols, however you may have been moved. [3]Therefore I want you to understand that no one speaking by the Spirit of God ever says "Jesus be cursed!" and no one can say "Jesus is Lord" except by the Holy Spirit.

Col 2:16–23 (§263–264)

[16]Therefore let no one pass judgment on you in questions of food and drink or with regard to a festival or a new moon or a sabbath. [17]These are only a shadow of what is to come; but the substance belongs to Christ. [18]Let no one disqualify you, insisting on self-abasement and worship of angels, taking his stand on visions, puffed up without reason by his sensuous mind, [19]and not holding fast to the Head, from whom the whole body, nourished and knit together through its joints and ligaments, grows with a growth that is from God.
[20]If with Christ you died to the elemental spirits of the universe, why do you live as if you still belonged to the world? Why do you submit to regulations, [21]"Do not handle, Do not taste, Do not touch" [22](referring to things which all perish as they are used), according to human precepts and doctrines? [23]These have indeed an appearance of wisdom in promoting rigor of devotion and self-abasement and severity to the body, but they are of no value in checking the indulgence of the flesh.

1 Thess 1:2–10 (§276)

[2]We give thanks to God always for you all, constantly mentioning you in our prayers, [3]remembering before our God and Father your work of faith and labor of love and steadfastness of hope in our Lord Jesus Christ. [4]For we know, brethren beloved by God, that he has chosen you; [5]for our gospel came to you not only in word, but also in power and in the Holy Spirit and with full conviction. You know what kind of men we proved to be among you for your sake. [6]And you became imitators of us and of the Lord, for you received the word in much affliction, with joy inspired by the Holy Spirit; [7]so that you became an example to all the believers in Macedonia and in Achaia. [8]For not only has the word of the Lord sounded forth from you in Macedonia and Achaia, but your faith in God has gone forth everywhere, so that we need not say anything. [9]For they themselves report concerning us what a welcome we had among you, and how you turned to God from idols, to serve a living and true God, [10]and to wait for his Son from heaven, whom he raised from the dead, Jesus who delivers us from the wrath to come.

● **Gal 4:8**
Eph 2   [11]Therefore remember that at one time you Gentiles in the flesh, called the uncircumcision by what is called the circumcision, which is made in the flesh by hands— [12]remember that you were at that time separated from Christ, alienated from the commonwealth of Israel, and strangers to the covenants of promise, having no hope and without God in the world. [13]But now in Christ Jesus you who once were far off have been brought near in the blood of Christ.

1 Thess 4   [5]not in the passion of lust like heathen who do not know God; . . .

● **Gal 4:9**
Col 2   [8]See to it that no one makes a prey of you by philosophy and empty deceit, according to human tradition, according to the elemental spirits of the universe, and not according to Christ.

● **Gal 4:11**
1 Cor 15   [58]Therefore, my beloved brethren, be steadfast, immovable, always abounding in the work of the Lord, knowing that in the Lord your labor is not in vain.

1 Thess 3   [5]For this reason, when I could bear it no longer, I sent that I might know your faith, for fear that somehow the tempter had tempted you and that our labor would be in vain.

¹²Brethren, I beseech you, become as I am, for I also have become as you are. You did me no wrong; ¹³you know it was because of a bodily ailment that I preached the gospel to you at first; ¹⁴and though my condition was a trial to you, you did not scorn or despise me, but received me as an angel of God, as Christ Jesus. ¹⁵What has become of the satisfaction you felt? For I bear you witness that, if possible, you would have plucked out your eyes and given them to me. ¹⁶Have I then become your enemy by telling you the truth? ¹⁷They make much of you, but for no good purpose; they want to shut you out, that you may make much of them. ¹⁸For a good purpose it is always good to be made much of, and not only when I am present with you. ¹⁹My little children, with whom I am again in travail until Christ be formed in you! ²⁰I could wish to be present with you now and to change my tone, for I am perplexed about you.

PRIMARY

1 Cor 2:1–5 (§76)

¹When I came to you, brethren, I did not come proclaiming to you the testimony of God in lofty words or wisdom. ²For I decided to know nothing among you except Jesus Christ and him crucified. ³And I was with you in weakness and in much fear and trembling; ⁴and my speech and my message were not in plausible words of wisdom, but in demonstration of the Spirit and of power, ⁵that your faith might not rest in the wisdom of men but in the power of God.

1 Cor 4:14–21 (§86)

¹⁴I do not write this to make you ashamed, but to admonish you as my beloved children. ¹⁵For though you have countless guides in Christ, you do not have many fathers. For I became your father in Christ Jesus through the gospel. ¹⁶I urge you, then, be imitators of me. ¹⁷Therefore I sent to you Timothy, my beloved and faithful child in the Lord, to remind you of my ways in Christ, as I teach them everywhere in every church. ¹⁸Some are arrogant, as though I were not coming to you. ¹⁹But I will come to you soon, if the Lord wills, and I will find out not the talk of these arrogant people but their power. ²⁰For the kingdom of God does not consist in talk but in power. ²¹What do you wish? Shall I come to you with a rod, or with love in a spirit of gentleness?

2 Cor 1:3–11 (§147)

³Blessed be the God and Father of our Lord Jesus Christ, the Father of mercies and God of all comfort, ⁴who comforts us in all our affliction, so that we may be able to comfort those who are in any affliction, with the comfort with which we ourselves are comforted by God. ⁵For as we share abundantly in Christ's sufferings, so through Christ we share abundantly in comfort too. ⁶If we are afflicted, it is for your comfort and salvation; and if we are comforted, it is for your comfort, which you experience when you patiently endure the same sufferings that we suffer. ⁷Our hope for you is unshaken; for we know that as you share in our sufferings, you will also share in our comfort.

⁸For we do not want you to be ignorant, brethren, of the affliction we experienced in Asia; for we were so utterly, unbearably crushed that we despaired of life itself. ⁹Why, we felt that we had received the sentence of death; but that was to make us rely not on ourselves but on God who raises the dead; ¹⁰he delivered us from so deadly a peril, and he will deliver us; on him we have set our hope that he will deliver us again. ¹¹You also must help us by prayer, so that many will give thanks on our behalf for the blessing granted us in answer to many prayers.

Phil 1:27–30 (§241)

²⁷Only let your manner of life be worthy of the gospel of Christ, so that whether I come and see you or am absent, I may hear of you that you stand firm in one spirit, with one mind striving side by side for the faith of the gospel, ²⁸and not frightened in anything by your opponents. This is a clear omen to them of their destruction, but of your salvation, and that from God. ²⁹For it has been granted to you that for the sake of Christ you should not only believe in him but also suffer for his sake, ³⁰engaged in the same conflict which you saw and now hear to be mine.

1 Thess 1:2–10 (§276)

²We give thanks to God always for you all, constantly mentioning you in our prayers, ³remembering before our God and Father your work of faith and labor of love and steadfastness of hope in our Lord Jesus Christ. ⁴For we know, brethren beloved by God, that he has chosen you; ⁵for our gospel came to you not only in word, but also in power and in the Holy Spirit and with full conviction. You know what kind of men we proved to be among you for your sake. ⁶And you became imitators of us and of the Lord, for you received the word in much affliction, with joy inspired by the Holy Spirit; ⁷so that you became an example to the all the believers in Macedonia and in Achaia. ⁸For not only has the word of the Lord sounded forth from you in Macedonia and Achaia, but your faith in God has gone forth everywhere, so that we need not say anything. ⁹For they themselves report concerning us what a welcome we had among you, and how you turned to God from idols, to serve a living and true God, ¹⁰and to wait for his Son from heaven, whom he raised from the dead, Jesus who delivers us from the wrath to come.

● **Gal 4:12**
1 Cor 11 ¹Be imitators of me, as I am of Christ.

● **Gal 4:13**
2 Cor 7 ⁵For even when we came into Macedonia, our bodies had no rest but we were afflicted at every turn— fighting without and fear within.

2 Cor 7 ⁷and not only by his coming but also by the comfort with which he was comforted in you, as he told us of your longing, your mourning, your zeal for me, so that I rejoiced still more.

2 Cor 10 ¹⁰For they say, "His letters are weighty and strong, but his bodily presence is weak, and his speech of no account."

2 Cor 12 ⁷And to keep me from being too elated by the abundance of revelations, a thorn was given me in the flesh, a messenger of Satan, to harass me, to keep me from being too elated.

Acts 16 ⁶And they went through the region of Phrygia and Galatia, having been forbidden by the Holy Spirit to speak the word in Asia.

● **Gal 4:14**
Gal 1 ⁸But even if we, or an angel from heaven, should preach to you a gospel contrary to that which we preached to you, let him be accursed.

● **Gal 4:17**
Gal 6 ¹²It is those who want to make a good showing in the flesh that would compel you to be circumcised, and only in order that they may not be persecuted for the cross of Christ. ¹³For even those who receive cir-cumcision do not themselves keep the law, but they desire to have you circumcised that they may glory in your flesh.

Phil 2 ²¹They all look after their own interests, not those of Jesus Christ.

● **Gal 4:19**
1 Cor 4 ¹⁵For though you have countless guides in Christ, you do not have many fathers. For I became your father in Christ Jesus through the gospel.

1 Thess 2 ⁷But we were gentle among you, like a nurse taking care of her children.

1 Thess 2 ¹¹for you know how, like a father with his children, we exhorted each one of you and encouraged you and charged you . . .

[21] Tell me, you who desire to be under law, do you not hear the law? [22] For it is written that Abraham had two sons, one by a slave and one by a free woman. [23] But the son of the slave was born according to the flesh, the son of the free woman through promise. [24] Now this is an allegory: these women are two covenants. One is from Mount Sinai, bearing children for slavery; she is Hagar. [25] Now Hagar is Mount Sinai in Arabia; she corresponds to the present Jerusalem, for she is in slavery with her children. [26] But the Jerusalem above is free, and she is our mother. [27] For it is written,

"Rejoice, O barren one who does not bear;

break forth and shout, you who are not in travail;

for the children of the desolate one are many more

than the children of her that is married."

[28] Now we, brethren, like Isaac, are children of promise. [29] But as at that time he who was born according to the flesh persecuted him who was born according to the Spirit, so it is now. [30] But what does the scripture say? "Cast out the slave and her son; for the son of the slave shall not inherit with the son of the free woman." [31] So, brethren, we are not children of the slave but of the free woman.

PRIMARY

Rom 9:6–13 (§36)

[6] But it is not as though the word of God had failed. For not all who are descended from Israel belong to Israel, [7] and not all are children of Abraham because they are his descendants; but "Through Isaac shall your descendants be named." [8] This means that it is not the children of the flesh who are the children of God, but the children of the promise are reckoned as descendants. [9] For this is what the promise said, "About this time I will return and Sarah shall have a son." [10] And not only so, but also when Rebecca had conceived children by one man, our forefather Isaac, [11] though they were not yet born and had done nothing either good or bad, in order that God's purpose of election might continue, not because of works but because of his call, [12] she was told, "The elder will serve the younger." [13] As it is written, "Jacob I loved, but Esau I hated."

2 Cor 3:12–18 (§157)

[12] Since we have such a hope, we are very bold, [13] not like Moses, who put a veil over his face so that the Israelites might not see the end of the fading splendor. [14] But their minds were hardened; for to this day, when they read the old covenant, that same veil remains unlifted, because only through Christ is it taken away. [15] Yes, to this day whenever Moses is read a veil lies over their minds; [16] but when a man turns to the Lord the veil is removed. [17] Now the Lord is the Spirit, and where the Spirit of the Lord is, there is freedom. [18] And we all, with unveiled face, beholding the glory of the Lord, are being changed into his likeness from one degree of glory to another; for this comes from the Lord who is the Spirit.

● **Gal 4:21–31**
Rom 4   [13] The promise to Abraham and his descendants, that they should inherit the world, did not come through the law but through the righteousness of faith. [14] If it is the adherents of the law who are to be the heirs, faith is null and the promise is void. [15] For the law brings wrath, but where there is no law there is no transgression.
    [16] That is why it depends on faith, in order that the promise may rest on grace and be guaranteed to all his descendants—not only to the adherents of the law but also to those who share the faith of Abraham, for he is the father of us all, [17] as it is written, "I have made you the father of many nations"—in the presence of the God in whom he believed, who gives life to the dead and calls into existence the things that do not exist.[18] In hope he believed against hope, that he should become the father of many nations; as he had been told, "So shall your descendants be." [19] He did not weaken in faith when he considered his own body, which was as good as dead because he was about a hundred years old, or when he considered the barrenness of Sarah's womb. [20] No distrust made him waver concerning the promise of God, but he grew strong in his faith as he gave glory to God, [21] fully convinced that God was able to do what he had promised. [22] That

is why his faith was "reckoned to him as righteousness." [23] But the words, "it was reckoned to him," were written not for his sake alone, [24] but for ours also. It will be reckoned to us who believe in him that raised from the dead Jesus our Lord, [25] who was put to death for our trespasses and raised for our justification.

Gal 3   [22] But the scripture consigned all things to sin, that what was promised to faith in Jesus Christ might be given to those who believe.

● **Gal 4:22**
Gen 21   [9] But Sarah saw the son of Hagar the Egyptian, whom she had borne to Abraham, playing with her son Isaac.

Gen 16   [15] And Hagar bore Abram a son; and Abram called the name of his son, whom Hagar bore, Ishmael.

● **Gal 4:25**
(Arabia) *read* for Sinai is a mountain in Arabia: p[46]SCG it vg cop(sa) Origen(Latin)

● **Gal 4:27**
Isa 54   [1] "Sing, O barren one, who did not bear;

break forth into singing and cry aloud,

you who have not been in travail!

For the children of the desolate one will be more than the children of her that is married, says the Lord."

● **Gal 4:28**
(we) *read* you: p[46]BD*G it (few) syr(pal) cop(sa) Irenaeus

● **Gal 4:30**
Gen 21   [10] So she said to Abraham, "Cast out this slave woman with her son; for the son of this slave woman shall not be heir with my son Isaac." [11] And the thing was very displeasing to Abraham on account of his son. [12] But God said to Abraham, "Be not displeased because of the lad and because of your slave woman; whatever Sarah says to you, do as she tells you, for through Isaac shall your descendants be named."

● **Gal 4:31**
Gal 3   [7] So you see that it is men of faith who are the sons of Abraham.

Gal 3   [29] And if you are Christ's, then you are Abraham's offspring, heirs according to promise.

5 For freedom Christ has set us free; stand fast therefore, and do not submit again to a yoke of slavery.

²Now I, Paul, say to you that if you receive circumcision, Christ will be of no advantage to you. ³I testify again to every man who receives circumcision that he is bound to keep the whole law. ⁴You are severed from Christ, you who would be justified by the law; you have fallen away from grace. ⁵For through the Spirit, by faith, we wait for the hope of righteousness. ⁶For in Christ Jesus neither circumcision nor uncircumcision is of any avail, but faith working through love. ⁷You were running well; who hindered you from obeying the truth? ⁸This persuasion is not from him who called you. ⁹A little leaven leavens the whole lump. ¹⁰I have confidence in the Lord that you will take no other view than mine; and he who is troubling you will bear his judgment, whoever he is. ¹¹But if I, brethren, still preach circumcision, why am I still persecuted? In that case the stumbling block of the cross has been removed. ¹²I wish those who unsettle you would mutilate themselves!

PRIMARY

Rom 2:25–29 (§11)
²⁵Circumcision indeed is of value if you obey the law; but if you break the law, your circumcision becomes uncircumcision. ²⁶So, if a man who is uncircumcised keeps the precepts of the law, will not his uncircumcision be regarded as circumcision? ²⁷Then those who are physically uncircumcised but keep the law will condemn you who have the written code and circumcision but break the law. ²⁸For he is not a real Jew who is one outwardly, nor is true circumcision something external and physical.

²⁹He is a Jew who is one inwardly, and real circumcision is a matter of the heart, spiritual and not literal. His praise is not from men but from God.

Rom 6:15–23 (§25)
¹⁵What then? Are we to sin because we are not under law but under grace? By no means! ¹⁶Do you not know that if you yield yourselves to any one as obedient slaves, you are slaves of the one whom you obey, either of sin, which leads to death, or of obedience, which leads to righteousness? ¹⁷But thanks be to God, that you who were once slaves of sin have become obedient from the heart to the standard of teaching to which you were committed, ¹⁸and, having been set free from sin, have become slaves of righteousness. ¹⁹I am speaking in human terms, because of your natural limitations. For just as you once yielded your members to impurity and to greater and greater iniquity, so now yield your members to righteousness for sanctification. ²⁰When you were slaves of sin, you were free in regard to righteousness. ²¹But then what return did you get from the things of which you are now ashamed? The end of those things is death. ²²But now that you have been set free from sin and have become slaves of God, the return you get is sanctification and its end, eternal life. ²³For the wages of sin is death, but the free gift of God is eternal life in Christ Jesus our Lord.

Rom 9:30–33 (§39)
³⁰What shall we say, then? That Gentiles who did not pursue righteousness have attained it, that is, righteousness through faith; ³¹but that Israel who pursued the righteousness which is based on law did not succeed in fulfilling that law. ³²Why? Because they did not pursue it through faith, but as if it were based on

works. They have stumbled over the stumbling stone, ³³as it is written,

"Behold, I am laying in Zion a stone that will make men stumble,
a rock that will make them fall;
and he who believes in him will not be put to shame."

1 Cor 5:6–8 (§88)
⁶Your boasting is not good. Do you not know that a little leaven leavens the whole lump? ⁷Cleanse out the old leaven that you may be a new lump, as you really are unleavened. For Christ, our paschal lamb, has been sacrificed. ⁸Let us, therefore, celebrate the festival, not with the old leaven, the leaven of malice and evil, but with the unleavened bread of sincerity and truth.

1 Cor 7:17–24 (§97)
¹⁷Only, let every one lead the life which the Lord has assigned to him, and in which God has called him. This is my rule in all the churches. ¹⁸Was any one at the time of his call already circumcised? Let him not seek to remove the marks of circumcision. Was any one at the time of his call uncircumcised? Let him not seek circumcision. ¹⁹For neither circumcision counts for anything nor uncircumcision, but keeping the commandments of God. ²⁰Every one should remain in the state in which he was called. ²¹Were you a slave when called? Never mind. But if you can gain your freedom, avail yourself of the opportunity. ²²For he who was called in the Lord as a slave is a freedman of the Lord. Likewise he who was free when called is a slave of Christ. ²³You were bought with a price; do not become slaves of men. ²⁴So, brethren, in whatever state each was called, there let him remain with God.

● **Gal 5:2**
Gal 6   ¹⁵For neither circumcision counts for anything, nor uncircumcision, but a new creation.

Acts 15   ¹But some men came down from Judea and were teaching the brethren, "Unless you are circumcised according to the custom of Moses, you cannot be saved." ²And when Paul and Barnabas had no small dissension and debate with them, Paul and Barnabas and some of the others were appointed to go up to Jerusalem to the apostles and the elders about this question.

● **Gal 5:3**
Gal 3   ¹²but the law does not rest on faith, for "He who does them shall live by them."

Gal 5   ¹⁴For the whole law is fulfilled in one word, "You shall love your neighbor as yourself."

Gal 6   ¹³For even those who receive circumcision do not themselves keep the law, but they desire to have you circumcised that they may glory in your flesh.

● **Gal 5:5**
Rom 8   ²²We know that the whole creation has been groaning in travail together until now; ²³and not only the creation, but we ourselves, who have the first fruits of the Spirit, groan inwardly as we wait for adoption as sons, the redemption of our bodies. ²⁴For in this hope we were saved. Now hope that is seen is not hope. For who hopes for what he sees? ²⁵But if we hope for what we do not see, we wait for it with patience.

Rom 15   ¹³May the God of hope fill you with all joy and peace in believing, so that by the power of the Holy Spirit you may abound in hope.

● **Gal 5:6**
Rom 2   ¹⁶on that day when, according to my gospel, God judges the secrets of men by Christ Jesus.

Gal 6   ¹⁵For neither circumcision counts for anything, nor uncircumcision, but a new creation.

1 Tim 1   ⁵whereas the aim of our charge is love that issues from a pure heart and a good conscience and sincere faith.

● **Gal 5:10**
Gal 3   ¹O foolish Galatians! Who has bewitched you, before whose eyes Jesus Christ was publicly portrayed as crucified?

● **Gal 5:11**
1 Cor 1   ²²For Jews demand signs and Greeks seek wisdom, ²³but we preach Christ crucified, a stumbling block to Jews and folly to Gentiles, . . .

Cf. 1 Cor 4:11–13; 2 Cor 4:7–12; 2 Cor 6:1–10; 2 Cor 11:21–29

Gal 6   ¹²It is those who want to make a good showing in the flesh that would compel you to be circumcised, and only in order that they may not be persecuted for the cross of Christ.

● **Gal 5:12**
Phil 3   ²Look out for the dogs, look out for the evil-workers, look out for those who mutilate the flesh.

[13]For you were called to freedom, brethren; only do not use your freedom as an opportunity for the flesh, but through love be servants of one another. [14]For the whole law is fulfilled in one word, "You shall love your neighbor as yourself." [15]But if you bite and devour one another take heed that you are not consumed by one another.

PRIMARY

Rom 6:15–23 (§25)

[15]What then? Are we to sin because we are not under law but under grace? By no means! [16]Do you not know that if you yield yourselves to any one as obedient slaves, you are slaves of the one whom you obey, either of sin, which leads to death, or of obedience, which leads to righteousness? [17]But thanks be to God, that you who were once slaves of sin have become obedient from the heart to the standard of teaching to which you were committed, [18]and, having been set free from sin, have become slaves of righteousness. [19]I am speaking in human terms, because of your natural limitations. For just as you once yielded your members to impurity and to greater and greater iniquity, so now yield your members to righteousness for sanctification.

[20]When you were slaves of sin, you were free in regard to righteousness. [21]But then what return did you get from the things of which you are now ashamed? The end of those things is death. [22]But now that you have been set free from sin and have become slaves of God, the return you get is sanctification and its end, eternal life. [23]For the wages of sin is death, but the free gift of God is eternal life in Christ Jesus our Lord.

Rom 13:8–10 (§55)

[8]Owe no one anything, except to love one another; for he who loves his neighbor has fulfilled the law. [9]The commandments, "You shall not commit adultery, You shall not kill, You shall not steal, You shall not covet," and any other commandment, are summed up in this sentence, "You shall love your neighbor as yourself." [10]Love does no wrong to a neighbor; therefore love is the fulfilling of the law.

Rom 13:11–14 (§56)

[11]Besides this you know what hour it is, how it is full time now for you to wake from sleep. For salvation is nearer to us now than when we first believed; [12]the night is far gone, the day is at hand. Let us then cast off the works of darkness and put on the armor of light; [13]let us conduct ourselves becomingly as in the day, not in reveling and drunkenness, not in debauchery and licentiousness, not in quarreling and jealousy. [14]But put on the Lord Jesus Christ, and make no provision for the flesh, to gratify its desires.

1 Cor 9:19–23 (§107)

[19]For though I am free from all men, I have made myself a slave to all, that I might win the more. [20]To the Jews I became as a Jew, in order to win Jews; to those under the law I became as one under the law—though not being myself under the law—that I might win those under the law. [21]To those outside the law I became as one outside the law—not being without law

toward God but under the law of Christ—that I might win those outside the law. [22]To the weak I became weak, that I might win the weak. I have become all things to all men, that I might by all means save some. [23]I do it all for the sake of the gospel, that I may share in its blessings.

1 Cor 16:13–14 (§141)

[13]Be watchful, stand firm in your faith, be courageous, be strong. [14]Let all that you do be done in love.

1 Thess 5:1–11 (§287)

[1]But as to the times and the seasons, brethren, you have no need to have anything written to you. [2]For you yourselves know well that the day of the Lord will come like a thief in the night. [3]When people say, "There is peace and security," then sudden destruction will come upon them as travail comes upon a woman with child, and there will be no escape. [4]But you are not in darkness, brethren, for that day to surprise you like a thief. [5]For you are all sons of light and sons of the day; we are not of the night or of darkness. [6]So then let us not sleep, as others do, but let us keep awake and be sober. [7]For those who sleep sleep at night, and those who get drunk are drunk at night. [8]But, since we belong to the day, let us be sober, and put on the breastplate of faith and love, and for a helmet the hope of salvation. [9]For God has not destined us for wrath, but to obtain salvation through our Lord Jesus Christ, [10]who died for us so that whether we wake or sleep we might live with him. [11]Therefore encourage one another and build one another up, just as you are doing.

● **Gal 5:13**
Gal 5 [1]For freedom Christ has set us free; stand fast therefore, and do not submit again to a yoke of slavery.

● **Gal 5:14**
Rom 3   [31]Do we then overthrow the law by this faith? By no means! On the contrary, we uphold the law.

Rom 10   [4]For Christ is the end of the law, that every one who has faith may be justified.

Gal 5   [3]I testify again to every man who receives circumcision that he is bound to keep the whole law.

Lev 19   [18]You shall not take vengeance or bear any grudge against the sons of your own people, but you shall love your neighbor as yourself: I am the Lord.

FORMAL ELEMENT:
VICE & VIRTUE LIST

[16]But I say, walk by the Spirit, and do not gratify the desires of the flesh. [17]For the desires of the flesh are against the Spirit, and the desires of the Spirit are against the flesh; for these are opposed to each other, to prevent you from doing what you would. [18]But if you are led by the Spirit you are not under the law. [19]Now the works of the flesh are plain: fornication, impurity, licentiousness, [20]idolatry, sorcery, enmity, strife, jealousy, anger, selfishness, dissension, party spirit, [21]envy, drunkenness, carousing, and the like. I warn you, as I warned you before, that those who do such things shall not inherit the kingdom of God. [22]But the fruit of the Spirit is love, joy, peace, patience, kindness, goodness, faithfulness, [23]gentleness, self-control; against such there is no law. [24]And those who belong to Christ Jesus have crucified the flesh with its passions and desires. [25]If we live by the Spirit, let us also walk by the Spirit. [26]Let us have no self-conceit, no provoking of one another, no envy of one another.

PRIMARY

See §6 for VICE LIST

2 Cor 6:1–10 (§165)

[1]Working together with him, then, we entreat you not to accept the grace of God in vain. [2]For he says,

"At the acceptable time I have listened to you,

and helped you on the day of salvation."
Behold, now is the acceptable time; behold, now is the day of salvation. [3]We put no obstacle in any one's way, so that no fault may be found with our ministry, [4]but as servants of God we commend ourselves in every way: through great endurance, in afflictions, hardships, calamities, [5]beatings, imprisonments, tumults, labors, watching, hunger; [6]by purity, knowledge, forbearance, kindness, the Holy Spirit, genuine love, [7]truthful speech, and the power of God; with the weapons of righteousness for the right hand and for the left; [8]in honor and dishonor, in ill repute and good repute. We are treated as impostors, and yet are true; [9]as unknown, and yet well known; as dying, and behold we live; as punished, and yet not killed; [10]as sorrowful, yet always rejoicing; as poor, yet making many rich; as having nothing, and yet possessing everything.

2 Cor 8:1–7 (§171)

[1]We want you to know, brethren, about the grace of God which has been shown in the churches of Macedonia, [2]for in a severe test of affliction, their abundance of joy and their extreme poverty have overflowed in a wealth of liberality on their part. [3]For they gave according to their means, as I can testify, and beyond their means, of their own free will, [4]begging us earnestly for the favor of taking part in the relief of the saints— [5]and this, not as we expected, but first they gave themselves to the Lord and to us by the will of God. [6]Accordingly we have urged Titus that as he had already made a beginning, he should also complete among you this gracious work. [7]Now as you excel in everything—in faith, in utterance, in knowledge, in all earnestness, and in your love for us—see that you excel in this gracious work also.

Eph 4:1–10 (§225)

[1]I therefore, a prisoner for the Lord, beg you to lead a life worthy of the calling to which you have been called, [2]with all lowliness and meekness, with patience, forbearing one another in love, [3]eager to maintain the unity of the Spirit in the bond of peace. [4]There is one body and one Spirit, just as you were called to the one hope that belongs to your call, [5]one Lord, one faith, one baptism, [6]one God and Father of us all, who is above all and through all and in all. [7]But grace was given to each of us according to the measure of Christ's gift. [8]Therefore it is said,

"When he ascended on high he led a host of captives,

and he gave gifts to men."
[9](In saying, "He ascended," what does it mean but that he had also descended into the lower parts of the earth? [10]He who descended is he who also ascended far above all the heavens, that he might fill all things.)

Phil 4:8–9 (§252)

[8]Finally, brethren, whatever is true, whatever is honorable, whatever is just, whatever is pure, whatever is lovely, whatever is gracious, if there is any excellence, if there is anything worthy of praise, think about these things. [9]What you have learned and received and heard and seen in me, do; and the God of peace will be with you.

Col 3:12–17 (§267)

[12]Put on then, as God's chosen ones, holy and beloved, compassion, kindness, lowliness, meekness, and patience, [13]forbearing one another and, if one has a complaint against another, forgiving each other; as the Lord has forgiven you, so you also must forgive. [14]And above all these put on love, which binds everything together in perfect harmony. [15]And let the peace of Christ rule in your hearts, to which indeed you were called in the one body. And be thankful. [16]Let the word of Christ dwell in you richly, as you teach and admonish one another in all wisdom, and as you sing psalms and hymns and spiritual songs with thankfulness in your hearts to God. [17]And whatever you do, in word or deed, do everything in the name of the Lord Jesus, giving thanks to God the Father through him.

SECONDARY

1 Thess 4:1–8 (§284)

[1]Finally, brethren, we beseech and exhort you in the Lord Jesus, that as you learned from us how you ought to live and to please God, just as you are doing, you do so more and more. [2]For you know what instructions we gave you through the Lord Jesus. [3]For this is the will of God, your sanctification: that you abstain from unchastity; [4]that each one of you know how to take a wife for himself in holiness and honor, [5]not in the passion of lust like heathen who do not know God; [6]that no man transgress, and wrong his brother in this matter, because the Lord is an avenger in all these things, as we solemnly forewarned you. [7]For God has not called us for uncleanness, but in holiness. [8]Therefore whoever disregards this, disregards not man but God, who gives his Holy Spirit to you.

● **Gal 5:16–17**
See Gal 3:1–5, Rom 7:14–25

● **Gal 5:18**
1 Tim 1   [9]understanding this, that the law is not laid down for the just but for the lawless and disobedient, for the ungodly and sinners, for the unholy and profane, for murderers of fathers and murderers of mothers, for manslayers, [10]immoral persons, sodomites, kidnappers, liars, perjurers, and whatever else is contrary to sound doctrine, . . .

Cf. Rom 8:1–8

● **Gal 5:19–21**
1 Tim 6   [4]he is puffed up with conceit, he knows nothing; he has a morbid craving for controversy and for disputes about words, which produce envy, dissension, slander, base suspicions, [5]and wrangling among men who are depraved in mind and bereft of the truth, imagining that godliness is a means of gain. [6]There is great gain in godliness with contentment; . . .

2 Tim 3   [2]For men will be lovers of self, lovers of money, proud, arrogant, abusive, disobedient to their parents, ungrateful, unholy, [3]inhuman, implacable, slanderers, profligates, fierce, haters of good, [4]treacherous, reckless, swollen with conceit, lovers of pleasure rather than lovers of God, . . .

Titus 3   [3]For we ourselves were once foolish, disobedient, led astray, slaves to various passions and pleasures, passing our days in malice and envy, hated by men and hating one another; . . .

● **Gal 5:21**
(envy) *add* murder: ACD G Koine Lect it vg syr cop(bo) Ambrosiaster

● **Gal 5:23**
See 1 Cor 7:9

Acts 24   [25]And as he argued about justice and self-control and future judgment, Felix was alarmed and said, "Go away for the present; when I have an opportunity I will summon you."

● **Gal 5:24**
See Gal 2:20

● **Gal 5:26**
Cf. 1 Cor 3:1–4

6 Brethren, if a man is overtaken in any trespass, you who are spiritual should restore him in a spirit of gentleness. Look to yourself, lest you too be tempted. [2] Bear one another's burdens, and so fulfil the law of Christ. [3] For if any one thinks he is something, when he is nothing, he deceives himself. [4] But let each one test his own work, and then his reason to boast will be in himself alone and not in his neighbor. [5] For each man will have to bear his own load.

[6] Let him who is taught the word share all good things with him who teaches.

PRIMARY

Rom 15:1-6 (§60)

[1] We who are strong ought to bear with the failings of the weak, and not to please ourselves; [2] let each of us please his neighbor for his good, to edify him. [3] For Christ did not please himself; but, as it is written, "The reproaches of those who reproached thee fell on me." [4] For whatever was written in former days was written for our instruction, that by steadfastness and by the encouragement of the scriptures we might have hope. [5] May the God of steadfastness and encouragement grant you to live in such harmony with one another, in accord with Christ Jesus, [6] that together you may with one voice glorify the God and Father of our Lord Jesus Christ.

1 Cor 2:6-16 (§77)

[6] Yet among the mature we do impart wisdom, although it is not a wisdom of this age or of the rulers of this age, who are doomed to pass away. [7] But we impart a secret and hidden wisdom of God, which God decreed before the ages for our glorification. [8] None of the rulers of this age understood this; for if they had, they would not have crucified the Lord of glory.

[9] But, as it is written,

"What no eye has seen, nor ear heard,
nor the heart of man conceived,

what God has prepared for those who love him," [10] God has revealed to us through the Spirit. For the Spirit searches everything, even the depths of God. [11] For what person knows a man's thoughts except the spirit of the man which is in him? So also no one comprehends the thoughts of God except the Spirit of God. [12] Now we have received not the spirit of the world, but the Spirit which is from God, that we might understand the gifts bestowed on us by God. [13] And we impart this in words not taught by human wisdom but taught by the Spirit, interpreting spiritual truths to those who possess the Spirit.

[14] The unspiritual man does not receive the gifts of the Spirit of God, for they are folly to him, and he is not able to understand them because they are spiritually discerned. [15] The spiritual man judges all things, but is himself to be judged by no one. [16] "For who has known the mind of the Lord so as to instruct him?" But we have the mind of Christ.

1 Cor 4:6-7 (§84)

[6] I have applied all this to myself and Apollos for your benefit, brethren, that you may learn by us not to go beyond what is written, that none of you may be puffed up in favor of one against another. [7] For who sees anything different in you? What have you that you did not receive? If then you received it, why do you boast as if it were not a gift?

1 Cor 9:1-14 (§105)

[1] Am I not free? Am I not an apostle? Have I not seen Jesus our Lord? Are not you my workmanship in the Lord? [2] If to others I am not an apostle, at least I am to you; for you are the seal of my apostleship in the Lord.

[3] This is my defense to those who would examine me. [4] Do we not have the right to our food and drink? [5] Do we not have the right to be accompanied by a wife, as the other apostles and the brothers of the Lord and Cephas? [6] Or is it only Barnabas and I who have no right to refrain from working for a living? [7] Who serves as a soldier at his own expense? Who plants a vineyard without eating any of its fruit? Who tends a flock without getting some of the milk?

[8] Do I say this on human authority? Does not the law say the same? [9] For it is written in the law of Moses, "You shall not muzzle an ox when it is treading out the grain." Is it for oxen that God is concerned? [10] Does he not speak entirely for our sake? It was written for our sake, because the plowman should plow in hope and the thresher thresh in hope of a share in the crop. [11] If we have sown spiritual good among you, is it too much if we reap your material benefits? [12] If others share this rightful claim upon you, do not we still more?

Nevertheless, we have not made use of this right, but we endure anything rather than put an obstacle in the way of the gospel of Christ. [13] Do you not know that those who are employed in the temple service get their food from the temple, and those who serve at the altar share in the sacrificial offerings? [14] In the same way, the Lord commanded that those who proclaim the gospel should get their living by the gospel.

2 Cor 2:5-11 (§151)

[5] But if any one has caused pain, he has caused it not to me, but in some measure—not to put it too severely— to you all. [6] For such a one this punishment by the majority is enough; [7] so you should rather turn to forgive and comfort him, or he may be overwhelmed by excessive sorrow. [8] So I beg you to reaffirm your love for him. [9] For this is why I wrote, that I might

---

● **Gal 6:1**

1 Cor 4　[21] What do you wish? Shall I come to you with a rod, or with love in a spirit of gentleness?

1 Thess 2　[7] But we were gentle among you, like a nurse taking care of her children.

● **Gal 6:2**

1 Cor 9　[21] To those outside the law I became as one outside the law—not being without law toward God but under the law of Christ —that I might win those outside the law.

2 Cor 8　[13] I do not mean that others should be eased and you burdened, [14] but that as a matter of equality your abundance at the present time should supply their want, so that their abundance may supply your want, that there may be equality.

test you and know whether you are obedient in everything. [10]Any one whom you forgive, I also forgive. What I have forgiven, if I have forgiven anything, has been for your sake in the presence of Christ, [11]to keep Satan from gaining the advantage over us; for we are not ignorant of his designs.

2 Cor 8:8–15 (§172)

[8]I say this not as a command, but to prove by the earnestness of others that your love also is genuine. [9]For you know the grace of our Lord Jesus Christ, that though he was rich, yet for your sake he became poor, so that by his poverty you might become rich. [10]And in this matter I give my advice: it is best for you now to complete what a year ago you began not only to do but to desire, [11]so that your readiness in desiring it may be matched by your completing it out of what you have. [12]For if the readiness is there, it is acceptable according to what a man has, not according to what he has not. [13]I do not mean that others should be eased and you burdened, [14]but that as a matter of equality your abundance at the present time should supply their want, so that their abundance may supply your want, that there may be equality. [15]As it is written, "He who gathered much had nothing over, and he who gathered little had no lack."

Eph 4:25–32 (§228)

[25]Therefore, putting away falsehood, let every one speak the truth with his neighbor, for we are members one of another. [26]Be angry but do not sin; do not let the sun go down on your anger, [27]and give no opportunity to the devil. [28]Let the thief no longer steal, but rather let him labor, doing honest work with his hands, so that he may be able to give to those in need. [29]Let no evil talk come out of your mouths, but only such as is good for edifying, as fits the occasion, that it may impart grace to those who hear. [30]And do not grieve the Holy Spirit of God, in whom you were sealed for the day of redemption. [31]Let all bitterness and wrath and anger and clamor and slander be put away from you, with all malice, [32]and be kind to one another, tenderhearted, forgiving one another, as God in Christ forgave you.

Phil 4:1–3 (§250)

[1]Therefore, my brethren, whom I love and long for, my joy and crown, stand firm thus in the Lord, my beloved.

[2]I entreat Euodia and I entreat Syntyche to agree in the Lord. [3]And I ask you also, true yokefellow, help these women, for they have labored side by side with me in the gospel together with Clement and the rest of my fellow workers, whose names are in the book of life.

1 Thess 5:12–22 (§288)

[12]But we beseech you, brethren, to respect those who labor among you and are over you in the Lord and admonish you, [13]and to esteem them very highly in love because of their work. Be at peace among yourselves. [14]And we exhort you, brethren, admonish the idle, encourage the fainthearted, help the weak, be patient with them all. [15]See that none of you repays evil for evil, but always seek to do good to one another and to all. [16]Rejoice always, [17]pray constantly, [18]give thanks in all circumstances; for this is the will of God in Christ Jesus for you. [19]Do not quench the Spirit, [20]do not despise prophesying, [21]but test everything; hold fast what is good, [22]abstain from every form of evil.

2 Thess 3:6–13 (§300)

[6]Now we command you, brethren, in the name of our Lord Jesus Christ, that you keep away from any brother who is living in idleness and not in accord with the tradition that you received from us. [7]For you yourselves know how you ought to imitate us; we were not idle when we were with you, [8]we did not eat any one's bread without paying, but with toil and labor we worked night and day, that we might not burden any of you. [9]It was not because we have not that right, but to give you in our conduct an example to imitate. [10]For even when we were with you, we gave you this command: If any one will not work, let him not eat. [11]For we hear that some of you are living in idleness, mere busybodies, not doing any work. [12]Now such persons we command and exhort in the Lord Jesus Christ to do their work in quietness and to earn their own living. [13]Brethren, do not be weary in well-doing.

2 Thess 3:14–15 (§301)

[14]If any one refuses to obey what we say in this letter, note that man, and have nothing to do with him, that he may be ashamed. [15]Do not look on him as an enemy, but warn him as a brother.

Phlm 15–20 (§308)

[15]Perhaps this is why he was parted from you for a while, that you might have him back for ever, [16]no longer as a slave but more than a slave, as a beloved brother, especially to me but how much more to you, both in the flesh and in the Lord. [17]So if you consider me your partner, receive him as you would receive me. [18]If he has wronged you at all, or owes you anything, charge that to my account. [19]I, Paul, write this with my own hand, I will repay it—to say nothing of your owing me even your own self. [20]Yes, brother, I want some benefit from you in the Lord. Refresh my heart in Christ.

● **Gal 6:3**
1 Cor 8   [2]If any one imagines that he knows something, he does not yet know as he ought to know.

● **Gal 6:4**
2 Cor 13   [5]Examine yourselves, to see whether you are holding to your faith. Test yourselves. Do you not realize that Jesus Christ is in you?—unless indeed you fail to meet the test!

● **Gal 6:5**
Rom 14   [12]So each of us shall give account of himself to God.

● **Gal 6:6**
Rom 15   [27]they were pleased to do it, and indeed they are in debt to them, for if the Gentiles have come to share in their spiritual blessings, they ought also to be of service to them in material blessings.

⁷Do not be deceived; God is not mocked, for whatever a man sows, that he will also reap. ⁸For he who sows to his own flesh will from the flesh reap corruption; but he who sows to the Spirit will from the Spirit reap eternal life. ⁹And let us not grow weary in well-doing, for in due season we shall reap, if we do not lose heart. ¹⁰So then, as we have opportunity, let us do good to all men, and especially to those who are of the household of faith.

PRIMARY

Rom 6:15–23 (§25)

¹⁵What then? Are we to sin because we are not under law but under grace? By no means! ¹⁶Do you not know that if you yield yourselves to any one as obedient slaves, you are slaves of the one whom you obey, either of sin, which leads to death, or of obedience, which leads to righteousness? ¹⁷But thanks be to God, that you who were once slaves of sin have become obedient from the heart to the standard of teaching to which you were committed, ¹⁸and, having been set free from sin, have become slaves of righteousness. ¹⁹I am speaking in human terms, because of your natural limitations. For just as you once yielded your members to impurity and to greater and greater iniquity, so now yield your members to righteousness for sanctification. ²⁰When you were slaves of sin, you were free in regard to righteousness. ²¹But then what return did you get from the things of which you are now ashamed? The end of those things is death. ²²But now that you have been set free from sin and have become slaves of God, the return you get is sanctification and its end, eternal life. ²³For the wages of sin is death, but the free gift of God is eternal life in Christ Jesus our Lord.

Rom 8:9–17 (§30)

⁹But you are not in the flesh, you are in the Spirit, if in fact the Spirit of God dwells in you. Any one who does not have the Spirit of Christ does not belong to him. ¹⁰But if Christ is in you, although your bodies are dead because of sin, your spirits are alive because of righteousness. ¹¹If the Spirit of him who raised Jesus from the dead dwells in you, he who raised Christ Jesus from the dead will give life to your mortal bodies also through his Spirit which dwells in you. ¹²So then, brethren, we are debtors, not to the flesh, to live according to the flesh—¹³for if you live according to the flesh you will die, but if by the Spirit you put to death the deeds of the body you will live. ¹⁴For all who are led by the Spirit of God are sons of God. ¹⁵For you did not receive the spirit of slavery to fall back into fear, but you have received the spirit of sonship. When we cry, "Abba! Father!" ¹⁶it is the Spirit himself bearing witness with our spirit that we are children of God, ¹⁷and if children, then heirs, heirs of God and fellow heirs with Christ, provided we suffer with him in order that we may also be glorified with him.

1 Cor 15:42–50 (§136)

⁴²So is it with the resurrection of the dead. What is sown is perishable, what is raised is imperishable. ⁴³It is sown in dishonor, it is raised in glory. It is sown in weakness, it is raised in power. ⁴⁴It is sown a physical body, it is raised a spiritual body. If there is a physical body, there is also a spiritual body. ⁴⁵Thus it is written, "The first man Adam became a living being"; the last Adam became a life-giving spirit. ⁴⁶But it is not the spiritual which is first but the physical, and then the spiritual. ⁴⁷The first man was from the earth, a man of dust; the second man is from heaven. ⁴⁸As was the man of dust, so are those who are of the dust; and as is the man of heaven, so are those who are of heaven. ⁴⁹Just as we have borne the image of the man of dust, we shall also bear the image of the man of heaven. ⁵⁰I tell you this, brethren: flesh and blood cannot inherit the kingdom of God, nor does the perishable inherit the imperishable.

2 Thess 3:6–13 (§300)

⁶Now we command you, brethren, in the name of our Lord Jesus Christ, that you keep away from any brother who is living in idleness and not in accord with the tradition that you received from us. ⁷For you yourselves know how you ought to imitate us; we were not idle when we were with you, ⁸we did not eat any one's bread without paying, but with toil and labor we worked night and day, that we might not burden any of you. ⁹It was not because we have not that right, but to give you in our conduct an example to imitate. ¹⁰For even when we were with you, we gave you this command: If any one will not work, let him not eat. ¹¹For we hear that some of you are living in idleness, mere busybodies, not doing any work. ¹²Now such persons we command and exhort in the Lord Jesus Christ to do their work in quietness and to earn their own living. ¹³Brethren, do not be weary in well-doing.

● **Gal 6:7**
1 Cor 9   ¹¹If we have sown spiritual good among you, is it too much if we reap your material benefits?

2 Cor 9   ⁶The point is this: he who sows sparingly will also reap sparingly, and he who sows bountifully will also reap bountifully.

● **Gal 6:8**
Rom 8   ⁶To set the mind on the flesh is death, but to set the mind on the Spirit is life and peace.

● **Gal 6:9**
Rom 2   ⁶For he will render to every man according to his works: . . .

Heb 12   ³Consider him who endured from sinners such hostility against himself, so that you may not grow weary or fainthearted.

● **Gal 6:10**
Rom 12   ¹⁸If possible, so far as it depends upon you, live peaceably with all.

FORMAL ELEMENT: SIGNATURE DEVICE

11 See with what large letters I am writing to you with my own hand. **12** It is those who want to make a good showing in the flesh that would compel you to be circumcised, and only in order that they may not be persecuted for the cross of Christ. **13** For even those who receive circumcision do not themselves keep the law, but they desire to have you circumcised that they may glory in your flesh. **14** But far be it from me to glory except in the cross of our Lord Jesus Christ, by which the world has been crucified to me, and I to the world. **15** For neither circumcision counts for anything, nor uncircumcision, but a new creation. **16** Peace and mercy be upon all who walk by this rule, upon the Israel of God.

17 Henceforth let no man trouble me; for I bear on my body the marks of Jesus.

PRIMARY

1 Cor 16:21–22 (§144)
21 I, Paul, write this greeting with my own hand. **22** If any one has no love for the Lord, let him be accursed. Our Lord, come!

Col 4:16–18a (§273)
16 And when this letter has been read among you, have it read also in the church of the Laodiceans; and see that you read also the letter from Laodicea. **17** And say to Archippus, "See that you fulfil the ministry which you have received in the Lord."

18 I, Paul, write this greeting with my own hand. Remember my fetters.

2 Thess 3:17 (§303)
17 I, Paul, write this greeting with my own hand. This is the mark in every letter of mine; it is the way I write.

SECONDARY

Rom 2:25–29 (§11)
25 Circumcision indeed is of value if you obey the law; but if you break the law, your circumcision becomes uncircumcision. **26** So, if a man who is uncircumcised keeps the precepts of the law, will not his uncircumcision be regarded as circumcision? **27** Then those who are physically uncircumcised but keep the law will condemn you who have the written code and circumcision but break the law. **28** For he is not a real Jew who is one outwardly, nor is true circumcision something external and physical. **29** He is a Jew who is one inwardly, and real circumcision is a matter of the heart, spiritual and not literal. His praise is not from men but from God.

1 Cor 7:17–24 (§97)
17 Only, let every one lead the life which the Lord has assigned to him, and in which God has called him. This is my rule in all the churches. **18** Was any one at the time of his call already circumcised? Let him not seek to remove the marks of circumcision. Was any one at the time of his call uncircumcised? Let him not seek circumcision. **19** For neither circumcision counts for anything nor uncircumcision, but keeping the commandments of God. **20** Every one should remain in the state in which he was called. **21** Were you a slave when called? Never mind. But if you can gain your freedom, avail yourself of the opportunity. **22** For he who was called in the Lord as a slave is a freedman of the Lord. Likewise he who was free when called is a slave of Christ. **23** You were bought with a price; do not become slaves of men. **24** So, brethren, in whatever state each was called, there let him remain with God.

1 Thess 2:1–8 (§277)
1 For you yourselves know, brethren, that our visit to you was not in vain; **2** but though we had already suffered and been shamefully treated at Philippi, as you know, we had courage in our God to declare to you the gospel of God in the face of great opposition. **3** For our appeal does not spring from error or uncleanness, nor is it made with guile; **4** but just as we have been approved by God to be entrusted with the gospel, so we speak, not to please men, but to please God who tests our hearts. **5** For we never used either words of flattery, as you know, or a cloak for greed, as God is witness; **6** nor did we seek glory from men, whether from you or from others, though we might have made demands as apostles of Christ. **7** But we were gentle among you, like a nurse taking care of her children. **8** So, being affectionately desirous of you, we were ready to share with you not only the gospel of God but also our own selves, because you had become very dear to us.

● **Gal 6:11**
Rom 16   **22** I Tertius, the writer of this letter, greet you in the Lord.

● **Gal :12–15**
Cf. Phlm 14

● **Gal 6:12–13**
Gal 4   **17** They make much of you, but for no good purpose; they want to shut you out, that you may make much of them.

Cf. Phil 1:17

● **Gal 6:12**
Gal 5   **11** But if I, brethren, still preach circumcision, why am I still persecuted? In that case the stumbling block of the cross has been removed.

Acts 15   **1** But some men came down from Judea and were teaching the brethren, "Unless you are circumcised according to the custom of Moses, you cannot be saved." **2** And when Paul and Barnabas had no small dissension and debate with them, Paul and Barnabas and some of the others were appointed to go up to Jerusalem to the apostles and the elders about this question.

● **Gal 6:13**
Gal 5   **3** I testify again to every man who receives circumcision that he is bound to keep the whole law.

Cf. Rom 2:17–24

Phil 3   **6** as to zeal a persecutor of the church, as to righteousness under the law blameless.

● **Gal 6:14**
Rom 3   **27** Then what becomes of our boasting? It is excluded. On what principle? On the principle of works? No, but on the principle of faith. **28** For we hold that a man is justified by faith apart from works of law. **29** Or is God the God of Jews only? Is he not the God of Gentiles also? Yes, of Gentiles also, **30** since God is one; and he will justify the circumcised on the ground of their faith and the uncircumcised through their faith. **31** Do we then overthrow the law by this faith? By no means! On the contrary, we uphold the law.

1 Cor 1   **26** For consider your call, brethren; not many of you were wise according to worldly standards, not many were powerful, not many were of noble birth; **27** but God chose what is foolish in the world to shame the wise, God chose what is weak in the world to shame the strong, **28** God chose what is low and despised in the world, even things that are not, to bring to nothing things that are, **29** so that no human being might boast in the presence of God. **30** He is the source of your life in Christ Jesus, whom God made our wisdom, our righteousness and sanctification and redemption; **31** therefore, as it is written, "Let him who boasts, boast of the Lord."

2 Cor 10   **13** But we will not boast beyond limit, but will keep to the limits God has apportioned us, to reach even to you. **14** For we are not overextending ourselves, as though we did not reach you; we were the first to come all the way to you with the gospel of Christ. **15** We do not boast beyond limit, in other men's labors; but our hope is that as your faith increases, our field among you may be greatly enlarged, **16** so that we may preach the gospel in lands beyond you, without boasting of work already done in another's field.

17 "Let him who boasts, boast of the Lord." **18** For it is not the man who commends himself that is accepted, but the man whom the Lord commends.

Gal 2   **20** I have been crucified with Christ; it is no longer I who live, but Christ who lives in me; and the life I now live in the flesh I live by faith in the Son of God, who loved me and gave himself for me.

Cf. Rom 15:18–19; 1 Cor 2:2; 2 Cor 4:4; Col 2:20

● **Gal 6:15**
2 Cor 5   **17** Therefore, if any one is in Christ, he is a new creation; the old has passed away, behold, the new has come.

Gal 5   **2** Now I, Paul, say to you that if you receive circumcision, Christ will be of no advantage to you.

Gal 5   **6** For in Christ Jesus neither circumcision nor uncircumcision is of any avail, but faith working through love.

● **Gal 6:17**
2 Cor 4   **10** always carrying in the body the death of Jesus, so that the life of Jesus may also be manifested in our bodies.

Col 1   **24** Now I rejoice in my sufferings for your sake, and in my flesh I complete what is lacking in Christ's afflictions for the sake of his body, that is, the church, . . .

LETTER STRUCTURE: CLOSING GRACE

[18]**The grace of our Lord Jesus Christ be with your spirit, brethren. Amen.**

PRIMARY

Rom 16:20b (§68)

The grace of our Lord Jesus Christ be with you.

1 Cor 16:23–24 (§145)

[23]The grace of the Lord Jesus be with you. [24]My love be with you all in Christ Jesus. Amen.

2 Cor 13:14 (§192)

[14]The grace of the Lord Jesus Christ and the love of God and the fellowship of the Holy Spirit be with you all.

Eph 6:23–24 (§236)

[23]Peace be to the brethren, and love with faith, from God the Father and the Lord Jesus Christ. [24]Grace be with all who love our Lord Jesus Christ with love undying.

Phil 4:23 (§255)

[23]The grace of the Lord Jesus Christ be with your spirit.

Col 4:18b (§274)

Grace be with you.

1 Thess 5:28 (§293)

[28]The grace of our Lord Jesus Christ be with you.

2 Thess 3:18 (§304)

[18]The grace of our Lord Jesus Christ be with you all.

Phlm 25 (§311)

[25]The grace of the Lord Jesus Christ be with your spirit.

● **Gal 6:18**
1 Tim 6   [21]. . . Grace be with you.

2 Tim 4   [22]The Lord be with your spirit. Grace be with you.

Titus 3   [15]. . . Grace be with you all.

LETTER STRUCTURE: SALUTATION

1 Paul, an apostle of Christ Jesus by the will of God,

To the saints who are also faithful in Christ Jesus:

[2]Grace to you and peace from God our Father and the Lord Jesus Christ.

PRIMARY

Rom 1:1–7 (§1)

[1]Paul, a servant of Jesus Christ, called to be an apostle, set apart for the gospel of God [2]which he promised beforehand through his prophets in the holy scriptures, [3]the gospel concerning his Son, who was descended from David according to the flesh [4]and designated Son of God in power according to the Spirit of holiness by his resurrection from the dead, Jesus Christ our Lord, [5]through whom we have received grace and apostleship to bring about the obedience of faith for the sake of his name among all the nations, [6]including yourselves who are called to belong to Jesus Christ;

[7]To all God's beloved in Rome, who are called to be saints:

Grace to you and peace from God our Father and the Lord Jesus Christ.

1 Cor 1:1–3 (§71)

[1]Paul, called by the will of God to be an apostle of Christ Jesus, and our brother Sosthenes,

[2]To the church of God which is at Corinth, to those sanctified in Christ Jesus, called to be saints together with all those who in every place call on the name of our Lord Jesus Christ, both their Lord and ours:

[3]Grace to you and peace from God our Father and the Lord Jesus Christ.

2 Cor 1:1–2 (§146)

[1]Paul, an apostle of Christ Jesus by the will of God, and Timothy our brother.

To the church of God which is at Corinth, with all the saints who are in the whole of Achaia:

[2]Grace to you and peace from God our Father and the Lord Jesus Christ.

Gal 1:1–5 (§193)

[1]Paul an apostle—not from men nor through man, but through Jesus Christ and God the Father, who raised him from the dead— [2]and all the brethren who are with me,

To the churches of Galatia:

[3]Grace to you and peace from God the Father and our Lord Jesus Christ, [4]who gave himself for our sins to deliver us from the present evil age, according to the will of our God and Father; [5]to whom be the glory for ever and ever. Amen.

Phil 1:1–2 (§237)

[1]Paul and Timothy, servants of Christ Jesus,

To all the saints in Christ Jesus who are at Philippi, with the bishops and deacons:

[2]Grace to you and peace from God our Father and the Lord Jesus Christ.

Col 1:1–2 (§256)

[1]Paul, an apostle of Christ Jesus by the will of God, and Timothy our brother,

[2]To the saints and faithful brethren in Christ at Colossae:

Grace to you and peace from God our Father.

1 Thess 1:1 (§275)

[1]Paul, Silvanus, and Timothy,

To the church of the Thessalonians in God the Father and the Lord Jesus Christ:

Grace to you and peace.

2 Thess 1:1–2 (§294)

[1]Paul, Silvanus, and Timothy,

To the church of the Thessalonians in God our Father and the Lord Jesus Christ:

[2]Grace to you and peace from God the Father and the Lord Jesus Christ.

Phlm 1–3 (§305)

[1]Paul, a prisoner for Christ Jesus, and Timothy our brother,

To Philemon our beloved fellow worker [2]and Apphia our sister and Archippus our fellow soldier, and the church in your house:

[3]Grace to you and peace from God our Father and the Lord Jesus Christ.

● **Eph 1:1–2**

1 Tim 1   [1]Paul, an apostle of Christ Jesus by command of God our Savior and of Christ Jesus our hope,

    [2]To Timothy, my true child in the faith:

    Grace, mercy, and peace from God the Father and Christ Jesus our Lord.

2 Tim 1   [1]Paul, an apostle of Christ Jesus by the will of God according to the promise of the life which is in Christ Jesus,

    [2]To Timothy, my beloved child:

    Grace, mercy, and peace from God the Father and Christ Jesus our Lord.

Titus 1   [1]Paul, a servant of God and an apostle of Jesus Christ, to further the faith of God's elect and their knowledge of the truth which accords with godliness, [2]in hope of eternal life which God, who never lies, promised ages ago [3]and at the proper time manifested in his word through the preaching with which I have been entrusted by command of God our Savior;

    [4]To Titus, my true child in a common faith:

Grace and peace from God the Father and Christ Jesus our Savior.

● **Eph 1:1**

Acts 18   [19]And they came to Ephesus, and he left them there; but he himself went into the synagogue and argued with the Jews.

(are) *add* at Ephesus: S^cAB^3 DG Koine Lect it vg syr cop Ambrosiaster; *text:* p^46S*B* Origen

LETTER STRUCTURE: BLESSING

[3]Blessed be the God and Father of our Lord Jesus Christ, who has blessed us in Christ with every spiritual blessing in the heavenly places, [4]even as he chose us in him before the foundation of the world, that we should be holy and blameless before him. [5]He destined us in love to be his sons through Jesus Christ, according to the purpose of his will, [6]to the praise of his glorious grace which he freely bestowed on us in the Beloved. [7]In him we have redemption through his blood, the forgiveness of our trespasses, according to the riches of his grace [8]which he lavished upon us. [9]For he has made known to us in all wisdom and insight the mystery of his will, according to his purpose which he set forth in Christ [10]as a plan for the fulness of time, to unite all things in him, things in heaven and things on earth.

[11]In him, according to the purpose of him who accomplishes all things according to the counsel of his will, [12]we who first hoped in Christ have been destined and appointed to live for the praise of his glory. [13]In him you also, who have heard the word of truth, the gospel of your salvation, and have believed in him, were sealed with the promised Holy Spirit, [14]which is the guarantee of our inheritance until we acquire possession of it, to the praise of his glory.

[15]For this reason, because I have heard of your faith in the Lord Jesus and your love toward all the saints, [16]I do not cease to give thanks for you, remembering you in my prayers, [17]that the God of our Lord Jesus Christ, the Father of glory, may give you a spirit of wisdom and of revelation in the knowledge of him, [18]having the eyes of your hearts enlightened, that you may know what is the hope to which he has called you, what are the riches of his glorious inheritance in the saints, [19]and what is the immeasurable greatness of his power in us who believe, according to the working of his great might [20]which he accomplished in Christ when he raised him from the dead and made him sit at his right hand in the heavenly places, [21]far above all rule and authority and power and dominion, and above every name that is named, not only in this age but also in that which is to come; [22]and he has put all things under his feet and has made him the head over all things for the church, [23]which is his body, the fulness of him who fills all in all.

PRIMARY

2 Cor 1:3–11 (§147)

[3]Blessed be the God and Father of our Lord Jesus Christ, the Father of mercies and God of all comfort, [4]who comforts us in all our affliction, so that we may be able to comfort those who are in any affliction, with the comfort with which we ourselves are comforted by God. [5]For as we share abundantly in Christ's sufferings, so through Christ we share abundantly in comfort too. [6]If we are afflicted, it is for your comfort and salvation; and if we are comforted, it is for your comfort, which you experience when you patiently endure the same sufferings that we suffer. [7]Our hope for you is unshaken; for we know that as you share in our sufferings, you will also share in our comfort.

[8]For we do not want you to be ignorant, brethren, of the affliction we experienced in Asia; for we were so utterly, unbearably crushed that we despaired of life itself. [9]Why, we felt that we had received the sentence of death; but that was to make us rely not on ourselves but on God who raises the dead; [10]he delivered us from so deadly a peril, and he will deliver us; on him we have set our hope that he will deliver us again. [11]You also must help us by prayer, so that many will give thanks on our behalf for the blessing granted us in answer to many prayers.

SECONDARY

Rom 8:28–30 (§33)

[28]We know that in everything God works for good with those who love him, who are called according to his purpose. [29]For those whom he foreknew he also predestined to be conformed to the image of his Son, in order that he might be the first-born among many brethren. [30]And those whom he predestined he also called; and those whom he called he also justified; and those whom he justified he also glorified.

● **Eph 1:3–23**
Cf. 1 Cor 15:20–28; 2 Cor 1:15–22; Phil 2:1–11; Col 1:15–20; 2 Thess 2:1–12

● **Eph 1:4**
Heb 4   [3]For we who have believed enter that rest, as he has said,
"As I swore in my wrath,
'They shall never enter my rest,'"
although his works were finished from the foundation of the world.

● **Eph 1:5**
Acts 13   [48]And when the Gentiles heard this, they were glad and glorified the word of God; and as many as were ordained to eternal life believed.

● **Eph 1:6–7**
Rom 3   [24]they are justified by his grace as a gift, through the redemption which is in Christ Jesus, [25]whom God put forward as an expiation by his blood, to be received by faith.

● **Eph 1:7**
Col 1   [14]in whom we have redemption, the forgiveness of sins.

Heb 9   [22]Indeed, under the law almost everything is purified with blood, and without the shedding of blood there is no forgiveness of sins.

Acts 2   [38]And Peter said to them, "Repent, and be baptized every one of you in the name of Jesus Christ for the forgiveness of your sins; and you shall receive the gift of the Holy Spirit."

Acts 20   [28]"Take heed to yourselves and to all the flock, in which the Holy Spirit has made you overseers, to care for the church of God which he obtained with the blood of his own Son."

● **Eph 1:10**
2 Cor 1   [20]For all the promises of God find their Yes in him. That is why we utter the Amen through him, to the glory of God.

Gal 4   [4]But when the time had fully come, God sent forth his Son, born of woman, born under the law, . . .

Titus 1   [3]and at the proper time manifested in his word through the preaching with which I have been entrusted by command of God our Savior; . . .

● **Eph 1:11**
Acts 2   [23]". . . this Jesus, delivered up according to the definite plan and foreknowledge of God, you crucified and killed by the hands of lawless men."

● **Eph 1:13–14**
Rom 4   [11]He received circumcision as a sign or seal of the righteousness which he had by faith while he was still uncircumcised. The purpose was to make him the father of all who believe without being circumcised and who thus have righteousness reckoned to them, . . .

2 Cor 1   [22]he has put his seal upon us and given us his Spirit in our hearts as a guarantee.

Rom 9:19–29 (§38)

[19] You will say to me then, "Why does he still find fault? For who can resist his will?" [20] But who are you, a man, to answer back to God? Will what is molded say to its molder, "Why have you made me thus?" [21] Has the potter no right over the clay, to make out of the same lump one vessel for beauty and another for menial use? [22] What if God, desiring to show his wrath and to make known his power, has endured with much patience the vessels of wrath made for destruction, [23] in order to make known the riches of his glory for the vessels of mercy, which he has prepared beforehand for glory, [24] even us whom he has called, not from the Jews only but also from the Gentiles? [25] As indeed he says in Hosea,

"Those who were not my people
I will call 'my people,'
and her who was not beloved
I will call 'my beloved.'"

[26] "And in the very place where it was said to them, 'You are not my people,'
they will be called 'sons of the living God.'"

[27] And Isaiah cries out concerning Israel: "Though the number of the sons of Israel be as the sand of the sea, only a remnant of them will be saved; [28] for the Lord will execute his sentence upon the earth with rigor and dispatch." [29] And as Isaiah predicted,

"If the Lord of hosts had not left us children, we would have fared like Sodom and been made like Gomorrah."

Gal 4:1–7 (§207)

[1] I mean that the heir, as long as he is a child, is no better than a slave, though he is the owner of all the estate; [2] but he is under guardians and trustees until the date set by the father. [3] So with us; when we were children, we were slaves to the elemental spirits of the universe. [4] But when the time had fully come, God sent forth his Son, born of woman, born under the law, [5] to redeem those who were under the law, so that we might receive adoption as sons. [6] And because you are sons, God has sent the Spirit of his Son into our hearts, crying, "Abba! Father!" [7] So through God you are no longer a slave but a son, and if a son then an heir.

Col 1:3–14 (§257)

[3] We always thank God, the Father of our Lord Jesus Christ, when we pray for you, [4] because we have heard of your faith in Christ Jesus and of the love which you have for all the saints, [5] because of the hope laid up for you in heaven. Of this you have heard before in the word of the truth, the gospel [6] which has come to you, as indeed in the whole world it is bearing fruit and growing—so among yourselves, from the day you heard and understood the grace of God in truth, [7] as you learned it from Epaphras our beloved fellow servant. He is a faithful minister of Christ on our behalf [8] and has made known to us your love in the Spirit.

[9] And so, from the day we heard of it, we have not ceased to pray for you, asking that you may be filled with the knowledge of his will in all spiritual wisdom and understanding, [10] to

lead a life worthy of the Lord, fully pleasing to him, bearing fruit in every good work and increasing in the knowledge of God. [11] May you be strengthened with all power, according to his glorious might, for all endurance and patience with joy, [12] giving thanks to the Father, who has qualified us to share in the inheritance of the saints in light. [13] He has delivered us from the dominion of darkness and transferred us to the kingdom of his beloved Son, [14] in whom we have redemption, the forgiveness of sins.

2 Thess 2:13–15 (§297)

[13] But we are bound to give thanks to God always for you, brethren beloved by the Lord, because God chose you from the beginning to be saved, through sanctification by the Spirit and belief in the truth. [14] To this he called you through our gospel, so that you may obtain the glory of our Lord Jesus Christ. [15] So then, brethren, stand firm and hold to the traditions which you were taught by us, either by word of mouth or by letter.

Phlm 4–7 (§306)

[4] I thank my God always when I remember you in my prayers, [5] because I hear of your love and of the faith which you have toward the Lord Jesus and all the saints, [6] and I pray that the sharing of your faith may promote the knowledge of all the good that is ours in Christ. [7] For I have derived much joy and comfort from your love, my brother, because the hearts of the saints have been refreshed through you.

---

2 Cor 5   [5] He who has prepared us for this very thing is God, who has given us the Spirit as a guarantee.

Gal 3   [2] Let me ask you only this: Did you receive the Spirit by works of the law, or by hearing with faith?

● **Eph 1:15**
Col 1   [4] because we have heard of your faith in Christ Jesus and of the love which you have for all the saints, . . .

(love) *omit* your love: p[46]S* AB cop(bo) Origen

● **Eph 1:18**
Acts 20   [32] "And now I commend you to God and to the word of his grace, which is able to build you up and to give you the inheritance among all those who are sanctified."

● **Eph 1:20**
Col 3   [1] If then you have been raised with Christ, seek the things that are above, where Christ is, seated at the right hand of God. [2] Set your minds on things

that are above, not on things that are on earth. [3] For you have died, and your life is hid with Christ in God. [4] When Christ who is our life appears, then you also will appear with him in glory.

Acts 2   [24] "But God raised him up, having loosed the pangs of death, because it was not possible for him to be held by it."

● **Eph 1:22–23**
Rom 12   [5] so we, though many, are one body in Christ, and individually members one of another.

1 Cor 12   [12] For just as the body is one and has many members, and all the members of the body, though many, are one body, so it is with Christ.

1 Cor 12   [27] Now you are the body of Christ and individually members of it.

Col 1   [18] He is the head of the body, the church; he is the beginning, the first-born from the dead, that in everything he might be pre-eminent.

Col 2   [19] and not holding fast to the Head, from whom the whole body, nourished and knit together through its joints and ligaments, grows with a growth that is from God.

Eph 4   [15] Rather, speaking the truth in love, we are to grow up in every way into him who is the head, into Christ, . . .

Eph 5   [23] For the husband is the head of the wife as Christ is the head of the church, his body, and is himself its Savior.

● **Eph 1:23**
Rom 11   [32] For God has consigned all men to disobedience, that he may have mercy upon all.

Eph 4   [12] to equip the saints for the work of ministry, for building up the body of Christ, . . .

Eph 5   [30] because we are members of his body.

2 And you he made alive, when you were dead through the trespasses and sins [2] in which you once walked, following the course of this world, following the prince of the power of the air, the spirit that is now at work in the sons of disobedience. [3] Among these we all once lived in the passions of our flesh, following the desires of body and mind, and so we were by nature children of wrath, like the rest of mankind. [4] But God, who is rich in mercy, out of the great love with which he loved us, [5] even when we were dead through our trespasses, made us alive together with Christ (by grace you have been saved), [6] and raised us up with him, and made us sit with him in the heavenly places in Christ Jesus, [7] that in the coming ages he might show the immeasurable riches of his grace in kindness toward us in Christ Jesus. [8] For by grace you have been saved through faith; and this is not your own doing, it is the gift of God— [9] not because of works, lest any man should boast. [10] For we are his workmanship, created in Christ Jesus for good works, which God prepared beforehand, that we should walk in them.

PRIMARY

Rom 3:21-26 (§14)

[21] But now the righteousness of God has been manifested apart from law, although the law and the prophets bear witness to it, [22] the righteousness of God through faith in Jesus Christ for all who believe. For there is no distinction; [23] since all have sinned and fall short of the glory of God, [24] they are justified by his grace as a gift, through the redemption which is in Christ Jesus, [25] whom God put forward as an expiation by his blood, to be received by faith. This was to show God's righteousness, because in his divine forbearance he had passed over former sins; [26] it was to prove at the present time that he himself is righteous and that he justifies him who has faith in Jesus.

Rom 3:27-31 (§15)

[27] Then what becomes of our boasting? It is excluded. On what principle? On the principle of works? No, but on the principle of faith. [28] For we hold that a man is justified by faith apart from works of law. [29] Or is God the God of Jews only? Is he not the God of Gentiles also? Yes, of Gentiles also, [30] since God is one; and he will justify the circumcised on the ground of their faith and the uncircumcised through their faith. [31] Do we then overthrow the law by this faith? By no means! On the contrary, we uphold the law.

Rom 6:1-10 (§23)

[1] What shall we say then? Are we to continue in sin that grace may abound? [2] By no means! How can we who died to sin still live in it? [3] Do you not know that all of us who have been baptized into Christ Jesus were baptized into his death? [4] We were buried therefore with him by baptism into death, so that as Christ was raised from the dead by the glory of the Father, we too might walk in newness of life.

[5] For if we have been united with him in a death like his, we shall certainly be united with him in a resurrection like his. [6] We know that our old self was crucified with him so that the sinful body might be destroyed, and we might no longer be enslaved to sin. [7] For he who has died is freed from sin. [8] But if we have died with Christ, we believe that we shall also live with him. [9] For we know that Christ being raised from the dead will never die again; death no longer has dominion over him. [10] The death he died he died to sin, once for all, but the life he lives he lives to God.

Rom 9:14-18 (§37)

[14] What shall we say then? Is there injustice on God's part? By no means! [15] For he says to Moses, "I will have mercy on whom I have mercy, and I will have compassion on whom I have compassion." [16] So it depends not upon man's will or exertion, but upon God's mercy. [17] For the scripture says to Pharaoh, "I have raised you up for the very purpose of showing my power in you, so that my name may be proclaimed in all the earth." [18] So then he has mercy upon whomever he wills, and he hardens the heart of whomever he wills.

Rom 11:1-6 (§44)

[1] I ask, then, has God rejected his people? By no means! I myself am an Israelite, a descendant of Abraham, a member of the tribe of Benjamin. [2] God has not rejected his people whom he foreknew. Do you not know what the scripture says of Elijah, how he pleads with God against Israel? [3] "Lord, they have killed thy prophets, they have demolished thy altars, and I alone am left, and they seek my life." [4] But what is God's reply to him? "I have kept for myself seven thousand men who have not bowed the knee to Baal." [5] So too at the present time there is a remnant, chosen by grace. [6] But if it is by grace, it is no longer on the basis of works; otherwise grace would no longer be grace.

Rom 11:17-24 (§48)

[17] But if some of the branches were broken off, and you, a wild olive shoot, were grafted in their place to share the richness of the olive tree, [18] do not boast over the branches. If you do boast, remember it is not you that support the root, but the root that supports you. [19] You will say, "Branches were broken off so that I might be grafted in." [20] That is true. They were broken off because of their unbelief, but you stand fast only through faith. So do not become proud, but stand in awe. [21] For if God did not spare the natural branches, neither will he spare you. [22] Note then the kindness and the severity of God: severity toward those who have fallen, but God's kindness to you, provided you continue in his kindness; otherwise you too will be cut off. [23] And even the others, if they do not persist in their unbelief, will be grafted in, for God has the power to graft them in again. [24] For if you have been cut from what is by nature a wild olive tree, and grafted, contrary to nature, into a cultivated olive tree, how much more will these natural branches be grafted back into their own olive tree.

1 Cor 3:1-4 (§78)

[1] But I, brethren, could not address you as spiritual men, but as men of the flesh, as babes in Christ. [2] I fed you with milk, not solid food; for you were not ready for it; and even yet you are not ready, [3] for you are still of the flesh. For while there is jealousy and strife among you, are you not of the flesh, and behaving like ordinary men? [4] For when one says, "I belong to Paul," and another, "I belong to Apollos," are you not merely men?

1 Cor 4:6-7 (§84)

[6] I have applied all this to myself and Apollos for your benefit, brethren, that you may learn by us not to go beyond what is written, that none

---

● **Eph 2:2-3**

Acts 26   [18] "to open their eyes, that they may turn from darkness to light and from the power of Satan to God, that they may receive forgiveness of sins and a place among those who are sanctified by faith in me."

● **Eph 2:3-4**

Titus 3   [3] For we ourselves were once foolish, disobedient, led astray, slaves to various passions and pleasures, passing our days in malice and envy, hated by men and hating one another; [4] but when the goodness and loving kindness of God our Savior appeared, [5] he saved us, not because of deeds done by us in righteousness, but in virtue of his own mercy, by the washing of regeneration and renewal in the Holy Spirit, [6] which he poured out upon us richly through Jesus Christ our Savior, [7] so that we might be justified by his grace and become heirs in hope of eternal life.

● **Eph 2:3**

Rom 1   [24] Therefore God gave them up in the lusts of their hearts to impurity, to the dishonoring of their bodies among themselves, [25] because they exchanged the truth about God for a lie and worshiped and served the creature rather than the Creator, who is blessed for ever! Amen.

[26] For this reason God gave them up to dishonorable passions. Their women exchanged natural relations for unnatural, [27] and the men likewise gave up natural relations with women and were consumed with passion for one another, men committing shameless acts with men and receiving in their own persons the due penalty for their error.

[28] And since they did not see fit to acknowledge God, God gave them up to a base mind and to improper conduct.

Rom 8   [9] But you are not in the flesh, you are in the Spirit, if in fact the Spirit of God dwells in you. Any one who does not have the Spirit of Christ does not belong to him. [10] But if Christ is in you, although your bodies are dead because of sin, your spirits are alive because of righteousness. [11] If the Spirit of him who raised Jesus from the dead dwells in you, he who raised Christ Jesus from the dead will give life to your mortal bodies also through his Spirit which dwells in you.

of you may be puffed up in favor of one against another. [7]For who sees anything different in you? What have you that you did not receive? If then you received it, why do you boast as if it were not a gift?

2 Cor 5:14–21 (§164)

[14]For the love of Christ controls us, because we are convinced that one has died for all; therefore all have died. [15]And he died for all, that those who live might live no longer for themselves but for him who for their sake died and was raised.

[16]From now on, therefore, we regard no one from a human point of view; even though we once regarded Christ from a human point of view, we regard him thus no longer. [17]Therefore, if any one is in Christ, he is a new creation; the old has passed away, behold, the new has come. [18]All this is from God, who through Christ reconciled us to himself and gave us the ministry of reconciliation; [19]that is, in Christ God was reconciling the world to himself, not counting their trespasses against them, and entrusting to us the message of reconciliation. [20]So we are ambassadors for Christ, God making his appeal through us. We beseech you on behalf of Christ, be reconciled to God. [21]For our sake he made him to be sin who knew no sin, so that in him we might become the righteousness of God.

Gal 2:15–21 (§199)

[15]We ourselves, who are Jews by birth and not Gentile sinners, [16]yet who know that a man is not justified by works of the law but through faith in Jesus Christ, even we have believed in Christ Jesus, in order to be justified by faith in Christ, and not by works of the law, because by works of the law shall no one be justified. [17]But if, in our endeavor to be justified in Christ, we ourselves were found to be sinners, is Christ then an agent of sin? Certainly not! [18]But if I build up again those things which I tore down, then I prove myself a transgressor. [19]For I through the law died to the law, that I might live to God. [20]I have been crucified with Christ; it is no longer I who live, but Christ who lives in me; and the life I now live in the flesh I live by faith in the Son of God, who loved me and gave himself for me. [21]I do not nullify the grace of God; for if justification were through the law, then Christ died to no purpose.

Phil 3:17–21 (§249)

[17]Brethren, join in imitating me, and mark those who so live as you have an example in us. [18]For many, of whom I have often told you and now tell you even with tears, live as enemies of the cross of Christ. [19]Their end is destruction, their god is the belly, and they glory in their shame, with minds set on earthly things. [20]But our commonwealth is in heaven, and from it we await a Savior, the Lord Jesus Christ, [21]who will change our lowly body to be like his glorious body, by the power which enables him even to subject all things to himself.

Col 2:8–15 (§262)

[8]See to it that no one makes a prey of you by philosophy and empty deceit, according to human tradition, according to the elemental spirits of the universe, and not according to Christ. [9]For in him the whole fulness of deity dwells bodily, [10]and you have come to fulness of life in him, who is the head of all rule and authority. [11]In him also you were circumcised with a circumcision made without hands, by putting off the body of flesh in the circumcision of Christ; [12]and you were buried with him in baptism, in which you were also raised with him through faith in the working of God, who raised him from the dead. [13]And you, who were dead in trespasses and the uncircumcision of your flesh, God made alive together with him, having forgiven us all our trespasses, [14]having canceled the bond which stood against us with its legal demands; this he set aside, nailing it to the cross. [15]He disarmed the principalities and powers and made a public example of them, triumphing over them in him.

Col 3:1–11 (§265–266)

[1]If then you have been raised with Christ, seek the things that are above, where Christ is, seated at the right hand of God. [2]Set your minds on things that are above, not on things that are on earth. [3]For you have died, and your life is hid with Christ in God. [4]When Christ who is our life appears, then you also will appear with him in glory.

[5]Put to death therefore what is earthly in you: fornication, impurity, passion, evil desire, and covetousness, which is idolatry. [6]On account of these the wrath of God is coming. [7]In these you once walked, when you lived in them. [8]But now put them all away: anger, wrath, malice, slander, and foul talk from your mouth. [9]Do not lie to one another, seeing that you have put off the old nature with its practices [10]and have put on the new nature, which is being renewed in knowledge after the image of its creator. [11]Here there cannot be Greek and Jew, circumcised and uncircumcised, barbarian, Scythian, slave, free man, but Christ is all, and in all.

2 Thess 2:1–12 (§296)

[1]Now concerning the coming of our Lord Jesus Christ and our assembling to meet him, we beg you, brethren, [2]not to be quickly shaken in mind or excited, either by spirit or by word, or by letter purporting to be from us, to the effect that the day of the Lord has come. [3]Let no one deceive you in any way; for that day will not come, unless the rebellion comes first, and the man of lawlessness is revealed, the son of perdition, [4]who opposes and exalts himself against every so-called god or object of worship, so that he takes his seat in the temple of God, proclaiming himself to be God. [5]Do you not remember that when I was still with you I told you this? [6]And you know what is restraining him now so that he may be revealed in his time. [7]For the mystery of lawlessness is already at work; only he who now restrains it will do so until he is out of the way. [8]And then the lawless one will be revealed, and the Lord Jesus will slay him with the breath of his mouth and destroy him by his appearing and his coming. [9]The coming of the lawless one by the activity of Satan will be with all power and with pretended signs and wonders, [10]and with all wicked deception for those who are to perish, because they refused to love the truth and so be saved. [11]Therefore God sends upon them a strong delusion, to make them believe what is false, [12]so that all may be condemned who did not believe the truth but had pleasure in unrighteousness.

2 Thess 2:16–17 (§298)

[16]Now may our Lord Jesus Christ himself, and God our Father, who loved us and gave us eternal comfort and good hope through grace, [17]comfort your hearts and establish them in every good work and word.

---

[12]So then, brethren, we are debtors, not to the flesh, to live according to the flesh— [13]for if you live according to the flesh you will die, but if by the Spirit you put to death the deeds of the body you will live.

Gal 5   [16]But I say, walk by the Spirit, and do not gratify the desires of the flesh. [17]For the desires of the flesh are against the Spirit, and the desires of the Spirit are against the flesh; for these are opposed to each other, to prevent you from doing what you would.

● **Eph 2:4**
Rom 2   [4]Or do you presume upon the riches of his kindness and forbearance and patience? Do you not know that God's kindness is meant to lead you to repentance?

● **Eph 2:7**
Titus 3   [4]but when the goodness and loving kindness of God our Savior appeared, . . .

● **Eph 2:9**
1 Cor 1   [29]so that no human being might boast in the presence of God.

2 Cor 10   [13]But we will not boast beyond limit, but will keep to the limits God has apportioned us, to reach even to you. [14]For we are not overextending ourselves, as though we did not reach you; we were the first to come all the way to you with the gospel of Christ. [15]We do not boast beyond limit, in other men's labors; but our hope is that as your faith increases, our field among you may be greatly enlarged, [16]so that we may preach the gospel in lands beyond you, without boasting of work already done in another's field. [17]"Let him who boasts, boast of the Lord."

2 Tim 1   [9]who saved us and called us with a holy calling, not in virtue of our works but in virtue of his own purpose and the grace which he gave us in Christ Jesus ages ago, . . .

Titus 3   [5]he saved us, not because of deeds done by us in righteousness, but in virtue of his own mercy, by the washing of regeneration and renewal in the Holy Spirit, . . .

● **Eph 2:10**
Titus 2   [14]who gave himself for us to redeem us from all iniquity and to purify for himself a people of his own who are zealous for good deeds.

[11] Therefore remember that at one time you Gentiles in the flesh, called the uncircumcision by what is called the circumcision, which is made in the flesh by hands— [12] remember that you were at that time separated from Christ, alienated from the commonwealth of Israel, and strangers to the covenants of promise, having no hope and without God in the world. [13] But now in Christ Jesus you who once were far off have been brought near in the blood of Christ. [14] For he is our peace, who has made us both one, and has broken down the dividing wall of hostility, [15] by abolishing in his flesh the law of commandments and ordinances, that he might create in himself one new man in place of the two, so making peace, [16] and might reconcile us both to God in one body through the cross, thereby bringing the hostility to an end. [17] And he came and preached peace to you who were far off and peace to those who were near; [18] for through him we both have access in one Spirit to the Father. [19] So then you are no longer strangers and sojourners, but you are fellow citizens with the saints and members of the household of God, [20] built upon the foundation of the apostles and prophets, Christ Jesus himself being the cornerstone, [21] in whom the whole structure is joined together and grows into a holy temple in the Lord; [22] in whom you also are built into it for a dwelling place of God in the Spirit.

PRIMARY

Rom 5:6–11 (§21)

[6] While we were still weak, at the right time Christ died for the ungodly. [7] Why, one will hardly die for a righteous man—though perhaps for a good man one will dare even to die. [8] But God shows his love for us in that while we were yet sinners Christ died for us. [9] Since, therefore, we are now justified by his blood, much more shall we be saved by him from the wrath of God. [10] For if while we were enemies we were reconciled to God by the death of his Son, much more, now that we are reconciled, shall we be saved by his life. [11] Not only so, but we also rejoice in God through our Lord Jesus Christ, through whom we have now received our reconciliation.

Rom 9:1–5 (§35)

[1] I am speaking the truth in Christ, I am not lying; my conscience bears me witness in the Holy Spirit, [2] that I have great sorrow and unceasing anguish in my heart. [3] For I could wish that I myself were accursed and cut off from Christ for the sake of my brethren, my kinsmen by race. [4] They are Israelites, and to them belong the sonship, the glory, the covenants, the giving of the law, the worship, and the promises; [5] to them belong the patriarchs, and of their race, according to the flesh, is the Christ. God who is over all be blessed for ever. Amen.

Rom 11:17–24 (§48)

[17] But if some of the branches were broken off, and you, a wild olive shoot, were grafted in their place to share the richness of the olive tree, [18] do not boast over the branches. If you do boast, remember it is not you that support the root, but the root that supports you. [19] You will say, "Branches were broken off so that I might be grafted in." [20] That is true. They were broken off because of their unbelief, but you stand fast only through faith. So do not become proud, but stand in awe. [21] For if God did not spare the natural branches, neither will he spare you. [22] Note then the kindness and the severity of God: severity toward those who have fallen, but God's kindness to you, provided you continue in his kindness; otherwise you too will be cut off. [23] And even the others, if they do not persist in their unbelief, will be grafted in, for God has the power to graft them in again. [24] For if you have been cut from what is by nature a wild olive tree, and grafted, contrary to nature, into a cultivated olive tree, how much more will these natural branches be grafted back into their own olive tree.

Rom 15:7–13 (§61)

[7] Welcome one another, therefore, as Christ has welcomed you, for the glory of God. [8] For I tell you that Christ became a servant to the circumcised to show God's truthfulness, in order to confirm the promises given to the patriarchs, [9] and in order that the Gentiles might glorify God for his mercy. As it is written,

"Therefore I will praise thee among the Gentiles,
　and sing to thy name";
[10] and again it is said,

● **Eph 2:11**

Rom 2　[28] For he is not a real Jew who is one outwardly, nor is true circumcision something external and physical. [29] He is a Jew who is one inwardly, and real circumcision is a matter of the heart, spiritual and not literal. His praise is not from men but from God.

Rom 4　[11] He received circumcision as a sign or seal of the righteousness which he had by faith while he was still uncircumcised. The purpose was to make him the father of all who believe without being circumcised and who thus have righteousness reckoned to them, [12] and likewise the father of the circumcised who are not merely circumcised but also follow the example of the faith which our father Abraham had before he was circumcised.

Gal 3　[15] To give a human example, brethren: no one annuls even a man's will, or adds to it, once it has been ratified. [16] Now the promises were made to Abraham and to his offspring. It does not say, "And to offsprings," referring to many; but, referring to one, "And to your offspring," which is Christ. [17] This is what I mean: the law, which came four hundred and thirty years afterward, does not annul a covenant previously ratified by God, so as to make the promise void. [18] For if the inheritance is by the law, it is no longer by promise; but God gave it to Abraham by a promise.

Phil 2　[1] So if there is any encouragement in Christ, any incentive of love, any participation in the Spirit, any affection and sympathy, [2] complete my joy by being of the same mind, having the same love, being in full accord and of one mind. [3] Do nothing from selfishness or conceit, but in humility count others better than yourselves. [4] Let each of you look not only to his own interests, but also to the interests of others. [5] Have this mind among yourselves, which is yours in Christ Jesus, [6] who, though he was in the form of God, did not count equality with God a thing to be grasped,

[7] but emptied himself, taking the form of a servant, being born in the likeness of men. [8] And being found in human form he humbled himself and became obedient unto death, even death on a cross. [9] Therefore God has highly exalted him and bestowed on him the name which is above every name, [10] that at the name of Jesus every knee should bow, in heaven and on earth and under the earth, [11] and every tongue confess that Jesus Christ is Lord, to the glory of God the Father.

Phlm　[8] Accordingly, though I am bold enough in Christ to command you to do what is required, [9] yet for love's sake I prefer to appeal to you—I, Paul, an ambassador and now a prisoner also for Christ Jesus— [10] I appeal to you for my child, Onesimus, whose father I have become in my imprisonment. [11] (Formerly he was useless to you, but now he is indeed useful to you and to me.) [12] I am sending him back to you, sending my very heart. [13] I would have been glad

"Rejoice, O Gentiles, with his peoples";
[11] and again,
"Praise the Lord, all Gentiles,
and let all the peoples praise him";
[12] and further Isaiah says,
"The root of Jesse shall come,
he who rises to rule the Gentiles;
in him shall the Gentiles hope."
[13] May the God of hope fill you with all joy and peace in believing, so that by the power of the Holy Spirit you may abound in hope.

1 Cor 3:5–9 (§79)

[5] What then is Apollos? What is Paul? Servants through whom you believed, as the Lord assigned to each. [6] I planted, Apollos watered, but God gave the growth. [7] So neither he who plants nor he who waters is anything, but only God who gives the growth. [8] He who plants and he who waters are equal, and each shall receive his wages according to his labor. [9] For we are God's fellow workers; you are God's field, God's building.

1 Cor 3:16–17 (§81)

[16] Do you not know that you are God's temple and that God's Spirit dwells in you? [17] If any one destroys God's temple, God will destroy him. For God's temple is holy, and that temple you are.

1 Cor 12:1–3 (§116)

[1] Now concerning spiritual gifts, brethren, I do not want you to be uninformed. [2] You know that when you were heathen, you were led astray to dumb idols, however you may have been moved. [3] Therefore I want you to understand that no one speaking by the Spirit of God ever says "Jesus be cursed!" and no one can say "Jesus is Lord" except by the Holy Spirit.

1 Cor 12:12–13 (§118)

[12] For just as the body is one and has many members, and all the members of the body, though many, are one body, so it is with Christ. [13] For by one Spirit we were all baptized into one body— Jews or Greeks, slaves or free—and all were made to drink of one Spirit.

2 Cor 5:14–21 (§164)

[14] For the love of Christ controls us, because we are convinced that one has died for all; therefore all have died. [15] And he died for all, that those who live might live no longer for themselves but for him who for their sake died and was raised.
[16] From now on, therefore, we regard no one from a human point of view; even though we once regarded Christ from a human point of view, we regard him thus no longer. [17] Therefore, if any one is in Christ, he is a new creation; the old has passed away, behold, the new has come. [18] All this is from God, who through Christ reconciled us to himself and gave us the ministry of reconciliation; [19] that is, in Christ God was reconciling the world to himself, not counting their trespasses against them, and entrusting to us the message of reconciliation. [20] So we are ambassadors for Christ, God making his appeal through us. We beseech you on behalf of Christ, be reconciled to God. [21] For our sake he made him to be sin who knew no sin, so that in him we might become the righteousness of God.

Gal 2:11–14 (§198)

[11] But when Cephas came to Antioch I opposed him to his face, because he stood condemned. [12] For before certain men came from James, he ate with the Gentiles; but when they came he drew back and separated himself, fearing the circumcision party. [13] And with him the rest of the Jews acted insincerely, so that even Barnabas was carried away by their insincerity. [14] But when I saw that they were not straightforward about the truth of the gospel, I said to Cephas before them all, "If you, though a Jew, live like a Gentile and not like a Jew, how can you compel the Gentiles to live like Jews?"

Gal 4:8–11 (§208)

[8] Formerly, when you did not know God, you were in bondage to beings that by nature are no gods; [9] but now that you have come to know God, or rather to be known by God, how can you turn back again to the weak and beggarly elemental spirits, whose slaves you want to be once more? [10] You observe days, and months, and seasons, and years! [11] I am afraid I have labored over you in vain.

Col 1:21–23 (§259)

[21] And you, who once were estranged and hostile in mind, doing evil deeds, [22] he has now reconciled in his body of flesh by his death, in order to present you holy and blameless and irreproachable before him, [23] provided that you continue in the faith, stable and steadfast, not shifting from the hope of the gospel which you heard, which has been preached to every creature under heaven, and of which I, Paul, became a minister.

---

to keep him with me, in order that he might serve me on your behalf during my imprisonment for the gospel; [14] but I preferred to do nothing without your consent in order that your goodness might not be by compulsion but of your own free will.
[15] Perhaps this is why he was parted from you for a while, that you might have him back for ever, [16] no longer as a slave but more than a slave, as a beloved brother, especially to me but how much more to you, both in the flesh and in the Lord. [17] So if you consider me your partner, receive him as you would receive me. [18] If he has wronged you at all, or owes you anything, charge that to my account. [19] I, Paul, write this with my own hand, I will repay it—to say nothing of your owing me even your own self. [20] Yes, brother, I want some benefit from you in the Lord. Refresh my heart in Christ.

● **Eph 2:12**
1 Thess 4   [13] But we would not have you ignorant, brethren, concerning those who are asleep, that you may not grieve as others do who have no hope.

● **Eph 2:15–16**
Gal 3   [28] There is neither Jew nor Greek, there is neither slave nor free, there is neither male nor female; for you are all one in Christ Jesus.

Col 3   [11] Here there cannot be Greek and Jew, circumcised and uncircumcised, barbarian, Scythian, slave, free man, but Christ is all, and in all.

● **Eph 2:17**
Acts 10   [36] "You know the word which he sent to Israel, preaching good news of peace by Jesus Christ (he is Lord of all). . . ."

● **Eph 2:18**
Rom 5   [2] Through him we have obtained access to this grace in which we stand, and we rejoice in our hope of sharing the glory of God.

● **Eph 2:19**
1 Tim 3   [15] if I am delayed, you may know how one ought to behave in the household of God, which is the church of the living God, the pillar and bulwark of the truth.

● **Eph 2:20–22**
1 Cor 6   [19] Do you not know that your body is a temple of the Holy Spirit within you, which you have from God? You are not your own; [20] you were bought with a price. So glorify God in your body.

3 For this reason I, Paul, a prisoner for Christ Jesus on behalf of you Gentiles— [2]assuming that you have heard of the stewardship of God's grace that was given to me for you, [3]how the mystery was made known to me by revelation, as I have written briefly. [4]When you read this you can perceive my insight into the mystery of Christ, [5]which was not made known to the sons of men in other generations as it has now been revealed to his holy apostles and prophets by the Spirit; [6]that is, how the Gentiles are fellow heirs, members of the same body, and partakers of the promise in Christ Jesus through the gospel.

[7]Of this gospel I was made a minister according to the gift of God's grace which was given me by the working of his power. [8]To me, though I am the very least of all the saints, this grace was given, to preach to the Gentiles the unsearchable riches of Christ, [9]and to make all men see what is the plan of the mystery hidden for ages in God who created all things; [10]that through the church the manifold wisdom of God might now be made known to the principalities and powers in the heavenly places. [11]This was according to the eternal purpose which he has realized in Christ Jesus our Lord, [12]in whom we have boldness and confidence of access through our faith in him. [13]So I ask you not to lose heart over what I am suffering for you, which is your glory.

Primary

Rom 1:1-7 (§1)

[1]Paul, a servant of Jesus Christ, called to be an apostle, set apart for the gospel of God [2]which he promised beforehand through his prophets in the holy scriptures, [3]the gospel concerning his Son, who was descended from David according to the flesh [4]and designated Son of God in power according to the Spirit of holiness by his resurrection from the dead, Jesus Christ our Lord, [5]through whom we have received grace and apostleship to bring about the obedience of faith for the sake of his name among all the nations, [6]including yourselves who are called to belong to Jesus Christ; [7]To all God's beloved in Rome, who are called to be saints:

Grace to you and peace from God our Father and the Lord Jesus Christ.

Rom 11:13-16 (§47)

[13]Now I am speaking to you Gentiles. Inasmuch then as I am an apostle to the Gentiles, I magnify my ministry [14]in order to make my fellow Jews jealous, and thus save some of them. [15]For if their rejection means the reconciliation of the world, what will their acceptance mean but life from the dead? [16]If the dough offered as first fruits is holy, so is the whole lump; and if the root is holy, so are the branches.

Rom 15:14-21 (§62)

[14]I myself am satisfied about you, my brethren, that you yourselves are full of goodness, filled with all knowledge, and able to instruct one another. [15]But on some points I have written to you very boldly by way of reminder, because of the grace given me by God [16]to be a minister of Christ Jesus to the Gentiles in the priestly service of the gospel of God, so that the offering of the Gentiles may be acceptable, sanctified by the Holy Spirit. [17]In Christ Jesus, then, I have reason to be proud of my work for God. [18]For I will not venture to speak of anything except what Christ has wrought through me to win obedience from the Gentiles, by word and deed, [19]by the power of signs and wonders, by the power of the Holy Spirit, so that from Jerusalem and as far round as Illyricum I have fully preached the gospel of Christ, [20]thus making it my ambition to preach the gospel, not where Christ has already been named, lest I build on another man's foundation, [21]but as it is written,

"They shall see who have never been told of him,

and they shall understand who have never heard of him."

1 Cor 9:15-18 (§106)

[15]But I have made no use of any of these rights, nor am I writing this to secure any such provision. For I would rather die than have any one deprive me of my ground for boasting. [16]For if I preach the gospel, that gives me no ground for boasting. For necessity is laid upon me. Woe to me if I do not preach the gospel! [17]For if I do this of my own will, I have a reward; but if not of my own will, I am entrusted with a commission. [18]What then is my reward? Just this: that in my preaching I may make the gospel free of charge, not making full use of my right in the gospel.

1 Cor 15:1-11 (§131)

[1]Now I would remind you, brethren, in what terms I preached to you the gospel, which you received, in which you stand, [2]by which you are saved, if you hold it fast —unless you believed in vain.

[3]For I delivered to you as of first importance what I also received, that Christ died for our sins in accordance with the scriptures, [4]that he was buried, that he was raised on the third day in accordance with the scriptures, [5]and that he appeared to Cephas, then to the twelve. [6]Then he appeared to more than five hundred brethren at one time, most of whom are still alive, though some have fallen asleep. [7]Then he appeared to James, then to all the apostles. [8]Last of all, as to one untimely born, he appeared also to me. [9]For I am the least of the apostles, unfit to be called an apostle, because I persecuted the church of God. [10]But by the grace of God I am what I am, and his grace toward me was not in vain. On the contrary, I worked harder than any of them, though it was not I, but the grace of God which is with me. [11]Whether then it was I or they, so we preach and so you believed.

2 Cor 4:1-6 (§158)

[1]Therefore, having this ministry by the mercy of God, we do not lose heart. [2]We have renounced disgraceful, underhanded ways; we refuse to practice cunning or to tamper with God's word, but by the open statement of the

---

● **Eph 3:1-13**
Cf. Rom 11:33-36; 1 Cor 2:6-16; 1 Cor 4:1-5; 2 Cor 11:1-6; 2 Cor 12:1-12; Gal 4:1-7; 2 Thess 2:1-12

● **Eph 3:1**
Eph 4　[1]I therefore, a prisoner for the Lord, beg you to lead a life worthy of the calling to which you have been called, . . .

Phil 1　[12]I want you to know, brethren, that what has happened to me has really served to advance the gospel, [13]so that it has become known throughout the whole praetorian guard and to all the rest that my imprisonment is for Christ; [14]and most of the brethren have been made confident in the Lord because of my imprisonment, and are much more bold to speak the word of God without fear.

[15]Some indeed preach Christ from envy and rivalry, but others from good will. [16]The latter do it out of love, knowing that I am put here for the defense of the gospel; [17]the former proclaim Christ out of partisanship, not sincerely but thinking to afflict me in my imprisonment. [18]What then? Only that in every way, whether in pretense or in truth, Christ is proclaimed; and in that I rejoice.

[19]Yes, and I shall rejoice. For I know that through your prayers and the help of the Spirit of Jesus Christ this will turn out for my deliverance, [20]as it is my eager expectation and hope that I shall not be at all ashamed, but that with full courage now as always Christ will be honored in my body, whether by life or by death.

Col 4　[3]and pray for us also, that God may open to us a door for the word, to declare the mystery of Christ, on account of which I am in prison, . . .

Col 4　[18]I, Paul, write this greeting with my own hand. Remember my fetters.

Phlm　[1]Paul, a prisoner for Christ Jesus, and Timothy our brother,
To Philemon our beloved fellow worker . . .

Phlm　[9]yet for love's sake I prefer to appeal to you— I, Paul, an ambassador and now a prisoner also for Christ Jesus . . .

2 Tim 1　[8]Do not be ashamed then of testifying to our Lord, nor of me his prisoner, but share in suffering for the gospel in the power of God, . . .

2 Tim 1　[12]and therefore I suffer as I do. But I am not ashamed, for I know whom I have believed, and I am sure that he is able to guard until that Day what has been entrusted to me.

2 Tim 1　[16]May the Lord grant mercy to the household of Onesiphorus, for he often refreshed me; he was not ashamed of my chains, . . .

truth we would commend ourselves to every man's conscience in the sight of God. [3]And even if our gospel is veiled, it is veiled only to those who are perishing. [4]In their case the god of this world has blinded the minds of the unbelievers, to keep them from seeing the light of the gospel of the glory of Christ, who is the likeness of God. [5]For what we preach is not ourselves, but Jesus Christ as Lord, with ourselves as your servants for Jesus' sake. [6]For it is the God who said, "Let light shine out of darkness," who has shone in our hearts to give the light of the knowledge of the glory of God in the face of Christ.

Gal 1:15–24 (§196)

[15]But when he who had set me apart before I was born, and had called me through his grace, [16]was pleased to reveal his Son to me, in order that I might preach him among the Gentiles, I did not confer with flesh and blood, [17]nor did I go up to Jerusalem to those who were apostles before me, but I went away into Arabia; and again I returned to Damascus.

[18]Then after three years I went up to Jerusalem to visit Cephas, and remained with him fifteen days. [19]But I saw none of the other apostles except James the Lord's brother. [20](In what I am writing to you, before God, I do not lie!) [21]Then I went into the regions of Syria and Cilicia. [22]And I was still not known by sight to the churches of Christ in Judea; [23]they only heard it said, "He who once persecuted us is now preaching the faith he once tried to destroy." [24]And they glorified God because of me.

Gal 2:1–10 (§197)

[1]Then after fourteen years I went up again to Jerusalem with Barnabas, taking Titus along with me. [2]I went up by revelation; and I laid before them (but privately before those who were of repute) the gospel which I preach among the Gentiles, lest somehow I should be running or had run in vain. [3]But even Titus, who was with me, was not compelled to be circumcised, though he was a Greek. [4]But because of false brethren secretly brought in, who

slipped in to spy out our freedom which we have in Christ Jesus, that they might bring us into bondage— [5]to them we did not yield submission even for a moment, that the truth of the gospel might be preserved for you. [6]And from those who were reputed to be something (what they were makes no difference to me; God shows no partiality)—those, I say, who were of repute added nothing to me; [7]but on the contrary, when they saw that I had been entrusted with the gospel to the uncircumcised, just as Peter had been entrusted with the gospel to the circumcised [8](for he who worked through Peter for the mission to the circumcised worked through me also for the Gentiles), [9]and when they perceived the grace that was given to me, James and Cephas and John, who were reputed to be pillars, gave to me and Barnabas the right hand of fellowship, that we should go to the Gentiles and they to the circumcised; [10]only they would have us remember the poor, which very thing I was eager to do.

Phil 1:12–18 (§239)

[12]I want you to know, brethren, that what has happened to me has really served to advance the gospel, [13]so that it has become known throughout the whole praetorian guard and to all the rest that my imprisonment is for Christ; [14]and most of the brethren have been made confident in the Lord because of my imprisonment, and are much more bold to speak the word of God without fear.

[15]Some indeed preach Christ from envy and rivalry, but others from good will. [16]The latter do it out of love, knowing that I am put here for the defense of the gospel; [17]the former proclaim Christ out of partisanship, not sincerely but thinking to afflict me in my imprisonment. [18]What then? Only that in every way, whether in pretense or in truth, Christ is proclaimed; and in that I rejoice.

Col 1:24–2:3 (§260)

[24]Now I rejoice in my sufferings for your sake, and in my flesh I complete what is lacking in Christ's afflictions for the sake of his body, that is, the church, [25]of which I became a

minister according to the divine office which was given to me for you, to make the word of God fully known, [26]the mystery hidden for ages and generations but now made manifest to his saints. [27]To them God chose to make known how great among the Gentiles are the riches of the glory of this mystery, which is Christ in you, the hope of glory. [28]Him we proclaim warning every man and teaching every man in all wisdom, that we may present every man mature in Christ. [29]For this I toil, striving with all the energy which he mightily inspires within me.

[2:1]For I want you to know how greatly I strive for you, and for those at Laodicea, and for all who have not seen my face, [2]that their hearts may be encouraged as they are knit together in love, to have all the riches of assured understanding and the knowledge of God's mystery, of Christ, [3]in whom are hid all the treasures of wisdom and knowledge.

1 Thess 2:1–8 (§277)

[1]For you yourselves know, brethren, that our visit to you was not in vain; [2]but though we had already suffered and been shamefully treated at Philippi, as you know, we had courage in our God to declare to you the gospel of God in the face of great opposition. [3]For our appeal does not spring from error or uncleanness, nor is it made with guile; [4]but just as we have been approved by God to be entrusted with the gospel, so we speak, not to please men, but to please God who tests our hearts. [5]For we never used either words of flattery, as you know, or a cloak for greed, as God is witness; [6]nor did we seek glory from men, whether from you or from others, though we might have made demands as apostles of Christ. [7]But we were gentle among you, like a nurse taking care of her children. [8]So, being affectionately desirous of you, we were ready to share with you not only the gospel of God but also our own selves, because you had become very dear to us.

Acts 23   [18]So he took him and brought him to the tribune and said, "Paul the prisoner called me and asked me to bring this young man to you, as he has something to say to you."

● **Eph 3:2–3**
1 Cor 15   [8]Last of all, as to one untimely born, he appeared also to me. [9]For I am the least of the apostles, unfit to be called an apostle, because I persecuted the church of God. [10]But by the grace of God I am what I am, and his grace toward me was not in vain. On the contrary, I worked harder than any of them, though it was not I, but the grace of God which is with me.

● **Eph 3:3**
Acts 9   [15]But the Lord said to him, "Go, for he is a chosen instrument of mine to carry my name before the Gentiles and kings and the sons of Israel. . . ."

Acts 22   [21]"And he said to me, 'Depart; for I will send you far away to the Gentiles.'"

Acts 26   [16]"But rise and stand upon your feet; for I have appeared to you for this purpose, to appoint you to serve and bear witness to the things in which you have seen me and to those in which I will appear to you, [17]delivering you from the people and from the Gentiles —to whom I send you . . ."

● **Eph 3:4**
1 Cor 11   [6]Even if I am unskilled in speaking, I am not in knowledge; in every way we have made this plain to you in all things.

● **Rom 3:5**
Rom 16   [25]Now to him who is able to strengthen you according to my gospel and the preaching of Jesus Christ, according to the revelation of the mystery which was kept secret for long ages . . .

● **Eph 3:7**
2 Cor 4   [1]Therefore, having this ministry by the mercy of God, we do not lose heart.

● **Eph 3:9**
(all men) *omit* all: S*A Origen

● **Eph 3:12**
Rom 5   [2]Through him we have obtained access to this grace in which we stand, and we rejoice in our hope of sharing the glory of God.

● **Eph 3:13**
2 Cor 4   [16]So we do not lose heart. Though our outer nature is wasting away, our inner nature is being renewed every day.

2 Tim 2   [10]Therefore I endure everything for the sake of the elect, that they also may obtain salvation in Christ Jesus with its eternal glory.

14For this reason I bow my knees before the Father, **15**from whom every family in heaven and on earth is named, **16**that according to the riches of his glory he may grant you to be strengthened with might through his Spirit in the inner man, **17**and that Christ may dwell in your hearts through faith; that you, being rooted and grounded in love, **18**may have power to comprehend with all the saints what is the breadth and length and height and depth, **19**and to know the love of Christ which surpasses knowledge, that you may be filled with all the fulness of God.

PRIMARY

Rom 8:31-39 (§34)

31What then shall we say to this? If God is for us, who is against us? **32**He who did not spare his own Son but gave him up for us all, will he not also give us all things with him? **33**Who shall bring any charge against God's elect? It is God who justifies; **34**who is to condemn? Is it Christ Jesus, who died, yes, who was raised from the dead, who is at the right hand of God, who indeed intercedes for us? **35**Who shall separate us from the love of Christ? Shall tribulation, or distress, or persecution, or famine, or nakedness, or peril, or sword? **36**As it is written,

"For thy sake we are being killed all the day long;
we are regarded as sheep to be slaughtered."

37No, in all these things we are more than conquerors through him who loved us. **38**For I am sure that neither death, nor life, nor angels, nor principalities, nor things present, nor things to come, nor powers, **39**nor height, nor depth, nor anything else in all creation, will be able to separate us from the love of God in Christ Jesus our Lord.

1 Cor 3:18-23 (§82)

18Let no one deceive himself. If any one among you thinks that he is wise in this age, let him become a fool that he may become wise. **19**For the wisdom of this world is folly with God. For it is written, "He catches the wise in their craftiness," **20**and again, "The Lord knows that the thoughts of the wise are futile." **21**So let no one boast of men. For all things are yours, **22**whether Paul or Apollos or Cephas or the world or life or death or the present or the future, all are yours; **23**and you are Christ's; and Christ is God's.

1 Cor 8:1-3 (§102)

1Now concerning food offered to idols: we know that "all of us possess knowledge." "Knowledge" puffs up, but love builds up. **2**If any one imagines that he knows something, he does not yet know as he ought to know. **3**But if one loves God, one is known by him.

2 Cor 4:16-5:5 (§161)

16So we do not lose heart. Though our outer nature is wasting away, our inner nature is being renewed every day. **17**For this slight momentary affliction is preparing for us an eternal weight of glory beyond all comparison, **18**because we look not to the things that are seen but to the things that are unseen; for the things that are seen are transient, but the things that are unseen are eternal.

5 **1**For we know that if the earthly tent we live in is destroyed, we have a building from God, a house not made with hands, eternal in the heavens. **2**Here indeed we groan, and long to put on our heavenly dwelling, **3**so that by putting it on we may not be found naked. **4**For while we are still in this tent, we sigh with anxiety; not that we would be unclothed, but that we would be further clothed, so that what is mortal may be swallowed up by life. **5**He who has prepared us for this very thing is God, who has given us the Spirit as a guarantee.

● **Eph 3:14-19**
Col 1   **9**And so, from the day we heard of it, we have not ceased to pray for you, asking that you may be filled with the knowledge of his will in all spiritual wisdom and understanding, **10**to lead a life worthy of the Lord, fully pleasing to him, bearing fruit in every good work and increasing in the knowledge of God. **11**May you be strengthened with all power, according to his glorious might, for all endurance and patience with joy, **12**giving thanks to the Father, who has qualified us to share in the inheritance of the saints in light. **13**He has delivered us from the dominion of darkness and transferred us to the kingdom of his beloved Son, **14**in whom we have redemption, the forgiveness of sins.

● **Eph 3:14**
(father) *add* of our Lord Jesus Christ: S^{c}DG Koine Lect it vg syr(pes har) Origen (Latin)

● **Eph 3:16**
Rom 9   **23**in order to make known the riches of his glory for the vessels of mercy, which he has prepared beforehand for glory, . . .

● **Eph 3:17**
Gal 2   **20**I have been crucified with Christ; it is no longer I who live, but Christ who lives in me; and the life I now live in the flesh I live by faith in the Son of God, who loved me and gave himself for me.

● **Eph 3:19**
Phil 4   **7**And the peace of God, which passes all understanding, will keep your hearts and your minds in Christ Jesus.

Col 2   **9**For in him the whole fulness of deity dwells bodily, **10**and you have come to fulness of life in him, who is the head of all rule and authority.

(you) *read* he: p^{46}B cop(sa)

Formal Element: Ascription

20 Now to him who by the power at work within us is able to do far more abundantly than all that we ask or think, 21 to him be glory in the church and in Christ Jesus to all generations, for ever and ever. Amen.

Primary

Rom 16:25–27 (§70)

25 Now to him who is able to strengthen you according to my gospel and the preaching of Jesus Christ, according to the revelation of the mystery which was kept secret for long ages 26 but is now disclosed and through the prophetic writings is made known to all nations, according to the command of the eternal God, to bring about the obedience of faith— 27 to the only wise God be glory for evermore through Jesus Christ! Amen.

Secondary

2 Cor 9:6–15 (§175)

6 The point is this: he who sows sparingly will also reap sparingly, and he who sows boun-tifully will also reap bountifully. 7 Each one must do as he has made up his mind, not reluctantly or under compulsion, for God loves a cheerful giver. 8 And God is able to provide you with every blessing in abundance, so that you may always have enough of everything and may provide in abundance for every good work. 9 As it is written,

"He scatters abroad, he gives to the poor;
his righteousness endures for ever."

10 He who supplies seed to the sower and bread for food will supply and multiply your resources and increase the harvest of your righteousness. 11 You will be enriched in every way for great generosity, which through us will produce thanksgiving to God; 12 for the rendering of this service not only supplies the wants of the saints but also overflows in many thanksgivings to God. 13 Under the test of this service, you will glorify God by your obedience in acknowledging the gospel of Christ, and by the generosity of your contribution for them and for all others; 14 while they long for you and pray for you, because of the surpassing grace of God in you. 15 Thanks be to God for his inexpressible gift!

Phil 4:10–20 (§253)

10 I rejoice in the Lord greatly that now at length you have revived your concern for me; you were indeed concerned for me, but you had no opportunity. 11 Not that I complain of want; for I have learned, in whatever state I am, to be content. 12 I know how to be abased, and I know how to abound; in any and all circumstances I have learned the secret of facing plenty and hunger, abundance and want. 13 I can do all things in him who strengthens me.

14 Yet it was kind of you to share my trouble. 15 And you Philippians yourselves know that in the beginning of the gospel, when I left Macedonia, no church entered into partnership with me in giving and receiving except you only; 16 for even in Thessalonica you sent me help once and again. 17 Not that I seek the gift; but I seek the fruit which increases to your credit. 18 I have received full payment, and more; I am filled, having received from Epaphroditus the gifts you sent, a fragrant offering, a sacrifice acceptable and pleasing to God. 19 And my God will supply every need of yours according to his riches in glory in Christ Jesus. 20 To our God and Father be glory for ever and ever. Amen.

● **Eph 3:20**

2 Cor 13   4 For he was crucified in weakness, but lives by the power of God. For we are weak in him, but in dealing with you we shall live with him by the power of God. Father; . . .

● **Eph 3:21**

Gal 1   5 to whom be the glory for ever and ever. Amen.

1 Tim 1   17 To the King of ages, immortal, invisible, the only God, be honor and glory for ever and ever. Amen.

2 Tim 4   18 . . . To him be the glory for ever and ever. Amen.

4 I therefore, a prisoner for the Lord, beg you to lead a life worthy of the calling to which you have been called, [2] with all lowliness and meekness, with patience, forbearing one another in love, [3] eager to maintain the unity of the Spirit in the bond of peace. [4] There is one body and one Spirit, just as you were called to the one hope that belongs to your call, [5] one Lord, one faith, one baptism, [6] one God and Father of us all, who is above all and through all and in all. [7] But grace was given to each of us according to the measure of Christ's gift. [8] Therefore it is said,

"When he ascended on high he led a host of captives,

and he gave gifts to men."

[9] (In saying, "He ascended," what does it mean but that he had also descended into the lower parts of the earth? [10] He who descended is he who also ascended far above all the heavens, that he might fill all things.)

PRIMARY

See §50 for CONFESSION

Rom 12:1–2 (§51)

[1] I appeal to you therefore, brethren, by the mercies of God, to present your bodies as a living sacrifice, holy and acceptable to God, which is your spiritual worship. [2] Do not be conformed to this world but be transformed by the renewal of your mind, that you may prove what is the will of God, what is good and acceptable and perfect.

1 Cor 1:10–17 (§73)

[10] I appeal to you, brethren, by the name of our Lord Jesus Christ, that all of you agree and that there be no dissensions among you, but that you be united in the same mind and the same judgment. [11] For it has been reported to me by Chloe's people that there is quarreling among you, my brethren. [12] What I mean is that each one of you says, "I belong to Paul," or "I belong to Apollos," or "I belong to Cephas," or "I belong to Christ." [13] Is Christ divided? Was Paul crucified for you? Or were you baptized in the name of Paul? [14] I am thankful that I baptized none of you except Crispus and Gaius; [15] lest any one should say that you were baptized in my name. [16] (I did baptize also the household of Stephanas. Beyond that, I do not know whether I baptized any one else.) [17] For Christ did not send me to baptize but to preach the gospel, and not with eloquent wisdom, lest the cross of Christ be emptied of its power.

2 Cor 10:1–6 (§176)

[1] I, Paul, myself entreat you, by the meekness and gentleness of Christ—I who am humble when face to face with you, but bold to you when I am away!—[2] I beg of you that when I am present I may not have to show boldness with such confidence as I count on showing against some who suspect us of acting in worldly fashion. [3] For though we live in the world we are not carrying on a worldly war, [4] for the weapons of our warfare are not worldly but have divine power to destroy strongholds. [5] We destroy arguments and every proud obstacle to the knowledge of God, and take every thought captive to obey Christ, [6] being ready to punish every disobedience, when your obedience is complete.

1 Thess 4:1–8 (§284)

[1] Finally, brethren, we beseech and exhort you in the Lord Jesus, that as you learned from us how you ought to live and to please God, just as you are doing, you do so more and more. [2] For you know what instructions we gave you through the Lord Jesus. [3] For this is the will of God, your sanctification: that you abstain from unchastity; [4] that each one of you know how to take a wife for himself in holiness and honor, [5] not in the passion of lust like heathen who do not know God; [6] that no man transgress, and wrong his brother in this matter, because the Lord is an avenger in all these things, as we solemnly forewarned you. [7] For God has not called us for uncleanness, but in holiness. [8] Therefore whoever disregards this, disregards not man but God, who gives his Holy Spirit to you.

2 Thess 2:1–12 (§296)

2 [1] Now concerning the coming of our Lord Jesus Christ and our assembling to meet him, we beg you, brethren, [2] not to be quickly shaken in mind or excited, either by spirit or by word, or by letter purporting to be from us, to the effect that the day of the Lord has come. [3] Let no one deceive you in any way; for that day will not come, unless the rebellion comes first, and the man of lawlessness is revealed, the son of perdition, [4] who opposes and exalts himself against every so-called god or object of worship, so that he takes his seat in the temple of God, proclaiming himself to be God. [5] Do you not remember that when I was still with you I told you this? [6] And you know what is restraining him now so that he may be revealed in his time. [7] For the mystery of lawlessness is already at work; only he who now restrains it will do so until he is out of the way. [8] And then the lawless one will be revealed, and the Lord Jesus will slay him with the breath of his mouth and destroy him by his appearing and his coming. [9] The coming of the lawless one by the activity of Satan will be with all power and with pretended signs and wonders, [10] and with all wicked deception for those who are to perish, because they refused to love the truth and so be saved. [11] Therefore God sends upon them a strong delusion, to make them believe what is false, [12] so that all may be condemned who did not believe the truth but had pleasure in unrighteousness.

Phlm 8–14 (§307)

[8] Accordingly, though I am bold enough in Christ to command you to do what is required, [9] yet for love's sake I prefer to appeal to you—I, Paul, an ambassador and now a prisoner also for Christ Jesus—[10] I appeal to you for my child, Onesimus, whose father I have become in my imprisonment. [11] (Formerly he was useless to you, but now he is indeed useful to you and to me.) [12] I am sending him back to you, sending my very heart. [13] I would have been glad to keep him with me, in order that he might serve me on your behalf during my imprisonment for the gospel; [14] but I preferred to do nothing without your consent in order that your goodness might not be by compulsion but of your own free will.

SECONDARY

Rom 12:3–8 (§52)

[3] For by the grace given to me I bid every one among you not to think of himself more highly than he ought to think, but to think with sober judgment, each according to the measure of faith which God has assigned him. [4] For as in one body we have many members, and all the members do not have the same function, [5] so we, though many, are one body in Christ, and individually members one of another. [6] Having

---

● **Eph 4:1–10**
Cf. Phil 4:10–20

● **Eph 4:1**
Eph 3 [1] For this reason I, Paul, a prisoner for Christ Jesus on behalf of you Gentiles . . .

Phil 1 [12] I want you to know, brethren, that what has happened to me has really served to advance the gospel, . . .

Phil 1 [27] Only let your manner of life be worthy of the gospel of Christ, so that whether I come and see you or am absent, I may hear of you that you stand firm in one spirit, with one mind striving side by side for the faith of the gospel, . . .

Col 1 [10] to lead a life worthy of the Lord, fully pleasing to him, bearing fruit in every good work and increasing in the knowledge of God.

Col 4 [18] I, Paul, write this greeting with my own hand. Remember my fetters.

Phlm [1] Paul, a prisoner for Christ Jesus, and Timothy our brother,
To Philemon our beloved fellow worker . . .

● **Eph 4:2**
2 Cor 8 [7] Now as you excel in everything—in faith, in utterance, in knowledge, in all earnestness, and in your love for us—see that you excel in this gracious work also.

Eph 4 [32] and be kind to one another, tenderhearted, forgiving one another, as God in Christ forgave you.

gifts that differ according to the grace given to us, let us use them: if prophecy, in proportion to our faith; ⁷if service, in our serving; he who teaches, in his teaching; ⁸he who exhorts, in his exhortation; he who contributes, in liberality; he who gives aid, with zeal; he who does acts of mercy, with cheerfulness.

1 Cor 12:4–13 (§117–118)

⁴Now there are varieties of gifts, but the same Spirit; ⁵and there are varieties of service, but the same Lord; ⁶and there are varieties of working, but it is the same God who inspires them all in every one. ⁷To each is given the manifestation of the Spirit for the common good. ⁸To one is given through the Spirit the utterance of wisdom, and to another the utterance of knowledge according to the same Spirit, ⁹to another faith by the same Spirit, to another gifts of healing by the one Spirit, ¹⁰to another the working of miracles, to another prophecy, to another the ability to distinguish between spirits, to another various kinds of tongues, to another the interpretation of tongues. ¹¹All these are inspired by one and the same Spirit, who apportions to each one individually as he wills.

¹²For just as the body is one and has many members, and all the members of the body, though many, are one body, so it is with Christ. ¹³For by one Spirit we were all baptized into one body— Jews or Greeks, slaves or free—and all were made to drink of one Spirit.

2 Cor 6:1–10 (§165)

¹Working together with him, then, we entreat you not to accept the grace of God in vain. ²For he says,

"At the acceptable time I have listened to you,

and helped you on the day of salvation."
Behold, now is the acceptable time; behold, now is the day of salvation. ³We put no obstacle in any one's way, so that no fault may be found with our ministry, ⁴but as servants of God we commend ourselves in every way: through great endurance, in afflictions, hardships, calamities, ⁵beatings, imprisonments, tumults, labors, watching, hunger; ⁶by purity, knowledge, forbearance, kindness, the Holy Spirit, genuine love, ⁷truthful speech, and the power of God; with the weapons of righteousness for the right hand and for the left; ⁸in honor and dishonor, in ill repute and good repute. We are treated as impostors, and yet are true; ⁹as un-

known, and yet well known; as dying, and behold we live; as punished, and yet not killed; ¹⁰as sorrowful, yet always rejoicing; as poor, yet making many rich; as having nothing, and yet possessing everything.

2 Cor 8:1–7 (§171)

¹We want you to know, brethren, about the grace of God which has been shown in the churches of Macedonia, ²for in a severe test of affliction, their abundance of joy and their extreme poverty overflowed in a wealth of liberality on their part. ³For they gave according to their means, as I can testify, and beyond their means, of their own free will, ⁴begging us earnestly for the favor of taking part in the relief of the saints— ⁵and this, not as we expected, but first they gave themselves to the Lord and to us by the will of God. ⁶Accordingly we have urged Titus that as he had already made a beginning, he should also complete among you this gracious work. ⁷Now as you excel in everything—in faith, in utterance, in knowledge, in all earnestness, and in your love for us—see that you excel in this gracious work also.

Gal 3:26–29 (§206)

²⁶for in Christ Jesus you are all sons of God, through faith. ²⁷For as many of you as were baptized into Christ have put on Christ. ²⁸There is neither Jew nor Greek, there is neither slave nor free, there is neither male nor female; for you are all one in Christ Jesus. ²⁹And if you are Christ's, then you are Abraham's offspring, heirs according to promise.

Gal 5:16–26 (§213)

¹⁶But I say, walk by the Spirit, and do not gratify the desires of the flesh. ¹⁷For the desires of the flesh are against the Spirit, and the desires of the Spirit are against the flesh; for these are opposed to each other, to prevent you from doing what you would. ¹⁸But if you are led by the Spirit you are not under the law. ¹⁹Now the works of the flesh are plain: fornication, impurity, licentiousness, ²⁰idolatry, sorcery, enmity, strife, jealousy, anger, selfishness, dissension, party spirit, ²¹envy, drunkenness, carousing, and the like. I warn you, as I warned you before, that those who do such things shall not inherit the kingdom of God. ²²But the fruit of the Spirit is love, joy, peace, patience, kindness, goodness, faithfulness, ²³gentleness, self-control; against such there is no law. ²⁴And

those who belong to Christ Jesus have crucified the flesh with its passions and desires.

²⁵If we live by the Spirit, let us also walk by the Spirit. ²⁶Let us have no self-conceit, no provoking of one another, no envy of one another.

Phil 1:27–30 (§241)

²⁷Only let your manner of life be worthy of the gospel of Christ, so that whether I come and see you or am absent, I may hear of you that you stand firm in one spirit, with one mind striving side by side for the faith of the gospel, ²⁸and not frightened in anything by your opponents. This is a clear omen to them of their destruction, but of your salvation, and that from God. ²⁹For it has been granted to you that for the sake of Christ you should not only believe in him but also suffer for his sake, ³⁰engaged in the same conflict which you saw and now hear to be mine.

Phil 4:8–9 (§252)

⁸Finally, brethren, whatever is true, whatever is honorable, whatever is just, whatever is pure, whatever is lovely, whatever is gracious, if there is any excellence, if there is anything worthy of praise, think about these things. ⁹What you have learned and received and heard and seen in me, do; and the God of peace will be with you.

Col 3:12–17 (§267)

¹²Put on then, as God's chosen ones, holy and beloved, compassion, kindness, lowliness, meekness, and patience, ¹³forbearing one another and, if one has a complaint against another, forgiving each other; as the Lord has forgiven you, so you also must forgive. ¹⁴And above all these put on love, which binds everything together in perfect harmony. ¹⁵And let the peace of Christ rule in your hearts, to which indeed you were called in the one body. And be thankful. ¹⁶Let the word of Christ dwell in you richly, as you teach and admonish one another in all wisdom, and as you sing psalms and hymns and spiritual songs with thankfulness in your hearts to God. ¹⁷And whatever you do, in word or deed, do everything in the name of the Lord Jesus, giving thanks to God the Father through him.

● **Eph 4:4–8**
1 Tim 2 ⁵For there is one God, and there is one mediator between God and men, the man Christ Jesus, . . .

1 Tim 3 ¹⁶Great indeed, we confess, is the mystery of our religion:
He was manifested in the flesh,
vindicated in the Spirit,
    seen by angels,
preached among the nations,
believed on in the world,
    taken up in glory.

● **Eph 4:7**
1 Cor 7 ⁷I wish that all were as I myself am. But each has his own special gift from God, one of one kind and one of another.

● **Eph 4:8–10**
Rom 10 ⁶But the righteousness based on faith says, Do not say in your heart, "Who will ascend into heaven?" (that is, to bring Christ down) ⁷ or "Who will descend into the abyss?" (that is, to bring Christ up from the dead). ⁸But what does it say? The word is near you, on your lips and in your heart (that is, the word of faith which we preach); . . .

● **Eph 4:8**
Ps 68 ¹⁸Thou didst ascend the high mount, leading captives in thy train, and receiving gifts among men,
even among the rebellious, that the Lord God may dwell there.

[11]And his gifts were that some should be apostles, some prophets, some evangelists, some pastors and teachers, [12]to equip the saints for the work of ministry, for building up the body of Christ, [13]until we all attain to the unity of the faith and of the knowledge of the Son of God, to mature manhood, to the measure of the stature of the fulness of Christ; [14]so that we may no longer be children, tossed to and fro and carried about with every wind of doctrine, by the cunning of men, by their craftiness in deceitful wiles. [15]Rather, speaking the truth in love, we are to grow up in every way into him who is the head, into Christ, [16]from whom the whole body, joined and knit together by every joint with which it is supplied, when each part is working properly, makes bodily growth and upbuilds itself in love.

PRIMARY

Rom 12:3–8 (§52)

[3]For by the grace given to me I bid every one among you not to think of himself more highly than he ought to think, but to think with sober judgment, each according to the measure of faith which God has assigned him. [4]For as in one body we have many members, and all the members do not have the same function, [5]so we, though many, are one body in Christ, and individually members one of another. [6]Having gifts that differ according to the grace given to us, let us use them: if prophecy, in proportion to our faith; [7]if service, in our serving; he who teaches, in his teaching; [8]he who exhorts, in his exhortation; he who contributes, in liberality; he who gives aid, with zeal; he who does acts of mercy, with cheerfulness.

1 Cor 2:6–16 (§77)

[6]Yet among the mature we do impart wisdom, although it is not a wisdom of this age or of the rulers of this age, who are doomed to pass away. [7]But we impart a secret and hidden wisdom of God, which God decreed before the ages for our glorification. [8]None of the rulers of this age understood this; for if they had, they would not have crucified the Lord of glory. [9]But, as it is written,

"What no eye has seen, nor ear heard,
   nor the heart of man conceived,

what God has prepared for those who love him," [10]God has revealed to us through the Spirit. For the Spirit searches everything, even the depths of God. [11]For what person knows a man's thoughts except the spirit of the man which is in him? So also no one comprehends the thoughts of God except the Spirit of God. [12]Now we have received not the spirit of the world, but the Spirit which is from God, that we might understand the gifts bestowed on us by God. [13]And we impart this in words not taught by human wisdom but taught by the Spirit, interpreting spiritual truths to those who possess the Spirit.

[14]The unspiritual man does not receive the gifts of the Spirit of God, for they are folly to him, and he is not able to understand them because they are spiritually discerned. [15]The spiritual man judges all things, but is himself to be judged by no one. [16]"For who has known the mind of the Lord so as to instruct him?" But we have the mind of Christ.

1 Cor 3:1–4 (§78)

[1]But I, brethren, could not address you as spiritual men, but as men of the flesh, as babes in Christ. [2]I fed you with milk, not solid food; for you were not ready for it; and even yet you are not ready, [3]for you are still of the flesh. For while there is jealousy and strife among you, are you not of the flesh, and behaving like ordinary men? [4]For when one says, "I belong to Paul," and another, "I belong to Apollos," are you not merely men?

1 Cor 12:4–11 (§117)

[4]Now there are varieties of gifts, but the same Spirit; [5]and there are varieties of service, but the same Lord; [6]and there are varieties of working, but it is the same God who inspires them all in every one. [7]To each is given the manifestation of the Spirit for the common good. [8]To one is given through the Spirit the utterance of wisdom, and to another the utterance of knowledge according to the same Spirit, [9]to another faith by the same Spirit, to another gifts of healing by the one Spirit, [10]to another the working of miracles, to another prophecy, to another the ability to distinguish between spirits, to another various kinds of tongues, to another the interpretation of tongues. [11]All these are inspired by one and the same Spirit, who apportions to each one individually as he wills.

1 Cor 12:14–26 (§119)

[14]For the body does not consist of one member but of many. [15]If the foot should say, "Because I am not a hand, I do not belong to the body," that would not make it any less a part of the body. [16]And if the ear should say, "Because I am not an eye, I do not belong to the body," that would not make it any less a part of the body. [17]If the whole body were an eye, where would be the hearing? If the whole body were an ear, where would be the sense of smell? [18]But as it is, God arranged the organs in the body, each one of them, as he chose. [19]If all

---

● **Eph 4:11–16**
1 Cor 1 [4]I give thanks to God always for you because of the grace of God which was given you in Christ Jesus, [5]that in every way you were enriched in him with all speech and all knowledge . . .

● **Eph 4:11**
1 Tim 5 [17]As for the rich in this world, charge them not to be haughty, nor to set their hopes on uncertain riches but on God who richly furnishes us with everything to enjoy.

Acts 13 [1]Now in the church at Antioch there were prophets and teachers, Barnabas, Simeon who was

called Niger, Lucius of Cyrene, Manaen a member of the court of Herod the tetrarch, and Saul.

Acts 15 [32]And Judas and Silas, who were themselves prophets, exhorted the brethren with many words and strengthened them.

Acts 15 [35]But Paul and Barnabas remained in Antioch, teaching and preaching the word of the Lord, with many others also.

● **Eph 4:12**
Eph 1 [23]which is his body, the fulness of him who fills all in all.

Eph 5 [30]because we are members of his body.

2 Tim 3 [16]All scripture is inspired by God and profitable for teaching, for reproof, for correction, and for training in righteousness, [17]that the man of God may be complete, equipped for every good work.

● **Eph 4:13–16**
Rom 16 [19]For while your obedience is known to all, so that I rejoice over you, I would have you wise as to what is good and guileless as to what is evil; . . .

were a single organ, where would the body be? [20]As it is, there are many parts, yet one body. [21]The eye cannot say to the hand, "I have no need of you," nor again the head to the feet, "I have no need of you." [22]On the contrary, the parts of the body which seem to be weaker are indispensable, [23]and those parts of the body which we think less honorable we invest with the greater honor, and our unpresentable parts are treated with greater modesty, [24]which our more presentable parts do not require. But God has so composed the body, giving the greater honor to the inferior part, [25]that there may be no discord in the body, but that the members may have the same care for one another. [26]If one member suffers, all suffer together; if one member is honored, all rejoice together.

1 Cor 12:27–31 (§120)

[27]Now you are the body of Christ and individually members of it. [28]And God has appointed in the church first apostles, second prophets, third teachers, then workers of miracles, then healers, helpers, administrators, speakers in various kinds of tongues. [29]Are all apostles? Are all prophets? Are all teachers? Do all work miracles? [30]Do all possess gifts of healing? Do all speak with tongues? Do all interpret? [31]But earnestly desire the higher gifts.

And I will show you a still more excellent way.

2 Cor 11:1–6 (§179)

[1]I wish you would bear with me in a little foolishness. Do bear with me! [2]I feel a divine jealousy for you, for I betrothed you to Christ to present you as a pure bride to her one husband. [3]But I am afraid that as the serpent deceived Eve by his cunning, your thoughts will be led astray from a sincere and pure devotion to Christ. [4]For if some one comes and preaches another Jesus than the one we preached, or if you receive a different spirit from the one you received, or if you accept a different gospel from the one you accepted, you submit to it readily enough. [5]I think that I am not in the least inferior to these superlative apostles. [6]Even if I am unskilled in speaking, I am not in knowledge; in every way we have made this plain to you in all things.

Gal 1:6–12 (§194)

[6]I am astonished that you are so quickly deserting him who called you in the grace of Christ and turning to a different gospel— [7]not that there is another gospel, but there are some who trouble you and want to pervert the gospel of Christ. [8]But even if we, or an angel from heaven, should preach to you a gospel contrary to that which we preached to you, let him be accursed. [9]As we have said before, so now I say again, If any one is preaching to you a gospel contrary to that which you received, let him be accursed.

[10]Am I now seeking the favor of men, or of God? Or am I trying to please men? If I were still pleasing men, I should not be a servant of Christ.

[11]For I would have you know, brethren, that the gospel which was preached by me is not man's gospel. [12]For I did not receive it from man, nor was I taught it, but it came through a revelation of Jesus Christ.

Phil 3:12–16 (§248)

[12]Not that I have already obtained this or am already perfect; but I press on to make it my own, because Christ Jesus has made me his own. [13]Brethren, I do not consider that I have made it my own; but one thing I do, forgetting what lies behind and straining forward to what lies ahead, [14]I press on toward the goal for the prize of the upward call of God in Christ Jesus. [15]Let those of us who are mature be thus minded; and if in anything you are otherwise minded, God will reveal that also to you. [16]Only let us hold true to what we have attained.

Col 2:16–19 (§263)

[16]Therefore let no one pass judgment on you in questions of food and drink or with regard to a festival or a new moon or a sabbath. [17]These are only a shadow of what is to come; but the substance belongs to Christ. [18]Let no one disqualify you, insisting on self-abasement and worship of angels, taking his stand on visions, puffed up without reason by his sensuous mind, [19]and not holding fast to the Head, from whom the whole body, nourished and knit together through its joints and ligaments, grows with a growth that is from God.

1 Thess 3:11–13 (§283)

[11]Now may our God and Father himself, and our Lord Jesus, direct our way to you; [12]and may the Lord make you increase and abound in love to one another and to all men, as we do to you, [13]so that he may establish your hearts unblamable in holiness before our God and Father, at the coming of our Lord Jesus with all his saints.

---

1 Cor 13   [11]When I was a child, I spoke like a child, I thought like a child, I reasoned like a child; when I became a man, I gave up childish ways.

1 Cor 14   [20]Brethren, do not be children in your thinking; be babes in evil, but in thinking be mature.

● **Eph 4:14**
2 Cor 4   [2]We have renounced disgraceful, underhanded ways; we refuse to practice cunning or to tamper with God's word, but by the open statement of the truth we would commend ourselves to every man's conscience in the sight of God.

2 Cor 11   [13]For such men are false apostles, deceitful workmen, disguising themselves as apostles of Christ.

1 Thess 2   [3]For our appeal does not spring from error or uncleanness, nor is it made with guile; . . .

● **Eph 4:15**
1 Cor 11   [3]But I want you to understand that the head of every man is Christ, the head of a woman is her husband, and the head of Christ is God.

Eph 1   [22]and he has put all things under his feet and has made him the head over all things for the church, [23]which is his body, the fulness of him who fills all in all.

Eph 5   [23]For the husband is the head of the wife as Christ is the head of the church, his body, and is himself its Savior.

FORMAL ELEMENT: VICE LIST

[17]Now this I affirm and testify in the Lord, that you must no longer live as the Gentiles do, in the futility of their minds; [18]they are darkened in their understanding, alienated from the life of God because of the ignorance that is in them, due to their hardness of heart; [19]they have become callous and have given themselves up to licentiousness, greedy to practice every kind of uncleanness. [20]You did not so learn Christ!—[21]assuming that you have heard about him and were taught in him, as the truth is in Jesus. [22]Put off your old nature which belongs to your former manner of life and is corrupt through deceitful lusts, [23]and be renewed in the spirit of your minds, [24]and put on the new nature, created after the likeness of God in true righteousness and holiness.

PRIMARY

Rom 1:29–32 (§6)

[29]They were filled with all manner of wickedness, evil, covetousness, malice. Full of envy, murder, strife, deceit, malignity, they are gossips, [30]slanderers, haters of God, insolent, haughty, boastful, inventors of evil, disobedient to parents, [31]foolish, faithless, heartless, ruthless. [32]Though they know God's decree that those who do such things deserve to die, they not only do them but approve those who practice them.

Rom 13:11–14 (§56)

[11]Besides this you know what hour it is, how it is full time now for you to wake from sleep. For salvation is nearer to us now than when we first believed; [12]the night is far gone, the day is at hand. Let us then cast off the works of darkness and put on the armor of light; [13]let us conduct ourselves becomingly as in the day, not in reveling and drunkenness, not in debauchery and licentiousness, not in quarreling and jealousy. [14]But put on the Lord Jesus Christ, and make no provision for the flesh, to gratify its desires.

1 Cor 5:9–13 (§89)

[9]I wrote to you in my letter not to associate with immoral men; [10]not at all meaning the immoral of this world, or the greedy and robbers, or idolaters, since then you would need to go out of the world. [11]But rather I wrote to you not to associate with any one who bears the name of brother if he is guilty of immorality or greed, or is an idolater, reviler, drunkard, or robber—not even to eat with such a one. [12]For what have I to do with judging outsiders? Is it not those inside the church whom you are to judge? [13]God judges those outside. "Drive out the wicked person from among you."

1 Cor 6:9–11 (§91)

[9]Do you not know that the unrighteous will not inherit the kingdom of God? Do not be deceived; neither the immoral, nor idolaters, nor adulterers, nor sexual perverts, [10]nor thieves, nor the greedy, nor drunkards, nor revilers, nor robbers will inherit the kingdom of God. [11]And such were some of you. But you were washed, you were sanctified, you were justified in the name of the Lord Jesus Christ and in the Spirit of our God.

2 Cor 12:19–21 (§188)

[19]Have you been thinking all along that we have been defending ourselves before you? It is in the sight of God that we have been speaking in Christ, and all for your upbuilding, beloved. [20]For I fear that perhaps I may come and find you not what I wish, and that you may find me not what you wish; that perhaps there may be quarreling, jealousy, anger, selfishness, slander, gossip, conceit, and disorder. [21]I fear that when I come again my God may humble me before you, and I may have to mourn over many of those who sinned before and have not repented of the impurity, immorality, and licentiousness which they have practiced.

Gal 5:16–26 (§213)

[16]But I say, walk by the Spirit, and do not gratify the desires of the flesh. [17]For the desires of the flesh are against the Spirit, and the desires of the Spirit are against the flesh; for these are opposed to each other, to prevent you from doing what you would. [18]But if you are led by the Spirit you are not under the law. [19]Now the works of the flesh are plain: fornication, impurity, licentiousness, [20]idolatry, sorcery, enmity, strife, jealousy, anger, selfishness, dissension, party spirit, [21]envy, drunkenness, carousing, and the like. I warn you, as I warned you before, that those who do such things shall not inherit the kingdom of God. [22]But the fruit

---

● Eph 4:17–24

Eph 5　[3]But fornication and all impurity or covetousness must not even be named among you, as is fitting among saints. [4]Let there be no filthiness, nor silly talk, nor levity, which are not fitting; but instead let there be thanksgiving. [5]Be sure of this, that no fornicator or impure man, or one who is covetous (that is, an idolater), has any inheritance in the kingdom of Christ and of God. [6]Let no one deceive you with empty words, for it is because of these things that the wrath of God comes upon the sons of disobedience. [7]Therefore do not associate with them, [8]for once you were darkness, but now you are light in the Lord; walk as children of light [9](for the fruit of light is found in all that is good and right and true), [10]and try to learn what is pleasing to the Lord. [11]Take no part in the unfruitful works of darkness, but instead expose them. [12]For it is a shame even to speak of the things that they do in secret; [13]but when anything is exposed by the light it

becomes visible, for anything that becomes visible is light. [14]Therefore it is said,

> "Awake, O sleeper, and arise from the dead,
> and Christ shall give you light."

1 Tim 1　[9]understanding this, that the law is not laid down for the just but for the lawless and disobedient, for the ungodly and sinners, for the unholy and profane, for murderers of fathers and murderers of mothers, for manslayers, [10]immoral persons, sodomites, kidnappers, liars, perjurers, and whatever else is contrary to sound doctrine, . . .

1 Tim 6　[4]he is puffed up with conceit, he knows nothing; he has a morbid craving for controversy and for disputes about words, which produce envy, dissension, slander, base suspicions, [5]and wrangling among men who are depraved in mind and bereft of the truth, imagining that godliness is a means of gain.

2 Tim 3　[2]For men will be lovers of self, lovers of money, proud, arrogant, abusive, disobedient to their parents, ungrateful, unholy, [3]inhuman, implacable, slanderers, profligates, fierce, haters of good, [4]treacherous, reckless, swollen with conceit, lovers of pleasure rather than lovers of God, . . .

Titus 3　[3]For we ourselves were once foolish, disobedient, led astray, slaves to various passions and pleasures, passing our days in malice and envy, hated by men and hating one another; . . .

● Eph 4:17–18

Gal 2　[15]We ourselves, who are Jews by birth and not Gentile sinners, . . .

Eph 4　[25]Therefore, putting away falsehood, let every one speak the truth with his neighbor, for we are members one of another. [26]Be angry but do not sin; do not let the sun go down on your anger, [27]and give no

of the Spirit is love, joy, peace, patience, kindness, goodness, faithfulness, ²³gentleness, self-control; against such there is no law. ²⁴And those who belong to Christ Jesus have crucified the flesh with its passions and desires.

²⁵If we live by the Spirit, let us also walk by the Spirit. ²⁶Let us have no self-conceit, no provoking of one another, no envy of one another.

Col 3:5–11 (§266)

⁵Put to death therefore what is earthly in you: fornication, impurity, passion, evil desire, and covetousness, which is idolatry. ⁶On account of these the wrath of God is coming. ⁷In these you once walked, when you lived in them. ⁸But now put them all away: anger, wrath, malice, slander, and foul talk from your mouth. ⁹Do not lie to one another, seeing that you have put off the old nature with its practices ¹⁰and have put on the new nature, which is being renewed in knowledge after the image of its creator. ¹¹Here there cannot be Greek and Jew, circumcised and uncircumcised, barbarian, Scythian, slave, free man, but Christ is all, and in all.

Secondary

Rom 1:18–28 (§4–5)

¹⁸For the wrath of God is revealed from heaven against all ungodliness and wickedness of men who by their wickedness suppress the truth. ¹⁹For what can be known about God is plain to them, because God has shown it to them. ²⁰Ever since the creation of the world his invisible nature, namely, his eternal power and deity, has been clearly perceived in the things that have been made. So they are without excuse; ²¹for although they knew God they did not honor him as God or give thanks to him, but they became futile in their thinking and their senseless minds were darkened. ²²Claiming to be wise, they became fools, ²³and exchanged the glory of the immortal God for images resembling mortal man or birds or animals or reptiles.

²⁴Therefore God gave them up in the lusts of their hearts to impurity, to the dishonoring of their bodies among themselves, ²⁵because they exchanged the truth about God for a lie and worshiped and served the creature rather than the Creator, who is blessed for ever! Amen. ²⁶For this reason God gave them up to dishonorable passions. Their women exchanged natural relations for unnatural, ²⁷and the men likewise gave up natural relations with women and were consumed with passion for one another, men committing shameless acts with men and receiving in their own persons the due penalty for their error. ²⁸And since they did not see fit to acknowledge God, God gave them up to a base mind and to improper conduct.

Rom 11:25–32 (§49)

²⁵Lest you be wise in your own conceits, I want you to understand this mystery, brethren: a hardening has come upon part of Israel, until the full number of the Gentiles come in, ²⁶and so all Israel will be saved; as it is written,

"The Deliverer will come from Zion,

he will banish ungodliness from Jacob";
²⁷"and this will be my covenant with them when I take away their sins."
²⁸As regards the gospel they are enemies of God, for your sake; but as regards election they are beloved for the sake of their forefathers. ²⁹For the gifts and the call of God are irrevocable. ³⁰Just as you were once disobedient to God but now have received mercy because of their disobedience, ³¹so they have now been disobedient in order that by the mercy shown to you they also may receive mercy. ³²For God has consigned all men to disobedience, that he may have mercy upon all.

1 Thess 4:1–8 (§284)

¹Finally, brethren, we beseech and exhort you in the Lord Jesus, that as you learned from us how you ought to live and to please God, just as you are doing, you do so more and more. ²For you know what instructions we gave you through the Lord Jesus. ³For this is the will of God, your sanctification: that you abstain from unchastity; ⁴that each one of you know how to take a wife for himself in holiness and honor ⁵not in the passion of lust like heathen who do not know God; ⁶that no man transgress, and wrong his brother in this matter, because the Lord is an avenger in all these things, as we solemnly forewarned you. ⁷For God has not called us for uncleanness, but in holiness. ⁸Therefore whoever disregards this, disregards not man but God, who gives his Holy Spirit to you.

---

opportunity to the devil. ²⁸Let the thief no longer steal, but rather let him labor, doing honest work with his hands, so that he may be able to give to those in need. ²⁹Let no evil talk come out of your mouths, but only such as is good for edifying, as fits the occasion, that it may impart grace to those who hear. ³⁰And do not grieve the Holy Spirit of God, in whom you were sealed for the day of redemption. ³¹Let all bitterness and wrath and anger and clamor and slander be put away from you, with all malice, ³²and be kind to one another, tenderhearted, forgiving one another, as God in Christ forgave you.

● **Eph 4:18**

Rom 11 ⁷What then? Israel failed to obtain what it sought. The elect obtained it, but the rest were hardened, ⁸as it is written,

"God gave them a spirit of stupor,
eyes that should not see and ears that should not hear,

down to this very day."
⁹And David says,
"Let their table become a snare and a trap,
a pitfall and a retribution for them;
¹⁰let their eyes be darkened so that they cannot see,
and bend their backs for ever."

Gal 4 ⁸Formerly, when you did not know God, you were in bondage to beings that by nature are no gods; . . .

2 Thess 2 ¹¹Therefore God sends upon them a strong delusion, to make them believe what is false, ¹²so that all may be condemned who did not believe the truth but had pleasure in unrighteousness.

Acts 17 ³⁰"The times of ignorance God overlooked, but now he commands all men everywhere to repent. . . ."

● **Eph 4:21**

Eph 3 ²assuming that you have heard of the stewardship of God's grace that was given to me for you, . . .

● **Eph 4:22**

Gal 3 ²⁷For as many of you as were baptized into Christ have put on Christ.

Eph 6 ¹¹Put on the whole armor of God, that you may be able to stand against the wiles of the devil.

Eph 6 ¹⁴Stand therefore, having girded your loins with truth, and having put on the breastplate of righteousness, . . .

1 Thess 5 ⁸But, since we belong to the day, let us be sober, and put on the breastplate of faith and love, and for a helmet the hope of salvation.

FORMAL ELEMENTS: VICE LIST
& GNOMIC SAYINGS

²⁵ Therefore, putting away falsehood, let every one speak the truth with his neighbor, for we are members one of another. ²⁶ Be angry but do not sin; do not let the sun go down on your anger, ²⁷ and give no opportunity to the devil. ²⁸ Let the thief no longer steal, but rather let him labor, doing honest work with his hands, so that he may be able to give to those in need. ²⁹ Let no evil talk come out of your mouths, but only such as is good for edifying, as fits the occasion, that it may impart grace to those who hear. ³⁰ And do not grieve the Holy Spirit of God, in whom you were sealed for the day of redemption. ³¹ Let all bitterness and wrath and anger and clamor and slander be put away from you, with all malice, ³² and be kind to one another, tenderhearted, forgiving one another, as God in Christ forgave you.

PRIMARY

See §227 for VICE LIST

See §53 for GNOMIC SAYINGS

SECONDARY

2 Thess 3:6–13 (§300)

⁶ Now we command you, brethren, in the name of our Lord Jesus Christ, that you keep away from any brother who is living in idleness and not in accord with the tradition that you received from us. ⁷ For you yourselves know how you ought to imitate us; we were not idle when we were with you, ⁸ we did not eat any one's bread without paying, but with toil and labor we worked night and day, that we might not burden any of you. ⁹ It was not because we have not that right, but to give you in our conduct an example to imitate. ¹⁰ For even when we were with you, we gave you this command: If any one will not work, let him not eat. ¹¹ For we hear that some of you are living in idleness, mere busybodies, not doing any work. ¹² Now such persons we command and exhort in the Lord Jesus Christ to do their work in quietness and to earn their own living. ¹³ Brethren, do not be weary in well-doing.

● **Eph 4:25**
Rom 12   ⁵ so we, though many, are one body in Christ, and individually members one of another.

1 Cor 12   ²² On the contrary, the parts of the body which seem to be weaker are indispensable, . . .

1 Cor 12   ²⁷ Now you are the body of Christ and individually members of it.

Eph 5   ³⁰ because we are members of his body.

● **Eph 4:28**
1 Cor 4   ¹² and we labor, working with our own hands. When reviled, we bless; when persecuted, we endure; . . .

Acts 20   ³⁵ "In all things I have shown you that by so toiling one must help the weak, remembering the words of the Lord Jesus, how he said, 'It is more blessed to give than to receive.'"

● **Eph 4:30**
Rom 4   ¹¹ He received circumcision as a sign or seal of the righteousness which he had by faith while he was still uncircumcised. The purpose was to make him the father of all who believe without being circumcised and who thus have righteousness reckoned to them, . . .

2 Cor 1   ²² he has put his seal upon us and given us his Spirit in our hearts as a guarantee.

Eph 1   ¹³ In him you also, who have heard the word of truth, the gospel of your salvation, and have believed in him, were sealed with the promised Holy Spirit, . . .

● **Eph 4:31**
Eph 4   ²² Put off your old nature which belongs to your former manner of life and is corrupt through deceitful lusts, . . .

Eph 5   ³ But fornication and all impurity or covetousness must not even be named among you, as is fitting among saints. ⁴ Let there be no filthiness, nor silly talk, nor levity, which are not fitting; but instead let there be thanksgiving. ⁵ Be sure of this, that no fornicator or impure man, or one who is covetous (that is, an idolater), has any inheritance in the kingdom of Christ and of God. ⁶ Let no one deceive you with empty words, for it is because of these things that the wrath of God comes upon the sons of disobedience. ⁷ Therefore do not associate with them, ⁸ for once you were darkness, but now you are light in the Lord; walk as children of light ⁹ (for the fruit of light is found in all that is good and right and true), ¹⁰ and try to learn what is pleasing to the Lord. ¹¹ Take no part in the unfruitful works of darkness, but instead expose them. ¹² For it is a shame even to speak of the things that they do in secret; ¹³ but when anything is exposed by the light it becomes visible, for anything that becomes visible is light. ¹⁴ Therefore it is said,
"Awake, O sleeper, and arise from the dead,
and Christ shall give you light."

● **Eph 4:32**
2 Cor 8   ⁷ Now as you excel in everything—in faith, in utterance, in knowledge, in all earnestness, and in your love for us—see that you excel in this gracious work also.

Eph 4   ² with all lowliness and meekness, with patience, forbearing one another in love, . . .

5 Therefore be imitators of God, as beloved children. ²And walk in love, as Christ loved us and gave himself up for us, a fragrant offering and sacrifice to God.

P<small>RIMARY</small>

1 Cor 5:6–8 (§88)

⁶Your boasting is not good. Do you not know that a little leaven leavens the whole lump? ⁷Cleanse out the old leaven that you may be a new lump, as you really are unleavened. For Christ, our paschal lamb, has been sacrificed. ⁸Let us, therefore, celebrate the festival, not with the old leaven, the leaven of malice and evil, but with the unleavened bread of sincerity and truth.

2 Cor 2:14–17 (§153)

¹⁴But thanks be to God, who in Christ always leads us in triumph, and through us spreads the fragrance of the knowledge of him everywhere. ¹⁵For we are the aroma of Christ to God among those who are being saved and among those who are perishing, ¹⁶to one a fragrance from death to death, to the other a fragrance from life to life. Who is sufficient for these things? ¹⁷For we are not, like so many, peddlers of God's word; but as men of sincerity, as commissioned by God, in the sight of God we speak in Christ.

● **Eph 5:1**

1 Cor 11   ¹Be imitators of me, as I am of Christ.

Phil 2   ⁵Have this mind among yourselves, which is yours in Christ Jesus, . . .

1 Thess 1   ⁶And you became imitators of us and of the Lord, for you received the word in much affliction, with joy inspired by the Holy Spirit; . . .

● **Eph 5:2**

Rom 8   ³²He who did not spare his own Son but gave him up for us all, will he not also give us all things with him?

Rom 12   ¹I appeal to you therefore, brethren, by the mercies of God, to present your bodies as a living sacrifice, holy and acceptable to God, which is your spiritual worship.

Gal 2   ²⁰I have been crucified with Christ; it is no longer I who live, but Christ who lives in me; and the life I now live in the flesh I live by faith in the Son of God, who loved me and gave himself for me.

Eph 5   ²⁵Husbands, love your wives, as Christ loved the church and gave himself up for her, . . .

Phil 2   ⁻¹⁷Even if I am to be poured as a libation upon the sacrificial offering of your faith, I am glad and rejoice with you all.

Phil 4   ¹⁸I have received full payment, and more; I am filled, having received from Epaphroditus the gifts you sent, a fragrant offering, a sacrifice acceptable and pleasing to God.

(loved us) *read* loved you: S*AB it(few) cop Clement (for us) *read* for you: B it(few) cop Origen

FORMAL ELEMENT: VICE LIST

3 But fornication and all impurity or covetousness must not even be named among you, as is fitting among saints. 4 Let there be no filthiness, nor silly talk, nor levity, which are not fitting; but instead let there be thanksgiving. 5 Be sure of this, that no fornicator or impure man, or one who is covetous (that is, an idolater), has any inheritance in the kingdom of Christ and of God. 6 Let no one deceive you with empty words, for it is because of these things that the wrath of God comes upon the sons of disobedience. 7 Therefore do not associate with them, 8 for once you were darkness, but now you are light in the Lord; walk as children of light 9 (for the fruit of light is found in all that is good and right and true), 10 and try to learn what is pleasing to the Lord. 11 Take no part in the unfruitful works of darkness, but instead expose them. 12 For it is a shame even to speak of the things that they do in secret; 13 but when anything is exposed by the light it becomes visible, for anything that becomes visible is light. 14 Therefore it is said,

   "Awake, O sleeper, and arise from the dead,

    and Christ shall give you light."

PRIMARY

See §227 for VICE LIST

SECONDARY

2 Cor 6:14–7:1 (§167)

14 Do not be mismated with unbelievers. For what partnership have righteousness and iniquity? Or what fellowship has light with darkness? 15 What accord has Christ with Belial? Or what has a believer in common with an unbeliever? 16 What agreement has the temple of God with idols? For we are the temple of the living God; as God said,

"I will live in them and move among them,
and I will be their God,
and they shall be my people.
17 Therefore come out from them,
and be separate from them, says the Lord,
and touch nothing unclean;
then I will welcome you,
18 and I will be a father to you,
and you shall be my sons and daughters,
says the Lord Almighty."

7 1 Since we have these promises, beloved, let us cleanse ourselves from every defilement of body and spirit, and make holiness perfect in the fear of God.

Phil 3:17–21 (§249)

17 Brethren, join in imitating me, and mark those who so live as you have an example in us. 18 For many, of whom I have often told you and now tell you even with tears, live as enemies of the cross of Christ. 19 Their end is destruction, their god is the belly, and they glory in their shame, with minds set on earthly things. 20 But our commonwealth is in heaven, and from it we await a Savior, the Lord Jesus Christ, 21 who will change our lowly body to be like his glorious body, by the power which enables him even to subject all things to himself.

1 Thess 5:1–11 (§287)

1 But as to the times and the seasons, brethren, you have no need to have anything written to you. 2 For you yourselves know well that the day of the Lord will come like a thief in the night. 3 When people say, "There is peace and security," then sudden destruction will come upon them as travail comes upon a woman with child, and there will be no escape. 4 But you are not in darkness, brethren, for that day to surprise you like a thief. 5 For you are all sons of light and sons of the day; we are not of the night or of darkness. 6 So then let us not sleep, as others do, but let us keep awake and be sober. 7 For those who sleep sleep at night, and those who get drunk are drunk at night. 8 But, since we belong to the day, let us be sober, and put on

the breastplate of faith and love, and for a helmet the hope of salvation. 9 For God has not destined us for wrath, but to obtain salvation through our Lord Jesus Christ, 10 who died for us so that whether we wake or sleep we might live with him. 11 Therefore encourage one another and build one another up, just as you are doing.

2 Thess 2:1–12 (§296)

1 Now concerning the coming of our Lord Jesus Christ and our assembling to meet him, we beg you, brethren, 2 not to be quickly shaken in mind or excited, either by spirit or by word, or by letter purporting to be from us, to the effect that the day of the Lord has come. 3 Let no one deceive you in any way; for that day will not come, unless the rebellion comes first, and the man of lawlessness is revealed, the son of perdition, 4 who opposes and exalts himself against every so-called god or object of worship, so that he takes his seat in the temple of God, proclaiming himself to be God. 5 Do you not remember that when I was still with you I told you this? 6 And you know what is restraining him now so that he may be revealed in his time. 7 For the mystery of lawlessness is already at work; only he who now restrains it will do so until he is out of the way. 8 And then the lawless one will be revealed, and the Lord Jesus will slay him with the breath of his mouth and destroy him by his appearing and his coming. 9 The coming of the lawless one by the activity of Satan will be with all power and with pretended signs and wonders, 10 and with all wicked deception for those who are to perish, because they refused to love the truth and so be saved. 11 Therefore God sends upon them a strong delusion, to make them believe what is false, 12 so that all may be condemned who did not believe the truth but had pleasure in unrighteousness.

● **Eph 5:3–14**
Cf. Eph 4:17–32

1 Tim 1 9 understanding this, that the law is not laid down for the just but for the lawless and disobedient, for the ungodly and sinners, for the unholy and profane, for murderers of fathers and murderers of mothers, for manslayers, 10 immoral persons, sodomites, kidnappers, liars, perjurers, and whatever else is contrary to sound doctrine, . . .

1 Tim 6 4 he is puffed up with conceit, he knows nothing; he has a morbid craving for controversy and for disputes about words, which produce envy, dissension, slander, base suspicions, 5 and wrangling among men who are depraved in mind and bereft of the truth, imagining that godliness is a means of gain.

2 Tim 3 2 For men will be lovers of self, lovers of money, proud, arrogant, abusive, disobedient to their parents, ungrateful, unholy, 3 inhuman, implacable, slanderers, profligates, fierce, haters of good, 4 treacherous, reckless, swollen with conceit, lovers of pleasure rather than lovers of God, . . .

Titus 3 3 For we ourselves were once foolish, disobedient, led astray, slaves to various passions and pleasures, passing our days in malice and envy, hated by men and hating one another; . . .

● **Eph 5:6**
Col 2 8 See to it that no one makes a prey of you by philosophy and empty deceit, according to human tradition, according to the elemental spirits of the universe, and not according to Christ.

● **Eph 5:8**
Acts 26 16 "But rise and stand upon your feet; for I have appeared to you for this purpose, to appoint you to serve and bear witness to the things in which you have seen me and to those in which I will appear to you, 17 delivering you from the people and from the Gentiles—to whom I send you 18 to open their eyes, that they may turn from darkness to light and from the power of Satan to God, that they may receive forgiveness of sins and a place among those who are sanctified by faith in me."

● **Eph 5:10**
Rom 8 8 and those who are in the flesh cannot please God.

Gal 1 10 Am I now seeking the favor of men, or of God? Or am I trying to please men? If I were still pleasing men, I should not be a servant of Christ.

Eph 4 1 I therefore, a prisoner for the Lord, beg you to lead a life worthy of the calling to which you have been called, . . .

1 Thess 2 4 but just as we have been approved by God to be entrusted with the gospel, so we speak, not to please men, but to please God who tests our hearts.

● **Eph 5:14**
Rom 13 11 Besides this you know what hour it is, how it is full time now for you to wake from sleep. For salvation is nearer to us now than when we first believed; . . .

¹⁵Look carefully then how you walk, not as unwise men but as wise, ¹⁶making the most of the time, because the days are evil. ¹⁷Therefore do not be foolish, but understand what the will of the Lord is. ¹⁸And do not get drunk with wine, for that is debauchery; but be filled with the Spirit, ¹⁹addressing one another in psalms and hymns and spiritual songs, singing and making melody to the Lord with all your heart, ²⁰always and for everything giving thanks in the name of our Lord Jesus Christ to God the Father.

PRIMARY

Rom 13:11–14 (§56)

¹¹Besides this you know what hour it is, how it is full time now for you to wake from sleep. For salvation is nearer to us now than when we first believed; ¹²the night is far gone, the day is at hand. Let us then cast off the works of darkness and put on the armor of light; ¹³let us conduct ourselves becomingly as in the day, not in reveling and drunkenness, not in debauchery and licentiousness, not in quarreling and jealousy. ¹⁴But put on the Lord Jesus Christ, and make no provision for the flesh, to gratify its desires.

Rom 14:5–12 (§58)

⁵One man esteems one day as better than another, while another man esteems all days alike. Let every one be fully convinced in his own mind. ⁶He who observes the day, observes it in honor of the Lord. He also who eats, eats in honor of the Lord, since he gives thanks to God; while he who abstains, abstains in honor of the Lord and gives thanks to God. ⁷None of us lives to himself, and none of us dies to himself. ⁸If we live, we live to the Lord, and if we die, we die to the Lord; so then, whether we live or whether we die, we are the Lord's. ⁹For to this end Christ died and lived again, that he might be Lord both of the dead and of the living.

¹⁰Why do you pass judgment on your brother? Or you, why do you despise your brother? For we shall all stand before the judgment seat of God; ¹¹for it is written,

"As I live, says the Lord, every knee shall bow to me,

and every tongue shall give praise to God."

¹²So each of us shall give account of himself to God.

1 Cor 10:23–11:1 (§111)

²³"All things are lawful," but not all things are helpful. "All things are lawful," but not all things build up. ²⁴Let no one seek his own good, but the good of his neighbor. ²⁵Eat whatever is sold in the meat market without raising any question on the ground of conscience. ²⁶For "the earth is the Lord's, and everything in it." ²⁷If one of the unbelievers invites you to dinner and you are disposed to go, eat whatever is set before you without raising any question on the ground of conscience. ²⁸(But if some one says to you, "This has been offered in sacrifice," then out of consideration for the man who informed you, and for conscience' sake— ²⁹I mean his conscience, not yours—do not eat it.) For why should my liberty be determined by another man's scruples? ³⁰If I partake with thankfulness, why am I denounced because of that for which I give thanks?

³¹So, whether you eat or drink, or whatever you do, do all to the glory of God. ³²Give no offense to Jews or to Greeks or to the church of God, ³³just as I try to please all men in everything I do, not seeking my own advantage, but that of many, that they may be saved. 11 ¹Be imitators of me, as I am of Christ.

1 Cor 14:13–19 (§126)

¹³Therefore, he who speaks in a tongue should pray for the power to interpret. ¹⁴For if I pray in a tongue, my spirit prays but my mind is unfruitful. ¹⁵What am I to do? I will pray with the spirit and I will pray with the mind also; I will sing with the spirit and I will sing with the mind also. ¹⁶Otherwise, if you bless with the spirit, how can any one in the position of an outsider say the "Amen" to your thanksgiving when he does not know what you are saying? ¹⁷For you may give thanks well enough, but the other man is not edified. ¹⁸I thank God that I speak in tongues more than you all; ¹⁹nevertheless, in church I would rather speak five words with my mind, in order to instruct others, than ten thousand words in a tongue.

1 Cor 14:26–33a (§128)

²⁶What then, brethren? When you come together, each one has a hymn, a lesson, a revelation, a tongue, or an interpretation. Let all things be done for edification. ²⁷If any speak in a tongue, let there be only two or at most three, and each in turn; and let one interpret. ²⁸But if there is no one to interpret, let each of them keep silence in church and speak to himself and to God. ²⁹Let two or three prophets speak, and let the others weigh what is said. ³⁰If a revelation is made to another sitting by, let the first be silent. ³¹For you can all prophesy one by one, so that all may learn and all be encouraged; ³²and the spirits of prophets are subject to prophets. ³³For God is not a God of confusion but of peace.

Col 3:12–17 (§267)

¹²Put on then, as God's chosen ones, holy and beloved, compassion, kindness, lowliness, meekness, and patience, ¹³forbearing one another and, if one has a complaint against another, forgiving each other; as the Lord has forgiven you, so you also must forgive. ¹⁴And above all these put on love, which binds everything together in perfect harmony. ¹⁵And let the peace of Christ rule in your hearts, to which indeed you were called in the one body. And be thankful. ¹⁶Let the word of Christ dwell in you richly, as you teach and admonish one another in all wisdom, and as you sing psalms and hymns and spiritual songs with thankfulness in your hearts to God. ¹⁷And whatever you do, in word or deed, do everything in the name of the Lord Jesus, giving thanks to God the Father through him.

● **Eph 5:15–18**

Gal 5   ²⁵If we live by the Spirit, let us also walk by the Spirit.

● **Eph 5:16**

1 Cor 7   ²⁶I think that in view of the present distress it is well for a person to remain as he is.

● **Eph 5:19**

1 Cor 14   ⁴⁰but all things should be done decently and in order.

Acts 16   ²⁵But about midnight Paul and Silas were praying and singing hymns to God, and the prisoners were listening to them, . . .

● **Eph 5:20**

1 Thess 5   ¹⁸give thanks in all circumstances; for this is the will of God in Christ Jesus for you.

Cf. 1 Tim 4   ⁴For everything created by God is good, and nothing is to be rejected if it is received with thanksgiving; . . .

FORMAL ELEMENT: HOUSEHOLD TABLE

²¹Be subject to one another out of reverence for Christ. ²²Wives, be subject to your husbands, as to the Lord. ²³For the husband is the head of the wife as Christ is the head of the church, his body, and is himself its Savior. ²⁴As the church is subject to Christ, so let wives also be subject in everything to their husbands. ²⁵Husbands, love your wives, as Christ loved the church and gave himself up for her, ²⁶that he might sanctify her, having cleansed her by the washing of water with the word, ²⁷that he might present the church to himself in splendor, without spot or wrinkle or any such thing, that she might be holy and without blemish. ²⁸Even so husbands should love their wives as their own bodies. He who loves his wife loves himself. ²⁹For no man ever hates his own flesh, but nourishes and cherishes it, as Christ does the church, ³⁰because we are members of his body. ³¹"For this reason a man shall leave his father and mother and be joined to his wife, and the two shall become one flesh." ³²This mystery is a profound one, and I am saying that it refers to Christ and the church; ³³however, let each one of you love his wife as himself, and let the wife see that she respects her husband.

6 ¹Children, obey your parents in the Lord, for this is right. ²"Honor your father and mother" (this is the first commandment with a promise), ³"that it may be well with you and that you may live long on the earth." ⁴Fathers, do not provoke your children to anger, but bring them up in the discipline and instruction of the Lord.

⁵Slaves, be obedient to those who are your earthly masters, with fear and trembling, in singleness of heart, as to Christ; ⁶not in the way of eyeservice, as men-pleasers, but as servants of Christ, doing the will of God from the heart, ⁷rendering service with a good will as to the Lord and not to men, ⁸knowing that whatever good any one does, he will receive the same again from the Lord, whether he is a slave or free. ⁹Masters, do the same to them, and forbear threatening, knowing that he who is both their Master and yours is in heaven, and that there is no partiality with him.

PRIMARY

Col 3:18–4:1 (§268)
¹⁸Wives, be subject to your husbands, as is fitting in the Lord. ¹⁹Husbands, love your wives, and do not be harsh with them. ²⁰Children, obey your parents in everything, for this pleases the Lord. ²¹Fathers, do not provoke

your children, lest they become discouraged. ²²Slaves, obey in everything those who are your earthly masters, not with eyeservice, as menpleasers, but in singleness of heart, fearing the Lord. ²³Whatever your task, work heartily, as serving the Lord and not men, ²⁴knowing that from the Lord you will receive the inheritance as your reward; you are serving the Lord Christ. ²⁵For the wrongdoer will be paid back for the wrong he has done, and there is no partiality. 4 ¹Masters, treat your slaves justly and fairly, knowing that you also have a Master in heaven.

SECONDARY

Rom 13:1–7 (§54)
¹Let every person be subject to the governing authorities. For there is no authority except from God, and those that exist have been instituted by God. ²Therefore he who resists the authorities resists what God has appointed, and those who resist will incur judgment. ³For rulers are not a terror to good conduct, but to bad. Would you have no fear of him who is in authority? Then do what is good, and you will receive his approval, ⁴for he is God's servant for your good. But if you do wrong, be afraid, for he does not bear the sword in vain; he is the servant of God to execute his wrath on the wrongdoer. ⁵Therefore one must be subject, not only to avoid God's wrath but also for the

---

● **Eph 5:22–6:9**
Titus 2 ⁹Bid slaves to be submissive to their masters and to give satisfaction in every respect; they are not to be refractory, ¹⁰nor to pilfer, but to show entire and true fidelity, so that in everything they may adorn the doctrine of God our Savior.

1 Pet 2 ¹³Be subject for the Lord's sake to every human institution, whether it be to the emperor as supreme, ¹⁴or to governors as sent by him to punish those who do wrong and to praise those who do right. ¹⁵For it is God's will that by doing right you should put to silence the ignorance of foolish men. ¹⁶Live as free men, yet without using your freedom as a pretext for evil; but live as servants of God. ¹⁷Honor all men. Love the brotherhood. Fear God. Honor the emperor. ¹⁸Servants, be submissive to your masters with all respect, not only to the kind and gentle but also to the overbearing. ¹⁹For one is approved if, mindful of God, he endures pain while suffering unjustly. ²⁰For what credit is it, if when you do wrong and are beaten for it you take it patiently? But if when you do right and suffer for it you take it patiently, you have God's approval. ²¹For to this you have been called, because Christ also suffered for you, leaving you an example,

that you should follow in his steps. ²²He committed no sin; no guile was found on his lips. ²³When he was reviled, he did not revile in return; when he suffered, he did not threaten; but he trusted to him who judges justly. ²⁴He himself bore our sins in his body on the tree, that we might die to sin and live to righteousness. By his wounds you have been healed. ²⁵For you were straying like sheep, but have now returned to the Shepherd and Guardian of your souls.
3 ¹Likewise you wives, be submissive to your husbands, so that some, though they do not obey the word, may be won without a word by the behavior of their wives, ²when they see your reverent and chaste behavior. ³Let not yours be the outward adorning with braiding of hair, decoration of gold, and wearing of fine clothing, ⁴but let it be the hidden person of the heart with the imperishable jewel of a gentle and quiet spirit, which in God's sight is very precious. ⁵So once the holy women who hoped in God used to adorn themselves and were submissive to their husbands, ⁶as Sarah obeyed Abraham, calling him lord. And you are now her children if you do right and let nothing terrify you.
⁷Likewise you husbands, live considerately with your wives, bestowing honor on the woman as the

weaker sex, since you are joint heirs of the grace of life, in order that your prayers may not be hindered.

● **Eph 5:22**
(subject) *omit* be subject: p⁴⁶B Origen

● **Eph 5:23**
Eph 1 ²²and he has put all things under his feet and has made him the head over all things for the church, ²³which is his body, the fulness of him who fills all in all.

Eph 4 ¹⁵Rather, speaking the truth in love, we are to grow up in every way into him who is the head, into Christ, . . .

Col 1 ¹⁸He is the head of the body, the church; he is the beginning, the first-born from the dead, that in everything he might be pre-eminent.

Col 2 ¹⁹and not holding fast to the Head, from whom the whole body, nourished and knit together through its joints and ligaments, grows with a growth that is from God.

sake of conscience. [6]For the same reason you also pay taxes, for the authorities are ministers of God, attending to this very thing. [7]Pay all of them their dues, taxes to whom taxes are due, revenue to whom revenue is due, respect to whom respect is due, honor to whom honor is due.

1 Cor 7:32–35 (§99)

[32]I want you to be free from anxieties. The unmarried man is anxious about the affairs of the Lord, how to please the Lord; [33]but the married man is anxious about worldly affairs, how to please his wife, [34]and his interests are divided. And the unmarried woman or girl is anxious about the affairs of the Lord, how to be holy in body and spirit; but the married woman is anxious about worldly affairs, how to please her husband. [35]I say this for your own benefit, not to lay any restraint upon you, but to promote good order and to secure your undivided devotion to the Lord.

1 Cor 11:2–16 (§112)

[2]I commend you because you remember me in everything and maintain the traditions even as I have delivered them to you. [3]But I want you to understand that the head of every man is Christ, the head of a woman is her husband, and the head of Christ is God. [4]Any man who prays or prophesies with his head covered dishonors his head, [5]but any woman who prays or prophesies with her head unveiled dishonors her head—it is the same as if her head were shaven. [6]For if a woman will not veil herself, then she should cut off her hair; but if it is disgraceful for a woman to be shorn or shaven, let her wear a veil. [7]For a man ought not to cover his head, since he is the image and glory of God; but woman is the glory of man. [8](For man was not made from woman, but woman from man. [9]Neither was man created for woman, but woman for man.) [10]That is why a woman ought to have a veil on her head, because of the angels. [11](Nevertheless, in the Lord woman is not independent of man nor man of woman; [12]for as woman was made from man, so man is now born of woman. And all things are from God.) [13]Judge for yourselves; is it proper for a woman to pray to God with her head uncovered? [14]Does not nature itself teach you that for a man to wear long hair is degrading to him, [15]but if a woman has long hair, it is her pride? For her hair is given to her for a covering. [16]If any one is disposed to be contentious, we recognize no other practice, nor do the churches of God.

1 Cor 14:33b–36 (§129)

As in all the churches of the saints, [34]the women should keep silence in the churches. For they are not permitted to speak, but should be subordinate, as even the law says. [35]If there is anything they desire to know, let them ask their husbands at home. For it is shameful for a woman to speak in church. [36]What! Did the word of God originate with you, or are you the only ones it has reached?

2 Cor 11:1–6 (§179)

[1]I wish you would bear with me in a little foolishness. Do bear with me! [2]I feel a divine jealousy for you, for I betrothed you to Christ to present you as a pure bride to her one husband. [3]But I am afraid that as the serpent deceived Eve by his cunning, your thoughts will be led astray from a sincere and pure devotion to Christ. [4]For if some one comes and preaches another Jesus than the one we preached, or if you receive a different spirit from the one you received, or if you accept a different gospel from the one you accepted, you submit to it readily enough. [5]I think that I am not in the least inferior to these superlative apostles. [6]Even if I am unskilled in speaking, I am not in knowledge; in every way we have made this plain to you in all things.

● **Eph 5:25**
Rom 8   [32]He who did not spare his own Son but gave him up for us all, will he not also give us all things with him?

Eph 5   [2]And walk in love, as Christ loved us and gave himself up for us, a fragrant offering and sacrifice to God.

Cf. Gal 2   [20]I have been crucified with Christ; it is no longer I who live, but Christ who lives in me; and the life I now live in the flesh I live by faith in the Son of God, who loved me and gave himself for me.

● **Eph 5:26**
Cf. Titus 2   [14]who gave himself for us to redeem us from all iniquity and to purify for himself a people of his own who are zealous for good deeds.

Cf. Titus 3   [5]he saved us, not because of deeds done by us in righteousness, but in virtue of his own mercy, by the washing of regeneration and renewal in the Holy Spirit, . . .

Cf. Acts 22   [16]"And now why do you wait? Rise and be baptized, and wash away your sins, calling on his name."

Cf. Heb 10   [22]Let us draw near with a true heart in full assurance of faith, with our hearts sprinkled clean from an evil conscience and our bodies washed with pure water.

● **Eph 5:27**
Eph 1   [4]even as he chose us in him before the foundation of the world, that we should be holy and blameless before him.

Cf. Col 1   [22]he has now reconciled in his body of flesh by his death, in order to present you holy and blameless and irreproachable before him, . . .

● **Eph 5:31**
Gen 2   [24]Therefore a man leaves his father and his mother and cleaves to his wife, and they become one flesh.

● **Eph 6:1**
(Lord) *omit* in the Lord: BD*G it (few) Marcion

● **Eph 6:2**
Exod 20   [12]"Honor your father and your mother, that your days may be long in the land which the Lord your God gives you."

● **Eph 6:3**
Deut 5   [16]"'Honor your father and your mother, as the Lord your God commanded you; that your days may be prolonged, and that it may go well with you, in the land which the Lord your God gives you.'"

● **Eph 6:5**
1 Tim 6   [1]Let all who are under the yoke of slavery regard their masters as worthy of all honor, so that the name of God and the teaching may not be defamed.

● **Eph 6:8**
Rom 2   [6]For he will render to every man according to his works: . . .

● **Eph 6:9**
Acts 10   [34]And Peter opened his mouth and said: "Truly I perceive that God shows no partiality. . . ."

FORMAL ELEMENT: "WATCH!" "STAND!"

[10]Finally, be strong in the Lord and in the strength of his might. [11]Put on the whole armor of God, that you may be able to stand against the wiles of the devil. [12]For we are not contending against flesh and blood, but against the principalities, against the powers, against the world rulers of this present darkness, against the spiritual hosts of wickedness in the heavenly places. [13]Therefore take the whole armor of God, that you may be able to withstand in the evil day, and having done all, to stand. [14]Stand therefore, having girded your loins with truth, and having put on the breastplate of righteousness, [15]and having shod your feet with the equipment of the gospel of peace; [16]besides all these, taking the shield of faith, with which you can quench all the flaming darts of the evil one. [17]And take the helmet of salvation, and the sword of the Spirit, which is the word of God.

PRIMARY

Rom 13:11–14 (§56)

[11]Besides this you know what hour it is, how it is full time now for you to wake from sleep. For salvation is nearer to us now than when we first believed; [12]the night is far gone, the day is at hand. Let us then cast off the works of darkness and put on the armor of light; [13]let us conduct ourselves becomingly as in the day, not in reveling and drunkenness, not in debauchery and licentiousness, not in quarreling and jealousy. [14]But put on the Lord Jesus Christ, and make no provision for the flesh, to gratify its desires.

1 Cor 16:13–14 (§141)

[13]Be watchful, stand firm in your faith, be courageous, be strong. [14]Let all that you do be done in love.

Col 4:2–4 (§269)

[2]Continue steadfastly in prayer, being watchful in it with thanksgiving; [3]and pray for us also, that God may open to us a door for the word, to declare the mystery of Christ, on account of which I am in prison, [4]that I may make it clear, as I ought to speak.

1 Thess 5:1–11 (§287)

[1]But as to the times and the seasons, brethren, you have no need to have anything written to you. [2]For you yourselves know well that the day of the Lord will come like a thief in the night. [3]When people say, "There is peace and security," then sudden destruction will come upon them as travail comes upon a woman with child, and there will be no escape. [4]But you are not in darkness, brethren, for that day to surprise you like a thief. [5]For you are all sons of light and sons of the day; we are not of the night or of darkness. [6]So then let us not sleep, as others do, but let us keep awake and be sober. [7]For those who sleep sleep at night, and those who get drunk are drunk at night. [8]But, since we belong to the day, let us be sober, and put on the breastplate of faith and love, and for a helmet the hope of salvation. [9]For God has not destined us for wrath, but to obtain salvation through our Lord Jesus Christ, [10]who died for us so that whether we wake or sleep we might live with him. [11]Therefore encourage one another and build one another up, just as you are doing.

2 Thess 2:13–17 (§297–298)

[13]But we are bound to give thanks to God always for you, brethren beloved by the Lord, because God chose you from the beginning to be saved, through sanctification by the Spirit and belief in the truth. [14]To this he called you through our gospel, so that you may obtain the glory of our Lord Jesus Christ. [15]So then, brethren, stand firm and hold to the traditions which you were taught by us, either by word of mouth or by letter.

[16]Now may our Lord Jesus Christ himself, and God our Father, who loved us and gave us eternal comfort and good hope through grace, [17]comfort your hearts and establish them in every good work and word.

SECONDARY

2 Cor 10:1–6 (§176)

[1]I, Paul, myself entreat you, by the meekness and gentleness of Christ—I who am humble when face to face with you, but bold to you when I am away!—[2]I beg of you that when I am present I may not have to show boldness with such confidence as I count on showing against some who suspect us of acting in worldly fashion. [3]For though we live in the world we are not carrying on a worldly war, [4]for the weapons of our warfare are not worldly but have divine power to destroy strongholds. [5]We destroy arguments and every proud obstacle to the knowledge of God, and take every thought captive to obey Christ, [6]being ready to punish every disobedience, when your obedience is complete.

2 Thess 2:1–12 (§296)

[1]Now concerning the coming of our Lord Jesus Christ and our assembling to meet him, we beg you, brethren, [2]not to be quickly shaken in mind or excited, either by spirit or by word, or by letter purporting to be from us, to the effect that the day of the Lord has come. [3]Let no one deceive you in any way; for that day will not come, unless the rebellion comes first, and the man of lawlessness is revealed, the son of perdition, [4]who opposes and exalts himself against every so-called god or object of worship, so that he takes his seat in the temple of God, proclaiming himself to be God. [5]Do you not remember that when I was still with you I told you this? [6]And you know what is restraining him now so that he may be revealed in his time. [7]For the mystery of lawlessness is already at work; only he who now restrains it will do so until he is out of the way. [8]And then the lawless one will be revealed, and the Lord Jesus will slay him with the breath of his mouth and destroy him by his appearing and his coming. [9]The coming of the lawless one by the activity of Satan will be with all power and with pretended signs and wonders, [10]and with all wicked deception for those who are to perish, because they refused to love the truth and so be saved. [11]Therefore God sends upon them a strong delusion, to make them believe what is false, [12]so that all may be condemned who did not believe the truth but had pleasure in unrighteousness.

● **Eph 6:10**
2 Tim 2 [1]You then, my son, be strong in the grace that is in Christ Jesus, . . .

● **Eph 6:11**
2 Cor 6 [7]truthful speech, and the power of God; with the weapons of righteousness for the right hand and for the left; . . .

● **Eph 6:12**
Gal 4 [3]So with us; when we were children, we were slaves to the elemental spirits of the universe.

Gal 4 [9]but now that you have come to know God, or rather to be known by God, how can you turn back again to the weak and beggarly elemental spirits, whose slaves you want to be once more?

Col 2 [8]See to it that no one makes a prey of you by philosophy and empty deceit, according to human tradition, according to the elemental spirits of the universe, and not according to Christ.

Col 2 [20]If with Christ you died to the elemental spirits of the universe, why do you live as if you still belonged to the world? Why do you submit to regulations, . . .

Acts 26 [16]"But rise and stand upon your feet; for I have appeared to you for this purpose, to appoint you to serve and bear witness to the things in which you have seen me and to those in which I will appear to you, [17]delivering you from the people and from the Gentiles—to whom I send you [18]to open their eyes, that they may turn from darkness to light and from the power of Satan to God, that they may receive forgiveness of sins and a place among those who are sanctified by faith in me."

(we) *read* you: p[46]BD*G it (some) syr(pes pal) Ambrosiaster

● **Eph 6:14**
Gal 5 [1]For freedom Christ has set us free; stand fast therefore, and do not submit again to a yoke of slavery.

● **Eph 6:15**
Acts 10 [36]"You know the word which he sent to Israel, preaching good news of peace by Jesus Christ (he is Lord of all). . . ."

FORMAL ELEMENT: REQUEST FOR PRAYER

18Pray at all times in the Spirit, with all prayer and supplication. To that end keep alert with all perseverance, making supplication for all the saints, 19and also for me, that utterance may be given me in opening my mouth boldly to proclaim the mystery of the gospel, 20for which I am an ambassador in chains; that I may declare it boldly, as I ought to speak.

PRIMARY

Rom 15:30–33 (§64)
30I appeal to you, brethren, by our Lord Jesus Christ and by the love of the Spirit, to strive together with me in your prayers to God on my behalf, 31that I may be delivered from the unbelievers in Judea, and that my service for Jerusalem may be acceptble to the saints, 32so that by God's will I may come to you with joy and be refreshed in your company. 33The God of peace be with you all. Amen.

Col 4:2–4 (§269)
2Continue steadfastly in prayer, being watchful in it with thanksgiving; 3and pray for us also, that God may open to us a door for the word, to declare the mystery of Christ, on account of which I am in prison, 4that I may make it clear, as I ought to speak.

1 Thess 5:25 (§290)
25Brethren, pray for us.

2 Thess 3:1–5 (§299)
1Finally, brethren, pray for us, that the word of the Lord may speed on and triumph, as it did among you, 2and that we may be delivered from wicked and evil men; for not all have faith. 3But the Lord is faithful; he will strengthen you and guard you from evil. 4And we have confidence in the Lord about you, that you are doing and will do the things which we command. 5May the Lord direct your hearts to the love of God and to the steadfastness of Christ.

SECONDARY

Rom 8:26–27 (§32)
26Likewise the Spirit helps us in our weakness; for we do not know how to pray as we ought, but the Spirit himself intercedes for us with sighs too deep for words. 27And he who searches the hearts of men knows what is the mind of the Spirit, because the Spirit intercedes for the saints according to the will of God.

Col 1:24–2:3 (§260)
24Now I rejoice in my sufferings for your sake, and in my flesh I complete what is lacking in Christ's afflictions for the sake of his body, that is, the church, 25of which I became a minister according to the divine office which was given to me for you, to make the word of God fully known, 26the mystery hidden for ages and generations but now made manifest to his saints. 27To them God chose to make known how great among the Gentiles are the riches of the glory of this mystery, which is Christ in you, the hope of glory. 28Him we proclaim warning every man and teaching every man in all wisdom, that we may present every man mature in Christ. 29For this I toil, striving with all the energy which he mightily inspires within me.

2 1For I want you to know how greatly I strive for you, and for those at Laodicea, and for all who have not seen my face, 2that their hearts may be encouraged as they are knit together in love, to have all the riches of assured understanding and the knowledge of God's mystery, of Christ, 3in whom are hid all the treasures of wisdom and knowledge.

• **Eph 6:18**
Phil 1   12I want you to know, brethren, that what has happened to me has really served to advance the gospel, 13so that it has become known throughout the whole praetorian guard and to all the rest that my imprisonment is for Christ; 14and most of the brethren have been made confident in the Lord because of my imprisonment, and are much more bold to speak the word of God without fear.
15Some indeed preach Christ from envy and rivalry, but others from good will. 16The latter do it out of love, knowing that I am put here for the defense of the gospel; 17the former proclaim Christ out of partisanship, not sincerely but thinking to afflict me in my imprisonment. 18What then? Only that in every way, whether in pretense or in truth, Christ is proclaimed; and in that I rejoice.
19Yes, and I shall rejoice. For I know that through your prayers and the help of the Spirit of Jesus Christ this will turn out for my deliverance, 20as it is my eager expectation and hope that I shall not be at all ashamed, but that with full courage now as always Christ will be honored in my body, whether by life or by death.

Phil 4   6Have no anxiety about anything, but in everything by prayer and supplication with thanksgiving let your requests be made known to God.

Col 4   18I, Paul, write this greeting with my own hand. Remember my fetters.

Phlm   1Paul, a prisoner for Christ Jesus, and Timothy our brother,
     To Philemon our beloved fellow worker . . .

Phlm   9yet for love's sake I prefer to appeal to you—I, Paul, an ambassador and now a prisoner also for Christ Jesus . . .

Phlm   22At the same time, prepare a guest room for me, for I am hoping through your prayers to be granted to you.

1 Tim 2   1First of all, then, I urge that supplications, prayers, intercessions, and thanksgivings be made for all men, . . .

• **Eph 6:19**
Eph 3   3how the mystery was made known to me by revelation, as I have written briefly.

Eph 3   9and to make all men see what is the plan of the mystery hidden for ages in God who created all things; 10that through the church the manifold wisdom of God might now be made known to the principalities and powers in the heavenly places.

• **Eph 6:20**
Eph 3   1For this reason I, Paul, a prisoner for Christ Jesus on behalf of you Gentiles . . .

Eph 4   1I therefore, a prisoner for the Lord, beg you to lead a life worthy of the calling to which you have been called, . . .

Acts 21   33Then the tribune came up and arrested him, and ordered him to be bound wih two chains. He inquired who he was and what he had done.

FORMAL ELEMENT: COMMENDATION

[21] **Now that you also may know how I am and what I am doing, Tychicus the beloved brother and faithful minister in the Lord will tell you everything.** [22] **I have sent him to you for this very purpose, that you may know how we are, and that he may encourage your hearts.**

PRIMARY

Rom 16:1-2 (§65)

[1] I commend to you our sister Phoebe, a deaconess of the church at Cenchreae, [2] that you may receive her in the Lord as befits the saints, and help her in whatever she may require from you, for she has been a helper of many and of myself as well.

1 Cor 16:10-12 (§140)

[10] When Timothy comes, see that you put him at ease among you, for he is doing the work of the Lord, as I am. [11] So let no one despise him. Speed him on his way in peace, that he may return to me; for I am expecting him with the brethren. [12] As for our brother Apollos, I strongly urged him to visit you with the other brethren, but it was not at all his will to come now. He will come when he has opportunity.

1 Cor 16:15-18 (§142)

[15] Now, brethren, you know that the household of Stephanas were the first converts in Achaia, and they have devoted themselves to the service of the saints; [16] I urge you to be subject to such men and to every fellow worker and laborer. [17] I rejoice at the coming of Stephanas and Fortunatus and Achaicus, because they have made up for your absence; [18] for they refreshed my spirit as well as yours. Give recognition to such men.

2 Cor 3:1-3 (§154)

[1] Are we beginning to commend ourselves again? Or do we need, as some do, letters of recommendation to you, or from you? [2] You yourselves are our letter of recommendation, written on your hearts, to be known and read by all men; [3] and you show that you are a letter from Christ delivered by us, written not with ink but with the Spirit of the living God, not on tablets of stone but on tablets of human hearts.

2 Cor 8:16-24 (§173)

[16] But thanks be to God who puts the same earnest care for you into the heart of Titus. [17] For he not only accepted our appeal, but being himself very earnest he is going to you of his own accord. [18] With him we are sending the brother who is famous among all the churches for his preaching of the gospel; [19] and not only that, but he has been appointed by the churches to travel with us in this gracious work which we are carrying on, for the glory of the Lord and to show our good will. [20] We intend that no one should blame us about this liberal gift which we are administering, [21] for we aim at what is honorable not only in the Lord's sight but also in the sight of men. [22] And with them we are sending our brother whom we have often tested and found earnest in many matters, but who is now more earnest than ever because of his great confidence in you. [23] As for Titus, he is my partner and fellow worker in your service; and as for our brethren, they are messengers of the churches, the glory of Christ. [24] So give proof, before the churches, of your love and of our boasting about you to these men.

Phil 2:19-24 (§245)

[19] I hope in the Lord Jesus to send Timothy to you soon, so that I may be cheered by news of you. [20] I have no one like him, who will be genuinely anxious for your welfare. [21] They all look after their own interests, not those of Jesus Christ. [22] But Timothy's worth you know, how as a son with a father he has served with me in the gospel. [23] I hope therefore to send him just as soon as I see how it will go with me; [24] and I trust in the Lord that shortly I myself shall come also.

Phil 2:25-3:1 (§246)

[25] I have thought it necessary to send to you Epaphroditus my brother and fellow worker and fellow soldier, and your messenger and minister to my need, [26] for he has been longing for you all, and has been distressed because you heard that he was ill. [27] Indeed he was ill, near to death. But God had mercy on him, and not only on him but on me also, lest I should have sorrow upon sorrow. [28] I am the more eager to send him, therefore, that you may rejoice at seeing him again, and that I may be less anxious. [29] So receive him in the Lord with all joy; and honor such men, [30] for he nearly died for the work of Christ, risking his life to complete your service to me.

3 [1] Finally, my brethren, rejoice in the Lord. To write the same things to you is not irksome to me, and is safe for you.

Col 4:7-9 (§271)

[7] Tychicus will tell you all about my affairs; he is a beloved brother and faithful minister and fellow servant in the Lord. [8] I have sent him to you for this very purpose, that you may know how we are and that he may encourage your hearts, [9] and with him Onesimus, the faithful and beloved brother, who is one of yourselves. They will tell you of everything that has taken place here.

Phlm 8-20 (§307-308)

[8] Accordingly, though I am bold enough in Christ to command you to do what is required, [9] yet for love's sake I prefer to appeal to you—I, Paul, an ambassador and now a prisoner also for Christ Jesus—[10] I appeal to you for my child, Onesimus, whose father I have become in my imprisonment. [11] (Formerly he was useless to you, but now he is indeed useful to you and to me.) [12] I am sending him back to you, sending my very heart. [13] I would have been glad to keep him with me, in order that he might serve me on your behalf during my imprisonment for the gospel; [14] but I preferred to do nothing without your consent in order that your goodness might not be by compulsion but of your own free will. [15] Perhaps this is why he was parted from you for a while, that you might have him back for ever, [16] no longer as a slave but more than a slave, as a beloved brother, especially to me but how much more to you, both in the flesh and in the Lord. [17] So if you consider me your partner, receive him as you would receive me. [18] If he has wronged you at all, or owes you anything, charge that to my account. [19] I, Paul, write this with my own hand, I will repay it—to say nothing of your owing me even your own self. [20] Yes, brother, I want some benefit from you in the Lord. Refresh my heart in Christ.

● **Eph 6:21**
Titus 3   [12] When I send Artemas or Tychicus to you, do your best to come to me at Nicopolis, for I have decided to spend the winter there.

● **Eph 6:22**
1 Cor 16   [18] for they refreshed my spirit as well as yours. Give recognition to such men.

LETTER STRUCTURE: CLOSING GRACE

[23] Peace be to the brethren, and love with faith, from God the Father and the Lord Jesus Christ. [24] Grace be with all who love our Lord Jesus Christ with love undying.

PRIMARY

Rom 16:20b (§68)

The grace of our Lord Jesus Christ be with you.

1 Cor 16:23–24 (§145)

[23] The grace of the Lord Jesus be with you. [24] My love be with you all in Christ Jesus. Amen.

2 Cor 13:14 (§192)

[14] The grace of the Lord Jesus Christ and the love of God and the fellowship of the Holy Spirit be with you all.

Gal 6:18 (§217)

[18] The grace of our Lord Jesus Christ be with your spirit, brethren. Amen.

Phil 4:23 (§255)

[23] The grace of the Lord Jesus Christ be with your spirit.

Col 4:18b (§274)

Grace be with you.

1 Thess 5:28 (§293)

[28] The grace of our Lord Jesus Christ be with you.

2 Thess 3:18 (§304)

[18] The grace of our Lord Jesus Christ be with you all.

Phlm 25 (§311)

[25] The grace of the Lord Jesus Christ be with your spirit.

● **Eph 6:24**

1 Tim 6   [21] Grace be with you.   2 Tim 4   [22] Grace be with you.   Titus 3   [15] Grace be with you all.

LETTER STRUCTURE: SALUTATION

1 **Paul and Timothy, servants of Christ Jesus,**

To all the saints in Christ Jesus who are at Philippi, with the bishops and deacons:

²**Grace to you and peace from God our Father and the Lord Jesus Christ.**

PRIMARY

Rom 1:1-7 (§1)

¹Paul, a servant of Jesus Christ, called to be an apostle, set apart for the gospel of God ²which he promised beforehand through his prophets in the holy scriptures, ³the gospel concerning his Son, who was descended from David according to the flesh ⁴and designated Son of God in power according to the Spirit of holiness by his resurrection from the dead, Jesus Christ our Lord, ⁵through whom we have received grace and apostleship to bring about the obedience of faith for the sake of his name among all the nations, ⁶including yourselves who are called to belong to Jesus Christ;

⁷To all God's beloved in Rome, who are called to be saints:

Grace to you and peace from God our Father and the Lord Jesus Christ.

1 Cor 1:1-3 (§71)

¹Paul, called by the will of God to be an apostle of Christ Jesus, and our brother Sosthenes,

²To the church of God which is at Corinth, to those sanctified in Christ Jesus, called to be saints together with all those who in every place call on the name of our Lord Jesus Christ, both their Lord and ours:

³Grace to you and peace from God our Father and the Lord Jesus Christ.

2 Cor 1:1-2 (§146)

¹Paul, an apostle of Christ Jesus by the will of God, and Timothy our brother.

To the church of God which is at Corinth, with all the saints who are in the whole of Achaia:

²Grace to you and peace from God our Father and the Lord Jesus Christ.

Gal 1:1-5 (§193)

¹Paul an apostle—not from men nor through man, but through Jesus Christ and God the Father, who raised him from the dead—²and all the brethren who are with me,

To the churches of Galatia:

³Grace to you and peace from God the Father and our Lord Jesus Christ, ⁴who gave himself for our sins to deliver us from the present evil age, according to the will of our God and Father; ⁵to whom be the glory for ever and ever. Amen.

Eph 1:1-2 (§218)

¹Paul, an apostle of Christ Jesus by the will of God,

To the saints who are also faithful in Christ Jesus:

²Grace to you and peace from God our Father and the Lord Jesus Christ.

Col 1:1-2 (§256)

¹Paul, an apostle of Christ Jesus by the will of God, and Timothy our brother,

²To the saints and faithful brethren in Christ at Colossae:

Grace to you and peace from God our Father.

1 Thess 1:1 (§275)

¹Paul, Silvanus, and Timothy,

To the church of the Thessalonians in God the Father and the Lord Jesus Christ:

Grace to you and peace.

2 Thess 1:1-2 (§294)

¹Paul, Silvanus, and Timothy,

To the church of the Thessalonians in God our Father and the Lord Jesus Christ:

²Grace to you and peace from God the Father and the Lord Jesus Christ.

Phlm 1-3 (§305)

¹Paul, a prisoner for Christ Jesus, and Timothy our brother,

To Philemon our beloved fellow worker ²and Apphia our sister and Archippus our fellow soldier, and the church in your house:

³Grace to you and peace from God our Father and the Lord Jesus Christ.

● **Eph 1:1-2**

1 Tim 1   ¹Paul, an apostle of Christ Jesus by command of God our Savior and of Christ Jesus our hope,

²To Timothy, my true child in the faith:

Grace, mercy, and peace from God the Father and Christ Jesus our Lord.

2 Tim 1   ¹Paul, an apostle of Christ Jesus by the will of God according to the promise of the life which is in Christ Jesus,

²To Timothy, my beloved child:

Grace, mercy, and peace from God the Father and Christ Jesus our Lord.

Titus 1   ¹Paul, a servant of God and an apostle of Jesus Christ, to further the faith of God's elect and their knowledge of the truth which accords with godliness, ²in hope of eternal life which God, who never lies, promised ages ago ³and at the proper time man-ifested in his word through the preaching with which I have been entrusted by command of God our Savior;

⁴To Titus, my true child in a common faith:

Grace and peace from God the Father and Christ Jesus our Savior.

● **Eph 1:1**

1 Thess 2   ²but though we had already suffered and been shamefully treated at Philippi, as you know, we had courage in our God to declare to you the gospel of God in the face of great opposition.

1 Tim 3   ¹The saying is sure: If any one aspires to the office of bishop, he desires a noble task. ²Now a bishop must be above reproach, the husband of one wife, temperate, sensible, dignified, hospitable, an apt teacher, . . .

1 Tim 3   ⁸Deacons likewise must be serious, not double-tongued, not addicted to much wine, not greedy for gain; ⁹they must hold the mystery of the faith with a clear conscience. ¹⁰And let them also be tested first; then if they prove themselves blameless let them serve as deacons.

Titus 1   ⁷For a bishop, as God's steward, must be blameless; he must not be arrogant or quick-tempered or a drunkard or violent or greedy for gain, . . .

Acts 16   ¹And he came also to Derbe and to Lystra. A disciple was there, named Timothy, the son of a Jewish woman who was a believer; but his father was a Greek.

Acts 16   ¹¹Setting sail therefore from Troas, we made a direct voyage ot Samothrace, and the following day to Neapolis, ¹²and from there to Philippi, which is the leading city of the district of Macedonia, and a Roman colony. We remained in this city some days; . . .

LETTER STRUCTURE: THANKSGIVING

³I thank my God in all my remembrance of you, ⁴always in every prayer of mine for you all making my prayer with joy, ⁵thankful for your partnership in the gospel from the first day until now. ⁶And I am sure that he who began a good work in you will bring it to completion at the day of Jesus Christ. ⁷It is right for me to feel thus about you all, because I hold you in my heart, for you are all partakers with me of grace, both in my imprisonment and in the defense and confirmation of the gospel. ⁸For God is my witness, how I yearn for you all with the affection of Christ Jesus. ⁹And it is my prayer that your love may abound more and more, with knowledge and all discernment, ¹⁰so that you may approve what is excellent, and may be pure and blameless for the day of Christ, ¹¹filled with the fruits of righteousness which come through Jesus Christ, to the glory and praise of God.

PRIMARY

See §2 for THANKSGIVING

● **Phil 1:3**

1 Tim 1   ¹²I thank him who has given me strength for this, Christ Jesus our Lord, because he judged me faithful by appointing me to his service, . . .

2 Tim 1   ³I thank God whom I serve with a clear conscience, as did my fathers, when I remember you constantly in my prayers.

Titus 1   ⁵This is why I left you in Crete, that you might amend what was defective, and appoint elders in every town as I directed you, . . .

● **Phil 1:5**

2 Cor 11   ⁸I robbed other churches by accepting support from them in order to serve you. ⁹And when I was with you and was in want, I did not burden any one, for my needs were supplied by the brethren who came from Macedonia. So I refrained and will refrain from burdening you in any way.

Phil 4   ¹⁵And you Philippians yourselves know that in the beginning of the gospel, when I left Macedonia, no church entered into partnership with me in giving and receiving except you only; ¹⁶for even in Thessalonica you sent me help once and again.

Phlm   ¹⁷So if you consider me your partner, receive him as you would receive me.

Acts 2   ⁴²And they devoted themselves to the apostles' teaching and fellowship, to the breaking of bread and the prayers.

Acts 16   ¹²and from there to Philippi, which is the leading city of the district of Macedonia, and a Roman colony. We remained in this city some days; ¹³and on the sabbath day we went outside the gate to the riverside, where we supposed there was a place of prayer; and we sat down and spoke to the women who had come together. ¹⁴One who heard us was a woman named Lydia, from the city of Thyatira, a seller of purple goods, who was a worshiper of God. The Lord opened her heart to give heed to what was said by Paul. ¹⁵And when she was baptized, with her household, she besought us, saying, "If you have judged me to be faithful to the Lord, come to my house and stay." And she prevailed upon us.

SECONDARY

Rom 15:14–21 (§62)

¹⁴I myself am satisfied about you, my brethren, that you yourselves are full of goodness, filled with all knowledge, and able to instruct one another. ¹⁵But on some points I have written to you very boldly by way of reminder, because of the grace given me by God ¹⁶to be a minister of Christ Jesus to the Gentiles in the priestly service of the gospel of God, so that the offering of the Gentiles may be acceptable, sanctified by the Holy Spirit. ¹⁷In Christ Jesus, then, I have reason to be proud of my work for God. ¹⁸For I will not venture to speak of anything except what Christ has wrought through me to win obedience from the Gentiles, by word and deed, ¹⁹by the power of signs and wonders, by the power of the Holy Spirit, so that from Jerusalem and as far round as Illyricum I have fully preached the gospel of Christ, ²⁰thus making it my ambition to preach the gospel, not where Christ has already been named, lest I build on another man's foundation, ²¹but as it is written,

● **Phil 1:6**

1 Cor 1   ⁷so that you are not lacking in any spiritual gift, as you wait for the revealing of our Lord Jesus Christ; ⁸who will sustain you to the end, guiltless in the day of our Lord Jesus Christ.

Phil 2   ¹⁶holding fast the word of life, so that in the day of Christ I may be proud that I did not run in vain or labor in vain.

1 Thess 5   ²For you yourselves know well that the day of the Lord will come like a thief in the night.

1 Thess 5   ⁴But you are not in darkness, brethren, for that day to surprise you like a thief.

2 Thess 2   ²not to be quickly shaken in mind or excited, either by spirit or by word, or by letter purporting to be from us, to the effect that the day of the Lord has come. ³Let no one deceive you in any way; for that day will not come, unless the rebellion comes first, and the man of lawlessness is revealed, the son of perdition, . . .

● **Phil 1:7**

2 Cor 1   ²³But I call God to witness against me—it was to spare you that I refrained from coming to Corinth.

2 Cor 11   ³¹The God and Father of the Lord Jesus, he who is blessed for ever, knows that I do not lie.

Eph 3   ¹For this reason I, Paul, a prisoner for Christ Jesus on behalf of you Gentiles . . .

Eph 4   ¹I therefore, a prisoner for the Lord, beg you to lead a life worthy of the calling to which you have been called, . . .

Col 4   ³and pray for us also, that God may open to us a door for the word, to declare the mystery of Christ, on account of which I am in prison, . . .

Col 4   ¹⁸I, Paul, write this greeting with my own hand. Remember my fetters.

Phlm   ¹Paul, a prisoner for Christ Jesus, and Timothy our brother,
To Philemon our beloved fellow worker . . .

"They shall see who have never been told of him,
and they shall understand who have never heard of him."

1 Thess 3:6–13 (§282–283)

⁶But now that Timothy has come to us from you, and has brought us the good news of your faith and love and reported that you always remember us kindly and long to see us, as we long to see you—⁷for this reason, brethren, in all our distress and affliction we have been comforted about you through your faith; ⁸for now we live, if you stand fast in the Lord. ⁹For what thanksgiving can we render to God for you, for all the joy which we feel for your sake before our God, ¹⁰praying earnestly night and day that we may see you face to face and supply what is lacking in your faith?

¹¹Now may our God and Father himself, and our Lord Jesus, direct our way to you; ¹²and may the Lord make you increase and abound in love to one another and to all men, as we do to you, ¹³so that he may establish your hearts unblamable in holiness before our God and Father, at the coming of our Lord Jesus with all his saints.

Phlm   ⁹yet for love's sake I prefer to appeal to you—I, Paul, an ambassador and now a prisoner also for Christ Jesus . . .

2 Tim 1   ⁸Do not be ashamed then of testifying to our Lord, nor of me his prisoner, but share in suffering for the gospel in the power of God, . . .

2 Tim 1   ¹²and therefore I suffer as I do. But I am not ashamed, for I know whom I have believed, and I am sure that he is able to guard until that Day what has been entrusted to me.

2 Tim 1   ¹⁶May the Lord grant mercy to the household of Onesiphorus, for he often refreshed me; he was not ashamed of my chains, . . .

Acts 21   ³³Then the tribune came up and arrested him, and ordered him to be bound wih two chains. He inquired who he was and what he had done.

● **Phil 1:10**

Phil 4   ⁸Finally, brethren, whatever is true, whatever is honorable, whatever is just, whatever is pure, whatever is lovely, whatever is gracious, if there is any excellence, if there is anything worthy of praise, think about these things.

● **Phil 1:11**

Rom 6   ²¹But then what return did you get from the things of which you are now ashamed? The end of those things is death. ²²But now that you have been set free from sin and have become slaves of God, the return you get is sanctification and its end, eternal life.

Rom 7   ⁴Likewise, my brethren, you have died to the law through the body of Christ, so that you may belong to another, to him who has been raised from the dead in order that we may bear fruit for God. ⁵While we were living in the flesh, our sinful passions, aroused by the law, were at work in our members to bear fruit for death.

Gal 5   ²²But the fruit of the Spirit is love, joy, peace, patience, kindness, goodness, faithfulness, . . .

[12]I want you to know, brethren, that what has happened to me has really served to advance the gospel, [13]so that it has become known throughout the whole praetorian guard and to all the rest that my imprisonment is for Christ; [14]and most of the brethren have been made confident in the Lord because of my imprisonment, and are much more bold to speak the word of God without fear.

[15]Some indeed preach Christ from envy and rivalry, but others from good will. [16]The latter do it out of love, knowing that I am put here for the defense of the gospel; [17]the former proclaim Christ out of partisanship, not sincerely but thinking to afflict me in my imprisonment. [18]What then? Only that in every way, whether in pretense or in truth, Christ is proclaimed; and in that I rejoice.

PRIMARY

Rom 1:16–17 (§3)

[16]For I am not ashamed of the gospel: it is the power of God for salvation to every one who has faith, to the Jew first and also to the Greek. [17]For in it the righteousness of God is revealed through faith for faith; as it is written, "He who through faith is righteous shall live."

Rom 16:17–20a (§67)

[17]I appeal to you, brethren, to take note of those who create dissensions and difficulties, in opposition to the doctrine which you have been taught; avoid them. [18]For such persons do not serve our Lord Christ, but their own appetites, and by fair and flattering words they deceive the hearts of the simple-minded. [19]For while your obedience is known to all, so that I rejoice over you, I would have you wise as to what is good and guileless as to what is evil; [20]then the God of peace will soon crush Satan under your feet.

1 Cor 4:14–21 (§86)

[14]I do not write this to make you ashamed, but to admonish you as my beloved children. [15]For though you have countless guides in Christ, you do not have many fathers. For I became your father in Christ Jesus through the gospel. [16]I urge you, then, be imitators of me. [17]Therefore I sent to you Timothy, my beloved and faithful child in the Lord, to remind you of my ways in Christ, as I teach them everywhere in every church. [18]Some are arrogant, as though I were not coming to you. [19]But I will come to you soon, if the Lord wills, and I will find out not the talk of these arrogant people but their power. [20]For the kingdom of God does not consist in talk but in power. [21]What do you wish? Shall I come to you with a rod, or with love in a spirit of gentleness?

2 Cor 10:1–6 (§176)

[1]I, Paul, myself entreat you, by the meekness and gentleness of Christ—I who am humble when face to face with you, but bold to you when I am away!—[2]I beg of you that when I am present I may not have to show boldness with such confidence as I count on showing against some who suspect us of acting in worldly fashion. [3]For though we live in the world we are not carrying on a worldly war, [4]for the weapons of our warfare are not worldly but have divine power to destroy strongholds. [5]We destroy arguments and every proud obstacle to the knowledge of God, and take every thought captive to obey Christ, [6]being ready to punish every disobedience, when your obedience is complete.

2 Cor 10:7–12 (§177)

[7]Look at what is before your eyes. If any one is confident that he is Christ's, let him remind himself that as he is Christ's, so are we. [8]For even if I boast a little too much of our authority, which the Lord gave for building you up and not for destroying you, I shall not be put to shame. [9]I would not seem to be frightening you with letters. [10]For they say, "His letters are weighty and strong, but his bodily presence is weak, and his speech of no account." [11]Let such people understand that what we say by letter when absent, we do when present. [12]Not that we venture to class or compare ourselves with some of those who commend themselves. But when they measure themselves by one another and compare themselves with one another, they are without understanding.

Gal 1:6–12 (§194)

[6]I am astonished that you are so quickly deserting him who called you in the grace of Christ and turning to a different gospel—[7]not that there is another gospel, but there are some who trouble you and want to pervert the gospel of Christ. [8]But even if we, or an angel from heaven, should preach to you a gospel contrary to that which we preached to you, let him be accursed. [9]As we have said before, so now I say again, If any one is preaching to you a gospel contrary to that which you received, let him be accursed.

[10]Am I now seeking the favor of men, or of God? Or am I trying to please men? If I were still pleasing men, I should not be a servant of Christ.

[11]For I would have you know, brethren, that the gospel which was preached by me is not man's gospel. [12]For I did not receive it from man, nor was I taught it, but it came through a revelation of Jesus Christ.

● **Phil 1:12**
2 Tim 2   [9]the gospel for which I am suffering and wearing fetters like a criminal. But the word of God is not fettered.

● **Phil 1:13**
Rom 15   [19]by the power of signs and wonders, by the power of the Holy Spirit, so that from Jerusalem and as far round as Illyricum I have fully preached the gospel of Christ, . . .

Eph 3   [1]For this reason I, Paul, a prisoner for Christ Jesus on behalf of you Gentiles . . .

Eph 4   [1]I therefore, a prisoner for the Lord, beg you to lead a life worthy of the calling to which you have been called, . . .

Phil 4   [22]All the saints greet you, especially those of Caesar's household.

Col 1   [24]Now I rejoice in my sufferings for your sake, and in my flesh I complete what is lacking in Christ's afflictions for the sake of his body, that is, the church, . . .

Col 4   [3]and pray for us also, that God may open to us a door for the word, to declare the mystery of Christ, on account of which I am in prison, . . .

Phlm   [1]Paul, a prisoner for Christ Jesus, and Timothy our brother,
To Philemon our beloved fellow worker . . .

Phlm   [9]yet for love's sake I prefer to appeal to you—I, Paul, an ambassador and now a prisoner also for Christ Jesus . . .

Acts 28   [30]And he lived there two whole years at his own expense, and welcomed all who came to him, . . .

● **Phil 1:14**
2 Thess 3   [4]And we have confidence in the Lord about you, that you are doing and will do the things which we command.

Acts 4   [31]And when they had prayed, the place in which they were gathered together was shaken; and they were all filled with the Holy Spirit and spoke the word of God with boldness.

Acts 28   [31]preaching the kingdom of God and teaching about the Lord Jesus Christ quite openly and unhindered.

● **Phil 1:15**
Rom 2   [8]but for those who are factious and do not obey the truth, but obey wickedness, there will be wrath and fury.

● **Phil 1:17**
2 Cor 4   [2]We have renounced disgraceful, underhanded ways; we refuse to practice cunning or to tamper with God's word, but by the open statement of the truth we would commend ourselves to every man's conscience in the sight of God.

1 Thess 2   [2]but though we had already suffered and been shamefully treated at Philippi, as you know, we had courage in our God to declare to you the gospel of God in the face of great opposition.

● **Phil 1:18**
Rom 10   [17]So faith comes from what is heard, and what is heard comes by the preaching of Christ.

1 Cor 15   [11]Whether then it was I or they, so we preach and so you believed.

[19]Yes, and I shall rejoice. For I know that through your prayers and the help of the Spirit of Jesus Christ this will turn out for my deliverance, [20]as it is my eager expectation and hope that I shall not be at all ashamed, but that with full courage now as always Christ will be honored in my body, whether by life or by death. [21]For to me to live is Christ, and to die is gain. [22]If it is to be life in the flesh, that means fruitful labor for me. Yet which I shall choose I cannot tell. [23]I am hard pressed between the two. My desire is to depart and be with Christ, for that is far better. [24]But to remain in the flesh is more necessary on your account. [25]Convinced of this, I know that I shall remain and continue with you all, for your progress and joy in the faith, [26]so that in me you may have ample cause to glory in Christ Jesus, because of my coming to you again.

Primary

Rom 14:5–12 (§58)

[5]One man esteems one day as better than another, while another man esteems all days alike. Let every one be fully convinced in his own mind. [6]He who observes the day, observes it in honor of the Lord. He also who eats, eats in honor of the Lord, since he gives thanks to God; while he who abstains, abstains in honor of the Lord and gives thanks to God. [7]None of us lives to himself, and none of us dies to himself. [8]If we live, we live to the Lord, and if we die, we die to the Lord; so then, whether we live or whether we die, we are the Lord's. [9]For to this end Christ died and lived again, that he might be Lord both of the dead and of the living. [10]Why do you pass judgment on your brother? Or you, why do you despise your brother? For we shall all stand before the judgment seat of God; [11]for it is written,

"As I live, says the Lord, every knee shall bow to me,

and every tongue shall give praise to God." [12]So each of us shall give account of himself to God.

2 Cor 4:7–12 (§159)

[7]But we have this treasure in earthen vessels, to show that the transcendent power belongs to God and not to us. [8]We are afflicted in every way, but not crushed; perplexed, but not driven to despair; [9]persecuted, but not forsaken; struck down, but not destroyed; [10]always carrying in the body the death of Jesus, so that the life of Jesus may also be manifested in our bodies. [11]For while we live we are always being given up to death for Jesus' sake, so that the life of Jesus may be manifested in our mortal flesh. [12]So death is at work in us, but life in you.

2 Cor 4:16–5:5 (§161)

[16]So we do not lose heart. Though our outer nature is wasting away, our inner nature is being renewed every day. [17]For this slight momentary affliction is preparing for us an eternal weight of glory beyond all comparison, [18]because we look not to the things that are seen but to the things that are unseen; for the things that are seen are transient, but the things that are unseen are eternal.

5 [1]For we know that if the earthly tent we live in is destroyed, we have a building from God, a house not made with hands, eternal in the heavens. [2]Here indeed we groan, and long to put on our heavenly dwelling, [3]so that by putting it on we may not be found naked. [4]For while we are still in this tent, we sigh with anxiety; not that we would be unclothed, but that we would be further clothed, so that what is mortal may be swallowed up by life. [5]He who has prepared us for this very thing is God, who has given us the Spirit as a guarantee.

2 Cor 5:6–10 (§162)

[6]So we are always of good courage; we know that while we are at home in the body we are away from the Lord, [7]for we walk by faith, not by sight. [8]We are of good courage, and we would rather be away from the body and at home with the Lord. [9]So whether we are at home or away, we make it our aim to please him. [10]For we must all appear before the judgment seat of Christ, so that each one may receive good or evil, according to what he has done in the body.

Eph 6:18–20 (§234)

[18]Pray at all times in the Spirit, with all prayer and supplication. To that end keep alert with all perseverance, making supplication for all the saints, [19]and also for me, that utterance may be given me in opening my mouth boldly to proclaim the mystery of the gospel, [20]for which I am an ambassador in chains; that I may declare it boldly, as I ought to speak.

Col 4:2–4 (§269)

[2]Continue steadfastly in prayer, being watchful in it with thanksgiving; [3]and pray for us also, that God may open to us a door for the word, to declare the mystery of Christ, on account of which I am in prison, [4]that I may make it clear, as I ought to speak.

2 Thess 3:1–5 (§299)

3 [1]Finally, brethren, pray for us, that the word of the Lord may speed on and triumph, as it did among you, [2]and that we may be delivered from wicked and evil men; for not all have faith. [3]But the Lord is faithful; he will strengthen you and guard you from evil. [4]And we have confidence in the Lord about you, that you are doing and will do the things which we command. [5]May the Lord direct your hearts to the love of God and to the steadfastness of Christ.

Phlm 21–22 (§309)

[21]Confident of your obedience, I write to you, knowing that you will do even more than I say. [22]At the same time, prepare a guest room for me, for I am hoping through your prayers to be granted to you.

● Phil 1:19–26
Phil 4 [12]I know how to be abased, and I know how to abound; in any and all circumstances I have learned the secret of facing plenty and hunger, abundance and want.

● Phil 1:19
2 Cor 1 [11]You also must help us by prayer, so that many will give thanks on our behalf for the blessing granted us in answer to many prayers.

Acts 16 [7]And when they had come opposite Mysia, they attempted to go into Bithynia, but the Spirit of Jesus did not allow them; . . .

● Phil 1:20
Rom 1 [16]For I am not ashamed of the gospel: it is the power of God for salvation to every one who has faith, to the Jew first and also to the Greek.

1 Cor 6 [20]you were bought with a price. So glorify God in your body.

● Phil 1:21
Rom 8 [10]But if Christ is in you, although your bodies are dead because of sin, your spirits are alive because of righteousness.

Gal 2 [20]I have been crucified with Christ; it is no longer I who live, but Christ who lives in me; and the life I now live in the flesh I live by faith in the Son of God, who loved me and gave himself for me.

Col 3 [4]When Christ who is our life appears, then you also will appear with him in glory.

● Phil 1:23
1 Cor 15 [23]But each in his own order: Christ the first fruits, then at his coming those who belong to Christ. [24]Then comes the end, when he delivers the kingdom to God the Father after destroying every rule and every authority and power.

● Phil 1:26
1 Cor 4 [19]But I will come to you soon, if the Lord wills, and I will find out not the talk of these arrogant people but their power. [20]For the kingdom of God does not consist in talk but in power. [21]What do you wish? Shall I come to you with a rod, or with love in a spirit of gentleness?

[27] Only let your manner of life be worthy of the gospel of Christ, so that whether I come and see you or am absent, I may hear of you that you stand firm in one spirit, with one mind striving side by side for the faith of the gospel, [28] and not frightened in anything by your opponents. This is a clear omen to them of their destruction, but of your salvation, and that from God. [29] For it has been granted to you that for the sake of Christ you should not only believe in him but also suffer for his sake, [30] engaged in the same conflict which you saw and now hear to be mine.

PRIMARY

Rom 2:6–11 (§8)

[6] For he will render to every man according to his works: [7] to those who by patience in well-doing seek for glory and honor and immortality, he will give eternal life; [8] but for those who are factious and do not obey the truth, but obey wickedness, there will be wrath and fury. [9] There will be tribulation and distress for every human being who does evil, the Jew first and also the Greek, [10] but glory and honor and peace for every one who does good, the Jew first and also the Greek. [11] For God shows no partiality.

Rom 12:3–8 (§52)

[3] For by the grace given to me I bid every one among you not to think of himself more highly than he ought to think, but to think with sober judgment, each according to the measure of faith which God has assigned him. [4] For as in one body we have many members, and all the members do not have the same function, [5] so we, though many, are one body in Christ, and individually members one of another. [6] Having gifts that differ according to the grace given to us, let us use them: if prophecy, in proportion to our faith; [7] if service, in our serving; he who teaches, in his teaching; [8] he who exhorts, in his exhortation; he who contributes, in liberality; he who gives aid, with zeal; he who does acts of mercy, with cheerfulness.

1 Cor 12:4–11 (§117)

[4] Now there are varieties of gifts, but the same Spirit; [5] and there are varieties of service, but the same Lord; [6] and there are varieties of working, but it is the same God who inspires them all in every one. [7] To each is given the manifestation of the Spirit for the common good. [8] To one is given through the Spirit the utterance of wisdom, and to another the utterance of knowledge according to the same Spirit, [9] to another faith by the same Spirit, to another gifts of healing by the one Spirit, [10] to another the working of miracles, to another prophecy, to another the ability to distinguish between spirits, to another various kinds of tongues, to another the interpretation of tongues. [11] All these are inspired by one and the same Spirit, who apportions to each one individually as he wills.

Gal 4:12–20 (§209)

[12] Brethren, I beseech you, become as I am, for I also have become as you are. You did me no wrong; [13] you know it was because of a bodily ailment that I preached the gospel to you at first; [14] and though my condition was a trial to you, you did not scorn or despise me, but received me as an angel of God, as Christ Jesus. [15] What has become of the satisfaction you felt? For I bear you witness that, if possible, you would have plucked out your eyes and given them to me. [16] Have I then become your enemy by telling you the truth? [17] They make much of you, but for no good purpose; they want to shut you out, that you may make much of them.

[18] For a good purpose it is always good to be made much of, and not only when I am present with you. [19] My little children, with whom I am again in travail until Christ be formed in you! [20] I could wish to be present with you now and to change my tone, for I am perplexed about you.

Col 2:4–7 (§261)

[4] I say this in order that no one may delude you with beguiling speech. [5] For though I am absent in body, yet I am with you in spirit, rejoicing to see your good order and the firmness of your faith in Christ.

[6] As therefore you received Christ Jesus the Lord, so live in him, [7] rooted and built up in him and established in the faith, just as you were taught, abounding in thanksgiving.

1 Thess 2:13–16 (§279)

[13] And we also thank God constantly for this, that when you received the word of God which you heard from us, you accepted it not as the word of men but as what it really is, the word of God, which is at work in you believers. [14] For you, brethren, became imitators of the churches of God in Christ Jesus which are in Judea; for you suffered the same things from your own countrymen as they did from the Jews, [15] who killed both the Lord Jesus and the prophets, and drove us out, and displease God and oppose all men [16] by hindering us from speaking to the Gentiles that they may be saved—so as always to fill up the measure of their sins. But God's wrath has come upon them at last!

Phlm 21–22 (§309)

[21] Confident of your obedience, I write to you, knowing that you will do even more than I say. [22] At the same time, prepare a guest room for me, for I am hoping through your prayers to be granted to you.

● **Phil 1:27**

2 Cor 1　[24] Not that we lord it over your faith; we work with you for your joy, for you stand firm in your faith.

Eph 4　[1] I therefore, a prisoner for the Lord, beg you to lead a life worthy of the calling to which you have been called, . . .

Phil 2　[24] and I trust in the Lord that shortly I myself shall come also.

Col 1　[10] to lead a life worthy of the Lord, fully pleasing to him, bearing fruit in every good work and increasing in the knowledge of God.

Acts 4　[32] Now the company of those who believed were of one heart and soul, and no one said that any of the things which he possessed was his own, but they had everything in common.

● **Phil 1:29**

2 Cor 1　[5] For as we share abundantly in Christ's sufferings, so through Christ we share abundantly in comfort too.

1 Thess 1　[4] Therefore we ourselves boast of you in the churches of God for your steadfastness and faith in all your persecutions and in the afflictions which you are enduring.

Acts 5　[41] Then they left the presence of the council, rejoicing that they were counted worthy to suffer dishonor for the name.

Acts 14　[22] strengthening the souls of the disciples, exhorting them to continue in the faith, and saying that through many tribulations we must enter the kingdom of God.

● **Phil 1:29–30**

Col 1　[24] Now I rejoice in my sufferings for your sake, and in my flesh I complete what is lacking in Christ's afflictions for the sake of his body, that is, the church, . . .

● **Phil 1:30**

Rom 15　[30] I appeal to you, brethren, by our Lord Jesus Christ and by the love of the Spirit, to strive together with me in your prayers to God on my behalf, [31] that I may be delivered from the unbelievers in Judea, and that my service for Jerusalem may be acceptble to the saints, [32] so that by God's will I may come to you with joy and be refreshed in your company.

1 Tim 4　[7] Have nothing to do with godless and silly myths. Train yourself in godliness; . . .

1 Tim 6　[12] Fight the good fight of the faith; take hold of the eternal life to which you were called when you made the good confession in the presence of many witnesses.

Acts 16　[22] The crowd joined in attacking them; and the magistrates tore the garments off them and gave orders to beat them with rods.

Formal Elements: Confession & Gnomic Sayings

2 So if there is any encouragement in Christ, any incentive of love, any participation in the Spirit, any affection and sympathy, [2]complete my joy by being of the same mind, having the same love, being in full accord and of one mind. [3]Do nothing from selfishness or conceit, but in humility count others better than yourselves. [4]Let each of you look not only to his own interests, but also to the interests of others. [5]Have this mind among yourselves, which is yours in Christ Jesus, [6]who, though he was in the form of God, did not count equality with God a thing to be grasped, [7]but emptied himself, taking the form of a servant, being born in the likeness of men. [8]And being found in human form he humbled himself and became obedient unto death, even death on a cross. [9]Therefore God has highly exalted him and bestowed on him the name which is above every name, [10]that at the name of Jesus every knee should bow, in heaven and on earth and under the earth, [11]and every tongue confess that Jesus Christ is Lord, to the glory of God the Father.

Primary

See §50 for Confession

See §53 for Gnomic Sayings

Secondary

Rom 5:6–11 (§21)
[6]While we were still weak, at the right time Christ died for the ungodly. [7]Why, one will hardly die for a righteous man—though perhaps for a good man one will dare even to die. [8]But God shows his love for us in that while we were yet sinners Christ died for us. [9]Since, therefore, we are now justified by his blood, much more shall we be saved by him from the wrath of God. [10]For if while we were enemies we were reconciled to God by the death of his Son, much more, now that we are reconciled, shall we be saved by his life. [11]Not only so, but we also rejoice in God through our Lord Jesus Christ, through whom we have now received our reconciliation.

Rom 15:1–6 (§60)
[1]We who are strong ought to bear with the failings of the weak, and not to please ourselves; [2]let each of us please his neighbor for his good, to edify him. [3]For Christ did not please himself; but, as it is written, "The reproaches of those who reproached thee fell on me." [4]For whatever was written in former days was written for our instruction, that by steadfastness and by the encouragement of the scriptures we might have hope. [5]May the God of steadfastness and encouragement grant you to live in such harmony with one another, in accord with Christ Jesus, [6]that together you may with one voice glorify the God and Father of our Lord Jesus Christ.

● **Phil 2:1**
See 1 Thess 2:7–8

2 Thess 1 [3]We are bound to give thanks to God always for you, brethren, as is fitting, because your faith is growing abundantly, and the love of every one of you for one another is increasing.

Phlm [9]yet for love's sake I prefer to appeal to you—I, Paul, an ambassador and now a prisoner also for Christ Jesus . . .

● **Phil 2:2**
Rom 2 [7]to those who by patience in well-doing seek for glory and honor and immortality, he will give eternal life; . . .

Rom 8 [6]To set the mind on the flesh is death, but to set the mind on the Spirit is life and peace.

1 Cor 1 [30]He is the source of your life in Christ Jesus, whom God made our wisdom, our righteousness and sanctification and redemption; . . .

Phil 4 [2]I entreat Euodia and I entreat Syntyche to agree in the Lord.

● **Phil 2:3**
Gal 5 [25]If we live by the Spirit, let us also walk by the Spirit.

Col 3 [12]Put on then, as God's chosen ones, holy and beloved, compassion, kindness, lowliness, meekness, and patience, . . .

● **Phil 2:6–11**
1 Tim 3 [16]Great indeed, we confess, is the mystery of our religion:
 He was manifested in the flesh,
 vindicated in the Spirit,
  seen by angels,

preached among the nations,
believed on in the world,
 taken up in glory.

2 Cor 8 [9]For you know the grace of our Lord Jesus Christ, that though he was rich, yet for your sake he became poor, so that by his poverty you might become rich.

● **Phil 2:7**
2 Cor 13 [4]For he was crucified in weakness, but lives by the power of God. For we are weak in him, but in dealing with you we shall live with him by the power of God.

Heb 2 [9]But we see Jesus, who for a little while was made lower than the angels, crowned with glory and honor because of the suffering of death, so that by the grace of God he might taste death for every one.

● **Phil 2:8**
1 Cor 10 [33]just as I try to please all men in everything I do, not seeking my own advantage, but that of many, that they may be saved.

Gal 3 [1]O foolish Galatians! Who has bewitched you, before whose eyes Jesus Christ was publicly portrayed as crucified?

Gal 6 [2]Bear one another's burdens, and so fulfil the law of Christ.

Heb 5 [8]Although he was a Son, he learned obedience through what he suffered; . . .

● **Phil 2:9–11**
Rom 10 [6]But the righteousness based on faith says, Do not say in your heart, "Who will ascend into heaven?" (that is, to bring Christ down) . . .

Eph 1 [20]which he accomplished in Christ when he raised him from the dead and made him sit at his right hand in the heavenly places, [21]far above all rule and authority and power and dominion, and above every name that is named, not only in this age but also in that which is to come; . . .

Col 3 [1]If then you have been raised with Christ, seek the things that are above, where Christ is, seated at the right hand of God.

Heb 1 [1]In many and various ways God spoke of old to our fathers by the prophets; [2]but in these last days he has spoken to us by a Son, whom he appointed the heir of all things, through whom also he created the world. [3]He reflects the glory of God and bears the very stamp of his nature, upholding the universe by his word of power. When he had made purification for sins, he sat down at the right hand of the Majesty on high, [4]having become as much superior to angels as the name he has obtained is more excellent than theirs.

Heb 12 [2]looking to Jesus the pioneer and perfecter of our faith, who for the joy that was set before him endured the cross, despising the shame, and is seated at the right hand of the throne of God.

● **Phil 2:9**
Rom 8 [11]If the Spirit of him who raised Jesus from the dead dwells in you, he who raised Christ Jesus from the dead will give life to your mortal bodies also through his Spirit which dwells in you.

Acts 2 [33]"Being therefore exalted at the right hand of God, and having received from the Father the promise of the Holy Spirit, he has poured out this which you see and hear."

● **Phil 2:11**
1 Cor 12 [3]Therefore I want you to understand that no one speaking by the Spirit of God ever says "Jesus be cursed!" and no one can say "Jesus is Lord" except by the Holy Spirit.

12Therefore, my beloved, as you have always obeyed, so now, not only as in my presence but much more in my absence, work out your own salvation with fear and trembling; **13**for God is at work in you, both to will and to work for his good pleasure.

PRIMARY

Rom 15:14–21 (§62)

14I myself am satisfied about you, my brethren, that you yourselves are full of goodness, filled with all knowledge, and able to instruct one another. **15**But on some points I have written to you very boldly by way of reminder, because of the grace given me by God **16**to be a minister of Christ Jesus to the Gentiles in the priestly service of the gospel of God, so that the offering of the Gentiles may be acceptable, sanctified by the Holy Spirit. **17**In Christ Jesus, then, I have reason to be proud of my work for God. **18**For I will not venture to speak of anything except what Christ has wrought through me to win obedience from the Gentiles, by word and deed, **19**by the power of signs and wonders, by the power of the Holy Spirit, so that from Jerusalem and as far round as Illyricum I have fully preached the gospel of Christ, **20**thus making it my ambition to preach the gospel, not where Christ has already been named, lest I build on another man's foundation, **21**but as it is written,

"They shall see who have never been told of him,
and they shall understand who have never heard of him."

1 Cor 14:37–40 (§130)

37If any one thinks that he is a prophet, or spiritual, he should acknowledge that what I am writing to you is a command of the Lord. **38**If any one does not recognize this, he is not recognized. **39**So, my brethren, earnestly desire to prophesy, and do not forbid speaking in tongues; **40**but all things should be done decently and in order.

2 Cor 7:13b–16 (§170)

And besides our own comfort we rejoiced still more at the joy of Titus, because his mind has been set at rest by you all. **14**For if I have expressed to him some pride in you, I was not put to shame; but just as everything we said to you was true, so our boasting before Titus has proved true. **15**And his heart goes out all the more to you, as he remembers the obedience of you all, and the fear and trembling with which you received him. **16**I rejoice, because I have perfect confidence in you.

2 Cor 13:5–10 (§190)

5Examine yourselves, to see whether you are holding to your faith. Test yourselves. Do you not realize that Jesus Christ is in you?— unless indeed you fail to meet the test! **6**I hope you will find out that we have not failed. **7**But we pray God that you may not do wrong— not that we may appear to have met the test, but that you may do what is right, though we may seem to have failed. **8**For we cannot do anything against the truth, but only for the truth. **9**For we are glad when we are weak and you are strong. What we pray for is your improvement. **10**I

write this while I am away from you, in order that when I come I may not have to be severe in my use of the authority which the Lord has given me for building up and not for tearing down.

Col 2:4–7 (§261)

4I say this in order that no one may delude you with beguiling speech. **5**For though I am absent in body, yet I am with you in spirit, rejoicing to see your good order and the firmness of your faith in Christ.

6As therefore you received Christ Jesus the Lord, so live in him, **7**rooted and built up in him and established in the faith, just as you were taught, abounding in thanksgiving.

2 Thess 2:13–15 (§297)

13But we are bound to give thanks to God always for you, brethren beloved by the Lord, because God chose you from the beginning to be saved, through sanctification by the Spirit and belief in the truth. **14**To this he called you through our gospel, so that you may obtain the glory of our Lord Jesus Christ. **15**So then, brethren, stand firm and hold to the traditions which you were taught by us, either by word of mouth or by letter.

Phlm 21–22 (§309)

21Confident of your obedience, I write to you, knowing that you will do even more than I say. **22**At the same time, prepare a guest room for me, for I am hoping through your prayers to be granted to you.

● **Phil 2:12**

1 Cor 5   **3**For though absent in body I am present in spirit, and as if present, I have already pronounced judgment . . .

2 Cor 7   **15**What accord has Christ with Belial? Or what has a believer in common with an unbeliever?

Col 2   **5**For though I am absent in body, yet I am with you in spirit, rejoicing to see your good order and the firmness of your faith in Christ.

1 Thess 2   **17**But since we were bereft of you, brethren, for a short time, in person not in heart, we endeavored the more eagerly and with great desire to see you face to face; . . .

Phlm   **21**Confident of your obedience, I write to you, knowing that you will do even more than I say.

● **Phil 2:13**

1 Thess 2   **13**And we also thank God constantly for this, that when you received the word of God which you heard from us, you accepted it not as the word of men but as what it really is, the word of God, which is at work in you believers.

[14]Do all things without grumbling or questioning, [15]that you may be blameless and innocent, children of God without blemish in the midst of a crooked and perverse generation, among whom you shine as lights in the world, [16]holding fast the word of life, so that in the day of Christ I may be proud that I did not run in vain or labor in vain. [17]Even if I am to be poured as a libation upon the sacrificial offering of your faith, I am glad and rejoice with you all. [18]Likewise you also should be glad and rejoice with me.

PRIMARY

Rom 12:1–2 (§51)

[1]I appeal to you therefore, brethren, by the mercies of God, to present your bodies as a living sacrifice, holy and acceptable to God, which is your spiritual worship. [2]Do not be conformed to this world but be transformed by the renewal of your mind, that you may prove what is the will of God, what is good and acceptable and perfect.

Rom 13:11–14 (§56)

[11]Besides this you know what hour it is, how it is full time now for you to wake from sleep. For salvation is nearer to us now than when we first believed; [12]the night is far gone, the day is at hand. Let us then cast off the works of darkness and put on the armor of light; [13]let us conduct ourselves becomingly as in the day, not in reveling and drunkenness, not in debauchery and licentiousness, not in quarreling and jealousy. [14]But put on the Lord Jesus Christ, and make no provision for the flesh, to gratify its desires.

1 Cor 1:4–9 (§72)

[4]I give thanks to God always for you because of the grace of God which was given you in Christ Jesus, [5]that in every way you were enriched in him with all speech and all knowledge— [6]even as the testimony to Christ was confirmed among you—[7]so that you are not lacking in any spiritual gift, as you wait for the revealing of our Lord Jesus Christ; [8]who will sustain you to the end, guiltless in the day of our Lord Jesus Christ. [9]God is faithful, by whom you were called into the fellowship of his Son, Jesus Christ our Lord.

1 Cor 15:12–19 (§132)

[12]Now if Christ is preached as raised from the dead, how can some of you say that there is no resurrection of the dead? [13]But if there is no resurrection of the dead, then Christ has not been raised; [14]if Christ has not been raised, then our preaching is in vain and your faith is in vain. [15]We are even found to be misrepresenting God, because we testified of God that he raised Christ, whom he did not raise if it is true that the dead are not raised. [16]For if the dead are not raised, then Christ has not been raised. [17]If Christ has not been raised, your faith is futile and you are still in your sins. [18]Then those also who have fallen asleep in Christ have perished. [19]If for this life only we have hoped in Christ, we are of all men most to be pitied.

2 Cor 1:12–14 (§148)

[12]For our boast is this, the testimony of our conscience that we have behaved in the world, and still more toward you, with holiness and godly sincerity, not by earthly wisdom but by the grace of God. [13]For we write you nothing but what you can read and understand; I hope you will understand fully, [14]as you have understood in part, that you can be proud of us as we can be of you, on the day of the Lord Jesus.

Col 1:21–23 (§259)

[21]And you, who once were estranged and hostile in mind, doing evil deeds, [22]he has now reconciled in his body of flesh by his death, in order to present you holy and blameless and irreproachable before him, [23]provided that you continue in the faith, stable and steadfast, not shifting from the hope of the gospel which you heard, which has been preached to every creature under heaven, and of which I, Paul, became a minister.

1 Thess 3:11–13 (§283)

[11]Now may our God and Father himself, and our Lord Jesus, direct our way to you; [12]and may the Lord make you increase and abound in love to one another and to all men, as we do to you, [13]so that he may establish your hearts unblamable in holiness before our God and Father, at the coming of our Lord Jesus with all his saints.

1 Thess 5:1–11 (§287)

[1]But as to the times and the seasons, brethren, you have no need to have anything written to you. [2]For you yourselves know well that the day of the Lord will come like a thief in the night. [3]When people say, "There is peace and security," then sudden destruction will come upon them as travail comes upon a woman with child, and there will be no escape. [4]But you are not in darkness, brethren, for that day to surprise you like a thief. [5]For you are all sons of light and sons of the day; we are not of the night or of darkness. [6]So then let us not sleep, as others do, but let us keep awake and be sober. [7]For those who sleep sleep at night, and those who get drunk are drunk at night. [8]But, since we belong to the day, let us be sober, and put on the breastplate of faith and love, and for a helmet the hope of salvation. [9]For God has not destined us for wrath, but to obtain salvation through our Lord Jesus Christ, [10]who died for us so that whether we wake or sleep we might live with him. [11]Therefore encourage one another and build one another up, just as you are doing.

1 Thess 5:23–24 (§289)

[23]May the God of peace himself sanctify you wholly; and may your spirit and soul and body be kept sound and blameless at the coming of our Lord Jesus Christ. [24]He who calls you is faithful, and he will do it.

● **Phil 2:15**
Eph 5　[27]that he might present the church to himself in splendor, without spot or wrinkle or any such thing, that she might be holy and without blemish.

Phlm　[10]I appeal to you for my child, Onesimus, whose father I have become in my imprisonment.

Acts 2　[40]And he testified with many other words and exhorted them, saying, "Save yourselves from this crooked generation."

Cf. Eph 1　[4]even as he chose us in him before the foundation of the world, that we should be holy and blameless before him.

Cf. Eph 5　[1]Therefore be imitators of God, as beloved children.

● **Phil 2:16**
1 Cor 1　[7]so that you are not lacking in any spiritual gift, as you wait for the revealing of our Lord Jesus Christ; [8]who will sustain you to the end, guiltless in the day of our Lord Jesus Christ.

2 Cor 1　[14]as you have understood in part, that you can be proud of us as we can be of you, on the day of the Lord Jesus.

Gal 2　[2]I went up by revelation; and I laid before them (but privately before those who were of repute) the gospel which I preach among the Gentiles, lest somehow I should be running or had run in vain.

2 Thess 2　[2]not to be quickly shaken in mind or excited, either by spirit or by word, or by letter purporting to be from us, to the effect that the day of the Lord has come. [3]Let no one deceive you in any way; for that day will not come, unless the rebellion comes first, and the man of lawlessness is revealed, the son of perdition, . . .

Cf. 1 Cor 15　[58]Therefore, my beloved brethren, be steadfast, immovable, always abounding in the work of the Lord, knowing that in the Lord your labor is not in vain.

Cf. Phil 1　[6]And I am sure that he who began a good work in you will bring it to completion at the day of Jesus Christ.

Cf. Phil 1　[10]so that you may approve what is excellent, and may be pure and blameless for the day of Christ, . . .

Cf. 1 Thess 3　[5]For this reason, when I could bear it no longer, I sent that I might know your faith, for fear that somehow the tempter had tempted you and that our labor would be in vain.

● **Phil 2:17–18**
Rom 12　[15]Rejoice with those who rejoice, weep with those who weep.

● **Phil 2:17**
Phil 4　[18]I have received full payment, and more; I am filled, having received from Epaphroditus the gifts you sent, a fragrant offering, a sacrifice acceptable and pleasing to God.

● **Phil 2:18**
Cf. Phil 3:1; 4:4; 4:8

FORMAL ELEMENT: COMMENDATION

[19]I hope in the Lord Jesus to send Timothy to you soon, so that I may be cheered by news of you. [20]I have no one like him, who will be genuinely anxious for your welfare. [21]They all look after their own interests, not those of Jesus Christ. [22]But Timothy's worth you know, how as a son with a father he has served with me in the gospel. [23]I hope therefore to send him just as soon as I see how it will go with me; [24]and I trust in the Lord that shortly I myself shall come also.

PRIMARY

Rom 16:1-2 (§65)

[1]I commend to you our sister Phoebe, a deaconess of the church at Cenchreae, [2]that you may receive her in the Lord as befits the saints, and help her in whatever she may require from you, for she has been a helper of many and of myself as well.

1 Cor 16:10-12 (§140)

[10]When Timothy comes, see that you put him at ease among you, for he is doing the work of the Lord, as I am. [11]So let no one despise him. Speed him on his way in peace, that he may return to me; for I am expecting him with the brethren.

[12]As for our brother Apollos, I strongly urged him to visit you with the other brethren, but it was not at all his will to come now. He will come when he has opportunity.

1 Cor 16:15-18 (§142)

[15]Now, brethren, you know that the household of Stephanas were the first converts in Achaia, and they have devoted themselves to the service of the saints; [16]I urge you to be subject to such men and to every fellow worker and laborer. [17]I rejoice at the coming of Stephanas and Fortunatus and Achaicus, be-cause they have made up for your absence; [18]for they refreshed my spirit as well as yours. Give recognition to such men.

2 Cor 3:1-3 (§154)

[1]Are we beginning to commend ourselves again? Or do we need, as some do, letters of recommendation to you, or from you? [2]You yourselves are our letter of recommendation, written on your hearts, to be known and read by all men; [3]and you show that you are a letter from Christ delivered by us, written not with ink but with the Spirit of the living God, not on tablets of stone but on tablets of human hearts.

2 Cor 8:16-24 (§173)

[16]But thanks be to God who puts the same earnest care for you into the heart of Titus. [17]For he not only accepted our appeal, but being himself very earnest he is going to you of his own accord. [18]With him we are sending the brother who is famous among all the churches for his preaching of the gospel; [19]and not only that, but he has been appointed by the churches to travel with us in this gracious work which we are carrying on, for the glory of the Lord and to show our good will. [20]We intend that no one should blame us about this liberal gift which we are administering, [21]for we aim at what is honorable not only in the Lord's sight but also in the sight of men. [0]And with them we are sending our brother whom we have often tested and found earnest in many matters, but who is now more earnest than ever because of his great confidence in you. [23]As for Titus, he is my partner and fellow worker in your service; and as for our brethren, they are messengers of the churches, the glory of Christ. [24]So give proof, before the churches, of your love and of our boasting about you to these men.

Eph 6:21-22 (§235)

[21]Now that you also may know how I am and what I am doing, Tychicus the beloved brother and faithful minister in the Lord will tell you everything. [22]I have sent him to you for this very purpose, that you may know how we are, and that he may encourage your hearts.

Col 4:7-9 (§271)

[7]Tychicus will tell you all about my affairs; he is a beloved brother and faithful minister and fellow servant in the Lord. [8]I have sent him to you for this very purpose, that you may know how we are and that he may encourage your hearts, [9]and with him Onesimus, the faithful and beloved brother, who is one of yourselves. They will tell you of everything that has taken place here.

Phlm 8-20 (§307-308)

[8]Accordingly, though I am bold enough in Christ to command you to do what is required, [9]yet for love's sake I prefer to appeal to you—I, Paul, an ambassador and now a prisoner also for Christ Jesus—[10]I appeal to you for my child, Onesimus, whose father I have become in my imprisonment. [11](Formerly he was useless to you, but now he is indeed useful to you and to me.) [12]I am sending him back to you, sending my very heart. [13]I would have been glad to keep him with me, in order that he might serve me on your behalf during my imprisonment for the gospel; [14]but I preferred to do nothing without your consent in order that your goodness might not be by compulsion but of your own free will. [15]Perhaps this is why he was parted from you for a while, that you might have him back for ever, [16]no longer as a slave but more than a slave, as a beloved brother, especially to me but how much more to you, both in the flesh and in the Lord. [17]So if you consider me your partner, receive him as you would receive me. [18]If he has wronged you at all, or owes you anything, charge that to my account. [19]I, Paul, write this with my own hand, I will repay it—to say nothing of your owing me even your own self. [20]Yes, brother, I want some benefit from you in the Lord. Refresh my heart in Christ.

● **Phil 2:19-24**

Phil 2   [25]I have thought it necessary to send to you Epaphroditus my brother and fellow worker and fellow soldier, and your messenger and minister to my need, [26]for he has been longing for you all, and has been distressed because you heard that he was ill. [27]Indeed he was ill, near to death. But God had mercy on him, and not only on him but on me also, lest I should have sorrow upon sorrow. [28]I am the more eager to send him, therefore, that you may rejoice at seeing him again, and that I may be less anxious. [29]So receive him in the Lord with all joy; and honor such men, [30]for he nearly died for the work of Christ, risking his life to complete your service to me.

Phil 4:   [2]I entreat Euodia and I entreat Syntyche to agree in the Lord. [3]And I ask you also, true yokefellow, help these women, for they have labored side by side with me in the gospel together with Clement and the rest of my fellow workers, whose names are in the book of life.

● **Phil 2:19**

1 Cor 4   [17]Therefore I sent to you Timothy, my beloved and faithful child in the Lord, to remind you of my ways in Christ, as I teach them everywhere in every church.

1 Thess 3   [2]and we sent Timothy, our brother and God's servant in the gospel of Christ, to establish you in your faith and to exhort you, . . .

Acts 16   [1]And he came also to Derbe and to Lystra. A disciple was there, named Timothy, the son of a Jewish woman who was a believer; but his father was a Greek.

● **Phil 2:21**

Gal 4   [17]They make much of you, but for no good purpose; they want to shut you out, that you may make much of them.

Gal 6   [12]It is those who want to make a good showing in the flesh that would compel you to be circumcised, and only in order that they may not be persecuted for the cross of Christ. [13]For even those who receive circumcision do not themselves keep the law, but they desire to have you circumcised that they may glory in your flesh.

2 Tim 4   [16]At my first defense no one took my part; all deserted me. May it not be charged against them!

● **Phil 2:24**

Phil 1   [27]Only let your manner of life be worthy of the gospel of Christ, so that whether I come and see you or am absent, I may hear of you that you stand firm in one spirit, with one mind striving side by side for the faith of the gospel, . . .

FORMAL ELEMENT: COMMENDATION

25I have thought it necessary to send to you Epaphroditus my brother and fellow worker and fellow soldier, and your messenger and minister to my need, 26for he has been longing for you all, and has been distressed because you heard that he was ill. 27Indeed he was ill, near to death. But God had mercy on him, and not only on him but on me also, lest I should have sorrow upon sorrow. 28I am the more eager to send him, therefore, that you may rejoice at seeing him again, and that I may be less anxious. 29So receive him in the Lord with all joy; and honor such men, 30for he nearly died for the work of Christ, risking his life to complete your service to me.

3 1Finally, my brethren, rejoice in the Lord. To write the same things to you is not irksome to me, and is safe for you.

PRIMARY

Rom 16:1–2 (§65)

[1]I commend to you our sister Phoebe, a deaconess of the church at Cenchreae, [2]that you may receive her in the Lord as befits the saints, and help her in whatever she may require from you, for she has been a helper of many and of myself as well.

1 Cor 16:10–12 (§140)

[10]When Timothy comes, see that you put him at ease among you, for he is doing the work of the Lord, as I am. [11]So let no one despise him. Speed him on his way in peace, that he may return to me; for I am expecting him with the brethren.

[12]As for our brother Apollos, I strongly urged him to visit you with the other brethren, but it was not at all his will to come now. He will come when he has opportunity.

1 Cor 16:15–18 (§142)

[15]Now, brethren, you know that the household of Stephanas were the first converts in Achaia, and they have devoted themselves to the service of the saints; [16]I urge you to be subject to such men and to every fellow worker and laborer. [17]I rejoice at the coming of Stephanas and Fortunatus and Achaicus, because they have made up for your absence; [18]for they refreshed my spirit as well as yours. Give recognition to such men.

2 Cor 3:1–3 (§154)

[1]Are we beginning to commend ourselves again? Or do we need, as some do, letters of recommendation to you, or from you? [2]You yourselves are our letter of recommendation, written on your hearts, to be known and read by all men; [3]and you show that you are a letter from Christ delivered by us, written not with ink but with the Spirit of the living God, not on tablets of stone but on tablets of human hearts.

2 Cor 8:16–24 (§173)

[16]But thanks be to God who puts the same earnest care for you into the heart of Titus. [17]For he not only accepted our appeal, but being himself very earnest he is going to you of his own accord. [18]With him we are sending the brother who is famous among all the churches for his preaching of the gospel; [19]and not only that, but he has been appointed by the churches to travel with us in this gracious work which we are carrying on, for the glory of the Lord and to show our good will. [20]We intend that no one should blame us about this liberal gift which we are administering, [21]for we aim at what is honorable not only in the Lord's sight but also in the sight of men. [22]And with them we are sending our brother whom we have often tested and found earnest in many matters, but who is now more earnest than ever because of his great confidence in you. [23]As for Titus, he is my partner and fellow worker in your service; and as for our brethren, they are messengers of the churches, the glory of Christ. [24]So give proof, before the churches, of your love and of our boasting about you to these men.

Eph 6:21–22 (§235)

[21]Now that you also may know how I am and what I am doing, Tychicus the beloved brother and faithful minister in the Lord will tell you everything. [22]I have sent him to you for this very purpose, that you may know how we are, and that he may encourage your hearts.

Col 4:7–9 (§271)

[7]Tychicus will tell you all about my affairs; he is a beloved brother and faithful minister and fellow servant in the Lord. [8]I have sent him to you for this very purpose, that you may know how we are and that he may encourage your hearts, [9]and with him Onesimus, the faithful and beloved brother, who is one of yourselves. They will tell you of everything that has taken place here.

Phlm 8–20 (§307–308)

[8]Accordingly, though I am bold enough in Christ to command you to do what is required, [9]yet for love's sake I prefer to appeal to you—I, Paul, an ambassador and now a prisoner also for Christ Jesus—[10]I appeal to you for my child, Onesimus, whose father I have become in my imprisonment. [11](Formerly he was useless to you, but now he is indeed useful to you and to me.) [12]I am sending him back to you, sending my very heart. [13]I would have been glad to keep him with me, in order that he might serve me on your behalf during my imprisonment for the gospel; [14]but I preferred to do nothing without your consent in order that your goodness might not be by compulsion but of your own free will. [15]Perhaps this is why he was parted from you for a while, that you might have him back for ever, [16]no longer as a slave but more than a slave, as a beloved brother, especially to me but how much more to you, both in the flesh and in the Lord. [17]So if you consider me your partner, receive him as you would receive me. [18]If he has wronged you at all, or owes you anything, charge that to my account. [19]I, Paul, write this with my own hand, I will repay it—to say nothing of your owing me even your own self. [20]Yes, brother, I want some benefit from you in the Lord. Refresh my heart in Christ.

● **Phil :25–30**

Phil 2   [19]I hope in the Lord Jesus to send Timothy to you soon, so that I may be cheered by news of you. [20]I have no one like him, who will be genuinely anxious for your welfare. [21]They all look after their own interests, not those of Jesus Christ. [22]But Timothy's worth you know, how as a son with a father he has served with me in the gospel. [23]I hope therefore to send him just as soon as I see how it will go with me; [24]and I trust in the Lord that shortly I myself shall come also.

● **Phil 2:30**

Phil 4   [14]Yet it was kind of you to share my trouble. [15]And you Philippians yourselves know that in the beginning of the gospel, when I left Macedonia, no church entered into partnership with me in giving and receiving except you only; [16]for even in Thessalonica you sent me help once and again. [17]Not that I seek the gift; but I seek the fruit which increases to your credit. [18]I have received full payment, and more; I am filled, having received from Epaphroditus the gifts you sent,

a fragrant offering, a sacrifice acceptable and pleasing to God.

● **Phil 3:1**

1 Thess 5   [16]Rejoice always, . . .

²Look out for the dogs, look out for evil-workers, look out for those who mutilate the flesh. ³For we are the true circumcision, who worship God in spirit, and glory in Christ Jesus, and put no confidence in the flesh. ⁴Though I myself have reason for confidence in the flesh also. If any other man thinks he has reason for confidence in the flesh, I have more: ⁵circumcised on the eighth day, of the people of Israel, of the tribe of Benjamin, a Hebrew born of Hebrews; as to the law a Pharisee, ⁶as to zeal a persecutor of the church, as to righteousness under the law blameless. ⁷But whatever gain I had, I counted as loss for the sake of Christ. ⁸Indeed I count everything as loss because of the surpassing worth of knowing Christ Jesus my Lord. For his sake I have suffered the loss of all things, and count them as refuse, in order that I may gain Christ ⁹and be found in him, not having a righteousness of my own, based on law, but that which is through faith in Christ, the righteousness from God that depends on faith; ¹⁰that I may know him and the power of his resurrection, and may share his sufferings, becoming like him in his death, ¹¹that if possible I may attain the resurrection from the dead.

PRIMARY

Rom 2:17–24 (§10)

¹⁷But if you call yourself a Jew and rely upon the law and boast of your relation to God ¹⁸and know his will and approve what is excellent, because you are instructed in the law, ¹⁹and if you are sure that you are a guide to the blind, a light to those who are in darkness, ²⁰a corrector of the foolish, a teacher of children, having in the law the embodiment of knowledge and truth—²¹you then who teach others, will you not teach yourself? While you preach against stealing, do you steal? ²²You who say that one must not commit adultery, do you commit adultery? You who abhor idols, do you rob temples? ²³You who boast in the law, do you dishonor God by breaking the law? ²⁴For, as it is written, "The name of God is blasphemed among the Gentiles because of you."

Rom 2:25–29 (§11)

²⁵Circumcision indeed is of value if you obey the law; but if you break the law, your circumcision becomes uncircumcision. ²⁶So, if a man who is uncircumcised keeps the precepts of the law, will not his uncircumcision be regarded as circumcision? ²⁷Then those who are physically uncircumcised but keep the law will condemn you who have the written code and circumcision but break the law. ²⁸For he is not a real Jew who is one outwardly, nor is true circumcision something external and physical. ²⁹He is a Jew who is one inwardly, and real circumcision is a matter of the heart, spiritual and not literal. His praise is not from men but from God.

Rom 3:21–26 (§14)

²¹But now the righteousness of God has been manifested apart from law, although the law and the prophets bear witness to it, ²²the righteousness of God through faith in Jesus Christ for all who believe. For there is no distinction; ²³since all have sinned and fall short of the glory of God, ²⁴they are justified by his grace as a gift, through the redemption which is in Christ Jesus, ²⁵whom God put forward as an expiation by his blood, to be received by faith. This was to show God's righteousness, because in his divine forbearance he had passed over former sins; ²⁶it was to prove at the present time that he himself is righteous and that he justifies him who has faith in Jesus.

Rom 3:27–31 (§15)

²⁷Then what becomes of our boasting? It is excluded. On what principle? On the principle of works? No, but on the principle of faith. ²⁸For we hold that a man is justified by faith apart from works of law. ²⁹Or is God the God of Jews only? Is he not the God of Gentiles also? Yes, of Gentiles also, ³⁰since God is one; and he will justify the circumcised on the ground of their faith and the uncircumcised through their faith. ³¹Do we then overthrow the law by this faith? By no means! On the contrary, we uphold the law.

Rom 9:30–33 (§39)

³⁰What shall we say, then? That Gentiles who did not pursue righteousness have attained it, that is, righteousness through faith; ³¹but that Israel who pursued the righteousness which is based on law did not succeed in fulfilling that law. ³²Why? Because they did not pursue it through faith, but as if it were based on works. They have stumbled over the stumbling stone, ³³as it is written,
"Behold, I am laying in Zion a stone that will make men stumble,
a rock that will make them fall;
and he who believes in him will not be put to shame."

Rom 10:1–4 (§40)

¹Brethren, my heart's desire and prayer to God for them is that they may be saved. ²I bear them witness that they have a zeal for God, but it is not enlightened. ³For, being ignorant of the righteousness that comes from God, and seeking to establish their own, they did not submit to God's righteousness. ⁴For Christ is the end of the law, that every one who has faith may be justified.

● **Phil 3:2**
Gal 5   ¹¹But if I, brethren, still preach circumcision, why am I still persecuted? In that case the stumbling block of the cross has been removed. ¹²I wish those who unsettle you would mutilate themselves!

● **Phil 3:3**
(Spirit) *read* worship by the Spirit of God: S*AB CDᶜG Koine Lect cop Origen; *omit* God: p⁴⁶ *text:* SᶜD* it vg syr Origen

● **Phil 3:4–7**
Acts 8   ³But Saul was ravaging the church, and entering house after house, he dragged off men and women and committed them to prison.

Acts 9   ⁵And he said, "Who are you, Lord?" And he said, "I am Jesus, whom you are persecuting...."

Acts 22   ⁴"I persecuted this Way to the death, binding and delivering to prison both men and women, ⁵as the high priest and the whole council of elders bear me witness. From them I received letters to the brethren, and I journeyed to Damascus to take those also who were there and bring them in bonds to Jerusalem to be punished."

Acts 23   ⁶But when Paul perceived that one part were Sadducees and the other Pharisees, he cried out in the council, "Brethren, I am a Pharisee, a son of Pharisees; with respect to the hope and the resurrection of the dead I am on trial."

Acts 26   ¹⁰"And I did so in Jerusalem; I not only shut up many of the saints in prison, by authority from the chief priests, but when they were put to death I cast my vote against them. ¹¹And I punished them often in all the synagogues and tried to make them blaspheme; and in raging fury against them, I persecuted them even to foreign cities."

● **Phil 3:6**
1 Cor 15   ⁹For I am the least of the apostles, unfit to be called an apostle, because I persecuted the church of God.

Gal 1   ²³they only heard it said, "He who once persecuted us is now preaching the faith he once tried to destroy."

● **Phil 3:8**
1 Cor 4   ¹³when slandered, we try to conciliate; we have become, and are now, as the refuse of the world, the off-scouring of all things.

2 Cor 5   ¹⁴For the love of Christ controls us, because we are convinced that one has died for all; therefore all have died. ¹⁵And he died for all, that those who live might live no longer for themselves but for him who for their sake died and was raised.

● **Phil 3:10–11**
Rom 6   ³Do you not know that all of us who have been baptized into Christ Jesus were baptized into his death? ⁴We were buried therefore with him by baptism into death, so that as Christ was raised from the dead by the glory of the Father, we too might walk in newness of life.

⁵For if we have been united with him in a death like his, we shall certainly be united with him in a resurrection like his.

1 Cor 15   ³For I delivered to you as of first importance what I also received, that Christ died for our sins in accordance with the scriptures, ⁴that he was buried, that he was raised on the third day in accordance with the scriptures, ⁵and that he appeared to Cephas, then to the twelve. ⁶Then he appeared to more than five hundred brethren at one time, most of whom are still alive, though some have fallen asleep. ⁷Then he appeared to James, then to all the apostles. ⁸Last of all, as to one untimely born, he appeared also to me. ⁹For I

Rom 11:1–6 (§44)

[1]I ask, then, has God rejected his people? By no means! I myself am an Israelite, a descendant of Abraham, a member of the tribe of Benjamin. [2]God has not rejected his people whom he foreknew. Do you not know what the scripture says of Elijah, how he pleads with God against Israel? [3]"Lord, they have killed thy prophets, they have demolished thy altars, and I alone am left, and they seek my life." [4]But what is God's reply to him? "I have kept for myself seven thousand men who have not bowed the knee to Baal." [5]So too at the present time there is a remnant, chosen by grace. [6]But if it is by grace, it is no longer on the basis of works; otherwise grace would no longer be grace.

1 Cor 1:26–31 (§75)

[26]For consider your call, brethren; not many of you were wise according to worldly standards, not many were powerful, not many were of noble birth; [27]but God chose what is foolish in the world to shame the wise, God chose what is weak in the world to shame the strong, [28]God chose what is low and despised in the world, even things that are not, to bring to nothing things that are, [29]so that no human being might boast in the presence of God. [30]He is the source of your life in Christ Jesus, whom God made our wisdom, our righteousness and sanctification and redemption; [31]therefore, as it is written, "Let him who boasts, boast of the Lord."

1 Cor 4:8–13 (§85)

[8]Already you are filled! Already you have become rich! Without us you have become kings! And would that you did reign, so that we might share the rule with you! [9]For I think that God has exhibited us apostles as last of all, like men sentenced to death; because we have become a spectacle to the world, to angels and to men. [10]We are fools for Christ's sake, but you are wise in Christ. We are weak, but you are strong. You are held in honor, but we in disrepute. [11]To the present hour we hunger and thirst, we are ill-clad and buffeted and homeless, [12]and we labor, working with our own hands. When reviled, we bless; when persecuted, we endure; [13]when slandered, we try to conciliate; we have become, and are now, as the refuse of the world, the off-scouring of all things.

2 Cor 3:4–6 (§155)

[4]Such is the confidence that we have through Christ toward God. [5]Not that we are competent of ourselves to claim anything as coming from us; our competence is from God, [6]who has made us competent to be ministers of a new covenant, not in a written code but in the Spirit; for the written code kills, but the Spirit gives life.

2 Cor 11:21b–29 (§183)

But whatever any one dares to boast of—I am speaking as a fool—I also dare to boast of that. [22]Are they Hebrews? So am I. Are they Israelites? So am I. Are they descendants of Abraham? So am I. [23]Are they servants of Christ? I am a better one—I am talking like a madman—with far greater labors, far more imprisonments, with countless beatings, and often near death. [24]Five times I have received at the hands of the Jews the forty lashes less one. [25]Three times I have been beaten with rods; once I was stoned. Three times I have been shipwrecked; a night and a day I have been adrift at sea; [26]on frequent journeys, in danger from rivers, danger from robbers, danger from my own people, danger from Gentiles, danger in the city, danger in the wilderness, danger at sea, danger from false brethren; [27]in toil and hardship, through many a sleepless night, in hunger and thirst, often without food, in cold and exposure. [28]And, apart from other things, there is the daily pressure upon me of my anxiety for all the churches. [29]Who is weak, and I am not weak? Who is made to fall, and I am not indignant?

Gal 1:13–14 (§195)

[13]For you have heard of my former life in Judaism, how I persecuted the church of God violently and tried to destroy it; [14]and I advanced in Judaism beyond many of my own age among my people, so extremely zealous was I for the traditions of my fathers.

Gal 2:15–21 (§199)

[15]We ourselves, who are Jews by birth and not Gentile sinners, [16]yet who know that a man is not justified by works of the law but through faith in Jesus Christ, even we have believed in Christ Jesus, in order to be justified by faith in Christ, and not by works of the law, because by works of the law shall no one be justified. [17]But if, in our endeavor to be justified in Christ, we ourselves were found to be sinners, is Christ then an agent of sin? Certainly not! [18]But if I build up again those things which I tore down, then I prove myself a´ transgressor. [19]For I through the law died to the law, that I might live to God. [20]I have been crucified with Christ; it is no longer I who live, but Christ who lives in me; and the life I now live in the flesh I live by faith in the Son of God, who loved me and gave himself for me. [21]I do not nullify the grace of God; for if justification were through the law, then Christ died to no purpose.

---

am the least of the apostles, unfit to be called an apostle, because I persecuted the church of God. [10]But by the grace of God I am what I am, and his grace toward me was not in vain. On the contrary, I worked harder than any of them, though it was not I, but the grace of God which is with me.

● Phil 3:10

Rom 1   [4]and designated Son of God in power according to the Spirit of holiness by his resurrection from the dead, Jesus Christ our Lord, . . .

2 Cor 4   [7]But we have this treasure in earthen vessels, to show that the transcendent power belongs to God and not to us. [8]We are afflicted in every way, but not crushed; perplexed, but not driven to despair; [9]persecuted, but not forsaken; struck down, but not destroyed; [10]always carrying in the body the death of Jesus, so that the life of Jesus may also be manifested in our bodies. [11]For while we live we are always being given up to death for Jesus' sake, so that the life of Jesus may be manifested in our mortal flesh. [12]So death is at work in us, but life in you.

2 Cor 6   [4]but as servants of God we commend ourselves in every way: through great endurance, in afflictions, hardships, calamities, [5]beatings, imprisonments, tumults, labors, watching, hunger; [6]by purity, knowledge, forbearance, kindness, the Holy Spirit, genuine love, [7]truthful speech, and the power of God; with the weapons of righteousness for the right hand and for the left; [8]in honor and dishonor, in ill repute and good repute. We are treated as impostors, and yet are true; [9]as unknown, and yet well known; as dying, and behold we live; as punished, and yet not killed; [10]as sorrowful, yet always rejoicing; as poor, yet making many rich; as having nothing, and yet possessing everything.

Col 3   [1]If then you have been raised with Christ, seek the things that are above, where Christ is, seated at the right hand of God.

● Phil 3:11

1 Cor 15   [16]For if the dead are not raised, then Christ has not been raised. [17]If Christ has not been raised, your faith is futile and you are still in your sins. [18]Then those also who have fallen asleep in Christ have perished. [19]If for this life only we have hoped in Christ, we are of all men most to be pitied.

1 Cor 15   [20]But in fact Christ has been raised from the dead, the first fruits of those who have fallen asleep. [21]For as by a man came death, by a man has come also the resurrection of the dead. [22]For as in Adam all die, so also in Christ shall all be made alive. [23]But each in his own order: Christ the first fruits, then at his coming those who belong to Christ. [24]Then comes the end, . . .

1 Cor 15   [49]Just as we have borne the image of the man of dust, we shall also bear the image of the man of heaven. [50]I tell you this, brethren: flesh and blood cannot inherit the kingdom of God, nor does the perishable inherit the imperishable.

1 Thess 4   [14]For since we believe that Jesus died and rose again, even so, through Jesus, God will bring with him those who have fallen asleep. [15]For this we declare to you by the word of the Lord, that we who are alive, who are left until the coming of the Lord, shall not precede those who have fallen asleep. [16]For the Lord himself will descend from heaven with a cry of command, with the archangel's call, and with the sound of the trumpet of God. And the dead in Christ will rise first; [17]then we who are alive, who are left, shall be caught up together with them in the clouds to meet the Lord in the air; and so we shall always be with the Lord.

[12] Not that I have already obtained this or am already perfect; but I press on to make it my own, because Christ Jesus has made me his own. [13] Brethren, I do not consider that I have made it my own; but one thing I do, forgetting what lies behind and straining forward to what lies ahead, [14] I press on toward the goal for the prize of the upward call of God in Christ Jesus. [15] Let those of us who are mature be thus minded; and if in anything you are otherwise minded, God will reveal that also to you. [16] Only let us hold true to what we have attained.

PRIMARY

1 Cor 9:24–27 (§108)

[24] Do you not know that in a race all the runners compete, but only one receives the prize? So run that you may obtain it. [25] Every athlete exercises self-control in all things. They do it to receive a perishable wreath, but we an imperishable. [26] Well, I do not run aimlessly, I do not box as one beating the air; [27] but I pommel my body and subdue it, lest after preaching to others I myself should be disqualified.

Eph 4:11–16 (§226)

[11] And his gifts were that some should be apostles, some prophets, some evangelists, some pastors and teachers, [12] to equip the saints for the work of ministry, for building up the body of Christ, [13] until we all attain to the unity of the faith and of the knowledge of the Son of God, to mature manhood, to the measure of the stature of the fulness of Christ; [14] so that we may no longer be children, tossed to and fro and carried about with every wind of doctrine, by the cunning of men, by their craftiness in deceitful wiles. [15] Rather, speaking the truth in love, we are to grow up in every way into him who is the head, into Christ, [16] from whom the whole body, joined and knit together by every joint with which it is supplied, when each part is working properly, makes bodily growth and upbuilds itself in love.

Col 3:1–4 (§265)

[1] If then you have been raised with Christ, seek the things that are above, where Christ is, seated at the right hand of God. [2] Set your minds on things that are above, not on things that are on earth. [3] For you have died, and your life is hid with Christ in God. [4] When Christ who is our life appears, then you also will appear with him in glory.

● **Phil 3:12**

1 Tim 6 [12] Fight the good fight of the faith; take hold of the eternal life to which you were called when you made the good confession in the presence of many witnesses.

2 Tim 4 [8] Henceforth there is laid up for me the crown of righteousness, which the Lord, the righteous judge, will award to me on that Day, and not only to me but also to all who have loved his appearing.

Heb 12 [1] Therefore, since we are surrounded by so great a cloud of witnesses, let us also lay aside every weight, and sin which clings so closely, and let us run with perseverance the race that is set before us, [2] looking to Jesus the pioneer and perfecter of our faith, who for the joy that was set before him endured the cross, despising the shame, and is seated at the right hand of the throne of God.

● **Phil 3:14**

2 Tim 1 [9] who saved us and called us with a holy calling, not in virtue of our works but in virtue of his own purpose and the grace which he gave us in Christ Jesus ages ago, . . .

2 Tim 4 [7] I have fought the good fight, I have finished the race, I have kept the faith.

● **Phil 3:15**

1 Cor 2 [6] Yet among the mature we do impart wisdom, although it is not a wisdom of this age or of the rulers of this age, who are doomed to pass away.

1 Cor 14 [20] Brethren, do not be children in your thinking; be babes in evil, but in thinking be mature.

Gal 1 [16] was pleased to reveal his Son to me, in order that I might preach him among the Gentiles, I did not confer with flesh and blood, . . .

Col 2 [19] and not holding fast to the Head, from whom the whole body, nourished and knit together through its joints and ligaments, grows with a growth that is from God.

Col 4 [12] Epaphras, who is one of yourselves, a servant of Christ Jesus, greets you, always remembering you earnestly in his prayers, that you may stand mature and fully assured in all the will of God.

[17]Brethren, join in imitating me, and mark those who so live as you have an example in us. [18]For many, of whom I have often told you and now tell you even with tears, live as enemies of the cross of Christ. [19]Their end is destruction, their god is the belly, and they glory in their shame, with minds set on earthly things. [20]But our commonwealth is in heaven, and from it we await a Savior, the Lord Jesus Christ, [21]who will change our lowly body to be like his glorious body, by the power which enables him even to subject all things to himself.

PRIMARY

Rom 2:6–11 (§8)

[6]For he will render to every man according to his works: [7]to those who by patience in well-doing seek for glory and honor and immortality, he will give eternal life; [8]but for those who are factious and do not obey the truth, but obey wickedness, there will be wrath and fury. [9]There will be tribulation and distress for every human being who does evil, the Jew first and also the Greek, [10]but glory and honor and peace for every one who does good, the Jew first and also the Greek. [11]For God shows no partiality.

1 Cor 15:42–50 (§136)

[42]So is it with the resurrection of the dead. What is sown is perishable, what is raised is imperishable. [43]It is sown in dishonor, it is raised in glory. It is sown in weakness, it is raised in power. [44]It is sown a physical body, it is raised a spiritual body. If there is a physical body, there is also a spiritual body. [45]Thus it is written, "The first man Adam became a living being"; the last Adam became a life-giving spirit. [46]But it is not the spiritual which is first but the physical, and then the spiritual. [47]The first man was from the earth, a man of dust; the second man is from heaven. [48]As was the man of dust, so are those who are of the dust; and as is the man of heaven, so are those who are of heaven. [49]Just as we have borne the image of the man of dust, we shall also bear the image of the man of heaven. [50]I tell you this, brethren: flesh and blood cannot inherit the kingdom of God, nor does the perishable inherit the imperishable.

Col 3:1–4 (§265)

[1]If then you have been raised with Christ, seek the things that are above, where Christ is, seated at the right hand of God. [2]Set your minds on things that are above, not on things that are on earth. [3]For your have died, and your life is hid with Christ in God. [4]When Christ who is our life appears, then you also will appear with him in glory.

1 Thess 4:13–18 (§286)

[13]But we would not have you ignorant, brethren, concerning those who are asleep, that you may not grieve as others do who have no hope. [14]For since we believe that Jesus died and rose again, even so, through Jesus, God will bring with him those who have fallen asleep. [15]For this we declare to you by the word of the Lord, that we who are alive, who are left until the coming of the Lord, shall not precede those who have fallen asleep. [16]For the Lord himself will descend from heaven with a cry of command, with the archangel's call, and with the sound of the trumpet of God. And the dead in Christ will rise first; [17]then we who are alive, who are left, shall be caught up together with them in the clouds to meet the Lord in the air; and so we shall always be with the Lord. [18]Therefore comfort one another with these words.

2 Thess 2:1–12 (§296)

[1]Now concerning the coming of our Lord Jesus Christ and our assembling to meet him, we beg you, brethren, [2]not to be quickly shaken in mind or excited, either by spirit or by word, or by letter purporting to be from us, to the effect that the day of the Lord has come. [3]Let no one deceive you in any way; for that day will not come, unless the rebellion comes first, and the man of lawlessness is revealed, the son of perdition, [4]who opposes and exalts himself against every so-called god or object of worship, so that he takes his seat in the temple of God, proclaiming himself to be God. [5]Do you not remember that when I was still with you I told you this? [6]And you know what is restraining him now so that he may be revealed in his time. [7]For the mystery of lawlessness is already at work; only he who now restrains it will do so until he is out of the way. [8]And then the lawless one will be revealed, and the Lord Jesus will slay him with the breath of his mouth and destroy him by his appearing and his coming. [9]The coming of the lawless one by the activity of Satan will be with all power and with pretended signs and wonders, [10]and with all wicked deception for those who are to perish, because they refused to love the truth and so be saved. [11]Therefore God sends upon them a strong delusion, to make them believe what is false, [12]so that all may be condemned who did not believe the truth but had pleasure in unrighteousness.

● **Phil 3:17**
Cf. 1 Cor 4:16; 1 Cor 11:1; Gal 4:12; Eph 5:1; Phil 4:8–9; 1 Thess 2:14; 2 Thess 3:7

● **Phil 3:18**
Rom 9   [2]that I have great sorrow and unceasing anguish in my heart.

1 Cor 5   [10]not at all meaning the immoral of this world, or the greedy and robbers, or idolaters, since then you would need to go out of the world.

● **Phil 3:19**
Rom 11   [26]and so all Israel will be saved; as it is written,
"The Deliverer will come from Zion,
he will banish ungodliness from Jacob"; . . .

Rom 14   [17]For the kingdom of God is not food and drink but righteousness and peace and joy in the Holy Spirit; . . .

1 Cor 6   [13]"Food is meant for the stomach and the stomach for food"—and God will destroy both one and the other. The body is not meant for immorality, but for the Lord, and the Lord for the body.

1 Cor 8   [8]Food will not commend us to God. We are no worse off if we do not eat, and no better off if we do.

Eph 5   [5]Be sure of this, that no fornicator or impure man, or one who is covetous (that is, an idolater), has any inheritance in the kingdom of Christ and of God.

[6]Let no one deceive you with empty words, for it is because of these things that the wrath of God comes upon the sons of disobedience.

1 Thess 2   [16]. . . But God's wrath has come upon them at last!

2 Thess 1   [9]They shall suffer the punishment of eternal destruction and exclusion from the presence of the Lord and from the glory of his might, [10]when he comes on that day to be glorified in his saints, and to be marveled at in all who have believed, because our testimony to you was believed.

2 Tim 3   [4]treacherous, reckless, swollen with conceit, lovers of pleasure rather than lovers of God, . . .

Titus 1   [12]One of themselves, a prophet of their own, said, "Cretans are always liars, evil beasts, lazy gluttons."

● **Phil 3:20–21**
2 Cor 5   [1]For we know that if the earthly tent we live in is destroyed, we have a building from God, a house not made with hands, eternal in the heavens. [2]Here indeed we groan, and long to put on our heavenly dwelling, . . .

Eph 2   [6]and raised us up with him, and made us sit with him in the heavenly places in Christ Jesus, . . .

Col 1   [5]because of the hope laid up for you in heaven. Of this you have heard before in the word of the truth, the gospel . . .

Col 3   [1]If then you have been raised with Christ, seek the things that are above, where Christ is, seated at the right hand of God.

● **Phil 3:20**
Eph 2   [6]and raised us up with him, and made us sit with him in the heavenly places in Christ Jesus, . . .

Eph 2   [12]remember that you were at that time separated from Christ, alienated from the commonwealth of Israel, and strangers to the covenants of promise, having no hope and without God in the world.

Titus 2   [13]awaiting our blessed hope, the appearing of the glory of our great God and Savior Jesus Christ, . . .

● **Phil 3:21**
Rom 16   [20]then the God of peace will soon crush Satan under your feet.

Cf. 1 Cor 15:24–25

2 Cor 4   [14]knowing that he who raised the Lord Jesus will raise us also with Jesus and bring us with you into his presence.

2 Cor 5   [4]For while we are still in this tent, we sigh with anxiety; not that we would be unclothed, but that we would be further clothed, so that what is mortal may be swallowed up by life.

4 Therefore, my brethren, whom I love and long for, my joy and crown, stand firm thus in the Lord, my beloved.

²I entreat Euodia and I entreat Syntyche to agree in the Lord. ³And I ask you also, true yokefellow, help these women, for they have labored side by side with me in the gospel together with Clement and the rest of my fellow workers, whose names are in the book of life.

PRIMARY

Rom 15:1-6 (§60)

¹We who are strong ought to bear with the failings of the weak, and not to please ourselves; ²let each of us please his neighbor for his good, to edify him. ³For Christ did not please himself; but, as it is written, "The reproaches of those who reproached thee fell on me." ⁴For whatever was written in former days was written for our instruction, that by steadfastness and by the encouragement of the scriptures we might have hope. ⁵May the God of steadfastness and encouragement grant you to live in such harmony with one another, in accord with Christ Jesus, ⁶that together you may with one voice glorify the God and Father of our Lord Jesus Christ.

1 Cor 4:6-7 (§84)

⁶I have applied all this to myself and Apollos for your benefit, brethren, that you may learn by us not to go beyond what is written, that none of you may be puffed up in favor of one against another. ⁷For who sees anything different in you? What have you that you did not receive? If then you received it, why do you boast as if it were not a gift?

2 Cor 2:5-11 (§151)

⁵But if any one has caused pain, he has caused it not to me, but in some measure—not to put it too severely— to you all. ⁶For such a one this punishment by the majority is enough; ⁷so you should rather turn to forgive and comfort him, or he may be overwhelmed by excessive sorrow. ⁸So I beg you to reaffirm your love for him. ⁹For this is why I wrote, that I might test you and know whether you are obedient in everything. ¹⁰Any one whom you forgive, I also forgive. What I have forgiven, if I have forgiven anything, has been for your sake in the presence of Christ, ¹¹to keep Satan from gaining the advantage over us; for we are not ignorant of his designs.

Gal 6:1-6 (§214)

¹Brethren, if a man is overtaken in any trespass, you who are spiritual should restore him in a spirit of gentleness. Look to yourself, lest you too be tempted. ²Bear one another's burdens, and so fulfil the law of Christ. ³For if any one thinks he is something, when he is nothing, he deceives himself. ⁴But let each one test his own work, and then his reason to boast will be in himself alone and not in his neighbor. ⁵For each man will have to bear his own load. ⁶Let him who is taught the word share all good things with him who teaches.

1 Thess 2:17-20 (§280)

¹⁷But since we were bereft of you, brethren, for a short time, in person not in heart, we endeavored the more eagerly and with great desire to see you face to face; ¹⁸because we wanted to come to you—I, Paul, again and again—but Satan hindered us. ¹⁹For what is our hope or joy or crown of boasting before our Lord Jesus at his coming? Is it not you? ²⁰For you are our glory and joy.

1 Thess 5:12-22 (§288)

¹²But we beseech you, brethren, to respect those who labor among you and are over you in the Lord and admonish you, ¹³and to esteem them very highly in love because of their work. Be at peace among yourselves. ¹⁴And we exhort you, brethren, admonish the idle, encourage the fainthearted, help the weak, be patient with them all. ¹⁵See that none of you repays evil for evil, but always seek to do good to one another and to all. ¹⁶Rejoice always, ¹⁷pray constantly, ¹⁸give thanks in all circumstances; for this is the will of God in Christ Jesus for you. ¹⁹Do not quench the Spirit, ²⁰do not despise prophesying, ²¹but test everything; hold fast what is good, ²²abstain from every form of evil.

Phlm 15-20 (§308)

¹⁵Perhaps this is why he was parted from you for a while, that you might have him back for ever, ¹⁶no longer as a slave but more than a slave, as a beloved brother, especially to me but how much more to you, both in the flesh and in the Lord. ¹⁷So if you consider me your partner, receive him as you would receive me. ¹⁸If he has wronged you at all, or owes you anything, charge that to my account. ¹⁹I, Paul, write this with my own hand, I will repay it—to say nothing of your owing me even your own self. ²⁰Yes, brother, I want some benefit from you in the Lord. Refresh my heart in Christ.

● **Phil 4:1**

Eph 6   ¹³Therefore take the whole armor of God, that you may be able to withstand in the evil day, and having done all, to stand.

Phil 1   ⁸For God is my witness, how I yearn for you all with the affection of Christ Jesus.

1 Thess 3   ⁸for now we live, if you stand fast in the Lord.

● **Phil 4:2**

Phil 2   ²complete my joy by being of the same mind, having the same love, being in full accord and of one mind.

● **Phil 4:3**

Rom 16   ³Greet Prisca and Aquila, my fellow workers in Christ Jesus, . . .

Rom 16   ⁹Greet Urbanus, our fellow worker in Christ, and my beloved Stachys.

Rom 16   ²¹Timothy, my fellow worker, greets you; so do Lucius and Jason and Sosipater, my kinsmen.

1 Cor 3   ⁹For we are God's fellow workers; you are God's field, God's building.

2 Cor 1   ²⁴Not that we lord it over your faith; we work with you for your joy, for you stand firm in your faith.

2 Cor 8   ²³As for Titus, he is my partner and fellow worker in your service; and as for our brethren, they are messengers of the churches, the glory of Christ.

Phil 2   ²⁵I have thought it necessary to send to you Epaphroditus my brother and fellow worker and fellow soldier, and your messenger and minister to my need, . . .

Col 4   ¹¹and Jesus who is called Justus. These are the only men of the circumcision among my fellow

workers for the kingdom of God, and they have been a comfort to me.

1 Thess 3   ²and we sent Timothy, our brother and God's servant in the gospel of Christ, to establish you in your faith and to exhort you, . . .

Phlm   ¹Paul, a prisoner for Christ Jesus, and Timothy our brother,
To Philemon our beloved fellow worker . . .

Phlm   ²⁴and so do Mark, Aristarchus, Demas, and Luke, my fellow workers.

Rev 3   ⁵He who conquers shall be clad thus in white garments, and I will not blot his name out of the book of life; I will confess his name before my Father and before his angels.

Rev 20   ¹⁵and if any one's name was not found written in the book of life, he was thrown into the lake of fire.

FORMAL ELEMENT: GNOMIC SAYINGS

⁴Rejoice in the Lord always; again I will say, Rejoice. ⁵Let all men know your forbearance. The Lord is at hand. ⁶Have no anxiety about anything, but in everything by prayer and supplication with thanksgiving let your requests be made known to God. ⁷And the peace of God, which passes all understanding, will keep your hearts and your minds in Christ Jesus.

PRIMARY

Rom 12:9–21 (§53)

⁹Let love be genuine; hate what is evil, hold fast to what is good; ¹⁰love one another with brotherly affection; outdo one another in showing honor. ¹¹Never flag in zeal, be aglow with the Spirit, serve the Lord. ¹²Rejoice in your hope, be patient in tribulation, be constant in prayer. ¹³Contribute to the needs of the saints, practice hospitality.

¹⁴Bless those who persecute you; bless and do not curse them. ¹⁵Rejoice with those who rejoice, weep with those who weep. ¹⁶Live in harmony with one another; do not be haughty, but associate with the lowly; never be conceited. ¹⁷Repay no one evil for evil, but take thought for what is noble in the sight of all. ¹⁸If possible, so far as it depends upon you, live peaceably with all. ¹⁹Beloved, never avenge yourselves, but leave it to the wrath of God; for it is written, "Vengeance is mine, I will repay, says the Lord." ²⁰No, "if your enemy is hungry, feed him; if he is thirsty, give him drink; for by so doing you will heap burning coals upon his head." ²¹Do not be overcome by evil, but overcome evil with good.

1 Cor 13:4–7 (§122)

⁴Love is patient and kind; love is not jealous or boastful; ⁵it is not arrogant or rude. Love does not insist on its own way; it is not irritable or resentful; ⁶it does not rejoice at wrong, but rejoices in the right. ⁷Love bears all things, believes all things, hopes all things, endures all things.

2 Cor 13:11–13 (§191)

¹¹Finally, brethren, farewell. Mend your ways, heed my appeal, agree with one another, live in peace, and the God of love and peace will be with you. ¹²Greet one another with a holy kiss. ¹³All the saints greet you.

Eph 4:25–32 (§228)

²⁵Therefore, putting away falsehood, let every one speak the truth with his neighbor, for we are members one of another. ²⁶Be angry but do not sin; do not let the sun go down on your anger, ²⁷and give no opportunity to the devil. ²⁸Let the thief no longer steal, but rather let him labor, doing honest work with his hands, so that he may be able to give to those in need. ²⁹Let no evil talk come out of your mouths, but only such as is good for edifying, as fits the occasion, that it may impart grace to those who hear. ³⁰And do not grieve the Holy Spirit of God, in whom you were sealed for the day of redemption. ³¹Let all bitterness and wrath and anger and clamor and slander be put away from you, with all malice, ³²and be kind to one another, tenderhearted, forgiving one another, as God in Christ forgave you.

Col 3:12–17 (§267)

¹²Put on then, as God's chosen ones, holy and beloved, compassion, kindness, lowliness, meekness, and patience, ¹³forbearing one another and, if one has a complaint against another, forgiving each other; as the Lord has forgiven you, so you also must forgive. ¹⁴And above all these put on love, which binds everything together in perfect harmony. ¹⁵And let the peace of Christ rule in your hearts, to which indeed you were called in the one body. And be thankful. ¹⁶Let the word of Christ dwell in you richly, as you teach and admonish one another in all wisdom, and as you sing psalms and hymns and spiritual songs with thankfulness in your hearts to God. ¹⁷And whatever you do, in word or deed, do everything in the name of the Lord Jesus, giving thanks to God the Father through him.

1 Thess 4:9–12 (§285)

⁹But concerning love of the brethren you have no need to have any one write to you, for you yourselves have been taught by God to love one another; ¹⁰and indeed you do love all the brethren throughout Macedonia. But we exhort you, brethren, to do so more and more, ¹¹to aspire to live quietly, to mind your own affairs, and to work with your hands, as we charged you; ¹²so that you may command the respect of outsiders,

1 Thess 5:12–22 (§288)

¹²But we beseech you, brethren, to respect those who labor among you and are over you in the Lord and admonish you, ¹³and to esteem them very highly in love because of their work. Be at peace among yourselves. ¹⁴And we exhort you, brethren, admonish the idle, encourage the fainthearted, help the weak, be patient with them all. ¹⁵See that none of you repays evil for evil, but always seek to do good to one another and to all. ¹⁶Rejoice always, ¹⁷pray constantly, ¹⁸give thanks in all circumstances; for this is the will of God in Christ Jesus for you. ¹⁹Do not quench the Spirit, ²⁰do not despise prophesying, ²¹but test everything; hold fast what is good, ²²abstain from every form of evil.

SECONDARY

1 Cor 7:32–35 (§99)

³²I want you to be free from anxieties. The unmarried man is anxious about the affairs of the Lord, how to please the Lord; ³³but the married man is anxious about worldly affairs, how to please his wife, ³⁴and his interests are divided. And the unmarried woman or girl is anxious about the affairs of the Lord, how to be holy in body and spirit; but the married woman is anxious about worldly affairs, how to please her husband. ³⁵I say this for your own benefit, not to lay any restraint upon you, but to promote good order and to secure your undivided devotion to the Lord.

2 Thess 3:16 (§302)

¹⁶Now may the Lord of peace himself give you peace at all times in all ways. The Lord be with you all.

● **Phil 4:4–7**

Phil 2   ¹So if there is any encouragement in Christ, any incentive of love, any participation in the Spirit, any affection and sympathy, ²complete my joy by being of the same mind, having the same love, being in full accord and of one mind. ³Do nothing from selfishness or conceit, but in humility count others better than yourselves. ⁴Let each of you look not only to his own interests, but also to the interests of others. ⁵Have this mind among yourselves, which is yours in Christ Jesus, . . .

Phil 4   ⁸Finally, brethren, whatever is true, whatever is honorable, whatever is just, whatever is pure, whatever is lovely, whatever is gracious, if there is any excellence, if there is anything worthy of praise, think about these things. ⁹What you have learned and received and heard and seen in me, do; and the God of peace will be with you.

● **Phil 4:4**

Phil 2   ¹⁸Likewise you also should be glad and rejoice with me.

Phil 3   ¹Finally, my brethren, rejoice in the Lord. To write the same things to you is not irksome to me, and is safe for you.

1 Thess 5   ¹⁶Rejoice always, . . .

● **Phil 4:6**

Eph 5   ²⁰always and for everything giving thanks in the name of our Lord Jesus Christ to God the Father.

1 Tim 2   ¹First of all, then, I urge that supplications, prayers, intercessions, and thanksgivings be made for all men, . . .

Fᴏʀᴍᴀʟ Eʟᴇᴍᴇɴᴛ: Vɪʀᴛᴜᴇ Lɪsᴛ

8Finally, brethren, whatever is true, whatever is honorable, whatever is just, whatever is pure, whatever is lovely, whatever is gracious, if there is any excellence, if there is anything worthy of praise, think about these things. 9What you have learned and received and heard and seen in me, do; and the God of peace will be with you.

Pʀɪᴍᴀʀʏ

2 Cor 6:1–10 (§165)

1Working together with him, then, we entreat you not to accept the grace of God in vain. 2For he says,

"At the acceptable time I have listened to you,

and helped you on the day of salvation."

Behold, now is the acceptable time; behold, now is the day of salvation. 3We put no obstacle in any one's way, so that no fault may be found with our ministry, 4but as servants of God we commend ourselves in every way: through great endurance, in afflictions, hardships, calamities, 5beatings, imprisonments, tumults, labors, watching, hunger; 6by purity, knowledge, forbearance, kindness, the Holy Spirit, genuine love, 7truthful speech, and the power of God; with the weapons of righteousness for the right hand and for the left; 8in honor and dishonor, in ill repute and good repute. We are treated as impostors, and yet are true; 9as unknown, and yet well known; as dying, and behold we live; as punished, and yet not killed; 10as sorrowful, yet always rejoicing; as poor, yet making many rich; as having nothing, and yet possessing everything.

2 Cor 8:1–7 (§171)

1We want you to know, brethren, about the grace of God which has been shown in the churches of Macedonia, 2for in a severe test of affliction, their abundance of joy and their extreme poverty have overflowed in a wealth of liberality on their part. 3For they gave according to their means, as I can testify, and beyond their means, of their own free will, 4begging us earnestly for the favor of taking part in the relief of the saints— 5and this, not as we expected, but first they gave themselves to the Lord and to us by the will of God. 6Accordingly we have urged Titus that as he had already made a beginning, he should also complete among you this gracious work. 7Now as you excel in everything—in faith, in utterance, in knowledge, in all earnestness, and in your love for us—see that you excel in this gracious work also.

Gal 5:16–26 (§213)

16But I say, walk by the Spirit, and do not gratify the desires of the flesh. 17For the desires of the flesh are against the Spirit, and the desires of the Spirit are against the flesh; for these are opposed to each other, to prevent you from doing what you would. 18But if you are led by the Spirit you are not under the law. 19Now the works of the flesh are plain: fornication, impurity, licentiousness, 20idolatry, sorcery, enmity, strife, jealousy, anger, selfishness, dissension, party spirit, 21envy, drunkenness, carousing, and the like. I warn you, as I warned you before, that those who do such things shall not inherit the kingdom of God. 22But the fruit of the Spirit is love, joy, peace, patience, kindness, goodness, faithfulness, 23gentleness, self-control; against such there is no law. 24And those who belong to Christ Jesus have crucified the flesh with its passions and desires.

25If we live by the Spirit, let us also walk by the Spirit. 26Let us have no self-conceit, no provoking of one another, no envy of one another.

Eph 4:1–10 (§225)

1I therefore, a prisoner for the Lord, beg you to lead a life worthy of the calling to which you have been called, 2with all lowliness and meekness, with patience, forbearing one another in love, 3eager to maintain the unity of the Spirit in the bond of peace. 4There is one body and one Spirit, just as you were called to the one hope that belongs to your call, 5one Lord, one faith, one baptism, 6one God and Father of us all, who is above all and through all and in all. 7But grace was given to each of us according to the measure of Christ's gift. 8Therefore it is said,

"When he ascended on high he led a host of captives,

and he gave gifts to men."

9(In saying, "He ascended," what does it mean but that he had also descended into the lower parts of the earth? 10He who descended is he who also ascended far above all the heavens, that he might fill all things.)

Col 3:12–17 (§267)

12Put on then, as God's chosen ones, holy and beloved, compassion, kindness, lowliness, meekness, and patience, 13forbearing one an-

---

● **Phil 4:8**
Phil 1   10so that you may approve what is excellent, and may be pure and blameless for the day of Christ,
. . .

● **Phil 4:9**
Rom 16   20then the God of peace will soon crush Satan under your feet.

1 Cor 4   16I urge you, then, be imitators of me.

1 Cor 11   1Be imitators of me, as I am of Christ.

other and, if one has a complaint against another, forgiving each other; as the Lord has forgiven you, so you also must forgive. [14]And above all these put on love, which binds everything together in perfect harmony. [15]And let the peace of Christ rule in your hearts, to which indeed you were called in the one body. And be thankful. [16]Let the word of Christ dwell in you richly, as you teach and admonish one another in all wisdom, and as you sing psalms and hymns and spiritual songs with thankfulness in your hearts to God. [17]And whatever you do, in word or deed, do everything in the name of the Lord Jesus, giving thanks to God the Father through him.

SECONDARY

Rom 10:14–17 (§42)

[14]But how are men to call upon him in whom they have not believed? And how are they to believe in him of whom they have never heard? And how are they to hear without a preacher? [15]And how can men preach unless they are sent? As it is written, "How beautiful are the feet of those who preach good news!" [16]But they have not all obeyed the gospel; for Isaiah says, "Lord, who has believed what he has heard from us?" [17]So faith comes from what is heard, and what is heard comes by the preaching of Christ.

Rom 12:1–2 (§51)

[1]I appeal to you therefore, brethren, by the mercies of God, to present your bodies as a living sacrifice, holy and acceptable to God, which is your spiritual worship. [2]Do not be conformed to this world but be transformed by the renewal of your mind, that you may prove what is the will of God, what is good and acceptable and perfect.

1 Cor 11:2–16 (§112)

[2]I commend you because you remember me in everything and maintain the traditions even as I have delivered them to you. [3]But I want you to understand that the head of every man is Christ, the head of a woman is her husband, and the head of Christ is God. [4]Any man who prays or prophesies with his head covered dishonors his head, [5]but any woman who prays or prophesies with her head unveiled dishonors her head—it is the same as if her head were shaven. [6]For if a woman will not veil herself, then she should cut off her hair; but if it is disgraceful for a woman to be shorn or shaven, let her wear a veil. [7]For a man ought not to cover his head, since he is the image and glory of God; but woman is the glory of man. [8](For man was not made from woman, but woman from man. [9]Neither was man created for woman, but woman for man.) [10]That is why a woman ought to have a veil on her head, because of the angels. [11](Nevertheless, in the Lord woman is not independent of man nor man of woman; [12]for as woman was made from man, so man is now born of woman. And all things are from God.) [13]Judge for yourselves; is it proper for a woman to pray to God with her head uncovered? [14]Does not nature itself teach you that for a man to wear long hair is degrading to him, [15]but if a woman has long hair, it is her pride? For her hair is given to her for a covering. [16]If any one is disposed to be contentious, we recognize no other practice, nor do the churches of God.

Eph 4:25–32 (§228)

[25]Therefore, putting away falsehood, let every one speak the truth with his neighbor, for we are members one of another. [26]Be angry but do not sin; do not let the sun go down on your anger, [27]and give no opportunity to the devil. [28]Let the thief no longer steal, but rather let him labor, doing honest work with his hands, so that he may be able to give to those in need. [29]Let no evil talk come out of your mouths, but only such as is good for edifying, as fits the occasion, that it may impart grace to those who hear. [30]And do not grieve the Holy Spirit of God, in whom you were sealed for the day of redemption. [31]Let all bitterness and wrath and anger and clamor and slander be put away from you, with all malice, [32]and be kind to one another, tenderhearted, forgiving one another, as God in Christ forgave you.

1 Thess 3:11–13 (§283)

[11]Now may our God and Father himself, and our Lord Jesus, direct our way to you; [12]and may the Lord make you increase and abound in love to one another and to all men, as we do to you, [13]so that he may establish your hearts unblamable in holiness before our God and Father, at the coming of our Lord Jesus with all his saints.

2 Thess 2:16–17 (§298)

[16]Now may our Lord Jesus Christ himself, and God our Father, who loved us and gave us eternal comfort and good hope through grace, [17]comfort your hearts and establish them in every good work and word.

---

2 Cor 13   [11]Finally, brethren, farewell. Mend your ways, heed my appeal, agree with one another, live in peace, and the God of love and peace will be with you.

1 Thess 5   [23]May the God of peace himself sanctify you wholly; and may your spirit and soul and body be kept sound and blameless at the coming of our Lord Jesus Christ.

2 Thess 3   [9]It was not because we have not that right, but to give you in our conduct an example to imitate.

2 Thess 3   [16]Now may the Lord of peace himself give you peace at all times in all ways. The Lord be with you all.

¹⁰I rejoice in the Lord greatly that now at length you have revived your concern for me; you were indeed concerned for me, but you had no opportunity. ¹¹Not that I complain of want; for I have learned, in whatever state I am, to be content. ¹²I know how to be abased, and I know how to abound; in any and all circumstances I have learned the secret of facing plenty and hunger, abundance and want. ¹³I can do all things in him who strengthens me.

¹⁴Yet it was kind of you to share my trouble. ¹⁵And you Philippians yourselves know that in the beginning of the gospel, when I left Macedonia, no church entered into partnership with me in giving and receiving except you only; ¹⁶for even in Thessalonica you sent me help once and again. ¹⁷Not that I seek the gift; but I seek the fruit which increases to your credit. ¹⁸I have received full payment, and more; I am filled, having received from Epaphroditus the gifts you sent, a fragrant offering, a sacrifice acceptable and pleasing to God. ¹⁹And my God will supply every need of yours according to his riches in glory in Christ Jesus. ²⁰To our God and Father be glory for ever and ever. Amen.

PRIMARY

Rom 8:31–39 (§34)

³¹What then shall we say to this? If God is for us, who is against us? ³²He who did not spare his own Son but gave him up for us all, will he not also give us all things with him? ³³Who shall bring any charge against God's elect? It is God who justifies; ³⁴who is to condemn? Is it Christ Jesus, who died, yes, who was raised from the dead, who is at the right hand of God, who indeed intercedes for us? ³⁵Who shall separate us from the love of Christ? Shall tribulation, or distress, or persecution, or famine, or nakedness, or peril, or sword? ³⁶As it is written,

"For thy sake we are being killed all the day long;

we are regarded as sheep to be slaughtered."
³⁷No, in all these things we are more than conquerors through him who loved us. ³⁸For I am sure that neither death, nor life, nor angels, nor principalities, nor things present, nor things to come, nor powers, ³⁹nor height, nor depth, nor anything else in all creation, will be able to separate us from the love of God in Christ Jesus our Lord.

Rom 12:1–2 (§51)

¹I appeal to you therefore, brethren, by the mercies of God, to present your bodies as a living sacrifice, holy and acceptable to God, which is your spiritual worship. ²Do not be conformed to this world but be transformed by the renewal of your mind, that you may prove what is the will of God, what is good and acceptable and perfect.

1 Cor 9:1–18 (§105–106)

¹Am I not free? Am I not an apostle? Have I not seen Jesus our Lord? Are not you my workmanship in the Lord? ²If to others I am not an apostle, at least I am to you; for you are the seal of my apostleship in the Lord.

³This is my defense to those who would examine me. ⁴Do we not have the right to our food and drink? ⁵Do we not have the right to be accompanied by a wife, as the other apostles and the brothers of the Lord and Cephas? ⁶Or is it only Barnabas and I who have no right to refrain from working for a living? ⁷Who serves as a soldier at his own expense? Who plants a vineyard without eating any of its fruit? Who tends a flock without getting some of the milk?

⁸Do I say this on human authority? Does not the law say the same? ⁹For it is written in the law of Moses, "You shall not muzzle an ox when it is treading out the grain." Is it for oxen that God is concerned? ¹⁰Does he not speak entirely for our sake? It was written for our sake, because the plowman should plow in hope and the thresher thresh in hope of a share in the crop. ¹¹If we have sown spiritual good among you, is it too much if we reap your material benefits? ¹²If others share this rightful claim upon you, do not we still more?

Nevertheless, we have not made use of this right, but we endure anything rather than put an obstacle in the way of the gospel of Christ. ¹³Do you not know that those who are employed in the temple service get their food from the temple, and those who serve at the altar share in the sacrificial offerings? ¹⁴In the same way, the Lord commanded that those who proclaim the gospel should get their living by the gospel.

¹⁵But I have made no use of any of these rights, nor am I writing this to secure any such provision. For I would rather die than have any one deprive me of my ground for boasting. ¹⁶For if I preach the gospel, that gives me no ground for boasting. For necessity is laid upon me. Woe to me if I do not preach the gospel! ¹⁷For if I do this of my own will, I have a reward; but if not of my own will, I am entrusted with a commission. ¹⁸What then is my reward? Just this: that in my preaching I may make the gospel free of charge, not making full use of my right in the gospel.

2 Cor 2:14–17 (§153)

¹⁴But thanks be to God, who in Christ always leads us in triumph, and through us spreads the fragrance of the knowledge of him everywhere. ¹⁵For we are the aroma of Christ to God among those who are being saved and among those who are perishing, ¹⁶to one a fragrance from death to death, to the other a fragrance from life to life. Who is sufficient for these things? ¹⁷For we are not, like so many, peddlers of God's word; but as men of sincerity, as commissioned by God, in the sight of God we speak in Christ.

● **Phil 4:10**

2 John   ⁴I rejoiced greatly to find some of your children following the truth, just as we have been commanded by the Father.

3 John   ³For I greatly rejoiced when some of the brethren arrived and testified to the truth of your life, as indeed you do follow the truth.

● **Phil 4:11**

1 Tim 6   ⁶There is great gain in godliness with contentment; ⁷for we brought nothing into the world, and we cannot take anything out of the world; ⁸but if we have food and clothing, with these we shall be content.

● **Phil 4:14–18**

2 Cor 8   ¹³I do not mean that others should be eased and you burdened, ¹⁴but that as a matter of equality your abundance at the present time should supply their want, so that their abundance may supply your want, that there may be equality. ¹⁵As it is written, "He who gathered much had nothing over, and he who gathered little had no lack."

2 Cor 6:1–10 (§165)

[1]Working together with him, then, we entreat you not to accept the grace of God in vain. [2]For he says,

"At the acceptable time I have listened to you,

and helped you on the day of salvation."
Behold, now is the acceptable time; behold, now is the day of salvation. [3]We put no obstacle in any one's way, so that no fault may be found with our ministry, [4]but as servants of God we commend ourselves in every way: through great endurance, in afflictions, hardships, calamities, [5]beatings, imprisonments, tumults, labors, watching, hunger; [6]by purity, knowledge, forbearance, kindness, the Holy Spirit, genuine love, [7]truthful speech, and the power of God; with the weapons of righteousness for the right hand and for the left; [8]in honor and dishonor, in ill repute and good repute. We are treated as impostors, and yet are true; [9]as unknown, and yet well known; as dying, and behold we live; as punished, and yet not killed; [10]as sorrowful, yet always rejoicing; as poor, yet making many rich; as having nothing, and yet possessing everything.

2 Cor 7:2–4 (§168)

[2]Open your hearts to us; we have wronged no one, we have corrupted no one, we have taken advantage of no one. [3]I do not say this to condemn you, for I said before that you are in our hearts, to die together and to live together. [4]I have great confidence in you; I have great pride in you; I am filled with comfort. With all our affliction, I am overjoyed.

2 Cor 11:7–11 (§180)

[7]Did I commit a sin in abasing myself so that you might be exalted, because I preached God's gospel without cost to you? [8]I robbed other churches by accepting support from them in order to serve you. [9]And when I was with you and was in want, I did not burden any one, for my needs were supplied by the brethren who came from Macedonia. So I refrained and will refrain from burdening you in any way. [10]As the truth of Christ is in me, this boast of mine shall not be silenced in the regions of Achaia. [11]And why? Because I do not love you? God knows I do!

2 Cor 12:1–10 (§185)

[1]I must boast; there is nothing to be gained by it, but I will go on to visions and revelations of the Lord. [2]I know a man in Christ who fourteen years ago was caught up to the third heaven—whether in the body or out of the body I do not know, God knows. [3]And I know that this man was caught up into Paradise—whether in the body or out of the body I do not know, God knows— [4]and he heard things that cannot be told, which man may not utter. [5]On behalf of this man I will boast, but on my own behalf I will not boast, except of my weaknesses. [6]Though if I wish to boast, I shall not be a fool, for I shall be speaking the truth. But I refrain from it, so that no one may think more of me than he sees in me or hears from me. [7]And to keep me from being too elated by the abundance of revelations, a thorn was given me in the flesh, a messenger of Satan, to harass me, to keep me from being too elated. [8]Three times I besought the Lord about this, that it should leave me; [9]but he said to me, "My grace is sufficient for you, for my power is made perfect in weakness." I will all the more gladly boast of my weaknesses, that the power of Christ may rest upon me. [10]For the sake of Christ, then, I am content with weaknesses, insults, hardships, persecutions, and calamities; for when I am weak, then I am strong.

Eph 3:20–21 (§224)

[20]Now to him who by the power at work within us is able to do far more abundantly than all that we ask or think, [21]to him be glory in the church and in Christ Jesus to all generations, for ever and ever. Amen.

Eph 5:1–2 (§229)

[1]Therefore be imitators of God, as beloved children. [2]And walk in love, as Christ loved us and gave himself up for us, a fragrant offering and sacrifice to God.

1 Thess 2:9–12 (§278)

[9]For you remember our labor and toil, brethren; we worked night and day, that we might not burden any of you, while we preached to you the gospel of God. [10]You are witnesses, and God also, how holy and righteous and blameless was our behavior to you believers; [11]for you know how, like a father with his children, we exhorted each one of you and encouraged you and charged you [12]to lead a life worthy of God, who calls you into his own kingdom and glory.

2 Thess 3:6–13 (§300)

[6]Now we command you, brethren, in the name of our Lord Jesus Christ, that you keep away from any brother who is living in idleness and not in accord with the tradition that you received from us. [7]For you yourselves know how you ought to imitate us; we were not idle when we were with you, [8]we did not eat any one's bread without paying, but with toil and labor we worked night and day, that we might not burden any of you. [9]It was not because we have not that right, but to give you in our conduct an example to imitate. [10]For even when we were with you, we gave you this command: If any one will not work, let him not eat. [11]For we hear that some of you are living in idleness, mere busybodies, not doing any work. [12]Now such persons we command and exhort in the Lord Jesus Christ to do their work in quietness and to earn their own living. [13]Brethren, do not be weary in well-doing.

● **Phil 4:15–16**
2 Cor 11   [8]I robbed other churches by accepting support from them in order to serve you.

Phil 1   [5]thankful for your partnership in the gospel from the first day until now.

● **Phil 4:16**
Acts 17   [1]Now when they had passed through Amphipolis and Apollonia they came to Thessalonica, where there was a synagogue of the Jews. [2]And Paul went in, as was his custom, and for three weeks he argued with them from the scriptures, . . .

● **Phil 4:19**
Rom 9   [23]in order to make known the riches of his glory for the vessels of mercy, which he has prepared beforehand for glory, . . .

Eph 3   [16]that according to the riches of his glory he may grant you to be strengthened with might through his Spirit in the inner man, . . .

LETTER STRUCTURE: GREETINGS

[21] Greet every saint in Christ Jesus. The brethren who are with me greet you. [22] All the saints greet you, especially those of Caesar's household.

PRIMARY

Rom 16:3-16 (§66)

[3] Greet Prisca and Aquila, my fellow workers in Christ Jesus, [4] who risked their necks for my life, to whom not only I but also all the churches of the Gentiles give thanks; [5] greet also the church in their house. Greet my beloved Epaenetus, who was the first convert in Asia for Christ. [6] Greet Mary, who has worked hard among you. [7] Greet Andronicus and Junias, my kinsmen and my fellow prisoners; they are men of note among the apostles, and they were in Christ before me. [8] Greet Ampliatus, my beloved in the Lord. [9] Greet Urbanus, our fellow worker in Christ, and my beloved Stachys. [10] Greet Apelles, who is approved in Christ. Greet those who belong to the family of Aristobulus. [11] Greet my kinsman Herodion. Greet those in the Lord who belong to the family of Narcissus. [12] Greet those workers in the Lord, Tryphaena and Tryphosa. Greet the beloved Persis, who has worked hard in the Lord. [13] Greet Rufus, eminent in the Lord, also his mother and mine. [14] Greet Asyncritus, Phlegon, Hermes, Patrobas, Hermas, and the brethren who are with them. [15] Greet Philologus, Julia, Nereus and his sister, and Olympas, and all the saints who are with them. [16] Greet one another with a holy kiss. All the churches of Christ greet you.

Rom 16:21-23 (§69)

[21] Timothy, my fellow worker, greets you; so do Lucius and Jason and Sosipater, my kinsmen. [22] I Tertius, the writer of this letter, greet you in the Lord. [23] Gaius, who is host to me and to the whole church, greets you. Erastus, the city treasurer, and our brother Quartus, greet you.

1 Cor 16:19-20 (§143)

[19] The churches of Asia send greetings. Aquila and Prisca, together with the church in their house, send you hearty greetings in the Lord. [20] All the brethren send greetings. Greet one another with a holy kiss.

2 Cor 13:11-13 (§191)

[11] Finally, brethren, farewell. Mend your ways, heed my appeal, agree with one another, live in peace, and the God of love and peace will be with you. [12] Greet one another with a holy kiss. [13] All the saints greet you.

Col 4:10-15 (§272)

[10] Aristarchus my fellow prisoner greets you, and Mark the cousin of Barnabas (concerning whom you have received instructions—if he comes to you, receive him), [11] and Jesus who is called Justus. These are the only men of the circumcision among my fellow workers for the kingdom of God, and they have been a comfort to me. [12] Epaphras, who is one of yourselves, a servant of Christ Jesus, greets you, always remembering you earnestly in his prayers, that you may stand mature and fully assured in all the will of God. [13] For I bear him witness that he has worked hard for you and for those in Laodicea and in Hierapolis. [14] Luke the beloved physician and Demas greet you. [15] Give my greetings to the brethren at Laodicea, and to Nympha and the church in her house.

1 Thess 5:26 (§291)

[26] Greet all the brethren with a holy kiss.

Phlm 23-24 (§310)

[23] Epaphras, my fellow prisoner in Christ Jesus, sends greetings to you, [24] and so do Mark, Aristarchus, Demas, and Luke, my fellow workers.

● **Phil 4:21-22**

2 Tim 4   [19] Greet Prisca and Aquila, and the household of Onesiphorus. [20] Erastus remained at Corinth; Trophimus I left ill at Miletus. [21] Do your best to come before winter. Eubulus sends greetings to you, as do Pudens and Linus and Claudia and all the brethren.

Titus 3   [15] All who are with me send greetings to you. Greet those who love us in the faith.

● **Phil 4:22**

Phil 1   [13] so that it has become known throughout the whole praetorian guard and to all the rest that my imprisonment is for Christ; . . .

LETTER STRUCTURE: CLOSING GRACE

[23]**The grace of the Lord Jesus Christ be with your spirit.**

PRIMARY

Rom 16:20b (§68)
    The grace of our Lord Jesus Christ be with you.

1 Cor 16:23–24 (§145)
    [23]The grace of the Lord Jesus be with you. [24]My love be with you all in Christ Jesus. Amen.

2 Cor 13:14 (§192)
    [14]The grace of the Lord Jesus Christ and the love of God and the fellowship of the Holy Spirit be with you all.

Gal 6:18 (§217)
    [18]The grace of our Lord Jesus Christ be with your spirit, brethren. Amen.

Eph 6:23–24 (§236)
    [23]Peace be to the brethren, and love with faith, from God the Father and the Lord Jesus Christ. [24]Grace be with all who love our Lord Jesus Christ with love undying.

Col 4:18b (§274)
    Grace be with you.

1 Thess 5:28 (§293)
    [28]The grace of our Lord Jesus Christ be with you.

2 Thess 3:18 (§304)
    [18]The grace of our Lord Jesus Christ be with you all.

Phlm 25 (§311)
    [25]The grace of the Lord Jesus Christ be with your spirit.

● **Phil 4:23**
1 Tim 6   [21] . . . Grace be with you.

2 Tim 4   [22] . . . Grace be with you.

Titus 3   [15] . . . Grace be with you all.

LETTER STRUCTURE: SALUTATION

1 Paul, an apostle of Christ Jesus by the will of God, and Timothy our brother, [2]To the saints and faithful brethren in Christ at Colossae:

Grace to you and peace from God our Father.

PRIMARY

Rom 1:1–7 (§1)

[1]Paul, a servant of Jesus Christ, called to be an apostle, set apart for the gospel of God [2]which he promised beforehand through his prophets in the holy scriptures, [3]the gospel concerning his Son, who was descended from David according to the flesh [4]and designated Son of God in power according to the Spirit of holiness by his resurrection from the dead, Jesus Christ our Lord, [5]through whom we have received grace and apostleship to bring about the obedience of faith for the sake of his name among all the nations, [6]including yourselves who are called to belong to Jesus Christ;

[7]To all God's beloved in Rome, who are called to be saints:

Grace to you and peace from God our Father and the Lord Jesus Christ.

1 Cor 1:1–3 (§71)

[1]Paul, called by the will of God to be an apostle of Christ Jesus, and our brother Sosthenes,

[2]To the church of God which is at Corinth, to those sanctified in Christ Jesus, called to be saints together with all those who in every place call on the name of our Lord Jesus Christ, both their Lord and ours:

[3]Grace to you and peace from God our Father and the Lord Jesus Christ.

2 Cor 1:1–2 (§146)

[1]Paul, an apostle of Christ Jesus by the will of God, and Timothy our brother.

To the church of God which is at Corinth, with all the saints who are in the whole of Achaia:

[2]Grace to you and peace from God our Father and the Lord Jesus Christ.

Gal 1:1–5 (§193)

[1]Paul an apostle—not from men nor through man, but through Jesus Christ and God the Father, who raised him from the dead— [2]and all the brethren who are with me,

To the churches of Galatia:

[3]Grace to you and peace from God the Father and our Lord Jesus Christ, [4]who gave himself for our sins to deliver us from the present evil age, according to the will of our God and Father; [5]to whom be the glory for ever and ever. Amen.

Eph 1:1–2 (§218)

[1]Paul, an apostle of Christ Jesus by the will of God,

To the saints who are also faithful in Christ Jesus:

[2]Grace to you and peace from God our Father and the Lord Jesus Christ.

Phil 1:1–2 (§237)

[1]Paul and Timothy, servants of Christ Jesus,

To all the saints in Christ Jesus who are at Philippi, with the bishops and deacons:

[2]Grace to you and peace from God our Father and the Lord Jesus Christ.

1 Thess 1:1 (§275)

[1]Paul, Silvanus, and Timothy,

To the church of the Thessalonians in God the Father and the Lord Jesus Christ:

Grace to you and peace.

2 Thess 1:1–2 (§294)

[1]Paul, Silvanus, and Timothy,

To the church of the Thessalonians in God our Father and the Lord Jesus Christ:

[2]Grace to you and peace from God the Father and the Lord Jesus Christ.

Phlm 1–3 (§305)

[1]Paul, a prisoner for Christ Jesus, and Timothy our brother,

To Philemon our beloved fellow worker [2]and Apphia our sister and Archippus our fellow soldier, and the church in your house:

[3]Grace to you and peace from God our Father and the Lord Jesus Christ.

● **Col 1:1–2**

1 Tim 1   [1]Paul, an apostle of Christ Jesus by command of God our Savior and of Christ Jesus our hope,

[2]To Timothy, my true child in the faith:

Grace, mercy, and peace from God the Father and Christ Jesus our Lord.

2 Tim 1   [1]Paul, an apostle of Christ Jesus by the will of God according to the promise of the life which is in Christ Jesus,

[2]To Timothy, my beloved child:

Grace, mercy, and peace from God the Father and Christ Jesus our Lord.

Titus 1   [1]Paul, a servant of God and an apostle of Jesus Christ, to further the faith of God's elect and their knowledge of the truth which accords with godliness, [2]in hope of eternal life which God, who never lies, promised ages ago [3]and at the proper time manifested in his word through the preaching with

which I have been entrusted by command of God our Savior;

[4]To Titus, my true child in a common faith:

Grace and peace from God the Father and Christ Jesus our Savior.

Acts 16   [1]And he came also to Derbe and to Lystra. A disciple was there, named Timothy, the son of a Jewish woman who was a believer; but his father was a Greek.

LETTER STRUCTURE: THANKSGIVING

³We always thank God, the Father of our Lord Jesus Christ, when we pray for you, ⁴because we have heard of your faith in Christ Jesus and of the love which you have for all the saints, ⁵because of the hope laid up for you in heaven. Of this you have heard before in the word of the truth, the gospel ⁶which has come to you, as indeed in the whole world it is bearing fruit and growing—so among yourselves, from the day you heard and understood the grace of God in truth, ⁷as you learned it from Epaphras our beloved fellow servant. He is a faithful minister of Christ on our behalf ⁸and has made known to us your love in the Spirit.

⁹And so, from the day we heard of it, we have not ceased to pray for you, asking that you may be filled with the knowledge of his will in all spiritual wisdom and understanding, ¹⁰to lead a life worthy of the Lord, fully pleasing to him, bearing fruit in every good work and increasing in the knowledge of God. ¹¹May you be strengthened with all power, according to his glorious might, for all endurance and patience with joy, ¹²giving thanks to the Father, who has qualified us to share in the inheritance of the saints in light. ¹³He has delivered us from the dominion of darkness and transferred us to the kingdom of his beloved Son, ¹⁴in whom we have redemption, the forgiveness of sins.

PRIMARY

See §2 for THANKSGIVING

● Col 1:3

1 Tim 1   ¹²I thank him who has given me strength for this, Christ Jesus our Lord, because he judged me faithful by appointing me to his service, . . .

2 Tim 1   ³I thank God whom I serve with a clear conscience, as did my fathers, when I remember you constantly in my prayers.

Titus 1   ⁵This is why I left you in Crete, that you might amend what was defective, and appoint elders in every town as I directed you, . . .

● Col 1:4–5

1 Cor 13   ¹³So faith, hope, love abide, these three; but the greatest of these is love.

Gal 5   ⁵For through the Spirit, by faith, we wait for the hope of righteousness. ⁶For in Christ Jesus neither circumcision nor uncircumcision is of any avail, but faith working through love.

Eph 1   ¹⁵For this reason, because I have heard of your faith in the Lord Jesus and your love toward all the saints, ¹⁶I do not cease to give thanks for you, remembering you in my prayers, ¹⁷that the God of our Lord Jesus Christ, the Father of glory, may give you a spirit of wisdom and of revelation in the knowledge of him, ¹⁸having the eyes of your hearts enlightened, that you may know what is the hope to which he has called you, what are the riches of his glorious inheritance in the saints, . . .

1 Thess 1   ³remembering before our God and Father your work of faith and labor of love and steadfastness of hope in our Lord Jesus Christ.

1 Thess 5   ⁸But, since we belong to the day, let us be sober, and put on the breastplate of faith and love, and for a helmet the hope of salvation.

● Col 1:5

Eph 1   ¹³In him you also, who have heard the word of truth, the gospel of your salvation, and have believed in him, were sealed with the promised Holy Spirit, . . .

Eph 2   ⁶and raised us up with him, and made us sit with him in the heavenly places in Christ Jesus, . . .

Phil 3   ²⁰But our commonwealth is in heaven, and from it we await a Savior, the Lord Jesus Christ, ²¹who will change our lowly body to be like his glorious body, by the power which enables him even to subject all things to himself.

Col 3   ¹If then you have been raised with Christ, seek the things that are above, where Christ is, seated at the right hand of God.

Titus 1   ²in hope of eternal life which God, who never lies, promised ages ago . . .

● Col 1:6

Rom 10   ¹⁸But I ask, have they not heard? Indeed they have; for
    "Their voice has gone out to all the earth, and their words to the ends of the world."

Col 1   ²³provided that you continue in the faith, stable and steadfast, not shifting from the hope of the gospel which you heard, which has been preached to every creature under heaven, and of which I, Paul, became a minister.

● Col 1:7

Col 4   ¹²Epaphras, who is one of yourselves, a servant of Christ Jesus, greets you, always remembering you earnestly in his prayers, that you may stand mature and fully assured in all the will of God. ¹³For I bear him witness that he has worked hard for you and for those in Laodicea and in Hierapolis.

Phlm   ²³Epaphras, my fellow prisoner in Christ Jesus, sends greetings to you, . . .

(on our) *read* your: SᶜC Dᶜ Koine Lect it(most) vg syr cop Ephraem; *text* p⁴⁶S*ABD (Greek) Ambrosiaster

● Col 1:9

Rom 15   ¹⁴I myself am satisfied about you, my brethren, that you yourselves are full of goodness, filled with all knowledge, and able to instruct one another.

Eph 1   ¹⁵For this reason, because I have heard of your faith in the Lord Jesus and your love toward all the saints, ¹⁶I do not cease to give thanks for you, remembering you in my prayers, ¹⁷that the God of our Lord Jesus Christ, the Father of glory, may give you a spirit of wisdom and of revelation in the knowledge of him, . . .

● Col 1:10

Rom 7   ⁴Likewise, my brethren, you have died to the law through the body of Christ, so that you may belong to another, to him who has been raised from the dead in order that we may bear fruit for God.

Gal 1   ¹⁰Am I now seeking the favor of men, or of God? Or am I trying to please men? If I were still pleasing men, I should not be a servant of Christ.

Gal 5   ²²But the fruit of the Spirit is love, joy, peace, patience, kindness, goodness, faithfulness, . . .

Eph 4   ¹I therefore, a prisoner for the Lord, beg you to lead a life worthy of the calling to which you have been called, . . .

Phil 1   ¹¹filled with the fruits of righteousness which come through Jesus Christ, to the glory and praise of God.

1 Thess 2   ⁴but just as we have been approved by God to be entrusted with the gospel, so we speak, not to please men, but to please God who tests our hearts.

1 Thess 2   ¹²to lead a life worthy of God, who calls you into his own kingdom and glory.

● Col 1:12

Eph 1   ¹⁸having the eyes of your hearts enlightened, that you may know what is the hope to which he has called you, what are the riches of his glorious inheritance in the saints, . . .

Col 3   ²⁴knowing that from the Lord you will receive the inheritance as your reward; you are serving the Lord Christ.

Acts 20   ³²"And now I commend you to God and to the word of his grace, which is able to build you up and to give you the inheritance among all those who are sanctified."

(us) *read* you: SB cop(sa) Ambrosiaster: *text:* AC DG Koine Lect it vg cop (bo) Origen (Latin) Ambrosiaster

● Col 1:13

Eph 2   ²in which you once walked, following the course of this world, following the prince of the power of the air, the spirit that is now at work in the sons of disobedience.

● Col 1:14

Eph 1   ⁷In him we have redemption through his blood, the forgiveness of our trespasses, according to the riches of his grace . . .

FORMAL ELEMENT: CONFESSION

15He is the image of the invisible God, the first-born of all creation; 16for in him all things were created, in heaven and on earth, visible and invisible, whether thrones or dominions or principalities or authorities—all things were created through him and for him. 17He is before all things, and in him all things hold together. 18He is the head of the body, the church; he is the beginning, the first-born from the dead, that in everything he might be pre-eminent. 19For in him all the fulness of God was pleased to dwell, 20and through him to reconcile to himself all things, whether on earth or in heaven, making peace by the blood of his cross.

PRIMARY

Rom 1:1–7 (§1)

¹Paul, a servant of Jesus Christ, called to be an apostle, set apart for the gospel of God ²which he promised beforehand through his prophets in the holy scriptures, ³the gospel concerning his Son, who was descended from David according to the flesh ⁴and designated Son of God in power according to the Spirit of holiness by his resurrection from the dead, Jesus Christ our Lord, ⁵through whom we have received grace and apostleship to bring about the obedience of faith for the sake of his name among all the nations, ⁶including yourselves who are called to belong to Jesus Christ;

⁷To all God's beloved in Rome, who are called to be saints:

Grace to you and peace from God our Father and the Lord Jesus Christ.

Rom 11:33–36 (§50)

³³O the depth of the riches and wisdom and knowledge of God! How unsearchable are his judgments and how inscrutable his ways!

³⁴"For who has known the mind of the Lord,
or who has been his counselor?"

³⁵"Or who has given a gift to him
that he might be repaid?"

³⁶For from him and through him and to him are all things. To him be glory for ever. Amen.

1 Cor 8:4–6 (§103)

⁴Hence, as to the eating of food offered to idols, we know that "an idol has no real existence," and that "there is no God but one." ⁵For although there may be so-called gods in heaven or on earth—as indeed there are many "gods" and many "lords"— ⁶yet for us there is one God, the Father, from whom are all things and for whom we exist, and one Lord, Jesus Christ, through whom are all things and through whom we exist.

1 Cor 15:1–11 (§131)

¹Now I would remind you, brethren, in what terms I preached to you the gospel, which you received, in which you stand, ²by which you are saved, if you hold it fast —unless you believed in vain.

³For I delivered to you as of first importance what I also received, that Christ died for our sins in accordance with the scriptures, ⁴that he was buried, that he was raised on the third day in accordance with the scriptures, ⁵and that he appeared to Cephas, then to the twelve. ⁶Then he appeared to more than five hundred brethren at one time, most of whom are still alive, though some have fallen asleep. ⁷Then he appeared to James, then to all the apostles. ⁸Last of all, as to one untimely born, he appeared also to me. ⁹For I am the least of the apostles, unfit to be called an apostle, because I persecuted the church of God. ¹⁰But by the grace of God I am what I am, and his grace toward me was not in vain. On the contrary, I worked harder than any of them, though it was not I, but the grace of God which is with me. ¹¹Whether then it was I or they, so we preach and so you believed.

Eph 4:1–10 (§225)

¹I therefore, a prisoner for the Lord, beg you to lead a life worthy of the calling to which you have been called, ²with all lowliness and meekness, with patience, forbearing one another in love, ³eager to maintain the unity of the Spirit in the bond of peace. ⁴There is one body and one Spirit, just as you were called to the one hope that belongs to your call, ⁵one Lord, one faith, one baptism, ⁶one God and Father of us all, who is above all and through all and in all. ⁷But grace was given to each of us according to the measure of Christ's gift. ⁸Therefore it is said,

"When he ascended on high he led a host of captives,
and he gave gifts to men."

⁹(In saying, "He ascended," what does it mean but that he had also descended into the lower parts of the earth? ¹⁰He who descended is he who also ascended far above all the heavens, that he might fill all things.)

Phil 2:1–11 (§242)

¹So if there is any encouragement in Christ, any incentive of love, any participation in the Spirit, any affection and sympathy, ²complete my joy by being of the same mind, having the same love, being in full accord and of one mind. ³Do nothing from selfishness or conceit, but in humility count others better than yourselves. ⁴Let each of you look not only to his own interests, but also to the interests of others. ⁵Have this mind among yourselves, which is yours in Christ Jesus, ⁶who, though he was in the form of God, did not count equality with God a thing to be grasped, ⁷but emptied himself, taking the form of a servant, being born in the likeness of men. ⁸And being found in human form he humbled himself and became obedient unto death, even death on a cross. ⁹Therefore God has highly exalted him and bestowed on him the name which is above every name, ¹⁰that at the name of Jesus every knee should bow, in heaven and on earth and under the earth, ¹¹and every tongue confess that Jesus Christ is Lord, to the glory of God the Father.

1 Thess 1:2–10 (§276)

²We give thanks to God always for you all, constantly mentioning you in our prayers, ³remembering before our God and Father your work of faith and labor of love and steadfastness of hope in our Lord Jesus Christ. ⁴For we know, brethren beloved by God, that he has chosen you; ⁵for our gospel came to you not only in word, but also in power and in the Holy Spirit and with full conviction. You know what kind of men we proved to be among you for your sake. ⁶And you became imitators of us and of the Lord, for you received the word in much affliction, with joy inspired by the Holy Spirit; ⁷so that you became an example to the all the believers in Macedonia and in Achaia. ⁸For not only has the word of the Lord sounded forth from you in Macedonia and Achaia, but your

---

● Col 1:15–16
2 Cor 4   ⁴In their case the god of this world has blinded the minds of the unbelievers, to keep them from seeing the light of the gospel of the glory of Christ, who is the likeness of God.

2 Cor 4   ¹⁸because we look not to the things that are seen but to the things that are unseen; for the things that are seen are transient, but the things that are unseen are eternal.

Col 3   ¹⁰and have put on the new nature, which is being renewed in knowledge after the image of its creator.

1 Tim 1   ¹⁷To the King of ages, immortal, invisible, the only God, be honor and glory for ever and ever. Amen.

1 Tim 2   ⁵For there is one God, and there is one mediator between God and men, the man Christ Jesus, . . .

● Col 1:16–17
Rom 11   ³⁶For from him and through him and to him are all things. To him be glory for ever. Amen.

● Col 1:17–18
Eph 1   ²¹far above all rule and authority and power and dominion, and above every name that is named, not only in this age but also in that which is to come; ²²and he has put all things under his feet and has made him the head over all things for the church, ²³which is his body, the fulness of him who fills all in all.

faith in God has gone forth everywhere, so that we need not say anything. ⁹For they themselves report concerning us what a welcome we had among you, and how you turned to God from idols, to serve a living and true God, ¹⁰and to wait for his Son from heaven, whom he raised from the dead, Jesus who delivers us from the wrath to come.

SECONDARY

Rom 5:6–11 (§21)

⁶While we were still weak, at the right time Christ died for the ungodly.

⁷Why, one will hardly die for a righteous man—though perhaps for a good man one will dare even to die. ⁸But God shows his love for us in that while we were yet sinners Christ died for us. ⁹Since, therefore, we are now justified by his blood, much more shall we be saved by him from the wrath of God. ¹⁰For if while we were enemies we were reconciled to God by the death of his Son, much more, now that we are reconciled, shall we be saved by his life. ¹¹Not only so, but we also rejoice in God through our Lord Jesus Christ, through whom we have now received our reconciliation.

Rom 8:28–30 (§33)

²⁸We know that in everything God works for good with those who love him, who are called according to his purpose. ²⁹For those whom he foreknew he also predestined to be conformed to the image of his Son, in order that he might be the first-born among many brethren. ³⁰And those whom he predestined he also called; and those whom he called he also justified; and those whom he justified he also glorified.

Rom 11:13–16 (§47)

¹³Now I am speaking to you Gentiles. Inasmuch then as I am an apostle to the Gentiles, I magnify my ministry ¹⁴in order to make my fellow Jews jealous, and thus save some of them. ¹⁵For if their rejection means the reconciliation of the world, what will their acceptance mean but life from the dead? ¹⁶If the dough offered as first fruits is holy, so is the whole lump; and if the root is holy, so are the branches.

1 Cor 15:20–28 (§133)

²⁰But in fact Christ has been raised from the dead, the first fruits of those who have fallen asleep. ²¹For as by a man came death, by a man has come also the resurrection of the dead. ²²For as in Adam all die, so also in Christ shall all be made alive. ²³But each in his own order: Christ the first fruits, then at his coming those who belong to Christ. ²⁴Then comes the end, when he delivers the kingdom to God the Father after destroying every rule and every authority and power. ²⁵For he must reign until he has put all his enemies under his feet. ²⁶The last enemy to be destroyed is death. ²⁷"For God has put all things in subjection under his feet." But when it says, "All things are put in subjection under him," it is plain that he is excepted who put all things under him. ²⁸When all things are subjected to him, then the Son himself will also be subjected to him who put all things under him, that God may be everything to every one.

1 Cor 15:42–50 (§136)

⁴²So is it with the resurrection of the dead. What is sown is perishable, what is raised is imperishable. ⁴³It is sown in dishonor, it is raised in glory. It is sown in weakness, it is raised in power. ⁴⁴It is sown a physical body, it is raised a spiritual body. If there is a physical body, there is also a spiritual body. ⁴⁵Thus it is written, "The first man Adam became a living being"; the last Adam became a life-giving spirit. ⁴⁶But it is not the spiritual which is first but the physical, and then the spiritual. ⁴⁷The first man was from the earth, a man of dust; the second man is from heaven. ⁴⁸As was the man of dust, so are those who are of the dust; and as is the man of heaven, so are those who are of heaven. ⁴⁹Just as we have borne the image of the man of dust, we shall also bear the image of the man of heaven. ⁵⁰I tell you this, brethren: flesh and blood cannot inherit the kingdom of God, nor does the perishable inherit the imperishable.

2 Cor 5:14–21 (§164)

¹⁴For the love of Christ controls us, because we are convinced that one has died for all; therefore all have died. ¹⁵And he died for all, that those who live might live no longer for themselves but for him who for their sake died and was raised.

¹⁶From now on, therefore, we regard no one from a human point of view; even though we once regarded Christ from a human point of view, we regard him thus no longer. ¹⁷Therefore, if any one is in Christ, he is a new creation; the old has passed away, behold, the new has come. ¹⁸All this is from God, who through Christ reconciled us to himself and gave us the ministry of reconciliation; ¹⁹that is, in Christ God was reconciling the world to himself, not counting their trespasses against them, and entrusting to us the message of reconciliation. ²⁰So we are ambassadors for Christ, God making his appeal through us. We beseech you on behalf of Christ, be reconciled to God. ²¹For our sake he made him to be sin who knew no sin, so that in him we might become the righteousness of God.

Eph 2:11–22 (§221)

¹¹Therefore remember that at one time you Gentiles in the flesh, called the uncircumcision by what is called the circumcision, which is made in the flesh by hands— ¹²remember that you were at that time separated from Christ, alienated from the commonwealth of Israel, and strangers to the covenants of promise, having no hope and without God in the world. ¹³But now in Christ Jesus you who once were far off have been brought near in the blood of Christ. ¹⁴For he is our peace, who has made us both one, and has broken down the dividing wall of hostility, ¹⁵by abolishing in his flesh the law of commandments and ordinances, that he might create in himself one new man in place of the two, so making peace, ¹⁶and might reconcile us both to God in one body through the cross, thereby bringing the hostility to an end. ¹⁷And he came and preached peace to you who were far off and peace to those who were near; ¹⁸for through him we both have access in one Spirit to the Father. ¹⁹So then you are no longer strangers and sojourners, but you are fellow citizens with the saints and members of the household of God, ²⁰built upon the foundation of the apostles and prophets, Christ Jesus himself being the cornerstone, ²¹in whom the whole structure is joined together and grows into a holy temple in the Lord; ²²in whom you also are built into it for a dwelling place of God in the Spirit.

● **Col 1:18**

Rom 12 ⁵so we, though many, are one body in Christ, and individually members of one another.

1 Cor 12 ¹²For just as the body is one and has many members, and all the members of the body, though many, are one body, so it is with Christ.

1 Cor 12 ²⁷Now you are the body of Christ and individually members of it.

Eph 4 ¹⁵Rather, speaking the truth in love, we are to grow up in every way into him who is the head, into Christ, . . .

Col 2 ¹⁹and not holding fast to the Head, from whom the whole body, nourished and knit together through its joints and ligaments, grows with a growth that is from God.

Cf. Eph 5 ²³For the husband is the head of the wife as Christ is the head of the church, his body, and is himself its Savior.

● **Col 1:19**

Col 2 ⁹For in him the whole fulness of deity dwells bodily, . . .

● **Col 1:20**

Rom 5 ¹⁸Then as one man's trespass led to condemnation for all men, so one man's act of righteousness leads to acquittal and life for all men.

1 Cor 15 ²²For as in Adam all die, so also in Christ shall all be made alive.

(cross) *add* through him: p⁴⁶SACDᶜ Koine(some) Lect syr cop(bo) Chrysostom; *text:* BD*G Koine (some) it vg cop(sa) Origen

21 And you, who once were estranged and hostile in mind, doing evil deeds, 22 he has now reconciled in his body of flesh by his death, in order to present you holy and blameless and irreproachable before him, 23 provided that you continue in the faith, stable and steadfast, not shifting from the hope of the gospel which you heard, which has been preached to every creature under heaven, and of which I, Paul, became a minister.

PRIMARY

Rom 12:1–2 (§51)

1 I appeal to you therefore, brethren, by the mercies of God, to present your bodies as a living sacrifice, holy and acceptable to God, which is your spiritual worship. 2 Do not be conformed to this world but be transformed by the renewal of your mind, that you may prove what is the will of God, what is good and acceptable and perfect.

1 Cor 1:26–31 (§75)

26 For consider your call, brethren; not many of you were wise according to worldly standards, not many were powerful, not many were of noble birth; 27 but God chose what is foolish in the world to shame the wise, God chose what is weak in the world to shame the strong, 28 God chose what is low and despised in the world, even things that are not, to bring to nothing things that are, 29 so that no human being might boast in the presence of God. 30 He is the source of your life in Christ Jesus, whom God made our wisdom, our righteousness and sanctification and redemption; 31 therefore, as it is written, "Let him who boasts, boast of the Lord."

2 Cor 4:13–15 (§160)

13 Since we have the same spirit of faith as he had who wrote, "I believed, and so I spoke," we too believe, and so we speak, 14 knowing that he who raised the Lord Jesus will raise us also with Jesus and bring us with you into his presence. 15 For it is all for your sake, so that as grace extends to more and more people it may increase thanksgiving, to the glory of God.

2 Cor 5:14–21 (§164)

14 For the love of Christ controls us, because we are convinced that one has died for all; therefore all have died. 15 And he died for all, that those who live might live no longer for themselves but for him who for their sake died and was raised.

16 From now on, therefore, we regard no one from a human point of view; even though we once regarded Christ from a human point of view, we regard him thus no longer. 17 Therefore, if any one is in Christ, he is a new creation; the old has passed away, behold, the new has come. 18 All this is from God, who through Christ reconciled us to himself and gave us the ministry of reconciliation; 19 that is, in Christ God was reconciling the world to himself, not counting their trespasses against them, and entrusting to us the message of reconciliation. 20 So we are ambassadors for Christ, God making his appeal through us. We beseech you on behalf of Christ, be reconciled to God. 21 For our sake he made him to be sin who knew no sin, so that in him we might become the righteousness of God. and ever. Amen.

Gal 1:6–12 (§194)

6 I am astonished that you are so quickly deserting him who called you in the grace of Christ and turning to a different gospel— 7 not that there is another gospel, but there are some who trouble you and want to pervert the gospel of Christ. 8 But even if we, or an angel from heaven, should preach to you a gospel contrary to that which we preached to you, let him be accursed. 9 As we have said before, so now I say again, If any one is preaching to you a gospel

---

● **Col 1:21**

Eph 2   1 And you he made alive, when you were dead through the trespasses and sins . . .

Eph 4   8 Therefore it is said,
"When he ascended on high he led a host of captives,
and he gave gifts to men."

● **Col 1:22**

Rom 5   10 For if while we were enemies we were reconciled to God by the death of his Son, much more, now that we are reconciled, shall we be saved by his life.

2 Cor 11   2 I feel a divine jealousy for you, for I betrothed you to Christ to present you as a pure bride to her one husband.

Eph 5   27 that he might present the church to himself in splendor, without spot or wrinkle or any such thing, that she might be holy and without blemish.

● **Col 1:23**

Rom 10   14 But how are men to call upon him in whom they have not believed? And how are they to believe in him of whom they have never heard? And how are they to hear without a preacher? 15 And how

contrary to that which you received, let him be accursed.

[10] Am I now seeking the favor of men, or of God? Or am I trying to please men? If I were still pleasing men, I should not be a servant of Christ.

[11] For I would have you know, brethren, that the gospel which was preached by me is not man's gospel. [12] For I did not receive it from man, nor was I taught it, but it came through a revelation of Jesus Christ.

Gal 4:8–11 (§208)

[8] Formerly, when you did not know God, you were in bondage to beings that by nature are no gods; [9] but now that you have come to know God, or rather to be known by God, how can you turn back again to the weak and beggarly elemental spirits, whose slaves you want to be once more? [10] You observe days, and months, and seasons, and years! [11] I am afraid I have labored over you in vain.

Eph 2:11–22 (§221)

[11] Therefore remember that at one time you Gentiles in the flesh, called the uncircumcision by what is called the circumcision, which is made in the flesh by hands— [12] remember that you were at that time separated from Christ, alienated from the commonwealth of Israel, and strangers to the covenants of promise, having no hope and without God in the world. [13] But now in Christ Jesus you who once were far off have been brought near in the blood of Christ. [14] For he is our peace, who has made us both one, and has broken down the dividing wall of hostility, [15] by abolishing in his flesh the law of commandments and ordinances, that he might create in himself one new man in place of the two, so making peace, [16] and might reconcile us both to God in one body through the cross, thereby bringing the hostility to an end. [17] And he came and preached peace to you who were far off and peace to those who were near; [18] for through him we both have access in one Spirit to the Father. [19] So then you are no longer strangers and sojourners, but you are fellow citizens with the saints and members of the household of God, [20] built upon the foundation of the apostles and prophets, Christ Jesus himself being the cornerstone, [21] in whom the whole structure is joined together and grows into a holy temple in the Lord; [22] in whom you also are built into it for a dwelling place of God in the Spirit.

Phil 4:8–9 (§252)

[8] Finally, brethren, whatever is true, whatever is honorable, whatever is just, whatever is pure, whatever is lovely, whatever is gracious, if there is any excellence, if there is anything worthy of praise, think about these things. [9] What you have learned and received and heard and seen in me, do; and the God of peace will be with you.

1 Thess 3:11–13 (§283)

[11] Now may our God and Father himself, and our Lord Jesus, direct our way to you; [12] and may the Lord make you increase and abound in love to one another and to all men, as we do to you, [13] so that he may establish your hearts unblamable in holiness before our God and Father, at the coming of our Lord Jesus with all his saints.

2 Thess 2:16–17 (§298)

[16] Now may our Lord Jesus Christ himself, and God our Father, who loved us and gave us eternal comfort and good hope through grace, [17] comfort your hearts and establish them in every good work and word.

---

can men preach unless they are sent? As it is written, "How beautiful are the feet of those who preach good news!" [16] But they have not all obeyed the gospel; for Isaiah says, "Lord, who has believed what he has heard from us?" [17] So faith comes from what is heard, and what is heard comes by the preaching of Christ.

Rom 11　　[13] Now I am speaking to you Gentiles. Inasmuch then as I am an apostle to the Gentiles, I magnify my ministry . . .

1 Cor 15　　[58] Therefore, my beloved brethren, be steadfast, immovable, always abounding in the work of the Lord, knowing that in the Lord your labor is not in vain.

Gal 5　　[1] For freedom Christ has set us free; stand fast therefore, and do not submit again to a yoke of slavery.

Eph 3　　[7] Of this gospel I was made a minister according to the gift of God's grace which was given me by the working of his power.

Phil 4　　[1] Therefore, my brethren, whom I love and long for, my joy and crown, stand firm thus in the Lord, my beloved.

Col 2　　[6] As therefore you received Christ Jesus the Lord, so live in him, [7] rooted and built up in him and established in the faith, just as you were taught, abounding in thanksgiving.

[24]Now I rejoice in my sufferings for your sake, and in my flesh I complete what is lacking in Christ's afflictions for the sake of his body, that is, the church, [25]of which I became a minister according to the divine office which was given to me for you, to make the word of God fully known, [26]the mystery hidden for ages and generations but now made manifest to his saints. [27]To them God chose to make known how great among the Gentiles are the riches of the glory of this mystery, which is Christ in you, the hope of glory. [28]Him we proclaim warning every man and teaching every man in all wisdom, that we may present every man mature in Christ. [29]For this I toil, striving with all the energy which he mightily inspires within me.

2 [1]For I want you to know how greatly I strive for you, and for those at Laodicea, and for all who have not seen my face, [2]that their hearts may be encouraged as they are knit together in love, to have all the riches of assured understanding and the knowledge of God's mystery, of Christ, [3]in whom are hid all the treasures of wisdom and knowledge.

PRIMARY

Rom 15:14–21 (§62)

[14]I myself am satisfied about you, my brethren, that you yourselves are full of goodness, filled with all knowledge, and able to instruct one another. [15]But on some points I have written to you very boldly by way of reminder, because of the grace given me by God [16]to be a minister of Christ Jesus to the Gentiles in the priestly service of the gospel of God, so that the offering of the Gentiles may be acceptable, sanctified by the Holy Spirit. [17]In Christ Jesus, then, I have reason to be proud of my work for God. [18]For I will not venture to speak of anything except what Christ has wrought through me to win obedience from the Gentiles, by word and deed, [19]by the power of signs and wonders, by the power of the Holy Spirit, so that from Jerusalem and as far round as Illyricum I have fully preached the gospel of Christ, [20]thus making it my ambition to preach the gospel, not where Christ has already been

named, lest I build on another man's foundation, [21]but as it is written,

"They shall see who have never been told of him,
and they shall understand who have never heard of him."

1 Cor 2:6–16 (§77)

[6]Yet among the mature we do impart wisdom, although it is not a wisdom of this age or of the rulers of this age, who are doomed to pass away. [7]But we impart a secret and hidden wisdom of God, which God decreed before the ages for our glorification. [8]None of the rulers of this age understood this; for if they had, they would not have crucified the Lord of glory. [9]But, as it is written,

"What no eye has seen, nor ear heard,
nor the heart of man conceived,
what God has prepared for those who love him," [10]God has revealed to us through the Spirit. For the Spirit searches everything, even the depths of God. [11]For what person knows a man's thoughts except the spirit of the man which is in him? So also no one comprehends the thoughts of God except the Spirit of God. [12]Now we have received not the spirit of the world, but the Spirit which is from God, that we might understand the gifts bestowed on us by God. [13]And we impart this in words not taught by human wisdom but taught by the Spirit, interpreting spiritual truths to those who possess the Spirit.

[14]The unspiritual man does not receive the gifts of the Spirit of God, for they are folly to him, and he is not able to understand them because they are spiritually discerned. [15]The spiritual man judges all things, but is himself to be judged by no one. [16]"For who has known the mind of the Lord so as to instruct him?" But we have the mind of Christ.

1 Cor 4:1–5 (§83)

[1]This is how one should regard us, as servants of Christ and stewards of the mysteries of God. [2]Moreover it is required of stewards that they be found trustworthy. [3]But with me it is a very small thing that I should be judged by you or by any human court. I do not even judge myself. [4]I am not aware of anything against myself, but I am not thereby acquitted. It is the

Lord who judges me. [5]Therefore do not pronounce judgment before the time, before the Lord comes, who will bring to light the things now hidden in darkness and will disclose the purposes of the heart. Then every man will receive his commendation from God.

2 Cor 4:1–6 (§158)

[1]Therefore, having this ministry by the mercy of God, we do not lose heart. [2]We have renounced disgraceful, underhanded ways; we refuse to practice cunning or to tamper with God's word, but by the open statement of the truth we would commend ourselves to every man's conscience in the sight of God. [3]And even if our gospel is veiled, it is veiled only to those who are perishing. [4]In their case the god of this world has blinded the minds of the unbelievers, to keep them from seeing the light of the gospel of the glory of Christ, who is the likeness of God. [5]For what we preach is not ourselves, but Jesus Christ as Lord, with ourselves as your servants for Jesus' sake. [6]For it is the God who said, "Let light shine out of darkness," who has shone in our hearts to give the light of the knowledge of the glory of God in the face of Christ.

2 Cor 4:7–12 (§159)

[7]But we have this treasure in earthen vessels, to show that the transcendent power belongs to God and not to us. [8]We are afflicted in every way, but not crushed; perplexed, but not driven to despair; [9]persecuted, but not forsaken; struck down, but not destroyed; [10]always carrying in the body the death of Jesus, so that the life of Jesus may also be manifested in our bodies. [11]For while we live we are always being given up to death for Jesus' sake, so that the life of Jesus may be manifested in our mortal flesh. [12]So death is at work in us, but life in you.

2 Cor 11:21b–29 (§183)

But whatever any one dares to boast of—I am speaking as a fool—I also dare to boast of that. [22]Are they Hebrews? So am I. Are they Israelites? So am I. Are they descendants of Abraham? So am I. [23]Are they servants of Christ? I am a better one—I am talking like a madman—with far greater labors, far more

---

● **Col 1:24–2:1**
1 Thess 3 [10]praying earnestly night and day that we may see you face to face and supply what is lacking in your faith?

● **Col 1:24**
Phil 1 [12]I want you to know, brethren, that what has happened to me has really served to advance the gospel, [13]so that it has become known throughout the whole praetorian guard and to all the rest that my imprisonment is for Christ; . . .

1 Thess 2 [2]but though we had already suffered and been shamefully treated at Philippi, as you know, we had courage in our God to declare to you the gospel of God in the face of great opposition.

2 Tim 1 [8]Do not be ashamed then of testifying to our Lord, nor of me his prisoner, but share in suffering for the gospel in the power of God, . . .

2 Tim 1 [12]and therefore I suffer as I do. But I am not ashamed, for I know whom I have believed, and I am sure that he is able to guard until that Day what has been entrusted to me.

2 Tim 1 [16]May the Lord grant mercy to the household of Onesiphorus, for he often refreshed me; he was not ashamed of my chains, . . .

2 Tim 2 [10]Therefore I endure everything for the sake of the elect, that they also may obtain salvation in Christ Jesus with its eternal glory.

● **Col 1:25–27**
Gal 1 [15]But when he who had set me apart before I was born, and had called me through his grace, [16]was pleased to reveal his Son to me, in order that I might preach him among the Gentiles, I did not confer with flesh and blood, . . .

imprisonments, with countless beatings, and often near death. [24]Five times I have received at the hands of the Jews the forty lashes less one. [25]Three times I have been beaten with rods; once I was stoned. Three times I have been shipwrecked; a night and a day I have been adrift at sea; [26]on frequent journeys, in danger from rivers, danger from robbers, danger from my own people, danger from Gentiles, danger in the city, danger in the wilderness, danger at sea, danger from false brethren; [27]in toil and hardship, through many a sleepless night, in hunger and thirst, often without food, in cold and exposure. [28]And, apart from other things, there is the daily pressure upon me of my anxiety for all the churches. [29]Who is weak, and I am not weak? Who is made to fall, and I am not indignant?

Eph 3:1–13 (§222)

[1]For this reason I, Paul, a prisoner for Christ Jesus on behalf of you Gentiles— [2]assuming that you have heard of the stewardship of God's grace that was given to me for you, [3]how the mystery was made known to me by revelation, as I have written briefly. [4]When you read this you can perceive my insight into the mystery of Christ, [5]which was not made known to the sons of men in other generations as it has now been revealed to his holy apostles and prophets by the Spirit; [6]that is, how the Gentiles are fellow heirs, members of the same body, and partakers of the promise in Christ Jesus through the gospel.

[7]Of this gospel I was made a minister according to the gift of God's grace which was given me by the working of his power. [8]To me, though I am the very least of all the saints, this grace is given, to preach to the Gentiles the unsearchable riches of Christ, [9]and to make all men see what is the plan of the mystery hidden for ages in God who created all things; [10]that through the church the manifold wisdom of God might now be made known to the principalities and powers in the heavenly places. [11]This was according to the eternal purpose which he has realized in Christ Jesus our Lord, [12]in whom we have boldness and confidence of access through our faith in him. [13]So I ask you not to lose heart over what I am suffering for you, which is your glory.

Phil 1:3–11 (§238)

[3]I thank my God in all my remembrance of you, [4]always in every prayer of mine for you all making my prayer with joy, [5]thankful for your partnership in the gospel from the first day until now. [6]And I am sure that he who began a good work in you will bring it to completion at the day of Jesus Christ. [7]It is right for me to feel thus about you all, because I hold you in my heart, for you are all partakers with me of grace, both in my imprisonment and in the defense and confirmation of the gospel. [8]For God is my witness, how I yearn for you all with the affection of Christ Jesus. [9]And it is my prayer that your love may abound more and more, with knowledge and all discernment, [10]so that you may approve what is excellent, and may be pure and blameless for the day of Christ, [11]filled with the fruits of righteousness which come through Jesus Christ, to the glory and praise of God.

Phil 1:12–18 (§239)

[12]I want you to know, brethren, that what has happened to me has really served to advance the gospel, [13]so that it has become known throughout the whole praetorian guard and to all the rest that my imprisonment is for Christ; [14]and most of the brethren have been made confident in the Lord because of my imprisonment, and are much more bold to speak the word of God without fear.

[15]Some indeed preach Christ from envy and rivalry, but others from good will. [16]The latter do it out of love, knowing that I am put here for the defense of the gospel; [17]the former proclaim Christ out of partisanship, not sincerely but thinking to afflict me in my imprisonment. [18]What then? Only that in every way, whether in pretense or in truth, Christ is proclaimed; and in that I rejoice.

1 Thess 2:1–8 (§277)

[1]For you yourselves know, brethren, that our visit to you was not in vain; [2]but though we had already suffered and been shamefully treated at Philippi, as you know, we had courage in our God to declare to you the gospel of God in the face of great opposition. [3]For our appeal does not spring from error or uncleanness, nor is it made with guile; [4]but just as we

have been approved by God to be entrusted with the gospel, so we speak, not to please men, but to please God who tests our hearts. [5]For we never used either words of flattery, as you know, or a cloak for greed, as God is witness; [6]nor did we seek glory from men, whether from you or from others, though we might have made demands as apostles of Christ. [7]But we were gentle among you, like a nurse taking care of her children. [8]So, being affectionately desirous of you, we were ready to share with you not only the gospel of God but also our own selves, because you had become very dear to us.

2 Thess 2:1–12 (§296)

[1]Now concerning the coming of our Lord Jesus Christ and our assembling to meet him, we beg you, brethren, [2]not to be quickly shaken in mind or excited, either by spirit or by word, or by letter purporting to be from us, to the effect that the day of the Lord has come. [3]Let no one deceive you in any way; for that day will not come, unless the rebellion comes first, and the man of lawlessness is revealed, the son of perdition, [4]who opposes and exalts himself against every so-called god or object of worship, so that he takes his seat in the temple of God, proclaiming himself to be God. [5]Do you not remember that when I was still with you I told you this? [6]And you know what is restraining him now so that he may be revealed in his time. [7]For the mystery of lawlessness is already at work; only he who now restrains it will do so until he is out of the way. [8]And then the lawless one will be revealed, and the Lord Jesus will slay him with the breath of his mouth and destroy him by his appearing and his coming. [9]The coming of the lawless one by the activity of Satan will be with all power and with pretended signs and wonders, [10]and with all wicked deception for those who are to perish, because they refused to love the truth and so be saved. [11]Therefore God sends upon them a strong delusion, to make them believe what is false, [12]so that all may be condemned who did not believe the truth but had pleasure in unrighteousness.

• **Col 1:26**
1 Cor 13   [2]And if I have prophetic powers, and understand all mysteries and all knowledge, and if I have all faith, so as to remove mountains, but have not love, I am nothing.

• **Col 1:27**
Rom 5   [2]Through him we have obtained access to this grace in which we stand, and we rejoice in our hope of sharing the glory of God.

Gal 2   [20]I have been crucified with Christ; it is no longer I who live, but Christ who lives in me; and the life I now live in the flesh I live by faith in the Son of God, who loved me and gave himself for me.

• **Col 1:28**
Phil 3   [15]Let those of us who are mature be thus minded; and if in anything you are otherwise minded, God will reveal that also to you.

Acts 20   [31]"Therefore be alert, remembering that for three years I did not cease night or day to admonish every one with tears."

• **Col 2:1**
Col 4   [13]For I bear him witness that he has worked hard for you and for those in Laodicea and in Hierapolis. [14]Luke the beloved physician and Demas greet you. [15]Give my greetings to the brethren at Laodicea, and to Nympha and the church in her house.

[16]And when this letter has been read among you, have it read also in the church of the Laodiceans; and see that you read also the letter from Laodicea. [17]And say to Archippus, "See that you fulfil the ministry which you have received in the Lord."

• **Col 2:2**
Col 4   [12]Epaphras, who is one of yourselves, a servant of Christ Jesus, greets you, always remembering you earnestly in his prayers, that you may stand mature and fully assured in all the will of God.

4I say this in order that no one may delude you with beguiling speech. **5**For though I am absent in body, yet I am with you in spirit, rejoicing to see your good order and the firmness of your faith in Christ.

6As therefore you received Christ Jesus the Lord, so live in him, **7**rooted and built up in him and established in the faith, just as you were taught, abounding in thanksgiving.

PRIMARY

Rom 16:17–20a (§67)

17I appeal to you, brethren, to take note of those who create dissensions and difficulties, in opposition to the doctrine which you have been taught; avoid them. **18**For such persons do not serve our Lord Christ, but their own appetites, and by fair and flattering words they deceive the hearts of the simple-minded. **19**For while your obedience is known to all, so that I rejoice over you, I would have you wise as to what is good and guileless as to what is evil; **20**then the God of peace will soon crush Satan under your feet.

1 Cor 1:4–9 (§72)

4I give thanks to God always for you because of the grace of God which was given you in Christ Jesus, **5**that in every way you were enriched in him with all speech and all knowledge— **6**even as the testimony to Christ was confirmed among you— **7**so that you are not lacking in any spiritual gift, as you wait for the revealing of our Lord Jesus Christ; **8**who will sustain you to the end, guiltless in the day of our Lord Jesus Christ. **9**God is faithful, by whom you were called into the fellowship of his Son, Jesus Christ our Lord.

1 Cor 16:13–14 (§141)

13Be watchful, stand firm in your faith, be courageous, be strong. **14**Let all that you do be done in love.

2 Cor 7:2–4 (§168)

2Open your hearts to us; we have wronged no one, we have corrupted no one, we have taken advantage of no one. **3**I do not say this to condemn you, for I said before that you are in our hearts, to die together and to live together. **4**I have great confidence in you; I have great pride in you; I am filled with comfort. With all our affliction, I am overjoyed.

2 Cor 11:1–6 (§179)

1I wish you would bear with me in a little foolishness. Do bear with me! **2**I feel a divine jealousy for you, for I betrothed you to Christ to present you as a pure bride to her one husband. **3**But I am afraid that as the serpent deceived Eve by his cunning, your thoughts will be led astray from a sincere and pure devotion to Christ. **4**For if some one comes and preaches another Jesus than the one we preached, or if you receive a different spirit from the one you received, or if you accept a different gospel from the one you accepted, you submit to it readily enough. **5**I think that I am not in the least inferior to these superlative apostles. **6**Even if I am unskilled in speaking, I am not in knowledge; in every way we have made this plain to you in all things.

Gal 1:6–12 (§194)

6I am astonished that you are so quickly deserting him who called you in the grace of Christ and turning to a different gospel— **7**not that there is another gospel, but there are some who trouble you and want to pervert the gospel of Christ. **8**But even if we, or an angel from heaven, should preach to you a gospel contrary to that which we preached to you, let him be accursed. **9**As we have said before, so now I say again, If any one is preaching to you a gospel contrary to that which you received, let him be accursed.

10Am I now seeking the favor of men, or of God? Or am I trying to please men? If I were

---

● **Col 2:4**

Rom 16   **18**For such persons do not serve our Lord Christ, but their own appetites, and by fair and flattering words they deceive the hearts of the simple-minded.

2 Cor 4   **2**We have renounced disgraceful, underhanded ways; we refuse to practice cunning or to tamper with God's word, but by the open statement of the truth we would commend ourselves to every man's conscience in the sight of God.

● **Col 2:5**

1 Cor 5   **3**For though absent in body I am present in spirit, and as if present, I have already pronounced judgment . . .

1 Cor 14   **40**but all things should be done decently and in order.

Acts 16   **5**So the churches were strengthened in the faith, and they increased in numbers daily.

● **Col 2:6–7**

Col 1   **23**provided that you continue in the faith, stable and steadfast, not shifting from the hope of the gospel which you heard, which has been preached to every creature under heaven, and of which I, Paul, became a minister.

still pleasing men, I should not be a servant of Christ. [11]For I would have you know, brethren, that the gospel which was preached by me is not man's gospel. [12]For I did not receive it from man, nor was I taught it, but it came through a revelation of Jesus Christ.

Eph 5:3–14 (§230)

[3]But fornication and all impurity or covetousness must not even be named among you, as is fitting among saints. [4]Let there be no filthiness, nor silly talk, nor levity, which are not fitting; but instead let there be thanksgiving. [5]Be sure of this, that no fornicator or impure man, or one who is covetous (that is, an idolater), has any inheritance in the kingdom of Christ and of God. [6]Let no one deceive you with empty words, for it is because of these things that the wrath of God comes upon the sons of disobedience. [7]Therefore do not associate with them, [8]for once you were darkness, but now you are light in the Lord; walk as children of light [9](for the fruit of light is found in all that is good and right and true), [10]and try to learn what is pleasing to the Lord. [11]Take no part in the unfruitful works of darkness, but instead expose them. [12]For it is a shame even to speak of the things that they do in secret; [13]but when anything is exposed by the light it becomes visible, for anything that becomes visible is light. [14]Therefore it is said,

> "Awake, O sleeper, and arise from the dead,
> and Christ shall give you light."

Phil 1:27–30 (§241)

[27]Only let your manner of life be worthy of the gospel of Christ, so that whether I come and see you or am absent, I may hear of you that you stand firm in one spirit, with one mind striving side by side for the faith of the gospel, [28]and not frightened in anything by your opponents. This is a clear omen to them of their destruction, but of your salvation, and that from God. [29]For it has been granted to you that for the sake of Christ you should not only believe in him but also suffer for his sake, [30]engaged in the same conflict which you saw and now hear to be mine.

1 Thess 2:1–8 (§277)

[1]For you yourselves know, brethren, that our visit to you was not in vain; [2]but though we had already suffered and been shamefully treated at Philippi, as you know, we had courage in our God to declare to you the gospel of God in the face of great opposition. [3]For our appeal does not spring from error or uncleanness, nor is it made with guile; [4]but just as we have been approved by God to be entrusted with the gospel, so we speak, not to please men, but to please God who tests our hearts. [5]For we never used either words of flattery, as you know, or a cloak for greed, as God is witness; [6]nor did we seek glory from men, whether from you or from others, though we might have made demands as apostles of Christ. [7]But we were gentle among you, like a nurse taking care of her children. [8]So, being affectionately desirous of you, we were ready to share with you not only the gospel of God but also our own selves, because you had become very dear to us.

2 Thess 2:13–15 (§297)

[13]But we are bound to give thanks to God always for you, brethren beloved by the Lord, because God chose you from the beginning to be saved, through sanctification by the Spirit and belief in the truth. [14]To this he called you through our gospel, so that you may obtain the glory of our Lord Jesus Christ. [15]So then, brethren, stand firm and hold to the traditions which you were taught by us, either by word of mouth or by letter.

● **Col 2:7**

1 Cor 11   [23]"All things are lawful," but not all things are helpful. "All things are lawful," but not all things build up.

1 Cor 15   [1]Now I would remind you, brethren, in what terms I preached to you the gospel, which you received, in which you stand, [2]by which you are saved, if you hold it fast —unless you believed in vain.

[3]For I delivered to you as of first importance what I also received, . . .

Eph 2   [20]built upon the foundation of the apostles and prophets, Christ Jesus himself being the cornerstone, . . .

Eph 2   [22]in whom you also are built into it for a dwelling place of God in the Spirit.

Eph 3   [17]and that Christ may dwell in your hearts through faith; that you, being rooted and grounded in love, . . .

Eph 4   [21]assuming that you have heard about him and were taught in him, as the truth is in Jesus.

⁸See to it that no one makes a prey of you by philosophy and empty deceit, according to human tradition, according to the elemental spirits of the universe, and not according to Christ. ⁹For in him the whole fulness of deity dwells bodily, ¹⁰and you have come to fulness of life in him, who is the head of all rule and authority. ¹¹In him also you were circumcised with a circumcision made without hands, by putting off the body of flesh in the circumcision of Christ; ¹²and you were buried with him in baptism, in which you were also raised with him through faith in the working of God, who raised him from the dead. ¹³And you, who were dead in trespasses and the uncircumcision of your flesh, God made alive together with him, having forgiven us all our trespasses, ¹⁴having canceled the bond which stood against us with its legal demands; this he set aside, nailing it to the cross. ¹⁵He disarmed the principalities and powers and made a public example of them, triumphing over them in him.

PRIMARY

Rom 6:1-10 (§23)

¹What shall we say then? Are we to continue in sin that grace may abound? ²By no means! How can we who died to sin still live in it? ³Do you not know that all of us who have been baptized into Christ Jesus were baptized into his death? ⁴We were buried therefore with him by baptism into death, so that as Christ was raised from the dead by the glory of the Father, we too might walk in newness of life. ⁵For if we have been united with him in a death like his, we shall certainly be united with him in a resurrection like his. ⁶We know that our old self was crucified with him so that the sinful body might be destroyed, and we might no longer be enslaved to sin. ⁷For he who has died is freed from sin. ⁸But if we have died with Christ, we believe that we shall also live with

him. ⁹For we know that Christ being raised from the dead will never die again; death no longer has dominion over him. ¹⁰The death he died he died to sin, once for all, but the life he lives he lives to God.

1 Cor 15:1-11 (§131)

¹Now I would remind you, brethren, in what terms I preached to you the gospel, which you received, in which you stand, ²by which you are saved, if you hold it fast —unless you believed in vain.

³For I delivered to you as of first importance what I also received, that Christ died for our sins in accordance with the scriptures, ⁴that he was buried, that he was raised on the third day in accordance with the scriptures, ⁵and that he appeared to Cephas, then to the twelve. ⁶Then he appeared to more than five hundred brethren at one time, most of whom are still alive, though some have fallen asleep. ⁷Then he appeared to James, then to all the apostles. ⁸Last of all, as to one untimely born, he appeared also to me. ⁹For I am the least of the apostles, unfit to be called an apostle, because I persecuted the church of God. ¹⁰But by the grace of God I am what I am, and his grace toward me was not in vain. On the contrary, I worked harder than any of them, though it was not I, but the grace of God which is with me. ¹¹Whether then it was I or they, so we preach and so you believed.

2 Cor 5:14-21 (§164)

¹⁴For the love of Christ controls us, because we are convinced that one has died for all; therefore all have died. ¹⁵And he died for all, that those who live might live no longer for themselves but for him who for their sake died and was raised.

¹⁶From now on, therefore, we regard no one from a human point of view; even though we once regarded Christ from a human point of view, we regard him thus no longer. ¹⁷Therefore, if any one is in Christ, he is a new creation;

the old has passed away, behold, the new has come. ¹⁸All this is from God, who through Christ reconciled us to himself and gave us the ministry of reconciliation; ¹⁹that is, in Christ God was reconciling the world to himself, not counting their trespasses against them, and entrusting to us the message of reconciliation. ²⁰So we are ambassadors for Christ, God making his appeal through us. We beseech you on behalf of Christ, be reconciled to God. ²¹For our sake he made him to be sin who knew no sin, so that in him we might become the righteousness of God.

2 Cor 11:1-6 (§179)

¹I wish you would bear with me in a little foolishness. Do bear with me! ²I feel a divine jealousy for you, for I betrothed you to Christ to present you as a pure bride to her one husband. ³But I am afraid that as the serpent deceived Eve by his cunning, your thoughts will be led astray from a sincere and pure devotion to Christ. ⁴For if some one comes and preaches another Jesus than the one we preached, or if you receive a different spirit from the one you received, or if you accept a different gospel from the one you accepted, you submit to it readily enough. ⁵I think that I am not in the least inferior to these superlative apostles. ⁶Even if I am unskilled in speaking, I am not in knowledge; in every way we have made this plain to you in all things.

2 Cor 11:16-21a (§182)

¹⁶I repeat, let no one think me foolish; but even if you do, accept me as a fool, so that I too may boast a little. ¹⁷(What I am saying I say not with the Lord's authority but as a fool, in this boastful confidence; ¹⁸since many boast of worldly things, I too will boast.) ¹⁹For you gladly bear with fools, being wise yourselves! ²⁰For you bear it if a man makes slaves of you, or preys upon you, or takes advantage of you, or puts on airs, or strikes you in the face. ²¹To my shame, I must say, we were too weak for that!

● **Col 2:8-15**

Gal 1　¹⁴and I advanced in Judaism beyond many of my own age among my people, so extremely zealous was I for the traditions of my fathers.

Eph 5　⁶Let no one deceive you with empty words, for it is because of these things that the wrath of God comes upon the sons of disobedience.

Col 2　²²(referring to things which all perish as they are used), according to human precepts and doctrines?

2 Thess 2　¹⁵So then, brethren, stand firm and hold to the traditions which you were taught by us, either by word of mouth or by letter.

2 Thess 3　⁶Now we command you, brethren, in the name of our Lord Jesus Christ, that you keep away from any brother who is living in idleness and not in accord with the tradition that you received from us.

● **Col 2:9**

Col 1　¹⁹For in him all the fulness of God was pleased to dwell, . . .

● **Col 2:10**

Eph 1　²¹far above all rule and authority and power and dominion, and above every name that is named, not only in this age but also in that which is to come; ²²and he has put all things under his feet and has made him the head over all things for the church, ²³which is his body, the fulness of him who fills all in all.

Eph 4　¹⁵Rather, speaking the truth in love, we are to grow up in every way into him who is the head, into Christ, . . .

Gal 2:15–21 (§199)

¹⁵We ourselves, who are Jews by birth and not Gentile sinners, ¹⁶yet who know that a man is not justified by works of the law but through faith in Jesus Christ, even we have believed in Christ Jesus, in order to be justified by faith in Christ, and not by works of the law, because by works of the law shall no one be justified. ¹⁷But if, in our endeavor to be justified in Christ, we ourselves were found to be sinners, is Christ then an agent of sin? Certainly not! ¹⁸But if I build up again those things which I tore down, then I prove myself a transgressor. ¹⁹For I through the law died to the law, that I might live to God. ²⁰I have been crucified with Christ; it is no longer I who live, but Christ who lives in me; and the life I now live in the flesh I live by faith in the Son of God, who loved me and gave himself for me. ²¹I do not nullify the grace of God; for if justification were through the law, then Christ died to no purpose.

Gal 3:21–29 (§205–206)

²¹Is the law then against the promises of God? Certainly not; for if a law had been given which could make alive, then righteousness would indeed be by the law. ²²But the scripture consigned all things to sin, that what was promised to faith in Jesus Christ might be given to those who believe.

²³Now before faith came, we were confined under the law, kept under restraint until faith should be revealed. ²⁴So that the law was our custodian until Christ came, that we might be justified by faith. ²⁵But now that faith has come, we are no longer under a custodian;

²⁶for in Christ Jesus you are all sons of God, through faith. ²⁷For as many of you as were baptized into Christ have put on Christ. ²⁸There is neither Jew nor Greek, there is neither slave nor free, there is neither male nor female; for you are all one in Christ Jesus. ²⁹And if you are Christ's, then you are Abraham's offspring, heirs according to promise.

Gal 4:8–11 (§208)

⁸Formerly, when you did not know God, you were in bondage to beings that by nature are no gods; ⁹but now that you have come to know God, or rather to be known by God, how can you turn back again to the weak and beggarly elemental spirits, whose slaves you want to be once more? ¹⁰You observe days, and months, and seasons, and years! ¹¹I am afraid I have labored over you in vain.

Eph 2:1–10 (§220)

¹And you he made alive, when you were dead through the trespasses and sins ²in which you once walked, following the course of this world, following the prince of the power of the air, the spirit that is now at work in the sons of disobedience. ³Among these we all once lived in the passions of our flesh, following the desires of body and mind, and so we were by nature children of wrath, like the rest of mankind. ⁴But God, who is rich in mercy, out of the great love with which he loved us, ⁵even when we were dead through our trespasses, made us alive together with Christ (by grace you have been saved), ⁶and raised us up with him, and made us sit with him in the heavenly places in Christ Jesus, ⁷that in the coming ages he might show the immeasurable riches of his grace in kindness toward us in Christ Jesus. ⁸For by grace you have been saved through faith; and this is not your own doing, it is the gift of God—⁹not because of works, lest any man should boast. ¹⁰For we are his workmanship, created in Christ Jesus for good works, which God prepared beforehand, that we should walk in them.

Phil 2:1–11 (§242)

¹So if there is any encouragement in Christ, any incentive of love, any participation in the Spirit, any affection and sympathy, ²complete my joy by being of the same mind, having the same love, being in full accord and of one mind. ³Do nothing from selfishness or conceit, but in humility count others better than yourselves. ⁴Let each of you look not only to his own interests, but also to the interests of others. ⁵Have this mind among yourselves, which is yours in Christ Jesus, ⁶who, though he was in the form of God, did not count equality with God a thing to be grasped, ⁷but emptied himself, taking the form of a servant, being born in the likeness of men. ⁸And being found in human form he humbled himself and became obedient unto death, even death on a cross. ⁹Therefore God has highly exalted him and bestowed on him the name which is above every name, ¹⁰that at the name of Jesus every knee should bow, in heaven and on earth and under the earth, ¹¹and every tongue confess that Jesus Christ is Lord, to the glory of God the Father.

1 Thess 2:1–8 (§277)

¹For you yourselves know, brethren, that our visit to you was not in vain; ²but though we had already suffered and been shamefully treated at Philippi, as you know, we had courage in our God to declare to you the gospel of God in the face of great opposition. ³For our appeal does not spring from error or uncleanness, nor is it made with guile; ⁴but just as we have been approved by God to be entrusted with the gospel, so we speak, not to please men, but to please God who tests our hearts. ⁵For we never used either words of flattery, as you know, or a cloak for greed, as God is witness; ⁶nor did we seek glory from men, whether from you or from others, though we might have made demands as apostles of Christ. ⁷But we were gentle among you, like a nurse taking care of her children. ⁸So, being affectionately desirous of you, we were ready to share with you not only the gospel of God but also our own selves, because you had become very dear to us.

● **Col 2:11**

Rom 2   ²⁸For he is not a real Jew who is one outwardly, nor is true circumcision something external and physical. ²⁹He is a Jew who is one inwardly, and real circumcision is a matter of the heart, spiritual and not literal. His praise is not from men but from God.

2 Cor 5   ⁴For while we are still in this tent, we sigh with anxiety; not that we would be unclothed, but that we would be further clothed, so that what is mortal may be swallowed up by life.

● **Col 2:12**

Acts 2   ²⁴"But God raised him up, having loosed the pangs of death, because it was not possible for him to be held by it."

● **Col 2:13**

Rom 6   ¹¹So you also must consider yourselves dead to sin and alive to God in Christ Jesus.

2 Cor 2   ¹⁴But thanks be to God, who in Christ always leads us in triumph, and through us spreads the fragrance of the knowledge of him everywhere.

[16] Therefore let no one pass judgment on you in questions of food and drink or with regard to a festival or a new moon or a sabbath. [17] These are only a shadow of what is to come; but the substance belongs to Christ. [18] Let no one disqualify you, insisting on self-abasement and worship of angels, taking his stand on visions, puffed up without reason by his sensuous mind, [19] and not holding fast to the Head, from whom the whole body, nourished and knit together through its joints and ligaments, grows with a growth that is from God.

PRIMARY

Rom 2:1-5 (§7)

[1] Therefore you have no excuse, O man, whoever you are, when you judge another; for in passing judgment upon him you condemn yourself, because you, the judge, are doing the very same things. [2] We know that the judgment of God rightly falls upon those who do such things. [3] Do you suppose, O man, that when you judge those who do such things and yet do them yourself, you will escape the judgment of God? [4] Or do you presume upon the riches of his kindness and forbearance and patience? Do you not know that God's kindness is meant to lead you to repentance? [5] But by your hard and impenitent heart you are storing up wrath for yourself on the day of wrath when God's righteous judgment will be revealed.

Rom 14:5-12 (§58)

[5] One man esteems one day as better than another, while another man esteems all days alike. Let every one be fully convinced in his own mind. [6] He who observes the day, observes it in honor of the Lord. He also who eats, eats in honor of the Lord, since he gives thanks to God; while he who abstains, abstains in honor of the Lord and gives thanks to God. [7] None of us lives to himself, and none of us dies to himself. [8] If we live, we live to the Lord, and if we die, we die to the Lord; so then, whether we live or whether we die, we are the Lord's. [9] For to this end Christ died and lived again, that he might be Lord both of the dead and of the living.

[10] Why do you pass judgment on your brother? Or you, why do you despise your brother? For we shall all stand before the judgment seat of God; [11] for it is written,

"As I live, says the Lord, every knee shall bow to me,

and every tongue shall give praise to God."

[12] So each of us shall give account of himself to God.

1 Cor 4:1-5 (§83)

[1] This is how one should regard us, as servants of Christ and stewards of the mysteries of God. [2] Moreover it is required of stewards that they be found trustworthy. [3] But with me it is a very small thing that I should be judged by you or by any human court. I do not even judge myself. [4] I am not aware of anything against myself, but I am not thereby acquitted. It is the Lord who judges me. [5] Therefore do not pronounce judgment before the time, before the Lord comes, who will bring to light the things now hidden in darkness and will disclose the purposes of the heart. Then every man will receive his commendation from God.

1 Cor 6:1-8 (§90)

[1] When one of you has a grievance against a brother, does he dare go to law before the unrighteous instead of the saints? [2] Do you not know that the saints will judge the world? And if the world is to be judged by you, are you incompetent to try trivial cases? [3] Do you not know that we are to judge angels? How much more, matters pertaining to this life! [4] If then you have such cases, why do you lay them before those who are least esteemed by the church? [5] I say this to your shame. Can it be that there is no man among you wise enough to

---

● **Col 2:16**

Rom 2   [1] Therefore you have no excuse, O man, whoever you are, when you judge another; for in passing judgment upon him you condemn yourself, because you, the judge, are doing the very same things.

Rom 14   [17] For the kingdom of God is not food and drink but righteousness and peace and joy in the Holy Spirit; . . .

1 Tim 4   [1] Now the Spirit expressly says that in later times some will depart from the faith by giving heed to deceitful spirits and doctrines of demons, [2] through the pretensions of liars whose consciences are seared, [3] who forbid marriage and enjoin abstinence from foods which God created to be received with thanksgiving by those who believe and know the truth.

● **Col 2:17**

Heb 8   [5] They serve a copy and shadow of the heavenly sanctuary; for when Moses was about to erect the tent, he was instructed by God, saying, "See that you make everything according to the pattern which was shown you on the mountain."

Heb 10   [1] For since the law has but a shadow of the good things to come instead of the true form of these realities, it can never, by the same sacrifices which are continually offered year after year, make perfect those who draw near.

● **Col 2:18**

Heb 12   [22] But you have come to Mount Zion and to the city of the living God, the heavenly Jerusalem, and to innumerable angels in festal gathering, [23] and to the assembly of the first-born who are enrolled in heaven, and to a judge who is God of all, and to the spirits of just men made perfect, [24] and to Jesus, the mediator of a new covenant, and to the sprinkled blood that speaks more graciously than the blood of Abel.

[25] See that you do not refuse him who is speaking. For if they did not escape when they refused him who warned them on earth, much less shall we escape if we

decide between members of the brotherhood, [6]but brother goes to law against brother, and that before unbelievers?

[7]To have lawsuits at all with one another is defeat for you. Why not rather suffer wrong? Why not rather be defrauded? [8]But you yourselves wrong and defraud, and that even your own brethren.

2 Cor 12:1-10 (§185)

[1]I must boast; there is nothing to be gained by it, but I will go on to visions and revelations of the Lord. [2]I know a man in Christ who fourteen years ago was caught up to the third heaven—whether in the body or out of the body I do not know, God knows. [3]And I know that this man was caught up into Paradise— whether in the body or out of the body I do not know, God knows— [4]and he heard things that cannot be told, which man may not utter. [5]On behalf of this man I will boast, but on my own behalf I will not boast, except of my weaknesses. [6]Though if I wish to boast, I shall not be a fool, for I shall be speaking the truth. But I refrain from it, so that no one may think more of me than he sees in me or hears from me. [7]And to keep me from being too elated by the abundance of revelations, a thorn was given me in the flesh, a messenger of Satan, to harass me,

to keep me from being too elated. [8]Three times I besought the Lord about this, that it should leave me; [9]but he said to me, "My grace is sufficient for you, for my power is made perfect in weakness." I will all the more gladly boast of my weaknesses, that the power of Christ may rest upon me. [10]For the sake of Christ, then, I am content with weaknesses, insults, hardships, persecutions, and calamities; for when I am weak, then I am strong.

Gal 2:11-14 (§198)

[11]But when Cephas came to Antioch I opposed him to his face, because he stood condemned. [12]For before certain men came from James, he ate with the Gentiles; but when they came he drew back and separated himself, fearing the circumcision party. [13]And with him the rest of the Jews acted insincerely, so that even Barnabas was carried away by their insincerity. [14]But when I saw that they were not straightforward about the truth of the gospel, I said to Cephas before them all, "If you, though a Jew, live like a Gentile and not like a Jew, how can you compel the Gentiles to live like Jews?"

Gal 4:8-11 (§208)

[8]Formerly, when you did not know God, you were in bondage to beings that by nature

are no gods; [9]but now that you have come to know God, or rather to be known by God, how can you turn back again to the weak and beggarly elemental spirits, whose slaves you want to be once more? [10]You observe days, and months, and seasons, and years! [11]I am afraid I have labored over you in vain.

Eph 4:11-16 (§226)

[11]And his gifts were that some should be apostles, some prophets, some evangelists, some pastors and teachers, [12]to equip the saints for the work of ministry, for building up the body of Christ, [13]until we all attain to the unity of the faith and of the knowledge of the Son of God, to mature manhood, to the measure of the stature of the fulness of Christ; [14]so that we may no longer be children, tossed to and fro and carried about with every wind of doctrine, by the cunning of men, by their craftiness in deceitful wiles. [15]Rather, speaking the truth in love, we are to grow up in every way into him who is the head, into Christ, [16]from whom the whole body, joined and knit together by every joint with which it is supplied, when each part is working properly, makes bodily growth and upbuilds itself in love.

---

reject him who warns from heaven. [26]His voice then shook the earth; but now he has promised, "Yet once more I will shake not only the earth but also the heaven." [27]This phrase, "Yet once more," indicates the removal of what is shaken, as of what has been made, in order that what cannot be shaken may remain. [28]Therefore let us be grateful for receiving a kingdom that cannot be shaken, and thus let us offer to God acceptable worship, with reverence and awe; [29]for our God is a consuming fire.

(visions) *read* what he has not seen: S^cCD^cG Koine Lect it (most) vg syr Origen: *text:* p^46 S*ABD* it (few) cop Marcion Origen

● **Col 2:19**
Rom 12   [5]so we, though many, are one body in Christ, and individually members one of another.

1 Cor 12   [12]For just as the body is one and has many members, and all the members of the body, though many, are one body, so it is with Christ.

1 Cor 12   [27]Now you are the body of Christ and individually members of it.

Eph 1   [22]and he has put all things under his feet and has made him the head over all things for the church, [23]which is his body, the fulness of him who fills all in all.

Eph 2   [21]in whom the whole structure is joined together and grows into a holy temple in the Lord; [22]in whom you also are built into it for a dwelling place of God in the Spirit.

Eph 4   [15]Rather, speaking the truth in love, we are to grow up in every way into him who is the head, into Christ, [16]from whom the whole body, joined and knit together by every joint with which it is supplied, when each part is working properly, makes bodily growth and upbuilds itself in love.

Eph 5   [23]For the husband is the head of the wife as Christ is the head of the church, his body, and is himself its Savior.

20If with Christ you died to the elemental spirits of the universe, why do you live as if you still belonged to the world? Why do you submit to regulations, **21**"Do not handle, Do not taste, Do not touch" **22**(referring to things which all perish as they are used), according to human precepts and doctrines? **23**These have indeed an appearance of wisdom in promoting rigor of devotion and self-abasement and severity to the body, but they are of no value in checking the indulgence of the flesh.

PRIMARY

Rom 6:11–14 (§24)

11So you also must consider yourselves dead to sin and alive to God in Christ Jesus. **12**Let not sin therefore reign in your mortal bodies, to make you obey their passions. **13**Do not yield your members to sin as instruments of wickedness, but yield yourselves to God as men who have been brought from death to life, and your members to God as instruments of righteousness. **14**For sin will have no dominion over you, since you are not under law but under grace.

1 Cor 3:1–4 (§78)

1But I, brethren, could not address you as spiritual men, but as men of the flesh, as babes in Christ. **2**I fed you with milk, not solid food; for you were not ready for it; and even yet you are not ready, **3**for you are still of the flesh. For while there is jealousy and strife among you, are you not of the flesh, and behaving like ordinary men? **4**For when one says, "I belong to Paul," and another, "I belong to Apollos," are you not merely men?

2 Cor 5:14–21 (§164)

14For the love of Christ controls us, because we are convinced that one has died for all; therefore all have died. **15**And he died for all, that those who live might live no longer for themselves but for him who for their sake died and was raised.

16From now on, therefore, we regard no one from a human point of view; even though we once regarded Christ from a human point of view, we regard him thus no longer. **17**Therefore, if any one is in Christ, he is a new creation; the old has passed away, behold, the new has come. **18**All this is from God, who through Christ reconciled us to himself and gave us the ministry of reconciliation; **19**that is, in Christ God was reconciling the world to himself, not counting their trespasses against them, and entrusting to us the message of reconciliation. **20**So we are ambassadors for Christ, God making his appeal through us. We beseech you on behalf of Christ, be reconciled to God. **21**For our sake he made him to be sin who knew no sin, so that in him we might become the righteousness of God.

Gal 2:15–21 (§199)

15We ourselves, who are Jews by birth and not Gentile sinners, **16**yet who know that a man is not justified by works of the law but through faith in Jesus Christ, even we have believed in Christ Jesus, in order to be justified by faith in Christ, and not by works of the law, because by works of the law shall no one be justified. **17**But if, in our endeavor to be justified in Christ, we ourselves were found to be sinners, is Christ then an agent of sin? Certainly not! **18**But if I build up again those things which I tore down, then I prove myself a transgressor. **19**For I through the law died to the law, that I might live to God. **20**I have been crucified with Christ; it is no longer I who live, but Christ who lives in me; and the life I now live in the flesh I live by faith in the Son of God, who loved me and gave himself for me. **21**I do not nullify the grace of God; for if justification were through the law, then Christ died to no purpose.

Gal 4:8–11 (§208)

8Formerly, when you did not know God, you were in bondage to beings that by nature are no gods; **9**but now that you have come to know God, or rather to be known by God, how can you turn back again to the weak and beggarly elemental spirits, whose slaves you want to be once more? **10**You observe days, and months, and seasons, and years! **11**I am afraid I have labored over you in vain.

● **Col 2:20–23**
Gal 6 **12**It is those who want to make a good showing in the flesh that would compel you to be circumcised, and only in order that they may not be persecuted for the cross of Christ. **13**For even those who receive circumcision do not themselves keep the law, but they desire to have you circumcised that they may glory in your flesh. **14**But far be it from me to glory except in the cross of our Lord Jesus Christ, by which the world has been crucified to me, and I to the world. **15**For neither circumcision counts for anything, nor uncircumcision, but a new creation.

Eph 2 **5**even when we were dead through our trespasses, made us alive together with Christ (by grace you have been saved), . . .

Phil 3 **10**that I may know him and the power of his resurrection, and may share his sufferings, becoming like him in his death, . . .

● **Col 2:20**
Gal 4 **3**So with us; when we were children, we were slaves to the elemental spirits of the universe.

● **Col 2:22**
Col 2 **8**See to it that no one makes a prey of you by philosophy and empty deceit, according to human tradition, according to the elemental spirits of the universe, and not according to Christ.

Titus 1 **14**instead of giving heed to Jewish myths or to commands of men who reject the truth.

● **Col 2:23**
Rom 13 **14**But put on the Lord Jesus Christ, and make no provision for the flesh, to gratify its desires.

1 Cor 9 **27**but I pommel my body and subdue it, lest after preaching to others I myself should be disqualified.

1 Tim 4 **1**Now the Spirit expressly says that in later times some will depart from the faith by giving heed to deceitful spirits and doctrines of demons, **2**through the pretensions of liars whose consciences are seared, **3**who forbid marriage and enjoin abstinence from foods which God created to be received with thanksgiving by those who believe and know the truth.

1 Tim 4 **8**for while bodily training is of some value, godliness is of value in every way, as it holds promise for the present life and also for the life to come.

3 If then you have been raised with Christ, seek the things that are above, where Christ is, seated at the right hand of God. [2] Set your minds on things that are above, not on things that are on earth. [3] For you have died, and your life is hid with Christ in God. [4] When Christ who is our life appears, then you also will appear with him in glory.

PRIMARY

Rom 6:11–14 (§24)

[11] So you also must consider yourselves dead to sin and alive to God in Christ Jesus.

[12] Let not sin therefore reign in your mortal bodies, to make you obey their passions. [13] Do not yield your members to sin as instruments of wickedness, but yield yourselves to God as men who have been brought from death to life, and your members to God as instruments of righteousness. [14] For sin will have no dominion over you, since you are not under law but under grace.

Rom 8:1–8 (§29)

[1] There is therefore now no condemnation for those who are in Christ Jesus. [2] For the law of the Spirit of life in Christ Jesus has set me free from the law of sin and death. [3] For God has done what the law, weakened by the flesh, could not do: sending his own Son in the likeness of sinful flesh and for sin, he condemned sin in the flesh, [4] in order that the just requirement of the law might be fulfilled in us, who walk not according to the flesh but according to the Spirit. [5] For those who live according to the flesh set their minds on the things of the flesh, but those who live according to the Spirit set their minds on the things of the Spirit. [6] To set the mind on the flesh is death, but to set the mind on the Spirit is life and peace. [7] For the mind that is set on the flesh is hostile to God; it does not submit to God's law, indeed it cannot; [8] and those who are in the flesh cannot please God.

1 Cor 15:51–58 (§137)

[51] Lo! I tell you a mystery. We shall not all sleep, but we shall all be changed, [52] in a moment, in the twinkling of an eye, at the last trumpet. For the trumpet will sound, and the dead will be raised imperishable, and we shall be changed. [53] For this perishable nature must put on the imperishable, and this mortal nature must put on immortality. [54] When the perishable puts on the imperishable, and the mortal puts on immortality, then shall come to pass the saying that is written:

"Death is swallowed up in victory."
[55] "O death, where is thy victory?
O death, where is thy sting?" [56] The sting of death is sin, and the power of sin is the law. [57] But thanks be to God, who gives us the victory through our Lord Jesus Christ.

[58] Therefore, my beloved brethren, be steadfast, immovable, always abounding in the work of the Lord, knowing that in the Lord your labor is not in vain.

2 Cor 4:13–15 (§160)

[13] Since we have the same spirit of faith as he had who wrote, "I believed, and so I spoke," we too believe, and so we speak, [14] knowing that he who raised the Lord Jesus will raise us also with Jesus and bring us with you into his presence. [15] For it is all for your sake, so that as grace extends to more and more people it may increase thanksgiving, to the glory of God.

Gal 2:15–21 (§199)

[15] We ourselves, who are Jews by birth and not Gentile sinners, [16] yet who know that a man is not justified by works of the law but through faith in Jesus Christ, even we have believed in Christ Jesus, in order to be justified by faith in Christ, and not by works of the law, because by works of the law shall no one be justified. [17] But if, in our endeavor to be justified in Christ, we ourselves were found to be sinners, is Christ then an agent of sin? Certainly not! [18] But if I build up again those things which I tore down, then I prove myself a transgressor. [19] For I through the law died to the law, that I might live to God. [20] I have been crucified with Christ; it is no longer I who live, but Christ who lives in me; and the life I now live in the flesh I live by faith in the Son of God, who loved me and gave himself for me. [21] I do not nullify the grace of God; for if justification were through the law, then Christ died to no purpose.

Eph 2:1–10 (§220)

[1] And you he made alive, when you were dead through the trespasses and sins [2] in which you once walked, following the course of this world, following the prince of the power of the air, the spirit that is now at work in the sons of disobedience. [3] Among these we all once lived in the passions of our flesh, following the desires of body and mind, and so we were by nature children of wrath, like the rest of mankind. [4] But God, who is rich in mercy, out of the great love with which he loved us, [5] even when we were dead through our trespasses, made us alive together with Christ (by grace you have been saved), [6] and raised us up with him, and made us sit with him in the heavenly places in

Christ Jesus, [7] that in the coming ages he might show the immeasurable riches of his grace in kindness toward us in Christ Jesus. [8] For by grace you have been saved through faith; and this is not your own doing, it is the gift of God— [9] not because of works, lest any man should boast. [10] For we are his workmanship, created in Christ Jesus for good works, which God prepared beforehand, that we should walk in them.

Phil 2:1–11 (§242)

[1] So if there is any encouragement in Christ, any incentive of love, any participation in the Spirit, any affection and sympathy, [2] complete my joy by being of the same mind, having the same love, being in full accord and of one mind. [3] Do nothing from selfishness or conceit, but in humility count others better than yourselves. [4] Let each of you look not only to his own interests, but also to the interests of others. [5] Have this mind among yourselves, which is yours in Christ Jesus, [6] who, though he was in the form of God, did not count equality with God a thing to be grasped, [7] but emptied himself, taking the form of a servant, being born in the likeness of men. [8] And being found in human form he humbled himself and became obedient unto death, even death on a cross. [9] Therefore God has highly exalted him and bestowed on him the name which is above every name, [10] that at the name of Jesus every knee should bow, in heaven and on earth and under the earth, [11] and every tongue confess that Jesus Christ is Lord, to the glory of God the Father.

1 Thess 4:13–18 (§286)

[13] But we would not have you ignorant, brethren, concerning those who are asleep, that you may not grieve as others do who have no hope. [14] For since we believe that Jesus died and rose again, even so, through Jesus, God will bring with him those who have fallen asleep. [15] For this we declare to you by the word of the Lord, that we who are alive, who are left until the coming of the Lord, shall not precede those who have fallen asleep. [16] For the Lord himself will descend from heaven with a cry of command, with the archangel's call, and with the sound of the trumpet of God. And the dead in Christ will rise first; [17] then we who are alive, who are left, shall be caught up together with them in the clouds to meet the Lord in the air; and so we shall always be with the Lord. [18] Therefore comfort one another with these words.

● **Col 3:2–4**

Phil 3   [20] But our commonwealth is in heaven, and from it we await a Savior, the Lord Jesus Christ, [21] who will change our lowly body to be like his glorious body, by the power which enables him even to subject all things to himself.

● **Col 3:2**

Col 1   [5] because of the hope laid up for you in heaven. Of this you have heard before in the word of the truth, the gospel . . .

● **Col 3:3–4**

Rom 6   [4] We were buried therefore with him by

baptism into death, so that as Christ was raised from the dead by the glory of the Father, we too might walk in newness of life.

● **Col 3:4**

(our) *read* your: p[46]SCD*G it vg cop(bo) Origen; *text:* BD[c] Koine Lect syr cop(sa) Origen

FORMAL ELEMENTS: VICE LIST & BAPTISMAL LITURGY

[5]Put to death therefore what is earthly in you: fornication, impurity, passion, evil desire, and covetousness, which is idolatry. [6]On account of these the wrath of God is coming. [7]In these you once walked, when you lived in them. [8]But now put them all away: anger, wrath, malice, slander, and foul talk from your mouth. [9]Do not lie to one another, seeing that you have put off the old nature with its practices [10]and have put on the new nature, which is being renewed in knowledge after the image of its creator. [11]Here there cannot be Greek and Jew, circumcised and uncircumcised, barbarian, Scythian, slave, free man, but Christ is all, and in all.

PRIMARY

See §6 for VICE LIST

1 Cor 12:12-13 (§118)

[12]For just as the body is one and has many members, and all the members of the body, though many, are one body, so it is with Christ. [13]For by one Spirit we were all baptized into one body— Jews or Greeks, slaves or free—and all were made to drink of one Spirit.

Gal 3:26-29 (§206)

[26]for in Christ Jesus you are all sons of God, through faith. [27]For as many of you as were baptized into Christ have put on Christ. [28]There is neither Jew nor Greek, there is neither slave nor free, there is neither male nor female; for you are all one in Christ Jesus. [29]And if you are Christ's, then you are Abraham's offspring, heirs according to promise.

Eph 4:17-32 (§227-228)

[17]Now this I affirm and testify in the Lord, that you must no longer live as the Gentiles do, in the futility of their minds; [18]they are darkened in their understanding, alienated from the life of God because of the ignorance that is in them, due to their hardness of heart; [19]they have become callous and have given themselves up to licentiousness, greedy to practice every kind of uncleanness. [20]You did not so learn Christ!— [21]assuming that you have heard about him and were taught in him, as the truth is in Jesus. [22]Put off your old nature which belongs to your former manner of life and is corrupt through deceitful lusts, [23]and be renewed in the spirit of your minds, [24]and put on the new nature, created after the likeness of God in true righteousness and holiness.

[25]Therefore, putting away falsehood, let every one speak the truth with his neighbor, for we are members one of another. [26]Be angry but do not sin; do not let the sun go down on your anger, [27]and give no opportunity to the devil. [28]Let the thief no longer steal, but rather let him labor, doing honest work with his hands, so that he may be able to give to those in need. [29]Let no evil talk come out of your mouths, but only such as is good for edifying, as fits the occasion, that it may impart grace to those who hear. [30]And do not grieve the Holy Spirit of God, in whom you were sealed for the day of redemption. [31]Let all bitterness and wrath and anger and clamor and slander be put away from you, with all malice, [32]and be kind to one another, tenderhearted, forgiving one another, as God in Christ forgave you.

Eph 5:3-14 (§230)

[3]But fornication and all impurity or covetousness must not even be named among you, as is fitting among saints. [4]Let there be no filthiness, nor silly talk, nor levity, which are not fitting; but instead let there be thanksgiving. [5]Be sure of this, that no fornicator or impure man, or one who is covetous (that is, an idolater), has any inheritance in the kingdom of Christ and of God. [6]Let no one deceive you with empty words, for it is because of these things that the wrath of God comes upon the sons of disobedience. [7]Therefore do not associate with them, [8]for once you were darkness, but now you are light in the Lord; walk as children of light [9](for the fruit of light is found in all that is good and right and true), [10]and try to learn what is pleasing to the Lord. [11]Take no part in the unfruitful works of darkness, but instead expose them. [12]For it is a shame even to speak of the things that they do in secret; [13]but when anything is exposed by the light it becomes visible, for anything that becomes visible is light. [14]Therefore it is said,

"Awake, O sleeper, and arise from the dead,
   and Christ shall give you light."

SECONDARY

Rom 2:1-5 (§7)

[1]Therefore you have no excuse, O man, whoever you are, when you judge another; for in passing judgment upon him you condemn yourself, because you, the judge, are doing the very same things. [2]We know that the judgment of God rightly falls upon those who do such things. [3]Do you suppose, O man, that when you judge those who do such things and yet do them yourself, you will escape the judgment of God? [4]Or do you presume upon the riches of his kindness and forbearance and patience? Do you not know that God's kindness is meant to lead you to repentance? [5]But by your hard and impenitent heart you are storing up wrath for yourself on the day of wrath when God's righteous judgment will be revealed.

Rom 6:11-14 (§24)

[11]So you also must consider yourselves dead to sin and alive to God in Christ Jesus.

[12]Let not sin therefore reign in your mortal bodies, to make you obey their passions. [13]Do not yield your members to sin as instruments of wickedness, but yield yourselves to God as men who have been brought from death to life, and

---

● **Col 3:5-11**

1 Tim 1   [9]understanding this, that the law is not laid down for the just but for the lawless and disobedient, for the ungodly and sinners, for the unholy and profane, for murderers of fathers and murderers of mothers, for manslayers, [10]immoral persons, sodomites, kidnappers, liars, perjurers, and whatever else is contrary to sound doctrine, . . .

1 Tim 6   [4]he is puffed up with conceit, he knows nothing; he has a morbid craving for controversy and for disputes about words, which produce envy, dissension, slander, base suspicions, [5]and wrangling among men who are depraved in mind and bereft of the truth, imagining that godliness is a means of gain.

2 Tim 3   [2]For men will be lovers of self, lovers of money, proud, arrogant, abusive, disobedient to their parents, ungrateful, unholy, [3]inhuman, implacable, slanderers, profligates, fierce, haters of good, [4]treacherous, reckless, swollen with conceit, lovers of pleasure rather than lovers of God, . . .

Titus 3   [3]For we ourselves were once foolish, disobedient, led astray, slaves to various passions and pleasures, passing our days in malice and envy, hated by men and hating one another; . . .

● **Col 3:6**

(coming) *add* upon the sons of disobedience: S ACDG Koine Lect it vg syr cop(bo) Clement; *text:* p46 B cop(sa) Clement

your members to God as instruments of righteousness. [14] For sin will have no dominion over you, since you are not under law but under grace.

Rom 8:9-17 (§30)

[9] But you are not in the flesh, you are in the Spirit, if in fact the Spirit of God dwells in you. Any one who does not have the Spirit of Christ does not belong to him. [10] But if Christ is in you, although your bodies are dead because of sin, your spirits are alive because of righteousness. [11] If the Spirit of him who raised Jesus from the dead dwells in you, he who raised Christ Jesus from the dead will give life to your mortal bodies also through his Spirit which dwells in you.

[12] So then, brethren, we are debtors, not to the flesh, to live according to the flesh— [13] for if you live according to the flesh you will die, but if by the Spirit you put to death the deeds of the body you will live. [14] For all who are led by the Spirit of God are sons of God. [15] For you did not receive the spirit of slavery to fall back into fear, but you have received the spirit of sonship. When we cry, "Abba! Father!" [16] it is the Spirit himself bearing witness with our spirit that we are children of God, [17] and if children, then heirs, heirs of God and fellow heirs with Christ, provided we suffer with him in order that we may also be glorified with him.

1 Cor 10:1-13 (§109)

[1] I want you to know, brethren, that our fathers were all under the cloud, and all passed through the sea, [2] and all were baptized into Moses in the cloud and in the sea, [3] and all ate the same supernatural food [4] and all drank the same supernatural drink. For they drank from the supernatural Rock which followed them, and the Rock was Christ. [5] Nevertheless with most of them God was not pleased; for they were overthrown in the wilderness.

[6] Now these things are warnings for us, not to desire evil as they did. [7] Do not be idolaters as some of them were; as it is written, "The people sat down to eat and drink and rose up to dance." [8] We must not indulge in immorality as some of them did, and twenty-three thousand fell in a single day. [9] We must not put the Lord to the test, as some of them did and were destroyed by serpents; [10] nor grumble, as some of them did and were destroyed by the Destroyer. [11] Now these things happened to them as a warning, but they were written down for our instruction, upon whom the end of the ages has come. [12] Therefore let any one who thinks that he stands take heed lest he fall. [13] No temptation has overtaken you that is not common to man. God is faithful, and he will not let you be tempted beyond your strength, but with the temptation will also provide the way of escape, that you may be able to endure it.

1 Cor 15:42-50 (§136)

[42] So is it with the resurrection of the dead. What is sown is perishable, what is raised is imperishable. [43] It is sown in dishonor, it is raised in glory. It is sown in weakness, it is raised in power. [44] It is sown a physical body, it is raised a spiritual body. If there is a physical body, there is also a spiritual body. [45] Thus it is written, "The first man Adam became a living being"; the last Adam became a life-giving spirit. [46] But it is not the spiritual which is first but the physical, and then the spiritual. [47] The first man was from the earth, a man of dust; the second man is from heaven. [48] As was the man of dust, so are those who are of the dust; and as is the man of heaven, so are those who are of heaven. [49] Just as we have borne the image of the man of dust, we shall also bear the image of the man of heaven. [50] I tell you this, brethren: flesh and blood cannot inherit the kingdom of God, nor does the perishable inherit the imperishable.

2 Cor 4:16-5:5 (§161)

[16] So we do not lose heart. Though our outer nature is wasting away, our inner nature is being renewed every day. [17] For this slight momentary affliction is preparing for us an eternal weight of glory beyond all comparison, [18] because we look not to the things that are seen but to the things that are unseen; for the things that are seen are transient, but the things that are unseen are eternal.

5 [1] For we know that if the earthly tent we live in is destroyed, we have a building from God, a house not made with hands, eternal in the heavens. [2] Here indeed we groan, and long to put on our heavenly dwelling, [3] so that by putting it on we may not be found naked. [4] For while we are still in this tent, we sigh with anxiety; not that we would be unclothed, but that we would be further clothed, so that what is mortal may be swallowed up by life. [5] He who has prepared us for this very thing is God, who has given us the Spirit as a guarantee.

1 Thess 4:1-8 (§284)

[1] Finally, brethren, we beseech and exhort you in the Lord Jesus, that as you learned from us how you ought to live and to please God, just as you are doing, you do so more and more. [2] For you know what instructions we gave you through the Lord Jesus. [3] For this is the will of God, your sanctification: that you abstain from unchastity; [4] that each one of you know how to take a wife for himself in holiness and honor [5] not in the passion of lust like heathen who do not know God; [6] that no man transgress, and wrong his brother in this matter, because the Lord is an avenger in all these things, as we solemnly forewarned you. [7] For God has not called us for uncleanness, but in holiness. [8] Therefore whoever disregards this, disregards not man but God, who gives his Holy Spirit to you.

● **Col 3:7**
Eph 2 [3] Among these we all once lived in the passions of our flesh, following the desires of body and mind, and so we were by nature children of wrath, like the rest of mankind.

Eph 5 [6] Let no one deceive you with empty words, for it is because of these things that the wrath of God comes upon the sons of disobedience.

● **Col 3:8**
Eph 4 [26] Be angry but do not sin; do not let the sun go down on your anger, . . .

Eph 4 [31] Let all bitterness and wrath and anger and clamor and slander be put away from you, with all malice, . . .

● **Col 3:9**
Eph 4 [25] Therefore, putting away falsehood, let

every one speak the truth with his neighbor, for we are members one of another.

● **Col 3:10**
Col 1 [15] He is the image of the invisible God, the first-born of all creation; . . .

● **Col 3:11**
Rom 10 [12] For there is no distinction between Jew and Greek; the same Lord is Lord of all and bestows his riches upon all who call upon him.

FORMAL ELEMENTS: VIRTUE LIST & GNOMIC SAYINGS

[12]Put on then, as God's chosen ones, holy and beloved, compassion, kindness, lowliness, meekness, and patience, [13]forbearing one another and, if one has a complaint against another, forgiving each other; as the Lord has forgiven you, so you also must forgive. [14]And above all these put on love, which binds everything together in perfect harmony. [15]And let the peace of Christ rule in your hearts, to which indeed you were called in the one body. And be thankful. [16]Let the word of Christ dwell in you richly, as you teach and admonish one another in all wisdom, and as you sing psalms and hymns and spiritual songs with thankfulness in your hearts to God. [17]And whatever you do, in word or deed, do everything in the name of the Lord Jesus, giving thanks to God the Father through him.

PRIMARY

See §53 for GNOMIC SAYINGS

See §252 for VIRTUE LIST

SECONDARY

Rom 15:1-6 (§60)

[1]We who are strong ought to bear with the failings of the weak, and not to please ourselves; [2]let each of us please his neighbor for his good, to edify him. [3]For Christ did not please himself; but, as it is written, "The reproaches of those who reproached thee fell on me." [4]For whatever was written in former days was written for our instruction, that by steadfastness and by the encouragement of the scriptures we might have hope. [5]May the God of steadfastness and encouragement grant you to live in such harmony with one another, in accord with Christ Jesus, [6]that together you may with one voice glorify the God and Father of our Lord Jesus Christ.

1 Cor 10:23-11:1 (§111)

[23]"All things are lawful," but not all things are helpful. "All things are lawful," but not all things build up. [24]Let no one seek his own good, but the good of his neighbor. [25]Eat whatever is sold in the meat market without raising any question on the ground of conscience. [26]For "the earth is the Lord's, and everything in it." [27]If one of the unbelievers invites you to dinner and you are disposed to go, eat whatever is set before you without raising any question on the ground of conscience. [28](But if some one says to you, "This has been offered in sacrifice," then out of consideration for the man who informed you, and for conscience' sake— [29]I mean his conscience, not yours—do not eat it.) For why should my liberty be determined by another man's scruples? [30]If I partake with thankfulness, why am I denounced because of that for which I give thanks?

[31]So, whether you eat or drink, or whatever you do, do all to the glory of God. [32]Give no offense to Jews or to Greeks or to the church of God, [33]just as I try to please all men in everything I do, not seeking my own advantage, but that of many, that they may be saved. 11 [1]Be imitators of me, as I am of Christ.

1 Cor 14:26-33a (§128)

[26]What then, brethren? When you come together, each one has a hymn, a lesson, a revelation, a tongue, or an interpretation. Let all things be done for edification. [27]If any speak in a tongue, let there be only two or at most three, and each in turn; and let one interpret. [28]But if there is no one to interpret, let each of them keep silence in church and speak to himself and to God. [29]Let two or three prophets speak, and let the others weigh what is said. [30]If a revelation is made to another sitting by, let the first be silent. [31]For you can all prophesy one by one, so that all may learn and all be encouraged; [32]and the spirits of prophets are subject to prophets. [33]For God is not a God of confusion but of peace.

Eph 5:15-20 (§231)

[15]Look carefully then how you walk, not as unwise men but as wise, [16]making the most of the time, because the days are evil. [17]Therefore do not be foolish, but understand what the will of the Lord is. [18]And do not get drunk with wine, for that is debauchery; but be filled with the Spirit, [19]addressing one another in psalms and hymns and spiritual songs, singing and making melody to the Lord with all your heart, [20]always and for everything giving thanks in the name of our Lord Jesus Christ to God the Father.

• **Col 3:12**

2 Cor 8   [7]Now as you excel in everything—in faith, in utterance, in knowledge, in all earnestness, and in your love for us—see that you excel in this gracious work also.

Eph 4   [24]and put on the new nature, created after the likeness of God in true righteousness and holiness.

Eph 4   [32]and be kind to one another, tenderhearted, forgiving one another, as God in Christ forgave you.

• **Col 3:13**

2 Cor 2   [7]so you should rather turn to forgive and comfort him, or he may be overwhelmed by excessive sorrow.

• **Col 3:14**

1 Cor 13   [13]So faith, hope, love abide, these three; but the greatest of these is love.

• **Col 3:15**

Phil 4   [7]And the peace of God, which passes all understanding, will keep your hearts and your minds in Christ Jesus.

• **Col 3:16**

Acts 16   [25]But about midnight Paul and Silas were praying and singing hymns to God, and the prisoners were listening to them, . . .

• **Col 3:17**

Rom 14   [6]He who observes the day, observes it in honor of the Lord. He also who eats, eats in honor of the Lord, since he gives thanks to God; while he who abstains, abstains in honor of the Lord and gives thanks to God.

FORMAL ELEMENT: HOUSEHOLD TABLE

[18]Wives, be subject to your husbands, as is fitting in the Lord. [19]Husbands, love your wives, and do not be harsh with them. [20]Children, obey your parents in everything, for this pleases the Lord. [21]Fathers, do not provoke your children, lest they become discouraged. [22]Slaves, obey in everything those who are your earthly masters, not with eyeservice, as men-pleasers, but in singleness of heart, fearing the Lord. [23]Whatever your task, work heartily, as serving the Lord and not men, [24]knowing that from the Lord you will receive the inheritance as your reward; you are serving the Lord Christ. [25]For the wrongdoer will be paid back for the wrong he has done, and there is no partiality.

4 [1]Masters, treat your slaves justly and fairly, knowing that you also have a Master in heaven.

PRIMARY

Eph 5:21–6:9 (§232)

[21]Be subject to one another out of reverence for Christ. [22]Wives, be subject to your husbands, as to the Lord. [23]For the husband is the head of the wife as Christ is the head of the church, his body, and is himself its Savior. [24]As the church is subject to Christ, so let wives also be subject in everything to their husbands. [25]Husbands, love your wives, as Christ loved the church and gave himself up for her, [26]that he might sanctify her, having cleansed her by the washing of water with the word, [27]that he might present the church to himself in splendor, without spot or wrinkle or any such thing, that she might be holy and without blemish. [28]Even so husbands should love their wives as their own bodies. He who loves his wife loves himself. [29]For no man ever hates his own flesh, but nourishes and cherishes it, as Christ does the church, [30]because we are members of his body. [31]"For this reason a man shall leave his father and mother and be joined to his wife, and the two shall become one flesh." [32]This mystery is a profound one, and I am saying that it refers to Christ and the church; [33]however, let each one of you love his wife as himself, and let the wife see that she respects her husband.

6 [1]Children, obey your parents in the Lord, for this is right. [2]"Honor your father and mother" (this is the first commandment with a promise), [3]"that it may be well with you and that you may live long on the earth." [4]Fathers, do not provoke your children to anger, but bring them up in the discipline and instruction of the Lord.

[5]Slaves, be obedient to those who are your earthly masters, with fear and trembling, in singleness of heart, as to Christ; [6]not in the way of eyeservice, as men-pleasers, but as servants of Christ, doing the will of God from the heart, [7]rendering service with a good will as to the Lord and not to men, [8]knowing that whatever good any one does, he will receive the same again from the Lord, whether he is a slave or free. [9]Masters, do the same to them, and forbear threatening, knowing that he who is both their Master and yours is in heaven, and that there is no partiality with him.

SECONDARY

Rom 13:1–7 (§54)

[1]Let every person be subject to the governing authorities. For there is no authority except from God, and those that exist have been instituted by God. [2]Therefore he who resists the authorities resists what God has appointed, and those who resist will incur judgment. [3]For rulers are not a terror to good conduct, but to bad. Would you have no fear of him who is in authority? Then do what is good, and you will receive his approval, [4]for he is God's servant for your good. But if you do wrong, be afraid, for he does not bear the sword in vain; he is the servant of God to execute his wrath on the

wrongdoer. [5]Therefore one must be subject, not only to avoid God's wrath but also for the sake of conscience. [6]For the same reason you also pay taxes, for the authorities are ministers of God, attending to this very thing. [7]Pay all of them their dues, taxes to whom taxes are due, revenue to whom revenue is due, respect to whom respect is due, honor to whom honor is due.

1 Cor 7:32–35 (§99)

[32]I want you to be free from anxieties. The unmarried man is anxious about the affairs of the Lord, how to please the Lord; [33]but the married man is anxious about worldly affairs, how to please his wife, [34]and his interests are divided. And the unmarried woman or girl is anxious about the affairs of the Lord, how to be holy in body and spirit; but the married woman is anxious about worldly affairs, how to please her husband. [35]I say this for your own benefit, not to lay any restraint upon you, but to promote good order and to secure your undivided devotion to the Lord.

1 Thess 4:1–8 (§284)

[1]Finally, brethren, we beseech and exhort you in the Lord Jesus, that as you learned from us how you ought to live and to please God, just as you are doing, you do so more and more. [2]For you know what instructions we gave you through the Lord Jesus. [3]For this is the will of God, your sanctification: that you abstain from unchastity; [4]that each one of you know how to take a wife for himself in holiness and honor [5]not in the passion of lust like heathen who do not know God; [6]that no man transgress, and wrong his brother in this matter, because the Lord is an avenger in all these things, as we solemnly forewarned you. [7]For God has not called us for uncleanness, but in holiness. [8]Therefore whoever disregards this, disregards not man but God, who gives his Holy Spirit to you.

● **Col 3:18–4:1**
See 1 Cor 11:3; 1 Cor 14:34

1 Tim 6　[1]Let all who are under the yoke of slavery regard their masters as worthy of all honor, so that the name of God and the teaching may not be defamed.

1 Pet 2　[13]Be subject for the Lord's sake to every human institution, whether it be to the emperor as supreme, [14]or to governors as sent by him to punish those who do wrong and to praise those who do right. [15]For it is God's will that by doing right you should put to silence the ignorance of foolish men. [16]Live as free men, yet without using your freedom as a pretext for evil; but live as servants of God. [17]Honor all men. Love the brotherhood. Fear God. Honor the emperor. [18]Servants, be submissive to your masters with all respect, not only to the kind and gentle but also to the overbearing. [19]For one is approved if, mindful of God, he endures pain while suffering unjustly. [20]For what credit is it, if when you do wrong and are beaten for it you take it patiently? But if when you do right and suffer for it you take it patiently, you have God's approval. [21]For to this you have been called, because Christ also suffered for you, leaving you an example, that you should follow in his steps. [22]He committed no

sin; no guile was found on his lips. [23]When he was reviled, he did not revile in return; when he suffered, he did not threaten; but he trusted to him who judges justly. [24]He himself bore our sins in his body on the tree, that we might die to sin and live to righteousness. By his wounds you have been healed. [25]For you were straying like sheep, but have now returned to the Shepherd and Guardian of your souls.

3 [1]Likewise you wives, be submissive to your husbands, so that some, though they do not obey the word, may be won without a word by the behavior of their wives, [2]when they see your reverent and chaste behavior. [3]Let not yours be the outward adorning with braiding of hair, decoration of gold, and wearing of fine clothing, [4]but let it be the hidden person of the heart with the imperishable jewel of a gentle and quiet spirit, which in God's sight is very precious. [5]So once the holy women who hoped in God used to adorn themselves and were submissive to their husbands, [6]as Sarah obeyed Abraham, calling him lord. And you are now her children if you do right and let nothing terrify you.

[7]Likewise you husbands, live considerately with your wives, bestowing honor on the woman as the weaker sex, since you are joint heirs of the grace of life, in order that your prayers may not be hindered.

● **Col 3:22**
1 Cor 7　[22]For he who was called in the Lord as a slave is a freedman of the Lord. Likewise he who was free when called is a slave of Christ.

● **Col 3:24**
Col 1　[22]he has now reconciled in his body of flesh by his death, in order to present you holy and blameless and irreproachable before him, . . .

Acts 20　[32]"And now I commend you to God and to the word of his grace, which is able to build you up and to give you the inheritance among all those who are sanctified."

● **Col 3:25**
Rom 2　[11]For God shows no partiality.

Rom 3　[22]. . . For there is no distinction; . . .

Rom 13　[4]for he is God's servant for your good. But if you do wrong, be afraid, for he does not bear the sword in vain; he is the servant of God to execute his wrath on the wrongdoer.

Acts 10　[34]And Peter opened his mouth and said: "Truly I perceive that God shows no partiality. . . ."

317

FORMAL ELEMENTS: REQUEST FOR PRAYER & "WATCH!" "STAND!"

[2]Continue steadfastly in prayer, being watchful in it with thanksgiving; [3]and pray for us also, that God may open to us a door for the word, to declare the mystery of Christ, on account of which I am in prison, [4]that I may make it clear, as I ought to speak.

PRIMARY

Rom 13:11-14 (§56)

[11]Besides this you know what hour it is, how it is full time now for you to wake from sleep. For salvation is nearer to us now than when we first believed; [12]the night is far gone, the day is at hand. Let us then cast off the works of darkness and put on the armor of light; [13]let us conduct ourselves becomingly as in the day, not in reveling and drunkenness, not in debauchery and licentiousness, not in quarreling and jealousy. [14]But put on the Lord Jesus Christ, and make no provision for the flesh, to gratify its desires.

Rom 15:30-33 (§64)

[30]I appeal to you, brethren, by our Lord Jesus Christ and by the love of the Spirit, to strive together with me in your prayers to God on my behalf, [31]that I may be delivered from the unbelievers in Judea, and that my service for Jerusalem may be acceptable to the saints, [32]so that by God's will I may come to you with joy and be refreshed in your company. [33]The God of peace be with you all. Amen.

1 Cor 16:13-14 (§141)

[13]Be watchful, stand firm in your faith, be courageous, be strong. [14]Let all that you do be done in love.

Eph 6:10-17 (§233)

[10]Finally, be strong in the Lord and in the strength of his might. [11]Put on the whole armor of God, that you may be able to stand against the wiles of the devil. [12]For we are not contending against flesh and blood, but against the principalities, against the powers, against the world rulers of this present darkness, against the spiritual hosts of wickedness in the heavenly places. [13]Therefore take the whole armor of God, that you may be able to withstand in the evil day, and having done all, to stand. [14]Stand therefore, having girded your loins with truth, and having put on the breastplate of righteousness, [15]and having shod your feet with the equipment of the gospel of peace; [16]besides all these, taking the shield of faith, with which you can quench all the flaming darts of the evil one. [17]And take the helmet of salvation, and the sword of the Spirit, which is the word of God.

Eph 6:18-20 (§234)

[18]Pray at all times in the Spirit, with all prayer and supplication. To that end keep alert with all perseverance, making supplication for all the saints, [19]and also for me, that utterance may be given me in opening my mouth boldly to proclaim the mystery of the gospel, [20]for which I am an ambassador in chains; that I may declare it boldly, as I ought to speak.

1 Thess 5:1-11 (§287)

[1]But as to the times and the seasons, brethren, you have no need to have anything written to you. [2]For you yourselves know well that the day of the Lord will come like a thief in the night. [3]When people say, "There is peace and security," then sudden destruction will come upon them as travail comes upon a woman with child, and there will be no escape. [4]But you are not in darkness, brethren, for that day to surprise you like a thief. [5]For you are all sons of light and sons of the day; we are not of the night or of darkness. [6]So then let us not sleep, as others do, but let us keep awake and be sober. [7]For those who sleep sleep at night, and those who get drunk are drunk at night. [8]But, since we belong to the day, let us be sober, and put on the breastplate of faith and love, and for a helmet the hope of salvation. [9]For God has not destined us for wrath, but to obtain salvation through our Lord Jesus Christ, [10]who died for us so that whether we wake or sleep we might live with him. [11]Therefore encourage one another and build one another up, just as you are doing.

1 Thess 5:25 (§290)

[25]Brethren, pray for us.

2 Thess 2:13-17 (§297-298)

[13]But we are bound to give thanks to God always for you, brethren beloved by the Lord, because God chose you from the beginning to be saved, through sanctification by the Spirit and belief in the truth. [14]To this he called you through our gospel, so that you may obtain the glory of our Lord Jesus Christ. [15]So then, brethren, stand firm and hold to the traditions which you were taught by us, either by word of mouth or by letter.

[16]Now may our Lord Jesus Christ himself, and God our Father, who loved us and gave us eternal comfort and good hope through grace, [17]comfort your hearts and establish them in every good work and word.

2 Thess 3:1-5 (§299)

[1]Finally, brethren, pray for us, that the word of the Lord may speed on and triumph, as it did among you, [2]and that we may be delivered from wicked and evil men; for not all have faith. [3]But the Lord is faithful; he will strengthen you and guard you from evil. [4]And we have confidence in the Lord about you, that you are doing and will do the things which we command. [5]May the Lord direct your hearts to the love of God and to the steadfastness of Christ.

SECONDARY

2 Cor 2:12-13 (§152)

[12]When I came to Troas to preach the gospel of Christ, a door was opened for me in the Lord; [13]but my mind could not rest because I did not find my brother Titus there. So I took leave of them and went on to Macedonia.

● **Col 4:2**

1 Thess 5   [6]So then let us not sleep, as others do, but let us keep awake and be sober.

Acts 1   [14]All these with one accord devoted themselves to prayer, together with the women and Mary the mother of Jesus, and with his brothers.

● **Col 4:3**

Eph 3   [1]For this reason I, Paul, a prisoner for Christ Jesus on behalf of you Gentiles . . .

Phil 1   [12]I want you to know, brethren, that what has happened to me has really served to advance the gospel, [13]so that it has become known throughout the whole praetorian guard and to all the rest that my imprisonment is for Christ; [14]and most of the brethren have been made confident in the Lord because of my imprisonment, and are much more bold to speak the word of God without fear.

[15]Some indeed preach Christ from envy and rivalry, but others from good will. [16]The latter do it out of love, knowing that I am put here for the defense of the gospel; [17]the former proclaim Christ out of partisanship, not sincerely but thinking to afflict me in my imprisonment. [18]What then? Only that in every way, whether in pretense or in truth, Christ is proclaimed; and in that I rejoice.

[19]Yes, and I shall rejoice. For I know that through your prayers and the help of the Spirit of Jesus Christ this will turn out for my deliverance, [20]as it is my eager expectation and hope that I shall not be at all ashamed, but that with full courage now as always Christ will be honored in my body, whether by life or by death.

Phil 4   [6]Have no anxiety about anything, but in everything by prayer and supplication with thanksgiving let your requests be made known to God.

Col 4   [18]I, Paul, write this greeting with my own hand. Remember my fetters.

Phlm   [1]Paul, a prisoner for Christ Jesus, and Timothy our brother,

To Philemon our beloved fellow worker . . .

Phlm   [9]yet for love's sake I prefer to appeal to you— I, Paul, an ambassador and now a prisoner also for Christ Jesus . . .

Phlm   [22]At the same time, prepare a guest room for me, for I am hoping through your prayers to be granted to you.

Acts 14   [27]And when they arrived, they gathered the church together and declared all that God had done with them, and how he had opened a door of faith to the Gentiles.

5Conduct yourselves wisely toward outsiders, making the most of the time. 6Let your speech always be gracious, seasoned with salt, so that you may know how you ought to answer every one.

PRIMARY

Rom 12:9–21 (§53)

9Let love be genuine; hate what is evil, hold fast to what is good; 10love one another with brotherly affection; outdo one another in showing honor. 11Never flag in zeal, be aglow with the Spirit, serve the Lord. 12Rejoice in your hope, be patient in tribulation, be constant in prayer. 13Contribute to the needs of the saints, practice hospitality.

14Bless those who persecute you; bless and do not curse them. 15Rejoice with those who rejoice, weep with those who weep. 16Live in harmony with one another; do not be haughty, but associate with the lowly; never be conceited. 17Repay no one evil for evil, but take thought for what is noble in the sight of all. 18If possible, so far as it depends upon you, live peaceably with all. 19Beloved, never avenge yourselves, but leave it to the wrath of God; for it is written, "Vengeance is mine, I will repay, says the Lord." 20No, "if your enemy is hungry, feed him; if he is thirsty, give him drink; for by so doing you will heap burning coals upon his head." 21Do not be overcome by evil, but overcome evil with good.

1 Cor 6:1–8 (§90)

1When one of you has a grievance against a brother, does he dare go to law before the unrighteous instead of the saints? 2Do you not know that the saints will judge the world? And if the world is to be judged by you, are you incompetent to try trivial cases? 3Do you not know that we are to judge angels? How much more, matters pertaining to this life! 4If then you have such cases, why do you lay them before those who are least esteemed by the church? 5I say this to your shame. Can it be that there is no man among you wise enough to decide between members of the brotherhood, 6but brother goes to law against brother, and that before unbelievers?

7To have lawsuits at all with one another is defeat for you. Why not rather suffer wrong? Why not rather be defrauded? 8But you yourselves wrong and defraud, and that even your own brethren.

1 Cor 14:13–25 (§126–127)

13Therefore, he who speaks in a tongue should pray for the power to interpret. 14For if I pray in a tongue, my spirit prays but my mind is unfruitful. 15What am I to do? I will pray with the spirit and I will pray with the mind also; I will sing with the spirit and I will sing with the mind also. 16Otherwise, if you bless with the spirit, how can any one in the position of an outsider say the "Amen" to your thanksgiving when he does not know what you are saying? 17For you may give thanks well enough, but the other man is not edified. 18I thank God that I speak in tongues more than you all; 19nevertheless, in church I would rather speak five words with my mind, in order to instruct others, than ten thousand words in a tongue.

20Brethren, do not be children in your thinking; be babes in evil, but in thinking be mature. 21In the law it is written, "By men of strange tongues and by the lips of foreigners will I speak to this people, and even then they will not listen to me, says the Lord." 22Thus, tongues are a sign not for believers but for unbelievers, while prophecy is not for unbelievers but for believers. 23If, therefore, the whole church assembles and all speak in tongues, and outsiders or unbelievers enter, will they not say that you are mad? 24But if all prophesy, and an unbeliever or outsider enters, he is convicted by all, he is called to account by all, 25the secrets of his heart are disclosed; and so, falling on his face, he will worship God and declare that God is really among you.

1 Cor 14:26–33a (§128)

26What then, brethren? When you come together, each one has a hymn, a lesson, a revelation, a tongue, or an interpretation. Let all things be done for edification. 27If any speak in a tongue, let there be only two or at most three, and each in turn; and let one interpret. 28But if there is no one to interpret, let each of them keep silence in church and speak to himself and to God. 29Let two or three prophets speak, and let the others weigh what is said. 30If a revelation is made to another sitting by, let the first be silent. 31For you can all prophesy one by one, so that all may learn and all be encouraged; 32and the spirits of prophets are subject to prophets. 33For God is not a God of confusion but of peace.

1 Thess 4:9–12 (§285)

9But concerning love of the brethren you have no need to have any one write to you, for you yourselves have been taught by God to love one another; 10and indeed you do love all the brethren throughout Macedonia. But we exhort you, brethren, to do so more and more, 11to aspire to live quietly, to mind your own affairs, and to work with your hands, as we charged you; 12so that you may command the respect of outsiders, and be dependent on nobody.

● **Col 4:5–6**
Gal 6   10So then, as we have opportunity, let us do good to all men, and especially to those who are of the household of faith.

Phil 1   12I want you to know, brethren, that what has happened to me has really served to advance the gospel, 13so that it has become known throughout the whole praetorian guard and to all the rest that my imprisonment is for Christ; . . .

● **Col 4:5**
Rom 13   7Pay all of them their dues, taxes to whom taxes are due, revenue to whom revenue is due, respect to whom respect is due, honor to whom honor is due.

Eph 5   15Look carefully then how you walk, not as unwise men but as wise, 16making the most of the time, because the days are evil.

Phil 1   13so that it has become known throughout the whole praetorian guard and to all the rest that my imprisonment is for Christ; . . .

1 Tim 3   7moreover he must be well thought of by outsiders, or he may fall into reproach and the snare of the devil.

● **Col 4:6**
Eph 4   29Let no evil talk come out of your mouths, but only such as is good for edifying, as fits the occasion, that it may impart grace to those who hear.

FORMAL ELEMENT: COMMENDATION

7Tychicus will tell you all about my affairs; he is a beloved brother and faithful minister and fellow servant in the Lord. 8I have sent him to you for this very purpose, that you may know how we are and that he may encourage your hearts, 9and with him Onesimus, the faithful and beloved brother, who is one of yourselves. They will tell you of everything that has taken place here.

PRIMARY

Rom 16:1–2 (§65)

1I commend to you our sister Phoebe, a deaconess of the church at Cenchreae, 2that you may receive her in the Lord as befits the saints, and help her in whatever she may require from you, for she has been a helper of many and of myself as well.

1 Cor 16:10–12 (§140)

10When Timothy comes, see that you put him at ease among you, for he is doing the work of the Lord, as I am. 11So let no one despise him. Speed him on his way in peace, that he may return to me; for I am expecting him with the brethren. 12As for our brother Apollos, I strongly urged him to visit you with the other brethren, but it was not at all his will to come now. He will come when he has opportunity.

1 Cor 16:15–18 (§142)

15Now, brethren, you know that the household of Stephanas were the first converts in Achaia, and they have devoted themselves to the service of the saints; 16I urge you to be subject to such men and to every fellow worker and laborer. 17I rejoice at the coming of Stephanas and Fortunatus and Achaicus, because they have made up for your absence; 18for they refreshed my spirit as well as yours. Give recognition to such men.

2 Cor 3:1–3 (§154)

1Are we beginning to commend ourselves again? Or do we need, as some do, letters of recommendation to you, or from you? 2You yourselves are our letter of recommendation,

written on your hearts, to be known and read by all men; 3and you show that you are a letter from Christ delivered by us, written not with ink but with the Spirit of the living God, not on tablets of stone but on tablets of human hearts.

2 Cor 8:16–24 (§173)

16But thanks be to God who puts the same earnest care for you into the heart of Titus. 17For he not only accepted our appeal, but being himself very earnest he is going to you of his own accord. 18With him we are sending the brother who is famous among all the churches for his preaching of the gospel; 19and not only that, but he has been appointed by the churches to travel with us in this gracious work which we are carrying on, for the glory of the Lord and to show our good will. 20We intend that no one should blame us about this liberal gift which we are administering, 21for we aim at what is honorable not only in the Lord's sight but also in the sight of men. 22And with them we are sending our brother whom we have often tested and found earnest in many matters, but who is now more earnest than ever because of his great confidence in you. 23As for Titus, he is my partner and fellow worker in your service; and as for our brethren, they are messengers of the churches, the glory of Christ. 24So give proof, before the churches, of your love and of our boasting about you to these men.

Eph 6:21–22 (§235)

21Now that you also may know how I am and what I am doing, Tychicus the beloved brother and faithful minister in the Lord will tell you everything. 22I have sent him to you for this very purpose, that you may know how we are, and that he may encourage your hearts.

Phil 2:19–24 (§245)

19I hope in the Lord Jesus to send Timothy to you soon, so that I may be cheered by news of you. 20I have no one like him, who will be genuinely anxious for your welfare. 21They all look after their own interests, not those of Jesus Christ. 22But Timothy's worth you know, how as a son with a father he has served with me in the gospel. 23I hope therefore to send him just as soon as I see how it will go with me; 24and I trust in the Lord that shortly I myself shall come also.

Phil 2:25–3:1 (§246)

25I have thought it necessary to send to you Epaphroditus my brother and fellow worker and fellow soldier, and your messenger and minister to my need, 26for he has been longing for you all, and has been distressed because you heard that he was ill. 27Indeed he was ill, near to death. But God had mercy on him, and not only on him but on me also, lest I should have sorrow upon sorrow. 28I am the more eager to send him, therefore, that you may rejoice at seeing him again, and that I may be less anxious. 29So receive him in the Lord with all joy; and honor such men, 30for he nearly died for the work of Christ, risking his life to complete your service to me.

3 1Finally, my brethren, rejoice in the Lord. To write the same things to you is not irksome to me, and is safe for you.

Phlm 8–20 (§307–308)

8Accordingly, though I am bold enough in Christ to command you to do what is required, 9yet for love's sake I prefer to appeal to you—I, Paul, an ambassador and now a prisoner also for Christ Jesus— 10I appeal to you for my child, Onesimus, whose father I have become in my imprisonment. 11(Formerly he was useless to you, but now he is indeed useful to you and to me.) 12I am sending him back to you, sending my very heart. 13I would have been glad to keep him with me, in order that he might serve me on your behalf during my imprisonment for the gospel; 14but I preferred to do nothing without your consent in order that your goodness might not be by compulsion but of your own free will.

15Perhaps this is why he was parted from you for a while, that you might have him back for ever, 16no longer as a slave but more than a slave, as a beloved brother, especially to me but how much more to you, both in the flesh and in the Lord. 17So if you consider me your partner, receive him as you would receive me. 18If he has wronged you at all, or owes you anything, charge that to my account. 19I, Paul, write this with my own hand, I will repay it—to say nothing of your owing me even your own self. 20Yes, brother, I want some benefit from you in the Lord. Refresh my heart in Christ.

● **Col 4:7**

Acts 20   4Sopater of Beroea, the son of Pyrrhus, accompanied him; and of the Thessalonians, Aristarchus and Secundus; and Gaius of Derbe, and Timothy; and the Asians, Tychicus and Trophimus.

● **Col 4:8**

1 Cor 16   18for they refreshed my spirit as well as yours. Give recognition to such men.

Titus 3   12When I send Artemas or Tychicus to you, do your best to come to me at Nicopolis, for I have decided to spend the winter there.

LETTER STRUCTURE: GREETINGS

[10] Aristarchus my fellow prisoner greets you, and Mark the cousin of Barnabas (concerning whom you have received instructions—if he comes to you, receive him), [11] and Jesus who is called Justus. These are the only men of the circumcision among my fellow workers for the kingdom of God, and they have been a comfort to me. [12] Epaphras, who is one of yourselves, a servant of Christ Jesus, greets you, always remembering you earnestly in his prayers, that you may stand mature and fully assured in all the will of God. [13] For I bear him witness that he has worked hard for you and for those in Laodicea and in Hierapolis. [14] Luke the beloved physician and Demas greet you. [15] Give my greetings to the brethren at Laodicea, and to Nympha and the church in her house.

PRIMARY

Rom 16:3–16 (§66)

[3] Greet Prisca and Aquila, my fellow workers in Christ Jesus, [4] who risked their necks for my life, to whom not only I but also all the churches of the Gentiles give thanks; [5] greet also the church in their house. Greet my beloved Epaenetus, who was the first convert in Asia for Christ. [6] Greet Mary, who has worked hard among you. [7] Greet Andronicus and Junias, my kinsmen and my fellow prisoners; they are men of note among the apostles, and they were in Christ before me. [8] Greet Ampliatus, my beloved in the Lord. [9] Greet Urbanus, our fellow worker in Christ, and my beloved Stachys. [10] Greet Apelles, who is approved in Christ. Greet those who belong to the family of Aristobulus. [11] Greet my kinsman Herodion. Greet those in the Lord who belong to the family of Narcissus. [12] Greet those workers in the Lord, Tryphaena and Tryphosa. Greet the beloved Persis, who has worked hard in the Lord. [13] Greet Rufus, eminent in the Lord, also his mother and mine. [14] Greet Asyncritus, Phlegon, Hermes, Patrobas, Hermas, and the brethren who are with them. [15] Greet Philologus, Julia, Nereus and his sister, and Olympas, and all the saints who are with them. [16] Greet one another with a holy kiss. All the churches of Christ greet you.

Rom 16:21–23 (§69)

[21] Timothy, my fellow worker, greets you; so do Lucius and Jason and Sosipater, my kinsmen.
[22] I Tertius, the writer of this letter, greet you in the Lord.
[23] Gaius, who is host to me and to the whole church, greets you. Erastus, the city treasurer, and our brother Quartus, greet you.

1 Cor 16:19–20 (§143)

[19] The churches of Asia send greetings. Aquila and Prisca, together with the church in their house, send you hearty greetings in the Lord. [20] All the brethren send greetings. Greet one another with a holy kiss.

2 Cor 13:11–13 (§191)

[11] Finally, brethren, farewell. Mend your ways, heed my appeal, agree with one another, live in peace, and the God of love and peace will be with you. [12] Greet one another with a holy kiss. [13] All the saints greet you.

Phil 4:21–22 (§254)

[21] Greet every saint in Christ Jesus. The brethren who are with me greet you. [22] All the saints greet you, especially those of Caesar's household.

1 Thess 5:26 (§291)

[26] Greet all the brethren with a holy kiss.

Phlm 23–24 (§310)

[23] Epaphras, my fellow prisoner in Christ Jesus, sends greetings to you, [24] and so do Mark, Aristarchus, Demas, and Luke, my fellow workers.

● Col 4:10–15
2 Tim 4　[19] Greet Prisca and Aquila, and the household of Onesiphorus. [20] Erastus remained at Corinth; Trophimus I left ill at Miletus. [21] Do your best to come before winter. Eubulus sends greetings to you, as do Pudens and Linus and Claudia and all the brethren.

Titus 3　[15] All who are with me send greetings to you. Greet those who love us in the faith.

● Col 4:10–12
Acts 19　[29] So the city was filled with the confusion; and they rushed together into the theater, dragging with them Gaius and Aristarchus, Macedonians who were Paul's companions in travel.

● Col 4:10–11
Acts 27　[2] And embarking in a ship of Adramyttium, which was about to sail to the ports along the coast of Asia, we put to sea, accompanied by Aristarchus, a Macedonian from Thessalonica.

● Col 4:10
2 Tim 4　[11] Luke alone is with me. Get Mark and bring him with you; for he is very useful in serving me.

Acts 4　[36] Thus Joseph who was surnamed by the apostles Barnabas (which means, Son of encouragement), a Levite, a native of Cyprus, . . .

Acts 12　[12] When he realized this, he went to the house of Mary, the mother of John whose other name was Mark, where many were gathered together and were praying.

Acts 13　[5] When they arrived at Salamis, they proclaimed the word of God in the synagogues of the Jews. And they had John to assist them.

Acts 13　[13] Now Paul and his company set sail from Paphos, and came to Perga in Pamphylia. And John left them and returned to Jerusalem; . . .

Acts 15　[37] And Barnabas wanted to take with them John called Mark.

Acts 15　[39] And there arose a sharp contention, so that they separated from each other; Barnabas took Mark with him and sailed away to Cyprus, . . .

● Col 4:12–13
Col 1　[7] as you learned it from Epaphras our beloved fellow servant. He is a faithful minister of Christ on our behalf . . .

● Col 4:12
Col 2　[2] that their hearts may be encouraged as they are knit together in love, to have all the riches of assured understanding and the knowledge of God's mystery, of Christ, . . .

● Col 4:13–15
Col 2　[1] For I want you to know how greatly I strive for you, and for those at Laodicea, and for all who have not seen my face, . . .

FORMAL ELEMENTS: ENFORCEMENT STATEMENTS & SIGNATURE DEVICE

[16]And when this letter has been read among you, have it read also in the church of the Laodiceans; and see that you read also the letter from Laodicea. [17]And say to Archippus, "See that you fulfil the ministry which you have received in the Lord."

[18]I, Paul, write this greeting with my own hand. Remember my fetters.

PRIMARY

1 Cor 14:37–40 (§130)

[37]If any one thinks that he is a prophet, or spiritual, he should acknowledge that what I am writing to you is a command of the Lord. [38]If any one does not recognize this, he is not recognized. [39]So, my brethren, earnestly desire to prophesy, and do not forbid speaking in tongues; [40]but all things should be done decently and in order.

1 Cor 16:21–22 (§144)

[21]I, Paul, write this greeting with my own hand. [22]If any one has no love for the Lord, let him be accursed. Our Lord, come!

Gal 6:11–17 (§216)

[11]See with what large letters I am writing to you with my own hand. [12]It is those who want to make a good showing in the flesh that would compel you to be circumcised, and only in order that they may not be persecuted for the cross of Christ. [13]For even those who receive circumcision do not themselves keep the law, but they desire to have you circumcised that they may glory in your flesh. [14]But far be it from me to glory except in the cross of our Lord Jesus Christ, by which the world has been crucified to me, and I to the world. [15]For neither circumcision counts for anything, nor uncircumcision, but a new creation. [16]Peace and mercy be upon all who walk by this rule, upon the Israel of God.

[17]Henceforth let no man trouble me; for I bear on my body the marks of Jesus.

1 Thess 5:27 (§292)

[27]I adjure you by the Lord that this letter be read to all the brethren.

2 Thess 3:14–15 (§301)

[14]If any one refuses to obey what we say in this letter, note that man, and have nothing to do with him, that he may be ashamed. [15]Do not look on him as an enemy, but warn him as a brother.

2 Thess 3:17 (§303)

[17]I, Paul, write this greeting with my own hand. This is the mark in every letter of mine; it is the way I write.

Phlm 21–22 (§309)

[21]Confident of your obedience, I write to you, knowing that you will do even more than I say. [22]At the same time, prepare a guest room for me, for I am hoping through your prayers to be granted to you.

● **Col 4:16–17**

Col 2   [1]For I want you to know how greatly I strive for you, and for those at Laodicea, and for all who have not seen my face, . . .

● **Col 4:17**

Phlm   [2]and Apphia our sister and Archippus our fellow soldier, and the church in your house: . . .

2 Tim 4   [5]As for you, always be steady, endure suffering, do the work of an evangelist, fulfil your ministry.

● **Col 4:18a**

Eph 3   [1]For this reason I, Paul, a prisoner for Christ Jesus on behalf of you Gentiles . . .

Phil 1   [12]I want you to know, brethren, that what has happened to me has really served to advance the gospel, [13]so that it has become known throughout the whole praetorian guard and to all the rest that my imprisonment is for Christ; [14]and most of the brethren have been made confident in the Lord because of my imprisonment, and are much more bold to speak the word of God without fear.

[15]Some indeed preach Christ from envy and rivalry, but others from good will. [16]The latter do it out of love, knowing that I am put here for the defense of the gospel; [17]the former proclaim Christ out of partisanship, not sincerely but thinking to afflict me in my imprisonment. [18]What then? Only that in every way, whether in pretense or in truth, Christ is proclaimed; and in that I rejoice.

[19]Yes, and I shall rejoice. For I know that through your prayers and the help of the Spirit of Jesus Christ this will turn out for my deliverance, [20]as it is my eager expectation and hope that I shall not be at all ashamed, but that with full courage now as always Christ will be honored in my body, whether by life or by death.

Col 4   [3]and pray for us also, that God may open to us a door for the word, to declare the mystery of Christ, on account of which I am in prison, . . .

Phlm   [1]Paul, a prisoner for Christ Jesus, and Timothy our brother,
   To Philemon our beloved fellow worker . . .

Phlm   [9]yet for love's sake I prefer to appeal to you— I, Paul, an ambassador and now a prisoner also for Christ Jesus . . .

LETTER STRUCTURE: CLOSING GRACE

Grace be with you.

PRIMARY

Rom 16:20b (§68)

The grace of our Lord Jesus Christ be with you.

1 Cor 16:23–24 (§145)

[23]The grace of the Lord Jesus be with you. [24]My love be with you all in Christ Jesus. Amen.

2 Cor 13:14 (§192)

[14]The grace of the Lord Jesus Christ and the love of God and the fellowship of the Holy Spirit be with you all.

Gal 6:18 (§217)

[18]The grace of our Lord Jesus Christ be with your spirit, brethren. Amen.

Eph 6:23–24 (§236)

[23]Peace be to the brethren, and love with faith, from God the Father and the Lord Jesus Christ. [24]Grace be with all who love our Lord Jesus Christ with love undying.

Phil 4:23 (§255)

[23]The grace of the Lord Jesus Christ be with your spirit.

1 Thess 5:28 (§293)

[28]The grace of our Lord Jesus Christ be with you.

2 Thess 3:18 (§304)

[18]The grace of our Lord Jesus Christ be with you all.

Phlm 25 (§311)

[25]The grace of the Lord Jesus Christ be with your spirit.

● **Col 4:18b**
1 Tim 6   [21]. . . Grace be with you.

2 Tim 4   [22]. . . Grace be with you.

Titus 3   [15]. . . Grace be with you all.

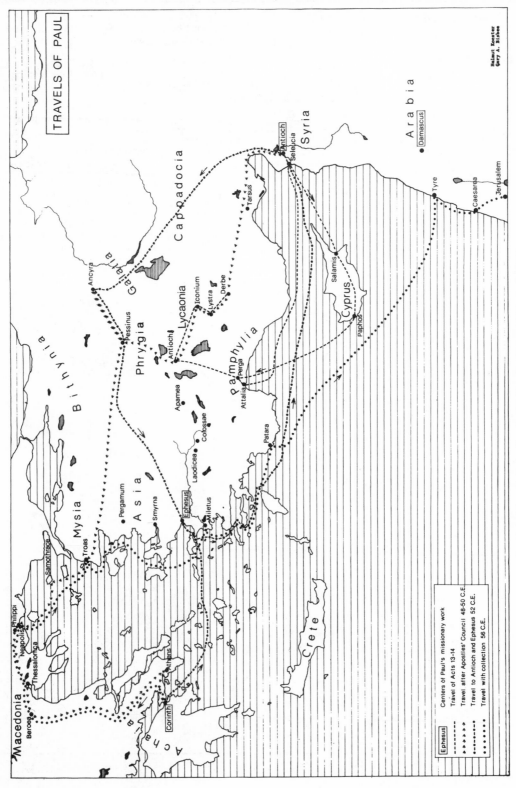

TRAVELS OF PAUL

Ephesus — Centers of Paul's missionary work
––––– Travel of Acts 13-14
→→→→ Travel after Apostles' Council 48-50 C.E.
•••••• Travel to Antioch and Ephesus 52 C.E.
•••••• Travel with collection 56 C.E.

Reprinted from *Introduction to the New Testament, Volume 2: History and Literature of Early Christianity*, by Helmut Koester (Philadelphia: Fortress Press, 1982), by permission of the publisher.

Helmut Koester
Gary A. Bibbee

LETTER STRUCTURE: SALUTATION

1 **Paul, Silvanus, and Timothy,**
To the church of the Thessalonians in
God the Father and the Lord Jesus Christ:
Grace to you and peace.

PRIMARY

Rom 1:1–7 (§1)
[1]Paul, a servant of Jesus Christ, called to be an apostle, set apart for the gospel of God [2]which he promised beforehand through his prophets in the holy scriptures, [3]the gospel concerning his Son, who was descended from David according to the flesh [4]and designated Son of God in power according to the Spirit of holiness by his resurrection from the dead, Jesus Christ our Lord, [5]through whom we have received grace and apostleship to bring about the obedience of faith for the sake of his name among all the nations, [6]including yourselves who are called to belong to Jesus Christ;
[7]To all God's beloved in Rome, who are called to be saints:
Grace to you and peace from God our Father and the Lord Jesus Christ.

1 Cor 1:1–3 (§71)
[1]Paul, called by the will of God to be an apostle of Christ Jesus, and our brother Sosthenes,
[2]To the church of God which is at Corinth, to those sanctified in Christ Jesus, called to be saints together with all those who in every place call on the name of our Lord Jesus Christ, both their Lord and ours:
[3]Grace to you and peace from God our Father and the Lord Jesus Christ.

2 Cor 1:1–2 (§146)
[1]Paul, an apostle of Christ Jesus by the will of God, and Timothy our brother.
To the church of God which is at Corinth, with all the saints who are in the whole of Achaia:
[2]Grace to you and peace from God our Father and the Lord Jesus Christ.

Gal 1:1–5 (§193)
[1]Paul an apostle—not from men nor through man, but through Jesus Christ and God the Father, who raised him from the dead— [2]and all the brethren who are with me,
To the churches of Galatia:
[3]Grace to you and peace from God the Father and our Lord Jesus Christ, [4]who gave himself for our sins to deliver us from the present evil age, according to the will of our God and Father; [5]to whom be the glory for ever and ever. Amen.

Eph 1:1–2 (§218)
[1]Paul, an apostle of Christ Jesus by the will of God,
To the saints who are also faithful in Christ Jesus:

[2]Grace to you and peace from God our Father and the Lord Jesus Christ.

Phil 1:1–2 (§237)
[1]Paul and Timothy, servants of Christ Jesus,
To all the saints in Christ Jesus who are at Philippi, with the bishops and deacons:
[2]Grace to you and peace from God our Father and the Lord Jesus Christ.

Col 1:1–2 (§256)
[1]Paul, an apostle of Christ Jesus by the will of God, and Timothy our brother,
[2]To the saints and faithful brethren in Christ at Colossae:
Grace to you and peace from God our Father.

2 Thess 1:1–2 (§294)
[1]Paul, Silvanus, and Timothy,
To the church of the Thessalonians in God our Father and the Lord Jesus Christ:
[2]Grace to you and peace from God the Father and the Lord Jesus Christ.

Phlm 1–3 (§305)
[1]Paul, a prisoner for Christ Jesus, and Timothy our brother,
To Philemon our beloved fellow worker [2]and Apphia our sister and Archippus our fellow soldier, and the church in your house:
[3]Grace to you and peace from God our Father and the Lord Jesus Christ.

● **1 Thess 1:1**
1 Tim 1   [1]Paul, an apostle of Christ Jesus by command of God our Savior and of Christ Jesus our hope,
[2]To Timothy, my true child in the faith:
Grace, mercy, and peace from God the Father and Christ Jesus our Lord.

2 Tim 1   [1]Paul, an apostle of Christ Jesus by the will of God according to the promise of the life which is in Christ Jesus,
[2]To Timothy, my beloved child:
Grace, mercy, and peace from God the Father and Christ Jesus our Lord.

Titus 1   [1]Paul, a servant of God and an apostle of Jesus Christ, to further the faith of God's elect and their knowledge of the truth which accords with godliness, [2]in hope of eternal life which God, who never lies, promised ages ago [3]and at the proper time manifested in his word through the preaching with which I have been entrusted by command of God our Savior;
[4]To Titus, my true child in a common faith:
Grace and peace from God the Father and Christ Jesus our Savior.

Acts 16   [1]And he came also to Derbe and to Lystra. A disciple was there, named Timothy, the son of a Jewish woman who was a believer; but his father was a Greek.

Acts 17   [1]Now when they had passed through Amphipolis and Apollonia, they came to Thessalonica, where there was a synagogue of the Jews. [2]And Paul went in, as was his custom, and for three weeks he argued with them from the scriptures, [3]explaining and proving that it was necessary for the Christ to suffer and to rise from the dead, and saying, "This Jesus, whom I proclaim to you, is the Christ." [4]And some of them were persuaded, and joined Paul and Silas; as did a great many of the devout Greeks and not a few of the leading women. [5]But the Jews were jealous, and taking some wicked fellows of the rabble, they gathered a crowd, set the city in an uproar, and attacked the house of Jason, seeking to bring them out to the people. [6]And when they could not find them, they dragged Jason and some of the brethren before the city authorities, crying, "These men who have turned the world upside down have come here also, [7]and Jason has received them; and they are all acting against the decrees of Ceasar, saying that there is another king, Jesus." [8]And the people and the city authorities were disturbed when they heard this. [9]And when they had taken security from Jason and the rest, they let him go.

LETTER STRUCTURE: THANKSGIVING
FORMAL ELEMENT: CONFESSION

1 We give thanks to God always for you all, constantly mentioning you in our prayers, ³remembering before our God and Father your work of faith and labor of love and steadfastness of hope in our Lord Jesus Christ. ⁴For we know, brethren beloved by God, that he has chosen you; ⁵for our gospel came to you not only in word, but also in power and in the Holy Spirit and with full conviction. You know what kind of men we proved to be among you for your sake. ⁶And you became imitators of us and of the Lord, for you received the word in much affliction, with joy inspired by the Holy Spirit; ⁷so that you became an example to the all the believers in Macedonia and in Achaia. ⁸For not only has the word of the Lord sounded forth from you in Macedonia and Achaia, but your faith in God has gone forth everywhere, so that we need not say anything. ⁹For they themselves report concerning us what a welcome we had among you, and how you turned to God from idols, to serve a living and true God, ¹⁰and to wait for his Son from heaven, whom he raised from the dead, Jesus who delivers us from the wrath to come.

PRIMARY

See §50 for CONFESSION

Rom 1:8-15 (§2)
⁸First, I thank my God through Jesus Christ for all of you, because your faith is proclaimed in all the world. ⁹For God is my witness, whom I serve with my spirit in the gospel of his Son, that without ceasing I mention you always in my prayers, ¹⁰asking that somehow by God's will I may now at last succeed in coming to you.

¹¹For I long to see you, that I may impart to you some spiritual gift to strengthen you, ¹²that is, that we may be mutually encouraged by each other's faith, both yours and mine. ¹³I want you to know, brethren, that I have often intended to come to you (but thus far have been prevented), in order that I may reap some harvest among you as well as among the rest of the Gentiles. ¹⁴I am under obligation both to Greeks and to barbarians, both to the wise and to the foolish: ¹⁵so I am eager to preach the gospel to you also who are in Rome.

1 Cor 1:4-9 (§72)
⁴I give thanks to God always for you because of the grace of God which was given you in Christ Jesus, ⁵that in every way you were enriched in him with all speech and all knowledge— ⁶even as the testimony to Christ was confirmed among you— ⁷so that you are not lacking in any spiritual gift, as you wait for the revealing of our Lord Jesus Christ; ⁸who will sustain you to the end, guiltless in the day of our Lord Jesus Christ. ⁹God is faithful, by whom you were called into the fellowship of his Son, Jesus Christ our Lord.

Phil 1:3-11 (§238)
³I thank my God in all my remembrance of you, ⁴always in every prayer of mine for you all making my prayer with joy, ⁵thankful for your partnership in the gospel from the first day until now. ⁶And I am sure that he who began a good work in you will bring it to completion at the day of Jesus Christ. ⁷It is right for me to feel thus about you all, because I hold you in my heart, for you are all partakers with me of grace, both in my imprisonment and in the defense and confirmation of the gospel. ⁸For God is my witness, how I yearn for you all with the affection of Christ Jesus. ⁹And it is my prayer that your love may abound more and more, with knowledge and all discernment, ¹⁰so that you

may approve what is excellent, and may be pure and blameless for the day of Christ, ¹¹filled with the fruits of righteousness which come through Jesus Christ, to the glory and praise of God.

Col 1:3-14 (§257)
³We always thank God, the Father of our Lord Jesus Christ, when we pray for you, ⁴because we have heard of your faith in Christ Jesus and of the love which you have for all the saints, ⁵because of the hope laid up for you in heaven. Of this you have heard before in the word of the truth, the gospel ⁶which has come to you, as indeed in the whole world it is bearing fruit and growing—so among yourselves, from the day you heard and understood the grace of God in truth, ⁷as you learned it from Epaphras our beloved fellow servant. He is a faithful minister of Christ on our behalf ⁸and has made known to us your love in the Spirit.

⁹And so, from the day we heard of it, we have not ceased to pray for you, asking that you may be filled with the knowledge of his will in all spiritual wisdom and understanding, ¹⁰to lead a life worthy of the Lord, fully pleasing to him, bearing fruit in every good work and increasing in the knowledge of God. ¹¹May you be strengthened with all power, according to his glorious might, for all endurance and patience with joy, ¹²giving thanks to the Father, who has qualified us to share in the inheritance of the saints in light. ¹³He has delivered us from the dominion of darkness and transferred us to the kingdom of his beloved Son, ¹⁴in whom we have redemption, the forgiveness of sins.

2 Thess 1:3-12 (§295)
³We are bound to give thanks to God always for you, brethren, as is fitting, because your faith is growing abundantly, and the love of every one of you for one another is increasing. ⁴Therefore we ourselves boast of you in the

---

● **1 Thess 1:2**
1 Thess 2   ¹³And we also thank God constantly for this, that when you received the word of God which you heard from us, you accepted it not as the word of men but as what it really is, the word of God, which is at work in you believers.

1 Tim 1   ¹²I thank him who has given me strength for this, Christ Jesus our Lord, because he judged me faithful by appointing me to his service, . . .

2 Tim 1   ³I thank God whom I serve with a clear conscience, as did my fathers, when I remember you constantly in my prayers.

Titus 1   ⁵This is why I left you in Crete, that you might amend what was defective, and appoint elders in every town as I directed you, . . .

● **1 Thess 1:3**
1 Cor 13   ¹³So faith, hope, love abide, these three; but the greatest of these is love.

Gal 5   ⁵For through the Spirit, by faith, we wait for the hope of righteousness. ⁶For in Christ Jesus neither circumcision nor uncircumcision is of any avail, but faith working through love.

See Eph 1:15-18

Col 1   ⁴because we have heard of your faith in Christ Jesus and of the love which you have for all the saints, ⁵because of the hope laid up for you in heaven. Of this you have heard before in the word of the truth, the gospel . . .

1 Thess 5   ⁸But, since we belong to the day, let us be sober, and put on the breastplate of faith and love, and for a helmet the hope of salvation.

● **1 Thess 1:4**
Rom 9   ¹¹though they were not yet born and had done nothing either good or bad, in order that God's purpose of election might continue, not because of works but because of his call, . . .

Rom 11   ⁷What then? Israel failed to obtain what it sought. The elect obtained it, but the rest were hardened, . . .

Eph 1   ⁴even as he chose us in him before the foundation of the world, that we should be holy and blameless before him.

Col 3   ¹²Put on then, as God's chosen ones, holy and beloved, compassion, kindness, lowliness, meekness, and patience, . . .

● **1 Thess 1:5-7**
Rom 15   ¹⁸For I will not venture to speak of anything except what Christ has wrought through me to win obedience from the Gentiles, by word and deed, ¹⁹by the power of signs and wonders, by the power of the Holy Spirit, so that from Jerusalem and as far round as Illyricum I have fully preached the gospel of Christ, . . .

● **1 Thess 1:5**
Gal 3   ²Let me ask you only this: Did you receive the Spirit by works of the law, or by hearing with faith? ³Are you so foolish? Having begun with the Spirit, are you now ending with the flesh? ⁴Did you experience so many things in vain?—if it really is in vain. ⁵Does he who supplies the Spirit to you and works miracles among you do so by works of the law, or by hearing with faith?

Gal 4   ¹²Brethren, I beseech you, become as I am, for I also have become as you are. You did me no wrong; ¹³you know it was because of a bodily ailment that I preached the gospel to you at first; ¹⁴and though my condition was a trial to you, you did not scorn or despise me, but received me as an angel of God, as Christ Jesus. ¹⁵What has become of the satisfaction you felt? For I bear you witness that, if possible, you would have plucked out your eyes and given them to me.

churches of God for your steadfastness and faith in all your persecutions and in the afflictions which you are enduring.

[5]This is evidence of the righteous judgment of God, that you may be made worthy of the kingdom of God, for which you are suffering—[6]since indeed God deems it just to repay with affliction those who afflict you, [7]and to grant rest with us to you who are afflicted, when the Lord Jesus is revealed from heaven with his mighty angels in flaming fire, [8]inflicting vengeance upon those who do not know God and upon those who do not obey the gospel of our Lord Jesus. [9]They shall suffer the punishment of eternal destruction and exclusion from the presence of the Lord and from the glory of his might, [10]when he comes on that day to be glorified in his saints, and to be marveled at in all who have believed, because our testimony to you was believed. [11]To this end we always pray for you, that our God may make you worthy of his call, and may fulfil every good resolve and work of faith by his power, [12]so that the name of our Lord Jesus may be glorified in you, and you in him, according to the grace of our God and the Lord Jesus Christ.

Phlm 4–7 (§306)

[4]I thank my God always when I remember you in my prayers, [5]because I hear of your love and of the faith which you have toward the Lord Jesus and all the saints, [6]and I pray that the sharing of your faith may promote the knowledge of all the good that is ours in Christ. [7]For I have derived much joy and comfort from your love, my brother, because the hearts of the saints have been refreshed through you.

Secondary

1 Cor 2:1–5 (§76)

[1]When I came to you, brethren, I did not come proclaiming to you the testimony of God in lofty words or wisdom. [2]For I decided to know nothing among you except Jesus Christ and him crucified. [3]And I was with you in weakness and in much fear and trembling; [4]and my speech and my message were not in plausible words of wisdom, but in demonstration of the Spirit and of power, [5]that your faith might not rest in the wisdom of men but in the power of God.

1 Cor 10:14–22 (§110)

[14]Therefore, my beloved, shun the worship of idols. [15]I speak as to sensible men; judge for yourselves what I say. [16]The cup of blessing which we bless, is it not a participation in the blood of Christ? The bread which we break, is it not a participation in the body of Christ? [17]Because there is one bread, we who are many are one body, for we all partake of the one bread.

[18]Consider the people of Israel; are not those who eat the sacrifices partners in the altar? [19]What do I imply then? That food offered to idols is anything, or that an idol is anything? [20]No, I imply that what pagans sacrifice they offer to demons and not to God. I do not want you to be partners with demons. [21]You cannot drink the cup of the Lord and the cup of demons. You cannot partake of the table of the Lord and the table of demons. [22]Shall we provoke the Lord to jealousy? Are we stronger than he?

Gal 4:8–11 (§208)

[8]Formerly, when you did not know God, you were in bondage to beings that by nature are no gods; [9]but now that you have come to know God, or rather to be known by God, how can you turn back again to the weak and beggarly elemental spirits, whose slaves you want to be once more? [10]You observe days, and months, and seasons, and years! [11]I am afraid I have labored over you in vain.

Phil 1:27–30 (§241)

[27]Only let your manner of life be worthy of the gospel of Christ, so that whether I come and see you or am absent, I may hear of you that you stand firm in one spirit, with one mind striving side by side for the faith of the gospel, [28]and not frightened in anything by your opponents. This is a clear omen to them of their destruction, but of your salvation, and that from God. [29]For it has been granted to you that for the sake of Christ you should not only believe in him but also suffer for his sake, [30]engaged in the same conflict which you saw and now hear to be mine.

Phil 3:17–21 (§249)

[17]Brethren, join in imitating me, and mark those who so live as you have an example in us. [18]For many, of whom I have often told you and now tell you even with tears, live as enemies of the cross of Christ. [19]Their end is destruction, their god is the belly, and they glory in their shame, with minds set on earthly things. [20]But our commonwealth is in heaven, and from it we await a Savior, the Lord Jesus Christ, [21]who will change our lowly body to be like his glorious body, by the power which enables him even to subject all things to himself.

2 Thess 2:13–15 (§297)

[13]But we are bound to give thanks to God always for you, brethren beloved by the Lord, because God chose you from the beginning to be saved, through sanctification by the Spirit and belief in the truth. [14]To this he called you through our gospel, so that you may obtain the glory of our Lord Jesus Christ. [15]So then, brethren, stand firm and hold to the traditions which you were taught by us, either by word of mouth or by letter.

---

1 Thess 2　[13]And we also thank God constantly for this, that when you received the word of God which you heard from us, you accepted it not as the word of men but as what it really is, the word of God, which is at work in you believers.

Acts 13　[52]And the disciples were filled with joy and with the Holy Spirit.

● **1 Thess 1:6–7**
1 Cor 8　[1]We want you to know, brethren, about the grace of God which has been shown in the churches of Macedonia, [2]for in a severe test of affliction, their abundance of joy and their extreme poverty have overflowed in a wealth of liberality on their part.

● **1 Thess 1:6**
1 Cor 11　[1]Be imitators of me, as I am of Christ.

Phil 3　[17]Brethren, join in imitating me, and mark those who so live as you have an example in us.

1 Thess 2　[14]For you, brethren, became imitators of the churches of God in Christ Jesus which are in Judea; for you suffered the same things from your own countrymen as they did from the Jews, . . .

2 Thess 3　[7]For you yourselves know how you ought to imitate us; we were not idle when we were with you, [8]we did not eat any one's bread without paying, but with toil and labor we worked night and day, that we might not burden any of you. [9]It was not because we have not that right, but to give you in our conduct an example to imitate.

● **1 Thess 1:7**
2 Cor 9　[2]for I know your readiness, of which I boast about you to the people of Macedonia, saying that Achaia has been ready since last year; and your zeal has stirred up most of them.

● **1 Thess 1:8**
Rom 10　[18]But I ask, have they not heard? Indeed they have; for
"Their voice has gone out to all the earth,
and their words to the ends of the world."

● **1 Thess 1:9**
1 Cor 12　[2]You know that when you were heathen, you were led astray to dumb idols, however you may have been moved.

Acts 14　[15]"Men, why are you doing this? We also are men, of like nature with you, and bring you good news, that you should turn from these vain things to a living God who made the heaven and the earth and the sea and all that is in them."

● **1 Thess 1:10**
Rom 5　[9]Since, therefore, we are now justified by his blood, much more shall we be saved by him from the wrath of God.

Col 1　[5]because of the hope laid up for you in heaven. Of this you have heard before in the word of the truth, the gospel . . .

Phil 3　[20]But our commonwealth is in heaven, and from it we await a Savior, the Lord Jesus Christ, . . .

1 Thess 4　[14]For since we believe that Jesus died and rose again, even so, through Jesus, God will bring with him those who have fallen asleep.

Titus 2　[13]awaiting our blessed hope, the appearing of the glory of our great God and Savior Jesus Christ, . . .

Acts 2　[24]"But God raised him up, having loosed the pangs of death, because it was not possible for him to be held by it."

2 For you yourselves know, brethren, that our visit to you was not in vain; [2]but though we had already suffered and been shamefully treated at Philippi, as you know, we had courage in our God to declare to you the gospel of God in the face of great opposition. [3]For our appeal does not spring from error or uncleanness, nor is it made with guile; [4]but just as we have been approved by God to be entrusted with the gospel, so we speak, not to please men, but to please God who tests our hearts. [5]For we never used either words of flattery, as you know, or a cloak for greed, as God is witness; [6]nor did we seek glory from men, whether from you or from others, though we might have made demands as apostles of Christ. [7]But we were gentle among you, like a nurse taking care of her children. [8]So, being affectionately desirous of you, we were ready to share with you not only the gospel of God but also our own selves, because you had become very dear to us.

PRIMARY

Rom 15:14–21 (§62)

[14]I myself am satisfied about you, my brethren, that you yourselves are full of goodness, filled with all knowledge, and able to instruct one another. [15]But on some points I have written to you very boldly by way of reminder, because of the grace given me by God [16]to be a minister of Christ Jesus to the Gentiles in the priestly service of the gospel of God, so that the offering of the Gentiles may be acceptable, sanctified by the Holy Spirit. [17]In Christ Jesus, then, I have reason to be proud of my work for God. [18]For I will not venture to speak of anything except what Christ has wrought through me to win obedience from the Gentiles, by word and deed, [19]by the power of signs and wonders, by the power of the Holy Spirit, so that from Jerusalem and as far round as Illyricum I have fully preached the gospel of Christ, [20]thus making it my ambition to preach the gospel, not where Christ has already been named, lest I build on another man's foundation, [21]but as it is written,

"They shall see who have never been told of him,
and they shall understand who have never heard of him."

Rom 16:17–20a (§67)

[17]I appeal to you, brethren, to take note of those who create dissensions and difficulties, in opposition to the doctrine which you have been taught; avoid them. [18]For such persons do not serve our Lord Christ, but their own appetites, and by fair and flattering words they deceive the hearts of the simple-minded. [19]For while your obedience is known to all, so that I rejoice over you, I would have you wise as to what is good and guileless as to what is evil; [20]then the God of peace will soon crush Satan under your feet.

1 Cor 4:14–21 (§86)

[14]I do not write this to make you ashamed, but to admonish you as my beloved children. [15]For though you have countless guides in Christ, you do not have many fathers. For I became your father in Christ Jesus through the gospel. [16]I urge you, then, be imitators of me. [17]Therefore I sent to you Timothy, my beloved and faithful child in the Lord, to remind you of my ways in Christ, as I teach them everywhere in every church. [18]Some are arrogant, as though I were not coming to you. [19]But I will come to you soon, if the Lord wills, and I will find out not the talk of these arrogant people but their power. [20]For the kingdom of God does not consist in talk but in power. [21]What do you wish? Shall I come to you with a rod, or with love in a spirit of gentleness?

1 Cor 9:15–18 (§106)

[15]But I have made no use of any of these rights, nor am I writing this to secure any such provision. For I would rather die than have any one deprive me of my ground for boasting. [16]For if I preach the gospel, that gives me no ground for boasting. For necessity is laid upon me. Woe to me if I do not preach the gospel! [17]For if I do this of my own will, I have a reward; but if not of my own will, I am entrusted with a commission. [18]What then is my reward? Just this: that in my preaching I may make the gospel free of charge, not making full use of my right in the gospel.

2 Cor 2:14–17 (§153)

[14]But thanks be to God, who in Christ always leads us in triumph, and through us spreads the fragrance of the knowledge of him everywhere. [15]For we are the aroma of Christ to God among those who are being saved and among those who are perishing, [16]to one a fragrance from death to death, to the other a fragrance from life to life. Who is sufficient for these things? [17]For we are not, like so many, peddlers of God's word; but as men of sincerity, as commissioned by God, in the sight of God we speak in Christ.

2 Cor 3:4–6 (§155)

[4]Such is the confidence that we have through Christ toward God. [5]Not that we are competent of ourselves to claim anything as coming from us; our competence is from God, [6]who has made us competent to be ministers of a new covenant, not in a written code but in the Spirit; for the written code kills, but the Spirit gives life.

2 Cor 4:1–6 (§158)

[1]Therefore, having this ministry by the mercy of God, we do not lose heart. [2]We have renounced disgraceful, underhanded ways; we refuse to practice cunning or to tamper with God's word, but by the open statement of the truth we would commend ourselves to every man's conscience in the sight of God. [3]And even if our gospel is veiled, it is veiled only to those who are perishing. [4]In their case the god of this world has blinded the minds of the unbelievers, to keep them from seeing the light of the gospel of the glory of Christ, who is the likeness of God. [5]For what we preach is not ourselves, but Jesus Christ as Lord, with ourselves as your servants for Jesus' sake. [6]For it is the God who said, "Let light shine out of darkness," who has shone in our hearts to give the light of the knowledge of the glory of God in the face of Christ.

2 Cor 6:1–10 (§165)

[1]Working together with him, then, we entreat you not to accept the grace of God in vain. [2]For he says,

"At the acceptable time I have listened to you,
and helped you on the day of salvation."

Behold, now is the acceptable time; behold, now is the day of salvation. [3]We put no obstacle in any one's way, so that no fault may be found with our ministry, [4]but as servants of God we commend ourselves in every way: through great endurance, in afflictions, hardships, ca-

---

● **1 Thess 2:1**

Acts 17   [1]Now when they had passed through Amphipolis and Apollonia they came to Thessalonica, where there was a synagogue of the Jews. [2]And Paul went in, as was his custom, and for three weeks he argued with them from the scriptures, . . .

● **1 Thess 2:2**

2 Cor 11   [21]. . . But whatever any one dares to boast of—I am speaking as a fool—I also dare to boast of that. [22]Are they Hebrews? So am I. Are they Israelites? So am I. Are they descendants of Abraham? So am I. [23]Are they servants of Christ? I am a better one—I am talking like a madman—with far greater labors, far more imprisonments, with countless beatings, and often near death. [24]Five times I have received at the

hands of the Jews the forty lashes less one. [25]Three times I have been beaten with rods; once I was stoned. Three times I have been shipwrecked; a night and a day I have been adrift at sea; [26]on frequent journeys, in danger from rivers, danger from robbers, danger from my own people, danger from Gentiles, danger in the city, danger in the wilderness, danger at sea, danger from false brethren; [27]in toil and hardship, through many a sleepless night, in hunger and thirst, often without food, in cold and exposure. [28]And, apart from other things, there is the daily pressure upon me of my anxiety for all the churches. [29]Who is weak, and I am not weak? Who is made to fall, and I am not indignant?

Acts 14   [5]When an attempt was made by both Gentiles and Jews, with their rulers, to molest them and to stone them, . . .

Acts 16   [19]But when her owners saw that their hope of gain was gone, they seized Paul and Silas and dragged them into the market place before the rulers; [20]and when they had brought them to the magistrates they said, "These men are Jews and they are disturbing our city. [21]They advocate customs which it is not lawful for us Romans to accept or practice." [22]The crowd joined in attacking them; and the magistrates tore the garments off them and gave orders to beat them with rods. [23]And when they had inflicted many blows upon them, they threw them into prison, charging the jailer to keep them safely. [24]Having received this charge, he put them into the inner prison and fastened their feet in the stocks.

lamities, [5]beatings, imprisonments, tumults, labors, watching, hunger; [6]by purity, knowledge, forbearance, kindness, the Holy Spirit, genuine love, [7]truthful speech, and the power of God; with the weapons of righteousness for the right hand and for the left; [8]in honor and dishonor, in ill repute and good repute. We are treated as impostors, and yet are true; [9]as unknown, and yet well known; as dying, and behold we live; as punished, and yet not killed; [10]as sorrowful, yet always rejoicing; as poor, yet making many rich; as having nothing, and yet possessing everything.

2 Cor 7:2–4 (§168)

[2]Open your hearts to us; we have wronged no one, we have corrupted no one, we have taken advantage of no one. [3]I do not say this to condemn you, for I said before that you are in our hearts, to die together and to live together. [4]I have great confidence in you; I have great pride in you; I am filled with comfort. With all our affliction, I am overjoyed.

2 Cor 10:1–6 (§176)

[1]I, Paul, myself entreat you, by the meekness and gentleness of Christ—I who am humble when face to face with you, but bold to you when I am away!—[2]I beg of you that when I am present I may not have to show boldness with such confidence as I count on showing against some who suspect us of acting in worldly fashion. [3]For though we live in the world we are not carrying on a worldly war, [4]for the weapons of our warfare are not worldly but have divine power to destroy strongholds. [5]We destroy arguments and every proud obstacle to the knowledge of God, and take every thought captive to obey Christ, [6]being ready to punish every disobedience, when your obedience is complete.

2 Cor 11:7–11 (§180)

[7]Did I commit a sin in abasing myself so that you might be exalted, because I preached God's gospel without cost to you? [8]I robbed other churches by accepting support from them in order to serve you. [9]And when I was with you and was in want, I did not burden any one, for my needs were supplied by the breth-

ren who came from Macedonia. So I refrained and will refrain from burdening you in any way. [10]As the truth of Christ is in me, this boast of mine shall not be silenced in the regions of Achaia. [11]And why? Because I do not love you? God knows I do!

2 Cor 12:14–18 (§187)

[14]Here for the third time I am ready to come to you. And I will not be a burden, for I seek not what is yours but you; for children ought not to lay up for their parents, but parents for their children. [15]I will most gladly spend and be spent for your souls. If I love you the more, am I to be loved the less? [16]But granting that I myself did not burden you, I was crafty, you say, and got the better of you by guile. [17]Did I take advantage of you through any of those whom I sent to you? [18]I urged Titus to go, and sent the brother with him. Did Titus take advantage of you? Did we not act in the same spirit? Did we not take the same steps?

Gal 4:12–20 (§209)

[12]Brethren, I beseech you, become as I am, for I also have become as you are. You did me no wrong; [13]you know it was because of a bodily ailment that I preached the gospel to you at first; [14]and though my condition was a trial to you, you did not scorn or despise me, but received me as an angel of God, as Christ Jesus. [15]What has become of the satisfaction you felt? For I bear you witness that, if possible, you would have plucked out your eyes and given them to me. [16]Have I then become your enemy by telling you the truth? [17]They make much of you, but for no good purpose; they want to shut you out, that you may make much of them. [18]For a good purpose it is always good to be made much of, and not only when I am present with you. [19]My little children, with whom I am again in travail until Christ be formed in you! [20]I could wish to be present with you now and to change my tone, for I am perplexed about you.

Phil 2:1–11 (§242)

[1]So if there is any encouragement in Christ, any incentive of love, any participation in the Spirit, any affection and sympathy, [2]complete my joy by being of the same mind, having the

same love, being in full accord and of one mind. [3]Do nothing from selfishness or conceit, but in humility count others better than yourselves. [4]Let each of you look not only to his own interests, but also to the interests of others. [5]Have this mind among yourselves, which is yours in Christ Jesus, [6]who, though he was in the form of God, did not count equality with God a thing to be grasped, [7]but emptied himself, taking the form of a servant, being born in the likeness of men. [8]And being found in human form he humbled himself and became obedient unto death, even death on a cross. [9]Therefore God has highly exalted him and bestowed on him the name which is above every name, [10]that at the name of Jesus every knee should bow, in heaven and on earth and under the earth, [11]and every tongue confess that Jesus Christ is Lord, to the glory of God the Father.

Col 2:4–7 (§261)

[4]I say this in order that no one may delude you with beguiling speech. [5]For though I am absent in body, yet I am with you in spirit, rejoicing to see your good order and the firmness of your faith in Christ.

[6]As therefore you received Christ Jesus the Lord, so live in him, [7]rooted and built up in him and established in the faith, just as you were taught, abounding in thanksgiving.

Phlm 8–14 (§307)

[8]Accordingly, though I am bold enough in Christ to command you to do what is required, [9]yet for love's sake I prefer to appeal to you—I, Paul, an ambassador and now a prisoner also for Christ Jesus— [10]I appeal to you for my child, Onesimus, whose father I have become in my imprisonment. [11](Formerly he was useless to you, but now he is indeed useful to you and to me.) [12]I am sending him back to you, sending my very heart. [13]I would have been glad to keep him with me, in order that he might serve me on your behalf during my imprisonment for the gospel; [14]but I preferred to do nothing without your consent in order that your goodness might not be by compulsion but of your own free will.

● **1 Thess 2:4**

1 Cor 4   [5]Therefore do not pronounce judgment before the time, before the Lord comes, who will bring to light the things now hidden in darkness and will disclose the purposes of the heart. Then every man will receive his commendation from God.

Gal 1   [10]Am I now seeking the favor of men, or of God? Or am I trying to please men? If I were still pleasing men, I should not be a servant of Christ.

Eph 3   [2]assuming that you have heard of the stewardship of God's grace that was given to me for you, . . .

1 Tim 1   [11]in accordance with the glorious gospel of the blessed God with which I have been entrusted.

● **1 Thess 2:5**

Acts 20   [33]"I coveted no one's silver or gold or apparel."

● **1 Thess 2:6**

Phlm   [8]Accordingly, though I am bold enough in Christ to command you to do what is required, . . .

● **1 Thess 2:7**

2 Tim 2   [24]And the Lord's servant must not be quarrelsome but kindly to every one, an apt teacher, forbearing, [25]correcting his opponents with gentleness.

Cf. 1 Cor 3   [2]I fed you with milk, not solid food; for you were not ready for it; and even yet you are not ready, . . .

Cf. 1 Cor 14   [20]Brethren, do not be children in your thinking; be babes in evil, but in thinking be mature.

Cf. 2 Cor 6   [13]In return—I speak as to children— widen your hearts also.

Cf. Gal 4   [19]My little children, with whom I am again in travail until Christ be formed in you!

Cf. Eph 5   [1]Therefore be imitators of God, as beloved children.

(gentle) *read* babes: p[65] SBC*D*G it vg cop(bo) Clement; *text:* AC[2]D[e] Koine Lect syr cop(sa) Clement

⁹For you remember our labor and toil, brethren; we worked night and day, that we might not burden any of you, while we preached to you the gospel of God. ¹⁰You are witnesses, and God also, how holy and righteous and blameless was our behavior to you believers; ¹¹for you know how, like a father with his children, we exhorted each one of you and encouraged you and charged you ¹²to lead a life worthy of God, who calls you into his own kingdom and glory.

PRIMARY

1 Cor 4:14-21 (§86)

¹⁴I do not write this to make you ashamed, but to admonish you as my beloved children. ¹⁵For though you have countless guides in Christ, you do not have many fathers. For I became your father in Christ Jesus through the gospel. ¹⁶I urge you, then, be imitators of me. ¹⁷Therefore I sent to you Timothy, my beloved and faithful child in the Lord, to remind you of my ways in Christ, as I teach them everywhere in every church. ¹⁸Some are arrogant, as though I were not coming to you. ¹⁹But I will come to you soon, if the Lord wills, and I will find out not the talk of these arrogant people but their power. ²⁰For the kingdom of God does not consist in talk but in power. ²¹What do you wish? Shall I come to you with a rod, or with love in a spirit of gentleness?

1 Cor 9:1-14 (§105)

¹Am I not free? Am I not an apostle? Have I not seen Jesus our Lord? Are not you my workmanship in the Lord? ²If to others I am not an apostle, at least I am to you; for you are the seal of my apostleship in the Lord.

³This is my defense to those who would examine me. ⁴Do we not have the right to our food and drink? ⁵Do we not have the right to be accompanied by a wife, as the other apostles and the brothers of the Lord and Cephas? ⁶Or is it only Barnabas and I who have no right to refrain from working for a living? ⁷Who serves as a soldier at his own expense? Who plants a vineyard without eating any of its fruit? Who

tends a flock without getting some of the milk? ⁸Do I say this on human authority? Does not the law say the same? ⁹For it is written in the law of Moses, "You shall not muzzle an ox when it is treading out the grain." Is it for oxen that God is concerned? ¹⁰Does he not speak entirely for our sake? It was written for our sake, because the plowman should plow in hope and the thresher thresh in hope of a share in the crop. ¹¹If we have sown spiritual good among you, is it too much if we reap your material benefits? ¹²If others share this rightful claim upon you, do not we still more?

Nevertheless, we have not made use of this right, but we endure anything rather than put an obstacle in the way of the gospel of Christ. ¹³Do you not know that those who are employed in the temple service get their food from the temple, and those who serve at the altar share in the sacrificial offerings? ¹⁴In the same way, the Lord commanded that those who proclaim the gospel should get their living by the gospel.

2 Cor 1:12-14 (§148)

¹²For our boast is this, the testimony of our conscience that we have behaved in the world, and still more toward you, with holiness and godly sincerity, not by earthly wisdom but by the grace of God. ¹³For we write you nothing but what you can read and understand; I hope you will understand fully, ¹⁴as you have understood in part, that you can be proud of us as we can be of you, on the day of the Lord Jesus.

2 Cor 11:7-11 (§180)

⁷Did I commit a sin in abasing myself so that you might be exalted, because I preached God's gospel without cost to you? ⁸I robbed other churches by accepting support from them in order to serve you. ⁹And when I was with you and was in want, I did not burden any one, for my needs were supplied by the brethren who came from Macedonia. So I refrained and will refrain from burdening you in any way. ¹⁰As the truth of Christ is in me, this boast of mine shall not be silenced in the regions of Achaia. ¹¹And why? Because I do not love you? God knows I do!

Phil 4:10-20 (§253)

¹⁰I rejoice in the Lord greatly that now at length you have revived your concern for me; you were indeed concerned for me, but you had no opportunity. ¹¹Not that I complain of want; for I have learned, in whatever state I am, to be content. ¹²I know how to be abased, and I know how to abound; in any and all circumstances I have learned the secret of facing plenty and hunger, abundance and want. ¹³I can do all things in him who strengthens me.

¹⁴Yet it was kind of you to share my trouble. ¹⁵And you Philippians yourselves know that in the beginning of the gospel, when I left Macedonia, no church entered into partnership with me in giving and receiving except you only; ¹⁶for even in Thessalonica you sent me help once and again. ¹⁷Not that I seek the gift; but I seek the fruit which increases to your credit. ¹⁸I have received full payment, and more; I am filled, having received from Epaphroditus the gifts you sent, a fragrant offering, a sacrifice acceptable and pleasing to God. ¹⁹And my God will supply every need of yours according to his riches in glory in Christ Jesus. ²⁰To our God and Father be glory for ever and ever. Amen.

2 Thess 3:6-13 (§300)

⁶Now we command you, brethren, in the name of our Lord Jesus Christ, that you keep away from any brother who is living in idleness and not in accord with the tradition that you received from us. ⁷For you yourselves know how you ought to imitate us; we were not idle when we were with you, ⁸we did not eat any one's bread without paying, but with toil and labor we worked night and day, that we might not burden any of you. ⁹It was not because we have not that right, but to give you in our conduct an example to imitate. ¹⁰For even when we were with you, we gave you this command: If any one will not work, let him not eat. ¹¹For we hear that some of you are living in idleness, mere busybodies, not doing any work. ¹²Now such persons we command and exhort in the Lord Jesus Christ to do their work in quietness and to earn their own living. ¹³Brethren, do not be weary in well-doing.

● **1 Thess 2:9**
Rom 12   ¹I appeal to you therefore, brethren, by the mercies of God, to present your bodies as a living sacrifice, holy and acceptable to God, which is your spiritual worship.

1 Cor 4   ¹²and we labor, working with our own hands. When reviled, we bless; when persecuted, we endure; . . .

2 Cor 12   ¹³For in what were you less favored than the rest of the churches, except that I myself did not burden you? Forgive me this wrong!

● **1 Thess 2:10**
Rom 7   ¹²So the law is holy, and the commandment is holy and just and good.

1 Cor 1   ³⁰He is the source of your life in Christ Jesus, whom God made our wisdom, our righteousness and sanctification and redemption; . . .

Eph 1   ⁴even as he chose us in him before the foundation of the world, that we should be holy and blameless before him.

Eph 5   ²⁷that he might present the church to himself in splendor, without spot or wrinkle or any such thing, that she might be holy and without blemish.

Col 1   ²²he has now reconciled in his body of flesh by his death, in order to present you holy and blameless and irreproachable before him, . . .

1 Thess 5   ²³May the God of peace himself sanctify you wholly; and may your spirit and soul and body be kept sound and blameless at the coming of our Lord Jesus Christ.

● **1 Thess 2:11**
1 Cor 3   ²I fed you with milk, not solid food; for you were not ready for it; and even yet you are not ready, . . .

1 Cor 14   ²⁰Brethren, do not be children in your thinking; be babes in evil, but in thinking be mature.

1 Cor 6   ¹³In return—I speak as to children—widen your hearts also.

Gal 4   ¹⁹My little children, with whom I am again in travail until Christ be formed in you!

Eph 5   ¹Therefore be imitators of God, as beloved children.

1 Thess 2   ⁷But we were gentle among you, like a nurse taking care of her children.

Phlm   ¹⁰I appeal to you for my child, Onesimus, whose father I have become in my imprisonment.

[13]And we also thank God constantly for this, that when you received the word of God which you heard from us, you accepted it not as the word of men but as what it really is, the word of God, which is at work in you believers. [14]For you, brethren, became imitators of the churches of God in Christ Jesus which are in Judea; for you suffered the same things from your own countrymen as they did from the Jews, [15]who killed both the Lord Jesus and the prophets, and drove us out, and displease God and oppose all men [16]by hindering us from speaking to the Gentiles that they may be saved—so as always to fill up the measure of their sins. But God's wrath has come upon them at last!

PRIMARY

Rom 10:1-4 (§40)
[1]Brethren, my heart's desire and prayer to God for them is that they may be saved. [2]I bear them witness that they have a zeal for God, but it is not enlightened. [3]For, being ignorant of the righteousness that comes from God, and seeking to establish their own, they did not submit to God's righteousness. [4]For Christ is the end of the law, that every one who has faith may be justified.

Rom 11:25-32 (§49)
[25]Lest you be wise in your own conceits, I want you to understand this mystery, brethren: a hardening has come upon part of Israel, until the full number of the Gentiles come in, [26]and so all Israel will be saved; as it is written,

"The Deliverer will come from Zion,
he will banish ungodliness from Jacob";
[27]"and this will be my covenant with them
when I take away their sins."

[28]As regards the gospel they are enemies of God, for your sake; but as regards election they are beloved for the sake of their forefathers. [29]For the gifts and the call of God are irrevocable. [30]Just as you were once disobedient to God but now have received mercy because of their disobedience, [31]so they have now been disobedient in order that by the mercy shown to you they also may receive mercy. [32]For God has consigned all men to disobedience, that he may have mercy upon all.

1 Cor 1:18-25 (§74)
[18]For the word of the cross is folly to those who are perishing, but to us who are being saved it is the power of God. [19]For it is written,

"I will destroy the wisdom of the wise,
and the cleverness of the clever I will thwart."

[20]Where is the wise man? Where is the scribe? Where is the debater of this age? Has not God made foolish the wisdom of the world? [21]For since, in the wisdom of God, the world did not know God through wisdom, it pleased God through the folly of what we preach to save those who believe. [22]For Jews demand signs and Greeks seek wisdom, [23]but we preach Christ crucified, a stumbling block to Jews and folly to Gentiles, [24]but to those who are called, both Jews and Greeks, Christ the power of God and the wisdom of God. [25]For the foolishness of God is wiser than men, and the weakness of God is stronger than men.

Gal 1:6-12 (§194)
[6]I am astonished that you are so quickly deserting him who called you in the grace of Christ and turning to a different gospel— [7]not that there is another gospel, but there are some who trouble you and want to pervert the gospel of Christ. [8]But even if we, or an angel from heaven, should preach to you a gospel contrary to that which we preached to you, let him be accursed. [9]As we have said before, so now I say again, If any one is preaching to you a gospel contrary to that which you received, let him be accursed.

[10]Am I now seeking the favor of men, or of God? Or am I trying to please men? If I were still pleasing men, I should not be a servant of Christ.

[11]For I would have you know, brethren, that the gospel which was preached by me is not man's gospel. [12]For I did not receive it from man, nor was I taught it, but it came through a revelation of Jesus Christ.

Gal 1:13-14 (§195)
[13]For you have heard of my former life in Judaism, how I persecuted the church of God violently and tried to destroy it; [14]and I advanced in Judaism beyond many of my own age among my people, so extremely zealous was I for the traditions of my fathers.

Phil 3:17-21 (§249)
[17]Brethren, join in imitating me, and mark those who so live as you have an example in us. [18]For many, of whom I have often told you and now tell you even with tears, live as enemies of the cross of Christ. [19]Their end is destruction, their god is the belly, and they glory in their shame, with minds set on earthly things. [20]But our commonwealth is in heaven, and from it we await a Savior, the Lord Jesus Christ, [21]who will change our lowly body to be like his glorious body, by the power which enables him even to subject all things to himself.

● **1 Thess 2:13**
Rom 10 [14]But how are men to call upon him in whom they have not believed? And how are they to believe in him of whom they have never heard? And how are they to hear without a preacher?

Rom 10 [18]But I ask, have they not heard? Indeed they have; for
"Their voice has gone out to all the earth,
and their words to the ends of the world."

1 Thess 1 [5]for our gospel came to you not only in word, but also in power and in the Holy Spirit and with full conviction. You know what kind of men we proved to be among you for your sake.

Cf. 1 Thess 1:2; 1 Thess 3:9

● **1 Thess 2:14**
Gal 4 [12]Brethren, I beseech you, become as I am, for I also have become as you are. You did me no wrong; . . .

Acts 17 [5]But the Jews were jealous, and taking some wicked fellows of the rabble, they gathered a crowd, set the city in an uproar, and attacked the house of Jason, seeking to bring them out to the people.

Acts 17 [13]But when the Jews of Thessalonica learned that the word of God was proclaimed by Paul at Beroea also, they came there too, stirring up and inciting the crowds.

Cf. 1 Cor 1:22-23; 1 Cor 4:16-17; 1 Cor 11:1; Phil 3:17; 1 Thess 1:6

● **1 Thess 2:15**
Rom 10 [21]But of Israel he says, "All day long I have held out my hands to a disobedient and contrary people."

Cf. Rom 16:17-18

Acts 2 [23]". . . this Jesus, delivered up according to the difinite plan and foreknowledge of God, you crucified and killed by the hands of lawless men."

Acts 7 [52]"Which of the prophets did not your fathers persecute? And they killed those who announced beforehand the coming of the Righteous One, whom you have now betrayed and murdered."

Acts 21 [13]Then Paul answered, "What are you doing, weeping and breaking my heart? For I am ready not only to be imprisoned but even to die at Jerusalem for the name of the Lord Jesus."

● **1 Thess 2:15-16**
2 Thess 2 [4]who opposes and exalts himself against every so-called god or object of worship, so that he takes his seat in the temple of God, proclaiming himself to be God.

2 Thess 2 [8]And then the lawless one will be revealed, and the Lord Jesus will slay him with the breath of his mouth and destroy him by his appearing and his coming.

● **1 Thess 2:16**
Acts 9 [23]When many days had passed, the Jews plotted to kill him, . . .

Acts 13 [45]But when the Jews saw the multitudes, they were filled with jealousy, and contradicted what was spoken by Paul, and reviled him.

Acts 13 [50]But the Jews incited the devout women of high standing and the leading men of the city, and stirred up persecution against Paul and Barnabas, and drove them out of their district.

Acts 14 [2]But the unbelieving Jews stirred up the Gentiles and poisoned their minds against the brethren.

Acts 14 [5]When an attempt was made by both Gentiles and Jews, with their rulers, to molest them and to stone them, . . .

Acts 14 [19]But Jews came there from Antioch and Iconium; and having persuaded the people, they stoned Paul and dragged him out of the city, supposing that he was dead.

Cf. Rom 1:18

FORMAL ELEMENT: APOSTOLIC VISIT

¹⁷But since we were bereft of you, brethren, for a short time, in person not in heart, we endeavored the more eagerly and with great desire to see you face to face; ¹⁸because we wanted to come to you—I, Paul, again and again—but Satan hindered us. ¹⁹For what is our hope or joy or crown of boasting before our Lord Jesus at his coming? Is it not you? ²⁰For you are our glory and joy.

PRIMARY

See §63 for APOSTOLIC VISIT

SECONDARY

2 Cor 2:12–13 (§152)

¹²When I came to Troas to preach the gospel of Christ, a door was opened for me in the Lord; ¹³but my mind could not rest because I did not find my brother Titus there. So I took leave of them and went on to Macedonia.

2 Cor 7:5–13a (§169)

⁵For even when we came into Macedonia, our bodies had no rest but we were afflicted at every turn— fighting without and fear within. ⁶But God, who comforts the downcast, comforted us by the coming of Titus, ⁷and not only by his coming but also by the comfort with which he was comforted in you, as he told us of your longing, your mourning, your zeal for me, so that I rejoiced still more. ⁸For even if I made you sorry with my letter, I do not regret it (though I did regret it), for I see that that letter grieved you, though only for a while. ⁹As it is, I rejoice, not because you were grieved, but because you were grieved into repenting; for you felt a godly grief, so that you suffered no loss through us. ¹⁰For godly grief produces a repentance that leads to salvation and brings no regret, but worldly grief produces death. ¹¹For see what earnestness this godly grief has produced in you, what eagerness to clear yourselves, what indignation, what alarm, what longing, what zeal, what punishment! At every point you have proved yourselves guiltless in the matter. ¹²So although I wrote to you, it was not on account of the one who did the wrong, nor on account of the one who suffered the wrong, but in order that your zeal for us might be revealed to you in the sight of God. ¹³Therefore we are comforted.

● **1 Thess 2:17–18**

Rom 1   ¹¹For I long to see you, that I may impart to you some spiritual gift to strengthen you, . . .

Rom 1   ¹³I want you to know, brethren, that I have often intended to come to you (but thus far have been prevented), in order that I may reap some harvest among you as well as among the rest of the Gentiles.

Phil 1   ²⁶so that in me you may have ample cause to glory in Christ Jesus, because of my coming to you again.

Col 2   ¹For I want you to know how greatly I strive for you, and for those at Laodicea, and for all who have not seen my face, . . .

Col 2   ⁵For though I am absent in body, yet I am with you in spirit, rejoicing to see your good order and the firmness of your faith in Christ.

● **1 Thess 2:18**

Phil 2   ²⁴and I trust in the Lord that shortly I myself shall come also.

2 Thess 2   ⁹The coming of the lawless one by the activity of Satan will be with all power and with pretended signs and wonders, . . .

● **1 Thess 2:19**

1 Cor 15   ²³But each in his own order: Christ the first fruits, then at his coming those who belong to Christ.

Phil 2   ¹⁶holding fast the word of life, so that in the day of Christ I may be proud that I did not run in vain or labor in vain.

Phil 4   ¹Therefore, my brethren, whom I love and long for, my joy and crown, stand firm thus in the Lord, my beloved.

1 Thess 3   ¹³so that he may establish your hearts unblamable in holiness before our God and Father, at the coming of our Lord Jesus with all his saints.

1 Thess 4   ¹⁵For this we declare to you by the word of the Lord, that we who are alive, who are left until the coming of the Lord, shall not precede those who have fallen asleep.

1 Thess 5   ²³May the God of peace himself sanctify you wholly; and may your spirit and soul and body be kept sound and blameless at the coming of our Lord Jesus Christ.

2 Thess 1   ⁴Therefore we ourselves boast of you in the churches of God for your steadfastness and faith in all your persecutions and in the afflictions which you are enduring.

3 Therefore when we could bear it no longer, we were willing to be left behind at Athens alone, [2] and we sent Timothy, our brother and God's servant in the gospel of Christ, to establish you in your faith and to exhort you, [3] that no one be moved by these afflictions. You yourselves know that this is to be our lot. [4] For when we were with you, we told you beforehand that we were to suffer affliction; just as it has come to pass, and as you know. [5] For this reason, when I could bear it no longer, I sent that I might know your faith, for fear that somehow the tempter had tempted you and that our labor would be in vain.

PRIMARY

See §34 for HARDSHIPS LIST

1 Cor 16:10–12 (§140)

[10] When Timothy comes, see that you put him at ease among you, for he is doing the work of the Lord, as I am. [11] So let no one despise him. Speed him on his way in peace, that he may return to me; for I am expecting him with the brethren.

[12] As for our brother Apollos, I strongly urged him to visit you with the other brethren, but it was not at all his will to come now. He will come when he has opportunity.

2 Cor 1:3–11 (§147)

[3] Blessed be the God and Father of our Lord Jesus Christ, the Father of mercies and God of all comfort, [4] who comforts us in all our affliction, so that we may be able to comfort those who are in any affliction, with the comfort with which we ourselves are comforted by God. [5] For as we share abundantly in Christ's sufferings, so through Christ we share abundantly in comfort too. [6] If we are afflicted, it is for your comfort and salvation; and if we are comforted, it is for your comfort, which you experience when you patiently endure the same sufferings that we suffer. [7] Our hope for you is unshaken; for we know that as you share in our sufferings, you will also share in our comfort.

[8] For we do not want you to be ignorant, brethren, of the affliction we experienced in Asia; for we were so utterly, unbearably crushed that we despaired of life itself. [9] Why, we felt that we had received the sentence of death; but that was to make us rely not on ourselves but on God who raises the dead; [10] he delivered us from so deadly a peril, and he will deliver us; on him we have set our hope that he will deliver us again. [11] You also must help us by prayer, so that many will give thanks on our behalf for the blessing granted us in answer to many prayers.

2 Cor 7:5–13a (§169)

[5] For even when we came into Macedonia, our bodies had no rest but we were afflicted at every turn— fighting without and fear within. [6] But God, who comforts the downcast, comforted us by the coming of Titus, [7] and not only by his coming but also by the comfort with which he was comforted in you, as he told us of your longing, your mourning, your zeal for me, so that I rejoiced still more. [8] For even if I made you sorry with my letter, I do not regret it (though I did regret it), for I see that that letter grieved you, though only for a while. [9] As it is, I rejoice, not because you were grieved, but because you were grieved into repenting; for you felt a godly grief, so that you suffered no loss through us. [10] For godly grief produces a repentance that leads to salvation and brings no regret, but worldly grief produces death. [11] For see what earnestness this godly grief has produced in you, what eagerness to clear yourselves, what indignation, what alarm, what longing, what zeal, what punishment! At every point you have proved yourselves guiltless in the matter. [12] So although I wrote to you, it was not on account of the one who did the wrong, nor on account of the one who suffered the wrong, but in order that your zeal for us might be revealed to you in the sight of God. [13] Therefore we are comforted.

Phil 2:19–24 (§245)

[19] I hope in the Lord Jesus to send Timothy to you soon, so that I may be cheered by news of you. [20] I have no one like him, who will be genuinely anxious for your welfare. [21] They all look after their own interests, not those of Jesus Christ. [22] But Timothy's worth you know, how as a son with a father he has served with me in the gospel. [23] I hope therefore to send him just as soon as I see how it will go with me; [24] and I trust in the Lord that shortly I myself shall come also.

Phil 4:10–20 (§253)

[10] I rejoice in the Lord greatly that now at length you have revived your concern for me; you were indeed concerned for me, but you had no opportunity. [11] Not that I complain of want; for I have learned, in whatever state I am, to be content. [12] I know how to be abased, and I know how to abound; in any and all circumstances I have learned the secret of facing plenty and hunger, abundance and want. [13] I can do all things in him who strengthens me.

[14] Yet it was kind of you to share my trouble. [15] And you Philippians yourselves know that in the beginning of the gospel, when I left Macedonia, no church entered into partnership with me in giving and receiving except you only; [16] for even in Thessalonica you sent me help once and again. [17] Not that I seek the gift; but I seek the fruit which increases to your credit. [18] I have received full payment, and more; I am filled, having received from Epaphroditus the gifts you sent, a fragrant offering, a sacrifice acceptable and pleasing to God. [19] And my God will supply every need of yours according to his riches in glory in Christ Jesus. [20] To our God and Father be glory for ever and ever. Amen.

2 Thess 1:3–12 (§295)

[3] We are bound to give thanks to God always for you, brethren, as is fitting, because your faith is growing abundantly, and the love of every one of you for one another is increasing. [4] Therefore we ourselves boast of you in the churches of God for your steadfastness and faith in all your persecutions and in the afflictions which you are enduring.

[5] This is evidence of the righteous judgment of God, that you may be made worthy of the kingdom of God, for which you are suffering— [6] since indeed God deems it just to repay with affliction those who afflict you, [7] and to grant rest with us to you who are afflicted, when the Lord Jesus is revealed from heaven with his mighty angels in flaming fire, [8] inflicting vengeance upon those who do not know God and upon those who do not obey the gospel of our Lord Jesus. [9] They shall suffer the punishment of eternal destruction and exclusion from the presence of the Lord and from the glory of his might, [10] when he comes on that day to be glorified in his saints, and to be marveled at in all who have believed, because our testimony to you was believed. [11] To this end we always pray for you, that our God may make you worthy of his call, and may fulfil every good resolve and work of faith by his power, [12] so that the name of our Lord Jesus may be glorified in you, and you in him, according to the grace of our God and the Lord Jesus Christ.

● **1 Thess 3:1**
Acts 17   [15] Those who conducted Paul brought him as far as Athens; and receiving a command for Silas and Timothy to come to him as soon as possible, they departed.

● **1 Thess 3:2**
Acts 16   [1] And he came also to Derbe and to Lystra. A disciple was there, named Timothy, the son of a Jewish woman who was a believer; but his father was a Greek.

● **1 Thess 3:3**
2 Thess 1   [4] Therefore we ourselves boast of you in the churches of God for your steadfastness and faith in all your persecutions and in the afflictions which you are enduring.

Acts 9   [16] ". . . for I will show him how much he must suffer for the sake of my name."

Acts 14   [22] strengthening the souls of the disciples, exhorting them to continue in the faith, and saying that through many tribulations we must enter the kingdom of God.

Cf. 1 Cor 4:17; 1 Cor 16:10; Phil 2:19; 1 Thess 1:6; 1 Thess 2:14

● **1 Thess 3:5**
1 Cor 7   [5] Do not refuse one another except perhaps by agreement for a season, that you may devote yourselves to prayer; but then come together again, lest Satan tempt you through lack of self-control.

Phil 2   [16] holding fast the word of life, so that in the day of Christ I may be proud that I did not run in vain or labor in vain.

Cf. Eph 6:21–22; Col 4:7–9; 1 Cor 15:58; Gal 6:1

⁶But now that Timothy has come to us from you, and has brought us the good news of your faith and love and reported that you always remember us kindly and long to see us, as we long to see you—⁷for this reason, brethren, in all our distress and affliction we have been comforted about you through your faith; ⁸for now we live, if you stand fast in the Lord. ⁹For what thanksgiving can we render to God for you, for all the joy which we feel for your sake before our God, ¹⁰praying earnestly night and day that we may see you face to face and supply what is lacking in your faith?

PRIMARY

2 Cor 1:3-11 (§147)

³Blessed be the God and Father of our Lord Jesus Christ, the Father of mercies and God of all comfort, ⁴who comforts us in all our affliction, so that we may be able to comfort those who are in any affliction, with the comfort with which we ourselves are comforted by God. ⁵For as we share abundantly in Christ's sufferings, so through Christ we share abundantly in comfort too. ⁶If we are afflicted, it is for your comfort and salvation; and if we are comforted, it is for your comfort, which you experience when you patiently endure the same sufferings that we suffer. ⁷Our hope for you is unshaken; for we know that as you share in our sufferings, you will also share in our comfort.

⁸For we do not want you to be ignorant, brethren, of the affliction we experienced in Asia; for we were so utterly, unbearably crushed that we despaired of life itself. ⁹Why, we felt that we had received the sentence of death; but that was to make us rely not on ourselves but on God who raises the dead; ¹⁰he delivered us from so deadly a peril, and he will deliver us; on him we have set our hope that he will deliver us again. ¹¹You also must help us by prayer, so that many will give thanks on our behalf for the blessing granted us in answer to many prayers.

2 Cor 7:5-13a (§169)

⁵For even when we came into Macedonia, our bodies had no rest but we were afflicted at every turn— fighting without and fear within. ⁶But God, who comforts the downcast, comforted us by the coming of Titus, ⁷and not only by his coming but also by the comfort with which he was comforted in you, as he told us of your longing, your mourning, your zeal for me, so that I rejoiced still more. ⁸For even if I made you sorry with my letter, I do not regret it (though I did regret it), for I see that that letter grieved you, though only for a while. ⁹As it is, I rejoice, not because you were grieved, but because you were grieved into repenting; for you felt a godly grief, so that you suffered no loss through us. ¹⁰For godly grief produces a repentance that leads to salvation and brings no regret, but worldly grief produces death. ¹¹For see what earnestness this godly grief has produced in you, what eagerness to clear yourselves, what indignation, what alarm, what longing, what zeal, what punishment! At every point you have proved yourselves guiltless in the matter. ¹²So although I wrote to you, it was not on account of the one who did the wrong, nor on account of the one who suffered the wrong, but in order that your zeal for us might be revealed to you in the sight of God. ¹³Therefore we are comforted.

Phlm 4-7 (§306)

⁴I thank my God always when I remember you in my prayers, ⁵because I hear of your love and of the faith which you have toward the Lord Jesus and all the saints, ⁶and I pray that the sharing of your faith may promote the knowledge of all the good that is ours in Christ. ⁷For I have derived much joy and comfort from your love, my brother, because the hearts of the saints have been refreshed through you.

● 1 Thess 3:6

1 Cor 1   ¹¹For it has been reported to me by Chloe's people that there is quarreling among you, my brethren.

1 Cor 16   ¹⁰When Timothy comes, see that you put him at ease among you, for he is doing the work of the Lord, as I am. ¹¹So let no one despise him. Speed him on his way in peace, that he may return to me; for I am expecting him with the brethren.

Phil 1   ¹⁸What then? Only that in every way, whether in pretense or in truth, Christ is proclaimed; and in that I rejoice.

Phil 4   ¹Therefore, my brethren, whom I love and long for, my joy and crown, stand firm thus in the Lord, my beloved.

1 Thess 2   ⁸So, being affectionately desirous of you, we were ready to share with you not only the gospel of God but also our own selves, because you had become very dear to us.

Acts 18   ⁵When Silas and Timothy arrived from Macedonia, Paul was occupied with preaching, testifying to the Jews that the Christ was Jesus.

● 1 Thess 3:7-8

Rom 11   ²⁰That is true. They were broken off because of their unbelief, but you stand fast only through faith. So do not become proud, but stand in awe.

1 Cor 15   ¹Now I would remind you, brethren, in what terms I preached to you the gospel, which you received, in which you stand, . . .

● 1 Thess 3:7

2 Thess 1   ⁴Therefore we ourselves boast of you in the churches of God for your steadfastness and faith in all your persecutions and in the afflictions which you are enduring.

● 1 Thess 3:9

1 Thess 1   ²We give thanks to God always for you all, constantly mentioning you in our prayers, . . .

1 Thess 1   ⁵for our gospel came to you not only in word, but also in power and in the Holy Spirit and with full conviction. You know what kind of men we proved to be among you for your sake.

1 Thess 2   ¹³And we also thank God constantly for this, that when you received the word of God which you heard from us, you accepted it not as the word of men but as what it really is, the word of God, which is at work in you believers.

● 1 Thess 3:10

Rom 1   ¹¹For I long to see you, that I may impart to you some spiritual gift to strengthen you, ¹²that is, that we may be mutually encouraged by each other's faith, both yours and mine.

Col 1   ²⁴Now I rejoice in my sufferings for your sake, and in my flesh I complete what is lacking in Christ's afflictions for the sake of his body, that is, the church, . . .

Col 2   ¹For I want you to know how greatly I strive for you, and for those at Laodicea, and for all who have not seen my face, . . .

FORMAL ELEMENT: PRAYER

[11] Now may our God and Father himself, and our Lord Jesus, direct our way to you; [12] and may the Lord make you increase and abound in love to one another and to all men, as we do to you, [13] so that he may establish your hearts unblamable in holiness before our God and Father, at the coming of our Lord Jesus with all his saints.

PRIMARY

1 Thess 5:23–24 (§289)

[23] May the God of peace himself sanctify you wholly; and may your spirit and soul and body be kept sound and blameless at the coming of our Lord Jesus Christ. [24] He who calls you is faithful, and he will do it.

2 Thess 2:16–17 (§298)

[16] Now may our Lord Jesus Christ himself, and God our Father, who loved us and gave us eternal comfort and good hope through grace, [17] comfort your hearts and establish them in every good work and word.

2 Thess 3:16 (§302)

[16] Now may the Lord of peace himself give you peace at all times in all ways. The Lord be with you all.

SECONDARY

Rom 12:1–2 (§51)

[1] I appeal to you therefore, brethren, by the mercies of God, to present your bodies as a living sacrifice, holy and acceptable to God, which is your spiritual worship. [2] Do not be conformed to this world but be transformed by the renewal of your mind, that you may prove what is the will of God, what is good and acceptable and perfect.

1 Cor 1:4–9 (§72)

[4] I give thanks to God always for you because of the grace of God which was given you in Christ Jesus, [5] that in every way you were enriched in him with all speech and all knowledge— [6] even as the testimony to Christ was confirmed among you— [7] so that you are not lacking in any spiritual gift, as you wait for the revealing of our Lord Jesus Christ; [8] who will sustain you to the end, guiltless in the day of our Lord Jesus Christ. [9] God is faithful, by whom you were called into the fellowship of his Son, Jesus Christ our Lord.

Phil 4:4–7 (§251)

[4] Rejoice in the Lord always; again I will say, Rejoice. [5] Let all men know your forbearance. The Lord is at hand. [6] Have no anxiety about anything, but in everything by prayer and supplication with thanksgiving let your requests be made known to God. [7] And the peace of God, which passes all understanding, will keep your hearts and your minds in Christ Jesus.

Col 1:21–23 (§259)

[21] And you, who once were estranged and hostile in mind, doing evil deeds, [22] he has now reconciled in his body of flesh by his death, in order to present you holy and blameless and irreproachable before him, [23] provided that you continue in the faith, stable and steadfast, not shifting from the hope of the gospel which you heard, which has been preached to every creature under heaven, and of which I, Paul, became a minister.

● **1 Thess 3:11–13**

1 Thess 5   [23] May the God of peace himself sanctify you wholly; and may your spirit and soul and body be kept sound and blameless at the coming of our Lord Jesus Christ. [24] He who calls you is faithful, and he will do it.

● **1 Thess 3:12**

Gal 2   [10] only they would have us remember the poor, which very thing I was eager to do.

1 Thess 4   [9] But concerning love of the brethren you have no need to have any one write to you, for you yourselves have been taught by God to love one another; . . .

2 Thess 1   [3] We are bound to give thanks to God always for you, brethren, as is fitting, because your faith is growing abundantly, and the love of every one of you for one another is increasing.

● **1 Thess 3:13**

Eph 1   [4] even as he chose us in him before the foundation of the world, that we should be holy and blameless before him.

Eph 5   [27] that he might present the church to himself in splendor, without spot or wrinkle or any such thing, that she might be holy and without blemish.

Phil 1   [10] so that you may approve what is excellent, and may be pure and blameless for the day of Christ, . . .

1 Thess 2   [19] For what is our hope or joy or crown of boasting before our Lord Jesus at his coming? Is it not you?

1 Thess 4   [15] For this we declare to you by the word of the Lord, that we who are alive, who are left until the coming of the Lord, shall not precede those who have fallen asleep.

2 Thess 1   [7] and to grant rest with us to you who are afflicted, when the Lord Jesus is revealed from heaven with his mighty angels in flaming fire, . . .

2 Thess 1   [10] when he comes on that day to be glorified in his saints, and to be marveled at in all who have believed, because our testimony to you was believed.

LETTER STRUCTURE: APPEAL

4 Finally, brethren, we beseech and exhort you in the Lord Jesus, that as you learned from us how you ought to live and to please God, just as you are doing, you do so more and more. ²For you know what instructions we gave you through the Lord Jesus. ³For this is the will of God, your sanctification: that you abstain from unchastity; ⁴that each one of you know how to take a wife for himself in holiness and honor ⁵not in the passion of lust like heathen who do not know God; ⁶that no man transgress, and wrong his brother in this matter, because the Lord is an avenger in all these things, as we solemnly forewarned you. ⁷For God has not called us for uncleanness, but in holiness. ⁸Therefore whoever disregards this, disregards not man but God, who gives his Holy Spirit to you.

PRIMARY

See §51 for APPEAL

SECONDARY

Rom 2:6–11 (§8)

⁶For he will render to every man according to his works: ⁷to those who by patience in well-doing seek for glory and honor and immortality, he will give eternal life; ⁸but for those who are factious and do not obey the truth, but obey wickedness, there will be wrath and fury. ⁹There will be tribulation and distress for every human being who does evil, the Jew first and also the Greek, ¹⁰but glory and honor and peace for every one who does good, the Jew first and also the Greek. ¹¹For God shows no partiality.

1 Cor 6:12–20 (§92)

¹²"All things are lawful for me," but not all things are helpful. "All things are lawful for me," but I will not be enslaved by anything.

¹³"Food is meant for the stomach and the stomach for food"—and God will destroy both one and the other. The body is not meant for immorality, but for the Lord, and the Lord for the body. ¹⁴And God raised the Lord and will also raise us up by his power. ¹⁵Do you not know that your bodies are members of Christ? Shall I therefore take the members of Christ and make them members of a prostitute? Never! ¹⁶Do you not know that he who joins himself to a prostitute becomes one body with her? For, as it is written, "The two shall become one flesh." ¹⁷But he who is united to the Lord becomes one spirit with him. ¹⁸Shun immorality. Every other sin which a man commits is outside the body; but the immoral man sins against his own body. ¹⁹Do you not know that your body is a temple of the Holy Spirit within you, which you have from God? You are not your own; ²⁰you were bought with a price. So glorify God in your body.

1 Cor 7:1–7 (§93)

¹Now concerning the matters about which you wrote. It is well for a man not to touch a woman. ²But because of the temptation to immorality, each man should have his own wife and each woman her own husband. ³The husband should give to his wife her conjugal rights, and likewise the wife to her husband. ⁴For the wife does not rule over her own body, but the husband does; likewise the husband does not rule over his own body, but the wife does. ⁵Do not refuse one another except perhaps by agreement for a season, that you may devote yourselves to prayer; but then come together again, lest Satan tempt you through lack of self-control. ⁶I say this by way of concession, not of command. ⁷I wish that all were as I myself am. But each has his own special gift from God, one of one kind and one of another.

1 Cor 7:12–16 (§96)

¹²To the rest I say, not the Lord, that if any brother has a wife who is an unbeliever, and she consents to live with him, he should not divorce her. ¹³If any woman has a husband who is an

unbeliever, and he consents to live with her, she should not divorce him. ¹⁴For the unbelieving husband is consecrated through his wife, and the unbelieving wife is consecrated through her husband. Otherwise, your children would be unclean, but as it is they are holy. ¹⁵But if the unbelieving partner desires to separate, let it be so; in such a case the brother or sister is not bound. For God has called us to peace. ¹⁶Wife, how do you know whether you will save your husband? Husband, how do you know whether you will save your wife?

1 Cor 7:36–38 (§100)

³⁶If any one thinks that he is not behaving properly toward his betrothed, if his passions are strong, and it has to be, let him do as he wishes: let them marry—it is no sin. ³⁷But whoever is firmly established in his heart, being under no necessity but having his desire under control, and has determined this in his heart, to keep her as his betrothed, he will do well. ³⁸So that he who marries his betrothed does well; and he who refrains from marriage will do better.

Phil 4:8–9 (§252)

⁸Finally, brethren, whatever is true, whatever is honorable, whatever is just, whatever is pure, whatever is lovely, whatever is gracious, if there is any excellence, if there is anything worthy of praise, think about these things. ⁹What you have learned and received and heard and seen in me, do; and the God of peace will be with you.

Col 1:21–23 (§259)

²¹And you, who once were estranged and hostile in mind, doing evil deeds, ²²he has now reconciled in his body of flesh by his death, in order to present you holy and blameless and irreproachable before him, ²³provided that you continue in the faith, stable and steadfast, not shifting from the hope of the gospel which you heard, which has been preached to every creature under heaven, and of which I, Paul, became a minister.

● **1 Thess 4:1**

1 Cor 7   ³²I want you to be free from anxieties. The unmarried man is anxious about the affairs of the Lord, how to please the Lord; . . .

1 Thess 4   ¹⁰and indeed you do love all the brethren throughout Macedonia. But we exhort you, brethren, to do so more and more, . . .

● **1 Thess 4:5**

1 Cor 15   ³⁴Come to your right mind, and sin no more. For some have no knowledge of God. I say this to your shame.

Gal 4   ⁸Formerly, when you did not know God, you were in bondage to beings that by nature are no gods; . . .

● **1 Thess 4:6**

1 Cor 5   ¹It is actually reported that there is immorality among you, and of a kind that is not found even among pagans; for a man is living with his father's wife.

● **1 Thess 4:8**

1 Cor 7   ¹⁷Only, let every one lead the life which the Lord has assigned to him, and in which God has called him. This is my rule in all the churches.

1 Cor 11   ¹⁶If any one is disposed to be contentious, we recognize no other practice, nor do the churches of God.

1 Cor 14   ³⁷If any one thinks that he is a prophet, or spiritual, he should acknowledge that what I am writing to you is a command of the Lord. ³⁸If any one does not recognize this, he is not recognized.

2 Thess 3   ¹⁴If any one refuses to obey what we say in this letter, note that man, and have nothing to do with him, that he may be ashamed.

Formal Element: Gnomic Sayings

[9]But concerning love of the brethren you have no need to have any one write to you, for you yourselves have been taught by God to love one another; [10]and indeed you do love all the brethren throughout Macedonia. But we exhort you, brethren, to do so more and more, [11]to aspire to live quietly, to mind your own affairs, and to work with your hands, as we charged you; [12]so that you may command the respect of outsiders, and be dependent on nobody.

Primary

See §53 for Gnomic Sayings

Secondary

Rom 13:8–10 (§55)

[8]Owe no one anything, except to love one another; for he who loves his neighbor has fulfilled the law. [9]The commandments, "You shall not commit adultery, You shall not kill, You shall not steal, You shall not covet," and any other commandment, are summed up in this sentence, "You shall love your neighbor as yourself." [10]Love does no wrong to a neighbor; therefore love is the fulfilling of the law.

Gal 5:13–15 (§212)

[13]For you were called to freedom, brethren; only do not use your freedom as an opportunity for the flesh, but through love be servants of one another. [14]For the whole law is fulfilled in one word, "You shall love your neighbor as yourself." [15]But if you bite and devour one another take heed that you are not consumed by one another.

Gal 6:1–6 (§214)

[1]Brethren, if a man is overtaken in any trespass, you who are spiritual should restore him in a spirit of gentleness. Look to yourself, lest you too be tempted. [2]Bear one another's burdens, and so fulfil the law of Christ. [3]For if any one thinks he is something, when he is nothing, he deceives himself. [4]But let each one test his own work, and then his reason to boast will be in himself alone and not in his neighbor. [5]For each man will have to bear his own load.

[6]Let him who is taught the word share all good things with him who teaches.

Col 4:5–6 (§270)

[5]Conduct yourselves wisely toward outsiders, making the most of the time. [6]Let your speech always be gracious, seasoned with salt, so that you may know how you ought to answer every one.

2 Thess 3:6–13 (§300)

[6]Now we command you, brethren, in the name of our Lord Jesus Christ, that you keep away from any brother who is living in idleness and not in accord with the tradition that you received from us. [7]For you yourselves know how you ought to imitate us; we were not idle when we were with you, [8]we did not eat any one's bread without paying, but with toil and labor we worked night and day, that we might not burden any of you. [9]It was not because we have not that right, but to give you in our conduct an example to imitate. [10]For even when we were with you, we gave you this command: If any one will not work, let him not eat. [11]For we hear that some of you are living in idleness, mere busybodies, not doing any work. [12]Now such persons we command and exhort in the Lord Jesus Christ to do their work in quietness and to earn their own living. [13]Brethren, do not be weary in well-doing.

● **1 Thess 4:9**

2 Cor 9   [1]Now it is superfluous for me to write to you about the offering for the saints, . . .

1 Thess 3   [12]and may the Lord make you increase and abound in love to one another and to all men, as we do to you, . . .

1 Thess 5   [1]But as to the times and the seasons, brethren, you have no need to have anything written to you.

Cf. 2 Cor 6   [6]by purity, knowledge, forbearance, kindness, the Holy Spirit, genuine love, . . .

Cf. Gal 5   [6]For in Christ Jesus neither circumcision nor uncircumcision is of any avail, but faith working through love.

Cf. Gal 5   [22]But the fruit of the Spirit is love, joy, peace, patience, kindness, goodness, faithfulness, . . .

Cf. Col 3   [14]And above all these put on love, which binds everything together in perfect harmony.

Cf. Phlm   [9]yet for love's sake I prefer to appeal to you—I, Paul, an ambassador and now a prisoner also for Christ Jesus . . .

● **1 Thess 4:10**

1 Thess 4   [1]Finally, brethren, we beseech and exhort you in the Lord Jesus, that as you learned from us how you ought to live and to please God, just as you are doing, you do so more and more.

● **1 Thess 4:11–12**

1 Cor 10   [27]If one of the unbelievers invites you to dinner and you are disposed to go, eat whatever is set before you without raising any question on the ground of conscience.

1 Cor 10   [31]So, whether you eat or drink, or whatever you do, do all to the glory of God. [32]Give no offense to Jews or to Greeks or to the church of God, [33]just as I try to please all men in everything I do, not seeking my own advantage, but that of many, that they may be saved.

1 Tim 2   [2]for kings and all who are in high positions, that we may led a quiet and peaceable life, godly and respectful in every way.

Acts 20   [34]"You yourselves know that these hands ministered to my necessities, and to those who were with me. [35]In all things I have shown you that by so toiling one must help the weak, remembering the words of the Lord Jesus, how he said, 'It is more blessed to give than to receive.'"

● **1 Thess 4:11**

Eph 4   [28]Let the thief no longer steal, but rather let him labor, doing honest work with his hands, so that he may be able to give to those in need.

Acts 18   [3]and because he was of the same trade he stayed with them, and they worked, for by trade they were tentmakers.

● **1 Thess 4:12**

1 Cor 14   [23]If, therefore, the whole church assembles and all speak in tongues, and outsiders or unbelievers enter, will they not say that you are mad?

[13] But we would not have you ignorant, brethren, concerning those who are asleep, that you may not grieve as others do who have no hope. [14] For since we believe that Jesus died and rose again, even so, through Jesus, God will bring with him those who have fallen asleep. [15] For this we declare to you by the word of the Lord, that we who are alive, who are left until the coming of the Lord, shall not precede those who have fallen asleep. [16] For the Lord himself will descend from heaven with a cry of command, with the archangel's call, and with the sound of the trumpet of God. And the dead in Christ will rise first; [17] then we who are alive, who are left, shall be caught up together with them in the clouds to meet the Lord in the air; and so we shall always be with the Lord. [18] Therefore comfort one another with these words.

PRIMARY

1 Cor 15:12–28 (§132–133)

[12] Now if Christ is preached as raised from the dead, how can some of you say that there is no resurrection of the dead? [13] But if there is no resurrection of the dead, then Christ has not been raised; [14] if Christ has not been raised, then our preaching is in vain and your faith is in vain. [15] We are even found to be misrepresenting God, because we testified of God that he raised Christ, whom he did not raise if it is true that the dead are not raised. [16] For if the dead are not raised, then Christ has not been raised. [17] If Christ has not been raised, your faith is futile and you are still in your sins. [18] Then those also who have fallen asleep in Christ have perished. [19] If for this life only we have hoped in Christ, we are of all men most to be pitied.

[20] But in fact Christ has been raised from the dead, the first fruits of those who have fallen asleep. [21] For as by a man came death, by a man has come also the resurrection of the dead. [22] For as in Adam all die, so also in Christ shall all be made alive. [23] But each in his own order: Christ the first fruits, then at his coming those who belong to Christ. [24] Then comes the end, when he delivers the kingdom to God the Father after destroying every rule and every authority and power. [25] For he must reign until he has put all his enemies under his feet. [26] The last enemy to be destroyed is death. [27] "For God has put all things in subjection under his feet." But when it says, "All things are put in subjection under him," it is plain that he is excepted who put all things under him. [28] When all things are subjected to him, then the Son himself will also be subjected to him who put all things under him, that God may be everything to every one.

1 Cor 15:51–58 (§137)

[51] Lo! I tell you a mystery. We shall not all sleep, but we shall all be changed, [52] in a moment, in the twinkling of an eye, at the last trumpet. For the trumpet will sound, and the dead will be raised imperishable, and we shall be changed. [53] For this perishable nature must put on the imperishable, and this mortal nature must put on immortality. [54] When the perishable puts on the imperishable, and the mortal puts on immortality, then shall come to pass the saying that is written:

"Death is swallowed up in victory."

[55] "O death, where is thy victory?

O death, where is thy sting?" [56] The sting of death is sin, and the power of sin is the law. [57] But thanks be to God, who gives us the victory through our Lord Jesus Christ.

[58] Therefore, my beloved brethren, be steadfast, immovable, always abounding in the work of the Lord, knowing that in the Lord your labor is not in vain.

2 Cor 4:13–15 (§160)

[13] Since we have the same spirit of faith as he had who wrote, "I believed, and so I spoke," we

---

● **1 Thess 4:13**

Rom 8 [24] For in this hope we were saved. Now hope that is seen is not hope. For who hopes for what he sees? [25] But if we hope for what we do not see, we wait for it with patience.

Eph 2 [12] remember that you were at that time separated from Christ, alienated from the commonwealth of Israel, and strangers to the covenants of promise, having no hope and without God in the world.

● **1 Thess 4:14**

1 Thess 1 [10] and to wait for his Son from heaven, whom he raised from the dead, Jesus who delivers us from the wrath to come.

● **1 Thess 4:15**

Phil 1 [21] For to me to live is Christ, and to die is gain. [22] If it is to be life in the flesh, that means fruitful labor for me. Yet which I shall choose I cannot tell. [23] I am hard pressed between the two. My desire is to depart and be with Christ, for that is far better. [24] But to remain in the flesh is more necessary on your account. [25] Convinced of this, I know that I shall remain and continue with you all, for your progress and joy in the faith, [26] so that in me you may have ample cause to glory in Christ Jesus, because of my coming to you again.

1 Thess 2 [19] For what is our hope or joy or crown of boasting before our Lord Jesus at his coming? Is it not you?

too believe, and so we speak, [14]knowing that he who raised the Lord Jesus will raise us also with Jesus and bring us with you into his presence. [15]For it is all for your sake, so that as grace extends to more and more people it may increase thanksgiving, to the glory of God.

2 Cor 4:16–5:5 (§161)

[16]So we do not lose heart. Though our outer nature is wasting away, our inner nature is being renewed every day. [17]For this slight momentary affliction is preparing for us an eternal weight of glory beyond all comparison, [18]because we look not to the things that are seen but to the things that are unseen; for the things that are seen are transient, but the things that are unseen are eternal.

5 [1]For we know that if the earthly tent we live in is destroyed, we have a building from God, a house not made with hands, eternal in the heavens. [2]Here indeed we groan, and long to put on our heavenly dwelling, [3]so that by putting it on we may not be found naked. [4]For while we are still in this tent, we sigh with anxiety; not that we would be unclothed, but that we would be further clothed, so that what is mortal may be swallowed up by life. [5]He who has prepared us for this very thing is God, who has given us the Spirit as a guarantee.

Phil 3:17–21 (§249)

[17]Brethren, join in imitating me, and mark those who so live as you have an example in us. [18]For many, of whom I have often told you and now tell you even with tears, live as enemies of the cross of Christ. [19]Their end is destruction, their god is the belly, and they glory in their shame, with minds set on earthly things. [20]But our commonwealth is in heaven, and from it we await a Savior, the Lord Jesus Christ, [21]who will change our lowly body to be like his glorious body, by the power which enables him even to subject all things to himself.

Col 3:1–4 (§265)

[1]If then you have been raised with Christ, seek the things that are above, where Christ is, seated at the right hand of God. [2]Set your minds on things that are above, not on things that are on earth. [3]For you have died, and your life is hid with Christ in God. [4]When Christ who is our life appears, then you also will appear with him in glory.

2 Thess 2:1–12 (§296)

[1]Now concerning the coming of our Lord Jesus Christ and our assembling to meet him, we beg you, brethren, [2]not to be quickly shaken in mind or excited, either by spirit or by word, or by letter purporting to be from us, to the effect that the day of the Lord has come. [3]Let no one deceive you in any way; for that day will not come, unless the rebellion comes first, and the man of lawlessness is revealed, the son of perdition, [4]who opposes and exalts himself against every so-called god or object of worship, so that he takes his seat in the temple of God, proclaiming himself to be God. [5]Do you not remember that when I was still with you I told you this? [6]And you know what is restraining him now so that he may be revealed in his time. [7]For the mystery of lawlessness is already at work; only he who now restrains it will do so until he is out of the way. [8]And then the lawless one will be revealed, and the Lord Jesus will slay him with the breath of his mouth and destroy him by his appearing and his coming. [9]The coming of the lawless one by the activity of Satan will be with all power and with pretended signs and wonders, [10]and with all wicked deception for those who are to perish, because they refused to love the truth and so be saved. [11]Therefore God sends upon them a strong delusion, to make them believe what is false, [12]so that all may be condemned who did not believe the truth but had pleasure in unrighteousness.

---

1 Thess 3   [13]so that he may establish your hearts unblamable in holiness before our God and Father, at the coming of our Lord Jesus with all his saints.

1 Thess 5   [23]May the God of peace himself sanctify you wholly; and may your spirit and soul and body be kept sound and blameless at the coming of our Lord Jesus Christ.

● **1 Thess 4:16–17**
Eph 2   [4]But God, who is rich in mercy, out of the great love with which he loved us, [5]even when we were dead through our trespasses, made us alive together with Christ (by grace you have been saved), [6]and raised us up with him, and made us sit with him in the heavenly places in Christ Jesus, . . .

● **1 Thess 4:16**
2 Thess 1   [7]and to grant rest with us to you who are afflicted, when the Lord Jesus is revealed from heaven with his mighty angels in flaming fire, . . .

2 Thess 1   [10]when he comes on that day to be glorified in his saints, and to be marveled at in all who have believed, because our testimony to you was believed.

● **1 Thess 4:17**
Cf. Acts 8   [39]And when they came up out of the water, the Spirit of the Lord caught up Philip; and the eunuch saw him no more, and went on his way rejoicing.

Formal Element: "Watch!" "Stand!"

5 But as to the times and the seasons, brethren, you have no need to have anything written to you. ²For you yourselves know well that the day of the Lord will come like a thief in the night. ³When people say, "There is peace and security," then sudden destruction will come upon them as travail comes upon a woman with child, and there will be no escape. ⁴But you are not in darkness, brethren, for that day to surprise you like a thief. ⁵For you are all sons of light and sons of the day; we are not of the night or of darkness. ⁶So then let us not sleep, as others do, but let us keep awake and be sober. ⁷For those who sleep sleep at night, and those who get drunk are drunk at night. ⁸But, since we belong to the day, let us be sober, and put on the breastplate of faith and love, and for a helmet the hope of salvation. ⁹For God has not destined us for wrath, but to obtain salvation through our Lord Jesus Christ, ¹⁰who died for us so that whether we wake or sleep we might live with him. ¹¹Therefore encourage one another and build one another up, just as you are doing.

Primary

See §56 for "Watch!" "Stand!"

Secondary

Rom 8:28–30 (§33)

²⁸We know that in everything God works for good with those who love him, who are called according to his purpose. ²⁹For those whom he foreknew he also predestined to be conformed to the image of his Son, in order that he might be the first-born among many brethren. ³⁰And those whom he predestined he also called; and those whom he called he also justified; and those whom he justified he also glorified.

Rom 9:19–29 (§38)

¹⁹You will say to me then, "Why does he still find fault? For who can resist his will?" ²⁰But who are you, a man, to answer back to God? Will what is molded say to its molder, "Why have you made me thus?" ²¹Has the potter no right over the clay, to make out of the same lump one vessel for beauty and another for menial use? ²²What if God, desiring to show his wrath and to make known his power, has endured with much patience the vessels of wrath made for destruction, ²³in order to make known the riches of his glory for the vessels of mercy, which he has prepared beforehand for glory, ²⁴even us whom he has called, not from the Jews only but also from the Gentiles? ²⁵As indeed he says in Hosea,

"Those who were not my people
I will call 'my people,'
and her who was not beloved
I will call 'my beloved.'"

²⁶"And in the very place where it was said to them, 'You are not my people,'
they will be called 'sons of the living God.'"

²⁷And Isaiah cries out concerning Israel: "Though the number of the sons of Israel be as the sand of the sea, only a remnant of them will be saved; ²⁸for the Lord will execute his sentence upon the earth with rigor and dispatch." ²⁹And as Isaiah predicted,

"If the Lord of hosts had not left us children,
we would have fared like Sodom and been
made like Gomorrah."

Rom 14:5–12 (§58)

⁵One man esteems one day as better than another, while another man esteems all days alike. Let every one be fully convinced in his own mind. ⁶He who observes the day, observes it in honor of the Lord. He also who eats, eats in honor of the Lord, since he gives thanks to God; while he who abstains, abstains in honor of the Lord and gives thanks to God. ⁷None of us lives to himself, and none of us dies to himself. ⁸If we live, we live to the Lord, and if we die, we die to the Lord; so then, whether we live or whether we die, we are the Lord's. ⁹For to this end Christ died and lived again, that he might be Lord both of the dead and of the living.

¹⁰Why do you pass judgment on your brother? Or you, why do you despise your brother? For we shall all stand before the judgment seat of God; ¹¹for it is written,

"As I live, says the Lord, every knee shall bow to me,
and every tongue shall give praise to God."

¹²So each of us shall give account of himself to God.

1 Cor 7:25–31 (§98)

²⁵Now concerning the unmarried, I have no command of the Lord, but I give my opinion as one who by the Lord's mercy is trustworthy. ²⁶I think that in view of the present distress it is well for a person to remain as he is. ²⁷Are you bound to a wife? Do not seek to be free. Are you free from a wife? Do not seek marriage. ²⁸But if you marry, you do not sin, and if a girl marries she does not sin. Yet those who marry will have worldly troubles, and I would spare you that. ²⁹I mean, brethren, the appointed time has grown very short; from now on, let those who have wives live as though they had none, ³⁰and those who mourn as though they were not mourning, and those who rejoice as though they were not rejoicing, and those who buy as though they had no goods, ³¹and those who deal with the world as though they had no dealings with it. For the form of this world is passing away.

2 Cor 10:1–6 (§176)

¹I, Paul, myself entreat you, by the meekness and gentleness of Christ—I who am humble when face to face with you, but bold to you when I am away!—²I beg of you that when I am present I may not have to show boldness with such confidence as I count on showing against some who suspect us of acting in worldly fashion. ³For though we live in the world we are not carrying on a worldly war, ⁴for the weapons of our warfare are not worldly but

---

● **1 Thess 5:1**
Acts 1   ⁷He said to them, "It is not for you to know times or seasons which the Father has fixed by his own authority."

● **1 Thess 5:2**
2 Cor 1   ¹⁴as you have understood in part, that you can be proud of us as we can be of you, on the day of the Lord Jesus.

Phil 1   ⁶And I am sure that he who began a good work in you will bring it to completion at the day of Jesus Christ.

Phil 1   ¹⁰so that you may approve what is excellent, and may be pure and blameless for the day of Christ, . . .

● **1 Thess 5:3**
Rom 8   ²²We know that the whole creation has been groaning in travail together until now; . . .

● **1 Thess 5:4**
Acts 26   ¹⁸"to open their eyes, that they may turn from darkness to light and from the power of Satan to God, that they may receive forgiveness of sins and a place among those who are sanctified by faith in me."

● **1 Thess 5:8**
1 Cor 13   ¹³So faith, hope, love abide, these three; but the greatest of these is love.

have divine power to destroy strongholds. [5]We destroy arguments and every proud obstacle to the knowledge of God, and take every thought captive to obey Christ, [6]being ready to punish every disobedience, when your obedience is complete.

Eph 1:3–23 (§219)
[3]Blessed be the God and Father of our Lord Jesus Christ, who has blessed us in Christ with every spiritual blessing in the heavenly places, [4]even as he chose us in him before the foundation of the world, that we should be holy and blameless before him. [5]He destined us in love to be his sons through Jesus Christ, according to the purpose of his will, [6]to the praise of his glorious grace which he freely bestowed on us in the Beloved. [7]In him we have redemption through his blood, the forgiveness of our trespasses, according to the riches of his grace [8]which he lavished upon us. [9]For he has made known to us in all wisdom and insight the mystery of his will, according to his purpose which he set forth in Christ [10]as a plan for the fulness of time, to unite all things in him, things in heaven and things on earth.

[11]In him, according to the purpose of him who accomplishes all things according to the counsel of his will, [12]we who first hoped in Christ have been destined and appointed to live for the praise of his glory. [13]In him you also, who have heard the word of truth, the gospel of your salvation, and have believed in him, were sealed with the promised Holy Spirit, [14]which is the guarantee of our inheritance until we acquire possession of it, to the praise of his glory.

[15]For this reason, because I have heard of your faith in the Lord Jesus and your love toward all the saints, [16]I do not cease to give thanks for you, remembering you in my prayers, [17]that the God of our Lord Jesus Christ, the Father of glory, may give you a spirit of wisdom and of revelation in the knowledge of him, [18]having the eyes of your hearts enlightened, that you may know what is the

hope to which he has called you, what are the riches of his glorious inheritance in the saints, [19]and what is the immeasurable greatness of his power in us who believe, according to the working of his great might [20]which he accomplished in Christ when he raised him from the dead and made him sit at his right hand in the heavenly places, [21]far above all rule and authority and power and dominion, and above every name that is named, not only in this age but also in that which is to come; [22]and he has put all things under his feet and has made him the head over all things for the church, [23]which is his body, the fulness of him who fills all in all.

Eph 5:3–14 (§230)
[3]But fornication and all impurity or covetousness must not even be named among you, as is fitting among saints. [4]Let there be no filthiness, nor silly talk, nor levity, which are not fitting; but instead let there be thanksgiving. [5]Be sure of this, that no fornicator or impure man, or one who is covetous (that is, an idolater), has any inheritance in the kingdom of Christ and of God. [6]Let no one deceive you with empty words, for it is because of these things that the wrath of God comes upon the sons of disobedience. [7]Therefore do not associate with them, [8]for once you were darkness, but now you are light in the Lord; walk as children of light [9](for the fruit of light is found in all that is good and right and true), [10]and try to learn what is pleasing to the Lord. [11]Take no part in the unfruitful works of darkness, but instead expose them. [12]For it is a shame even to speak of the things that they do in secret; [13]but when anything is exposed by the light it becomes visible, for anything that becomes visible is light. [14]Therefore it is said,

"Awake, O sleeper, and arise from the dead,
and Christ shall give you light."

Phil 2:14–18 (§244)
[14]Do all things without grumbling or questioning, [15]that you may be blameless and inno-

cent, children of God without blemish in the midst of a crooked and perverse generation, among whom you shine as lights in the world, [16]holding fast the word of life, so that in the day of Christ I may be proud that I did not run in vain or labor in vain. [17]Even if I am to be poured as a libation upon the sacrificial offering of your faith, I am glad and rejoice with you all. [18]Likewise you also should be glad and rejoice with me.

2 Thess 2:1–12 (§296)
[1]Now concerning the coming of our Lord Jesus Christ and our assembling to meet him, we beg you, brethren, [2]not to be quickly shaken in mind or excited, either by spirit or by word, or by letter purporting to be from us, to the effect that the day of the Lord has come. [3]Let no one deceive you in any way; for that day will not come, unless the rebellion comes first, and the man of lawlessness is revealed, the son of perdition, [4]who opposes and exalts himself against every so-called god or object of worship, so that he takes his seat in the temple of God, proclaiming himself to be God. [5]Do you not remember that when I was still with you I told you this? [6]And you know what is restraining him now so that he may be revealed in his time. [7]For the mystery of lawlessness is already at work; only he who now restrains it will do so until he is out of the way. [8]And then the lawless one will be revealed, and the Lord Jesus will slay him with the breath of his mouth and destroy him by his appearing and his coming. [9]The coming of the lawless one by the activity of Satan will be with all power and with pretended signs and wonders, [10]and with all wicked deception for those who are to perish, because they refused to love the truth and so be saved. [11]Therefore God sends upon them a strong delusion, to make them believe what is false, [12]so that all may be condemned who did not believe the truth but had pleasure in unrighteousness.

---

2 Cor 6 [7]truthful speech, and the power of God; with the weapons of righteousness for the right hand and for the left; . . .

Gal 5 [5]For through the Spirit, by faith, we wait for the hope of righteousness. [6]For in Christ Jesus neither circumcision nor uncircumcision is of any avail, but faith working through love.

Col 1 [4]because we have heard of your faith in Christ Jesus and of the love which you have for all the saints,

[5]because of the hope laid up for you in heaven. Of this you have heard before in the word of the truth, the gospel . . .

1 Thess 1 [3]remembering before our God and Father your work of faith and labor of love and steadfastness of hope in our Lord Jesus Christ.

● **1 Thess 5:9**
Rom 1 [18]For the wrath of God is revealed from heaven against all ungodliness and wickedness of men who by their wickedness suppress the truth.

Rom 3 [24]they are justified by his grace as a gift, through the redemption which is in Christ Jesus, . . .

Rom 6 [18]and, having been set free from sin, have become slaves of righteousness.

Rom 11 [32]For God has consigned all men to disobedience, that he may have mercy upon all.

Gal 3 [22]But the scripture consigned all things to sin, that what was promised to faith in Jesus Christ might be given to those who believe.

FORMAL ELEMENT: GNOMIC SAYINGS

[12]But we beseech you, brethren, to respect those who labor among you and are over you in the Lord and admonish you, [13]and to esteem them very highly in love because of their work. Be at peace among yourselves. [14]And we exhort you, brethren, admonish the idle, encourage the faint-hearted, help the weak, be patient with them all. [15]See that none of you repays evil for evil, but always seek to do good to one another and to all. [16]Rejoice always, [17]pray constantly, [18]give thanks in all circumstances; for this is the will of God in Christ Jesus for you. [19]Do not quench the Spirit, [20]do not despise prophesying, [21]but test everything; hold fast what is good, [22]abstain from every form of evil.

PRIMARY

See §53 for GNOMIC SAYINGS

SECONDARY

1 Cor 14:1–5 (§124)

[1]Make love your aim, and earnestly desire the spiritual gifts, especially that you may prophesy. [2]For one who speaks in a tongue speaks not to men but to God; for no one understands him, but he utters mysteries in the Spirit. [3]On the other hand, he who prophesies speaks to men for their upbuilding and encouragement and consolation. [4]He who speaks in a tongue edifies himself, but he who prophesies edifies the church. [5]Now I want you all to speak in tongues, but even more to prophesy. He who prophesies is greater than he who speaks in tongues, unless some one interprets, so that the church may be edified.

1 Cor 14:37–40 (§130)

[37]If any one thinks that he is a prophet, or spiritual, he should acknowledge that what I am writing to you is a command of the Lord.

[38]If any one does not recognize this, he is not recognized. [39]So, my brethren, earnestly desire to prophesy, and do not forbid speaking in tongues; [40]but all things should be done decently and in order.

1 Cor 16:15–18 (§142)

[15]Now, brethren, you know that the household of Stephanas were the first converts in Achaia, and they have devoted themselves to the service of the saints; [16]I urge you to be subject to such men and to every fellow worker and laborer. [17]I rejoice at the coming of Stephanas and Fortunatus and Achaicus, because they have made up for your absence; [18]for they refreshed my spirit as well as yours. Give recognition to such men.

Gal 6:1–6 (§214)

[1]Brethren, if a man is overtaken in any trespass, you who are spiritual should restore him in a spirit of gentleness. Look to yourself, lest you too be tempted. [2]Bear one another's burdens, and so fulfil the law of Christ. [3]For if any one thinks he is something, when he is nothing, he deceives himself. [4]But let each one test his own work, and then his reason to boast will be in himself alone and not in his neighbor. [5]For each man will have to bear his own load.

[6]Let him who is taught the word share all good things with him who teaches.

Eph 5:15–20 (§231)

[15]Look carefully then how you walk, not as unwise men but as wise, [16]making the most of the time, because the days are evil. [17]Therefore do not be foolish, but understand what the will of the Lord is. [18]And do not get drunk with wine, for that is debauchery; but be filled with the Spirit, [19]addressing one another in psalms and hymns and spiritual songs, singing and making melody to the Lord with all your heart, [20]always and for everything giving thanks in the name of our Lord Jesus Christ to God the Father.

2 Thess 3:6–13 (§300)

[6]Now we command you, brethren, in the name of our Lord Jesus Christ, that you keep away from any brother who is living in idleness and not in accord with the tradition that you received from us. [7]For you yourselves know how you ought to imitate us; we were not idle when we were with you, [8]we did not eat any one's bread without paying, but with toil and labor we worked night and day, that we might not burden any of you. [9]It was not because we have not that right, but to give you in our conduct an example to imitate. [10]For even when we were with you, we gave you this command: If any one will not work, let him not eat. [11]For we hear that some of you are living in idleness, mere busybodies, not doing any work. [12]Now such persons we command and exhort in the Lord Jesus Christ to do their work in quietness and to earn their own living. [13]Brethren, do not be weary in well-doing.

2 Thess 3:14–15 (§301)

[14]If any one refuses to obey what we say in this letter, note that man, and have nothing to do with him, that he may be ashamed. [15]Do not look on him as an enemy, but warn him as a brother.

Phlm 15–20 (§308)

[15]Perhaps this is why he was parted from you for a while, that you might have him back for ever, [16]no longer as a slave but more than a slave, as a beloved brother, especially to me but how much more to you, both in the flesh and in the Lord. [17]So if you consider me your partner, receive him as you would receive me. [18]If he has wronged you at all, or owes you anything, charge that to my account. [19]I, Paul, write this with my own hand, I will repay it—to say nothing of your owing me even your own self. [20]Yes, brother, I want some benefit from you in the Lord. Refresh my heart in Christ.

● **1 Thess 5:12–13**

1 Cor 9   [1]Am I not free? Am I not an apostle? Have I not seen Jesus our Lord? Are not you my workmanship in the Lord? [2]If to others I am not an apostle, at least I am to you; for you are the seal of my apostleship in the Lord.

Heb 13   [7]Remember your leaders, those who spoke to you the word of God; consider the outcome of their life, and imitate their faith.

Heb 13   [17]Obey your leaders and submit to them; for they are keeping watch over your souls, as men who will have to give account. Let them do this joyfully, and not sadly, for that would be of no advantage to you.

● **1 Thess 5:12**

1 Tim 5   [17]As for the rich in this world, charge them not to be haughty, nor to set their hopes on uncertain riches but on God who richly furnishes us with everything to enjoy.

FORMAL ELEMENT: PRAYER

[23]May the God of peace himself sanctify you wholly; and may your spirit and soul and body be kept sound and blameless at the coming of our Lord Jesus Christ. [24]He who calls you is faithful, and he will do it.

PRIMARY

1 Thess 3:11–13 (§283)

[11]Now may our God and Father himself, and our Lord Jesus, direct our way to you; [12]and may the Lord make you increase and abound in love to one another and to all men, as we do to you, [13]so that he may establish your hearts unblamable in holiness before our God and Father, at the coming of our Lord Jesus with all his saints.

2 Thess 2:16–17 (§298)

[16]Now may our Lord Jesus Christ himself, and God our Father, who loved us and gave us eternal comfort and good hope through grace, [17]comfort your hearts and establish them in every good work and word.

2 Thess 3:16 (§302)

[16]Now may the Lord of peace himself give you peace at all times in all ways. The Lord be with you all.

SECONDARY

1 Cor 1:4–9 (§72)

[4]I give thanks to God always for you because of the grace of God which was given you in Christ Jesus, [5]that in every way you were enriched in him with all speech and all knowledge— [6]even as the testimony to Christ was confirmed among you— [7]so that you are not lacking in any spiritual gift, as you wait for the revealing of our Lord Jesus Christ; [8]who will sustain you to the end, guiltless in the day of our Lord Jesus Christ. [9]God is faithful, by whom you were called into the fellowship of his Son, Jesus Christ our Lord.

● **1 Thess 5:23–24**

Rom 15   [13]May the God of hope fill you with all joy and peace in believing, so that by the power of the Holy Spirit you may abound in hope.

1 Thess 3   [11]Now may our God and Father himself, and our Lord Jesus, direct our way to you; [12]and may the Lord make you increase and abound in love to one another and to all men, as we do to you, [13]so that he may establish your hearts unblamable in holiness before our God and Father, at the coming of our Lord Jesus with all his saints.

● **1 Thess 5:23**

Rom 15   [33]The God of peace be with you all. Amen.

1 Cor 7   [15]But if the unbelieving partner desires to separate, let it be so; in such a case the brother or sister is not bound. For God has called us to peace.

1 Cor 14   [33]For God is not a God of confusion but of peace.

Col 1   [22]he has now reconciled in his body of flesh by his death, in order to present you holy and blameless and irreproachable before him, . . .

1 Thess 2   [10]You are witnesses, and God also, how holy and righteous and blameless was our behavior to you believers; . . .

1 Thess 2   [19]For what is our hope or joy or crown of boasting before our Lord Jesus at his coming? Is it not you?

1 Thess 4   [15]For this we declare to you by the word of the Lord, that we who are alive, who are left until the coming of the Lord, shall not precede those who have fallen asleep.

● **1 Thess 5:24**

2 Cor 1   [18]As surely as God is faithful, our word to you has not been Yes and No.

2 Cor 10   [13]But we will not boast beyond limit, but will keep to the limits God has apportioned us, to reach even to you.

FORMAL ELEMENT:
REQUEST FOR PRAYER

²⁵ Brethren, pray for us.

PRIMARY

Rom 15:30–33 (§64)

³⁰I appeal to you, brethren, by our Lord Jesus Christ and by the love of the Spirit, to strive together with me in your prayers to God on my behalf, ³¹that I may be delivered from the unbelievers in Judea, and that my service for Jerusalem may be acceptble to the saints, ³²so that by God's will I may come to you with joy and be refreshed in your company. ³³The God of peace be with you all. Amen.

Eph 6:18–20 (§234)

¹⁸Pray at all times in the Spirit, with all prayer and supplication. To that end keep alert with all perseverance, making supplication for all the saints, ¹⁹and also for me, that utterance may be given me in opening my mouth boldly to proclaim the mystery of the gospel, ²⁰for which I am an ambassador in chains; that I may declare it boldly, as I ought to speak.

Col 4:2–4 (§269)

²Continue steadfastly in prayer, being watchful in it with thanksgiving; ³and pray for us also, that God may open to us a door for the word, to declare the mystery of Christ, on account of which I am in prison, ⁴that I may make it clear, as I ought to speak.

2 Thess 3:1–5 (§299)

¹Finally, brethren, pray for us, that the word of the Lord may speed on and triumph, as it did among you, ²and that we may be delivered from wicked and evil men; for not all have faith. ³But the Lord is faithful; he will strengthen you and guard you from evil. ⁴And we have confidence in the Lord about you, that you are doing and will do the things which we command. ⁵May the Lord direct your hearts to the love of God and to the steadfastness of Christ.

● **1 Thess 5:25**

2 Cor 1　¹¹You also must help us by prayer, so that many will give thanks on our behalf for the blessing granted us in answer to many prayers.

Phil 4　⁶Have no anxiety about anything, but in everything by prayer and supplication with thanksgiving let your requests be made known to God.

Phlm　²²At the same time, prepare a guest room for me, for I am hoping through your prayers to be granted to you.

Heb 13　¹⁸Pray for us, for we are sure that we have a clear conscience, desiring to act honorably in all things. ¹⁹I urge you the more earnestly to do this in order that I may be restored to you the sooner.

LETTER STRUCTURE: GREETINGS

26 Greet all the brethren with a holy kiss.

PRIMARY

Rom 16:3–16 (§66)

3 Greet Prisca and Aquila, my fellow workers in Christ Jesus, 4 who risked their necks for my life, to whom not only I but also all the churches of the Gentiles give thanks; 5 greet also the church in their house. Greet my beloved Epaenetus, who was the first convert in Asia for Christ. 6 Greet Mary, who has worked hard among you. 7 Greet Andronicus and Junias, my kinsmen and my fellow prisoners; they are men of note among the apostles, and they were in Christ before me. 8 Greet Ampliatus, my beloved in the Lord. 9 Greet Urbanus, our fellow worker in Christ, and my beloved Stachys. 10 Greet Apelles, who is approved in Christ. Greet those who belong to the family of Aristobulus. 11 Greet my kinsman Herodion. Greet those in the Lord who belong to the family of Narcissus. 12 Greet those workers in the Lord, Tryphaena and Tryphosa. Greet the beloved Persis, who has worked hard in the Lord. 13 Greet Rufus, eminent in the Lord, also his mother and mine. 14 Greet Asyncritus, Phlegon, Hermes, Patrobas, Hermas, and the brethren who are with them. 15 Greet Philologus, Julia, Nereus and his sister, and Olympas, and all the saints who are with them. 16 Greet one another with a holy kiss. All the churches of Christ greet you.

Rom 16:21–23 (§69)

21 Timothy, my fellow worker, greets you; so do Lucius and Jason and Sosipater, my kinsmen.

22 I Tertius, the writer of this letter, greet you in the Lord.

23 Gaius, who is host to me and to the whole church, greets you. Erastus, the city treasurer, and our brother Quartus, greet you.

1 Cor 16:19–20 (§143)

19 The churches of Asia send greetings. Aquila and Prisca, together with the church in their house, send you hearty greetings in the Lord. 20 All the brethren send greetings. Greet one another with a holy kiss.

2 Cor 13:11–13 (§191)

11 Finally, brethren, farewell. Mend your ways, heed my appeal, agree with one another, live in peace, and the God of love and peace will be with you. 12 Greet one another with a holy kiss. 13 All the saints greet you.

Phil 4:21–22 (§254)

21 Greet every saint in Christ Jesus. The brethren who are with me greet you. 22 All the saints greet you, especially those of Caesar's household.

Col 4:10–15 (§272)

10 Aristarchus my fellow prisoner greets you, and Mark the cousin of Barnabas (concerning whom you have received instructions—if he comes to you, receive him), 11 and Jesus who is called Justus. These are the only men of the circumcision among my fellow workers for the kingdom of God, and they have been a comfort to me. 12 Epaphras, who is one of yourselves, a servant of Christ Jesus, greets you, always remembering you earnestly in his prayers, that you may stand mature and fully assured in all the will of God. 13 For I bear him witness that he has worked hard for you and for those in Laodicea and in Hierapolis. 14 Luke the beloved physician and Demas greet you. 15 Give my greetings to the brethren at Laodicea, and to Nympha and the church in her house.

Phlm 23–24 (§310)

23 Epaphras, my fellow prisoner in Christ Jesus, sends greetings to you, 24 and so do Mark, Aristarchus, Demas, and Luke, my fellow workers.

● **1 Thess 5:26**

2 Tim 4　19 Greet Prisca and Aquila, and the household of Onesiphorus. 20 Erastus remained at Corinth; Trophimus I left ill at Miletus. 21 Do your best to come before winter. Eubulus sends greetings to you, as do Pudens and Linus and Claudia and all the brethren.

Titus 3　15 All who are with me send greetings to you. Greet those who love us in the faith.

FORMAL ELEMENT:
ENFORCEMENT STATEMENT

27 I adjure you by the Lord that this letter be read to all the brethren.

PRIMARY

1 Cor 14:37-40 (§130)

37 If any one thinks that he is a prophet, or spiritual, he should acknowledge that what I am writing to you is a command of the Lord. 38 If any one does not recognize this, he is not recognized. 39 So, my brethren, earnestly desire to prophesy, and do not forbid speaking in tongues; 40 but all things should be done decently and in order.

Col 4:16-18a (§273)

16 And when this letter has been read among you, have it read also in the church of the Laodiceans; and see that you read also the letter from Laodicea. 17 And say to Archippus, "See that you fulfil the ministry which you have received in the Lord."

18 I, Paul, write this greeting with my own hand. Remember my fetters.

2 Thess 3:14-15 (§301)

14 If any one refuses to obey what we say in this letter, note that man, and have nothing to do with him, that he may be ashamed. 15 Do not look on him as an enemy, but warn him as a brother.

Phlm 21-22 (§309)

21 Confident of your obedience, I write to you, knowing that you will do even more than I say. 22 At the same time, prepare a guest room for me, for I am hoping through your prayers to be granted to you.

LETTER STRUCTURE: CLOSING GRACE

[28]**The grace of our Lord Jesus Christ be with you.**

PRIMARY

Rom 16:20b (§68)
The grace of our Lord Jesus Christ be with you.

1 Cor 16:23–24 (§145)
[23]The grace of the Lord Jesus be with you. [24]My love be with you all in Christ Jesus. Amen.

2 Cor 13:14 (§192)
[14]The grace of the Lord Jesus Christ and the love of God and the fellowship of the Holy Spirit be with you all.

Gal 6:18 (§217)
[18]The grace of our Lord Jesus Christ be with your spirit, brethren. Amen.

Eph 6:23–24 (§236)
[23]Peace be to the brethren, and love with faith, from God the Father and the Lord Jesus Christ. [24]Grace be with all who love our Lord Jesus Christ with love undying.

Phil 4:23 (§255)
[23]The grace of the Lord Jesus Christ be with your spirit.

Col 4:18b (§274)
Grace be with you.

2 Thess 3:18 (§304)
[18]The grace of our Lord Jesus Christ be with you all.

Phlm 25 (§311)
[25]The grace of the Lord Jesus Christ be with your spirit.

● **1 Thess 5:28**
1 Tim 6   [21]. . . Grace be with you.

2 Tim 4   [22]. . . Grace be with you.

Titus 3   [15]. . . Grace be with you all.

LETTER STRUCTURE: SALUTATION

1 **Paul, Silvanus, and Timothy,**
To the church of the Thessalonians in
God our Father and the Lord Jesus Christ:
²**Grace to you and peace from God the**
Father and the Lord Jesus Christ.

PRIMARY

Rom 1:1-7 (§1)
¹Paul, a servant of Jesus Christ, called to be
an apostle, set apart for the gospel of God
²which he promised beforehand through his
prophets in the holy scriptures, ³the gospel
concerning his Son, who was descended from
David according to the flesh ⁴and designated
Son of God in power according to the Spirit of
holiness by his resurrection from the dead,
Jesus Christ our Lord, ⁵through whom we have
received grace and apostleship to bring about
the obedience of faith for the sake of his name
among all the nations, ⁶including yourselves
who are called to belong to Jesus Christ;
⁷To all God's beloved in Rome, who are
called to be saints:
Grace to you and peace from God our
Father and the Lord Jesus Christ.

1 Cor 1:1-3 (§71)
¹Paul, called by the will of God to be an
apostle of Christ Jesus, and our brother
Sosthenes,
²To the church of God which is at Corinth,

to those sanctified in Christ Jesus, called to be
saints together with all those who in every place
call on the name of our Lord Jesus Christ, both
their Lord and ours:
³Grace to you and peace from God our
Father and the Lord Jesus Christ.

2 Cor 1:1-2 (§146)
¹Paul, an apostle of Christ Jesus by the will
of God, and Timothy our brother.
To the church of God which is at Corinth,
with all the saints who are in the whole of
Achaia:
²Grace to you and peace from God our
Father and the Lord Jesus Christ.

Gal 1:1-5 (§193)
¹Paul an apostle—not from men nor
through man, but through Jesus Christ and
God the Father, who raised him from the
dead— ²and all the brethren who are with me,
To the churches of Galatia:
³Grace to you and peace from God the
Father and our Lord Jesus Christ, ⁴who gave
himself for our sins to deliver us from the
present evil age, according to the will of our
God and Father; ⁵to whom be the glory for ever
and ever. Amen.

Eph 1:1-2 (§218)
¹Paul, an apostle of Christ Jesus by the will
of God,
To the saints who are also faithful in Christ
Jesus:

²Grace to you and peace from God our
Father and the Lord Jesus Christ.

Phil 1:1-2 (§237)
¹Paul and Timothy, servants of Christ Jesus,
To all the saints in Christ Jesus who are at
Philippi, with the bishops and deacons:
²Grace to you and peace from God our
Father and the Lord Jesus Christ.

Col 1:1-2 (§256)
¹Paul, an apostle of Christ Jesus by the will
of God, and Timothy our brother,
²To the saints and faithful brethren in
Christ at Colossae:
Grace to you and peace from God our
Father.

1 Thess 1:1 (§275)
¹Paul, Silvanus, and Timothy,
To the church of the Thessalonians in God the
Father and the Lord Jesus Christ:
Grace to you and peace.

Phlm 1-3 (§305)
¹Paul, a prisoner for Christ Jesus, and
Timothy our brother,
To Philemon our beloved fellow worker
²and Apphia our sister and Archippus our
fellow soldier, and the church in your house:
³Grace to you and peace from God our
Father and the Lord Jesus Christ.

● **1 Thess 1:1**
1 Tim 1 ¹Paul, an apostle of Christ Jesus by
command of God our Savior and of Christ Jesus our
hope,
²To Timothy, my true child in the faith:
Grace, mercy, and peace from God the Father and
Christ Jesus our Lord.

2 Tim 1 ¹Paul, an apostle of Christ Jesus by the will
of God according to the promise of the life which is in
Christ Jesus,
²To Timothy, my beloved child:
Grace, mercy, and peace from God the Father and
Christ Jesus our Lord.

Titus 1 ¹Paul, a servant of God and an apostle of
Jesus Christ, to further the faith of God's elect and
their knowledge of the truth which accords with
godliness, ²in hope of eternal life which God, who
never lies, promised ages ago ³and at the proper time
manifested in his word through the preaching with
which I have been entrusted by command of God our
Savior;
⁴To Titus, my true child in a common faith:
Grace and peace from God the Father and Christ
Jesus our Savior.

Acts 16 ¹And he came also to Derbe and to Lystra. A
disciple was there, named Timothy, the son of a
Jewish woman who was a believer; but his father was a
Greek.

Acts 17 ¹Now when they had passed through
Amphipolis and Apollonia they came to Thessalonica, where there was a synagogue of the Jews. ²And
Paul went in, as was his custom, and for three weeks he
argued with them from the scriptures, . . .

LETTER STRUCTURE: THANKSGIVING

³We are bound to give thanks to God always for you, brethren, as is fitting, because your faith is growing abundantly, and the love of every one of you for one another is increasing. ⁴Therefore we ourselves boast of you in the churches of God for your steadfastness and faith in all your persecutions and in the afflictions which you are enduring.

⁵This is evidence of the righteous judgment of God, that you may be made worthy of the kingdom of God, for which you are suffering—⁶since indeed God deems it just to repay with affliction those who afflict you, ⁷and to grant rest with us to you who are afflicted, when the Lord Jesus is revealed from heaven with his mighty angels in flaming fire, ⁸inflicting vengeance upon those who do not know God and upon those who do not obey the gospel of our Lord Jesus. ⁹They shall suffer the punishment of eternal destruction and exclusion from the presence of the Lord and from the glory of his might, ¹⁰when he comes on that day to be glorified in his saints, and to be marveled at in all who have believed, because our testimony to you was believed. ¹¹To this end we always pray for you, that our God may make you worthy of his call, and may fulfil every good resolve and work of faith by his power, ¹²so that the name of our Lord Jesus may be glorified in you, and you in him, according to the grace of our God and the Lord Jesus Christ.

PRIMARY

See §2 for THANKSGIVING

SECONDARY

2 Cor 1:3–11 (§147)

³Blessed be the God and Father of our Lord Jesus Christ, the Father of mercies and God of all comfort, ⁴who comforts us in all our affliction, so that we may be able to comfort those who are in any affliction, with the comfort with which we ourselves are comforted by God. ⁵For as we share abundantly in Christ's sufferings, so through Christ we share abundantly in comfort too. ⁶If we are afflicted, it is for your comfort and salvation; and if we are comforted, it is for your comfort, which you experience when you patiently endure the same sufferings that we suffer. ⁷Our hope for you is unshaken; for we know that as you share in our sufferings, you will also share in our comfort.

⁸For we do not want you to be ignorant, brethren, of the affliction we experienced in Asia; for we were so utterly, unbearably crushed that we despaired of life itself. ⁹Why, we felt that we had received the sentence of death; but that was to make us rely not on ourselves but on God who raises the dead; ¹⁰he delivered us from so deadly a peril, and he will deliver us; on him we have set our hope that he will deliver us again. ¹¹You also must help us by prayer, so that many will give thanks on our behalf for the blessing granted us in answer to many prayers.

Phil 1:27–30 (§241)

²⁷Only let your manner of life be worthy of the gospel of Christ, so that whether I come and see you or am absent, I may hear of you that you stand firm in one spirit, with one mind striving side by side for the faith of the gospel, ²⁸and not frightened in anything by your opponents. This is a clear omen to them of their destruction, but of your salvation, and that from God. ²⁹For it has been granted to you that for the sake of Christ you should not only believe in him but also suffer for his sake, ³⁰engaged in the same

conflict which you saw and now hear to be mine.

Phil 3:17–21 (§249)

¹⁷Brethren, join in imitating me, and mark those who so live as you have an example in us. ¹⁸For many, of whom I have often told you and now tell you even with tears, live as enemies of the cross of Christ. ¹⁹Their end is destruction, their god is the belly, and they glory in their shame, with minds set on earthly things. ²⁰But our commonwealth is in heaven, and from it we await a Savior, the Lord Jesus Christ, ²¹who will change our lowly body to be like his glorious body, by the power which enables him even to subject all things to himself.

Phil 4:10–20 (§253)

¹⁰I rejoice in the Lord greatly that now at length you have revived your concern for me; you were indeed concerned for me, but you had no opportunity. ¹¹Not that I complain of want; for I have learned, in whatever state I am, to be content. ¹²I know how to be abased, and I know how to abound; in any and all circumstances I have learned the secret of facing plenty and hunger, abundance and want. ¹³I can do all things in him who strengthens me.

¹⁴Yet it was kind of you to share my trouble. ¹⁵And you Philippians yourselves know that in the beginning of the gospel, when I left Macedonia, no church entered into partnership with me in giving and receiving except you only; ¹⁶for even in Thessalonica you sent me help once and again. ¹⁷Not that I seek the gift; but I seek the fruit which increases to your credit. ¹⁸I have received full payment, and more; I am filled, having received from Epaphroditus the gifts you sent, a fragrant offering, a sacrifice acceptable and pleasing to God. ¹⁹And my God will supply every need of yours according to his riches in glory in Christ Jesus. ²⁰To our God and Father be glory for ever and ever. Amen.

● **2 Thess 1:3**

1 Thess 3   ¹²and may the Lord make you increase and abound in love to one another and to all men, as we do to you, . . .

1 Thess 4   ⁹But concerning love of the brethren you have no need to have any one write to you, for you yourselves have been taught by God to love one another; . . .

Cf. 2 Thess 2:13

1 Tim 1   ²To Timothy, my true child in the faith: Grace, mercy, and peace from God the Father and Christ Jesus our Lord.

2 Tim 1   ³I thank God whom I serve with a clear conscience, as did my fathers, when I remember you constantly in my prayers.

Titus 1   ⁵This is why I left you in Crete, that you might amend what was defective, and appoint elders in every town as I directed you, . . .

● **2 Thess 1:4**

2 Cor 7   ⁴I have great confidence in you; I have great pride in you; I am filled with comfort. With all our affliction, I am overjoyed.

● **2 Thess 1:5–10**

Cf. Rom 12:14–21

● **2 Thess 1:5**

1 Thess 2   ¹²to lead a life worthy of God, who calls you into his own kingdom and glory.

Acts 14   ²²strengthening the souls of the disciples, exhorting them to continue in the faith, and saying that through many tribulations we must enter the kingdom of God.

● **2 Thess 1:6**

2 Cor 7   ⁵For even when we came into Macedonia, our bodies had no rest but we were afflicted at every turn—fighting without and fear within.

● **2 Thess 1:7**

1 Cor 3   ¹³each man's work will become manifest; for the Day will disclose it, because it will be revealed with fire, and the fire will test what sort of work each one has done.

1 Thess 3   ¹³so that he may establish your hearts unblamable in holiness before our God and Father, at the coming of our Lord Jesus with all his saints.

1 Thess 4   ¹⁶For the Lord himself will descend from

heaven with a cry of command, with the archangel's call, and with the sound of the trumpet of God. And the dead in Christ will rise first; . . .

Cf. 2 Thess 2:8

● **2 Thess 1:8**

Rom 2   ⁸but for those who are factious and do not obey the truth, but obey wickedness, there will be wrath and fury.

● **2 Thess 1:9**

Col 1   ¹¹May you be strengthened with all power, according to his glorious might, for all endurance and patience with joy, . . .

● **2 Thess 1:10**

1 Cor 15   ²³But each in his own order: Christ the first fruits, then at his coming those who belong to Christ.

1 Thess 2   ¹⁹For what is our hope or joy or crown of boasting before our Lord Jesus at his coming? Is it not you?

Cf. 1 Thess 5:23; 2 Thess 2:1; 2 Thess 2:8

● **2 Thess 1:11**

Cf. Gal 5:6

Letter Structure: Appeal
Formal Element: Gnomic Sayings

2 Now concerning the coming of our Lord Jesus Christ and our assembling to meet him, we beg you, brethren, [2]not to be quickly shaken in mind or excited, either by spirit or by word, or by letter purporting to be from us, to the effect that the day of the Lord has come. [3]Let no one deceive you in any way; for that day will not come, unless the rebellion comes first, and the man of lawlessness is revealed, the son of perdition, [4]who opposes and exalts himself against every so-called god or object of worship, so that he takes his seat in the temple of God, proclaiming himself to be God. [5]Do you not remember that when I was still with you I told you this? [6]And you know what is restraining him now so that he may be revealed in his time. [7]For the mystery of lawlessness is already at work; only he who now restrains it will do so until he is out of the way. [8]And then the lawless one will be revealed, and the Lord Jesus will slay him with the breath of his mouth and destroy him by his appearing and his coming. [9]The coming of the lawless one by the activity of Satan will be with all power and with pretended signs and wonders, [10]and with all wicked deception for those who are to perish, because they refused to love the truth and so be saved. [11]Therefore God sends upon them a strong delusion, to make them believe what is false, [12]so that all may be condemned who did not believe the truth but had pleasure in unrighteousness.

Primary

See §53 for Gnomic Sayings

Rom 12:1-2 (§51)
[1]I appeal to you therefore, brethren, by the mercies of God, to present your bodies as a living sacrifice, holy and acceptable to God, which is your spiritual worship. [2]Do not be conformed to this world but be transformed by the renewal of your mind, that you may prove what is the will of God, what is good and acceptable and perfect.

1 Cor 1:10-17 (§73)
[10]I appeal to you, brethren, by the name of our Lord Jesus Christ, that all of you agree and that there be no dissensions among you, but that you be united in the same mind and the same judgment. [11]For it has been reported to me by Chloe's people that there is quarreling among you, my brethren. [12]What I mean is that each one of you says, "I belong to Paul," or "I belong to Apollos," or "I belong to Cephas," or "I belong to Christ." [13]Is Christ divided? Was Paul crucified for you? Or were you baptized in the name of Paul? [14]I am thankful that I baptized none of you except Crispus and Gaius; [15]lest any one should say that you were baptized in my name. [16](I did baptize also the household of Stephanas. Beyond that, I do not know whether I baptized any one else.) [17]For Christ did not send me to baptize but to preach the gospel, and not with eloquent wisdom, lest the cross of Christ be emptied of its power.

2 Cor 10:1-6 (§176)
[1]I, Paul, myself entreat you, by the meekness and gentleness of Christ—I who am humble when face to face with you, but bold to you when I am away!—[2]I beg of you that when I am present I may not have to show boldness with such confidence as I count on showing against some who suspect us of acting in worldly fashion. [3]For though we live in the world we are not carrying on a worldly war, [4]for the weapons of our warfare are not worldly but have divine power to destroy strongholds. [5]We destroy arguments and every proud obstacle to the knowledge of God, and take every thought captive to obey Christ, [6]being ready to punish every disobedience, when your obedience is complete.

Eph 4:1-10 (§225)
[1]I therefore, a prisoner for the Lord, beg you to lead a life worthy of the calling to which you have been called, [2]with all lowliness and meekness, with patience, forbearing one another in love, [3]eager to maintain the unity of the Spirit in the bond of peace. [4]There is one body and one Spirit, just as you were called to the one hope that belongs to your call, [5]one Lord, one faith, one baptism, [6]one God and Father of us all, who is above all and through all and in all. [7]But grace was given to each of us according to the measure of Christ's gift. [8]Therefore it is said,

"When he ascended on high he led a host of captives,
and he gave gifts to men."

[9](In saying, "He ascended," what does it mean but that he had also descended into the lower parts of the earth? [10]He who descended is he who also ascended far above all the heavens, that he might fill all things.)

1 Thess 4:1-8 (§284)
[1]Finally, brethren, we beseech and exhort you in the Lord Jesus, that as you learned from us how you ought to live and to please God, just as you are doing, you do so more and more. [2]For you know what instructions we gave you through the Lord Jesus. [3]For this is the will of God, your sanctification: that you abstain from unchastity; [4]that each one of you know how to take a wife for himself in holiness and honor [5]not in the passion of lust like heathen who do not know God; [6]that no man transgress, and wrong his brother in this matter, because the Lord is an avenger in all these things, as we solemnly forewarned you. [7]For God has not called us for uncleanness, but in holiness. [8]Therefore whoever disregards this, disregards not man but God, who gives his Holy Spirit to you.

● 2 Thess 2:1
1 Thess 2 [19]For what is our hope or joy or crown of boasting before our Lord Jesus at his coming? Is it not you?

1 Thess 3 [13]so that he may establish your hearts unblamable in holiness before our God and Father, at the coming of our Lord Jesus with all his saints.

1 Thess 5 [23]May the God of peace himself sanctify you wholly; and may your spirit and soul and body be kept sound and blameless at the coming of our Lord Jesus Christ.

2 Thess 1 [10]when he comes on that day to be glorified in his saints, and to be marveled at in all who have believed, because our testimony to you was believed.

● 2 Thess 2:2
1 Cor 1 [8]who will sustain you to the end, guiltless in the day of our Lord Jesus Christ.

1 Cor 1 [14]I am thankful that I baptized none of you except Crispus and Gaius; . . .

1 Cor 5 [5]you are to deliver this man to Satan for the destruction of the flesh, that his spirit may be saved in the day of the Lord Jesus.

Phil 1 [6]And I am sure that he who began a good work in you will bring it to completion at the day of Jesus Christ.

Phil 1 [10]so that you may approve what is excellent, and may be pure and blameless for the day of Christ, . . .

Phil 2 [16]holding fast the word of life, so that in the day of Christ I may be proud that I did not run in vain or labor in vain.

2 Tim 2 [18]who have swerved from the truth by holding that the resurrection is past already. They are upsetting the faith of some.

● 2 Thess 2:3
1 Cor 7 [31]. . . For the form of this world is passing away.

Eph 5 [6]Let no one deceive you with empty words, for it is because of these things that the wrath of God comes upon the sons of disobedience.

1 Tim 4 [1]Now the Spirit expressly says that in later times some will depart from the faith by giving heed to deceitful spirits and doctrines of demons, . . .

● 2 Thess 2:4
1 Cor 8 [5]For although there may be so-called gods in heaven or on earth—as indeed there are many "gods" and many "lords"— [6]yet for us there is one God, the Father, from whom are all things and for whom we exist, and one Lord, Jesus Christ, through whom are all things and through whom we exist.

1 Cor 10 [7]Do not be idolaters as some of them were; as it is written, "The people sat down to eat and drink and rose up to dance."

● 2 Thess 2:5
1 Thess 3 [4]For when we were with you, we told you beforehand that we were to suffer affliction; just as it has come to pass, and as you know.

Acts 20 [29]"I know that after my departure fierce wolves will come in among you, not sparing the flock; [30]and from among your own selves will arise men speaking perverse things, to draw away the disciples after them."

Phlm 8–14 (§307)

[8]Accordingly, though I am bold enough in Christ to command you to do what is required, [9]yet for love's sake I prefer to appeal to you—I, Paul, an ambassador and now a prisoner also for Christ Jesus— [10]I appeal to you for my child, Onesimus, whose father I have become in my imprisonment. [11](Formerly he was useless to you, but now he is indeed useful to you and to me.) [12]I am sending him back to you, sending my very heart. [13]I would have been glad to keep him with me, in order that he might serve me on your behalf during my imprisonment for the gospel; [14]but I preferred to do nothing without your consent in order that your goodness might not be by compulsion but of your own free will.

SECONDARY

Rom 1:18–23 (§4)

[18]For the wrath of God is revealed from heaven against all ungodliness and wickedness of men who by their wickedness suppress the truth. [19]For what can be known about God is plain to them, because God has shown it to them. [20]Ever since the creation of the world his invisible nature, namely, his eternal power and deity, has been clearly perceived in the things that have been made. So they are without excuse; [21]for although they knew God they did not honor him as God or give thanks to him, but they became futile in their thinking and their senseless minds were darkened. [22]Claiming to be wise, they became fools, [23]and exchanged the glory of the immortal God for images resembling mortal man or birds or animals or reptiles.

1 Cor 15:20–28 (§133)

[20]But in fact Christ has been raised from the dead, the first fruits of those who have fallen asleep. [21]For as by a man came death, by a man has come also the resurrection of the dead. [22]For as in Adam all die, so also in Christ shall all be made alive. [23]But each in his own order: Christ the first fruits, then at his coming those who belong to Christ. [24]Then comes the end, when he delivers the kingdom to God the Father after destroying every rule and every authority and power. [25]For he must reign until he has put all his enemies under his feet. [26]The last enemy to be destroyed is death. [27]"For God has put all things in subjection under his feet." But when it says, "All things are put in subjection under him," it is plain that he is excepted who put all things under him. [28]When all things are subjected to him, then the Son himself will also be subjected to him who put all things under him, that God may be everything to every one.

2 Cor 11:12–15 (§181)

[12]And what I do I will continue to do, in order to undermine the claim of those who would like to claim that in their boasted mission they work on the same terms as we do. [13]For such men are false apostles, deceitful workmen, disguising themselves as apostles of Christ. [14]And no wonder, for even Satan disguises himself as an angel of light. [15]So it is not strange if his servants also disguise themselves as servants of righteousness. Their end will correspond to their deeds.

Eph 6:10–17 (§233)

[10]Finally, be strong in the Lord and in the strength of his might. [11]Put on the whole armor of God, that you may be able to stand against the wiles of the devil. [12]For we are not contending against flesh and blood, but against the principalities, against the powers, against the world rulers of this present darkness, against the spiritual hosts of wickedness in the heavenly places. [13]Therefore take the whole armor of God, that you may be able to withstand in the evil day, and having done all, to stand. [14]Stand therefore, having girded your loins with truth, and having put on the breastplate of righteous-ness, [15]and having shod your feet with the equipment of the gospel of peace; [16]besides all these, taking the shield of faith, with which you can quench all the flaming darts of the evil one. [17]And take the helmet of salvation, and the sword of the Spirit, which is the word of God.

Phil 3:17–21 (§249)

[17]Brethren, join in imitating me, and mark those who so live as you have an example in us. [18]For many, of whom I have often told you and now tell you even with tears, live as enemies of the cross of Christ. [19]Their end is destruction, their god is the belly, and they glory in their shame, with minds set on earthly things. [20]But our commonwealth is in heaven, and from it we await a Savior, the Lord Jesus Christ, [21]who will change our lowly body to be like his glorious body, by the power which enables him even to subject all things to himself.

1 Thess 4:13–18 (§286)

[13]But we would not have you ignorant, brethren, concerning those who are asleep, that you may not grieve as others do who have no hope. [14]For since we believe that Jesus died and rose again, even so, through Jesus, God will bring with him those who have fallen asleep. [15]For this we declare to you by the word of the Lord, that we who are alive, who are left until the coming of the Lord, shall not precede those who have fallen asleep. [16]For the Lord himself will descend from heaven with a cry of command, with the archangel's call, and with the sound of the trumpet of God. And the dead in Christ will rise first; [17]then we who are alive, who are left, shall be caught up together with them in the clouds to meet the Lord in the air; and so we shall always be with the Lord. [18]Therefore comfort one another with these words.

● 2 Thess 2:6

Rom 8   [18]I consider that the sufferings of this present time are not worth comparing with the glory that is to be revealed to us. [19]For the creation waits with eager longing for the revealing of the sons of God; [20]for the creation was subjected to futility, not of its own will but by the will of him who subjected it in hope; [21]because the creation itself will be set free from its bondage to decay and obtain the glorious liberty of the children of God. [22]We know that the whole creation has been groaning in travail together until now; [23]and not only the creation, but we ourselves, who have the first fruits of the Spirit, groan inwardly as we wait for adoption as sons, the redemption of our bodies.

● 2 Thess 2:8

Rom 2   [8]but for those who are factious and do not obey the truth, but obey wickedness, there will be wrath and fury. [9]There will be tribulation and distress for every human being who does evil, the Jew first and also the Greek, . . .

1 Thess 4   [16]For the Lord himself will descend from heaven with a cry of command, with the archangel's call, and with the sound of the trumpet of God. And the dead in Christ will rise first; . . .

2 Thess 1   [7]and to grant rest with us to you who are afflicted, when the Lord Jesus is revealed from heaven with his mighty angels in flaming fire, . . .

1 Tim 6   [14]I charge you to keep the commandment unstained and free from reproach until the appearing of our Lord Jesus Christ; . . .

2 Tim 1   [10]and now has manifested through the appearing of our Savior Christ Jesus, who abolished death and brought life and immortality to light through the gospel.

2 Tim 4   [1]I charge you in the presence of God and of Christ Jesus who is to judge the living and the dead, and by his appearing and his kingdom: . . .

2 Tim 4   [8]Henceforth there is laid up for me the crown of righteousness, which the Lord, the righteous judge, will award to me on that Day, and not only to me but also to all who have loved his appearing.

Titus 2   [13]awaiting our blessed hope, the appearing of the glory of our great God and Savior Jesus Christ.

● 2 Thess 2:9

2 Cor 4   [4]In their case the god of this world has blinded the minds of the unbelievers, to keep them from seeing the light of the gospel of the glory of Christ, who is the likeness of God.

2 Cor 12   [12]The signs of a true apostle were performed among you in all patience, with signs and wonders and mighty works.

● 2 Thess 2:10

Rom 1   [25]because they exchanged the truth about God for a lie and worshiped and served the creature rather than the Creator, who is blessed for ever! Amen.

1 Cor 1   [18]For the word of the cross is folly to those who are perishing, but to us who are being saved it is the power of God.

1 Tim 2   [4]who desires all men to be saved and to come to the knowledge of the truth.

● 2 Thess 2:11

Rom 11   [8]as it is written,
"God gave them a spirit of stupor,
eyes that should not see and ears that should not hear,
down to this very day."

2 Tim 4   [4]and will turn away from listening to the truth and wander into myths.

[13]But we are bound to give thanks to God always for you, brethren beloved by the Lord, because God chose you from the beginning to be saved, through sanctification by the Spirit and belief in the truth. [14]To this he called you through our gospel, so that you may obtain the glory of our Lord Jesus Christ. [15]So then, brethren, stand firm and hold to the traditions which you were taught by us, either by word of mouth or by letter.

PRIMARY

Rom 5:1-5 (§20)

[1]Therefore, since we are justified by faith, we have peace with God through our Lord Jesus Christ. [2]Through him we have obtained access to this grace in which we stand, and we rejoice in our hope of sharing the glory of God. [3]More than that, we rejoice in our sufferings, knowing that suffering produces endurance, [4]and endurance produces character, and character produces hope, [5]and hope does not disappoint us, because God's love has been poured into our hearts through the Holy Spirit which has been given to us.

1 Cor 1:4-9 (§72)

[4]I give thanks to God always for you because of the grace of God which was given you in Christ Jesus, [5]that in every way you were enriched in him with all speech and all knowledge— [6]even as the testimony to Christ was confirmed among you— [7]so that you are not lacking in any spiritual gift, as you wait for the revealing of our Lord Jesus Christ; [8]who will sustain you to the end, guiltless in the day of our Lord Jesus Christ. [9]God is faithful, by whom you were called into the fellowship of his Son, Jesus Christ our Lord.

1 Cor 16:13-14 (§141)

[13]Be watchful, stand firm in your faith, be courageous, be strong. [14]Let all that you do be done in love.

Eph 1:3-23 (§219)

[3]Blessed be the God and Father of our Lord Jesus Christ, who has blessed us in Christ with every spiritual blessing in the heavenly places, [4]even as he chose us in him before the foundation of the world, that we should be holy and blameless before him. [5]He destined us in love to be his sons through Jesus Christ, according to the purpose of his will, [6]to the praise of his glorious grace which he freely bestowed on us in the Beloved. [7]In him we have redemption through his blood, the forgiveness of our trespasses, according to the riches of his grace [8]which he lavished upon us. [9]For he has made known to us in all wisdom and insight the mystery of his will, according to his purpose which he set forth in Christ [10]as a plan for the fulness of time, to unite all things in him, things in heaven and things on earth.

[11]In him, according to the purpose of him who accomplishes all things according to the counsel of his will, [12]we who first hoped in Christ have been destined and appointed to live for the praise of his glory. [13]In him you also, who have heard the word of truth, the gospel of your salvation, and have believed in him, were sealed with the promised Holy Spirit, [14]which is the guarantee of our inheritance until we acquire possession of it, to the praise of his glory.

[15]For this reason, because I have heard of your faith in the Lord Jesus and your love toward all the saints, [16]I do not cease to give thanks for you, remembering you in my prayers, [17]that the God of our Lord Jesus Christ, the Father of glory, may give you a spirit of wisdom and of revelation in the knowledge of him, [18]having the eyes of your hearts enlightened, that you may know what is the hope to which he has called you, what are the riches of his glorious inheritance in the saints, [19]and what is the immeasurable greatness of his power in us who believe, according to the working of his great might [20]which he accomplished in Christ when he raised him from the dead and made him sit at his right hand in the heavenly places, [21]far above all rule and authority and power and dominion, and above every name that is named, not only in this age but also in that which is to come; [22]and he has put all things under his feet and has made him the head over all things for the church, [23]which is his body, the fulness of him who fills all in all.

Phil 4:8-9 (§252)

[8]Finally, brethren, whatever is true, whatever is honorable, whatever is just, whatever is pure, whatever is lovely, whatever is gracious, if there is any excellence, if there is anything worthy of praise, think about these things. [9]What you have learned and received and heard and seen in me, do; and the God of peace will be with you.

Col 1:15-20 (§258)

[15]He is the image of the invisible God, the first-born of all creation; [16]for in him all things were created, in heaven and on earth, visible and invisible, whether thrones or dominions or principalities or authorities—all things were created through him and for him. [17]He is before all things, and in him all things hold together. [18]He is the head of the body, the church; he is the beginning, the first-born from the dead, that in everything he might be preeminent. [19]For in him all the fulness of God was pleased to dwell, [20]and through him to reconcile to himself all things, whether on earth or in heaven, making peace by the blood of his cross.

Col 1:21-23 (§259)

[21]And you, who once were estranged and hostile in mind, doing evil deeds, [22]he has now reconciled in his body of flesh by his death, in order to present you holy and blameless and irreproachable before him, [23]provided that you continue in the faith, stable and steadfast, not shifting from the hope of the gospel which you heard, which has been preached to every creature under heaven, and of which I, Paul, became a minister.

Col 2:4-7 (§261)

[4]I say this in order that no one may delude you with beguiling speech. [5]For though I am absent in body, yet I am with you in spirit, rejoicing to see your good order and the firmness of your faith in Christ.

[6]As therefore you received Christ Jesus the Lord, so live in him, [7]rooted and built up in him and established in the faith, just as you were taught, abounding in thanksgiving.

1 Thess 5:1-11 (§287)

[1]But as to the times and the seasons, brethren, you have no need to have anything written to you. [2]For you yourselves know well that the day of the Lord will come like a thief in the night. [3]When people say, "There is peace and security," then sudden destruction will come upon them as travail comes upon a woman with child, and there will be no escape. [4]But you are not in darkness, brethren, for that day to surprise you like a thief. [5]For you are all sons of light and sons of the day; we are not of the night or of darkness. [6]So then let us not sleep, as others do, but let us keep awake and be sober. [7]For those who sleep sleep at night, and those who get drunk are drunk at night. [8]But, since we belong to the day, let us be sober, and put on the breastplate of faith and love, and for a helmet the hope of salvation. [9]For God has not destined us for wrath, but to obtain salvation through our Lord Jesus Christ, [10]who died for us so that whether we wake or sleep we might live with him. [11]Therefore encourage one another and build one another up, just as you are doing.

● **2 Thess 2:13**

2 Thess 1   [3]We are bound to give thanks to God always for you, brethren, as is fitting, because your faith is growing abundantly, and the love of every one of you for one another is increasing.

● **2 Thess 2:14**

Rom 2   [7]to those who by patience in well-doing seek for glory and honor and immortality, he will give eternal life; . . .

Phil 3   [21]who will change our lowly body to be like his glorious body, by the power which enables him even to subject all things to himself.

● **2 Thess 2:15**

Rom 6   [17]But thanks be to God, that you who were once slaves of sin have become obedient from the heart to the standard of teaching to which you were committed, . . .

1 Cor 11   [2]I commend you because you remember me in everything and maintain the traditions even as I have delivered them to you.

Gal 5   [1]For freedom Christ has set us free; stand fast therefore, and do not submit again to a yoke of slavery.

2 Thess 3   [6]Now we command you, brethren, in the name of our Lord Jesus Christ, that you keep away from any brother who is living in idleness and not in accord with the tradition that you received from us.

FORMAL ELEMENT: PRAYER

¹⁶Now may our Lord Jesus Christ himself, and God our Father, who loved us and gave us eternal comfort and good hope through grace, ¹⁷comfort your hearts and establish them in every good work and word.

PRIMARY

1 Thess 3:11-13 (§283)

¹¹Now may our God and Father himself, and our Lord Jesus, direct our way to you; ¹²and may the Lord make you increase and abound in love to one another and to all men, as we do to you, ¹³so that he may establish your hearts unblamable in holiness before our God and Father, at the coming of our Lord Jesus with all his saints.

1 Thess 5:23-24 (§289)

²³May the God of peace himself sanctify you wholly; and may your spirit and soul and body be kept sound and blameless at the coming of our Lord Jesus Christ. ²⁴He who calls you is faithful, and he will do it.

2 Thess 3:16 (§302)

¹⁶Now may the Lord of peace himself give you peace at all times in all ways. The Lord be with you all.

SECONDARY

2 Cor 1:3-11 (§147)

³Blessed be the God and Father of our Lord Jesus Christ, the Father of mercies and God of all comfort, ⁴who comforts us in all our affliction, so that we may be able to comfort those who are in any affliction, with the comfort with which we ourselves are comforted by God. ⁵For as we share abundantly in Christ's sufferings, so through Christ we share abundantly in comfort too. ⁶If we are afflicted, it is for your comfort and salvation; and if we are comforted, it is for your comfort, which you experience when you patiently endure the same sufferings that we suffer. ⁷Our hope for you is unshaken; for we know that as you share in our sufferings, you will also share in our comfort.

⁸For we do not want you to be ignorant, brethren, of the affliction we experienced in Asia; for we were so utterly, unbearably crushed that we despaired of life itself. ⁹Why, we felt that we had received the sentence of death; but that was to make us rely not on ourselves but on God who raises the dead; ¹⁰he delivered us from so deadly a peril, and he will deliver us; on him we have set our hope that he will deliver us again. ¹¹You also must help us by prayer, so that many will give thanks on our behalf for the blessing granted us in answer to many prayers.

Col 1:21-23 (§259)

²¹And you, who once were estranged and hostile in mind, doing evil deeds, ²²he has now reconciled in his body of flesh by his death, in order to present you holy and blameless and irreproachable before him, ²³provided that you continue in the faith, stable and steadfast, not shifting from the hope of the gospel which you heard, which has been preached to every creature under heaven, and of which I, Paul, became a minister.

• **2 Thess 2:16-17**

1 Thess 5   ²³May the God of peace himself sanctify you wholly; and may your spirit and soul and body be kept sound and blameless at the coming of our Lord Jesus Christ. ²⁴He who calls you is faithful, and he will do it.

2 Thess 3   ¹⁶Now may the Lord of peace himself give you peace at all times in all ways. The Lord be with you all.

• **2 Thess 2:16**

Titus 3   ⁷so that we might be justified by his grace and become heirs in hope of eternal life.

• **2 Thess 2:17**

Eph 2   ¹⁰For we are his workmanship, created in Christ Jesus for good works, which God prepared beforehand, that we should walk in them.

1 Thess 4   ¹⁸Therefore comfort one another with these words.

1 Thess 5   ¹¹Therefore encourage one another and build one another up, just as you are doing.

FORMAL ELEMENT:
REQUEST FOR PRAYER

3 Finally, brethren, pray for us, that the word of the Lord may speed on and triumph, as it did among you, ²and that we may be delivered from wicked and evil men; for not all have faith. ³But the Lord is faithful; he will strengthen you and guard you from evil. ⁴And we have confidence in the Lord about you, that you are doing and will do the things which we command. ⁵May the Lord direct your hearts to the love of God and to the steadfastness of Christ.

PRIMARY

Rom 15:30–33 (§64)
³⁰I appeal to you, brethren, by our Lord Jesus Christ and by the love of the Spirit, to strive together with me in your prayers to God on my behalf, ³¹that I may be delivered from the unbelievers in Judea, and that my service for Jerusalem may be acceptable to the saints, ³²so that by God's will I may come to you with joy and be refreshed in your company. ³³The God of peace be with you all. Amen.

Eph 6:18–20 (§234)
¹⁸Pray at all times in the Spirit, with all prayer and supplication. To that end keep alert with all perseverance, making supplication for all the saints, ¹⁹and also for me, that utterance may be given me in opening my mouth boldly to proclaim the mystery of the gospel, ²⁰for which I am an ambassador in chains; that I may declare it boldly, as I ought to speak.

Col 4:2–4 (§269)
²Continue steadfastly in prayer, being watchful in it with thanksgiving; ³and pray for us also, that God may open to us a door for the word, to declare the mystery of Christ, on account of which I am in prison, ⁴that I may make it clear, as I ought to speak.

1 Thess 5:25 (§290)
²⁵Brethren, pray for us.

● **2 Thess 3:2**
Acts 17   ⁵But the Jews were jealous, and taking some wicked fellows of the rabble, they gathered a crowd, set the city in an uproar, and attacked the house of Jason, seeking to bring them out to the people.

● **2 Thess 3:3**
1 Cor 1   ⁹God is faithful, by whom you were called into the fellowship of his Son, Jesus Christ our Lord.

1 Cor 10   ¹³No temptation has overtaken you that is not common to man. God is faithful, and he will not let you be tempted beyond your strength, but with the temptation will also provide the way of escape, that you may be able to endure it.

2 Cor 1   ¹⁸As surely as God is faithful, our word to you has not been Yes and No.

Eph 6   ¹⁰Finally, be strong in the Lord and in the strength of his might. ¹¹Put on the whole armor of God, that you may be able to stand against the wiles of the devil.

Eph 6   ¹³Therefore take the whole armor of God, that you may be able to withstand in the evil day, and having done all, to stand.

Phil 4   ⁶Have no anxiety about anything, but in everything by prayer and supplication with thanksgiving let your requests be made known to God.

Col 1   ¹¹May you be strengthened with all power, according to his glorious might, for all endurance and patience with joy, . . .

Phlm   ²²At the same time, prepare a guest room for me, for I am hoping through your prayers to be granted to you.

● **2 Thess 3:4**
2 Cor 7   ¹⁶What agreement has the temple of God with idols? For we are the temple of the living God; as God said,
    "I will live in them and move among them,
    and I will be their God,
    and they shall be my people."

● **2 Thess 3:5**
Rom 15   ⁵May the God of steadfastness and encouragement grant you to live in such harmony with one another, in accord with Christ Jesus, . . .

[6]Now we command you, brethren, in the name of our Lord Jesus Christ, that you keep away from any brother who is living in idleness and not in accord with the tradition that you received from us. [7]For you yourselves know how you ought to imitate us; we were not idle when we were with you, [8]we did not eat any one's bread without paying, but with toil and labor we worked night and day, that we might not burden any of you. [9]It was not because we have not that right, but to give you in our conduct an example to imitate. [10]For even when we were with you, we gave you this command: If any one will not work, let him not eat. [11]For we hear that some of you are living in idleness, mere busybodies, not doing any work. [12]Now such persons we command and exhort in the Lord Jesus Christ to do their work in quietness and to earn their own living. [13]Brethren, do not be weary in well-doing.

PRIMARY

1 Cor 9:1–14 (§105)

[1]Am I not free? Am I not an apostle? Have I not seen Jesus our Lord? Are not you my workmanship in the Lord? [2]If to others I am not an apostle, at least I am to you; for you are the seal of my apostleship in the Lord.

[3]This is my defense to those who would examine me. [4]Do we not have the right to our food and drink? [5]Do we not have the right to be accompanied by a wife, as the other apostles and the brothers of the Lord and Cephas? [6]Or is it only Barnabas and I who have no right to refrain from working for a living? [7]Who serves as a soldier at his own expense? Who plants a vineyard without eating any of its fruit? Who tends a flock without getting some of the milk?

[8]Do I say this on human authority? Does not the law say the same? [9]For it is written in the law of Moses, "You shall not muzzle an ox when it is treading out the grain." Is it for oxen that God is concerned? [10]Does he not speak entirely for our sake? It was written for our sake, because the plowman should plow in hope and the thresher thresh in hope of a share in the crop. [11]If we have sown spiritual good among you, is it too much if we reap your material benefits? [12]If others share this rightful claim upon you, do not we still more?

Nevertheless, we have not made use of this right, but we endure anything rather than put an obstacle in the way of the gospel of Christ. [13]Do you not know that those who are employed in the temple service get their food from the temple, and those who serve at the altar share in the sacrificial offerings? [14]In the same way, the Lord commanded that those who proclaim the gospel should get their living by the gospel.

2 Cor 11:7–11 (§180)

[7]Did I commit a sin in abasing myself so that you might be exalted, because I preached God's gospel without cost to you? [8]I robbed other churches by accepting support from them in order to serve you. [9]And when I was with you and was in want, I did not burden any one, for my needs were supplied by the brethren who came from Macedonia. So I refrained and will refrain from burdening you in any way. [10]As the truth of Christ is in me, this boast of mine shall not be silenced in the regions of Achaia. [11]And why? Because I do not love you? God knows I do!

Phil 3:17–21 (§249)

[17]Brethren, join in imitating me, and mark those who so live as you have an example in us. [18]For many, of whom I have often told you and now tell you even with tears, live as enemies of the cross of Christ. [19]Their end is destruction, their god is the belly, and they glory in their shame, with minds set on earthly things. [20]But our commonwealth is in heaven, and from it we await a Savior, the Lord Jesus Christ, [21]who will change our lowly body to be like his glorious body, by the power which enables him even to subject all things to himself.

1 Thess 2:9–12 (§278)

[9]For you remember our labor and toil, brethren; we worked night and day, that we might not burden any of you, while we preached to you the gospel of God. [10]You are witnesses, and God also, how holy and righteous and blameless was our behavior to you believers; [11]for you know how, like a father with his children, we exhorted each one of you and encouraged you and charged you [12]to lead a life worthy of God, who calls you into his own kingdom and glory.

1 Thess 4:9–12 (§285)

[9]But concerning love of the brethren you have no need to have any one write to you, for you yourselves have been taught by God to love one another; [10]and indeed you do love all the brethren throughout Macedonia. But we exhort you, brethren, to do so more and more, [11]to aspire to live quietly, to mind your own affairs, and to work with your hands, as we charged you; [12]so that you may command the respect of outsiders, and be dependent on nobody.

1 Thess 5:12–22 (§288)

[12]But we beseech you, brethren, to respect those who labor among you and are over you in the Lord and admonish you, [13]and to esteem them very highly in love because of their work. Be at peace among yourselves. [14]And we exhort you, brethren, admonish the idle, encourage the fainthearted, help the weak, be patient with them all. [15]See that none of you repays evil for evil, but always seek to do good to one another and to all. [16]Rejoice always, [17]pray constantly, [18]give thanks in all circumstances; for this is the will of God in Christ Jesus for you. [19]Do not quench the Spirit, [20]do not despise prophesying, [21]but test everything; hold fast what is good, [22]abstain from every form of evil.

● **2 Thess 3:6**

Rom 6   [17]But thanks be to God, that you who were once slaves of sin have become obedient from the heart to the standard of teaching to which you were committed, . . .

1 Cor 7   [6]I say this by way of concession, not of command.

1 Cor 7   [10]To the married I give charge, not I but the Lord, that the wife should not separate from her husband . . .

1 Cor 7   [12]To the rest I say, not the Lord, that if any brother has a wife who is an unbeliever, and she consents to live with him, he should not divorce her.

1 Cor 11   [2]I commend you because you remember me in everything and maintain the traditions even as I have delivered them to you.

1 Cor 11   [23]For I received from the Lord what I also delivered to you, that the Lord Jesus on the night when he was betrayed took bread, . . .

1 Cor 15   [3]For I delivered to you as of first importance what I also received, that Christ died for our sins in accordance with the scriptures, . . .

Col 2   [6]As therefore you received Christ Jesus the Lord, so live in him, [7]rooted and built up in him and established in the faith, just as you were taught, abounding in thanksgiving.

2 Thess 2   [15]So then, brethren, stand firm and hold to the traditions which you were taught by us, either by word of mouth or by letter.

● **2 Thess 3:7**

Cf. 1 Cor 4:6; 1 Cor 11:1; Gal 4:12; 1 Thess 1:6

● **2 Thess 3:8**

Acts 18   [3]and because he was of the same trade he stayed with them, and they worked, for by trade they were tentmakers.

Cf. 1 Cor 4   [12]and we labor, working with our own hands. When reviled, we bless; when persecuted, we endure; . . .

Cf. 2 Cor 12   [13]For in what were you less favored than the rest of the churches, except that I myself did not burden you? Forgive me this wrong!

[14]Here for the third time I am ready to come to you. And I will not be a burden, for I seek not what is yours but you; for children ought not to lay up for their parents, but parents for their children. [15]I will most gladly spend and be spent for your souls. If I love you the more, am I to be loved the less? [16]But granting that I myself did not burden you, I was crafty, you say, and got the better of you by guile.

Cf. Gal 6   [5]For each man will have to bear his own load.

Cf. Eph 4   [28]Let the thief no longer steal, but rather let him labor, doing honest work with his hands, so that he may be able to give to those in need.

● **2 Thess 3:11**

1 Tim 5   [13]Besides that, they learn to be idlers, gadding about from house to house, and not only idlers but gossips and busybodies, saying what they should not.

FORMAL ELEMENT:
ENFORCEMENT STATEMENT

[14] If any one refuses to obey what we say in this letter, note that man, and have nothing to do with him, that he may be ashamed. [15] Do not look on him as an enemy, but warn him as a brother.

PRIMARY

1 Cor 14:37–40 (§130)

[37] If any one thinks that he is a prophet, or spiritual, he should acknowledge that what I am writing to you is a command of the Lord. [38] If any one does not recognize this, he is not recognized. [39] So, my brethren, earnestly desire to prophesy, and do not forbid speaking in tongues; [40] but all things should be done decently and in order.

Col 4:16–18a (§273)

[16] And when this letter has been read among you, have it read also in the church of the Laodiceans; and see that you read also the letter from Laodicea. [17] And say to Archippus, "See that you fulfil the ministry which you have received in the Lord." [18] I, Paul, write this greeting with my own hand. Remember my fetters.

1 Thess 5:27 (§292)

[27] I adjure you by the Lord that this letter be read to all the brethren.

Phlm 21–22 (§309)

[21] Confident of your obedience, I write to you, knowing that you will do even more than I say. [22] At the same time, prepare a guest room for me, for I am hoping through your prayers to be granted to you.

SECONDARY

1 Cor 5:9–13 (§89)

[9] I wrote to you in my letter not to associate with immoral men; [10] not at all meaning the immoral of this world, or the greedy and robbers, or idolaters, since then you would need to go out of the world. [11] But rather I wrote to you not to associate with any one who bears the name of brother if he is guilty of immorality or greed, or is an idolater, reviler, drunkard, or robber—not even to eat with such a one. [12] For what have I to do with judging outsiders? Is it not those inside the church whom you are to judge? [13] God judges those outside. "Drive out the wicked person from among you."

2 Cor 2:5–11 (§151)

[5] But if any one has caused pain, he has caused it not to me, but in some measure—not to put it too severely— to you all. [6] For such a one this punishment by the majority is enough; [7] so you should rather turn to forgive and comfort him, or he may be overwhelmed by excessive sorrow. [8] So I beg you to reaffirm your love for him. [9] For this is why I wrote, that I might test you and know whether you are obedient in everything. [10] Any one whom you forgive, I also forgive. What I have forgiven, if I have forgiven anything, has been for your sake in the presence of Christ, [11] to keep Satan from gaining the advantage over us; for we are not ignorant of his designs.

Gal 6:1–6 (§214)

[1] Brethren, if a man is overtaken in any trespass, you who are spiritual should restore him in a spirit of gentleness. Look to yourself, lest you too be tempted. [2] Bear one another's burdens, and so fulfil the law of Christ. [3] For if

any one thinks he is something, when he is nothing, he deceives himself. [4] But let each one test his own work, and then his reason to boast will be in himself alone and not in his neighbor. [5] For each man will have to bear his own load.

[6] Let him who is taught the word share all good things with him who teaches.

1 Thess 5:12–22 (§288)

[12] But we beseech you, brethren, to respect those who labor among you and are over you in the Lord and admonish you, [13] and to esteem them very highly in love because of their work. Be at peace among yourselves. [14] And we exhort you, brethren, admonish the idle, encourage the fainthearted, help the weak, be patient with them all. [15] See that none of you repays evil for evil, but always seek to do good to one another and to all. [16] Rejoice always, [17] pray constantly, [18] give thanks in all circumstances; for this is the will of God in Christ Jesus for you. [19] Do not quench the Spirit, [20] do not despise prophesying, [21] but test everything; hold fast what is good, [22] abstain from every form of evil.

Phlm 15–20 (§308)

[15] Perhaps this is why he was parted from you for a while, that you might have him back for ever, [16] no longer as a slave but more than a slave, as a beloved brother, especially to me but how much more to you, both in the flesh and in the Lord. [17] So if you consider me your partner, receive him as you would receive me. [18] If he has wronged you at all, or owes you anything, charge that to my account. [19] I, Paul, write this with my own hand, I will repay it—to say nothing of your owing me even your own self. [20] Yes, brother, I want some benefit from you in the Lord. Refresh my heart in Christ.

● **2 Thess 3:14–15**

Rom 12 [17] Repay no one evil for evil, but take thought for what is noble in the sight of all. [18] If possible, so far as it depends upon you, live peaceably with all.

Rom 15 [1] We who are strong ought to bear with the failings of the weak, and not to please ourselves; [2] let each of us please his neighbor for his good, to edify him. [3] For Christ did not please himself; but, as it is written, "The reproaches of those who reproached

thee fell on me." [4] For whatever was written in former days was written for our instruction, that by steadfastness and by the encouragement of the scriptures we might have hope. [5] May the God of steadfastness and encouragement grant you to live in such harmony with one another, in accord with Christ Jesus, [6] that together you may with one voice glorify the God and Father of our Lord Jesus Christ.

[7] Welcome one another, therefore, as Christ has welcomed you, for the glory of God.

1 Cor 7 [7] I wish that all were as I myself am. But each has his own special gift from God, one of one kind and one of another.

1 Cor 11 [16] If any one is disposed to be contentious, we recognize no other practice, nor do the churches of God.

Phlm [8] Accordingly, though I am bold enough in Christ to command you to do what is required, [9] yet for love's sake I prefer to appeal to you—I, Paul, an ambassador and now a prisoner also for Christ Jesus . . .

FORMAL ELEMENT: PRAYER

16 Now may the Lord of peace himself give you peace at all times in all ways. The Lord be with you all.

PRIMARY

1 Thess 3:11–13 (§283)

11 Now may our God and Father himself, and our Lord Jesus, direct our way to you; 12 and may the Lord make you increase and abound in love to one another and to all men, as we do to you, 13 so that he may establish your hearts unblamable in holiness before our God and Father, at the coming of our Lord Jesus with all his saints.

1 Thess 5:23–24 (§289)

23 May the God of peace himself sanctify you wholly; and may your spirit and soul and body be kept sound and blameless at the coming of our Lord Jesus Christ. 24 He who calls you is faithful, and he will do it.

2 Thess 2:16–17 (§298)

16 Now may our Lord Jesus Christ himself, and God our Father, who loved us and gave us eternal comfort and good hope through grace, 17 comfort your hearts and establish them in every good work and word.

SECONDARY

Rom 15:30–33 (§64)

30 I appeal to you, brethren, by our Lord Jesus Christ and by the love of the Spirit, to strive together with me in your prayers to God on my behalf, 31 that I may be delivered from the unbelievers in Judea, and that my service for Jerusalem may be acceptble to the saints, 32 so that by God's will I may come to you with joy and be refreshed in your company. 33 The God of peace be with you all. Amen.

● **2 Thess 3:16**
Rom 15   13 May the God of hope fill you with all joy and peace in believing, so that by the power of the Holy Spirit you may abound in hope.

1 Cor 7   15 But if the unbelieving partner desires to separate, let it be so; in such a case the brother or sister is not bound. For God has called us to peace.

1 Cor 14   33 For God is not a God of confusion but of peace.

FORMAL ELEMENT: SIGNATURE DEVICE

[17]I, Paul, write this greeting with my own hand. This is the mark in every letter of mine; it is the way I write.

PRIMARY

1 Cor 16:21–22 (§144)

[21]I, Paul, write this greeting with my own hand. [22]If any one has no love for the Lord, let him be accursed. Our Lord, come!

Gal 6:11–17 (§216)

[11]See with what large letters I am writing to you with my own hand. [12]It is those who want to make a good showing in the flesh that would compel you to be circumcised, and only in order that they may not be persecuted for the cross of Christ. [13]For even those who receive circumcision do not themselves keep the law, but they desire to have you circumcised that they may glory in your flesh. [14]But far be it from me to glory except in the cross of our Lord Jesus Christ, by which the world has been crucified to me, and I to the world. [15]For neither circumcision counts for anything, nor uncircumcision, but a new creation. [16]Peace and mercy be upon all who walk by this rule, upon the Israel of God.

[17]Henceforth let no man trouble me; for I bear on my body the marks of Jesus.

Col 4:16–18a (§273)

[16]And when this letter has been read among you, have it read also in the church of the Laodiceans; and see that you read also the letter from Laodicea. [17]And say to Archippus, "See that you fulfil the ministry which you have received in the Lord."

[18]I, Paul, write this greeting with my own hand. Remember my fetters.

● **2 Thess 3:17**

2 Thess 2   [2]not to be quickly shaken in mind or excited, either by spirit or by word, or by letter purporting to be from us, to the effect that the day of the Lord has come.

2 Thess 2   [15]So then, brethren, stand firm and hold to the traditions which you were taught by us, either by word of mouth or by letter.

LETTER STRUCTURE: CLOSING GRACE

[18]The grace of our Lord Jesus Christ be with you all.

PRIMARY

Rom 16:20b (§68)
The grace of our Lord Jesus Christ be with you.

1 Cor 16:23–24 (§145)
[23]The grace of the Lord Jesus be with you. [24]My love be with you all in Christ Jesus. Amen.

2 Cor 13:14 (§192)
[14]The grace of the Lord Jesus Christ and the love of God and the fellowship of the Holy Spirit be with you all.

Gal 6:18 (§217)
[18]The grace of our Lord Jesus Christ be with your spirit, brethren. Amen.

Eph 6:23–24 (§236)
[23]Peace be to the brethren, and love with faith, from God the Father and the Lord Jesus Christ. [24]Grace be with all who love our Lord Jesus Christ with love undying.

Phil 4:23 (§255)
[23]The grace of the Lord Jesus Christ be with your spirit.

Col 4:18b (§274)
Grace be with you.

1 Thess 5:28 (§293)
[28]The grace of our Lord Jesus Christ be with you.

Phlm 25 (§311)
[25]The grace of the Lord Jesus Christ be with your spirit.

● **2 Thess 3:18**
1 Tim 6　[21]. . . Grace be with you.

2 Tim 4　[22]. . . Grace be with you.

Titus 3　[15]. . . Grace be with you all.

LETTER STRUCTURE: SALUTATION

1 Paul, a prisoner for Christ Jesus, and Timothy our brother,
To Philemon our beloved fellow worker [2]and Apphia our sister and Archippus our fellow soldier, and the church in your house:
[3]Grace to you and peace from God our Father and the Lord Jesus Christ.

PRIMARY

Rom 1:1–7 (§1)
[1]Paul, a servant of Jesus Christ, called to be an apostle, set apart for the gospel of God [2]which he promised beforehand through his prophets in the holy scriptures, [3]the gospel concerning his Son, who was descended from David according to the flesh [4]and designated Son of God in power according to the Spirit of holiness by his resurrection from the dead, Jesus Christ our Lord, [5]through whom we have received grace and apostleship to bring about the obedience of faith for the sake of his name among all the nations, [6]including yourselves who are called to belong to Jesus Christ;
[7]To all God's beloved in Rome, who are called to be saints:
Grace to you and peace from God our Father and the Lord Jesus Christ.

1 Cor 1:1–3 (§71)
[1]Paul, called by the will of God to be an apostle of Christ Jesus, and our brother Sosthenes,
[2]To the church of God which is at Corinth, to those sanctified in Christ Jesus, called to be saints together with all those who in every place call on the name of our Lord Jesus Christ, both their Lord and ours:
[3]Grace to you and peace from God our Father and the Lord Jesus Christ.

2 Cor 1:1–2 (§146)
[1]Paul, an apostle of Christ Jesus by the will of God, and Timothy our brother.
To the church of God which is at Corinth, with all the saints who are in the whole of Achaia:
[2]Grace to you and peace from God our Father and the Lord Jesus Christ.

Gal 1:1–5 (§193)
[1]Paul an apostle—not from men nor through man, but through Jesus Christ and God the Father, who raised him from the dead— [2]and all the brethren who are with me,
To the churches of Galatia:
[3]Grace to you and peace from God the Father and our Lord Jesus Christ, [4]who gave himself for our sins to deliver us from the present evil age, according to the will of our God and Father; [5]to whom be the glory for ever and ever. Amen.

Eph 1:1–2 (§218)
[1]Paul, an apostle of Christ Jesus by the will of God,
To the saints who are also faithful in Christ Jesus:
[2]Grace to you and peace from God our Father and the Lord Jesus Christ.

Phil 1:1–2 (§237)
[1]Paul and Timothy, servants of Christ Jesus,
To all the saints in Christ Jesus who are at Philippi, with the bishops and deacons:
[2]Grace to you and peace from God our Father and the Lord Jesus Christ.

Col 1:1–2 (§256)
[1]Paul, an apostle of Christ Jesus by the will of God, and Timothy our brother,
[2]To the saints and faithful brethren in Christ at Colossae:
Grace to you and peace from God our Father.

1 Thess 1:1 (§275)
[1]Paul, Silvanus, and Timothy,
To the church of the Thessalonians in God the Father and the Lord Jesus Christ:
Grace to you and peace.

2 Thess 1:1–2 (§294)
[1]Paul, Silvanus, and Timothy,
To the church of the Thessalonians in God our Father and the Lord Jesus Christ:
[2]Grace to you and peace from God the Father and the Lord Jesus Christ.

● **Phlm 1–3**
1 Tim 1   [1]Paul, an apostle of Christ Jesus by command of God our Savior and of Christ Jesus our hope,
[2]To Timothy, my true child in the faith:
Grace, mercy, and peace from God the Father and Christ Jesus our Lord.

2 Tim 1   [1]Paul, an apostle of Christ Jesus by the will of God according to the promise of the life which is in Christ Jesus,

[2]To Timothy, my beloved child:
Grace, mercy, and peace from God the Father and Christ Jesus our Lord.

Titus 1   [1]Paul, a servant of God and an apostle of Jesus Christ, to further the faith of God's elect and their knowledge of the truth which accords with godliness, [2]in hope of eternal life which God, who never lies, promised ages ago [3]and at the proper time manifested in his word through the preaching with which I have been entrusted by command of God our Savior;

[4]To Titus, my true child in a common faith:
Grace and peace from God the Father and Christ Jesus our Savior.

● **Phlm 2**
Phil 2   [25]I have thought it necessary to send to you Epaphroditus my brother and fellow worker and fellow soldier, and your messenger and minister to my need, . . .

2 Tim 2   [3]Share in suffering as a good soldier of Christ Jesus.

LETTER STRUCTURE: THANKSGIVING

4I thank my God always when I remember you in my prayers, 5because I hear of your love and of the faith which you have toward the Lord Jesus and all the saints, 6and I pray that the sharing of your faith may promote the knowledge of all the good that is ours in Christ. 7For I have derived much joy and comfort from your love, my brother, because the hearts of the saints have been refreshed through you.

PRIMARY

Rom 1:8–15 (§2)

8First, I thank my God through Jesus Christ for all of you, because your faith is proclaimed in all the world. 9For God is my witness, whom I serve with my spirit in the gospel of his Son, that without ceasing I mention you always in my prayers, 10asking that somehow by God's will I may now at last succeed in coming to you. 11For I long to see you, that I may impart to you some spiritual gift to strengthen you, 12that is, that we may be mutually encouraged by each other's faith, both yours and mine. 13I want you to know, brethren, that I have often intended to come to you (but thus far have been prevented), in order that I may reap some harvest among you as well as among the rest of the Gentiles. 14I am under obligation both to Greeks and to barbarians, both to the wise and to the foolish: 15so I am eager to preach the gospel to you also who are in Rome.

1 Cor 1:4–9 (§72)

4I give thanks to God always for you because of the grace of God which was given you in Christ Jesus, 5that in every way you were enriched in him with all speech and all knowledge— 6even as the testimony to Christ was confirmed among you— 7so that you are not lacking in any spiritual gift, as you wait for the revealing of our Lord Jesus Christ; 8who will sustain you to the end, guiltless in the day of our Lord Jesus Christ. 9God is faithful, by whom you were called into the fellowship of his Son, Jesus Christ our Lord.

Phil 1:3–11 (§238)

3I thank my God in all my remembrance of you, 4always in every prayer of mine for you all making my prayer with joy, 5thankful for your partnership in the gospel from the first day until now. 6And I am sure that he who began a good work in you will bring it to completion at the day of Jesus Christ. 7It is right for me to feel thus about you all, because I hold you in my heart, for you are all partakers with me of grace, both in my imprisonment and in the defense and confirmation of the gospel. 8For God is my witness, how I yearn for you all with the affection of Christ Jesus. 9And it is my prayer that your love may abound more and more, with knowledge and all discernment, 10so that you may approve what is excellent, and may be pure and blameless for the day of Christ, 11filled with the fruits of righteousness which come through Jesus Christ, to the glory and praise of God.

Col 1:3–14 (§257)

3We always thank God, the Father of our Lord Jesus Christ, when we pray for you, 4because we have heard of your faith in Christ Jesus and of the love which you have for all the saints, 5because of the hope laid up for you in heaven. Of this you have heard before in the word of the truth, the gospel 6which has come to you, as indeed in the whole world it is bearing fruit and growing—so among yourselves, from the day you heard and understood the grace of God in truth, 7as you learned it from Epaphras our beloved fellow servant. He is a faithful minister of Christ on our behalf 8and has made known to us your love in the Spirit.

9And so, from the day we heard of it, we have not ceased to pray for you, asking that you may be filled with the knowledge of his will in all spiritual wisdom and understanding, 10to lead a life worthy of the Lord, fully pleasing to him, bearing fruit in every good work and increasing in the knowledge of God. 11May you be strengthened with all power, according to his glorious might, for all endurance and patience with joy, 12giving thanks to the Father, who has qualified us to share in the inheritance of the saints in light. 13He has delivered us from the dominion of darkness and transferred us to the kingdom of his beloved Son, 14in whom we have redemption, the forgiveness of sins.

1 Thess 1:2–10 (§276)

2We give thanks to God always for you all, constantly mentioning you in our prayers, 3remembering before our God and Father your work of faith and labor of love and steadfastness of hope in our Lord Jesus Christ. 4For we know, brethren beloved by God, that he has chosen you; 5for our gospel came to you not only in word, but also in power and in the Holy Spirit and with full conviction. You know what kind of men we proved to be among you for your sake. 6And you became imitators of us and of the Lord, for you received the word in much affliction, with joy inspired by the Holy Spirit; 7so that you became an example to the all the believers in Macedonia and in Achaia. 8For not only has the word of the Lord sounded forth from you in Macedonia and Achaia, but your faith in God has gone forth everywhere, so that we need not say anything. 9For they themselves report concerning us what a welcome we had among you, and how you turned to God from idols, to serve a living and true God, 10and to wait for his Son from heaven, whom he raised from the dead, Jesus who delivers us from the wrath to come.

2 Thess 1:3–12 (§295)

3We are bound to give thanks to God always for you, brethren, as is fitting, because your faith is growing abundantly, and the love of every one of you for one another is increasing. 4Therefore we ourselves boast of you in the churches of God for your steadfastness and faith in all your persecutions and in the afflictions which you are enduring.

5This is evidence of the righteous judgment of God, that you may be made worthy of the kingdom of God, for which you are suffering— 6since indeed God deems it just to repay with affliction those who afflict you, 7and to grant rest with us to you who are afflicted, when the Lord Jesus is revealed from heaven with his mighty angels in flaming fire, 8 inflicting vengeance upon those who do not know God and upon those who do not obey the gospel of our Lord Jesus. 9They shall suffer the punishment of eternal destruction and exclusion from the presence of the Lord and from the glory of his might, 10when he comes on that day to be glorified in his saints, and to be marveled at in all who have believed, because our testimony to you was believed. 11To this end we always pray for you, that our God may make you worthy of his call, and may fulfil every good resolve and work of faith by his power, 12so that the name of our Lord Jesus may be glorified in you, and you in him, according to the grace of our God and the Lord Jesus Christ.

● **Phlm 4**

1 Tim 1   12I thank him who has given me strength for this, Christ Jesus our Lord, because he judged me faithful by appointing me to his service, . . .

2 Tim 1   3I thank God whom I serve with a clear conscience, as did my fathers, when I remember you constantly in my prayers.

Titus 1   5This is why I left you in Crete, that you might amend what was defective, and appoint elders in every town as I directed you, . . .

● **Phlm 6–7**

1 Thess 3   7for this reason, brethren, in all our distress and affliction we have been comforted about you through your faith; . . .

● **Phlm 6**

Phil 1   9And it is my prayer that your love may abound more and more, with knowledge and all discernment, . . .

(our) *read* yours: p61SG Koine it (some) vg syr cop Chrysostom; *text:* ACD Lect (some) it (few) Ambrosiaster

● **Phlm 7**

1 Cor 16   18for they refreshed my spirit as well as yours. Give recognition to such men.

Cf. 2 Cor 1:3–7

2 Cor 7   4I have great confidence in you; I have great pride in you; I am filled with comfort. With all our affliction, I am overjoyed.

2 Cor 7   13Therefore we are comforted.

Phlm   20Yes, brother, I want some benefit from you in the Lord. Refresh my heart in Christ.

LETTER STRUCTURE: APPEAL
FORMAL ELEMENT: COMMENDATION

8Accordingly, though I am bold enough in Christ to command you to do what is required, 9yet for love's sake I prefer to appeal to you—I, Paul, an ambassador and now a prisoner also for Christ Jesus—10I appeal to you for my child, Onesimus, whose father I have become in my imprisonment. 11(Formerly he was useless to you, but now he is indeed useful to you and to me.) 12I am sending him back to you, sending my very heart. 13I would have been glad to keep him with me, in order that he might serve me on your behalf during my imprisonment for the gospel; 14but I preferred to do nothing without your consent in order that your goodness might not be by compulsion but of your own free will.

PRIMARY

See §51 for APPEAL

See §65 for COMMENDATION

SECONDARY

Rom 13:8-10 (§55)

8Owe no one anything, except to love one another; for he who loves his neighbor has fulfilled the law. 9The commandments, "You shall not commit adultery, You shall not kill, You shall not steal, You shall not covet," and any other commandment, are summed up in this sentence, "You shall love your neighbor as yourself." 10Love does no wrong to a neighbor; therefore love is the fulfilling of the law.

Gal 5:1-15 (§211-212)

1For freedom Christ has set us free; stand fast therefore, and do not submit again to a yoke of slavery.

2Now I, Paul, say to you that if you receive circumcision, Christ will be of no advantage to you. 3I testify again to every man who receives circumcision that he is bound to keep the whole law. 4You are severed from Christ, you who would be justified by the law; you have fallen away from grace. 5For through the Spirit, by faith, we wait for the hope of righteousness. 6For in Christ Jesus neither circum- cision nor uncircumcision is of any avail, but faith working through love. 7You were running well; who hindered you from obeying the truth? 8This persuasion is not from him who called you. 9A little leaven leavens the whole lump. 10I have confidence in the Lord that you will take no other view than mine; and he who is troubling you will bear his judgment, whoever he is. 11But if I, brethren, still preach circumcision, why am I still persecuted? In that case the stumbling block of the cross has been removed. 12I wish those who unsettle you would mutilate themselves!

13For you were called to freedom, brethren; only do not use your freedom as an opportunity for the flesh, but through love be servants of one another. 14For the whole law is fulfilled in one word, "You shall love your neighbor as yourself." 15But if you bite and devour one another take heed that you are not consumed by one another.

● **Phlm 8-9**
1 Cor 7　6I say this by way of concession, not of command.

1 Cor 7　10To the married I give charge, not I but the Lord, that the wife should not separate from her husband . . .

1 Cor 7　12To the rest I say, not the Lord, that if any brother has a wife who is an unbeliever, and she consents to live with him, he should not divorce her.

1 Cor 7　25Now concerning the unmarried, I have no command of the Lord, but I give my opinion as one who by the Lord's mercy is trustworthy.

2 Cor 8　8I say this not as a command, but to prove by the earnestness of others that your love also is genuine.

2 Thess 3　6Now we command you, brethren, in the name of our Lord Jesus Christ, that you keep away from any brother who is living in idleness and not in accord with the tradition that you received from us.

2 Thess 3　10For even when we were with you, we gave you this command: If any one will not work, let him not eat.

2 Thess 3　12Now such persons we command and exhort in the Lord Jesus Christ to do their work in quietness and to earn their own living.

● **Phlm 9**
Rom 12　9Let love be genuine; hate what is evil, hold fast to what is good; 10love one another with brotherly affection; outdo one another in showing honor.

Eph 3　1For this reason I, Paul, a prisoner for Christ Jesus on behalf of you Gentiles . . .

Phil 1　12I want you to know, brethren, that what has happened to me has really served to advance the gospel, 13so that it has become known throughout the whole praetorian guard and to all the rest that my imprisonment is for Christ; 14and most of the brethren have been made confident in the Lord because of my imprisonment, and are much more bold to speak the word of God without fear.

15Some indeed preach Christ from envy and rivalry, but others from good will. 16The latter do it out of love, knowing that I am put here for the defense of the gospel; 17the former proclaim Christ out of partisanship, not sincerely but thinking to afflict me in my imprisonment. 18What then? Only that in every way, whether in pretense or in truth, Christ is proclaimed; and in that I rejoice.

19Yes, and I shall rejoice. For I know that through your prayers and the help of the Spirit of Jesus Christ this will turn out for my deliverance, 20as it is my eager expectation and hope that I shall not be at all ashamed, but that with full courage now as always Christ will be honored in my body, whether by life or by death.

Col 4　3and pray for us also, that God may open to us a door for the word, to declare the mystery of Christ, on account of which I am in prison, . . .

Col 4　18I, Paul, write this greeting with my own hand. Remember my fetters.

Phlm　1Paul, a prisoner for Christ Jesus, and Timothy our brother,
To Philemon our beloved fellow worker . . .

● **Phlm 10**
1 Cor 4　14I do not write this to make you ashamed, but to admonish you as my beloved children. 15For though you have countless guides in Christ, you do not have many fathers. For I became your father in Christ Jesus through the gospel.

2 Cor 6　13In return—I speak as to children—widen your hearts also.

Gal 4　19My little children, with whom I am again in travail until Christ be formed in you!

Eph 5　1Therefore be imitators of God, as beloved children.

Phil 2　22But Timothy's worth you know, how as a son with a father he has served with me in the gospel.

● **Phlm 11**
2 Tim 4　11Luke alone is with me. Get Mark and bring him with you; for he is very useful in serving me.

● **Phlm 13**
Phil 2　30for he nearly died for the work of Christ, risking his life to complete your service to me.

● **Phlm 14**
1 Cor 7　6I say this by way of concession, not of command.

1 Cor 7　35I say this for your own benefit, not to lay any restraint upon you, but to promote good order and to secure your undivided devotion to the Lord.

2 Cor 9　7Each one must do as he has made up his mind, not reluctantly or under compulsion, for God loves a cheerful giver.

1 Tim 6　2Those who have believing masters must not be disrespectful on the ground that they are brethren; rather they must serve all the better since those who benefit by their service are believers and beloved.
Teach and urge these duties.

FORMAL ELEMENT: COMMENDATION

15Perhaps this is why he was parted from you for a while, that you might have him back for ever, 16no longer as a slave but more than a slave, as a beloved brother, especially to me but how much more to you, both in the flesh and in the Lord. 17So if you consider me your partner, receive him as you would receive me. 18If he has wronged you at all, or owes you anything, charge that to my account. 19I, Paul, write this with my own hand, I will repay it—to say nothing of your owing me even your own self. 20Yes, brother, I want some benefit from you in the Lord. Refresh my heart in Christ.

PRIMARY

See §65 for COMMENDATION

SECONDARY

Rom 13:8–10 (§55)

8Owe no one anything, except to love one another; for he who loves his neighbor has fulfilled the law. 9The commandments, "You shall not commit adultery, You shall not kill, You shall not steal, You shall not covet," and any other commandment, are summed up in this sentence, "You shall love your neighbor as yourself." 10Love does no wrong to a neighbor; therefore love is the fulfilling of the law.

1 Cor 7:17–24 (§97)

17Only, let every one lead the life which the Lord has assigned to him, and in which God has called him. This is my rule in all the churches. 18Was any one at the time of his call already circumcised? Let him not seek to remove the marks of circumcision. Was any one at the time of his call uncircumcised? Let him not seek circumcision. 19For neither circumcision counts for anything nor uncircumcision, but keeping the commandments of God. 20Every one should remain in the state in which he was called. 21Were you a slave when called? Never mind. But if you can gain your freedom, avail yourself of the opportunity. 22For he who was called in the Lord as a slave is a freedman of the Lord. Likewise he who was free when called is a slave of Christ. 23You were bought with a price; do not become slaves of men. 24So, brethren, in whatever state each was called, there let him remain with God.

Gal 6:1–6 (§214)

1Brethren, if a man is overtaken in any trespass, you who are spiritual should restore him in a spirit of gentleness. Look to yourself, lest you too be tempted. 2Bear one another's burdens, and so fulfil the law of Christ. 3For if any one thinks he is something, when he is nothing, he deceives himself. 4But let each one test his own work, and then his reason to boast will be in himself alone and not in his neighbor. 5For each man will have to bear his own load.

6Let him who is taught the word share all good things with him who teaches.

Eph 4:25–32 (§228)

25Therefore, putting away falsehood, let every one speak the truth with his neighbor, for we are members one of another. 26Be angry but do not sin; do not let the sun go down on your anger, 27and give no opportunity to the devil. 28Let the thief no longer steal, but rather let him labor, doing honest work with his hands, so that he may be able to give to those in need. 29Let no evil talk come out of your mouths, but only such as is good for edifying, as fits the occasion, that it may impart grace to those who hear. 30And do not grieve the Holy Spirit of God, in whom you were sealed for the day of redemption. 31Let all bitterness and wrath and anger and clamor and slander be put away from you, with all malice, 32and be kind to one another, tenderhearted, forgiving one another, as God in Christ forgave you.

Col 3:12–17 (§267)

12Put on then, as God's chosen ones, holy and beloved, compassion, kindness, lowliness, meekness, and patience, 13forbearing one another and, if one has a complaint against another, forgiving each other; as the Lord has forgiven you, so you also must forgive. 14And above all these put on love, which binds everything together in perfect harmony. 15And let the peace of Christ rule in your hearts, to which indeed you were called in the one body. And be thankful. 16Let the word of Christ dwell in you richly, as you teach and admonish one another in all wisdom, and as you sing psalms and hymns and spiritual songs with thankfulness in your hearts to God. 17And whatever you do, in word or deed, do everything in the name of the Lord Jesus, giving thanks to God the Father through him.

1 Thess 5:12–22 (§288)

12But we beseech you, brethren, to respect those who labor among you and are over you in the Lord and admonish you, 13and to esteem them very highly in love because of their work. Be at peace among yourselves. 14And we exhort you, brethren, admonish the idle, encourage the fainthearted, help the weak, be patient with them all. 15See that none of you repays evil for evil, but always seek to do good to one another and to all. 16Rejoice always, 17pray constantly, 18give thanks in all circumstances; for this is the will of God in Christ Jesus for you. 19Do not quench the Spirit, 20do not despise prophesying, 21but test everything; hold fast what is good, 22abstain from every form of evil.

● **Phlm 17–20**

Rom 12   21Do not be overcome by evil, but overcome evil with good.

● **Phlm 17**

Rom 14   1As for the man who is weak in faith, welcome him, but not for disputes over opinions.

Rom 15   7Welcome one another, therefore, as Christ has welcomed you, for the glory of God.

Phil 1   5thankful for your partnership in the gospel from the first day until now.

Phil 4   15And you Philippians yourselves know that in the beginning of the gospel, when I left Macedonia, no church entered into partnership with me in giving and receiving except you only; . . .

● **Phlm 20**

Phlm   7For I have derived much joy and comfort from your love, my brother, because the hearts of the saints have been refreshed through you.

FORMAL ELEMENTS: APOSTOLIC VISIT & ENFORCEMENT STATEMENT

[21]Confident of your obedience, I write to you, knowing that you will do even more than I say. [22]At the same time, prepare a guest room for me, for I am hoping through your prayers to be granted to you.

PRIMARY

See §63 for APOSTOLIC VISIT

1 Cor 14:37–40 (§130)
[37]If any one thinks that he is a prophet, or spiritual, he should acknowledge that what I am writing to you is a command of the Lord. [38]If any one does not recognize this, he is not recognized. [39]So, my brethren, earnestly desire to prophesy, and do not forbid speaking in tongues; [40]but all things should be done decently and in order.

Col 4:16–18a (§273)
[16]And when this letter has been read among you, have it read also in the church of the Laodiceans; and see that you read also the letter from Laodicea. [17]And say to Archippus, "See that you fulfil the ministry which you have received in the Lord."
[18]I, Paul, write this greeting with my own hand. Remember my fetters.

1 Thess 5:27 (§292)
[27]I adjure you by the Lord that this letter be read to all the brethren.

2 Thess 3:14–15 (§301)
[14]If any one refuses to obey what we say in this letter, note that man, and have nothing to do with him, that he may be ashamed. [15]Do not look on him as an enemy, but warn him as a brother.

SECONDARY

Rom 15:30–33 (§64)
[30]I appeal to you, brethren, by our Lord Jesus Christ and by the love of the Spirit, to strive together with me in your prayers to God on my behalf, [31]that I may be delivered from the unbelievers in Judea, and that my service for Jerusalem may be accebtble to the saints, [32]so that by God's will I may come to you with joy and be refreshed in your company. [33]The God of peace be with you all. Amen.

Eph 6:18–20 (§234)
[18]Pray at all times in the Spirit, with all prayer and supplication. To that end keep alert with all perseverance, making supplication for all the saints, [19]and also for me, that utterance may be given me in opening my mouth boldly to proclaim the mystery of the gospel, [20]for which I am an ambassador in chains; that I may declare it boldly, as I ought to speak.

Phil 1:19–26 (§240)
[19]Yes, and I shall rejoice. For I know that through your prayers and the help of the Spirit of Jesus Christ this will turn out for my deliverance, [20]as it is my eager expectation and hope that I shall not be at all ashamed, but that with full courage now as always Christ will be honored in my body, whether by life or by death. [21]For to me to live is Christ, and to die is gain. [22]If it is to be life in the flesh, that means fruitful labor for me. Yet which I shall choose I cannot tell. [23]I am hard pressed between the two. My desire is to depart and be with Christ, for that is far better. [24]But to remain in the flesh is more necessary on your account. [25]Convinced of this, I know that I shall remain and continue with you all, for your progress and joy in the faith, [26]so that in me you may have ample cause to glory in Christ Jesus, because of my coming to you again.

Phil 1:27–30 (§241)
[27]Only let your manner of life be worthy of the gospel of Christ, so that whether I come and see you or am absent, I may hear of you that you stand firm in one spirit, with one mind striving side by side for the faith of the gospel, [28]and not frightened in anything by your opponents. This is a clear omen to them of their destruction, but of your salvation, and that from God. [29]For it has been granted to you that for the sake of Christ you should not only believe in him but also suffer for his sake, [30]engaged in the same conflict which you saw and now hear to be mine.

Phil 2:12–13 (§243)
[12]Therefore, my beloved, as you have always obeyed, so now, not only as in my presence but much more in my absence, work out your own salvation with fear and trembling; [13]for God is at work in you, both to will and to work for his good pleasure.

Phil 2:19–24 (§245)
[19]I hope in the Lord Jesus to send Timothy to you soon, so that I may be cheered by news of you. [20]I have no one like him, who will be genuinely anxious for your welfare. [21]They all look after their own interests, not those of Jesus Christ. [22]But Timothy's worth you know, how as a son with a father he has served with me in the gospel. [23]I hope therefore to send him just as soon as I see how it will go with me; [24]and I trust in the Lord that shortly I myself shall come also.

Col 4:2–4 (§269)
[2]Continue steadfastly in prayer, being watchful in it with thanksgiving; [3]and pray for us also, that God may open to us a door for the word, to declare the mystery of Christ, on account of which I am in prison, [4]that I may make it clear, as I ought to speak.

1 Thess 5:25 (§290)
[25]Brethren, pray for us.

2 Thess 3:1–5 (§299)
[1]Finally, brethren, pray for us, that the word of the Lord may speed on and triumph, as it did among you, [2]and that we may be delivered from wicked and evil men; for not all have faith. [3]But the Lord is faithful; he will strengthen you and guard you from evil. [4]And we have confidence in the Lord about you, that you are doing and will do the things which we command. [5]May the Lord direct your hearts to the love of God and to the steadfastness of Christ.

● **Phlm 22**
Rom 1   [11]For I long to see you, that I may impart to you some spiritual gift to strengthen you, . . .

LETTER STRUCTURE: GREETINGS

23Epaphras, my fellow prisoner in Christ Jesus, sends greetings to you, **24**and so do Mark, Aristarchus, Demas, and Luke, my fellow workers.

PRIMARY

Rom 16:3–16 (§66)

³Greet Prisca and Aquila, my fellow workers in Christ Jesus, ⁴who risked their necks for my life, to whom not only I but also all the churches of the Gentiles give thanks; ⁵greet also the church in their house. Greet my beloved Epaenetus, who was the first convert in Asia for Christ. ⁶Greet Mary, who has worked hard among you. ⁷Greet Andronicus and Junias, my kinsmen and my fellow prisoners; they are men of note among the apostles, and they were in Christ before me. ⁸Greet Ampliatus, my beloved in the Lord. ⁹Greet Urbanus, our fellow worker in Christ, and my beloved Stachys. ¹⁰Greet Apelles, who is approved in Christ. Greet those who belong to the family of Aristobulus. ¹¹Greet my kinsman Herodion. Greet those in the Lord who belong to the family of Narcissus. ¹²Greet those workers in the Lord, Tryphaena and Tryphosa. Greet the beloved Persis, who has worked hard in the Lord. ¹³Greet Rufus, eminent in the Lord, also his mother and mine. ¹⁴Greet Asyncritus, Phlegon, Hermes, Patrobas, Hermas, and the brethren who are with them. ¹⁵Greet Philologus, Julia, Nereus and his sister, and Olympas, and all the saints who are with them. ¹⁶Greet one another with a holy kiss. All the churches of Christ greet you.

Rom 16:21–23 (§69)

²¹Timothy, my fellow worker, greets you; so do Lucius and Jason and Sosipater, my kinsmen.

²²I Tertius, the writer of this letter, greet you in the Lord.

²³Gaius, who is host to me and to the whole church, greets you. Erastus, the city treasurer, and our brother Quartus, greet you.

1 Cor 16:19–20 (§143)

¹⁹The churches of Asia send greetings. Aquila and Prisca, together with the church in their house, send you hearty greetings in the Lord. ²⁰All the brethren send greetings. Greet one another with a holy kiss.

2 Cor 13:11–13 (§191)

¹¹Finally, brethren, farewell. Mend your ways, heed my appeal, agree with one another, live in peace, and the God of love and peace will be with you. ¹²Greet one another with a holy kiss. ¹³All the saints greet you.

Phil 4:21–22 (§254)

²¹Greet every saint in Christ Jesus. The brethren who are with me greet you. ²²All the saints greet you, especially those of Caesar's household.

Col 4:10–15 (§272)

¹⁰Aristarchus my fellow prisoner greets you, and Mark the cousin of Barnabas (concerning whom you have received instructions—if he comes to you, receive him), ¹¹and Jesus who is called Justus. These are the only men of the circumcision among my fellow workers for the kingdom of God, and they have been a comfort to me. ¹²Epaphras, who is one of yourselves, a servant of Christ Jesus, greets you, always remembering you earnestly in his prayers, that you may stand mature and fully assured in all the will of God. ¹³For I bear him witness that he has worked hard for you and for those in Laodicea and in Hierapolis. ¹⁴Luke the beloved physician and Demas greet you. ¹⁵Give my greetings to the brethren at Laodicea, and to Nympha and the church in her house.

1 Thess 5:26 (§291)

²⁶Greet all the brethren with a holy kiss.

● Phlm 23

2 Tim 4   ¹⁹Greet Prisca and Aquila, and the household of Onesiphorus. ²⁰Erastus remained at Corinth; Trophimus I left ill at Miletus. ²¹Do your best to come before winter. Eubulus sends greetings to you, as do Pudens and Linus and Claudia and all the brethren.

Titus 3   ¹⁵All who are with me send greetings to you. Greet those who love us in the faith.

● Phlm 24

2 Tim 4   ¹⁰For Demas, in love with this present world, has deserted me and gone to Thessalonica; Crescens has gone to Galatia, Titus to Dalmatia.

Acts 12   ¹²When he realized this, he went to the house of Mary, the mother of John whose other name was Mark, where many were gathered together and were praying.

Acts 19   ²⁹So the city was filled with the confusion; and they rushed together into the theater, dragging with them Gaius and Aristarchus, Macedonians who were Paul's companions in travel.

Acts 27   ²And embarking in a ship of Adramyttium, which was about to sail to the ports along the coast of Asia, we put to sea, accompanied by Aristarchus, a Macedonian from Thessalonica.

LETTER STRUCTURE: CLOSING GRACE

25 The grace of the Lord Jesus Christ be with your spirit.

PRIMARY

Rom 16:20b (§68)
The grace of our Lord Jesus Christ be with you.

1 Cor 16:23–24 (§145)
²³The grace of the Lord Jesus be with you. ²⁴My love be with you all in Christ Jesus. Amen.

2 Cor 13:14 (§192)
¹⁴The grace of the Lord Jesus Christ and the love of God and the fellowship of the Holy Spirit be with you all.

Gal 6:18 (§217)
¹⁸The grace of our Lord Jesus Christ be with your spirit, brethren. Amen.

Eph 6:23–24 (§236)
²³Peace be to the brethren, and love with faith, from God the Father and the Lord Jesus Christ. ²⁴Grace be with all who love our Lord Jesus Christ with love undying.

Phil 4:23 (§255)
²³The grace of the Lord Jesus Christ be with your spirit.

Col 4:18b (§274)
Grace be with you.

1 Thess 5:28 (§293)
²⁸The grace of our Lord Jesus Christ be with you.

2 Thess 3:18 (§304)
¹⁸The grace of our Lord Jesus Christ be with you all.

● **Phlm 25**
1 Tim 6   ²¹. . . Grace be with you.

2 Tim 4   ²². . . Grace be with you.

Titus 3   ¹⁵. . . Grace be with you all.

● References are to sections.

● References are to sections.

● References are to sections.

• References are to sections.

● References are to sections.

● References are to sections.

● References are to sections.